HANDBOOK OF
RESEARCH DESIGN
&
SOCIAL
MEASUREMENT
6TH EDITION

This book is dedicated in honor of Sara Jennifer Salkind—
An uncommon young woman of valor, integrity, and courage.

And to the memory of John C. Wright—

*To laugh often and much; To win the respect of intelligent people and
the affection of children; To earn the appreciation of honest critics and
endure the betrayal of false friends; To appreciate beauty, to find the best in
others; To leave the world a bit better, whether by a healthy child, a garden
patch, or a redeemed social condition; To know that even one life has
breathed easier because you have lived. This is to have succeeded.*

—Ralph Waldo Emerson

DELBERT C. MILLER
late of Indiana University, Bloomington
NEIL J. SALKIND
University of Kansas

HANDBOOK OF
RESEARCH
DESIGN
&
SOCIAL
MEASUREMENT
6TH EDITION

Sage Publications
International Educational and Professional Publisher
Thousand Oaks ■ London ■ New Delhi

For information:

Sage Publications, Inc.
2455 Teller Road
Thousand Oaks, California 91320
E-mail: order@sagepub.com

Sage Publications Ltd.
6 Bonhill Street
London EC2A 4PU
United Kingdom

Sage Publications India Pvt. Ltd.
M-32 Market
Greater Kailash I
New Delhi 110 048 India

Printed in the United States of America

Library of Congress Cataloging-in-Publication Data

Handbook of research design and social measurement.— 6th ed. / edited
by Delbert C. Miller (deceased), Neil J. Salkind.
        p.   cm.
Rev. ed. of: Handbook of research design and social measurement /
    Delbert C. Miller. 5th ed. ©1991.
    Includes bibliographical references and index.
    ISBN 0-7619-2045-5 (cloth)
    ISBN 0-7619-2046-3 (paperback)
    1. Social sciences—Research.   2. Sociometry.   I. Miller, Delbert
Charles, 1913-   . II. Salkind, Neil J.   III. Miller, Delbert Charles, 1913-   .
Handbook of research design and social measurement. 5th ed.
    H62 .M44   2002
    302′.072—dc21   2001006672

02   03   04   05   06   10   9   8   7   6   5   4   3   2   1

Acquiring Editor: C. Deborah Laughton
Editorial Assistant: Veronica Novak
Production Editor: Diana E. Axelsen
Copy Editor: A. J. Sobczak
Typesetter/Designer: Janelle LeMaster
Indexer: Mary Mortensen
Cover Designer: Ravi Balasuriya

CONTENTS

PART 3   APPLIED AND EVALUATION RESEARCH

PART 4   QUALITATIVE RESEARCH

John W. Creswell and Raymond C. Maietta

PART 5
GUIDES TO METHODS AND TECHNIQUES OF COLLECTING DATA IN LIBRARY, FIELD, AND LABORATORY SETTINGS: SOCIAL SCIENCE DATA LIBRARIES AND RESEARCH CENTERS

PART 6 GUIDE TO STATISTICAL ANALYSIS OF SOCIAL SCIENCE DATA

PART 7   ASSESSING SOCIAL VARIABLES: SCALES AND INDEXES

PART 8   RESEARCH PROPOSAL, FUNDING, BUDGETING, REPORTING, AND CAREER PLANNING

PREFACE

This sixth edition of the *Handbook of Research Design and Social Measurement* is the most extensive revision in the history of the book. We have continued to emphasize the tools that social scientists need to become familiar with and that enable them to conduct high-quality empirical research; however, we also recognize that sociologists need to become familiar with the fast-changing, information-rich world.

Like earlier editions, this sixth edition of the *Handbook* remains a carefully designed sourcebook for all the research steps in social research investigation. It seeks to provide guidance for research in the social and behavioral sciences and such applied professions as journalism, education, social work, and business. Researchers in hotel administration, health services, public health, city management, and law enforcement may also find it applicable to their problems.

With this edition, the *Handbook* celebrates more than three decades of service to social and behavioral science researchers. It has been used in three different ways.

1. It serves as an independent reference handbook for social and behavioral science researchers. As a reference work, this volume includes digests of useful knowledge that social and behavioral science researchers need as a guide to their research requirements. For that reason, the contents cover searches of periodicals, useful sourcebooks, bibliographies, computer programs, many of the most important scales and sources of scales, sources of funding and publication, and much more. The purpose is to place in the *Handbook* enough information so that experienced researchers can find digests of material not taught in the days of their graduate training, as well as information that may be used by any researcher.

This revision also recognizes the value of qualitative research methods and devotes an entire chapter to that end.

2. It can be used as a supplement to social science methods texts for teachers who wanted to provide their students with basic information about social science research and how it is organized. At least one entire part of the book—Part 8 in this volume—focuses on professional development, including grant writing, professional organizations, employment, research institutes, and professional writing and communication.

3. Finally, as a textbook, it provides step-by-step instructions for students' research training. It begins where every basic researcher—student or professional—begins in finding a creative idea, a middle-range theory, and initial hypotheses. It proceeds through design, proposal, collection and analysis of data, and finally writing, reporting, publication, and utilization of research skills.

For applied and evaluation researchers, an orientation to the practical problems to be faced in their research assignments is outlined. The activities and objectives of basic, applied, and evaluation research are delineated. The way that such problems may be handled by theory and methodological tools is described.

While trying to maintain the standards of earlier editions, this revised edition contains a great deal of new material, including the following:

- A comprehensive introduction to qualitative methods, including a review of existing computer applications for collecting and analyzing data
- New and more current reviews and commentaries that replace excerpts that are dated or no longer relevant
- Thousands of new references on the assessment of important sociological variables, as well as references to such topics as statistical analysis, computer applications, and specific topics
- Updated information about the use of computers and online research techniques, including beginning and intermediate material about the Internet and its use by the modern research scientist
- A review of some of the most popular statistical analysis software packages available today
- Extensive coverage of institutional review board activities and procedures
- Discussion and guidelines regarding ethical practices in social and behavioral sciences research
- Abstracts, citations, and grouping by topical focus of the past five years of the *American Sociological Review, Social Psychology Quarterly,* and *American Journal of Sociology.*
- Extensive coverage of how to prepare manuscripts for publication, including a list of all journals covered by *Sociological Abstracts,* along with the editorial office address and URL for each entry
- Expansion of social indicators to include international coverage
- An extensive Table of Contents and, for the first time in the history of the book, a comprehensive index

This edition was started as a collaboration between Professors Delbert C. Miller and Neil J. Salkind. Much to the sorrow of everyone who has been associated with this book over these many years, Professor Miler passed away as the revision was just beginning. This revision is inspired by his vision of what a resource this book could be to so many beginning and advanced researchers. It is both necessary and appropriate to include Professor Miller's acknowledgments from the fifth edition of the *Handbook:*

In the years behind me are three teachers of sociology who inspired me with the same thought: Social data are natural data. Their study can and should follow the contours of the scientific method. After two years of high school teaching as an instructor of physical science and mathematics, I became a student of the social sciences. I went back to the university to learn about social research. I must now salute Read Bain, my M.A. mentor at Miami University; F. Stuart Chapin, my Ph.D. mentor at the University of Minnesota; and his student, George A. Lundberg, who became my teacher and department head at the University of Washington. All carried the vision of the sociometric scale as a crucial element in social measurement. This book itself was born with that vision in a classroom during a course in social measurement at Pennsylvania State University. It has been nurtured by me for 31 years at Indiana University. Every research article in the *American Sociological Review,* official organ of the American Sociological Association, has been examined for the scales used and classified as to type, frequency, and trend from 1951 to 1987. The Summary Notes can be found in this and previous editions of the *Handbook.*

It is to Dr. Miller that I owe a great deal, for having allowed me the opportunity to participate in this revision. I hope that the value of the book measures up to his past contributions.

ACKNOWLEDGMENTS

Any author is foolish to think that he or she is the reason a book goes from an idea to the bookshelf, and with a revision of this magnitude, it may be even more so the case. C. Deborah Laughton, my editor, was absolutely ready to support the authors in any way necessary or imaginable to see that the manuscript was completed. If this book sees any success, it is to a large extent due to her professionalism, competence, and sincere concern for her authors. In this time of editors changing companies and jobs as often as the seasons, it's reassuring to know that some in the publishing business still believe in continuity and integrity. To her, I am most grateful.

I would also like to especially thank A. J. Sobczak and Diana Axelsen. A. J. is a copy editor in name but much more than that in practice. He verified facts, sought out references, suggested organizational changes, and made sure that every section number was where it should be and every modifier left undangling. He was a source of advice and constant encouragement. Diana managed the production process, transformed the manuscript, and made it into an attractive and useful book. Her patience throughout the process, attention to detail, and gentle encouragement show in these pages. Janelle LeMaster designed the interior of the book and handled the complex typesetting with great aplomb.

Finally, we would like to thank all the reviewers: Michael L. Vasu, North Carolina State University; Dan Berkowitz, University of Iowa; Dan Cover, Furman University; Barry L. Johnson, Brigham Young University; Jianhong Liu, Rhode Island College; David M. Klein, University of Notre Dame; Ronald H. Heck, University of Hawaii at Manoa; David Lopez-Lee, University of Southern California; and Marja J. Verhoef, University of Calgary.

Neil J. Salkind
University of Kansas
Lawrence, Kansas 66044

PART 1

INTRODUCTION: UNDERSTANDING BASIC, APPLIED, AND EVALUATION RESEARCH

Part 1 defines the characteristics of basic, applied, and evaluation research and includes a brief discussion of the three types of research. The opportunities and limitations that characterize each of these approaches are also described.

Researchers interested in behavioral or organizational problems can focus their inquiries in three different directions. These are generally called *basic*, *applied*, and *evaluation* research, although each can be found under other names depending on the context within which they are used. For example, basic research is often called *pure* or *experimental research*, and applied research often appears under the terminology of *policy research* and *action research*. Finally, evaluation research sometimes is referred to as *assessment* or *appraisal research*, and even as *social accounting*.

Although a variety of terms are used to describe each of the three, we will be using *basic*, *applied*, and *evaluation* throughout the *Handbook of Research Design and Social Measurement*.

Table 1.1 illustrates some of the differences between basic, applied, and evaluation research by providing the defining characteristics of each, organized by the following categories: the nature of the problem addressed, the goal of the research, the underlying or guiding theory, and appropriate techniques used in a research setting.

Table 1.1	**RESEARCH DESIGN ORIENTATIONS**		
Defining Characteristic	*Basic*	*Applied*	*Evaluation*
The nature of the problem	Basic scientific investigation seeks new knowledge about social phenomena, hoping to establish general principles and theories with which to explain them	Applied research seeks to understand how basic research can help alleviate a demanding social problem and provides policymakers with well-grounded guides to remedial action	Evaluative research assesses outcomes of treatments applied to social problems or the outcomes of prevailing practices
The goal of the research	To produce new knowledge, including the discovery of the nature of the relationships between variables	To explore the value of basic knowledge in an applied setting that can be useful to a policymaker who seeks to eliminate or alleviate a social problem	To provide an accurate accounting of a treatment program applied to a social problem
The underlying theory	Selection of a theory to guide hypothesis testing	Selection of a theory, guidelines, or intuitive hunches to explore the dynamics of a social system	Selection of a theory to fit the problem under assessment
The appropriate techniques	Theory formulation, hypothesis testing using the experimental and quasi-experimental methods, sampling, data collection techniques, statistical treatment of data, and validation or rejection of hypotheses	Very similar to basic research, only in a setting where the implications of the research are immediately obvious	Use of conventional techniques appropriate to the question

A careful review of the contents of Table 1.1 reveals several threads that connect the three types of research. For example, where basic research seeks new knowledge in the answers to fundamental questions about social phenomena, applied research hopes to show how this knowledge can be used to address a pressing problem. Evaluative research, on the other hand, is involved in making judgments about the value or merit of a program.

Each type of research can be conducted independently, but the value of any one type must be judged in the light of the results of the other two. An increasing number of researchers, however, find themselves in different camps. Although the divergent goals of each type of investigation commit researchers to differing research orientations and researchers feel strongly about the worth of their own kinds of research, each type must be understood by all social and behavior researchers to best answer most research questions.

The greater the mastery that the researcher has of basic knowledge, theory, design, and methodological techniques and general application, the greater the opportunities will be for answering a particular research question accurately. This is true whether the task is problem discovery and definition, discovering design possibilities, collection and treatment of data, or the final testing of a hypothesis.

Although this handbook is disposed primarily toward understanding basic research, therefore, references will be made to the important areas of applied and evaluation research (especially in Parts 2 and 3) where social practitioners live and their ideas are tested daily. Rossi and Wright (1985) have defined the reciprocal relationship between the research fields as follows:

> We also anticipate that basic research will continue to benefit from the substantive and technical advances made by applied researchers as the latter attempt to tackle even more complicated applied research tasks. There is no doubt that much technical and substantive knowledge flows the other way as well. A discipline that does not have an applied side loses a certain richness of theory and method. An applied field that loses touch with its basic discipline also runs a risk of parochialism and overly narrow attention to policy-makers' definitions of social problems and their most feasible solutions. (p. 76)

Reference

Rossi, Peter H., & Wright, James D. (1985). Evaluation research: An assessment. In Linda H. Aiken & Barbara H. Kehrer (Eds.), *Evaluation Studies Review Annual* (Vol. 10). Beverly Hills, CA: Sage.

1.2 THE ORIENTATION AND COMMITMENT OF THE BASIC RESEARCHER

Most researchers who conduct basic research define their goal as that of advancing knowledge or the understanding of basic scientific phenomena. Any immediate and obvious utility is secondary to the primary objective of science, which is to describe the world as it exists, without any necessary regard for how it might be changed. Although most would agree that all knowledge, whether it validates a hypothesis or not, eventually will be useful, it is always useful to know what may be "true" and what is not true. Consistent with this theme is a statement by Hans Selye, an endocrinologist who developed the modern concept of stress and studied the effects of stress on the body, that he has always felt that many great scientists who have made numerous valuable contributions were motivated primarily not by curiosity or a great desire to serve humanity, but by an emotional reluctance to accept defeat.

The way to this basic knowledge presents numerous challenges. In the real world, a large number of social variables are found to be highly related to each other, and unambiguous causal relationships are difficult to establish. Theories and explanations abound for the same phenomenon, and biases and ideological differences among researchers are part of the very methodological approaches that are to lead us to the answers we seek.

So why do social researchers commit themselves to working with such uncertain, shifting, confusing, and exasperating concepts and ideas? Many welcome the challenge of working in new scientific fields, the origins of which are only a scant century old. Others like the social science orientation toward what they consider the most important problems of our time and see the social sciences as holding the promise for a solution. Some researchers respect the integrity of the scientific method and the mathematical and conceptual tools that demand intellectual discipline and integrity.

Committed social researchers continue to pursue knowledge, whatever the outcome. The questions most often asked examine relationships and attempt to fit such generic propositions as "given certain conditions, if X were changed, then Y can be expected to change as well." As good scientists, these researchers attempt to replicate and affirm findings, and with each increase in predictive power, the value of the knowledge and of the discipline increases and the closer the outcomes come to the "true" state of affairs. When a policymaker demands basic data from the social sciences and these data are indispensable, social science moves forward and a theory and data intertwine with research, strengthening theory. Social study then becomes social science.

THE ORIENTATION AND COMMITMENT OF THE APPLIED RESEARCHER **1.3**

Applied researchers seek knowledge that can be used to solve pressing social and organizational problems. This knowledge, which is often an extension of basic research, should be valid, descriptive, and informative as to how change may be accomplished.

Policy analysts or action researchers often believe that much of the knowledge we have about social science phenomena has not been generated using the appropriate methodological tools. Consequently, accurate interpretation of the dynamic behavior underlying social organizations is somewhat limited. Nevertheless, most applied researchers would accept the "applied mind-set" in which every effort is made to use research data in applied settings.

1.3.1 A Typology of Applied Research

Rubin (1983) developed a typology of the social scientists who do applied social research, shown in Table 1.2. He describes the four types as follows:

Table 1.2		
	Focus Upon Policy Implications	*Focus Upon Data Gathering and Data Interpretation*
Concern With Social Processes	Policy Analyst	Evaluation Researcher
Concern With Social Outcomes	Social Monitor	Data Analyst

- A *policy analyst* studies social processes and describes what policy alternatives exist to solve an existing problem
- An *evaluation researcher* studies social processes to determine if a program or project is accomplishing what it is intended to accomplish
- A *social monitor* examines outcomes data to discover patterns that require some organizational or government action
- A *data analyst* uses and refines methodological tools to interpret outcome data, often using advanced statistical procedures

An applied researcher may be called on to fill any one of or all the above roles, depending on the desires of the person seeking help as well as the demands of the question under consideration. In addition, all applied researchers should bear some responsibility for understanding research methodology as well as determining the cost of gathering information versus its value as part of the decision-making process.

Universities offer some courses in applied research, but the most likely place to learn its techniques is in the research activity of social science institutes. There, learning takes place through work in internships, apprenticeships, and staff entry-level positions (see Part 8). Professional schools such as schools of business, social work, and education are receptive to applied research that is "useful in theory and practice." Many individual professors can be found in the midst of "practical" research in those schools.

Reference

Rubin, Herbert J. (1983). *Applied social research.* Columbus, OH: Charles E. Merrill.

1.3.2 The Applied Researcher as Intruder

The applied researcher is often (for better or worse) seen as an agent of change in an often relatively closed social system. Everyone seems curious about what the researcher is doing, what he or she is looking for, and why he or she "lurks around" and asks so many questions. Others start asking questions, such as "What do you expect to find?" "What are you trying to do?" "Are you going to put us on a couch, Doc?" and "Is management trying to speed us up?"

Supervisors may refuse to cooperate or may cooperate with sullen indifference. If top management does not wholeheartedly support the research, there can be endless difficulty. Any researcher weathering a hostile environment may find coping very difficult, and this is why we encourage our colleagues to participate actively in the applied research process, to help build an understanding and tolerance for it.

The researcher carries the thought, "I am trying to help improve the well-being of the individuals involved in the organization. Why are the employees and supervisors so defensive? Why are they so suspicious of my research?" These questions should focus the goals of the applied researcher and clarify the purpose of any perceived intrusions. The researcher should attempt to answer these questions, then provide a rationale for the study to gain the full approval of employees as well as management.

1.3.3 Future Training Needs for Applied Researchers

The American Sociological Association (ASA) is fully aware of the need to reassess the capability of sociology to make knowledge available that relates to productive goals and to furnish knowledge that is valuable to the evaluation and policy-making process. The ASA regularly sponsors workshops on directions in applied sociology. For information and or eligibility standards, consult the ASA about specific programs at www.asanet.org/ or

American Sociological Association
1307 New York Avenue, NW—Suite 700
Washington, DC 20005
Phone: (202) 383-9005
Fax: (202) 638-0882
TDD: (202) 872-0486
e-mail: executive.office@asanet.org

Methodological training now stresses skills in computer analysis and mastery of the software required to analyze data adequately and to fully answer the research questions that were first posed. Evaluation and policy-making research also have a high priority.

It must be remembered that applied research training and basic research training are not mutually exclusive endeavors, especially in the training of social scientists. They are highly complementary, and well-trained social science researchers can participate effectively in both applied and basic research. In fact, the best applied researchers possess solid training in basic research. The primary differences are the question being asked and the goal of the research—not necessarily the method selected to investigate the problem at hand.

Most federal funding goes toward the training of applied behavioral scientists and applied researchers. In recent years, because of changes in federal policy, both basic research (which traditionally has been underfunded) and applied research have received increasing funding.

1.3.4 The Growing Presence of Applied Research Organizations

The growing interest in applied research and sociological practice is evidenced by the growth in numbers of sociological practitioners, sociological practice organizations, and applied research itself. The Sociological Practice Association or SPA (www.socpractice.org/) focuses on the application of sociology and is more than 20 years old. The SPA is a community of practitioners and scholars in which members combine their skills in intervention with research, technology, and critical analysis. The mission of the SPA is to

- Promote the application of sociological knowledge for individual and social change through scholarly and educational activities
- Develop opportunities for the employment and utilization of sociological practitioners
- Provide a common meeting ground for sociological practitioners, allied professionals, and interested scholars and students
- Promote training and educational opportunities to further sociological practice
- Advance theory, research, and methods for improving the utilization of sociological approaches to change

As an indication of the continually growing interest in applied sociology, the SPA now publishes *The Sociological Practice: A Journal of Clinical and Applied Sociology*, which includes articles, essays, and practice and research reports concerned with the clinical uses of sociology. The first issue (March 1999) contained the following articles.

"Introductory Statement: Philosophy and Future Direction," by John G. Bruhn

"Tomorrow's Most Challenging Practice Issues: 21st Century Surprises," by Arthur B. Shostak

"Installing Circuit Breakers: Mechanisms to Avoid Sexual Harassment in the Workplace," by John Marker

"Gambling, Drugs, and Sex: New Drug Trends and Addictions in Honolulu, Hawaii, 1998," by Gordon James Knowles

"What Sociologists Do and Where They Do It—The NSF Survey on Sociologists' Work Activities and Workplaces," by Robert J. Dotzler and Ross Koppel

"Book Review: *Developmental Theories of Crime and Delinquency*," edited by Terence P. Thornberry, reviewed by Blake Nelson

Other organizations that focus on applied sociology include the Commission on Applied and Clinical Sociology (www.sociologycommission.org), whose purpose is "to develop, promote, and support quality sociological education and practice in applied and clinical areas," and the Society for Applied Sociology or SAS (www.appliedsoc.org/), which "is an international organization for professionals involved in applying sociological knowledge in a wide variety of settings." The purposes of the SAS are

- To provide a forum for sociologists and others interested in applying sociological knowledge
- To enhance understanding of the interrelationship between sociological knowledge and sociological practice
- To increase the effectiveness of applied sociological research and training

1.4 THE ORIENTATION AND COMMITMENT OF THE EVALUATION RESEARCHER

Evaluation involves assessment of the strengths and weaknesses of programs, policies, personnel, products, and organizations in an effort to improve their effectiveness. Evaluation researchers are called in when the effectiveness of a policy or program needs to be assessed.

An integral part of undertaking any evaluation exercise is to judge whether the activity being studied is worthwhile. Edward Suchman (1967) defined a set of criteria that can assist in that judgment.

- Level of effort or activity
- Level of performance or accomplishment
- Adequacy or impact of the program
- Efficiency or output relative to input
- Specification of conditions of effectiveness of the program

According to Suchman, the first two criteria are *evaluative* and are concerned with the determination of the relationship between activities and effects. The second two criteria are administrative in nature, dealing with a judgment about the size and cost of the effort relative to the effects. The last criterion is concerned with increased knowledge or understanding, irrespective of effect.

The current political climate and relatively recent importance placed on accountability point to applied sociologists' need for resources. Evaluators can turn to the American Evaluation Association (www.eval.org/), an international professional association of evaluators who focus on "the application and exploration of program evaluation, personnel evaluation, technology, and many other forms of evaluation." Its mission is to

- Improve evaluation practices and methods
- Increase evaluation use
- Promote evaluation as a profession
- Support the contribution of evaluation to the generation of theory and knowledge about effective human action

Reference

Suchman, Edward A. (1967). *Evaluative research, principles and practice in public service and social action programs.* New York: Russell Sage Foundation.

GENERAL READINGS ON BASIC, APPLIED, AND EVALUATION RESEARCH **1.5**

Throughout this handbook, you will be introduced to hundreds of references about different topics that are vital to research methods in the social sciences. The following is a sampling of important and interesting references for the topics of basic, applied, and evaluation research.

1.5.1 Basic Research

Bailey, Kenneth D. (1997). *Research methods for creating a just world: Overcoming barriers to inclusion in social research.* Los Angeles: University of California, Society for the Study of Social Problems.

Blessing, Lusienne T. M., & Chakrabarti, Amaresh. (1999). *A design research methodology.* Godalming, Surrey, UK: Springer Verlag London.

Dyer, James A. (1996). *The art and science of survey research.* In Timothy J. Flanagan & Dennis R. Longmire (Eds.), *Americans view crime and justice: A national public opinion survey.* Thousand Oaks, CA: Sage.

Lacy, Michael G. (1997). Efficiently studying rare events: Case-control methods for sociologists. *Sociological Perspectives, 40,* 129-154.

Tabachnick, Barbara G., & Fidell, Linda S. (2000). *Computer-assisted research design and analysis.* Needham Heights, MA: Allyn and Bacon.

1.5.2 Applied Research

Bechofer, Frank, & Paterson, Lindsay. (2000). *Principles of research design in social sciences.* New York: Routledge.

Grunow, Dieter. (1995). The research design in organization studies: Problems and prospects. *Organization Science, 6,* 93-103.

Kenny, David A. (1996). The design and analysis of social-interaction research. *Annual Review of Psychology, 47,* 59-86.

Narver, Betty Jane. (1999). Applied research: Entrepreneurial style. *Metropolitan Universities: An International Forum, 10,* 57-64.

1.5.3 Evaluation Research

Greene, Jay P., & Peterson, Paul E. (1996). *Methodological issues in evaluation research: The Milwaukee school choice plan* (Occasional Paper 4). Cambridge, MA: Harvard University, Department of Government.

LaFond, Colette, Toomey, Traci L., Rothstein, Catherine, Wagenaar, Alexander C., & Manning, Willard. (2000). Policy evaluation research: Measuring the independent variables. *Evaluation Review, 24,* 92-101.

Toffolon Weiss, Melissa M., Bertrand, Jane T., & Terrell, Stanley S. (1999). The results framework—An innovative tool for program planning and evaluation. *Evaluation Review, 23,* 336-359.

Watt, James H. (1999). Internet systems for evaluation research. *New Directions for Evaluation, 84,* 23-43.

PART 2

BASIC RESEARCH DESIGN

Part 2 emphasizes the discipline of basic research as the common denominator of all research, whether the research be basic, applied, or evaluative in nature. Guides are presented that include the first steps in the sequence of a planned research proposal: selection and definition of a sociological problem, description of the relationship of the problem to a theoretical framework, formulation of working hypotheses (including null and research), design of the experiment or inquiry, and sampling procedures.

Certain elements must be included in the outline or plan of action for a social science research endeavor before the actual fieldwork or laboratory work is undertaken. Each of the individual guides in this part of the *Handbook of Research Design and Social Measurement* has been selected to assist in planning the five main steps. Parts 3 (Applied and Evaluation Research), 5 (Guides to Methods and Techniques of Collecting Data), and 6 (Guide to Statistical Analysis and Computer Resources) also provide sets of guides that expand and further develop the main points listed here.

What follows is a point by point guide showing how to create an acceptable research proposal. You can even use what follows as a checklist to help keep track of progress in your proposal development.

I. Identifying and Describing the Sociological Problem
   A. Present a clear statement of the problem, with important and relevant concepts defined where necessary.
   B. Illustrate how the problem is amenable to being investigated through the use of a treatment or test.
   C. Describe the significance of the problem with reference to one or more of the following criteria:
      1. It represents an issue or issues that is/are particularly timely in basic importance.
      2. The question under consideration can be shown to relate to a practical problem.
      3. Outcomes may have significant implications for a wide audience.
      4. The problem at hand relates to an influential or critical population.
      5. The completed work would fill a gap in the research literature.
      6. The completed work would permit generalization to broader principles of social interaction or general theory.
      7. The definition of an important concept or relationship would be refined.
      8. The results will have implications for a wide range of practical problems.
      9. Results in the past have been equivocal, and replication of the experiment is needed.
      10. New or better instrumentation for observing and analyzing data will be developed.
      11. Opportunities for gathering data, restricted by the limited time available for gathering particular data, are increased.

II. The Theoretical Framework
   A. Describe the relationship of the problem or research questions to a theoretical framework.
   B. Demonstrate how the problem statement is related to previous research and how the previous research narrows the current set of questions being asked.

III. The Hypotheses
   A. Clearly state the null and research or alternate hypotheses. Present alternate research hypotheses considered feasible within the framework of the theory.
   B. Define the degree of risk you are willing to take by assigning a significance or Type I level.
   C. Define concepts or variables in operational terms.
      1. Independent and dependent variables should be operationally defined.
      2. The specific instruments used to assess these variables should be identified and, if possible, samples included in the appendix.
      3. Psychometric data including reliability and validity about the instruments should be provided and discussed.
   D. Describe possible shortcomings and their consequences.

IV. Design of the Experiment
   A. Describe the specific experimental design, with particular attention to all variables and whether the variables are to be tested, controlled, or ignored.
   B. Define threats to internal and external validity and how they will be accounted for.
   C. Specify statistical tests.
      1. Specify the level of confidence at which each null hypothesis will be tested.
      2. Determine the power of tests, given the research hypothesis.
V. Sampling Procedures
   A. Describe the experimental and control samples.
   B. Define and specify the population for which the research hypotheses are relevant.
      1. Explain how sample size will be determined and the type of sample that will be selected.
   C. Specify the method of drawing or selecting sample(s).
   D. Estimate relative costs of collecting data given the various sizes and types of samples.
VI. Data Collection
   A. Estimate data collection time. If appropriate, be sure to specify
      1. Number of questions to be asked of each respondent.
      2. Approximate time needed for interview.
      3. Schedule as it has been constructed to this time.
      4. Preliminary testing of interview and results.
      5. Alternative plan for specifying adequate time and place should 1-4 above go awry.
   B. Include the following in description of interview procedures if appropriate.
      1. Means of obtaining information (i.e., by direct interview, all or part by mail, telephone, or other means).
      2. Description of special training for interviewer.
VII. Analysis of Results
   A. Specify method of analysis for each research hypothesis.
      1. Statistical software packages to be used.
      2. Use of tables, etc., with illustration by example.
      3. Use of graphic techniques and tables that are to be used.
VIII. Discussion and Interpretation of Results
   A. Discuss how data relate to hypotheses.
   B. Discuss alternative plans for analysis.
   C. Shortcomings of current research and possible solutions.
   D. Ideas for future research.
IX. Format and Publication or Reporting Plans
   A. Proposal should conform to the style of the journal or institution for which it is intended; usually, this will be the *Publication Manual of the American Psychological Association* (5th ed., 2001) or the *American Sociological Association Style Guide* (2nd ed., 1997).
   B. Completion of final document according to department and graduate school requirements.
   C. Selection of appropriate journals for submission with regard to specific journal submission guidelines.

2.2 FORMULATING A RESEARCH PROBLEM

The first step in the design of research is the selection of a question that has its roots in an interesting theoretical argument. The range of potential topics for social research is as broad as the range of social behavior, and although this fact does not make it easier for the researcher to make a choice, it does represent a very large universe of ideas to explore. In addition, no researcher ever ignores his or her personal life and professional experiences as the source for an idea that leads to a research question.

The greatest of discoveries often begin as ideas formulated not in the confines of the classroom or laboratory but on the trail during a walk or during the solitary early morning hours.

Selection of a problem represents a commitment of time, money, and energy, and it is not unusual for a researcher to dedicate 6 months to a year to finding a specific problem and formulating the question that will then lead to a research study. It may take many years to conduct the research and even longer to see it through to publication.

The significance of a problem and the precision with which the research question is formulated cannot be underestimated in the role they both play for helping to contribute to the body of knowledge in a particular field. The obvious question is "How can this significance be foreseen for research not yet undertaken?" To a great extent, this is the challenge that faces all researchers and why the quality of the research question initially asked is so important. The competent and experienced researcher is very familiar with the research literature and can identify what needs to be done next to further answer the more general and theoretical questions. A rich array of theory and methodology is available in which the proposed problem can be cast.

The student (or any researcher, for that matter) should be led through the process of identifying interesting and potentially productive problems during training. The following set of general points provides suggestions for how to find a research topic (including master's thesis or dissertation research activities) and the accompanying research design.

1. Identify interesting topics in the first set of courses that you take (which are usually core or required courses).
2. Ask questions and incorporate the answers into the body of knowledge you acquire during your coursework.
3. Consider your own experiences and personal characteristics and qualities, such as your potential professional growth and future career interests, the ability and interests of the faculty with whom you are working, your ability and desire to work with a specific professor, and the availability of resources (money, equipment, etc.) to complete your work.

As you continue your coursework and begin to feel more comfortable as an aspiring researcher, be sure to do the following:

1. Enroll in seminars through which you hope to experience intellectual growth.
2. Examine carefully how others (especially more advanced graduate students) have approached research problems and the steps they have taken to get where they are in their careers.
3. Initiate small research projects in the direction of your interests (usually under the supervision of a faculty member, either as an original study or one related to what the faculty member might be doing).
4. Discuss suggested topics with your adviser, examining which unexplored areas of the field should be studied, what previous research has been done, and what relevant literature bears upon the specific question being asked.
5. Attend professional conferences whenever possible; although these might be in distant cities and your resources might be limited, remember that graduate students for years have been sharing rooms (and having a great deal of fun) and learning at the same time.

This set of suggestions assumes that the student takes his or her work seriously and is not simply going through the motions to "knock out a thesis," but instead is planning a scholarly career. From a thesis may emerge published articles that will provide the base for the researcher's reputation in the field and the springboard for future growth and contributions.

There are no shortcuts to becoming a competent researcher. It involves a great deal of time and practice in every sense of the word. An increasing number of experiences in different settings leads to enhanced competence. A suggested place to start, especially for the naïve researcher, is a replication of existing work. Social science needs this kind of research badly in acquiring cumulative evidence, especially when the results of previous research are equivocal. The student may utilize secondary data to enrich research and to minimize expenditures of time and other resources.

Several books can help novice researchers select important problems worthy of research. Two of them are identified below.

Further Readings on Formulating a Research Problem

Creswell, John W. (1994). *Research design: Qualitative and quantitative approaches.* Thousand Oaks, CA: Sage.

Denzin, Norman K., & Lincoln, Yvonna S. (2000). *Handbook of qualitative research.* Thousand Oaks, CA: Sage.

2.3 EVALUATING RESEARCH STUDIES

An integral part of preparing any research proposal is reviewing the existing literature. You'll learn more about how to do this in Part 4 of the *Handbook of Research Design and Social Measurement.* Here, the focus is on the criteria one should use when evaluating the research studies included in one's review and used as a basis for the rationale for the study one wants to complete. To be an effective researcher, you need a critical eye for the outstanding features as well as the deficits of any one piece of research.

The following list of questions should help guide you through the process of evaluating a research report and in writing a literature review.

The Review of Previous Research

1. How closely is the literature reviewed in the study related to previous literature?
2. Is the review recent? Are there any outstanding references (those of vital conceptual significance) left out?

The Problem and Purpose

3. Can you understand the statement of the problem?
4. Is the purpose of the study clearly stated?
5. Is the study's purpose tied to the literature that is reviewed?
6. Is there a conceptual rationale to which the hypotheses are grounded?
7. Is there a rationale for why the study is an important one to do?

The Hypothesis

8. Are the research hypotheses clearly and explicitly stated?
9. Do the hypotheses state a clear association between variables?
10. Are the hypotheses grounded in theory or in a review and presentation of relevant literature?
11. Are the hypotheses testable?

The Method

12. Are both the independent and dependent variables clearly defined?
13. Are the definitions and descriptions of the variables complete?
14. Is it clear how the study was conducted?
15. Are there adequate reliability and validity data regarding the dependent variables?

The Sample

16. Was the sample selected in such a way that you think it is representative of the population?
17. Is it clear where the sample comes from and how it was selected?
18. How similar are the subjects in the study to those that have been used in other, similar studies?

Results and Discussion

19. Does the author relate the results to the review of literature?
20. Are the results related to the hypothesis?
21. Is the discussion of the results consistent with the results?
22. Does the discussion provide closure to the initial hypothesis that the author presents?

References

23. Is the list of references current?
24. Are the references consistent in their format?
25. Are the references complete?
26. Does the list of references reflect some of the most important reference sources in the field?
27. Does each reference cited in the body of the paper appear in the reference list?

General Comments About the Report

28. Is it clearly written and understandable?
29. Is the language unbiased (nonsexist and relatively culture-free)?
30. What are the strengths and weaknesses of the research?
31. What are the primary implications of the research?
32. What would you do to improve the research?

2.3.1 Useful and Beneficial Attributes of a "Good" Research Problem

How does one judge the value of a research problem? Ask these seven questions as they apply to the topics you have under consideration.

1. Is the problem concerned with basic concepts, such that the knowledge produced will be cumulative and build on an existing body of knowledge?
2. Will the investigation of the research problem result in a testing of some theoretical formulation?
3. Does the research problem allow for the careful specification of the variables involved and use of the most precise and appropriate methods available?
4. Will an investigation of the research problem result in a contribution to methodology by the discovery, development, or refinement of practicable tools, techniques, or methods?
5. Will the research problem utilize the relevant concepts, theories, evidence, and techniques from the discipline or subdiscipline of interest?
6. Will the integration of this single study into a planned program of related research produce results that are more meaningful than those achieved prior to the integration?
7. Will there be opportunity for the training of additional research scientists?

2.4 ELEMENTS OF RESEARCH DESIGN

When selecting a problem for possible research consideration, the complete research design and all its elements must be considered and formally evaluated. Table 2.1 lists dimensions of the research design that need to be considered throughout the process of selecting a problem, asking the question, framing the hypothesis, and completing the experiment. The following pages provide guides for many of these design decisions. The choice of a research design is of great importance because it influences all the outcomes of the study.

Table 2.1 IMPORTANT FACTORS IN DETERMINING CHARACTERISTICS OF THE RESEARCH DESIGN

Research Element	Choices
Type of underlying theory	• General theory • Middle-range theory • Suppositions
Study design	• Pre-experimental (survey) • Experimental • Quasi-experimental
Access to organizations and respondents	• Requires permission of individuals • Requires permission of organizational officials
Degree of control over the social system being studied	• No control • Partial control • Complete control
Type of data available	• Case and observational studies only • Quantitative analysis only • Quantitative supplemented with case and observational studies • Other (historical, cross-cultural, etc.)
Temporal dimension	• Cases from a single society at a single period (cross-sectional) • Cases from a single society at many periods (time series or longitudinal) • Cases from many societies at a single period (comparative cross-cultural) • Cases from many societies at different periods (comparative longitudinal)
Sample or universe to be studied	• Individuals in a role within a group • Pair of interrelated group members (dyad) • Primary group (30 or less) • Secondary group (31 or more) • Tertiary group (crowd, public, etc.) • State, nation, or society
Sample size	• Single or few cases • Small sample (under 30) • Large sample (more than 30)
Data source	• Original data to be collected by the researcher • Archived or secondary data in hand • Archived or secondary data to be collected
Data gathering method	• Direct observation • Interviews • Questionnaire • Test or some other form of measurement

Research Element	Choices
Number of independent variables	• One • More than one
Number of dependent variables	• One • More than one
Level of measurement	• Nominal • Ordinal • Interval • Ratio
Selection of scales to assess dependent variable	• Presence of reliability and validity data • Absence of reliability and validity data
Characteristics of dependent variable(s)	• Normally distributed • Not normally distributed
Duration of study	• Brief (less than 6 months) • Long term (more than 6 months)
Resources required for completion of study	• Funds required • No funds required

SOURCE: Adapted in part from Matilda White Riley, *Sociological Research: A Case Approach* (New York: Harcourt, Brace & World, 1963).

CHOOSING A RESEARCH DESIGN　2.5

Empirical research in social science proceeds in a variety of settings and contexts. The choice of a design setting for any research project is generally of vital concern to the researcher, who seeks to determine the validity of a hypothesis and how best to discover evidence to either accept or reject it. Social phenomena are almost always complex, and control of the relevant variables that contribute to that complexity is difficult at best.

The major question then becomes, "What design will best ascertain associations or causal paths among all the relevant variables?" How the research design goes about answering that question may well determine the future outcome of the study. It will most certainly determine the amounts of time, money, and other resources required for the study.

The general guideline to "start strong" should supersede any other design consideration. Every effort must be made to select a design setting using a population characterized by a *large* amount of variability in both the independent and dependent variables. In general, the more variability, the more likely it is that differences between groups will be detectable. In addition, for any research project, *insurance* is important and may be secured by combining case analysis with any other research design. Intense examination of extreme cases at the tails of a distribution may reveal polarized relationships that suggest new hypotheses, designs, and analyses of the data.

Table 2.2 presents a summary of the many different types of designs used in basic and applied research. It describes the type of design, its central characteristics, and the outcomes that are possible. You may find many of these similar. The one (or combination) you select will be a function primarily of the nature of the research question you are asking and the hypothesis that reflects that question.

Table 2.2 THE DIFFERENT DESIGNS USED IN BASIC AND APPLIED RESEARCH

Type of Research Design Setting	Central Characteristics	Prospective Outcomes

1. Descriptive survey
  a. Cross-sectional study
    Examples: U.S. decennial census; James A. Davis, *Undergraduate Career Decisions*; Peter M. Blau & O. D. Duncan, *The American Occupational Structure*
 	
  b. Longitudinal study
    Examples: Greg J. Duncan & James N. Morgan (Eds.), *Five Thousand American Families*
	Concerned with information generally obtained by interview or mailed questionnaire. Other sources include official reports or statistics. Occasionally, data banks of other researchers provide appropriate information. Requires an effort to procure 100% enumeration of the sample under study. Time series are produced showing social or behavioral changes over varying periods of time.	A sizable volume of information that can be classified by type, frequency, and measures of central tendency.
		Expense of the survey will be very large if the population is substantial. Final yield: data that may be analyzed for numerous relationships.
		Standardized data capable of comparative analysis over successive time intervals in which longitudinal studies examine age changes and cross-sectional studies examine age differences.

2. Sample survey *Examples:* Gallup, Harris, and Roper polls of public opinion; *Current Population Surveys*, Bureau of the Census; William H. Sewell & Robert M. Hauser, *Education, Occupation, and Earnings*	Deals with only a fraction of a total population. Sampling methods are employed to provide a sample that is an accurate representation of the total population. Test hypotheses may be established. To ensure validity, researcher will utilize techniques for scaling, pay careful attention to questionnaire wording and presentation, and include questions on personal background and other potentially useful variables.	Data may be analyzed for simple relationships between two variables. Multivariate analysis may involve factor analysis, matrix analysis, and multiple discriminant analysis. Both quantitative and qualitative data are analyzed with appropriate parametric or nonparametric methods.
3. Field studies *Examples:* Robert Lynd & Helen Lynd, *Middletown* and *Middletown in Transition*; August B. Hollingshead, *Elmtown's Youth: The Impact of Social Classes on Adolescents* and *Elmtown's Youth* and *Elmtown Revisited*; William F. Whyte, *Street Corner Society*; Phillip E. Hammond (Ed.), *Sociologists at Work*	Concerned primarily with processes and patterns under investigation of a single group, family, institution, organization, or community. Emphasis is on the social structure (i.e., interrelationships of parts of the structure and social interaction taking place). Attempts observations of social interactions or investigates thoroughly the reciprocal perceptions and attitudes of people playing interdependent roles. Direct and participant observation, interview, and scaling techniques are often employed.	Data gathered enable many hypotheses to be tested that would not be amenable to testing with survey data. Greater control is achieved by focusing on a subgroup of larger population. Sociological products such as processes, patterns, roles, attitudes, and values become available.
4. Case studies of persons *Examples:* Elizabeth Eddy, *Becoming a Teacher: The Passage to Professional Status*; Erwin O. Smigel, *The Wall Street Lawyer*; W. F. Cottrell, *The Railroader*	Usually refers to relatively intensive analysis of a single instance of a phenomenon being investigated. Investigator interviews individuals or studies life history documents to gain insight into behavior. Attempts to discover unique features and common traits shared by all persons in a given classification. Cases may be grouped by type to discover uniformities.	Data can be assembled to provide insight into conditioning of relationships and causative factors. Personality and socialization processes can be identified. Concepts can be tested and discovered. Cases can be coded and statistical tests applied to provide associations between variables.

Type of Research Design Setting	Central Characteristics	Prospective Outcomes
5. Combined survey and case study *Examples:* E. W. Burgess & Leonard S. Cottrell, Jr., *Predicting Success or Failure in Marriage*; Alfred C. Kinsey & Associates, *Sexual Behavior in the Human Male* and *Sexual Behavior in the Human Female*	Survey methodology is combined with study of specific cases to illuminate relationships first portrayed in a correlational pattern and then interpreted through case study to display processes and patterns. Cases are selected after a survey reveals those that are high or low on a criterion variable or those that display significant characteristics.	Relationships accompanied by process and pattern data revealing personal socialization in greater depth. Two data banks assembled: statistical data and case analysis data.
6. Prediction studies *Examples:* Sheldon Glueck & Eleanor Glueck, *Predicting Delinquency and Crime*; Paul Horst, *The Prediction of Personal Adjustment* (see especially Paul Wallin, "The Prediction of Individual Behavior From Case Studies")	Purpose is to estimate, in advance of participation, the level of an individual's performance in a given activity. Search is made of a population to find factors to serve as basis for prediction of such outcomes as success or failure in marriage, degree of success on parole, finding potential delinquents at an early age, school success, or criminal behavior. A discrete dependent variable is often sought, such as stable marriage vs. broken (divorced) marriage, law abiding vs. criminal behavior, delinquent vs. nondelinquent boys and girls, or academic achievers vs. academic nonachievers.	Relationships between a number of factors and a prediction criterion are determined. Selected factors are weighted in the construction of prognostic tables. Prognostic tables are utilized to make predictions.
7. Controlled experiments (with major types being laboratory, "natural," and field experiment) a. Laboratory *Example:* Robert Bales, *Personality and Interpersonal Behavior*	Investigator creates a situation with the exact conditions wanted and in which he or she controls some and manipulates other variables. Investigator observes and measures the effect of manipulation of independent variables on dependent variables in a situation in which other relevant factors are controlled or, if appropriate, ignored.	Relationships found can be considered more precise as a result of controlling "interfering" variables.
b. "Natural" experiments (such as cross-sectional or ex post facto). *Example:* F. S. Chapin, *Experimental Designs in Sociological Research*	Researcher capitalizes on some ongoing changes in the normal community setting and studies their effect in an experimental design. A treatment or social program may be given to one group of persons and their personal adjustment compared with that of a group of persons without such a program. Matching of groups makes the two groups homogeneous when selected factors are held constant by matching.	Discovers and exposes causal relationships under controlled conditions. Statements of greater rigor are made possible and increased validity of social treatments or programs is demonstrated.
c. Field experiment *Example:* J. G. Miller, *Experiments in Social Process*	Involves manipulation of conditions by the experimenter in order to determine possible causal relations. Maximum variation in the independent and dependent variables is built into the structure of the design. Experimental and control groups are established, holding constant factors believed to interfere with the relationship under study.	Independent variable (treatment) is capable of wide variation; a sensitive or definitive criterion variable is found. Matching data provide the strongest possible control. A causal pattern may be inferred with high confidence.

References

Bales, Robert. (1969). *Personality and interpersonal behavior.* New York: Holt, Rinehart, and Winston.

Blau, Peter M., & Duncan, O. D. (1967). *The American occupational structure.* New York: Wiley.

Burgess, E. W., & Cottrell, Leonard S., Jr. (1998). *Predicting success or failure in marriage.* London: Routledge/Thoemmes Press.

Chapin, F. S. (1974). *Experimental designs in sociological research* (Rev. ed.). Westport, CT: Greenwood.

Cottrell, Fred W. (1971). *The Railroader.* New York: Irvington.

Davis, James A. (1965). *Undergraduate career decisions: Correlates of occupational choice.* Chicago: Aldine.

Duncan, Greg J., & Morgan, James N. (Eds.). (1980). *Five thousand American families: Vol. 8. Analyses of the first eleven years of the Panel Study of Income Dynamics.* Ann Arbor, MI: Survey Research Center, Institute for Social Research, University of Michigan.

Eddy, Elizabeth. (1969). *Becoming a teacher: The passage to professional status.* New York: Teachers College Press.

Glueck, Sheldon, & Glueck, Eleanor. (1959). *Predicting delinquency and crime.* Cambridge, MA: Harvard University Press.

Hammond, Phillip E. (Ed.). (1964). *Sociologists at work: Essays on the craft of social research.* New York: Basic Books.

Hollingshead, August B. (1948). *Elmtown's youth: The impact of social classes on adolescents.* New York: Wiley.

Hollingshead, August B. (1975). *Elmtown's youth and Elmtown revisited.* New York: Wiley.

Horst, Paul. (1941). *The prediction of personal adjustment: A survey of logical problems and research techniques, with illustrative application to problems of vocational selection, school success, marriage, and crime.* New York: Social Science Research Council.

Kinsey, Alfred C., & Associates. (1998). *Sexual behavior in the human female.* Bloomington: Indiana University Press.

Kinsey, Alfred C., Pomeroy, Wardell B., & Martin, Clyde E. (1998). *Sexual behavior in the human male.* Bloomington: Indiana University Press.

Lynd, Robert, & Lynd, Helen. (1975). *Middletown: A study in American culture.* New York: Harcourt, Brace.

Lynd, Robert, & Lynd, Helen. (1982). *Middletown in transition: A study of cultural conflicts.* New York: Harcourt Brace Jovanovich.

Miller, James Grier. (Ed.). (1950). *Experiments in social process: A symposium on social psychology.* New York: McGraw-Hill.

Sewell, William H., & Hauser, Robert M. (1975). *Education, occupation, and earnings: Achievement in the early career.* New York: Academic Press.

Smigel, Erwin O. (1969). *The Wall Street lawyer, a professional organization man?* Bloomington: Indiana University Press.

U.S. Department of Commerce, Bureau of the Census. (various years). *Current population survey.* Washington, DC: Author.

Whyte, William F. (1993). *Street corner society: The social structure of an Italian slum.* Chicago: University of Chicago Press.

Further Readings on Research Design and Selecting a Research Problem

Allwood, Carl Martin, & Barmark, Jan. (1999). The role of research problems in the process of research. *Social Epistemology, 13,* 59-83.

Bailey, Kenneth D. (1999). *Methods of social research.* Collingdale, PA: Diane.

Bechofer, Frank, & Paterson, Lindsay. (2000). *Principles of research design in social sciences.* New York: Routledge.

Garratt, Dean, & Hodkinson, Phil. (1998). Can there be criteria for selecting research criteria? A hermeneutical analysis of an inescapable dilemma. *Qualitative Inquiry, 4,* 515-539.

Grunow, Dieter. (1995). The research design in organization studies: Problems and prospects. *Organization Science, 6,* 93-103.

Hazen, Dan, Horrell, Jeffrey, & Merrill-Oldham, Jan. (1998). *Selecting research collections for digitization.* Washington, DC: Council on Library and Information Resources.

Mitchell, Mark, & Jolley, Janina. (1995). *Research design explained.* Fort Worth: Harcourt College Publishers.

Reiser, Stanley Joel, & Bulger, Ruth Ellen. (1997). The social responsibilities of biological scientists. *Science and Engineering Ethics, 3,* 137-143.

Sasaki, Masamichi. (1995). Research design of cross-national attitudinal surveys. *Behaviormetrika, 22,* 99-114.

Tabachnick, Barbara G., & Fidell, Linda S. (2000). *Computer-assisted research design and analysis.* Needham Heights, MA: Allyn and Bacon.

HOW SCIENCE IS BUILT 2.6

This guide sets forth the canons of science as seen by the behavioral researcher and should be used as a set of signposts to point the direction of and identify the possible difficulties inherent in any scientific exploration. It's like a digest of the philosophy that researchers carry with them, use in their work, and live by amid the ups and downs of a life conducting research.

The three brief essays that follow describe (a) the importance of conceptual definitions and theory formulation in the construction of scientific knowledge (DiRenzo), (b) assumptions underlying the application of the scientific method (Sjoberg and Nett), and (c) dilemmas of the researcher and the distinctiveness of behavioral science (Kaplan). They are all well worth reading as you begin your thinking about research topics and professional activities you would like to pursue.

▶ Importance of Conceptual Definition and Theory Formulation

Gordon J. DiRenzo

Scientific investigation seeks to explain the phenomena it studies in our world of experience; by establishing general principles with which to explain them, hopefully, science can predict such phenomena. The principles of science are stated ultimately in what are known as theories. To explain the facts of reality, scientists require an organized system of concepts. A "science without concepts" is an impossibility—as unthinkable as any form of rational activity without concepts would be. Yet, to say that concepts are indispensable to science is merely to presuppose or to make possible the problems, namely, the definition and formation of the required scientific elements.

Initially, in scientific inquiry, description of phenomena may be stated in a nontechnical vocabulary. The growth of a discipline soon involves the development of a system of speculation, more or less abstract, of concepts and corresponding terminology. Nevertheless, even after decades of definition, and redefinition, many of the fundamental terms in the sciences are far from being distinguished by a universally accepted definition—as much within as outside of particular disciplines. For example, to name just three of the pivotal concepts of the behavioral sciences, there are several denotations for "society," "culture," and "personality." How scientific and technical concepts are introduced and how they function in the scientific process are the central questions here.

Conceptual definition and theory formulation go hand in hand as necessary steps in one unified process of scientific research. The analysis of concepts is but one phase—a fundamental requisite—of that complex process of scientific inquiry which culminates in theory. Concepts, thus, are the irreducible elements of theory or theoretical systems, as the term "theory" has come to be understood more particularly in the behavioral sciences. The more precise and refined the conceptual elements, the more precise and refined the theory.

The question to which we are addressing ourselves is a fundamental one for all areas of scientific inquiry.

SOURCE: From Gordon J. DiRenzo (Ed.) (1967), *Concepts, Theory, and Explanation in the Behavioral Sciences* (New York: Random House). Reprinted with permission.

▶ Assumptions Underlying the Application of the Scientific Method

Gideon Sjoberg and Roger Nett

A minimum set of assumptions (often left unstated) which underlie the application of the scientific method are (1) that there exists a definite order of recurrence of events, (2) that knowledge is superior to ignorance, (3) that a communication tie, based upon sense impressions, exists between the scientist and "external reality" (the so-called "empirical assumption"), and (4) that there are cause-and-effect relationships within the physical and the social orders. Moreover, (5) there are certain "observer" assumptions: (a) that the observer is driven to attain knowledge by his desire to ameliorate human conditions, (b) that the observer has the capacity to conceptually relate observations and impute meanings to events, and (c) that society will sustain the observer in his pursuit of knowledge. These assumptions, which the scientist more or less takes for granted, are in the last analysis largely understandable as "functional fictions." Their usefulness in the acquisition of knowledge is the primary raison d'être.

The Assumption of Order in the "Natural" World

Science, insofar as it seeks to generalize and predict, depends upon the existence of some degree of order in the physical or social world under study. That which it cannot describe as a manifestation of regularity it must define as some describable departure from regularity. Such reasoning assumes that events are ordered along certain dimensions. To be sure, all systems of knowledge rest upon the assumption of order in the universe, but this may be of greater significance for science than for other systems of knowledge. After all, scientists spend most of their time differentiating among classes of relative uniformity and relating these one to another. Even within a rapidly changing, revolutionary system there is a degree of order. And change itself displays patterns that can be described and analyzed.

The assumption of order leads the social scientist, if he is to remain a scientist, to eschew historicism. Those who advocate the historicist position in its extreme form assume that every cultural system must be studied as a separate entity and that, moreover, no regularities obtain across cultures. Of course, even the historicist admits there is a uniformity of sorts, for he recognizes that each system has its own laws of development.

The notion of order is closely related to the concept of a "natural universe." In our sketch of the history of science, we observed that a major breakthrough occurred when scholars were able to conceive of the physical and social environments in naturalistic terms, that is, as functioning independently of factors in the spiritual realm. This was an essential step in modern man's development of the means to manipulate and positively control aspects of the social and physical spheres.

In light of the evidence, it would be a mistake to confuse scientifically based knowledge with wisdom, as did some of the utopian thinkers of the nineteenth century. Wisdom involves sound ethical direction, the exercise of good taste, and distinguishing the worthwhile from the not so worthwhile.

The scientific method (in the narrow sense) does not tell us how to use empirically verified knowledge other than to further the ends of science; however, by utilizing more of the empirically validated knowledge and less of the unverified and often flat knowledge of other epistemologies the cause of humanity may be advanced.

SOURCE: From Gideon Sjoberg and Roger Nett (1968), *A Methodology for the Social Researcher* (New York: Harper & Row), pp. 30-31. Reprinted by permission of Waveland Press, Inc. 1968 (reissued 1997). All rights reserved.

▶ Dilemmas of the Researcher and the Distinctiveness of Behavioral Science

Abraham Kaplan

Dilemmas

In the conduct of inquiry we are continuously subjected to pulls in opposite directions: to search for data or to formulate hypotheses, to construct theories or to perform experiments, to focus on general laws or on individual cases, to conduct molar studies or molecular ones, to engage in synthesis or in analysis. It is seldom of much help, in the concrete, to be told that we must do both. In the constraints of specific problematic situations these are genuine dilemmas. But they are a species of what have come to be known as existential dilemmas: not characteristic of some special historical situation but intrinsic to the pursuit of truth. We do not make a choice of the lesser of two evils and abide by the unhappy outcome. The problems which the existential dilemmas pose cannot be solved at all, but only coped with; which is to say, we learn to live with them. "We need hard workers and empiricism, not inspiration," it is urged with good reason. But equally good reason can also be given for the converse. The fact is, we need all we can get. This state of affairs is in no way peculiar to behavioral science. Its methodology, as I see it, is not different from that of any other science whatever. If this identity is contemplated in speaking of "the scientific method," I warmly approve of the usage.

The Specialty of Behavioral Science

What is distinctive of behavioral science, therefore, is basically its subject-matter; the techniques that the subject-matter permits or demands are only derivative. If some single discriminant of this subject-matter is called for, I believe the most generally applicable one is that suggested by C. W. Morris: the use of "signs." Behavioral science deals with those processes in which symbols, or at any rate meanings, play an essential part. Just how broadly "meaning" is to be construed, and how much of animal behavior it comprises even in its broadest construction, are questions which need not trouble us here. There is no doubt that behavioral science spills over into biology however we choose to circumscribe its limits. But this difficulty is more administrative (for foundations, librarians, and deans) than methodological.

What is significant here is that the data for behavioral science are not sheer movements but actions—that is, acts performed in a perspective which gives them meaning or purpose. Plainly, it is of crucial importance that we distinguish between the meaning of the act to the actor (or to other people, including ourselves, reacting with him) and its meaning to us as scientists, taking the action as subject-matter. I call these, respectively, act meaning and action meaning. I shall return to this distinction later; for the present, we may note that behavioral science is involved in a double process of interpretation, and it is this which is responsible for such of its techniques as are distinctive. The behavioral scientist must first arrive at an act meaning, that is, construe what conduct a particular piece of behavior represents; and then he must search for the meaning of the interpreted action, its interconnections with other actions or circumstances. He must first see the act of marking a ballot or operating a machine as the action of casting a vote, and then pursue his study of voting behavior.

Now although interpretation for act meanings usually involves special techniques, these are subject to the same methodological norms that govern interpretation for action meanings (and thereby other sciences as well). We interpret speech-acts (in our own language) without any special effort—indeed, usually without any awareness at all of the acts as acts (we do not hear the words, but what is said). Yet every such interpretation is a hypothesis, every reply an experiment —we may, after all, have misunderstood. When it comes to interpreting foreign languages, and in general to interpreting the patterns of another culture, the situation becomes clearer, though it is essentially no different. Some implications of this state of affairs will be explored in connection with the role of "verstehen" in behavioral science. The point I am making here is that the behavioral scientist seeks to understand behavior in just the same sense that the physicist, say, seeks to understand nuclear processes. The difference is not that there are two kinds of understanding but that the behavioral scientist has two different things to understand: for instance, a psychiatrist needs to understand why a patient makes certain noises (to tell his therapist how much he hates him), and why he says the things he does (because he has not yet worked through the transference). Admittedly, we have special ways of understanding noises, because we are ourselves human; but for the same reason, we also have special ways of interpreting light waves, but need quite other techniques for radio waves. The point is that even what we see is not always to be believed. Every technique is subject to validation, and the same norms apply to all of them.

SOURCE: Abraham Kaplan (1964), *The Conduct of Inquiry* (San Francisco: Chandler), pp. 30-33. Reprinted with permission of Transaction Publishers.

Further Readings on the Scientific Method and Scientific Theory

Carey, Stephen S. (1997). *A beginner's guide to scientific method.* Belmont, CA: Wadsworth.

Gruender, David. (1998). Values and the philosophy of science. *Protosociology, 12,* 319-333.

Gustavsen, Bjorn. (1996). Is theory useful? *Concepts and Transformation, 1,* 63-77.

Klovdahl, Alden S. (1995). Levels of protection: Confidentiality in network research. *BMS, Bulletin de Methodologie Sociologique, 48,* 120-132.

Lee, Jeffrey A. (1999). *The scientific endeavor.* Menlo Park, CA: Benjamin Cummings.

Longhin, Luigi. (1998). The objectivity of scientific knowledge in the intersystemic approach. *Fenomenologia e Societa, 21,* 74-90.

Nola, Robert, & Sankey, Howard. (1999). *After Popper, Kuhn and Feyerabend: Recent issues in theories of scientific method*. Norwood, NJ: Kluwer Academic.

Poole, Darryl G., & Pickard, Ruth B. (1986). *Disciplinary change and sociological practice: An historical and integrative view*. Paper presented at the meeting of the American Sociological Association.

Sklar, Lawrence. (Ed.). (1999). *The philosophy of science: Vol. 2. The nature of scientific theory*. New York: Garland.

Taylor, Jan. (1987). Retrieval and reconstruction: A sense of purpose for the social sciences. *New Zealand Sociology, 2*, 98-111.

Weinberg, Steven. (1995). The methods of science . . . and those by which we live. *Academic Questions, 8*, 7-13.

THE IMPACT OF SOCIOLOGICAL THEORY ON EMPIRICAL RESEARCH 2.7

Few researchers in the social sciences would doubt that their basic and empirical research have an important and complex and almost symbiotic relationship. For example, Robert K. Merton, in the excerpt that follows this section, describes the impact that theories can have on empirical research and says that the "notion of directed research implies that, in part, empirical inquiry is so organized that if and when empirical uniformities are discovered, they have direct consequences for a theoretic system."

Note the functions of theory that Merton sets forth. The researcher must often formulate "middle-range" or miniature theories that will link hypotheses to a more inclusive, larger theory. On the same relationship, Zetterberg (1954) has written that our purpose is to create general theories and that miniature theories help to identify and generate convenient research problems. These miniature theories "will in part be made up by means of miniature theories, experimental evidence supporting a miniature theory will support also the inclusive theory of which the miniature theory is a special case" (p. 15).

Other scholars from different disciplines recognize the importance of the theory-data relationship as well. Milton Friedman, a Nobel Laureate in economics, has listed the following criteria for significant theory:

A theory is "simpler" the less initial knowledge is needed to make a prediction within a given field of phenomena; it is the more "fruitful" the more precise the resulting prediction, the wider the area within which the theory yields predictions, and the more additional lines for further research it suggests. . . . The only relevant test of the validity of a hypothesis is comparison of prediction with experience. (Friedman, 1953, p. 10)

References

Friedman, Milton. (1953). The methodology of positive economics. In *Essays in positive economics*. Chicago: University of Chicago Press.

Merton, Robert K. (1957). The bearing of sociological theory on empirical research. In *Social theory and social structure*. Glencoe, IL: Free Press.

Zetterberg, Hans L. (1954). *On theory and verification in sociology*. New York: Tressler.

▶ Empirical Generalizations in Sociology

Robert K. Merton

Not infrequently it is said that the object of sociological theory is to arrive at statements of so-cial uniformities. This is an elliptical assertion and hence requires clarification. For there are two types of statements of sociological uniformities that differ significantly in their bearing on theory. The first of these is the empirical generalization: an isolated proposition summarizing observed uniformities of relationships between two or more variables.[1] The sociological literature abounds with such generalizations that have not been assimilated to sociological theory. Thus, Engel's "laws" of consumption may be cited as examples. So, too, the Halbwachs' finding that la-borers spend more per adult unit for food than white-collar employees of the same income class.[2] Such generalizations may be of greater or less precision, but this does not affect their logi-cal place in the structure of inquiry. The Groves-Ogburn finding, for a sample of American cities, that "cities with a larger percentage engaged in manufacturing also have, on the average, slightly larger percentages of young persons married" has been expressed in an equation indi-cating the degree of this relationship. Although propositions of this order are essential in empiri-cal research, a miscellany of such propositions only provides the raw materials for sociology as a discipline. The theoretic task, and the orientation of empirical research toward theory, first be-gins when the bearing of such uniformities on a set of interrelated propositions is tentatively es-tablished. The notion of directed research implies that, in part,[3] empirical inquiry is so organized that if and when empirical uniformities are discovered, they have direct consequences for a theo-retic system. Insofar as the research is directed, the rationale of findings is set forth before the findings are obtained.

Sociological Theory

The second type of sociological generalization, the so-called scientific law, differs from the foregoing inasmuch as it is a statement of invariance derivable from a theory. The paucity of such laws in the sociological field perhaps reflects the prevailing bifurcation of theory and empirical research. Despite the many volumes dealing with the history of sociological theory and despite the plethora of empirical investigations, sociologists (including the writer) may discuss the logi-cal criteria of sociological laws without citing a single instance that fully satisfies these criteria.[4]

Approximations to these criteria are not entirely wanting. To exhibit the relations of empirical generalizations to theory and to set forth the functions of theory, it may be useful to examine a fa-miliar case in which such generalizations were incorporated into a body of substantive theory. Thus, it has long been established as a statistical uniformity that, in a variety of populations, Cath-olics have a lower suicide rate than Protestants.[5] In this form the uniformity posed a theoretical problem. It merely constituted an empirical regularity that would become significant for theory only if it could be derived from a set of other propositions, a task that Durkheim set himself. If we restate his theoretic assumptions in formal fashion, the paradigm of his theoretic analysis be-comes clear:

- Social cohesion provides support to group members subjected to acute stresses and anxi-eties.
- Suicide rates are functions of unrelieved anxieties and stresses to which persons are sub-jected.
- Catholics have greater social cohesion than Protestants.
- Therefore, lower suicide rates should be anticipated among Catholics than among Protes-tants.[6]

This case serves to locate the place of empirical generalizations in relation to theory and to illustrate the several functions of theory.

1. It indicates that theoretic pertinence is not inherently present or absent in empirical generalizations but appears when the generalization is conceptualized in abstractions of higher order (Catholicism–social cohesion–relieved anxieties–suicide rate) that are embodied in more general statements of relationships.[7] What was initially taken as an isolated uniformity is restated as a relation, not between religious affiliation and behavior, but between groups with certain conceptualized attributes (social cohesion) and the behavior. The *scope* of the original empirical finding is considerably extended, and several seemingly disparate uniformities are seen to be interrelated (thus differentials in suicide rates between married and single persons can be derived from the same theory).

2. Once having established the theoretic pertinence of a uniformity by deriving it from a set of interrelated propositions, we provide for the *cumulation* both of theory and of research findings. The differentials-in-suicide-rate uniformities add confirmation to the set of propositions from which they—and other uniformities—have been derived. This is a major function of *systematic theory*.

3. Whereas the empirical uniformity did not lend itself to the drawing of diverse consequences, the reformulation gives rise to various consequences in fields of conduct quite remote from that of suicidal behavior. For example, inquiries into obsessive behavior, morbid preoccupations, and other maladaptive behavior have found these also to be related to inadequacies of group cohesion.[8] The conversion of empirical uniformities into theoretic statements thus increases the *fruitfulness* of research through the successive exploration of implications.

4. By providing a rationale, the theory introduces a *ground for prediction* that is more secure than mere empirical extrapolation from previously observed trends. Thus, should independent measures indicate a decrease of social cohesion among Catholics, the theorist would predict a tendency toward increased rates of suicide in this group. The atheoretic empiricist would have no alternative, however, but to predict on the basis of extrapolation.

5. The foregoing list of functions presupposes one further attribute of theory that is not altogether true of the Durkheim formulation and which gives rise to a general problem that has peculiarly beset sociological theory, at least, up to the present. If theory is to be productive, it must be sufficiently *precise to be determinate*. Precision is an integral element of the criterion of *testability*. The prevailing pressure toward the utilization of statistical data in sociology, whenever possible, to control and test theoretic inferences has a justifiable basis, when we consider the logical place of precision in disciplined inquiry.

The more precise the inferences (predictions) that can be drawn from a theory, the less the likelihood of *alternative* hypotheses that will be adequate to these predictions. In other words, precise predictions and data serve to reduce the *empirical* bearing upon research of the *logical* fallacy of affirming the consequent.[9] It is well known that verified predictions derived from a theory do not prove or demonstrate that theory; they merely supply a measure of confirmation, for it is always possible that alternative hypotheses drawn from different theoretic systems can also account for the predicted phenomena.[10] But those theories that admit of precise predictions confirmed by observation take on strategic importance since they provide an initial basis for choice between competing hypotheses. In other words, precision enhances the likelihood of approximating a "crucial" observation or experiment.

The internal coherence of a theory has much the same function, for if a variety of empirically confirmed consequences are drawn from one theoretic system, this reduces the likelihood that competing theories can adequately account for the same data. The integrated theory sustains a larger measure of confirmation than is the case with distinct and unrelated hypotheses, thus accumulating a greater weight of evidence.

Both pressures—toward precision and logical coherence—can lead to unproductive activity, particularly in the social sciences. Any procedure can be abused as well as used. A premature insistence on precision at all costs may sterilize imaginative hypotheses. It may lead to a reformulation of the scientific problem in order to permit measurement with, at times, the result that the subsequent materials do not bear on the initial problem in hand.[11] In the search for precision, care must be taken to see that significant problems are not thus inadvertently blotted from view. Similarly, the pressure for logical consistency has at times invited logomachy and sterile theorizing, inasmuch as the assumptions contained in the system of analysis are so far removed from empirical referents or involve such high abstractions as not to permit of empirical inquiry.[12] But warrant for these criteria of inquiry is not vitiated by such abuses.

Notes

1. This usage of the term "empirical" is common, as Dewey notes. In this context, "*empirical* means that the subject-matter of a given proposition which has existential inference, represents merely a set of uniform confunctions of traits repeatedly observed to exist, without any understanding of *why* the confunction occurs; without a theory which states its rationale." John Dewey, *Logic: The Theory of Inquiry* (New York: Henry Holt, 1938), 305.

2. See a considerable collection of such uniformities summarized by C. C. Zimmerman, *Consumption and Standards of Living* (New York: Van Nostrand, 1936), 55ff.

3. "In part," if only because it stultifies the possibilities of obtaining fertile new findings to confine researches *wholly* to the test of predetermined hypotheses. Hunches originating in the course of the inquiry that may not have immediately obvious implications for a broader theoretic system may eventuate in the discovery of empirical uniformities that can later be incorporated into a theory. For example, in the sociology of political behavior, it has been recently established that the larger the number of social cross-pressures to which voters are subjected, the less interest they exhibit in a presidential election (P. F. Lazarsfeld, Bernard Berelson, and Hazel Gaudet, *The People's Choice* [New York: Duell, Sloan & Pearce, 1944], 56-64). This finding, which was wholly unanticipated when the research was first formulated, may well initiate new lines of systematic inquiry into political behavior, even though it is not yet integrated into a generalized theory. Fruitful empirical research not only tests theoretically derived hypotheses; it also originates new hypotheses. This might be termed the "serendipity" component of research, i.e., the discovery, by chance or sagacity, of valid results that were not sought for.

4. E.g., see the discussion by George A. Lundberg, "The Concept of Law in the Social Sciences," *Philosophy of Science* 5 (1938): 189-203, which affirms the possibility of such laws without including any case in point. The book by K. D. Har, *Social Laws* (Chapel Hill: University of North Carolina Press, 1930), does not fulfill the promise implicit in the title. A panel of social scientists discussing the possibility of obtaining social laws finds it difficult to instance cases. Herbert Blumer, *An Appraisal of Thomas and Znaniecki's The Polish Peasant in Europe and America* (New York: Social Science Research Council, 1939), 142-50.

5. It need hardly be said that this statement assumes that education, income, nationality, rural-urban residence, and other factors that might render this finding spurious have been held constant.

6. We need not examine further aspects of this illustration, e.g. (1) the extent to which we have adequately stated the premises implicit in Durkheim's interpretation; (2) the supplementary theoretic analysis that would take these premises not as given but as problematic; (3) the grounds on which the potentially infinite regression of theoretic interpretations is halted at one rather than another point; (4) the problems involved in the introduction of such intervening variables as social cohesion that are not directly measured; (5) the extent to which the premises have been empirically confirmed; (6) the comparatively low order of abstraction represented by this illustration; and (7) the fact that Durkheim derived several empirical generalizations from this same set of hypotheses.

7. Veblen has put this with typical cogency: "All this may seem like taking pains about trivialities. But the data with which any scientific inquiry has to do are trivialities in some other bearing than that one in which they are of account." Thorstein Veblen, *The Place of Science in Modern Civilization* (New York: Russell & Russell, 1961), 42.

8. See, e.g., Elton Mayo, *Human Problems of an Industrial Civilization* (New York: Macmillan, 1933), 113 and passim. The theoretical framework utilized in the studies of industrial morale by Whitehead, Roethlisberger, and Disckson stemmed appreciably from the Durkheim formulation, as the authors testify.

9. The paradigm of "proof through prediction" is, of course, logically fallacious: If *A* (hypothesis), then *B* (prediction).

B is observed.

Therefore, *A* is true.

This is not overdisturbing for scientific research, inasmuch as other than formal criteria are involved.

10. As a case in point, consider that different theorists had predicted war and internecine conflict on a large scale at midcentury. Sorokin and some Marxists, for example, set forth this prediction on the basis of quite distinct theoretic systems. The actual outbreak of large-scale conflicts does not in itself enable us to choose between these schemes of analysis, if only because the observed fact is consistent with both. Only if the predictions had been so *specified*, had been so precise, that the actual occurrences coincided with the one prediction and not with the other, would a determinate test have been instituted.

11. Stuart A. Rice comments on this tendency in public opinion research; see *Eleven Twenty-six: A Decade of Social Science Research*, ed. Louis Wirth (Chicago: University of Chicago, 1940), 167.

12. It is this practice to which Walker refers, in the field of economics, as "theoretic blight." E. Ronald Walker, *From Economic Theory to Policy* (Chicago: University of Chicago, 1943), chap. 4.

SOURCE: From Robert K. Merton (1957), "The Bearing of Sociological Theory on Empirical Research," in *Social Theory and Social Structure* (Glencoe, IL: Free Press), pp. 95-99. Copyright 1949 by The Free Press, copyright 1957 by The Free Press, A Corporation. Reprinted with permission of the publisher.

BRIDGING THE GAP BETWEEN THE LANGUAGES OF THEORY AND RESEARCH `2.8`

Countless advisers have told their students that words have meaning, and that students should say what they mean and mean what they say. This is no more true than when one starts dealing with the language of research and the associated jargon that we have all had to deal with. Especially when it comes to theory and the research that investigates it, language plays a particularly important role, as discussed below by Blalock.

▶ Causal Inferences in Non-Experimental Research

Hubert M. Blalock, Jr.

1. Owing to the inherent nature of the scientific method, there is a gap between the languages of theory and research. Causal inferences belong on the theoretical level, whereas actual research can only establish covariations and temporal sequences.

2. As a result, we can never actually demonstrate causal laws empirically. This is true even where experimentation is possible. Causal laws are working assumptions of the scientist, involving hypothetical statements of the if-then variety.

3. One admits that causal thinking belongs completely on the theoretical level and that causal laws can never be demonstrated empirically. But this does not mean that it is not helpful to think causally and to develop causal models that have implications that are indirectly testable. In working with these models it will be necessary to make use of a whole series of untestable simplifying assumptions, so that even when a given model yields correct empirical predictions, this does not mean that its correctness can be demonstrated.

Reality, or at least our perception of reality, admittedly consists of ongoing processes. No two events are ever exactly repeated, nor does any object or organism remain precisely the same from one moment to the next.[1] And yet, if we are ever to understand the nature of the real world, we must act and think as though events are repeated and as if objects do have properties that remain constant for some period of time, however short. Unless we permit ourselves to make such simple types of assumptions, we shall never be able to generalize beyond the simple and unique event.

4. The point we are emphasizing is that no matter how elaborate the design, certain simplifying assumptions must always be made. In particular, we must at some point assume that the effects of confounding factors are negligible. Randomization helps to rule out some of such variables, but the plausibility of this particular kind of simplifying assumption is always a question of degree. We wish to underscore this fact in order to stress the underlying similarity between the logic of making causal inferences on the basis of experimental and nonexperimental designs.

Note

1. This particular point is emphasized in Karl Pearson's classic, *The Grammar of Science* (New York: Meridian, 1957), chap. 5.

SOURCE: From Hubert M. Blalock, Jr. (1964), *Causal Inferences in Non-Experimental Research* (Chapel Hill: University of North Carolina Press), pp. 172-73, 6-7, and 26. Reprinted with permission.

Further Readings on Social Theory

Jacobsen, Chanoch, & Bronson, Richard. (1995). Computer simulations and empirical testing of sociological theory. *Sociological Methods and Research*, *23*, 479-506.

McLennan, Gregor. (1995). After postmodernism—back to sociological theory? *Sociology*, *29*, 117-132.

Ritzer, George. (1999). *Modern sociological theory*. New York: McGraw-Hill.

Ritzer, George. (2000). *Classical sociological theory* (3rd ed.). Boston: McGraw-Hill.

Wallace, Ruth A., & Wolf, Alison. (1999). *Contemporary sociological theory: Expanding the classical tradition*. Upper Saddle River, NJ: Prentice Hall.

Zeitlin, Irving M. (1996). *Ideology and the development of sociological theory*. Upper Saddle River, NJ: Prentice Hall.

2.9 CRITERIA FOR JUDGING THE USEFULNESS OF A HYPOTHESIS

Unless a hypothesis can be tested, it is useless. In the following section, William J. Goode and Paul K. Hatt present a step-by-step method for evaluating hypotheses against a set of criteria. Note that there is an emphasis that a hypothesis should be related to a body of theory.

To be complete in our thinking however, we also have to attend to the verification of the results of the test of the hypothesis. Zetterberg has stated three criteria for the acceptance of a working hypothesis, that

1. the empirical data were found to be arranged in the manner predicted by the working hypothesis,
2. we question the null hypothesis within a certain range of probability, and
3. we have disproved alternate hypotheses to the one that is being tested.

▶ **Methods in Social Research**

William J. Goode and Paul K. Hatt

1. *The hypotheses must be conceptually clear.* The concepts should be clearly defined, operationally if possible. Moreover, they should be definitions that are commonly accepted and communicable rather than the products of a "private world."

What to do: One simple device for clarifying concepts is to write out a list of the concepts used in the research outline. Then try to define them (a) in words, (b) in terms of particular operations (index calculations, types of observations, etc.), and (c) with reference to other concepts to be found in previous research. Talk over each concept with fellow students and other researchers in the field. It will often be found that supposedly simple concepts contain many meanings. Then it is possible to decide which is the desired referent.

2. *Hypotheses should have empirical referents.* It has also been previously pointed out that scientific concepts must have an ultimate empirical referent. No usable hypothesis can embody moral judgments. Such statements as "criminals are no worse than businessmen," "women should pursue a career," or "capitalists exploit their workers" are no more usable hypotheses than is the familiar proposition that "pigs are well named because they are so dirty" or the classical question, "How many yards of buttermilk are required to make a pair of breeches for a black bull?" In other words, while a hypothesis may involve the study of value judgments, such a goal must be separated from a moral preachment or a plea for acceptance of one's values.

What to do: First, analyze the concepts that express attitudes rather than describe or refer to empirical phenomena. Watch for key words such as "ought," "should," "bad," etc. Then transform the notions into more useful concepts. "Bad parents" is a value term, but the researcher may have a definite description in mind: parents who follow such practices as whimsical and arbitrary authoritarianism, inducing psychic insecurity in the child, failure to give love, etc. "Should" is also a value term, but the student may simply mean, "If women do not pursue a career, we can predict emotional difficulties when the children leave home, or we can predict that the society will not be able to produce as much goods," etc. When, instead, we find that our referent is simply a vague feeling and we cannot define the operations needed to observe it, we should study the problem further and discover what it is that we really wish to investigate.

3. *The hypotheses must be specific.* That is, all the operations and predictions indicated by it should be spelled out. The possibility of actually testing the hypothesis can thus be appraised. Often hypotheses are expressed in such general terms, and with so grandiose a scope, that they are simply not testable. Because of their magnitude, such grand ideas are tempting because they seem impressive and important. It is better for the student to avoid such problems and instead develop his skills upon more tangible notions.

By making all the concepts and operations explicit is meant not only conceptual clarity but a description of any indexes to be used. Thus, to hypothesize that the degree of vertical social mobility is decreasing in the United States requires the use of indexes. [At present there are many operational definitions of the status levels that define mobility. Therefore, the hypothesis must include a statement of the index that is to be used; see Part 6 for available indexes.]

Such specific formulations have the advantage of assuring that research is practicable and significant, in advance of the expenditure of effort. It furthermore increases the validity of the results, since the broader the terms the easier it is to fall into the trap of using selective evidence. The fame of most prophets and fortune-tellers lies in their ability to state predictions so that almost any occurrence can be interpreted as a fulfillment. We can express this in almost statistical terms: the more specific the prediction, the smaller the chance that the prediction will actually be borne out as a result of mere accident. Scientific predictions or hypotheses must, then, avoid the trap of selective evidence by being as definite and specific as possible.

What to do: Never be satisfied with a general prediction, if it can be broken into more precise subhypotheses. The general prediction of war is not enough, for example: we must specify time, place, and participants. Predicting the general decline of a civilization is not a hypothesis for testing a theory. Again, we must be able to specify and measure the forces, specify the meaning and time of decline, the population segments involved, etc. Often this can be done by conceptual analysis and the formulation of related hypotheses: e.g., we may predict that urbanization is accompanied by a decline in fertility. However, we gain in precision if we attempt to define our indexes of urbanization; specify which segments will be affected, and how much (since in the United States the various ethnic and religious segments are affected differently); specify the amount of fertility decline, and the type (percentage childless, net reproduction rate, etc.). Forming subhypotheses (1) clarifies the relationship between the data sought and the conclusions; and (2) makes the specific research task more manageable.

4. *Hypotheses should be related to available techniques.* Earlier, the point was repeatedly made that theory and method are not opposites. The theorist who does not know what techniques are available to test his hypotheses is in a poor way to formulate usable questions.

This is not to be taken as an absolute injunction against the formulation of hypotheses that at present are too complex to be handled by contemporary technique. It is merely a sensible requirement to apply to any problem in its early stages in order to judge its researchability.

There are some aspects of the impossible hypothesis that may make its formulation worth while. If the problem is significant enough as a possible frame of reference, it may be useful whether or not it can be tested at the time. The socioeconomic hypotheses of Marx, for example, were not proved by his data. The necessary techniques were not available either then or now. Nevertheless, Marxian frameworks are an important source of more precise, smaller, verifiable propositions. This is true for much of Emile Durkheim's work on suicide. His related formulations concerning social cohesion have also been useful. The work of both men has been of paramount importance to sociology, even though at the time their larger ideas were not capable of being handled by available techniques.

Furthermore, posing the impossible question may stimulate the growth of technique. Certainly some of the impetus toward modern developments in technique has come from criticisms against significant studies that were considered inadequate because of technical limitations. In any serious sociological discussion, research frontiers are continuously challenged by the assertion that various problems "ought" to be investigated even though the investigations are presently impossible.

What to do: Look for research articles on the subject being investigated. Make a list of the various techniques that have been used to measure the factors of importance in the study. If you are unable to locate any discussion of technique, you may find it wiser to do research on the necessary research techniques. You may, instead, decide that this lack of techniques means your problem is too large and general for your present resources.

Some items, such as stratification or race attitudes, have been studied by many techniques. Try to discover why one technique is used in one case and not in another. Note how refinements in technique have been made, and see whether one of these may be more useful for your purposes. Look for criticisms of previous research, so as to understand the weaknesses in the procedures followed.

Again, other problems may have been studied with few attempts at precise measurement. Study the literature to see why this is the case. Ascertain whether some subareas (for example, of religious behavior) may be attacked with techniques used in other areas (for example, attitude measurement, stratification measures, research on choice making, etc.).

5. *The hypothesis should be related to a body of theory.* This criterion is one which is often overlooked by the beginning student. He is more likely to select subject matter that is "interesting," without finding out whether the research will really help to refute, qualify, or support any ex-

isting theories of social relations. A science, however, can be cumulative only by building on an existing body of fact and theory. It cannot develop if each study is an isolated survey.

Although it is true that the clearest examples of crescive theoretical development are to be found in the physical and biological sciences, the process can also be seen in the social sciences. One such case is the development of a set of generalizations concerning the social character of intelligence. The anthropological investigations at the end of the nineteenth century uncovered the amazing variety of social customs in various societies, while demonstrating conclusively that there were a number of common elements in social life: family systems, religious patterns, an organization of the socialization process, etc.

The French school of sociology, including Lucien Lévy-Bruhl, Emile Durkheim, Marcel Mauss, Henri Hubert, and others, formulated a series of propositions, at the turn of the century, which suggested that the intellectual structure of the human mind is determined by the structure of the society. That is, perception and thought are determined by society, not alone by the anatomical structure of our eyes, ears, and other senses. Modes of thought vary from society to society. Some of these formulations were phrased in an extreme form that need not concern us now, and they were often vague. Nevertheless, the idea was growing that the intelligence of a Polynesian native could not be judged by European standards; his thinking was qualitatively, not merely quantitatively, different.

At the same time, however, better techniques were being evolved for measuring "intelligence," which came to be standardized in the form of scores on various IQ tests. When these were applied to different groups it became clear that the variation in IQ was great; children of Italian immigrants made lower grades on such tests, as did Negroes. Northern Negroes made higher grades than whites from many Southern states. American children of Chinese and Japanese parents made rather high scores. Since it was generally assumed that these tests measured "innate intelligence," these data were sometimes generalized to suggest that certain "racial" groups were by nature inferior and others superior.

However, such conclusions were opposed on rational grounds, and liberal sentiments suggested that they be put to the test. There were, then, two major sets of conclusions, one suggesting that intelligence is in the main determined by social experience, the other suggesting that the IQ is innately determined. To test such opposing generalizations, a research design was needed for testing logical expectations in more specific situations. If, for example, it is true that the intelligence of individuals who are members of "inferior" groups is really determined biologically, then changes in their environments should not change their IQ. If, on the other hand, the social experience is crucial, we should expect that such changes in social experience would result in definite patterns of IQ change.

Further deductions are possible. If identical twins are separated and are placed in radically different social experiences at an early age, we might expect significant differences in IQ. Or, if a group of rural Negro children moves from the poor school and social experience of the South to the somewhat more stimulating environment of the North, the group averages would be expected to change somewhat. Otto Klineberg, in a classic study, carried out the latter research. He traced Negro children of various ages after they had moved to the North and found that, in general, the earlier the move to the North occurred, the greater the average rise in the IQ. The later the move, the smaller the increase. Even if one assumes that the "better," more able, and more daring adult Negroes made this move, this does not explain the differences by time of movement. Besides, of course, the subjects were children at the time of the migration.[1]

In this research design a particular result was predicted by a series of deductions from a larger set of generalizations. Further, the prediction was actually validated. In justice to the great number of scholars who have been engaged in refining and developing IQ tests, it should be mentioned that other tests and investigations of a similar order have been carried out by many anthropologists, sociologists, and social psychologists. They do not invalidate the notion that IQ is based in part on "innate" abilities, but they do indicate that to a great extent these abilities must be stimulated by certain types of experience in order to achieve high scores on such tests.

From even so sketchy an outline of a theoretical development as the foregoing is, it can be seen that when research is systematically based upon a body of existing theory, a genuine contribution in knowledge is more likely to result. In other words, to be worth doing, a hypothesis must not only be carefully stated, but it should possess theoretical relevance.

What to do: First, of course, cover the literature relating to your subject. If it is impossible to do so, then your hypothesis probably covers too much ground. Second, try to abstract from the literature the way in which various propositions and sets of propositions relate to one another (for example, the literature relating to Sutherland's theory of differential association in criminology, the conditions for maximum morale in factories, or the studies of prediction of marital adjustment). Third, ascertain whether you can deduce any of the propositions, including your own hypothesis, from one another or from a small set of major statements. Fourth, test it by some theoretical model, such as Merton's "Paradigm for Functional Analysis in Sociology" (*Social Theory and Social Structure*, pp. 50-54), to see whether you have left out major propositions and determinants. Fifth, especially compare your own set of related propositions with those of some classic author, such as Weber on bureaucracy or Durkheim on suicide. If you find this task of abstraction difficult, compare instead with the propositions of these men as explained by a systematic interpreter such as Talcott Parsons in his *Structure of Social Action*. What is important is that, whatever the source of your hypothesis, it must be logically derivable from and based upon a set of related sociological propositions.

Note

1. Otto Klineberg, *Negro Intelligence and Selective Migration* (New York: Columbia University Press, 1935).

SOURCE: William J. Goode and Paul K. Hatt (1962), *Methods in Social Research* (New York: McGraw-Hill), pp. 68-73.

Readings on Theory and Research

Fawcett, Jacqueline. (1999). *Relationship of theory and research*. Philadelphia: F. A. Davis.

Gelso, Charles J., & Hayes, Jeffrey A. (1998). *The psychotherapy relationship: Theory, research, and practice*. New York: John Wiley & Sons.

Mongardini, Carlo, & Tabboni, Simonetta. (Eds.). *Robert K. Merton and contemporary sociology*. Unpublished manuscript, Department of Political Studies, University Roma "La Sapienza."

2.10 SCIENCE: SIMULTANEOUSLY OBSERVATIONAL, EXPERIMENTAL, AND HISTORICAL

Determining what method to use to investigate a particular research question of interest is always a challenge to the beginning scientist. Decisions regarding whether historical analysis, statistical sampling, qualitative structured observation, controlled experimentation, or other techniques are needed are difficult and depend to a large extent on the experience of the researchers who are involved.

In the following, Raymond Siever, a physical scientist, describes varieties and styles of science and stresses the importance of the problem and its relation to the scientific method.

▶ **Science: Observational, Experimental, Historical**

Raymond Siever

A question that has concerned many scientists for about as long as sciences started to differentiate from each other is, "Are there different sciences or is there just one science?" A related question can be put, "Is there a scientific method, or are there many scientific methods?" Discussion of these points is usually obfuscated by the speaker's background, in particular, what science he happens to be doing at the moment. It also, of course, is characteristically confused by mixing subject matter with the way in which an investigation is carried out. I will give my idea of how the different conventional groupings of sciences relate to each other and propose some answers to the question of whether there is just one science or many. It is not that these ideas are new. It is more that we need to remind ourselves of our philosophical underpinnings, especially now that branches of science have become more specialized and yet at the same time have joined together in attacks on complex systems.

Observational Versus Experimental

The distinction between an observational science and an experimental science is often made. In this context in some people's language, the word "observational" is associated with the thought "solely descriptive" and the word "experimental" is usually associated with an analytical approach. There is an extension of these associations by which some scientists, thereby qualifying themselves as superior, imply that there is "good" or "bad" science by linking observational with bad and experimental with good. This choice of terms is dictated by diplomacy within the scientific community, for it is not good policy to refer to work that one's colleagues in another field are doing as bad; it is much better simply to call it "descriptive." We all know that there are appropriate uses for the words bad and good, but properly only as applied to an individual piece of work.

There are, of course, other terms that we are familiar with. There are the "hard" sciences and, by implication I suppose, the "soft" sciences. We also know that a good many other words have been juxtaposed to distinguish between "two cultures" within science (Table 2.1). Without trying to wreck diplomacy, it is worthwhile to point out just how these words, observational, descriptive, experimental, analytical, are being used.

It must be taken as given, I think, that all sciences observe and describe. An example is one product of science that has been with us for a long time, the heat flow equation, an equation that is fundamentally based on simple observation. The laws that Newton first formulated for heat flow are simpler than the more elegant mathematical statements that we now use. But this elegant formulation with which we are able to do so much rests on rather elementary kinds of observations. So it is silly to speak of a nonobservational or a nondescriptive science.

There are said to be scientists who describe things and do not wish to make any analysis of them. They say description for its own sake is worthwhile science. It is true, of course, that many sciences in their early stages of development are characterized by an extraordinarily high ratio of data collecting to data analysis. This rarely implies that those who accumulate the data are not thinking about what they are describing or trying to integrate it into some pattern. It is obvious that those who describe are making a choice of what to describe and that analysis is involved in the selection of the object to be described. We ordinarily do not consider it science for somebody to observe everything that could be catalogued about a particular process, phenomenon, object, or other, though the point may be argued, and probably will be when the first man lands on the moon.

There is no denying that the scientific population includes some who do describe for its own sake, who admit that description is their only goal. As such they bear the same relationship to science as the inventory-taker does to business. But most who solely describe will say that they are

Table 2.1	WORDS THAT HAVE BEEN USED TO DESCRIBE DIFFERENCES AMONG THE SCIENCES

Analytical	Descriptive
Experimental	Observational
Soft	Hard
Nonmathematical	Mathematical
Good	Bad
Interesting	Dull
"Stamp collecting"	Crucial experimentation
Classical	Modern
The general equation	The encyclopedic monograph
Rigorous	Inexact
Easy	Difficult
Exploding	Mined out

only temporarily so engaged, that they are always working toward the goal of analysis (usually put off to some future time).

If it is true that description for its own sake, without any analysis of what to describe or how to integrate it after description, is not what we usually call science, then we really cannot speak of a descriptive or nondescriptive science. When some scientists say of another scientist's work or of another field within science, "It's descriptive," they really mean that it is not science.

The kind of statement made above may also be interpreted to mean, with good grace, that the proportion of description to analysis is high compared to those in some other field. The proportion varies, of course, with the stage of development of the field and it varies, obviously, with the person. Even within a field that is largely beyond the stage where description is in a high ratio to analysis, the invention of a new instrument can lead to new kinds of observations, temporarily producing a great abundance of data relative to analysis.

If one of the major objects of scientific endeavor is to make general laws from specific observation, then it must also be granted that the endeavor is more or less difficult. Physics has come to be, by and large, the domain of those who work where generalizations are relatively easy to make from limited data (though no one would claim physics as an easy field in terms of mental effort). Another way to put it is that the data have small variance and the generalizations are very good. It is also true that in certain fields, of which perhaps the social sciences are the most obvious example, the data have such high variance that the generalizations are either difficult or almost impossible to make. This inevitably leads to differences in the overall logical structure of disciplines. A great many parts of physics are tied together with a strong interconnecting network of fundamental physical theory from which all other parts can be derived, so-called first principles. On the other hand we have fields, such as some areas of engineering, where empiricism is the order of the day simply because there is no generally valid group of first principles from which to operate.

Experiment and Science

Experiments have always been associated with science, and have rightly been considered the most powerful tools of science. Our vision of experiment is largely based on those that have been done in physics and chemistry. But there are a number of ways in which one can look at experiments. They can be divided into controlled and uncontrolled experiments. Alternatively, we can formulate experimentation as either natural or artificial. The artificial experiment we all know about; one chooses the starting materials and conditions of the experiment, then one observes the process in action or the final results.

The natural experiment we are somewhat less familiar with, except for those of us whose primary interest lies in biology, the earth sciences, or astronomy. We may ask what would have happened had Newton one day seen the mythical apple on the ground, somewhat overripe, partly eaten, and decayed. From such an observation, could he have extracted a generalization on gravity? I think it not improbable that he might have, but perhaps at a much greater cost in time and effort and with much less assurance. Many geochemists, for example, have to go about analyzing chemical processes on the earth in a special way. It would be as if someone who wanted to find out what was going on in an elementary chemistry laboratory would go to the laboratory when no one was in it, analyze what he found in the sink, and analyze what he found in the sewer leading from the laboratory. Noting how the laboratory is equipped he could make some deductions as to the experiments that were performed and guess what the starting reagents might have been. So natural experimentation has built into it restricted control and limited information on the nature of the starting materials. Natural experimentation, of course, has the same restrictions as artificial experimentation; one must pick the right observational parameters.

The natural experiment can be refined by looking at separable parts of it or by choosing the chance event that has resulted in a specially controlled or restricted experiment. In a multivariate situation we look for the occasional place or time when the variables are fewer. Those who have spent a good deal of time looking for controlled natural experiments can speak with feeling about the rarity or impossibility of finding the perfectly controlled natural experiment. They all have defects. And so those who work with such data seem always to be trying to draw some generalizations from rather poor experiments.

Restrictions on artificial experimentation possibilities in science are many. The first restriction is the largeness of some systems. Scaling factors are not always available or adequate to reduce the system in size for examination in the laboratory. The two most notable sciences in this regard are astronomy and geology. Here again, restricted bits and pieces of these large systems can be removed and taken to the laboratory, but the interrelatedness of the system itself cannot be reproduced.

The complexity and interrelatedness of some systems restrict the experiment. Warren Weaver (1955) applied the words "strongly coupled" and "weakly coupled" to the sciences. Weaver applied these terms to differentiate the natural from the social sciences, but I think the point can equally be taken to differentiate among the natural sciences. Some aspects of the study of the oceans, for example, the general oceanic circulation, appear to be relatively weakly coupled, in that one considers a few interactions between the motion of the planet, its atmosphere, and the heat budget of the earth and the oceans. Another branch of oceanography, ecology, is a very strongly coupled science. Ecology in the ocean is so strongly coupled that it is difficult even to distinguish the variables from each other. It appears that most natural phenomena of large scale on the earth's surface are rather strongly coupled in the sense that the variables are not separable either for experimental or analytical purposes.

There are, of course, large-scale artificial experiments that have been done and have revealed a great deal of information. I would class the modern air and water pollution disaster as an obvious, though socially evil, experiment. I can offer more examples: Bomb-C^{14} spread through the atmosphere and exchanged with the ocean to give us a much better picture of the circulation of CO_2 and its equilibrium between the ocean and the atmosphere than we had had previously. Attempts to counter the current pollution of the Great Lakes may be an experiment in reversibility; we have the social hope but scientific uncertainty that the Lakes can be cleaned up. Whether reversible or not, the pollution and the counter measures are certainly giving us a good deal of scientific (or engineering?) information.

In the past, social taboos have prevented a whole class of experiments, but it now seems that even these have broken down at some times, most notably with Nazi so-called "experimentation" in some concentration camps. There have been suggestions that warfare in Viet Nam involves certain experimental tests of new equipment and ideas. But it is still largely true that, for scientists, areas considered important in biological experimentation are taboo for what we consider good and sufficient social reasons.

Simulated or "hypothetical" experiments and systems analysis have been used to circumvent social control or for large systems that cannot be taken to the laboratory. But such "experiments" are only as good as the first principles that allow them to be carried on in the mind alone. Theoretical physics is a clear choice for the field in which such experiments have great value. But in most of the world of scientific practice, scientists use hypothetical experiments as a prelude to actual experimentation or further observation. One does not perform hypothetical experiments for their own sake. We grant that as teachers we have frequent recourse to such devices. As research workers in science they are of little value of and for themselves.

It appears then, that experimental science is of many different kinds, that though the nature of experiment is the same no matter where one sees it, the controls may vary and the ability to observe different parts of the experiment may be limited, and finally that there are experiments that simply cannot be done for social reasons.

Historical Versus Nonhistorical Science

This topic, a recurring theme in the dialogue on the nature of science (Nagel, 1952), has been explored recently by G. G. Simpson (1963) and R. A. Watson (1966). It appears to me that there is no fundamental difference between historical and nonhistorical science except as it may be economically profitable or culturally desirable to determine as exactly as possible what happened at a certain place and time. Thus we really do not care, as Watson puts it, exactly how the Grand Canyon of the Colorado River was formed. We only care how the generic class of Grand Canyons forms and has formed in the past, assuming that canyon-cutting was not a unique event. This is true in the same way that a chemist does not care what the particular numbers of an individual experiment are. His only concern is in repeating and generalizing that experiment so that the results from his or anybody else's operation of the same kind will fall into the same pattern. In fact, one rarely sees the particular numbers of any experiment. The raw data are of little interest except as an intermediate stage in the calculation of the quantities that are usually of true interest, quantities the significance of which has been established by earlier scientific studies. So, though we measure a particular mass and volume, we quote the important number as the density.

We may differentiate the historical sciences from the so-called nonhistorical sciences by the time scale of the processes involved. Though a chemical reaction has a "history," that history is usually faster than most processes we consider "historical." Even slow chemical reactions are extraordinarily fast compared to geological processes. In astronomy, too, a great many processes are very slow, although there are others that are fast. But even the history of a chemical reaction can be of major importance, for the study of chemical kinetics is just this. Again, though it is a historical event, the chemist studying the course of a reaction is rarely interested in any particular one performed at any particular time in his laboratory, but rather in the general repeatable experiment that anyone can do.

What is different about historical sciences is that many times only one natural experiment is observable, or so few that generalization is difficult if not impossible. We have on this earth, apparently, only one example of organic macroevolution. The general appearance of oxygen in the earth's primitive atmosphere probably happened only once. In modern times, the change in our lives caused by the development of the atomic bomb could happen only once. If the essence of experiment, whether artificial or natural, is that it be repeatable and that one needs at least one degree of freedom in order to make an average or to generalize, then we are destroyed by the uniqueness of some events. That is not to say, of course, that they are unique in the universe; they are only unique as far as our observational capabilities are concerned. It is for this reason that there is interest among biologists about the possibilities of some form of life on the moon or on Mars. They are simply seeking the additional experiment. Almost worse than the unique experiment is the availability of a very few experiments with a high variance. We have on the Earth only a few continents. In the development of the structure of the North American continent there have been only a few major evolutionary patterns of geosynclines and mountain chain evolution on the borders of the continent. There are only a few terrestrial planets. The social sciences to some extent are plagued by the same. There are as yet only a few nations that have atomic bombs.

Styles in Science

Each scientist selects the discipline he works in for a variety of reasons, but many styles can be found in all. I use the word "style" because, as has already become apparent, I reject the notion that there are different kinds of science, or scientific disciplines. There are many different personalities that go into science, and each of these personality types has his own way of doing things, as pointed out by Kurie (1953) and Eiduson (1962). Though there may be some correlation between personality and the discipline selected, I do not wish to discuss that issue.

Style is a word that has many meanings, ranging from a particular historical "school" in any subject (for example, "classical style") to a designation of a particular approach to any intellectual effort that is the product of the interaction of a personality with his time and his subject. It is the latter meaning of the word that I will use exclusively. Styles are probably related to personality, but they are always modified by the field in which that person works. An obvious recent example of different styles is that given by the contrast in the addresses of two recent Nobel laureates in physics, Richard Feynman (1966) and Julian Schwinger (1966). Here two men working in the same field of physics reveal very different styles of tackling the same kind of problem and writing about it.

We can recognize and tag some of the more distinctive styles that are common to all fields. We recognize that some of these are cross-coupled and one may indulge in several styles at different periods or as the mood strikes:

- the rigorous formalist
- the brilliant phenomenologist
- the painstaking laboratory methodologist and his equivalent, the careful, detailed field observer
- the quick and dirty cream skimmer
- the niche-lover or horizontal monopolist
- the subgeneralist or vertical monopolist
- the dilettante and his brother, the versatile virtuoso, separated by the difference between success and failure
- the older, wiser generalist

This is a parlor game that anyone can play and apply to his friends and colleagues.

Value judgments are usually made about the relative worth of various stylists' contributions. But it is probably so that all of these styles are necessary for science to advance, for everyone leans on everyone else. There is some danger at the present time that there will be too much emphasis on certain styles in picking the leaders of science, and that style will be confused with discipline and with fundamental ability of the individual to make advances in science. Pluralism and diversity make for more interest in science as they do elsewhere in life. But let us have differences in style and subject and recognize that invidious distinctions between "kinds" of science serve only to build hierarchies of position and privilege.

References

Eiduson, Bernice T. *Their Psychological World.* New York: Basic Books, 1962.

Feynman, Richard P. "The Development of the Space-Time View of Quantum Electrodynamics." *Science* 153 (1966): 699-708.

Kurie, L. S. "Problems of the Scientific Career." *Scientific Monthly* 74 (1953). (Reprinted in *Readings in the Philosophy of Science*, edited by H. Feigle and M. Brodbeck, 688-700. New York: Appleton-Century-Crofts, 1953.)

Nagel, Ernest. *The Structure of Science.* New York: Harcourt, Brace, & World, 1961.

Schwinger, Julian. "Relativistic Quantum Field Theory." *Science* 153 (1966): 949-53.

Simpson, G. G. "Historical Science." In *The Fabric of Geology*, edited by C. C. Albritton, Jr., 24-27. Reading, MA: Addison-Wesley, 1963.

Watson, R. A. "Is Geology Different: A Critical Discussion of 'The Fabric of Geology.'" *Philosophy of Science* 33 (1966): 172-85.

Weaver, Warren. "Science and People." *Science* 122 (1955): 1255-59.

SOURCE: From Raymond Siever (1968), "Science: Observational, Experimental, Historical," *American Scientist*, 56, 70-77. Copyright by *Sigma Xi*, Princeton, NJ.

2.11 GUIDES FOR DESIGN, MODEL BUILDING, AND LARGE-SCALE RESEARCH

What follows are readings that address the practice of building large-scale empirical studies. To start, "Some Observations on Study Design" by Samuel A. Stouffer is regarded as one of the single most useful statements of design requirements for large-scale social investigations.

Model building has become an integral part of scientific work. Section 2.12, "The Role of Models in Research Design," describes various types of models that are currently used.

Edward A. Suchman, in "General Considerations of Research Design" (Section 2.13), lists some realistic appraisals often needed when ideal plans must be compromised.

Factors affecting the internal and external validity of a research design are described in Section 2.14, which includes part of a classic monograph on experimental design by Donald T. Campbell and Julian C. Stanley. Large-scale group research has grown in volume and in scope.

Finally, Section 2.15 reviews the various types of sampling, including the types, brief descriptions of them, and the advantages and disadvantages of each one.

▸ Some Observations on Study Design

Samuel A. Stouffer

We must be clear in our own minds what proof consists of, and we must, if possible, provide dramatic examples of the advantages of relying on something more than plausibility. And the heart of our problem lies in study design in advance, such that the evidence is not capable of a dozen alternative interpretations.

Basically, I think it is essential that we always keep in mind the model of a controlled experiment, even if in practice we may have to deviate from an ideal model. Take the simple accompanying diagram.

	Before	After	After-Before
Experimental Group	x_1	x_2	$d = x_2 - x_1$
Control Group	x'_1	x'_2	$d = x'_2 - x'_1$

The test of whether a difference d is attributable to what we think it is attributable to is whether d is significantly larger than d'.

We used this model over and over again during the war to measure the effectiveness of orientation films in changing soldiers' attitudes. These experiences are described in Volume III of our *Studies in Social Psychology in World War II* (Hovland, Lumsdaine, & Sheffield, 1949).

One of the troubles with using this careful design was that the effectiveness of a single film when thus measured turned out to be so slight. If, instead of using the complete experimental design, we simply took an unselected sample of men and compared the attitudes of those who said they had seen a film with those who said they had not, we got much more impressive differences. This was more rewarding to us, too, for the management wanted to believe the films were powerful medicine. The gimmick was the selective fallibility of memory. Men who correctly remembered seeing the films were likely to be those most sensitized to their message. Men who were bored or indifferent may have actually seen them but slept through them or just forgot.

Most of the time we are not able or not patient enough to design studies containing all four cells as in the diagram above. Sometimes we have only the top two cells, as in the accompanying diagram.

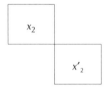

In this situation we have two observations of the same individuals or groups taken at different times. This is often a very useful design. In the army, for example, we could take a group of recruits, ascertain their attitudes, and restudy the same men later. From this we could tell whose attitudes changed and in what direction. (It was almost always for the worse, which did not endear us to the army!) But exactly what factors in the early training period were most responsible for deterioration of attitudes could only be inferred indirectly.

The panel study is usually more informative than a more frequent design, which might be pictured thus:

Here at one point in time we have one sample, and at a later point in time we have another sample. We observe that our measure, say, the mean, is greater for the recent sample than for the earlier one. But we are precluded from observing which men or what type of men shifted. Moreover, there is always the disturbing possibility that the populations in our two samples were initially different; hence the differences might not be attributable to conditions taking place in the time interval between the two observations. Thus we would study a group of soldiers in the United States and later ask the same questions of a group of soldiers overseas. Having matched the two groups of men carefully by branch of service, length of time in the army, rank, etc., we hoped that the results of the study would approximate what would be found if the same men could have been studied twice. But this could be no more than a hope. Some important factors could not be adequately controlled, for example, physical conditions. Men who went overseas were initially in better shape on the average than men who had been kept behind; but, if the follow-up study was in the tropics, there was a chance that unfavorable climate already had begun to take its toll. And so it went. How much men overseas changed called for a panel study as a minimum if we were to have much confidence in the findings.

A very common attempt to get the result of a controlled experiment without paying the price is with the design that might be as shown in the accompanying diagram. This is usually what we get with correlation analysis. We have two or more groups of men whom we study at the same point in time.

Thus we have men in the infantry and men in the air corps and compare their attitudes. How much of the difference between x'_2 and x_1 we can attribute to experience in a given branch of service and how much is a function of attributes of the men selected for each branch we cannot know assuredly. True, we can try to rule out various possibilities by matching; we can compare men from the two branches with the same age and education, for example. But there is all too often a wide-open gate through which other uncontrolled variables can march.

Sometimes, believe it or not, we have only one cell:

$$x_2$$

When this happens, we do not know much of anything. But we can still fill pages of social science journals with "brilliant analysis" if we use plausible conjecture in supplying missing cells from our imagination. Thus we may find that the adolescent today has wild ideas and conclude that society is going to the dogs. We fill in the dotted cell representing our own yesterdays with hypothetical data, where x_1 represents us and x_2 our offspring. The tragicomic part is that most of the public, including, I fear, many social scientists, are so acculturated that they ask for no better data.

I do not intend to disparage all research not conforming to the canons of the controlled experiment. I think that we will see more of full experimental design in sociology and social psychology in the future than in the past. But I am well aware of the practical difficulties of its execution, and I know that there are numberless important situations in which it is not feasible at all. What I am arguing for is awareness of the limitations of a design in which crucial cells are missing.

Sometimes by forethought and patchwork we can get approximations that are useful if we are careful to avoid overinterpretation. Let me cite an example:

In Europe during the war the army tested the idea of putting an entire platoon of Negro soldiers into a white infantry outfit. This was done in several companies. The Negroes fought beside white soldiers. After several months we were asked to find out what the white troops thought about the innovation. We found that only 7 percent of the white soldiers in companies with Negro platoons said that they disliked the idea very much, whereas 62 percent of the white soldiers in divisions without Negro troops said they would dislike the idea very much if it were tried in their outfits. We have:

Now, were these white soldiers who fought beside Negroes men who were naturally more favorable to Negroes than the cross section of white infantrymen? We did not think so, since, for example, they contained about the same proportion of southerners. The point was of some importance, however, if we were to make the inference that actual experience with Negroes reduced hostility from 62 to 7 percent. As a second-best substitute, we asked the white soldiers in companies with Negro platoons if they could recall how they felt when the innovation was first proposed. It happens that 67 percent said they were initially opposed to the idea. Thus we could tentatively fill in a missing cell and conclude that, under the conditions obtaining, there probably had been a marked change in attitude.

Even if this had been a perfectly controlled experiment, there was still plenty of chance to draw erroneous inferences. The conclusions apply only to situations closely approximating those of the study. It happens, for example, that the Negroes involved were men who volunteered to leave rear-area jobs for combat duty. If other Negroes had been involved, the situation might have been different. Moreover, they had white officers. One army colonel who saw this study and whom I expected to ridicule it because he usually opposed innovations, surprised me by offering congratulations. "This proves," he said, "what I have been arguing in all my thirty years in the army—that niggers will do all right if you give 'em white officers!" Moreover, the study applied only to combat experiences. Other studies would be needed to justify extending the findings to noncombat or garrison duty. In other words, one lone study, however well designed, can be a very dangerous thing if it is exploited beyond its immediate implications.

Now experiments take time and money, and there is no use denying that we in social science cannot be as prodigal with the replications as the biologist who can run a hundred experiments simultaneously by growing plants in all kinds of soils and conditions. The relative ease of experimentation in much—not all—of natural science goes far to account for the difference in quality of proof demanded by physical and biological sciences, on the one hand, and social scientists, on the other.

Though we cannot always design neat experiments when we want to, we can at least keep the experimental model in front of our eyes and behave cautiously when we fill in missing cells with dotted lines. But there is a further and even more important operation we can perform in the interest of economy. That lies in our choice of the initial problem.

Reference

Hovland, Carl I., Lumsdaine, Arthur, & Sheffield, Fred D. (1949). *Experiments on mass communication.* Princeton, NJ: Princeton University Press.

SOURCE: From Samuel A. Stouffer (1950), "Some Observations on Study Design," *American Journal of Sociology, 55,* 356-359. Copyright 1950 by the University of Chicago. Reprinted with permission.

2.12 THE ROLE OF MODELS IN RESEARCH DESIGN

Model building is an integral part of the social sciences because models guide both theory development and research design. Model building has been accentuated and accelerated by many forces in contemporary life. Models seem appropriate to the worlds of computers, biotechnology, and automation, and they have conferred new status on the scientist in government, industry, and the military. Models are also very important to social scientists because they provide a framework through which important questions are investigated.

To further emphasize the importance of this activity in the social sciences, the act of modeling has taken on the status of a verb ("model") representing an action. Although we still have "model building," the activity is more often represented as "modeling," and the language of social science now includes such terms as *game models (gaming), simulation models, mathematical models, trend models, stochastic models, laboratory models, information* and *cybernetic models, causal* and *path models,* and many more. Even theory itself is being fractionalized into *theoretical models.*

All these terms stand for a closed system from which are generated predictions (or hypotheses) that, when made, require some kind of empirical test. Researchers should be encouraged to use models when they can assist in identifying significant variables in such a way that tests of hypotheses can be defined more sharply.

In trying to bring some order to the variety of models, one soon discovers that there is a great deal of overlap, and that widely different usages exist. There is no common agreement on the classification of models, but in the following description, five categories of models and their variants are set out (Lave & March, 1975).

1. Physical models
2. Theoretical models
3. Mathematical models
4. Mechanical models
5. Symbolic interactionist models

Whenever possible, the researcher should be guided by the following rules in the design and use of models:

1. We must first understand as completely as possible the system to be modeled.
2. Only the important parts of a system, and their controls, can be modeled.
3. Wherever possible, constants, rates, and relationships in the model must be empirically measured and not taken from the literature.
4. The modeling exercise and the resultant simulations are regarded as tools to be used to further our understanding of how the system works (Hobbie, 1980).

References

Hobbie, James E. (Ed.). (1980). *Lymnology of tundra ponds, Barrow, Alaska.* Stroudsburg, PA: Hutchinson & Ross.

Lave, Charles A., & March, James G. (1975). *An introduction to models in the social sciences.* New York: Harper & Row.

2.12.1 Physical Models

A physical model is a concrete object fashioned to look like the phenomenon the model is being used to represent. These objects incorporate static or structural properties. For example, skeletons, organs, molecules, atoms, small-scale buildings, airplanes, and air tunnels all can be represented by physical models. Perhaps the most famous model in contemporary science is the double-helix model showing the structuring of the DNA code gene that governs human reproduction. Pilot operating models introduce dynamic system patterns to represent functioning mechanisms in many fields.

A cognitive function is performed by the physical model in almost every field of science and branch of technology, from sewing to architecture and aeronautical engineering. Sociology has made limited use of physical models, but F. S. Chapin has experimented with models to demonstrate institutions and social space, and D. C. Miller has worked with models of group and power relations.

Further Reading on Physical Models

O'Meara, Tim. (1997). Causation and the struggle for a science of culture. *Current Anthropology, 38,* 399-418.

2.12.2 Theoretical Models

The term *model* is often used loosely to refer to any scientific theory phrased in symbolic or formal styles. If there is any value in using *theory* and *model* as synonymous terms (and many social scientists would not agree), it probably exists when a theory is set forth as a set of postulations, with the relations among the parts clearly specified or exhibited.

Further Readings on Theoretical Models

Dubin, Robert. (1969). *Theory building: A practical guide to the construction and testing of theoretical models.* New York: Free Press.

Land, Kenneth C. (1971). Formal theory. In Herbert L. Costner (Ed.), *Sociological methodology 1971.* San Francisco: Jossey-Bass.

Lave, Charles A., & March, James G. (1975). *An introduction to models in the social sciences.* New York: Harper & Row.

2.12.3 Mathematical Models

The term *mathematical model,* when applied to the social sciences, refers to the use of mathematical equations to depict the behavior of persons, groups, communities, states, or nations. Common use of mathematics can be observed in trend, causal, path, stochastic, and game models.

For example, one type of mathematical model, a *trend model,* refers to the fitting of time series data to equations or curves postulated as change principles or laws. *Causal* and *path models* involve the construction of a simplified model of social reality in which variables are presumed to act in a causal sequence. The most important variables affecting some dependent (outcome) variable or criterion are sought and arranged according to their influence or impact. All other variables entering into the causal system are regarded as residuals.

The term *stochastic model* refers to a probability construction in which a sequence of behavioral events occurs in time and to which are assigned probabilities for the joint occurrence of such events. Such models deal with "stochastic processes."

Game models rest on a mathematical theory that pertains to the determination of optimum strategies in a competitive situation (game of strategy) involving two or more individuals or parties. Games of strategy, in contrast to games in which the outcome depends only on chance, are games in which the outcome depends also, or entirely, on the moves chosen by the individual players.

Further Readings on Mathematical Models

Backman, Olof, & Edling, Christofer. (1999). Mathematics matters: On the absence of mathematical models in quantitative sociology. *Acta Sociologica*, *42*, 69-78.

Manfredi, Piero. (1994). Mathematical models for communication: An introduction. *European Journal of Population*, *10*, 384-386.

2.12.4 Mechanical Models

In the social sciences, mechanical models use concepts from physics and engineering to provide analogues for social behavior. Increasingly, interest has grown in these machine models as extensions of the concern with mathematical models, because they are based on mathematical language and symbolic logic. The general computer model is the focus of the machine model, and the terms *computer-simulated model* and *electronic-simulated model* are also used.

The *computer-simulated model* focuses on the use of a computer program to provide a test of a set of constructs that are internally consistent and have presumed explanatory power to derive generalizable propositions from the empirical data. The postulates of the model can be programmed into the computer (making the computer program the theory), and the computer will calculate the behavior that the program (i.e., theory) dictates.

Microanalytic simulation models are used to examine the effects of various kinds of policies on the demographic structure of the population, saving and tax behavior, income security during retirement, social class differences in health and disease, and numerous other aspects of the population and its well-being. The microanalytic simulation system (MASS) was originally developed by Guy Orcutt of Yale University. It is a computer approach to capturing many of the complexities of a nation's social and economic structure. It is sophisticated enough to handle research problems as complex as the real-life events that affect the economic lives of whole populations of human beings: marrying and divorcing, giving birth, changing residence, becoming unemployed and finding new jobs, retiring, and dying. Research involving general simulation modeling to capture very large sets of human behaviors is still rare.

Further Reading on Mechanical Models

Panel to Evaluate Microsimulation Models for Social Welfare Programs. (1991). *Improving information for social policy decisions: The uses of microsimulation modeling* (2 vols., edited by Constance F. Citro & Eric A. Hanushek). Washington, DC: National Academy Press.

2.12.5 Symbolic Interactionist Models

Symbolic interactionist models address themselves to the meanings that actors give to the symbols they use or encounter. In social interaction, cues to behavior are transmitted by word and gesture, and behavior constantly changes as transactions occur. Some symbolic interactionist models are simple constructs involving few persons; others are more elaborate and use computers to seek out patterns and generalizations. All models tend to be simulation models; that is, they are based on contrived situations or structured concepts that are isomorphic to reality situations.

Laboratory models (a type of symbolic interactionist model) involve contrived situations simulating groups or organizations in which actors play roles that are either structured or unstructured, according to the design of the researcher. Generally, such behavior is observed in a closed environment where observation and recording devices can be employed. Well-known examples can be cited from the small group laboratory. Somewhat less attention has been given to the organization in the laboratory, but research is increasing rapidly.

Information and *cybernetic models* depict the input, flow, and result of information within communication systems. Such models may range from mechanical to symbolic interactionist, where meaning becomes more significant. The most common analogue is human intelligence, and we observe growing use of supercomputers to mimic that trait.

Further Readings on Symbolic Interactionist Models

Manis, Jerome G., & Meltzer, Bernard N. (Eds.). (1967). *Symbolic interaction: A reader in social psychology.* Boston: Allyn and Bacon.
Schneider, Anne L., Snyder Joy, Zoann, & Hopper, Melanie. (1993). Rational and symbolic models of attitudes toward AIDS policy. *Social Science Quarterly*, 74, 349-366.

GENERAL CONSIDERATIONS OF RESEARCH DESIGN `2.13`

Below, Edward A. Suchman qualifies what the role of research design is in the scientific process and emphasizes that there are several ways to do the "right" thing.

▶ The Principles of Research Design

Edward A. Suchman

1. It seems to us futile to argue whether or not a certain design is "scientific." The design is *the plan of study* and, as such, is present in all studies, uncontrolled as well as controlled and subjective as well as objective. It is not a case of scientific or not scientific, but rather one of good or less good design. The degree of accuracy desired, the level of "proof" aimed at, the state of existing knowledge, etc., all combine to determine the amount of concern one can have with the degree of "science" in one's design.

2. The proof of hypotheses is never definitive. The best one can hope to do is to make more or less plausible a series of alternative hypotheses. In most cases multiple explanations will be operative. Demonstrating one's own hypotheses does not rule out alternative hypotheses and vice versa.

3. There is no such thing as a single "correct" design. Different workers will come up with different designs favoring their own methodological and theoretical predispositions. Hypotheses can be studied by different methods using different designs.

4. All research design represents a compromise dictated by the many practical considerations that go into social research. None of us operates except on limited time, money, and personnel budgets. Further limitations concern the availability of data and the extent to which one can impose upon one's subjects. A research design must be *practical*.

5. A research design is not a highly specific plan to be followed without deviation, but rather a series of guideposts to keep one headed in the right direction. One must be prepared to discard (although not too quickly) hypotheses that do not work out and to develop new hypotheses on the basis of increased knowledge. Furthermore, any research design developed in the office will inevitably have to be changed in the face of field considerations.

SOURCE: From Edward A. Suchman (1954), "The Principles of Research Design," in *An Introduction to Social Research*, edited by John T. Doby, with the assistance of Edward A. Suchman, John C. McKinney, Roy G. Francis, and John P. Dean (New York: Stackpole). Reprinted by permission of Edward A. Suchman and the Stackpole Company.

2.14 FACTORS JEOPARDIZING INTERNAL AND EXTERNAL VALIDITY OF RESEARCH DESIGNS

Perhaps the most important publication in the past 50 years relative to understanding research design and planning experiments is that of Donald T. Campbell and Julian C. Stanley, excerpted below. Their conceptualization of internal and external validity as critical evaluative constructs and associated threats opened the door to efficient and concise assessment of experimental designs.

Internal validity is the quality of an experimental design such that any outcomes or effects can be attributed to the manipulation of the independent variable. *External validity* is the quality of an experimental design such that the results are generalizable to different settings. As might already be obvious, there is a trade-off between the two. For example, it is impossible to have a very high degree of internal validity and have much generalizability, just as it is very difficult to have little control (or low interval validity) and be able to generalize to other samples. The balance between the two depends most upon the experimental question being asked (expressed as a hypothesis) and the risk that the researcher is willing to take.

▶ **Experimental and Quasi-Experimental Designs for Research**

Donald T. Campbell and Julian C. Stanley

Fundamental to this listing is a distinction between *internal validity* and *external validity*. *Internal validity* is the basic minimum without which any experiment is uninterpretable: Did in fact the experimental treatments make a difference in this specific experimental instance? *External validity* asks the question of generalizability: To what populations, settings, treatment variables, and measurement variables can this effect be generalized? Both types of criteria are obviously important, even though they are frequently at odds in that features increasing one may jeopardize the other. While *internal validity* is the *sine qua non*, and while the question of *external validity*, like the question of inductive inference, is never completely answerable, the selection of designs strong in both types of validity is obviously our ideal.

Relevant to *internal validity*, eight different classes of extraneous variables will be presented; these variables, if not controlled in the experimental design, might produce effects confounded with the effect of the experimental stimulus. They represent the effects of:

1. *History*, the specific events occurring between the first and second measurement in addition to the experimental variable.
2. *Maturation*, processes within the respondents operating as a function of the passage of time per se (not specific to the particular events), including growing older, growing hungrier, growing more tired, and the like.

3. *Testing*, the effects of taking a test upon the scores of a second testing.
4. *Instrumentation*, in which changes in the calibration of a measuring instrument or changes in the observers or scores used may produce changes in the obtained measurements.
5. *Statistical regression*, operating where groups have been selected on the basis of their extreme scores.
6. Biases resulting in differential *selection* of respondents for the comparison groups.
7. *Experimental mortality*, or differential loss of respondents from the comparison groups.
8. *Selection-maturation interaction*, etc., which in certain of the multiple-group quasi-experimental designs is confounded with, i.e., might be mistaken for, the effect of the experimental variable.

The factors jeopardizing *external validity* or *representativeness* are:

9. The *reactive* or *interaction effect of testing*, in which a pretest might increase or decrease the respondent's sensitivity or responsiveness to the experimental variable and thus make the results obtained for a pretested population unrepresentative of the effects of the experimental variable for the unpretested universe from which the experimental respondents were selected.
10. The *interaction* effects of *selection* biases and the *experimental variable*.
11. *Reactive effects of experimental arrangements*, which would preclude generalization about the effect of the experimental variable upon persons being exposed to it in nonexperimental settings.

The value of such a list is that it gives the researcher some cautions before finalizing a design. To increase the degree of accuracy desired, these factors cannot be ignored. What is put into a research design directs what will come out after the data are collected and analyzed.

SOURCE: From Donald T. Campbell and Julian C. Stanley (1966), *Experimental and Quasi-Experimental Designs for Research* (Chicago: Rand McNally), pp. 5-6.

Further Readings on Internal and External Validity

Barr, Judith T. (Ed.). (1996). *Clinical effectiveness in allied health practices: Critical literature review.* Collingdale, PA: Diane.
Braver, Sanford L., & Smith, Melanie C. (1996). Maximizing both external and internal validity in longitudinal true experiments with voluntary treatments: The "combined modified" design. *Evaluation and Program Planning, 19,* 287-300.
Durlak, Joseph A. (1998). Why program implementation is important. *Journal of Prevention and Intervention in the Community, 17,* 5-18.
Garaway, G. B. (1997). Evaluation, validity, and values. *Evaluation and Program Planning, 20,* 1-5.
Kirk, Jerome, & Miller, Marc L. (1999). *Reliability and validity in qualitative research.* Thousand Oaks, CA: Sage.

SAMPLING 2.15

A sample is a set of subjects selected from a population. The goal of sampling is to select a sample where the sampling error (or difference between sample and population characteristics) is minimized. That way, the sample best represents the population of interest, and generalizability, a hallmark of science and particularly inferential statistics (see Part 6), is maximized as well.

Sampling problems may be divided into those that affect (a) the definition of the population, (b) the size of the sample, or (c) the representativeness of the sample. In regard to the definition of the population, the important problem is to decide to which group the researcher wishes to generalize his or her findings. In regard to size of the sample, consideration must be given to the persistent disappearance of cases (called mortality) and should be foreseen as clearly as possible. Dummy tables help provide for such planning. In addition, the sample size must be large enough for there to be sufficient power in the statistical analysis, but not so large as to waste resources. The third and perhaps most intricate sampling problem arises in connection with the method of securing a representative sample. The essential requirement of any sample is that it is as representative as possible of the population or universe from which it is taken.

Three methods of sampling are commonly used: *random sampling*, *stratified sampling*, and *judgmental* or *purposive sampling*.

2.15.1 Random Sampling

A random sample is one that is drawn in such a way that every member of the population has an equal chance and independent chance of being included. The most rigorous method of random sampling employs a table of random numbers. A number is assigned to each member of the population. Members of the population are included in the sample if their numbers are selected using a table of random numbers; numbers are chosen in succession until a sample of predetermined size is drawn. Another method is to write the names or numbers of the members of a population on cards or disks, shuffle these, and then draw.

With the increasing popularity of such programs as SPSS, a sample can be selected with little effort, as shown in Figure 2.1. The cases with a diagonal line through the row number have been selected for the sample.

Systematic sampling is a convenient alternative method, not exactly equivalent to random sampling but often close enough for practical purposes. Systematic sampling takes every *n*th item in the population, beginning at some random member in the population. It is performed by dividing the population by the size of the desired sample to arrive at *n*, selecting a starting point, then selecting every *n*th name. For example, if you wanted to select a sample of 20 from a population of 200, you would divide 100 by 20 to arrive at 5, and then select every 5th name on the list, starting at some random name on the list.

2.15.2 Stratified Sampling

The aforementioned methods assume that the composition of the total group is not known, and that a representative sample will be best approximated by a strictly random selection or a selection by regular intervals. In some cases the composition of the total group with respect to some significant characteristics is known (exactly or approximately) before the sample is selected. The paramount criterion is that when a population characteristic (such as gender or social class) is related to the dependent variable, then the sample needs to be stratified on that characteristic.

For example, we may know the exact ratio of men to women in the population and that sex differences are related to the variables we wish to test. In such cases researchers can increase the chances of selecting a representative sample by selecting subsamples proportionate in size to the significant characteristics of the total population. Thus they can select a sample that is mathematically absolutely representative with regard to some significant characteristics. The numerous forms of stratified random sampling techniques are shown in Table 2.3.

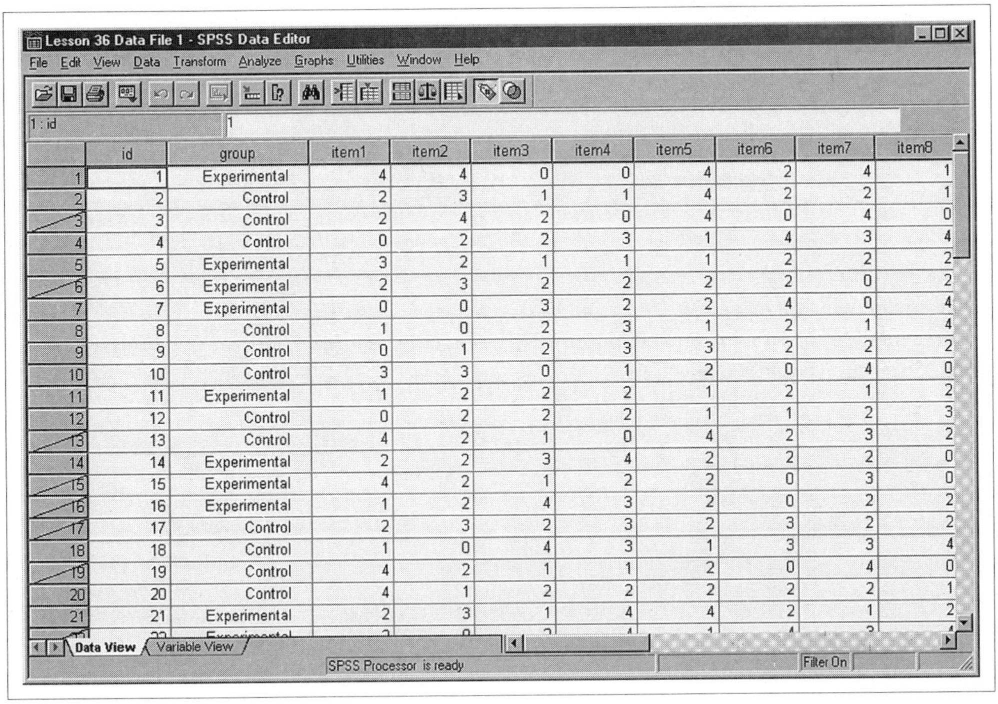

	id	group	item1	item2	item3	item4	item5	item6	item7	item8
1	1	Experimental	4	4	0	0	4	2	4	1
2	2	Control	2	3	1	1	4	2	2	1
3	3	Control	2	4	2	0	4	0	4	0
4	4	Control	0	2	2	3	1	4	3	4
5	5	Experimental	3	2	1	1	1	2	2	2
6	6	Experimental	2	3	2	2	2	2	0	2
7	7	Experimental	0	0	3	2	2	4	0	4
8	8	Control	1	0	2	3	1	2	1	4
9	9	Control	0	1	2	3	3	2	2	2
10	10	Control	3	3	0	1	2	0	4	0
11	11	Experimental	1	2	2	2	1	2	1	2
12	12	Control	0	2	2	2	1	1	2	3
13	13	Control	4	2	1	0	4	2	3	2
14	14	Experimental	2	2	3	4	2	2	2	0
15	15	Experimental	4	2	1	2	2	0	3	0
16	16	Experimental	1	2	4	3	2	0	2	2
17	17	Control	2	3	2	3	2	3	2	2
18	18	Control	1	0	4	3	1	3	3	4
19	19	Control	4	2	1	1	2	0	4	0
20	20	Control	4	1	2	2	2	2	2	1
21	21	Experimental	2	3	1	4	4	2	1	2

Figure 2.1. SPSS Computer Screen Illustrating Random Sampling

2.15.3 Judgmental or Purposive Sampling

When practical considerations preclude the use of probability sampling, researchers may seek a representative sample by other (nonprobability) means. They may look for a subgroup that is typical of the population as a whole. Observations are then restricted to this subgroup, and conclusions from the data obtained are generalized to the total population. An example would be the choice of a particular state or county as a barometer of an election outcome, relying upon the results of past elections as evidence of the representativeness of the sample for the state or nation.

Sampling errors and biases cannot be computed for such samples. For this reason, judgmental sampling should be restricted to the following situations: (a) when the possible errors are not serious and (b) when probability sampling is practically impossible. Data from judgmental samples at best suggest or indicate conclusions, but in general they cannot be used as the basis of statistical testing procedures.

2.15.4 An Overview of Sampling Techniques

The three forms of sampling discussed above do not exhaust the range of sampling procedures. Table 2.3 lists such types as multistage random sampling, cluster, stratified cluster, and repetitive sampling.

Table 2.3 A REVIEW OF SAMPLING TECHNIQUES

Type of Sampling	Brief Description	Advantages	Disadvantages
A. Simple random	1. Assign to each population member a unique number 2. Select sample items by use of random numbers	1. Requires minimum knowledge of population in advance 2. Free of possible classification errors 3. Easy to analyze data and compute errors	1. Does not make use of the researcher's knowledge of the population 2. Larger errors for same sample size than in stratified sampling
B. Systematic	1. Uses natural ordering or order in the population 2. Select random starting point between 1 and the nearest integer to the sampling ratio (N/n) 3. Select items at interval of nearest integer to sampling ratio	1. If population is ordered with respect to the pertinent property, the method gives a stratification effect and hence reduces variability compared with simple random sampling 2. Simplicity of drawing sample	1. If sampling interval is related to a periodic ordering of the population, increased variability may be introduced 2. Estimates of error are likely to be high where there is a stratification effect
C. Multistage random	Use a form of random sampling in each of the sampling stages where there are at least two stages	1. Sampling lists, identification, and numbering required only for members of sampling units selected in sample 2. If sampling units are geographically defined, cuts down field costs (e.g., travel)	1. Errors likely to be larger than in random or systematic sampling for the same sample size 2. Errors increase as the number of sampling units selected decreases
1. With probability proportionate to size	Select sampling units with probability proportionate to their size	1. Reduces variability	1. Lack of knowledge of size of each sampling unit before selection increases variability
D. Stratified 1. Proportionate	Select from every sampling unit at other than last stage a random sample proportionate to the size of the sampling unit	1. Ensures representativeness with respect to the property that forms basis of classifying units; therefore yields less variability than simple random or multistage random sampling 2. Decreases chance of failing to include members of the population because of the classification process 3. Characteristics of each stratum can be estimated, and hence comparisons can be made	1. Requires accurate information on the proportion of population in each stratum, otherwise increases error 2. If stratified lists are not available, may be costly to prepare them; possibility of faulty classification and hence increase in variability
2. Optimum allocation	Same as proportionate except sample is proportionate to variability within strata as well as their size	1. Less variability for same sample size than proportionate	1. Requires knowledge of variability of pertinent characteristic within strata

Type of Sampling	Brief Description	Advantages	Disadvantages
E. Cluster	Select sampling units by some forms of random sampling: ultimate units are groups; select these at random and take a complete count of each	1. If clusters are geographically defined, yields lowest field costs 2. Requires listing only individuals in selected clusters 3. Characteristics of clusters as well as those of the population can be estimated 4. Can be used for subsequent samples, because clusters, not individuals, are selected, and substitution of individuals may be permissible	1. Larger errors for comparable size than other probability samples 2. Requires ability to assign each member of the population uniquely to a cluster; inability to do so may result in duplication or omission of individuals
F. Stratified cluster	Select clusters at random from every sampling unit	1. Reduces variability of plain cluster sampling	1. Disadvantages of stratified sampling added to those of cluster sampling 2. Because cluster properties may change, advantage of stratification may be reduced and make sample unusable for later research
G. Repetitive: multiple or sequential	Two or more samples of any of the above types are taken, using results from earlier samples to design later ones, or determine if they are necessary	1. Provides estimates of population characteristics that facilitate efficient planning of succeeding sample, therefore reduces error of final estimate 2. In the long run, reduces number of observations required	1. Complicates administration of fieldwork 2. More computation and analysis required than in nonrepetitive sampling 3. Sequential sampling can be used only where a very small sample can approximate representativeness and where the number of observations can be increased conveniently at any stage of the research
H. Judgment	Select a subgroup of the population that, on the basis of available information, can be judged to be representative of the total population; take a complete count or subsample of this group	1. Reduces cost of preparing sample and fieldwork, because ultimate units can be selected so that they are close together	1. Variability and bias of estimates cannot be measured or controlled 2. Requires strong assumptions or considerable knowledge of population and subgroup selected
I. Quota	Classify population by pertinent properties; determine desired proportion of sample from each class; fix quotas for each observer	1. Same as above 2. Introduces some stratification effect	1. Introduces bias of observers' classification of subjects and nonrandom selection within classes

SOURCE: Adapted from Russell Ackoff (1953), *The Design of Social Research* (Chicago: University of Chicago Press), p. 124.

▶ Selecting Samples

Russell Ackoff

From practical as well as purely scientific purposes it is necessary to use selection procedures whose errors are measurable. A procedure should be capable of characterization relative to bias and variability. The fundamental procedure satisfying these conditions is simple random sampling, a method in which each individual has an equal chance of being selected. Simple random sampling is performed with the aid of random numbers, while systematic sampling is a variation which proceeds from a random start to select elements at a preset interval.

By breaking the population into subgroups, we may select a sample in stages as follows. If a random sample is selected at each stage, we have a multistage random sample. If a complete count of sampling units is taken at one stage other than the last, we have a stratified sample. If a complete count is made at the last stage, we have a cluster sample. The probability of selecting any subgroup may be made proportionate to some function of the size of the subgroup, and the number of units selected from any subgroup may also be made proportionate to some such function. Proportionate sampling tends to reduce sampling errors. Stratification and clustering can be combined to yield efficient samples, particularly where stratification and/or clustering is based on geographic properties (i.e., in area sampling). Area sampling reduces the complexity of preparing sampling lists and permits the clustering of subjects so that they come in bunches.

In double sampling a first sample can be used to provide information which can in turn be used to design an efficient second sample. Such sampling can also be used to reduce the number of observations required, on the average, for coming to a conclusion. When double sampling is generalized, it yields sequential sampling, a method of drawing one item or set of items at a time and using the data obtained to decide whether to continue sampling or not.

The ultimate basis for selecting a sampling procedure should be the minimization of the cost of getting the sample and the expected cost of errors which may result from using the method. Expert assistance should be employed in making such evaluations.

The above sampling chart [Table 2.3] summarizes in a very brief way the description, advantages, and disadvantages of the various sampling procedures discussed.

SOURCE: From Russell Ackoff (1953), *The Design of Social Research* (Chicago: University of Chicago Press), pp. 123-126.

Further Readings on Sampling

Abbott, Andrew, & Barman, Emily. (1997). Sequence comparison via alignment and Gibbs sampling: A formal analysis of the emergence of the modern sociological article. *Sociological Methodology*, 27, 47-87.

Handwerker, W. Penn, & Wozniak, Danielle F. (1997). Sampling strategies for the collection of cultural data: An extension of Boas's answer to Galton's problem. *Current Anthropology, 38*, 869-875.

Maisel, Richard, & Persell, Caroline H. (1995). *How sampling works.* Boston: Pine Forge Press.

Rosnow, Ralph L., & Rosenthal, Robert. (2001). *Beginning behavioral research: A conceptual primer* (4th ed.). Upper Saddle River, NJ: Prentice Hall.

Valliant, Richard L., Dorfman, Alan H., & Royall, Richard M. (2000). *Finite population sampling and inference: A prediction approach.* New York: John Wiley and Sons.

SELECTED BIBLIOGRAPHY ON
BASIC RESEARCH AND RESEARCH DESIGN 2.16

Ackoff, Russell L. (1953). *The design of social research*. Chicago: University of Chicago Press.

Ader, Herman J., & Mellenbergh, Gideon J. (1999). *Research methodology on the social, behavioral, and life sciences: Designs, models, and methods*. Thousand Oaks, CA: Sage.

Alwin, Duane F. (Ed.). (1978). *Survey design and analysis*. Beverly Hills, CA: Sage.

Armer, Michael, & Grimshaw, Allen (Eds.). (1973). *Comparative social research: Methodological problems and strategies*. New York: Wiley.

Blalock, Hubert M., Jr. (1984). *Basic dilemmas in the social sciences*. Beverly Hills, CA: Sage.

Blessing, Lusienne T. M., & Chakrabarti, Amaresh. (1999). *A design research methodology*. Godalming, Surrey, UK: Springer-Verlag.

Bordens, Kenneth S., & Abbott, Bruce B. (1998). *Research design and methods: A process approach*. Mountain View, CA: Mayfield.

Brinberg, David, & McGrath, Joseph E. (1985). *Validity and the research process*. Beverly Hills, CA: Sage.

Fielding, Nigel G. (1988). *Actions and structure: Research methods and social theory*. Newbury Park, CA: Sage.

Grunow, Dieter. (1995). The research design in organization studies: Problems and prospects. *Organization Science*, 6, 93-103.

Hakim, Catherine. (1987). *Research design*. Winchester, MA: Allen & Unwin.

Jensen, Paul A. (1999). *Models and methods in operations research*. Upper Saddle River, NJ: Prentice Hall.

Kenny, David A. (1996). The design and analysis of social-interaction research. *Annual Review of Psychology*, 47, 59-86.

Kuehl, Robert O. (1999). *Statistical principles of research design and analysis*. Pacific Grove, CA: Brooks/Cole.

Lieberson, Stanley. (1985). *Making it count: The improvement of social research and theory*. Berkeley: University of California Press.

Strauss, Anselm, & Corbin, Juliet. (1990). *Basics of qualitative research: Grounded theory procedures and techniques*. Newbury Park, CA: Sage.

PART 3

APPLIED AND EVALUATION RESEARCH

Part 3 describes how both applied and evaluation researchers confront operational or policy-making problems. Unlike in basic research, the research problem is often not chosen by the researcher, but is given to the researcher by an administrator or legislator who needs help now.

The applied researcher moves in to confront the problem head-on; the evaluation researcher must evaluate the end product of a program or process. Both types of research offer very important research challenges. In this part we look at the technical and social considerations with which applied and evaluation researchers must grapple. Cost and effectiveness are constant criteria by which their work is judged, and as you will see later in this part, they are often used in evaluating the effectiveness of a policy.

A RATIONALE FOR APPLIED SOCIOLOGY
AS IT RELATES TO POLICY-MAKING 3.1

Applied sociology has received greatly renewed interest because of the growth of employment opportunities outside universities combined with a tight academic market. Moreover, over the past two decades social science has been found to be increasingly useful in applied social science research in support of social programs of a wide variety. Why applied sociology?

Otto Larsen, former director of Social and Economic Sciences at the National Science Foundation, explains the role of social scientists in policy-making:

> Scientists do not make public policies, elected officials do. Research from social and behavioral research can and does inform the decision-making process through a variety of mechanisms. For example, the National Research Council of the National Academy of Sciences is regularly consulted for advice on policy matters. Its committees and panels draw heavily on the research of the social and behavioral sciences as they evaluate programs and deal with such concerns as energy, taxation, biomedical technologies, environmental monitoring, alcohol abuse, protection of individual privacy, aging, noise abatement, child development, and changes in fertility and mortality. The same is true of the many Presidential Commissions such as those dealing with violence, obscenity, population, or crime. Organizations outside government also use social science data to inform and advise the policy process. For example, under the auspices of the Hoover Institution at Stanford University, a distinguished set of scholars, mainly economists and political scientists, provides a review and analysis of major domestic and international issues in a book, *The United States in the 1980s*, edited by Peter Duignan and Alvin Rabushka. (Larsen, 1981, p. 8)

Peter Rossi believes that social science departments have a major opportunity to serve as suppliers of social science expertise through bidding on applied social science contracts: "As an organized discipline, we have to build linkages to the applied social science world, apprising the contracting agencies and the research industry that sociology has something to offer and to our own colleagues and students that applied social research is a career that is exciting and interesting" (Rossi, 1980, p. 20).

Writing as chairman of the Committee on Professional Opportunities in Applied Sociology of the American Sociological Association, Howard E. Freeman points to the current status of applied sociology:

> Applied sociology has long roots in the discipline; certainly since the 1930's there have been numerous declarations by outstanding sociologists about the need to apply the findings of social research, conferences about the importance of applied work, and books documenting the utility of sociological studies. Further, applied sociology has been growing within the discipline as evidenced by the increase in extra university employment and career opportunities, possibilities for research support, and graduate training opportunities. The 1980 Guide to Graduate Departments of Sociology lists over 100 departments offering courses and special programs in applied sociology; some of the larger profit and nonprofit research organizations employ more sociologists than many sociology departments; and Federal support for basic research is only a small fraction of current applied research funding. (Freeman, 1980, p. 1; see also Study Project of Social Research and Development, 1978)

All applied social science training programs must teach that to influence policymakers, a number of factors must be taken into account. Leonard Saxe writes:

> Successful use of social science by policymakers is dependent on a host of factors. These include how problems are defined, the credibility of the researchers, the nature of the argument developed by the researchers, the quality and availability of the research evidence, the ability of analysts to communicate their ideas and research findings, and the timeliness of the policymakers' interest in the issue. (Saxe, 1987, p. 226)

References

Freeman, Howard E. (1980). *Footnotes* (American Sociological Association), p. 1.

Larsen, Otto. (1981, March). Need for continuing support for social sciences. *Footnotes* (American Sociological Association), p. 8.

Rossi, Peter. (1980, August). *Footnotes* (American Sociological Association), p. 20.

Saxe, Leonard. (1987). Policymakers' use of social science research. In William R. Shadish, Jr., & Charles S. Reichardt, eds., *Evaluation Studies Review Annual* (Vol. 12). Newbury Park, CA: Sage.

Study Project of Social Research and Development. (1978). *Study project report: Vol. 1. The federal investment in knowledge of social problems.* Washington, DC: National Academy of Sciences.

3.1.1 The Future of Applied Sociology: A Presidential View

Stan Capela is the 2000-2001 president of the Society of Applied Sociologists. He offers the following view regarding the direction of this field during the first 10 years of the new millennium.

▶ Applied Sociology: Where Do We Go From Here?

Stan Capela

This is the first of a series of presidential columns on the state of applied sociology. Every month I will devote some time on the state of applied sociology as well as where it fits in the scheme of things.

At the recent Unity Conference there was a lot of discussion around where applied sociology should go in the 21st century. In trying to answer the question I had to decide on the relevance of this question to three different groups. The first group is the practicing sociologist who works outside of the academy. The second includes academics that have to educate our students and provide them with the skills necessary to compete in the open market. The third is the student who is trying to decide if sociology is relevant and worthy of study in the hopes of landing a job once they graduate.

If I were addressing the practicing sociologist I assume he or she would want to know where the future work of the applied sociologist will be in the future. Is it in research? Is it as an evaluator? Is it in government? If I were talking to the academic I would have to provide some information on what skills will be required in the future and how best to translate the information in a way that an academic can apply it in a classroom setting. As for the students, they want to know where the jobs are.

During my tenure at HeartShare Human Services as the MIS Director I have found the future of the applied sociologist to be that of the facilitator. Specifically, when one works in an organizational setting the CEO often looks to someone to identify the problem and come up with a solution. In many instances the CEO wants you to convene a group of people who have their own vested interests and have them work as a group to problem solve and reach a consensus. In many instances you deal with a group of people from a variety of disciplines who look to make sure that whatever the solution is it would impact on them in a negative way and clearly shifts the blame to someone else.

Applied sociologists work well in such a setting because very often they possess group process skills. Second, they understand the importance of language in reaching consensus. More importantly, the theoretical bases upon which they collect information and analyze situations often present themselves in a nonthreatening way that fosters consensus building. In the final analysis if the applied sociologist is able to use their theoretical base as a foundation and if they can present the information in an understandable format they can go a long way in playing a key role in a variety of organizational settings.

What do you think? How can you expand on this thought? Forward your comments and hopefully we can build on this idea and ultimately meet the needs of the different constituencies in our field.

SOURCE: From Stan Capela (2000), *Applied Sociology: Where Do We Go From Here?*, Newsletter, Society of Applied Sociologists. Reprinted with permission.

APPLIED RESEARCH DESIGN   3.2

In contrast with basic research, applied sociological research has many important differences, with new rules and demands.

1. The applied researcher must address a pressing problem presented by some client (be it public or private). The client may be the researcher's boss in a business, government, or service organization, or the client may be an outside organization seeking the services of a professor or a consulting management or research agency. The client is often a government or private funding agency. Each wants the same thing: useful knowledge serving to answer a question that is being faced by policymakers.

2. The researcher must be a translator between the academic discipline in which he or she works and the world of action. Major demands come from the world of action, including concern with timeliness, action, use of everyday language and concepts, ever-present involvement of special interests, conflict, and struggles over resources (Coleman, 1972).

3. The researcher must decide whether it is important to find a relationship between action findings and theory. Academic researchers are usually under rather heavy pressures to publish their work with scientific standing. Patterns of hypothesis testing based on a guiding theory must then be followed. This requirement will influence the design toward basic research standards, but the demand for practical policy guidance will always be a strong opposing pull.

4. The researcher is paid by the client, and the work is evaluated by the results obtained in solving or alleviating the management (as policy) problem.

The late Professor Samuel Stouffer of Harvard University, who directed large-scale research on the American soldier for the U.S. Army in World War II, used to say, "If I get the chance to do ten percent basic research while carrying out the operational research for the U.S. Army, I shall be happy." His success with both types of research was certified by the commendation of General George Marshall of the U.S. Army as well as the praise of American sociologists and psychologists for the superb four volumes known as *The American Soldier* (see Stouffer, 1947, 1949). For this bridging of basic and applied research, *The American Soldier* is a model.

All researchers, basic and applied, need funds, and more funds usually can be secured for applied research than for basic research given the federal government's mandate to make "good" on what it supports. In other words, the results of applied research often answer straightforward and obvious questions. In addition, the ability to provide research designs that capitalize on combinations of basic and practical goals is desirable and very attractive to policymakers and gatekeepers.

References

Coleman, James S. (1972). *Policy research in the social sciences*. Morristown, NJ: General Learning Press.

Stouffer, Samuel A. (1947, 1949). *Studies in social psychology: The American soldier* (4 vols.). Princeton, NJ: Princeton University Press.

3.3 FITTING AN APPLIED RESEARCH DESIGN TO A PROBLEM

An applied research design must be able to interpret behavior embedded in a complex social system. The researcher begins by trying to conceptualize the parts of the system under investigation, its boundaries, its interface with other systems, the feedback loops, and other subsystems to which it may be connected. The key questions then become two:

- How do we achieve specific ends in the system?
- What key causal factors are involved?

Analysis begins with location of situational factors. It progresses to a definition of existing psychological and behavioral responses. Interpersonal factors such as perceptions, norms, values, evaluations, and goals must be mapped as participants interact. Then a theory of intervention must be designed to manipulate situational factors through policy and structural changes. After intervention, evaluation should be undertaken.

Chris Argyris (1985; Argyris, Putnam, & Smith, 1985) has pointed out that practitioners need to consider what kind of knowledge individuals require and use while acting. People make sense of their world by organizing data into patterns, storing them in their heads, and retrieving them whenever they need them. Social scientists can help ensure that the knowledge they produce will be usable by organizing these behavioral patterns in the form of maps for action.

Argyris fashions action maps that set out factors in a given problem situation and traces the participants as they cooperate and conflict. The sequence of steps includes the pressures the participants report with their successes and failures as they try to cope, and their outcome behavior.

References

Argyris, Chris. (1985). Making knowledge more relevant to practice: Maps for action. In Edward E. Lawler III & Associates, *Doing research that is useful for theory and practice* (pp. 79-106). San Francisco: Jossey-Bass.

Argyris, Chris, Putnam, Robert, & Smith, Diana McLain. (1985). *Action science: Concepts, methods, and skills for research and intervention*. San Francisco: Jossey-Bass.

3.4 THE MOOD OF THE ACADEMIC RESEARCHER ENGAGED IN APPLIED RESEARCH

Academics in applied research can get caught up in ambivalent feelings. J. Richard Hackman (1985) says it well:

First, despite my intellectual confidence that new conceptual and methodological approaches are required in organizational behavior, experimenting with those approaches occasionally makes me feel as if my deviations from traditional ways of pursuing scientific values were somehow heretic and sinful. Second, when one is trying to do something which one does not know how to do and for which there are no ready models, failure is always a real possibility and is probably more likely than success. Such ambivalence tends to be accompanied by anxiety, which, in turn, can block intellectual work and make it hard to get anything done, let alone something new and possibly interesting. But ambivalence and anxiety are also reputed to be the precursors of creativity, so there is always hope that something worthwhile will emerge if one sticks with it long enough.

These, then, are the kinds of questions and issues, both emotional and intellectual, that I am wrestling with these days as I continue to try to develop practical theories of individual and group performance effectiveness. I am finding the challenges—to my imagination and to my courage—substantial. (pp. 148-149)

Reference

Hackman, J. Richard. (1985). In Edward E. Lawler III & Associates, *Doing research that is useful in theory and practice* (pp. 148-149). San Francisco: Jossey-Bass.

THE APPLICATION OF SUCCESSFUL APPLIED RESEARCH THROUGH POLICY ANALYSIS 3.5

The use of policy analysis as a tool of social and behavioral researchers is perhaps one of the best examples of applied research. Here, basic data is taken and applied to real-world policy problems and evaluated following a set of evaluative criteria. What follows is an excerpt from an example of such an evaluation (focusing on a discussion of various day care options) including these evaluative criteria and how they applied.

▶ Policy Analysis

Ron Haskins

One answer that has become increasingly popular in recent years in tools to help make decisions about the relative merits of one public policy or another is the use of something called *policy analysis*. Though policy analysis is not a new field (MacRae, 1976; Nagel, 1977), the application of policy analysis tools to social problems is, if not new, at least a growing concern among psychologists, educators and other social scientists. As the papers in this volume demonstrate, the large and somewhat disparate group of researchers and other professionals who focus on children and their families has begun to pay explicit attention to the public policy implications of their work. The purpose of this introductory chapter is to outline a particular approach to the examination of problems dealt with by social policy.

What Is Policy Analysis?

MacRae and Wilde (1979) have defined policy analysis as "the use of reason and evidence to choose the best policy among a number of alternatives" (p. 4). This definition, like many others (Rein, 1976; Titmuss, 1974), emphasizes the application of reason and evidence to policy alternatives. In these respects, policy analysis has much in common with social science. The use of reason implies that decisions will be based on some explicit set of criteria that are themselves defended as appropriate for the case at hand. Whim, personal prejudice, and political belief, then, must be minimized and subjugated to the rules of logic and inference.

An important element in attempts to subdue whim and prejudice while emphasizing logic is the application of evidence to selection among policy alternatives. Though social science research constitutes an important type of evidence it is by no means the only type that the analyst can use. The history of a social problem often supplies evidence that should be taken into account, as does demographic information. Nor can the analyst afford to be bounded by the confines of a favored academic discipline. Indeed, there is no current problem of social policy—health care, day care, income maintenance, education—for which one discipline can supply all the relevant evidence.

To take child care as an example, any moderately complete analysis of the problem and its potential solutions would consider the history of child care in the United States, provide an economic description of the current child care market, and examine the sociological and psychological effects of various types of child care on children and families. Such an analysis is, of necessity, interdisciplinary. *Interdisciplinary*, another term much in vogue, refers to nothing more than an activity which uses the information and techniques from more than one discipline. The term rolls easily off many tongues, but when developmentalists begin to deal with benefit-cost analysis, trade-offs, and externalities, while economists begin to consider early experience, the development of aggression, and the complexities of gene-environment interaction, interdisciplinary activities take on a concrete meaning, and professionals quickly realize the depth and importance of evidence and techniques about which they have received little formal training. But if evidence refuses to recognize the artificial boundaries of the scientific disciplines, analysts have no choice but to expand their perspective and overcome the prejudices of their own disciplines.

A Model of Policy Analysis

Having defined policy analysis, I would like now to outline a specific approach to analysis that promises some reasonable possibility of successfully attacking social problems. Although the sketch offered here must be brief, I mean to provide a concrete set of proposals that, taken together, constitute a concise but comprehensive method for analyzing social problems, selecting a solution, and communicating that solution to those who can cause it to be enacted and implemented.

This model consists of five distinct steps: analyzing the problem situation, specifying the analysis criteria, generating alternative strategies, synthesizing information to select a policy alternative, and examining the feasibility of the policy alternative selected. In expanding somewhat on each of these five steps of the analysis model, examples will be drawn from day-care policy. Although examples might have been taken from any of various policy problems, day care was chosen because of its timeliness and because it provides particularly clear and rich illustrations of steps in the model.

Analysis of the Problem Situation

Most problem situations arise because of changes in demographic features of society, the breakdown of traditional patterns of behavior, the gradual evolution of new values and attitudes, or technological innovation. The outcome of these forces is that some group sees an opportunity for advancement, believes that its current situation is threatened, or perceives an unfulfilled need. In this stage of analysis, an historical perspective is often helpful. In fact, one might argue that understanding the problem situation is impossible without examining the problem's origin and, if appropriate, previous attempts to deal with the problem. History informs the present and, in so doing, offers important insights to both the nature of a policy problem and its potential solutions. Analysis of the problem situation must also include a review of groups that want to implement a particular policy and groups that may be affected by a policy. This review will show that often the groups most concerned see a threatened value or an opportunity to promote an important value.

For many policy problems, defining the problem situation should also include an examination of current state and federal policies that influence the situation. Almost every problem that affects children and families has been dealt with in some way by state or federal laws. Previous and current government activity, then, is an integral part of the problem situation and must be taken into account if the analyst is to avoid creating policies that actually oppose one another. Further, as will be argued later, examining the outcomes of current policies can yield important insights for devising new policies.

Finally, an important product of a thorough analysis of the problem situation should be a clear and comprehensive statement of the problem which the analysis aims to attack. This statement may well differ from that held by the analyst when review of the problem situation began. Indeed, one particularly important justification for analysis of the problem situation is that thorough analysis often changes the analyst's understanding of the problem, its causes, and its potential solutions. Such changes constitute a restatement of the problem in a form more consonant with historical facts and more comprehensive in its understanding of which groups are interested in, and affected by, the policy.

Generating Policy Alternatives

The analyst is now in position to generate alternative strategies. The objective of this stage of analysis is to identify an extensive list of potential policies addressed to the problem situation and then to eliminate alternatives that seem clearly infeasible.

There are at least four sources of ideas for identifying policy alternatives. One of the most important of these is history. As indicated previously, the historical background of a policy problem will often suggest a number of policy alternatives. Some of these may actually have been attempted at some level of government; others will have been proposed by particular individuals or groups but never enacted; still others will occur to the analyst who is familiar with the policy problem and its background. A second source of ideas of policy alternatives is the practices and policies of other countries. Particularly with regard to social programs, such as child care, income supports, and health, many European countries have a long history of progressive and effective policies (Kamerman & Kahn, 1978).

Social sciences research may also provide suggestions for policy alternatives. Especially significant in this regard are the income maintenance experiments (New Jersey, Gary, Iowa/North Carolina, and Seattle/Denver) which have provided massive information on the effects of a guaranteed income. Various papers published from these studies concern the use of child care by working mothers, the use of social services, school achievement of children, the consumption of health care, and so on. This type of information can be used to evaluate the effects of income maintenances strategy that has been advocated as a basic solution to many social problems (Keniston, 1977; National Academy of Sciences, 1976)—on each of these policy concerns.

The fourth source an analyst should examine in generating policy alternatives is the particular strategies favored by interest groups, prominent research or policy organizations, and powerful public figures, including politicians. Policy alternatives supported by individuals or groups may be spelled out in particular detail in a public speech, written report, or pamphlet.

Once these policy alternatives have been identified, the analyst may want to eliminate some because they are too costly, too impractical, or too strongly opposed by powerful individuals or groups. In any case, the final list of policy alternatives is now subjected to the critical stage of policy selection.

Specifying Valuative Criteria

As Quade (1975) and others point out, policy analysis grew out of systems research, operations research, and public administration. Many of the problems to which these analytic methods have been applied were technological—building highways, conducting war, sending men into space. As various groups and individuals now apply these methods to social problems, and especially to child and family policy, it becomes increasingly clear that difficulties abound. A basic cause of these difficulties is that the solution of human social problems involves *the synthesis of values.* By this I mean simply that various groups enter the policy arena with competing needs, interests, claims, and rights.

How are these incommensurables to be resolved? As I shall argue, analysts of social policy can answer this question by using analysis criteria. The important point to be made here is that values necessarily play a powerful—even preeminent—role in the analysis of child and family policies. Thus, a primary characteristic of analysis models for social policy must be some means of making values explicit and, where necessary, choosing among competing values. If, as MacRae and Wilde (1979) argue, policy analysis is the process of using "reason and evidence to choose the best policy" (p. 4), valuative criteria are the heart of policy analysis because they are the yardstick by which we judge the worth of policy alternatives.

A number of these valuative criteria are universal; i.e., they can and should be considered in the analysis of most social policies. Four examples of these universal criteria are horizontal and vertical equity, efficiency, preference satisfaction, and stigma.

Horizontal and Vertical Equity.   Horizontal equity involves the equal treatment of equals. For example, all children have the right to adequate health care and education. Vertical equity involves the unequal treatment of unequal individuals and groups. To satisfy the criterion of vertical equity, a policy must result in redistribution of resources in such a way as to provide greater benefits to the poor than to the rich. The criteria of horizontal and vertical equity, like most valuative criteria, are not accepted as a primary objective of social policy by all political groups. Liberals and conservatives agree that a society should have some fairly substantial difference in financial reward across job categories in order to maintain incentives for increasing productivity.

Efficiency.   A second important valuation criterion, not completely separable from vertical equity, is efficiency. *Efficiency* is defined as that use of resources which will produce the maximum benefit. By this criterion, a policy is less desirable if another policy would produce, on the whole, greater benefits. Needless to say, the word "benefits" does not have clear meaning in these definitions. What is a benefit? Who receives the benefit? In what units can it be measured?

Economists have devised a method that provides a partial answer to these questions. Benefit-cost analysis has the potential to maximize efficiency by expressing both the benefits and costs of a program in dollars. Except for a few complications, such as opportunity costs (MacRae & Wilde, 1979), the measurement of program costs is usually straightforward. Thus, we can usually measure in dollars what expenditures were made, or are planned or estimated, for a given social program. But measuring the benefits of a social program is often more difficult. In what units can we measure the value of a ten-point IQ gain produced by a preschool program? Of 1,000 single women placed in jobs by a training program? Of 10,000 children from poor families receiving a balanced lunch? Of a 10 percent reduction in infant mortality?

The criterion of efficiency should play a primary role in all policy decisions. Since everyone gains in the long run when public funds are spent efficiently, there would seem to be little reason for anyone to quarrel with this criterion. It must be admitted, however, that the intended outcome of many social policies cannot be easily measured; this problem limits ability to apply the efficiency criterion.

Preference Satisfaction.   In a society that values freedom and often avoids government intervention on the grounds that it limits individual choice, preference satisfaction must be considered a fundamental criterion in that individuals are better off when policy helps them satisfy their own preferences. As with the case of efficiency, few will disagree that this criterion is important.

At least two complications, however, make this criterion quite difficult to maximize. First, preferences can best be satisfied when individuals are able to buy the goods and services they prefer. For example, many individuals and families in our society do not have enough money to satisfy basic preferences.

Second, it is obvious that not everyone has the same preferences and that the preferences of some individuals and groups may be in conflict.

Stigma.   As used here, *stigma* means that a policy results in recipients being labeled as different in some negative way from citizens not affected by the policy. The value underlying this criterion is that all citizens have a right to benefit from government programs without their fellow citizens attributing deficits, weaknesses, or pathology to the participants' characters.

It seems wise to minimize stigma, not just because it violates the privacy of families, but because it may contribute to prolonging the very conditions a given policy aims to ameliorate. Although persuasive evidence is not available, it seems reasonable to argue that when parents or children are constantly reminded of their inferior status and dependence on public largesse, they may come to resent such treatment, to have their self-esteem damaged, and to develop a sense of hopelessness (see, for example, Rainwater, 1970). In any case, it seems unwise to risk these effects of policy where they can be avoided.

Policy-Specific Criteria

In addition to the universal criteria just discussed, every policy problem will have idiosyncratic criteria appropriate to that particular problem. These criteria are typically ones that concern the specific objectives of a given policy and that allow comparison of particular strategies or alternative programs designed to address the problem.

For example, in referring again to day-care policy in order to illustrate this type of criteria, we can identify a number of important dimensions along which day-care policies might be compared. Two general types of criteria, each having a number of more specific criteria, are effects of child care on children's development and effects on the family. Regarding the former, the analyst should consider the effects on intellectual development, social development, and health. Regarding the latter, the analyst might consider effects on the mother-child relation, on employment of mothers, on marital satisfaction, and on the mother's sense of accomplishment and fulfillment. These, of course, are not the only possible criteria for assessing the effects of day care, but they illustrate the point that the analysis should include criteria tailored specifically to the policy problem at hand.

In addition to universal and policy-specific criteria, one other criterion merits attention. Nearly every policy has effects that were neither planned nor anticipated. These consequences associated with the policy may be either positive or negative. In either case, the experienced analyst may be able to anticipate them and thereby avoid or capitalize on these associated effects.

Feasibility.   Feasibility—or the probability that a policy will actually be carried out—has already played a role at the stage of generating policy alternatives. In that case, it was recommended that after generating an exhaustive set of policy options, the analyst could save considerable time and trouble by eliminating from further consideration any policies that were clearly infeasible.

After selecting the policy of choice, feasibility again becomes a primary consideration. Indeed, as MacRae and Wilde (1979) note, when the policy option has been selected, much work remains to be done. In particular, it is now necessary to devise a plan for enactment and a plan for implementation of the policy.

Enactment.   Having selected the best policy option, the analyst must now consider ways in which the policy of choice can actually receive legislative support. In so doing, the analyst may in some cases adopt more of an advocacy role. Of course, whether an advocacy role is appropriate depends in large measure on the analyst's position—the citizen or analyst is usually free to become an advocate; an analyst employed by a firm or the government may not be free to play this role.

Implementation.   Even if a policy is enacted, its actual effect on children and families cannot be assumed until the policy has been implemented. Excellent policy ideas and sufficient funding can be foiled at a number of points between the federal or state level and the site of service delivery.

First, and perhaps most important, is the way legislative directives are translated into actual policy by the writing of administrative regulations and guidelines. These guidelines will determine to a large degree how funds are distributed, reports are written, and services are delivered. Thus, the analyst must pay careful attention to the way these guidelines are written and be prepared to offer assistance where possible and to protest obvious flaws in the guidelines where necessary.

Closely related to the problem of guidelines is the administering agency selected to implement the policy. In some cases, the administering agency will have played an important role in writing the legislation, but even in such cases the agency may write and enforce guidelines in such a way as to give its staff maximum flexibility in policy implementation. Thus, it is not surprising that an agency which is hostile to a given policy can often subvert the intent of the legislation. Indeed, a favored device of presidents and high administrative officials for killing a policy they oppose is to assign it to an agency that also opposes the policy.

A third serious problem with implementation is that individuals or groups hostile to the policy but with insufficient political strength to block the legislation may be able to subvert implementation. Techniques that can be applied to this end are legion—including both techniques just outlined. In addition, congressional foes may be able to delay implementation by blocking either the appropriation or authorization of the policy's funding.

Fourth, a number of policies fail at the level of implementation because the technology or knowledge needed to ensure success is not available.

Policy Selection: The Synthesis of Information

The various policy alternatives can now be compared by estimating their effects as measured by each of the criteria. The analyst uses social science research, historical information, and best guesses to make these estimates.

Of course, quantitative estimates are preferable, but given the present state of knowledge, it is often impossible to reach such estimates with any degree of precision. Hence, one often must use techniques that have not been traditional in social science. An example of such a technique is the Delphi procedure (Linstone & Turoff, 1975). In this procedure, experts are asked to estimate the quantitative value of a particular policy's effect on some variable. The experts' individual estimates are shared with the entire group of experts, and they are then asked to make a second quantitative estimate. Obviously, this procedure attempts to encourage agreement between experts—the underlying assumption being that convergence among experts is the best way to estimate the value of a variable that is not well understood.

We can refer to the decision matrix (shown in the following illustration where policy alternatives are compared across the evaluative criteria that we just discussed).

	Horizontal Equity	Vertical Equity	Efficiency	Preference Satisfaction	Stigma	Feasibility	Enactment	Implementation	Policy-Specific Criteria
Status Quo									
Policy Alternative 1									
Policy Alternative 2									

The first policy alternative is always to maintain the *status quo*. MacRae and Wilde (1979) recommend that this alternative, which they refer to as *do nothing*, be included in all analyses to serve as a kind of baseline against which to compare the effects of other policies. Of course, we should keep in mind that for virtually any policy problem that affects children and families, the option of maintaining the *status quo* does not refer to a situation free of government intervention. In fact, many levels of government are already involved in most problems that affect children and families. Thus, the *status quo* alternative means that current government policy will continue to operate.

References

Kamerman, S. B., & Kahn, A. J. (Eds.). *Family policy: Government and families in fourteen countries.* New York: Columbia University Press, 1978.

Keniston, K. *All our children: The American family under pressure.* New York: Harcourt Brace Jovanovich, 1977.

Linstone, U. A., & Turoff, M. (Eds.). *The Delphi method: Techniques and applications.* Reading, Mass.: Addison-Wesley, 1975.

MacRae, D. *The social function of social science.* New Haven: Yale University Press, 1976.

MacRae, D., & Wilde, J. A. *Policy analysis for public decisions.* North Scituate, Mass.: Duxbury Press, 1979.

Nagel, S. S. (1977). *Operations research methods.* Beverly Hills, CA: Sage.

National Academy of Sciences. *Toward a national policy for children and families.* Washington, D.C.: Author, 1976.

Quade, E. S. *Analysis for public decisions.* New York: Elsevier, 1975.

Rainwater, L. *Behind ghetto walls: Black families in a federal slum.* Chicago: Aldine, 1970.

Rein, M. *Social science and public policy.* New York: Penguin, 1976.

Titmuss, R. M. *Social policy: An introduction.* New York: Pantheon Books, 1974.

SOURCE: From Ron Haskins (1980), *Care and education of young children in America: Policy, politics, and social science* (Norwood, NJ: Ablex). Reprinted with permission.

3.6 BIBLIOGRAPHY ON APPLIED SOCIOLOGY, KNOWLEDGE UTILIZATION, POLICY-MAKING, AND EVALUATION

3.6.1 Applied Sociology

Anderson, R. J., and Sharrock, W. W. (Eds.). (1984). *Applied sociological perspectives*. New York: Routledge.

Birchenall, Joan. (1998). *Sociology applied to nursing*. Philadelphia, PA: W. B. Saunders.

Brown, William R. (1984, August). *An assessment of teaching applied sociology*. Paper presented at the annual meeting of the American Sociological Association, San Antonio, TX.

Clute, William T. (1986). Student consultants: Teaching applied sociology in substantive courses. *Teaching Sociology, 14,* 196-199.

Freeman, Howard E. (Ed.). (In press). *Applied sociology*. Ann Arbor, MI: Books on Demand.

Freudenburg, William R., & Keating, Kenneth M. (1985). Applying sociology to policy: Social science and the environmental impact statement. *Rural Sociology, 50,* 578-604.

Green, Charles S., III, & Salem, Richard G. (1982). The nonsociologist as applied sociologist: Teaching undergraduates applied sociology as ethical practice. *Teaching Sociology, 11,* 32-46.

Johnson, Doyle Paul, Brown, William R., Hage, Jerald, Lyson, Thomas A., Orthner, Dennis K., Paulson, Steven K., Squires, Gregory D., & Wimberley, Ronald D. (1987). The challenge of training in applied sociology. *American Sociologist, 18,* 356-368.

Kelly, Robert F. (1986). Teaching graduate applied sociology through internships: Program development, management, and problems. *Teaching Sociology, 14,* 234-242.

Kenig, Sylvia. (1992). *Who plays? Who pays? Who cares? A case study in applied sociology, political economy, and the community mental health centers movement*. Amityville, NY: Baywood.

Kimmel, Allan J. (1988). *Ethics and values in applied social research* (Vol. 12). Thousand Oaks, CA: Sage.

Lazarsfeld, Paul, & Reitz, Jeffery G. (In press). *An introduction to applied sociology*. Ann Arbor, MI: Books on Demand.

Maneker, Jerry S. (1994). *Applied sociology: Sociological understanding and its application*. Lanham, MD: University Press of America.

Olsen, Marvin E., & Micklin, Michael. (Eds.). (1981). *Handbook of applied sociology: Frontiers of contemporary research*. New York: Praeger.

Park, Betty Jean. (1982). The Center for the Study of Local Issues: A vehicle for applied sociology. *Teaching Sociology, 11,* 105-112.

Parsons, Talcott. (1997). *Essays on sociological theory: Pure and applied*. New York: Free Press.

Petrus, Gene, & Adamek, Raymond J. (1988). Taking the role of the other: An aid to marketing applied sociology. *Teaching Sociology, 16,* 25-32.

Popenoe, David. (2000). *Sociology*. Upper Saddle River, NJ: Prentice Hall.

Porter, M. (1998). *Psychology and sociology applied to medicine*. Camden Town, UK: Churchill-Livingstone.

Sherohman, James. (1982, August-September). *Applied sociology and social work*. Paper presented at the annual meeting of the American Sociological Association, Detroit, MI.

Steele, Stephen F., & Iutcovich, Joyce M. (Eds.). (1997). *Directions in applied sociology: Presidential addresses of the Society for Applied Sociology, 1985-1995*. London: Arnold.

Steele, Stephen F., Scarsisbrick-Hauser, Annemarie, & Hauser, William J. (1998). *Solution-centered sociology: Addressing problems through applied sociology*. Thousand Oaks, CA: Sage.

Sullivan, Thomas. (1991). *Applied sociology: Research and critical thinking.* Upper Saddle River, NJ: Prentice-Hall.

Tepperman, Lorne, & Blaine, Jenny. (1999). *Think twice! Sociology looks at current social issues.* Upper Saddle River, NJ: Prentice-Hall.

Wallace, Richard Cheever. (1988). A capstone course in applied sociology. *Teaching Sociology, 16,* 34-40.

Ward, Lester F. (1999). *Applied sociology.* Temecula, CA: Reprint Services Corporation.

Watts, W. David, Short, A., & Schultz, C. (1982). Applied sociology and the current crisis. *Teaching Sociology, 11,* 47-61.

Wright, R., Dubois, William, & Bacon, Allyn. (2000). *Applying sociology: Making a better world.* Needham Heights, MA: Allyn and Bacon.

Yiannakis, Andrew, & Greendorfer, Susan L. (Eds.). (1992). *Applied sociology of sport.* Champaign, IL: Human Kinetics.

3.6.2 Knowledge Utilization

Backer, Thomas E., & Shaperman, Julie. (1992). Knowledge utilization and foundations supporting health research and demonstrations: Initial explorations. *Knowledge: Creation, Diffusion, and Utilization, 14,* 386-400.

Beker, Jerome, & Eisikovits, Zvi C. (Eds.). (1991). *Knowledge utilization in residential care and youth care practice.* Washington, DC: Child Welfare League of America, Inc.

Cernada, George P. (1982). *Knowledge in action: A guide to research utilization.* Amityville, NY: Baywood.

Guiltinan, Joseph P., & Achabal, Dale. (1986). *AMA Winter Educators' Conference, 1986: Marketing Education: Knowledge Development, Dissemination, and Utilization.* Ann Arbor, MI: Books on Demand.

Havelock, Ronald G., & Guskin, Alan E. (1971). *Planning for Innovation Through Dissemination and Utilization of Knowledge.* Ann Arbor, MI: Center for Research on Utilization of Scientific Knowledge.

Hess, T. M. (Ed.). (1990). *Aging and cognition: Knowledge organization and utilization.* New York: Elsevier Science.

Hultman, Glenn, & Horberg, Cristina Robertson. (1998). Knowledge competition and personal ambition: A theoretical framework for knowledge utilization and action in context. *Science Communication, 19,* 328-348.

Kiresuk, Thomas J. (1992). The evaluation of knowledge utilization: Placebo and nonspecific effects, dynamical systems, and chaos theory. *Journal of the American Society for Information Science, 44,* 235-241.

Paisley, William. (1992). Knowledge utilization: The role of new communication technologies. *Journal for the American Society of Information Science, 44,* 222-234.

Wong, Kenneth K. (1998). Laying the groundwork for a new generation of policy research: Commentary on "Knowledge utilization in educational policy and politics," Spotlight on Student Success No. 302. *Educational Administration Quarterly, 34,* 141-146.

3.6.3 Policy-Making/Policy Analysis

Anderson, James E. (2000). *Public policymaking: An introduction* (4th ed.). Boston: Houghton Mifflin.

Bardach, Eugene. (2000). *A practical guide for policy analysis: The eightfold path to more effective problem solving.* New York: Seven Bridges Press.

Berman, David R. (1982). *American government, politics, and policymaking.* Pacific Palisades, CA: Palisades Publishers.

Burns, Tom R., & Ueberhorst, Reinhard. (1988). *Creative democracy: Systemic conflict resolution and policymaking in a world of high science and technology.* Westport, CT: Greenwood.

De-Greene, Kenyon B. (Ed.). (1992). *A systems based approach to policymaking.* Norwood, NJ: Kluwer Academic Publishers.

Friedelbaum, Stanley. (1988). *Human rights in the states: New directions in constitutional policymaking.* Westport, CT: Greenwood.

Janis, Irving L. (1989). *Crucial decisions: Leadership in policymaking and crisis management.* New York: Free Press.

Longest, Beaufort B. (1998). *Health policymaking in the United States.* Chicago: Health Administration Press.

Meehan, Eugene J. (1990). *Ethics for policymaking: A methodological analysis.* Westport, CT: Greenwood.

Mezey, Susan G. (1996). *Children in court: Public policymaking and federal court decisions.* Albany: State University of New York Press.

Protess, D., & McCombs, M. (Eds.). (1991). *Agenda setting: Readings on media, public opinion and policymaking.* Mahwah, NJ: Lawrence Erlbaum.

Prunty, John J. (1984). *A critical reformulation of educational policy analysis.* New York: State Mutual Book & Periodical Service.

Rich, Michael J. (1992). *Federal policymaking and the poor: National goals, local choices, and distributional outcomes.* Princeton, NJ: Princeton University Press.

Ross, Robert S. (Ed.). (1992). *China, the United States and the Soviet Union: Tripolarity and policymaking in the Cold War.* Armonk, NY: M. E. Sharpe.

Schmitz, David F., & Jespersen, T. Christopher. (Eds.). (1999). *Architects of the American century: Individuals and institutions in twentieth-century U.S. foreign policymaking.* Chicago: Imprint Publications.

Sharkansky, Ira. (1999). *Ambiguity, coping and governance: Israeli experiences in politics, religion and policymaking.* Westport, CT: Greenwood.

Shepard, N. Alan. (1984). *A policy analysis of professional development and personnel preparation for serving special populations.* Columbus, OH: Center for Education and Training for Employment.

Stokey, Edith, & Zeckhauser, Richard. (1978). *A primer for policy analysis.* New York: W. W. Norton and Company.

3.6.4 Evaluation Basic Primers

Ackerman, Marc J. (1995). *Clinician's guide to child custody evaluations.* New York: John Wiley and Sons.

Alkin, Marvin C., & Jacobsen, Phyllis. (1985). *A guide for evaluation decision makers.* Lima, OH: Books on Demand.

Boruch, Robert F. (1997). *Randomized experiments for planning and evaluation: A practical guide.* Thousand Oaks, CA: Sage.

Davitz, Joel Robert, & Davitz, Lois Leiderman. (1996). *Evaluating research proposals: A guide for the behavioral sciences.* Englewood Cliffs, NJ: Prentice Hall.

Fink, Arlene. (1992). *Evaluation fundamentals: Guiding health programs, research and policy.* Newbury Park, CA: Sage.

Giardino, Angelo P., Christian, Cindy W., & Giardino, Eileen R. (1997). *A practical guide to the evaluation of child physical abuse and neglect.* Thousand Oaks, CA: Sage.

Giardino, Angelo P., Finkel, Martin A., Giardino, Eileen R., Seidl, Toni, & Ludwig, Stephen. (1992). *A practical guide to the evaluation of sexual abuse in the prepubertal child.* Newbury Park, CA: Sage.

Korte, Nic. (1999). *A guide for the technical evaluation of environmental data.* Lancaster, PA: Technomic.

Ogles, Benjamin M., Lambert, Michael J., & Masters, Kevin S. (1996). *Assessing outcome in clinical practice.* Boston: Allyn and Bacon.

Patrick, John. (1992). *Training: Research and practice.* London: Academic Press.

Patton, Michael Quinn. (1997). *Utilization-focused evaluation: The new century text.* Thousand Oaks, CA: Sage.

Rice, Marilyn, & Valdivia, Leonel. (1991). A simple guide for design, use and evaluation of educational materials. *Health Education Quarterly, 18,* 79-85.

Rubin, Frances. (1995). *A basic guide to evaluation for development workers.* Oxford, UK: Oxfam Publishing.

Simon, Robert I. (Ed.). (1995). *Posttraumatic stress disorder in litigation: Guidelines for forensic assessment.* Washington, DC: American Psychiatric Press.

Stahl, Philip Michael. (1994). *Conducting child custody evaluations: A comprehensive guide.* Thousand Oaks, CA: Sage.

3.6.5 Examples of Evaluation

Al-Sharideh, Khalid. (1999). *Modernization and socio-cultural transformation in Saudi Arabia: An evaluation.* Unpublished doctoral dissertation, Kansas State University.

Altus, Deborah E., & Mathews, R. Mark. (1999). A case study evaluation of the homecare suite: A new long-term care option for elders. *Journal of Housing for the Elderly, 13,* 115-125.

Arts, Wil, Hermkens, Piet, & Van-Wijck, Peter. (1999). Modernisation theory, income evaluation, and the transition in Eastern Europe. *International Journal of Comparative Sociology, 40,* 61-78.

Atim, Chris. (1999). Social movements and health insurance: A critical evaluation of voluntary, non-profit insurance schemes with case studies from Ghana and Cameroon. *Social Science and Medicine, 48,* 881-896.

Berk, Richard A., & de-Leeuw, Jan. (1999). An evaluation of California's inmate classification system using a generalized regression discontinuity design. *Journal of the American Statistical Association, 94,* 1045-1052.

Birnbacher, Dieter. (1999). Quality of life—Evaluation or description? *Ethical Theory and Moral Practice, 2,* 25-36.

Bode, Maarten. (1998). Social structure and change: Vol. 1. Theory and method. An evaluation of the work of M. N. Srinivas. *Contributions to Indian Sociology* (New Series), *32,* 558-559.

Bogner, Franz X., & Wiseman, Michael. (1998). Environmental perception of Swiss and Bavarian pupils: An empirical evaluation. *Revue Suisse de Sociologie, 24,* 547-566.

Bonta, James, Wallace, Capretta-Suzanne, & Rooney, Jennifer. (2000). Can electronic monitoring make a difference? An evaluation of three Canadian programs. *Crime and Delinquency, 46,* 61-75.

Calloway, Michael O., & Nadlicki, Terri M. (2000, April). *Research and learning: Using theories of social capital to guide health policy and evaluation.* Paper presented at the annual meeting of the Southern Sociological Society, New Orleans, LA.

Cannon, Julie Ann Harms. (1996). The social construction of knowledge: An evaluation of the works of Dorothy E. Smith and Patricia Hill Collins. *Humanity and Society, 20,* 9-24.

Chodos, Howard. (1998). Theory and metatheory in the evaluation of Marxism: A review essay. *Critical Sociology, 24,* 156-166.

Craglia, Massimo, Haining, Robert, & Wiles, Paul. (2000). A comparative evaluation of approaches to urban crime pattern analysis. *Urban Studies, 37*, 711-729.

Dalenberg, Constance J. (1999). Overcoming obstacles to just evaluation and successful prosecution of multivictim cases. *Journal of Aggression Maltreatment and Trauma, 2*, 141-162.

Dumaine, Marian Lee. (1998). *An evaluation of coping ability as a guide to the treatment of persons diagnosed with schizophrenia and substance abuse.* Unpublished doctoral dissertation, Florida International University, Miami.

Farrell, Graham, & Buckley, Alistair. (1999). Evaluation of a UK police domestic violence unit using repeat victimisation as a performance indicator. *Howard Journal of Criminal Justice, 38*, 42-52.

Ferligoj, Anuska, & Hlebec, Valentina. (1999). Evaluation of social network measurement instruments. *Social Networks, 21*, 111-130.

Foddy, William. (1998). An empirical evaluation of in-depth probes used to pretest survey questions. *Sociological Methods and Research, 27*, 103-132.

Gavazzi, Stephen M., Wasserman, Deborah, Partridge, Charles, & Sheridan, S. (2000). The Growing Up FAST diversion program: An example of juvenile justice program development for outcome evaluation. *Aggression and Violent Behavior, 5*, 159-175.

Gransky, Laura A., & Patterson, Marisa E. (1999). A discussion of Illinois' gang free prison: Evaluation results. *Corrections Management Quarterly, 3*, 30-42.

Green Mazerolle, Lorraine, Ready, Justin, Terrill, William, & Waring, Elin. (2000). Problem-oriented policing in public housing: The Jersey City evaluation. *Justice Quarterly, 17*, 129-158.

Harris, Philip W., & Jones, Peter R. (1999). Differentiating delinquent youths for program planning and evaluation. *Criminal Justice and Behavior, 26*, 403-434.

Hatley, Heather Lynne. (1999). *The influences of managed care on certified nurse midwives: An evaluation of health system change.* Unpublished doctoral dissertation, University of Wisconsin, Madison.

Henderson, Harold, German, Victor F., Panter, A. T., Huba, G. J., Rohweder, Catherine, Zalumas, Jacqueline, Wolfe, Leslie, Uldall, Karina K., Lalonde, Bernadette, Henderson, Ron, Driscoll, Mary, Martin, Sara, Duggan, Sandra, Rahiman, Afsaneh, & Melchior, Lisa A. (1999). Systems change resulting from HIV/AIDS education and training: A cross-cutting evaluation of nine innovative projects. *Evaluation and the Health Professions, 22*, 405-426.

Henry, Gary T., & Julnes, George. (1998). Values and realist evaluation. *New Directions for Evaluation, 78*, 53-71.

Holmila, Marja. (1999). Public policy and program evaluation. *Acta Sociologica, 42*, 97-99.

Jasso, Guillermina, & Wegener, Bernd. (1999). Gender and country differences in the sense of justice: Justice evaluation, gender earnings gap, and earnings functions in thirteen countries. *International Journal of Comparative Sociology, 40*, 94-116.

Julnes, George, & Mark, Melvin M. (1998). Evaluation as sensemaking: Knowledge construction in a realist world. *New Directions for Evaluation, 78*, 33-52.

Khan, M.-Adil. (1998). Evaluation capacity building: An overview of current status, issues, and options. *Evaluation, 4*, 310-328.

Klein, Susan Shurberg. (1992). Sharing the best: Finding better ways for the federal government to use evaluation to guide the dissemination of promising and exemplary education solutions. *Evaluation and Program Planning, 16*, 213-217.

Koskinen, Ilpo. (2000). Plans, evaluation, and accountability at the workplace. *Sociological Research Online.* Retrieved February 4, 2000, from the World Wide Web: http://www.socresonline.org.uk

Kuehne, Valerie-Shahariw. (1999). Building intergenerational communities through research and evaluation. *Generations, 22*, 82-87.

Kyudd, Sally Anna. (1999). *A case study of program planning and evaluation in assisting Montserratian evacuees and British government officials in natural disaster planning.* Unpublished doctoral dissertation, Rutgers State University.

Latkin, Carl A., & Knowlton, Amy R. (2000). New directions in HIV prevention among drug users: Settings, norms, and network approaches to AIDS prevention (SNNAAP); a social influence approach. *Advances in Medical Sociology*, 7, 261-287.

Leon, Ana M., Dziegielewski, Sophia F., & Tubiak, Christine. (1999). A program evaluation of a juvenile halfway house: Considerations for strengthening program components. *Program Planning and Evaluation*, 22, 141-152.

Loveday, Barry. (1999). Tough on crime or tough on the causes of crime? An evaluation of Labour's crime and disorder legislation. *Crime Prevention and Community Safety—An International Journal*, 1, 7-24.

Mason, George P. (1999). *The Congress of Industrial Organizations and the rise of American industrial unionism: A re-evaluation of the record.* Paper presented at the annual meeting of the American Sociological Association.

Mears, Daniel P. (1998). Evaluation issues confronting juvenile justice sentencing reforms: A case study of Texas. *Crime and Delinquency*, 44, 443-462.

Mears, Daniel Preston. (2000). *Evaluating juvenile justice reform: An analysis of prosecutorial discretion and determinate sentencing in Texas.* Unpublished doctoral dissertation, University of Texas, Austin.

Miller, J. Mitchell. (1999). Administrative police training for an emerging democracy: An evaluation of the Moscow Police Command College—a research note. *American Journal of Criminal Justice*, 23, 267-276.

Moore, Melanie, Blumstein, Philip, & Schwarz, Pepper. (1998). The power of motherhood: A contextual evaluation of family resources. *Free Inquiry in Creative Sociology*, 26, 111-117.

Neuhauser, Linda, Schwab, Michael, Syme, S. Leonard, Bieber, Michelle, & Obarski, Susan King. (1998). Community participation in health promotion: Evaluation of California wellness guide. *Health Promotion International*, 13, 211-222.

O'Sullivan, Rita G., & O'Sullivan, John M. (1998). Evaluation voices: Promoting evaluation from within programs through collaboration. *Evaluation and Program Planning*, 21, 21-29.

Rossi, Peter H. (1997). Advances in quantitative evaluation 1987-1996. *New Directions for Evaluation*, 76, 57-68.

Rowe, Gene, & Frewer, Lynn J. (2000). Public participation methods: A framework for evaluation. *Science, Technology, and Human Values*, 25, 3-29.

Shapiro, Jeremy P., Welker, Carolyn J., & Pierce, Janice L. (1999). An evaluation of residential treatment for youth with mental health and delinquency-related problems. *Residential Treatment for Children and Youth*, 17, 33-48.

Slizyk, Jeanne. (2000, April). *Program evaluation of a program to assist victims of domestic violence.* Paper presented at the annual meeting of the Southern Sociological Society, New Orleans, LA.

Stall, Ron D., Paul, Jay B., Barrett, Donald C., Crosby, G. Michael, & Bein, Edward. (1999). An outcome evaluation to measure changes in sexual risk taking among gay men undergoing substance abuse disorder treatment. *Journal of Studies on Alcohol*, 60, 837-845.

Stockmann, Reinhard. (1999). The implementation of dual vocational training structures in developing countries: An evaluation of "dual projects" assisted by the German Agency for Technical Cooperation. *International Journal of Sociology*, 29, 29-65.

Van Goor, H., & Stuiver, B. (1998). Can weighting compensate for nonresponse bias in a dependent variable? An evaluation of weighting methods to correct for substantive bias in a mail survey among Dutch municipalities. *Social Science Research*, 27, 481-499.

Van Hees, Alma. (1999). Halt: Early prevention and repression; recent developments and research. *European Journal on Criminal Policy and Research*, 7, 405-416.

Voas, R. B., Marques, P. R., Tippetts, A. S., & Beirness, D. J. (1999). The Alberta Interlock Program: The evaluation of a province-wide program on DUI recidivism. *Addiction*, 94, 1849-1859.

Wagner, Peter. (1999). After justification: Repertoires of evaluation and the sociology of modernity. *European Journal of Social Theory*, 2, 341-357.

Williams, James L., Rodeheaver, Daniel G., & Huggins, Denise W. (1999). A comparative evaluation of a new generation jail. *American Journal of Criminal Justice*, 23, 223-246.

Wilson, Barbara Renee. (1999). *Evaluation of the Family Support Worker Program.* Unpublished doctoral dissertation, University of Minnesota.

Wilson, Steve T. (2000). *Minority police officers, police discrimination and the police subculture: An evaluation of prior studies and a proposal for future research.* Paper presented at the annual meeting of the Southern Sociological Society.

Yeboah, David. (2000). The evaluation of New Zealand's Habilitation Centre's pilot program. *Journal of Criminal Justice*, 28, 227-235.

3.6.6 Applications of Knowledge Utilization

Berlin, Donna F., & White, Arthur L. (1992, April). *Action research as a solution to the problem of knowledge utilization.* Paper presented at the annual meeting of the American Educational Research Association, San Francisco.

Cousins, J. Bradley, & Leithwood, Kenneth A. (1992). Enhancing knowledge utilization as a strategy for school improvement. *Knowledge: Creation, Diffusion, and Utilization*, 14, 305-332.

Datta, Lois Ellin. (1992). A grass roots perspective on legislating knowledge utilization: The Seventh Annual Howard Davis Memorial Lecture, April 1992. *Knowledge: Creation, Diffusion, and Utilization*, 14, 291-304.

Elpers, J. R. (1989). Development and utilization of incentive systems for mental health operations: Successful and unsuccessful knowledge utilization in California and Los Angeles. *Journal of Mental Health Administration*, 16, 9-20.

Nelson, Scott J. (1989). Values and priorities: Their effect on knowledge utilization in public mental health programs. *Journal of Mental Health Administration*, 16, 44-49.

Peterson, Paul D., & Quasim, Lyle. (1989). Using strategy to promote knowledge utilization and change in community mental health systems. *Journal of Mental Health Administration*, 16, 29-36.

Sorensen, James E. (1989). Collaboration among state and local mental health organizations: Examples of knowledge utilization. *Journal of Mental Health Administration*, 16, 3-8.

3.7 EVALUATION RESEARCH AS A PROCESS

Every attempt to reduce or eliminate a social problem involves a theory, a program, and usually a large amount of money. The effectiveness of programs to reduce crime and delinquency, combat drug addiction, conquer health problems, and improve neighborhoods and communities and the quality of life generally—all pose problems of evaluation. Because these problems are so important to national and community life and are so costly, evaluation has been given a high priority and evaluation research is increasing.

Edward Suchman (1967) has written:

Evaluation always starts with some value, either explicit or implicit—for example, it is good to live a long time; then a goal is formulated derived from this value. The selection of goals is usually preceded by or concurrent with "*value formation.*" An example of "*goal-setting*" would be the statement that fewer people should develop coronary disease, or that not so many people should die from cancer. Goal-setting forces are always in competition with each other for money, resources, and effort.

There next has to be some way of "*measuring goal attainment.*" If we set as our goal that fewer people should die from cancer, then we need some means of discovering how many are presently dying from cancer (for example, vital statistics). The nature of the evaluation will depend largely on the type of measure we have available to determine the attainment of our objective. The next step in the process is the identification of some kind of "goal-attaining activity." In the case of cancer, for example, a program of cancer-detection activities aimed at early detection and treatment might be considered. Then the goal-attaining activity is put into operation. Diagnostic centers are set up and people urged to come in for check-ups.

Then, at some point, we have the *assessment* of this goal-directed operation. This stage includes the evaluation of the degree to which the operating program has achieved the predetermined objectives. As stated previously, this assessment may be scientifically done or it may not.

Finally, on the basis of the assessment, a *judgment* is made as to whether the goal-directed activity was worthwhile. This brings us back to value formation. Someone now may say that it is "good" to have cancer diagnostic centers. At the end of the evaluation process, we may get a new value, or we may reaffirm, reassess, or redefine an old value. For example, if the old value was "it is good to live a long time," the new value might be, "it is good to live until 100 if you remain healthy; but if you can't remain healthy it's better not to live past eighty."

Reference

Suchman, Edward A. (1967). *Evaluative research, principles and practice in public service and social action programs*. New York: Russell Sage Foundation.

3.7.1. Design and Implementation of Evaluation Models

One way in which many social and behavioral science disciplines has changed is an increased call for accountability. One of the ways this has been expressed is through the design and implementation of evaluation models and strategies. In the following excerpt, Rossi and Wright discuss the role of evaluation in the assessment of programmatic outcomes and how evaluation has developed as a scientific approach to the answer of whether a program is effective.

▶ **Evaluation Research: An Assessment**

Peter H. Rossi and James D. Wright

Evaluation research came into prominence as an applied social scientific activity during the Great Society programs of the mid-1960s. The distinctive feature of the past 25 years is the explicit recognition among policymakers and public administrators that evaluations could be conducted systematically using social scientific research methods and could produce results that had more use and validity than the judgmental approaches used previously. During the Great Society era, Congress authorized many new programs and systematic evaluations were mandated in several of the more important pieces of legislation.[1]

The new administrative agencies set up to implement many of these programs were partially staffed by social scientists who had strong interests in applied work. The entire gamut of the social scientific disciplines was involved. Economists had a strong foothold in the Office of Economic Opportunity; sociologists, psychologists, and educators were ensconced in the Office of Education (later the Department of Education); the Department of Health, Education and Welfare (now Health and Human Services) was big enough to accommodate members of all of the social scientific disciplines in critical positions; and the Department of Labor's Manpower Research Division was also generous, providing opportunities for all.

The interdisciplinary character of this new social scientific activity was especially noteworthy. Economists, sociologists, psychologists, and educational researchers often found themselves bidding on the same contracts in competition with each other, a process that facilitated the transfer of knowledge, craft lore, and mutual respect across disciplinary boundaries. Research firms and institutes previously dominated by one discipline broadened their outlooks by hiring professionals from other social sciences, mainly in order to increase their competitive edge. Interdisciplinary professional societies were also founded, e.g., the Evaluation Research Society and the Evaluation Network.[2]

University-based social scientific researchers were slow to take advantage of the new opportunities for research funding, even though the topics involved were often of central interest, a reflection of the indifference (even hostility) to applied work that has characterized the academic social science departments until very recently (Raizen & Rossi 1981, Rossi & Wright 1983, Rossi et al. 1978). Private entrepreneurs, however, were quicker to notice and exploit the new emphasis on evaluation. Some existing firms that had not been particularly interested in the social sciences opened subsidiaries that could compete for social research contracts (e.g., Westinghouse). Others greatly expanded their social science research sections (e.g., the Rand Corporation). In addition, literally hundreds of new firms appeared on the scene, a handful of which became spectacular successes during the "golden years" (e.g., Abt Associates).[3]

By the middle of the 1970s, some 500-600 private firms existed primarily to bid on contracts for applied social research. As in other areas of corporate activity, a few firms garnered the majority of the available funds. For example, in the period 1975-1980, 6 large research firms received over 60% of the evaluation funds expended by the Department of Education (Raizen & Rossi 1981).

An additional large number of firms sprang up to bid on contracts for evaluation and other applied social research activities at the state and local levels. These research opportunities were neither as well funded as those on the federal level nor were the tasks as intellectually or technically challenging. There was (and continues to be) enough evaluation "business" on the state and local levels, however, to provide the essential "bread and butter" for a very large number of small-scale job shops.

Some of the existing university-based research institutes with histories of large-scale social research also prospered during this period. The National Opinion Research Center at the University of Chicago and the Survey Research Center at the University of Michigan both grew enormously in size. Their staffs eventually came to dwarf most academic departments in the relevant fields. New academic research organizations also were started to take advantage of the funding opportunities offered through the grant and contract mechanism.

A corresponding growth took place on the conceptual side of evaluation research. The publication in 1966 of Donald T. Campbell and Julian Stanley's seminal work on research designs useful in the evaluation of educational programs created an entirely new vocabulary for the taxonomy of research designs and for the discussion of validity issues. It also made the randomized, controlled experimental paradigm the method of choice for causal analyses. Both of these emphases came to dominate large portions of the evaluation field for the next decade. Evaluation research was initially seen as, quintessentially, the assessment of programs' net effects. Correspondingly, the main problem in designing evaluation research was to specify appropriate *ceteris paribus* conditions that would permit valid estimates of these net effects. Within this framework, the randomized, controlled experiment became the ruling paradigm for evaluation research. The conceptual foundations had been developed many decades earlier, and this approach had been the ruling research paradigm in both psychology and biology for many years. The special contribution made during the period under current review was that the paradigm was taken out of the laboratory and into the field, and it was combined with the sample survey in studies designed to test the effects of the proposed programs. To many social scientists of a technocratic bent, the randomized field experiment promised to replace our bumbling trial-and-error approaches to forging social policy with a more self-consciously rational "experimenting society" (Campbell 1969).

By the early 1970s, an impressive number of large-scale experiments had been funded and started. These experiments covered a wide variety of topics: income maintenance plans intended to replace the existing welfare benefits system: housing allowances that might stimulate the market to produce better housing for the poor; health insurance plans that would not create perverse medical-care price effects; and so on through a veritable laundry list of field experiments. Ironically, most of them were designed and run by economists, members of a field not noted for its tradition of experimental work.

The realization quickly emerged, however, that randomized, controlled experiments could only be done correctly under very limited circumstances and that the demand for evaluation covered many programs that simply could not be assessed in this way. Not only were there frequent ethical and legal limitations to randomization, but many existing programs that had full (or almost full) coverage of their intended beneficiary populations could not be assessed using controlled experiments because there was no way to create appropriate control groups. It also turned out that field experiments took a long time—3 to 5 years or more—from design to final report, a delay that was simply intolerable given the much shorter time horizons of most policymakers and public administrators.

Campbell and Stanley (1966) had provided one possible solution to this dilemma by coining the term *quasi-experiments* and using it to cover evaluation research designs that do not rely on randomization to form controls. Although they explicitly recognized the inferior validity of data generated in this way, they also discussed the conditions under which valid causal inferences could be drawn from evaluation studies using such designs. Their treatment of quasi-experimental research designs certainly stimulated the use of such designs in evaluation studies, sometimes under conditions that Campbell and Stanley explicitly stated were potentially fatal. Indeed, the vast majority of the evaluations that have been carried out have been quasi-experiments, rather than randomized, "true" experiments, mainly because the latter have proven difficult, if not impossible, to implement in real world settings.

But even quasi-experimental designs have their limitations. For one thing, while not as expensive or time-consuming as "true" experiments, a well-conducted quasi-experiment may demand more funds, time and talent than are available. Another problem is that many of the more sophisticated quasi-experimental designs (in particular, interrupted time series designs) require long time series of data—ideally, series that contain a long run of observations prior to the introduction of a policy intervention and that continue for several years after that. Concerning the first, the necessary data often do not exist; and, concerning the second, the old problem of timeliness reappears. A final problem, of course—one Campbell and Stanley discussed in detail—is that there are potential threats to the validity of any quasi-experimental design. In using such designs, one always runs some risk of mistaking various artifacts for true program effects. Hence, quasi-experiments are almost always vulnerable to critical attack; witness the rancorous controversies surrounding some of the major educational evaluations (e.g., McLaughlin 1975, Mosteller & Moynihan 1972, Rossi & Wright 1982).

Due to the many evident problems of both experimental and quasi-experimental approaches to evaluation research, the need for methods of evaluation that were timely, relatively inexpensive, and responsive to many program administrators' and officials' fears that evaluations would somehow "do them in" quickly became apparent. This statement applies especially to evaluations that were mandated by Congress and that the program agencies themselves were supposed to conduct. Indeed, Congress—coupling its newfound enthusiasm for evaluations with a seriously flawed understanding of the time, talent and funding needed to carry out evaluations of even minimum quality—often imposed evaluation tasks on program agencies that far exceeded the agencies' research capacities and then provided funds that were grossly inadequate to accomplish them.

The need for evaluations that could be carried out by technically unsophisticated persons and that would be timely and useful to program administrators fueled a strong interest in qualitative approaches to evaluation research (Patton 1980, Scriven 1977, Guba & Lincoln 1981, House 1980). Qualitative research methods have always had some following in all of the social sciences, especially in sociology. Their special attraction in sociology is their presumed ability to stay close to reality and to promote an understanding of social processes through intimate familiarity with field conditions. In addition, for evaluation purposes, qualitative methods seemed to have the attractive triple advantages of being inexpensive, timely, and responsive to administrators' needs. These approaches were especially attractive to program sponsors and operators because they appeared to be flexible enough to cope with social programs that, once implemented, tend to vary sharply from one locale to another not only in their goals but also in the benefits and services that are actually delivered. The goals for some broad-spectrum programs (e.g., Model Cities) were not clearly defined by Congress or the administering agencies. Each operating agency thus defined its own goals and often changed them frequently (Kaplan 1973, Williams 1980). The appeal, at least initially, of qualitative approaches to evaluation is that they apparently had the potential to be sensitive to the nuances of ill-defined and constantly evolving program goals.

The great boom in evaluation ended in 1981 when the Reagan administration began to dismantle the social programs that had been developed over the previous 20 years. The extensive manpower research program of the Department of Labor was reduced to almost nothing and there were similar (although less drastic) cuts in the Departments of Health and Human Services, Education, and Agriculture, among others. The immediate consequence was a drastic reduction in the amount of federal money available for applied social research.

Ironically, the Reagan cutbacks occurred just as more and more academic departments began to discover that there was a nonacademic market for newly minted PhDs. Openings for evaluation researchers were a large component of this market. The American Sociological Association held an extremely well-attended conference in Washington, D.C., in 1981 (Freeman et al. 1983) on the appropriate training for careers in applied sociology. Many graduate departments throughout the country began programs to train applied researchers of all kinds, and there was an evident interest among at least some prominent sociologists. Indeed, both presidents of the American Sociological Association in 1980 and 1981 devoted their presidential addresses to applied work (Rossi 1981, Whyte 1982).

The Intellectual Harvest of the Golden Years of Evaluation

The frenzied growth of evaluation research during the 1960s and 1970s produced a real increment in our knowledge about the relevant social problems and a decided increase in the technical sophistication of research in the social sciences. Both of these developments have already had some impact on the social sciences and will be increasingly valuable to our fields in the future.

The Large-Scale Field Experiments of the "Golden Age"

Perhaps the most impressive substantive and technical achievements of the entire Golden Age were those of the large-scale field experiments. Most of these experiments were initially funded by the Office of Economic Opportunity and, upon the demise of that agency, by the Department of Health, Education and Welfare.

On the technical side, these experiments combined both sample survey techniques and classical experimental designs. Experimental and control groups were created by sampling open communities and then randomly allocating sampled households to experimental and control groups. Interviews with experimental and control households were then undertaken, using traditional sample survey techniques to measure responses to the experimental treatments. Looked upon as surveys, these experiments were long-term panels with repeated measurements of the major dependent (i.e., outcome) variables. Measures were taken as often as once a month in some of the experiments and extended over periods of up to five years. Viewed as experiments, the studies were factorial ones in which important parameters of the treatments were systematically varied.

Perhaps the best-known of the field experiments during the Golden Age were those designed to test various forms of the "negative income tax" (NIT) as a means of maintaining a reasonable income floor for poor households. All told, there were five such experiments in the United States and one in Canada.

Fixing Up Nonexperimental Designs

The discussion so far has been fairly narrowly focused on randomized experimental designs for impact assessment because (a) the technically most successful impact assessments were carried out using that design and therefore (b) the randomized, controlled experimental paradigm has dominated the evaluation scene for the last two decades. As detailed above, however, there are good reasons at least to modify the experimental paradigm, chief among them being that for most social programs evaluation must perforce use nonexperimental methods.

There are many reasons why randomized experimental designs cannot be used in some evaluation studies. First, ongoing programs that cover most or all of their intended target populations simply do not admit of believable controls. For example, an estimated 5-10% of the persons eligible for Old Age and Survivors Insurance (Social Security) benefits have not applied for them. These nonapplicants cannot realistically serve as controls for estimating the effects of social security benefits, however, because the self-selection factors are undoubtedly strong. Comparing persons receiving social security benefits with those who are eligible but, for whatever reasons, have not applied for them violates the *ceteris paribus* condition.

Second, some programs, such as Head Start, fail to reach significantly large proportions of the eligible population—perhaps as much as 25% of the Head Start example. These children are not reached by the Head Start program because parents have not allowed their children to enroll or because the school systems involved have too few poor children to support Head Start projects. Clearly, strong self-selection factors are at work, and hence, contrasting Head Start participants with eligible nonparticipants would not hold constant important differences between the two groups.

Finally, it would be ethically unthinkable to use randomization in the evaluation of some programs. For example, a definitive way of estimating the relative effectiveness of private and public high schools would be to assign adolescents to one or the other randomly and observe the outcome over an extended period of time. Obviously, there is no way that either policymakers or parents would allow such an evaluation to take place.

Thus, many of the evaluation studies of the past two decades have employed something other than classical randomized experimental designs. Unfortunately, these evaluations have not been technically successful on the whole. Each of the major nonexperimental evaluations has been shrouded in controversy—controversy that arises out of the political implications of the findings but that often centers on the technical inadequacies of the designs employed. Thus, Coleman's (1966) attempt to sort out schools' effects on achievement by analyzing a cross-sectional survey of thousands of students from hundreds of high schools was criticized mainly because of the statistical models he used (Mosteller & Moynihan 1972). Similarly, an evaluation (Westinghouse Learning Corporation 1969) of the long-lasting effects of participating in Head Start came under fire (Campbell & Erlebacher 1970) because the researchers compared youngsters who had attended Head Start preschools with "comparable" children who had not. According to the study's critics, confounding self-selection factors were undoubtedly at work that made the two groups incomparable in important respects.

The problem of administrative or self-selection of program participants and non-participants is at the heart of nonexperimental evaluation designs' vulnerability to criticism. To illustrate this point, we can consider Coleman and his associates' (1982) recent study of academic achievement in public and private (mostly Catholic) high schools. The critical comparisons in such a study are clearly plagued by self-selection factors: whether a child attends the Catholic parochial high schools or the public high schools cannot by any stretch of the imagination be considered a random choice. Parents often make the choice alone, although they sometimes consult the child; they make their education decisions on the basis of factors such as their anticipated income, their commitment to their religious group and its ideology, their assessments of their child's intellectual capabilities, the relative reputations of the local high schools, and so on. Nor are parents and child the only forces involved. Parochial high schools exercise judgment about whom they want to admit, selecting students on the basis of factors like their previous educational experience, the kind of curriculum the child or parents want, and the child's reputation as a behavioral problem. Some of these factors are probably related to high school achievement; the extent to which these factors independently affect such achievement would confound any *simple* comparisons between the achievement scores of parochial and public high school students.

Obviously, one way out of the problem is to hold constant statistically those factors relating both to achievement and to school choice. The difficulties of doing so, however, are also obvious. First, it is necessary to specify the relevant factors correctly, a task that is usually difficult because of the absence of empirically grounded theory to aid in that specification. Secondly, if the element of choice is one of those factors (as in this example), it *cannot* be held constant since choice exists for one group but not for the other; in the present case, that is, non-Catholics would not have the option of sending their children to parochial schools. [See Rossi & Wright (1982) for a more detailed critique of Coleman along these lines.]

A potentially fruitful solution to this problem has recently been suggested by the econometricians (Goldberger 1980, Barnow et al. 1980, Berk & Ray 1982). They propose that researchers construct explicit models of the decision process and incorporate these models into structural equation systems as a means of holding constant the self-selection process. Although these proposals are somewhat more attractive than the usual approach of adding independent variables to a regression equation, they are still largely irrelevant because the appropriate decision models cannot be constructed except in special circumstances.

Another important development in the methodology used in nonexperimental evaluations has been the application of time series models to the assessment of the net effects of large-scale programs. [These models were originally developed in economic forecasting (Pindyck & Rubinfeld 1976) and subsequently applied specifically to evaluation problems (McCleary & Hay 1980, Cook & Campbell 1979).] First suggested by Campbell & Stanley (1966) as "interrupted time series" designs, the application of time series models has made it possible to assess the impact of new large-scale programs or the effects of modifying existing ones without recourse to classical randomized experiments. This approach is limited to programs that have long time series of data on their outcomes available and whose onset can be definitely located in time as, for example, with the enactment of new legislation.

Among the best-known interrupted time series evaluations are the various assessments of the Massachusetts Bartley-Fox gun law (G. L. Pierce & Bowers 1979, Deutsch & Alt 1977, Hay & McCleary 1979). This law imposed a mandatory penalty for carrying guns without a license, with the objective of reducing the use of guns in crimes. Using time series models, the researchers modeled the trends in gun-related crimes before the Bartley-Fox law went into effect and compared the resulting projections with the trends observed after the law was enacted. The findings suggest that the law led to only a slight reduction in the use of guns in crimes. The times series models used (Box-Jenkins models) are composed of a family of frameworks, each differing from the others in its assumptions about the kinds of time-dependent processes at work. To some degree, the choice among models is a judgment call, a condition that has led to polemical exchanges among independent researchers about the law's true effects (e.g., Hay & McCleary 1979, Deutsch 1979).

The two developments just discussed have implications for sociology that go considerably beyond evaluation research per se. The conceptualization of the self-selection problem in evaluation research has direct applications to most sociological research that relies on cross-sectional studies. The data analysis problems encountered are identical, so solutions developed in the evaluation field have immediate applications in the many sociological studies in which self-selection issues complicate the interpretation of findings.

Time series of critical data are available on many of the substantive areas of interest to sociologists. Aggregate data on crime rates go back almost 50 years; unemployment rates have been available on a monthly basis for almost 40 years; and so on.

Research on program implementation is primarily research in public administration. Although good examples are rare, in principle it is no more difficult to test several alternative ways of delivering a program than to test several alternative programs; indeed, the two problems are formally identical. That implementation issues are often critical is widely recognized (Williams & Elmore 1976, Pressman & Wildavsky 1973, W. S. Pierce 1981), but the importance of research on the issues involved has not received the attention it deserves.

The Future of Evaluation Research:
An Addendum by Delbert C. Miller

Since the above assessment of evaluation research was written by Rossi and Wright in 1984, evaluation research has suffered a decline in fiscal support. The decline began to be evident as early as 1980, in the political climate imposed by the Reagan administration. Personnel of the U.S. General Accounting Office recently reported the following.

1. Between 1980 and 1984, the number of professional staff in all agency evaluation units decreased by 22%, from about 1,500 to about 1,200. In contrast, the total number of staff in these agencies decreased by only 6% during this period.
2. Between 1980 and 1984, funds for program evaluation were reduced by 37%, compared with a 4% increase for the agencies as a whole.
3. Information loss and distortion of findings were reported as the result of lack in assessment. These failures were shown to be most serious in the areas of defense, the environment, and labor and personnel (Chelimsky et al. 1989).

The future of evaluation research, in spite of recent declines, is promising.

> Reducing the federal deficit and promoting public confidence in the federal government are two top concerns the incoming Congress and administration must face. Crucial to both is the availability of timely, technically sound information for legislative oversight, for program management, and for public awareness. Information for the first audience—Congress—answers questions about how money is being spent and managed, and what results have been achieved. Information for the second audience—program managers—answers questions about what needs to be done to comply with the law and to achieve greatest effectiveness and efficiency of opera-

tions. Information for the third audience—the public—answers questions about what it is getting for its money.

Program evaluation is an essential tool in providing information to all three audiences. (Chelimsky et al. 1989, p. 25)

These needs will not go away. If anything, as old social demands increase in severity and new social needs arise, and as budgets rise by the multibillions of dollars, evaluation research becomes ever more important to Congress, to program managers, and to the public. And the need for evaluation is not limited to the federal government; it is equally important for state and city governments.

Evaluation appears to have become part of the tools of government. Private research agencies will continue to receive important contracts for program assessment. Therefore, there will probably be a continuing need for personnel well trained in the social sciences to staff the research projects that will be undertaken, and sociologists may continue to find employment in evaluation research.

The accompanying list of the literature cited by Rossi and Wright is an outstanding compilation of both evaluation methodology and evaluation studies of social programs.

Notes

1. Especially important were the evaluations mandated in the 1964 Elementary and Secondary School Education Act (McLaughlin 1975), in the Housing and Urban Development budget authorization of 1970 calling for the experimental evaluation of a proposed housing allowance program (Struyk & Bendick 1981), and in the enabling legislation for the Department of Labor's Comprehensive Employment Training Program (Rossi et al. 1980). Evaluation research is found today in all major fields of social intervention, including health, mental health, criminal justice, housing, and handicapped children and their families. The Department of Defense has used evaluation research increasingly.

2. A tabulation of the primary disciplines of the members of the Evaluation Research Society (Evaluation Research Society 1979) nicely illustrates the interdisciplinary character of the evaluation research field. Herewith, the breakdown of membership by field: psychology 47%; sociology 10%; economics 4%; political science 6%; education 15%; and other 18%.

3. Some of the spectacular successes of those prosperous times, of course, have been greatly diminished by the reverses of today's harder times. At its height, Abt Associates employed more PhDs in the social sciences than any one of the Boston area universities and more than most combinations of universities. In the past few years, its PhD workforce has been reduced by almost 50%.

Literature Cited*

American Institutes for Research. 1977. *Evaluation of the Impact of the EASA Title 7 Spanish/English Bilingual Education Program.* Vols. 1-3. Palo Alto, CA: Am. Inst. Res.

American Institutes for Research. 1980. *The National Evaluation of the PUSH for Excellence Project.* Washington, DC: Am. Inst. Res.

Barnow, B. S., Cain, G. G., Goldberger, A. S. 1980. Issues in the analysis of selectivity bias. In *Evaluation Studies Review Annual,* vol. 5, ed. E. W. Stormsdorfer, G. Farkas, 43-59. Beverly Hills, CA: Sage.

Bawden, D. L., Harrar, W. S., eds. 1978. *Rural Income Maintenance Experiment: Final Report.* 6 vols. Madison, WI: Inst. Res. Poverty.

Berk, R. A., Ray, S. C. 1982. Selection biases in sociological data. *Social Science Research* 11(4): 352-98.

Bernstein, I., Freeman, H. 1975. *Academic and Entrepreneurial Research.* New York: Russell Sage Foundation.

Bradbury, K., Downs, A., eds. 1981. *Do Housing Allowances Work?* Washington, DC: Brookings Inst.

Campbell, D. T. A phenomenology of the other one: Corrigible, hypothetical, and critical. In *Human Action,* ed. W. Mischel, 1, 41-69.

---

*Some items on this list were cited in part of the original publication not excerpted here.

Campbell, D. T., Erlebacher, A. 1970. How regression artifacts in quasi-experiments can mistakenly make compensatory education look harmful. In *The Disadvantaged Child*, ed. J. Helmuth, 185-210. New York: Brunner-Mazel.

Campbell, D. T., Stanley, J. C. 1966. *Experimental and Quasi-Experimental Designs for Research*. Skokie, IL: Rand McNally.

Chelimsky, E. C., Cordray, D., Datta, L. 1989. Federal evaluation: The pendulum has swung too far. *Evaluation Practice* 10(2):24-28.

Chen, H., Rossi, P. H. 1982. Evaluating with sense: The theory driven approach. *Evaluation Review* 7(3):283-302.

Coleman, J. C. 1966. *Equality of Educational Opportunity*. Washington, DC: USGPO.

Coleman, J. C., Hoffer, T., Kilgore, S. 1982. *High School Achievement: Public, Catholic and Private Schools Compared*. New York: Basic.

Cook, T. D., Campbell, D. T. 1979. *Quasi-Experimentation: Design and Analysis Issues for Field Settings*. Chicago: Rand McNally.

Cronbach, L. J. 1982. *Designing Evaluations of Educational and Social Programs*. San Francisco: Jossey-Bass.

Cronbach, L. J., Ambron, S. R., Dornbusch, S. M., Hess, R. D., Hornik, R. C., Phillips, D. C. 1980. *Toward Reform of Program Evaluation*. San Francisco: Jossey-Bass.

Davidson, W. S., et al. 1981. *Evaluation Strategies in Criminal Justice*. New York: Pergamon.

Deutsch, S. J. 1979. Lies, damned lies and statistics: A rejoinder to the comment by Hay and McCleary. *Evaluation Quarterly* 3(2):315-28.

Deutsch, S. J., Alt, F. B. 1977. The effect of Massachusetts' gun control law on gun-related crimes in the city of Boston. *Evaluation Quarterly* 1(3):543-67.

Deutscher, I. 1977. Toward avoiding the goal trap in evaluation research. In *Readings in Evaluation Research*, ed. F. G. Caro, 108-22. New York: Russell Sage Foundation.

Evaluation Research Society. 1979. *Membership Directory*. Columbus, OH: Evaluation Research Society.

Fairweather, G. W., Tornatzky, L. G. 1977. *Experimental Methods for Social Policy Research*. New York: Pergamon.

Freeman, H., Dynes, R., Rossi, P. H., Whyte, W. F., eds. 1983. *Applied Sociology*. San Francisco: Jossey-Bass.

Friedman, J., Weinberg, D., eds. 1982. *The Great Housing Experiment*. Beverly Hills, CA: Sage.

Friesema, H. P., Caporaso, J., Goldstein, G., Lineberry, R., McCleary, R. 1979. *Aftermath*. Beverly Hills, CA: Sage.

Goldberger, A. S. 1980. Linear regression after selection. *Journal of Econometrics* 15(12):357-66.

Gramlich, E. M., Koshel, P. P. 1975. *Educational Performance Contracting: An Evaluation of an Experiment*. Washington, DC: Brookings Institution.

Guba, E. G., Lincoln, Y. S. 1981. *Effective Evaluation*. San Francisco: Jossey-Bass.

Hamilton, W. L. 1979. *A Social Experiment in Program Administration: The Housing Allowance Administrative Agency Experiment*. Cambridge, MA: Abt.

Hay, R., Jr., McCleary, R. 1979. Box-Tiao time series models for impact assessment: A comment on the recent work of Deutsch and Alt. *Evaluation Quarterly* 3(2):277-314.

House, E. 1980. *Evaluating with Validity*. Beverly Hills, CA: Sage.

Kaplan, M. 1973. *Urban Planning in the 1960's: A Design for Irrelevancy*. New York: Praeger.

Kelling, G. L., Pate, T., Dieckman, D., Brown, C. E. 1974. *The Kansas City Preventive Patrol Experiment: A Technical Report*. Washington, DC: Police Foundation.

Kershaw, D., Fair, J. 1975. *The New Jersey-Pennsylvania Income Maintenance Experiment*. Vol. 1. New York: Academic Press.

Manderscheid, R. W., Greenwald, M. 1983. Trends in employment of sociologists. In *Applied Sociology*, ed. H. E. Freeman, R. R. Dynes, P. H. Rossi, W. F. Whyte, 51-62. San Francisco: Jossey-Bass.

Manpower Demonstration Research Corporation Board of Directors. 1980. *Summary and Findings of the National Supported Work Demonstration*. Cambridge, MA: Ballinger.

McCleary, R., Hay, R. A., Jr. 1980. *Applied Time Series Analysis*. Beverly Hills, CA: Sage.

McLaughlin, M. W. 1975. *Evaluation and Reform: The Elementary and Secondary Education Act of 1965*. Cambridge, MA: Ballinger.

Moffitt, R. A. 1979. The labor supply response in the Gary experiment. *Journal of Human Resources* 14(4):477-87.

Mosteller, F., Moynihan, D. P., eds. 1972. *On Equality of Educational Opportunity.* New York: Vintage.

Nathan, R., Cook, R. F., Rawlins, V. L. 1981. *Public Service Employment: A Field Evaluation.* Washington, DC: Brookings Institution.

Newhouse, J. P., Rolph, J. E., Mori, B., Murphy, M. 1980. The effects of deductibles on the demand for medical care services. *Journal of the American Statistical Association* 75(371):525-32.

Patton, M. 1980. *Qualitative Evaluation Methods.* Beverly Hills, CA: Sage.

Pierce, G. L., Bowers, W. J. 1979. *The Impact of the Bartley-Fox Gun Law on Crime in Massachusetts.* Boston: Center for Applied Social Research, Northeastern University.

Pierce, W. S. 1981. *Bureaucratic Failure and Public Expenditures.* New York: Academic.

Pindyck, R. S., Rubinfeld, D. L. 1976. *Econometric Models and Economic Forecasts.* New York: McGraw-Hill.

Pressman, J., Wildavsky, A. 1972. *Implementation.* Berkeley: University of California Press.

Raizen, S., Rossi, P. H. 1981. *Program Evaluation in Education.* Washington, DC: National Academy of Sciences-National Resource Council.

Robins, P. K., Spiegelman, R. G., Weiner, S., Bell, J. G., eds. 1980. *A Guaranteed Annual Income: Evidence from a Social Experiment.* New York: Academic.

Rossi, P. H. 1978. Issues in the evaluation of human services delivery. *Evaluation Quarterly* 2:573-99.

Rossi, P. H. 1981. Presidential address: The challenge and opportunities of applied social research. *American Sociological Review* 45(6):889-904.

Rossi, P. H. 1982. Pussycats, weasels, or percherons? Current prospects for the social sciences under the Reagan regime. *Evaluation News* 40(1):12-27.

Rossi, P. H., Berk, R. A., Lenihan, K. 1980. *Money, Work and Crime.* New York: Academic.

Rossi, P. H., Berk, R. A., Lenihan, K. 1982. Saying it wrong with figures. *American Journal of Sociology* 88(2):390-92.

Rossi, P. H., Freeman, H. E. 1982. *Evaluation: A Systematic Approach.* 2nd ed. Beverly Hills, CA: Sage.

Rossi, P. H., Lyall, K. 1974. *Reforming Public Welfare.* New York: Russell Sage Foundation.

Rossi, P. H., Wright, J. D. 1982. Best schools—Better discipline or better students? *American Journal of Education* 91(1):79-89.

Rossi, P. H., Wright, J. D. 1983. Applied social science. *Contemporary Sociology* 12(2):148-51.

Rossi, P. H., Wright, J. D., Wright, S. R. 1978. The theory and practice of applied social research. *Evaluation Quarterly* 2(2):171-91.

Scriven, M. 1977. *Evaluation Thesaurus.* 3rd ed. Inverness, CA: Edgepress.

Struyk, R. J., Bendick, M., Jr. 1981. *Housing Vouchers for the Poor.* Washington, DC: Urban Institute.

Tornatzky, L., Fergus, E., Avellar, J., Fairweather, G., Fleischer, M. 1980. *Innovation and Social Process: A National Experiment in Implementing Social Technology.* New York: Pergamon.

Watts, H. W., Rees, A. 1976. *The New Jersey Income-Maintenance Experiment.* Vols. 2, 3. New York: Academic.

Watts, H. W., Skidmore, F. 1981. A critical review of the program as social experiment. In Bradbury & Downs 1981, pp. 33-65.

Weiss, R., Rein, M. 1970. The evaluation of broad-aimed programs: Experimental design, its difficulties, and an alternative. *Administrative Science Quarterly* 15(1):97-109.

Westinghouse Learning Corporation. 1969. *The Impact of Head Start.* Athens, OH: Westinghouse Learning Corporation & Ohio University.

Whyte, W. F. 1982. Presidential address: Social questions of resolving human problems. *American Sociological Review* 47(1):1-12.

Williams, W. 1980. *Government by Agency: Lessons from the Social Program Grants-in-Aid Experience.* New York: Academic.

Williams, W., Elmore, R. F. 1976. *Social Program Implementation.* New York: Academic.

Williams, W., Elmore, R., Hall, J., Jung, R., Kirst, M., Machmanus, S. 1982. *Studying Implementation: Methodological and Substantive Issues.* New York: Chatham.

Wright, J. D., Rossi, P. H., Wright, S. R., Weber-Burdin, E. 1979. *After the Clean-Up: Long Range Effects of Natural Disasters.* Beverly Hills, CA: Sage.

Zeisel, H. 1982. Evaluation of an experiment. *American Journal of Sociology* 88(2):378-89.

SOURCE: From Peter H. Rossi and James D. Wright (1984), "Evaluation Research: An Assessment," *Annual Review of Sociology,* 10, 332-352. Reprinted by permission of the Annual Review, www.AnnualReviews. org.

3.7.2 Defining Evaluation and a Comparison of Internal and External Evaluation

Evaluation, according to Sonnichsen (2000), is the process of collecting and analyzing evidence, then disseminating the findings to identified audiences so that policy and programmatic judgments and decisions can be made.

Traditionally, most evaluations have been external in nature, performed by an evaluator selected from outside the organization, but this has changed. One of the major advantages of internal evaluation, in today's environment of tighter budget constraints, is the lower costs associated usually with internal evaluations. Several other factors also come into play.

Sonnichsen (2000) presents the following comparison of internal and external evaluation, including the advantages and disadvantages.

	Internal Evaluations	External Evaluations
Advantages	• Commitment to the organization • Knowledge of the organization's personnel and operations • Quick response to evaluation requests • Greater perceived credibility by organizational components • Function as an institutional memory • Frequent client contact • Support of the decision-making process • Access to data • Lower costs • Greater ability to observe the organization's operations • Flexibility to assume other than evaluation tasks on short notice • Greater ability to monitor recommendation implementation • Potential to educate organization regarding value of evaluation • Serve as change agents • Continuity of evaluation effort	• May possess superior evaluation skills • Perceived as more independent • Bring fresh perspective to organizational issues • Greater objectivity • Less susceptible to co-optation • Can objectively assess organization-wide programs that may include the internal evaluators as participants
Disadvantages	• Possible lack of power in the organization • Possible lack of independence • Ethical dilemmas • Burden of additional tasks • Perceived organizational bias • May lack technical evaluation expertise	• Lack knowledge of the organization • Limited access to organizational data • More expensive

Reference

Sonnichsen, R. (2000). *High impact internal evaluation: A practitioner's guide to evaluating and consulting inside organizations*. Thousand Oaks, CA: Sage.

3.7.3 The Sequence of Evaluation

Regardless of what it is that evaluators evaluate (such as programs, policies, organizations, products, or individuals), and be the evaluation internal or external, the sequence of steps tends to remain the same. Sonnichsen (2000) outlines a series of steps (see table on previous page) that should take place in any internal evaluation that, for the most part, can be applied to external evaluations as well.

This "methodical sequence of the significant components required for an internal evaluation" almost guarantees a thorough and complete set of outcomes. The following sequence, easily modified depending upon one's particular problem at hand, is an excellent starting point.

▶ Significant Components of an Internal Evaluation

Richard Sonnichsen

1. Study initiation
   - Opening memorandum. Contains sufficient information to convey, to interested stakeholders and the evaluation staff, the commencement of the evaluation
   - Authority
   - Purpose
   - Deadlines
   - Team members
   - Administrative requirements
   - Computerized control log entries
   - Meetings with affected executives and managers
   - Notification of department heads and appropriate stakeholders
   - Contacts with subject matter experts
2. Literature search
   - Review both organizational policies and paperwork and the substantive literature
3. Formulation phase
   - Develop issues and frame evaluation questions
4. Evaluation plan
   - Prepare workplan
   - Design evaluation
   - Prepare design matrix
5. Data collection and analysis
   - Determine quality and availability of data
   - Ascertain precision needed in evaluative data
   - Resolve quantitative and qualitative data collection strategies
   - Decide on random or purposeful sampling methodologies
   - Plan and match appropriate statistical and analytical tools to anticipated data
6. Communicating evaluation results
   - Determine if report will be written
   - Prepare appropriate briefings
   - Resolve dissemination procedures for evaluation findings
7. Write recommendations
   - Identify options if appropriate
8. Closing procedures
   - Workpaper preparation
   - Retention and disposition of workpapers
   - Report annotation
   - Classified material handling (if necessary)
   - Control log updating
9. Follow-up
   - After six months, determine the status of suggested changes, approved recommendations, and attempt to measure impact of the evaluation

SOURCE: From Richard Sonnichsen (2000), *High Impact Internal Evaluation: A Practitioner's Guide to Evaluating and Consulting Inside Organizations* (Thousand Oaks, CA: Sage). Reprinted with permission.

3.7.4 The Concept of Forms in the Evaluation Process

John Owen and Patricia Rogers (1999) have created what they refer to as a meta-model of evaluation that is based on five evaluation forms, each with a "defining orientation and a focus on a set of common issues, which provide guidance for the planning and conduct of investigations."

These five categories or forms are

- Proactive
- Clarificative
- Interactive
- Monitoring
- Impact

As you will shortly see, they can all be compared across a variety of criteria including the purpose of the evaluation, the issues the different forms address, the approach taken during the evaluation, the major focus of the evaluation, and others. Table 3.1 organizes these five forms of evaluation as a function of these criteria.

Reference

Owen, John M., & Rogers, Patricia. (1999). *Program evaluation: Forms and approaches*. London: Sage.

3.7.5 Selected References on Evaluation Research

Sage Publications continues a very active publication effort in the field of evaluation, with coverage of theory, method, and utilization. The student or researcher interested in operational aspects of evaluation research should first examine volumes in the Program Evaluation Kit and then continue with the readings listed in this section for other selected examples of evaluation research focused on specific problems. The "general references" are directed to the student who seeks a fuller understanding of theory, method, and research advances.

Interest in evaluation research is exploding, both in scope and in publication. One good starting point is the ERIC Clearinghouse on Assessment and Evaluation, which can be found at http://ericae.net. Here, you can find entire books, journal articles, and other resources on assessment, evaluation, and associated research topics.

3.7.5.1 Program Evaluation Kit (Sage Publications)

This kit, first published in 1978 with Joan L. Herman as series editor, provides information on many different techniques for evaluating many different types of programs.

- Volume 1—*Evaluator's Handbook* (1988) by Joan L. Herman, Lynn Lyons Morris, and Carol Taylor Fitz-Gibbon. This first volume is the heart of the Program Evaluation Kit and provides a broad overview of evaluation planning and a practical guide to designing and managing programs.
- Volume 2—*How to Focus an Evaluation* (1988) by Brian Stecher and W. Alan Davis. This volume provides a broad overview of evaluation planning and a practical guide to designing and managing programs.
- Volume 3—*How to Design a Program Evaluation* (1988) by Carol Taylor Fitz-Gibbon and Lynn Lyons Morris. This volume reflects the tremendous explosion of interest in this vital area of the

Table 3.1 EVALUATION FORMS: ORIENTATION, TYPICAL ISSUES, AND KEY APPROACHES

	Proactive Evaluation	Clarificative Evaluation	Interactive Evaluation	Monitoring Evaluation	Impact Evaluation
Orientation	Synthesis	Clarification	Improvement	Justification/fine tuning	Justification/accountability
Typical issues	• Is there a need for the program? • What do we know about this problem that the program will address? • What is recognized as best practice in this area? • Have there been other attempts to find solutions to this problem? • What does the relevant research or conventional wisdom tell us about this problem? • What do we know about the problem that the program will address? • What could we find out from external sources to rejuvenate an existing policy or program?	• What are the intended outcomes, and how is the program designed to achieve them? • What is the underlying rationale for this program? • What program elements need to be modified to maximize the intended outcomes? • Is the program plausible? • Which aspects of this program are amenable to a subsequent monitoring or impact assessment?	• What is this program trying to achieve? • How is this service going? • Is the delivery working? • Is delivery consistent with the program plan? • How could delivery be changed to make it more effective? • How could this organization be changed so as to make it more effective?	• Is the program reaching the target population? • Is implementation meeting program benchmarks? • How is implementation going between sites? • How is implementation now compared with a month ago? • Are our costs rising or falling? • How can we fine-tune the program to make it more efficient? • How can we fine-tune the program to make it more effective? • Is there a program site that needs attention to ensure more effective delivery?	• Has the program been implemented as planned? • Have the stated goals of the program been achieved? • Have the needs of those served by the program been achieved? • What are the unintended outcomes? • Does the implementation strategy lead to intended outcomes? • How do differences in implementation affect program outcomes? • Has the program been cost-effective?

Key approaches	• Needs assessment • Research review • Review of best practice (benchmarking)	• Evaluability assessment • Logic/theory development • Accreditation	• Responsive • Action research • Quality review • Developmental • Empowerment	• Component analysis • Devolved performance assessment • Systems analysis	• Objectives based • Process-outcome studies • Needs based • Goal free • Performance audit
State of program	None	Development	Development	Settled	Settled
Major focus	Program context	All elements	Delivery	Delivery/outcomes	Delivery/outcomes
Timing [vis-à-vis program delivery]	Before	During	During	During	After
Assembly of evidence	Review of documents and databases, site visits, and other interactive methods. Focus groups, nominal groups, and Delphi technique useful for needs assessments.	Generally relies on combination of document analysis, interview, and observation. Findings include program plan and implications for organization. Can lead to improved morale.	Relies on intensive on-site studies, including observation. Degree of data structure depends on approach. May invoke providers and program participants.	Systems approach requires availability of Management Information Systems (MIS), the use of indicators, and the meaningful use of performance information.	Traditionally required use of preordinate research designs, where possible the use of treatment and control groups, and the use of tests and other quantitative data. Studies of implementation generally require observational data. Determining all the outcomes requires use of more exploratory methods and the use of qualitative evidence.

evaluation process and recognizes that deciding what to evaluate is a complex negotiation process that involves many different factors.

■ Volume 4—*How to Use Qualitative Methods in Evaluation* (1988) by Michael Quinn Patton. Introduces the reader to qualitative approaches.

■ Volume 5—*How to Assess Program Implementation* (1988) by Jean A. King, Lynn Lyons Morris, and Carol Taylor Fitz-Gibbon. Extensively revised to reflect modern views of program implementation, this volume introduces the variety of functions served by implementation studies and the roles played by qualitative and quantitative data.

■ Volume 6—*How to Measure Attitudes* (1988) by Marlene E. Henerson, Lynn Lyons Morris, and Carol Taylor Fitz-Gibbon. An important part of any evaluation process, this book focuses on the assessment of attitudes.

■ Volume 7—*How to Measure Performance and Use Tests* (1988) by Lynn Lyons Morris, Carol Taylor Fitz-Gibbon, and Elaine Lindheim. The evaluator's role in performance measurement is a critical element, and this volume focuses on ways an evaluator can select, develop, and analyze tests.

■ Volume 8—*How to Analyze Data* (1988) by Carol Taylor Fitz-Gibbon and Lynn Lyons Morris. This is a basic introduction to a variety of elementary statistical techniques, including those for summarizing data, for examining differences between groups, and for examining relationships between two measures.

■ Volume 9—*How to Communicate Evaluation Findings* (1988) by Lynn Lyons Morris, Carol Taylor Fitz-Gibbon, and Marie E. Freeman. This volume includes examples from a wide range of disciplines and shows the reader how to communicate results to users and stakeholders throughout the evaluation process.

3.7.5.2 Other Sage Publications in Evaluation

The Evaluation Studies Review Annuals are published by Sage Publications. Information on them is available at www.sagepub.com. The series includes the following volumes:

Volume 1: edited by Gene V. Glass (1976, 704 pages)
Volume 2: edited by Marcia Guttentag with Shalom Saar (1977, 736 pages)
Volume 3: edited by Thomas D. Cook and Associates (1978, 783 pages)
Volume 4: edited by Lee Sechrest, Stephen G. West, Melinda A. Phillips, Robin Redner, and William Yeaton (1979, 768 pages)
Volume 5: edited by Ernst W. Stromsdorfer and George Farkas (1980, 800 pages)
Volume 6: edited by Howard E. Freeman and Marian A. Solomon (1981, 769 pages)
Volume 7: edited by Ernest R. House and Associates (1982, 752 pages)
Volume 8: edited by Richard J. Light (1983, 672 pages)
Volume 9: edited by Ross F. Conner, David G. Altman, and Christine Jackson (1984, 752 pages)
Volume 10: edited by Linda H. Aiken and Barbara H. Kehrer (1985, 650 pages)
Volume 11: edited by David S. Cordray and Mark W. Lipsey (1986-1987, 757 pages)
Volume 12: edited by William R. Shadish, Jr., and Charles S. Reichardt (1988, 704 pages)

3.7.5.3 Selected Examples of Evaluation Research

Covello, Vincent. (Ed.). (1980). *Poverty and public policy: An evaluation of social science research.* Rochester, NY: Schenkman.

Creemers, B. P. (Ed.). (1985). *Evaluation research in education.* Philadelphia, PA: Taylor and Francis.

Fults, Gail J. (1992). *How participatory evaluation research affects management control process of a multinational nonprofit organization.* New York: Garland.

Glaser, Daniel. (1987). *Evaluation research and decision guidance for correctional, addiction treatment, mental health, education, and other people changing agencies.* Piscataway: Transaction Publishers.

Houser, Rick. (1998). *Counseling and educational research: Evaluation and application.* Thousand Oaks, CA: Sage.

Irden, Ellen R. (1996). *Evaluation research articles from start to finish.* Thousand Oaks, CA: Sage.

Lomand, Turner C. (1999). *Social science research: A cross section of journal articles for discussion and evaluation.* Los Angeles: Pyrczak Publishing.

Malaney, Gary D. (Ed.). (1999). *Student affairs research, evaluation, and assessment: Structure and practice in an era of change.* San Francisco: Jossey-Bass.

Pollard, William. (1986). *Bayesian statistics for evaluation research: An introduction.* Beverly Hills, CA: Sage.

Swerver, S. (1995). *Climate change research: Evaluation and policy implications.* New York: Elsevier Science.

Teichler, Ulrich, & Maiworm, Friedhelm, (1997). *The ERAMUS experience: Major findings of the ERAMUS Evaluation Research Project.* Brussels, Belgium: Commission of the European Communities.

Vance, Mary. (1987). *Evaluation research (social action programs): Monographs.* Monticello, VA: Vance Bibliographies.

3.7.5.4 General References for Evaluation Studies

Boggio, Giorgio (Ed.). (1982). *Evaluation of research and development.* Norwood, NJ: Kluwer Academic.

Buchanan, Nina K., & Feldhusen, John F. (Eds.). (1991). *Conducting research and evaluation in gifted education: A handbook of methods and applications.* New York: Teachers College Press.

Burgess, Robert G. (1992). *Educational research and evaluation: For policy and practice?* Philadelphia, PA: Taylor and Francis.

DIANE Publishing Company. (1992). *Drugs in the workplace: Research and evaluation data.* Collingdale: Author.

Fink, Arlene. (1992). *Evaluation fundamentals: Improving health programs, research, and policies.* Thousand Oaks, CA: Sage.

Frizzell, Leon A. (1984). *Evaluation of research reports: Bioeffects literature reviews.* Laurel: American Institute of Ultrasound in Medicine.

Hadley, Robert G., & Mitchell, Lynda K. (1994). *Counseling research and program evaluation.* Pacific Grove, CA: Brooks/Cole.

Hoorweg, Jan, & Neimeijer, Rudo. (1988). *Intervention in child nutrition: Evaluation studies in Kenya.* New York: Routledge.

Ladbury, John E. (1999). *Evaluation of the NASA Langley Research Center Mode-Stirred Chamber Facility.* Washington, DC: Government Printing Office.

Meyer, Michael M., & Fienberg, Stephen E. (Eds.). (1992). *Assessing evaluation studies: The case of bilingual education.* Ann Arbor, MI: Books on Demand.

Milinki, Andrea K. (Ed.). (1999). *Cases in qualitative research: Research reports for discussion and evaluation.* Los Angeles: Pyrczak Publishing.

Oman, Ray C., & Masters, Bill. (1987). *Implementing change in organizations, based on analysis and evaluation studies: A bibliography.* Monticello, VA: Vance Bibliographies.

Pond, D. J. (1998). *Evaluation of human factors research for ultrasonic inservice inspection.* Washington, DC: Government Printing Office.

Rudman, Jack. (1994). *Director of research and evaluation.* Sysosset: National Learning Corporation.

Schulenburg, J. Matthias. (Ed.). (in press). *The influence of economic evaluation studies on health care decision making: A European survey.* Burke, CA: IOS Press.

Wells, Kathleen. (1991). *Family preservation services: Research and evaluation.* Thousand Oaks, CA: Sage.

Windsor, M., Lange, K., & Mohr, V. (1994). *Evaluation of the Fisheries and Aquaculture Research Programme, 1988-1992.* Brussels: Commission of the European Communities.

3.7.5.5 Specialized Evaluation Journals

The following journals are all published by Sage Publications. Information is available on them at www.sagepub.com.

Evaluation: The International Journal of Theory, Research, and Practice
Evaluation and the Health Professions
Evaluation Review: A Journal of Applied Social Research

The following evaluation journals are published as noted.

Evaluation Practice (JAI Press)
New Directions for Evaluation (Jossey-Bass)
Evaluation and Program Planning (Pergamon)
Journal of Policy Analysis and Management (John Wiley)
Canadian Journal of Program Evaluation (University of Calgary Press)
Evaluation Journal of Australia (Australian Evaluation Society)
Educational Evaluation and Policy Analysis (American Educational Research Association)
Assessment and Evaluation in Higher Education (Carfax Publishing Ltd.)

3.7.5.6 The Survey Kit

What follows are the references included in the Sage Survey Kit, a collection of books published by Sage Publications in 1995 that treats the essential topics related to using surveys to collect data.

Bourque, L., & Fielder, E. P. *How to conduct self-administered and mail surveys.*
Fink, A. *How to analyze survey data.*
Fink, A. *How to ask survey questions.*
Fink, A. *How to design surveys.*
Fink, A. *How to report on surveys.*
Fink, A. *How to sample in surveys.*
Fink, A. *The survey handbook.*
Fink, A. *The survey kit.*
Frey, J., & Oishi, S. M. *How to conduct interviews by telephone and in person.*
Litwin, M. *How to measure survey reliability and validity.*

3.7.5.7 Professional Organizations for Program Evaluators and Policy Analysts

American Evaluation Association at www.eval.org
Association for Public Policy Analysis and Management at www.appam.org
Canadian Evaluation Association at www.evaluationcanada.ca/

Australian Evaluation Association at www.aes.asn.au
European Evaluation Association at www.europeanevaluation.org
United Kingdom Evaluation Association at www.evaluation.org.uk
Italian Evaluation Association at www.valutazione.it

3.7.6 Selected Bibliography on Evaluation

Airasian, Peter W., & Gullickson, Arlen R. (1997). *Teacher self-evaluation tool kit.* Thousand Oaks, CA: Corwin Press.

Awasthi, Dinesh N., & Sebastian, Jose. (1996). *Evaluation of entrepreneurship development programmes.* New Delhi: Sage India.

Barker, Cornelius L., & Searchwell, Claudette J. (1998). *Writing meaningful teacher evaluations—right now! The principal's quick start reference guide.* Thousand Oaks, CA: Corwin Press.

Berk, Richard A., & Rossi, Peter H. (1990). *Thinking about program evaluation.* Newbury Park, CA: Sage.

Bickman, Leonard, & Rog, Debra J. (1995). *Children's mental health services: Research, policy, and evaluation.* Thousand Oaks, CA: Sage.

Blenkin, Geva M., & Kelly, A. V. (1994). *The National Curriculum and early learning: An evaluation.* London: Paul Chapman Publishing.

Borders, L. Dianne, & Drury, Sandra M. (1992). *Counseling programs.* Thousand Oaks, CA: Corwin Press.

Boruch, Robert F. (1997). *Randomized experiments for planning and evaluation: A practical guide.* Thousand Oaks, CA: Sage.

Bright, George W., Uprichard, A. Edward, & Jetton, Janice H. (1993). *Mathematics programs: A guide to evaluation.* Thousand Oaks, CA: Corwin Press.

Card, Josefina J. (1993). *Handbook of adolescent sexuality and pregnancy: Research and evaluation instruments.* Newbury Park, CA: Sage.

Chattopadhyay, Manabendu, Maiti, Pradip, & Rakshit, Mihir. (1996). *Planning and economic policy in India: Evaluation and lessons for the future.* New Delhi: Sage India.

Chelimsky, Eleanor, & Shadish, William R. (1997). *Evaluation for the 21st century: A handbook.* Thousand Oaks, CA: Sage.

Chen, Huey-Tsyh. (1994). *Theory-driven evaluations.* Thousand Oaks, CA: Sage.

Clarke, Alan. (1999). *Evaluation research: An introduction to principles, methods and practice.* London: Sage.

Dale, Reider. (1998). *Evaluation frameworks for development programmes and projects.* New Delhi: Sage India.

Edwards, Ward, & Newman, J. Robert. (1982). *Multiattribute evaluation.* Beverly Hills, CA: Sage.

Evaluation and the health professions [journal published by Sage Publications].

Evaluation review: A journal of applied social research [journal published by Sage Publications].

Evaluation: The international journal of theory, research, and practice [journal published by Sage Publications].

Fetterman, David M. (2000). *Foundation of empowerment evaluation.* Thousand Oaks, CA: Sage.

Fetterman, David M., Kaftarian, Shakeh J., & Wandersman, Abraham. (1995). *Empowerment evaluation: Knowledge and tools for self-assessment and accountability.* Thousand Oaks, CA: Sage.

Fink, Arlene. (1993). *Evaluation fundamentals: Guiding health programs, research, and policy.* Thousand Oaks, CA: Sage.

Fink, Arlene. (1995). *Evaluation for education and psychology.* Thousand Oaks, CA: Sage.

Finkel, Martin A., & Giardino, Angelo P. (Eds.). (2001). *Medical evaluation of child sexual abuse: A practical guide* (2nd ed.). Thousand Oaks, CA: Sage.

Fitz-Gibbon, Carol Taylor, & Morris, Lynn Lyons. (1988). *How to design a program evaluation.* Newbury Park, CA: Sage.

Fowler, Floyd J., Jr. (1995). *Improving survey questions: Design and evaluation.* Thousand Oaks, CA: Sage.

Freeman, Howard E., Rossi, Peter H., & Sandefur, Gary D. (1993). *Workbook for evaluation: A systematic approach.* Newbury Park, CA: Sage.

Giardino, Angelo P., Christian, Cindy W., & Giardino, Eileen R. (1997). *A practical guide to the evaluation of child physical abuse and neglect.* Thousand Oaks, CA: Sage.

Giardino, Angelo P., Finkel, Martin A., Giardino, Eileen R., Seidl, Toni, & Ludwig, Stephen. (1992). *A practical guide to the evaluation of sexual abuse in the prepubertal child.* Newbury Park, CA: Sage.

Gil, Libia. (2001). *Principal peer evaluation: Promoting success from within.* Thousand Oaks, CA: Corwin Press.

Glasman, Naftaly S. (1994). *Making better decisions about school problems: How administrators use evaluation to find solutions.* Thousand Oaks, CA: Corwin Press.

Gould, Jonathan W. (1998). *Conducting scientifically crafted child custody evaluations.* Thousand Oaks, CA: Sage.

Grembowski, David. (2001). *The practice of health program evaluation.* Thousand Oaks, CA: Sage.

Guba, Egon G., & Lincoln, Yvonna S. (1989). *Fourth generation evaluation.* Thousand Oaks, CA: Sage.

Hambleton, Robin, & Thomas, Huw. (1995). *Urban policy evaluation: Challenge and change.* London: Paul Chapman Publishing.

Herman, Joan L. (1988). *Program evaluation kit.* Newbury Park, CA: Sage.

Herman, Joan L., & Winters, Lynn. (1992). *Tracking your school's success: A guide to sensible evaluation.* Thousand Oaks, CA: Corwin Press.

Hilton, N. Zoe. (1993). *Legal responses to wife assault: Current trends and evaluation.* Newbury Park, CA: Sage.

Holloway, Jacky, Lewis, Jenny, & Mallory, Geoff. (1995). *Performance measurement and evaluation.* London: Sage.

House, Ernest R. (1993). *Professional evaluation: Social impact and political consequences.* Newbury Park, CA: Sage.

House, Ernest R., & Howe, Kenneth R. (1999). *Values in evaluation and social research.* Thousand Oaks, CA: Sage.

Houser, Rick. (1998). *Counseling and educational research: Evaluation and application.* Thousand Oaks, CA: Sage.

Imrie, Rob, & Thomas, Huw. (1999). *British urban policy: An evaluation of the urban development corporations.* London: Sage.

Jenny, Carole. (1996). *Medical evaluation of physically and sexually abused children.* Thousand Oaks, CA: Sage.

Kosecoff, Jacqueline, & Fink, Arlene. (1983). *Evaluation basics: A practitioner's manual.* Beverly Hills, CA: Sage.

Kushner, Saville. (2000). *Personalizing evaluation.* London: Sage.

Love, Arnold J. (1991). *Internal evaluation: Building organizations from within.* Newbury Park, CA: Sage.

Millman, Jason. (1981). *Handbook of teacher evaluation.* Beverly Hills, CA: Sage.

Millman, Jason. (1997). *Grading teachers, grading schools: Is student achievement a valid evaluation measure?* Thousand Oaks, CA: Corwin Press.

Millman, Jason, & Darling-Hammond, Linda. (1991). *The new handbook of teacher evaluation: Assessing elementary and secondary school teachers.* Thousand Oaks, CA: Corwin Press.

Mohr, Lawrence B. (1996). *Impact analysis for program evaluation.* Thousand Oaks, CA: Sage.

Morris, Lynn Lyons, Fitz-Gibbon, Carol Taylor, & Freeman, Marie E. (1988). *How to communicate evaluation findings.* Newbury Park, CA: Sage.

Mullins, Terry W. (1994). *Staff development programs: A guide to evaluation.* Thousand Oaks, CA: Corwin Press.

Mundry, Susan, Britton, Edward, Raizen, Senta, & Loucks-Horsley, Susan. (2000). *Designing successful professional meetings and conferences in education: Planning, implementation, and evaluation.* Thousand Oaks, CA: Corwin Press.

Newman, Dianna L., & Brown, Robert D. (1996). *Applied ethics for program evaluation.* Thousand Oaks, CA: Sage.

Olson, Mary W., & Miller, Samuel D. (1993). *Reading and language arts programs: A guide to evaluation.* Thousand Oaks, CA: Corwin Press.

O'Sullivan, Rita G., & Tennant, Cheryl V. (1993). *Programs for at-risk students: A guide to evaluation.* Thousand Oaks, CA: Corwin Press.

Owen, John M., & Rogers, Patricia. (1999). *Program evaluation: Forms and approaches.* London: Sage.

Padaki, Vijay. (1995). *Development intervention and programme evaluation: Concepts and cases.* New Delhi: Sage India.

Patton, Michael Quinn. (1983). *Practical evaluation.* Beverly Hills, CA: Sage.

Patton, Michael Quinn. (1988). *How to use qualitative methods in evaluation.* Newbury Park, CA: Sage.

Patton, Michael Quinn. (1991). *Family sexual abuse: Frontline research and evaluation.* Newbury Park, CA: Sage.

Patton, Michael Quinn. (1997). *Utilization-focused evaluation: The new century text.* Thousand Oaks, CA: Sage.

Patton, Michael Quinn. (2002). *Qualitative research and evaluation methods.* Thousand Oaks, CA: Sage.

Pawson, Ray, & Tilley, Nicholas. (1997). *Realistic evaluation.* London: Sage.

Peterson, Kenneth D. (2000). *Teacher evaluation: A comprehensive guide to new directions and practices* (2nd ed.). Thousand Oaks, CA: Corwin Press.

Pietrzak, Jeanne, Ramler, Malia, Renner, Tany, Ford, Lucy, & Gilbert, Neil. (1990). *Practical program evaluation: Examples from child abuse prevention.* Newbury Park, CA: Sage.

Robson, Colin. (1999). *Small scale evaluations: Principles and practice.* London: Sage.

Rossi, Peter H., Freeman, Howard E., & Lipsey, Mark W. (1999). *Evaluation* (6th ed.). Thousand Oaks, CA: Sage.

Rutman, Leonard, & Mowbray, George. (1983). *Understanding programme evaluation.* London: Sage.

Sanders, James R., & The Joint Committee on Standards for Educational Evaluation. (1994). *The Program Evaluation Standards: How to assess evaluations of educational programs.* Thousand Oaks, CA: Sage.

Schinke, Steven P., Botvin, Gilbert J., & Orlandi, Mario A. (1991). *Substance abuse in children and adolescents: Evaluation and intervention.* Newbury Park, CA: Sage.

Schram, Barbara. (1997). *Creating small scale social programs.* Thousand Oaks, CA: Sage.

Scriven, Michael. (1991). *Evaluation thesaurus.* Newbury Park, CA: Sage.

Shadish, William R., Cook, Thomas D., & Leviton, Laura C. (1993). *Foundations of program evaluation: Theories of practice.* Newbury Park, CA: Sage.

Shah, A. M., Baviskar, B. S., & Ramaswamy, E. A. (1996). *Social structure and change: Vol. 1. Theory and method—an evaluation of the work of M. N. Srinivas.* New Delhi: Sage India.

Shaw, Ian. (1999). *Qualitative evaluation.* London: Sage.

Shaw, Ian, & Lishman, Joyce. (1999). *Evaluation and social work practice.* London: Sage.

Sonnichsen, Richard. (2000). *High impact internal evaluation: A practitioner's guide to evaluating and consulting inside organizations.* Thousand Oaks, CA: Sage.

Stahl, Philip Michael. (1994). *Conducting child custody evaluations: A comprehensive guide.* Thousand Oaks, CA: Sage.

Stahl, Philip Michael. (1999). *Complex issues in child custody evaluation.* Thousand Oaks, CA: Sage.

Stecher, Brian, & Davis, W. Alan. (1988). *How to focus an evaluation.* Newbury Park, CA: Sage.

Stufflebeam, Daniel L. (1988). *The personnel evaluation standards: How to assess systems for evaluating educators.* Thousand Oaks, CA: Corwin Press.

Torres, Rosalie T., Preskill, Hallie, & Piontek, Mary E. (1996). *Evaluation strategies for communicating and reporting: Enhancing learning in organizations.* Thousand Oaks, CA: Sage.

Vallecorsa, Ada L., deBettencourt, Laurie U., & Garriss, Elizabeth. (1992). *Special education programs: A guide to evaluation.* Thousand Oaks, CA: Corwin Press.

Veale, James. (2001). *Practical evaluation for collaborative services: Goals, processes, tools, and reporting systems for school-based programs.* Thousand Oaks, CA: Corwin Press.

Yuan, Ying-Ying T., & Rivest, Michele. (1990). *Preserving families: Evaluation resources for practitioners and policymakers.* Newbury Park, CA: Sage.

3.8 ETHICAL PRACTICES IN RESEARCH

Ethics in research are, and should be, of primary concern for any individual who undertakes research. Almost all professional organizations have a published code of ethics, and very early in any graduate training, this code should be discussed so that every element is fully understood by all who participate in research. Following is the American Sociological Association's Code of Ethics, reprinted with its permission.

▶ American Sociological Association Code of Ethics

Introduction

The American Sociological Association's (ASA's) Code of Ethics sets forth the principles and ethical standards that underlie sociologists' professional responsibilities and conduct. These principles and standards should be used as guidelines when examining everyday professional activities. They constitute normative statements for sociologists and provide guidance on issues that sociologists may encounter in their professional work.

ASA's Code of Ethics consists of an Introduction, a Preamble, five General Principles, and specific Ethical Standards. This Code is also accompanied by the Rules and Procedures of the ASA Committee on Professional Ethics which describe the procedures for filing, investigating, and resolving complaints of unethical conduct.

The Preamble and General Principles of the Code are aspirational goals to guide sociologists toward the highest ideals of sociology. Although the Preamble and General Principles are not enforceable rules, they should be considered by sociologists in arriving at an ethical course of action and may be considered by ethics bodies in interpreting the Ethical Standards.

The Ethical Standards set forth enforceable rules for conduct by sociologists. Most of the Ethical Standards are written broadly in order to apply to sociologists in varied roles, and the application of an Ethical Standard may vary depending on the context. The Ethical Standards are not exhaustive. Any conduct that is not specifically addressed by this Code of Ethics is not necessarily ethical or unethical.

Membership in the ASA commits members to adhere to the ASA Code of Ethics and to the Policies and Procedures of the ASA Committee on Professional Ethics. Members are advised of this obligation upon joining the Association and that violations of the Code may lead to the imposition of sanctions, including termination of membership. ASA members subject to the Code of Ethics may be reviewed under these Ethical Standards only if the activity is part of or affects their work-related functions, or if the activity is sociological in nature. Personal activities having no connection to or effect on sociologists' performance of their professional roles are not subject to the Code of Ethics.

Preamble

This Code of Ethics articulates a common set of values upon which sociologists build their professional and scientific work. The Code is intended to provide both the general principles and the rules to cover professional situations encountered by sociologists. It has as its primary goal the welfare and protection of the individuals and groups with whom sociologists work. It is the individual responsibility of each sociologist to aspire to the highest possible standards of conduct in research, teaching, practice, and service.

The development of a dynamic set of ethical standards for a sociologist's work-related conduct requires a personal commitment to a lifelong effort to act ethically; to encourage ethical behavior by students, supervisors, supervisees, employers, employees, and colleagues; and to consult with others as needed concerning ethical problems. Each sociologist supplements, but does not violate, the values and rules specified in the Code of Ethics based on guidance drawn from personal values, culture, and experience.

General Principles

The following General Principles are aspirational and serve as a guide for sociologists in determining ethical courses of action in various contexts. They exemplify the highest ideals of professional conduct.

Principle A: Professional Competence

Sociologists strive to maintain the highest levels of competence in their work; they recognize the limitations of their expertise; and they undertake only those tasks for which they are qualified by education, training, or experience. They recognize the need for ongoing education in order to remain professionally competent; and they utilize the appropriate scientific, professional, technical, and administrative resources needed to ensure competence in their professional activities. They consult with other professionals when necessary for the benefit of their students, research participants, and clients.

Principle B: Integrity

Sociologists are honest, fair, and respectful of others in their professional activities—in research, teaching, practice, and service. Sociologists do not knowingly act in ways that jeopardize either their own or others' professional welfare. Sociologists conduct their affairs in ways that inspire trust and confidence; they do not knowingly make statements that are false, misleading, or deceptive.

Principle C: Professional and Scientific Responsibility

Sociologists adhere to the highest scientific and professional standards and accept responsibility for their work. Sociologists understand that they form a community and show respect for other sociologists even when they disagree on theoretical, methodological, or personal approaches to professional activities. Sociologists value the public trust in sociology and are concerned about their ethical behavior and that of other sociologists that might compromise that trust. While endeavoring always to be collegial, sociologists must never let the desire to be collegial outweigh their shared responsibility for ethical behavior. When appropriate, they consult with colleagues in order to prevent or avoid unethical conduct.

Principle D: Respect for People's Rights, Dignity, and Diversity

Sociologists respect the rights, dignity, and worth of all people. They strive to eliminate bias in their professional activities, and they do not tolerate any forms of discrimination based on age; gender; race; ethnicity; national origin; religion; sexual orientation; disability; health conditions; or marital, domestic, or parental status. They are sensitive to cultural, individual, and role differences in serving, teaching, and studying groups of people with distinctive characteristics. In all of their work-related activities, sociologists acknowledge the rights of others to hold values, attitudes, and opinions that differ from their own.

Principle E: Social Responsibility

Sociologists are aware of their professional and scientific responsibility to the communities and societies in which they live and work. They apply and make public their knowledge in order to contribute to the public good. When undertaking research, they strive to advance the science of sociology and to serve the public good.

Ethical Standards

1. Professional and Scientific Standards

Sociologists adhere to the highest possible technical standards that are reasonable and responsible in their research, teaching, practice, and service activities. They rely on scientifically and professionally derived knowledge; act with honesty and integrity; and avoid untrue, deceptive, or undocumented statements in undertaking work-related functions or activities.

2. Competence

   (a) Sociologists conduct research, teach, practice, and provide service only within the boundaries of their competence, based on their education, training, supervised experience, or appropriate professional experience.
   (b) Sociologists conduct research, teach, practice, and provide service in new areas or involving new techniques only after they have taken reasonable steps to ensure the competence of their work in these areas.
   (c) Sociologists who engage in research, teaching, practice, or service maintain awareness of current scientific and professional information in their fields of activity, and undertake continuing efforts to maintain competence in the skills they use.
   (d) Sociologists refrain from undertaking an activity when their personal circumstances may interfere with their professional work or lead to harm for a student, supervisee, human subject, client, colleague, or other person to whom they have a scientific, teaching, consulting, or other professional obligation.

3. Representation and Misuse of Expertise

    (a) In research, teaching, practice, service, or other situations where sociologists render professional judgments or present their expertise, they accurately and fairly represent their areas and degrees of expertise.

    (b) Sociologists do not accept grants, contracts, consultation, or work assignments from individual or organizational clients or sponsors that appear likely to require violation of the standards in this Code of Ethics. Sociologists dissociate themselves from such activities when they discover a violation and are unable to achieve its correction.

    (c) Because sociologists' scientific and professional judgments and actions may affect the lives of others, they are alert to and guard against personal, financial, social, organizational, or political factors that might lead to misuse of their knowledge, expertise, or influence.

    (d) If sociologists learn of misuse or misrepresentation of their work, they take reasonable steps to correct or minimize the misuse or misrepresentation.

4. Delegation and Supervision

    (a) Sociologists provide proper training and supervision to their students, supervisees, or employees and take reasonable steps to see that such persons perform services responsibly, competently, and ethically.

    (b) Sociologists delegate to their students, supervisees, or employees only those responsibilities that such persons, based on their education, training, or experience, can reasonably be expected to perform either independently or with the level of supervision provided.

5. Nondiscrimination

Sociologists do not engage in discrimination in their work based on age; gender; race; ethnicity; national origin; religion; sexual orientation; disability; health conditions; marital, domestic, or parental status; or any other applicable basis proscribed by law.

6. Non-exploitation

    (a) Whether for personal, economic, or professional advantage, sociologists do not exploit persons over whom they have direct or indirect supervisory, evaluative, or other authority such as students, supervisees, employees, or research participants.

    (b) Sociologists do not directly supervise or exercise evaluative authority over any person with whom they have a sexual relationship, including students, supervisees, employees, or research participants.

7. Harassment

Sociologists do not engage in harassment of any person, including students, supervisees, employees, or research participants. Harassment consists of a single intense and severe act or of multiple persistent or pervasive acts which are demeaning, abusive, offensive, or create a hostile professional or workplace environment. Sexual harassment may include sexual solicitation, physical advance, or verbal or non-verbal conduct that is sexual in nature. Racial harassment may include unnecessary, exaggerated, or unwarranted attention or attack, whether verbal or non-verbal, because of a person's race or ethnicity.

8. Employment Decisions

Sociologists have an obligation to adhere to the highest ethical standards when participating in employment related decisions, when seeking employment, or when planning to resign from a position.

8.01 Fair Employment Practices

(a) When participating in employment-related decisions, sociologists make every effort to ensure equal opportunity and fair treatment to all full- and part-time employees. They do not discriminate in hiring, promotion, salary, treatment, or any other conditions of employment or career development on the basis of age; gender; race; ethnicity; national origin; religion; sexual orientation; disability; health conditions; marital, domestic, or parental status; or any other applicable basis proscribed by law.

(b) When participating in employment-related decisions, sociologists specify the requirements for hiring, promotion, tenure, and termination and communicate these requirements thoroughly to full- and part-time employees and prospective employees.

(c) When participating in employment-related decisions, sociologists have the responsibility to be informed of fair employment codes, to communicate this information to employees, and to help create an atmosphere upholding fair employment practices for full- and part-time employees.

(d) When participating in employment-related decisions, sociologists inform prospective full- and part-time employees of any constraints on research and publication and negotiate clear understandings about any conditions that may limit research and scholarly activity.

8.02 Responsibilities of Employees

(a) When seeking employment, sociologists provide prospective employers with accurate and complete information on their professional qualifications and experiences.

(b) When leaving a position, permanently or temporarily, sociologists provide their employers with adequate notice and take reasonable steps to reduce negative effects of leaving.

9. Conflicts of Interest

Sociologists maintain the highest degree of integrity in their professional work and avoid conflicts of interest and the appearance of conflict. Conflicts of interest arise when sociologists' personal or financial interests prevent them from performing their professional work in an unbiased manner. In research, teaching, practice, and service, sociologists are alert to situations that might cause a conflict of interest and take appropriate action to prevent conflict or disclose it to appropriate parties.

9.01 Adherence to Professional Standards

Irrespective of their personal or financial interests or those of their employers or clients, sociologists adhere to professional and scientific standards in

(1) the collection, analysis, or interpretation of data;
(2) the reporting of research;
(3) the teaching, professional presentation, or public dissemination of sociological knowledge; and
(4) the identification or implementation of appropriate contractual, consulting, or service activities.

9.02 Disclosure

Sociologists disclose relevant sources of financial support and relevant personal or professional relationships that may have the appearance of or potential for a conflict of interest to an employer or client, to the sponsors of their professional work, or in public speeches and writing.

9.03 Avoidance of Personal Gain

(a) Under all circumstances, sociologists do not use or otherwise seek to gain from information or material received in a confidential context (e.g., knowledge obtained from reviewing a manuscript or serving on a proposal review panel), unless they have authorization to do so or until that information is otherwise made publicly available.

(b) Under all circumstances, sociologists do not seek to gain from information or material in an employment or client relationship without permission of the employer or client.

9.04 Decisionmaking in the Workplace

In their workplace, sociologists take appropriate steps to avoid conflicts of interest or the appearance of conflicts, and carefully scrutinize potentially biasing affiliations or relationships. In research, teaching, practice, or service, such potentially biasing affiliations or relationships include, but are not limited to, situations involving family, business, or close personal friendships or those with whom sociologists have had strong conflict or disagreement.

9.05 Decisionmaking Outside of the Workplace

In professional activities outside of their workplace, sociologists in all circumstances abstain from engaging in deliberations and decisions that allocate or withhold benefits or rewards from individuals or institutions if they have biasing affiliations or relationships. These biasing affiliations or relationships are:

(1) current employment or being considered for employment at an organization or institution that could be construed as benefiting from the decision;

(2) current officer or board member of an organization or institution that could be construed as benefiting from the decision;

(3) current employment or being considered for employment at the same organization or institution where an individual could benefit from the decision;

(4) a spouse, domestic partner, or known relative who as an individual could benefit from the decision; or

(5) a current business or professional partner, research collaborator, employee, supervisee, or student who as an individual could benefit from the decision.

10. Public Communication

Sociologists adhere to the highest professional standards in public communications about their professional services, credentials and expertise, work products, or publications, whether these communications are from themselves or from others.

10.01 Public Communications

(a) Sociologists take steps to ensure the accuracy of all public communications. Such public communications include, but are not limited to, directory listings; personal resumes or curriculum vitae; advertising; brochures or printed matter; interviews or comments to the media; statements in legal proceedings; lectures and public oral presentations; or other published materials.

(b) Sociologists do not make public statements that are false, deceptive, misleading, or fraudulent, either because of what they state, convey, or suggest or because of what they omit, concerning their research, practice, or other work activities or those of persons or organizations with which they are affiliated. Such activities include, but are not limited to, false or deceptive statements concerning sociologists'

    (1) training, experience, or competence;

    (2) academic degrees;

    (3) credentials;

    (4) institutional or association affiliations;

    (5) services;

    (6) fees; or

    (7) publications or research findings. Sociologists do not make false or deceptive statements concerning the scientific basis for, results of, or degree of success from their professional services.

(c) When sociologists provide professional advice or comment by means of public lectures, demonstrations, radio or television programs, prerecorded tapes, printed articles, mailed material, or other media, they take reasonable precautions to ensure that

    (1) the statements are based on appropriate research, literature, and practice; and

    (2) the statements are otherwise consistent with this Code of Ethics.

10.02 Statements by Others

(a) Sociologists who engage or employ others to create or place public statements that promote their work products, professional services, or other activities retain responsibility for such statements.

(b) Sociologists make reasonable efforts to prevent others whom they do not directly engage, employ, or supervise (such as employers, publishers, sponsors, organizational clients, members of the media) from making deceptive statements concerning their professional research, teaching, or practice activities.

(c) In working with the press, radio, television, or other communications media or in advertising in the media, sociologists are cognizant of potential conflicts of interest or appearances of such conflicts (e.g., they do not provide compensation to employees of the media), and they adhere to the highest standards of professional honesty (e.g., they acknowledge paid advertising).

11. Confidentiality

Sociologists have an obligation to ensure that confidential information is protected. They do so to ensure the integrity of research and the open communication with research participants and to protect sensitive information obtained in research, teaching, practice, and service. When gathering confidential information, sociologists should take into account the long-term uses of the information, including its potential placement in public archives or the examination of the information by other researchers or practitioners.

11.01 Maintaining Confidentiality

(a) Sociologists take reasonable precautions to protect the confidentiality rights of research participants, students, employees, clients, or others.

(b) Confidential information provided by research participants, students, employees, clients, or others is treated as such by sociologists even if there is no legal protection or privilege to do so. Sociologists have an obligation to protect confidential information, and not allow information gained in confidence from being used in ways that would unfairly compromise research participants, students, employees, clients, or others.

(c) Information provided under an understanding of confidentiality is treated as such even after the death of those providing that information.

(d) Sociologists maintain the integrity of confidential deliberations, activities, or roles, including, where applicable, that of professional committees, review panels, or advisory groups (e.g., the ASA Committee on Professional Ethics).

(e) Sociologists, to the extent possible, protect the confidentiality of student records, performance data, and personal information, whether verbal or written, given in the context of academic consultation, supervision, or advising.

(f) The obligation to maintain confidentiality extends to members of research or training teams and collaborating organizations who have access to the information. To ensure that access to confidential information is restricted, it is the responsibility of researchers, administrators, and principal investigators to instruct staff to take the steps necessary to protect confidentiality.

(g) When using private information about individuals collected by other persons or institutions, sociologists protect the confidentiality of individually identifiable information. Information is private when an individual can reasonably expect that the information will not be made public with personal identifiers (e.g., medical or employment records).

11.02 Limits of Confidentiality

(a) Sociologists inform themselves fully about all laws and rules which may limit or alter guarantees of confidentiality. They determine their ability to guarantee absolute confidentiality and, as appropriate, inform research participants, students, employees, clients, or others of any limitations to this guarantee at the outset consistent with ethical standards set forth in 11.02(b).

(b) Sociologists may confront unanticipated circumstances where they become aware of information that is clearly health- or life-threatening to research participants, students, employees, clients, or others. In these cases, sociologists balance the importance of guarantees of confidentiality with other principles in this Code of Ethics, standards of conduct, and applicable law.

(c) Confidentiality is not required with respect to observations in public places, activities conducted in public, or other settings where no rules of privacy are provided by law or custom. Similarly, confidentiality is not required in the case of information available from public records.

11.03 Discussing Confidentiality and Its Limits

(a) When sociologists establish a scientific or professional relationship with persons, they discuss
(1) the relevant limitations on confidentiality, and
(2) the foreseeable uses of the information generated through their professional work.

(b) Unless it is not feasible or is counter-productive, the discussion of confidentiality occurs at the outset of the relationship and thereafter as new circumstances may warrant.

11.04 Anticipation of Possible Uses of Information

(a) When research requires maintaining personal identifiers in data bases or systems of records, sociologists delete such identifiers before the information is made publicly available.

(b) When confidential information concerning research participants, clients, or other recipients of service is entered into data bases or systems of records available to persons without the prior consent of the relevant parties, sociologists protect anonymity by not including personal identifiers or by employing other techniques that mask or control disclosure of individual identities.

(c) When deletion of personal identifiers is not feasible, sociologists take reasonable steps to determine that appropriate consent of personally-identifiable individuals has been obtained before they transfer such data to others or review such data collected by others.

11.05 Electronic Transmission of Confidential Information

Sociologists use extreme care in delivering or transferring any confidential data, information, or communication over public computer networks. Sociologists are attentive to the problems of maintaining confidentiality and control over sensitive material and data when use of technological innovations, such as public computer networks, may open their professional and scientific communication to unauthorized persons.

11.06 Anonymity of Sources

(a) Sociologists do not disclose in their writings, lectures, or other public media confidential, personally identifiable information concerning their research participants, students, individual or organizational clients, or other recipients of their service which is obtained during the course of their work, unless consent from individuals or their legal representatives has been obtained.

(b) When confidential information is used in scientific and professional presentations, sociologists disguise the identity of research participants, students, individual or organizational clients, or other recipients of their service.

11.07 Minimizing Intrusions on Privacy

(a) To minimize intrusions on privacy, sociologists include in written and oral reports, consultations, and public communications only information germane to the purpose for which the communication is made.

(b) Sociologists discuss confidential information or evaluative data concerning research participants, students, supervisees, employees, and individual or organizational clients only for appropriate scientific or professional purposes and only with persons clearly concerned with such matters.

11.08 Preservation of Confidential Information

(a) Sociologists take reasonable steps to ensure that records, data, or information is preserved in a confidential manner consistent with the requirements of this Code of Ethics, recognizing that ownership of records, data, or information may also be governed by law or institutional principles.

(b) Sociologists plan so that confidentiality of records, data, or information is protected in the event of the sociologist's death, incapacity, or withdrawal from the position or practice.

(c) When sociologists transfer confidential records, data, or information to other persons or organizations, they obtain assurances that the recipients of the records, data, or information will employ measures to protect confidentiality at least equal to those originally pledged.

12. Informed Consent

Informed consent is a basic ethical tenet of scientific research on human populations. Sociologists do not involve a human being as a subject in research without the informed consent of the subject or the subject's legally authorized representative, except as otherwise specified in this Code. Sociologists recognize the possibility of undue influence or subtle pressures on subjects that may derive from researchers' expertise or authority, and they take this into account in designing informed consent procedures.

12.01 Scope of Informed Consent

(a) Sociologists conducting research obtain consent from research participants or their legally authorized representatives

  (1) when data are collected from research participants through any form of communication, interaction, or intervention; or

  (2) when behavior of research participants occurs in a private context where an individual can reasonably expect that no observation or reporting is taking place.

(b) Despite the paramount importance of consent, sociologists may seek waivers of this standard when

  (1) the research involves no more than minimal risk for research participants, and

  (2) the research could not practicably be carried out were informed consent to be required. Sociologists recognize that waivers of consent require approval from institutional review boards or, in the absence of such boards, from another authoritative body with expertise on the ethics of research. Under such circumstances, the confidentiality of any personally identifiable information must be maintained unless otherwise set forth in 11.02(b).

(c) Sociologists may conduct research in public places or use publicly available information about individuals (e.g., naturalistic observations in public places, analysis of public records, or archival research) without obtaining consent. If, under such circumstances, sociologists have any doubt whatsoever about the need for informed consent, they consult with institutional review boards or, in the absence of such boards, with another authoritative body with expertise on the ethics of research before proceeding with such research.

(d) In undertaking research with vulnerable populations (e.g., youth, recent immigrant populations, the mentally ill), sociologists take special care to ensure that the voluntary nature of the research is understood and that consent is not coerced. In all other respects, sociologists adhere to the principles set forth in 12.01(a)-(c).

(e) Sociologists are familiar with and conform to applicable state and federal regulations and, where applicable, institutional review board requirements for obtaining informed consent for research.

12.02 Informed Consent Process

(a) When informed consent is required, sociologists enter into an agreement with research participants or their legal representatives that clarifies the nature of the research and the responsibilities of the investigator prior to conducting the research.

(b) When informed consent is required, sociologists use language that is understandable to and respectful of research participants or their legal representatives.

(c) When informed consent is required, sociologists provide research participants or their legal representatives with the opportunity to ask questions about any aspect of the research, at any time during or after their participation in the research.

(d) When informed consent is required, sociologists inform research participants or their legal representatives of the nature of the research; they indicate to participants that their participation or continued participation is voluntary; they inform participants of significant factors that may be expected to influence their willingness to participate (e.g., possible risks and benefits of their participation); and they explain other aspects of the research and respond to questions from prospective participants. Also, if relevant, sociologists explain that refusal to participate or withdrawal from participation in the research involves no penalty, and they explain any foreseeable consequences of declining or withdrawing. Sociologists explicitly discuss confidentiality and, if applicable, the extent to which confidentiality may be limited as set forth in 11.02(b).

(e) When informed consent is required, sociologists keep records regarding said consent. They recognize that consent is a process that involves oral and/or written consent.

(f) Sociologists honor all commitments they have made to research participants as part of the informed consent process except where unanticipated circumstances demand otherwise as set forth in 11.02(b).

12.03 Informed Consent of Students and Subordinates

When undertaking research at their own institutions or organizations with research participants who are students or subordinates, sociologists take special care to protect the prospective subjects from adverse consequences of declining or withdrawing from participation.

12.04 Informed Consent with Children

(a) In undertaking research with children, sociologists obtain the consent of children to participate, to the extent that they are capable of providing such consent, except under circumstances where consent may not be required as set forth in 12.01(b).

(b) In undertaking research with children, sociologists obtain the consent of a parent or a legally authorized guardian. Sociologists may seek waivers of parental or guardian consent when (1) the research involves no more than minimal risk for the research participants, and (2) the research could not practicably be carried out were consent to be required, or (3) the consent of a parent or guardian is not a reasonable requirement to protect the child (e.g., neglected or abused children).

(c) Sociologists recognize that waivers of consent from a child and a parent or guardian require approval from institutional review boards or, in the absence of such boards, from another authoritative body with expertise on the ethics of research. Under such circumstances, the confidentiality of any personally identifiable information must be maintained unless otherwise set forth in 11.02(b).

12.05 Use of Deception in Research

(a) Sociologists do not use deceptive techniques
    (1) unless they have determined that their use will not be harmful to research participants; is justified by the study's prospective scientific, educational, or applied value; and that equally effective alternative procedures that do not use deception are not feasible, and
    (2) unless they have obtained the approval of institutional review boards or, in the absence of such boards, with another authoritative body with expertise on the ethics of research.

(b) Sociologists never deceive research participants about significant aspects of the research that would affect their willingness to participate, such as physical risks, discomfort, or unpleasant emotional experiences.

(c) When deception is an integral feature of the design and conduct of research, sociologists attempt to correct any misconception that research participants may have no later than at the conclusion of the research.

(d) On rare occasions, sociologists may need to conceal their identity in order to undertake research that could not practically be carried out were they to be known as researchers. Under such circumstances, sociologists undertake the research if it involves no more than minimal risk for the research participants and if they have obtained approval to proceed in this manner from an institutional review board or, in the absence of such boards, from another authoritative body with expertise on the ethics of research. Under such circumstances, confidentiality must be maintained unless otherwise set forth in 11.02(b).

12.06 Use of Recording Technology

Sociologists obtain informed consent from research participants, students, employees, clients, or others prior to videotaping, filming, or recording them in any form, unless these activities involve simply naturalistic observations in public places and it is not anticipated that the recording will be used in a manner that could cause personal identification or harm.

13. Research Planning, Implementation, and Dissemination

Sociologists have an obligation to promote the integrity of research and to ensure that they comply with the ethical tenets of science in the planning, implementation, and dissemination of research. They do so in order to advance knowledge, to minimize the possibility that results will be misleading, and to protect the rights of research participants.

13.01 Planning and Implementation

(a) In planning and implementing research, sociologists minimize the possibility that results will be misleading.

(b) Sociologists take steps to implement protections for the rights and welfare of research participants and other persons affected by the research.

(c) In their research, sociologists do not encourage activities or themselves behave in ways that are health- or life-threatening to research participants or others.

(d) In planning and implementing research, sociologists consult those with expertise concerning any special population under investigation or likely to be affected.

(e) In planning and implementing research, sociologists consider its ethical acceptability as set forth in the Code of Ethics. If the best ethical practice is unclear, sociologists consult with institutional review boards or, in the absence of such review processes, with another authoritative body with expertise on the ethics of research.

(f) Sociologists are responsible for the ethical conduct of research conducted by them or by others under their supervision or authority.

13.02 Unanticipated Research Opportunities

If during the course of teaching, practice, service, or non-professional activities, sociologists determine that they wish to undertake research that was not previously anticipated, they make known their intentions and take steps to ensure that the research can be undertaken consonant with ethical principles, especially those relating to confidentiality and informed consent. Under such circumstances, sociologists seek the approval of institutional review boards or, in the absence of such review processes, another authoritative body with expertise on the ethics of research.

13.03 Offering Inducements for Research Participants

Sociologists do not offer excessive or inappropriate financial or other inducements to obtain the participation of research participants, particularly when it might coerce participation. Sociologists may provide incentives to the extent that resources are available and appropriate.

13.04 Reporting on Research

(a) Sociologists disseminate their research findings except where unanticipated circumstances (e.g., the health of the researcher) or proprietary agreements with employers, contractors, or clients preclude such dissemination.

(b) Sociologists do not fabricate data or falsify results in their publications or presentations.

(c) In presenting their work, sociologists report their findings fully and do not omit relevant data. They report results whether they support or contradict the expected outcomes.

(d) Sociologists take particular care to state all relevant qualifications on the findings and interpretation of their research. Sociologists also disclose underlying assumptions, theories, methods, measures, and research designs that might bear upon findings and interpretations of their work.

(e) Consistent with the spirit of full disclosure of methods and analyses, once findings are publicly disseminated, sociologists permit their open assessment and verification by other responsible researchers with appropriate safeguards, where applicable, to protect the anonymity of research participants.

(f) If sociologists discover significant errors in their publication or presentation of data, they take reasonable steps to correct such errors in a correction, a retraction, published errata, or other public fora as appropriate.

(g) Sociologists report sources of financial support in their written papers and note any special relations to any sponsor. In special circumstances, sociologists may withhold the names of specific sponsors if they provide an adequate and full description of the nature and interest of the sponsor.

(h) Sociologists take special care to report accurately the results of others' scholarship by using correct information and citations when presenting the work of others in publications, teaching, practice, and service settings.

13.05 Data Sharing

(a) Sociologists share data and pertinent documentation as a regular practice. Sociologists make their data available after completion of the project or its major publications, except where proprietary agreements with employers, contractors, or clients preclude such accessibility or when it is impossible to share data and protect the confidentiality of the data or the anonymity of research participants (e.g., raw field notes or detailed information from ethnographic interviews).

(b) Sociologists anticipate data sharing as an integral part of a research plan whenever data sharing is feasible.

(c) Sociologists share data in a form that is consonant with research participants' interests and protect the confidentiality of the information they have been given. They maintain the confidentiality of data, whether legally required or not; remove personal identifiers before data are shared; and if necessary use other disclosure avoidance techniques.

(d) Sociologists who do not otherwise place data in public archives keep data available and retain documentation relating to the research for a reasonable period of time after publication or dissemination of results.

(e) Sociologists may ask persons who request their data for further analysis to bear the associated incremental costs, if necessary.

(f) Sociologists who use data from others for further analyses explicitly acknowledge the contribution of the initial researchers.

14. Plagiarism

(a) In publications, presentations, teaching, practice, and service, sociologists explicitly identify, credit, and reference the author when they take data or material verbatim from another person's written work, whether it is published, unpublished, or electronically available.

(b) In their publications, presentations, teaching, practice, and service, sociologists provide acknowledgment of and reference to the use of others' work, even if the work is not quoted verbatim or paraphrased, and they do not present others' work as their own whether it is published, unpublished, or electronically available.

15. Authorship Credit

(a) Sociologists take responsibility and credit, including authorship credit, only for work they have actually performed or to which they have contributed.

(b) Sociologists ensure that principal authorship and other publication credits are based on the relative scientific or professional contributions of the individuals involved, regardless of their status. In claiming or determining the ordering of authorship, sociologists seek to reflect accurately the contributions of main participants in the research and writing process.

(c) A student is usually listed as principal author on any multiple authored publication that substantially derives from the student's dissertation or thesis.

16. Publication Process

Sociologists adhere to the highest ethical standards when participating in publication and review processes when they are authors or editors.

16.01 Submission of Manuscripts for Publication

(a) In cases of multiple authorship, sociologists confer with all other authors prior to submitting work for publication and establish mutually acceptable agreements regarding submission.

(b) In submitting a manuscript to a professional journal, book series, or edited book, sociologists grant that publication first claim to publication except where explicit policies allow multiple submissions. Sociologists do not submit a manuscript to a second publication until after an official decision has been received from the first publication or until the manuscript is withdrawn. Sociologists submitting a manuscript for publication in a journal, book series, or edited book can withdraw a manuscript from consideration up until an official acceptance is made.

(c) Sociologists may submit a book manuscript to multiple publishers. However, once sociologists have signed a contract, they cannot withdraw a manuscript from publication unless there is reasonable cause to do so.

16.02 Duplicate Publication of Data

When sociologists publish data or findings that they have previously published elsewhere, they accompany these publications by proper acknowledgment.

16.03 Responsibilities of Editors

(a) When serving as editors of journals or book series, sociologists are fair in the application of standards and operate without personal or ideological favoritism or malice. As editors, sociologists are cognizant of any potential conflicts of interest.

(b) When serving as editors of journals or book series, sociologists ensure the confidential nature of the review process and supervise editorial office staff, including students, in accordance with practices that maintain confidentiality.

(c) When serving as editors of journals or book series, sociologists are bound to publish all manuscripts accepted for publication unless major errors or ethical violations are discovered after acceptance (e.g., plagiarism or scientific misconduct).

(d) When serving as editors of journals or book series, sociologists ensure the anonymity of reviewers unless they otherwise receive permission from reviewers to reveal their identity. Editors ensure that their staff conform to this practice.

(e) When serving as journal editors, sociologists ensure the anonymity of authors unless and until a manuscript is accepted for publication or unless the established practices of the journal are known to be otherwise.

(f) When serving as journal editors, sociologists take steps to provide for the timely review of all manuscripts and respond promptly to inquiries about the status of the review.

17. Responsibilities of Reviewers

(a) In reviewing material submitted for publication, grant support, or other evaluation purposes, sociologists respect the confidentiality of the process and the proprietary rights in such information of those who submitted it.

(b) Sociologists disclose conflicts of interest or decline requests for reviews of the work of others where conflicts of interest are involved.

(c) Sociologists decline requests for reviews of the work of others when they believe that the review process may be biased or when they have questions about the integrity of the process.

(d) If asked to review a manuscript, book, or proposal they have previously reviewed, sociologists make it known to the person making the request (e.g., editor, program officer) unless it is clear that they are being asked to provide a reappraisal.

18. Education, Teaching, and Training

As teachers, supervisors, and trainers, sociologists follow the highest ethical standards in order to ensure the quality of sociological education and the integrity of the teacher-student relationship.

18.01 Administration of Education Programs

(a) Sociologists who are responsible for education and training programs seek to ensure that the programs are competently designed, provide the proper experiences, and meet all goals for which claims are made by the program.

(b) Sociologists responsible for education and training programs seek to ensure that there is an accurate description of the program content, training goals and objectives, and requirements that must be met for satisfactory completion of the program.

(c) Sociologists responsible for education and training programs take steps to ensure that graduate assistants and temporary instructors have the substantive knowledge required to teach courses and the teaching skills needed to facilitate student learning.

(d) Sociologists responsible for education and training programs have an obligation to ensure that ethics are taught to their graduate students as part of their professional preparation.

18.02 Teaching and Training

(a) Sociologists conscientiously perform their teaching responsibilities. They have appropriate skills and knowledge or are receiving appropriate training.

(b) Sociologists provide accurate information at the outset about their courses, particularly regarding the subject matter to be covered, bases for evaluation, and the nature of course experiences.

(c) Sociologists make decisions concerning textbooks, course content, course requirements, and grading solely on the basis of educational criteria without regard for financial or other incentives.

(d) Sociologists provide proper training and supervision to their teaching assistants and other teaching trainees and take reasonable steps to ensure that such persons perform these teaching responsibilities responsibly, competently, and ethically.

(e) Sociologists do not permit personal animosities or intellectual differences with colleagues to foreclose students' or supervisees' access to these colleagues or to interfere with student or supervisee learning, academic progress, or professional development.

19. Contractual and Consulting Services

(a) Sociologists undertake grants, contracts, or consultation only when they are knowledgeable about the substance, methods, and techniques they plan to use or have a plan for incorporating appropriate expertise.

(b) In undertaking grants, contracts, or consultation, sociologists base the results of their professional work on appropriate information and techniques.

(c) When financial support for a project has been accepted under a grant, contract, or consultation, sociologists make reasonable efforts to complete the proposed work on schedule.

(d) In undertaking grants, contracts, or consultation, sociologists accurately document and appropriately retain their professional and scientific work.

(e) In establishing a contractual arrangement for research, consultation, or other services, sociologists clarify, to the extent feasible at the outset, the nature of the relationship with the individual, organizational, or institutional client. This clarification includes, as appropriate, the nature of the services to be performed, the probable uses of the services provided, possibilities for the sociologist's future use of the work for scholarly or publication purposes, the timetable for delivery of those services, and compensation and billing arrangements.

20. Adherence to the Code of Ethics

Sociologists have an obligation to confront, address, and attempt to resolve ethical issues according to this Code of Ethics.

20.01 Familiarity with the Code of Ethics

Sociologists have an obligation to be familiar with this Code of Ethics, other applicable ethics codes, and their application to sociologists' work. Lack of awareness or misunderstanding of an ethical standard is not, in itself, a defense to a charge of unethical conduct.

20.02 Confronting Ethical Issues

(a) When sociologists are uncertain whether a particular situation or course of action would violate the Code of Ethics, they consult with other sociologists knowledgeable about ethical issues, with ASA's Committee on Professional Ethics, or with other organizational entities such as institutional review boards.

(b) When sociologists take actions or are confronted with choices where there is a conflict between ethical standards enunciated in the Code of Ethics and laws or legal requirements, they make known their commitment to the Code and take steps to resolve the conflict in a responsible manner by consulting with colleagues, professional organizations, or the ASA's Committee on Professional Ethics.

20.03 Fair Treatment of Parties in Ethical Disputes

(a) Sociologists do not discriminate against a person on the basis of his or her having made an ethical complaint.

(b) Sociologists do not discriminate against a person based on his or her having been the subject of an ethical complaint. This does not preclude taking action based upon the outcome of an ethical complaint.

20.04 Reporting Ethical Violations of Others

When sociologists have substantial reason to believe that there may have been an ethical violation by another sociologist, they attempt to resolve the issue by bringing it to the attention of that individual if an informal resolution appears appropriate or possible, or they seek advice about whether or how to proceed based on this belief, assuming that such activity does not violate any confidentiality rights. Such action might include referral to ASA's Committee on Professional Ethics.

20.05 Cooperating with Ethics Committees

Sociologists cooperate in ethics investigations, proceedings, and resulting requirements of the American Sociological Association. In doing so, they make reasonable efforts to resolve any issues of confidentiality. Failure to cooperate may be an ethics violation.

20.06 Improper Complaints

Sociologists do not file or encourage the filing of ethics complaints that are frivolous and are intended to harm the alleged violator rather than to protect the integrity of the discipline and the public.

NOTE: This code of ethics was approved by ASA membership in the spring of 1997. Reprinted by permission of the American Sociological Association.

3.8.1 The Institutional Review Process

Every academic and research institution that accepts funds from federal agencies (which are most leading institutions and almost all universities and colleges) as a regular practice reviews proposals to conduct experiments using human subjects. These reviews are conducted by institutional review boards (or IRBs), whose membership consists of some combination of staff members, faculty, student representatives, and administrators. In general, no matter who is conducting research (be it undergraduate or graduate students, or faculty), researchers are required to submit an application for approval.

For example at the Mankato Campus of the Minnesota State University (MSU), the Mankato Institutional Review Board for the Protection of Human Subjects in Research (IRB) is a standing committee of the university composed of faculty, administrators, health professionals, and community members. The IRB is responsible for protecting the rights and welfare of human research subjects or participants. The IRB administrator is the staff person responsible for providing the resources and support needed by the IRB. At MSU, the dean of graduate studies and research is the IRB administrator.

3.8.1.1 Sample IRB Documents

As a model for the process, what follows is a copy of the documents distributed by the IRB at the University of Kansas, where the IRB is called the Advisory Committee on Human Experimentation (documents are reprinted with permission of that IRB). These documents provide an excellent model for those institutions that may not yet have a well-organized review practice.

▶ University of Kansas IRB Documents*

INSTRUCTIONS FOR SUBMITTING PROPOSALS TO
THE UNIVERSITY OF KANSAS
ADVISORY COMMITTEE ON HUMAN EXPERIMENTATION
(ACHE)

University of Kansas
Lawrence, KS 66045-7563

Email applications may be submitted. See page 10 of the instructions for details.

*Reprinted by permission of the University of Kansas Advisory Committee on Human Experimentation.

Who Must Apply for ACHE Approval (and Why)?

The National Research Act of 1974/1983 (PL 93-348) dictates that, in order for institutions to be eligible for behavioral or biomedical research grants from federal sources (e.g., The Department of Health and Human Services and its various research institutes), an Institutional Review Board (IRB) must be established and maintained to review research involving human subjects. The charge of this IRB is to protect the rights of those subjects participating in such research at this institution. The IRB for the University of Kansas is the Advisory Committee on Human Experimentation (ACHE). The University must also have an approved Multiple Project Assurance which sets forth the responsibilities of the University, the researchers, and the IRB with respect to human subjects research. Our Multiple Project Assurance may be found at http://www.research.ukans.edu. ACHE must review proposals for research involving human subjects if the research:

(1) is in any way sponsored by the University (e.g., affiliated with the University in name), or
(2) is conducted by, or under the direction of, any employee or agent of the University as part of their institutional responsibilities, or
(3) is conducted by, or under the direction of, any employee or agent of the University using University facilities or property, or
(4) involves the use of the institution's non-public information to contact or identify participants or prospective participants.

Investigators conducting research with human subjects that meets any of these conditions must prepare proposals of that research and submit them to ACHE for approval. ACHE's review of the proposals is guided by the Code of Federal Regulations (Title 45, Part 46), which sets the minimum standards for protection of human subjects.

When to Submit

Proposals for ACHE approval can be submitted at any time. During the academic year, ACHE works continuously on the review of proposals and meets on a monthly basis, usually in the first week of each month. Research proposals that are received by the 15th of each month will be acted upon at the meeting that takes place during the following month.

For example, if a proposal needing a full committee review is submitted by October 15th, a committee decision concerning that proposal will be reached during the November meeting. A proposal submitted on the 16th of October, however, is not guaranteed committee action until the December meeting. Thus, the turnaround interval for committee action on a reviewed proposal can be as brief as three weeks, or as long as six weeks. Note that if the 15th of the month falls on a weekend or holiday, the deadline for receipt of a proposal is extended to 5:00 p.m. on the next full work day.

ACHE recommends that lead time for committee approval be figured into the schedule for the conduct of research, especially since committee action (i.e., discussion and vote on approval of the project) is not necessarily equivalent to or a guarantee of committee approval. Furthermore, it should be noted that the same turnaround schedule cannot be guaranteed during the summer months, because some of the committee members are on nine-month University contracts, and are thus unavailable to review projects or attend meetings during the summer months.

What to Submit

Proposals are submitted using the ACHE application form. The form is available from the ACHE office or from your department, or can be emailed to you.

The most current version of the application will have "1/98" typed on the upper left hand corner of the face page. Proposals submitted to ACHE typically consist of two parts.

Part 1:   The ACHE application, which includes four pages (a face page, a checklist page, a description page, and an abstract page). A copy of the application follows the text of this manual. IBM or MacIntosh versions of the application formatted for popular word processors are also available on disk from the ACHE office. Send or bring a blank 3.5" diskette to the ACHE office and we will return it with the application in the format requested. ACHE can send you the Instructions and application via email upon your request.

Part 2:   Appendices may also be submitted with the application. Appendices contain supplementary information regarding the application, which usually include (but are not limited to) a copy of the written consent form (if applicable) to be used in the conduct of the research, and copies of any additional supplementary materials (surveys, questionnaires, assessment materials, etc.) that will be used in the conduct of the research. However, the PI should feel free to include any materials that (s)he believes will assist the committee in evaluating the application.

Each of these two parts of an ACHE proposal is discussed in the sections that follow.

Part 1: The ACHE Application

The ACHE application is attached at the end of this manual. Please use this form for any new submissions.

Page 1.   The face page contains the formalities of the ACHE application. The space for the ACHE application number at the top right of the face page should be left blank.

1. Name of Investigator(s).   All investigators should be listed here. In projects with more than one investigator, correspondence about the proposal will be addressed to the investigator who signs as the first investigator. From here on, this person is referred to as the principal investigator (PI). The PI will be KU faculty, student, or staff. If the PI is neither faculty nor staff, a KU faculty supervisor or sponsor will be needed to sign off on the form (see item 5 on the next page). Students, therefore, need to have a faculty supervisor or sponsor. The faculty supervisor/sponsor is considered to be ultimately responsible for the proper conduct of the project with respect to the protection of human subjects.

Tutorial: All researchers, including the faculty supervisor for a project, must complete the online tutorial for conducting research involving human subjects before the project can receive ACHE approval. You may access the tutorial at www.research.ukans.edu/tutor.

2. Department Affiliation.   Please indicate the campus department (if applicable) with which the PI is affiliated.

3. Campus or Home Mailing Address.   This is the address to which correspondence concerning the proposal will be sent. If possible, please give a campus address, so that ACHE may use campus mail for delivery of this correspondence. If you have an email address, you should provide that also as email correspondence allows much faster turnaround on project review and approval than surface mail.

4. Phone Number(s).   Please provide a campus number (if applicable) and home telephone number at which the PI can be reached. These allow the coordinator to contact the PI in case there is a technical problem with the application.

5. Name of Faculty Member Responsible for Project.   Research projects submitted to ACHE must have a faculty sponsor. If the PI is not a KU faculty member or faculty-equivalent please indicate the faculty member who will be sponsoring the research.

6. Type of Investigator and Nature of Activity.   If the PI applying for ACHE approval is faculty or staff, the top part of this item should be filled out, indicating the status of the PI and whether the research is to be submitted for internal or external funding. If a KU/KUCR account number has been assigned to this project, please provide that number. If the PI is a student, fill out the bottom part of this item.

7. Title of Investigation.   Please give a brief title for the project. Brief titles facilitate correspondence and record keeping. If this is a funded project or an application for a funded

project, is the ACHE project title the same as that submitted to the funding organization? If not, please give that title as well.

8. Individuals Other Than Faculty, Staff, or Students at Kansas University. If applicable, check the box and indicate the names of other non-KU personnel that may be participating in the conduct of this research.

9. Certifications. The PI and any other personnel involved in the conduct of the research should sign the bottom of the face page, thus affirming familiarity with the policies of ACHE and the professional codes of ethical conduct with respect to human subjects. This is an important step. ACHE cannot process applications that are not signed by the faculty sponsor and all participating investigators. Please note that by submitting the application via email or hard copy you are certifying that you have read, understand, and will comply with the policies and procedures of the University of Kansas regarding human subjects in research and that you subscribe to the standards and will adhere to the policies and procedures of the ACHE.

Page 2. Please fill out the name of the PI and the proposal title at the top of this page. The space following the "ACHE #." is for office use and should be left blank.

10. Checklist. The checklist allows ACHE to rapidly screen applications for possible expedited or exempt conditions. Please read and answer Yes or No to items 10a to 10m carefully. Failure to do so accurately may result in delays in the processing or approval of your proposal. The section "Other Supporting Materials," should be noted if item 10c., about cooperating institutions, is checked "yes." If item 10k is marked "yes," then copies of the instruments to be used in the research (or a detailed description of the instruments) must be attached as an appendix. These materials will be retained in ACHE files concerning this project.

Use of Audio and Video Recording

For projects in which audio and/or video recording is intended, your abstract and consent form should explain who will have access to the tapes, security measures you will take to protect the privacy of subjects recorded, and what you will do with the tapes upon completion of your project (e.g., erase them, retain them for future research, etc.).

Payment to Subjects

Please note that if the research involves payment to subjects (i.e., if item 10b is marked "yes"), such payment is considered to be appropriate only if it is meant to compensate subjects for costs incurred as part of participation in the research (e.g., travel, time, etc.). PIs should not use payment schemes that may be potentially coercive.

11. Approximate Number of Subjects to Be Involved in the Research. Please indicate the number of subjects from whom you are planning to collect data.

Page 3. Information about the project purpose, proposed subjects, and selection procedures helps the committee discern the potential benefits to be derived from the research, whether the proposed population is especially vulnerable or at risk, and whether the processes for subject selection are equitable and sensitive to issues of confidentiality and privacy.

12. Project Purpose(s). Please describe briefly, and without jargon, the purpose of the project described in the application. Please use only the space provided.

13. Describe the Proposed Subjects. Please indicate any special criteria for including or excluding subjects involved in the proposed research. For example, if subjects are to be included in the project only if they are from a particular age group, racial group, or gender, please indicate this here. Additionally, if there is some medical attribute (e.g., Alzheimer's

Disease, heart disease, etc.) or physical [*sic*] (e.g., marathon runners, bicyclists, weight lifters) that characterizes the subjects to be included in the study, please indicate this here as well.

Subject Selection Considerations

14. Describe How the Subjects Are to Be Selected. Please indicate how you will gain access to and recruit these subjects for participation in the project. For example, if subjects are to be recruited randomly (by mail or telephone), through one of the on-campus subject pools, through PSYCH. 104 mass screening, or through a cooperating institution, please indicate the particulars here. Please note that investigators who wish to recruit subjects who are clients of an organization (clinic, hospital, etc.) should have that organization ascertain subjects' interest rather than just obtain a list of client names from the organization without the consent of the clients. Investigators may ask the organization to distribute the consent form or introductory letter and have interested subjects contact the investigator directly or through the organization. This method protects the privacy of prospective subjects.

Page 4. This is an important part of the application. Although proposals assigned to committee review will be read and considered in their entirety by only three members of ACHE, pages 2 to 4 of such proposals are distributed to all members of the committee prior to the monthly meeting. Thus, the abstract will be seen by all members of the committee and so it should be complete and provide an accurate description of the proposed project. Many of the problems the committee encounters in evaluating proposals arise from difficulties in understanding what is being proposed. Often, the committee must request clarification before reaching a final decision with respect to a proposal. With clear abstracts and generic language, many of these problems can be avoided.

15. Abstract of the Proposed Procedures. The abstract should be a succinct overview of the project. Please describe the procedures to be employed in the project. The ACHE committee is comprised of professionals from various academic and nonacademic fields. Therefore, it is important that the procedures be described in terms that can be understood by such an audience. Describe the procedures in the space provided, without jargon, abbreviations, or technical terminology. If you must use technical terms, please define or explain them so that someone not knowledgeable about your field can understand them.

Part 2: Appendices

Supplementary materials should be attached to the applications as appendices. These supporting materials often include the following items.

Copies of Research Instruments

If applicable (usually, if item 10k on the page 2 of the application has been checked "yes"), copies of instruments (assessments, scales, questionnaires, surveys, protocols, etc.) that are to be used in the proposed research are attached in appendices. If the instruments or protocols cannot be attached themselves, a detailed description of the instruments may suffice.

Informed Consent Form

If written informed consent is being used, a copy of the consent form that will be used in the research should be attached. According to the federal code of regulations (45 CFR 46), the consent form must include the following items when appropriate and applicable:

a. A statement of the purpose of the research and a brief description of procedures to be followed.

b. A description of any reasonably foreseeable discomforts or risks (psychological, sociological, or physical) to the subjects. If more than minimal risk is involved in the project, a statement concerning the Kansas Tort Claims Act should be included. Minimal risk means that the probability and magnitude of harm or discomfort anticipated in the research are not greater in and of themselves than those ordinarily encountered in daily life or during the performance of routine physical or psychological examinations or tests. The Kansas Tort Claims Act reads as follows:

> "In the event of injury, the Kansas Tort Claims Act provides for compensation if it can be demonstrated that the injury was caused by the negligent or wrongful act or omission of a state employee acting within the scope of his/her employment."

c. A description of the benefits for the subjects or others which may be reasonably expected from the research.

d. A disclosure of alternative procedures that would be advantageous to the subject. (This is usually only applicable to research involving experimental medical treatments.)

e. A statement that participation is voluntary. This should include an assurance that participation may be discontinued at any time, and that refusal to participate in, or withdraw participation from, the project will result in no penalty or loss of benefits to which the subject is otherwise entitled.

f. A statement describing the extent (if any) to which the confidentiality of records through which the subject can be identified will be protected.

g. An indication of the commitment in time required to participate in the study.

h. An offer to answer any inquiries concerning the project, and information concerning whom to contact in case questions arise after the data collection session is completed. This is usually done by providing the name of the PI, the departmental affiliation, and the telephone number(s) on the consent form.

i. Signatures

  (1) The subject's signature, if appropriate (e.g., the subject is of legal age, the subject is competent to understand and provide informed consent). If individuals who are not of legal age (under 18 years) may be inadvertently recruited for participation in the project (e.g., when subjects are obtained from University subject pools), the following should appear below the signature: "With my signature, I affirm that I am at least 18 years of age."

  (2) If the subject's signature is not appropriate, the signature of the parent or guardian (again, if of legal age), and the name of the subject.

j. Reference to any written explanations given to subjects to be followed if this explanation does not appear on the consent form.

k. An affirmation under the signature stating that, "With my signature I acknowledge that I have received a copy of this consent form to keep."

l. Add to the consent form/introductory letter the faculty supervisor's name, department, and department phone number.

Please note that, if the consent form is longer than a single page, then page numbers should be provided that indicate the entire length of the form on each of the pages (e.g., "Page 1 of 3," "Page 2 of 3," etc.). Copies of acceptable consent forms are provided for illustrative purposes with this packet.

If oral informed consent is being proposed for use, the PI should consult directions and regulations for documenting oral consent in the Federal Regulations (45 CFR 46.117.b.2). This typically involves submission of a text or script of the consent procedures, the presence of a witness, and a summary description of the research provided for subjects.

Assent Procedures

In research with children or other participants for whom the ability to give informed consent is otherwise compromised, it is usually appropriate to obtain some form of agreement, or "assent" to participation in the data collection sessions. For example, even though children or individuals with developmental disabilities cannot provide informed consent for participation in research, a researcher should still describe the procedures in language that can be understood by the subjects, and obtain their verbal "agreement" to participate. If an assent procedure is to be used, a prototype of the "script" of this procedure should be included in the appendices of the application.

Surveys and Questionnaires

For mail surveys or questionnaires that are completely anonymous in nature, signed informed consent can often be waived. However, in the place of informed consent under such circumstances, an appropriate "letter of introduction" should accompany the survey. The letter of introduction should include the critical aspects of the informed consent form (e.g., risk-benefit statements, assurances of voluntary participation and confidentiality of responses, etc.). The letter should also include a statement that, by returning the questionnaire, the respondent indicates his or her consent to participate in the study. A copy of the letter of introduction should be included in the appendices.

If investigators wish to use the Internet or electronic mail to conduct surveys some extra precautions are necessary. Because respondents' electronic addresses are typically provided when they return such surveys by e-mail, PIs should devise a plan for stripping such information to maintain the confidentiality and anonymity of respondents' names. Also, it is possible that, through intent or accident, someone other than the intended recipient may see the subject's response. The investigator should therefore inform subjects that, while effort will be made to protect subjects' privacy, security and confidentiality of participants' responses cannot be guaranteed.

Other Supporting Materials

Often, some of the concerns of the committee can be addressed by the inclusion of supporting letters from responsible individuals at institutions (schools, clinics, health care facilities, branches of law enforcement, etc.) that are involved or cooperating in the research. These letters might provide an indication of their willingness to cooperate in the conduct of the research, or their granting of permission to project personnel for access to subject populations located at such institutions. The letter may also indicate that such individuals have reviewed or (if applicable) have secured approval of the research protocol within that institution.

How Much to Submit

Investigators must submit: ONE copy of the entire completed ACHE application (pages 1-4) plus consent form(s) and all appendix materials.

Where to Submit

If submitting proposals by U.S. mail, send them to Mr. David Hann, ACHE Coordinator, 233 Youngberg Hall, University of Kansas, Lawrence, KS 66045-7563. Email applications may be submitted. Student researchers must email their application to their faculty supervisor, who looks at the application then forwards it to: dhann@ukans.edu. Please note that supporting materials that cannot be emailed must be provided to the ACHE office by hand delivery or surface mail.

Campus mail submissions may be addressed to David Hann at ACHE, 233 Youngberg Hall. Proposals may be delivered directly to Mr. Hann in his office at 233 Youngberg Hall. His telephone number is (785) 864-7429. Do not send ACHE submissions to the chair of the committee; this will result in a delay of processing the proposal.

On What Bases Are ACHE Proposals Evaluated?

General Issues of Subject Protection

Given the fundamental charge of the committee, there are particular aspects of the proposal to which ACHE will be attending. By law, ACHE can only grant approval to projects that satisfy certain requirements. PIs who anticipate evaluation on these requirements and attend to them in their proposals will encounter markedly fewer problems during the ACHE approval process. The requirements for approval (as paraphrased from the Code of Federal Regulations) include the following:

Risks to subjects are minimized. This is the first and foremost concern in the review of application by ACHE. What potential risks, stresses, or discomforts (if any) will be incurred by participation in this project? Has the PI taken steps in the design or procedures of the study to reduce the possibility of these risks or discomforts?

Risks to subjects are reasonable in relation to anticipated benefits. Do the benefits, if any, to be derived from this research outweigh the risks posed by this research to the subjects?

Informed consent will be sought from each subject (or the subject's legal representative) and documented. Are subjects fully informed of the risks and benefits of participation in the research? Are subjects informed of their basic rights in participating (e.g., withdrawal without penalty)? Are all of the appropriate aspects of informed consent included? If not, have the omissions been adequately justified? If the subjects themselves are unable to give informed consent, has consent been acquired from the appropriate responsible person(s), and has an assent procedure been provided? Is there adequate provision for the documentation of informed consent by the PI? Please note that the most common form of difficulty encountered by ACHE in granting approval of projects involves technical problems with informed consent forms (e.g., all the necessary aspects listed in Consent Form Requirements are not included).

Adequate provisions for monitoring data to insure the safety of subjects. Is the research monitored so that previously unforeseen risks come to the attention of the PI? This section also includes the monitoring of data in the case that individual subjects are identified as being at risk for medical or psychological problems. For example, in the course of research on exercise physiology, a PI might discover the presence of a heart murmur; in the course of psychological research on depression, a PI might discover a subject who is at some risk for suicide. What provisions, if any, are made for subjects who are identified as being at risk during the conduct of this research?

Adequate provisions to protect the privacy of subjects and maintain confidentiality. To what degree are subjects' responses protected with respect to confidentiality and anonymity? Will subjects' names be associated with their data? Who will have access to materials (e.g., data sheets, audio recordings or videotapes) through which subjects might be identified? Will response sheets be kept in a safe place? What are the plans for disposition of materials through which subjects might be identified when the study is finished? Appropriate additional safeguards for subjects who are especially vulnerable. [*sic*] Have adequate additional provisions been made to protect the rights of those subjects who might be especially vulnerable to coercion or undue influence? Federal law specifically mentions children, those with physical illness or psychological disorders, or those who are economically or educationally disadvantaged, as being members of this class. Are there any circumstances in the proposed research under which subjects might feel coerced to participate?

ACHE Policy on Experiments Involving Deception of Subjects

ACHE acknowledges that it is occasionally necessary to use deception in a research design in order to protect or strengthen the scientific integrity of an investigation. However, because participants are deliberately misinformed concerning the actual purposes or procedures of the research in such cases, ACHE considers such research to not meet the general requirement for informed consent as stated in the Code of Federal Regulations (45 CFR 46.116.a.1). This part of the law delineates the basic elements of informed consent, and states that in seeking informed consent, the following information shall be provided to each subject:

> . . . an explanation of the purposes of the research and . . . a description of the procedures to be followed . . .

Please note that federal law does not necessarily restrict the concept of "informed consent" to the consent form that subjects sign at the start of a study.

The Code of Federal Regulations, however, does provide for instances in which informed consent can be altered or waived. Under this federal law (45 CFR 46.116.d.1-4), this can occur only if all of the following conditions are met:

(1) The research involves no more than minimal risk to the subjects;
(2) The waiver or alteration [of consent] will not adversely affect the rights and welfare of the subjects;
(3) The research could not practicably be carried out without the waiver or alteration [of consent]; and
(4) Whenever appropriate, the subjects will be provided with additional pertinent information after participation.

Therefore, investigators proposing research to ACHE in which participants are misinformed concerning the study's procedures or purposes during the course of data collection must address how their proposals meet these conditions. This requirement may be met in a number of ways. However, in order to address these issues and facilitate review of such proposals, ACHE recommends that proposals for research involving deception include the following elements:

a. Justification for the Deception.   The justification should address condition 3 listed above. Investigators should provide specific and cogent reasons why fully informed consent is not appropriate for this study, and/or the manner in which fully informed consent threatens the integrity of the research.

b. Explicit Statement of No Risk/Minimal Risk.   This statement should address conditions 1 and 2 listed on the previous page. Investigators should provide a statement affirming that the proposed research presents no more than minimal risk to the participants. Federal law (45 CFR 46.102.g) defines "minimal risk" as follows:

> "Minimal risk" means that the risks of harm anticipated in the proposed research are not greater, considering probability and magnitude, than those ordinarily encountered in daily life or during the performance of routine physical or psychological examinations or tests.

c. Description of Debriefing. Procedures for debriefing should address condition 4, listed above. Subjects should be informed that deception took place, and should be appropriately informed as to the actual purpose of the research, and the role of the deception in protecting the integrity of the research. Finally, subjects should also be reminded of their right to withdraw from the study at this time; this can be accomplished through a range of various procedures, extending from the inclusion of a simple statement to that effect in the debriefing, to having the participant sign a second informed consent form at the end of the study.

It is noted that the text of the Code of Federal Regulations allows for the possibility that circumstances may arise in which debriefing may not be judged to be "appropriate." ACHE allows for this possibility, but PIs should note that requests to omit such debriefing in research involving deception should be strongly justified.

Although proposals involving deception must meet the conditions for alteration of informed consent, signed informed consent is still required to meet the requirements described in 45 CFR 46.116.a.2-8. Note that the informed consent form may not contain misinformation, may not be used as part of the deception, and may not be used as a means for manipulating subjects' behavior.

The committee has directed the Coordinator to refrain from sending applications to them that are not complete. Therefore, applicants submitting deception research applications without adequate debriefing procedures will be asked to provide them before the applications are sent on to the committee for review.

The Review Procedure

Over 500 proposals for research are received by ACHE each calendar year. About 40% to 50% of these projects arrive at the start of each of the semesters. That is, in the first two months of each semester, ACHE may process up to 100 applications. The remaining applications are processed over the course of the rest of the year. When ACHE proposals are received, they go through a review process that is detailed in the Assurance Statement filed by the University with the U.S. Department of Health and Human Services.

Screening for Exempt and Expedited Projects

The ACHE coordinator and/or the ACHE chair first screens the proposals to determine whether they fit the description of projects that are exempt from IRB (committee) review, or whether they might be afforded an expedited review.

Exempt Review. A proposal may be considered exempt from full committee review if the research being conducted falls into one or more of the following categories, as specified by the federal regulations:

(1) Research conducted in established or commonly accepted educational settings, involving normal educational practices, such as (a) research on regular and special education instructional strategies, or (b) research on the effectiveness of or the comparison among instructional techniques, curricula, or classroom management methods.
(2) Research involving the use of educational tests (cognitive, diagnostic, aptitude, achievement), if information taken from these sources is recorded in such a manner that subjects cannot be identified, directly or through identifiers linked to the subjects.
(3) Research involving survey or interview procedures, except where all of the following exist:
  (a) responses are recorded in such a manner that the human subjects can be identified, directly or through identifiers linked to the subjects, and
  (b) the subject's responses, if they became known outside the research, could reasonably place the subject at risk for criminal or civil liability or be damaging to the subject's financial standing or employability, and

(c) the research deals with sensitive aspects of the subject's own behavior, such as illegal conduct, drug use, sexual behavior, or use of alcohol.

Note that "Exempt" means that the project may be reviewed by the coordinator and/or the committee chair, not that the project may be carried out with no review or approval by ACHE.

Expedited Review. Expedited approval may be granted for certain specific classes of projects defined by the Code of Federal Regulations. Most often, PIs can receive expedited approvals for three classes of projects:

(1) projects that have been previously approved by ACHE, in which minor protocol changes have been made, or
(2) projects that have been previously approved by ACHE, and whose approval date exceeds one year. In this latter case, the expedited approval takes the form of an "update."
(3) some projects not exempt but which involve no more than minimal risk, as described in 45 CFR 46.110 (f) (1-7).

If a proposal fits one of these categories (which are strictly defined by the Federal Code of Regulations: 45 CFR 46), and the application meets criteria for approval, approval notification is sent out immediately to the PI. Upon receipt of this notification, the PI may begin the research.

Committee Review

Proposals that do not fit either the exempt or expedited-review categories are assigned to three committee members for review. The committee members receive the full application plus appendices, and return their recommendations and comments concerning the proposal to the coordinator. These recommendations and comments are compiled and integrated by the central ACHE office, and then presented to the full committee at the monthly meeting. At that meeting, all projects sent out for review are open for discussion and voted on. Results of that committee vote and the commentary from the reviewers are forwarded to the PI.

Forms of Committee Action

The outcome of the ACHE review can take several forms. Each of these particular actions is discussed below.

Disapproval. Projects are disapproved when the committee judges the risk to human subjects participating in such experiments to be unacceptable. The acceptability of the risk is determined by the judgment of the cost/benefit ratio of the research. Thus, higher levels of risk will be tolerated for research in which the potential benefit is judged to be higher; the opposite is true for research that presents no obvious benefit. PIs should note that only a very small percentage of projects reviewed by ACHE are disapproved.

Failure on the part of the PI to adequately describe the project in the abstract portion of the application is often the cause for disapproval, since it is here that the PI must describe screening, safety precautions, and contingency plans to meet adverse reactions from subjects to project procedures, as well as to describe the procedures in layperson's terms without technical jargon.

Not Approved. In some cases, not enough information is provided to allow the committee to determine the degree of risk to which subjects will be exposed. This occurs when critical information is omitted from the application. Thus, the application does not describe the project in detail adequate to allow a judgment of either approval, contingency, or disapproval. Occasionally, the cause for a failure to approve lies in the use of technical jargon which neither reviewers nor prospective subjects may understand. In such a case, the PI must submit the needed information so the proposal may be considered at the monthly meeting.

Approval Upon Meeting Contingencies. ACHE may withhold approval of the application, contingent upon a request from the committee for clarification of some point concerning the project, or for changes to the consent form or materials involved in the research. The PI then must respond to the request. Depending on the number of contingencies involved in the project, the determination of whether the response is adequate will be made by either the chair and/or coordinator, or the opinion of other ACHE members may be sought. If the response adequately meets the contingencies set by the committee, an approval is generated for the project.

Approval. Finally, ACHE may approve the application. The approval is usually accompanied by an evaluation of risk for the subjects involved: (a) the subjects will not be at risk, (b) the subjects will be at minimal risk, or (c) the subjects will be at some risk, but the potential benefit from the research outweighs the risk to the subjects. Upon notification of such approval, the PI may begin the research. The department chair and Faculty sponsor (if any) is also notified in the case of such an approval.

Updates and Continuing Review of Approved Projects

Please note that Federal Regulations limit the tenure of ACHE approvals to one year. Therefore, even approved projects are subject to what NIH calls "continuing review." Before the anniversary of each project's approval, the PI will receive a notice from the ACHE office that the approval is about to expire, and is prompted for information concerning the proposal with respect to "updating" or extending ACHE approval of the project for another year.

If the project is continuing, but the PI envisions that major changes will be made to the approved protocol, the project must be reviewed by the full committee. If the project is continuing as proposed, or is continuing with only minor changes to the protocol, then an expedited approval can usually be granted to update the approval for another year. PIs should note, however, that NIH has recently emphasized the need for thorough continuing review and monitoring of approved projects. Thus, projects that have been previously subject to full IRB review may be reviewed again by the full IRB prior to updating the approval.

At the very least, ACHE will require a copy of the consent form currently in use before issuing an expedited (updated) approval. Finally, if the PI reports that an approved project has been completed, that project will be designated Inactive and the ACHE documentation of that project will be archived.

Consent Form Requirements

These are reprinted here for your convenience in use with the provided consent form examples, which have superscripts referring to the required items. The consent form must include the following items when appropriate and applicable: Remove the superscript numbers from your working document.

1. A statement of the purpose of the research and a brief description of procedures to be followed. Identify any procedures that can be classified as experimental in nature; that is, not well proven or established.
2. A description of any reasonably foreseeable discomforts or risks to the subjects (psychological, sociological, or physical).
3. Inclusion of the Kansas Tort Claims Act statement when more than minimal risk is involved. The statement to be included if the risk is more than minimal is as follows: "In the event of injury, the Kansas Tort Claims Act provides for compensation if it can be demonstrated that

the injury was caused by the negligent or wrongful act or omission of a state employee acting within the scope of his/her employment."

4. A description of benefits for the subjects or others which may be reasonably expected from the research.
5. A disclosure of alternative procedures that would be advantageous to the subject. (Usually applicable only to research involving medical treatments.)
6. An offer to answer any inquiries concerning the project and whom to contact, including phone number and address (questions concerning the procedures, purpose or subject's rights).
7. A statement that participation is voluntary, that participation may be discontinued at any time and that refusal to participate or the decision to discontinue participation will be without penalty or loss of benefits to which the subject is otherwise entitled.
8. A statement describing the extent, if any, to which confidentiality of records identifying the subject will be maintained.
9. Name of principal investigator(s) and their departments and telephone number(s).
10. Name of subject if other than the one giving consent (i.e., if subjects are not capable of giving informed consent).
11. Signature of subject (if appropriate).
12. If subjects are under 18 years of age, or have limited capacity to give informed consent, consent from the parent/guardian is required.
13. Reference to any written explanations given to subjects of procedures to be followed if this explanation does not appear on the consent form.
14. An indication of the time commitment for participation in the study.
15. If the subject pool is likely to have individuals under the age of 18 and they are not to be included, the following shall appear below the signature: "With my signature I affirm that I am at least 18 years of age."
16. The Committee requires that the following should be included: "With my signature I acknowledge that I have received a copy of this consent form to keep." This could be placed under the signature line.
17. When the length of a consent form exceeds one page, a page number format indicating the total number of pages of the consent form (e.g., "1 of 3," "2 of 3," "3 of 3") should be used.
18. The consent form must include the faculty supervisor's name, department, and department phone number.

Examples of Informed Consent Statements

Note: Preceding these two illustrative examples is a list of the requirements for informed consent forms. The superscripts that appear throughout these examples correspond to the superscripted requirements or elements of informed consent that appear on that list.

Example #1: A Project Involving Minimal Risk

The Department of _____ at the University of Kansas[9] supports the practice of protection for human subjects participating in research. The following information is provided for you to decide whether you wish to participate in the present study. You should be aware that even if you agree to participate, you are free to withdraw at any time without penalty.[7]

We are interested in studying the effects of media on how people view themselves, their problems, and their futures. You will be participating in two sessions that will involve filling out some questionnaires, watching some videotaped materials, talking with the researcher, and doing some written and verbal tasks.[1] It is estimated that this will take no more than two hours of your time.[14]

The content of the videotapes and questions concerns _____, and so there is a chance that you might feel slightly uncomfortable with some of the materials and topics addressed in the research.[2] Although participation will not directly benefit you, we believe that the information will be useful in evaluating the effects of media on viewers.[4]

Your participation is solicited although strictly voluntary.[7] We assure you that your name will not be associated in any way with the research findings.[8] The information will be identified only by a code number.[8]

If you would like additional information concerning this study before or after it is complete, please feel free to contact me by phone or mail.[6]

Sincerely,

John Doe,[9]
Principal Investigator
Human Studies Dept.
200 Fisher Hall
University of Kansas
Lawrence, KS 66045
785 864 _____[9]

J.D. Smythe, Ph.D.[18]
Faculty Supervisor
Human Studies Dept.
200 Fisher Hall
University of Kansas
Lawrence, KS 66045
785 864 _____

_____[11]

Signature of subject agreeing to participate

With my signature I affirm that I am at least 18 years of age[15] and have received a copy of the consent form to keep.[16]

(Note: Items 3, 5, 10, and 12 are not applicable to the above consent form.)

Example #2: A Project Involving More Than Minimal Risk

The Department of _____ at the University of Kansas[9] supports the practice of protection for human subjects participating in research. The following information is provided for you to decide whether you wish to participate in the present study. You should be aware that even if you agree to participate, you are free to withdraw at any time without affecting opportunities for participation in other projects offered by this department.[7]

This study is involved with flexibility in eight selected joints and the improvement after involvement in a weekly low intensity aerobics exercise program. This study will also measure your ability to move in your daily activities, test your balance, equilibrium and other skills in order to determine if the low intensity aerobics program will improve your ability to walk and move about and to pursue your daily activities.[1]

Measurement of joint flexibility will be with a standard goniometer, a device that measures the angle of your joint, and with the "Sit and Reach" test, a test designed to measure flexibility in your legs and lower back. Measurement of various skills related to walking about will be observed as you attempt to perform them based upon our instructions.[1] This will require approximately 1 hour of your time three days a week for six weeks.[14]

This experimental investigation is being conducted by an experienced and trained graduate student in exercise physiology at the University of Kansas. All procedures have been approved by an advisor in the Department of _____. We do solicit your participation but it is strictly voluntary.[7] Do not hesitate to ask any questions about the study before, during, or after the research is complete.[6] Be assured that your name will not be associated with the research findings in any way.[8] Names will be deleted from all research data before use.

The expected benefits associated with your participation include information concerning your present state of flexibility and ability to move about freely. There is also the possibility (but no promise) that there will be a noticeable improvement in these areas after participation in the program.[4]

The discomforts and/or risks are minimal and include the possibility of initially experiencing slight soreness and/or stiffness that frequently accompanies the initiation of exercise. There is little chance of injury other than accidental incidents that accompany any physical activity.[2] However, the following information is provided in accordance with HEW regulations.

"In the event of injury, the Kansas Tort Claims Act provides for compensation if it can be demonstrated that the injury was caused by the negligent or wrongful act or omission of a state employee acting within the scope of his/her employment."[3]

Please sign your consent with full knowledge of the nature and purpose of the procedures, the benefits you may expect, and the discomforts and/or risks which may be encountered. I appreciate your assistance.

John Doe,[9]
Principal Investigator
Human Studies Dept.
200 Fisher Hall
University of Kansas
Lawrence, KS 66045
785 864 _____[9]

J. D. Smythe, Ph.D.[18]
Faculty Supervisor
Human Studies Dept.
200 Fisher Hall
University of Kansas
Lawrence, KS 66045
785 864 _____

_____ [11]
Subject's Signature

With my signature I acknowledge that I have received a copy of the consent form to keep.[16]

(Note: Items 5, 10, and 12 are not applicable to the above consent form.)

Omission of any of the listed items for the informed consent must either be explicitly defended or must be obviously clear within the context of the application. See the Code of Federal Regulations (45 CFR 46.116 and 117) for discussion of examples of situations in which specific items are not applicable and/or appropriate.

The examples given above are modified and edited versions of two consent forms actually submitted to the Committee. They are illustrations rather than models.

1/98

ACHE #_____ (to be assigned)
UNIVERSITY OF KANSAS
Advisory Committee on Human Experimentation
Application for Project Approval

1. Name of Investigator(s)
2. Department Affiliation
3. a. Campus or Home Mailing Address:
   b. email address:
4. Phone Number(s): (a) Campus: _____ (b) Home: _____
5. Name of Faculty Member Responsible for Project:

6. Type of investigator and nature of activity. (Check appropriate categories)
_____ Faculty or staff of University of Kansas
_____ Project to be submitted for extramural funding; Agency: _____
KU/KUCR project number: _____ (to be completed by ACHE)

(ACHE must compare *all* protocols in grant applications with the protocols in the corresponding ACHE application)

_____ Project to be submitted for intramural funding; Source: _____
_____ Project unfunded
_____ Other
_____ Student at University of Kansas: ____ Graduate ____ Undergraduate ____ Special
_____ Thesis _____ Dissertation
_____ Class project (number & title of class): _____
_____ Independent study (name of faculty supervisor): _____
_____ Other (please explain):
_____ Investigators not from the Lawrence campus but using subjects obtained through the University of Kansas

7. a. Title of investigation: _____
   b. Title of sponsored project, if different from above: _____

8. Individuals other than faculty, staff, or students at the Kansas University. Please identify investigators and research group:
_____
_____

9. Certifications:

By submitting this application via email or hard copy I am certifying that I have read, understand, and will comply with the policies and procedures of the University of Kansas regarding human subjects in research. I subscribe to the standards and will adhere to the policies and procedures of the ACHE.
and
I am familiar with the published guidelines for the ethical treatment of subjects associated with my particular field of study.

Date: _____   Date: _____

Signature: _____   Signature: _____
        First Investigator   *Faculty Supervisor*

Signature: _____   Signature: _____
        Second Investigator   *Third Investigator*

Principal Investigator: _____   ACHE #: _____

Project Title: _____

10. Please answer the following questions with regard to the research activity proposed:

(Please write "Yes"or "No.")   If answering Yes, be sure to provide details on the abstract and consent form.

Does the research involve:

_____ a. drugs or other controlled substances?

_____ b. payment of subjects for participation?

_____ c. access to subjects through a cooperating institution?

_____ d. substances taken internally by or applied externally to the subjects?

_____ e. mechanical or electrical devices (e.g., electrodes) applied to the subjects?

_____ f. fluids (e.g., blood) or tissues removed from the subjects?

_____ g. subjects experiencing stress (physiological or psychological)?

_____ h. deception of subjects concerning any aspect of purposes or procedures (misleading or withheld information)?

_____ i. subjects who could be judged to have limited freedom of consent (e.g., minors, developmentally delayed persons, or those institutionalized)?

_____ j. any procedure or activities that might place the subjects at risk (psychological, physical, or social)?

_____ k. use of _____ interviews, _____ surveys, _____ questionnaires, _____ audio or _____ video recordings?   (check all that apply)

_____ l. data collection over a period greater than one year?

_____ m. a written consent form will be used?
Note: ACHE makes the final determination on waiver of consent form.

11.   Approximate number of subjects to be involved in the research: _____

Complete the following questions on this page. Please do not use continuation sheets.

12.   Project Purpose(s):

_____

_____

13.   Describe the proposed subjects (age, sex, race, or other special characteristics).

_____

14.   Describe how the subjects are to be selected. (If subjects are to be recruited from a cooperating institution, such as a clinic or other service organization be aware that subjects' names and other private information, such as medical diagnosis, may not be obtained without the subjects' written permission.)

_____

_____

15.   Abstract of the proposed procedures in the project (must be complete on this page).

_____

_____

_____

_____

(Here is where you must provide details about Yes answers to items under question 10a through 10m of the application: drugs, cooperating institutions, security measures and post-project plans for tapes, questionnaires, surveys, and other data, and detailed debriefing procedures for deception projects.)

Submit one complete application to ACHE, 233 Youngberg Hall. Be sure to include consent forms, questionnaires, and other applicable supporting documents.

3.8.1.2. The IRB Tutor

As part of the training program for IRB applicants, the University of Kansas has created an online tutorial which addresses the critical issues that IRB applicants need to know about as they apply for approval. This can be found at www.research.ukans.edu/tutor.

3.8.1.3 Automating the IRB Process

Active research institutions have hundreds or thousands of reviews to conduct annually. Given the many steps in the process as described above, any type of assistance in record creation and keeping is usually very welcomed.

PRO_IRB™ is one such tool. It is a Microsoft Access™–based Institutional Review Board software application providing productivity and compliance assurance tools for managing the IRB process. Among its features are that it

- Helps plan and control meeting agenda, record meeting actions, and generate notification letters of IRB meeting actions
- Allows for recording and creates a permanent record of Serious Adverse Events, IND Reports, and MedWatch numbers and automatically places the study on the agenda for on-site and user-specified event types
- Features an Informed Consent Checklist for review of the FDA (or custom) required elements
- Automatically generates letters identifying all Informed Consent modifications required and provides for follow-up on receipt of a revised Informed Consent form
- Generates notification letters of Continuing Review and provides for follow-up on receipt of a progress or final report
- Provides for recording protocol revisions and other changes and automatically places the study on the agenda
- Allows for the reporting and querying of studies

For example, in Figure 3.1, you can see the PRO_IRB™ screen that shows the checklist one follows in the initial evaluation of a proposal.

PRO_IRB™ can be ordered from ProIRB Plus, Inc., 6020 44th Ave. North, St. Petersburg, FL 33709. A PowerPoint demonstration slide show can be downloaded from www. proirb.com/proirb_present.htm. The cost of PRO_IRB™ is $3,995 for a single user, with various plans for multiple users and maintenance contracts.

3.8.1.4 The National Association of IRB Managers

The National Association of IRB Managers offers courses and certification in IRB management. The association can be contacted at www.naim.org/ or (404) 766-9890.

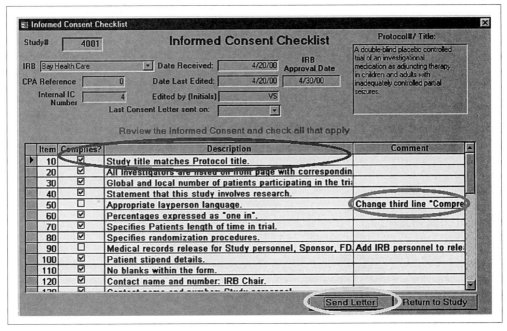

Figure 3.1.   A Sample Screen From PRO_IRB

3.8.2 The IRB Reference Book

Perhaps the most complete reference on institutional review boards is the *The IRB Reference Book* (2001), edited by Michelle Russell-Einhorn and T. Puglisi. The following table of contents shows the extensive historical perspective as well as the treatment of practical issues with which most IRB administrators and board members should be concerned.

Foreword
Preface

Chapter One: Introductory Message
A. Welcome to IRB Members
B. Non-Affiliated Members and Non-Scientists
C. What Is a Research Protocol?
D. Diagram of a Research Protocol

Chapter Two: Historical Background
A. Nuremberg Code
B. American Concerns for Human Subjects in the 1950s and 1960s
C. U.S. Public Health Service Syphilis Study (1932-1972)
D. The Belmont Report
E. The Development of Federal Human Subject Regulations
F. The 1990s and Beyond
G. Chapter References
     History of Human Subject Protections Timeline

Chapter Three: Federal Oversight of Human Subject Research

A. Federal Oversight of Human Subject Research
B. The Office for Human Research Protections (OHRP)
C. The Food and Drug Administration (FDA)
D. Oversight of Gene Transfer Research
E. Other Federal "Common Rule" Agencies
F. Chapter References
   Engagement of Institutions in Research (OPRR, 1/99)
   Engagement of Pharmaceutical Companies in HHS-Supported Research
   Human Subject Research Subcommittee Roster (OPRR, 12/99)

Chapter Four: Definitions

A. Citing the Federal Policy
B. Glossary of Frequently Used Terms

Chapter Five: Applying the Regulations

A. When Do the Federal Regulations Apply?
B. What Constitutes a Human Subject?
C. What Constitutes Research?
D. When Is Research Exempt?
E. Chapter References
   Decision Tree for Definition of Human Subject
   Decision Tree for Exempt Research
   Emergency Medical Care (OPRR Reports 91-01)
   Exemption for Public Benefit and Service Programs (OPRR, 12/97)
   Repositories, Tissue Storage Activities, Data Banks (OPRR, 11/97, 8/96, 5/97)

Chapter Six: Creating an IRB

A. Creating an IRB
B. Membership Requirements
C. Educating the Research Community
D. Administrative Resources
E. Chapter References
   Procedures for Registering Institutional Review Boards and Filing Federalwide Assurances
      of Protection for Human Subjects
   Required Education in the Protection of Human Subjects (NIH, 6/5/2000)
   Frequently Asked Questions About the Requirement for
   Education in the Protection of Human Subjects (NIH)
   PHS Policy on Instruction in the Responsible Conduct of Research (RCR)

Chapter Seven: IRB Mechanics and Operations

A. Authority of an IRB
B. Required Documentation of IRB Findings and Determinations
C. Quorum
D. Voting
E. Teleconferencing for Meetings and Votes
F. IRB Records
G. Internal Reporting Mechanisms

Chapter Eleven: Subject Recruitment

A. Subject Recruitment
B. Coercion and Undue Influence
C. Advertising
D. Use of Medical Records
E. Internet Recruitment
F. Recruitment Incentives for Investigators
G. Compensation and Incentives for Participation
H. Recruitment Checklist: Helpful Hints
I. Chapter References
   FDA Information Sheets: Recruiting Study Subjects
   FDA Information Sheets: Payment to Research Subjects
   FDA Information Sheets: Screening Tests Prior to Study Enrollment

Chapter Twelve: Privacy and Confidentiality

A. General Concerns
B. Genetic Research
C. Certificates of Confidentiality (COC)
D. Chapter References
   Certificate of Confidentiality: Privacy Protection for Research Subjects
   NIH Guidelines for Research Involving Recombinant DNA Molecules

Chapter Thirteen: Behavioral and Social Science Research

A. Applying the Regulations to Behavioral and Social Science Research
B. Risks to Subjects in Social and Behavioral Research
C. IRB Review of Social and Behavioral Research
D. Minimal Risk Social and Behavioral Research
E. Current Challenges for Social Science IRBs

Chapter Fourteen: Special Mechanisms for Monitoring Research

A. Data and Safety Monitoring Boards (DSMBs)
B. Consent Monitors
C. Random Audits
D. Chapter References
   Data and Safety Monitoring for Phase I and Phase II Trials, NIH 2000290
   NIH Policy for Data and Safety Monitoring, 1998

Chapter Fifteen: The Food and Drug Administration, the IRB, and Human Subject Protections

A. FDA and DHHS Regulations: A Comparison
B. Definitions
C. FDA Process
D. Emergency Use
E. Informed Consent
F. Eligibility for Expedited Review
G. Vulnerable Populations
H. Unanticipated Problems and Adverse Events
I. Conflicts of Interest
J. FDA Inspections
K. Sanctions for Regulation Non-Compliance—What Can the FDA Do?

The IRB Reference Book can be purchased from

PriceWaterhouseCoopers LLP
1900 K Street, N.W., Suite 900
Washington, D.C. 20006

The cost is $295 per copy.

SOURCE: Russell-Einhorn, Michelle, & Puglisi, T. (Eds). (2001). *The IRB Reference Book*. Washington, DC: Price- WaterhouseCoopers. Reprinted by permission.

Further Readings on Informed Consent

Akabayashi, A. Fetters. (2000). Paying for informed consent. *Journal of Medical Ethics*, 26, 212-214.

Chastain, Garvin, & Landrum, Eric R. (Eds.). (1999). *Protecting human subjects: Departmental subject pools and institutional review boards.* Washington, DC: American Psychological Association.

Hecht, Jeffrey B. (1995). *The institutional review board in social science research.* Paper presented at the annual meeting of the Mid-Western Educational Research Association, Chicago.

Kuther, Tara L. (1999). Competency to provide informed consent in older adulthood. *Gerontology and Geriatrics Education*, 20, 15-30.

Miller, Catherine. (1995). Protection of human subjects of research in Canada. *Health Law Review*, 4, 8-16.

Parascandola, Mark, Rusnak, Eileen, Saunders, Carol A., & Sugar, Alan M. (2000). *Foundations of human subject protection.* Wellesley, MA: Center for Clinical Research Practice.

Pinals, D. A., & Appelbaum, P. S. (2000). The history and current status of competence and informed consent in psychiatric research. *The Israel Journal of Psychiatry and Related Sciences*, 37, 82-94.

Sieber, Joan E. (Ed.). (1984). *NIH readings on the protection of human subjects in behavioral and social science research.* Westport, CT: Greenwood.

Sieber, Joan E. (1992). *Planning ethically responsible research.* Newbury Park, CA: Sage.

Stephens, John Patrick. (2000). Is this informed consent? *Psychiatric Bulletin*, 24, 154.

White, G. (2000). Informed consent. *The American Journal of Nursing*, 100, 83.

PART 4

QUALITATIVE RESEARCH

John W. Creswell
Raymond C. Maietta

INTRODUCTORY COMMENTS

Neil J. Salkind

Qualitative research methods are often used when the scientist is interested in obtaining detailed and rich knowledge of a specific phenomenon. These methods include the five categories of procedures defined by Creswell and Maietta in this part of the *Handbook of Research Design and Social Measurement*. In this part they cover narrative research, phenomenology, grounded theory research, ethnography, and case studies. Within each of these sections they explore the key elements of each method and discuss how the methods can be used to answer questions best suited to qualitative methods. In addition, this part of the handbook includes extensive coverage of software that is available for analyzing data collected within a qualitative framework.

One very important point to make, especially for the beginning researcher, is that qualitative research methods, while somewhat more recent in their development than the corresponding quantitative methods covered in the earlier parts of this book, are not alternatives to quantitative methods. They are not another way to answer the same question. Instead, they constitute a relatively new way to answer a different type of question, one characterized by a unique approach with a different set of underlying assumptions reflecting a different worldview of how individuals and group behavior can best be studied.

Sections 4.1 through 4.11 of this part were written by John W. Creswell, Professor, Department of Educational Psychology, University of Nebraska–Lincoln, and Raymond C. Maietta, President, ResearchTalk, Bohemia, New York.

Conventional wisdom in conducting qualitative research is to keep the approach flexible and open-ended to learn the meanings and views held by participants in a study. Over the years, this mandate has meant that individuals submitting proposals for funding, graduate students negotiating studies with faculty committees, and inquirers submitting articles for publication are often criticized for a lack of systematic procedures that describe their proposal or research study. With the "postmodern" turn in qualitative inquiry (Denzin & Lincoln, 2000)—an approach that emphasizes researcher self-consciousness, minimizes attention to methods, and relative findings—the openness of qualitative research is further encouraged.

Few would argue, however, that qualitative inquirers do not use tested procedures in collecting and analyzing data. Granted, some procedures are less structured and systematic than others, but some procedures are in place and analysis of data does occur (Creswell, 1994). This is especially the case when researchers analyze large databases and when inquirers use qualitative computer programs for their data analysis.

The purpose of this part of the handbook is to review systematic approaches available for conducting inquiry in qualitative research. We focus on five procedures of inquiry and seven computer software programs for qualitative data analysis. These five approaches are

- Narrative research
- Phenomenology
- Grounded theory
- Ethnography
- Case study research

In the discussion of each approach we will briefly trace its origin, provide a definition, examine the variants, identify key elements, and advance major procedures for using the approach when conducting a study. Keeping with the same theme of systematic inquiry, we next explore seven software computer packages that have gained popularity in social science research and that will provide a systematic approach to qualitative inquiry. These are

- ATLAS.it
- ETHNOGRAPH5
- HyperRESEARCH 2.5
- Classic 4N (or NUD*IST Version 4.0)
- N5 (NUD*IST Version 5.0)
- NVIVO-QSR
- WinMAX

Our intent is to provide a state-of-the-art discussion about each package and to review each on the basis of eight criteria. These criteria are (a) ease of integration, (b) type of data, (c) ability to read and review text, (d) reflective writing, (e) categorization, (f) analysis inventory and assessment, (g) quantitative data, and (h) merging projects.

4.2 SYSTEMATIC INQUIRY APPROACHES

Those undertaking a qualitative study have a baffling number of inquiry approaches from which to choose. We can gain a sense of this diversity by examining several classifications or typologies. One of the more popular classifications is provided by Tesch (1990), who organized 18 approaches into 4 branches of a flowchart, classifying these approaches based on the central interest of the investigator. Wolcott (1992) classified approaches into a tree diagram, with branches of the tree designating 25 strategies for data collection. Miller and Crabtree (1992) organized 18 types according to the domain of human life of concern to the researcher, such as a focus on the individual, the social world, or the culture. In the field of education, Jacob (1987) categorized all qualitative research into traditions, such as ecological psychology, symbolic interactionism, and holistic ethnography. Lancy (1993) organized qualitative inquiry into discipline perspectives, such as anthropology, sociology, biology, cognitive psychology, and history. Denzin and Lincoln (2000) identified several strategies of inquiry that researchers use for collecting and analyzing empirical materials. They presented performance ethnography, the case study, ethnography, interpretive practice, grounded theory, life history, new histories, testimonials, participatory action research, and clinical models as important inquiry strategies.

The qualitative researcher today has a baffling array of inquiry approaches from which to choose. We will selectively discuss five approaches for which we have found systematic procedures available in recent books. Some inquiry approaches are still emerging and developing, and we did not find the procedures as clearly articulated as we needed for our discussion here. In selecting our five approaches, we were also cognizant of those frequently used in social science research and popularly reported in journals across the social and human sciences.

Furthermore, our selection was based on an interest in identifying approaches from different social science traditions so as to encourage qualitative researchers to look beyond their own discipline into procedures that have worked in other fields. To this end, we have selected narrative research from the humanities, phenomenology from psychology and philosophy, grounded theory from sociology, ethnography from anthropology and sociology, and case studies from the human and social science and applied areas such as evaluation research.

4.3 A CONCEPTUAL OVERVIEW OF FIVE INQUIRY APPROACHES

From these sketches of each tradition, we can identify fundamental differences among these types of qualitative research. Table 4.1 presents several dimensions. At a most fundamental level, the five differ in what they are trying to accomplish: their focus, or the primary objective of the study. Exploring stories of a life is different from generating a theory or describing the behavior of a cultural group. Moreover, although overlaps exist in discipline origin, some traditions have fewer interdisciplinary traditions (e.g., grounded theory from sociology; ethnography from anthropology and sociology), while others have a broad base of disciplinary evolution (e.g., narrative and case study). Data collection processes vary from an emphasis on specific forms (e.g., more observations in ethnography; more interviews in grounded theory) to a wide range of forms (e.g., multiple types of data collected in case study research to provide the in-depth case picture). The differences are most marked at the data analysis stage. Not only is the distinction one of specificity of the analysis phase (e.g., grounded theory most specific; narrative less well defined) but the number of steps to be undertaken also varies (e.g., see the extensive steps in phenomenology and the few steps in ethnography).

Table 4.1 ▾ FIVE INQUIRY APPROACHES IN QUALITATIVE RESEARCH

Dimensions	Narrative Research	Phenomenology	Grounded Theory	Ethnography	Case Study
Focus	Collecting the stories of lived experiences	Understanding the essence of experiences surrounding a phenomenon	Developing a theory grounded in data from the field	Describing and interpreting a cultural and social group	Developing an in-depth analysis of a single case or multiple cases
Discipline origin	Literature History Psychology Sociology Anthropology	Philosophy Sociology Psychology	Sociology	Cultural anthropology Sociology	Political science Sociology Evaluation Urban studies Other social sciences
Data collection	Primarily interviews and documents	Long interviews with up to 10 people	Interviews with 20-30 individuals to "saturate" categories and detail a theory	Primarily observations and interviews, with additional artifacts, during extended time in the field (e.g., 6 months to 1 year)	Multiple sources: documents, archival records, interviews, observations, physical artifacts, quantitative data
Data analysis	Stories Restories Themes Description of context	Statements Meanings Meaning themes General descriptions of the experience	Open coding Axial coding Selective coding	Description Thematic analysis Interpretation	Description Themes Assertions
Narrative form	Chronological story of an individual life	A description of the "essence" of the experience	A theory or theoretical model	A description of the cultural behavior of a group or individual	In-depth study of a "case" or multiple "cases"

The result of each tradition, its narrative form, takes shape from all the processes before it. A detailed picture of an individual's stories forms the basis of narrative, and a description of the "essence" of the experience of the phenomenon becomes a phenomenology. A theory, often portrayed in a visual model, emerges in grounded theory; a holistic view of a social-cultural group or system results in an ethnography; and an in-depth study of a bounded system or a "case" (or several "cases") becomes a case study. From this overview, we now turn to narrative research as a systematic approach to qualitative inquiry.

NARRATIVE RESEARCH   4.4

Despite substantial interest in narrative research, its methods or procedures in qualitative inquiry are still being developed and are infrequently discussed in the literature (Errante, 2000). In narrative research, inquirers describe the lives of individuals, collect and tell stories about people's lives, and write narratives of individual experiences (Connelly & Clandinin, 1990). As a distinct form of qualitative research, narrative typically focuses on studying a single person, gathering data through the collection of stories, reporting individual experiences, and presenting the meaning of those experiences for the individual.

Narrative research is popular across the social sciences. The "narrative turn," as Riessman (1993) calls it, embraces all the human sciences, so that this form of research is not the providence of any specific field of study. Writers in literature, history, anthropology, sociology, sociolinguistics, and education all lay claim to narrative and have developed discipline-specific approaches. Like the art and science of portraiture discussed recently in the social sciences (Lawrence-Lightfoot & Davis, 1997), this design involves drawing portraits of individuals, documenting their voices and their visions within a social and cultural context. Within the field of education, for example, Clandinin and Connelly (2000) provide the first overview of narrative research for the field of education. In their informative, classic article "Stories of Experience and Narrative Inquiry" (Connelly & Clandinin, 1990), they cite many social science applications of narrative, elaborate on the process of collecting narrative field notes, and discuss the writing and structure of a narrative study. This article expands their earlier discussion about narrative within the context of teaching and learning in classrooms (Connelly & Clandinin, 1988). More recently. these two authors expanded their ideas in a text titled *Narrative Inquiry* (Clandinin & Connelly, 2000), openly espousing "what narrative researchers do" (p. 48).

The popularity of narrative is due to several factors. Cortazzi (1993) suggests that there is an interest in personal reflection, what people know, and empowering individuals to talk about their personal experiences. For example, women tell stories to children, adolescent girls, and their own female associates (Degh, 1995). This interest has culminated in a growing list of interdisciplinary social scientists who have offered procedural guidance for narrative reports as a form of qualitative research (e.g., see the psychologists Lieblich, Tuval-Mashiach, and Zilber, 1998; the sociologist Cortazzi, 1993; and Riessman, 1993). Interdisciplinary efforts at narrative research have also been encouraged by the *Narrative Study of Lives* annual series that began in 1993 (e.g., Josselson & Lieblich, 1993).

4.4.1 Variants

With so many different authors addressing narrative research, it is understandable that it is expressed in many variants. Today narrative may be considered an overarching category for a variety of research practices (see, e.g., Casey, 1995/1996). Each type of narrative assumes a slightly different approach. Four of these types will be discussed: biography, life history, teacher and student approaches, and theoretical perspectives (see Creswell, 2002, for a more extensive discussion of narrative forms).

4.4.1.1 Biography

Who writes and records the story of the individual is a basic distinction in narrative research. A biography is a form of narrative study in which the researcher writes and records the experiences of another person's life. Typically, biographies are constructed from records and archives (Angrosino, 1989), although researchers may use other sources of information as well (e.g., interviews, photographs). In an autobiography, the narrative account is written and recorded by the individual who is the subject of the study. Autobiographies are less frequently found in educational research, although recently, accounts of teachers as professionals are being reported (Connelly & Clandinin, 1990).

4.4.1.2 Life History

In anthropology, life history examples portray an individual's entire life. A life history is a narrative study of an individual's entire life experiences. Anthropologists, for example, engage in life history research to learn about the individual's life within the context of a culture-sharing group. Often the focus includes turning points or significant events in the life of an individual (Angrosino, 1989). Narrative studies, however, typically do not involve the account of an entire life and instead focus on an episode or single event in the individual's life. A personal experience story is a narrative study of an individual's personal experience found in single or multiple episodes, private situations, or communal folklore (Denzin, 1989). Clandinin and Connelly (2000) broaden the personal experience story to be both personal and social, and they have conveyed this stance as the essence of the experiences reported about teachers and teaching in schools.

4.4.1.3 Teacher and Student Narratives

Another type of narrative focuses on who provides the story. This factor is especially relevant in education, where educators have been the focus of narrative studies (Creswell, 2002). For example, teachers' stories are personal accounts by teachers of their own personal classroom experiences. A popular form of narrative in education, teachers' stories have been reported extensively to capture the lives of teachers as professionals and to examine learning in classrooms (e.g., see Connelly & Clandinin, 1988, 1999). Other narrative studies focus on students in the classroom. In children's stories, the children in classrooms are asked to present, orally or in writing, their own stories about their learnings (e.g., see Ollerenshaw & Creswell, 2000). The types of individuals in educational settings who can provide stories are extensive, including administrators, school board members, custodians and food service workers, and other educational personnel.

4.4.1.4 Theoretically Oriented Narratives

A final choice that shapes the character of a narrative is whether and to what extent the researcher uses a theoretical lens in developing the narrative. A theoretical lens suggests that a guiding perspective or ideology provides an organizing structure for a study in which the researcher advocates for groups or individuals. This lens may be to advocate for Latin Americans using *testimonios*, report the stories of women using a feminist lens (e.g., Personal Narratives Group, 1989), or collect the stories of marginalized individuals. In all these examples, the narrative researcher provides a "voice" for individuals whose voices may not be heard in the research literature.

4.4.2 Key Elements in Narrative Research

Despite the many forms of narrative inquiry, several common characteristics fit many studies. The inquirer emphasizes the importance of learning from participants in a setting. This learning occurs through individual stories told by an individual or several individuals. For Clandinin and Connelly (2000), these stories report personal experiences in narrative inquiry (what the individual experiences) as well as social experiences (the individual interacting with others). This focus on experience draws on the philosophical thoughts of John Dewey, who saw that an individual's experience was a central lens for understanding a person. One aspect of Dewey's thinking was to view experience as continuous (Clandinin & Connelly, 2000), with one experience leading to another. The stories constitute the data, which the researcher typically gathers through interviews or informal conversations. These stories, called field texts (Clandinin & Connelly, 2000), provide the raw data for researchers to analyze as they "retell" or "restory" the story based on narrative elements such as the problem, characters, setting, actions, and resolution (Ollerenshaw & Creswell, 2000). Restorying is the process of gathering stories, analyzing them for key elements of the story (e.g., time, place, plot, and scene), and then rewriting the stories to place them within a chronological sequence. Often when individuals tell a story, this sequence is missing or not logically developed; by restorying, the researcher provides a causal link among ideas. In restorying the participant's story and by telling the themes, the narrative researcher includes rich detail about the setting or context of the participant's experiences. This setting in narrative research may include friends, family, the workplace, home, a social organization, or school—the context in which a story physically occurs.

A story in narrative research is a first-person oral telling or retelling of events related to the personal or social experiences of an individual. Often these stories have a beginning, a middle, and an end. Similar to basic elements found in good novels, these aspects involve a predicament, conflict, or struggle; a protagonist or character; and a sequence with implied causality (i.e., a plot) during which the predicament is resolved in some fashion (Carter, 1993). In a more general sense, the story might include the elements typically found in novels, such as time, place, plot, and scene (Connelly & Clandinin, 1990). Researchers narrate the story and often identify themes or categories that emerge from it. Thus, the qualitative data analysis may be both a description of the story and themes that emerge from it. In addition, the researcher often writes into the reconstituted story a chronology of events that describes the individual's past, present, and future experiences, lodged within specific settings or contexts. Cortazzi (1993) suggests that it is the chronology of narrative research, with an emphasis on sequence, that sets narrative apart from other genres of research.

Throughout this process of collecting and analyzing data, the researcher collaborates with the participant by checking the story and negotiating the meaning of the database. Within the participant's story may also be an interweaved story of the researcher as she or he gains insight into herself or himself. In addition, researchers collaborate with participants by actively involving them in the inquiry as it unfolds. This collaboration may include many elements in the research process, from formulating the central phenomena to be examined, to the types of field texts that will yield helpful information, to the final written "restoried" rendition of the individual's experiences by the researcher. Collaboration involves negotiating relationships between the researcher and the participant to lessen the potential gap between the narrative told and the narrative reported. It also may include explaining the purpose of the inquiry to the participant, negotiating transitions from gathering data to writing the story, and arranging ways to involve participants in a study (Clandinin & Connelly, 2000).

4.4.3 Procedures Used in Narrative Research

The elements below play central roles in the general procedures for conducting narrative research and serve to illustrate the process.

1. Identify a research problem that focuses on learning or exploring the personal or social stories of an individual's (or sometimes more than one individual's) lived experiences. The intent of this study is for the researcher to provide a detailed rendering of the stories.

2. Select one or more individuals who have stories to tell and spend considerable time gathering their stories through interviews and documents that they might provide. Have the individuals record their stories in a journal or diary, or observe the individuals and record field notes. Collect letters sent by the individuals; assemble stories about the individuals from family members; gather documents such as memos or official correspondence about the individual; or obtain photographs, memory boxes (collection of items that trigger memories), and other personal-family-social artifacts. Record the individuals' life experiences (e.g., dance, theater, music, film, art, and literature) (Clandinin & Connelly, 2000).

3. Collect their stories and then "restory" them into a sequence that indicates a chronology of experiences. This chronology would include a discussion of the past, present, and future of the core idea

in their story. It typically includes rich context material so that the story is positioned within the setting in which it occurs. Moreover, in addition to simply telling the participants' story, you might include themes that arise from the story to provide a richer discussion of the meaning of their story.

4. Collaborate with participants during this process by actively involving them in your research. They might help shape the questions that you ask, search for data that support their stories, work with you to analyze the information, and assist in writing the final research report.

PHENOMENOLOGY 4.5

Whereas narrative research reports the life experiences of a single individual, a phenomenological study describes the meaning for several individuals of the lived experiences surrounding a concept or a phenomenon. Phenomenologists explore the structures of consciousness in human experiences (Polkinghorne, 1989). It has roots in the philosophical perspectives of Edmund Husserl (1859-1938) and philosophical discussions by Heidegger, Sartre, and Merleau-Ponty (Spiegelberg, 1982), and it has been used in the social and human sciences, especially in sociology (Borgatta & Borgatta, 1992; Swingewood, 1991), psychology (Giorgi, 1985; Polkinghorne, 1989, 1994), nursing and the health sciences (Nieswiadomy, 1993; Oiler, 1986), and education (Tesch, 1988).

The history of phenomenology started with the German mathematician Edmund Husserl and his extensive writings addressing phenomenological philosophy from 1913 until his retirement (Stewart & Mickunas, 1990). Husserl's ideas were abstract, and, as late as 1945, Merleau-Ponty (1962) raised the question, "What is phenomenology?" in his *Phenomenology of Perception*. In fact, Husserl was known to call any project currently under way "phenomenology" (Natanson, 1973).

Husserl emphasized many points (Moustakas, 1994; Natanson, 1973). Researchers search for the essential, invariant structure (or essence) or the central underlying meaning of the experience. They emphasize the intentionality of consciousness, in which experiences contain both an outward appearance and inward consciousness based on memory, image, and meaning. Phenomenological data analysis proceeds through the methodology of reduction, the analysis of specific statements and themes, and a search for all possible meanings. The researcher also sets aside all prejudgments, brackets his or her experiences (a return to "natural science"), and relies on intuition, imagination, and universal structures to obtain a picture of the experience.

From these philosophic tenets, four themes are discernible (Stewart & Mickunas, 1990).

1. *A return to the traditional tasks of philosophy.*   By the end of the 19th century, philosophy had become limited to exploring a world by empirical means, an approach called "scientism." The return to the traditional tasks of philosophy is a return to the Greek philosophy of a search for wisdom before philosophy became enamored with empirical science.

2. *A philosophy without presuppositions.*   Phenomenology's approach is to suspend all judgments about what is real, the "natural attitude," until they are founded on a more certain basis. This suspension is called "epoche" by Husserl.

3. *The intentionality of consciousness.*   This idea is that consciousness is always directed toward an object. Reality of an object then is inextricably related to one's consciousness of it. Reality, according to Husserl, is not divided into "subjects" and "objects," thus shifting the Cartesian duality to the meaning of an object that appears in consciousness.

4. *The refusal of the subject-object dichotomy.* This theme flows naturally from the intentionality of consciousness. The reality of an object is perceived only within the meaning of the experience of an individual.

4.5.1 Variants

The individuals who embrace these tenets and carry them forward in intellectual thought come from many social sciences areas, especially sociology and psychology, and they form different philosophical camps, such as reflective/transcendental phenomenology, dialogical phenomenology, empirical phenomenology, existential phenomenology, hermeneutic phenomenology, and social phenomenology (Barritt, 1986; Tesch, 1990). We will briefly mention social phenomenology and focus attention on psychological phenomenology as expressed through empirical/transcendental phenomenology.

The sociological perspective, social phenomenology, owes much to Schutz, who articulated the essence of phenomenology for studying social acts (Swingewood, 1991). Schutz was interested in how ordinary members of society constitute the world of everyday life, especially how individuals consciously develop meaning out of social interactions (people interacting with each other). As an extension of Schutz's thinking, Garfinkel called this approach ethnomethodology, a way to examine how individuals in society make meaning of their everyday life. Often drawing on ethnography and cultural themes, ethnomethodology relied on methods of analyzing everyday talk (Swingewood, 1991).

The psychological approach also focuses on the meaning of experiences, but it has found individual experiences, not group experiences, to be central. As presented in the *Duquesne Studies in Phenomenology*, the central tenets of this thinking are

> to determine what an experience means for the persons who have had the experience and are able to provide a comprehensive description of it. From the individual descriptions, general or universal meanings are derived, in other words, the essences of structures of the experience. (Moustakas, 1994, p. 13)

Moustakas (1994) proceeds to elaborate a type of phenomenology, "transcendental phenomenology," which traces back to Husserl but places more emphasis on bracketing out the researcher's preconceptions (i.e., epoche) and developing universal structures based on "what" people experience and "how."

4.5.2 Key Elements in Phenomenological Research

The conduct of psychological phenomenology has been addressed in a number of writings, including Dukes (1984), Tesch (1990), Giorgi (1985, 1994), Polkinghorne (1989), and Moustakas (1994), and there is general consensus about how to proceed (Oiler, 1986). But these methods, "based on phenomenological principles . . . function as general guidelines or outlines, and researchers are expected to develop plans of study especially suited to understanding the particular experiential phenomenon that is the object of their study" (Polkinghorne, 1989, p. 44). With this caveat in mind, we will summarize the major procedural elements in using phenomenology.

Researchers need to understand the philosophical perspectives behind the approach, especially the concept of studying how people experience a phenomenon. The concept of "epoche" is central, where researchers bracket their own preconceived ideas about the phenomenon to understand it through the voices of the informants (Field & Morse, 1985). Investigators write research questions that explore the meaning of that experience for individuals, and they ask individuals to describe their everyday "lived" experiences. They then collect data from individuals who have experienced the phenomenon under investigation. Typically this information is collected through long interviews (augmented with researcher self-reflection and previously developed descriptions from artistic works) with groups of informants ranging in size from 5 to 25 members (Polkinghorne, 1989). This information is further analyzed by developing broad themes about the individuals' experiences and constructing a detailed description that presents the "essence" of the phenomenon for the individuals being studied. The reader of the report should come away with the feeling that "I understand better what it is like for someone to experience that" (Polkinghorne, 1989, p. 46).

4.5.3 Procedures for Conducting a Phenomenological Study

The elements become central features in the procedures for conducting a phenomenological study. In these steps, the phenomenological analysis is generally similar for all psychological phenomenologists who discuss the methods (Moustakas, 1994; Polkinghorne, 1989).

1. *Identify a central phenomenon to study (e.g., the meaning of grief) and study the "essence" of the experience*—the common meanings ascribed by people to the phenomenon.

2. *Ask central research questions that focus on capturing this meaning.* For example, a phenomenologist might ask, "What meaning do individuals ascribe to grief? What is grief to them, and what is the context in which they experience it?"

3. *Collect data primarily through interviews*, although a wide range of data collection can occur through observations and study of documents, artifacts, music, and poetry (see Lauterbach, 1993, for an example of multiple forms of data collection).

4. *Analyze data by following the procedural steps identified by Moustakas (1994).* These steps begin with identifying "significant statements," short phrases of individuals (or in the researcher's words) that capture the meaning of the phenomenon under examination.

5. *Reduce the numerous significant statements to meaning units or themes.* In this process, the researcher looks for overlapping and redundant significant statements, then combines them into a small number of meaning units or themes that describe the meaning for the individual.

6. *Analyze the context in which the individuals experienced the meaning units or themes.* It is important in phenomenology to identify not only what the individuals experienced (called by Moustakas [1994] the textual description) but also the context, the setting, or the situation in which they experienced it (called the structural experience).

7. *Reflect on personal experiences you have had with the phenomenon.* Only some phenomenologists use this procedure. It involves reflecting on and actively writing about your own experiences. These written passages typically involve identifying how the researcher experienced the phenomenon and the contexts in which this experience occurred.

8. *Write a detailed analysis of the "essence" of the experience for the participants.* From an analysis of the significant statements, the meaning units, the analysis of what was experienced (the textual description), and how it was experienced (the structural description), the researcher writes a detailed analysis of the "essence" of the experience for the individuals participating in the study. Sometimes these descriptions are analyzed separately for individuals possessing different characteristics, such as for men or women (Riemen, 1986). The idea is for the phenomenologist to end a study with this

"essence" that captures the common experiences of the participants and the setting in which they experienced it. This passage can include the researcher's own experiences with the phenomenon.

4.6 GROUNDED THEORY RESEARCH

A phenomenological study emphasizes the common meaning of an experience for a number of individuals. In contrast, the intent of a grounded theory study is to generate or discover a theory that explains a concept, process, or interaction among individuals. In grounded theory, researchers primarily collect interview data, make multiple visits to the field, develop and interrelate categories of information, and write theoretical propositions or hypotheses or present a visual picture of the theory.

Two sociologists, Barney Glaser and Anselm Strauss, first articulated grounded theory research in 1967 and later elaborated on it through subsequent books (Glaser, 1978; Glaser & Strauss, 1967; Strauss, 1987; Strauss & Corbin, 1990, 1998). In contrast to the a priori theoretical orientation in sociology, they held that theories should be "grounded" in data from the field, especially in the actions, interactions, and social processes of people. Despite a rich history of collaboration between Glaser and Strauss that produced such works as *Awareness of Dying* (Glaser & Strauss, 1965) and *Time for Dying* (Glaser & Strauss, 1968), they have differed in recent years. Glaser has criticized Strauss's approach to grounded theory (Glaser, 1992). Despite the differences, both Glaser and Strauss have continued to independently author books about their approaches, and grounded theory has gained popularity in sociology, nursing, education, and other social science fields. More recently, Charmaz (2000) has advocated for a "constructivist" approach to grounded theory, thus introducing yet another perspective into the conversation about procedures.

4.6.1. Variants

From this historical sketch, we can see that perspectives about conducting grounded theory research have differed depending on the advocate for a particular approach. Three dominant designs are discernible: the systematic procedure advanced by Strauss and Corbin (1990, 1998); the emerging design, associated with Glaser (1992); and the constructivist approach, espoused by Charmaz (1990, 2000).

4.6.1.1 The Systematic Design

The systematic design for grounded theory is widely used in social science research, and it is associated with the detailed, rigorous procedures of Strauss and Corbin (1990) and elaborated in their second edition on techniques and procedures for developing grounded theory (Strauss & Corbin, 1998). As a procedural guide, it is much more prescribed than the original conceptualization of grounded theory in 1967 (Glaser & Strauss, 1967). A systematic design in grounded theory emphasizes the use of data analysis steps of open, axial, and selective coding, and the development of a logic paradigm or a visual picture of the theory generated.

In open coding, the researcher identifies several categories (or themes) found in the data. Within each category are properties that might be considered subcategories. These properties are dimensionalized in grounded theory to show the extreme possibilities on a continuum of the property. For example, the committee or department chair, as a provider (category), engages in funding faculty (a property), that consists of possibilities on a continuum of substantial funds ranging from start-up seed money to lesser travel money (dimensionalized property).

In axial coding, the grounded theorist selects one open coding category, positions it at the center of the process (or interaction) being explored (as the core phenomenon), and then relates it to other categories. These other categories are the causal conditions (factors that influence the core phenomenon), strategies (actions taken in response to the core phenomenon), contextual and intervening conditions (broad and specific situational factors that influence the strategies), and consequences (outcomes from using the strategies). This phase often involves drawing a diagram, called a coding paradigm, that interrelates the categories.

In selective coding, grounded theorists write a theory about the interrelationship of the categories in the axial coding model. This theory provides an abstract explanation for the process being studied in the research. Procedurally, it is the process of integrating and refining the theory (Strauss & Corbin, 1998) through such techniques as writing out the story line that interconnects the categories and sorting through personal memos about theoretical ideas. In a story line, a researcher might examine how certain factors influence the phenomenon leading to the use of specific strategies with certain outcomes.

Use of these three coding procedures means that systematic grounded theorists use set procedures to develop their theory, rely on analyzing their data for specific types of categories in axial coding, and use diagrams to present their theories (Creswell, 2002). A grounded theory study using this approach might end with hypotheses (called propositions by Strauss and Corbin [1998]) that make explicit the relationship among categories in the axial coding process.

4.6.1.2 The Emerging Design

Although Glaser participated with Strauss in the initial book on grounded theory (Glaser & Strauss, 1967), Glaser has written an extensive critique of the Strauss approach. In this critique, Glaser (1992) feels that Strauss with his colleague, Corbin, have overly emphasized rules and procedures, a preconceived framework for categories, and theory verification rather than theory generation (see Babchuk [1996, 1997] for a thorough review of how grounded theory has been used over the years and continues to be used). Glaser, on the other hand, has stressed the importance of letting a theory emerge from the data rather than using specific, preset categories (Glaser, 1992) such as seen in the axial coding paradigm (e.g., causal conditions, content, intervening condition, strategies, and consequences). Moreover, in Glaser's perspective, the objective of a grounded theory study is for the author to explain a "basic social process." This explanation involves the constant comparative coding procedures of comparing incident to incident and incident to category, as well as category to category. The focus is on connecting categories and emerging theory, not on simply describing categories. In the end, the researcher builds a theory and discusses the relationship among categories without specifying a diagram or picture.

The more flexible, less prescribed form of grounded theory research, as advanced by Glaser (1992), can be distilled into several major ideas.

1. Grounded theory exists at the most abstract conceptual level rather than the least abstract level, as found in life histories and simple data presentations.
2. A theory is grounded in the data and is not forced into categories.
3. A good grounded theory must meet four central criteria: fit, work, relevance, and modifiability. A theory carefully induced from a substantive area will fit the realities in the eyes of participants, practitioners, and researchers. If a grounded theory works, it will explain the variations in behavior of participants. If the theory fits and works, it has relevance. The theory should not be "written in stone" and should be modified when new data are obtained.

4.6.1.3 *The Constructivist Design*

The constructivist design has been articulated by Kathy Charmaz (see Charmaz, 1990, 2000) as a philosophical position between the more positivist (i.e., more quantitative) stance of Glaser, Strauss, and Corbin, and that of postmodern researchers (i.e., those who challenge the importance of methods). With a focus on the subjective meanings ascribed by participants in a study, Charmaz is more interested in the views, values, beliefs, feelings, assumptions, and ideologies of individuals than in gathering facts and describing acts. She suggests that any vestiges that obscure experiences, such as complex terms or jargon, diagrams, or conceptual maps detract from grounded theory and represent an attempt to gain power in their use. She advocates using active codes, such as "recasting life." Moreover, a grounded theory procedure does not minimize the role of the researcher in the process. The researcher makes decisions about the categories throughout the process (Charmaz, 1990). The researcher brings certain questions to the data along with a "store of sociological concepts" (p. 1165). The researcher also brings values, experiences, and priorities. Furthermore, any conclusions developed by grounded theorists are, according to Charmaz (2000), suggestive, incomplete, and inconclusive.

4.6.2 Key Elements in Grounded Theory Research

Grounded theorists seek to develop a broad explanation for a process, an interaction, or an action among individuals. To do this, they do not rely on existing theories but instead generate or develop themes (or categories) themselves. Although different sources of information might be used to develop these theories, grounded theorists often rely on individual interviews in which participants can describe their experiences in detail. Individuals are chosen based on their theoretical relevance, which means that they are people who can contribute direct insight into the theory being generated because they have experienced the phenomenon being studied. Researchers typically make several visits "to the field" to collect interview data, typically conducting 20-30 interviews to saturate the categories (meaning that further interviews would not likely yield more information). These categories represent units of information composed of events, happenings, and instances (Strauss & Corbin, 1990). Researchers also collect and analyze observations and documents, but these data forms are not the norm.

While the researcher collects data, the process of data analysis begins. In fact, an image for data collection in a grounded theory study is a "zigzag" process—out to the field to gather information, analyze the data, back to the field to gather more information, analyze the data, and so forth. The participants interviewed are theoretically chosen—in theoretical sampling—to help the researcher best form the theory. How many passes one makes to the field depends on whether the categories of information become "saturated" and whether the theory is elaborated in all of its complexity. This process of taking information from data collection and comparing it with emerging categories is called the constant comparative method of data analysis.

The result of this process of data collection and analysis is a theory, a substantive-level theory, written by the researchers close to a specific problem or population of people. The centerpiece of grounded theory research is the developm en t or generation of a "theory" closely related to the context of the phenomenon being studied. Strauss and Corbin (1994), for example, mention that a theory is a plausible relationship among concepts and sets of concepts. This "theory," developed by the researcher, is articulated toward the end of a study and can assume the form of a narrative statement (Strauss & Corbin, 1990), a visual picture (Morrow & Smith, 1995), or a series of hypotheses or propositions (Creswell & Brown, 1992). In the entire process, memoing plays a central role: The researcher writes memos about the emerging theory as it evolves and helps to shape the theory from the data.

4.6.3 Procedures Used in Grounded Theory Research

The procedures discussed here rely heavily on Strauss and Corbin (1990, 1998), who have indicated the most systematic approach to grounded theory research. For the researcher, they also provide procedural guidelines for a rigorous, systematic grounded theory study.

1. *Use grounded theory to generate a broad explanation.* This approach is useful if you want to develop a broad explanation or theory for a situation or concept when present explanations are inadequate because they do not capture the complexity of the situation or apply to individuals you wish to study. A grounded theory design is appropriate when you want to develop or modify a theory, explain a process, or generate a general abstraction of the interaction and action of people. As such, it offers a macro-analytic picture of social situations rather than a detailed micro-analytic picture.

2. *Explore a process or actions or interactions among individuals.* At the heart of grounded theory research is a process that you would like to explain. Thus, you need to identify a tentative process to examine in your grounded theory study. This process may change and emerge during your study, but a preliminary idea of the process is identified at this step. This process should naturally follow from your research problem and research questions that you seek to answer. It also needs to involve people who are acting or interacting in identifiable steps or with a sequence in their interactions.

3. *Ask a central question that requires developing a theory.* The central research question asked in grounded theory is often intended to specify an explanation for some process or interaction. For example, a grounded theorist in marketing might ask "What explanation exists for tourists' reaction to a historical site?" A grounded theorist in education might ask "What process explains why academic change takes places in colleges and universities?" In both these examples, the grounded theorist seeks to explain a theory of a process.

4. *Collect data primarily through interviews with individuals who can help you develop your theory, individuals who have experienced the process you are studying.* Grounded theorists use many forms of data, but many researchers rely on interviews to best capture the experiences of individuals in their own words. A characteristic of grounded theory research is that the inquirer collects data more than once and keeps returning to data sources for more information throughout a study until the categories are saturated and the theory is fully developed. There is no precise timeline for this process, and researchers need to make the decision as to when they have developed their categories and the theory. One general rule in graduate student research and interviewing is to collect at least 20 to 30 interviews during data collection (Creswell, 1998). This general guideline, of course, may change if the researcher collects multiple sources of data, such as observations, documents, and his or her own personal memos.

5. *Use the three-step systematic procedure of coding presented by Strauss and Corbin (1990, 1998).* The process of analyzing data, according to Strauss and Corbin (1990, 1998), consists of open coding, axial coding, and selective coding. The process of coding data occurs during data collection so that the researcher can determine what data to collect next. It typically begins with the identification of open coding categories and using the constant comparative approach to compare data to incidents and incidents to categories until a category is saturated. A reasonable number of categories is 10, but this number depends on the extent of the database and the complexity of the process being explored.

From open coding the researcher proceeds to axial coding and the development of a coding paradigm. This involves the process of selecting a core category from the open coding possibilities and positioning it at the center of the axial coding process. From here the researcher will likely return to data collection or re-analyze data to identify several categories of information that relate to the core category: causal conditions (What caused it?), intervening and contextual categories (What were the contextual or setting factors that influenced it?), strategies (What did people do in response to it?), and consequences (What were the outcomes of what people did?). This information can be assembled in the form of a coding paradigm or visual picture of the process. In drawing this picture, the researcher indicates with arrows the direction of the process.

The final process of coding is selective coding, in which the researcher begins to develop his or her theory. This involves interrelating the categories in the coding paradigm. It may involve refining the axial coding paradigm and presenting it as a model or theory of the process. It may include writing propositions that provide testable ideas to be further explored, although varied perspectives exist about whether the researcher or someone else might test the propositions or use them in practice. Theory can then be presented as a series of propositions or subpropositions. This stage may also involve writing a story, a narrative that describes the interrelationships among categories.

6. *End with propositions or relationship statements about the categories in the theoretical model.* The grounded theory project often ends with the presentation of the theoretical model in a figure or in the identification of specific hypotheses that draw together categories in the theoretical model (e.g., how the causes influence the core category, which, in turn, influences the strategies). These hypotheses may be written in a formal directional hypothesis form (e.g., "The more signs of distress by faculty, the more department chairs will engage in supportive roles and actively look for mentors for junior faculty"). The hypotheses may also be stated more as a discussion, with statements that link together the categories in the model to provide a description of the relationships.

4.7 THE ETHNOGRAPHY

Although a grounded theory study develops a theory from examining many individuals, these people may not have shared patterns of behavior because they do not interact on an ongoing basis. Studying a group of individuals who have developed shared patterns calls for an ethnography. An ethnography is a description and interpretation of a cultural or social group or system. The researcher examines the group's observable and learned patterns of behavior, customs, and ways of life (Harris, 1968). As both a process and an outcome of research (Agar, 1980), an ethnography is a product of research and typically is found in a lengthy journal article or a book. As a process, ethnography involves extended observation of the group, typically through participant observation, in which the researcher is immersed in the day-to-day lives of the people, or through one-on-one interviews with members of the group. Researchers study the meanings of the behavior, language, and interactions of the culture-sharing group.

Ethnography has its genesis in cultural anthropology conducted by early-20th-century anthropologists such as Boas, Malinowski, Radcliffe-Brown, and Mead and in their studies of comparative cultures. Although the researchers took the natural sciences as a model for research, they differed from traditional scientific approaches through the firsthand collection of data concerning existing "primitive" cultures (Atkinson & Hammersley, 1994). In the 1920s and 1930s, sociologists such as Park, Dewey, and Mead at the University of Chicago adapted anthropological field methods to the study of cultural groups in the United States (Bogdan & Biklen, 1992). Recently, scientific approaches to ethnography have expanded to include "schools" or subtypes of ethnography with different theoretical orientations and aims, such as structural functionalism, symbolic interactionism, cultural and cognitive anthropology, feminism, Marxism, ethnomethodology, critical theory, cultural studies, and postmodernism (Atkinson & Hammersley, 1994). This has led to a distinct lack of orthodoxy in ethnography and has resulted in pluralistic approaches to the description and interpretation of a cultural or social groups.

4.7.1 Variants

There are many variants to ethnography, such as a confessional ethnography, life history, autoethnography, feminist ethnography, and ethnographic novels (Denzin, 1997; LeCompte, Preissle, & Tesch, 1993; Van Maanen, 1988). Two forms popular in the social sciences will be emphasized here: the realist ethnography and the critical ethnography.

4.7.1.1 A Realist Ethnography

This form of ethnography is a traditional approach used by cultural anthropologists. Characterized by Van Maanen (1988), it reflects a particular stance taken by the researcher toward the individuals being studied. A realist ethnography is an objective account of the situation, typically written in the third-person point of view, reporting objectively on the information learned from participants at a field site. According to Van Maanen (1988), in this ethnographic design

- The realist ethnographer narrates the study in a third-person dispassionate voice and reports on what is observed or heard from participants. The ethnographer does not offer personal reflections in the research report and remains in the background as an omniscient reporter of the "facts."
- Reports objective data in a measured style uncontaminated by personal bias, political goals, and judgment. The researcher may provide mundane details of everyday life among the people studied. The ethnographer also uses standard categories for cultural description (e.g., family life, work life, social networks, status systems).
- The ethnographer produces the participants' views through closely edited quotations and has the final word on how the culture is to be interpreted and presented.

4.7.1.2 Critical Ethnography

When Denzin (1997) spoke of the twin crises of representation and legitimation, he was responding to profound changes in American society, such as becoming more multinational, joining a world economy, and changing demographics that included more racial groups. These factors have created a system of power, prestige, privilege, and authority that serves to marginalize individuals in society who are from different classes, races, and genders. With roots in German thinking of the 1920s, the historical problems of domination, alienation, and social struggle are now playing out within social science research.

Ethnography now incorporates a "critical" approach (Carspecken, 1995; Carspecken & Apple, 1992; Thomas, 1993) by including an advocacy perspective. Critical ethnographies are a type of ethnographic research in which the authors advocate for the emancipation of groups marginalized in society (Thomas, 1993). Critical researchers typically are politically minded individuals who seek, through their research, to advocate against inequality and domination (Carspecken & Apple, 1992). For example, critical ethnographers might study schools that provide privileges to certain types of students, create inequitable situations among members of different social classes, and perpetuate the pattern of boys "speaking up" and girls being silent participants in class.

The major components of a critical ethnography are summarized as including a value-laden orientation, empowering people by giving them more authority, challenging the status quo, and addressing concerns about power and control. More specific characteristics are as follows (see Denzin, 1997).

- The critical ethnographer studies social issues of power, empowerment, inequality, inequity, dominance, repression, hegemony, and victimization.

- Researchers conduct critical ethnographies so that their studies do not further marginalize the individuals being studied. Thus, the inquirers collaborate with and actively involve participants, negotiate the final written report, use care in entering and leaving a site, and reciprocate by giving back to the people being studied.

- The critical ethnographer is self-conscious about his or her interpretation, recognizing that interpretations reflect one's own history and culture, and thus they can be only tentative and questioning, subject to how readers as well as participants will view the account.

- Critical researchers position themselves in the text and are reflexive and self-aware of their role. They do not remain in the background, and they identify their biases and values. They also acknowledge views and distinguish among textual representations by the author, the participants, and the reader. No longer is the ethnographer an "objective" observer as in the realist approach.

- This non-neutral position for the critical researcher also means that he or she will be an advocate for change to help transform society so that people are less oppressed and marginalized.

- In the end, the critical ethnographic report will be a "messy, multilevel, multimethod" approach to inquiry, full of contradictions, imponderables, and tensions.

4.7.2 Key Elements of an Ethnography

As discussed by Hammersley and Atkinson (1995), Wolcott (1987, 1994), and Fetterman (1989), the ethnographer begins the study by looking at people in interaction in ordinary settings and by attempting to discern pervasive patterns such as life cycles, events, and cultural themes. "Culture" is an amorphous term, not something "lying about" (Wolcott, 1987, p. 41), but something the researcher attributes to a group as he or she looks for patterns of daily living. It is inferred from the words and actions of members of the group and is assigned to this group by the researcher. It consists of looking for what people do (behaviors), what they say (language), and some tension between what they really do and what they ought to do and what they make and use (artifacts) (Spradley, 1980). Thus, ethnographers gather artifacts and physical trace evidence; find stories, rituals, and myths; or uncover cultural themes. Such themes are diverse, as illustrated in Winthrop's (1991) *Dictionary of Concepts in Cultural Anthropology* and Fetterman's (1989) themes of structure and function as a guide to research of social organizations. Structure refers to the social structure or configuration of the group, such as the kinship or political structure of the sociocultural group. Function refers to patterns in the social relations among members of the group that help regulate behavior.

To establish these patterns, ethnographers engage in extensive work in the "field," called fieldwork. They gather information through observations, interviews, and materials that will be helpful in developing a portrait and establishing "cultural rules" of the culture-sharing group. Ethnographers are sensitive to fieldwork issues (Hammersley & Atkinson, 1995) such as gaining access to the group through gatekeepers, individuals who can provide access to a research site. The ethnographer locates key informants, individuals who provide useful insights into the group and can direct the researcher to information and contacts. The field researcher is also concerned about reciprocity between the investigator and the subjects being studied, planning that something will be returned to the people being studied in exchange for their information and reactivity.

Ethnographers are also sensitive to the impact of the researcher on the site and the people being studied. In accord with ethical standards, the ethnographer makes his or her presence known so that deception about the purpose or intent of the study is not practiced. Showing sensitivity to these field issues, the procedures in ethnography call for a detailed description of the culture-sharing group or individual, an analysis of the culture-sharing group by themes or perspectives, and some interpretation of the culture-sharing group for meanings of social interaction and generalizations about human social life (Wolcott, 1994). The amounts of weight researchers give to these three aspects vary. The final product of this effort is a holistic cultural portrait of the social group that incorporates both the views of the actors in the group (emic) and the interpretation of the research from views about human social life in a social science perspective (etic). By holistic, we mean that the ethnographer attempts to describe as much as possible about a cultural system or social group. This might include the group's history, religion, politics, economy, and environment (Fetterman, 1989). With a cultural portrait, the ethnographer provides an overview of the entire cultural scene by pulling together all aspects learned about the group and showing its complexity.

4.7.3 Procedures in Conducting an Ethnography

As with all qualitative inquiry, there is no single way to conduct an ethnography, although current writings provide more guidance to this approach than ever (for example, see the excellent overview found in Wolcott, 1999).

1. *Study a culture-sharing group.*   The most important first step in conducting research is to identify why you are undertaking a study, which form of design you plan to use, and how your intent relates to your research problem. In all forms of ethnographies, these factors need to be identified. The intent of your research and the type of problem you seek to study differs significantly if you plan to conduct a realist versus a critical ethnography. For a realist ethnography, the focus is on understanding a culture-sharing group and using the group to develop a deeper understanding of a cultural theme. The culture-sharing group may be an entire school, for example, or a single classroom. The themes may include such topics as enculturation, acculturation, socialization, institutionalized education, learning and cognition, and child and adult development (LeCompte et al., 1993). In a critical ethnography, the intent changes dramatically from those used in a realist or case study project. A critical ethnographer seeks to address an inequity in society or some part of it, plans to use the research to advocate and call for changes, and typically identifies a specific issue (e.g., inequality, dominance, oppression, empowerment) to study.

2. *Locate a setting in which to study this group.*   Because ethnographers spend a lengthy time with participants, gaining their trust, finding individuals to act as "gatekeepers" who can help open a site, being respectful of individuals and places, and reciprocating with individuals at a site are all important facets of this research. Initially, it is important that the researcher identify individuals and sites that can help understand a cultural theme or that can help emancipate individuals.

3. *Ask questions about the shared patterns of behavior, beliefs, and language.*   The research questions asked by an ethnographer tend to probe the culture-sharing aspects of the group of people. Questions such as "What are the patterns of language used by gang members?" or "What behaviors do 'punkers' use in high schools" start the process of understanding a culture-sharing group.

4. *Develop a description of the culture-sharing group and analyze data for themes that indicate shared patterns.*   In all ethnographic designs, the researcher will engage in the general process of developing a description, analyzing data for themes, and providing an interpretation of the meaning of the information collected. These are typical data analysis and interpretation procedures found in all qualitative studies; however, within these procedures the different types of ethnographic design vary in their approach. In a realist ethnography, the researcher must consider a balance among description,

analysis, and interpretation so that each becomes an important element of the analysis. Moreover, the researcher needs to both consider in his or her interpretation how he or she learned about the cultural theme studied and actively reflect back on what information existed in the literature and how this new study added to the understanding of the cultural theme. In a critical ethnography, the description, analysis, and interpretation are shaped to focus on the "critical" issue being explored in the study. Specifically, the researcher should interpret findings in view of the changes that need to occur and to advocate for improvements in the lives of the participants. Critical ethnographers often will advance a plan for change with specific steps that need to occur.

4.8   THE CASE STUDY

Although either the culture-sharing group or specific individuals within it might be considered a "case," the case study approach to qualitative inquiry is focused less on discerning patterns of the group and more on an in-depth description of a process, a program, an event, or an activity. Some consider "the case" an object of study (Stake, 1995), and others consider it a methodology (e.g., Merriam, 1988). In either situation, case study is an exploration of a "bounded system" or a case (or multiple cases), over time, through detailed, in-depth data collection involving multiple sources of information and rich in context.

The case study approach is familiar to social scientists because of its popularity in psychology (Freud), medicine (case analysis of a problem), law (case law), or political science (case reports). Case study research has a long, distinguished history across many disciplines. Hamel (1993) traces the origin of modern social science case studies through anthropology and sociology. He cites anthropologist Malinowski's study of the Trobriand Islands, French sociologist LePlay's study of families, and the case studies of the University of Chicago Department of Sociology in the 1920s and 1930s (e.g., Thomas and Znaniecki's study, *The Polish Peasant in Europe and America* [1918-1920/1958]) as antecedents of qualitative case study research. Today, the case study writer has a large array of texts and approaches from which to choose to develop a case study. Yin (1989), for example, espouses both quantitative and qualitative approaches to case study development and discusses exploratory and descriptive qualitative case studies. Merriam (1998) advocates a general approach to qualitative case studies in the field of education. Hamel (1993), a sociologist, provides a historical and problem-centered discussion of qualitative case studies. Stake (1995) systematically establishes procedures for case study research and cites them extensively in his example of "Harper School."

4.8.1   Variants

Case studies may be selected because they are unusual and have merit in and of themselves. When the case itself is of interest, it is called an intrinsic case. The study of a bilingual school illustrates this form of a case study (Stake, 2000). Alternatively, the focus of a qualitative study may be on a specific issue, with a case used to illustrate the issue. This type of case is considered to be an instrumental case, because it serves a purpose of illustrating a particular issue. The case study by Asmussen and Creswell (1995) portrays an instrumental case of a campus used to portray reactions to a gunman incident.

Case studies may also include multiple cases; this type is called a collective case study (Stake, 1995). Multiple cases are described and compared to provide insight into an issue. Several schools, for example, might be studied to illustrate alternative approaches to school choice for students. Finally, case study researchers may select several cases (a collective case study), with multiple cases illustrating a specific issue. When several cases are studied, the researcher selects the cases purposefully to illustrate typical examples of cases or representative cases. Although qualitative researchers do not intend to generalize findings, researchers using a multiple or collective case study often make claims about generalization. When this is done, the inquirer needs to select representative cases for inclusion in the qualitative study.

4.8.2 Key Elements of a Case Study

A case in a case study is a bounded system, bounded by time and place, and the case may be a program, an event, an activity, or individuals. For example, the researcher might select for study several programs (a multi-site study) or a single program (within-site study). The "case" may be a single individual, several individuals separately or in a group, a program, events, or activities (e.g., a teacher, several teachers, the implementation of a new math program). The "case" may represent a process consisting of a series of steps (e.g., a college curriculum process) that form a sequence of activities. To learn about these systems, researchers collect multiple sources of information including observations, interviews, audiovisual material, and documents and reports. The researcher seeks to develop an "in-depth" understanding of the case(s) through collecting multiple forms of data (e.g., pictures, scrapbooks, videotapes, and e-mails).

Providing this in-depth understanding requires studying only a few cases, because for each additional case examined, the researcher has less time to devote to exploring the depths of any one case. Setting the context of the case involves situating the case within its setting, which may be a physical setting or the social, historical, and economic situation. The researcher also locates the "case" or "cases" within their larger context, such as geographical, political, social, or economic settings (e.g., the family constellation consisting of grandparents, siblings, and "adopted" family members).

4.8.3 Procedures for Conducting a Case Study

Several procedures are available for conducting case studies (see Merriam, 1998; Stake, 1995). This discussion will rely primarily on Stake's (1995) approach to conducting a single or multiple case study.

1. *Provide an in-depth study of a bounded system.*   To use case study procedures, the researcher must be interested in developing an in-depth discussion and analysis of a bounded system. To establish this analysis, the researcher must determine the type of case that will best yield information about an issue or whether the case is important in itself.

2. *Ask questions about an issue under examination or about the details of a case that is of unusual interest.*   The research question asked addresses either an issue or a problem or a case. For example, a researcher might ask, "What is meant by professionalism for teachers in five schools of education?" In this example, the focus is on learning about the issue (an instrumental case study) and using the five schools as multiple cases to understand the issue. Alternatively, a case study researcher might ask, "What process unfolded during the teaching of a distance education course for deaf students?" The focus in this case study is on learning about an unusual case that is of intrinsic interest in its own right.

3. *Gather multiple forms of data to develop in-depth understanding.*   Because a hallmark of a case study is an in-depth portrait of the case, the qualitative researcher gathers multiple forms of data. These forms might include interviews, observations, documents, and audiovisual materials. The extent and complexity of the data mark a case study as different from many forms of qualitative re-

search. For example, Yin (1989) recommends six types of information: documentation, archival records, interviews, direct observations, participant-observations, and physical artifacts.

4. *Describe the case in detail and provide an analysis of issues or themes that the case presents.* Data analysis involves developing a detailed description of the case. This might be presented as a chronology of events or a detailed rendering of information about people, places, and activities involved in the case. Further data analysis typically includes developing issues or themes (Stake, 1995) that develop when the researcher studies the case. These issues add complexity to the case analysis. One popular pattern of analysis for the qualitative researcher of collective case studies is for the inquirer to analyze within each case for themes and across all cases for themes that are either common or different. This procedure is called within-case and across-case theme development. Analysis of this data can be a holistic analysis of the entire case or an embedded analysis of a specific aspect of the case (Yin, 1989).

5. *In both description and issue development, situate the case within its context or setting.* In the analysis, the case study researcher situates the case within its context so that the case description and themes are related to the specific activities and situations involved in the case. This might involve a focus on the organization, the day-to-day activities, or the people and places involved in the case, or a detailed presentation of demographic information about the people or the site. This analysis is rich in the context or setting in which the case presents itself (Merriam, 1988). From this analysis, the investigator narrates the study through techniques such as a chronology, major events followed by an up-close description, or a detailed perspective about a few incidents.

6. *Make an interpretation of the meaning of the case analysis.* The researcher interprets the meaning of the case, whether that meaning comes from learning about the issue of the case (instrumental case) or learning about an unusual situation (intrinsic case). In the final interpretive phase, the researcher reports, as Lincoln and Guba (1985) suggest, the "lessons learned" from the case.

4.9 QUALITATIVE DATA ANALYSIS SOFTWARE

In each systematic approach discussed thus far, we have highlighted procedures that qualitative researchers might use in conducting their studies. This systematic procedure is further encouraged by the use of computer packages that are helpful in developing a detailed analysis of data in qualitative projects. In recent years, a number of books have addressed the advantages and disadvantages of computer data analysis software programs (Fielding & Lee, 1998, Fisher, 1997; Tesch, 1990; Weaver & Atkinson, 1995; Weitzman & Miles, 1995).

These programs enable qualitative researchers to systematically analyze text or image files, categorize and code information, build descriptions and themes, sort and locate important data segments, and provide visual displays of codes and categories. With the refinements and continual development of these software programs, qualitative researchers have little basis for a comparative analysis of the programs and how they might be used in procedures of qualitative approaches. To address this deficiency, we present here and evaluate seven programs using eight key criteria that lie at the base of several approaches to qualitative data analysis. Unquestionably, all the programs have features useful in conducting narrative research, phenomenological inquiry, grounded theory studies, ethnographies, and case studies. In addition, they all possess a rich history of software development by researchers and demonstrate a commitment to future work in this area. The packages and companies who produce them, including Web sites, are listed below.

ATLAS.ti—developed by
    Scientific Software
    Thomas Muhr
    www.atlasti.de

ETHNOGRAPH5—developed by
    Qualis Research
    John Seidel
    www.qualisresearch.com

HyperRESEARCH 2.5—developed by
    ResearchWare
    Sharlene Hesse-Biber, T. Scott Kinder, Paul Dupuis, Ann Dupuis, and Richard Gaskin
    www.researchware.com

Classic N4—developed by Qualitative Solutions and Research (QSR). (It is the new name for what you may know as NUD*IST or N4.)
    Lyn and Tom Richards
    www.qsrinternational.com

N5—developed by QSR
    Lyn and Tom Richards
    www.qsrinternational.com

NVIVO—developed by QSR
    Lyn and Tom Richards
    www.qsrinternational.com

WinMAX
    Anne and Udo Kuckartz
    www.winmax.de

The work of Tesch (1990), Weitzman and Miles (1995), Fielding and Lee (1998), Weitzman (2000), and Fielding (2001) informs the structure and content of this section of Part 4. Our concern is to present a balanced perspective and to examine each program as software offering many possibilities for the user.

Our approach is not to declare a "best" program that covers the universe of qualitative data analysis software but instead to select a few programs and allow you to assess the strengths and weaknesses of each. Features that fit with a breadth of qualitative approaches shape the discussion. We emphasize how qualitative researchers can integrate software into their desired qualitative analysis approach. As shown in Table 4.2, we use a threefold classification scheme—evaluations of how "flexible, fluid," "comfortable," and "helpful" each program is—to summarize our assessment of how easily users can integrate each aspect of the programs into their analysis styles. Think of the table as a usability scale.

Flexible, fluid indicates that this feature of the program is easy to use, clear, and designed in a way consistent with qualitative thinking and computer convenience features. A flexible, fluid program generally is the most user-friendly.

Comfortable indicates that this aspect of the program is well designed and easy to integrate into work with qualitative data. Compared to flexible, fluid it is not as carefully fitted to qualitative approaches. A comfortable program, therefore, generally is not as user-friendly as a flexible, fluid program.

Table 4.2   A COMPARISON OF QUALITATIVE SOFTWARE PROGRAMS

	ATLAS.ti	ETHNOGRAPH5	HyperRESEARCH 2.5	Classic N4	N5	NVIVO	WinMAX
Ease of integration							
Windows or Macintosh	Windows	Windows	Both	Both	Windows	Windows	Windows
Getting started	Comfortable	Flexible, fluid	Flexible, fluid	Helpful	Helpful	Helpful	Flexible, fluid
Working through	Flexible, fluid	Flexible, fluid	Flexible, fluid	Comfortable	Comfortable	Comfortable	Comfortable
Type of data							
Text	Comfortable	Comfortable	Helpful	Helpful	Comfortable	Flexible, fluid	Flexible, fluid
Multimedia	Flexible, fluid	None	Flexible, fluid	None	None	Helpful	None
Read and review text							
Highlight and relate quotations	Flexible, fluid	Helpful	Helpful	Helpful	Helpful	Comfortable	Helpful
Text search	Flexible, fluid	Helpful	Flexible, fluid	Flexible, fluid	Flexible, fluid	Flexible, fluid	Flexible, fluid
Memo writing							
Memo system integration	Comfortable	Flexible, fluid	Comfortable	Comfortable	Comfortable	Comfortable	Comfortable
Memo system access	Flexible, fluid	Comfortable	Comfortable	Comfortable	Comfortable	Comfortable	Flexible, fluid
Categorization							
Code book	Flexible, fluid	Flexible, fluid	Comfortable	Comfortable	Comfortable	Comfortable	Comfortable
Code application	Flexible, fluid	Flexible, fluid	Flexible, fluid	Helpful	Helpful	Comfortable	Flexible, fluid
Code display	Flexible, fluid	Flexible, fluid	Comfortable	Helpful	Helpful	Comfortable	Comfortable
Review and adjust codes	Flexible, fluid	Flexible, fluid	Comfortable	Flexible, fluid	Flexible, fluid	Flexible, fluid	Flexible, fluid
Analysis inventory and assessment							
Sort and filter	Flexible, fluid	Comfortable	Flexible, fluid	Helpful	Helpful	Comfortable	Comfortable
Concept combination tool	Flexible, fluid	Comfortable	Flexible, fluid	Comfortable	Flexible, fluid	Flexible, fluid	Flexible, fluid
Conceptual map	Flexible, fluid	None	Helpful	None	None	Comfortable	None
Demographic comparison	Comfortable	Flexible, fluid	Flexible, fluid	Flexible, fluid	Flexible, fluid	Flexible, fluid	Flexible, fluid
Quantitative data							
Import	Comfortable	Flexible, fluid	Flexible, fluid	Flexible, fluid	Flexible, fluid	Flexible, fluid	Flexible, fluid
Export	Comfortable	Flexible, fluid	Flexible, fluid	Comfortable	Comfortable	Flexible, fluid	Flexible, fluid
Merging projects	Flexible, fluid	Comfortable	Flexible, fluid	Flexible, fluid	Flexible, fluid	Separate program	Comfortable

Helpful indicates that the user can accomplish this goal with the software but in a style that is more in line with the design of a particular software package as opposed to common thinking in qualitative data methodology terms. A helpful program is the most limited of the three categories.

The content of this review is based on work of ten consultants at ResearchTalk Inc., individuals who use and teach about qualitative research techniques and software. From our field testing of the packages and observations during consultation sessions with qualitative researchers, we have solicited comments from users, and from these comments, we have assembled a picture of what the qualitative process looks and feels like with different qualitative data analysis software packages. Admittedly, this review is subjective and will change as new features are added to the programs and as their tests and applications yield useful evaluative feedback.

4.9.1 Making Informed Decisions

We begin with the need to make informed decisions before purchasing and using software. We find that most scholars still have limited access to detailed, objective information about the differences between major software packages. Marketing and word of mouth remain main avenues for information. We find these sources to be less than reliable. Marketing material is written and approved by producers of the product. Some companies are better versed in marketing strategies than others. A recent advertisement from QSR, the creators of Classic N4, N5, and NVIVO, claims that NVIVO signifies a "New Generation" in qualitative software, yet a careful look at its features reveals little within the package that is new to the world of qualitative software, with the ability to use rich text the primary novelty. The change from Classic N4 to NVIVO makes the latter's features closely resemble features and approaches that have existed in ATLAS.ti, ETHNOGRAPH5, HyperRESEARCH 2.5, and WinMAX. Our current generation of qualitative software offers a range of attractive options for qualitative researchers seeking to integrate software into their analysis without overwhelming their unique process.

Several of your colleagues may be using qualitative software. Their advice certainly can be useful but should not be used exclusively. As discussed here, all the packages addressed do well in meeting the goals of qualitative researchers, but in very different ways. These variations may suit the preferences of one person more than another for very quirky reasons. Consider this seriously. Eventually the package should sit in the background as your energy is directed by the content of what you read, observe, and note. In addition, your colleagues' choices may have been made with an eye toward a limited range of options and/or prior to the release of several of the current versions and upgrades. We meet people who avoid ETHNOGRAPH5 because a colleague voiced discomfort with experiences with ETHNOGRAPH. However, we frequently find that people who are disappointed with ETHNOGRAPH used an earlier version, sometimes even the DOS version. Much progress has been made with ETHNOGRAPH5 since that time. Several other products also have changed. N5 is new to the market. Scientific Software frequently releases free upgrades that offer valuable features. ResearchWare will have released HyperRESEARCH 2.5 before the appearance of this discussion in print, which motivates our discussion of it rather than HyperRESEARCH 2.0.

4.9.2 Eight Criteria for Assessing Software Programs

We organize our comparison around eight key factors critical to analysis of qualitative data with software. Important questions about interaction during each phase of qualitative analysis that we address are presented here:

1. *Ease of integration.* A software package needs to be easy to use at all stages in the process of its use. This criterion relates to the ease of both "getting started" in using the software and "working through" qualitative analysis with different software packages.
2. *Type of data.* Two popular forms of qualitative data are text data and audiovisual materials. Each software package is assessed in terms of the use of "text" data and multimedia (e.g., videotape) data.
3. *Read and review text.* Finding specific text is an important step for a qualitative researcher. For each software package, the process of highlighting and relating quotations and the ease in searching for text and text strings are reviewed.
4. *Memo writing.* A process often involved in qualitative data analysis is to write memos to yourself that you use in analysis. Each package will be assessed in terms of its memo writing capability and the ease of retrieving memos for use.
5. *Categorization.* Categorizing data into codes and more broadly into themes is central to many data analysis procedures. Software needs to be reviewed for the process of using a codebook, applying codes, displaying codes, and reviewing and adjusting codes.
6. *Analysis inventory and assessment.* Various analysis procedures in qualitative research call for using specific codes or making connections among the codes to facilitate data analysis. Each software package can be reviewed for sorting and filtering capabilities, use of connecting codes, assessing code combinations, mapping concepts, and interacting with demographic information.
7. *Quantitative data.* The flexibility of qualitative analysis appears when you can integrate or combine quantitative data with qualitative data. Each package is reviewed for its capability to import and export quantitative data.
8. *Merging projects.* Although qualitative researchers often work alone during data analysis, there are times when multiple researchers work at different computers and need to merge their work. The software programs can be reviewed for their capability to merge data from different projects.

4.9.2.1 Ease of Integration

A core set of operations driven around reviewing, categorizing, and labeling text and images forms the foundation of both major qualitative traditions and qualitative software packages. What we as qualitative researchers must do when we come to software is integrate the program into our existing strategies for questioning and discovery. We can and should weigh the pros and cons and decide what or what not to implement and how.

Before using software, consider the following questions: What is your qualitative research knowledge and experience? What is your level of computer expertise? Do you even like computers? These and other issues further argue for finding a package you can integrate well with your individual style. This review of how easily you can integrate a specific package into your qualitative analysis approach focuses on three main points:

1. The language, logic, and layout of the package
2. The degree to which the package takes advantage of existing computer facilities such as drag-and-drop, multiple select, and right mouse clicks
3. The supporting documentation that comes with the package

After mention of which packages work with which computer platforms, we apply the above criteria to two phases of interaction with qualitative data, "getting started" and "working through."

HyperRESEARCH 2.5 and Classic N4 are the only packages we reviewed that are built for both Windows or Macintosh platforms. HyperRESEARCH 2.5 files can simply be shared across both platforms, and QSR provides a program that can convert files from one platform to the other. Weitzman (2000) also reports that even the most powerful PC programs sold today run well with the aid of PC emulators on Macintosh machines currently available.

Getting Started

One of the most common questions we are asked is "How long will it take me to get started with my new qualitative software package?" This question is difficult to answer, and we find some differences in how quickly people become comfortable with different packages. The best packages in this regard tend to feature a clear interface, a simple and familiar language for qualitative analysis, user-friendly options for performing tasks, and helpful supporting materials.

The language and design of ETHNOGRAPH5 are very straightforward. The codebook is accessed via a button that has a picture of a book on it. Text can be copied, formatted, and entered into your project via the ETHNOGRAPH5 editor. Right mouse clicks and button options appear in sensible places and provide access to key operations. ETHNOGRAPH5's manual is very clearly written. An appendix provides an insightful overview of the qualitative analysis process.

HyperRESEARCH 2.5 is built around case cards. All code and annotation work relevant to a specific case (each unit of analysis) is linked to its case card. This setup allows easy review of issues connected to one participant in your study or quick comparative exploration across participants. The language is consistent with traditional qualitative analysis language, and both the manual and help menus are carefully and clearly written. WinMax works with four main arenas for interaction: list of texts, list of codes, list of coded segments, and working text. Each section can be open on its own or in combination with any other. Initial work is directed via interaction with your list of texts and list of codes. Although the WinMAX manual can be hard to follow, the help menus direct you to steps necessary to achieve your goals.

ATLAS.ti can initially intimidate new users. We find that the primary source of this confusion is that ATLAS.ti offers several different options for how to perform any function you need to use. Once you figure out your most comfortable style and understand that ATLAS.ti allows you to perform a similar set of key actions to key objects (documents, quotations, codes, and memos) in your project, you can quickly find comfort with the program. For the most part, ATLAS.ti's language is clear. The network diagram uses terms that can be uncomfortable, such as "import neighbors," used to bring linked quotes and codes into the diagram. Although the manual that comes with the package can be frustrating, the extended manual (which you can print from the CD that loads the software) and help menus are useful. ATLAS.ti takes the most advantage of computer convenience features like drag-and-drop, right mouse click, and multiple select.

The good news is that once you adapt to a QSR product, you are probably very comfortable with and loyal to it. We find that the major issue with QSR products is that initial and continued use involves integration of a language and software structure that is less consistent with the language and organization of qualitative traditions than any other product we feature here. These concerns make QSR products the most difficult to integrate into your analysis and computer use style. The foundation of each QSR product—Classic N4, N5, and NVIVO—is built with a structure unique to QSR and a language that is often difficult for qualitative researchers to adopt. Within NVIVO, memos are written as document or node links. "Nodes," "Explorers," "Index Searches," and "Assay Scope" are just a few terms that users find disconnected from their normal language for qualitative analysis. In addition, codes and memos are organized into a node structure within each package. Nodes can be either free or in an index tree. Nodes within the index tree section are assigned addresses that are used for coding and questioning throughout Classic N4 and to a lesser degree within N5 and NVIVO. In NVIVO and N5, project pads are places where central functions are found.

The language and structure of QSR products add more distraction to new users than enhancement to the research process. The vast majority of goals achieved with QSR products are accomplished in other products with less cumbersome language and with interface organization that is less awkward. The supporting material for all products meets mixed reception, but it has improved. We find that once you are oriented to these products, you can perform a sound, interesting, insightful analysis.

Working Through

We discuss the fit of a package after initial orientation here. Does it get better or worse as you use or work through the package? ETHNOGRAPH5 and HyperRESEARCH 2.5 are the most consistent in convenient use and orientation throughout the life of a project. This strength results from clean interfaces and from well-written and organized supporting materials.

The main dilemma for initial ATLAS.ti users concerns orientation to its layout and design. We find that once an understanding of these factors is established, users achieve comfort and can progress sensibly through the remainder of their interaction with the program. As your understanding and interaction with the language and organization of QSR products increase, so do your comfort and ability to grasp later features. You begin to see how the structure is built to provide access to inventory and analysis tools used later in a project.

WinMAX users report initial disorientation when they begin to pursue issues of connection and attempt to answer questions about the work they have done. This confusion is alleviated once they realize that documents and codes about which they are curious must first be clicked and activated before questions are initiated by clicking within the coded segment section and reports requested via the file menu.

4.9.2.2 Type of Data

Text

It is important to know both how to format a document and the benefits and detriments to following format suggestions offered by developers. All programs read ASCII text. You can simply type your text and save as ASCII for any of them to read your text. As discussed below, NVIVO can read rich text, and WinMAX has features that work well for researchers working with open-ended responses to structured questions of a survey.

NVIVO allows you to use documents that contain color, bold, italic, underline, and other formatting via its ability to read rich text documents. In addition, you can mark several levels of structured sections that allow you to easily reference predefined sections of discussion such as those that are common in structured interviews and meetings that follow the same form session to session. Coloring documents, however, does not allow you to search for all "red" text, and QSR has reported that researchers with larger databases can experience problems within NVIVO. NVIVO offers character-based coding.

WinMAX will allow the use of rich text in its next version. Currently, it has a document feature that aids researchers using open-ended responses to questionnaires. You can prepare your text in one word-processed document that contains each person's response. Markers you place throughout the document allow WinMAX to recognize both all responses from each person in your study and each person's response to each of your open-response questions. WinMAX also offers character-based coding.

ATLAS.ti, ETHNOGRAPH5, and N5 read ASCII text and allow you to insert consistent labels on structured sections of text that can be recognized for automatic sorting of each topic in each document. Incorporation of text into your project is also straightforward. N5 lets you decide the smallest character for coding as you enter the document: either lines, sentences, or paragraphs. ETHNOGRAPH5 allows you to code by line. ATLAS.ti offers character-based coding. ATLAS.ti's next version will allow the use of rich text and other more dynamic document formats.

Although HyperRESEARCH 2.5 has few requirements and challenges for document format, it does not currently have the ability to recognize the end of key sections of discussion within your data files. This limitation creates challenges for researchers working with structured data. HyperRESEARCH 2.5 offers character-based coding. Classic N4 requires you to determine the size of "text units," the smallest amount of text to be coded, for your documents. Lines, sentences, or paragraphs are the most common options for text units. Classic N4 requires you to place hard returns at the ends of lines, sentences, or paragraphs upon document format (this can be accomplished with relative ease via either "edit-replace" or "save as text only with line breaks"). In addition, you have the option to insert headers (which are brief document summaries) and/or sections (used for structured discussions) into the body of your document. Users report that steps required to access these features can be more involved than they desire.

Multimedia Data

The use of multimedia data is a key area that will continue to develop in the coming years. In particular, you may soon witness the ability to see or have your video or your audio file run with concurrent text streaming. In the meantime, ATLAS.ti, HyperRESEARCH 2.5, and NVIVO currently allow you to work with multimedia files. ATLAS.ti and HyperRESEARCH 2.5 offer a greater degree of interaction with these files.

ATLAS.ti and HyperRESEARCH 2.5 provide flexible options for use of graphic, audio, and video files. Neither program contains facilities for you to digitize (create computer files of) your data, but they read a range of file types for each file format. After your multimedia data are entered into the program, you can code entire files or parts of the graphic, audio, or video file. Coded segments can be reviewed during an examination of items coded to one category or while exploring a range of co-occurrence options such as overlapping segments or one topic inside another.

NVIVO also allows you to use graphic, audio, or video files, but with a much less flexible requirement. Multimedia files must first be broken into "data-bites." Before you enter the file into your project, you decide the size and break points of larger graphic files and enter those parts into the program. Each data-bite must be coded in its entirety, resulting in a loss of fine coding ability. ETHNOGRAPH5, Classic N4, N5, and WinMAX do not currently offer the ability to introduce multimedia files.

4.9.2.3 Read and Review Text

Upon review of your documents, you may find quotations that deserve highlighting, sometimes without any link to specific code categories or memos. This practice can be particularly useful early in an analysis to simply recognize powerful quotations, but it can be adopted throughout your data review. Think of this exercise as marking participant statements with a highlighter pen.

Highlight and Relate Quotations

ATLAS.ti and NVIVO offer explicit functions that provide for this task. ATLAS.ti's options for "quote-work" are particularly powerful, as they easily link to its network diagram feature. ATLAS.ti considers quotes you mark as equal in status to your data documents, codes, and memos. You can mark a segment of text as a "free quote." Free quotes can be reviewed in isolation and left "free" or can be linked to a code or memo later in a project. In addition, ATLAS.ti's hyperlink feature lets you link connected quotes from a discussion that can be displayed in a network diagram. In a study of life satisfaction, one of our male respondents made a range of statements about his philosophy on how to treat people in his life. Some of his statements were about why treating everyone with respect comes back to benefit you later in life. At other points in his interview, he discussed life events that provided evidence of less than decent treatment of people in his life. At one point he discussed how his extra-marital affair was a good thing for his wife. When you hyperlink these statements, you can label the connection between them as discussions or criticisms of each other. Once labeled, each quote can be displayed in a network diagram to visually represent the ebbs and flows of the discussion.

NVIVO supports non-code marking of text through a link feature. "Node links" connect quote segments from different documents. They are contained in what NVIVO calls a node extract, which is essentially an unnamed code. These extracts can be named at any point in a project, and the status can be changed to make the original node extract a code. ETHNOGRAPH5, HyperRESEARCH 2.5, Classic N4, N5, and WinMAX contain easy options to begin to emulate these features. The trick is to simply name a code category "interesting quotes" or "contradictory statements" and then code quotes to these categories. Although this is not a perfect option, this practice ensures that you do not lose the observations about these quotes.

Text Search

One of the things computers do well is find patterns of text strings (words). All the packages we discuss can do that. The packages that do it better can not only search but also store results, mark results in the same way a code is marked, allow these results to be included in questions, allow you to store and explore context, and give you counts of word finds.

ATLAS.ti, HyperRESEARCH 2.5, the QSRs, and WinMAX accomplish the major goals we set for text searching. Classic N4 and N5 cannot give pure counts of word instances because they can only mark a text unit (QSR term for the smallest unit to be coded, either a line, paragraph, or sentence). If text units contain more than one instance of a search string, counts would register only one instance.

ETHNOGRAPH5 is primitive in comparison to the other packages in this regard. ETHNO-GRAPH5 can search for words only one at a time within an individual data document. If you elect to code "found" search strings, you must do so manually. The positive aspect here is that you are forced to read and consider each instance. The other packages can all mark codes automatically via a process commonly called autocoding. You can also opt to decide what instances should be coded one by one in the other packages.

4.9.2.4 Memo Writing

Note writing is a critical aspect of several qualitative analysis approaches. We consider two major issues in regard to memo writing. First, we discuss how well integrated the memo system is within each program. Second, we discuss how readily you can retrieve memos you have written.

Memo System Integration

A well-integrated memo system invites notes about an entire research project, about the analysis process, on individual data documents, on codes, on specific text, on conceptual maps—basically anywhere that written insight can benefit a project. ETHNOGRAPH5 offers a wide range of flexibility for memo writing. Free-standing memos on any topic can be composed, and there are opportunities to write memos on any document and referencing any text selection. Memos written on specific text sit in the data document with an icon showing their presence. Clicking on the icon allows access and editing. ATLAS.ti offers "comments" that can be written to any object in the project and memos that can be free-standing or linked to any quotation in your data. As in ETHNOGRAPH5, margin icons for memos allow access for editing. Users would like to see more direct pathways to link more than one quotation to the same memo and to classify memo types.

HyperRESEARCH 2.5 handles memos as annotations. Annotations can be linked to codes applied to text segments. There is no dedicated memo list. The link to codes on case card design initially appears limiting, but easy work-around strategies such as creation of a "general annotations" card for general topic memos and a document annotation memo at the top of each document case card can satisfy most memo writing needs. WinMAX allows memo placement on code categories and linked to any text instance. Similar to HyperRESEARCH 2.5, this apparent limitation can be overcome with work-around tricks such as creating mock codes to hold discussions of specific topics. Document memos can be written as text memos at the top of a document and linked to a code called "document memos."

In Classic N4 and N5, memos are attached to either a document or a node. Nodes should be considered containers that hold codes, memos, both, or neither. This use of nodes allows you to make a node that can hold a memo of any type, like a grounded theory analysis audit trail. Annotations can also be written on any selection of text; however, the annotation actually becomes text that exists in your data document, thus altering the original content and structure of your data. At times, decision making on where to put a memo can be challenging.

NVIVO memo strategies are either liked or not liked. Every memo is considered its own document, equal in status to your data, which can be coded. Some researchers find this liberating, while others find it to be circular and unnecessary. Memos can be included as links within documents. Icons for memos appear in the body text and can be clicked for access and editing. Our clients who use NVIVO ask for appearance of the word "memo" and a dedicated list of memos like those that appear in ETHNOGRAPH5, ATLAS.ti, and WinMAX.

Memo System Access

We find that researchers' major source of frustration with memo writing is retrieving memos they have written. Dedicated memo lists facilitate memo access. The ability to retrieve memo text as it links to codes and code combinations, without first having to code memo text, provides recovery for those who find themselves asking "Where did I put that note?"

ETHNOGRAPH5 offers the most thoroughly linked memo system. It contains an isolated, sortable memo list and the ability to request memo text written in concert with any code or code combination without document text. This facility permits focused examination of written notes. ATLAS.ti offers a memo list you can sort and filter, and it can show memo notes along with code and code combination reports. WinMAX has a dedicated memo list that can be filtered by any document, code, or code combination. Memos written to specific text can be accessed when that text is retrieved via code review in both ATLAS.ti and WinMax.

HyperRESEARCH 2.5, Classic N4, N5, and NVIVO do not have dedicated memo lists. Classic N4 and N5 have memo buttons that can be clicked with any highlighted code or document. Annotations are stored within documents and have their own home in the node explorer. HyperRESEARCH 2.5 allows isolated retrieval of annotations as a single click option in a report request. NVIVO offers options to group and focus on only memos, and it shows memo icons along with text retrieval at any code or code combination report.

4.9.2.5 Categorization

We use the term "categorization" to address work that qualitative researchers do to identify categories, themes, codes, and "bucket categories." You should expect to see the word "code" within each package. Qualitative software "codes" can be used to represent any type of categorization you need to do to your data, even if you simply want to mark the most interesting examples of what is coded to a category. You can make a "code" called "interesting stuff." This example demonstrates the kind of flexibility you should feel when working with your codes, whether you are in a codebook, applying codes, working with code displays, or reviewing and adjusting coded text.

Codebook

Codebooks should be built to accommodate adjustments. Changes to code names, definitions, and location should be easy to make (Fielding, 2001). Codebooks should provide the ability for focused work on the code list itself. The look of the codebook is also critical, especially during code application. ATLAS.ti and ETHNOGRAPH5 both incorporate flexible views of your codebook when taking an isolated look at your codes and displaying your code list while you apply codes. It is easy to display and edit definitions of codes. Codes can be combined easily. Changes to code names, definitions, and hierarchical relationships between codes can be made very easily. ATLAS.ti adds detailed, straightforward, and accessible sorting and filtering of your code list. ETHNOGRAPH5 offers options for sorting your codebook.

HyperRESEARCH 2.5's code list editor serves as its codebook. It is easy to use, and you can easily make adjustments such as renaming, deleting, and merging codes with a right mouse or control click. The main drawback of the code list editor is that it does not provide an option for a structured code list. If you want to organize a list of all actors in a study, you need to begin the name of each category with the word "actor" ("actor-friends," "actor-parents") in order to group the codes in the same location. Codebooks in both NVIVO and WinMAX are built to arrange codes hierarchically. Codes can be moved to become a subcategory of a different code by simply dragging and dropping. Making changes to names and definitions and combining codes is straightforward, although WinMAX does not have a specific code definition box—instead, you can write definitions in code memos, which might be awkward for some. Our clients report that, compared to ETHNOGRAPH5 and ATLAS.ti, code work and code display in both WinMAX and NVIVO are too structured.

Classic N4 and N5 provide a helpful, basic environment for building and presenting codes. Code names and definitions are easy to create and alter. Combining codes is done via cut-and-paste activities, rather than a simple merge or combine option. As in NVIVO and WinMAX, the code list is hierarchical in nature, but it is more uncomfortable to use because node addresses accompany names. You cut and attach codes to move them between subcategories rather than performing a more straightforward drag-and-drop as in WinMAX and NVIVO.

Code Application

Qualitative software's life is long enough for us to now be fairly demanding about basic tasks like code application and deletion. Codes should be easily visible alongside document text. Different users should be able to find different options for how they decide to apply codes: right mouse clicks, drag-and-drop, multiple select, and so on. Removing code applications should require only a few mouse clicks.

ATLAS.ti offers a wide range of easy-to-use and flexible options for applying either newly created or existing codes. You can drag-and-drop from a code list to a highlighted section. You can highlight text and right mouse click or use buttons or menu options. To remove a code application, you can right click the code in the margin display and "unlink" it.

ETHNOGRAPH5's quick code and code set options are easily used and accessed after you highlight text via buttons or a right mouse click. Code applications can be removed easily by clicking on a code marker and eliminating the code from the code set.

HyperRESEARCH 2.5 code application is very straightforward, flexible, and fast. You can create new codes easily and multiple select to apply more than one code at a time. Right mouse and control click options for MAC make code applications more convenient. Removing code references is less straightforward. You have to move off the document text to the case card for the person whose text you are reading.

WinMAX code references can be added and deleted quickly within WinMAX. With text highlighted, you can click on categories one by one to quickly apply codes. You can delete codes by right clicking on the code indicator in the margin area. Coding could be even more user friendly if drag-and-drop and right mouse options were available for coding. WinMax is also the only program to offer a "code-with-weight" option. You can apply a weight score of 1-100 to any code application. Weight scores are reported back upon code retrieval.

NVIVO's coding facilities are the easiest of all QSR products. You can drag-and-drop from a code list, and new codes are easily created. Initial negotiation with NVIVO's coder can be clumsy, but users adapt to it quickly. Strategies to use multiple selection of codes before application are disappointing.

Coding in N5 is more convenient than in Classic N4 but still awkward compared to ATLAS.ti, ETHNOGRAPH5, HyperRESEARCH 2.5, NVIVO, and WinMAX. Applying and deleting codes in both Classic N4 and N5 is impaired without an active on-screen display of codes, a reliance on node addresses, and the fact that the programs still takes less advantage of drag-and-drop, multiple select, and other convenience factors than they could.

Code Display

One strategy researchers use when coding transcripts and conducting fieldwork without computers is to use colored pencils to mark a bracket around text to signify where a code application would begin and end. Then the researcher writes the name of the code(s) that the section addressed next to the bracket. Qualitative software packages offer different versions of code displays that are available either as you work or on request after you have coded segments of text. ATLAS.ti and ETHNOGRAPH5 combine easy-to-read and easy-to-understand code displays with the ability to activate each code reference to reflect your thinking about specific code applications and/or categories. This ability to activate, query, and alter your recorded thoughts on code work captures the ongoing flow of qualitative thought on concepts integral to your project. This feature is what we point to as "state of the art" in this area.

ATLAS.ti offers a margin area display of codes to the right side of document text. You can choose font type and size for the margin display. When you apply a code to a segment of text, two things happen. First, a bracket appears that shows the start and stop point of the section. Second, the code(s) you selected appear(s) next to the bracket.

You can right click on each code in the margin area to access information about the category and record notes about it. An information display will show when a code was made, when it was last modified, and its current comment. Editing a comment lets you build running commentary about a specific category. The same right mouse click on a code in the margin area will allow you to view and work within a network diagram that contains that code. You can also view all other quotes coded to that category or remove a code reference with the unlink feature.

ETHNOGRAPH5 displays code names above the code segments where they are applied and shows the range of lines the code is applied to in the right margin. You can double click a displayed code to edit the code in its code set window, which allows you to delete the code from the segment or add another code to this section of text. You can change or expand the definition of the code or view it in the code family tree to group the code in relationship to other codes. You also have the option to display all code sets for a given document while you work with or review its codes. This feature provides a window to co-occurrences that may inform your analysis.

HyperRESEARCH 2.5 "Codes in Context" appear to the left of document text. They appear at the beginning of a code segment and display exact start and stop points of codes segments only when a code is selected. The code display is visual only; you cannot click on the code markers for more information or to make changes to information about the code. Code instances also display on individual case cards to show sequences and frequency of codes for each case in your study.

NVIVO displays codes as "code stripes" to the right of document text. Colored brackets mark the beginning and end of code segments. Codes applied to the same segments appear in a horizontal line. As in HyperRESEARCH 2.5, the code display is visual only, so it cannot be used interactively. NVIVO's code stripes also do not scroll up and down in sync with the document text.

WinMAX shows the start and end points of code segments, and it displays code names only when you move to a code segment indicator. You can click on a code segment indicator to delete that code reference, but no further work with or information about the category is available.

Classic N4 and N5 do not offer code displays that update and build as you work. You can request "examine coding" while you work; however, this feature does not indicate start and stop points of coded segments. You can also request a report with "code stripes" that allows you to select up to 26 codes to show in display. "Code stripes" appear in the right margin. Stripes are not code names but alphabetic codes that are defined in a key at the top of the code stripe report. Code indicators in "Code Stripe Reports" and "Examine Coding" are inactive.

Review and Adjust Codes

Taking multiple passes at coded data and adjusting work as you move along is critical to careful qualitative analysis. When reviewing and adjusting codes, you should be able to easily move back to original text and have full access to the same features you had while first reviewing documents. Most programs accommodate this process well.

ATLAS.ti, HyperRESEARCH 2.5, QSRs, and WinMAX all allow you to move back to your original text while you review the contents of a code category. This direct access lets you easily think more deeply about the logic behind your codes and coding and to adjust codes as you deem necessary. You can remove code references, add new codes to sections you review, and use the memo features of the program.

ETHNOGRAPH5 does not let you adjust code applications while you review code category contents. There is, however, an easy facility to add and delete coding from a document as you decide on changes. ETHNOGRAPH5 has another review feature worth noting. As you review each segment coded to a category, you can "mark" instances. "Marking" serves to distinguish select segments. After you mark segments, you can print or transfer to a word processor only the marked segments.

4.9.2.6 Analysis Inventory and Assessment

Qualitative research requires easy access to information on what has been done to date. Ideally, you should regularly assess the status of code lists, items coded to codes, and written notes. This practice teaches you about each item and enables you to question and perhaps change your current analysis strategies. Qualitative software packages contain several features to facilitate satisfying your curiosity about what your work with your data means. Here we discuss sort and filter abilities, concept combination tools, conceptual maps, and the ability to do demographic comparisons.

Sort and Filter

This section details the options and uses of sort and filter facilities in qualitative data analysis packages. Qualitative analysis often requires looking at information from different angles. You might elect to view only statements by women or focus on only a specific set of codes. Sorting codes or memos can help provide an inventory of what exists in your project and changes to these items across the life of your analysis. Fortunately, sorting and filtering is something computers do well.

ATLAS.ti has convenient sort and filter options for each of its main items in your project. You can sort documents, quotes, codes, and memos alphabetically, by recent usage, by date of creation, by volume of text, or by inclusion in network diagrams to gain perspective on relationships among these items. Filtering of the same set of items invites careful focus on key points of inquiry.

HyperRESEARCH 2.5 sorts codes on case cards and annotations attached to them. Although not as thoroughly integrated as the sort and filter options within ATLAS.ti, HyperRESEARCH 2.5 does provide convenient exploration of connections between documents and codes through filtering. You can literally turn on documents and/or codes to focus on only one set of items at a time.

NVIVO and WinMax permit filtering of codes and documents in similar ways to ATLAS.ti and HyperRESEARCH 2.5. WinMax allows you to activate any number of codes, documents, and demographic variables and to filter memos to focus only on items of interest to you. The filtering tools in NVIVO are similar and useful, but they are difficult to find, buried under "set" sections of document and node tabs of your main project pad. Sort options are not as extensive in either NVIVO or WinMax as in ATLAS.ti and HyperRESEARCH 2.5.

Filters in ETHNOGRAPH5 are straightforward. Although they do not literally turn items on and off as in ATLAS.ti, HyperRESEARCH 2.5, NVIVO, and WinMAX, they are very easy to use when you examine items referenced at any one code or combination of codes. Access to memos and work with codes in your codebook is made more dynamic by detailed sort options. Classic N4 and N5 do not have extensive sorting facilities within either package. Filtering is accommodated via a restrict option on searches of code relationships but does not turn project items on or off.

Concept Combination Tool

We use the term "connecting codes" to discuss the range of tools within qualitative software that allow you to make and assess connections among different codes. Each program has its own method that basically assesses how your applied codes relate to one another. Query Tools, Search Procedures, Hypothesis Testers, Index Search Operators, and Logic Machines all let you pursue the ways codes combine to inform your analysis. Our evaluation of these tools reveals a solid group of performers that provide you with powerful aids to analysis. Dynamic code results in ATLAS.ti, iterative questioning ("system closure" according to Richards and Richards [1994]), and matrix searches where you can pursue connection between and among several subcategories of two different codes create a strong field of concept combination tools. Although not readily accommodating matrix and iterative searching, ETHNOGRAPH5's search procedure tool deserves recognition for its clear organization and direct access.

ATLAS.ti contributes super-codes to the arena of concept combination. Super-codes are dynamic results of searches. If you ask ATLAS.ti to show the places where a code for friends appears within a code for issues of self and save that result as a super-code, you never need to run that search again. Super-codes should be considered live results. Coding updates that create more results to your original query are kept track of in your code list for easy retrieval. ATLAS.ti lets you question connections between subcategories of codes and supports iterative questioning.

HyperRESEARCH 2.5's "Select by Criteria" for codes and cases lets you easily pursue a range of connections between codes and cases. The hypothesis tester lets you ask involved questions of connection that can be pursued via the iterative questioning facilities of the other programs, but not with the explicit language of if-then statements and reports that goals are attained.

N5 offers a powerful range of question options that afford rich exploration of concept connections, including iterative searching and matrix connections, and provides a new organization and graphic diagrams to clear confusion that existed in Classic N4. Like ATLAS.ti, ETHNOGRAPH5, and WinMAX, NVIVO condenses search options into a single window that lets you assess code connection and text search at once for an entire data set or a focused look at only part of a data set. The logic machine of WinMAX is convenient and flexible. It invites iterative questioning and searching connections between subcategories in an easy-to-use single window.

ETHNOGRAPH5's search procedures do not accommodate matrix searches of the members of two different code families. Iterative questioning is possible only by saving results of a first search as a new data document and coding the entire text to a code named for the search you performed, which is a bit cumbersome. ETHNOGRAPH5's search procedure window, however, is the least difficult to learn. Its straightforward design and accessibility score high points. Classic N4's Index Search operators are powerful and incorporate a range of question options, including iterative questions and matrix searches; however, its organization and language are challenging.

Conceptual Map

As your analysis progresses, the ability to diagram observed relationships and to pursue connections between documents, quotes, codes, and memos can assist theory building (Weitzman, 2000). ATLAS.ti, HyperRESEARCH 2.5, and NVIVO are the only programs we discuss that offer conceptual mapping facilities. Here we discuss the degree to which the conceptual map feature is integrated throughout the program, how easy it is to use, and how attractive the display is.

ATLAS.ti features a network diagram that is well integrated throughout the program and incorporates major objects of your analysis. Network diagrams can be built from within their own window or through menu prompts. Options for creation of diagrams prove fruitful. You can build connections while reviewing text by using the hyperlink feature or while working within document, quote, code, and memo lists. For the individual who does not care about diagrams, this avenue to network building is easier to access and understand. Connections between items in a diagram can be labeled with a selection of preset options within ATLAS.ti or personalized options created by the user. You can also change the color and shape of icons in the model. The introduction of quotations onto tiles within the diagram encourages strong links between concepts and real data. It also presents opportunities for visually shifting quotations referenced at a code to further pursue what you can learn from that category. To use the network feature of ATLAS.ti, you will need to be familiar with the language of the network tool.

NVIVO's models invite diagramming connections between codes, memos, documents, and attribute characteristics. The conceptual map display is attractive and flexible. You can label arrows that connect items in the model and can change the color and shape of icons in the model. You cannot include individual quotes in the model, but you have direct access to the text referenced at codes within your model via a right mouse click. Access to models is not as thoroughly integrated as in ATLAS.ti.

HyperRESEARCH 2.5 includes a "code map" that lets you draw connections between code categories. Its appearance is unappealing, however, and interaction with it is a bit unwieldy. Action buttons that direct what you want to do, such as "move" a code, must be clicked before you can perform simple functions such as shifting a code in the map from one area to another. In addition, the code map is not as deeply integrated as those in ATLAS.ti and NVIVO. Documents, memos, and quotations are not included as items that can appear in the diagram and, diagram records can be built only from within the code map. ETHNOGRAPH5, Classic N4, N5, and WinMAX do not contain conceptual mapping–network diagram features. In Classic N4 and N5, you can transfer code items to conceptual mapping programs Inspiration and Decision Explorer.

Demographic Comparisons

You can assess patterns of discussion along demographic lines within qualitative software. At a minimum, programs let you record demographics by coding all the text of a document, such as "female" or "male." Some programs have easy-to-understand entry windows. Most programs also hold the results of demographic searches for later query.

ETHNOGRAPH5's face sheet is ideal. After easily entering demographics into the program, you can ask for comparison along demographic lines and save the results. NVIVO's attribute entry window is designed in similar ways to those of ETHNOGRAPH5 and WinMAX and is very easy to use. All three packages allow you to easily focus questions on specific values of demographic variables and save these results.

HyperRESEARCH 2.5, Classic N4, and N5 do not have dedicated windows for entry of demographic characteristics, but they do offer table import options and manual procedures that are not difficult to follow. In all three programs, demographic results are saved for later questioning only when demographics are entered as codes. You can record demographics in ATLAS.ti via its "family" feature and narrow question results with a textbase selection directed to only one demographic category, but the results of queries focusing on demographic families are not saved.

4.9.2.7 *Quantitative Data*

Work with quantitative data within qualitative software has moved onto relatively equal footing rather quickly. All programs allow import and export of quantitative data in table formats. You can import demographic-attribute characteristics for your sample to compare how code applications differ by groups of interest. You can export code counts and/or absence or presence of codes and even transfer these tables to quantitative packages for more involved statistical analysis, if desired.

ETHNOGRAPH5, HyperRESEARCH 2.5, Classic N4, N5, NVIVO, and WinMAX all allow you to move to and from quantitative and spreadsheet packages with direct links to document IDs in these programs. With the exception of Classic N4 and N5, frequencies of codes can also be easily displayed within each program. NVIVO's "profile of codes," which brings this report to your screen, can be slow to produce.

ATLAS.ti's quantitative option is strong and well structured. The code-document table within ATLAS.ti is easy to understand and quick to produce. However, ATLAS.ti links documents within your hermeneutic unit to quantitative programs by using ATLAS.ti's internal document number rather than document IDs you set within either a spreadsheet or a statistical package. This mismatch means you have to do manual matching of ATLAS.ti PD numbers and document IDs in your stats package. Classic N4 and N5 both offer options for table outputs. They do not provide pure code instance reports and require specific organization of codes within the "node explorer" to produce absence or presence of coding reports.

4.9.2.8 *Merging Projects*

Merging projects is an area where user desires continue to exceed current technology. Users want merge procedures that are lower maintenance than what is currently available. Currently, you must carefully monitor who works on what sections of a project and ensure that exact language is used for like items in each project—a practice that is recommended. Some programs allow different strategies for teamwork with their merge design; others are less flexible in this regard. As progress is made in this area, we will see more straightforward procedures that allow a more flexible work strategy for different researchers on the same project and more precise procedures for ensuring that the work of each user is properly tagged in each project.

ATLAS.ti, Classic N4, and N5 all offer merge options that provide flexibility for team members' work strategy. You can either divide documents among team members using the same set of codes or have all members work with the same documents and different sets of codes. However, multiple merges and changes to division-of-labor strategies can prove problematic. HyperRESEARCH 2.5 lets you copy and paste selected parts of one project to another but is less efficient when you attempt to merge a large portion or the entire project.

Both ETHNOGRAPH5 and WinMAX have easy-to-use merge facilities; however, having multiple people work on the same documents, each with her or his own set of unique codes, is not supported, although it is a common strategy for research teams. QSR has just introduced MERGE for NVIVO as a separate product. Although the timing of its release did not allow us to test it extensively, we can tell you that its functions would earn it the classification "flexible, fluid."

4.10 CONCLUSION

With this review of the software packages, we are recommending that software is merely a tool. As with any tool, your choice should be an individual one. Consider what is most important to you as a qualitative researcher to have and not have in a program, then make choices accordingly. You as a researcher are responsible for the depth and quality of your analysis and must be cognizant of the effects of software use on your analysis. Researchers must report qualitative analysis techniques not simply as applications of software but as tools that facilitate systematic data analysis. In a similar way, qualitative inquiry approaches will continue to develop with systematic procedures. Locating data analysis procedures that provide specific, systematic direction is difficult. Although all approaches adhere to a set of common practices in qualitative research, the approaches differ in their data collection, analysis, and form of writing.

We need to encourage flexibility of approaches yet provide guidance for those conducting studies so that they do not have to innovate in their approaches and re-create techniques already in place and tested by others. Both inquiry approaches and computer programs need to be revisited periodically with the thought of updating procedures and computer applications. Both systematic techniques and computer programs enhance the rigor of qualitative research and increase the sophistication of qualitative reports.

4.11 REFERENCES

Agar, M. H. (1980). *The professional stranger: An informal introduction to ethnography.* San Diego: Academic Press.

Angrosino, M. V. (1989). *Documents of interaction: Biography, autobiography, and life history in social science perspective.* Gainesville: University of Florida Press.

Asmussen, K. J., & Creswell, J. W. (1995). Campus response to a student gunman. *Journal of Higher Education, 66*(5), 575-591.

Atkinson, P., & Hammersley, M. (1994). Ethnography and participant observation. In N. K. Denzin & Y. S. Lincoln (Eds.), *Handbook of qualitative research* (pp. 248-261). Thousand Oaks, CA: Sage.

Babchuk, W. A. (1996). *Glaser or Strauss? Grounded theory and adult education.* Paper presented at the Midwest Research-to-Practice Conference in Adult, Continuing and Community Education, University of Nebraska–Lincoln.

Babchuk, W. A. (1997). *The rediscovery of grounded theory: Strategies for qualitative research in adult education.* Unpublished doctoral dissertation, University of Nebraska–Lincoln.

Barritt, L. (1986). Human sciences and the human image. *Phenomenology and Pedagogy, 4*(3), 14-22.

Bogdan, R. C., & Biklen, S. K. (1992). *Qualitative research for education: An introduction to theory and methods.* Boston: Allyn and Bacon.

Borgatta, E. F., & Borgatta, M. L. (Eds.). (1992). *Encyclopedia of sociology* (Vol. 4). New York: Macmillan.

Carspecken, P. F. (1995). *Critical ethnography in educational research: A theoretical and practical guide.* London: Routledge.

Carspecken, P. F., & Apple, M. (1992). Critical qualitative research: Theory, methodology, and practice. In M. D. LeCompte, W. L. Millroy, & J. Preissle (Eds.), *The handbook of qualitative research in education* (pp. 507-553). San Diego: Academic Press.

Carter, K. (1993). The place of a story in the study of teaching and teacher education. *Educational Researcher, 22*(1), 5-12, 18.

Casey, K. (1995/1996). The new narrative research in education. *Review of Research in Education, 21*, 211-253.

Charmaz, K. (1990). "Discovering" chronic illness: Using grounded theory. *Social Science Medicine, 30*, 1161-1172.

Charmaz, K. (2000). Grounded theory: Objectivist and constructivist methods. In N. K. Denzin & Y. S. Lincoln (Eds.), *Handbook of qualitative research* (2nd ed., pp. 509-535). Thousand Oaks, CA: Sage.

Clandinin, D. J., & Connelly, F. M. (2000). *Narrative inquiry: Experience and story in qualitative research*. San Francisco: Jossey-Bass.

Connelly, F. M., & Clandinin, D. J. (1988). *Teachers as curriculum planners: Narratives of experience*. New York: Teachers College Press.

Connelly, F. M., & Clandinin, D. J. (1990). Stories of experience and narrative inquiry. *Educational Researcher, 19*(5), 2-14.

Connelly, F. M., & Clandinin, D. J. (1999). *Shaping a professional identity*. New York: Teachers College Press.

Cortazzi, M. (1993). *Narrative analysis*. London: Falmer.

Creswell, J. W. (1994). *Research design: Qualitative and quantitative approaches*. Thousand Oaks, CA: Sage.

Creswell, J. W. (1998). *Qualitative inquiry and research design: Choosing among five traditions*. Thousand Oaks, CA: Sage.

Creswell, J. W. (2002). *Educational research: Planning, conducting, and evaluating quantitative and qualitative research*. Columbus, OH: Merrill/Prentice-Hall.

Creswell, J. W., & Brown, M. L. (1992). How chairpersons enhance faculty research: A grounded theory study. *The Review of Higher Education, 16*(1), 41-62.

Degh, L. (1995). *Narratives in society: A performer-centered study of narration*. Helsinki: Suomalainen Tiedeakatemia, Academia Scientiarum Fennica.

Denzin, N. K. (1989). *Interpretive biography*. Newbury Park, CA: Sage.

Denzin, N. K. (1997). *Interpretive ethnography*. Thousand Oaks, CA: Sage.

Denzin, N., & Lincoln, Y. (2000). *Handbook of qualitative research* (2nd ed.). Thousand Oaks, CA: Sage.

Dukes, S. (1984). Phenomenological methodology in the human sciences. *Journal of Religion and Health, 23*(3), 197-203.

Errante, A. (2000). But sometimes you're not part of the story: Oral histories and ways of remembering and telling. *Educational Researcher, 29*, 16-27.

Fetterman, D. M. (1989). *Ethnography: Step by step*. Newbury Park, CA: Sage.

Field, P. A., & Morse, J. M. (1985). *Nursing research: The application of qualitative approaches*. Rockville, MD: Aspen Systems.

Fielding, N. G. (2001). Computer applications in qualitative research. In P. Atkinson, A. Coffey, S. Delamont, J. Lofland, & L. Lofland (Eds.), *Handbook of ethnography* (pp. 453-467). Thousand Oaks, CA: Sage.

Fielding, N. G., & Lee, R. M. (1998). *Computer analysis and qualitative research*. Thousand Oaks, CA: Sage.

Fisher, M. (1997). *Qualitative computing: Using software for qualitative data analysis*. Aldershot, UK: Avebury.

Giorgi, A. (Ed.). (1985). *Phenomenology and psychological research*. Pittsburgh, PA: Duquesne University Press.

Giorgi, A. (1994). A phenomenological perspective on certain qualitative research methods. *Journal of Phenomenological Psychology, 25*(2), 190-220.

Glaser, B. G. (1978). *Theoretical sensitivity*. Mill Valley, CA: Sociology Press.

Glaser, B. G. (1992). *Basics of grounded theory analysis*. Mill Valley, CA: Sociology Press.

Glaser, B., & Strauss, A. (1965). *Awareness of dying*. Chicago: Aldine.

Glaser, B., & Strauss, A. (1967). *The discovery of grounded theory*. Chicago: Aldine.

Glaser, B., & Strauss, A. (1968). *Time for dying*. Chicago: Aldine.

Hamel, J. (1993). *Case study methods*. Newbury Park, CA: Sage.

Hammersley, M., & Atkinson, P. (1995). *Ethnography: Principles in practice* (2nd ed.). New York: Routledge.

Harris, M. (1968). *The rise of anthropological theory: A history of theories of culture*. New York: T. Y. Crowell.

Jacob, E. (1987). Qualitative research traditions: A review. *Review of Educational Research, 57*(1), 1-50.

Josselson, R., & Lieblich, A. (Eds.). (1993). *The narrative study of lives* (Vol. 1). Newbury Park, CA: Sage.

Lancy, D. F. (1993). *Qualitative research in education: An introduction to the major traditions*. New York: Longman.

Lauterbach, S. S. (1993). In another world: A phenomenological perspective and discovery of meaning in mothers' experience with death of a wished-for baby: Doing phenomenology. In P. L. Munhall & C. O. Boyd (Eds.), *Nursing research: A qualitative perspective* (pp. 133-179). New York: National League for Nursing Press.

Lawrence-Lightfoot, S., & Davis, J. H. (1997). *The art and science of portraiture*. San Francisco: Jossey-Bass.

LeCompte, M. D., Preissle, J., & Tesch, R. (1993). *Ethnography and qualitative design in educational research* (2nd ed.). San Diego: Academic Press.

Lieblich, A., Tuval-Mashiach, R., & Zilber, T. (1998). *Narrative research: Reading, analysis, and interpretation*. Thousand Oaks, CA: Sage.

Lincoln, Y. S., & Guba, E. G. (1985). *Naturalistic inquiry*. Beverly Hills, CA: Sage.

Merleau-Ponty, M. (1962). *Phenomenology of perception* (C. Smith, Trans.). London: Routledge & Kegan Paul.

Merriam, S. B. (1988). *Case study research in education: A qualitative approach*. San Francisco: Jossey-Bass.

Merriam, S. R. (1998). *Qualitative research and case study applications in education*. San Francisco: Jossey-Bass.

Miller, W. L., & Crabtree, B. F. (1992). Primary care research: A multimethod typology and qualitative road map. In B. F. Crabtree & W. L. Miller, *Doing qualitative research* (pp. 3-28). Newbury Park, CA: Sage.

Morrow, S. L., & Smith, M. L. (1995). Constructions of survival and coping by women who have survived childhood sexual abuse. *Journal of Counseling Psychology, 42*(1), 24-33.

Moustakas, C. (1994). *Phenomenological research methods*. Thousand Oaks, CA: Sage.

Natanson, M. (Ed.). (1973). *Phenomenology and the social sciences*. Evanston, IL: Northwestern University Press.

Nieswiadomy, R. M. (1993). *Foundations of nursing research* (2nd ed.). Norwalk, CT: Appleton & Lange.

Oiler, C. J. (1986). Phenomenology: The method. In P. L. Munhall & C. J. Oiler (Eds.), *Nursing research: A qualitative perspective* (pp. 69-82). Norwalk, CT: Appleton-Century-Crofts.

Ollerenshaw, J. A., & Creswell, J. W. (2000). *Data analysis in narrative research: A comparison of two "restorying" approaches*. Paper presented at the annual meeting of the American Educational Research Association, New Orleans, LA.

Personal Narratives Group. (1989). *Interpreting women's lives*. Bloomington: Indiana University Press.

Polkinghorne, D. E. (1989). Phenomenological research methods. In R. S. Valle & S. Halling (Eds.), *Existential-phenomenological perspectives in psychology* (pp. 41-60). New York: Plenum.

Polkinghorne, D. E. (1994). Reaction to special section on qualitative research in counseling process and outcome. *Journal of Counseling Psychology, 41*(4), 510-512.

Richards, T., & Richards, L. (1994). Using computers in qualitative analysis. In N. K. Denzin & Y. S. Lincoln (Eds.), *Handbook of qualitative research* (pp. 445-462). Thousand Oaks, CA: Sage.

Riemen, D. J. (1986). The essential structure of a caring interaction: Doing phenomenology. In P. M. Munhall & C. J. Oiler (Eds.), *Nursing research: A qualitative perspective* (pp. 85-105). Norwalk, CT: Appleton-Century-Crofts.

Riessman, C. K. (1993). *Narrative analysis*. Newbury Park, CA: Sage.

Spiegelberg, H. (1982). *The phenomenological movement* (3rd ed.). The Hague: Martinus Nijhoff.

Spradley, J. P. (1980). *Participant observation*. New York: Holt, Rinehart & Winston.

Stake, R. (1995). *The art of case study research*. Thousand Oaks, CA: Sage.

Stake, R. E. (2000). Case studies. In N. K. Denzin & Y. S. Lincoln (Eds.), *Handbook of qualitative research* (2nd ed., pp. 435-454). Thousand Oaks, CA: Sage.

Stewart, D., & Mickunas, A. (1990). *Exploring phenomenology: A guide to the field and its literature* (2nd ed.). Athens: Ohio University Press.

Strauss, A. (1987). *Qualitative analysis for social scientists*. New York: Cambridge University Press.

Strauss, A., & Corbin, J. (1990). *Basics of qualitative research: Grounded theory procedures and techniques*. Newbury Park, CA: Sage.

Strauss, A., & Corbin, J. (1994). Grounded theory methodology: An overview. In N. Denzin & Y. Lincoln (Eds.), *Handbook of qualitative research* (pp. 273-285). Thousand Oaks, CA: Sage.

Strauss, A., & Corbin, J. (1998). *Basics of qualitative research: Grounded theory procedures and techniques* (2nd ed.). Thousand Oaks, CA: Sage.

Swingewood, A. (1991). *A short history of sociological thought*. New York: St. Martin's.

Tesch, R. (1988). *The contribution of a qualitative method: Phenomenological research*. Unpublished manuscript, Qualitative Research Management, Santa Barbara, CA.

Tesch, R. (1990). *Qualitative research: Analysis types and software tools*. Bristol, PA: Falmer.

Thomas, J. (1993). *Doing critical ethnography*. Newbury Park, CA: Sage.

Thomas, W. I., & Znaniecki, F. (1958). *The Polish peasant in Europe and America*. New York: Dover. (Original work published 1918-1920)

Van Maanen, J. (1988). *Tales of the field: On writing ethnography*. Chicago: The University of Chicago Press.

Weaver, A., & Atkinson, P. (1995). *Microcomputing and qualitative data analysis.* Aldershot, UK: Avebury.

Weitzman, E. A. (2000). Software and qualitative research. In N. K. Denzin & Y. S. Lincoln (Eds.), *Handbook of qualitative research* (2nd ed., pp. 803-820). Thousand Oaks, CA: Sage.

Weitzman, E. A., & Miles, M. B. (1995). *Computer programs for qualitative data analysis.* Thousand Oaks, CA: Sage.

Winthrop, R. H. (1991). *Dictionary of concepts in cultural anthropology.* Westport, CT: Greenwood.

Wolcott, H. F. (1987). On ethnographic intent. In G. Spindler & L. Spindler (Eds.), *Interpretive ethnography of education: At home and abroad* (pp. 37-57). Hillsdale, NJ: Lawrence Erlbaum.

Wolcott, H. F. (1992). Posturing in qualitative research. In M. D. LeCompte, W. L. Millroy, & J. Preissle (Eds.), *The handbook of qualitative research in education* (pp. 3-52). San Diego: Academic Press.

Wolcott, H. F. (1994). *Transforming qualitative data: Description, analysis, and interpretation.* Thousand Oaks, CA: Sage.

Wolcott, H. F. (1999). *Ethnography: A way of seeing.* Walnut Creek, CA: AltaMira.

Yin, R. K. (1989). *Case study research: Design and method.* Newbury Park, CA: Sage.

4.12 QUALITATIVE RESEARCH METHODOLOGY: A NEW PERSPECTIVE

During the introduction to this part, we discussed how qualitative research methodologies are often used when researchers are interested in obtaining more authentic information about some phenomenon than that which would be available using more conventional quantitative techniques. The following article, reprinted with permission, discusses the context in which these new forms of research emerged and the promises and perils they present. This is an interesting look into the past along with some speculation about the future.

▶ **The New Frontier in Qualitative Research Methodology**

Elliot W. Eisner

First, I would like to thank the members of the Qualitative SIG [Special Interest Group] for asking me to deliver this address on the occasion of the SIG's 10th anniversary. When the first meeting of the SIG convened in Washington, D.C., a decade ago, there was a small band of AERA members in attendance. Since then, the SIG, qualitative research methods, and the field of educational research in general has come a long way. You have helped make that happen. I am here this evening to help celebrate your achievements and to reflect on where we are today.

The theme of my remarks focuses on the promise and perils of the new frontier in qualitative research methodology. I will be addressing the following questions: What is the new frontier and why is it being explored? What promise does it hold for improving the quality of education? What are its perils? And, finally, where do we go from here?

The new frontier in qualitative research methodology refers to research efforts that explore new assumptions about cognition, the meaning of research, and how new research methods might broaden and complement traditional ways of thinking about and doing educational research. Conventional approaches to educational research, those employing statistical procedures and the use of correlation and experimental designs, have in the past provided the paradigmatic conditions for the conduct of research. To do research was to use such procedures. An entire technical language has been created and batteries of statistical procedures invented to draw dependable conclusions from data. These procedures and the assumptions on which they rest are quite alive and healthy, but they no longer are the exclusive—perhaps not even the dominant—orientation to educational research. But why is this exploration occurring?

The emergence of what I have referred to as the "new frontier" secured its impetus from several sources, not least of which is a dissatisfaction with the constraints of operationalism and the legacies of positivism and behaviorism. Research conducted under the influence of these theories of meaning and behavior is often extremely reductive in character. In the opinion of many researchers, the theories leave out more than they include. Operationalism, for example, requires the measurement of variables, and although measurement can be a precise way to describe some aspects of the world, as a form of description it by no means exhausts the ways in which the countenance of the world or its details can be represented. Increasingly, researchers are becoming aware of the fact that form and content cannot be severed; *how* one chooses to describe something imposes constraints on *what* can be described.

As for behaviorism, neither stimulus response theory rooted in Thorndike's (Jonich, 1968) legacy to American psychology nor Watson's (1925) was ever adequate for understanding how or what the world means to those who inhabit it—perhaps especially children. For humans, meaning matters and values and intentions count. Humans live in a contingent world and form purposes that shift and alter depending on the meanings those contingencies have fostered. Indeed, as constructivism has increased in saliency as a way to understand how humans made sense of the world, behaviorism as an approach to individual psychology has seemed less and less relevant. The dominant philosophical and psychological orientations of the first 50 years of the 20th century left out, in the views of many educational researchers, too much that mattered.

Other sources of discontent developed from a growing interest in what Schwab referred to as the practical. In his classic paper (1969), given at this annual meeting in 1969, Schwab advanced a view of knowledge which at that time had little saliency among educational researchers. The view that he advanced pertained to the centrality of practical knowledge in the context of action. For Schwab, teaching and curriculum development were, above all else, practical activities. By practical he meant what Aristotle meant: Practical activities are activities aimed at making good decisions, not activities seeking truth. Practical activities dealt with contingencies, not with causal laws. Practical activities made use of theory, but as a rule of thumb, not as a rule. Practical activities required deliberation and at their best exemplified what the Greeks called *phronesis*, a concept that referred not simply to knowledge but to wise moral choice.

Schwab's emphasis on the practical adumbrated for educational researchers another way of thinking about how we come to know. As those of you who are familiar with Aristotle's theory of knowledge will know, Aristotle distinguished between three types of knowledge (McKeon, 1941). The first pertained to theoretical knowledge, knowledge that could, in principle, be secured on phenomena that were of necessity; that is, phenomena that had to be the way they were because they could be no other way. I speak here of fields such as mathematics, astronomy, physics, and other sciences whose subject matters were knowable by their necessary and sufficient conditions; subject matters whose locus of movement, Aristotle tells us, resides within themselves.

Practical knowledge, as I have indicated, is contingent knowledge; it depends on context. Perhaps its architectonic exemplification is located in the art of politics. Human activities in general cannot, in Aristotelian terms, be understood in the ways in which the stars can be.

The third form of knowledge is productive knowledge. For Aristotle, productive knowledge is knowledge of how to make something: tables, symphonies, paintings, or poems. Its most vivid manifestation is displayed in the arts.

The point that researchers derived from Schwab's presentation is that knowledge need not be defined solely in the positivistic terms that had for so long dominated the conduct of educational research and that theory itself had limited utility in the domain of practice. Theory is general, whereas action always occurs in the particular. Knowing what to do requires practical knowledge; theoretical knowledge provides a backdrop.

At about the time that Schwab presented his paper, there was also a growing interest in cognitive pluralism and cracks were beginning to appear in foundationalism. This interest was spurred by developments in philosophy—Rorty's (1979) work for example—and in feminism and multiculturalism. The traditional desiderata of "hard" data and "rigor" (the etymology of rigor refers to stiff) were both regarded as very "male" criteria, and these were criteria that were less than attractive to feminists. There was more to understanding the world than a male to take on its necessary and sufficient features. These sources of both dissatisfaction and interest led to a return to the study of cases and to attention to particularity. This attention led researchers back to schools and to the fine-grained study of educational phenomena. Among the first in education to cut new ground were Jackson (1990) in *Life in Classrooms* and Smith (1968) in *The Complexities of the Urban Classroom.*

Interest in cases, initially at least, persuaded more than a few traditional researchers to regard qualitative research as merely reconnaissance efforts that set the stage for "real" research—the kind they did. After all, they reasoned, what could you learn from a case that applied to nothing but itself? Yet, the study of cases has had a long history in human intellectual thought. Toulmin (1990), for example, pointed out with brilliant clarity that interest in the particular preceded what is usually regarded as the advent of modern science in the mid-17th century. Galileo's focus on the quantitative description of relationships helped shift our conception of what science was about. This shift in conception refocused attention from the timely to the timeless, from the local to the universal, from the oral to the written, from the particular to the general, from the qualitative to the quantitative. By the late 1940s and 1950s, according to Toulmin, interest in the timely, the local, the particular, and the oral began to reemerge. Indeed it has.

These new interests are, I think, expressed most publicly in the saliency of qualitative research in the growth of the qualitative SIG, and in the emergence of experimental formats at the AERA annual meeting in the publication of qualitative research journals, texts, and handbooks. If you look at the subject index in the AERA annual meeting program, you will find that qualitative research is among the largest categories on that list. It is exceeded by subjects such as teacher education and school reform, but some of these domains have a timely and a temporary character to them. Indeed, one can trace the saliency of qualitative research by tracing the number of listings in each of the annual meetings over the last decade. In 1991, there were 22 papers dealing with qualitative research in the AERA annual meeting program; in 1992 there were 32, 18 in 1993, 27 in 1994, 50 in 1995, and 55 in 1996. This year there are 45.

I said that the emergence of the new frontier emanated from discontent with older paradigms, with a growing interest in cognitive pluralism, and in new ways of thinking about the nature of research itself. One of these new approaches is the more recent interest in arts-based research. As you will know, when qualitative research emerged as a viable and definable option for educational researchers, the first tendency was to look to ethnography as the form within which to do such research. This looking to ethnography is, of course, altogether understandable. Ethnography is the child of anthropology, and anthropology is a member of the social sciences. The move from one social science to another is far less wrenching than a move from a social science to an arts- or humanities-based approach to research. The idea that the arts could provide a basis for doing research is itself regarded by more than a few as an oxymoronic notion. Yet, increasingly, researchers are recognizing that scientific inquiry is a species of research. Research is not merely a species of social science. Virtually any careful, reflective, systematic study of phenomena undertaken to advance human understanding can count as a form of research. It all depends on how that work is pursued.

My point here is that this particular period in the history of the American educational research community—the period in which we are working—displays a remarkable degree of exploratory inclinations. Younger scholars especially, although not exclusively, are trying to invent new forms that they believe are better suited for studying the educational worlds they care about. Arts-based research is one of the newer developments in the educational research community, and I am happy to say that all three of the AERA-sponsored arts-based research institutes that have been offered over the past 4 years have been oversubscribed.

Thus far, my remarks have been designed to provide an overview of the evolution of qualitative research in the American educational research community. I must tell you, however, that interest in qualitative research methods and more pointedly in new ways of thinking about matters of meaning is in no way restricted to the field of education. Social scientists and others working in other domains share similar interests. Yeasty new developments are a part of our intellectual landscape. Consider, for example, the work of Schepper-Hughes (1992) in anthropology, of Becker (1990) in sociology, and of Sternberg (1988) in psychology, not to mention the newer forms that have emerged in all of the fine arts. As I said, these are yeasty times.

It is time now for us to shift our focus and to ask about the promise of these new developments in qualitative research. What might this new frontier have to offer?

One of the consequences of the new frontier in educational research methodology is so ubiquitous it might be invisible. I speak of the idea that the emergence of alternative conceptions of knowledge and method have problematized traditional views of what research entails and have escalated our consciousness of its unexamined assumptions. If the whole world were purple, we would not be able to see a thing. It is by virtue of contrast, contrast that is both qualitative and in more customary terms ideational, that helps us notice the all too familiar. When everybody is quantifying the world, it looks as though there are no other options. When everyone requires random selection of a sample from a population as a condition for generalization, it looks as though that idea is made in heaven. When almost everyone conceptualizes validity in terms of its four canonical conditions, the meaning of validity becomes a kind of catechism that novices memorize.

The fact of new ways of doing research and the presence of nontraditional conceptions of knowledge open up the debate. Such a debate was one that I engaged in with Howard Gardner at the 1996 AERA meeting regarding the possibility that a novel might be an acceptable form for a doctoral dissertation (Eisner, 1996). Gardner took the negative view, not simply to engage in debate but because he believed it. I took the positive view for the same reason. The fact that there was a debate on such an issue is itself important. Who would have predicted a decade ago that fiction might be considered a legitimate form for a Ph.D. dissertation (although I must tell you that I am advised by my esteemed colleague and one of the world's leading organizational theorists, James G. March, that in his view most of what goes on at AERA is fiction!). Nevertheless, the presence of alternatives literally forces us to seek justification, and in so doing we become more conscious of the uses and limits of tradition. To the extent to which our consciousness is heightened, we will all be more likely to know what we are doing. That is no mean accomplishment.

A second promising development in the new frontier is the use and exploration of narrative. As you undoubtably know, Bruner (1985) made a distinction between paradigmatic modes of knowing and narrative modes of knowing. The former seek truth; the latter seek verisimilitude, or truthlike observations. In the former, you mean what you say. In the latter you mean more than you say. Narrative relates to the telling of stories and to the sharing of experience. To the extent that experience itself can be conceived of as the primary medium of education, stories are among the most useful means for sharing what one has experienced. Narrative—which means a telling—makes it possible for others to have access not only to our own lives when our stories are about them but also to the lives of others. Narrative, when well crafted, is a spur to imagination, and through our imaginative participation in the worlds that we create we have a platform for seeing what might be called our "actual worlds" more clearly. Furthermore, when narrative is well crafted, empathic forms of understanding are advanced.

Let me say a word about empathy. Traditionally, emotion was regarded as a contaminant to understanding. To be emotional was to lose control. Rationality at its best was cool and disinterested; it did not traffic in feeling. Indeed, one of the intractable legacies of the enlightenment was the separation of body from mind, a separation that is alive and well in the subtexts of school curricula and in our conceptions of human ability. What narrative does for us is to put us there, it helps us secure a sense of how it feels to be an associate professor at 46 with a wife who nags and cajoles him about his position in the university and, indeed, in life. In *Who's Afraid of Virginia Woolf?* Albee (1962) shows us, not merely tells us. The narratives of Mailer (*The Armies of the Night*, 1968) and Capote (*In Cold Blood*, 1965) give us a glimpse into the world of war and murder. Narratives "get at"—and I use that phrase consciously—what can neither be said in number nor disclosed in literal text.

I believe that schools and classrooms, families and communities, and the practice of teaching and administration need to be understood every bit as much in the terms that narrative make possible as in terms defined through correlation coefficients, F ratios, or t-tests. This assertion of mine is not to be interpreted as a rejection of statistical approaches to research. What it does reject is the view that such approaches are the only legitimate ones.

The point here is that humans have used storied forms to inform since humans have been able to communicate. In a sense, ethnography is a refinement of those stories and fine art is the quintessential achievement of creating congruence between form and content in the telling.

A third promise of the new frontier has to do with the opportunities that it provides to those engaged in the research enterprise to play to their strengths. By this I mean that methods and aptitudes interact. Not every research form is good for every player. The availability of qualitative research methods in the fullness of their possibilities offers researchers opportunities to select a way of working that fits their interests, is congruent with what they wish to study, plays to their strengths, exploits their aptitudes, and gives them a chance to find a place in the sun.

Some researchers will, of course, be happily content with calculation and statistical analysis. All the more power to them. Again, the game here concerns not the construction of our own new hegemony but the expansion of the resources considered legitimate for studying the educational world. By having available modes of inquiry that exploit the representational capacities of language and image, the possibilities for graduate students and for professors alike to find their bliss in the pantheon of research methods are increased. I am all for that. And I know that you are as well.

A fourth promise of the new frontier pertains to something not indigenous or unique to it, but which, nevertheless, has come along with it. What I am referring to is the notion of collaboration. The feminists were among the first to call our attention to status differential between researchers and teachers in the conduct of research and the cost of such differential in really finding out about the situations we wish to understand. As a result, we have been urged from many quarters to regard teachers and school administrators not as subjects (a very telling term indeed) but as partners in a common enterprise, an enterprise that recognizes the distinctive contributions that different individuals working in different sectors of the educational enterprise are capable of making. Insider knowledge, or in anthropological terms, emic knowledge, is more likely to be shared when collaboration takes place. Such collaboration, at its best, initiates with the conceptualization process and not only at the data-gathering process.

Authentic collaboration, from my perspective, will require much more than good will between researchers and teachers. It will require a redefinition of the teacher's role so that teachers have significant opportunities—especially time—to engage in collaboration. If the school is to be a center of inquiry for students, it will need to be a center for inquiry for the professional staff as well.

If the potential virtues that I have described are within the realm of possibility, what we must ask, are the perils? What do we need to look out for? Let me turn to these questions now.

Before I get to the substance of my concerns, I want to tell you first that the list of issues that I will identify is longer than the list I have just completed. Some of these concerns you may regard as ill placed or badly conceived. Nevertheless, they are my concerns and I share them with you tonight.

My aim this evening is to avoid being Pollyannish while at the same time to avoid being discouraging. My aim is to put on your plate issues that I worry about, that I have not been able to resolve, that I believe are important for the future of qualitative research. My hope is that these concerns will give you something to chew on—and to get rid of if necessary. In short, my intentions are entirely constructive.

Let me identify some practical perils that I myself have faced. The most obvious is the difficulty publishing nontext material. My own presidential address at AERA a few years ago included the playing of a videotape that was essential to the point that I was making about the cognitive functions of nonlinguistic forms. When the piece was published in the *Educational Researcher* (Eisner, 1993), as you might expect, the very form central to my case could not be included. Similar difficulties have occurred in the uses I have made of sections from films such as *Dead Poets Society* and *School Colors* and from music selections such as Beethoven's hallelujah chorus from *Christ on the Mount of Olives*. Journals have no mechanism for sharing such material. Perhaps in the future, CD-ROMs will be available to remedy this problem, but at the present it is still a problem.

Another practical concern relates to the fact that little or no tradition in the use of nonconventional forms of research exists in most universities and, as a result, there is often little faculty expertise that students can draw upon. This is not an unusual condition. Innovation, by definition, is new; and when something is new, experience is limited. Those who want to use film as a major vehicle in doing educational research not only need access to a camera; they also need an understanding of how films are made, and unless the school or department is sympathetic to such an approach and has the resources available, the prospects for such work are dim. The absence of guidance leaves students on their own without the skills needed to use the medium well. The result can be a visual disaster, even though the intention is a noble one and the display of courage beyond question. The price paid for innovation is having to pick up what you can here and there and knit it together as best you can. It is certainly a problem worth addressing, especially in a university. I mention it here because it impacts the quality of research that individuals will be able to do.

Related to the relationship between innovation and experience is the discomfort people feel from not knowing how to appraise work that does not fit conventional paradigms. How should a novel, prepared as a piece of educational research, be appraised? Who should do the appraisal? What criteria are appropriate? How should one appraise a multimedia dissertation? Are criteria pertaining to validity and reliability, generalizability and stability, appropriate? If not, what criteria are?

We can learn something about these matters from the arts. You will recall that Van Gogh sold one work in his lifetime, and Stravinsky was booed off the stage when the *Rite of Spring* was first performed in 1913. New forms may require new criteria, and new criteria evolve through the efforts of those who can help interpret the meaning of the work. Critics in the arts do this as a normal part of their work when in those rare moments such innovative work emerges.

In addition to the foregoing more or less practical problems, there are some significant theoretical problems. Consider, for example, the fact that there are qualitative researchers who are quite reluctant to provide an analytic or theoretical interpretation of the situations they have described in their work. The argument is that works of art stand alone; after all, the author of a play does not provide a theoretical explication of the meaning of the play to the audience who beholds it. The play is manifested in language, action, and stage set. Plays are supposed to carry their own ineffable meanings, and the audience gets them or does not.

The criteria applicable to plays are analogized to educational research. I have problems with the analogy. Our work must go well beyond what a good journalist—or even a good writer—is able to do. After all, we are expected to bring to the educational situation a theoretical and analytical background in the field of education. That background must count for something in the way in which phenomena are characterized, analyzed, and assessed. It is the use of that background and the tools secured in acquiring it that provides the distinctively educational added value to our work.

In short, I am saying that I believe that except for very exceptional cases, it is unlikely that uninterpreted qualitative material will satisfy our colleagues or be optimally useful to those who work in the schools. Our challenge is learning how to make such interpretations without sacrificing the quality and character of the writing that we have done. One good model, to my way of thinking, is found in Jackson's (1993) essay describing his former algebra teacher, Mrs. Teresa Henze. In his essay, Jackson creates a remarkable rapprochement between the vividly descriptive and the philosophically analytic. The two are successfully united. I believe that we need more of that kind of work and, indeed, kinds that are yet to be envisioned. Again, good description, even very good description, is not likely to be enough.

Another concern that I have relates to the use of ambiguity in narrative and other forms of qualitative research. In literary circles, ambiguity has a positive, constructive contribution to make to the overall character of the story. At the same time, ambiguity creates uncertainty regarding the phenomena to which the story refers, hence making it difficult for readers to know with reasonable precision the point being conveyed. I feel a tension in these two pulls: the pull toward precision and the pull toward the productive consequences of ambiguity. I have no way at this moment to resolve the tension. I only want to acknowledge the dilemma that I feel in wanting to afford readers opportunities to imaginatively participate in the educational situations described without, at the same time, creating work that functions essentially as a Rorschach inkblot test.

Still another concern relates to what might be called "indefensible relativism." By indefensible, I refer to the attitude that is taken by some researchers that since interpretations are always personal, any interpretation is as defensible as any other. The logical implication of this view is that there is no basis whatsoever for making judgments about either the quality of the work or its meaning. Even if "truth" is given up as a regulative ideal in qualitative research or in a constructivist conception of knowledge, one need not be saddled by a view that provides no basis for assessing the quality of the work. Rorty (1979), for example, gives up truth but pursues what he calls "edification." Put another way, what good work should do in philosophy and elsewhere is to enrich and enliven the conversation. There should be a sense that it is moving forward, that we seem to be getting somewhere. Novelty for its own sake and relativism in assessment leaves us, I am afraid, rudderless. How should work in the new frontier be assessed? What criteria seem appropriate? How can we separate the wheat from the chaff? If a correspondence theory of truth will no longer do, what criteria will? These are some of the concerns I have about the basis for judgments about the quality of qualitative research.

What exacerbates this condition is the fact that in qualitative research—and it must also be said about most quantitative studies—the raw data upon which, say, a narrative was created are unavailable to a reader. For all practical purposes, there are no archives that house such material and even when there are, the material is at least once removed from the researcher's experience and is in fact only a pale representation of the situations or individuals it purports to describe. Thus, in qualitative studies we are at the mercy of the writer or filmmaker, at least to a large extent.

I am certainly aware of matters of triangulation, structural corroboration, referential adequacy, and other moves designed to check unwarranted conclusions or generalizations. Nevertheless, the bottom line is that the spin that is given to the description of a situation is the researcher's, and precisely how much spin is given is extremely difficult to know. These issues are ones I believe we need to think about.

Related to the issue of spin and personal interpretation is the matter of persuasiveness. All research efforts, whether in the qualitative or in the quantitative domain, seek to persuade. The question that must be addressed is the basis for the persuasiveness. Both advertising and propaganda are also aimed at persuading people to believe this or that. How shall we think about persuasiveness? What constitutes legitimate persuasiveness in qualitative research?

One answer to this question is one that Barone and I (1997) gave in our chapter on arts-based research in AERA's forthcoming *Handbook on Complementary Methods for Educational Research*. That answer was that what arts-based educational research seeks is not so much conclusions that readers come to believe but the number and quality of the questions that the work raises. Frankly, this answer—and it is our answer—is only half satisfying. Is there a way to ground persuasiveness in some kind of evidence or analysis without resorting to the same reductive procedures that motivated the move away from them? Put another way, can we have our evidentiary base and still maintain the sometime imaginative and poetic quality of well-crafted qualitative research? The questions that I have raised are by no means easy to answer, and I do not want to appear from this podium as if I had answers to them. These are issues that I worry about. They are issues that those of us working in the qualitative domain cannot afford to ignore. If we ignore them, they will be called to our attention by those who do not share our methodological proclivities.

Let me move now to another issue that is related to the troubles with relativism that I alluded to earlier. It has to do with the concept of "expertise." As you well know, we live at a time in which the notion of expertise, especially in a context that values collaboration, is regarded with suspicion. Expertise like connoisseurship seems to many to smack of elitism and to privilege the few. In an age in which so-called democratic tendencies pervade all levels of the research enterprise, the idea that someone has special competence to notice and interpret is often regarded as authoritarian. I must confess that I am not ready to give up either the concept of expertise or of authority. There is a distinction made in the sociological literature between ascribed authority and achieved authority. The former results from being assigned to a position in a hierarchy. The latter is secured through competence. Relativistic views of merit marginalize expertise because judgments about educational states of affairs are reduced to preferences or "mere" opinions.

I believe that in qualitative research, as in many other fields, expertise in knowing the subject matter that is being addressed—whether it is the Italians of Boston (Whyte, 1943), the fundamentalists of the American Midwest (Peshkin, 1986), or the young children who populated a Boston classroom (Kozol, 1968)—matters. Qualitative research designed to illuminate, for example, the quality of art or music teaching needs researchers who know something not only about art and music but about their teaching. I find that quite often matters of content quality are neglected in descriptions of classrooms. It is almost as if the content being taught and the pedagogical practices related to it do not matter. Expertise does matter, and doctoral programs preparing qualitative researchers would do well to provide opportunities for researchers to achieve the expertise they need to say something useful about the teaching of various subjects in the school.

I turn now to questions of generalization. One of the recurrent questions raised about the study of cases pertains to the generalizability of the findings. In doing case studies, are we, as Geertz (1983) would have it, simply hearing from another community or subculture, or is there something to be learned from the study of the case that generalizes to other situations?

As you well know, the canonical procedure for generalization in statistically driven studies requires the random selection of a sample from a population as a condition for determining levels of probability regarding the relationship between the findings in the sample and the population from which it was randomly selected. The logic of the enterprise is impeccable. Because in qualitative research we typically do not randomly select populations—for the most part they are convenience samples—how shall we think about generalization?

It seems to me that what qualitative research yields is a set of observations or images that facilitate the search and discovery process when examining other situations, including other classrooms and schools. This is what Powell, Cohen, and Farrar (1985) give us when, in *The Shopping Mall High School*, they tell us about the treaties that are formed between high school students and their teachers that are not limited to the particular high school they studied. They provide us with a frame for not only looking at classrooms and schools but for speculating on why such agreements would be made in the first place. Given the compromises high school teachers must make to cope with the magnitude of the demands that confront them each day, such agreements between students and teachers are understandable.

The conception of "treaty" that Powell et al. (1985) advanced serves as a schema for locating similar treaties in other schools and for deepening our understanding of the kinds of interpersonal collusion that makes life bearable for both students and teachers.

Is this heuristic use of ideas and images developed from qualitative research so different from the generalizing practices of quantitative research? I think not. Although the logic of statistical generalization seems unassailable with respect to the populations from which findings on samples were drawn that logic does not necessarily apply to other populations. First, the features of a population a researcher would need to know to determine whether the findings derived from another population are likely to apply to it are simply unavailable. Seldom are the boundary conditions for a finding or a theory specified. What we do, and wisely so, is to use findings derived from quantitative studies analogically or heuristically. In fact, we do not really know whether, for example, findings derived from a study in 1994 are applicable to a supposedly comparable population in 1997. The passage of time may matter. Furthermore, the population to which we are generalizing may or may not possess the features of the population originally studied. In short, quantitative researchers using statistical methods wind up using their findings in ways that are not unlike the ways in which qualitative researchers use theirs. Humans are not only tool-using animals, they are not only symbol-using animals; they are generalizing animals. We all generalize from N's of one and make adjustments that seem appropriate in the process. To do this we think analogically and metaphorically, and settle for plausibility.

I bring my remarks to a close by talking a bit about what the promise and perils of the new frontier mean for the future of educational research.

From my perspective, I see little likelihood that the advances that have been made, particularly in qualitative research, will be rescinded and that the world of research methodology will return to the traditional habits it displayed in the 1950s and 1960s. The practices that have emerged in the conduct of educational research are a part of a larger, more general movement, one that embraces pluralism in method and diversity in conceptions of knowledge. At the same time, I do not see the epistemological orientations that characterize our own views about inquiry widely embraced by the American public. The public continues to be goaded into a horse race view of academic performance, and for horse races, digits are much more effective than narratives. Put another way, when push comes to shove, the measurement of academic performance through testing will continue to be the way to go.

The reasons measured outcomes of schooling are attractive relate, I believe, to the fact that a meritocratic-social orientation of the kind that we have in America depends on comparison, and comparison is made very difficult when the idiosyncratic characteristics of individual performance are made salient. We prefer for purposes of comparison all students running down the same track, measured by the same tests, and whose performance is reported out to the third or fourth decimal place. I do not see qualitative forms of assessment changing that practice in our schools. Besides, quantitative methods are less labor intensive and less ambiguous. Numbers provide a false security—but a security nevertheless.

What I also see is a much greater acceptance in the research community of qualitative research than we have known before. Hardly a week goes by that I do not receive an announcement of four or five new books on qualitative research methods that have recently been published. The interest is widespread, to the point that some of our more traditionally oriented colleagues are concerned.

And with respect to our more traditionally oriented colleagues, I sense that for a significant portion, the selection of a method or orientation to the conduct of research is more than a methodological choice, it is a reflection of a personality disposition. Someone once said that the world can be divided into people who like San Francisco and those who like Los Angeles. The world might also be divided between those who prefer qualitative research and those who prefer quantitative approaches. Frankly, my hope is that the field will develop hybrid forms of research that use different approaches within the same study. As I said earlier, I have no interest in creating a new hegemony. I welcome pluralism within the field at large and, indeed, within studies themselves.

I began my remarks this evening congratulating you for the genuinely important leadership you have provided to the field. I meant what I said. I have tried this evening to identify both the promising features of the new frontier and those that seem to me to pose problems we must address. I am confident that they will be addressed. They are not only important; they are interesting. Your work has made it far easier for younger colleagues to do qualitative research in the field of education than it was for some of you when you were getting started. Cutting new ground is never easy. It takes courage and it's risky. But durability is one sign of vitality, so what better way to certify the durability of our work than to come together this evening to celebrate our 10th anniversary.

References

Albee, E. (1962). *Who's afraid of Virginia Woolf?* New York: Atheneum.

Barone, T., & Eisner, E. (1997). *Handbook on complementary methods for educational research* (Richard Yeager, Ed.). Washington, DC: AERA.

Becker, H. (1990). Performance science. *Social Problems, 37*(1), 117-132.

Bruner, J. (1985). Narrative and paradigmatic modes of thought. In E. Eisner (Ed.), *Learning and teaching the ways of knowing: Eighty-fourth yearbook of the National Society for the Study of Education, Part II.* Chicago: University of Chicago Press.

Capote, T. (1965). *In cold blood.* New York: Random House.

Eisner, E. (1993). Forms of understanding and the future of educational research. *Educational Researcher, 22*(7), 5-11.

Eisner, E. (1996). Should a novel count as a dissertation in education? *Research in the Teaching of English, 30*(4), 403-427.

Geertz, C. (1983). *Local knowledge: Further essays in interpretive anthropology.* New York: Basic Books.

Jackson, P. (1990). *Life in classrooms.* New York: Teachers College Press.

Jackson, P. (1993). *Untaught lessons.* New York: Teachers College Press.

Jonich, G. (1968). *The same positivist.* Middletown, CT: Wesleyan University Press.

Kozol, J. (1968). *Death at an early age.* New York: Bantam Books.

McKeon, R. (1941). *The basic works of Aristotle.* New York: Random House.

Mailer, N. (1968). *The armies of the night.* New York: New American Library.

Peshkin, A. (1986). *God's choice.* Chicago: University of Chicago Press.

Powell, A., Cohen, D., & Farrar, E. (1985). *Shopping mall high school.* Boston: Houghton Mifflin.

Rorty, R. (1979). *Philosophy and the mirror of nature.* Princeton, NJ: Princeton University Press.

Schepper-Hughes, N. (1992). *Death without weeping.* Berkeley: University of California Press.

Schwab, J. (1969). The practical: A language for curriculum. *School Review, 72.*

Smith, L. (1968). *The complexities of an urban classroom.* New York: Holt, Rinehart and Winston.

Sternberg, R. (1988). *The triangle of love.* New York: Basic Books.

Toulmin, S. R. (1990). *Cosmopolis.* New York: Free Press.

Watson, J. (1925). *Behaviorism.* New York: W. W. Norton.

Whyte, W. (1943). *Street corner society.* Chicago: University of Chicago Press.

SOURCE: From E. Eisner (1997), "The New Frontier in Qualitative Research Methodology," *Qualitative Inquiry, 3,* 259-273.

4.13 FURTHER RESOURCES FOR QUALITATIVE RESEARCHERS

4.13.1 Further Readings

Anzul, Margaret, Evans, Judith F., King, Rita, & Tellier-Robinson, Dora. (2001). Moving beyond a deficit perspective with qualitative research methods. *Exceptional Children, 67,* 235-249.

Berg, Bruce Lawrence. (2000). *Qualitative research methods for the social sciences.* Needham Heights, MA: Allyn and Bacon.

Bernard, H. Russell. (2000). *Social research methods: Qualitative and quantitative approaches.* Thousand Oaks, CA: Sage.

Campbell, Kim Sydow. (1999). Collecting information: Qualitative research methods for solving workplace problems. *Technical Communication: Journal of the Society for Technical Communication, 46,* 532-545.

Creswell, John W. (1994). *Research design: Qualitative and quantitative approaches.* Thousand Oaks, CA: Sage.

Dana, Nancy-Fichtman, & Dana, Thomas M. (1994, April). *Holistic perspectives on the teaching of qualitative research methods.* Paper presented at the annual meeting of the American Educational Research Association, New Orleans, LA.

Denzin, Norman K., & Lincoln, Yvonna S. (1995). Transforming qualitative research methods. *Journal of Contemporary Ethnography, 24,* 349-358.

Frey, Lawrence R., Anderson, Shawny, & Friedman, Paul G. (1998). The status of instruction in qualitative communication research methods. *Communication Education, 47,* 246-260.

Krane, Vikki, Andersen, Mark B., & Strean, William B. (1997). Issues of qualitative research methods and presentation. *Journal of Sport and Exercise Psychology, 19,* 213-218.

Lavender, Tony, & Lake, Nick. (2000). Qualitative research methods in psychiatric rehabilitation. *Psychiatric Rehabilitation Skills, 4,* 321-339.

Lindlof, Thomas R. (1994). *Qualitative communications research methods.* Thousand Oaks, CA: Sage.

MacKay, Kathleen A., & Schuh, John H. (1991). Practical issues associated with qualitative research methods. *Journal of College Student Development, 32,* 424-432.

McLean, Les, Myers, Margaret, Smillie, Carol, & Vaillancourt, Dale. (1997). Qualitative research methods: An essay review [Electronic version]. *Education Policy Analysis Archives, 5*(13). Retrieved August 28, 2001, from http://epaa.asu.edu/epaa/v5n13/

Miller, Steven I., & Fredricks, Marcel. (1996). *Qualitative research methods: Social epistemology and practical inquiry.* New York: Peter Lang.

Morse, Janice M. (Ed.). (1993). *Critical issues in qualitative research methods.* Newbury Park, CA: Sage.

Page, Reba N. (1997). A thought about curriculum in qualitative research methods. *International Journal of Qualitative Studies in Education, 10*, 171-173.

Patton, Michael Quinn. (2002). *Qualitative research and evaluation methods* (3rd ed.). Thousand Oaks, CA: Sage.

Robinson, Rhonda S., & Driscoll, Marcy P. (1993, January). *Qualitative research methods workshops: An introduction, definitions. Readings on qualitative research: An annotated bibliography.* Paper presented at the Association for Educational Communications and Technology Sponsored by the Research and Theory Division, New Orleans, LA.

Smithmier, Angela. (1996, June). *The "double bind" of re-presentation in qualitative research methods.* Paper presented at the Qualitative Research in Education Conference, St. Paul, MN.

Smith-Sebasto, N. J. (2000). Potential guidelines for conducting and reporting environmental education research: Qualitative methods of inquiry. *Environmental Education Research, 6*, 9-26.

Steen, Mangen. (1999). Qualitative research methods in cross-national settings. *International Journal of Social Research Methodology, 2*, 109-124.

Strauss, Anselm L., & Corbin, Juliet M. (1998). *Basics of qualitative research: Techniques and procedures for developing grounded theory* (2nd ed.). Thousand Oaks, CA: Sage.

Taylor, Steven J., & Bogdan, Robert. (1998). *Introduction to qualitative research methods: A guidebook and resource.* New York: John Wiley and Sons.

Westbrook, Lynn. (1994). Qualitative research methods: A review of major stages, data analysis techniques, and quality controls. *Library and Information Science Research, 16*, 241-254.

Whitt, Elizabeth J. (1991). Artful science: A primer on qualitative research methods. *Journal of College Student Development, 32*, 406-415.

4.13.2 Societies and Associations

Association for Qualitative Research at www.aqrp.co.uk/

ES R C Qualitative Data Archival Resource Centre at www.essex.ac.uk/qualidata/

International Institute for Qualitative Methodology at www.ualberta.ca/~iiqm/

Qualitative Research Consultants Association at www.qrca.org/

Qualitative Research Interest Group (QRIG) at www.upa.pdx.edu/QRIG/

Society for the Study of Symbolic Interaction (http://sun.soci.niu.edu/~sssi/) is a social science professional organization of scholars interested in qualitative, especially interactionist, research.

4.13.3 Qualitative Research E-mail Discussion Groups

Discussion groups or bulletin boards and listservs are becoming an increasingly useful way to share information among academics and others. Professor Judith Preissle from the University of Georgia (jude@arches.uga.edu) has assembled a very useful list of these discussion groups along with directions how to join them. The list, reprinted with her permission, is shown below. See Part 6 of this volume for more information about discussion groups and listservs.

QUALRS-L@listserv.uga.edu: Qualitative Research for the Human Sciences. To subscribe, send this message to listserv@listserv.uga.edu: subscribe QUALRS-L yourname. For help, contact Judith Preissle, jude@arches.uga.edu, or check http://listserv.uga.edu/archives/qualrs-l.html

QUALNET@listserv.bc.edu: Qualitative Research in Management and Organization Studies. To subscribe, send this message to majordomo@listserv.bc.edu: subscribe qualnet. For help, contact Ted Gaiser, Gaiser@bcvms.bc.edu

ATLAS-TI@atlasti.de: Topics on the text analysis, text management, and theory building program ATLAS/ti. To subscribe, send a one-line message to listserv@atlasti.DE: SUB ATLAS-TI yourfirstname yourlastname your institution. For help, contact Thomas Muhr, muhr@atlasti.de

QUAL-SOFTWARE@jiscmail.ac.uk: a list on qualitative analysis computer programs. To subscribe, send this message to jiscmail@jiscmail.ac.uk: join qual-software yourname. For help, contact qual-software-request@jiscmail.ac.uk

QSR-Forum@qsr.com.au (Qualitative Solutions and Research), for the qualitative analysis programs NUD*IST and NVIVO. To subscribe, send a message to mailing-list-request@qsr.com.au with the words SUBSCRIBE QSR-FORUM in the main body of the text. For help, contact list-master@qsr.com.au

QUAL-L@scu.edu.au: Qualitative Research List, initiated to serve folks at Penn State, but immediately attracted a broader audience. To subscribe, send this message to listproc@scu.edu.au: subscribe QUAL-L firstname lastname. For help, contact Bob Dick, bdick@scu.edu.au

SOURCE: Judith Preissle, University of Georgia, unpublished document. Adapted with permission.

4.13.4 Other Online Resources for Qualitative Research in the Human Sciences

METHODS@cios.org: a list for social science research methods instructors. To subscribe, send this message to comserve@cios.org: join methods yourname. For help, contact support@cios.org

PSYCH-NARRATIVE@massey.ac.nz: a discussion of narrative in everyday life. To subscribe, send this message to majordomo@massey.ac.nz: subscribe psych-narrative. For help, contact Andy Lock, A.J.Lock@massey.ac.nz

Ethno@cios.org: Ethnomethodology/conversation analysis. To subscribe, send this message to comserve@cios.org: join ethno yourname. For help, contact support@cios.org

IVSA@pdomain.uwindsor.ca: International Visual Sociology Association. To subscribe, send this message to listserv@pdomain.uwindsor.ca: subscribe ivsa yourname. For help, contact Dr. Veronika Mogyorody, mogy@uwindsor.ca

VISCOM@listserv.temple.edu: Visual Communications Discussion List. To subscribe, send this message to listserv@listserv.temple.edu: subscribe viscom yourname. For help, contact Jay Ruby, v5293e@vm.temple.edu

EVALTALK@bama.ua.edu: American Evaluation Association Discussion List. To subscribe, send this message to listserv@bama.ua.edu: subscribe evaltalk yourname. For help, contact owner-evaltalk@bama.ua.edu

ARLIST-L@scu.edu.au: Action Research Mailing List. To subscribe, send this message to listproc@scu.edu.au: subscribe ARLIST-L Lastname. For help, contact Bob Dick, bdick@scu.edu.au

XTAR@listproc.appstate.edu: Teacher Researchers list. To subscribe, send this message to listproc@listserv.appstate.edu: subscribe xtar yourname. For help, contact blantonwe@conrad.appstate.edu, jmm@am.appstate.edu, or combstm@conrad.appstate.edu

GOVTEVAL@nasionet.net: Public Sector Program Evaluation. To subscribe, send this message to majordomo@nasionet.net: subscribe govteval [your email address]. For help, contact Dr. Arunaselam Rasappan, artd@ppp.nasionet.net

H-ORALHIST@h-net.msu.edu: H-Net/Oral History Association Discussion List on Oral History. To subscribe, send this message to listserv@h-net.msu.edu: subscribe H-ORALHIST firstname lastname affiliation. For help, contact Jeff Charnley, Charnle2@pilot.msu.edu

BIOG-METHODS@mailbase.ac.uk: Biographical Methods for the Social Sciences. To subscribe, send this message to mailbase@mailbase.ac.uk: join BIOG-METHODS lastname. For help, contact biog-methods-request@mailbase.ac.uk

AELACTION@ael.org: Appalachia Educational discussion list on action research in classrooms. To subscribe, send this message to majordomo@aelliot.ael.org: subscribe aelaction your e-mail address. For help, contact owner-aelaction@aelliot.ael.org

Q-METHOD@listserv.kent.edu: Q Methodology discussion list on this broad approach to the study of subjectivity. To subscribe, send this message to listserv@listserv.kent.edu: subscribe Q-METHOD yourname. For help, contact Q-Method-request@listserv.kent.edu

ARMNET-L@scu.edu.au: Action research methodology network. To subscribe, send this message to listproc@scu.edu.au: subscribe ARMNET-L firstname lastname. For help, contact Bob Dick, bdick@scu.edu.au

Ethnography-in-education@mailbase.ac.uk: use of ethnographic research methods in education. To subscribe, send this message to mailbase@mailbase.ac.uk: join ethnography-in-education firstname lastname. For help, contact ethnography-in-education-request@mailbase.ac.uk

OnlineRsch@onelist.com: discussion of ethics and methodology in online research, including sociology, anthropology, and other related disciplines. To subscribe, send a message to OnlineRsch-subscribe@onelist.com; nothing necessary in the body of the message. For help, contact OnlineRsch-owner@onelist.com

PART 5

GUIDES TO METHODS
AND TECHNIQUES OF
COLLECTING DATA IN LIBRARY, FIELD,
AND LABORATORY SETTINGS:
SOCIAL SCIENCE DATA LIBRARIES
AND RESEARCH CENTERS

The collection of data is a crucial step in the execution of a good research design because the quality of the research often rests upon the quality of the data. In this part of the *Handbook of Research Design and Social Measurement*, the methods and techniques of social research are presented according to their common situses of research: library, field, and laboratory. Advantages and disadvantages of principal methods are pointed out, and guides to the construction of questionnaires, interviews, and scales are provided.

Section 5.21 provides a listing of social science data archives. These social science archives are available to research scholars and offer many excellent opportunities for research. With the advent of the Internet and easy remote access to most sites, much of the documentation that used to be available only to those located within close proximity to libraries is now available to almost anyone. The collecting of data is expensive, and the ability to use data that already have been collected offers the possibility of superior research at a greatly lowered cost. The guide to the U.S. Census and Bureau of Labor Statistics is especially thorough, revealing the rich mine of data available to social researchers and making it more usable.

Finally, directories of social science research centers in the United States, in England, and throughout the world are presented in section 5.22. A list of important research associations and institutes affiliated with the International Sociological Association may also provide valuable contact points for determining the status of current research and discovering comparative research advances in various fields.

The collection of data occurs in a designed inquiry only after a long series of steps, including the following:

1. definition of the problem,
2. construction of the theoretical framework,
3. stating of hypotheses,
4. establishment of the design of inquiry, and
5. determination of sampling procedures.

This section introduces the most common methods of social science research and presents a brief set of instructions for the construction of questionnaires, interviews, and scales. These instructions will assist the researcher in evaluating the appropriate method for his or her particular problem; he or she should consult methods books listed in the various bibliographies in this section for a thorough explanation of each method or technique.

Before we begin our listing and discussion of techniques and resources, it is important to turn to methods, which are the handmaidens of designed inquiry. It is important to distinguish carefully among four terms: *methodology*, *site*, *method*, and *technique*.

Methodology (regarding the collection of data) is a body of knowledge that describes and analyzes methods, indicating their limitations and resources, clarifying their presuppositions and consequences, and relating their potentialities to research advances. In this part of the *Handbook*, the methods of social science are first examined to set forth the advantages and disadvantages of each. The aim is to help researchers understand the process of gathering data and what their choices of methods entail.

Site refers to the place in which the data are gathered. For most sciences, the most used sites are the library, the field, and the laboratory.

Method refers to the specific means of gathering data that are common to all sciences or to a significant part of them. Methods include such procedures as the making of observations and measurements, performing experiments, building models and theories, providing explanations, and making predictions. The social sciences often use documentary analysis, the questionnaire, and the personal interview.

Technique refers to specific procedures that are used in a given method. For example, the field method worker may employ such techniques as use of sociometric scales to measure social variables and personality inventories to identify personal traits. The research worker, such as a demographer, may draw heavily on statistical documents and use various statistical techniques to describe relationships or gain statistical control over the data.

Regarding the relationship between methods and the content of one's efforts, wise counsel is offered by Muzafer Sherif (1967):

> No procedure and no technique for data collection are powerful or effective in their own right. The theory should be the *guide* for fruitful research. The techniques are powerful tools for data collection, if—and only if—they are appropriate in terms of the nature and characteristics of the *problems*. And *significant problems* can be formulated only after gaining substantial familiarity with the universe of discourse and not before. (pp. 55-56)

Table 5.1 presents an outline of methods and techniques as employed in the three sites: library, field, and laboratory. Aids are presented for the most common methods and techniques. Later in this part is a list of reference books that describe various methods and techniques in detail.

Table 5.1 **OUTLINE OF COMMON RESEARCH METHODS AND TECHNIQUES IN THREE SITES**

Site	Methods	Techniques
Library	1. Analysis of historical records: primary records—letters, diaries, etc.; secondary interpretations of events	• Recording of notes • Content analysis • Tape and film review and analysis
	2. Analysis of documents: statistical and nonstatistical records of formal agencies	• Statistical compilations and manipulations • Reference and abstract guides • Microfilm, microfiche searches
	3. Literature search for theory and previous research in books, journals, and monographs	• Computer information probes
Field	1. Mail questionnaire	• Identification of social and economic background of respondents • Use of sociometric scales to ascertain such variables as social status, group structure, community and social participation, leadership activity, and family adjustment • Use of attitude scales to measure morale
	2. Personal interview and structured interview schedule	• Interviewer uses a detailed schedule with open and closed questions • Sociometric scales may be used
	3. Focused interview	• Interviewer focuses attention on a given experience and its effects; knows in advance what topics or questions he or she wishes to cover
	4. Free story interview	• Respondent is urged to talk freely about the subjects treated in the study
	5. Group interview	• Small groups of respondents are interviewed simultaneously; any of the above techniques may be used
	6. Telephone survey	• Used as a survey technique for information and for discerning opinion • May be used for follow-up of a questionnaire mailing to increase the return rate
	7. Case study and life history	• For case study, cross-sectional collection of data for intensive analysis of a person, emphasizing personal and social factors in socialization • For life history, longitudinal collection of data of intensive character, also emphasizing socialization over an extended period of time
	8. Nonparticipant direct observation	• Use of standard score cards and observational behavior scales
	9. Participant observation	• Interactional recording; possible use of tape recorders and photographic techniques
	10. Mass observation	• Recording mass or collective behavior by observation and interview using independent observers in public places
Laboratory	Small group study of random behavior, play, problem solving, or stress behavior of individuals and/or groups; organizational and role analysis	• Use of contrived and nonconstructed situations, confederates, audiovisual recording devices, and observers behind one-way mirror

Table 5.2 CHOOSING AMONG RESEARCH TECHNIQUES		
Problem	*Approach*	*Research Technique*
To obtain reliable information under controlled conditions	Test people in a laboratory	Laboratory experiment, simulation
To find out how people behave in public	Watch them	Natural observation
To find out how people behave in private	Ask them to keep diaries	Personal documents
To learn what people think	Ask them	Interview, questionnaire, attitude scale
To find out where people go	Chart their movements	Behavioral mapping, trace measures
To identify personality traits or assess mental abilities	Administer a standardized test	Psychological testing
To identify trends in verbal material	Systematic tabulation	Content analysis
To understand an unusual event	Detailed and lengthy investigation	Case study

SOURCE: Adapted from Robert Sommers and Barbara B. Sommers (1986), *A Practical Guide to Behavioral Research*, 2nd ed. (New York: Oxford University Press), p. 8.

Robert and Barbara B. Sommers (1986) have developed some helpful rules of thumb, presented in Table 5.2, for selecting among the methods. Note that these authors begin with a brief inventory of research inquiries and describe appropriate approaches and research techniques. They point out that

> observation is well suited for what people do in public. For private behavior, the personal diary is more appropriate. The experiment is an immensely powerful tool for deciding between alternative explanations of a phenomenon. It is less useful, however, for studying natural behavior or opinions. With opinions and attitudes the questionnaire and interview are very efficient. (p. 8)

Although these rules are very helpful, keep in mind that the method one uses to answer a question often depends heavily on the way that question is being asked and the content that provides the focus of the question.

References

Sherif, Muzafer. (1967). In Gordon J. DiRenzo (Ed.), *Concepts, theory, and explanation in the social sciences*. New York: Random House.

Sommers, Robert, & Sommers, Barbara B. (1986). *A practical guide to behavioral research* (2nd ed.). New York: Oxford University Press.

5.2 A REVIEW OF PRINT AND ONLINE SOCIAL SCIENCE RESEARCH RESOURCES

The research question that motivates further research can come from a variety of sources, but most often it comes from the history of the topic. When such is the case, a search of the scientific literature becomes paramount. Social scientists often minimize this step because sometimes they mistakenly believe that their problems are so novel that past literature will not apply. All too often, they simply do not give enough importance to the way in which their work will help build on past research to validate a hypothesis or theory and thus increase the accumulation of findings. They underestimate past work and sell short the future requirements of their science.

Physical and biological scientists dare not take such risks because they know that fellow scientists will quickly detect these faults in scientific work. Social scientists have to learn that they cannot do so with impunity.

The resources for conducting a literature search are great and marvelous. They fall into four categories: indexes to periodical literature, computer-assisted reference services, microfilm-microfiche-microprint media, and specialized sourcebooks.

The following indexes are of most value to social scientists. They are described in the order in which they are usually consulted: *Social Sciences Index*, *Social Sciences Citation Index (SSCI)*, *Current Index to Journals in Education*, and *Population Index*.

5.2.1 *Social Sciences Index*

Social Sciences Index is a cumulative index to English-language periodicals. The main body of the index consists of author and subject entries to periodicals in the fields of addiction studies, anthropology, area studies, community health and medical care, corrections, criminal justice, criminology, economics, environmental studies, ethics, family studies, gender studies, geography, gerontology, international relations, law, minority studies, planning and public administration, policy sciences, political science, psychiatry, psychology, public welfare, social work, sociology, and urban studies. In addition, there is an author listing of citations to book reviews following the main body of the index. The *Index* is published by H. W. Wilson and includes more than 607,000 abstracts, with more than 47,000 being added annually. It appears both in print and in an electronic version. The print version is available from H. W. Wilson (www.hwwilson.com) at 1-800-367-6770.

The online/CD version is available through Silver Platter at www.silverplatter.com/. This index, which is published quarterly with bound cumulation each year, has a fairly long history. It began in 1907 as the *International Index*; in 1955, its name was changed, and it continued as the *Social Science and Humanities Index*. The growing body of knowledge necessitated a division of the index into a separate *Social Sciences Index* and a *Humanities Index* in 1974. This division continues today. The periodicals listed below are those of interest to the sociologist.

Table 5.3 shows all 524 journals currently abstracted in *Social Sciences Index*, along with the URL or Web address, the address of the editorial office, and when the journal was first abstracted (and when last abstracted, if pertinent).

(text continues on p. 239)

Table 5.3 SELECTED JOURNALS INDEXED IN SOCIAL SCIENCES INDEX

Title	URL	Editorial Address
Acta Sociologica	www.tandf.co.uk/journals/tfs/00016993.html	Acta Sociologica, Haskoli Islands, Adalbygging, Sudurgotu, IS-101 Reykjavik, Iceland E-mail: acta@hi.is
Addictive Behaviors	www.elsevier.com/locate/addictbeh	The Boulevard, Langford Lane, East Park, Kidlington, Oxford, OXB 1GB, United Kingdom E-mail: nlinfo-f@elsevier.nl Fax: 44-1865-843010
Administration in Social Work	www.haworthpressinc.com	10 Alice St., Binghamton, NY 13904-1580 E-mail: getinfo@haworthpressinc.com Phone: 607-722-5857; Fax: 607-722-6362
Administrative Science Quarterly	www.johnson.cornell.edu/ASQ/asq.html	20 Thornwood Drive, Suite 100, Ithaca, NY 14850-1265 E-mail: asq_journal@cornell.edu Phone: 607-254-7143; Fax: 607-254-7100
Adolescence		3089C Clairemont D Ste 383, San Diego, CA 92117 Phone: 858-571-1414
Africa (London, England)	www.ed.ac.uk/journals/africa.html22	George Sq., Edinburgh, Midlothian, EH8 9LF, United Kingdom E-mail: journals@eup.ed.ac.uk Phone: 44-131-650-6207; Fax: 44-131-662-0053
Africa Report	www.ide.go.jp/English/index4.html	42 Ichigaya-Honmura-cho, Shinjuku-ku, Tokyo, 162-0845, Japan E-mail: info@ide.go.jp Phone: 81-3-3353-1640; Fax: 81-3-3226-8475
Africa Today	www.africa.co.uk	601 N Morton St., Bloomington, IN 47404 E-mail: journals@indiana.edu Phone: 800-842-6796; Fax: 812-855-8507
African Studies Review	www.sas.upenn.edu/African_Studies/Home_Page/ASA_Menu.html	Rutgers, The State University of New Jersey, 132 George St., New Brunswick, NJ 08901-1400 E-mail: ckoch@emory.edu Phone: 732-932-8173; Fax: 732-932-3394
Age and Ageing	http://ageing.oupjournals.org	Great Clarendon St., Oxford, OX2 6DP, United Kingdom E-mail: jnl.info@oup.co.uk Phone: 44-1865-267907; Fax: 44-1865-267835

(continued)

Table 5.3   Continued

Title	URL	Editorial Address
Ageing and Society	www.cup.cam.ac.uk	Edinburgh Bldg., Shaftesbury Rd., Cambridge, CB2 2RU, United Kingdom E-mail: information@cup.cam.ac.uk Fax: 44-1223-315052
AIDS & Public Policy Journal	www.upgbooks.com	17100 Cole Rd., Ste. 312, Hagerstown, MD 31740 E-mail: orders@upgbooks.com Phone: 800-654-8188; Fax: 301-582-2406
Alcohol Research & Health	www.niaaa.nih.gov	6000 Executive Blvd., Bethesda, MD 20892-7003 Phone: 301-443-3860; Fax: 301-480-1726
American Anthropologist	www.ameranthassn.org/ameranth.htm	4350 N. Fairfax Dr., Ste. 640, Arlington, VA 22203-1620 Phone: 703-528-1902
American Behavioral Scientist	www.sagepub.com	2455 Teller Rd., Thousand Oaks, CA 91320 E-mail: info@sagepub.com Phone: 805-499-0721; Fax: 805-499-0871
American City & County	www.intertec.com	9800 Metcalf Ave., Overland Park, KS 66212-2216 E-mail: subs@intertec.com Phone: 770-955-2500; Fax: 770-955-0400
American Demographics	www.demographics.com/publications/ad	11 River Bend Dr. S, Box 4949, Stamford, CT 06907-0949 E-mail: subs@demographics.com Phone: 203-358-9900; Fax: 203-358-5811
American Ethnologist	www.ameranthassn.org/aespubs.htm	4350 N. Fairfax Dr., Ste. 640, Arlington, VA 22203-1620 Phone: 703-528-1902
American Indian Culture and Research Journal	www.sscnet.ucla.edu/esp/aisc/index.html	3220 Campbell Hall, P.O. Box 951548, Los Angeles, CA 90095-1548 E-mail: aisc@ucla.edu Phone: 310-206-7508; Fax: 310-206-7060
American Journal of Community Psychology	www.wkap.nl	233 Spring St., New York, NY 10013-1578 Phone: 212-620-8000; Fax: 212-463-0742
American Journal of Drug and Alcohol Abuse	www.dekker.com	270 Madison Ave., New York, NY 10016 Phone: 212-696-9000; Fax: 212-685-4540

American Journal of Family Therapy	www.tandf.co.uk/journals/pp/01926187.html	11 New Fetter Ln., London, EC4P 4EE, United Kingdom E-mail: info@taylorandfrancis.com Phone: 215-625-8900; Fax: 215-625-2940
American Journal of International Law	www.asil.org	2223 Massachusetts Ave., NW, Washington, DC 20008-2864 Phone: 202-939-6000; Fax: 202-797-713
American Journal of Orthopsychiatry	www.amerortho.org/ajo.htm	330 Seventh Ave., 18th Fl., New York, NY 10001 E-mail: amerortho@aol.com Phone: 212-564-5930; Fax: 212-564-6180
American Journal of Physical Anthropology	www.wiley.com/0002-9483	605 Third Ave., New York, NY 10158 E-mail: subinfo@jwiley.com Phone: 212-850-6645; Fax: 212-850-6021
American Journal of Political Science	www.wise.edu/wisconsinpress	2537 Daniels St., Madison, WI 53718-6772 Phone: 608-224-3880; Fax: 608-224-3883
American Journal of Psychiatry	ajp.psychiatryonline.org	1400 K St., NW, Ste. 1101, Washington, DC 20005 E-mail: order@appi.org Phone: 202-682-6020; Fax: 202-789-2648
American Journal of Psychotherapy	www.ajp.org	Belfer Education Center, 1300 Morris Park Ave., Rm. 402, Bronx, NY 10461-1602 Phone: 718-430-3503; Fax: 718-430-8907
American Journal of Public Health	www.apha.org	1015 15th St., NW, Washington, DC 20005 Phone: 202-777-2462; Fax: 202-777-2532
American Journal of Sociology	www.journals.uchicago.edu/AJS	University of Chicago Press, Journals Division, P.O. Box 37005, Chicago, IL 60637 E-mail: j-orders@press.uchicago.edu Phone: 773-753-3347; Fax: 773-753-0811
American Political Science Review	www.ssc.msu.edu/~apsr	1527 New Hampshire Ave., NW, Washington, DC 20036-1206 E-mail: apsa@apsanet.org Phone: 202-483-2512; Fax: 202-483-2657
American Politics Quarterly	www.sagepub.com	2455 Teller Rd., Thousand Oaks, CA 91320 E-mail: info@sagepub.com Phone: 805-499-0721; Fax: 805-499-0871

(continued)

Table 5.3 Continued

Title	URL	Editorial Address
American Prospect	www.prospect.org	5 Broad St., Boston, MA 02109 E-mail: info@prospect.org Phone: 617-547-2950; Fax: 617-547-3896
American Psychologist	www.apa.org/journals/amp.html	750 First St., NE, Washington, DC 20002-4242 E-mail: subscriptions@apa.org Phone: 202-336-5600; Fax: 202-336-5568
American Sociological Review	www.asanet.org	1307 New York Ave., NW, Ste. 700, Washington, DC 20005-4701 E-mail: publications@asanet.org Phone: 202-383-4701; Fax: 202-638-0882
Amicus Journal	www.nrdc.org	40 W. 20th St., 11th Fl., New York, NY 10011 E-mail: amicus@nrdc.org Phone: 212-727-2700; Fax: 212-727-1773
Annals of the Association of American Geographers	www.aag.org	1710 Sixteenth Street NW, Washington, DC 20009-3198 E-mail: annals@aag.org Phone: 202-234-1450; Fax: 202-234-2744
Annual Review of Anthropology	www.AnnualReviews.org/allenpress.com	4139 El Camino Way, Box 10139, Palo Alto, CA 94303-0139 E-mail: service@annurev.org and orders@allenpress.com Phone: 650-493-4400; Fax: 650-424-0910
Annual Review of Psychology	www.biomedical.annualreviews.org	4139 El Camino Way, Box 10139, Palo Alto, CA 94303-0139 E-mail: service@annurev.org and orders@allenpress.com Phone: 650-493-4400; Fax: 650-424-0910
Annual Review of Sex Research	www.ssc.wisc.edu/ssss	P.O. Box 208, Mt. Vernon, IA 52314 E-mail: thesociety@worldnet.att.net Phone: 319-895-8407; Fax: 319-895-6203
Annual Review of Sociology	www.annualreviews.orgwww.allenpress.com	4139 El Camino Way, Box 10139, Palo Alto, CA 94303-0139 E-mail: service@annurev.org and orders@allenpress.com Phone: 650-493-4400; Fax: 650-424-0910
Anthropological Quarterly	www.cua.edu/www/cupr-bin/hfs.cgi/66/catholic/aqu.ch	620 Michigan Ave., NE, Washington, DC 20064 E-mail: cua-press@cua.edu Phone: 202-319-5052; Fax: 202-319-4985

Journal	Website	Contact
Anthropology & Education Quarterly	www.ameranthassn.org/caepubs.htm	4350 N. Fairfax Dr., Ste. 640, Arlington, VA 22203-1620 Phone: 703-528-1902
Archives of Sexual Behavior	www.wkap.nl	233 Spring St., New York, NY 10013-1578 Phone: 212-620-8000; Fax: 212-463-0742
Armed Forces and Society	www.transactionpub.com	Department 3092, Rutgers University, New Brunswick, NJ 08903 E-mail: trans@transactionpub.com Phone: 732-445-2280; Fax: 732-445-3138
Asian Survey	www.ucpress.edu/journals	2000 Center St., Ste. 303, Berkeley, CA 94704-1223 E-mail: journals@ucop.edu Phone: 510-643-7154
Australian Journal of Anthropology	www.allenpress.com	c/o Dept. of Anthropology, Univ. of Sydney, Sydney, NSW, 2006, Australia E-mail: orders@allenpress.com Phone: 61-2-93515489
Aztlan	www.sscnet.ucla.edu/esp	UCLA Chicano Studies Research Center, 2307 Murphy Hall, P.O. Box 951544, Los Angeles, CA 90095-1544 E-mail: aztlan@csrc.ucla.edu Phone: 310-825-2642; Fax: 310-206-1784
Behavior Therapy	www.aabt.org	305 Seventh Ave., Ste. 16A, New York, NY 1000
Behavioral Health Management		1629 Euclid Ave., Ste. 1200, Cleveland, OH 44114-3003 Phone: 216-522-9700; Fax: 216-522-9707
Behavioral Neuroscience	www.apa.org/journals/bne.html	750 First St., NE, Washington, DC 20002-4242 E-mail: subscriptions@apa.org Phone: 202-336-5600; Fax: 202-336-5568
Behaviour Research and Therapy	www.elsevier.nl	P.O. Box 800, Kidlington, Oxon, OX5 1DX, United Kingdom E-mail: nlinfo-f@elsevier.nl, usinfo-f@elsevier.com, and forinfo-kyf04035@niftyserve.or.jp Phone: 44-1865-843000; Fax: 44-1865-843010
Beijing Review	www.ihep.ac.cn	24 Baiwanzhuang Rd., Beijing, 100037, China Phone: 86-10-8315599; Fax: 86-10-8314318
Bioethics	www.blacksci.co.uk	108 Cowley Rd., Oxford, OX4 1JF, United Kingdom E-mail: jnlinfo@blackwellpublishers.co.uk Phone: 44-1865-791100; Fax: 44-1865-791347

(continued)

Table 5.3   Continued

Title	URL	Editorial Address
Black Scholar	www.theblackscholar.org	P.O. Box 2869, Oakland, CA 94609 Phone: 510-547-6633
Boston College Environmental Affairs Law Review	www.bc.edu/bc_org/avp/law/lwsch/envirrev.html	885 Centre St., Newton, MA 02159 Phone: 617-552-4354
British Journal of Criminology	http://www3.oup.co.uk/crimin	Great Clarendon St., Oxford, OX2 6DP, United Kingdom E-mail: jnl.info@oup.co.uk Phone: 44-1865-267907
British Journal of Political Science	www.cup.org/journals/CUPJNLS.html	Edinburgh Bldg., Shaftesbury Rd., Cambridge, CB2 2RU, United Kingdom E-mail: information@cup.cam.ac.uk Fax: 44-1223-315052
British Journal of Psychology	www.bps.org.uk/index.cfm.	St. Andrews House, 48 Princess Rd. E, Leicester, LE1 7DR, United Kingdom Phone: 44-166-254-9568; Fax: 44-166-247-0787
British Journal of Sociology	www.tandf.co.uk/journals	11 New Fetter Ln., London, EC4P 4EE, United Kingdom E-mail: routledge@carfax.co.uk Phone: 44-20-7583-9855; Fax: 44-20-7842-2298
Brookings Papers on Economic Activity	www.brook.edu/press/journals.htm	1775 Massachusetts Ave., NW, Washington, DC 20036-2188 Phone: 202-797-6255; Fax: 202-797-6195
Business & Professional Ethics Journal		P.O. Box 15017, Gainesville, FL 32604 Phone: 352-392-2084; Fax: 352-392-5577
Business Ethics	www.blackwellpublishers.co.uk	108 Cowley Rd., Oxford, OX4 1JF, United Kingdom E-mail: jnlinfo@blackwellpublishers.co.uk Phone: 44-1865-791100; Fax: 44-1865-791347
Business Ethics Quarterly	www.bgsu.edu/pdc	Bowling Green, OH 43403-0189 E-mail: pdc@bgnet.bgsu.edu Phone: 419-372-2419; Fax: 419-372-6987
Cambridge Journal of Economics	http://www3.oup.co.uk/social	Great Clarendon St., Oxford, OX2 6DP, United Kingdom E-mail: jnl.info@oup.co.uk Phone: 44-1865-267907; Fax: 44-1865-267835

Canadian Geographer	www.uwindsor.ca/faculty/socsci/geog/cag/index.html	Burnside Hall, McGill University, 805 Sherbrooke St. W, Montreal, PQ, H3A 2K6, Canada Phone: 514-398-4946
Canadian Geographic	www.canadiangeographic.ca	39 McArthur Ave., Ottawa, ON, K1L 8L7, Canada E-mail: regs@cangeo.ca Phone: 613-745-4629; Fax: 613-744-0947
Canadian Journal of Criminology	http://home.istar.ca/~ccja/angl	383 Parkdale Ave., Ste. 304, Ottawa, ON, K1Y 4R4, Canada E-mail: ccja@istar.ca Phone: 613-725-3715; Fax: 613-725-3720
Canadian Journal of Economics	www.blackwellpublishers.co.uk	350 Main St., Malden, MA 02148 E-mail: brander@commerce.ubc.ca Phone: 781-388-8200; Fax: 781-388-8232
Canadian Journal of Experimental Psychology	www.cpa.ca	151 Slater St., Ste. 205, Ottawa, ON, K1P 5H3, Canada E-mail: m_singer@umanitoba.ca Phone: 613-237-2144; Fax: 613-237-1674
Canadian Journal of Political Science	www.uottawa.ca/associations/cpsa-acsp	260 Dalhousie St., Ste. 204, Ottawa, ON, K1N 7E4, Canada Phone: 1-613-562-1202; Fax: 1-613-241-0019
Capital & Class	www.cseweb.org.uk	25 Horsell Rd., London, N5 1XL, United Kingdom E-mail: cseoffice@gn.apc.org Phone: 44-171-607-9615; Fax: 44-171-607-9615
Child Abuse & Neglect	www.elsevier.nl/locate/chiabuneg	The Boulevard, Langford Ln., East Park, Kidlington, Oxford, OXB 1GB, United Kingdom E-mail: nlinfo-f@elsevier.nl, usinfo-f@elsevier.com, and forinfo-kyf04035@niftyserve.or.jp Fax: 44-1865-843010
Child and Adolescent Social Work Journal	www.wkap.nl/journalhome.htm/0738-0151	233 Spring St., New York, NY 10013-1578 E-mail: kluwer@wkap.com, services@wkap.nl, and info@plenum.com Phone: 212-620-8085; Fax: 212-463-0742
Child Development	www.srcd.org/cd.html	University of Michigan, 505 E. Huron St., Ste. 301, Ann Arbor, MI 48104-1567 E-mail: cdev@umich.edu Phone: 734-998-7310; Fax: 734-998-7282

(continued)

Table 5.3   Continued

Title	URL	Editorial Address
Child Welfare	www.cwla.org/pubs	440 First St., NW, 3rd Fl., Washington, DC 20001-2085 E-mail: cwla@pmds.com Phone: 202-638-2952; Fax: 202-638-4004
Children & Youth Services Review	www.childwelfare.com/kids/cysr.htm and www.elsevier.com/locate/childyouth	School of Public Policy and Social Research, University of California, Los Angeles, 3250 Public Policy Bldg., Los Angeles, CA 90095-1656
Chinese Law and Government	www.mesharpe.com/clg_main.htm	80 Business Park Dr., Armonk, NY 10504 E-mail: mesinfo@usa.net Phone: 914-273-1800; Fax: 914-273-2106
Chinese Sociology and Anthropology	www.mesharpe.com/csa_main.htm	80 Business Park Dr., Armonk, NY 10504 E-mail: mesinfo@usa.net Phone: 914-273-1800; Fax: 914-273-2106
Chinese Studies in History	www.mesharpe.com/csh_main.htm	80 Business Park Dr., Armonk, NY 10504 E-mail: mesinfo@usa.net Phone: 914-273-1800; Fax: 914-273-2106
Clinical Social Work Journal	www.cswf.org/cswj/cswj_main.htm and www.plenum.com	233 Spring St., New York, NY 10013-1578 E-mail: kluwer@wkap.com, services@wkap.com, and info@plenum.com Phone: 212-620-8000; Fax: 212-463-0742
Cognitive Psychology	www.academicpress.com/cogpsych	525 B Street, Suite 1900, San Diego, CA 92101-4495 E-mail: apjcs@harcourt.com Phone: 800-321-5068; 619-231-0926; Fax: 800-225-6030 (from U.S. or Canada) or 1-407-363-9661(from outside U.S. or Canada)
Commentary	www.commentarymagazine.com	165 E. 56th St., New York, NY 10022 Phone: 212-751-4000; Fax: 212-751-1174
Communication Quarterly	www.jmu.edu/orgs/eca/products.htm	Candice Thomas-Maddox, Executive DirectorOhio University-Lancaster 1570 Granville PikeLancaster, OH 43130 E-mail: thomas@ohiou.edu Phone: 740/654-6711 ext. 657

Communication Research	www.sagepub.com	2455 Teller Rd., Thousand Oaks, CA 91320 E-mail: info@sagepub.com Phone: 805-499-0721; Fax: 805-706-0871
Communist and Post-Communist Studies	www.elsevier.com/locate/postcomstud	The Boulevard, Langford Ln., East Park, Kidlington, Oxford, OXB 1GB, United Kingdom E-mail: nlinfo-f@elsevier.nl, usinfo-f@elsevier.com, and forinfo-kyf04035@niftyserve.or.jp Fax: 44-1865-843010
Community Mental Health Journal	www.wkap.nl/journalhome.htm/0010-3853	233 Spring St., New York, NY 10013-1578 E-mail: kluwer@wkap.com, services@wkap.nl, and info@plenum.com Phone: 212-620-8000; Fax: 212-463-0742
Comparative Political Studies	www.sagepub.com	2455 Teller Rd., Thousand Oaks, CA 91320 E-mail: info@sagepub.com Phone: 805-499-0721; Fax: 805-499-0871
Comparative Politics	web.gc.cuny.edu/jcp/index.htm	Graduate School and University CenterCity University of New York, 365 Fifth Avenue, New York, NY 10016-4309 Email: comppol@gc.cuny.edu Phone: 212-817-8686; Fax: 212-817-1645
Comparative Strategy	www.tandf.co.uk/journals/tf/01495933.html	11 New Fetter Ln., London EC4P 4EE, United Kingdom Phone: +44-0-7583-9855; Fax: +44-0-7842-2298
Computers in Human Behavior	www.elsevier.com/locate/comphumbeh	The Boulevard, Langford Ln., East Park, Kidlington, Oxford, OXB 1GB, United Kingdom E-mail: nlinfo-f@elsevier.nl, usinfo-f@elsevier.com, and forinfo-kyf04035@niftyserve.or.jp Fax: 44-1865-843010
Congressional Digest	www.congressionaldigest.com	3231 P St. NW, Washington, DC 20007 E-mail: info@congressionaldigest.com Phone: 202-333-7332Fax: 202-625-6670
Congressional Quarterly Weekly Report	www.cq.com	1414 22nd St., NW, Washington, DC 20037 Phone: 202-887-8500 or 800-432-2250; Fax: 202-728-1863

(continued)

Table 5.3 Continued

Title	URL	Editorial Address
Contemporary Economic Policy	www.3.oup.co.uk/coneco	2001 Evans Rd., Cary, NC 27513 E-mail: jnlorders@oup-usa.org Phone: 800-852-7323; Fax: 919-677-1714
Contemporary Sociology	www.asanet.org/pubs/journsub.html	1307 New York Avenue, NW, Suite 700, Washington, DC 20005-4701Email: subscriptions@asanet.orgPhone: 202.383.9005; Fax: 202.638.0882
Corrections Today	www.corrections.com/aca/cortoday	American Correctional Association, 4380 Forbes Boulevard, Lanham, MD 20706-4322 E-mail: jeffw@aca.org Phone: 800-222-5646
CQ Weekly	www.library.cqpress.com	CQ Press, 1414 22nd St., N.W. Washington, D.C. 20037 E-mail: customerservice@cqpress.com Phone: 1-800-638-1710Fax: 202-887-6706
Creativity Plus	www.staff.uiuc.edu/~s-nagel	PSODSIMKM Center, 711 Ashton Ln. S, Champaign, IL 61820 E-mail: s-nagel@uiuc.edu Phone: 217-333-4401; Fax: 217-352-3037
Crime & Delinquency	www.sagepub.com	2455 Teller Rd., Thousand Oaks, CA 91320 E-mail: info@sagepub.com Phone: 805-499-0721; Fax: 805-499-0871
Crime and Justice	www.press.uchicago.edu/Complete/Series/CJ.html	University of Chicago Press, Journals Division, P.O. Box 37005, Chicago, IL 60637 E-mail: j-orders@press.uchicago.edu Phone: 773-753-3347; Fax: 773-753-0811
Crime Law and Social Change	www.wkap.nl/kapis/CGI-BIN/WORLD/journalhome.htm?0925-4994	Kluwer Academic/Plenum Publishers, 233 Spring Street, New York, NY 10013-1578 E-mail: info@plenum.com Phone: (+1) 212 620 8000 Fax: (+1) 212 463 0742
Criminal Justice Ethics	www.lib.jjay.cuny.edu/cje	John Jay College of Criminal Justice, City University of New York, 899 Tenth Ave., New York, NY 10019-1029 E-mail: cjejj@cunyvm.cuny.edu Phone: 212-237-8033; Fax: 212-237-8901

Journal	Website	Contact
Criminal Justice Review	www.gsu.edu/~wwwcjr	Georgia State University, P.O. Box 4018, Atlanta, GA 30302-4018 E-mail: cjr@gsu.edu Phone: 404-651-3660Fax: 404-651-3658
Criminology	www.asc41.com/publications.html	Department of Criminology & Criminal Justice, University of Missouri-St. Louis, 8001 Natural Bridge Road, St. Louis, MO 63121 E-mail: bbursik@umsl.edu Phone: 314-516-7238; Fax: 314-516-7239 (fax)
Critical Studies in Media Communication	www.natcom.org	1765 N St., NW, Washington, DC 20036 E-mail: weadie@natcom.org Phone: 202-464-4622
Cross-Cultural Research	www.sage.co.uk	2455 Teller Rd., Thousand Oaks, CA 91320 E-mail: libraries@sagepub.com Phone: 805-499-0721; Fax: 805-499-0871
Cultural Anthropology	bernard.pitzer.edu/~cultanth	4350 N. Fairfax Dr., Ste. 640, Arlington, VA 22203-1620 E-mail: cultanth@email.pitzer.edu Phone: 703-528-1902
Current Anthropology	www.journals.uchicago.edu/CA/home.html	University of Chicago Press, Journals Division, P.O. Box 37005, Chicago, IL 60637 E-mail: j-orders@press.uchicago.edu Phone: 773-753-3347; Fax: 773-753-0811
Current Sociology	www.ucm.es/info/isa/cs.htm	Department of Sociology, University of Alberta, Edmonton, Alberta T6G 2H4, Canada Email: cursoc@gpu.srv.ualberta.ca Phone &Fax: 1-780-492 0470
Death Studies	www.taylorandfrancis.com	11 New Fetter Ln., London, EC4P 4EE, United Kingdom E-mail: info@taylorandfrancis.com Phone: 215-625-8900; Fax: 215-625-2940
Demography	www.popassoc.org/publications.html	8630 Fenton St., Ste. 722, Silver Spring, MD 20910-3812 E-mail: info@popassoc.org Phone: 301-565-6710; Fax: 301-565-7850
Developmental Policy	www.staff.uiuc.edu/~s-nagel	PSODSIMKM Center, 711 Ashton Ln. S, Champaign, IL 61820 E-mail: s-nagel@uiuc.edu Phone: 217-333-4401; Fax: 217-352-3037

(continued)

Table 5.3   Continued

Title	URL	Editorial Address
Developmental Psychology	www.apa.org/journals/dev.html	750 First St., NE, Washington, DC 20002-4242 E-mail: subscriptions@apa.org Phone: 202-336-5600; Fax: 202-336-5568
Dissent	www.dissentmagazine.org	310 Riverside Dr., Ste. 1201, New York, NY 10025 E-mail: editors@dissentmagazine.org Phone: 212-316-3120; Fax: 212-316-3145
East European Quarterly		Box 29 Regent Hall, University of Colorado, Boulder, Co, 80309
Economic Development and Cultural Change	www.journals.uchicago.edu/EDCC	University of Chicago Press, Journals Division, P.O. Box 37005, Chicago, IL 60637 E-mail: j-orders@press.uchicago.edu Phone: 773-753-3347; Fax: 773-753-0811
Economic Development Quarterly	www.sagepub.com	2455 Teller Rd., Thousand Oaks, CA 91320 E-mail: info@sagepub.com Phone: 805-499-0721; Fax: 805-499-0871
Economic Inquiry	ei.oupjournals.org	Great Clarendon Street, Oxford OX2 6DP, U.K. E-mail: jnl.info@oup.co.uk Phone: +44 (0)1865 267907; Fax: +44 (0)1865 2674
	www.blackwellpublishers.co.uk	108 Cowley Rd., Oxford, OX4 1JF, United Kingdom E-mail: jnlinfo@blackwellpublishers.co.uk Phone: 44-1865-791100; Fax: 44-1865-791347
Economy and Society	www.tandf.co.uk/journals/routledge/03085147.html	29 W. 35th St., New York NY 10001 Phone: 212-216-7800; Fax: 212-564-7854
Educational and Psychological Measurement	www.sagepub.com	2455 Teller Rd., Thousand Oaks, CA 91320 E-mail: info@sagepub.com Phone: 805-499-0721; Fax: 805-499-0871
Environment and Planning A	www.envplan.com	Sales Department, Pion Limited, 207 Brondesbury Park, London NW2 5JN, UK E-mail: wwwsales@pion.co.uk Phone: 44-20-8459-0066; Fax: 44-20-8451-6454

Journal	Website	Contact Information
Environmental Politics	www.frankcass.com/jnls/ep.htm	Crown House, 47 Chase Side, London, N14 5BP, United Kingdom E-mail: info@frankcass.com Phone: 44-20-8599-8866; Fax: 44-20-8599-0984
Ethics	www.journals.uchicago.edu/Ethics/home.html	University of Chicago Press, Journals Division, P.O. Box 37005, Chicago, IL 60637 E-mail: j-orders@press.uchicago.edu Phone: 773-753-3347; Fax: 773-753-0811
Ethics and the Environment	www.phil.uga.edu/eande	Journals Division, Indiana University Press, 601 North Morton Street, Bloomington, IN 47404 E-mail: journals@indiana.edu Phone: 812-855-9449
Ethnic and Racial Studies	www.tandf.co.uk/journals/routledge/01419870.html	29 W. 35th St., New York, NY 10001 Phone: 212-216-7800; Fax: 212-564 7854
Ethnic Groups	www.sirs.com	P.O. Box 272348, Boca Raton, FL 33427-2348 E-mail: custserve@sirs.com Phone: 561-994-0079; Fax: 561-994-4704
Ethnohistory	www.dukeupress.edu	P.O. Box 90660, Durham, NC 27708-0660 E-mail: amylee@acpub.acup.duke.edu Phone: 919-687-3600; Fax: 919-688-3524
Ethnology	www.pitt.edu/~ethnolog	Department of Anthropology, University of Pittsburgh, Pittsburgh, PA 15260 E-mail: ethnolog@pitt.edu Phone: 412-648-7503; Fax: 412-648-7535
Europe-Asia Studies	www.tandf.co.uk/journals/carfax/09668136.html	P.O. Box 25, Abingdon, OX14 3UE, United Kingdom E-mail: enquiries@carfax.co.uk Phone: 44-1235-401000; Fax: 44-1235-401550
European Economic Review	www.elsevier.com/locate/euroecorev	P.O. Box 211, 1000 AE Amsterdam, The Netherlands E-mail: j.dirkmaat@elsevier.nl Phone: 31-20-485-3911; Fax: 31-20-485-3598
Evaluation Review	www.sagepub.com	2455 Teller Rd., Thousand Oaks, CA 91320 E-mail: info@sagepub.com Phone: 805-499-0721; Fax: 805-499-0871

(continued)

Table 5.3   Continued

Title	URL	Editorial Address
Explorations in Economic History	www.academicpress.com/eeh	525 B Street, Suite 1900, San Diego, CA 92101-4495 E-mail: apjcs@harcourt.com Phone: 800-321-5068; 619-231-0926; Fax: 800-225-6030 (from U.S. or Canada) or 1-407-363-9661 (from outside U.S. or Canada)
Families in Society	www.alliance1.org	E-mail: isabel@manticore.ca Phone: 905-945-7221; Fax: 905-945-8486
Family Relations	ncfr.allenpress.com	810 E. Tenth, Lawrence, KS 66044 E-mail: acg@allenpress.com Phone: 785-843-1235; Fax: 785-843-1274
Far Eastern Economic Review	www.feer.com	E-mail: review@feer.com Phone: 852-2508-4338; Fax: 852-2503-1549
FBI Law Enforcement Bulletin	www.fbi.gov/publications/leb/leb.htm	E-mail: leb@fbiacademy.edu Phone: 703-632-1952; Fax: 703-632-1968
Feminist Review	www.tandf.co.uk/journals/routledge/01417789.html	29 W. 35th St., New York NY 10001 Phone: 212-216-7800; Fax: 212-564-7854
Feminist Studies	www.inform.umd.edu/FemStud	Dept. of Women's Studies, University of Maryland, College Park, MD 20742 E-mail: femstud@umail.umd.edu Phone: 301-405-7415; Fax: 301-314-9190
Finance & Development	www.worldbank.org/fandd	700 Nineteenth Street, N.W., Washington, DC 20431 E-mail: fandd@imf.org Phone: 202-623-8300; Fax: 202- 623-6149
Foreign Affairs	www.foreignaffairs.org	58 E. 68th St., New York, NY 10021 E-mail: foraff@cfr.org Fax: 212-861-2759
Foreign Policy	www.foreignpolicy.com	1779 Massachusetts Ave., NW, Washington, DC 20036 Phone: 202-862-7940; Fax: 202-463-7914

Forum for Applied Research and Public Policy	forum.ra.utk.edu	University of Tennessee, EERC, 311 Conference Building, Knoxville, TN 37996-4134 E-mail: forum@eerc.gw.utk.edu Phone: 423-974-4251; Fax: 423-974-8491
Gender & Society	www.sagepub.com	2455 Teller Rd., Thousand Oaks, CA 91320 E-mail: info@sagepub.com Phone: 805-499-0721; Fax: 805-499-0871
Generations	www.asaging.org/generations/gen.html	American Society on Aging, 833 Market St., Suite 511, San Francisco, CA 94103 E-mail: info@asaging.org Phone: 415-974-9600; Fax: 415-974-0300
Geography	www.geographyshop.org.uk/details/journ/journg.html	160 Solly St., Sheffield, S1 4BF, United Kingdom E-mail: ga@geography.org.uk Phone: 44-114-296-0088; Fax: 44-114-296-7176
Government and Opposition	les.man.ac.uk/government/journals/gov-opp	Government and Opposition, London School of Economics, Houghton Street, London, WC2A 2AE, UK. Tel/Fax: +44 -0171-405-5991
Health & Social Work	www.naswpress.org/publications/journals/health/hswintro.html	750 First Street NE, Ste. 700, Washington, DC 20002-4241 E-mail: press@naswdc.org Phone: 202-408-8600; 800-638-8799
Health Care Financing Review	www.hcfa.gov/pubforms/ordpub.htm	7500 Security Boulevard, C3-24-07, Baltimore, MD 21244-1850E-mail: lwolf@hcfa.gov Phone: 410-786-6572; Fax: 410-786-6511
Hispanic Journal of Behavioral Sciences	www.sagepub.com	2455 Teller Rd., Thousand Oaks, CA 91320 E-mail: info@sagepub.com Phone: 805-499-0721; Fax: 805-499-0871
Human Communication Research	www3.oup.co.uk/humcom	2001 Evans Rd., Cary, NC 27513 E-mail: jnlorders@oup-usa.org Phone: 800-852-7323; Fax: 919-677-1714
Human Ecology	maxweber.hunter.cuny.edu/anthro/ecology.html	Department of Anthropology, Hunter College of The City University of New York, 695 Park Avenue, New York, NY 10021 E-mail: dbates@shiva.hunter.cuny.edu

(continued)

Table 5.3 Continued

Title	URL	Editorial Address
Human Organization	www.sfaa.net/ho	P.O. Box 2436, Oklahoma City, OK 73101-2436 E-mail: info@sfaa.net Phone: 405-843-5113; Fax: 405-843-8553
Human Relations	www.sagepub.com	2455 Teller Rd., Thousand Oaks, CA 91320 E-mail: info@sagepub.com Phone: 805-499-0721; Fax: 805-499-0871
Human Rights Journal	www.law.harvard.edu/studorgs/hrj	Harvard Human Rights Journal, Pound Hall 403, Harvard Law School, Cambridge, MA 02138 E-mail: HLSHRJ@law.harvard.edu Phone: 617-495-8318
Human Rights Quarterly	muse.jhu.edu/journals/human_rights_quarterly	Johns Hopkins University Press, 2715 North Charles St., Baltimore, MD 21218-4363 E-mail: muse@muse.jhu.edu Phone: 410-516-6989; Fax: 410-516-6968
International Journal of Aging and Human Development	www.baywood.com/search/PreviewJournal.asp?qsRecord=5	Baywood Publishing Company, Inc., 26 Austin Ave., Box 337, Amityville, NY 11701E-mail: info@baywood.com Phone: 631-691-1270; Fax: 631-691-1770
International Journal of Comparative Sociology (Leiden, Netherlands)	www.yorku.ca/faculty/academic/ishwaran/ijcs.htm	E.J. Brill, 24 Hudson Street, Kinderhook, NY 12106 E-mail: 103740.2612@compuserve.com Phone: 800-962-4406 ext. 11; Fax: 518-758-1959
International Journal of Eating Disorders	www.interscience.wiley.com/jpages/0276-3478	605 Third Avenue, New York, New York 10158-0012 E-mail: subinfo@wiley.com Phone: 212-850-6645; Fax: 212-850-6021
International Journal of Group Psychotherapy	www.guilford.com/cartscript.cgi?page=periodicals/jngr.htm&cart_id=	72 Spring Street, New York, NY 10012 E-mail: info@guilford.com Phone: 800-365-7006 or 212-431-9800; Fax: 212-966-6708
International Journal of Mental Health	www.mesharpe.com/imh_main.htm	80 Business Park Dr., Armonk, NY 10504 E-mail: mesinfo@usa.net Phone: 1-800-541-6563 or 914-273-1800; Fax: 914-273-2106

Journal	Web Address	Contact
International Journal of Middle East Studies	uk.cambridge.org/journals/meswww.umich.edu/~iinet/cmenas/ijmes/ijmes.htm	Edinburgh Bldg., Shaftesbury Rd., Cambridge, CB2 2RU, United Kingdom E-mail: information@cup.cam.ac.uk Fax: 44-1223-315052
International Journal of Offender Therapy and Comparative Criminology	www.sagepub.co.uk/journals/details/j0011.html	2455 Teller Rd., Thousand Oaks, CA 91320 E-mail: info@sagepub.com Phone: 805-499-0721; Fax: 805-499-0871
International Journal of Sociology	www.mesharpe.com/ijs_main.htm	80 Business Park Dr., Armonk, NY 10504 E-mail: mesinfo@usa.net Phone: 1-800-541-6563 or 914-273-1800; Fax: 914-273-2106
International Journal of the Sociology of Law	www.academicpress.com/www/journal/slnojs.htm	525 B Street, Suite 1900, San Diego, CA 92101-4495 E-mail: apjcs@harcourt.com Phone: 800-321-5068; 619-231-0926; Fax: 800-225-6030 (from U.S. or Canada) or 1-407-363-9661 (from outside U.S. or Canada)
International Journal of Urban and Regional Research	www.blackwellpublishers.co.uk/journals/IJURR/descript.htm	Cowley Rd., Oxford, OX4 1JF, United Kingdom E-mail: jnlinfo@blackwellpublishers.co.uk Phone: 44-1865-791100; Fax: 44-1865-791347
International Labour Review	www.ilo.org/public/english/support/publ/revue	4, route des Morillons, CH-1211 Geneva 22, Switzerland E-mail: pubvente@ilo.org Phone: 41-22-799-6111; Fax: 41-22-798-6358
International Organization	mitpress.mit.edu/journal-home.tcl?issn=00208183	Five Cambridge Center, Cambridge, MA 02142 E-mail: journals-orders@mit.edu Phone: 617-253-2889; Fax: 617-577-1545
International Political Science Review	www.sagepub.com	2455 Teller Rd., Thousand Oaks, CA 91320 E-mail: info@sagepub.com Phone: 805-499-0721; Fax: 805-499-0871
International Review of Social History	uk.cambridge.org/journals/ish/ishifc.htm	Edinburgh Bldg., Shaftesbury Rd., Cambridge, CB2 2RU, United Kingdom E-mail: information@cup.cam.ac.uk Fax: 44-1223-315052
International Security	mitpress.mit.edu/ISEC	Five Cambridge Center, Cambridge, MA 02142 E-mail: journals-orders@mit.edu Phone: 617-253-2889; Fax: 617-577-1545

(continued)

Table 5.3   Continued

Title	URL	Editorial Address
International Social Science Journal	www.unesco.org/issj	Dr David Makinson, International Social Science Journal, SHS/SRP UNESCO, 1 rue Miollis, 75732 Paris Cedex 15, France E-mail: d.makinson@unesco.org Phone: 33 1 45 68 38 28, Fax: 33 1 45 68 57 24
International Social Work	www.sagepub.com	2455 Teller Rd., Thousand Oaks, CA 91320 E-mail: info@sagepub.com Phone: 805-499-0721; Fax: 805-499-0871
International Studies Quarterly	www.public.iastate.edu/~isq	Cowley Rd., Oxford, OX4 1JF, United Kingdom E-mail: jnlinfo@blackwellpublishers.co.uk Phone: 44-1865-791100; Fax: 44-1865-791347
Israel Studies	muse.jhu.edu/journals/is	The Ben-Gurion Research Center, Ben-Gurion University of the Negev, IsraelIndiana University Press,601 North Morton Street, Bloomington, IN 47404 USA E-mail: journals@indiana.edu Phone: 812-855-9449; Fax: 812-855-8507
Journal of Abnormal Child Psychology	www.wkap.nl/journalhome.htm/0091-0627	233 Spring St., New York, NY 10013-1578 E-mail: kluwer@wkap.com, services@wkap.nl, and info@plenum.com Phone: 212-620-8085; Fax: 212-463-0742
Journal of Abnormal Psychology	www.apa.org/journals/abn.html	American Psychological Association, 750 First St., NE, Washington, DC 20002-4242 Phone: 800-374-2721 or 202-336-5500
ournal of Adolescence	www.academicpress.com/adolescence	525 B Street, Suite 1900, San Diego, CA 92101-4495 E-mail: apjcs@harcourt.com Phone: 800-321-5068; 619-231-0926; Fax: 800-225-6030 (from U.S. or Canada) or 1-407-363-9661 (from outside U.S. or Canada)
Journal of Aging Studies	www.elsevier.com/locate/jaging	P.O. Box 945, New York, N.Y. 10159-0945 E-mail: usinfo-f@elsevier.com Phone: +1 212 633 3730 or 1-888-4ES-INFO (437-4636); Fax: (+1) 212 633 3680

Journal	Website	Contact
Journal of American-East Asian Relations	www.imprint-chicago.com/jrnlamerestasrel.htm	Imprint Publications, Inc., 230 E. Ohio St. Suite 300, Chicago, Illinois 60611 E-mail: jespersen@imprint-chicago.com Phone: 312-337-9268; fax: 312-337-9622
Journal of Anthropological Research	www.unm.edu/~jar	Anthropology Bldg., Room 240, University of New Mexico, Albuquerque, NM 87131 E-mail: lstraus@unm.edu Phone: 505-277-4544; Fax: 505-277-0874
Journal of Applied Behavior Analysis	www.envmed.rochester.edu/wwwrap/behavior/jaba/jabahome.htm	Department of Human Development, 1000 Sunnyside Ave., University of Kansas, Lawrence, KS 66045-2133 E-mail: jabamlw@myexcel.com Phone: 785-843-0008; Fax: 785-843-5909
Journal of Applied Gerontology	www.sagepub.com	2455 Teller Rd., Thousand Oaks, CA 91320 E-mail: info@sagepub.com Phone: 805-499-0721; Fax: 805-499-0871
Journal of Applied Psychology	www.apa.org	750 First St., NE, Washington, DC 20002-4242 E-mail: subscriptions@apa.org Phone: 202-336-5600; Fax: 202-336-5568
Journal of Asian and African Studies	www.yorku.ca/faculty/academic/ishwaran/jaas.htm	E. J. Brill US, 24 Hudson Street, Kinderhook, NY 12106 Email: 103740.2612@compuserve.com Phone: 1-800-962-4406 ext. 11; Fax: 518-758-1959
Journal of Black Psychology	www.sagepub.com	2455 Teller Rd., Thousand Oaks, CA 91320 E-mail: info@sagepub.com Phone: 805-499-0721; Fax: 805-499-0871
Journal of Black Studies	www.sagepub.com	2455 Teller Rd., Thousand Oaks, CA 91320 E-mail: info@sagepub.com Phone: 805-499-0721; Fax: 805-499-0871
Journal of Broadcasting & Electronic Media	www.beaweb.org/jobem.html	212 Grehan Bldg., University of Kentucky, Lexington, KY 40506-0042 E-mail: lindlof@pop.uky.edu Phone: 859-257-4242; Fax: 859-323-3168
Journal of Clinical Psychology	www.interscience.wiley.com/jpages/0021-9762	E-mail: subinfo@wiley.com Phone: 212-850-6645; Fax: 212-850-6021

(continued)

Table 5.3 Continued

Title	URL	Editorial Address
Journal of Communication	joc.oupjournals.org	2001 Evans Rd., Cary, NC 27513 E-mail: jnlorders@oup-usa.org Phone: 800-852-7323; Fax: 919-677-1714
Journal of Community Health	www.wkap.nl/journalhome.htm/0094-5145	233 Spring Street, New York, NY 10013-1578 E-mail: info@plenum.com Phone: 212-620-8000; Fax: 212-463-0742
Journal of Comparative Psychology	www.apa.org/journals/com.html	750 First St., NE, Washington, DC 20002-4242 E-mail: subscriptions@apa.org Phone: 202-336-5600; Fax: 202-336-5568
Journal of Consulting and Clinical Psychology	www.apa.org/journals/ccp.html	American Psychological Association, 750 First St., NE, Washington, DC 20002-4242 Phone: 800-374-2721 or 202-336-5500
Journal of Contemporary Ethnography	www.sagepub.com	2455 Teller Rd., Thousand Oaks, CA 91320 E-mail: info@sagepub.com Phone: 805-499-0721; Fax: 805-499-0871
Journal of Counseling & Development	www.counseling.org/journals	American Counseling Association, 5999 Stevenson Avenue, Alexandria, Virginia 22304-3300 Phone: 703-823-9800; Fax: 703-823-0252
Journal of Counseling Psychology	www.apa.org/journals/cou.html	750 First St., NE, Washington, DC 20002-4242 E-mail: subscriptions@apa.org Phone: 202-336-5600; Fax: 202-336-5568
Journal of Criminal Justice and Popular Culture	www.albany.edu/scj/jcjpc	University at Albany, School of Criminal Justice, Draper Hall #213, 135 Western Avenue, Albany, NY 12222 Phone: 518-442-5210; Fax: 518-442-5212
Journal of Cross-Cultural Psychology	www.fit.edu/CampusLife/clubs-org/iaccp/JCCP/jccp.html	2455 Teller Rd., Thousand Oaks, CA 91320 E-mail: info@sagepub.com Phone: 805-499-0721; Fax: 805-499-0871
Journal of Democracy	muse.jhu.edu/journals/journal_of_democracy	The Johns Hopkins University Press, 2715 North Charles Street, Baltimore, MD 21218-4363 Phone: 410-516-6900; Fax: 410-516-6968

Journal	Website	Contact
Journal of Divorce & Remarriage	www.haworthpressinc.com	10 Alice St., Binghamton, NY 13904 E-mail: getinfo@haworthpressinc.com Phone: 607-722-5857; Fax: 607-722-6362
Journal of Drug Issues	www2.criminology.fsu.edu/~jdi	Florida State University, School of Criminology and Criminal Justice, 634 West Call Street, Tallahassee, FL32306 E-mail: jdi@garnet.fsu.edu Phone: 850-644-7368; 850-644-9614
Journal of Economic Geography	jeg.oupjournals.org	Great Clarendon Street, Oxford OX2 6DP, U.K. E-mail: jnl.info@oup.co.uk Phone: +44 (0)1865 267907; Fax: +44 (0)1865 267485
Journal of Economic Issues	www.orgs.bucknell.edu/afee/jei	Department of Economics, University of Nevada, Reno, NV 89557
Journal of Economic Literature	www.aeaweb.org/journal.html	Graduate School of Business, Stanford University, 518 Memorial Way, Rm. S319, Stanford, CA 94305-5015 Phone: 650-724-5546
Journal of Economic Theory	www.academicpress.com/jet	525 B Street, Suite 1900, San Diego, CA 92101-4495 E-mail: apjcs@harcourt.com Phone: 800-321-5068; 619-231-0926; Fax: 800-225-6030 (from U.S. or Canada) or 1-407-363-9661 (from outside U.S. or Canada)
Journal of Ethnicity in Substance Abuse (formerly Drugs & Society)	www.haworthpressinc.com/store/product.asp?sku=J233	10 Alice St. Binghamton, NY 13904 E-mail: getinfo@haworthpressinc.com Phone: 607-722-5857; Fax: 607-722-6362
Journal of Environmental Economics and Management	www.academicpress.com/www/journal/ee.htm	525 B Street, Suite 1900, San Diego, CA 92101-4495 E-mail: apjcs@harcourt.com Phone: 800-321-5068; 619-231-0926; Fax: 800-225-6030 (from U.S. or Canada) or 1-407-363-9661 (from outside U.S. or Canada)
Journal of Experimental Child Psychology	www.academicpress.com/jecp	525 B Street, Suite 1900, San Diego, CA 92101-4495 E-mail: apjcs@harcourt.com Phone: 800-321-5068; 619-231-0926; Fax: 800-225-6030 (from U.S. or Canada) or 1-407-363-9661 (from outside U.S. or Canada)
Journal of Experimental Psychology: Animal Behavior Processes	www.apa.org/journals/xan.html	750 First St., NE, Washington, DC 20002-4242 E-mail: subscriptions@apa.org Phone: 202-336-5600Fax: 202-336-5568

(continued)

Table 5.3   Continued

Title	URL	Editorial Address
Journal of Experimental Psychology. General	www.apa.org/journals/xge.html	750 First St., NE, Washington, DC 20002-4242 E-mail: subscriptions@apa.org Phone: 202-336-5600Fax: 202-336-5568
ournal of Experimental Psychology. Human Perception and Performance	www.apa.org/journals/xhp.html	750 First St., NE, Washington, DC 20002-4242 E-mail: subscriptions@apa.org Phone: 202-336-5600; Fax: 202-336-5568
Journal of Experimental Psychology. Learning, Memory and Cognition	www.apa.org/journals/xlm.html	750 First St., NE, Washington, DC 20002-4242 E-mail: subscriptions@apa.org Phone: 202-336-5600; Fax: 202-336-5568
Journal of Experimental Social Psychology	www.academicpress.com/jesp	525 B Street, Suite 1900, San Diego, CA 92101-4495 E-mail: apjcs@harcourt.com Phone: 800-321-5068; 619-231-0926; Fax: 800-225-6030 (from U.S. or Canada) or 1-407-363-9661 (from outside U.S. or Canada)
Journal of Family History	www.sagepub.com	2455 Teller Rd., Thousand Oaks, CA 91320 E-mail: info@sagepub.com Phone: 805-499-0721; Fax: 805-499-0871
Journal of Family Issues	www.sagepub.com	2455 Teller Rd., Thousand Oaks, CA 91320 E-mail: info@sagepub.com Phone: 805-499-0721; Fax: 805-499-0871
Journal of Family Psychology	www.apa.org/journals/fam.html	750 First St., NE, Washington, DC 20002-4242 E-mail: subscriptions@apa.org Phone: 202-336-5600Fax: 202-336-5568
Journal of Family Violence	www.nisso.nl/Tijdschr/jofv.htm	233 Spring Street, New York, NY 10013-1578 E-mail: info@plenum.com Phone: 212-620-8000; Fax: 212-463-0742
Journal of Homosexuality	www.nisso.nl/Tijdschr/johom.htm	10 Alice St. Binghamton, NY 13904 E-mail: getinfo@haworthpressinc.com Phone: 607-722-5857; Fax: 607-722-6362

Journal	Website	Contact
Journal of Humanistic Psychology	www.sagepub.com	2455 Teller Rd., Thousand Oaks, CA 91320 E-mail: info@sagepub.com Phone: 805-499-0721; Fax: 805-499-0871
Journal of Interdisciplinary Studies	www.jisonline.org	IIR 1065 Pine Bluff Dr., Pasadena, CA 91107-1751
Journal of International Affairs	jia.sipa.columbia.edu/journal.html	Box 4, International Affairs Bldg., 420 West 118th St., Columbia University, New York, NY 10027 Phone: 212-854-4775; Fax: 212-662-0398
Journal of International Economics	www.haas.berkeley.edu/~jie	Haas School of Business, Berkeley, CA USA 94720-1900 E-mail jie@hass.berkeley.edu Fax: 510-643-1048
Journal of Interpersonal Violence	www.sagepub.com	2455 Teller Rd., Thousand Oaks, CA 91320 E-mail: info@sagepub.com Phone: 805-499-0721; Fax: 805-499-0871
Journal of Labor Economics	www.journals.uchicago.edu/JOLE/home.html	University of Chicago Press, Journals Division, P.O. Box 37005, Chicago, IL 60637 E-mail: j-orders@press.uchicago.edu Phone: 773-753-3347; Fax: 773-753-0811
Journal of Labor Research	www.thelockeinstitute.org/jolr.html	The Locke Institute, 4084 University Drive, Suite 103, Fairfax, Virginia 22030-6812 E-mail: info@TheLockeInstitute.org Phone: 703-934-6934; Fax: 703-352-9747
Journal of Latin American Anthropology	www.northwestern.edu/jlaa	Northwestern University, Department of Anthropology, 1810 Hinman Avenue, Evanston, IL 60208-1310
Journal of Leisure Research	rptsweb.tamu.edu/Journals/JLR/index.html	Department. of Recreation, Park & Tourism Sciences, Texas A&M University, 2261 TAMU, College Station, TX 77843-2261 Phone: 979-845-5334; Fax: 979-845-0446
Journal of Marital and Family Therapy	www.aamft.org/resources/jmft_menu.htm	Texas Tech University Marriage and Family Therapy Program, Box 41162, Lubbock, TX 79409-1162 E-mail: JMFT@hs.ttu.edu
Journal of Marriage and the Family	http://ncfr.allenpress.com/ncfronline/?request=index-html	Allen Press, Inc., 810 East Tenth, Lawrence, KS 66044 E-mail: webmaster@allenpress.com Phone: 800-627-0326 or 785-843-1234; Fax: 785-843-1244

(continued)

Table 5.3 **Continued**

Title	URL	Editorial Address
Journal of Medical Ethics	jme.bmjjournals.com	BMJ Publishing Group, BMA HouseTavistock Square, London, WC1H 9JR, United Kingdom E-mail: subscriptions@bmjgroup.com Phone: 44 (0) 20 7383 6270; Fax: +44 (0) 20 7383 6402
Journal of Memory and Language	www.academicpress.com/jml	525 B Street, Suite 1900, San Diego, CA 92101-4495 E-mail: apjcs@harcourt.com Phone: 800-321-5068; 619-231-0926; Fax: 800-225-6030 (from U.S. or Canada) or 1-407-363-9661 (from outside U.S. or Canada)
Journal of Nonverbal Behavior	www.wkap.nl/journalhome.htm/0191-5886	233 Spring St., New York, NY 10013-1578 E-mail: kluwer@wkap.com, services@wkap.nl, and info@plenum.com Phone: 212-620-8085; Fax: 212-463-0742
ournal of Offender Rehabilitation	bubl.ac.uk/journals/soc/jofreh	10 Alice St. Binghamton, NY 13904 E-mail: getinfo@haworthpressinc.com Phone: 607-722-5857; Fax: 607-722-6362
Journal of Peace Research	www.sagepub.com	2455 Teller Rd., Thousand Oaks, CA 91320 E-mail: info@sagepub.com Phone: 805-499-0721; Fax: 805-499-0871
Journal of Personality	www.blackwellpub.com/journals/JOPY/descript.htm	108 Cowley Rd., Oxford, OX4 1JF, United Kingdom E-mail: jnlinfo@blackwellpublishers.co.uk Phone: 44-1865-791100; Fax: 44-1865-791347
Journal of Personality and Social Psychology	www.apa.org/journals/psp.html	750 First St., NE, Washington, DC 20002-4242E-mail: subscriptions@apa.org Phone: 202-336-5600; Fax: 202-336-5568
Journal of Policy Analysis and Management	qsilver.queensu.ca/appam/services/jpam	School of Public Affairs, Van Munching Hall, University of Maryland, College Park, MD 20742
Journal of Political Economy	www.journals.uchicago.edu/JPE/home.html	University of Chicago Press, Journals Division, P.O. Box 37005, Chicago, IL 60637 E-mail: j-orders@press.uchicago.edu Phone: 773-753-3347; Fax: 773-753-0811

Journal	Website	Contact
Journal of Research in Crime and Delinquency	www.sagepub.com	2455 Teller Rd., Thousand Oaks, CA 91320 E-mail: info@sagepub.com Phone: 805-499-0721; Fax: 805-499-0871
Journal of Sociology and Social WelfareSchool of Social Work	www.wmich.edu/hhs/Newslettersjournals/jssw	1903 W. Michigan Ave, Kalamazoo, MI 49008-5354 E-mail: macdonald@wmich.edu Phone: 616-387-3205; Fax: 616-387-3217
Journal of Speech, Language, and Hearing Research	164.109.82.203/resources/journals/JSLHR-index.cfm	American Speech-Language-Hearing Association, 10801 Rockville Pike, Rockville, MD 20852 Phone: 800-638-8255
Journal of Studies on Alcohol	www.rci.rutgers.edu/~cas2/journal	Rutgers Center of Alcohol Studies, P.O. Box 969, Piscataway, NJ 08855-0969
Journal of the American Academy of Child and Adolescent Psychiatry	www.jaacap.com	Children's Memorial Hospital, 2300 Children's Plaza #156, Chicago, IL 60614-3394
Journal of the American Geriatrics Society	www.blackwellscience.com/journals/geriatrics/index.html	108 Cowley Rd., Oxford, OX4 1JF, United Kingdom E-mail: jnlinfo@blackwellpublishers.co.uk Phone: 44-1865-791100; Fax: 44-1865-791347
Journal of the American Planning Association	www.japa.pdx.edu	American Planning Association, 122 South Michigan Avenue, Suite 1600, Chicago, IL 60603-6107 Fax: 312-431-9985
Journal of the Experimental Analysis of Behavior	www.envmed.rochester.edu/wwwrap/behavior/jeab/jeabhome.htm	Devonia Stein, JEAB, Department of Psychology, Indiana University, Bloomington, Indiana 47405-1301 E-mail: jeab@indiana.edu Phone: 812-339-4718; FAX: 812-855-4691
ournal of Third World Studies	www.wiu.edu/users/mfmbk/atws/journal.htm	Journal of Third World Studies P.O. Box 1232, Americus, Georgia 31709
Journal of Urban Affairs	www.udel.edu/uaa/journal.html	College of Public Service, St. Louis University, McGannon Hall, Ste. 232, 3750 Lindell Blvd., St. Louis, MO 63108-3342
Kyklos	www.unibas.ch/kykloswww.blackwellpublishers.co.uk/asp/journal.asp?ref=0023-5962 www.blackwellpublishers.co.uk	108 Cowley Rd., Oxford, OX4 1JF, United Kingdom E-mail: jnlinfo@blackwellpublishers.co.uk Phone: 44-1865-791100; Fax: 44-1865-791347
Land Economics	www.wisc.edu/wisconsinpress/journals/landecon.html	1930 Monroe St., 3rd Floor, Madison, WI 53711-2059 E-mail: journals@uwpress.wisc.edu Phone: 608 263-0668; Fax: 608 263-1173

(continued)

Table 5.3 Continued

Title	URL	Editorial Address
Latin American Perspectives	www.sagepub.com	2455 Teller Rd., Thousand Oaks, CA 91320 E-mail: info@sagepub.com E-mail: Phone: 805-499-0721; Fax: 805-499-0871
Latin American Politics and Society	www.rienner.com/laps.htm	1800 30th St., Boulder, CO 80301 E-mail: questions@reinner.com Phone: 303-444-6684; Fax: 303-444-0824
Law and Contemporary Problems	www.law.duke.edu/journals/lcp	Law & Contemporary Problems Duke University School of Law, Box 90364, Durham, NC 27708-0364 E-mail: publications@law.duke.edu Phone: 919-613-7109; Fax: 919-919-681-8460
Learning and Motivation	www.academicpress.com/l&m	525 B Street, Suite 1900, San Diego, CA 92101-4495 E-mail: apjcs@harcourt.com Phone: 800-321-5068; 619-231-0926; Fax: 800-225-6030 (from U.S. or Canada) or 1-407-363-9661 (from outside U.S. or Canada)
Media, Culture & Society	www.sagepub.com	2455 Teller Rd., Thousand Oaks, CA 91320 E-mail: info@sagepub.com E-mail: Phone: 805-499-0721; Fax: 805-499-0871
Medical Anthropology Quarterly	www.cudenver.edu/sma/medical_anthropology_quarterly.htm	Department of Anthropology, 114 Macbride Hall, University of Iowa, Iowa City, IA 52242-1322 E-mail: mac-marshall@uiowa.edu
Milbank Quarterly	www.milbank.org/quarterly.html	Blackwell Publishers, Journals Department, 350 Main Street, Malden, MA 02148 E-mail: subscrip@blackwellpub.com Phone: 800-835-6770; Fax: 781-388-8232
Modern China	www.sagepub.com	2455 Teller Rd., Thousand Oaks, CA 91320 E-mail: info@sagepub.com E-mail: Phone: 805-499-0721; Fax: 805-499-0871
Oxford Economic Papers	oep.oupjournals.org	Great Clarendon Street, Oxford, OX2 6DP, UK E-mail: jnl.info@oup.co.uk Phone: +44 (0)1865 267907; Fax: +44 (0)1865 267485

Parliamentary Affairs	http://www3.oup.co.uk/parlij	Great Clarendon Street, Oxford, OX2 6DP, UK E-mail: jnl.info@oup.co.uk Phone: +44 (0)1865 267907; Fax: +44 (0)1865 267485
Personality and Social Psychology Bulletin	www.spsp.org/pspb.htm	2455 Teller Rd., Thousand Oaks, CA 91320 E-mail: info@sagepub.com Phone: 805-499-0721; Fax: 805-499-0871
Philosophy of the Social Sciences	www.sagepub.com	2455 Teller Rd., Thousand Oaks, CA 91320 E-mail: info@sagepub.com Phone: 805-499-0721; Fax: 805-499-0871
Policy Review (online)	www.policyreview.org	Subscriptions Department, P.O. Box #653, Shrub Oak, NY 10588; Policy Review; 818 Connecticut Avenue, NW Suite #601, Washington, DC 20006 E-mail: polrev@hoover.stanford.edu Phone: 202.466.6730; Fax: 202.466.6733
Policy Studies Journal	www.siu.edu/~psj/welcome.html	Policy Studies Organization, 711 South Ashton Ln., Champaign, IL 61820
Political Science Quarterly	www.psqonline.org	475 Riverside Dr., Ste. 1274, New York, NY 10115-1274 E-mail: aps@psqonline.org Phone: 212-870-2500; Fax: 212-870-2202
Politics & Society	www.sagepub.com	2455 Teller Rd., Thousand Oaks, CA 91320 E-mail: info@sagepub.com Phone: 805-499-0721; Fax: 805-499-0871
Population Bulletin	www.prb.org//Content/NavigationMenu/PRB/AboutPRB/Population_Bulletin2/Population_Bulletin.htm	Population Reference Bureau, 1875 Connecticut Ave., NW, Ste. 520, Washington, DC 20009-5728 E-mail: popref@prb.org Phone: 800-877-9881 or 202-483-1100; Fax: 202-328-3937
Presidential Studies Quarterly	www.sagepub.com	2455 Teller Rd., Thousand Oaks, CA 91320 E-mail: info@sagepub.com Phone: 805-499-0721; Fax: 805-499-0871
Professional Psychology, Research and Practice	www.apa.org/journals/pro.html	750 First St., NE, Washington, DC 20002-4242 Phone: 800-374-2721 or 202-336-5500
Psychological Bulletin	www.apa.org/journals/bul.html	750 First St., NE, Washington, DC 20002-4242 Phone: 800-374-2721 or 202-336-5500

(continued)

Table 5.3 Continued

Title	URL	Editorial Address
Psychological Review	www.apa.org/journals/rev.html	750 First St., NE, Washington, DC 20002-4242 Phone: 800-374-2721 or 202-336-5500
Psychology and Aging	www.apa.org/journals/pag.html	750 First St., NE, Washington, DC 20002-4242 Phone: 800-374-2721 or 202-336-5500
Psychology of Women Quarterly	www.blackwellpublishers.co.uk/journals/PWQ/society.htm	Blackwell Publishers, Journals Department, 350 Main St., Malden, MA 02148 E-mail: lmos@aol.com Phone: 781-388-8200; Fax: 781-388-8232
Psychology Today	www.psychologytoday.com	49 East 21st St., 11th Fl., New York, NY 10010 Phone: 800-234-8361; 212-260-7210
Public Health Reports	phr.oupjournals.org	2001 Evans Rd., Cary, NC 27513 Phone: 919-677-0977, ext. 6686 or 800-852-7323 (toll-free in USA/Canada); Fax: 919-677-1714
Research on Aging	www.sagepub.com	2455 Teller Rd., Thousand Oaks, CA 91320 E-mail: info@sagepub.com Phone: 805-499-0721; Fax: 805-499-0871
Russian Politics and Law	www.mesharpe.com/rup_main.htm	M. E. Sharpe, 80 Business Park Dr., Armonk, NY 10504 Phone: 800-5416563; Fax: 914-273-2106
Social Science and Medicine	www.elsevier.nl/inca/publications/store/3/1/5	The Boulevard, Langford Ln., East Park, Kidlington, Oxford, OXB 1GB, United Kingdom E-mail: nlinfo-f@elsevier.nl, usinfo-f@elsevier.com, and forinfo-kyf04035@niftyserve.or.jp Fax: 44-1865-843010
Social Security Bulletin	www.ssa.gov/policy/pubs/SSB	
Sociological Perspectives	www.csus.edu/psa/journal.html	Berkeley Way, Berkeley, CA 94720-5812 E-mail: journals@ucop.edu Phone: 510-643-7154; Fax: 510-642-9917

Journal	Website	Address
The American Economic Review	www.aeaweb.org/aer	2014 Broadway, Ste. 305, Nashville, TN 37203 E-mail: aeainfo@ctrvax.vanderbilt.edu Phone: 615-322-2595
The American Enterprise	www.theamericanenterprise.org	The American Enterprise, Pof Box 7144, Bensenville, IL 60106-7144 E-mail: ccoyle@aei.org Phone: 888-295-9007
The American Journal of Economics and Sociology	www.babson.edu/ajes	350 Main St., Malden, MA 02148 E-mail: subscrip@blackwellpub.com Phone: 781-388-8200; Fax: 781-388-8232
The American Journal of Psychiatry	ajp.psychiatryonline.org	1400 K St., NW, Ste. 1101, Washington, DC 20005 E-mail: order@appi.org Phone: 202-682-6020; Fax: 202-789-2648
The American Journal of Psychoanalysis	www.wkap.nl/journalhome.htm/0002-9548	233 Spring St., New York, NY 10013-1578 E-mail: kluwer@wkap.com and services@wkap.nl Phone: 212-620-8000; Fax: 212-463-0742
The American Journal of Psychology	www.press.uillinois.edu/journals/ajp.html	1325 S Oak St., Champaign, IL 61820-6903 Phone: 217-333-0950; Fax: 217-244-8082
The American Statistician	www.amstat.org/publications/tas	1429 Duke St., Alexandria, VA 22314-3415 E-mail: journals@amstat.org Phone: 703-684-1221 or 888-231-3473 (toll free); Fax: 703-684-2037
The Annals of the American Academy of Political and Social Science	www.asc.upenn.edu/aapss/annals.html	2455 Teller Rd., Thousand Oaks, CA 91320 E-mail: info@sagepub.com Phone: 805-499-0721; Fax: 805-499-0871
The Canadian Review of Sociology and Anthropology	artsandscience.concordia.ca/socanth/CSAA/crsae.htm	Concordia University, 1455 boul de Maisonneuve Ouest, Montreal, QC, H3G 1M8, Canada E-mail: csaa@vax2.concordia.ca Phone: 514-848-8780; Fax: 514-848-4539
The China Quarterly	www.uk.cambridge.org/journals/cqy	Edinburgh Bldg., Shaftesbury Rd., Cambridge, CB2 2RU, United Kingdom E-mail: information@cup.cam.ac.uk Phone: 44-1223-312393; Fax: 44-1223-315052

(continued)

Table 5.3   Continued

Title	URL	Editorial Address
The Counseling Psychologist	www.sagepub.com	2455 Teller Rd., Thousand Oaks, CA 91320 E-mail: info@sagepub.com Phone: 805-499-0721; Fax: 805-499-0871
The Criminologist	www.asc41.com	1314 Kinnear Rd., Columbus, OH 43212-1156 E-mail: asc41@compuserve.com Phone: 614-292-9207; Fax: 614-292-6767
The Economic History Review	www.blackwellpublishers.co.uk	108 Cowley Rd., Oxford, OX4 1JF, United Kingdom E-mail: jnlinfo@blackwellpublishers.co.uk Phone: 44-1865-791100; Fax: 44-1865-791347
The Economic Journal	www.res.org.uk/econ.html	108 Cowley Rd., Oxford, OX4 1JF, United Kingdom E-mail: jnlinfo@blackwellpublishers.co.uk Phone: 44-1865-791100; Fax: 44-1865-791347
The Futurist	www.wfs.org/futurist.htm	7910 Woodmont Avenue, Suite 450, Bethesda, MD 20814 E-mail: sechard@wfs.org Phone: 800-989-8274 or 301-656-8274; Fax: 301-951-0394
The Geographical Journal	www.rgs.org/category.php?page=8publgeo	1 Kensington Gore, London SW7 2AR, England, UK E-mail: infor@rgs.org Phone: +44 (0)20 7591 3025; Fax: +44 (0)20 7591 3021
The Geographical Magazine	www.rgs.org/category.php?page=8publgeo	1 Kensington Gore, London SW7 2AR, England, UK E-mail: infor@rgs.org Phone: +44 (0)20 7591 3025; Fax: +44 (0)20 7591 3021
The Gerontologist	gerontologist.gerontologyjournals.org	The Gerontological Society of America, 1030 15th Street, NW, Suite 250, Washington, DC 20005-1503 E-mail: geron@geron.org Phone: 202-842-1275; Fax: 202-842-1150
The International Journal of Social Psychiatry	www.ijsp.co.uk	The Maudsley Hospital, 101 Denmark Hill, London. SE5 8AZ, United Kingdom Tel: 0171 740 5095

Journal	Website	Contact
The Journal of Applied Behavioral Science	www.sagepub.com	2455 Teller Rd., Thousand Oaks, CA 91320 E-mail: info@sagepub.com Phone: 805-499-0721; Fax: 805-499-0871
The Journal of Child Psychology and Psychiatry and Allied Disciplines	uk.cambridge.org/journals/cpp	Cambridge University Press, Edinburgh Building, Shaftesbury Road, Cambridge CB2 2RU E-mail: directcustserve@cup.cam.ac.uk Phone: +44 (0)1223 312393; Fax: +44 (0)1223 315052
The Journal of Conflict Resolution	www.sagepub.com	2455 Teller Rd., Thousand Oaks, CA 91320 E-mail: info@sagepub.com Phone: 805-499-0721; Fax: 805-499-0871
The Journal of Criminal Law & Criminology	www.press.uillinois.edu/journals/jclc.html	1325 S Oak St., Champaign, IL 61820-6903 Phone: 217-333-0950; Fax: 217-244-8082
The Journal of Development Studies	www.frankcass.com/jnls/jds.htm	Frank Cass & Co. Ltd, Crown House, 47 Chase Side, Southgate, London N14 5BP, UK E-mail: editors@frankcass.com Phone: +44 (0)20 8920 2100; Fax: +44 (0)20 8447 8548
The Journal of General Psychology	www.heldref.org/html/body_gen.html	Heldref Publications, 1319 Eighteenth St., NW, Washington, DC 20036-1802 E-mail: subscribe@heldref.org Phone: 202-296-6267; Fax: 202-296-5149
The Journal of Genetic Psychology	www.heldref.org	Heldref Publications, 1319 Eighteenth St., NW, Washington, DC 20036-1802 E-mail: subscribe@heldref.org Phone: 202-296-6267; Fax: 202-296-5149
The Journal of Human Resources	www.ssc.wisc.edu/jhr/home.html	1930 Monroe St., 3rd floor, Madison, WI 53711-2059 E-mail: journals@uwpress.wisc.edu Phone: 608 263-0668; Fax: 608 263-1173
The Journal of Law & Economics	www.journals.uchicago.edu/JLE/home.html	University of Chicago Press, Journals Division, P.O. Box 37005, Chicago, IL 60637 E-mail: j-orders@press.uchicago.edu Phone: 773-753-3347; Fax: 773-753-0811
The Journal of Politics	www.utexas.edu/utpress/journals/jjop.html	Journals Division, University of Texas Press, P.O. Box 7819, Austin, TX 78713-7819E-mail: journals@uts.cc.utexas.edu Phone: 512-471-4531; Fax: 512-320-0668

(continued)

| Table 5.3 | Continued |

Title	URL	Editorial Address
The Journal of Sex Research	www.ssc.wisc.edu/sss/jsr.htm	Department of Sociology, 1180 Observatory Drive, University of Wisconsin, Madison, WI 53706-1393 E-mail: jsexrsch@ssc.wisc.edu Phone: 608-262-1276; Fax: 608-265-8664
The Journal of Social Issues	www.blackwellpublishers.co.uk/journals/JSI	108 Cowley Rd., Oxford, OX4 1JF, United Kingdom E-mail: jnlinfo@blackwellpublishers.co.uk Phone: 44-1865-791100; Fax: 44-1865-791347
The Journal of Social, Political and Economic Studies	www.mankind.org/ssartlst.mgi?mgiToken=48OKQG4242C2RBJ33M	PO Box 34070 Washington DC 20043 Phone: 202-371-2700; Fax: 202-371-1523
The Journal of Social Psychology	www.heldref.org/html/body_soc.html	Heldref Publications, 1319 Eighteenth St., NW, Washington, DC 20036-1802 E-mail: subscribe@heldref.org Phone: 202-296-6267; Fax: 202-296-5149
The Political Quarterly	www.yale.edu/ypq	P.O. Box 203245, New Haven, CT 06520
The Prison Journal	www.sagepub.com	2455 Teller Rd., Thousand Oaks, CA 91320 E-mail: info@sagepub.com Phone: 805-499-0721; Fax: 805-499-0871
The Professional Geographer	typhoon.sdsu.edu/PG/home.html	1710 Sixteenth St., NW, Washington, DC 20009-3198 E-mail: hbaker@aag.org Phone: 202-234-1450; Fax 202-234-2744
The Public Opinion Quarterly	www.journals.uchicago.edu/POQ/home.html	University of Chicago Press, Journals Division, P.O. Box 37005, Chicago, IL 60637 E-mail: j-orders@press.uchicago.edu Phone: 773-753-3347; Fax: 773-753-0811
The Quarterly Journal of Economics	mitpress.mit.edu/catalog/item/default.asp?type=4&tid=8	MIT Press, Five Cambridge Center, Cambridge, MA 02142-1493 E-mail: mitpress-order-inq@mit.edu Phone: 800-3560343; Fax: 617-625-6660
The Rand Journal of Economics	www.rje.org	1700 Main St., Santa Monica, CA 90401 E-mail: rje@rand.org Phone: 310-393-0411

Journal	Web address	Publisher/Contact
The Review of Economics and Statistics	mitpress.mit.edu/catalog/item/default.asp?sid=8EBD1CAA-2D78-4E10-87C8-DFAB1157D48C&ttype=4&tid=17	MIT Press, Five Cambridge Center, Cambridge, MA 02142-1493E-mail: mitpress-order-inq@mit.eduPhone: 800-3560343; Fax: 617-625-6660
The Review of Politics	www.nd.edu/~rop	P.O. Box B, Notre Dame, IN 46556-0762Phone: 219-631-6623; Fax: 219-631-3103
The Sociological Quarterly	www.uiowa.edu/~tsq	Department of Sociology, University of Iowa, Iowa City, IA 52242E-mail: tsq@uiowa.eduPhone: 319-335-3982; Fax: 319-335-2509
The Wilson Quarterly	wwics.si.edu/OUTREACH/WQ/QUARTERL.HTM	The Wilson Quarterly, P.O. Box 420406, Palm Coast, Fl. 32142-0406E-mail: WQsubs@palmcoastd.comPhone: 800-829-5108
Urban Affairs Review	www.sagepub.com	2455 Teller Rd., Thousand Oaks, CA 91320E-mail: info@sagepub.comE-mail: Phone: 805-499-0721; Fax: 805-499-0871
Urban Studies	www.tandf.co.uk/journals/carfax/00420980.html	11 New Fetter Ln., London, EC4P 4EE, United KingdomE-mail: info@taylorandfrancis.comPhone: 215-625-8900; Fax: 215-625-2940
Washington Quarterly	www.twq.com	MIT Press, Five Cambridge Center, Cambridge, MA 02142-1493E-mail: mitpress-order-inq@mit.eduPhone: 800-3560343; Fax: 617-625-6660
Women & Environments	www.utoronto.ca/iwsgs/we.mag	IWSGS, New College, University of Toronto, 40 Willcocks St., Toronto, M5S 1C6, Ontario, CanadaE-mail: we.mag@utoronto.caPhone: 416-978-5259; Fax: 416-946-5561
Women & Politics	www.american.edu/wandp	Women & Politics Institute, School of Public Affairs, American University, 4400 Massachusetts Ave. NW, Washington, DC 20016 E-mail: wandp@american.edu Phone: 202-885-2903; Fax: 202-885-2967
Women's Studies Quarterly	www.rit.edu/~wsqwww	The Feminist Press at CUNY, City College/CUNY, The Graduate Center, 365 Fifth Ave., New York, NY 10016 E-mail: jnzgsl@rit.edu Phone: 212-817-1593; Fax: 212-817-1593
Working USA	www.mesharpe.com/usa_main.htm	80 Business Park Dr., Armonk, NY 10504 E-mail: mesinfo@usa.net Phone: 914-273-1800; Fax: 914-273-2106

(continued)

Table 5.3 Continued

Title	URL	Editorial Address
World Policy Journal	www.worldpolicy.org/journal	66 Fifth Ave., 9th Fl., New York, NY 10011 Phone: 212-229-5808; Fax: 212-807-1153
World Watch	www.worldwatch.org/mag	1776 Massachusetts Ave., NW, Washington, DC 20036-1904 E-mail: worldwatch@worldwatch.org and wwpub@worldwatch.org Phone: 202-452-1999; Fax: 202-296-7365
Youth & Society	www.sagepub.com	2455 Teller Rd., Thousand Oaks, CA 91320 E-mail: info@sagepub.com Phone: 805-499-0721; Fax: 805-499-0871

NOTE: Information about other journals can be found in Ulrich's Periodicals Directory (www.bowker.com/bowkerweb/catalog2001/prod00047.htm) and at www.publist.com, among other library resources.

5.2.2 *Social Sciences Citation Index (SSCI)*

SSCI is a calendar-year index begun in 1956 that continues currently and provides access to current and past bibliographic information, author abstracts, and references found in more than 1,700 scholarly social sciences journals covering more than 50 disciplines. Items from more than 5,700 science and technology journals are also included. *SSCI* is available in several different formats including Internet and intranet via the ISI Web of Science, which has weekly updates from 1956 to the present; a CD-ROM including author abstracts that is updated monthly and is available to 1992; and online via Social SciSearch, which has weekly updates from 1972 to the present.

Perhaps the most useful feature of *SSCI* is the cited reference searching, which allows you to search for articles that cite particular sources. For example, if you know of a particular author, you can search on that author's name and see what publications he or she is cited in. This is a perfect way to construct a bibliography around a particular scholar's work.

SSCI is available both in print and in various forms electronically and is published by ISI, 3501 Market Street, Philadelphia, PA 19104 USA, (800) 336-4474 or 215-386-0100, e-mail: sales@isinet.com.

The substantive areas covered by *SSCI* are anthropology, area studies, business, communication, criminology and penology, demography, economics, education and educational research, environmental studies, ergonomics, ethnic studies, family studies, geography, geriatrics and gerontology, health policy and services, history and philosophy of science, history of social sciences, industrial relations and labor, information science and library science, international relations, language and linguistics, law, management, medicine, law, nursing, philosophy, planning and development, political science, psychiatry, psychology (applied biological, clinical, developmental, educational, experimental, mathematics, psychoanalysis, and social), public administration, public environmental and occupational rehabilitation, social issues, social sciences (biomedical), social sciences (interdisciplinary), social sciences (mathematical, methods), social work, sociology, special education, substance abuse, transportation, urban studies, and women's studies.

5.2.2.1 *Searching Using SSCI*

Using *SSCI* is a relatively simple affair. In a citation index, the subject of a search is represented by the beginning of the reference rather than by a word or subject heading. Consequently, searching is independent of special nomenclatures or artificial languages. The searcher starts with a reference or an author he or she has identified through a footnote, book, encyclopedia, or conventional word or subject index. He or she then searches for the particular author's name. After locating the author's name, the searcher checks to see which of several possible references best fits his or her particular interest. Under the year, journal, volume, and page number of the selected reference, the searcher then looks to see who has currently cited this work. After noting the bibliographic citation of authors citing the work, the searcher then turns to the Source Index section and obtains complete bibliographic data for the works found.

The fundamental question one can answer quickly through the *SSCI* is, "Where and by whom has this paper been cited in the literature?" The *SSCI* is also used by scientists to determine whether their work has been applied or criticized by others. It can facilitate feedback in the communication cycle. Any author may choose to ignore citations to his or her own work and still use the index to retrieve publications that cite works by other social scientists. The *SSCI* can be used to identify researchers currently working on special problems or to determine whether a paper has been cited, whether there has been a review of a subject, or whether a concept has been applied, a theory confirmed, or a method improved. Because indications of corrections are published in the *SSCI*, it is also useful as an aid in following particular articles. Only the user's imagination limits the extent to which the *SSCI* can be useful for the scientist and librarian. Among the many questions that the user of *SSCI* can answer are these:

- Has this paper been cited?
- Has there been a review on this subject?
- Has this theory been confirmed?
- Has this work been extended?
- Has this method been improved?
- Has this suggestion been tried?
- Is this idea really original?
- Was this "to be published" paper published, and where?
- Where is the full paper for this preliminary communication?
- Has this technical report been published in a journal?
- Have subsequent errata and correction notes been published?
- Where are the data for an introduction to this paper?
- Where are the raw data for a review article on this subject?
- Is there sufficient new information to warrant updating a chapter in a book?
- What are the raw data for an analytical historical network diagram?
- Who else is working in this field?
- Are there data to delineate this field of study?
- What are some potential new markets for this product?
- Has this theory or concept been applied to a new field?
- What published work originated from this organization?
- Has this article been abstracted in primary journals?
- What are all the current works in which this person is primary author?
- What are all the current works in which this person is secondary author?
- What other works has this person written?
- Has this person's work been compiled?

5.2.3 *Current Index to Journals in Education (CIJE)*

The *CIJE* Source Journal Database (at www.oryxpress.com/cije.htm) is published by the Oryx Press and is a monthly guide to current periodical literature in education, covering articles published in approximately 980 major educational and education-related journals. *CIJE* is sponsored by the Educational Resources Information Center (ERIC), which is administered by the U.S. Department of Education, National Library of Education, Office of Educational Research and Improvement (OERI), 400 Maryland Ave, SW, Washington, DC 20202, (800) 424-1616.

5.2.4 *Population Index*

Population Index (http://popindex.princeton.edu/) has been published since 1935 and is the primary reference tool for the world's population literature. It presents an annotated bibliography of recently published books, journal articles, working papers, and other materials on population topics. It covers the bibliography of demographic research for demographers, and the online version contains 46,035 abstracts of demographic literature published in *Population Index* in the period 1986-1999. As of this writing, there is no longer a print version available. Along with the approximately 400 journals surveyed on a regular basis, many other periodicals covering biological, geographical, economic, and sociological literature are reviewed by scanning the principal bibliographic journals for each discipline, including *Biological Abstracts, Current Contents: Social and Behavioral Sciences, Current Geographical Publications, Geographical Abstracts: Human Geography, Journal of Economic Literature, PAIS International in Print*, and *Sociological Abstracts*.

The bibliography is arranged by subject. Citations appear only once and are classified according to the guidelines described in the headnotes to each section. Citations are arranged alphabetically by first author under the appropriate subject headings. Cross-references are provided by subject; the relevant citation numbers are listed at the end of each subject section following the phrase "[See also titles . . .]." Appropriate geographical and author indexes are published with each issue and cumulatively for each annual volume. In addition, cumulative indexes have been published by G. K. Hall & Co. of Boston for the years 1935-1968 and 1969-1981.

5.2.5 *Sociological Abstracts*

Sociological Abstracts is a print and online product published by Cambridge Scientific Abstracts (www.csa.com/), 7200 Wisconsin Avenue, Suite 601, Bethesda, MD 20814, (301) 961-6700. The CD-ROM product is available from Silver Platter (www.silverplatter.com/). It is published monthly, with approximately 2,500 new records added each month, and contained more than 500,000 records as of June 1999.

Sociological Abstracts describes research articles published in 20 major information areas (from 1963 through the present) including anthropology, business, collective behavior, community development, disaster studies, education, environmental studies, gender studies, gerontology, law and penology, marriage and family studies, medicine and health, racial interactions, social psychology, social work, sociological theory, stratification, substance abuse, urban studies, and violence.

For each abstract, information on the following fields (by code) is available as well.

Field Code	*Contents*
AB	Abstract
IS	ISSN
AF	Author Affiliation
LA	Language
AN	Accession Number
LC	Library of Congress Control Number
AU	Author
NT	Notes
CD	CODEN
TO	Original Title
CL	Classification
PB	Publisher
CP	Country of Publication
PT	Publication Type
DE	Descriptors
PY	Publication Year
IB	ISBN
SO	Source
ID	Identifiers
IT	Title

Sociological Abstracts is fundamental for interdisciplinary research in social science issues and for practitioners seeking the sociological perspective on various disciplines. *Sociological Abstracts* also contains book, chapter, and association paper abstracts, as well as book, film, and software review citations.

If copies of association papers presented at sociological conferences are available from *Sociological Abstracts*, that is indicated in the Note field of each abstract. For additional information, contact *Sociological Abstracts*, LLC at P.O. Box 22206, San Diego, CA 92192-0206, (800) 752-3945 or at info@mail.socabs.com. *Sociological Abstracts* is also indexed by subject and by author. A cumulative index for each volume is published as the last (eighth) issue of the year and includes a table of contents, a subject index, a periodical index, a monograph index, an author index, and a list of abbreviations.

Sociofile on CD-ROM includes citations and abstracts from more than 1,800 periodicals in sociology and related fields from 1974 on. It includes abstracts of journal articles published in *Sociological Abstracts* since 1974 and the enhanced bibliographic citations for relevant dissertations added since 1986. The *Social Planning Policy and Development Abstracts* database is included, with detailed journal article abstracts since 1980.

5.2.6 *Psychological Abstracts*

Psychological Abstracts (at www.apa.org/psycinfo/products/psycabs.html) is published by the American Psychological Association and does for psychology what *Sociological Abstracts* does for the wider field of social science.

Social scientists often work in similar areas, so the sociological researcher is as likely to find as much information in a related set of abstracts as in one from his or her own discipline. Also, because abstracting services tend to operate independently, there may be a certain degree of overlap, as well as a certain degree of independence between what references cite results in any one search. *Psychological Abstracts* is produced monthly and contains summaries (abstracts, bibliographic information, and indexing) of English-language journal articles, technical reports, book chapters, and books in the field of psychology. *Psychological Abstracts* contains 21 major content classifications (and their subclassifications) as follows. The organization code is shown for each area as well.

2100 General Psychology
2140 History & Systems
2200 Psychometrics & Statistics & Methodology
    2220 Tests & Testing
    2221 Sensory & Motor Testing
    2222 Developmental Scales & Schedules
    2223 Personality Scales & Inventories
    2224 Clinical Psychological Testing
    2225 Neuropsychological Assessment
    2226 Health Psychology Testing
    2227 Educational Measurement
    2228 Occupational & Employment Testing
    2229 Consumer Opinion & Attitude Testing
    2240 Statistics & Mathematics
    2260 Research Methods & Experimental Design
2300 Human Experimental Psychology
    2320 Sensory Perception
    2323 Visual Perception

2326 Auditory & Speech Perception
2330 Motor Processes
2340 Cognitive Processes
2343 Learning & Memory
2346 Attention
2360 Motivation & Emotion
2380 Consciousness States
2390 Parapsychology
2400 Animal Experimental & Comparative Psychology
2420 Learning & Motivation
2440 Social & Instinctive Behavior
2500 Physiological Psychology & Neuroscience
2510 Genetics
2520 Neuropsychology & Neurology
2530 Electrophysiology
2540 Physiological Processes
2560 Psychophysiology
2580 Psychopharmacology
2600 Psychology & the Humanities
2610 Literature & Fine Arts
2630 Philosophy
2700 Communication Systems
2720 Linguistics & Language & Speech
2750 Mass Media Communications
2800 Developmental Psychology
2820 Cognitive & Perceptual Development
2840 Psychosocial & Personality Development
2860 Gerontology
2900 Social Processes & Social Issues
2910 Social Structure & Organization
2920 Religion
2930 Culture & Ethnology
2950 Marriage & Family
2953 Divorce & Remarriage
2956 Childrearing & Child Care
2960 Political Processes & Political Issues
2970 Sex Roles & Women's Issues
2980 Sexual Behavior & Sexual Orientation
2990 Drug & Alcohol Usage (Legal)
3000 Social Psychology
3020 Group & Interpersonal Processes
3040 Social Perception & Cognition
3100 Personality Psychology
3120 Personality Traits & Processes
3140 Personality Theory
3143 Psychoanalytic Theory
3200 Psychological & Physical Disorders
3210 Psychological Disorders
3211 Affective Disorders
3213 Schizophrenia & Psychotic States

3215 Neuroses & Anxiety Disorders
3217 Personality Disorders
3230 Behavior Disorders & Antisocial Behavior
3233 Substance Abuse & Addiction
3236 Criminal Behavior & Juvenile Delinquency
3250 Developmental Disorders & Autism
3253 Learning Disorders
3256 Mental Retardation
3260 Eating Disorders
3270 Speech & Language Disorders
3280 Environmental Toxins & Health
3290 Physical & Somatoform & Psychogenic Disorders
3291 Immunological Disorders
3293 Cancer
3295 Cardiovascular Disorders
3297 Neurological Disorders & Brain Damage
3299 Vision & Hearing & Sensory Disorders
3300 Health & Mental Health Treatment & Prevention
3310 Psychotherapy & Psychotherapeutic Counseling
3311 Cognitive Therapy
3312 Behavior Therapy & Behavior Modification
3313 Group & Family Therapy
3314 Interpersonal & Client Centered & Humanistic Therapy
3315 Psychoanalytic Therapy
3340 Clinical Psychopharmacology
3350 Specialized Interventions
3351 Clinical Hypnosis
3353 Self-Help Groups
3355 Lay & Paraprofessional & Pastoral Counseling
3357 Art & Music & Movement Therapy
3360 Health Psychology & Medicine
3361 Behavioral & Psychological Treatment of Physical Illness
3363 Medical Treatment of Physical Illness
3365 Promotion & Maintenance of Health & Wellness
3370 Health & Mental Health Services
3371 Outpatient Services
3373 Community & Social Services
3375 Home Care & Hospice
3377 Nursing Homes & Residential Care
3379 Inpatient & Hospital Services
3380 Rehabilitation
3383 Drug & Alcohol Rehabilitation
3384 Occupational & Vocational Rehabilitation
3385 Speech & Language Therapy
3386 Criminal Rehabilitation & Penology
3400 Professional Psychological & Health Personnel Issues
3410 Professional Education & Training
3430 Professional Personnel Attitudes & Characteristics
3450 Professional Ethics & Standards & Liability
3470 Impaired Professionals

3500 Educational Psychology
    3510 Educational Administration & Personnel
    3530 Curriculum & Programs & Teaching Methods
    3550 Academic Learning & Achievement
    3560 Classroom Dynamics & Student Adjustment & Attitudes
    3570 Special & Remedial Education
    3575 Gifted & Talented
    3580 Educational/Vocational Counseling & Student Services
3600 Industrial & Organizational Psychology
    3610 Occupational Interests & Guidance
    3620 Personnel Management & Selection & Training
    3630 Personnel Evaluation & Job Performance
    3640 Management & Management Training
    3650 Personnel Attitudes & Job Satisfaction
    3660 Organizational Behavior
    3670 Working Conditions & Industrial Safety
3700 Sport Psychology & Leisure
    3720 Sports
    3740 Recreation & Leisure
3800 Military Psychology
3900 Consumer Psychology
    3920 Consumer Attitudes & Behavior
    3940 Marketing & Advertising
4000 Engineering & Environmental Psychology
    4010 Human Factors Engineering
    4030 Lifespace & Institutional Design
    4050 Community & Environmental Planning
    4070 Environmental Issues & Attitudes
    4090 Transportation
4100 Intelligent Systems
    4120 Artificial Intelligence & Expert Systems
    4140 Robotics
    4160 Neural Networks
4200 Forensic Psychology & Legal Issues
    4210 Civil Rights & Civil Law
    4230 Criminal Law & Criminal Adjudication
    4250 Mediation & Conflict Resolution
    4270 Crime Prevention
    4290 Police & Legal Personnel

5.2.7 PsycINFO

PsycINFO (at www.apa.org/psycinfo/about/) is the electronic version of *Psychological Abstracts* and covers 1,646 journals. It covers the same major areas as does *Psychological Abstracts* (the corresponding print version) and contains more than 1,000,000 records.

5.2.8 *Current Contents in the Social Behavioral Sciences*

Current Contents is published by the Institute for Scientific Information at ISI, 3501 Market Street, Philadelphia, PA 19104 USA, (800) 336-4474 or 215-386-0100, e-mail: sales@isinet.com. It is a source of complete bibliographic information from articles, editorials, meeting abstracts, commentaries, and all other items recently published in editions of more than 1,620 journals in the social and behavioral sciences. The list of journals in the social and behavioral sciences is available starting at the home page at http://sunweb.isinet.com.

Current Contents is available in several formats (all described in links from www.isinet.com/isi/products), including

- Internet and intranet via Current Contents Connect®
- Diskette and FTP via Current Contents Desktop™ and Current Contents on Diskette®, and
- Distribution partners via CC Search® at www.isinet.com/isi/products/cc/formats/ccsearch

5.2.9 *Annual Review of Sociology*

Annual Review of Sociology, published by Annual Reviews at http://soc.annualreviews.org/ and 4139 El Camino Way, P.O. Box 10139, Palo Alto, CA, 94303-0139, USA (800-523-8635 or 650-493-4400), publishes annual reviews in many different social and biomedical fields, with each volume consisting of invited chapters from noted authorities in the field. All the volumes from 1984 through 2000 are available online in various forms. The full text of each chapter is available from 1996 through 2000; before 1996, only the tables of contents are available. The publisher will send the following information electronically at no charge:

- Notification that a new issue of AR Sociology is online
- Complete table of contents for new or future issues
- Special announcements from Annual Reviews

The authors and titles of articles for the *Annual Review of Sociology* for the years 1996 through 2001 are as follows.

1996

"Steady Work: An Academic Memoir" by Seymour Martin Lipset

"Talking Back to Sociology: Distinctive Contributions of Feminist Methodology" by Marjorie L. DeVault

"Gender in the Welfare State" by Ann Orloff

"Adult Child-Parent Relationships" by Diane N. Lye

"Mass Media Effects on Violent Behavior" by Richard B. Felson

"Focus Groups" by David L. Morgan

"Gender Inequality and Higher Education" by Jerry A. Jacobs

"Law and Inequality: Race, Gender . . . and, of Course, Class" by Carroll Seron and Frank Munger

"Computer Networks as Social Networks: Collaborative Work, Telework, and Virtual Community" by Barry Wellman, Janet Salaff, Dimitrina Dimitrova, Laura Garton, Milena Gulia, and Caroline Haythornthwaite

"Comparative Medical Systems" by David Mechanic and David A. Rochefort

"What Do Interlocks Do? An Analysis, Critique, and Assessment of Research on Interlocking Directorates" by Mark S. Mizruchi

"The Division of Household Labor" by Beth Anne Shelton and Daphne John

"Cultural and Social-Structural Explanations of Cross-National Psychological Differences" by Carmi Schooler

"An Introduction to Categorical Data Analysis" by Douglas Sloane and S. Philip Morgan

"Innovations in Experimental Design I. Attitude Surveys" by Paul M. Sniderman and Douglas B. Grob

"Market Transition and Societal Transformation in Reforming State Socialism" by Victor Nee and Rebecca Matthews

"From Marxism to Postcommunism: Socialism Desires and East European Rejections" by Michael D. Kennedy and Naomi Galtz

"Gender and Crime: Toward a Gendered Theory of Female Offending" by Darrell Steffensmeier and Emilie Allan

1997

"On the Virtues of the Old Institutionalism" by Arthur L. Stinchcombe

"The Savings and Loan Debacle, Financial Crime, and the States" by K. Calavita, R. Tillman, and H. N. Pontell

"Modeling the Relationships Between Macro Forms of Social Control" by Allen E Liska

"Growing up American: The Challenge Confronting Immigrant Children and Children of Immigrants" by Min Zhou

"Feminist Theory and Sociology: Underutilized Contributions for Mainstream Theory" by Janet Saltzman Chafetz

"Poverty and Inequality Among Children" by Daniel T. Lichter

"The First Injustice: Socioeconomic Disparities, Health Services Technology, and Infant Mortality" by Steven L. Gortmaker and Paul H. Wise

"Sociological Perspectives on Medical Ethics and Decision-Making" by Robert Zussman

"Sociological Rational Choice Theory" by Michael Hechter and Satoshi Kanazawa

"The Changing Organizational Context of Professional Work" by Kevin T. Leicht and Mary L. Fennell

"The Measurement of Age, Age Structuring, and the Life Course" by Richard A. Settersten, Jr., and Karl Ulrich Mayer

"Culture and Cognition" by Paul Dimaggio

"The Family Responsive Workplace" by Jennifer L. Glass and Sarah Beth Estes

"New Forms of Work Organization" by Vicki Smith

"Sociology of Markets" by John Lie

"Politics and Culture: A Less Fissured Terrain" by Mabel Berezin

"Identity Construction: New Issues, New Directions" by Karen A. Cerulo

"New Social Movements: A Critical Review" by Nels A. Pichardo

"Women's Employment and the Gain to Marriage: The Specialization and Trading Model" by Valerie Kincade Oppenheimer

"People's Accounts Count: The Sociology of Accounts" by Terri L. Orbuch

"The Legal Environments of Organizations" by Lauren B. Edelman and Mark C. Suchman

1998

"Social Capital: Its Origins and Applications in Modern Sociology" by Alejandro Portes

"Fundamentalism et al: Conservative Protestants in America" by Robert D. Woodberry and Christian S. Smith

"Network Forms of Organization" by Joel M. Podolny and Karen L. Page

"Reactions Toward the New Minorities of Western Europe" by Thomas F. Pettigrew

"Social Memory Studies: From 'Collective Memory' to the Historical Sociology of Mnemonic Practices" by Jeffrey K. Olick and Joyce Robbins

"Computerization of the Workplace" by Beverly H. Burris

"Globalization and Democracy" by Kathleen C. Schwartzman

"Social Dilemmas: The Anatomy of Cooperation" by Peter Kollock

"Breakdown Theories of Collective Action" by Bert Useem

"Warmer and More Social: Recent Developments in Cognitive Social Psychology" by Norbert Schwarz

"Diffusion in Organizations and Social Movements: From Hybrid Corn to Poison Pills" by David Strang and Sarah A. Soule

"Alcohol, Drugs, and Violence" by Robert Nash Parker and Kathleen Auerhahn

"Commensuration as a Social Process" by Wendy Nelson Espel and Mitchell L. Stevens

"Measuring Meaning Structures" by John W. Mohr

"Was It Worth the Effort? The Outcomes and Consequences of Social Movements" by Marco G. Giugni

"Intermarriage and Homogamy: Causes, Patterns, Trends" by Matthijs Kalmijn

"Ethnic and Nationalist Violence" by Rogers Brubaker and David D. Laitin

"Contemporary Developments in Sociological Theory: Current Projects and Conditions of Possibility" by Charles Camic and Neil Gross

"Using Computers to Analyze Ethnographic Field Data: Theoretical and Practical Considerations" by Daniel Dohan and Martín Sánchez-Jankowski

"Sociological Work in Japan" by Keiko Nakao

"Narrative Analysis—Or Why (and How) Sociologists Should Be Interested in Narrative" by Roberto Franzosi

1999

"Looking Back at 25 Years of Sociology and the *Annual Review of Sociology*" by Neil J. Smelser

"The Sociology of Entrepreneurship" by Patricia H. Thornton

"Women's Movements in the Third World: Identity, Mobilization, and Autonomy" by R. Ray and A. C. Korteweg

"Sexuality in the Workplace: Organizational Control, Sexual Harassment, and the Pursuit of Pleasure" by Christine L. Williams, Patti A. Giuffre, and Kirsten Dellinger

"What Has Happened to the U.S. Labor Movement? Union Decline and Renewal" by Dan Clawson and Mary Ann Clawson

"Ownership Organization and Firm Performance" by David L. Kang and Aage B. Sørensen

"Declining Violent Crime Rates in the 1990s: Predicting Crime Booms and Busts" by Gary LaFree

"Gender and Sexual Harassment" by Sandy Welsh

"The Gender System and Interaction" by Cecilia L. Ridgeway and Lynn Smith-Lovin

"Bringing Emotions into Social Exchange Theory" by Edward J. Lawler and Shane R. Thye

"Aphorisms and Clichés: The Generation and Dissipation of Conceptual Charisma" by Murray S. Davis

"The Dark Side of Organizations: Mistake, Misconduct, and Disaster" by Diane Vaughan

"Feminization and Juvenilization of Poverty: Trends, Relative Risks, Causes, and Consequences" by Suzanne M. Bianchi

"The Determinants and Consequences of Workplace Sex and Race Composition" by Barbara F. Reskin, Debra B. McBrier, and Julie A. Kmec

"Recent Developments and Current Controversies in the Sociology of Religion" by Darren E. Sherkat and Christopher G. Ellison

"Cultural Criminology" by Jeff Ferrell

"Is South Africa Different? Sociological Comparisons and Theoretical Contributions From the Land of Apartheid" by Gay Seidman

"Politics and Institutionalism: Explaining Durability and Change" by Elisabeth S. Clemens and James M. Cook

"Social Networks and Status Attainment" by Nan Lin

"Socioeconomic Position and Health: The Independent Contribution of Community Socioeconomic Context" by Stephanie A. Robert

"A Retrospective on the Civil Rights Movement: Political and Intellectual Landmarks" by Aldon D. Morris

"Artistic Labor Markets and Careers" by Pierre-Michel Menger

"Perspectives on Technology and Work Organization" by Jeffrey K. Liker, Carol J. Haddad, and Jennifer Karlin

"Organizational Innovation and Organizational Change" by J. T. Hage

"Inequality in Earnings at the Close of the Twentieth Century" by Martina Morris and Bruce Western

"The Estimation of Causal Effects From Observational Data" by Christopher Winship and Stephen L. Morgan

2000

"Cohabitation in the United States: An Appraisal of Research Themes, Findings, and Implications" by Pamela J. Smock

"Double Standards for Competence: Theory and Research" by Martha Foschi

"The Changing Nature of Death Penalty Debates" by Michael L. Radelet and Marian J. Borg

"Wealth Inequality in the United States" by Lisa A. Keister and Stephanie Moller

"Crime and Demography: Multiple Linkages, Reciprocal Relations" by Scott J. South and Steven F. Messner

"Ethnicity and Sexuality" by Joane Nagel

"Prejudice, Politics, and Public Opinion: Understanding the Sources of Racial Policy Attitudes" by Maria Krysan

"Race and Race Theory" by Howard Winant

"States and Markets in an Era of Globalization" by Sen Ó Riain

"Volunteering" by John Wilson

"How Welfare Reform Is Affecting Women's Work" by Mary Corcoran, Sandra K. Danziger, Ariel Kalil, and Kristin S. Seefeld

"Fertility and Women's Employment in Industrialized Nations" by Karin L. Brewster and Ronald R. Rindfuss

"Political Sociological Models of the U.S. New Deal" by Jeff Manza

"The Trend in Between-Nation Income Inequality" by Glenn Firebaugh

"Nonstandard Employment Relations: Part-time, Temporary and Contract Work" by Arne L. Kalleberg

"Social Psychology of Identities" by Judith A. Howard

"Schools and Communities: Ecological and Institutional Dimensions" by Richard Arum

"Racial and Ethnic Variations in Gender-Related Attitudes" by Emily W. Kane

"Multilevel Modeling for Binary Data" by Guang Guo and Hongxin Zhao

"A Space for Place in Sociology" by Thomas F. Gieryn

"Wealth and Stratification Processes" by Seymour Spilerman

"The Choice-Within-Constraints New Institutionalism and Implications for Sociology" by Paul Ingram and Karen Clay

"Poverty Research and Policy for the Post-Welfare Era" by Alice O'Connor

"Closing the 'Great Divide': New Social Theory on Society and Nature" by Michael Goldman and Rachel A. Schurman

"Socialism and the Transition in East and Central Europe: The Homogeneity Paradigm, Class, and Economic Inefficiency" by Linda Fuller

"Framing Processes and Social Movements: An Overview and Assessment" by Robert D. Benford and David A. Snow

"Feminist State Theory: Applications to Jurisprudence, Criminology, and the Welfare State" by Lynne A. Haney

"Pathways to Adulthood in Changing Societies: Variability and Mechanisms in Life Course Perspective" by Michael J. Shanahan

"A Sociology for the Second Great Transformation?" by Michael Burawoy

"Agenda for Sociology at the Start of the Twenty-First Century" by Michael Hechter

"What I Don't Know About My Field But Wish I Did" by Douglas S. Massey

"Family, State, and Child Well-Being" by Sara McLanahan

"Getting It Right: Sex and Race Inequality in World Organizations" by Barbara F. Reskin

"Whither the Sociological Study of Crime?" by Robert J. Sampson

"On Granularity" by Emanuel Schegloff

"How Do Relations Store Histories?" by Charles Tilly

2001

"Violence and the Life Course: The Consequences of Victimization for Personal and Social Development" by Ross Macmillan

"Urban Poverty After *The Truly Disadvantaged*: The Rediscovery of the Family, the Neighborhood, and Culture" by Mario Luis Small and Katherine Newman

"Cases and Biographies: An Essay on Routinization and the Nature of Comparison" by Carol A. Heimer

"Education and Stratification in Developing Countries: A Review of Theories and Research" by Claudia Buchmann and Emily Hannum

"The Great Agricultural Transition: Crisis, Change, and Social Consequences of Twentieth Century U.S. Farming" by Linda Lobao and Katherine Meyer

"Religious Nationalism and the Problem of Collective Representation" by Roger Friedland

"Socioeconomic Status and Class in Studies of Fertility and Health in Developing Countries" by Kenneth A. Bollen, Jennifer L. Glanville, and Guy Stecklov

"Sport and Society" by Robert E. Washington and David Kare

"U.S. Social Policy in Comparative and Historical Perspective: Concepts, Images, Arguments, and Research Strategies" by Edwin Amenta, Chris Bonastia, and Neal Caren

"Is Globalization Civilizing, Destructive or Feeble? A Critique of Five Key Debates in the Social Science Literature" by Mauro F. Guillén

"Religious Pluralism and Religious Participation" by Mark Chaves and Philip S. Gorski

"Collective Identity and Social Movements" by Francesca Polletta and James M. Jasper

"Social Implications of the Internet" by Paul DiMaggio, Eszter Hargittai, W. Russell Neuman, and John P. Robinson

"The Scale of Justice: Observations on the Transformation of Urban Law Practice" by John P. Heinz, Robert L. Nelson, and Edward O. Laumann

"Conceptualizing Stigma" by Bruce G. Link and Jo C. Phelan

"Sociological Miniaturism: Seeing the Big Through the Small in Social Psychology" by John F. Stolte, Gary Alan Fine, and Karen S. Cook

"Birds of a Feather: Homophily in Social Networks" by Miller McPherson, Lynn Smith-Lovin, and James M. Cook

"Early Traditions of African-American Sociological Thought" by Alford A. Young, Jr., and Donald R. Deskins, Jr.

"Hate Crime: An Emergent Research Agenda" by Donald P. Green, Laurence H. McFalls, and Jennifer K. Smith

5.2.10 *American Sociological Review*

The *American Sociological Review* is published by the American Sociological Association at www.asanet.org and 1307 New York Avenue, NW, Suite 700, Washington, DC 20005-4701, (202) 383-9005. It contains works of interest to the discipline in general, new theoretical developments, results of research that advance understanding of fundamental social processes, and important methodological innovations. JSTOR (at www.jstor.org/journals/00031224.html) has the issues from 1936 to 1995 available online.

The authors and titles of articles for the *American Sociological Review* for the years 1996 through 2000 are as follows.

1995

"Hiroshima, the Holocaust, and the Politics of Exclusion: 1994 Presidential Address" by William A. Gamson

"Spousal Alternatives and Marital Dissolution" by Scott J. South and Kim M. Lloyd

"Gender and Family Businesses in Rural China" by Barbara Entwisle, Gail E. Henderson, Susan E. Short, Jill Bouma, and Zhai Fengying

"Changes in Gender Role Attitudes and Perceived Marital Quality" by Paul R. Amato and Alan Booth

"Policy Alternatives and Political Change: Work, Family, and Gender on the Congressional Agenda, 1945-1990" by Paul Burstein, R. Marie Bricher, and Rachel L. Einwohner

"Religious Participation in Early Adulthood: Age and Family Life Cycle Effects on Church Membership" by Ross M. Stolzenberg, Mary Blair-Loy, and Linda J. Waite

"The Epidemiology of Social Stress" by R. Jay Turner, Blair Wheaton, and Donald A. Lloyd

"Education, Social Liberalism, and Economic Conservatism: Attitudes Toward Homeless People" by Jo Phelan, Bruce G. Link, Ann Stueve, and Robert E. Moore

"Global Self-Esteem and Specific Self-Esteem: Different Concepts, Different Outcomes" by Morris Rosenberg, Carmi Schooler, Carrie Schoenbach, and Florence Rosenberg

"Class and Class Conflict in Six Western Nations" by Jonathan Kelley and M. D. R. Evans

"A Comparative Study of Working-Class Disorganization: Union Decline in Eighteen Advanced Capitalist Countries" by Bruce Western

"Friendship Among the French Financial Elite" by Charles Kadushin

"Education and the Dual Labor Market for Japanese Men" by Arthur Sakamoto and Daniel A. Powers

"An Extension of the Sorensen-Kalleberg Theory of the Labor Market Matching and Attainment Processes" by Scott R. Eliason

"The Stopping and Spacing of Childbirths and Their Birth-History Predictors: Rational-Choice Theory and Event-History Analysis" by Kazuo Yamaguchi and Linda R. Ferguson

"The Spatial Diffusion of Fertility: A Cross-Sectional Analysis of Counties in the American South, 1940" by Stewart E. Tolnay

"Career Mobility and the Communist Political Order" by Andrew G. Walder

"The Programmatic Emergence of the Social Security State" by Alexander Hicks, Joya Misra, and Tang Nah Ng

"Unemployment and the Incarceration of Pretrial Defendants" by Stewart J. D'Alessio and Lisa Stolzenberg

"The Individualist Polity and the Prevalence of Professionalized Psychology: A Cross-National Study" by David John Frank, John W. Meyer, and David Miyahara

"Engendering the Worlds of Labor: Women Workers, Labor Markets, and Production Politics in the South China Economic Miracle" by Ching Kwan Lee

"The Persistence of Gender Inequality in Earnings in the German Democratic Republic" by Annemette Sorensen and Heike Trappe

"The Gender Gap in Workplace Authority: A Cross-National Study" by Erik Olin Wright, Janeen Baxter, and Gunn Elisabeth Birkelund

"Gender and Values" by Ann M. Beutel and Margaret Mooney Marini

"Sex Differences in Distress: Real or Artifact?" by John Mirowsky and Catherine E. Ross

"The Friendly and Predatory Acquisition of Large U.S. Corporations in the 1960s: The Other Contested Terrain" by Donald Palmer, Brad M. Barber, Xueguang Zhou, and Yasemin Soysal

"Networks of Power or the Finance Conception of Control? Comment on Palmer, Barber, Zhou, and Soysal" by Neil Fligstein

"The Finance Conception of Control—'The Theory That Ate New York?' Reply to Fligstein" by Donald Palmer, Brad M. Barber, and Xueguang Zhou

"Organizational Evolution in a Multinational Context: Entries of Automobile Manufacturers in Belgium, Britain, France, Germany, and Italy" by Michael T. Hannan, Glenn R. Carroll, Elizabeth A. Dundon, and John Charles Torres

"Cultivating an Institutional Ecology of Organizations: Comment on Hannan, Carroll, Dundon, and Torres" by Joel A. C. Baum and Walter W. Powell

"Theory Building and Cheap Talk About Legitimation: Reply to Baum and Powell" by Michael T. Hannan and Glenn R. Carroll

"Habermas, Goffman, and Communicative Action: Implications for Professional Practice" by James J. Chriss

"The Question of Caste in Modern Society: Durkheim's Contradictory Theories of Race, Class, and Sex" by Jennifer M. Lehmann

"Prejudice as a Response to Perceived Group Threat: Population Composition and Anti-Immigrant and Racial Prejudice in Europe" by Lincoln Quillian

"The Institutional Environment: Implications for Race and Gender Inequality in the U.S. Labor Market" by John J. Beggs

"Interdependence and Reintegrative Social Control: Labeling and Reforming 'Inappropriate' Parents in Neonatal Intensive Care Units" by Carol A. Heimer and Lisa R. Staffen

"Criminal Careers in the Short-Term: Intra-Individual Variability in Crime and Its Relation to Local Life Circumstances" by Julie Horney, D. Wayne Osgood, and Ineke Haen Marshall

"Income Inequality, Development, and Dualism: Results From an Unbalanced Cross-National Panel" by Francois Nielsen and Arthur S. Alderson

"Democracy and Demographic Inheritance: The Influence of Modernity and Proto-Modernity on Political and Civil Rights, 1965 to 1980" by Edward M. Crenshaw

"The Links Between Education and Health" by Catherine E. Ross and Chia-ling Wu

"When Bigger Is Not Better: Family Size, Parental Resources, and Children's Educational Performance" by Douglas B. Downey

"The Influence of School Enrollment and Accumulation on Cohabitation and Marriage in Early Adulthood" by Arland Thornton, William G. Axinn, and Jay D. Teachman

Comments and Replies

"Making Gender Visible" by Barbara J. Risman and Myra Marx Ferree

"Rights and Interests: Raising the Next Generation" by James S. Coleman

"The Protestant Ethic and the Spirit of Bureaucracy" by Philip S. Gorski

"Rational Choice Versus Cultural Explanations of the Efficiency of the Prussian Tax System" by Edgar Kiser and Joachim Schneider

"Conceptualizing Regional Differences in Eighteenth-Century England" by Rosemary L. Hopcroft

"What's in a Name? Sociological Explanation and the Problem of Place" by Margaret R. Somers

"The Democratic Class Struggle in the United States, 1948-1992" by Michael Hout, Clem Brooks, and Jeff Manza

"Union Democracy, Radical Leadership, and the Hegemony of Capital" by Judith Stepan-Norris and Maurice Zeitlin

"The Political Economy of Business Failures Across the American States, 1970-1985: The Impact of Reagan's New Federalism" by Don Sherman Grant II

"The Structural Embeddedness of Business Decisions: The Migration of Manufacturing Plants in New York State, 1960 to 1985" by Frank P. Romo and Michael Schwartz

"Organizational Mortality in a Declining Social Movement: The Demise of Peace Movement Organizations in the End of the Cold War Era" by Bob Edwards and Sam Marullo

"Distinctive African American Names: An Experimental, Historical, and Linguistic Analysis of Innovation" by Stanley Lieberson and Kelly S. Mikelson

"American Indian Ethnic Renewal: Politics and the Resurgence of Identity" by Joane Nagel

"Economic Determinants of Democracy" by Edward N. Muller

"Income Inequality and Democratization Revisited: Comment on Muller" by Kenneth A. Bollen and Robert W. Jackman

"Income Inequality and Democratization: Reply to Bollen and Jackman" by Edward N. Muller

1996

"1995 Presidential Address: The Responsive Community: A Communitarian Perspective" by Amitai Etzioni

"Principals and Agents, Colonists and Company Men: The Decay of Colonial Control in the Dutch East Indies" by Julia Adams

"Do Private Schools Force Public Schools to Compete?" by Richard Arum

"Is Bigger Better? Explaining the Relationship Between Organization Size and Job Rewards" by Arne L. Kallenberg and Mark E. Van Buren

"Keiretsu Networks and Corporate Performance in Japan" by James R. Lincoln, Michael L. Gerlach, and Christina L. Ahmadijan

"Commitment in Exchange Relations: Test of a Theory of Relational Cohesion" by Edward J. Lawler and Jeongkoo Yoon

"On 'Realization' in Everyday Life: The Forecasting of Bad News as a Social Relation" by Douglas W. Maynard

"Concessions, Repression, and Political Protest in the Iranian Revolution" by Karen Rasler

"Structural Opportunity and Perceived Opportunity in Social-Movement Theory: The Iranian Revolution of 1979" by Charles Kurzman

Comments and Replies

"Comment: Entropy and Popular Culture: Product Diversity in the Popular Music Recording Industry" by Peter J. Alexander

"Reply: Measuring Industry Concentration, Diversity and Innovation in Popular Music" by Richard A. Peterson and David G. Berger

"Editor's Comment: The Editorial Transition Begins"

"Testing a Dynamic Model of Social Composition: Diversity and Change in Voluntary Groups" by J. Miller McPherson and Thomas Rotolo

"Mobilizing Local Religious Markets: Religious Pluralism in the Empire State, 1855 to 1865" by Roger Finke, Avery M. Guest, and Rodney Stark

"Self-Employment and Earnings of Immigrants" by Alejandro Portes and Min Zhou

"Immigrant Self-Employment: The Family as Social Capital and the Value of Human Capital" by Jimy M. Sanders and Victor Nee

"The Dynamics and Dilemmas of Collective Action" by Douglas D. Heckathorn

"Nucleus and Shield: The Evolution of Social Structure in the Iterated Prisoner's Dilemma" by Bjorn Lomborg

"Power in Networks of Substitutable and Complementary Exchange Relations: A Rational Choice Model and an Analysis of Power Centralization" by Kazuo Yamaguchi

Comments and Replies

"Comment: Cooperation Under Uncertainty: What Is New, What Is True, and What Is Important" by Jonathan Bendor, Roderick Kramer, and Piotr Swistak

"Comment: Cooperative Strategies in Low-Noise Environments" by Edward B. Reeves and Timothy C. Pitts

"Reply: The Logic and Practice of Generosity" by Peter Kollock

"Socioeconomic Achievement in the Life Course of Disadvantaged Men: Military Service as a Turning Point, Circa 1940-1965" by Robert J. Sampson and John H. Laub

"New Kid in Town: Social Capital and the Life Course Effects of Family Migration on Children" by John Hagan, Ross MacMillan, and Blair Wheaton

"Effects of Family Instability, Income, and Income Instability on the Risk of a Premarital Birth" by Lawrence L. Wu

"Life After Welfare: Women, Work, and Repeat Dependency" by Kathleen Mullan Harris

"Not for Widows Only: Institutional Policies and the Formative Years of Aid to Dependent Children" by Nancy K. Cauthen and Edwin Amenta

"Making Claims as Workers or Wives: The Distribution of Social Security Benefits" by Madonna Harrington Meyer

"Interests and Symbols in Post-Communist Political Culture: The Case of Hungary" by Szonja Szelenyi, Ivan Szelenyi, and Winifred R. Poster

"Images of Protest: Dimensions of Selection Bias in Media Coverage of Washington Demonstrations, 1982 and 1991" by John D. McCarthy, Clark McPhail, and Jackie Smith

"A Test of Durkheim's Theory of Suicide—Without Committing the 'Ecological Fallacy'" by Frans van Poppel and Lincoln H. Day

"The World System Paradigm as General Theory of Development: A Cross-National Test" by Ronan Van Rossem

"A Re-Evaluation of the Economic Consequences of Divorce" by Richard R. Peterson

"The Economic Consequences of Divorce Are Still Unequal: Comment on Peterson" by Lenore J. Weitzman

"Statistical Errors, Faulty Conclusions, Misguided Policy: Reply to Weitzman" by Richard R. Peterson

"Reconsidering the Declining Significance of Race: Racial Differences in Early Career Wages" by A. Silvia Cancio, T. David Evans, and David J. Maume, Jr.

"Appropriate Tests of Racial Wage Discrimination Require Controls for Cognitive Skill: Comment on Cancio, Evans, and Maume" by George Farkas and Keven Vicknair

"Cognitive Skills and Racial Wage Inequality: Reply to Farkas and Vicknair" by David J. Maume, Jr., A. Silvia Cancio, and T. David Evans

"Racial Economic Subordination and White Gain in the U.S. South" by Donald Tomaskovic-Devey and Vincent J. Roscigno

"Poverty, Segregation, and Race Riots: 1960-1993" by Susan Olzak, Suzanne Shanahan, and Elizabeth H. McEneaney

"The Effect of Changes in Interracial Income Inequality and Educational Attainment on Changes in Arrest Rates for African Americans and Whites, 1957 to 1990" by Gary LaFree and Kriss A. Drass

"Routine Activities and Individual Deviant Behavior" by D. Wayne Osgood, Janet K. Wilson, Patrick M. O'Malley, Jerald G. Bachman, and Lloyd D. Johnston

"Markets as Politics: A Political-Cultural Approach to Market Institutions" by Neil Fligstein

"The Sources and Consequences of Embeddedness for the Economic Performance of Organizations: The Network Effect" by Brian Uzzi

"Economic Behavior in Institutional Environments: The Corporate Merger Wave of the 1980s" by Linda Brewster Stearns and Kenneth D. Allan

"Dignity in the Workplace Under Participative Management: Alienation and Freedom Revisited" by Randy Hodson

"Market Transition and the Persistence of Power: The Changing Stratification System of Urban China" by Yanjie Bian and John R. Logan

"Homeboys, Babies, Men in Suits: The State of the Reproduction of Male Dominance" by Lynne Haney

"Using Racial and Ethnic Concepts: The Critical Case of the Very Young Children" by Debra Van Ausdale and Joe R. Feagin

"The Two Faces of Governance: Responses to Legal Uncertainty in U.S. Firms, 1955-1985" by John R. Sutton and Frank Dobbin

"Exploring the Limits of the New Institutionalism: The Causes and Consequences of Illegitimate Organizational Change" by Matthew S. Kraatz and Edward J. Zajac

"The Effect of Social Relationships on Psychological Well-Being: Are Men and Women So Different?" by Debra Umberson, Meichu D. Chen, James S. House, Kristine Hopkins, and Ellen Slaten

"An Interactive Model of Religiosity Inheritance: The Importance of Family Context" by Scott M. Myers

"Emotional Reactions and Status in Groups" by Michael J. Lovaglia and Jeffrey A. Houser

"'Anything But Heavy Metal': Symbolic Exclusion and Musical Dislikes" by Bethany Bryson

"Changing Highbrow Taste: From Snob to Omnivore" by Richard A. Peterson and Roger M. Kern

"Memory as a Cultural System: Abraham Lincoln in World War II" by Barry Schwartz

"Rethinking Stratification From a Feminist Perspective: Gender, Race, and Class in Mainstream Textbooks" by Myra Marx Ferree and Elaine J. Hall

"Perceptions of Racial Group Competition: Extending Blumer's Theory of Group Position to a Multiracial Social Context" by Lawrence Bobo and Vincent L. Hutchings

"The Impact of Protestant Fundamentalism on Educational Attainment" by Alfred Darnell and Darren E. Sherkat

"From Warre to Tyranny: Lethal Conflict and the State" by Mark Cooney

"Institutional Change and Job-Shift Patterns in Urban China, 1949 to 1994" by Xueguang Zhou, Nancy Brandon Tuma, and Phyllis Moen

"Bringing Strong Ties Back In: Indirect Ties, Network Bridges, and Job Searches in China" by Yanjie Bian

"Structural Change, Labor Market Turbulence, and Labor Market Outcomes" by Thomas A. DiPrete and K. Lynn Nonnemaker

"Prelates and Princes: Aristocratic Marriages, Canon Law Prohibitions, and Shifts in Norms and Patterns of Domination in the Central Middle Ages" by Ivan Ermakoff

"The Spread of Sharecropping in Tuscany: The Political Economy of Transaction Costs" by Rebecca Jean Emigh

"Culture and Conflict: The Portrayal of Blacks in U.S. Children's Picture Books Through the Mid- and Late-Twentieth Century" by Bernice A. Pescosolido, Elizabeth Grauerholz, and Melissa A. Milkie

"Rethinking Racism: Toward a Structural Interpretation" by Eduardo Bonilla-Silva

"Sociology's Asociological 'Core': An Examination of Textbook Sociology in Light of the Sociology of Scientific Knowledge" by Michael Lynch and David Bogen

"Tools for Intuition About Sample Selection Bias and Its Correction" by Ross M. Stolzenberg and Daniel A. Relles

"Gender, Children, and Social Contact: The Effects of Childrearing for Men and Women" by Allison Munch, Miller McPherson, and Lynn Smith-Lovin

"Living in Single-Parent Households: An Investigation of the Same-Sex Hypothesis" by Brian Powell and Douglas B. Downey

"Sexual Contact Between Children and Adults: A Life Course Perspective" by Christopher R. Browning and Edward O. Laumann

"Social Stratification Across Three Generations: New Evidence From the Wisconsin Longitudinal Study" by John Robert Warren and Robert M. Hauser

"Cultural and Educational Careers: The Dynamics of Social Reproduction" by Karen Aschaffenburg and Ineke Maas

"The Gender Gap in Earnings at Career Entry" by Margaret Mooney Marini and Pi-Ling Fan

"Are Young Black Men Really Less Willing to Work?" by Stephen M. Petterson

"Social Structure and Personality Under Conditions of Radical Social Change: A Comparative Analysis of Poland and Ukraine" by Melvin L. Kohn, Kazimierz M. Slomczynski, Krystyna Janicka, Valeri Khmelko, Bogdan W. Mach, Vladimir Paniotto, Wojciech Zaborowski, Roberto Gutierrez, and Cory Heyman

"National Context, Parental Socialization, and Religious Belief: Results From 15 Nations" by Jonathan Kelley and Nan Dirk De Graaf

"Labeling Mental Illness: The Effects of Received Services and Perceived Stigma on Life Satisfaction" by Sarah Rosenfield

"Resources and Relationships: Social Networks and Mobility in the Workplace" by Joel M. Podolny and James Baron

"Who Cares? Toward an Integrated Theory of Altruistic Behavior" by John Wilson and Marc Musick

"All Women Benefit in an Integrated Labor Market: The Macro-Level Effects of Occupational Gender Integration on Gender Earnings Equality" by Reeve Vanneman, David A. Cotter, JoAnn DeFiore, Joan M. Hermsen, and Brenda Marsteller Kowalewski

"The Changing Logic of Political Citizenship: Cross-National Acquisition of Women's Suffrage Rights 1890-1990" by Francisco Ramirez, Yasemin Soysal, and Suzanne Elise Shanahan

"American Sociological Association Elections, 1975-1996: Exploring Explanations for 'Feminization'" by Rachel A. Rosenfeld, David Cunningham, and Kathryn Schmidt

"Political Generations, Micro-Cohorts, and the Transformation of Social Movements" by Nancy Whittier

"The Sequencing of Social Movements" by Debra C. Minkoff

"The Impacts of Social Movements on the Political Process: A Study of the Civil Rights Movement and Black Electoral Politics in Mississippi" by Kenneth T. Andrews

"International Press Coverage of East German Protest Events, 1989" by Carol Mueller

Comment and Reply

"Power in Exchange Networks: Critique of a New Theory" by Barry N. Markovsky, David Willer, Brent Simpson, and Michael Lovaglia

"Reply: The Logic of the New Theory and the Logic of Selective Ignorance" by Kazuo Yamaguchi

"An Asian Route to Capitalism: Religious Economy and the Origins of Self-Transforming Growth in Japan" by Randall Collins

"Educational Credentials and Promotion Chances in Japanese and American Organizations" by Hiroshi Ishida, Seymour Spilerman, and Kuo-Hsien Su

"Sifting and Sorting: Personal Contacts and Hiring in a Retail Bank" by Roberto M. Fernandez and Nancy Weinberg

"Bigger May Be Better, But Is Older Wiser?: Dynamics of Age and Size in the New York Life Insurance Industry" by James Ranger-Moore

"Collective Memory and Cultural Constraint: Holocaust Myth and Rationality in German Politics" by Jeffrey K. Olick and Daniel Levy

"Social Cleavages and Political Alignments: U.S. Presidential Elections, 1960-1992" by Clem Brooks and Jeff Manza

"Probing the Character of Norms: A Factorial Survey Analysis of the Norms of Political Action" by Guillermina Jasso and Karl-Dieter Opp

"Self-Esteem Enhancement Through Fertility?: Addressing Issues of Socioeconomic Prospects, Gender, and Mutual Influence" by Gary L. Oates

"Population Dynamics and Economic Development: The Differential Effects of Age-Specific Population Growth Rates on Per Capita Economic Growth in Developing Countries" by Edward M. Crenshaw, Ansari Z. Ameen, and Matthew Christenson

1998

"1997 Presidential Address: The Rational and the Ambivalent in the Social Sciences" by Neil Smelser

"Leaving the 'Hood: Residential Mobility Between Black, White, and Integrated Neighborhoods" by Scott J. South and Kyle D. Crowder

"Race and Violent Crime in the Suburbs" by Allen E. Liska, John R. Logan, and Paul E. Bellair

"Immigration, Race, and Riot: The 1992 Los Angeles Uprising" by Albert Bergesen and Max Herman

"Social Networks, Gender, and Immigrant Incorporation: Resources and Constraints" by Jacqueline Maria Hagan

"Temporal Differentiation in the Occupational Mobility of Immigrant and Native-Born Latina Workers" by Dowell Myers and Cynthia J. Cranford

"Modeling Durkheim on the Micro Level: A Study of Youth Suicidality" by Thorolfur Thorlindsson and Thoroddur Bjarnason

"Editor's Note"

Exchange on Overreporting of U.S. Church Attendance

"Comment: The Case of the Phantom Episcopalians" by Theodore Caplow

"Comment: What Church Officials' Reports Don't Show: Another Look at Church Attendance Data" by Michael Hout and Andrew Greeley

"Comment: When Surveys Lie and People Tell the Truth: How Surveys Oversample Church Attenders" by Robert D. Woodberry

"Reply: Overreporting Church Attendance in America: Evidence That Demands the Same Verdict" by C. Kirk Hadaway, Penny Long Marler, and Mark Chaves

"A Review of Church Attendance Measures" by Tom W. Smith

"Data Collection Mode and Social Desirability Bias in Self-Reported Religious Attendance" by Stanley Presser and Linda Stinson

"Hazards of the Market: The Continuity and Dissolution of Interorganizational Market Relationships" by Wayne E. Baker, Robert R. Faulkner, and Gene A. Fisher

"Gatekeeping in Action: Editorial Conferences and Assessments of Newsworthiness" by Steven E. Clayman and Ann Reisner

"Bureaucratic Authority in the 'Company of Equals': The Interactional Management of Medical Peer Review" by Elizabeth A. Boyd

"Trajectories of Change in Criminal Offending: Good Marriages and the Desistance Process" by John H. Laub, Daniel S. Nagin, and Robert J. Sampson

"Effects of Parental Divorce on Mental Health Throughout the Life Course" by Andrew J. Cherlin, P. Lindsay Chase-Lansdale, and Christine McRae

"The Consequences of Premarital Fatherhood" by Steven L. Nock

"Educational Homogamy in 65 Countries: The Explanation of Differences in Openness With Country-Level Explanatory Variables" by Jeroen Smits, Wout Ultee, and Jan Lammers

"The Homogenization and Differentiation of 'Hate Crime' Law in the U.S., 1978-1995: An Analysis of Innovation and Diffusion in the Criminalization of Bigotry" by Ryken Grattet, Valerie Jenness, and Theodore R. Curry

"Beyond Individual Differences: Social Differentiation from First Principles" by Noah Mark

"How Do Status Beliefs Develop? The Role of Resources and Interactional Experience" by Cecilia L. Ridgeway, Elizabeth Heger Boyle, Kathy Kuipers, and Dawn Robinson

"Creating Status Characteristics" by Murray Webster and Stuart J. Hysom

"The Legitimation and Delegitimation of Power and Prestige Orders" by Joseph Berger, Cecilia Ridgeway, M. Hamit Fisek, and Robert Z. Norman

"How Much Does Childhood Poverty Affect the Life Chances of Children?" by Greg Duncan, Wei-Jun J. Yeung, Jeanne Brooks-Gunn, and Judith Smith

"Early Failure in the Labor Market: Childhood and Adolescent Predictors of Unemployment in the Transition to Adulthood" by Avshalom Caspi, Bradley R. Entner Wright, Terrie E. Moffitt, and Phil A. Silva

"Global Attitude Measurement: An Assessment of the World Values Survey Postmaterialism Scale" by Randall MacIntosh

"Detection and Determinants of Bias in Subjective Measures" by Kenneth Bollen and Pamela Paxton

"Glass Ceiling Effect or Cohort Effect? A Longitudinal Study of the Gender Earnings Gap for Engineers, 1982 to 1989" by Laurie A. Morgan

"Becoming a Gendered Body: Practices of Preschools" by Karin A. Martin

"How White Attitudes Vary With the Racial Composition of Local Populations: Numbers Count" by Marylee C. Taylor

"Assessing the Oppositional Culture Explanation for Racial/Ethnic Differences in School Performance" by James W. Ainsworth-Darnell and Douglas B. Downey

"Racial Disparities in Official Assessments of Juvenile Offenders: Atributional Stereotypes as Mediating Mechanisms" by George S. Bridges and Sara Steen

"Neighborhood Context and the Risk of Childbearing Among Metropolitan-Area Black Adolescents" by Clea A. Sucoff and Dawn M. Upchurch

"Self-Esteem, Delinquent Peers, and Delinquency: A Test of the Self-Enhancement Thesis" by Sung Joon Jang and Terence P. Thornberry

"Strong Legacies and Weak Markets: Bulgarian State-Owned Enterprises During Early Transition" by Kenneth I. Spenner, Olga O. Suhomlinova, Sten A. Thore, Kenneth C. Land, and Derek C. Jones

"Socially Embedded Consumer Transactions: For What Kinds of Purchases Do People Most Often Use Networks?" by Paul DiMaggio and Hugh Louch

"The Evolution of Trust and Cooperation Between Strangers: A Computational Model" by Michael W. Macy and John Skvoretz

"The Paradox of Redistribution and Strategies of Equality: Welfare State Institutions, Inequality, and Poverty in the Western Countries" by Walter Korpi and Joakim Palme

"Gender, the Welfare State, and Public Employment: A Comparative Study of Seven Industrialized Countries" by Janet C. Gornick and Jerry A. Jacobs

"And Then There Were More? The Effect of Organizational Sex Composition on the Hiring and Promotion of Managers" by Lisa E. Cohen, Joseph P. Broschak, and Heather A. Haveman

"Raising the Bar: The Gender Stratification of Law-Firm Capital" by Fiona M. Kay and John Hagan

"National Context, Social Change, and Sex Differences in Suicide Rates" by Fred C. Pampel

Comment and Reply

"Comment: Religious Pluralism in Contemporary U.S. Counties" by Daniel V. A. Olson

"Reply: Religious Choice and Competition" by Roger Finke and Rodney Stark

"Church Culture as a Strategy of Action in the Black Community" by Mary Pattillo-McCoy

"The Continuing Significance of Race Revisited: A Study of Race, Class, and Quality of Life in America, 1972 to 1996" by Michael Hughes and Melvin E. Thomas

"Conservative Protestant Childrearing: Authoritarian or Authoritative?" by W. Bradford Wilcox

"The Impact of Family Religious Life on the Quality of Mother-Child Relations" by Lisa D. Pearce and William G. Axinn

"Normative Versus Social Constructivist Processes in the Allocation of Citations: A Network-Analytic Model" by Stephane Baldi

"Sex Differences in Research Productivity: New Evidence About an Old Puzzle" by Yu Xie and Kimberlee A. Shauman

"Network Structure and Emotion in Exchange Relations" by Edward J. Lawler and Joengkoo Yoon

Comments and Replies

"Comment: Suicide and Religion: Did Durkheim Commit the Ecological Fallacy, or Did van Poppel and Day Combine Apples and Oranges?" by Miles Simpson

"Reply: Reply to Simpson" by Frans van Poppel and Lincoln H. Day

"Comment: The Loglinear Modeling of Interstate Migration: Some Additional Considerations" by Ge Lin and Yu Xie

"Reply: The Simple Virtues of Descriptive Modeling" by David B. Grusky, Jerald R. Herting, and Stephen E. Van Rompaey

1999

"Editor's Comment: The *ASR* in 1999 and Beyond"

"Creating a Capital Investment Welfare State: The New American Exceptionalism?" by Jill Quadagno

"Children of the Cultural Revolution: The State and the Life Course in the People's Republic of China" by Xueguang Zhou and Liren Hou

"Comment on Zhou and Hou: A Negative Life Event With Positive Consequences?" by Kevin Chen and Xiaonong Cheng

"The State, Courts, and Maternity Policies in U.S. Organizations: Specifying Institutional Mechanisms" by Doug Guthrie and Louise Marie Roth

"Organizational Mediation of Project-Based Labor Markets: Talent Agencies and the Careers of Screenwriters" by William T. Bielby and Denise D. Bielby

"Revolving Doors Reexamined: Occupational Sex Segregation Over the Life Course" by Tak Wing Chan

"Regional Origin and Family Disruption in Northern Cities: The Role of Context" by Stewart E. Tolnay and Kyle D. Crowder

"Neighborhood Effects on Family Formation: Concentrated Poverty and Beyond" by Scott J. South and Kyle D. Crowder

"How Much Injustice Is There in the World? Two New Justice Indexes" by Guillermina Jasso

"Editor's Comment: Introducing the New *ASR* Editors"

"Sibship Size and Intellectual Development: Is the Relationship Causal?" by Guang Guo and Leah K. VanWey

"Comment: Sibship Size and Academic Achievement: What We Now Know and What We Still Need to Know" by Meredith Phillips

"Comment: Much Ado About Siblings: Change Models, Sibship Size, and Intellectual Development" by Douglas B. Downey, Brian Powell, Lala Carr Steelman, and Shana Pribesh

"Reply: The Effects of Closely Spaced and Widely Spaced Sibship Size on Intellectual Development" by Guang Guo and Leah K. VanWey

"Rebel Without a Cause or Effect: Birth Order and Social Attitudes" by Jeremy Freese, Brian Powell, and Lala Carr Steelman

"Bilingualism and the Academic Achievement of First- and Second-Generation Asian Americans: Accommodation With or Without Assimilation?" by Ted Mouw and Yu Xie

"Has There Been an Intercohort Decline in Verbal Ability? Theory and Evidence" by James A. Wilson and Walter R. Gove

"Further Discussion of the Evidence for an Intercohort Decline in Education-Adjusted Vocabulary" by Norval D. Glenn

"Aging Versus Cohort Interpretations of Intercohort Differences in GSS Vocabulary Scores" by Duane F. Alwin and Ryan J. McCammon

"Reply: The Age-Period-Cohort Conumdrum and Verbal Ability: Empirical Relationships and Their Interpretation" by James A. Wilson and Walter R. Gove

"Utility of Health Data From Social Surveys: Is There a Gold Standard for Measuring Morbidity?" by Kenneth F. Ferraro and Melissa M. Farmer

"Real in Their Consequences: A Sociological Approach to Understanding the Association Between Psychotic Symptoms and Violence" by Bruce G. Link, John Monahan, Ann Stueve, and Francis T. Cullen

"Editor's Comment: A Note from the New *ASR* Editors"

"The Ties That Bind: Principles of Cohesion in Cohabitation and Marriage" by Julie Brines and Kara Joyner

"Collective Violence and Group Solidarity: Evidence From a Feuding Society" by Roger V. Gould

"Genre Memories and Memory Genres: A Dialogical Analysis of May 8, 1945 Commemorations in the Federal Republic of Germany" by Jeffrey K. Olick

"The Architecture of Small Networks: Strong Interaction and Dynamic Organization in Small Social Systems" by Thomas S. Smith and Gregory T. Stevens

"The Structuring of Organizational Populations" by David N. Barron

"Immigrant Groups in the Suburbs: A Reexamination of Suburbanization and Spatial Assimilation" by Richard D. Alba, John R. Logan, Brian J. Stults, Gilbert Marzan, and Wenquan Zhang

"'Property Values Drop When Blacks Move in Because . . .': Racial and Socioeconomic Determinants of Neighborhood Desirability" by David R. Harris

"Embeddedness in the Making of Financial Capital: How Social Relations and Networks Benefit Firms Seeking Financing" by Brian Uzzi

"The Coupling of the Symbolic and the Technical in an Institutionalized Context: The Negotiated Order of the GAO's Audit Reporting Process" by Onker N. Basu, Mark W. Dirsmith, and Parveen P. Gupta

"Building the Iron Cage: Determinants of Managerial Intensity in the Early Years of Organizations" by James N. Baron, Michael T. Hannan, and M. Diane Burton

"Economic Hardship Across the Life Course" by John Mirowsky and Catherine E. Ross

"Comment: Fueling the Politics of Age: On Economic Hardship Across the Life Course" by Melissa A. Hardy and Lawrence E. Hazelrigg

"Reply: Economic Hardship Declines With Age" by John Mirowsky and Catherine E. Ross

"In Search of Smoking Guns: What Makes Income Inequality Vary Over Time in Different Countries?" by Bjorn Gustafsson and Mats Johansson

"Income Inequality, Development, and Dependence: A Reconsideration" by Arthur S. Alderson and Francois Nielsen

"Beyond Social Capital: Spatial Dynamics of Collective Efficacy for Children" by Robert J. Sampson, Jeffrey D. Morenoff, and Felton Earls

"Parental Networks, Social Closure, and Mathematics Learning: A Test of Coleman's Social Capital Explanation of School Effects" by Stephen L. Morgan and Aage B. Sorensen

"Opening the Debate on Closure and Schooling Outcomes: Comment on Morgan and Sorensen" by William J. Carbonaro

"Conceptualizing and Measuring School Social Networks: Comment on Morgan and Sorensen" by Maureen T. Hallinan and Warren N. Kubitschek

"Theory, Measurement, and Specification Issues in Models of Network Effects on Learning: Reply to Carbonaro and to Hallinan and Kubitschek" by Stephen L. Morgan and Aage B. Sorensen

"Explaining Deindustrialization: Globalization, Failure, or Success?" by Arthur S. Anderson

"Developing Difference: Social Organization and the Rise of the Auto Industries of South Korea, Taiwan, Spain, and Argentina" by Nicole Woolsey Biggart and Mauro F. Guillen

"Bureaucracy and Growth: A Cross-National Analysis of the Effects of 'Weberian' State Structures on Economic Growth" by Peter Evans and James E. Rauch

"Boon or Bane? Reassessing the Productivity of Foreign Direct Investment" by Indra de Soysa and John R. Oneal

"The Social Inheritance of Divorce: Effects of Parent's Family Type in Postwar Germany" by Andreas Diekmann and Henriette Engelhardt

"The Effect of Marriage and Divorce on Women's Economic Well-Being" by Pamela J. Smock, Wendy D. Manning, and Sanjiv Gupta

"Americans' Increasing Belief in Life After Death: Religious Competition and Acculturation" by Andrew M. Greeley and Michael Hout

"Religious Congregations and Welfare Reform: Who Will Take Advantage of 'Charitable Choice'?" by Mark Chaves

"A Historical Note on Whites' Beliefs About Racial Inequality" by Howard Schuman and Maria Krysan

"Choice Shift and Group Polarization" by Noah E. Friedkin

"Power in Negotiated and Reciprocal Exchange" by Linda D. Molm, Gretchen Peterson, and Nobuyuki Takahashi

"Comment: Is 'Race' Essential?" by Mara Loveman

"Reply: The Essential Social Fact of Race" by Eduardo Bonilla-Silva

2000

"The Hidden Abode: Sociology as Analysis of the Unexpected" by Alejandro Portes

"Modernization, Cultural Change, and the Persistence of Traditional Values" by Ronald Inglehart and Wayne E. Baker

"The Web of Group Affiliations Revisited: Social Life, Postmodernism, and Sociology" by Bernice A. Pescosolido and Beth A. Rubin

"Trade Globalization Since 1975: Waves of Integration in the World-System" by Christopher Chase-Dunn, Yukio Kawano, and Benjamin D. Brewer

"The Nation-State and the Natural Environment Over the Twentieth Century" by David John Frank, Ann Hironaka, and Evan Schofer

"World Society, the Nation-State, and Environmental Protection: Comment on Frank, Hironaka, and Schofer" by Frederick H. Buttel

"Environmentalism as a Global Institution: Reply to Buttel" by David John Frank, Ann Hironaka, and Evan Schofer

"Lost in the Storm: The Sociology of the Black Working Class, 1850 to 1990" by Hayward Derrick Horton, Beveryly Lundy Allen, Cedric Herring, and Melvin E. Thomas

"Historicizing the Secularization Debate: Church, State, and Society in Late Medieval and Early Modern Europe (ca. 1300 to 1700)" by Philip S. Gorski

"Editor's Comment: *ASR*, 2000 to 2002"

"Did Socialism Fail to Innovate? A Natural Experiment of the Two Zeiss Companies" by Bruce Kogut and Udo Zander

"Politics and Life Chances in a State Socialist Regime: Dual Career Paths Into the Urban Chinese Elite, 1949 to 1996" by Andrew G. Walder, Bobai Li, and Donald J. Treiman

"Why Not Ascription? Organizations' Employment of Male and Female Managers" by Barbara F. Reskin and Debra Branch McBrier

"Gender and the New Inequality: Explaining the College/Non-College Wage Gap" by Leslie McCall

"Bad Jobs in America: Standard and Nonstandard Employment Relations and Job Quality in the United States" by Arne L. Kalleberg, Barbara F. Reskin, and Ken Hudson

"Early Work Histories of Urban Youth" by Doris R. Entwisle, Karl L. Alexander, and Linda Steffel Olson

"The Longitudinal Effects of Group Tenure Composition on Turnover" by Jesper B. Sorensen

Comment and Reply

"Comment: Unveiling the Hidden Glass Ceiling: An Analysis of the Cohort Effect Claim" by John C. Alessio and Julie Andrzejewski

"Reply: Is Engineering Hostile to Women? An Analysis of Data From the 1993 National Survey of College Graduates" by Laurie A. Morgan

"Partisan Governance, Women's Employment, and the Social Democratic Service State" by Evelyne Huber and John D. Stephens

"Family Change, Employment Transitions, and the Welfare State: Household Income Dynamics in the United States and Germany" by Thomas A. DiPrete and Patricia McManus

"Demographic Transition in Ecological Focus" by Edward M. Crenshaw, Matthew Christenson, and Doyle Ray Oakey

"Class Inequality and Social Mobility in Northern Ireland, 1973 to 1996" by Richard Breen

"A Status Value Theory of Power in Exchange Relations" by Shane R. Thye

"A New Solution to the Collective Action Problem: The Paradox of Voter Turnout" by Satoshi Kanazawa

"Biological Limits of Gender Construction" by J. Richard Udry

"Is Biology Destiny? Birth Weight and Life Chances" by Dalton Conley and Neil G. Bennett

Comment and Reply

"Comment: Still Missing the Feminist Revolution? Inequalities of Race, Class, and Gender in Introductory Sociology Textbooks" by Jeff Manza and Debbie Van Schyndel

"Reply: Gender Stratification and Paradigm Change" by Myra Marx Ferree and Elaine J. Hall

"Civil Rights Liberalism and the Suppression of a Republican Political Realignment in the United States, 1972 to 1996" by Clem Brooks

"Wage Wars: Institutional Politics, WPA Wages, and the Struggle for U.S. Social Policy" by Edwin Amenta and Drew Halfmann

"Work as a Turning Point in the Life Course of Criminals: A Duration Model of Age, Employment, and Recidivism" by Christopher Uggen

"The Structural Context of Homicide: Accounting for Racial Differences in Process" by Lauren J. Krivo and Ruth D. Peterson

"Routes to Children's Economic Recovery After Divorce: Are Cohabitation and Remarriage Equivalent?" by Donna Ruane Morrison and Amy Rittualo

"The Contingent Meaning of Neighborhood Stability for Residents' Psychological Well-Being" by Catherine E. Ross, John R. Reynolds, and Karlyn J. Geis

"Core Networks and Tie Activation: What Kinds of Routine Networks Allocate Resources in Nonroutine Situations?" by Dalton Conley and Neil G. Bennett

"Events, Instruments, and Reporting Errors" by Jennifer Dykema and Nora Cate Schaeffer

"Editor's Comment: A Short Note on Long Papers"

"The Market That Antitrust Built: Public Policy, Private Coercion, and Railroad Acquisitions, 1825 to 1922" by Frank Dobbin and Timothy J. Dowd

"Leveraging the State: Private Money and the Development of Public Education for Blacks" by David Strong, Pamela Barnhouse Walters, Brian Driscoll, and Scott Rosenberg

"Revenge as Sanction and Solidarity Display: An Analysis of Vendettas in Nineteenth-Century Corsica" by Roger V. Gould

"Ethnicity and Sentencing Outcomes in U.S. Federal Courts: Who Is Punished More Harshly?" by Darrell Steffensmeier and Stephen Demuth

"Job Relocation and the Racial Gap in Unemployment in Detroit and Chicago, 1980 to 1990" by Ted Mouw

"Analyzing Educational Careers: A Multinomial Transition Model" by Richard Breen and Jan O. Jonsson

Comment and Reply

"Comment: Temporal and Regional Variation in the Strength of Educational Homogamy" by James M. Raymo and Yu Xie

"Reply: More or Less Educational Homogamy? A Test of Different Versions of Modernization Theory Using Cross-Temporal Evidence for 60 Countries" by Jeroen Smits, Wout Ultee, and Jan Lammers

"History Repeats Itself, but How? City Character, Urban Tradition, and the Accomplishment of Place" by Marvey Molotch, William Freudenburg, and Krista E. Paulsen

"Surviving Closure: Post-Rejection Adaptation and Plurality in Science" by H. M. Collins

"Using the Literature: Reference Networks, Reference Contexts, and the Social Structure of Scholarship" by Lowell L. Hargens

"The Effects of Science on National Economic Development, 1970 to 1990" by Evan Schofer, Francisco O. Ramirez, and John W. Meyer

"Migration and Infant Death: Assimilation or Selective Migration Among Puerto Ricans?" by Nancy S. Landale, R. S. Oropesa, and Bridget K. Gorman

"The Significance of Socioeconomic Status in Explaining the Racial Gap in Chronic Health Conditions" by Mark D. Hayward, Eileen M. Crimmins, Toni P. Miles, and Yu Yang

5.2.11 PsycARTICLES

PsycARTICLES (at www.apa.org/psycarticles/) is a new electronic database that contains the full text articles from the following 43 journals.

American Psychologist
Behavioural Neuroscience
Canadian Journal of Behavioral Science
Canadian Journal of Experimental Psychology
Canadian Psychological Association
Canadian Psychology
Consulting Psychology Journal: Practice and Research
Cultural Diversity and Ethnic Minority Psychology
Developmental Psychology
Emotion
European Psychologist
Experimental and Clinical Psychopharmacology
Group Dynamics: Theory, Research, and Practice
Health Psychology
History of Psychology
Journal of Abnormal Psychology
Journal of Applied Psychology
Journal of Comparative Psychology
Journal of Consulting and Clinical Psychology
Journal of Counseling Psychology
Journal of Educational Psychology
Journal of Experimental Psychology: Animal Behavior Processes
Journal of Experimental Psychology: Applied
Journal of Experimental Psychology: General
Journal of Experimental Psychology: Human Perception and Performance
Journal of Experimental Psychology: Learning, Memory and Cognition
Journal of Family Psychology
Journal of Occupational Health Psychology

Journal of Personality and Social Psychology
Neuropsychology
Prevention & Treatment
Professional Psychology: Research and Practice
Psychoanalytic Psychology: A Journal of Theory, Practice, Research, and Criticism
Psychological Assessment
Psychological Bulletin
Psychological Methods
Psychological Review
Psychology and Aging
Psychology of Addictive Behaviors
Psychology of Men and Masculinity
Psychology, Public Policy, and Law
Rehabilitation Psychology
Review of General Psychology

5.2.12 Federal Government Educational Resources

The federal government operates the following electronic sources of reference information on education and related fields at www.ed.gov/EdRes/EdFed/.

5.2.12.1 Regional Comprehensive Assistance Centers

Regional Comprehensive Assistance Centers (at www.ed.gov/EdRes/EdFed/EdTechCtrs.html) consist of 15 separate Comprehensive Centers that are part of a network of organizations providing assistance and information nationwide. Their role in this network is to help states, school districts, and schools in meeting the needs of children served under the Elementary and Secondary Education Act (ESEA), including children in high-poverty areas, migratory children, immigrant children, children with limited English proficiency, neglected or delinquent children, homeless children and youth, Indian children, children with disabilities, and, where applicable, Alaska Native children and Native Hawaiian children (Title XIII of ESEA). The Comprehensive Centers focus on assisting Title I schoolwide programs and helping local education agencies.

5.2.12.2 Educational Resources Information Center (ERIC)

Educational Resources Information Center (ERIC) (at www.ed.gov/EdRes/EdFed/ERIC.html) is a nationwide information network that acquires, catalogs, summarizes, and provides access to education information from all sources. The database and ERIC document collections are housed in about 3,000 locations worldwide, including most major public and university library systems. ERIC produces a variety of publications and provides extensive user assistance, including AskERIC, an electronic question answering service for teachers on the Internet. AskERIC Virtual Library (at http://askeric.org/) is a personalized Internet-based service providing education information to teachers, librarians, counselors, administrators, parents, and anyone interested in education throughout the United States. It includes collections of lesson plans, ERIC searches, mailing lists, and AskERIC Infoguides.

Also associated with the ERIC system is *Early Childhood Research & Practice* (at www.ecrp.uiuc.edu/), an Internet journal on the development, care, and education of young children. The National

Parent Information Network (at http://npin.org/) provides information and communications support to parents and parent support organizations.

The ERIC system includes 16 subject-specific clearinghouses, the ERIC Processing and Reference facility, and ACCESS ERIC, which provides introductory services and other valuable resources for any social or behavioral scientist. Perhaps the most used part of the ERIC system are the primary and secondary clearinghouses. An ERIC Clearinghouse collects, abstracts, and indexes education materials for the ERIC database, responds to requests for information in its subject specific areas, and produces special publications on current research, programs, and practices. There are 16 such clearinghouses, each containing huge amounts of information, with descriptions and electronic locations as follows. Note that these clearinghouses are as different in their format and collections as are the subjects on which they focus. They can be accessed through the main ERIC Web site provided above.

- Adult, Career, and Vocational Education (at http://ericacve.org/) includes all levels and settings of adult, continuing, career, and vocational/technical education.
- Assessment and Evaluation (at http://ericae.net/) provides information focusing on educational assessment and test use.
- Community Colleges (at www.gseis.ucla.edu/ERIC/eric.html) covers development, administration, and evaluation of 2-year public and private community and junior colleges, technical institutes, and 2-year branch university campuses.
- Counseling and Student Services (at http://ericcass.uncg.edu/) includes information on preparation, practice, and supervision of counselors at all educational levels and in all settings, as well as theoretical development of counseling and student services.
- Disabilities and Gifted Education (at http://ericec.org/) covers all aspects of the education and development of the disabled and gifted, including identification, assessment, intervention, and enrichment, both in special settings and in mainstreamed settings.
- Educational Management (at http://eric.uoregon.edu/) covers all aspects of the governance, leadership, administration, and structure of public and private educational organizations at the elementary and secondary levels, including the provision of physical facilities for their operation.
- Elementary and Early Childhood Education (at http://ericeece.org/) covers the physical, cognitive, social, educational, and cultural development of children from birth through early adolescence.
- Higher Education (at www.eriche.org/) addresses college and university problems, programs, students, curricular and instructional programs, and institutional research.
- Information and Technology (at http://ericir.syr.edu/ithome/) covers educational technology and library and information science at all levels.
- Languages and Linguistics (at www.cal.org/ericcll/) covers languages and language sciences, including all aspects of second language instruction and learning in all commonly and uncommonly taught languages.
- Reading, English, and Communication (at www.indiana.edu/~eric_rec/) covers aspects of reading, English, and communication (verbal and nonverbal), preschool through college.
- Rural Education and Small Schools (at www.ael.org/eric/) covers economic, cultural, and social conditions related to educational programs and practices for rural residents; American Indians/Alaska Natives, Mexican Americans, and migrants; educational practices and programs in all small schools; and outdoor education.
- Science, Mathematics, and Environmental Education (at www.ericse.org/) covers all aspects and levels of science, mathematics, and environmental education.
- Social Studies/Social Science Education (at www.indiana.edu/~ssdc/eric_chess.htm or http://ericso.indiana.edu) monitors issues concerning the teaching and learning of history, geography, civics, economics, and other subjects in social studies/social sciences.

- ▪▪ Teaching and Teacher Education (at www.ericsp.org/) covers teacher recruitment, selection, licensing, certification, training, preservice and inservice preparation, evaluation, retention, and retirement. Also covers all aspects of health, physical education, recreation, and dance.

- ▪▪ Urban Education (at http://eric-web.tc.columbia.edu/) includes information on programs and practices in urban area schools; education of African American and Hispanic youth; theory and practice of educational equity; and urban and minority experiences, social institutions, and services.

Adjunct ERIC Clearinghouses are associated with the specific ERIC Clearinghouse and perform some of or all the following functions in their subject areas: identifying and acquiring significant literature within their scope area for the ERIC database, providing reference and referral services, providing technical assistance, maintaining or contributing to Web sites, and producing publications. Adjunct ERIC Clearinghouses receive funding from sponsors outside the ERIC system. These adjunct clearinghouses include the following.

- ▪▪ Child Care (at http://nccic.org/) includes information on child care linkages and serves as a mechanism for supporting quality, comprehensive services for children and families. It is sponsored by the National Child Care Information Center (NCCIC).

- ▪▪ Clinical Schools (at www.aacte.org/Eric/pro_dev_schools.htm) provides information on clinical schools, professional development schools, partner schools, professional practice schools, and similar institutions. It is sponsored by the American Association for Colleges for Teacher Education.

- ▪▪ Educational Opportunity (at www.trioprograms.org/clearinghouse/) provides information to help increase access to high-quality resources for individuals, parents, and organizations interested in ways and means to enable low-income, first-generation, and disabled students to attend college. It is supported by the Council for Opportunity in Education.

- ▪▪ Entrepreneurship Education (at www.celcee.edu/) indexes, abstracts, and disseminates information about entrepreneurship education and makes those resources available to the education community. It is sponsored by the Center for Entrepreneurial Leadership.

- ▪▪ ESL Literacy Education (at www.cal.org/ncle/) addresses aspects of literacy education for adults and out-of-school youth with limited English proficiency. It is sponsored by the National Clearinghouse for ESL Literacy Education.

- ▪▪ The National Law-Related Education Resource Center (at www.abanet.org/publiced/nlrc.html), which serves as an ERIC adjunct clearinghouse, collects and disseminates information on law-related education (LRE) programs and resources, substantive legal topics, funding sources, and teacher and resource leader training opportunities.

- ▪▪ Service Learning (at http://nicsl.jaws.umn.edu/ or www.nicsl.coled.umn.edu) provides information about service-learning programs, including organizations, people, calendar events, and literature/multimedia materials. It is sponsored by the National Service-Learning Clearinghouse.

- ▪▪ Test Collection (at http://ericae.net/testcol.htm) prepares descriptions of commercially available and noncommercially available tests, checklists, instruments, questionnaires, and other assessment and evaluation tools. The Test Locator is a joint project of the ERIC Clearinghouse on Assessment and Evaluation, the Library and Reference Services Division of the Educational Testing Service, the Buros Institute of Mental Measurements at the University of Nebraska in Lincoln, the Region III Comprehensive Center at George Washington University, and Pro-Ed test publishers.

- ▪▪ United States–Japan Studies (at www.indiana.edu/~japan/) covers all aspects of teaching and learning about Japanese society and culture.

The National Clearinghouse for Educational Facilities (www.edfacilities.org) is affiliated with the ERIC system. It acquires, manages, and disseminates information related to educational facilities and serves as a resource for school staff and others who plan, construct, and maintain educational facilities.

The ERIC Document Reproduction Service (EDRS) produces and sells microfiche and paper copies of documents abstracted by ERIC. It offers back collections of ERIC documents, annual subscriptions, cumulative indexes, and other ERIC-related products.

The Oryx Press publishes *Current Index to Journals in Education* (*CIJE*), the *Thesaurus of ERIC Descriptors*, and other ERIC products.

The United States Government Printing Office (www.access.gpo.gov/) publishes an extensive number of informative documents.

The Eisenhower National Clearinghouse and Regional Consortia (at www.mathsciencenetwork. org/connect.htm) provides technical assistance and professional development on issues in math and science education. The clearinghouse in each of 10 regions provides services important to its region and to the nation as a whole.

5.2.12.3. Equity Assistance Centers

Each of the 10 equity assistance centers (a directory can be found at www.ed.gov/EdRes/EdFed/ equity.html) is funded by the U.S. Department of Education under Title IV of the 1964 Civil Rights Act. The centers provide assistance in the areas of race, gender, and national origin equity to public school districts as a means of promoting equal educational opportunities.

5.2.12.4 National Research and Development Centers

The National Research and Development Centers (at www.ed.gov/offices/OERI/ResCtr.html) address nationally significant problems and issues through support of university-based national educational research and development centers. The centers address specific topics such as early childhood development and learning, student learning and achievement, cultural and linguistic diversity and second language learning, postsecondary improvement, adult learning, and education policy.

5.2.12.5 Regional Educational Laboratories

Each of the 10 regional educational laboratories (a directory can be found at www.ed.gov/ EdRes/EdFed/RegLab.html) works to help educators and policymakers solve education problems in their states and districts. The labs research education issues, print publications, and provide training programs to teachers and administrators. Each lab puts out a catalog of its publications, covering a wide range of topics such as teaching strategies, school improvement, and parental involvement.

5.2.12.6 Regional Technology in Education Consortia (R*TEC)

The Regional Technology in Education Consortia (R*TEC) (at www.rtec.org/) program helps states, local educational agencies, teachers, school library and media personnel, administrators, and other education entities successfully integrate technologies into kindergarten through 12th grade (K-12) classrooms, library media centers, and other educational settings, including adult literacy centers.

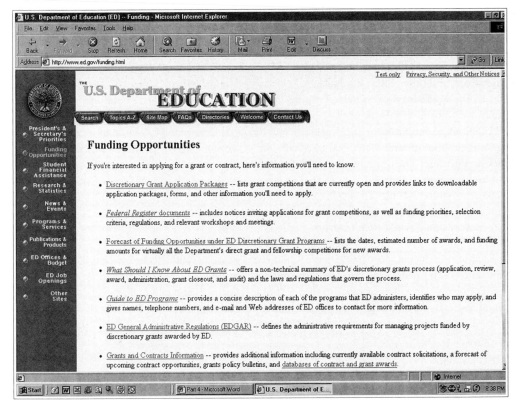

Figure 5.1. The U.S. Department of Education Web Site

5.2.12.7 Special Education and Rehabilitative Services

The Assistive Technology Funding and Systems Change Project (ATFSCP) (at www.ed.gov/ EdRes/EdFed/specedrs.html) provides training, technical assistance, and information on assistive technology funding and systems change issues nationwide. The goal of the project is to provide advocates with the knowledge and skills necessary to improve access to assistive technology devices and services for individuals with disabilities.

5.2.12.8 Star Schools Program Sites

The Star Schools Program (at www.ed.gov/EdRes/EdFed/Star.html) encourages improved instruction in mathematics, science, and foreign languages. It also supports improved literacy skills and vocational education. Through the use of telecommunications, it targets the underserved, including the disadvantaged, illiterate and limited-English populations, and individuals with disabilities.

United States Department of Education programs can be identified and examined at the department's Web site at http://search.ed.gov/csi/ (shown in Figure 5.1).

5.2.13 Child Development Abstracts & Bibliography

Child Development Abstracts & Bibliography (CDAB) (at www.srcd.org) was published by the Society for Research in Child Development from 1927 to 2001 and is a collection of abstracts culled from more than 300 different journals in the areas of sociology, psychology, pediatrics, social work, anthropology, nursing, and education, among others. The abstracts are organized into the areas of biology, personality and social psychology, cognition, psychiatry, theory and methodology, and education. The journal also published book notices.

5.2.14 POPLINE

POPLINE (POPulation information onLINE), located at www.jhuccp.org/popline/, is the world's largest bibliographic database on population, family planning, and related health issues. It contains citations with abstracts for more than 275,000 records. It is maintained by the Population Information Program at the Johns Hopkins School of Hygiene and Public Health. Online POPLINE is updated each month; POPLINE CD-ROM is updated every 6 months. Approximately 10,000 records are added annually. POPINFORM is updated every 2 weeks.

UNITED STATES BUREAU OF THE CENSUS AND OTHER FEDERAL SOURCES OF INFORMATION 5.3

The results of the decennial census survey (at www.census.gov) is perhaps one of the most ambitious and richest sources of data available to researchers and is now available online. Perhaps the best place to begin a search for census information is with the American FactFinder (at http://factfinder.census.gov/servlet/BasicFactsServlet). This is a gateway to a huge amount of census-related information and offers easy access to reference sets, data sets, maps, and more.

Updates for the decennial census through its Current Population Survey, American Housing Survey, and Survey of Income and Program Participation are available through Current Population Reports at www.census.gov/population/www and www.census.gov/hhes/www. They include information on

- Marital status
- Households and families
- School enrollment
- Educational attainment
- Fertility
- Age
- Computer use
- Family economics
- Child care arrangements
- Health care
- Population estimates and projections
- Income and poverty

The results of the 2000 Census are still being compiled. The products from this analysis are summarized in Table 5.4, which lists the estimated date of availability of each product and the media on which it will be available.

CenStats (at www.census.gov/apsd/www/censtats.html), which is now free to use, is a tool for accessing data from the U.S. Census. Hundreds of databases are available through CenStats. A sample listing of some titles for just the A category is given on page 274.

Table 5.4 RELEASE AND AVAILABILITY OF 2000 CENSUS DATA

Planned Date of First Release	Availability	Title
March–April 2001	Available on the Internet and CD-ROM	Census 2000 Redistricting Data Summary File
State data: April 2001 National data: November 2001	Available on the Internet	Quick Tables (population and housing characteristics)
State data: April 2001 National data: December 2001	Available on the Internet	Geographic Comparison Tables (population and housing characteristics)
June–September 2001	Available on the Internet, CD-ROM, and paper	Congressional District Demographic Profile (population totals and selected population and housing characteristics in a single table for congressional districts only).
June–September 2001	Available on the Internet, CD-ROM, and paper	Demographic Profile (population totals and selected population and housing characteristics in a single table)
State data: June 2001 National data: June–July 2002	Available on the Internet and CD-ROM	Summary File 1 population counts for 63 race categories and Hispanic or Latino Population counts for many detailed race and Hispanic or Latino categories and American Indian and Alaska Native tribes Selected population and housing characteristics
July 2001	Available on CD-ROM	Race and Hispanic or Latino Summary File on CD-ROM
State data: September 2001 National data: May 2002	Available on the Internet and CD-ROM	Summary File 2 population and housing characteristics iterated for many detailed race and Hispanic or Latino categories and American Indian and Alaska Native tribes (Urban/rural data are on the final national file—this is the only difference from the advance national file.)

December 2001	Available on the Internet, CD-ROM, and paper	Demographic Profile (demographic, social, economic, and housing characteristics presented in three separate tables)
December 2001	Available on the Internet, CD-ROM, and paper	Congressional District Demographic Profile (demographic, social, economic, and housing characteristics presented in three separate tables for congressional districts only)
January 2002	Available on the Internet and paper	Census 2000: Summary Population and Housing Characteristics
June 2002	Available on the Internet	Quick Tables (table with population and housing characteristics)
June 2002	Available on the Internet and CD-ROM	Summary File 3 (includes population counts for ancestry groups and selected population and housing characteristics)
July 2002	Available on the Internet	Geographic Comparison Tables (population and housing characteristics for a list of geographic areas, e.g., all counties in a state)
October 2002	Available on the Internet and CD-ROM	Summary File 4 (population and housing characteristics for Hispanic or Latino categories, American Indian and Alaska Native tribes, and ancestry groups)
2002	Available on CD-ROM	Public Use Microdata Sample (PUMS) Files (including 1% and 5% samples of the nation and states as well as substate areas where appropriate)
December 2002–March 2003	(release subject to policy decisions on access and confidentiality)	Advanced Query Function (user specifies contents of tabulations from full microdata file; includes safeguards against disclosure of identifying information about individuals and housing units)
2003	Available on the Internet and paper	Census 2000: Population and Housing Unit Totals
2003	Available on the Internet and CD-ROM	Congressional District Data Summary File (includes 100% and sample data for the redistricted 108th Congress)

Abbreviation and Acronym Glossary
Access Data Tools
Accommodation and Foodservices sector (Economic Census)
Acquisition Management/Procurement Activities
Address List Review-Local Update (LUCA)
Adjusted Data: 1990 Official (Unadjusted) and Adjusted Census Data
Administrative and Support and Waste Management and Remediation Services sector
    (Economic Census)
Advance Monthly Retail Sales
Advisory Committees
African Americans:
    —Businesses
    —Minority Links for Media
    —People
Age Data
Age Search Information
Aging/Elderly Population Data
Agricultural Census
AIDS/HIV Surveillance (Acquired Immunodeficiency Syndrome/Human
    Immunodeficiency Virus)
American Community Survey (ACS)
American FactFinder (Economic Census, American Community Survey,
    1990 Decennial Census, Census 2000 Dress Rehearsal, and Maps)
American Housing Survey (AHS)
American Indians and Alaska Natives:
    —Businesses
    —Geographic Area Programs
    —Minority Links for Media
    —People
    —Tribal Governments
American Samoa (Outlying Area)
Ancestry Data
Annual Capital Expenditures Survey (ACES)
Annual Retail Trade Survey
Annual Survey of Manufactures (ASM)
Annual Wholesale Trade Survey
Apportionment Data
Arts and Entertainment Industries (Annual Estimates)
Arts, Entertainment, and Recreation sector (Economic Census)
Asians and Pacific Islanders:
    —Businesses
    —Minority Links for Media
    —People
Ask the Experts
Assets and Expenditures Survey
Assets of State and Local Governments:
    —Governments
    —Retirement Systems
At-home Workers/Working At Home Data
Atlanta Regional Office
Automated Export System (AES)

Additional data sources include the following.

The Administration on Aging focuses on services to the aging. It also collects state data on the elderly as well as poverty numbers. Additional information can be found at www.aoa.dhhs.gov/.

The American Housing Survey (www.census.gov/hhes/www/ahs.html) collects data on the nation's housing, including apartments, single-family homes, mobile homes, and vacant housing units; household characteristics; income; housing and neighborhood quality; housing costs; equipment and fuels; size of housing units; and recent movers. National data are collected every other year, and data for each of 46 selected Metropolitan Statistical Areas (MSAs) are collected about every 4 years, with an average of 12 MSAs included each year.

The Current Population Survey provides monthly surveys of the labor force and annual demographic surveys of income, poverty, benefits, and other social characteristics, with data available for the nation, states, large metropolitan areas, and selected central cities. Addtitional information can be found at www.bls.census.gov/cps/cpsmain.htm.

Demographics USA (published by Trade Dimensions, with description at www.tradedimensions.com/p_demographics.html) provides current estimates of population by age and sex, racial percentages, number of households, household income, per capita income, employment by occupation, and employment by industry.

Disability Statistics provides a summary of national data on the characteristics of the disabled, including broad type of disability, employment, education, and income. Additional information is available at www.census.gov/hhes/www/disability/html.

Employment and Earnings (http://stats.bls.gov/cesee.htm) reports monthly employment and unemployment statistics cross-classified by socioeconomic characteristics.

The Federal Bureau of Investigation (FBI) provides a summary of crime for the nation and large metropolitan areas. Information is available on the Web at www.fbi.gov/. The FBI's Uniform Crime Reports provide annual crime data by crime type for the nation, states, counties, and cities with populations of at least 10,000. They can be found at www.fbi.gov/ucr/ucr.htm.

The *Geographic Profile of Employment and Unemployment* reports annual employment and unemployment data for Census regions, divisions, states, metropolitan areas, and selected cities. More information is available at http://stats.bls.gov/opub/gp/gpappend.htm

The Department of Housing and Urban Development provides national, regional, and metropolitan area data on new homes sales and occasionally on rent. Additional information is available at http://huduser.org/.

The Immigration and Naturalization Service provides annual national immigration data by country of origin and immigrant characteristics. Additional information is available at www.usdoj.gov/ins/.

Money magazine's "Best Places to Live" rates 300 metropolitan areas. Individual ratings are given for crime, housing, weather, education, economy, health, transit, and cultural factors. Additional information is available at www.money.com/money/depts/real_estate/bplive.

The *National Vital Statistics Report* (www.cdc.gov/nchs/products/pubs/pubd/nvsr/nvsr.htm), formerly the *Monthly Vital Statistics Report* (www.cdc.gov/nchs/products/pubs/pubd/mvsr/mvsr.htm), provides monthly national and state birth, death, marriage, and divorce figures starting from July, 1994. Mortality statistics are categorized by age, race, sex, and disease on a national level. Additional information is available at the two Web sites.

The National Archive of Computerized Data on Aging reports the National Institute on Aging data tapes on aging. Most surveys predate the 1990 Census. Additional information is available at www.icpsr.umich.edu/nacda/.

The National Center for Education Statistics publishes the *Digest of Education Statistics*, which provides national data on schools including enrollment, numbers of teachers, finances, and educational outcomes. Additional information is available at www.ed.gov/NCES/ or http://nces.ed/gov.

The National Center for Health Statistics classifies birth statistics by various factors, death statistics classified by cause, marriages, and divorces. Additional information is available at www.cdc.gov/nchs.

The National Compensation Survey provides weekly earnings of office and plant staff for large metropolitan areas. The same information formerly was provided by the Occupational Compensation Survey. Additional information is available at http://stats.bls.gov/ocshome.htm.

The *Places Rated Almanac* (IDG Books, 1999) rates MSAs as possible places for relocation.

School district estimates of poverty include Census Bureau data on total population, school-age population, and school-age children living in poverty. Additional information is available at www.census.gov/hhes/www/saipe/schooltoc.html.

Small Area Income and Poverty Estimates contains annual estimates of median household income, the percentage of people living in poverty, and numbers of children living in poverty for states and counties. Additional information is available at www.census.gov/hhes/www/saipe.html.

The *Statistical Abstract of the United States* (at www.census.gov/prod/www/statistical-abstract-us.html) presents comprehensive data on a broad set of categories describing the population of the United States.

The Administration on Aging maintains a site containing statistical information on older persons. It presents the current profile of the aging population, projections to 2050, and estimates of states' aging populations. Additional information is available at www.aoa.dhhs.gov/aoa/stats/statpage.html.

The *Statistical Yearbook of Immigration* details national and state immigration trends by country of origin of immigrants.

USA Counties lists population and housing variables including age, ancestry, race, education, income, and poverty for each county in the United States. It provides economic data for the private sector (manufacturing, wholesale trade, retail trade, service industries) as well as government employment and finance. Non-Census data include federal funds, current employment data from the Bureau of Labor Statistics, election data through 1992, Social Security beneficiaries, and vital statistics (births, marriages, and deaths). Additional information is available at http://govinfo.kerr.orst.edu/usaco-stateis.html.

U.S. Populations (National Institutes of Health) contains annual county population estimates by 5-year age groups, race, and sex from 1973 to 1996. Additional information is available at www-seer.ims.nci.nih.gov/USPops. The data are compressed and must be downloaded.

Vital Statistics of the United States is an annual publication of the National Center for Health Statistics containing detailed birth and death statistics for the United States, states, regions, metropolitan areas, counties, and cities. Additional information can be found at www.cdc.gov/nchs/nvss.htm.

The Bureau of the Census maintains a huge FAQ (*f*requently *a*sked *q*uestions and answers) repository. The questions relate to the Census and how data are accessed and used. The repository is located at www.census.gov/dmd/www/faqquest.htm.

5.3.1 How to Access Census Bureau Data

There are many different ways to access Census Bureau data, and the process is easier than ever before. The following sections outline where the various census data sets can be found.

5.3.1.1 *Online Access*

Most Census Bureau data are available through the Census Bureau's Internet home page located at www.census.gov.

5.3.1.2 *Community Availability*

Census Bureau data can be accessed in other media through the more than 1,800 state and local organizations participating in Data Center Programs, through 32 national and local minority organizations that are part of the National Census Information Center Program, and through 1,400 public and university libraries designated as federal depository libraries. In addition, Census Bureau reports and CD-ROMs are available for public use and review at 12 regional offices around the country. These are as follows. Note that these 12 regional offices are also the location of other federal offices and depositories.

Atlanta Regional Office
U.S. Bureau of the Census
101 Marietta Street, Suite 3200
Atlanta, GA 30303-2700
(404) 730-3832
TDD Number (404) 730-3963

Boston Regional Office
Bureau of the Census
Two Copley Place, Suite 301
P.O. Box 9108
Boston, MA 02117-9108
(617) 424-0510

Charlotte Regional Office
901 Center Park Drive, Suite 106
Charlotte, NC 28217-2935
(704) 344-6142

Chicago Regional Office
Chicago Regional Census Center
111 W. Jackson Blvd., Suite 400
Chicago, IL. 60604
(312) 353-9191
Fax: (312) 353-8957

Dallas Regional Office
6303 Harry Hines, Suite 210
Dallas, TX 75235
214-640-4400

Denver Regional Office
6900 West Jefferson Ave.
Lakewood, CO 80235
(303) 969-6750

Detroit Regional Office
Crowne Pointe Plaza
25900 Greenfield, Suite 400
Oak Park, MI 48237
(248) 968-2100

Kansas City Regional Office
Regional Census Center
10015 N. Executive Hills Blvd.
Kansas City, MO 64153
(816) 801-2050

Los Angeles Regional Office
15350 Sherman Way, Suite 300
Van Nuys, CA 91406-4224
(818) 904-6393
Fax: (818) 904-6427

New York Regional Office
26 Federal Plaza, Rm. 37-130
New York, NY 10278
(212) 264-3860
Fax: (212) 264-3862

Philadelphia Regional Office
1601 Market Street, 21st Floor
Philadelphia, PA 19103-2395
(215) 656-7550

Seattle Regional Office
U.S. Bureau of the Census
700 5th Ave., Suite 5100, Key Tower
Seattle, WA 98104-5018
(206) 553-5837 or
(800) 233-3308

5.3.1.3 CD-ROMs

Census Bureau products are available for sale through the Census Bureau's Customer Service Center, the U.S. Government Printing Office, and other sales outlets.

5.3.1.4 Other Sources

Many other governmental agencies and private companies provide Census Bureau data and offer various services related to using Census Bureau information or products. These include, among others, the state agencies that work with the Census Bureau to develop population estimates and projections, the U.S. Department of Commerce's International Trade Administration and STAT-USA for information on foreign trade, the National Archives and Records Administration for access to records of past censuses for genealogical research, and private companies that provide geographic information system products and services related to the Census Bureau's TIGER/Line Files.

5.3.2 Bureau of Labor Statistics

The Bureau of Labor Statistics (BLS) (at http://stats.bls.gov/) is a fact-finding agency engaged in the collection, interpretation, and dissemination of economic information. It conducts research on employment, human resources, prices, wages and industrial relations, productivity, safety and health, and economic growth. In many of these areas, the bureau has experience dating back to 1884. The bureau's goals are to measure the economy through producing and disseminating timely, accurate, and relevant information in its areas of expertise and to improve accuracy, efficiency, and relevance of economic measures and program outputs through increased application of state-of-the-art statistical techniques, economic concepts, technology, and management processes.

Relevant publications for the social and behavioral researcher (most of which are available online) include

- *The Editor's Desk*
- News releases from BLS
- *Information Services*
- *Monthly Labor Review Online*
- *Compensation and Working Conditions*
- *The National Compensation Survey: Compensation Statistics for the 21st Century*
- *Occupational Outlook Quarterly*
- *Career Guides*
- *Occupational Outlook Handbook*
- *Career Guide to Industries*
- *Issues in Labor Statistics*
- *Job Leavers*
- BLS bulletins
- *BLS Handbook of Methods*
- *Report on the American Workforce*
- *Major Programs of the BLS*
- *Report on the Youth Labor Force*
- *Geographic Profile*
- National Compensation Survey bulletins
- Additional bulletins
- *Catalog of BLS Publications*
- Career information
- BLS research papers

As do other federal agencies, the BLS offers data on a variety of different topics. The most often requested series of data as of 2000 are as follows.

Employment

Civilian labor force (seasonally adjusted)
Civilian employment (seasonally adjusted)
Civilian unemployment (seasonally adjusted)
Total non-farm payroll employment (seasonally adjusted)
Unemployment rate (seasonally adjusted)
Average hourly earnings (unadjusted)
Average weekly hours (unadjusted)

Productivity

Output per hour—nonfarm business productivity
Nonfarm business unit labor costs
Nonfarm business real hourly compensation
Private nonfarm business—multifactor productivity

Price indexes

CPI for all urban consumers (CPI-U) 1982-84 = 100 (unadjusted)
CPI for all urban consumers (CPI-U) 1967 = 100 (unadjusted)
CPI for urban wage earners and clerical workers (CPI-W) 1982-84 = 100 (unadjusted)

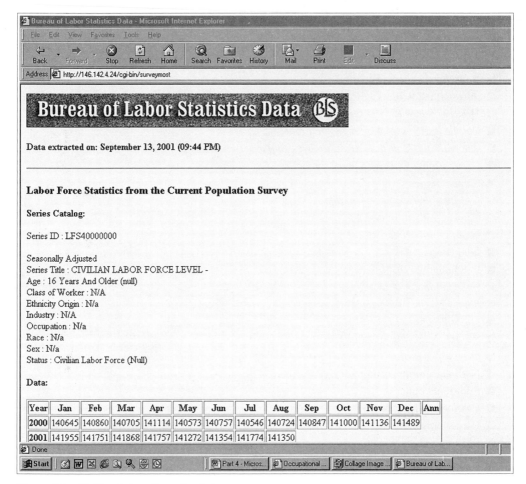

Figure 5.2. Civilian Labor Force Statistics

CPI-U less food and energy (unadjusted)

CPI-W less food and energy (unadjusted)

PPI finished goods 1982 = 100 (unadjusted)

PPI finished goods less food and energy (unadjusted)

PPi finished goods—energy (unadjusted)

PPI finished goods—food (unadjusted)

U.S. import index—all (unadjusted)

U.S. export index—all (unadjusted)

Compensation

Employment cost index (ECI) civilian (unadjusted)

ECI private (unadjusted)

ECI private wage and salaries (unadjusted)

Figure 5.2 shows the results of requesting one of these series of data, the employment statistics for the civilian labor force for 2000 and 2001.

FEDSTATS 5.4

FedStats (at www.fedstats.gov/) summarizes the statistics reported by more than 70 agencies in the United States federal government. The Federal Interagency Council on Statistical Policy maintains this site to provide easy access to the full range of statistics and information produced by these agencies for public use. This is a vast source of data on almost every sociological variable of interest. The agencies included and their associated URLs are listed in Table 5.5.

DATA MINING THROUGH FEDERAL RESOURCES 5.5

FERRET (Federal Electronic Research and Review Extraction Tool) is a sophisticated data mining tool developed and supported by the U.S. Bureau of the Census in collaboration with the Bureau of Labor Statistics. It permits both the novice and the expert to extract data for national, state, and metropolitan areas from census and government files. It can be found at http://ferret.bls.census.gov/cgi-bin/ferret. Once you subscribe, you can select the type of data you want to download, such as School Enrollment Supplement or Fertility and Birth Expectations Supplement. The data are then delivered electronically in one of many different formats that can be chosen, and they can be manipulated as needed.

5.5.1 PAIS International Database

PAIS International database (521 West 43rd Street, New York, NY 10036-4396, (212) 736-6629, www.pais.org/) contains information about journal articles, government reports and documents, and books pertaining to political science, international relations, economics, government, law, business, demography, and public affairs. The editors of PAIS review more than 1,800 journals, 6,000 books, and thousands of Web sites and electronic documents annually to classify some 12,000 to 14,000 items. Perhaps the most useful feature of this Internet site is that when available, each of the journals listed is linked to the home page for that journal.

5.5.2 ATLA Religion Database

ATLA Religion Database is the premier index to journal articles, book reviews, and collections of essays in all fields of religion. This comprehensive bibliographic database spans 50 years. Selected records go back as far as 1818. The more than 1 million records in the database include 366,000 journal articles, 14,500 multiauthor works containing 192,000 essays, 357,000 book reviews, and 1,461 journal titles. About 600 journals are currently indexed, and the material spans 35 languages and 128,000 cross-referenced subject headings in the electronic thesaurus. The journals covered include *Faith and Mission*, *Saturday Review*, and *Behavior and Philosophy*.

Table 5.5	AGENCIES FOR WHICH DATA ARE AVAILABLE THROUGH FEDSTATS	
Agency	Home Page URL	Federal Department
Administration for Children and Families	www.acf.dhhs.gov/	Health and Human Services
Administration on Aging	www.aoa.dhhs.gov/	Health and Human Services
Agency for Health Care Policy and Research	www.ahcpr.gov/	Health and Human Services
Agency for International Development	www.info.usaid.gov/	Independent agency
Agency for Toxic Substances and Disease Registry	www.atsdr.cdc.gov/atsdrhome.html	Health and Human Services
Agricultural Research Service	www.ars.usda.gov/	Agriculture
Animal and Plant Health Inspection Service	www.aphis.usda.gov/	Agriculture
Army Corps of Engineers	www.usace.army.mil/	Defense
Bureau of Economic Analysis	www.bea.doc.gov/	Commerce
Bureau of Justice Statistics	www.ojp.usdoj.gov/bjs/	Justice
Bureau of Labor Statistics	www.bls.gov/	Labor
Bureau of Land Management	www.blm.gov/	Interior
Bureau of the Census	www.census.gov/	Commerce
Bureau of Transportation Statistics	www.bts.gov/	Transportation
Center for Mental Health Service	www.mentalhealth.org/	Health and Human Services
Center for Substance Abuse Prevention	www.samhsa.gov/csap/index.htm	Health and Human Services
Center for Substance Abuse Treatment	www.samhsa.gov/csat/csat.htm	Health and Human Services
Centers for Disease Control and Prevention	www.cdc.gov/	Health and Human Services
Central Intelligence Agency	www.odci.gov/	Independent agency
Community Planning and Development	www.hud.gov/offices/cpd	Housing and Urban Development
Consumer Product Safety Commission	www.cpsc.gov/	Independent agency
Department of Agriculture	www.usda.gov/	Agriculture
Department of Energy	www.energy.gov/	Energy
Department of Health and Human Services	www.os.dhhs.gov/	Health and Human Services
Department of Housing and Urban Development	www.hud.gov/	Housing and Urban Development
Department of Veterans Affairs	www.va.gov/index.htm	Independent agency
Directorate for Information Operations and Reports	www.fedstats.gov/key_stats/DIORkey.html	Office of the Secretary of Defense
Drug Enforcement Administration	www.usdoj.gov/dea/	Justice
Economic Research Service	www.ers.usda.gov/	Agriculture

Agency	Home Page URL	Federal Department
Employment and Training Administration	www.doleta.gov/	Labor
Employment Standards Administration	www.dol.gov/dol/esa	Labor
Energy Information Administration	www.eia.doe.gov/	Energy
Environmental Protection Agency	www.epa.gov/	Independent agency
Equal Employment Opportunity Commission	www.eeoc.gov/	Independent agency
Federal Aviation Administration	www.faa.gov/	Transportation
Federal Bureau of Investigation	www.fbi.gov/	Justice
Federal Bureau of Prisons	www.bop.gov/	Justice
Federal Communications Commission	www.fcc.gov/	Independent agency
Federal Deposit Insurance Corporation	www.fdic.gov/	Independent agency
Federal Highway Administration	www.fhwa.dot.gov/	Transportation
Federal Interagency Forum on Child and Family Statistics	www.childstats.gov/	Interagency
Federal Railroad Administration	www.dot.gov:80/dotinfo/fra/welcome.html	Transportation
Federal Reserve Board	www.federalreserve.gov/	Independent agency
Federal Transit Administration	www.fta.dot.gov/	Transportation
Food Nutrition and Consumer Service	www.fns.usda.gov/fncs/	Agriculture
Foreign Agricultural Service	www.fas.usda.gov/	Agriculture
Forest Service	www.fs.fed.us/	Agriculture
Health Care Financing Administration	www.hcfa.gov/	Health and Human Services
Health Resources and Services Administration	www.hrsa.dhhs.gov/	Health and Human Services
Immigration and Naturalization Service	www.ins.usdoj.gov/	Justice
Indian Health Service	www.ihs.gov/	Health and Human Services
Internal Revenue Service—Statistics of Income Division	www.irs.ustreas.gov/prod/tax_stats/	Treasury
International Trade Administration	www.ita.doc.gov/	Commerce
Maritime Administration	www.marad.dot.gov/	Transportation
Mine Safety and Health Administration	www.msha.gov/	Labor
Minerals Management Service	www.mms.gov/	Interior
National Aeronautics and Space Administration	www.nasa.gov/	Independent agency
National Agricultural Statistics Service	www.usda.gov/nass/	Agriculture
National Biological Service	www.nbs.gov/	Interior

(continued)

Table 5.5   Continued

Agency	Home Page URL	Federal Department
National Cancer Institute	www.nci.nih.gov	Health and Human Services
National Center for Education Statistics	www.ed.gov/NCES/	Education
National Center for Health Statistics	www.cdc.gov/nchs/	Health and Human Services
National Eye Institute	www.nei.nih.gov/	Health and Human Services
National Heart, Lung, and Blood Institute	www.nhlbi.nih.gov/index.htm	Health and Human Services
National Highway Traffic Safety Administration	www.nhtsa.dot.gov/	Transportation
National Institute of Allergy and Infectious Disease	www.niaid.nih.gov/	Health and Human Services
National Institute of Arthritis and Musculoskeletal and Skin Disease	www.nih.gov/niams/	Health and Human Services
National Institute of Child Health and Human Development	www.nichd.nih.gov/	Health and Human Services
National Institute of Dental and Craniofacial Research	www.nidcr.nih.gov/	Health and Human Services
National Institute of Diabetes and Digestive and Kidney Diseases	www.niddk.nih.gov/	Health and Human Services
National Institute of Environmental Health Sciences	www.niehs.nih.gov/	Health and Human Services
National Institute of Neurological Disorders and Stroke	www.ninds.nih.gov/	Health and Human Services
National Institute of Nursing Research	www.nih.gov/ninr/	Health and Human Services
National Institute on Aging	www.nih.gov/nia/	Health and Human Services
National Institute on Alcohol Abuse and Alcoholism	www.niaaa.nih.gov/	Health and Human Services
National Institute on Deafness and Other Communication Disorders	www.nidcd.nih.gov	Health and Human Services
National Institute on Drug Abuse	www.nida.nih.gov/	Health and Human Services
National Institutes of Health	www.nih.gov/	Health and Human Services
National Marine Fisheries Service	ww.nmfs.noaa.gov	Commerce
National Oceanic and Atmospheric Administration	www.noaa.gov/	Commerce
National Science Foundation Science Resources Studies	www.nsf.gov/sbe/srs/stats.htm	Independent agency
Natural Resources Conservation Service	www.nrcs.usda.gov/	Agriculture
Occupational Safety and Health Administration	www.osha.gov/	Labor
Office of Federal Housing Enterprise Oversight	www.ofheo.gov/	Housing and Urban Development
Office of Management and Budget	www.whitehouse.gov/OMB/index.html	Executive Office of the President

Agency	Home Page URL	Federal Department
Office of Policy Development and Research	www.huduser.org/	Housing and Urban Development
Office of Public and Indian Housing	www.hud.gov/pih/pih.html	Housing and Urban Development
Office of Public Health and Science	www.surgeongeneral.gov/ophs/	Health and Human Services
Office of Scientific and Technical Information	www.doe.gov/osti/ostipg.html	Energy
Office of the Assistant Secretary for Environment, Safety and Health	http://tis.eh.doe/gov/portal/home.htm	Energy
Office of the Assistant Secretary for Housing	www.hud.gov	Housing and Urban Development
Office of the Assistant Secretary for Planning and Evaluation	http://aspe.os.dhhs.gov/	Health and Human Services
Office of the Director of the National Institute of Health	www.nih.gov/icd/od/index.htm	Health and Human Services
Office of the Secretary of Defense, Deputy Assistant Secretary for Administration	www.defenselink.mil/	Defense
Office of the Secretary of Transportation	www.dot.gov/ost/	Transportation
Small Business Administration	www.sba.gov/	Independent agency
Social Security Administration Office of Policy	www.ssa.gov/policy/	Social Security Administration
Stat-USA	www.stat-usa.gov/	Commerce
Substance Abuse and Mental Health Services Administration	www.samhsa.gov/	Health and Human Services
United States Customs Service	www.customs.treas.gov/	Treasury
United States Fish and Wildlife Service	www.fws.gov/	Interior
United States Geological Survey	www.usgs.gov/	Interior

GENERAL DATABASES OF BIBLIOGRAPHIC MATERIAL 5.6

There are virtually thousands of databases of bibliographic material available for perusal. Many are available in print, but increasingly they appear online. Almost every major institution of higher learning makes such a list available through both on- and off-campus access. In fact, these sources of information are often available to the public at large: It is not necessary to have faculty, staff, or student status. Contact your reference librarian to see what is available at your institution.

A sample of such databases is shown in Table 5.6. For the most part, these are proprietary, with their contents owned by the company that produces them and then licensed to institutions that make the contents available to users.

Table 5.6	A SELECTION OF BIBLIOGRAPHIC DATABASES AVAILABLE AT MOST MAJOR RESEARCH INSTITUTIONS

Database	Description
UnCover	UnCover is an electronic database that provides access to citations of more than eight million articles published since 1988 in almost 18,000 journals. The journals (most of which are in English) represent a range of disciplines (presently 51% sciences, 38% social sciences, and 11% humanities).
INFOTRAC®	The Infotrac® database provides citations to individual articles, citations with abstracts (summaries), and in many cases the full text of articles.
Congressional Universe	Congressional Universe, published by the Congressional Information Service (CIS), a subsidiary of LEXIS®-NEXIS®, provides access to information on the United States Congress, federal legislation and regulations, and related information. It also includes links to the Web sites of selected news and other organizations that provide background information and analysis. The time period covered varies greatly among the different categories of information, with the earliest being 1968. Coverage for many categories begins during the 1980s or 1990s.
CommSearch (2nd ed.)	The CommSearch database contains (a) the full texts covering the years 1991-1995 of the 6 scholarly journals published by the National Communication Association and (b) a searchable index up through the end of 1995 of these 6 journals as well as 18 other journals in the fields of communication studies and mass communications.
Arts & Humanities Citation Index	The Arts & Humanities Citation Index Compact Disc Edition covers more than 1,200 of the world's most significant arts and humanities journals, spanning more than 25 disciplines and covering the years from 1975 to the present.
Social Sciences Citation Index	The compact disc edition covers 1,700 of the world's most significant social sciences journals, spanning 60 disciplines, from 1981 to the present.
Science Citation Index	The compact disc edition provides access to more than 3,300 of the world's leading science and technical journals in a broad range of scientific subjects.
Anthropological Literature	Anthropological Literature contains the index (from 1984 to the present) to periodicals and edited works from the Tozzer Library at Harvard University. (The source is updated annually.) The primary subject emphases are archaeology, linguistics, and all branches of anthropology. Articles from related fields such as sociology, history, geography, and human genetics are also indexed. Although the source includes international publications, articles in languages other than Germanic, Romance, Scandinavian, or Slavic are indexed only if a title in one of the aforementioned languages is provided. Obituaries are indexed. Book, film, and video reviews; interviews; and conference reports are not indexed.
LEXIS®-NEXIS® Academic Universe	LEXIS®-NEXIS® Academic Universe provides full-text access to general and specialty news sources that are useful for company, business, industry, financial, demographic, policy, and market research. Legal sources include federal and state case law, law reviews, codes, statutes, and patent research.
EHRAF (electronic Human Relations Area Files)	EHRAF provides access to the full text of book chapters, articles, and unpublished materials on various ethnic, national, cultural, and religious groups. It is an important research tool for anthropologists and other social scientists.

Statistical Universe   Statistical Universe indexes and abstracts a wide range of statistics from the U.S. government, the world's most important and prolific publisher of statistics. Federal agencies produce a continuous flow of facts and figures on virtually every aspect of life in America and on most matters of worldwide concern. Statistical Universe is the most comprehensive source of federal statistics. It provides detailed abstracts, indexing, and locator information for all statistical reports of general research value issued by the federal government since the early 1960s. In some cases the full text of the publication is included. Statistical Universe also includes hyperlinks to all key statistical data available on federal agency Web sites as well as to the hundreds of reports stored within the Universe service itself.

Oxford English Dictionary   The *Oxford English Dictionary* (*OED*) records the history and development of the English language from its origins up to the past few years, with new editions providing updates. The *OED* describes both modern definitions of words and the historical development of their forms and meaning.

JSTOR   JSTOR (Journal Storage Project) is an ongoing project of some 200 libraries and other nonprofit organizations, designed to provide electronic access to the full text of core academic journals in a variety of disciplines. More information about the JSTOR project, including a list of journals and dates of coverage, can be found at www.jstor.org/ about.

INSPEC   INSPEC covers the world's published literature on all aspects of electronics, electrical engineering, physics, computers, and control and information technology. INSPEC scans approximately 4,200 journals and 1,000 conference proceedings, books, reports, and dissertations. The coverage spans 1989 to the present.

USING SEARCH ENGINES   5.7

Online research would not be possible without the use of search engines. Search engines allow researchers to enter search terms; the engine then lists Web pages on which information about the terms might be found. Search engines work by regularly sending out "spiders"—programs that search for newly appearing Web pages—and then cataloging the contents of these pages.

Searchenginewatch.com is a useful collection of information about search engines and links to the hundreds that are available, organized by category such as major search engines, specialty search engines, metacrawlers, regional search engines, news search engines, kids' search engines, multimedia search engines, and search utilities. It also contains hundred of links to related sites and a free newsletter subscription service. The following is a list of other search engines.

iLor (www.ilor.com/): The results of a search using iLor are quite different from those of other search engines. When the cursor arrow is placed over a search result, an option menu appears that provides options such as opening the results in a separate window or placing them on a list to save for later use.

Northern Light (www.nlsearch.com): In addition to its index of Web pages, Northern Light also searches (through pay-per-view) articles from periodicals and books not generally available on the Web. It sorts its results into topic headings.

Google (www.google.com): This is currently the most popular search engine. Google uses PageRank™, a system for ranking Web pages developed by Google founders Larry Page and Sergey Brin at Stanford University. PageRank relies on the democratic nature of the Web by using its link structure as an indicator of an individual page's value. Google interprets a link from page A to page B as a "vote," by page A, for page B. High-quality sites receive a higher PageRank, which Google remembers each time it conducts a search.

Internet Sleuth (www.isleuth.com): Internet Sleuth is a 3,000-strong collection of specialized on-line databases that can also simultaneously utilize up to six other search sites for Web pages, news, and other types of information.

Dogpile (www.dogpile.com): This metasearch site can go through 13 Web search engines and more than two dozen online news services or other types of sources. It sorts the results by the search engine that found them.

Ask Jeeves (www.ask.com or www.askjeeves.com): An excellent beginner's site that is also good for anyone's general queries, Ask Jeeves leads the user through questions to help narrow the search and simultaneously searches six other search sites for relevant Web pages.

Excite (www.excite.com): Excite is good for searches on broad general topics and adds extras, such as a simultaneous search of the Web, news headlines, sports scores, and company information. It then groups the relevant results on a single page.

AltaVista (www.altavista.net): AltaVista is quick and provides very detailed results in its search of more than 250 million Web pages.

Yahoo (www.yahoo.com): A human-compiled directory of Web sites, Yahoo doesn't help search for the contents of individual Web pages, but it is excellent for researching broad general topics.

Lycos (www.lycos.com): Lycos provides a good selection of advanced search capabilities, including the ability to search for specific media types (e.g., JPEG files, Java scripts). Its advanced search, Lycos Pro, provides even more options.

HotBot (www.hotbot.com): This is the search site of *Wired* magazine, whose search engine Inktomi also powers Snap.com's and Yahoo's Web searches. It is an excellent tool for finding specific in-formation. In addition to a thorough and up-to-date index, it provides an easy interface for con-structing precise search queries.

Metacrawler (www.metacrawler.com): This is a metasearch site that simultaneously searches Yahoo, Excite, and five other search engines, then aggregates the results.

5.8 MICROFICHE AS AN ARCHIVAL MEDIUM

Even though many periodicals and almost all newspapers appear in electronic format online, some books, newspapers, magazines, scientific journals, and doctoral dissertations are still available as mi-crofiche. This format has many advantages, such as packing a lot of information in an incredibly small space, and it is archivally desirable.

Interlibrary loans can fill researchers' needs anywhere in the United States. University Microfilms International (UMI) makes available journal articles and issue reprints of nearly 10,000 magazines and journals, by article or issue and in single or multiple copies. All the major journals in sociology and the social and behavioral sciences generally can be obtained for a fee. Every periodical cited in the UMI catalog is available either on paper or in microform (microfilm or microfiche). For further infor-mation, contact the UMI Article Reprint Department, 300 North Zeeb Rd., Ann Arbor, MI 48106. In England, the address is 18 Bedford Row, London WCIR 4EJ.

For a full list of available microforms see *Guide to Microforms in Print 2000*. This is an annual pub-lication listing author, subject, price, type of microform, and publisher. It is about 2,000 pages in length and is published by K. J. Saur in Munchen, Germany (online at www.saur.de/).

ONLINE COMPUTER LIBRARY CENTER 5.9

Online Computer Library Center (OCLC), at www.oclc.org/home/, operates a computer network used by more than 2,400 libraries in the United States and Canada, of which more than 300 are U.S. federal libraries. Founded in 1967 as the Ohio College Library Center, it has grown rapidly into an international center for library automation. To reflect its broadened geographic scope, the name was changed in 1977 to OCLC Inc., OCLC being the acronym by which it had already become known throughout the world. More than 3,800 remote computer terminals in the network are linked to OCLC's computer center in Dublin, Ohio. The OCLC is available only to institutions, through which individuals can use the resource.

Libraries use the OCLC system to catalog books, order custom-prined catalog cards, maintain location information on library materials, and arrange for interlibrary lending of materials. The files contain more than 6 million records of books and other library materials such as U.S. government documents.

The researcher can use a terminal to check bibliographic information (e.g., author, title), find out whether his or her library owns the item, or locate items in other libraries. Most college and university libraries do not charge for these services. OCLC can be contacted at OCLC Online Computer Library Center, Inc., 6565 Frantz Road, Dublin, OH 43017-3395, USA, telephone (614) 764-6000 or 1-800-848- 5878, fax (614) 764-6096, e-mail oclc@oclc.org.

DOCUMENTARY RESOURCES AVAILABLE IN LIBRARIES 5.10

Social science researchers commonly use various reference books, bibliographies, databases, and other materials. Some of the most useful of these are listed below.

5.10.1 Statistical Sources

5.10.1.1 Statistical Abstract of the United States

Statistical Abstract of the United States 2000 is the most current edition of the publication of the Government Printing Office and is available online (www.census.gov/prod/www/statistical-abstract-us.html) in .pdf (portable document format) and organized into the sections listed below. It contains an interactive index for locating particular information. The combination of it being electronically accessible and having search capabilities should make familiarization with it a requirement for any researcher.

Section 1. Population
Section 2. Vital Statistics
Section 3. Health and Nutrition

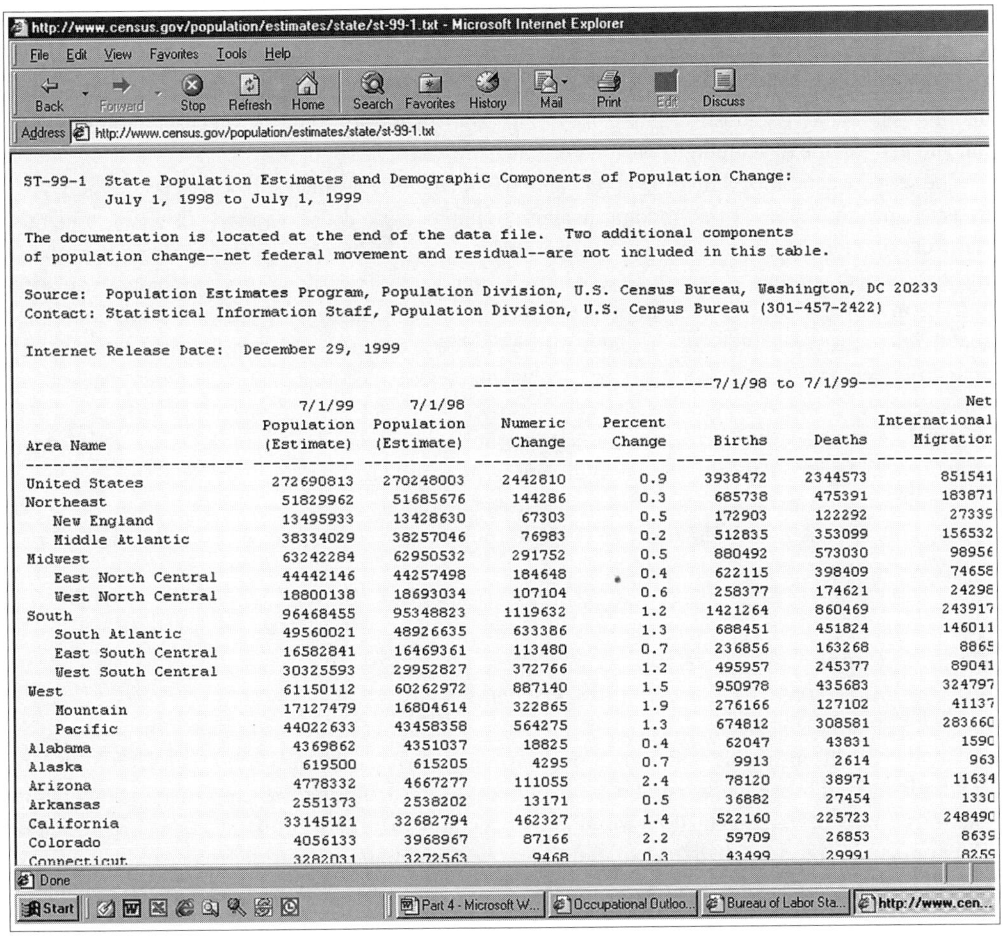

ST-99-1 State Population Estimates and Demographic Components of Population Change: July 1, 1998 to July 1, 1999

The documentation is located at the end of the data file. Two additional components of population change--net federal movement and residual--are not included in this table.

Source: Population Estimates Program, Population Division, U.S. Census Bureau, Washington, DC 20233
Contact: Statistical Information Staff, Population Division, U.S. Census Bureau (301-457-2422)

Internet Release Date: December 29, 1999

Area Name	7/1/99 Population (Estimate)	7/1/98 Population (Estimate)	7/1/98 to 7/1/99 Numeric Change	Percent Change	Births	Deaths	Net International Migration
United States	272690813	270248003	2442810	0.9	3938472	2344573	851541
Northeast	51829962	51685676	144286	0.3	685738	475391	183871
New England	13495933	13428630	67303	0.5	172903	122292	27339
Middle Atlantic	38334029	38257046	76983	0.2	512835	353099	156532
Midwest	63242284	62950532	291752	0.5	880492	573030	98956
East North Central	44442146	44257498	184648	0.4	622115	398409	74658
West North Central	18800138	18693034	107104	0.6	258377	174621	24298
South	96468455	95348823	1119632	1.2	1421264	860469	243917
South Atlantic	49560021	48926635	633386	1.3	688451	451824	146011
East South Central	16582841	16469361	113480	0.7	236856	163268	8865
West South Central	30325593	29952827	372766	1.2	495957	245377	89041
West	61150112	60262972	887140	1.5	950978	435683	324797
Mountain	17127479	16804614	322865	1.9	276166	127102	41137
Pacific	44022633	43458358	564275	1.3	674812	308581	283660
Alabama	4369862	4351037	18825	0.4	62047	43831	1590
Alaska	619500	615205	4295	0.7	9913	2614	963
Arizona	4778332	4667277	111055	2.4	78120	38971	11634
Arkansas	2551373	2538202	13171	0.5	36882	27454	1330
California	33145121	32682794	462327	1.4	522160	225723	248490
Colorado	4056133	3968967	87166	2.2	59709	26853	8639
Connecticut	3282031	3272563	9468	0.3	43499	29991	8259

Figure 5.3. Sample Screen From the Population Estimates Program Web Site

5.10.1.2 State Population Estimates

The Population Estimates Program (www.census.gov/population/www/estimates/statepop.html) each year produces, for each state, total population estimates, estimates by age and sex, and estimates by race and Hispanic origin. The release of total population estimates at the end of the calendar year also includes demographic components of change. In the spring, the program releases population by age and sex, presenting tables for different age groupings as well as single year of age. A third release in the summer presents estimates by age, sex, race, and Hispanic origin. All estimates are for the resident population unless noted otherwise. The reference date for state estimates is July 1. Figure 5.3 shows a sample screen from this site, containing general information, by state, regarding population estimates.

5.10.1.3. Historical Statistics of the United States: Colonial Times to 1970

Historical Statistics of the United States: Colonial Times to 1970 (produced by the U.S. Department of Commerce, Bureau of the Census, and published by Kraus International in 1989 and by Basic

Books in a 1976 edition) is available from the Superintendent of Documents, P.O. Box 371954, Pittsburgh, PA 15250-7954. This is a two-volume set, updating and expanding the second edition, *Historical Statistics of the United States, Colonial Times to 1957*. The bicentennial edition includes more than 12,500 time series, mostly annual, providing a statistical history of U.S. social, economic, political, and geographic development during periods from 1610 to 1970.

The series are organized in 24 chapters and 50 subchapters on such subjects as population, vital statistics, health, labor, prices, income, welfare, climate, agriculture, forestry, fisheries, minerals, construction, housing, manufactures, transportation, communications, energy, commerce, banking, and government, among others, plus a separate chapter devoted to colonial and pre-federal statistics. Accompanying text cites sources, defines technical terms, and includes discussion of methodology, qualifications, and reliability of the data. Also included are a time-period index, indicating which time series begin within specified 10- or 20-year time segments, and a detailed alphabetical subject index.

Data later than 1970 are presented for many of the series in annual issues of the *Statistical Abstract of the United States*. A special historical appendix in each *Statistical Abstract*, beginning with the 1975 edition, links the historical series to specific tables.

This collection is also available on a CD-ROM, published in 1997 by Cambridge University Press (http://www.cup.org).

5.10.1.4. County and City Extra: Annual Metro, City, and County Data Book

The tenth edition of this text, for 2000, was edited by Deirdre A. Gaquin with Katherine A. DeBrandt and published by Bernan Press (www.bernan.com/). The *County and City Extra* contains data for every U.S. state, county, metropolitan area, and congressional district, as well as for cities with populations of more than 25,000. Subjects covered include population by age and race; housing; education; income and poverty; crime; manufacturing, trade, and services; and government finances. Maps, rankings, and explanatory notes supplement data tables.

5.10.1.5. Business Statistics of the United States

The sixth edition of *Business Statistics of the United States*, edited by Linz Audain and Cornelia J. Strawser, was published in 2000 by Bernan Press (www.bernan.com/). It contains more than 2,000 data series covering virtually every aspect of the U.S. economy, including gross domestic product, employment, production, prices, productivity, international trade, money supply, and interest rates. As in previous editions, it fully incorporates historical data revisions released by government agencies.

5.10.1.6. Sourcebook of Criminal Justice Statistics

The most recent version, *Sourcebook of Criminal Justice Statistics: 1999*, was edited by Kathleen Maguire and Ann Pastore. This product of the Bureau of Justice Statistics, U.S. Department of Justice, is published by Bernan Press (www.bernan.com/). It contains statistical information on crime and criminal justice in the United States. Information is presented by regions, states, and cities. The various data series illustrate the broad range of issues of concern to the U.S. criminal justice system. Tables and figures provide statistics, and the text covers topics such as prison populations, characteristics and sentences of inmates, public attitudes toward crime, the various types of criminal justice agencies and employees, and workload of agency personnel. Explanatory appendices, annotated sources, and a list of publishers complete the detailed overview.

5.10.1.7. A Statistical Portrait of the United States

This volume, the first edition of which was published in 1998 by Bernan Press (www.bernan.com/) and edited by Mark S. Littman, illustrates demographic, social, and economic trends in U.S. society using interpretive text, charts, and tables. Chapters cover population, immigration, labor force, income, education, crime, voting patterns, recreation and leisure, the environment, and trends in government taxing and spending. Detailed tables present up to 25 years of data.

5.10.1.8. World Bank Atlas

World Bank Atlas: 2001, 33rd Edition is a product of the World Bank and was published in 2001 by Bernan Press (www.bernan.com/). The atlas, tables, charts, and colorful maps illustrate the development themes of people, economy, environment, states and markets, world view, and global links. Text, maps, and references appear in English, French, and Spanish.

5.10.1.9. The Municipal Year Book

The 2001 edition of *The Municipal Year Book* was published by the International City/County Management Association. It is an authoritative reference book on municipal governments covering such topics as the role of city governments, including education, housing, welfare, and health. The listings for separate municipal governments make it possible to compare any city with other cities on hundreds of items.

5.10.1.10 UNESCO Statistical Yearbook

This yearbook, the most recent edition of which was published in 1999 by Bernan Press (www.bernan.com/), is a product of the United Nations Educational, Scientific, and Cultural Organization (UNESCO). This major reference book has been revised annually, but a 2000 edition was not published because UNESCO's Statistics Office was in the process of moving from Paris to Montreal and could not gather the data for the yearbook. This edition provides key statistical information on education, science, technology, and communication in almost 200 countries. Topics covered worldwide include the following.

Population: Tables outline population by area and density from 1960 through 1976 and estimate major areas from 1970 to 1999.

Education: Summary tables for all levels of education are cited, and public expenditure on education is given at the current market prices and by level of education.

Science and technology: Labor power is inventoried for various areas of research and experimental development, and expenditures in the field are totaled.

Libraries: Libraries' holdings are summarized by category of library collections, borrowers, works loaned out, current expenditures, and personnel.

Publishing: Book production is delineated by number of titles published, language, number of copies, subject groups, translations, and authors; totals of newspapers and other periodicals, paper production, and paper consumption are aggregated.

Media: Seating capacity and annual attendance at theaters are given; radio/TV tables provide statistical information on transmitters, receivers, and programs.

5.10.1.11 Digest of Education Statistics

The most recent (2000) edition of this book was edited by Charlene Hoffman and Thomas Snyder. It is a product of the National Center for Education Statistics, U.S. Department of Education, and published by Bernan Press (www.bernan.com/). It provides statistical information on the whole range of American education. Coverage ranges from kindergarten through graduate school, and it is based on data from both government and private sources. Chapters break down information at all levels of education, elementary and secondary education, federal programs for education and related activities, outcomes of education, international comparisons of education, and learning resources and technology. Supplemental sections on population trends, attitudes toward education, education characteristics of the labor force, government finances, and economic trends provide the background needed to evaluate education data.

5.10.1.12 Education Statistics of the United States

The third edition of this source was published in 2001 by Bernan Press (www.bernan.com/) and edited by Katherine A. DeBrandt and Deirdre A. Gaquin. It brings together the most sought-after data from many sources of education statistics. Unique to this volume are educational data for the more than 3,100 U.S. counties.

Data are presented—along with brief analysis—in four groups of tables that present size and composition of enrollment, educational attainment, education characteristics by state, and county education data. The data in these tables are cross-classified by such socioeconomic variables as age, race, sex, marital status, earnings, labor force status, grade level, college attendance, and dropout rates.

County and state data for public schools for the 1995-1996 school year, previously untabulated, can be found along with state-level data for private elementary and secondary schools. International comparisons and historical tables dating back as far as 1940 are also included.

5.10.1.13 Almanac of Higher Education

The *1999 NEA Almanac of Higher Education* was published in 2000 by the National Education Association. It provides a summary of issues and data regarding higher education, including sections written by various authors covering faculty salaries, workload and performance, part-time faculty at community colleges, technology issues related to collective bargaining, fiscal prospects, benefits and retirement, and worklife issues of support personnel.

5.10.1.14 The International Handbook of Universities

This handbook, the most recent issue of which came out in 2001, is from the British publisher Palgrave. It is a guide to more than 7,300 higher education institutions in more than 175 countries.

More than 1,000 new entries have been added since the last edition. Each entry offers the name of the institution and full postal address; telephone, fax, e-mail, and telegraphic numbers and Web sites; all faculties, colleges, schools, institutes, and departments within the institutions, with numbers of staff and students and the fields of study offered; a brief historical background; information on the academic year, admission requirements, and tuition fees; degrees and diplomas offered at each level of study; student services, special facilities (e.g., museums), and publications; size and breakdown of academic staff; student enrollment figures, including foreign students; and principal academic and administrative officers with their own contact details.

5.10.1.15 *Commonwealth Universities Yearbook*

Palgrave also published this source, the most recent edition of which came out in 2000. It provides profiles of more than 600 universities in 36 countries or regions of the British Commonwealth, including the former British colony of Hong Kong. Each profile includes such facts and figures as foundation date, history, and location; library holdings; academic year with term or semester dates; statistics with a detailed breakdown of all staff and the student population; application procedures and educational requirements for entry into first degree courses; titles, course lengths, and admission requirements for first and higher degrees; language of instruction and availability of remedial courses; tuition fees, including international fees for postgraduate courses; and financial aid, including academic awards, scholarships, and bursaries.

National guides identify study options in larger countries at the undergraduate, postgraduate, and doctoral levels. A series of national introductions—illustrated with maps—provides an overview of several of the countries covered in the yearbook. These introductions summarize important background information, including academic year, pre-university education, application and admission procedures, financial issues, staff and student demographics, and references to further sources of information.

5.10.2 Bibliographies

International bibliography of the social sciences: Vol. 45. International bibliography of anthropology. (2001). New York: Routledge.
International bibliography of the social sciences: Vol. 49. International bibliography of anthropology. (2001). New York: Routledge.

5.10.3 Dictionaries and Glossaries

Champion, Dean J. (2001). *Dictionary of American criminal justice: Key terms and major Supreme Court cases.* London: Fitzroy Dearborn.

> This is a two-part dictionary. Part 1 uses an interdisciplinary approach to explain the American criminal justice system. Terms are drawn from such disciplines as criminology, criminal justice, corrections, probation/parole, juvenile justice, and policing. Many definitions are accompanied by examples from the research literature, illustrating how the terms apply in particular contexts. Also included are listings of leading theorists of criminology, a synopsis of their major theoretical contributions, and extracts from their written works. Part 2 provides examples that demonstrate the concepts of the dictionary in action. The dictionary includes the most recent and significant U.S. Supreme Court cases.

Lawson, Tony, & Garrod, Joan. (2001). *Dictionary of sociology*. London: Fitzroy Dearborn.

> The *Dictionary of Sociology* provides an introduction to the debates and issues in which sociologists engage. Key concepts in areas such as social stratification, crime and deviance, culture and identity, mass media, power and politics, and religion are defined and explained. Each entry begins with a clear one-sentence definition and goes on to provide illustrative examples of the concept or an introduction to the major points in support or criticism of it. The length of the entry usually depends on the relative importance of the concept and often depends on the degree of controversy it arouses.

Slattery, Martin. (Ed.). (2001). *Key ideas in sociology*. London: Fitzroy Dearborn.

> *Key Ideas in Sociology* provides a review of prominent sociological thinkers of the past two centuries—their lives, their main ideas, and their influence on further thinking and practice in sociology.

5.10.4 Encyclopedias

Magill, Frank N. (Ed.). (1996). *International encyclopedia of government and politics*. London: Fitzroy Dearborn.

> The *International Encyclopedia of Government and Politics* examines the scope of the science and practice of politics. The encyclopedia covers 13 major fields: civil rights and liberties; comparative government; economic issues; functions of government; history of government and politics; international government and politics; law and jurisprudence; local and regional government; military; political philosophy; politics (general); religion and government; and types of government.

Magill, Frank N. (Ed.). (2001). *International encyclopedia of sociology*. London: Fitzroy Dearborn.

> The *International Encyclopedia of Sociology* provides the general reader or student with an insight into the main topics and concerns of sociology. It contains 335 signed articles, a comprehensive glossary of terms, annotated bibliographies, and subject and general indices. A closing bibliography by Alan Sica offers a context of general readings for the individual entries.

Ness, Immanuel, & Ciment, James. (Eds.). (2000). *Encyclopedia of global population and demographics*. London: Fitzroy Dearborn.

> This up-to-date and comprehensive encyclopedia focuses on the population in each of the 194 countries of the world. Emphasis is on the world's population at the end of the 20th century and on predictions for the next 50 years. This will be the authoritative source of information for students, scholars, librarians, government officials, and journalists.

5.10.5 Guides to the Literature

Herron, Nancy L. (Ed.). (1996). *The social sciences: A cross-disciplinary guide to selected sources* (2nd ed.) (Library and Information Science Text Series). Englewood, CO: Libraries Unlimited.

> This is a guide to social science resources, useful for practicing librarians and students in library science and the social sciences. This second edition contains 1,043 annotated citations, arranged in sections on general social sciences, established disciplines, emerging disciplines including psychology and education, and the related disciplines of geography and communication.

Mitchie, J. (2001). *A reader's guide to the social sciences*. London: Fitzroy Dearborn.

> *A Reader's Guide to the Social Sciences* concentrates on economics, political economy, politics, sociology, law, management and business, psychology and organizational psychology, organizational behavior, human geography, international relations, and research and analysis methods in the social sciences. It contains more than 800 entries.

5.10.6 Handbooks, Sourcebooks, and Reviews

Berger, Charles R., & Chaffee, Steven H. (1987). *Handbook of communication science*. Newbury Park, CA: Sage.

Borgatta, Edgar F., & Cook, Karen S. (Eds.). (1988). *The future of sociology*. Thousand Oaks, CA: Sage.

GUIDES FOR SELECTION AND CONSTRUCTION OF QUESTIONNAIRES   5.11

The mail questionnaire is a list of questions used to obtain information or opinion that is mailed to potential respondents who have been chosen in some designated manner. The respondents are asked to complete the questionnaire and return it by mail.

This means of gathering information is very popular because it promises to secure data at a minimum expenditure of time and expense. The popularity of the method is often defeated because many respondents are overburdened by the number of questionnaires that reach them. In the competition for their time, respondents increasingly examine the purpose of the study, the sponsorship, the utility of findings to them, the time required to fill out the questionnaire, the quality and readability of the type, and perhaps the quality of the paper.

The all-important factor of return rates tends to differ dramatically. Table 5.7 is a brief summary of 19 studies, showing the population questioned, the aim and date of the questionnaire, the length of the questionnaire and number sent, the number and percentage of questionnaires returned, and the number of follow-ups. As you can see, the percentage of questionnaires returned varied greatly.

5.11.1 Advantages and Disadvantages of the Mail Questionnaire

Every researcher who chooses the mail questionnaire should consider its value in a highly competitive environment in which the majority of respondents probably will not complete and return the questionnaire. The researcher should examine carefully the advantages and disadvantages described below. The disadvantages are shown first to emphasize their importance. If the advantages override these disadvantages and if the method fits the study, then the questionnaire is appropriate. A guide to questionnaire construction and a guide to techniques for increasing the percentage of returned questionnaires follow the lists of advantages and disadvantages.

Table 5.7 SAMPLE OF QUESTIONNAIRES WITH DIFFERENT CHARACTERISTICS AND RATES OF RETURN

Population	Aim of Questionnaire	Length	Number Sent	Number Returned	Percentage Returned	Number of Follow-Ups	Research Agent
Members of the Ohio Genealogical Society, Summit County Chapter			221	115	52		
First- and third-year students at the University of Maryland at College Park	To examine relationships between perceptions of diversity and overall satisfaction	100 items		566	60	Mail and phone call	
Health care professionals in Rutherford, Tennessee	To study substance abuse among health care professionals		1,817	775	43		
College graduates of Johnson County Community College (Kansas) who completed career programs during the previous academic year	To assess institutional effectiveness			515	95		
Head librarians at each of Ohio's 21 adult prisons	To gather data about Ohio's prison libraries and the librarians who are responsible for them	36 items	21	12	57		
Tennessee farmers	To study the present social condition of rural society			531	75		
Terminees from Job Training Partnership Act programs in Tennessee			2,462		29.4	Two mailings	
Teachers from a Florida metropolitan school district	To study attrition in the teaching profession		310		53		
Vocational trainers at 15 vocational centers in Taiwan	To determine if the satisfaction of the trainers was related to in-service experience, age, job title, method of teaching, education level, factory experience, and teacher training.		649	420	64.7		

Alabama state representatives and senators	To examine how Alabama legislators' ratings of news media for job-relevant information correlate with their views on news media adversary and consensus agent roles		140	82	59		
Entry-level postbaccalaureate degree graduates	To determine whether graduates' perceptions of the professional role of the physical therapist and of self in that role changed after employment had begun and whether a relationship exists between these perceptions and job satisfaction		15		93		
Members of the American Society on the Abuse of Children	To examine the prevalence of career burnout for child sexual abuse therapists (1995)	Maslach Burnout Inventory, Personal Boundary Questionnaire, Flexibility subscale of the California Psychological Inventory, and demographic data	600	206	40	None reported	Dissertation study by Barton Jay Trentham
Female college graduates	To investigate the impact of self-esteem and intrapsychic conflicts on women's achievement motivation and work involvement	Hoffman's inventory, Hazan and Shaver's measure, Rosenberg and Hampilo's scales, the Work Involvement Index, the achievement scale of the Adjective Check List, Sadd's Fear of Succes scale, and a demographic and standard of living questionnaire	453		30	None reported	Dissertation study by Daniella Dankner

(continued)

Table 5.7 Continued

Population	Aim of Questionnaire	Length	Number Sent	Number Returned	Percentage Returned	Numbe of Follow-Ups	Research Agent
Louisiana state judges	To examine attitudes regarding child custody and visitation issues			190	31		
Residents of San Francisco and Santa Cruz Counties	To investigate citizen response to the 1989 Loma Prieta earthquake emergency			1,652	46		
New Jersey parents divorced between 1984 and 1987	To investigate satisfaction with court-mandated custody arrangements			112	11		
School psychologists in Wisconsin	To investigate involvement in service delivery activities related to AIDS education and prevention in schools		150		61		
Physicians	To investigate nonresponse bias and the usefulness of follow-up mailings		408		35		
Students at a large university in the Southeast	To examine the simple effects and interactions among four response rate inducements						

5.11.1.1 Disadvantages of the Mail Questionnaire

As noted by Wallace (1954), researchers have discovered the following disadvantages of using mail questionnaires.

1. The problem of nonreturns must be addressed.
   a. Response rates to mail questionnaires sent by private and relatively unskilled persons usually do not exceed 50%.
   b. Intensive follow-up efforts are required to increase returns.

2. Those who answer the questionnaire may differ significantly from nonrespondents, thereby biasing the sample.
   a. Nonrespondents become a collection of individuals about whom virtually nothing is known.
   b. Special efforts must be made (registered letters, telephone calls, personal interviews, and so on) to assess how nonrespondents compare with respondents.
   c. The most thorough of follow-up efforts bring the researcher up against persons who cannot be located, who may be inaccessible, or who are unreachable. The residual group of "no response" or "refuse to answer" can be considerable.

5.11.1.2 Advantages of the Mail Questionnaire

As noted by Wallace (1954), the following are advantages of using a mail questionnaire.

1. It permits wide coverage for minimum expenditure of both money and effort.
2. It affords wider geographic contact.
3. It reaches people who are difficult to locate and interview.
4. It provides greater coverage, which may yield greater validity through larger and more representative samples.
5. It permits more considered answers.
6. It is more effective in situations in which the respondent has to check information.
7. It is more effective in situations in which group consultations would give more valid information.
8. It provides greater uniformity in the manner in which questions are posed.
9. It gives respondents a sense of privacy.
10. It affords a simple means of continual reporting over time.
11. It lessens the interviewer effect.

Reference

Wallace, David. (1954). A case for—and against—mail questionnaires. *Public Opinion Quarterly*, 18, 40-52.

5.11.2 Guide to Questionnaire Design and Construction

Questionnaires take a great deal of time and energy to develop, but when designed and administered correctly, they provide a significant and accurate assessment. What follows is a list of important points to consider in the design and construction of a questionnaire. (See Lazarsfeld [1972], esp. chap. 8, and Dillman [1978] for further information.)

1. Reclarify the relationship of the method to the problem and hypotheses. Obtain a thorough grasp of the area to be studied and a clear understanding of the objectives of the study and the nature of the data needed.

In a *descriptive* inquiry the investigator seeks to estimate as precisely and comprehensively as possible a problem area, and in an *explanatory* inquiry of a theoretical type the investigator seeks to test some particular hypothesis about the determinants of a dependent variable or factor. In either type, economy and efficiency are important criteria. The rule is to gather the data you need but not more than is needed. Know how you will use and analyze your data. Construct dummy tables now if possible and challenge their adequacy for describing the possible distributions or relationships that are related to the problem or hypotheses.

2. Formulate the questions. Take the following points into account in building your questionnaire.

1. Keep the language appropriate to the level of the respondent. Interviews given only to specialized respondents can use the terminology with which they are familiar, but interviews given to the general public must use everyday language.

2. Use words that have the same meaning for everyone. For example, a questionnaire involving American and British respondents might ask "How often do you have tea?" Americans would probably think of tea as a drink. The British would likely think of tea in this question as referring to a light afternoon meal.

3. Avoid long questions. When questions are too long, they often become ambiguous and confusing.

4. Do not assume a priori that your respondents possess factual information or firsthand opinions. A mother may be able to report what books her child reads, but the child must be questioned to find out how he or she feels about reading those books.

5. Establish the frame of reference you have in mind. For example, instead of asking "How many magazines do you read?", use the question "Which magazines do you read?"

6. In forming a question, either suggest all possible alternatives to the respondent or don't suggest any. For example, rather than asking "Do you think the husband should help with dressing and feeding the small children when he's home?" ask instead "Do you think the husband should help with dressing and feeding the small children when he's home, or do you think it's the wife's job in any case?" or "Who should dress and feed the small children when the husband is home?"

7. Protect a respondent's ego. For example, don't ask "Do you know the name of the chief justice of the Supreme Court?" Instead, ask "Do you happen to know the name of the chief justice of the Supreme Court?"

8. If you are asking about an unpleasant experience, give your respondents a chance to express positive feelings first so that they are not put in an unfavorable light. For example, don't ask "What don't you like about X?" Instead, or first, ask "What do you like about X?"

9. Decide whether you need a direct question, an indirect question, or an indirect question followed by a direct one. For example, a direct question might be "Do you ever steal on the job?" An indirect one might ask "Do you know of anyone who has stolen on the job?"

10. Decide whether the question should be open (allowing for a range of answers) or closed (allowing for only one or a few answers). For example, an open question might be "It is believed that some people in this community have too much power. Do you think this is true? Who are they?" A closed one might be "It is believed that some people in this community have too much power. Is this statement true or false?"

11. Decide whether general or specific questions are needed. Although it may be enough to ask "How well did you like the book?", it may be preferable to ask "Have you recommended the book to anyone?"

12. Avoid ambiguous wording such as "Do you like what you do?" An alternative is to ask "Do you like writing nonfiction?"

13. Avoid biased or leading questions such as "Did you exercise your right as an American citizen to vote in the last election?" Instead ask "Did you vote in the last election?"

14. Phrase questions so that they are not unnecessarily objectionable. For example, rather than asking "Did you graduate from high school?", ask "What is the highest grade in school you completed?"

15. Decide whether a personal or impersonal question will obtain the better response. For example, "Are conditions satisfactory or not satisfactory where you work?" might not receive as useful a response as "Are you satisfied or dissatisfied with working conditions in the plant where you work?"

16. Questions should be limited to a simple idea or a single reference. For example, don't ask, "Do you favor or oppose increased job security and the guaranteed annual wage?" Instead, break the questions apart, asking "Do you favor or oppose increased job security?" and "Do you favor or oppose a guaranteed annual wage?"

3. *Organize the questionnaire.*   The order in which questions are asked is very important. Take the following into account in organizing your questions:

1. Start with easy questions that the respondent will enjoy answering.
   a. Don't start with age, occupation, or marital status.
   b. Ask questions to arouse interest.

2. Don't condition answers to subsequent questions by preceding ones.
   a. Go from the general to the specific.
   b. Go from easier questions to more difficult ones.

3. Use the sequence of questions to protect the respondent's ego. Save personal questions such as those about income for later.

4. Decide whether one or several questions will best obtain the information desired.

5. With free-answer questions, it is sometimes helpful to have the questions in pairs, asking for the pros and cons of a particular issue.

6. Open-ended questions, which require the most thought and writing, should be kept to a minimum. Generally these should be placed at the end to ensure that the closed questions will be answered.

7. Topics and questions should be arranged so that they make the most sense to the respondent. The aim is to secure a sequence that is natural and easy for the respondent.

4. Pretest the questionnaire. Easily corrected errors will show up when the questionairre is pretested. This is an essential step in quality control.

1. Select and interview a number of respondents representative of those you expect to survey. Encourage them to ask any questions that they have as they respond to your items. Watch for misunderstanding, ambiguity, and defensiveness. Ask how they would restate questions that are difficult to understand or to answer.

2. Never omit pretesting!

3. Select paper and typeface carefully. The use of a good-quality typeface can produce a mimeographed questionnaire on good paper that looks like a printed copy.

4. Consider how you can present the strongest possible sponsorship. The person, persons, or group that will support your efforts through a cover letter is important.

5. Examine each of the techniques discussed in section 5.12 for increasing the return rate of the questionnaire and decide which will maximize returns for you. Refer to the examples of question wording above. Note how open and closed questions are phrased. Table 5.8 presents a summary of ways to increase response rates. The methods themselves are discussed in section 5.12.

References

Dillman, Don A. (1978). Writing questions. Chap. 3 in *Mail and telephone surveys: The total design method*. New York: Wiley-Interscience.

Lazarsfeld, Paul F. (1972). *Qualitative analysis: Historical and critical essays*. Boston: Allyn & Bacon.

5.11.3 Using Outside Sources to Construct Questionnaires

The increasing importance of accurate information and the economy of questionnaires has led many companies to provide for online design of questionnaires. These questionnaires can be within Web sites on the Internet.

For example, QuestionBuilder (at www.questionbuilder.com/) allows for the construction of a questionnaire that can then be offered through a Web site or shared through e-mail. Some of the varied uses to which this technology can be put are Web-based surveys, custom questionnaires, online research, data gathering, Web site evaluation, market analysis, polling surveys, and e-mail surveys.

5.12 TECHNIQUES FOR INCREASING RESPONSE RATES

NCS Pearson (at www.ncs.com/ncscorp/top/wedo/index.htm) suggests the following guidelines for increasing the rate of return for questionnaires (available at www.ncspearson.com/ncscorp/research/97-1.htm).

Table 5.8 TECHNIQUES FOR INCREASING PERCENTAGE OF RETURNS

Method	Possible Increase in Percentage of Returns	Optimal Conditions
Follow-up	50	More than one follow-up may be needed. Returns may be increased by using double postcards, with the most important questions on follow-ups. The telephone often can be used effectively for follow-up. Researcher should find out if the respondent needs another copy of the questionnaire (it may have been destroyed or misplaced). Sewell and Shaw report an 87.2% return on 9,007 questionnaires from parents of Wisconsin high school students, using three waves of mailed questionnaires and a final telephone interview. American Sociological Review 33 (April 1968): 193.
Sponsor	17	John K. Norton found that people the respondent knew produced the best results. A state headquarters received the second best rate. Others, in order of highest rate of return to lowest, were a lower-status person in a similar field, a publishing firm, a college professor or student, and a private association or foundation.
Length	22	If a questionnaire is short, then the shorter the better. A double postcard should produce the best results. If the questionnaire is more than 10 pages at the minimum, length may cease to be a factor. Sewell and Shaw used a double postcard in the study reported.
Introductory letter	7	An altruistic appeal seems to have better results than the idea that the respondent may receive something good from it.
Type of questions	13	Questionnaires asking for objective information receive the best rate, and questionnaires asking for subjective information receive the worst.

SOURCE: Retrieved August 20, 2001, from www.ncspearson.com. Adapted with permission.

A Well-Designed Form

One of the easiest ways to increase mail survey response rates is to use a well-designed, attractive, easy-to-complete survey. In general, making survey forms easier to complete often increases the likelihood that the forms will be returned.

Additional Mailings

Several activities fall under the heading of additional mailings, including pre-notification, commitment cards, reminder postcards, and remailing surveys.

Pre-Notification and Commitment Cards. Pre-notification usually involves a postcard or letter that explains the impending survey delivery and requests participation. Commitment cards ask potential respondents to return a postcard indicating they will participate in the survey. Results of a recent study (Duhan & Wilson, 1990) indicate that pre-notification cards provided a response rate of 32.3% and the commitment card resulted in a response rate of 20.4%.

Reminder Cards.   Reminder postcards are sent to survey recipients roughly 1 week after the initial survey mailing. This card serves as a thank you to those who responded and a reminder to those who haven't. Experience with these cards suggests they are very helpful. Findings range from a 10% increase to a response nearly equaling that of the initial mailing.

Remailing Surveys.   Remailing surveys entails distributing a second survey to either the entire respondent base or to nonresponders only. Two studies provide considerable evidence of the benefit of using this approach. In one (Von Reisen, 1979), a remail improved response rates from 39.5% to 50.0%. The other showed an increase from 38.8% to 52.9% (Etzel & Walker, 1974).

Type of Mail

The type of mail used to distribute and receive the survey has been found to affect response rates. Research on different mail types and postage types indicates that they do have an impact on response rates (although there are frequently other variables involved).

Certified mail seems to be helpful for a lengthy survey. In a study of the impact of certified mail (Ford, McLaughlin, & Williamson, 1992), varying questionnaire lengths were tested in combination with a certified mail process. The results indicated that certified mail had little effect with short surveys; however, the response rate for certified mail was nearly double that of regular mail for long surveys (i.e., 33.3% vs. 17.8%).

Express mail also has been found to positively affect response rates, especially for executives and business respondents. In one study, when express mail was used for both the mailing and the return of the survey, a response rate of 52% was achieved, compared to a response rate of 26% for the group receiving and returning surveys via regular U.S. mail (Kallis & Gigleriano, 1992). Although express service costs much more than regular U.S. mail, it can be appropriate for highly sensitive surveys for which the response rate is expected to be low. Conceivably, the use of express mail conveys the importance of the survey to the potential respondent.

Finally, including return postage rather than requiring respondents to provide their own has been shown to increase response rates significantly. In addition, using stamps on return envelopes has been shown to be better than using business reply mail. Depending on volume, however, the incremental return gained by stamping the return envelopes may be more than outweighed by the cost.

Kanuk and Berenson (1975) and Linsky (1975) believe that the cover letter is one of the few direct opportunities to influence respondents and motivate. They suggest that the cover letter should be taken seriously, but unfortunately they provide no clear recommendations on how to proceed. A cover letter should explain the importance of the survey and any potential benefits to the respondent. Although Linsky (1975) reports one study that saw an increase of 12.7% (from 29.8% to 42.5%) by including an explanation of the purpose and importance of the survey, he reports another where a similar explanation reduced responses. He also reports that appeals to help the researcher can be counterproductive.

Heberlein and Baumgartner's (1978) review, though not specifically addressing cover letter types, found a significant effect for the salience of the survey, with more salient surveys receiving higher response rates. Using the cover letter to increase the survey salience by providing information on the value of the survey should increase response rates. Harvey's (1987) review summarizes the effects of cover letters as inconclusive. Specifically, Harvey reports two reviews indicating that cover letters appealing for assistance increase response rates; however, he also reports a study in which a cover letter appealing for assistance decreased response rates. Finally, Dillman (1991) argues that the cover letter is important in increasing response rates but provides no data or recommendations on how to proceed.

Telephone Follow-Up

When personnel are well trained, telephone follow-up can effectively increase response rates. The personal contact can serve to underscore the importance of the survey and communicate the importance of respondents' input. Unfortunately, this process frequently is more expensive than the increase in returns warrants.

Incentives

The use of incentives is a heavily researched area in response rate literature. Although several meta-analyses came to different conclusions, published reviews paint a clear picture with respect to two issues: First, incentives are effective in increasing the response rates for mail surveys, and second, promised incentives are not as effective as enclosed incentives. Although these two findings are almost universal, the effects of incentive size are less clear.

Some of the evidence on the role of incentive value is conflicting. Some authors propose that each one-cent increase in prepaid incentive will increase the response by 1%. Others propose a model of diminishing returns rather than a general linear trend. Finally, one review provides data that do not show a linear or increasing trend in response rates with increasing incentives. The bulk of the data suggest that there is some merit in increasing the value of the incentive; however, this issue is far from settled.

Specific recommendations on the amount to include reflect social exchange theory, which suggests people do not like to feel obligated to others and will, therefore, be motivated to behave in ways that reduce obligations. Including a small token in a survey theoretically is enough to have potential respondents feel obligated to respond. A token cannot be so large, however, as to suggest payment for services rendered. Based on this theory and empirical research, a common suggestion is that a $.50 incentive may increase response rates up to 50%. A $1 incentive often produces fewer responses because the dollar is large enough to be perceived as a payment for services rendered.

References

Following are references to the studies identified in the above text as well as other articles that may be of interest.

Armstrong, J. S., & Lusk, E. J. (1987). Return postage in mail surveys: A meta-analysis. *Public Opinion Quarterly, 51,* 233-248.

Church, A. H. (1993). Estimating the effect of incentives on mail survey response rates: A meta-analysis. *Public Opinion Quarterly, 57,* 62-79.

Dillman, D. A. (1991). The design and administration of mail surveys. *Annual Review of Sociology, 17,* 225-249.

Dillman, D. A., Sinclair, M. D., & Clark, J. R. (1993). Effects of questionnaire length, respondent friendly design, and a difficult question on response rates for occupant-addressed census mail surveys. *Public Opinion Quarterly, 57,* 289-304.

Dommeyer, C. (1988). How form of the monetary incentive affects mail survey response. *Journal of the Market Research Society, 30,* 379-385.

Duhan, D. F., & Wilson, D. R. (1990, May). Pre-notification and industrial survey response. *Industrial Marketing Management,* 95-105.

Etzel, M. J., & Walker, B. J. (1974). Effects of alternative follow-up procedures on mail survey response rates. *Journal of Applied Psychology, 59,* 219-220.

Ford, R. C., McLaughlin, F., & Williamson, S. (1992, November). Using certified mail in industrial research. *Industrial Marketing Management*, 281-285.

Fox, R., Crask, M. R., & Jonghoon, K. (1988). Mail survey response rate: A meta-analysis of selected techniques for inducing responses. *Public Opinion Quarterly*, 52, 467-491.

Harvey, L. (1987). Factors affecting response rates to mailed questionnaires: A comprehensive review of the literature. *Journal of the Market Research Society*, 29, 341-353.

Heberlein, T. A., & Baumgartner, R. (1978). Factors affecting response rates to mailed questionnaires: A quantitative analysis of the published literature. *American Sociological Review*, 43, 447-462.

Hopkins, K. D., & Gullickson, A. R. (1992). Response rates in survey research: A meta-analysis of the effects of monetary gratuities. *Journal of Experimental Education*, 61, 52-62.

Kallis, M. J., & Gigleriano, J. J. (1992, February). Improving mail response rates with express mail. *Industrial Marketing Management*, 1-4.

Kanuk, L., & Berenson, C. (1975). Mail surveys and response rates: A review. *Journal of Marketing Research*, 12, 440-453.

Linsky, A. (1975). Stimulating responses to mailed questionnaires: A review. *Public Opinion Quarterly*, 39, 82-101.

London, S. J., & Dommeyer, C. J. (1992, August). Increasing response to industrial mail surveys. *Industrial Marketing Management*, 235-241.

Schlegelmilch, B. B., & Diamantopoulos, A. (1991). Pre-notification and mail survey response rates: A quantitative integration of the literature. *Journal of the Market Research Society*, 33, 243-255.

Von Reisen, D. R. (1979). Postcard reminders vs. replacement questionnaires and mail survey response rates from a professional population. *Journal of Business Research*, 7, 1-7.

Yammarino, F. J., Skinner, S. L., & Childers, T. L. (1991). Understanding mail survey response behavior: Meta-analysis. *Public Opinion Quarterly*, 55, 613-639.

Yu, J., & Cooper, H. (1983). A quantitative review of research design effects on response rates to questionnaires. *Journal of Marketing Research*, 20, 36-44.

SOURCE: This section is adapted from "Increasing Response Rates," an article first published in January 1997. Retrieved August 20, 2001, from www.ncspearson.com/ncscorp/research/97-1.htm. Adapted with permission.

Further Readings on Factors Affecting Response Rates to Questionnaires

Altschuld, James W., Thomas, Phyllis M., McColskey, Wendy H., Smith, Dennis W., Wiesman, D., & Lower, M. (1992). Mailed evaluation questionnaires: Replications of a 96 percent return rate procedure. *Evaluation and Program Planning*, 15, 239-246.

Biner, Paul M., & Kidd, Heath J. (1994). The interactive effects of monetary incentive justification and questionnaire length on mail survey response rates. *Psychology and Marketing*, 11, 483-492.

Boser, Judith A., & Clark, Sheldon B. (1992, April). *Desirable mail questionnaire characteristics in teacher education research*. Paper presented at the annual meeting of the American Educational Research Association, April, San Francisco.

Christensen, Maribeth. (1997). An interdisciplinary theoretical framework for the mailed questionnaire process and the development of a theory on immediacy and salience as significant variables of response rates. *Dissertation Abstracts International*, 57, 4779B.

Cole, Cornette, Palmer, Randall, & Schwanz, Dennis. (1997). *Improving the mail return rates of SASS surveys: A review of the literature* (Working paper series). Washington, DC: U.S. Department of Education, Office of Educational Research and Improvement, National Center for Education Statistics.

Crompton, J. L., & Tian, Cole S. (1999). What response rate can be expected from questionnaire surveys that address park and recreation issues? *Journal of Park and Recreation Administration, 17,* 60-72.

Day, Neil Atherton, Dunt, David R., & Day, Susan. (1995). Maximizing response to surveys in health program evaluation at minimum cost using multiple methods: Mail, telephone, and visit. *Evaluation Review, 19,* 436-450.

Enger, John M., Shain, Russell E., Manning, Tom, Talbert, Lonnie E., & Wright, Don E. (1992, November). *Response rate effects of three questionnaire formats.* Paper presented at the annual meeting of the Mid-South Education Research Association, Knoxville, TN.

Enger, John M., & others. (1993, April). *Survey questionnaire format effect on response rate and cost per return.* Paper presented at the annual meeting of the American Educational Research Association, Atlanta, GA.

Fisher, M. R. (1996). Estimating the effect of nonresponse bias on angler surveys. *Transactions of the American Fisheries Society, 125,* 118-126.

Groves, Bruce W., & Olsson, Roy H., Jr. (2000). Response rates to surveys with self-addressed stamped envelopes versus a self-addressed label. *Psychological Reports, 86,* 1226-1228.

Hare, S., Price, J. H., Flynn, M. G., & King, K. A. (1998). Increasing return rates of a mail survey to exercise professionals using a modest monetary incentive. *Perceptual and Motor Skills, 86,* 217-218.

Harvey, Lee. (1987). Factors affecting response rates to mailed questionnaires: A comprehensive literature review. *Journal of the Market Research Society, 29,* 341-353.

MacGregor, Elizabeth, & McNamara, John R. (1995). Comparison of return procedures involving mailed versus student-delivered parental consent forms. *Psychological Reports, 77,* 1113-1114.

Newton, Kate, Stein, Samuel M., & Lucey, Clare. (1998). Influence of mailing strategies on response to questionnaires. *Psychiatric Bulletin, 22,* 692-694.

Paolo, Anthony M., Bonaminio, Giulia A., Gibson, Cheryl, Partridge, Ty, & Kallail, Ken. (2000). Response rate comparisons of e-mail- and mail-distributed student evaluations. *Teaching and Learning in Medicine, 12,* 81-84.

Parthasarathy, Anuradha, & others. (1995, April). *Effects of respondents' socioeconomic status and timing and amount of incentive payment on mailed questionnaire response rates.* Paper presented at the annual meeting of the American Educational Research Association, San Francisco.

Shahar, E., Bisgard, K. M., & Folsom, A. R. (1993). Response to mail surveys: Effect of a request to explain refusal to participate. The ARIC Study Investigators. *Epidemiology, 4,* 480-482.

Vogel, P. A., Skjostad, K., & Eriksen, L. (1992). Influencing return rate by mail of alcoholics' questionnaires at follow-up by varying lottery procedures and questionnaire lengths: Two experimental studies. *European Journal of Psychiatry, 6,* 213-222.

Westcott, S. Wickes, III, & others. (1995, May). *Evaluating reasons for low response from mail surveys: AIR 1995 annual forum paper.* Paper presented at the annual forum of the Association for Institutional Research, Boston.

GUIDES FOR SELECTION AND USE OF PERSONAL INTERVIEWS AS UTILIZED IN FIELD RESEARCH   5.13

The interview is a personal contact between an interviewer and a respondent, usually in the home or office of the respondent. The interview can range from a highly structured situation with a planned series of questions to a very informal talk with no structure except for some areas of discussion desired by the interviewer. The degrees of freedom pose both opportunity and danger: opportunity to explore many subjects with intensity, but with the danger that the interview may not yield the appropriate data. Interviews often are not susceptible to codification and comparability.

The researcher may not appreciate that every open-ended question will take considerable interview time. The analysis of open-ended questions requires a code guide and careful independent observers to establish the validity and reliability of the coding for each question. If the researcher must employ open-ended questions, he or she should choose a few with care and with the precise aims of the study in mind. If hypotheses are to be tested, the researcher should make sure that the questions bear directly upon them. Open-ended questions are appropriate and powerful under conditions that require probing of attitude and reaction formations and ascertaining information that is interlocked in a social system or personality structure.

In general, interviews should be kept within a 45-minute time span. Public opinion interviewers have reported that most respondents begin to weary and show less interest in the interview at this point. It is true that some respondents will "wake up" as the interview proceeds, and there are examples of 6- and 8-hour interviews in the literature. These long interviews are exceptional and can occur only under specially prepared conditions.

Interviews may take three forms: the *structured interview schedule*, the *focused interview*, and the *free story*. These forms and their characteristics are shown in Table 5.1 in section 5.1. Common techniques that may be employed include the use of scales to measure social factors, attitudes, and personality traits. Secret ballots and panel techniques are often employed.

The guide that follows identifies advantages and disadvantages of the personal interview. It is recommended for use as a checklist; the researcher can mark those advantages that are important or essential with a plus sign and those that will negatively affect his or her use of the interview with a minus sign. This can provide an adequate basis for choosing or rejecting the personal interview.

Other field methods are available, including the group interview, telephone interview, case study and life history, direct observation, participant observation, and mass observation. Guides have not been prepared for these methods, but appended to this section is a list of references that describe in detail all the methods and techniques.

The researcher should check the advantages important for his or her study, check the disadvantages that cannot be overcome, and appraise the choice. He or she should then reconsider documentary analysis, a mail questionnaire, a telephone interview, observation, or other methods suggested in Table 5.1.

5.13.1 Advantages of the Personal Interview

Researchers have identified numerous advantages of the personal interview, 14 of which are listed below.

1. Personal interviews usually yield a high percentage of returns because most people are willing to cooperate.

2. Personal interviews can be made to yield an almost perfect sample of the general population (if targeted appropriately) because practically everyone can be reached by and can respond to this approach.

3. The information secured is more likely to be correct than that secured by other techniques because the interviewer can clear up seemingly inaccurate answers by explaining the questions to the informants. If the latter deliberately falsify replies, the interviewer may be trained to spot such cases and use special devices to get the truth.

4. The interviewer can collect supplementary information about the informant's personal characteristics and environment that is valuable in interpreting results and evaluating the representativeness of the persons surveyed.

5. Scoring and test devices can be used, the interviewer acting as experimenter to establish accurate records of the subject.

6. Visual material to which the informant is to react can be presented.

7. Return visits to complete items on the schedule or to correct mistakes usually can be made without annoying the informant. Thus greater numbers of usable returns are assumed than when other methods are employed.

8. The interviewer may note more spontaneous reactions than would be the case if a written form were mailed out for the informant to mull over.

9. The interviewer usually can control which person or persons answer the questions, whereas in mail surveys several members of the household may confer before questions are answered. Group discussions can be held with the personal interview method if desired.

10. The personal interview may take long enough to allow the informant to become oriented to the topic under investigation. Thus, recall of relevant material is facilitated.

11. Questions about which the informant is likely to be sensitive can be carefully sandwiched in by the interviewer. By observing the informant's reactions, the investigator can change the subject if necessary or explain the survey problem further if it appears that the interviewee is about to rebel. In other words, a delicate situation usually can be handled more effectively in a personal interview than through other survey techniques.

12. More of the informant's time can be taken for the survey than would be the case if the interviewer were not present to elicit and record the information.

13. For cases in which a printed schedule is not used (compare disadvantage 2, below), the language of the survey can be adapted to the ability or educational level of the person interviewed. Therefore, it is comparatively easy to avoid misinterpretations or misleading questions.

14. The length of the interview does not affect refusal rates.

5.13.2 Disadvantages of the Personal Interview

In contrast to the advantages noted above, the following are disadvantages of personal interviews.

1. High costs are associated with all phases of the interview operations, such as salaries and travel expenses.

2. Lower response rates are being reported, especially in large metropolitan areas, where increases in personal and property crimes have altered the lifestyles of residents. Locked central entrances to apartment buildings and a greater concern among residents about opening their doors to strangers prevent interviewing in many multi-unit dwellings. There is also an increasing reticence to admit strangers into single-family dwellings in areas with high crime rates. In addition, some interviewers refuse to enter areas perceived to be dangerous. In large metropolitan areas, the final proportion of respondents who are located and consent to an interview has been shown to decline to a rate close to 50% (Groves & Kahn, 1979).

The above disadvantages focus more attention on the telephone survey (to be described in the following section). Consideration is also being given to a combination of data collection methods utilizing the mail questionnaire, telephone survey, and personal interview where indicated. For example, if the largest possible return is sought, a personal interview may be required as the follow-up to round out the sample after telephone and mail inquiries have exhausted their usefulness.

3. Unless personal interviewers are properly trained and supervised, data may be inaccurate and incomplete. A few poor enumerators may make a much higher percentage of returns unusable than if informants filled out the interview forms and mailed them to survey headquarters.

4. The personal interview usually takes more time than the telephone interview, providing that the persons who can be reached by telephone are a representative sample of the population to be

covered by the survey. A telephone inquiry is no substitute for a personal interview given the one-to-one rich and detailed responses that can more easily result from any personal interaction.

5. If the interview is to be conducted in the respondent's home during the day, the majority of informants will be housewives. If a response is to be obtained from a male member of the household, most of the fieldwork must be done in the evening or on weekends. Because only an hour or two can be used for evening interviewing, the personal interview method requires a large staff if studies need contacts with the working population.

6. The human equation may distort the returns. Interviewers with a certain bias, for example, may unconsciously ask questions so as to secure confirmation of their views. This is particularly true for opinion studies. To prevent such coloring of questions, most opinion surveyors instruct their interviewers to ask questions exactly as they are printed in the schedule.

7. Researchers should be aware that funding agencies may be reluctant to make grants to projects relying heavily on the personal interview. Given all the disadvantages, especially those associated with higher costs and lower response rates, the applicant for a grant may be placed on the defensive.

Reference

Groves, Robert M., & Kahn, Robert L. (1979). *Surveys by telephone: A national comparison with personal interviews.* New York: Academic Press.

Further Readings on Personal Interviews

Baker, Reginald P. (1992). New technology in survey research: Computer-assisted personal interviewing (CAPI). *Social Science Computer Review, 10,* 145-157.

Bongers, I.M.B., & van Oers, J.A.M. (1998). Mode effects on self-reported alcohol use and problem drinking: Mail questionnaires and personal interviewing compared. *Journal of Studies on Alcohol, 59,* 280-285.

Buetow, Stephen A., Douglas, Robert M., Harris, Peter, & McCulloch, Colin. (1996). Computer-assisted personal interviews: Development and experience of an approach in Australian general practice. *Social Science Computer Review, 14,* 205-212.

Cacciola, John S., Alterman, Arthur I., Rutherford, Megan J., McKay, James R., & Janssen, Denise May. (1999). Comparability of telephone and in-person structured clinical interview for DSM-III-R (SCID). *Assessment, 6,* 235-242.

Caldwell, David F., & Burger, Jerry M. (1998). Personality characteristics of job applicants and success in screening interviews. *Personnel Psychology, 51,* 119-136.

Collesano, Stephen Paul. (1986). Personal and telephone interviews: Comparison for trend data. *Disseration Abstracts International, 47,* 329A.

Lynn, Peter, Turner, Rachel, & Smith, Patten. (1998). Assessing the effects of an advance letter for a personal interview survey. *Journal of the Market Research Society, 40,* 265-272.

Reuband, Karl Heinz. (1992). On third persons in the interview situation and their impact on responses. *International Journal of Public Opinion Research, 4,* 269-274.

Schwarz, Shirley P., & others. (1991). Reasons for changing answers: An evaluation using personal interviews. *Journal of Educational Measurement, 28,* 163-171.

Wilson, K., Roe, B., & Wright, L. (1998). Telephone or face-to-face interviews? A decision made on the basis of a pilot study. *International Journal of Nursing Studies, 35,* 314-321.

DESCRIPTION OF AND INSTRUCTIONS FOR PREPARATION OF A TELEPHONE INTERVIEW SURVEY

5.14

With increasing frequency, social science researchers are utilizing the telephone for social investigation. Among the reasons for this trend are the following:

1. Almost all residences in the United States now have telephones. It is estimated that almost 100% of all persons in a cross-sectional sample can be reached by telephone. The probability of social class bias stemming from telephone availability has greatly diminished (Dillman, 1978).
2. Personal interview costs have risen greatly, and telephone surveys can be made at significantly lower costs—in some cases, only 45% to 65% of personal interview costs (Groves, 1980).
3. Personal interviews are incurring falling response rates in large cities, and telephone interviewing is competitive in response rates achieved on national populations. Telephone survey response rates are running only 5-10% lower than those of comparable in-person surveys (Groves, 1980).

The rapid emergence of the telephone as a survey research tool means that the social science community has relatively little information about telephone surveys. Among the unknowns are the following: (a) what response rates to expect for various populations, (b) how long different people will be willing to stay on the telephone with an interviewer, and (c) the unique requirements of telephone interviews in contrast with the familiar mail and personal interview surveys.

5.14.1 Instructions for the Telephone Interview[1]

The telephone interview contrasts sharply with the mail questionnaire. Telephone interviews depend entirely on verbal communication, and the interviewer must build rapport with the respondent in an interchange during which neither sees the other. Unlike in face-to-face interviews, the telephone interviewer cannot use visual aids to help explain questions and cannot observe respondents' facial expressions for hints that something is misunderstood.

The design of the telephone questionnaire must be shaped to meet the needs of three groups: respondents, interviewers, and coders.

5.14.1.1 Respondents

Responding to a telephone interview is difficult. Respondents may be called to the telephone unexpectedly and asked to do something—respond to the interviewer's questions—they do not fully understand. They may be in the midst of another activity, such as preparing dinner, playing a game, reading the newspaper, listening to the radio, or watching TV. Their feelings may range from frustration, suspicion, and anxiety to downright hostility. Subtle ways must be found to discourage respondents from beginning or continuing with other activities that may distract their attention from the interview. "Getting through" the interview may mean that the respondent needs time to get used to the interviewer's way of speaking, understanding different words and the meanings of questions, and so on. Being interviewed by telephone is a new experience for many people, and the respondent may need time to think through answers. Most respondents need support and encouragement.

5.14.1.2 Interviewers

The successful interviewer must secure completion of a telephone questionnaire with information that is accurate and that can be recorded accurately. The interviewer must determine who in the household is eligible to respond and get this person on the phone. The first few seconds are crucial in determining whether or not a successful interview will take place. The interviewer may be faced with such questions as "How do I know you are who you say you are?", "What are you trying to sell?", and "I don't know anything about you or your product—why don't you call someone else?" They may also offer excuses for not participating in the interview or of getting rid of the interviewer, such as "I have a call that I am expecting—you will have to hang up now. Can you call later?"

Interviewers must "prove" their personal legitimacy and the worth of their projects, and they must stimulate respondents to begin the interview. As the interview proceeds, the interviewer must move the conversation from question to question, write answers while mentally preparing to ask the next question, listen intently for any changes of mood, record unsolicited comments, hold the telephone receiver, and turn the pages of the questionnaire.

5.14.1.3. Coders

Methods of facilitating rapid data compilation are important. Precoding identifies each possible response on the questionnaire. Precoding marks and additional instructions for coders usually do not interfere with the requirements of the interviewer. Some important steps include the following.

1. Prepare the telephone questionnaire so that all questions are straightforward, unambiguous, and carefully ordered. Begin the questionnaire with items central to the topic that seem easy to answer, interesting, and socially important. All topical questions should be asked before questions relating to personal characteristics.
2. A well-constructed questionnaire will maximize the probability that interviewers will administer it in exactly the same fashion to each respondent. Each response category is assigned an identifying number that is used to represent it on a computer data file. The final version should be carefully pretested, possibly with interviewers role-playing the interviewer-respondent interchange.
3. The most difficult part of conducting telephone surveys is combining, for administration of the survey, all elements of the research design. Each act of preparation is oriented to the single critical act of the initial interviewing.

The following list of activities (adapted from Dillman, 1978), to be completed before interviewing begins, will help prevent oversights and organizational failures.

5.14.1.4 A Telephone Survey Checklist

What follows is a simple checklist that should help any researcher in preparing for a telephone interview.

Step 1: Selecting a Sample
_____ Names, street addresses, and telephone numbers are drawn from directories and typed onto gummed labels and attached to the cover page of each questionnaire [or]

_____ Random numbers are generated by computer (or manually from a table) and printed on lists for distribution to interviewers

Step 2: Facilities and Equipment
_____ Access to telephones is arranged. In some cases, cell phones may be less expensive to use; this depends in part on the amount of long distance calling to be done

_____ Telephones are checked to be sure they are in working order

____ Access to leased lines is arranged (if needed)

____ Chairs and tables are assembled (if needed)

____ Boxes are acquired and labeled to use for sorting questionnaires into appropriate categories (e.g., refusals, completions, and callbacks)

Step 3: Computer-Related Needs (if immediate data processing is planned)

____ Arrange access to computers (including laptops and personal digital assistants such as Palm Pilots)

____ Decide the analysis programs to be used and set up format statements for their use

____ Do preliminary computer runs with "dummy" data to check for errors in analysis programs

Step 4: Materials

____ Questionnaires are designed

____ They are duplicated

____ They are assembled

____ The cover page and selection procedures (if any) are added

____ A directory listing is attached to the cover page (if applicable)

____ Questionnaires are randomized for distribution to interviewers

____ A sheet with answers to questions respondents might ask is produced and duplicated

____ The "Rules Book" for interviewing is duplicated

____ Special dialing instructions are duplicated (if needed)

____ Pencils and notepads, thumbtacks, rubber bands, and other miscellaneous supplies are acquired

____ All the above are placed at each interviewing station

Step 5: Prenotification or Advance Letter

____ Letters are printed, personalized, and stuffed into envelopes

____ Each letter is mailed 3 to 5 days before an interviewer is likely to call

Step 6: Personnel and Training

Interviewers and coders are

____ Hired,

____ Trained, and

____ Scheduled

____ Supervisory personnel are scheduled

____ Persons to check questionnaires for completeness are scheduled

Step 7: Other Resources and Needs

____ Telephone directories are acquired that cover the study area (to aid in checking possible errors)

____ Researchers notify relevant officials that the survey is in progress

Note

1. This section is based on Dillman (1978, pp. 200-281). Users of telephone surveys are encouraged to consult this thorough treatment, which includes advice on constructing and administering a telephone survey.

References

Dillman, Don A. (1978). Mail and telephone surveys: The total design method. New York: Wiley-Interscience.

Groves, Robert M. (1980). Telephone helps solve survey problems. *Newsletter of the Institute of Social Research* (University of Michigan), 6(1).

Further Readings on Telephone Interviews

Bachofen, Martin, Nakagawa, Akiko, Marks, Isaac M., Park, Je Min, Greist, John H., Baer, Lee, Wenzel, Keith W., Parkin, Richard J., & Dottl, Susan L. (1999). Home self assessment and self-treatment on obsessive-compulsive disorder using a manual and a computer-conducted telephone interview: Replication of a U.K.-U.S.study. *Journal of Clinical Psychiatry, 60,* 545-549.

Blair, Ed. (1989). An experimental comparison of telephone and personal health interview surveys. *Public Opinion Quarterly, 53,* 145-146.

Bowen, Gary L. (1994). Estimating the reduction in nonresponse bias from using a mail survey as a backup for nonrespondents to a telephone interview survey. *Research on Social Work Practice, 4,* 115-128.

Fournier, Louise, & Kovess, Vivianne. (1993). A comparison of mail and telephone interview strategies for mental health surveys. *Canadian Journal of Psychiatry, 38,* 525-533.

Greenfield, Thomas K., Midanik, Lorraine T., & Rogers, John D. (2000). Effects of telephone versus face-to-face interview modes on reports of alcohol consumption. *Addiction, 95,* 277-284.

Katz, Elinor. (1993, April). *A critical analysis of interview, telephone, and mail survey designs.* Paper presented at the annual meeting of the American Educational Research Association, Atlanta, GA.

Maynard, Douglas W., & Schaeffer, Nora Cate. (1997). Keeping the gate: Declinations of the request to participate in a telephone survey interview. *Sociological Methods and Research, 26,* 34-79.

Moore, Robert John. (2000). Achieving understanding in the standardized interview: A conversation analytic study of talk in telephone surveys. *Dissertation Abstracts International, 60,* 3142A.

Tran, Thanh V. (1995). Telephone interview timing and measurement properties of well-being in a sample of elderly Hispanics. *Journal of Social Service Research, 20,* 29-47.

Wester, Fred. (1996). Telephone polls in social research: Methods, techniques, interview practice. *Communications, 21,* 507-508.

5.15 A COMPARISON OF TELEPHONE SURVEYS WITH PERSONAL INTERVIEWS

The development of telephone interviews and procedures for sampling households by means of random-digit dialing may be the most important innovation in survey research since the introduction of multistage probability sampling. Comparisons of telephone surveys with personal interviews raise several important questions.

1. Are telephone responses as reliable and as valid as those given in personal interviews?   There is no simple answer to this question, even when all conditions of sample and survey content are held constant—and that is almost impossible. Hard data are available, however, in regard to such important matters as sample coverage, selection of respondents in households, overall rates of response and nonresponse, and validity of response.

With almost 100% of all households in the United States reachable by telephone, the overall coverage of telephone samples begins to approach the levels typically obtained by personal interviews of an area probability sample of households.

The selection of respondents within sample households must be done at the time of the interview. In personal interview surveys, household selection is done by using a full listing of household members. In telephone surveys, the procedure can be simplified by using a grid corresponding to different numbers of male and female adults. The telephone interviewer determines the total number of adults in the household and the number of them who are women. Use of the grid then indicates the individual selected as respondent. Use of this procedure has shown it yielding an error in selection in about 10% of the sample households (Groves & Kahn, 1979).

The response rate of national telephone surveys remains at least 5 percentage points lower than that expected in personal surveys. This relationship has been rather stable despite numerous changes in training interviewers, monitoring and feedback procedures, and techniques of introducing the survey to respondents (Groves, Lyberg, & Massey, 1988).

2. *Are there systematic differences in the content or depth of the answers people give by telephone and those they give in person?* Consistent differences in interviewing speed between telephone and personal modes have been noted by researchers. The faster pace of telephone interviews is associated with differences in both the number and the type of responses to open-ended items. Some people begin telephone interviews but do not complete them. A lower response rate (5% lower) has already been noted for the telephone interview. Despite these differences, very few response discrepancies have been found between the two sets of data that were large enough to be considered statistically significant.

Many studies have concentrated on reports of embarrassing or sensitive data. These studies generally have found no or only slight differences between telephone and personal interviews. Most results vary because of differences in research design, populations studied, or kinds of data collected. A general statement is inappropriate.

There is a real concern about rapport between respondent and interviewer in the telephone survey. Nonresponse rates suggest that respondents find the telephone interview to be a less rewarding experience and more of a chore than the personal interview. A first priority for future research should be given to telephone techniques to establish motivation and trust equal to that in face-to-face surveys.

3. *Are there large gains in efficiency when sample households are interviewed by telephone?* Personnel needs for a national telephone survey are smaller than those for an equivalent personal interview survey. Take the case of a personal interview survey requiring 200 interviewers, each conducting 7 or 8 interviews. National telephone surveys are often conducted in the same amount of time using 30-40 interviewers, each doing 40-50 interviews. Supervisory and coordinating staff are similarly reduced. Clearly, cost advantages exist for telephone interviewing. (For a comparative analysis of costs for a mail questionnaire, a personal interview, and a telephone survey, see part 8, section 11.3.)

Efficiency results from having questionnaires of the telephone survey coded soon after they are taken. Interviewer errors discovered during coding are quickly detected and corrected. Interviewers can receive feedback on interview behavior quickly, and the results can be obtained promptly.

Increasingly, sampling is being done by random-digit dialing (RDD), which involves direct selection of numbers listed in telephone books. Generally, a set of randomly chosen digits corresponds to a working telephone number. This means that a random sample can be quickly and easily located, and even the equivalent of pre-notification can be used. The telephone subscriber answers his or phone to hear a recording of an introduction to the survey, followed by the voice of an interviewer who will collect the actual data.

Table 5.9 CHOOSING AMONG THE MAIL QUESTIONNAIRE, PERSONAL INTERVIEW, AND TELEPHONE SURVEY			
Factors Influencing Coverage and Information Secured	*Mailed Questionnaire*	*Personal Interview*	*Telephone Survey*
Lowest relative cost	1	3	2
Highest percentage of returns	3	1	2
Highest accuracy of information	2	1	3
Largest sample coverage	3	1	3
Completeness, including sensitive material	3	1	2
Overall reliability and validity	2	1	3
Time required to secure information	3	2	1

NOTE: 1 = most favorable ranking, 2 = intermediate ranking, and 3 = least favorable ranking.

References

Groves, Robert M., & Kahn, Robert L. (1979). *Surveys by telephone.* New York: Academic Press.

Groves, Robert M., Lyberg, Lys, & Massey, James. (1988). *Telephone survey methodology.* New York: John Wiley & Sons.

5.16 CHOOSING AMONG THE MAIL QUESTIONNAIRE, PERSONAL INTERVIEW, AND TELEPHONE SURVEY

The choice of a mode of collecting data involves many factors. The projection of results expected is speculative, because in one sense every sample and the conditions surrounding it are unique. Even changes in world events during administration can make a difference. If the researcher is prepared to utilize many follow-ups or a combination of methods, then a higher response rate can be expected.

Table 5.9 presents an evaluation of the modes of data collection, covering eight important factors. The researcher must determine which among these factors are most important in choosing a design, then select an option, keeping its strengths and drawbacks in mind.

Cost is, of course, always a high priority. Table 5.9 shows that the mailed questionnaire is the cheapest, the telephone survey is of intermediate cost, and the personal survey is the most expensive. If the telephone survey involves substantial long-distance calling, however, the cost figures change quickly to give telephoning a less favorable position in comparison with the personal survey. (For additional discussion of comparative costs, see Part 8.)

Note that cost is in inverse relation to almost all the other factors when comparing the mailed questionnaire with the personal interview. The personal interview, unless compared with the other methods at its most vulnerable conditions, easily leads in desirable factors. The telephone survey yields a consistent set of rankings in the intermediate and most favorable ranges. This accounts for its growing popularity.

A personal interview, whenever possible and reasonable, is always the researcher's preference. There are, however, some significant comparisons to be made between mail and telephone surveys. A mail survey is preferable when survey costs are a concern, the intended respondents have busy schedules and are difficult to reach, questions are sensitive and of a personal nature, and the survey is lengthy or complex. A telephone survey is preferable when survey results are needed quickly, respondents need to be qualified, and the sample being surveyed is small.

Further Readings on Surveys

Faria, A. J., Dickinson, John R., & Filipic, Timothy V. (1990). The effect of telephone versus letter prenotification on mail survey response rate, speed, quality and cost. *Journal of the Market Research Society, 32,* 551-568.

Frey, James H. (1983). *Survey research by telephone.* Newbury Park, CA: Sage.

Leftwich, Wade. (1993). How researchers can win friends and influence politicians. *American Demographics, 15,* 9.

Mohebi, Ed, & Hechter, Edward. (1993). Telemarketing: Faster, better, cheaper. *Bank Marketing, 25,* 36-38.

Okun, Jill. (1987). Lead generation media usage in business-to-business. *Direct Marketing, 50,* 142-146, 208-211.

Riche, Martha F. (1990). A bigger role for telephone interviews. *American Demographics, 12,* 17.

Savini, Gloria. (1989). When two technologies meet. *Direct Marketing, 51,* 54-58.

THE PANEL TECHNIQUE AS A RESEARCH INSTRUMENT 5.17

Social scientists are currently giving a great deal of attention to methods for analyzing time-related data. It has been noted that all the social science disciplines have moved from static to dynamic models. The panel technique is an important research instrument in dynamic models, and so much attention is now being given to it that it seems almost to have been rediscovered.

Definition. The panel technique involves interviewing the same group of people on two or more occasions. It is used primarily for studying changes in behavior or attitudes through repeated interviews ("waves"). Most panel studies contain a set of core questions or observations that are repeated for all or nearly all the waves. Considerable supplementary material may be obtained at each wave or in different waves, to be used in interpreting changes found in the core questions.

Uses. The panel is used in many areas of investigation, such as political polls, occupational and income trends and movements, consumer habits, and mass communications. Two major kinds of panels are those that focus mainly on attitudes and opinions and those that deal mainly with factual material regarding economic, consumption, communications, and other behavior.

Panel studies focusing on opinion and attitude changes generally have a limited number of waves, usually ranging from two to four and rarely exceeding seven. Because they seek specifically to pin down a particular fact or a reason for the changes noted, they are ordinarily restricted to the study of short-range changes of specific attitudes.

5.17.1 Advantages of the Panel Technique

The researcher has two options in searching for short-range changes of specific attitudes. First, information involving facts or experiences during the course of time can be obtained from a *single* contact with a respondent. Such questions as "For whom did you intend to vote one month ago?" and "Have you recently made a change in your job?" may be asked. The information obtained may be inaccurate because the recipient may not remember correctly, the question is deceptive, or both. Based as it is on *repeated* contact, the panel technique can be trusted to be more reliable and valid, with a number of distinct advantages. Zeisel (1957) has listed these advantages, and they are presented in Table 5.10.

5.17.2 Difficulties Inherent in the Panel Technique

Two basic difficulties inherent in the use of the panel technique are panel mortality and reinterviewing bias.

1. *Mortality* is the loss of panel members as a result of the difficulty of reaching the same person for two or more contacts or because of the respondent's refusal of continuous cooperation. Because different sections of the panel may show different mortality rates, some danger of a biased sample arises.
2. *Reinterviewing bias* is the effect of repeated discussions on certain topics on the respondent's behavior or attitude toward these very topics. The fact of being interviewed repeatedly may in itself induce changes of opinion.

5.17.2.1 Panel Mortality

There is bound to be a loss of panel members over time—and the longer the time, the greater the loss. The main reason for failure to reinterview is the respondent's temporary absence from the original place of interview or a complete change of address. This problem can be overcome in part by recording both home and business addresses at the time of the first interview and by persistent efforts to reach the respondent at the time of repeat interviews. If telephone interviewing has been the manner of contact, then a mailed questionnaire or a personal interview may be tried. A certified letter may increase response.

Mortality bias is a concern that increases with the loss of panel members. Mortality does not occur at random. It is well known, for example, that younger people and people in large cities, as well as people in the lower income brackets, have higher mobility than do older, small-town, and upper-class respondents. The researcher must find out in each case whether such a bias exists. Most efforts to do this center on nonrespondents. A vigorous effort is made to secure as many reinterviews as possible, using different approaches and persistence. When returns are secured from the previously nonrespondent group, the researcher carefully analyzes response data to see if mortality bias has been introduced and how serious it may be for interpreting the findings.

A consumer panel study reported in *Response Analysis* in 1986 ("Sampler," 1987) indicated that the panel technique can be effective in securing replies of at least 67% of the respondents from wave 1 to wave 2 in a given sample. The study was made of consumers in a worldwide chain of retail stores operated by the U.S. Navy for military personnel and their dependents. The research involved four interviewing periods in two locations during the first 8 months of 1986. Two research questions were posed: How willing are the customers to participate as panelists? and What percentage of panelists complete their assignments through three waves of interviewing?

Specially trained interviewers went to two store locations and sought consumers willing to participate. Some 94% of those asked agreed to be panelists. A total of 2,190 mail questionnaires were sent in the first wave; 1,989 were completed and returned for a 57% return rate. A second wave showed

Table 5.10 REPEATED CROSS-SECTIONS TECHNIQUE VERSUS PANEL TECHNIQUE

Cross-Sections Technique	*Panel Technique*
1. Recording changes	
In comparing, for example, the proportion of users of XX-branded soap at two different periods, one obtains the difference in the total proportion of users at each interview: the net change.	In addition to the net change, one obtains an accurate picture of the number and direction of individual shifts, which, when added together, account for the net change.
2. Reasons for observed changes	
For instance, whether or not a certain type of propaganda has influenced a person's political attitude. This is difficult to ask and to answer.	By analyzing separately those who were exposed to a certain piece of propaganda and those who were not, the panel can ascertain whether the number and direction of attitude changes are different for the two groups.
3. Amount of information collected	
Because the respondents differ from survey to survey, the researcher does not know any more about each respondent than can be gathered in any one interview.	Repeated interviews with the same respondents yield an ever-increasing amount of information. A three-interview panel study might yield 2 or 3 hours' worth of information about each member of the panel.
4. Data referring to time periods	
One-interview surveys will yield accurate results if the question refers to the time instant at which the interview takes place. If respondents are to recall events that extend over a time period, they must rely on memory. Such data are almost always required if certain research concepts are to be defined: If we want to find out a person's reading habits or whether he or she is a regular listener to a certain radio program, we must rely entirely on the respondent's memory and judgment.	Only through use of a panel can one avoid reliance on the respondent's memory if the goal is to collect data that refer to an extended period of time. Repeated interviews yield objective data on the consistency and fluctuations of habits and attitudes. Such distinctions as that between "regular" versus "nonregular" listeners can be made accurately and reliably.
5. Reliability of results	
The statistical significance of observed changes from survey to survey depends on the size and structure of the particular sample.	In most cases an observed change in a panel will be of higher statistical significance than a change of equal size observed in repeated cross-sections that equal the panel in size and structure.

SOURCE: Adapted from Hans Zeisel (1957), *Say It With Figures* (4th ed.) (New York: Harper & Row), pp. 217-218. Copyright © 1957 by Harper & Row.

that once panelists completed the first questionnaire, they were more likely to remain in the study. A return rate of 78% was received on the second wave. For wave 3, a $10 gift certificate was offered to customers who completed all three waves. Wave 3 respondents posted an 89% return. Senior Vice President Al Vogel of *Response Analysis*, who designed and directed the study, believes that the completion rate at any stage in the study could have been dramatically affected by changes in the incentive.

5.17.3 Reinterviewing Bias

Bias may be introduced by reinterviewing simply because the first interview may have heightened the respondent's attention. He or she then may have given more thought to the topic and thereby changed an opinion. The increasing familiarity gained by reinterviewing may add to the biasing of respondents' opinions.

To detect the presence of such bias, the researcher may interview a control group that is parallel to the panel. At the time of the first panel interview, a field sample that matches the structure of the panel is interviewed on the same topic. At the time of the second panel interview, a different field sample is interviewed as a control. In this way, any resulting bias can be discovered by comparing any changes within the panel with changes between the two field samples.

These two principal sources of error in panel studies, mortality and reinterviewing bias, demand attention. Studies have shown, however, that neither of these two factors seriously endangers the use of the panel. It is a highly promising and powerful tool in the field of social research.

A number of important decisions must be made in designing a panel study. Each of these is briefly described in Table 5.11.

References

"Sampler." (1987, September). *Response Analysis, 47*, 2.

Zeisel, Hans. (1957). *Say it with figures* (4th ed.). New York: Harper & Row.

5.17.3.1 Further Readings on Panel Techniques, Panel Studies, and Where These Methods Are Used

Alwin, Duane F. (1992). Information transmission in the survey interview: Number of response categories and the reliability of attitude measurement. In Peter V. Marsden (Ed.), *Sociological Methodology*. Washington, DC: American Sociological Association.

Alwin, Duane F., & Krosnick, Jon A. (1991). Aging, cohorts, and the stability of sociopolitical orientations over the life span. *American Journal of Sociology, 97*, 169-195.

Arzeimer, Kai, & Klein, Markus. (1999). The effect of material incentives on return rate, panel attrition and sample composition of a mail panel survey. *International Journal of Public Opinion Research, 11*, 368-377.

Bamberg, Sebastian, & Schmidt, Peter. (1998). Changing travel-mode choice as rational choice: Results from a longitudinal intervention study. *Rationality and Society, 10*, 223-252.

Barreiros, Lidia. (1995). The European Community Household Panel (ECHP): Its design, scientific and policy purposes. *Innovation, 8*, 41-52.

Choi, Namkee G. (1994a). Changes in labor force activities and income of the elderly before and after retirement: A longitudinal analysis. *Journal of Sociology and Social Welfare, 21*, 5-26.

Choi, Namkee G. (1994b). Racial differences in timing and factors associated with retirement. *Journal of Sociology and Social Welfare, 21*, 31-52.

Choi, Namkee G. (1999a). Living arrangements and household compositions of elderly couples and singles: A comparison of Hispanics and blacks. *Journal of Gerontological Social Work, 31*, 41-61.

Table 5.11 PROBLEMS OF ADMINISTRATION OF PANEL STUDIES AND SUGGESTIONS FOR DEALING WITH THEM

Administration Problem	Suggestion
1. Number of waves	
The choice of number of waves must consider the extent of cooperativeness on the part of the respondents. They may become bored, annoyed, or irritated by repeated interviews. Repeated interviewing is expensive—like cheap energy, cheap interviewing is gone.	The number of waves usually should be reduced to the minimum.
2. Interval between waves	
The decision regarding the interval between waves is governed by the factors of freshness of memory, type of information desired, and the speed with which a situation changes. If too long an interval elapses, the panel member may suffer a loss of memory of previous events that may distort answers to questions.	The type of information desired is the most important factor in determining the appropriate interval. Consumer panels ordinarily run waves at intervals of 1 or 2 weeks. Political panels ordinarily have waves 1 to 2 months apart. In an exciting political campaign or a political crisis, short intervals are preferable.
3. Sample size	
Sampling error can be reduced with larger samples, but using larger samples increases cost. A larger sample size can compensate for dropout mortality anticipated prior to the first wave (for example, use 1,200 potential participants in the original sample so that a desired 1,000 are available for interview). The problem here is that the original nonresponders may differ from the group that is interviewed.	Check sampling error associated with different sample sizes. Within the limitations imposed by cost, the researcher can either try to reduce the original mortality by repeated callbacks or try to obtain a sample of the original nonresponders.
4. Sample type: quota vs. area	
Quota samples have the advantage of being easier and cheaper to use than area samples. If respondents could be selected on the streets according to specific quota requirements, the speed and cost would be very desirable. After obtaining respondents' names and addresses, researchers could conduct interviews the next time in respondents' homes. This has not proved feasible because much of the original sample is lost for various reasons. The area sample is subject to considerably less mortality.	Whenever possible, personal interview panels should be conducted on an area basis in the home.

(continued)

Table 5.11 Continued

Administration Problem	Suggestion

5. Incentive

An incentive of some sort is needed to obtain the respondents' cooperation and participation. This is especially true in a panel study involving respondents' cooperation over fairly long periods and many waves of reinterviewing. The researcher faces the problem of first securing and then sustaining cooperation.

Two major incentives are usually effective, depending on the type of sponsor and the panel respondents. These are tangible (money, premiums) or prestigious (sponsorship, ego enhancement) incentives.

Consumer panels often use some sort of tangible reward such as points redeemable for premiums. Consider a small monetary payment.

Government and educationally sponsored panels often stress prestige and duty as a citizen to assist in advancing knowledge or improving society.

6. Type of interview: personal, telephone, mail

Personal interviews have been most common in panel studies, but this is the most expensive form of interview and is becoming more expensive. Telephone interviewing is becoming more common because the telephone is almost universally available at the home or work address. It is more difficult to get many kinds of sensitive information and attitudinal data by telephone.

The mail interview involves two problems not present in personal or telephone interviews: Mail interviews become impractical when the interval between waves is important, because there is no control over the time factor, and mail interviews are open to the very real possibility of a bias introduced by a discussion of answers with family members or neighbors.

The telephone interview is gaining in popularity as expenses of personal interviewing rise. New techniques and interview skills are making telephone interviewing more reliable and valid.

Mail interviews are to be avoided unless the telephone or personal interview is not feasible. The mail interview has some merit where it is not safe to enter areas of the city or where sensitive data are difficult to secure.

Choi, Namkee G. (1999b). Racial differences in the contribution of wife's earnings to family income distribution. *Journal of Poverty, 3*, 33-51.

Dex, Shirley, Robson, Paul, & Wilkinson, Frank. (1999). The characteristics of the low paid: A cross-national comparison. *Work, Employment and Society, 13*, 503-524.

Dey, Eric L. (1997). Undergraduate political attitudes: Peer influence in changing social contexts. *Journal of Higher Education, 68*, 398-413.

Dillbeck, Michael C., Banus, Carole Bandy, Polanzi, Craig, & Landrith, Garland S., III. (1988). Test of a field model of consciousness and social change: The transcendental meditation and TM-Sidhi program and decreased urban crime. *Journal of Mind and Behavior, 9*, 457-486.

Dirven, Jan Henk, & Berghman, Jos. (1995). The evolution of income poverty in the Netherlands: Results from the Dutch Socio-Economic Panel Survey. *Innovation, 8*, 75-94.

Ellis, Robert A., & Herrman, Margaret S. (1985). The stigmatization hypothesis re-examined: The social reaction to career-oriented college women. *Sociology and Social Research, 69*, 527-547.

Habich, Roland, & Speder, Zsolt. (1999). Income dynamics in three societies. *Szociologiai Szemel, 3*, 3-27.

Hamilton, Jack. (1994). What is marketing research? *Sotsiologicheski Issledovaniya, 1*, 109-120.

Haveman, Robert, Wolfe, Barbara, & Wilson, Kathryn. (1997). Childhood poverty and adolescent schooling and fertility outcomes: Reduced-form and structural estimates. In Greg J. Duncan & Jeanne Brooks-Gunn (Eds.), *Consequences of growing up poor* (pp. 419-460). New York: Russell Sage Foundation.

Havens, Betty, Hall, Madelyn, & Shapiro, Evelyn. (1998, July). *Self-care, informal care, and formal care in the face of aging and health reform.* Paper presented at the International Sociological Association meetings, Montreal.

Hunt, Marjorie E. (1997). A comparison of family of origin factors between children of alcoholics and children of non-alcoholics in a longitudinal panel. *American Journal of Drug and Alcohol Abuse*, 23, 597-613.

Ivie, Rachel L., Gimbel, Cynthia, & Elder, Glen H., Jr. (1991). Military experience and attitudes in later life in contextual influences across forty years. *Journal of Political and Military Sociology*, 19, 101-117.

Jagodzinski, Wolfgang, Kuhnel, Steffen M., & Schmidt, Peter. (1987). Is there a "Socratic effect" in nonexperimental panel studies? Consistency of an attitude toward guestworkers. *Sociological Methods and Research*, 15, 259-302.

Johnson, David R. (1988). Panel analysis in family studies. *Journal of Marriage and the Family*, 50, 949-955.

Jowell, Roger, Hedges, Barry, Lynn, Peter, Farrant, Graham, & Heath, Anthony. (1993). The 1992 British election: The failure of the polls. *Public Opinion Quarterly*, 57, 238-263.

Kaase, Max. (1986). The micro-/macro-puzzle of empirical social research. Some notes on the problem of aggregate stability with individual instability in panel studies. *Kolner Zeitschrift fur Soziologie und Sozialpsychologie*, 38, 209-222.

Kalton, Graham, & Citro, Constance F. (1995). Panel surveys: Adding the fourth dimension. *Innovation*, 8, 25-39.

Kitson, Gay C., & Morgan, Leslie A. (1990). The multiple consequences of divorce: A decade in review. *Journal of Marriage and the Family*, 52, 913-924.

Klein, Thomas. (1987). A new index for measuring individual versus structural change in panel surveys. *Zeitschrift fur Soziologie*, 16, 145-154.

Krohn, Marvin D., & Thornberry, Terence P. (1999). Retention of minority populations in panel studies of drug use. *Drugs and Society*, 14, 185-207.

Krosnick, Jon A. (1991). The stability of political preferences: Comparisons of symbolic and nonsymbolic attitudes. *American Journal of Political Science*, 35, 547-576.

Link, Bruce G., & Shrout, Patrick E. (1992). Spurious associations in longitudinal research. *Research in Community and Mental Health*, 7, 301-321.

Macintyre, Sally. (1992). The effects of family position and status on health. *Social Science and Medicine*, 35, 453-464.

Marsh, Herbert W. (1993). Stability of individual differences in multiwave panel studies: Comparison of Simplex models and one-factor models. *Journal of Educational Measurement*, 30, 157-183.

Mayer, Karl Ulrich. (2000). Promises fulfilled? A review of 20 years of life course research. *Archives Europeenes de Sociologie*, 41, 259-282.

Mayer, Lawrence S. (1986). Statistical inferences for cross-lagged panel models without the assumption of normal errors. *Social Science Research*, 15, 28-42.

Mayer, Lawrence S., & Carroll, Steven S. (1987). Testing for lagged, cotemporal, and total dependence in cross-lagged panel analysis. *Sociological Methods and Research*, 16, 187-217.

Mayer, Lawrence S., & Carroll, Steven S. (1988). Measures of dependence for cross-lagged panel models. *Sociological Methods and Research*, 17, 93-120.

McBroom, William H. (1988). Sample attrition in panel studies: A research note. *International Review of Modern Sociology*, 18, 231-245.

Mecsko, Lisa A., & Dunkelberger, John E. (1995). Influence of aspirations and background characteristics on educational attainments of college agricultural graduates. *A Review of County Health Councils, 33*(6), 1-6.

Mueller, Charles W., & Parcel, Toby L. (1986). Ascription, dimensions of authority, and earnings: The case of supervisors. *Research in Social Stratification and Mobility, 5,* 199-222.

Ribisl, Kurt M., Walton, Maureen A., Mowbray, Carol T., Luke, Douglas A., Davidson, William S., II, & Bootsmiller, Bonnie J. (1996). Minimizing participant attrition in panel studies through the use of effective retention and tracking strategies: Review and recommendations. *Evaluation and Program Planning, 19,* 1-25.

Rose, David. (1995). Household panel studies: An overview. *Innovation, 8,* 7-24.

Schupp, Jurgen, & Wagner, Gert G. (1995). The German socio-economic panel: A database for longitudinal international comparisons. *Innovation, 8,* 95-108.

Scott, Jacqueline. (1995). Using household panels to study micro-social change. *Innovation, 8,* 61-73.

Snyder, Leslie B. (1991). Modeling dynamic communication processes with event history analysis. *Communication Research, 18,* 464-486.

Taris, Toon W. (1996). Modeling nonresponse in multiwave panel studies using discrete-time Markov models. *Quality and Quantity, 30,* 189-203.

Taris, Toon W. (1997). On selectivity of nonresponse in discrete-time multi-wave panel studies. *Quality and Quantity, 31,* 79-94.

Taylor, Marcia Freed, & Schaber, Gaston. (1995). An integrated longitudinal database for comparative analysis: The panel. *Innovation, 8,* 53-59.

Toth, Istvan Gyorgy. (1995). The first two waves of the Hungarian Household Panel: Methods and results. *Innovation, 8,* 109-121.

Trivellato, Ugo. (1999). Issues in the design and analysis of panel studies: A cursory review. *Quality and Quantity, 33,* 339-352.

Wang, Jichuan, & Fisher, James H. (1994). Comments on "Estimating macro-relationships using micro-data: One-stage approach." *Sociological Methods and Research, 22,* 520-531.

Willits, Fern K., & Crider, Donald M. (1988). Transition to adulthood and attitudes toward traditional morality: A two-panel study. *Youth and Society, 20,* 88-105.

Zapf, Wolfgang. (1994). Transformation in the former GDR and the sociological theory of modernization. *Berliner Journal fur Sociologie, 4,* 295-305.

Zeh, Jurgen. (1989). Social control by public opinion. A sociological reflection on an issue in communication science. *Publizistik, 34,* 29-45.

5.18 GUIDES FOR THE SELECTION AND CONSTRUCTION OF SOCIAL SCALES AND INDEXES

Scaling techniques play a major role in the construction of instruments for collecting standardized, measurable data. Scales and indexes are significant because they provide quantitative measures that are amenable to greater precision, statistical manipulation, and explicit interpretation. Before constructing a new scale, however, it is important to conduct a very careful survey of the literature to ascertain if an appropriate scale already is available to measure the dependent or independent variables in a given study. The general rule is this: The available scale should be used if it has qualities of validity, reliability, and utility (in that order of priority). With such a scale, comparative and accumulative research is possible. The need to develop a new scale can almost be considered a disciplinary failure unless the variable represents a factor never before considered as open to measurement. This discussion begins, therefore, at the point at which the literature has not revealed an appropriate scale and the researcher decides to construct an index or scale.

How does one "think up" a number of indicators to be used in empirical research? This question is answered by Paul F. Lazarsfeld and Morris Rosenberg (1962) as follows:

> The first step seems to be the creation of a rather vague image or construct that results from the author's immersion in all the detail of a theoretical problem. The creative act may begin with the perception of many disparate phenomena as having some underlying characteristic in common. Or the author may have observed certain regularities and is trying to account for them. In any case, the concept, when first created, is some vaguely conceived entity that makes the observed relations meaningful. Next comes a stage in which the concept is specified by elaborate discussion of the phenomena out of which it emerged. We develop "aspects," "components," "dimensions," or similar specifications. They are sometimes derived logically from the overall concept, or one aspect is deduced from another, or empirically observed correlations between them are reported. The concept is shown to consist of a complex combination of phenomena, rather than a simple and directly observable item. In order to incorporate the concept into a research design, observable indicators of it must be selected. (p. 15)

The terms *indexes* and *scales* are often used interchangeably to refer to all sorts of measures, absolute or relative, single or composite, the product of simple or elaborate techniques of measurement.

Indexes may be very simple. For example, one way to measure morale is to ask the direct question, "How would you rate your morale? Very good, good, fair, poor, or very poor?" This might be refined slightly so that the responses are placed on a numerical scale. Note that there are nine points on the following scale.

very good		good		fair		poor		very poor
1	2	3	4	5	6	7	8	9

The basis for construction is logical inference, and the use of a numerical scale requires the assumption of a psychological continuity that the respondent can realistically act upon in self-rating. Face validity usually is asserted for such a scale, although it would be possible to make tests of relations with criteria such as work performance, absenteeism, lateness, amount of drinking, and hours of sleep.

A composite index is one of a set of measures, with each composite index formed by combining simple indexes. For example, morale may be considered as a composite of many dimensions. Four measures can be combined by such questions as the following:

How satisfied are you with your job?
How satisfied are you with your company or organization?
How satisfied are you in your personal life?
How satisfied are you with your community?

Response choices of *very good, good, fair, poor,* and *very poor* may be offered for each question, with respective weights of 5, 4, 3, 2, and 1. A range from 4 to 20 points is possible. Such a composite index may improve precision, reliability, and validity.

Rigor is introduced as greater attention is paid to tests of validity and reliability. At a certain point, a given means of measurement reaches its limit of improvement, and a more refined technique becomes necessary for greater precision. Many scaling techniques concern themselves with linearity and equal intervals or equal-appearing intervals. This means that the scale follows a straight-line model and that a scoring system is devised, preferably based on interchangeable units and subject to statistical manipulation. This is a major attribute of the Thurstone attitude scaling technique.

Unidimensionality or homogeneity is another desired attribute. A scale that is unidimensional or homogeneous measures only one dimension and not some mixture of factors. This is a prime concern of the Guttman scaling technique. Reproducibility is a characteristic that enables the researcher to predict the pattern of a respondent's answers by knowing only the total scale score. This attribute is built into Guttman scaling techniques.

The intensity of feeling is introduced in the Likert technique. The respondent usually is asked to indicate his or her feelings on a 5-point scale ranging from *strongly agree* to *strongly disagree*. Tests of item discrimination are applied.

There is no single method that combines the advantages of all these techniques. It is therefore important that we understand their respective purposes and the differences between them.

Reference

Lazarsfeld, Paul F., & Rosenberg, Morris. (Eds.). (1962). *The language of social research: A reader in the methodology of social research.* Glencoe, IL: Free Press.

5.18.1 Thurstone Equal-Appearing Interval Scale

Nature: This scale consists of a number of items whose positions on the scale have been determined previously by a ranking operation performed by judges. The subject selects the responses that best describe how he or she feels.

Utility: This scale approximates an interval level of measurement. This means that the distance between any two numbers on the scale is of known size. Parametric and nonparametric statistics may be applied. See part 6 for more information about such statistics.

Construction:

1. The investigator gathers several hundred statements conceived to be related to the attitude being investigated.
2. A large number of judges (50-300) independently classify the statements in 11 groups, ranging from *most favorable* to *neutral* to *least favorable*.
3. The scale value of a statement is computed as the median position to which it is assigned by the group of judges.
4. Statements that have too broad a spread are discarded as ambiguous or irrelevant.
5. The scale is formed by selecting items that are evenly spread along the scale from one extreme to the other.

Examples

▶ Duggan, Ashley, Hess, Brian, Morgan, Deanna, Kim, Sooyean, & Wilson, Katherine. (1999, April). *Measuring students' attitude toward educational use of the Internet.* Paper presented at the annual conference of the American Educational Research Association, Montreal, Canada.

Student attitudes toward the Internet were investigated in a study designed to develop an instrument that would provide a quantitative measure of the attitudes undergraduates have toward educational uses of the Internet. The study also investigated some behavioral correlates of student attitudes. The responses of 395 undergraduates to some form of the scale were used to construct the measure. Statements soliciting attitudes toward educational use of the Internet were written in two formats: the Thurstone equal-appearing interval scale and the Likert-type summated rating scale. These pilot scales were administered with a social desirability response scale to ensure that students did not respond to scale items in a socially desirable manner. The final form, administered to 188 students, was an 18-item Likert-format "Attitude Toward Educational Uses of the Internet" (ATEUI) scale that yielded a high internal consistency. Several behavioral correlates lent some credence to the scale's construct validity. Favorable attitudes were associated with (a) keeping track of valuable educational Internet sites; (b) sharing information found on the Internet with friends; (c) choosing classes that use the Internet; (d) greater frequency of Internet use, both in general and for educational purposes; (e) a greater number of reasons for using the Internet in education; and (f) a greater number of Internet features used. There were no differences between men and women or in class standing in ATEUI responses. Future research that considers using the ATEUI should continue to obtain new behavioral correlates of the domain.

▶ Fukuhara, S., Keller, S. D., Kaasa, J. E., Ware, J. E., Jr., Leplege, A., Gandek, B., Sanson-Fisher, R. W., Aaronson, N. K., Sullivan, M., Alonso, J., Wood-Dauphinee, S., Apolone G., Bjorner, J. B., Brazier, J., & Bullinger, M. (1998). Testing the equivalence of translations of widely used response choice labels: Results from the IQOLA Project. *Journal of Clinical Epidemiology, 51,* 933-944.

The similarity in meaning assigned to response choice labels from the SF-36 Health Survey (SF-36) was evaluated across countries. Convenience samples of judges (range = 10 to 117; median = 48) from 13 countries rated translations of response choice labels, using a variation of the Thurstone method of equal-appearing intervals. Judges marked a point on a 10-cm line representing the magnitude of a response choice label (e.g., *good* relative to the anchors of *poor* and *excellent*). Ratings were evaluated to determine the ordinal consistency of response choice labels within a response scale, the degree to which differences between adjacent response choice labels were equal interval, and the amount of variance that was due to response choice label, country, judge, and interaction between response choice label and country. Results confirmed the hypothesized ordering of response choice labels. The percentage of ordinal pairs ranged from 88.7% to 100% (median = 98.2%) across countries and response scales. Examination of the average magnitudes of response choice labels supported the "quasi-interval" nature of the scales. Analysis of variance (ANOVA) results supported the generalizability of response choice magnitudes across countries; labels explained 64% to 77% of the variance in ratings, and country explained 1% to 3%. These results support the equivalence of SF-36 response choice labels across countries. Departures from the assumption of equal intervals, when observed, were similar across countries and were greatest for the two response scales that were recalibrated under standard SF-36 scoring. Results provide justification for scoring translations of individual items using standard SF-36 scoring. Whether these items form the same scales in other countries as they do in the United States was evaluated with tests of scaling assumptions.

▶ Lattin, James M. (1990). A minimum-cost network-flow solution to the Case V Thurstone scaling problem. *Psychometrika, 55,* 353-370.

Presents an approach for determining unidimensional scale estimates that are insensitive to limited inconsistencies in paired comparisons data. The solution procedure, shown to be a minimum-cost network-flow problem, is presented in conjunction with a sensitivity diagnostic that assesses the influence of a single pairwise comparison on traditional Thurstone scale estimates. When distortion was indicated in the data, the network technique appeared to be more successful than Thurstone scaling in preserving the interval scale properties of the estimates.

▶ Schriesheim, Chester A., & Novelli, Luke, Jr. (1989). A comparative test of the interval-scale properties of magnitude estimation and Case III scaling and recommendations for equal-interval frequency response anchors. *Educational and Psychological Measurement, 49*, 59-74.

Differences between recommended sets of equal-interval response anchors derived from scaling techniques using magnitude estimations and Thurstone Case III pair-comparison treatment of complete ranks were compared. Differences in results for 205 undergraduates reflected differences in the samples as well as in the tasks and computational algorithms.

▶ Yen, Wendy M. (1986). The choice of scale for educational measurement: An IRT perspective. *Journal of Educational Measurement, 23*, 299-325.

Two methods of constucting equal-interval scales for educational achievement are discussed: Thurstone's absolute scaling method and item response theory. Alternative criteria for choosing a scale are contrasted. It is argued that clearer criteria are needed for judging the appropriateness and usefulness of alternative scaling procedures.

5.18.1.1 Readings on Thurstone Equal-Interval Scales

Duggan, Ashley, Hess, Brian, Morgan, Deanna, Kim, Sooyean, & Wilson, Katherine. (1999, April). *Measuring students' attitude toward educational use of the Internet.* Paper presented at the annual conference of the American Educational Research Association, Montreal, Canada.

Fukuhara, S., Keller, S. D., Kaasa, J. E., Ware, J. E., Jr., Leplege, A., Gandek, B., Sanson-Fisher, R. W., Aaronson, N. K., Sullivan, M., Alonso, J., Wood-Dauphinee, S., Apolone G., Bjorner, J. B., Brazier, J., & Bullinger, M. (1998). Testing the equivalence of translations of widely used response choice labels: Results from the IQOLA Project. *Journal of Clinical Epidemiology, 51*, 933-944.

Lattin, James M. (1990). A minimum-cost network-flow solution to the Case V Thurstone scaling problem. *Psychometrika, 55*, 353-370.

Schriesheim, Chester A., & Novelli, Luke, Jr. (1989). A comparative test of the interval-scale properties of magnitude estimation and Case III scaling and recommendations for equal-interval frequency response anchors. *Educational and Psychological Measurement, 49*, 59-74.

Yen, Wendy M. (1986). The choice of scale for educational measurement: An IRT perspective. *Journal of Educational Measurement, 23*, 299-325.

5.18.2 Likert-Type Scale

Nature: This is a summated scale consisting of a series of items to which the subject responds. The respondent indicates agreement or disagreement with each item on an intensity scale. The Likert technique produces an ordinal scale that generally requires nonparametric statistics.

Utility: This scale is highly reliable when it comes to a rough ordering of people with regard to a particular attitude or attitude complex. The score includes a measure of intensity as expressed on each statement.

Construction:

1. The investigator assembles a large number of items considered relevant to the attitude being investigated and clearly either favorable or unfavorable.
2. These items are administered to a group of subjects representative of those with whom the questionnaire is to be used.

3. The responses to the various items are scored in such a way that a response indicative of the most favorable attitude is given the highest score.
4. Each individual's total score is computed by adding his or her item scores.
5. The responses are analyzed to determine which items differentiate most clearly between the highest and lowest quartiles of total scores.
6. The items that differentiate best (at least six) are used to form a scale.

Examples

▶ Belmonte-Serrano, M. A., Beltran, Fabregat J., & Paz, Furio M. (1996). A comparative study of HAQ questionnaires—versions of 20 and 8 items—with Likert scale and visual analogue scale in rheumatoid arthritis patients. *Revista Espanola de Reumatologia, 23,* 83-88.

The purposes of this study were to perform a cross-validation of the Spanish versions of the disability scale of the Stanford Health Assessment Questionnaire (HAQ) versus Pincus's reduced version of 8 items (MHAQ) and to compare the visual analogue scale (VAS) against the verbal ordinal type (Likert) as instruments to assess pain and global health in rheumatic patients. A questionnaire with the 20 items of the HAQ and both types of scales was given to rheumatoid arthritis patients. The value of the 8 items of the MHAQ was obtained from the original data, as a subset of the HAQ itself. The HAQ and MHAQ showed an excellent internal consistency (alpha = .9) and good criterion and construct validity. The HAQ and MHAQ were highly and significantly correlated, both regarding total scores ($r = .88, p < .001$) and for each of the subscales (r values ranging from .57 to .87, $p < .001$). The mean score for the MHAQ was 31.2% lower than that obtained with the HAQ ($p < .001$). The study found a significant, moderate, and similar correlation of the HAQ and the MHAQ with the Steinbrocker functional capacity and both types of scales measuring pain and health status. The study of the pain and global health scales showed good correlation between Likert and VAS types for both variables ($r = .77$ and $r = .50, p < .001$). Likert and VAS scales had a highly linear relationship ($p < .0001$). In general, it was found that the MHAQ is as suitable as the HAQ; however, the marked difference of mean scores between the two questionnaires makes it impossible to use them indistinctly. The significant correlation and high linearity found between Likert and VAS scales, both for pain and for global health status, suggests that it is possible to use the equivalency values of the Likert scales as a surrogate for missing values in the VAS scales.

▶ Cheung, K. C., & Mooi, L. C. (1994). A comparison between the rating scale model and dual scaling for Likert scales. *Applied Psychological Measurement, 18,* 1-13.

Problems relating to existence of interval scales, dimensionality of a trait, and patterns of item response functions were approached through contrasting scaling methods: item response theory modeling and dual scaling. Similarity of the methods was established through a study of 326 female junior college students in Singapore who completed a Likert-type scale.

▶ Gu, Yongqui, & others. (1995). How often is often? Reference ambiguities of the Likert-scale in language learning strategy research. *Occasional Papers in English Language Teaching, 5,* 19-35.

This article, based on personal experience, examines the ambiguities of the Likert-type 5-point scale in learning strategy elicitation. Four parallel questionnaires consisting of the same batch of 20 items taken from the Oxford scale (1990) were administered among a group of 120 tertiary level, non-English majors in China. Questionnaire 1 used the Oxford scale without specifying dimensions of reference. Questionnaire 2 told the respondents to choose their answers by comparing with their peers in the same grade. Questionnaire 3 asked them to select their present behavioral frequency as compared with their own past learning experience in secondary schools. In questionnaire 4, subjects were told to check off the relevant frequency of a behavior by comparing its frequency of occurrence with that of other language skills. Results showed that out of the 20 items used, 13 were significantly different among the four questionnaires. Methodological implications for questionnaire research are discussed in the article, and suggestions for future research are proposed.

▶ Hassan, Abdel Moneim Ahmed, & Shrigley, Robert L. (1984). Designing a Likert scale to measure chemistry attitudes. *School Science and Mathematics, 84*, 659-669.

This article brings together the principles of designing Likert-type attitude scales and demonstrates the procedure through the development of a chemistry attitude scale. Design procedures and validity and reliability of the scale are each discussed, with a data summary for the 20-item chemistry scale.

▶ Smith-Sebasto, N. J., & D'Costa, Ayres. (1995). Designing a Likert-type scale to predict environmentally responsible behavior in undergraduate students: A multistep process. *Journal of Environment Education, 27*, 14-20.

Describes an attempt to develop a reliable and valid instrument to assess the relationship between locus of control of reinforcement and environmentally responsible behavior. Presents a six-step psychometric process used to develop the Environmental Action Internal Control Index (EAICI) for undergraduate students. Contains 54 references.

5.18.2.1 Readings on Likert-Type Scales

Belmonte-Serrano, M. A., Beltran, Fabregat J., & Paz, Furio M. (1996). A comparative study of HAQ questionnaires—versions of 20 and 8 items—with Likert scale and visual analogue scale in rheumatoid arthritis patients. *Revista Espanola de Reumatologia, 23*, 83-88.

Cheung, K. C., & Mooi, L. C. (1994). A comparison between the rating scale model and dual scaling for Likert scales. *Applied Psychological Measurement, 18*, 1-13.

Gu, Yongqui, & others. (1995). How often is often? Reference ambiguities of the Likert-scale in language learning strategy research. *Occasional Papers in English Language Teaching, 5*, 19-35.

Hassan, Abdel Moneim Ahmed, & Shrigley, Robert L. (1984). Designing a Likert scale to measure chemistry attitudes. *School Science and Mathematics, 84*, 659-669.

Smith-Sebasto, N. J., & D'Costa, Ayres. (1995). Designing a Likert-type scale to predict environmentally responsible behavior in undergraduate students: A multistep process. *Journal of Environment Education, 27*, 14-20.

5.18.3 Guttman Scale Analysis

Nature: The Guttman technique attempts to determine the unidimensionality of a scale. Only items meeting the criterion of reproducibility are acceptable as scalable. If a scale is unidimensional, then a person who has a more favorable attitude than another should respond to each statement with a favorableness score equal to or greater than that of the other person.

Utility: Each score corresponds to a highly similar response pattern or scale type. It is one of the few scales where the score can be used to predict the response pattern to all statements. Only a few state-

Table 5.12 PATTERNS OF RESPONSES IN GUTTMAN SCALE ANALYSIS

Respondent	Item 7	Item 5	Item 1	Item 8	Item 2	Item 4	Item 6	Item 3	Score
7	Yes	Yes	Yes	Yes	Yes	Yes	Yes	—	7
9	Yes	Yes	Yes	Yes	Yes	Yes	Yes	—	7
1	Yes	Yes	Yes	—	Yes	Yes	—	Yes	6
10	Yes	Yes	Yes	Yes	Yes	Yes	—	—	6
13	Yes	Yes	Yes	Yes	Yes	Yes	—	—	6
3	Yes	Yes	Yes	Yes	Yes	—	—	—	5
2	Yes	Yes	Yes	Yes	—	—	—	—	4
6	Yes	Yes	Yes	Yes	—	—	—	—	4
8	Yes	Yes	Yes	—	—	Yes	—	—	4
14	Yes	Yes	Yes	Yes	—	—	—	—	4
5	Yes	Yes	Yes	—	—	—	—	—	3
4	Yes	Yes	—	—	—	—	—	—	2
11	—	—	—	—	Yes	—	—	—	1
12	Yes	—	—	—	—	—	—	—	1

ments (5 to 10) are needed to provide a range of scalable responses. Note the analysis presented in Table 5.12, which shows how 14 subjects responded with a "Yes" to several statements and how scores reflect a given pattern of response.

Construction:

1. Select statements that are felt to apply to the measurable objective.
2. Test statements on a sample population (about 100).
3. Discard statements with more than 80% agreement or disagreement.
4. Order respondents from those having the most favorable responses to those having the fewest favorable responses. Order from left to right.
5. Order statements from those having the most favorable responses to those having the fewest favorable responses. Order from left to right.
6. Discard statements that fail to discriminate between favorable respondents and unfavorable respondents.
7. Calculate coefficient of reproducibility.
   a. Calculate the number of errors (favorable responses that do not fit pattern)
   b. Reproducibility = 1 − (number of errors/number of responses)
   c. If reproducibility equals .90 or greater, a unidimensional scale is said to exist.
8. Score each respondent by the number of favorable responses or response patterns.

Examples

▶ Burgin, Robert. (1989). Guttman scale analysis: An application to library science. *Library and Information Science Research*, *11*, 47-57.

Outlines the general techniques of Guttman scale analysis and briefly describes its uses in social science research. To illustrate the potential application to library science, a Guttman scale of restrictiveness in dealing with overdue books was developed, and data from a 1986 survey of public libraries were fitted into the scale.

▶ Kramer, Deirdre A. (1983, November). *A developmental investigation of relativistic and dialectical thought.* Paper presented at the Annual Scientific Meeting of the Gerontological Society, San Francisco.

Post-formal operational thought is characterized by both relativism and dialecticism. To examine age differences across adulthood in relativistic and dialectical thought, and to determine whether formal operations are necessary but not sufficient for these forms of thought, 20 young (mean age, 19.6), 20 middle-aged (mean age, 46.2), and 20 older (mean age, 68.5) adults were administered three cognitive tasks. The Ammons Quick Test was administered to determine the presence of comparable verbal intelligence. Subsequently, subjects were administered four formal operations tasks: separation of variables; three measures of coordination of two frames of reference; and two lifelike dilemmas, to which they were asked to react. Reactions to the dilemmas were placed into four categories of thought (formalistic-mechanistic, relativistic, awareness of contradictions, and integration of contradictions into a dialectical whole). Analysis of the results showed that older adults scored significantly higher on the Quick Test than young adults, with middle-aged adults falling between those two groups. On formal operations tasks, performance was intact across adulthood. On the lifelike dilemmas, older adults showed significantly less rejection and more acceptance of relativistic and dialectical thought. Guttman scale analysis showed that formal operations were necessary but not sufficient for dialectical thought. The findings provide potential support for the hypothesis that dialectical thought is post-formal operational.

▶ Lange, A., Kooiman, K., Huberts, L., & Van Oostendorp, E. (1995). Childhood unwanted sexual events and degree of psychopathology of psychiatric patients: Research with a new anamnestic questionnaire (the CHUSE). *Acta Psychiatrica Scandinavica, 92,* 441-446.

By means of a recently constructed anamnestic instrument, the Childhood Unwanted Sexual Events (CHUSE) questionnaire, the incidence of childhood experiences with sexual threat and/or abuse was investigated among 152 female psychiatric patients. The construction and applicability of the questionnaire are described. A Guttman scale analysis showed a unidimensional construct (severity of the sexual abuse) for the CHUSE. Within this psychiatric population, sexually abused women reported significantly more psychopathological symptoms than nonabused women. The correlation between severity of the abuse and severity of the psychopathological symptoms was investigated. The use of questionnaires concerning sexual abuse was compared with the more common interview techniques. Suggestions for future research are given.

▶ Stempel, Guiod H., III. (1982). A Guttman scale analysis of the Burger Court's press decisions. *Journalism Quarterly, 59,* 256-259.

Analyzes Supreme Court votes on 47 press-related cases and shows that they form a scalable universe that is unidimensional. The author suggests that the dimension is political predisposition.

▶ Von Korff, M., Ormel, J., Keefe, F. J., & Dworkin, S. F. (1992). Grading the severity of chronic pain. *Pain, 50,* 133-149.

This research develops and evaluates a simple method of grading the severity of chronic pain, for use in general population surveys and studies of primary care pain patients. Measures of pain intensity, disability, persistence, and recency of onset were tested for their ability to grade chronic pain severity in a longitudinal study of primary care back pain ($n = 1,213$), headache ($n = 779$), and temporomandibular disorder pain ($n = 397$) patients. A Guttman scale analysis showed that pain intensity and disability measures formed a reliable hierarchical scale. Pain intensity measures appeared to scale the lower range of global severity, whereas disability measures appeared to scale the upper range of global severity. Recency of onset and days in pain in the prior 6 months did not scale with pain intensity or disability. Using simple scoring rules, pain severity was graded into four hierarchical classes: Grade I, low disability-low intensity; Grade II, low disability-high intensity; Grade III, high disability-moderately limiting; and Grade IV, high disability-severely limiting. For each pain site, Chronic Pain Grade measured at baseline showed a highly statistically significant and monotonically increasing relationship with unemployment rate, pain-related functional limitations, depression, fair to poor self-rated health, frequent use of opioid analgesics, and frequent pain-related doctor visits both at baseline and at 1-year follow-up. Days in pain was related to these variables, but not as strongly as Chronic Pain Grade. Recent onset cases (first onset within the prior 3 months) did not show differences in psychological and behavioral dysfunction when compared to those with less recent onset. Using longitudinal data from a population-based study ($n = 803$), Chronic Pain Grade at baseline predicted the presence of pain in the prior 2 weeks as well as Chronic Pain Grade and pain-related functional limitations at 3-year follow-up. Grading chronic pain as a function of pain intensity and pain-related disability may be useful when a brief ordinal measure of global pain severity is required. Pain persistence, measured by days in pain in a fixed time period, provides useful additional information.

5.18.3.1 Readings on Guttman Scales

Burgin, Robert. (1989). Guttman scale analysis: An application to library science. *Library and Information Science Research*, 11, 47-57.

Gordon, Raymond L. (1977). *Unidimensional scaling of social variables*. Riverside, NJ: Free Press.

Kramer, Deirdre A. (1983, November). *A developmental investigation of relativistic and dialectical thought*. Paper presented at the Annual Scientific Meeting of the Gerontological Society, San Francisco.

Lange, A., Kooiman, K., Huberts, L., & Van Oostendorp, E. (1995). Childhood unwanted sexual events and degree of psychopathology of psychiatric patients: Research with a new anamnestic questionnaire (the CHUSE). *Acta Psychiatrica Scandinavica*, 92, 441-446.

Lin, Nan. (1976). *Foundations of social research*. New York: McGraw-Hill.

Stempel, Guiod H., III. (1982). A Guttman scale analysis of the Burger Court's press decisions. *Journalism Quarterly*, 59, 256-259.

Von Korff, M., Ormel, J., Keefe, F. J., & Dworkin, S. F. (1992). Grading the severity of chronic pain. *Pain*, 50, 133-149.

5.18.4 Scale Discrimination Technique

Nature: This technique seeks to develop a set of items that meet the requirements of a unidimensional scale, possess equal-appearing intervals, and measure intensity. Aspects of the construction of Thurstone's equal-appearing intervals, Likert's summated scales, and Guttman's scale analysis are combined in this technique, developed by Edwards and Kilpatrick.

Utility: Three distinct advantages of separate scaling techniques are combined. The interval scale quality of the Thurstone technique can be achieved. The discriminability between respondents and the addition of an intensity measure are derived from the Likert technique, and unidimensionality from the Guttman technique. Caution: Item analysis will eliminate items in the middle of the scale.

Construction:

1. The investigator selects a large number of statements that are thought to apply to the attitude being measured.
2. Items that are ambiguous or too extreme are discarded.
3. The statements are given to judges, who evaluate the favorableness of each statement and place it in 1 of 11 categories.
4. Half of the items with the greatest scatter, or variance, are discarded.
5. Scores are assigned to the remaining items as the median of the judges' scores.
6. The statements are devised in the form of a summated scale and given to a new set of judges.
7. An item analysis is performed to determined which questions discriminate best between the lowest and highest quartiles.
8. Twice the number of items that are wanted in the final scale are selected. From each scale interval, the statements that discriminate best are selected.
9. These statements are divided in half, and the halves are submitted to separate test groups.
10. Coefficients of reproducibility are determined for each test group; those that are .90 or above are used.

Examples

▶ Crist, D. A., Rickard, H. D., Prentice, Dunn S., & Barker, H. R. (1989). The Relaxation Inventory: Self-report scales of relaxation training effects. *Journal of Personality Assessment, 53,* 716-726.

The development of a self-report measure to assess the effects of relaxation training was examined. A rigorous statistical method of scale construction consisting of a modification of the scale discrimination technique was employed, resulting in a 45-item questionnaire representing three orthogonally derived scales. The three scales—physiological tension, physical assessment, and cognitive tension—demonstrated adequate internal consistency with KR20 reliability coefficients of .89, .95, and .81, respectively. In a second study of predictive validity, 40 individuals were randomly assigned to one of four conditions: relaxation training, tension inducement, pre-post control, or postcontrol. Univariate analysis of variance indicated significant findings for each of the three dimensions of the inventory. The physiological tension scale detected significant increases in tension following tension inducement, whereas the physical assessment scale and cognitive tension scale detected increases in relaxation following relaxation training. Recommendations were made for future research on the inventory.

▶ Foster, Don. (1991). *Social psychology in South Africa.* Johannesburg, South Africa: Lexicon.

Most of the basic methods of attitude measurement were developed in the United States during the 1920s and 1930s. They include the social distance scale, Thurstone's equal-appearing interval scale, the Likert form of scaling, and Katz and Braly's assessment of stereotypes. The scale discrimination technique was developed in the 1940s. It was only later that another popular method, the semantic differential, was developed. Most of these methods have been used in South Africa, and each of them are discussed in turn, using, where applicable, a South African example of the method.

▶ Killian, Kieran, Watson, Richard, Otis, Joceline, St. Amand, Timothy A., & O'Byrne, Paul M. (2000). Symptom perception during acute bronchoconstriction. *American Journal of Respiratory and Critical Care Medicine, 162,* 490-496.

The hypothesis underlying the study was that some of the variability in symptom intensity seen during acute bronchoconstriction may result from varying intensities of several stimuli, yielding several sensations that can be identified by specific descriptive expressions (symptoms). A total of 232 subjects inhaled methacholine in doubling concentrations to a 20% decrease in FEV1, or 64 mg/ml. The study identified the prevalence of dyspnea, nonspecific discomfort associated with the act of breathing, and 10 specific symptom expressions. Each symptom intensity was rated in Borg scale units. The contribution of the specific symptoms to the intensity of dyspnea is illustrated in the following equation ($r = 0.84$): Dyspnea = 0.44 + 0.19 Difficult breathing + 0.41 Chest tightness + 0.20 Breathlessness + 0.14 Labored breathing + 0.11 Chest pain. Dyspnea was more intense with bronchoconstriction, baseline pulmonary impairment, weight, and sex (being female). Dyspnea was less intense with age (being older) and as airway responsiveness to methacholine increased ($p < 0.05$ for all factors). Chest tightness and chest pain were at polar extremes on the discrimination scale (i.e., easily discriminated); chest tightness and difficult and labored breathing were not easily discriminated.

▶ Velozo, C. A., Magalhaes, L. C., Pan, A. W., & Leiter, P. (1995). Functional scale discrimination at admission and discharge: Rasch analysis of the Level of Rehabilitation Scale-III. *Archives of Physical Medicine and Rehabilitation, 76,* 705-712.

The purpose of this study was to determine the construct validity of the Level of Rehabilitation Scale-III (LORS-III) with a special focus on this instrument's capability to discriminate rehabilitation inpatient activities of daily living (ADL)/mobility and communication/cognition ability at admission and discharge. Rasch analysis of existing data sets in the LORS-III American Data System (LADS) was performed. Existing admission and discharge data from 3,056 rehabilitation inpatients (musculo-skeletal injury, cerebrovascular accident, multiple injuries/diseases, brain injury, neuromuscular disorder, and spinal cord injury) were entered into LADS between April 1992, and January 1993. LORS-III consists of 17 measurement areas representing abilities in ADL, mobility, communication, cognition, and memory. Fourteen of the measurement areas are concurrently scored by a nurse and a specified rehabilitation therapist, resulting in a total of 31 items. Consistent with findings reported for other functional status measures, the analysis indicated that the LORS-III consists of two unidimensional scales, an ADL/mobility scale and a communication/cognition scale. Although all scales fit the Rasch measurement model, the ADL/mobility scale used at admission was most appropriately targeted to the ability level of the sample. At discharge, the ADL scale generally was too easy because the ability level of the sample moved upward toward functional independence. The communication/cognition scale at both admission and discharge showed a similar "ceiling" effect. These findings indicate the importance of determining the measurement qualities of functional status measures for both admission and discharge ratings. Analyses, such as Rasch, can provide a logical direction for instrument refinement.

5.18.4.1 Readings on Scale Discrimination

Crist, Dwayne A., Rickard, Henry C., Prentice, Dunn Steven, & Barker, Harry R. (1989). The Relaxation Inventory: Self-report scales of relaxation training effects. *Journal of Personality Assessment, 53,* 716-726.

Foster, Don. (1991). *Social psychology in South Africa.* Johannesburg, South Africa: Lexicon.

Killian, Kieran, Watson, Richard, Otis, Joceline, St. Amand, Timothy A., & O'Byrne, Paul M. (2000). Symptom perception during acute bronchoconstriction. *American Journal of Respiratory and Critical Care Medicine, 162,* 490-496.

Velozo, C. A., Magalhaes, L. C., Pan, A. W., & Leiter, P. (1995). Functional scale discrimination at admission and discharge: Rasch analysis of the Level of Rehabilitation Scale-III. *Archives of Physical Medicine and Rehabilitation, 76,* 705-712.

5.18.5 Rating Scales

Nature: This technique, based on personal judgments, seeks to obtain an evaluation or a quantitative judgment of personality, group, or institutional characteristics. The rater places the person or object being rated at some point along a continuum or in one of an ordered series of categories. A numerical value is attached to the point or the category.

Utility: Rating scales can be used to assess attitudes, values, norms, social activities, and social structural features.

Construction:

1. The continuum to be measured is divided into an optimal number of scale divisions (approximately five to seven).
2. The continuum should have no breaks or divisions.
3. The positive and negative poles should be alternated.
4. Each trait is introduced with a question to which the rater can give an answer.
5. Descriptive adjectives or phrases are used to define different points on the continuum.
6. The investigator should decide beforehand on the probable extremes of the trait to be found in the group in which the scale is to be used.
7. Only universally understood descriptive terms should be used.
8. The end phrases should not be so extreme in meaning as to be avoided by the raters.
9. Descriptive phrases need to be evenly spaced.
10. During pretesting, the investigator asks respondents to raise any questions they have about the ratings and the different points on the continuum if they are unclear.
11. Assigned numerical values are used to score.

Examples

▶ Linacre, John M. (1999). Investigating rating scale category utility. *Journal of Outcome Measurement, 3,* 103-122.

Suggests eight guidelines to help an analyst investigate whether rating-scale categories are cooperating to produce observations on which valid measurement can be based. Presents these guidelines in the context of Rasch analysis and illustrates their use.

▶ Varner, Roy V., Chen, Y. Richard, Swann, Alan C., & Moeller, Frederick G. (2000). The Brief Psychiatric Rating Scale as an acute inpatient outcome measurement tool: A pilot study. *Journal of Clinical Psychiatry, 61,* 418-421.

Because guidelines for length of stay at psychiatric hospitals may have an unacceptable impact on patient outcome at discharge, a valid measurement tool is needed to evaluate significant patient change during brief hospitalization (typically 7 days) and to provide early prediction of unfavorable short-term outcome. This study examines the utility of the Brief Psychiatric Rating Scale (BPRS) as such a tool. During a 2-month testing period, the BPRS was administered to 87 adults successively admitted to an acute general psychiatric inpatient unit at admission, with administrations at 2 days, 7 days, and weekly thereafter until discharge. Total BPRS scores and four subscores were used in the data analysis, which included paired t tests and correlation analyses. Mean BPRS total scores demonstrated significant ($p < .001$) patient improvement at days 2, 7, and 14 of the hospital stay. Changes in subscores and their relationship to eventual outcome varied across diagnostic groups. The BPRS thus appears to be a useful inpatient outcome measure because it is capable of demonstrating significant change during stays of 1 week or less. Subscale scores may provide more specific prediction of change and may help clarify outcome in individual patients who show insignificant change in total score.

▶ Ward, M. M., Marx, A. S., & Barry, N. N. (2000). The rating scale preference measure as an evaluative measure in systemic lupus erythematosus. *Lupus*, *9*, 696-701.

Preference measures may be useful tools to assess patients' overall health-related quality of life. In a prospective longitudinal observational study of changes in the symptoms and clinical disease activity of 23 patients, the authors studied the validity and sensitivity to change of the rating scale preference measure in patients with systemic lupus erythematosus (SLE) and compared its properties with those of the patient global assessment of SLE activity. Patients were assessed every 2 weeks for up to 40 weeks. Construct validity was assessed by the strength of correlations between changes over time in the rating scale preference measure and patient global assessment and changes in the physician global assessment, Systemic Lupus Activity Measure (SLAM), European Consensus Lupus Activity Measure (ECLAM), the British Isles Lupus Assessment Group index (BILAG), and Systemic Lupus Erythematosus Disease Activity Index (SLEDAI). Changes in the rating scale were more highly correlated with changes in each of these standards than were changes in the patient global assessment, demonstrating the construct validity of this measure. Sensitivity to change was measured using the 2-week interval of greatest change in either the physician global assessment or the SLE activity measures as standards. The rating scale preference measure was less sensitive to change than was the patient global assessment when tested against four different standards. The sensitivity to change of the rating scale was less than half that of the patient global assessment when either the SLAM or ECLAM was used as the standard. Although these results support the validity of the rating scale as a measure of health-related quality of life in patients with SLE, its limited sensitivity to change may make it less attractive as an endpoint measure in clinical trials.

▶ Wright, Benjamin D., & Masters, Geofferey N. (1982). *Rating scale analysis*. Chicago: MESA.

This book discusses the construction of variables and development of measures. It begins by outlining the qualities a number must meet before it qualifies as a measure of something. The basis is the measurement philosophy of G. Rasch. The first requirement for making good measures is good raw material. To achieve the possibility of comparisons, the data must contain the possibility of a single variable along which persons can be measured. Chapter 2 presents a set of data that must be inspected, and techniques for inspecting the data are reviewed. In chapter 3, five different models for measuring are described, each of which was developed for a particular type of data. There are other models in the measurement literature, but these, all members of a family, are used because they meet the standards set for measurement. Chapter 4 shows how to use these models to get results, describing four different estimation procedures: PROX, PAIR, UCON, and CON. The quality control of variables is discussed in chapter 5. Chapters 6, 7, and 8 then illustrate the use of the techniques discussed, using four different data sets that were collected to measure drug use, fear of crime, knowledge of elementary physics, and child development.

5.18.5.1 Readings on Rating Scales

Linacre, John M. (1999). Investigating rating scale category utility. *Journal of Outcome Measurement*, *3*, 103-122.

Varner, Roy V., Chen, Y. Richard, Swann, Alan C., & Moeller, Frederick G. (2000). The Brief Psychiatric Rating Scale as an acute inpatient outcome measurement tool: A pilot study. *Journal of Clinical Psychiatry, 61*, 418-421.

Ward, M. M., Marx, A. S., & Barry, N. N. (2000). The rating scale preference measure as an evaluative measure in systemic lupus erythematosus. *Lupus, 9*, 696-701.

Wright, Benjamin D., & Masters, Geofferey N. (1982). *Rating scale analysis.* Chicago: MESA.

5.18.6 Latent Distance Scales

Nature: Analysis of these scales is based on a probability model that attempts to apply to qualitative data the principles of factor analysis, providing ordinal information. The basic postulate is that there exists a set of latent classes such that the manifest relationship between any two or more items on a questionnaire can be accounted for by the existence of these latent classes and by these alone.

Utility: Latent class analysis provides a description of categorical latent (unobserved) variables from an analysis of the structure of the relationships among several categorical manifest (observed) variables. This method is commonly called categorical data analogue to factor analysis.

Construction:

1. The investigator lists questions believed to be related to the latent attitude.
2. Answers to questions are dichotomized in terms of positive-negative, favorable-unfavorable, and so on.
3. The proportion of respondents who demonstrate the latent attitude in each response is calculated.
4. Items are arranged in terms of their manifest marginals.
5. The latent class frequencies are computed through inverse-probability procedures.
6. Response patterns are ranked in terms of average latent position, or an index is used to characterize each response pattern.

Examples

▶ Eshima, Nobuoki. (1991). Latent scalogram analysis. *Behaviormetrika, 20*, 1-21.

In scientific research, response structures are often more complex than those assumed under the latent distance model, an extension of the scalogram analysis proposed by Guttman (1950). Scaling models for these response structures are reviewed and compared, then expanded to develop latent scalogram analysis. Model selection procedures in both exploratory and confirmatory contexts are utilized in extracting both linear and branching hierarchical structures. Dynamic interpretation of latent scales is offered from a mathematical viewpoint, and a method for interpreting the proportions of latent scales is proposed. Numerical analysis shows the efficiency of this approach for deriving a simple latent structure based on binary data and for interpreting the extracted structure.

▶ Eshima, Nobuoki, & Asano, Chooichiro. (1988). On latent distance analysis and the MLE algorithm. *Behaviormetrika, 24*, 25-32.

Discusses Lazarsfeld and Henry's (1968) proposal of latent distance analysis, in which all the binary items (yes/no) are dominated by a common factor and each individual in a population responds to each item with a response probability, depending on the level of the latent factor. An algorithm is proposed that does not give any improper solution after transforming the latent response parameters to the logistic form and applying the new method of maximum likelihood estimation (MLE). The actual data analysis is provided.

▶ Mellenbergh, Gideon J. (1994). A unidimensional latent trait model for continuous item responses. *Multivariate Behavioral Research*, 29, 223-236.

A general linear latent trait model for continuous item responses is described. The special unidimensional case for continuous item response is K. G. Jöreskog's model of congeneric item response. The correspondence between models for continuous and dichotomous item responses is shown to be closer than usually supposed.

▶ Pascual, Leone Juan, & Baillargeon, Raymond. (1994). Developmental measurement of mental attention. *International Journal of Behavioral Development*, 17, 161-200.

Presents a dialectical constructivist model of mental attention and of working memory that is used to explicate research participants' processing in misleading test items. A set of 10 theoretical structural predictions were semantically derived that stipulated relations between mental attentional resources and the varied mental demands of items, as they jointly codetermine probable performance. These predictions were evaluated using a known family of ordered latent class models. A group of 616 children (aged 5-14 years) was tested. Results show that (a) data fit Lazarsfeld's latent distance model, providing initial support for the 10 predictions; (b) the M-power of children (latent mental-power classes), when assessed behaviorally, may increase with age in a discrete manner and have the potential to generate interval scales of measurement; and (c) what statisticians often consider "error of measurement" appears (in part) to be signal, not noise.

▶ Windle, Michael, & Dumenci, Leyent. (1998). An investigation of maternal and adolescent depressed mood using a latent trait-state model. *Journal of Research on Adolescence*, 8, 461-484.

A study using a latent trait-state model to study aspects of maternal and adolescent depressed mood found that maternal depression was predicted by lower family income, lower family cohesion, lower perceived social support, and higher parental role stress. The study also found that adolescent-trait depression was predicted by lower perceived family support, lower grade point average, more stressful life events, and female gender.

5.18.6.1 Readings on Latent Distance Scales

Eshima, Nobuoki. (1991). Latent scalogram analysis. *Behaviormetrika*, 20, 1-21.

Eshima, Nobuoki, & Asano, Chooichiro. (1988). On latent distance analysis and the MLE algorithm. *Behaviormetrika*, 24, 25-32.

Guttman, L. (1950). The basis for scalogram analysis. In S. A. Stouffer with the Social Science Research Council (Eds.), *Studies in social psychology in World War II: Vol. 4. Measurement and prediction*. Princeton, NJ: Princeton University Press.

Langeheine, Rolf, & Rost, Jürgen. (Eds.). (1988). *Latent trait and latent class models*. New York: Plenum.

Lazarsfeld, Paul F., & Henry, Neil W. (1968). *Latent structure analysis*. Boston: Houghton Mifflin.

Mellenbergh, Gideon J. (1994). A unidimensional latent trait model for continuous item responses. *Multivariate Behavioral Research*, 29, 223-236.

Pascual, Leone Juan, & Baillargeon, Raymond. (1994). Developmental measurement of mental attention. *International Journal of Behavioral Development*, 17, 161-200.

Windle, Michael, & Dumenci, Leyent. (1998). An investigation of maternal and adolescent depressed mood using a latent trait-state model. *Journal of Research on Adolescence*, 8, 461-484.

5.18.7 Paired Comparisons

Nature: This technique seeks to determine psychological values of qualitative stimuli without knowledge of any corresponding respondent values. By asking respondents to select the more favorable of a pair of statements or objects across a set of several pairs, an attempt is made to order the statements or objects along a continuum. This is sometimes called the forced-choices technique.

Utility: Ordering by paired comparisons is a relatively rapid process for securing a precise and relative positioning along a continuum. Comparative ordering generally increases reliability and validity over arbitrary rating methods.

Construction:

1. The investigator selects statements that relate to the attribute being measured.
2. The statements are arranged in all possible combinations of pairs as follows, with the number of combinations equal to $N(N - 1)/2$, where N is the number of statements.
3. Judges are asked to select which statement of each pair is the more favorable.
4. The proportion of judgments each statement received over every other statement is calculated.
5. The proportions are totaled for each statement.
6. The proportions are translated into standardized scale values.
7. An internal consistency check is applied by computing the absolute average discrepancy.
8. Statements are presented to respondents, who are asked to indicate favorableness or unfavorableness of each statement.
9. A respondent's score is the median of his or her favorable responses.

Examples

▶ Eisenberg, L. S., & Dirks, D. D. (1995). Reliability and sensitivity of paired comparisons and category rating in children. *Journal of Speech and Hearing Research, 38,* 1157-1167.

Children's subjective judgments of speech clarity using the methods of paired comparisons and category rating were evaluated in this investigation. Eighty children with normal hearing between the ages of 4 and 8 years judged the clarity of sentences that were systematically bandpass-filtered using conditions that increased intelligibility as estimated by the Articulation Index. Subjects were classified into four age groups (4, 5, 6, and 7-8 years olds), with 20 subjects per group. With use of materials and training methods suitable for children, judgments were obtained via the two psychophysical procedures (10 subjects per age group for each procedure). Results indicated that children 5 years of age and older were able to make reliable clarity judgments using either procedure; however, the method of paired comparisons was more sensitive than category rating in detecting differences between the bandpass-filtered conditions.

▶ Eisenberg, Laurie S., Dirks, Donald D., & Gornbein, Jeffrey A. (1997). Subjective judgments of speech clarity measured by paired comparisons and category rating. *Ear and Hearing, 18,* 294-306.

The purpose of this study was to compare listeners' subjective judgments of speech clarity via paired comparisons and category rating using stimulus conditions that varied in the relative spacing between stimulus items, producing either a wide or narrow range of performance. Subjective judgments of speech clarity were measured in 12 normal-hearing (Experiment 1) and 8 hearing-impaired adults (Experiment 2). Sentences processed by six bandpass filters that increased monotonically in Articulation Index (AI) estimates constituted the stimuli to be judged. Using subsets of three filters from the group of six, subjective judgments were additionally obtained for stimulus conditions in which the performance ranges were wide (large differences in AI) and narrow (small differences in AI). Results showed that speech clarity judgments obtained by paired comparisons and category rating were highly related to the AI estimates for both normal-hearing and hearing-impaired subjects. When the performance range was wide, both methods provided similar judgments for the normal-hearing subjects. For the hearing-impaired subjects, paired comparisons were more sensitive than category rating. When the performance range was narrow, paired comparisons were more sensitive than category rating in differentiating between filters for both groups of subjects. This difference was less obvious for the normal-hearing subjects when paired comparison data were converted to a scale comparable to the category ratings. Large between-subject variability was evident for the hearing-impaired subjects on the psychophysical scaling procedures, most notably for category rating. The researchers concluded that when judging the clarity among stimulus items for which performance varied over a wide range, category rating and paired comparisons provided comparable judgments for normal-hearing listeners. For conditions in which perceptual differences between stimulus items were restricted either by the choice of conditions or by the effects of sensorineural hearing loss, the method of paired comparisons was more sensitive.

5.18.7.1 Readings on Paired Comparisons

Bonebright, T. L. (1996). An investigation of data collection methods for auditory stimuli: Paired comparisons versus a computer sorting task. *Behavior Research Methods, Instruments, & Computers, 28,* 275-278.

Bossuyt, P. (1990). *A comparison of probabilistic unfolding theories for paired comparisons data.* New York: Springer Verlag.

David, H. A. (1963). *The method of paired comparisons.* Port Jervis, NY: Lubrecht and Cramer.

Eisenberg, L. S., & Dirks, D. D. (1995). Reliability and sensitivity of paired comparisons and category rating in children. *Journal of Speech and Hearing Research, 38,* 1157-1167.

Eisenberg, Laurie S., Dirks, Donald D., & Gornbein, Jeffrey A. (1997). Subjective judgments of speech clarity measured by paired comparisons and category rating. *Ear and Hearing, 18,* 294-306.

5.18.8 Semantic Differential

Nature: The semantic differential seeks to measure the meaning of an object to an individual. The subject is asked to rate a given concept (e.g., "African American," "Republican," "wife," "me as I would like to be," "me as I am") on a series of 7-point, bipolar rating scales. Any concept can be rated, whether a political issue, a person, an institution, or a work of art. The 7-point scales include such bipolar scales as the following: (a) fair-unfair, clean-dirty, good-bad, valuable-worthless; (b) large-small, strong-weak, heavy-light; and (c) active-passive, fast-slow, hot-cold (as shown in Table 5.13). The rating is made according to the respondent's perception of the relatedness or association of the adjective to the word or concept. The three subgroups measure the following three dimensions of attitude: (a) the individual's evaluation of the object or concept being rated, corresponding to the favorable-unfavorable dimension of more traditional attitude scales; (b) the individual's perception of the potency or power of the object or concept; and (c) the individual's perception of the activity of the object or concept.

Utility: A 100-item test can be administered in about 10-15 minutes. A 400-item test takes about an hour. The semantic differential may be adapted to the study of numerous phenomena through choice of concepts and scales. It may be useful in constructing and analyzing sociometric scales.

Table 5.13 EXAMPLE OF A SEMANTIC DIFFERENTIAL SCALE

Fifteen concepts: Love, Child, My Doctor, Me, My Job, Mental Sickness, My Mother, Peace of Mind, Fraud, My Spouse, Self-Control, Hatred, My Father, Confusion, Sex. Each concept was rated on the following 10 scales:

valuable	___:	___:	___:	___:	___:	___:	___:	worthless
clean	___:	___:	___:	___:	___:	___:	___:	dirty
tasty	___:	___:	___:	___:	___:	___:	___:	distasteful
large	___:	___:	___:	___:	___:	___:	___:	small
strong	___:	___:	___:	___:	___:	___:	___:	weak
deep	___:	___:	___:	___:	___:	___:	___:	shallow
fast	___:	___:	___:	___:	___:	___:	___:	slow
active	___:	___:	___:	___:	___:	___:	___:	passive
hot	___:	___:	___:	___:	___:	___:	___:	cold
tense	___:	___:	___:	___:	___:	___:	___:	relaxed

SOURCE: This semantic differential scale was used in a study reported by Charles E. Osgood and Zella Luria (1954), "A Blind Analysis of a Case of Multiple Personality Using the Semantic Differential," *Journal of Abnormal and Social Psychology, 49,* 579-591. For detailed information, see James G. Snider and Charles E. Osgood (Eds.) (1969), *Semantic Differential Technique: A Sourcebook* (Hawthorne, NY: Aldine).

Construction:

1. The investigator prepares a list of concepts appropriate to the theory guiding the variable to be measured.
2. Pairs of polar adjectives are selected on a priori grounds.
3. Selection of adjectives is determined empirically by asking different groups (comparative or experimental-control design) to take prescribed orientations in responding to an adjective-rating task. For example, members of one group of respondents could be asked to rate as they believe a person would rate the concept if he or she held a positive attitude; other respondents could be asked to rate as they believe a person would rate the concept if he or she held a strong negative attitude. Respondents are given the standard instructions for using the semantic differential form. Data are analyzed, and adjective pairs are selected that distinguish clearly between the groups.
4. New groups of respondents are selected who take prescribed orientations in rating the concepts. Data are analyzed.

Examples

▶ Bishop, J. Joe. (1999, April). *Locating Czech democracy: A semantic differential analysis of the meaning of democracy among students and teachers in three types of secondary schools.* Paper presented at the Midwest Sociological Society Meeting, Minneapolis, MN.

The study explored the meanings of democracy held by teachers and students in each of the three types of secondary schools in an emerging democracy (the Czech Republic) by locating the meaning in multidimensional semantic space. Data were collected during 2 months of fieldwork conducted in the Czech Republic during the fall of 1997. Students and teachers representative of three different types of schools in one large city, two medium-sized cities, and one small town were asked to think about the type of government the Czech Republic had while they completed a semantic differential scale composed of 57 bipolar adjectives. Factor analysis was used to represent the adjective pairs as a smaller number of variable factors. Results indicated significant age differences on the evaluative factor; sex differences on the potency and stability factors; school-level differences on the evaluative, potency, and stability factors; and a social class/prestige difference on the stability factor. No significant difference was found on the pervasiveness factor.

▶ Cogliser, Claudia C., & Schriesheim, Chester A. (1994). Development and application of a new approach to testing the bipolarity of semantic differential items. *Educational and Psychological Measurement, 54,* 594-605.

A method of testing semantic differential scales for bipolarity was developed using a new conception of bipolarity that does not require unidimensionality. Assessment of Fielder's Least Preferred Coworker instrument with 63 college student subjects using multidimensional scaling revealed its significant departures from bipolarity.

▶ Hayashi, Naoki, Yamashina, Mitsuru, Ishige, Naoko, Taguchi, Hisako, Igarashi, Yoshito, Hiraga, Masashi, & Inoue, Yukiyo. (2000). Perceptions of schizophrenic patients and their therapists: Application of the semantic differential technique to evaluate the treatment relationship. *Comprehensive Psychiatry, 41,* 197-205.

This study is an attempt to evaluate the treatment relationship with schizophrenic patients by examining the patients' and their therapists' perceptions of themselves and each other, which are hypothesized to reflect features of the relationship. A sample of 158 schizophrenic patients and 11 psychiatrists who each maintained a supportive relationship with the patients as a therapist estimated their perceptions using the semantic differential (SD) technique with 17 adjective pairs. Eight composite scales with sufficient internal consistency were constructed from the estimations. The interrelationship among the perceptual elements, which was represented by correlation analysis of the composite scale scores, seemed consistent with the researchers' clinical experience. A factor-analytic study of the scales yielded three orthogonal factors that could be assumed to characterize the treatment relationship. The patient-therapist cooperation factor indicated the degree of trust between the two participants, supposedly the affective or relational aspect of the therapeutic alliance. The therapist passivity factor reflected the therapist's passive role-taking and the clinical stability of the patient. The patient strength factor was related to the condition-related and characterological strength of the patient. It was demonstrated that the estimations performed by patients and therapists were valid and useful for evaluation of the treatment relationship in the current status.

5.18.8.1 *Readings on Semantic Differential Scales*

Bishop, J. Joe. (1999, April). *Locating Czech democracy: A semantic differential analysis of the meaning of democracy among students and teachers in three types of secondary schools.* Paper presented at the Midwest Sociological Society Meeting, Minneapolis, MN.

Cogliser, Claudia C., & Schriesheim, Chester A. (1994). Development and application of a new approach to testing the bipolarity of semantic differential items. *Educational and Psychological Measurement, 54,* 594-605.

Hayashi, Naoki, Yamashina, Mitsuru, Ishige, Naoko, Taguchi, Hisako, Igarashi, Yoshito, Hiraga, Masashi, & Inoue, Yukiyo. (2000). Perceptions of schizophrenic patients and their therapists: Application of the semantic differential technique to evaluate the treatment relationship. *Comprehensive Psychiatry, 41,* 197-205.

Moss, Claude S. (2001). *Dreams, images and fantasy: A semantic differential casebook.* Ann Arbor, MI: Books on Demand.

Osgood, Charles E., & Luria, Zella. (1954). A blind analysis of a case of multiple personality using the semantic differential. *Journal of Abnormal and Social Psychology, 49,* 579-591.

Osgood, Charles E., Suci, George J., & Tannenbaum, Percy H. (1957). *The measurement of meaning.* Urbana: University of Illinois Press.

Schriesheim, Chester A., & others. (1994). The equal-interval nature of semantic differential scales: An empirical investigation using Fiedler's Least Preferred Coworker (LPC) scale and magnitude estimation and Case III scaling procedures. *Educational and Psychological Measurement, 54,* 253-262.

Snider, James G., & Osgood, Charles E. (Eds.). (1969). *Semantic differential technique: A sourcebook.* Hawthorne, NY: Aldine.

5.19 GUIDE TO DATABASES OF COLLECTED DATA FOR THE SOCIAL SCIENCE RESEARCHER

Several online databases are available to social science researchers, most of which are proprietary in nature. This section of Part 5 describes those online resources through which researchers can access information about existing databases.

5.19.1 *Gale Directory of Databases*

The *Gale Directory of Databases* includes profiles on more than 12,500 databases. For each, it provides contact information, description, subject, geographic coverage, availability, and cost.

5.19.2 ProQuest® Information and Learning

ProQuest Information and Learning (formerly Bell and Howell) at www.umi.com/ focuses on collecting, organizing, and distributing information to researchers, faculty, and students in libraries, government, universities, and schools in more than 160 countries. Most of the sources are available only through university, college, and research institutions. An extensive collection of Web-based databases is available, including the following.

- ProQuest provides summaries of articles from more than 8,000 publications, with many in full text, full image format.

- UMI Dissertation Services publishes and archives dissertations and theses and sells copies on demand.

- Books on Demand™ provides information on obtaining out-of-print book titles using searches on fields that include keyword, author, title, subject, and ISBN. More than 150,000 titles are available. Thousands of topics and subject areas are covered, and books come from publishers such as Harvard University Press, Yale University Press, and Princeton University Press.

- The Newspapers in Microform catalog (NIM) lists more than 7,000 newspapers available in microform, and the Serials in Microform catalog (SIM) offers a comprehensive selection of periodicals, journals, and other serial literature in microform available anywhere. The SIM catalog lists more than 20,000 periodicals and 250 key newspapers.

:: UMI Research Collections contain original documentation of important papers. Under sociology and social work, the following materials are available:

> Charles Abrams: Papers and Files
>
> The Jane Addams Papers, 1860-1960
>
> American Culture Series II (ACS II): Anthropology and Sociology
>
> The John Beecher Papers, 1899-1972
>
> Crime & Juvenile Delinquency; Abstracts on Crime & Juvenile Delinquency
>
> The Caroline H. Dall Papers, 1811-1917
>
> English Poor Laws, 1639-1890
>
> Records of the Fair Employment Practice Committee, 1941-1946
>
> Friends Association for Abolishing State Regulation of Vice, 1873-1910;
>   Friends Association for the Promotion of Social Purity, 1910-1926
>
> Housing and Urban Affairs
>
> Emily Howland Papers
>
> Massachusetts Charitable Fire Society Papers, 1792-1970
>
> Massachusetts Historical Society Collections
>
> The Social Reform Papers of John James McCook
>
> The Missionary Society of Connecticut Papers, 1759-1948
>
> Oneida Community: Books, Pamphlets and Serials, 1834-1972
>
> Personal Papers Collections
>
> Quaker Official Correspondence: Home and Abroad, 1681-1881
>
> Rehabilitation and Handicapped Literature
>
> Royal Maternity Charity Minutes, 1761-1949
>
> Goldwin Smith Papers, 1823-1910
>
> The Peter Smith Papers, 1763-1850; The Gerrit Smith Papers, 1775-1924
>
> *The War Cry*, 1881-1981

For example, one area in the Crime & Juvenile Delinquency section includes 40,000 in-depth abstracts of studies published in more than 180 professional journals and also includes abstracts of material from books, pamphlets, monographs, federal and state documents, dissertations, case studies, task force findings, and statistical analyses. The collection spans a broad range of research topics, including criminal law, criminal courts, juvenile law, juvenile courts, criminal justice reform, law enforcement and the police, crime and the adult offender, correction, probation, prisons and parole, prison reform, drug abuse, and related social issues.

In addition to Web-based databases, ProQuest also provides access to the following databases. The Digital Vault™ includes scanned documents.

:: Genealogy & Local History Online is a tool for professional genealogical researchers and individuals tracing information on family lineage and local history.

:: Gerritsen Collection—Women's History Online provides an international view into the lives and experiences of women in the public and private arena from 1543 to 1945.

:: American Periodical Series Online contains four million pages relating to U.S. trends from 1741 to 1900.

:: ABI/INFORM Archive allows the user to search business journals (to 1986) for information on marketing, accounting, management, advertising, ethics, strategies, and other topics.

:: Access to H. Wilson Databases includes Social Sciences PlusText Social, which provides abstract-and-index coverage of more than 400 titles from Wilson's Social Sciences Index, with cover-to-cover full text and page images of more than 200 titles. Coverage begins in 1994. This database is also available on CD-ROM, with coverage from 1986 for citations and 1989 for full image.

■■ Education PlusText is useful to teachers, professors, students, and parents alike, with indexing and abstracts from 427 publications included in Wilson's Education Abstracts database. The file comprises leading publications in a wide range of specialties, including adult education, literacy standards, home schooling, and competency-based education. Education PlusText links more than 150 of the 427 indexed publications with full-text and full-image access; coverage begins in 1994.

■■ Applied Science & Technology contains all the journals in the Wilson index—some 450 titles—including full bibliographic citations plus abstracts of 40 to 100 words for each article. Users can go straight from citation to full image for more than 100 of the top journals; the full images are complete with all the graphs, diagrams, and illustrations so vital to scientific and technical literature. Coverage begins in 1994, with image coverage from 1997 forward. The CD-ROM version is updated monthly, with coverage from 1994 forward.

■■ ProQuest Full-Text Newspapers, easily accessible through ProQuest®, provides indexing and searchable ASCII full text for some 150 key national and international papers. From the citations of interest, users can move straight to full text in a single, seamless operation.

■■ ProQuest News & Magazines™ is the one-stop source for the materials that public library patrons are most likely to want—some 1,400 periodicals and regional newspapers. Virtually every general-reference periodical in the ProQuest® databases is included, as well as a package of newspapers tailored specifically to particular geographic locations.

■■ The General Reference Periodicals database contains more than 2,000 titles, some 1,000 of them in searchable ASCII full text or full image. It combines the titles in ProQuest Information and Learning's renowned Periodical Abstracts™ database with others carefully selected by panels of librarians. Some of the titles available and of interest to sociologists and other social and behavioral scientists are the following:

Administration in Social Work
AIDS & Public Policy Journal
The American Spectator
Annual Review of Sociology
Anthropological Quarterly
Behavior and Social Issues
Behavioral Science
The British Journal of Sociology
British Journal of Sociology of Education
Canadian Journal of Criminology
Canadian Public Policy
Child Abuse & Neglect
Child Welfare
Contemporary Sociology
Corrections Today
Criminology
Demography
Dissent
Economic Development and Cultural Change
The Economist
Ethnology
Families in Society
Family Process
Foreign Policy
Gender, Place and Culture
Governing
Growth and Change

Harvard International Review
Historian: A Journal of History
Human Organization
Information Management Journal
International Journal of Public Opinion Research
International Political Science Review
Journal of Aging & Social Policy
The Journal of Social Issues
Latin American Politics and Society
Monthly Labor Review
The Nation
National Review
New York Times Magazine
Occupational Outlook Quarterly
Organization & Environment
Peace Review
Planning
Policy Studies Review
Rolling Stone
Russian Social Science Review
Sage Family Studies Abstracts
SIECUS Report
Social Forces
Social Theory and Practice
Social Work
Social Work Research
Socialism and Democracy
Sociological Inquiry
Sociology of Education
Technology Review
Time
Triquarterly
The UNESCO Courier
U.S. Department of State Dispatch
Video Review
The Washington Monthly
Wired
World Politics

SOCIAL SCIENCE DATA ARCHIVES IN THE UNITED STATES   5.20

Many institutions are data archives, responsible for collecting, storing, and sharing data obtained from a wide variety of sources. These data sets make possible research in which new questions are asked and the often prohibitive expense of collecting data is avoided. Data archives in addition to those listed here can be found at Social Science Data Archives (http://osiris.colorado.edu/SOC/RES/data.html).

5.20.1 The Inter-University Consortium for Political and Social Research

The Inter-University Consortium for Political and Social Research (ICPSR, at www.icpsr.umich. edu/), established in 1962, essentially is a vast archive of data. The results of numerous studies and a huge number of facts are potentially available to every researcher in the world. The ICPSR is a federation of more than 400 colleges and universities worldwide. Each makes available data sets that are often not fully explored by the researchers who collect them. Through the ICPSR they are made available for continuing study by others. Many of the major studies of the Institute for Social Research at the University of Michigan are in the ICPSR archive. Major studies of the National Opinion Research Center's General Social Survey also are available.

Frequently requested data sets in the huge archive are those from the decennial census of the United States from the beginning of its history until 2000. The ICPSR also has a vast array of data sets on social phenomena occurring in more than 130 countries. These data sets are relevant to political science, sociology, economics, education, history, mass communication, psychology—the full range of social science disciplines. The ICPSR issues several publications that are helpful to researchers (see www.icpsr.umich.edu/ORG/Publications/pubs-email.html) as well as maintaining several e-mail lists that keep interested researchers informed regarding the status of particular data sets and new developments.

The data sets are organized into the following 18 subject areas:

> Census enumerations
> Community, urban studies
> Conflict, aggression, violence, wars
> Economic behavior, attitudes
> Education
> Elites and leadership
> Geography and environment
> Government structures, policies
> Health care, facilities
> Instructional packages
> International systems
> Legal systems
> Legislative, deliberative bodies
> Mass political behavior, attitudes
> Organizational behavior
> Publication-related archive
> Social indicators
> Social institutions, behavior

Each of these, in turn, has extensive levels of further definition. For example, under the general heading of social indicators, data are further segmented into those for the United States. Figure 5.4 shows the characteristics of one of these data sets, portrayed in an Excel file, for the *CBS Morning News* shopping habits and lifestyles poll, January 1989.

For each data set, the following variables are included:

> Abstract and study number
> Title
> Principal investigator(s)

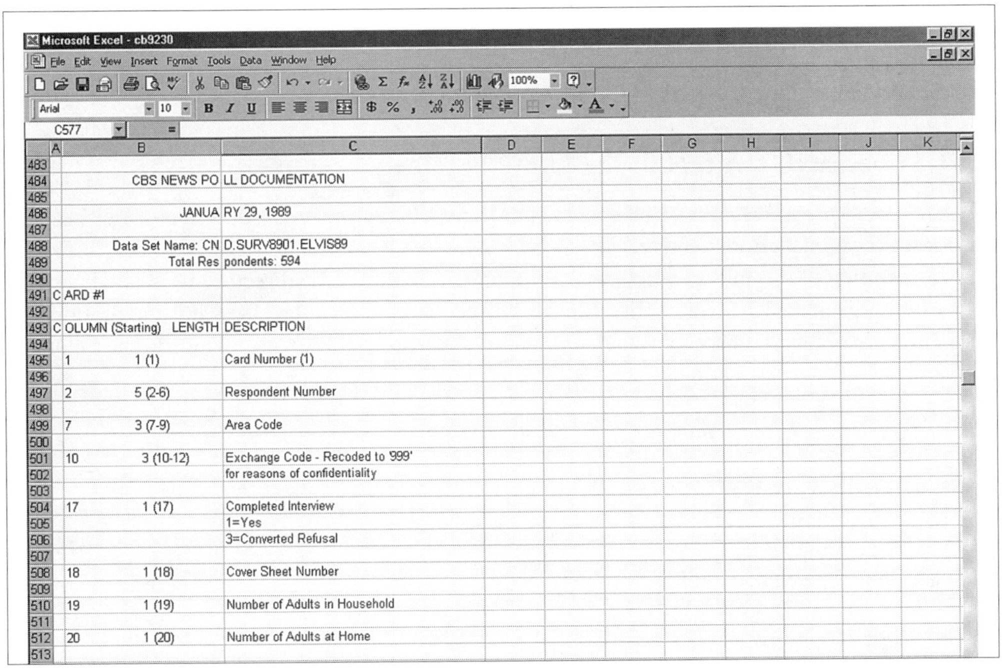

Figure 5.4. Data From the *CBS Morning News* Shopping Habits and Lifestyles Poll, January 1989

Summary

Extent of collection

Data type

Time period

Date of collection

Data source

Data format

Sampling

Universe

Date added

Date updated

Inquiries about the ICPSR and its data holdings and services should be addressed to Executive Director, Inter-University Consortium for Political and Social Research, P.O. Box 1248, Ann Arbor, MI 48106. The e-mail address is netmail@icpsr.umich.edu. Individual and group memberships are available. See the Web site for information on joining.

5.20.2 Center for Demography and Ecology

The Center for Demography and Ecology at the University of Wisconsin (www.ssc.wisc.edu/cde/datalib/collect.htm) is a multidisciplinary faculty research cooperative for social scientific demographic research. Membership includes sociologists, rural sociologists, economists, epidemiologists, and statisticians. It is also the location of a collection of data archive links that list the name of the archive, its URL, and a brief description.

5.21 DIRECTORIES OF SOCIAL SCIENCE RESEARCH CENTERS

5.21.1 Research Centers in the United States

The *Research Centers Directory*, published by Gale Research, reports on the programs, facilities, publications, educational efforts, and services of North America's leading nonprofit research institutes. The 28th edition of this indispensable source (published in 2001; the directory is updated periodically with supplements) describes more than 13,000 centers and includes URLs and e-mail addresses where available. Subject, geographic, personal name, and master indexes are included. The following areas are covered:

1. Agriculture, home economics, and nutrition
2. Astronomy
3. Business, economics, and transportation
4. Conservation
5. Education
6. Engineering and technology
7. Government and public affairs
8. Labor and industrial relations
9. Law
10. Life sciences
11. Mathematics
12. Physical and earth sciences
13. Regional and area studies
14. Social sciences, humanities, and religion (376 centers listed, including centers for research in anthropology, communications, human development, population, religion, sociology, history, ethnic folklore, linguistics, journalism, creativity, family studies, behavior, and race relations)
15. Multidisciplinary programs
16. Research coordinating offices

The typical directory entry shown below, for Columbia University, illustrates the information provided.

> 2750 Columbia University
> Center for the Social Sciences (1976)
> (formerly Bureau of Applied Science)
> Founded 1937
> 8th Level, 420 West 118th St.
> New York, New York 10027
> Dr. Jonathan R. Cole, Director; Phone (212) 280-3093

Integral unit of graduate faculties of Columbia University. Supported by parent institution, U.S. government, state and local agencies, foundations, non-profit social organizations, and industry. Staff: 41 research professionals, 7 supporting professionals, 20 graduate research assistants, 15 others, plus research fellows, interns, and part-time student interviewers, coders, and statistical clerks.

Principal fields of research: Public and elite opinion formation; political behavior; international comparative studies; manpower and populations; sociology of professions; formal organizations; community studies and evaluation of social programs. Also collects cases of application of social research to practical problems, codifies social research methods, develops new methods for study of aggregate aspects of mass social behavior, and provides empirical social science research training for graduate students and visiting foreign scholar. Maintains its own IBM data processing equipment.

Research results published in books, monographs, professional journals, project reports, and graduate student doctoral dissertations. Publication: *CSS Newsletter* (tri-annually). Also a Preprint Series, a Reprint Series, and Impact on Policy Monograph Series. Holds periodic seminars on social and political problems and applications of social science research methodology.

5.21.2 *International Research Centers Directory*

The *International Research Centers Directory* also is published by Gale Research, with the 28th edition in 2001. It provides access to government, university, independent, nonprofit, and commercial research and development activities in countries worldwide. Entries include the English and local name of the center, full mail and electronic addresses, a personal contact, organizational affiliates, staff, description of the research program, publications, services, and more. Master, subject, and country indexes are provided.

IMPORTANT RESEARCH ASSOCIATIONS AND INSTITUTES AFFILIATED WITH THE INTERNATIONAL SOCIOLOGICAL ASSOCIATION 5.22

This guide should assist research scholars who wish to communicate with other sociological researchers around the world. The list is not definitive, and not all research organizations are affiliated with the International Sociological Association. Many members belong to the older International Institute of Sociology, and scholars should try to contact that group's members as well to have a more complete channel of communication.

5.22.1 Members of the International Sociological Association

A blank entry in the table means that information is not available.

Name and Year Admitted Into the ISA	Contact Information	President
American Sociological Association (1950)	1307 New York Ave. NW, Suite 700 Washington, DC 20005-4701 USA Tel.: 1-202-833-9005 Fax: 1-202-638-0882 E-mail: executive.office@asanet.org www.asanet.org	Joe R. Feagin
Armenian Sociological Association (1993)	Armenian National Academy of Sciences Aram Str 44 Yerevan 375010 ARMENIA Tel.: 374-2-530571 Fax: 374-2-505947 E-mail: root@socio.arminco.com	Gevork Pogosian
Associaçao de Antropólogos e Sociologos de Angola	CP 16.648 Luanda ANGOLA	

(continued)

Name and Year Admitted Into the ISA	Contact Information	President
Associaçao Portuguesa de Sociologia	Instituto de Ciencias Sociais Edificio ISCTE, Ala Sul, 1 Andar Ave das Forças Armadas 1600 Lisboa PORTUGAL Tel.: 351-1-7995017 Fax: 351-1-7964953	
Asociación Colombiana de Sociología	Apartado Aéreo 90525 Santafé de Bogotá COLOMBIA Tel.: 57-1-2359912 Fax: 57-1-2356685	
Mexicana de Sociología	Torre de Humanidades, 9° Piso 04510 Mexico DF MEXICO Tel.: 52-5-6230218 Fax: 52-5-6161733 E-mail: regina@servidor.unam.mx	
Asociación Venezolana de Sociología (1953)	Espacio Abierto Investigadores Universidad del Zulia Apartado 15288 Maracaibo VENEZUELA	Roberto Briceño-Leon
Association Canadienne Sociologues & Anthropologues de Langue Français (1965)	06, Place d'Youville, Bur. B-10 Montréal, QUE H2Y 2B6 CANADA Tel.: 1-514-8414050 Fax: 1-514-8414015 acsalf@inrs-culture.uquebec.ca	Jacques Hamel hamelja@socio.umontreal.ca
Association Tunisienne de Sociologie (1995)	Faculté Sciences Humaines 94 Blvd du 9 Avril 1007 Tunis TUNISIA Tel.: 216-1-264797 Fax: 216-1-567551	Boutaleb Mohamed Nejib
Association of Mongolian Sociologists	Mongolian State University Ulan-Bator-46 MONGOLIA	
Associazione Italiana di Sociologia	Università degli Studi Roma Tre Facoltà di Scienze della Formazione Dip. Scienze dell'educazione V. Castro Pretorio, 20 00185 Roma (RM) ITALY Tel.: 06/492291 Fax: 06/4463722 Tel.: 39-2-7674351 Fax: 39-2-76015104 E-mail: rciprian@educ.uniroma3.it www.cisi.unito.it/associazioni/ais/	Laura Balbo bal@dns.unife.it

Name and Year Admitted Into the ISA	Contact Information	President
Australian Sociological Association (1965)	Social Science RMIT University Melbourne 3000 AUSTRALIA Tel.: 61-3-96603016 Fax: 61-3-96391885 E-mail: Katy Richmond, Secretary of TASA, k.richmond@latrobe.edu.au	Stephen Crook
Azerbaijanian Sociological Association	Prospect Inshatchilalar 581-9-3 370065 Baku AZERBAIJAN Tel.: 99412-325125 Fax: 99412-313457 E-mail: azsocas@azdata.net	
Belgian Sociological Association (1973)	c/o: Prof. B. Bawin-Legros Dept. Sciences Sociales Univ Liege Bd du Rectorat, 7 B31 bte 45 4000 Liege BELGIUM Tel.: 32-4-3663172 Fax: 32-4-3663178 E-mail: bbawin@ulg.ac.be	Erik Henderickx
British Sociological Association (1951)	Unit 3G Mountjoy Research Centre Stockton Road Durham DH1 3HR UNITED KINGDOM Tel.: 44-191-3830839 Fax: 44-191-3830782 E-mail: enquiries@britsoc.org.uk	Sara Arber
Bulgarian Sociological Association (1959)	5 Legue Street Sofia 1000 BULGARIA Tel.: 359-2-884181, 359-2-884035 Fax: 359-2-207102	Petar-Emil Mitevpmitev@bulnet.bg
Canadian Sociology and Anthropology Association/ La société canadienne de sociologie et d'anthropologie (1967)	Univ Concordia 1455 de Maisonneuve Blvd, West, LB-615 Montreal, QUE H3G 1M8 CANADA Tel.: 1-514-8488780 Fax: 1-514-8484539 csaa@vax2.concordia.ca	Vanaja Dhruvarajan vanaja.dhruvarajan @uwinnipeg.ca
Chinese Sociological Association	Institute of Sociology Chinese Acad. Social Sciences 5, Jian Guo Men Nei Da Jie Beijing 100732 CHINA Tel.: 86-1-5336250 Fax: 86-1-5336249	

(continued)

Name and Year Admitted Into the ISA	Contact Information	President
Croatian Sociological Association	Department of Sociology University of Zagreb D. Sajala, 3 41000 Zagreb CROATIA Tel.: 385-41-620007 Fax: 385-41-513834	
Dansk Sociologforening (1953)	Linnésgade 22 361 Copenhagen K DENMARK Tel.: 45-35323280 Fax: 45-35323940	Carsten Stroby Jensensoccsj@pc.ibt.dk
Deutsche Gesellschaft für Soziologie (1950)	Institut für Soziologie Ludwig-Maximilian-Universität Konradstrasse 680801 München GERMANY Tel.: 49-89-2180-3428 Fax: 49-89-2180-2922 E-mail: ls.allmendinger@lrz.uni-muenchen.de	Jutta Allmendinger
Estonian Academic Union of Sociologists (1991)	c/o Mikko Lagerspetz, President Estonian Institute of Humanities Salme 1210413 Tallinn ESTONIA Tel.: 372-6-416422Fax: 372-6-416423 E-mail: mikko@ehi.ee	Mikko Lagerspetz
Federación Española de Sociología (1980)	Alfonso XII, 18 - 528014 Madrid SPAIN Tel. & Fax: 34-915232741 E- mail: fes@iesam.csic.es	M. Angeles DuránAsociación Madrileña de Sociología
Hellenic Sociological Association (1989)	3 Plateia Agion Theodoron 105 61 Athens GREECE	Yiannis Panoussis
Hungarian Sociological Association (1964)	Benczur 33 1068 Budapest HUNGARY Tel.: 36-1-3225265 Fax: 36-1-3221843 E-mail: mszt@mtapti.hu	
Indian Sociological Society (1958)	Institute of Social Sciences 8 Nelson Mandela Road New Delhi 110070 INDIA Tel.: 91-11-6121902 Fax: 91-11-6137027 E-mail: iss@nda.vsnl.net.in	B. S. Baviskar
Institut de Sociologie	27 Rue Tran Xuan SoanHanoi Vietnam 8 Tel.: 84-4-261630 Fax: 84-4-261631	

Name and Year Admitted Into the ISA	Contact Information	President
Israel Sociological Society (1950)	Department of Sociology and Anthropology University of Haifa Mount Carmel Haifa 31905 ISRAEL Tel.: 972-4-8249650 Fax: 972-4-8240819 E-mail: issta@post.tau.ac.il	
Japan Sociological Society (1950)	Department of Sociology University of Tokyo 7-3-1 Hongo, Bunkyo-ku Tokyo 113-0033 JAPAN Tel.: 81-3-58418933 Fax: 81-3-58418932	Otohiko Hasumi
Korean Sociological Association	Miju-Harvard Officetel, 904 Pongchon-dong 875-7, Kwanak-ku Seoul 151-050 KOREA Tel.: 82-2-8718747 Fax: 82-2-8718748 E-mail: tksa@chollian.net http://soback.kornet.nm.kr/~ksa/	
Latvian Sociological Association	Latvian Academy of Sciences 19 Turgeneva Str Riga LV-1940 LATVIA Tel.: 371-2-227110 Fax: 371-2-210806 E-mail: atabuns@ac.lza.lv	
Lithuanian Sociological Society	Inst. Philosophy, Sociology & Law The Lithuanian Academy of Sciences Saltoniskiu 58 232600 Vilnius LITHUANIA Tel.: 370-2-624083 Fax: 370-2-610989	
Masaryk Czech Sociological Association (1993)	Husova 4 110 00 Praha 1 CZECH REPUBLIC Tel.: 420-2-66310612 Fax: 420-2-66310404 E-mail: rendlova@gw.czso.cz	Eliska Rendlova
Nederlandse Sociologische Vereniging (NSV) (1950)	NVMC-SISWO Plantage Muidergracht 4 1018 TV Amsterdam NETHERLANDS Tel.: 31-20-5270641 Fax: 31-20-6229430 E-mail: ganzeboom@cc.ruu.nl www.fsw.ruu.nl/soc/HG/nsv/index.htm	H. Ganzeboom

(continued)

Name and Year Admitted Into the ISA	Contact Information	President
Nigerian Anthropological-Sociological Association .	Dept. Sociology Ogun State University PMB 2002 Ago-Iwoye NIGERIA Tel.: 234-37-350680 Fax: 234-37-431966	
Norwegian Sociological Association (1957)	Munthes gate 31 0367 Oslo NORWAY E-mail: nsf@isaf.no www.isaf.no/nsf	Tore Lindbekk
Osterreichische Gesellschaft für Soziologie	Institut für Soziologie Universität Linz Altenbergerstrasse 69 A-4040 Linz AUSTRIA Tel.: 43-7322468242 Fax: 43-7322468243 www.soz.uni-linz.ac.at/oegs/	Josef Gunz josef.gunz@jk.uni-linz.ac.at
Polish Sociological Association (1956)	Nowy Swiat 7200-330 Warsaw POLAND Tel. & Fax: 48-22-267737 E-mail: pts@ifispan.waw.pl	Andrzej Kojder
Romanian Sociological Association (1992)	1 Schitu Magureanu St., Sector 5 70081 Bucarest ROMANIA Tel.: 40-1-3126618F ax: 40-1-3100284 E-mail: octav_m@yahoo.com	Ilie Badescu isogep@dial.kappa.ro
Russian Sociological Society (1958)	Krzhizhanovskogo 24/35 b.5 117259 Moscow RUSSIA Tel.: 7-095-7190971 Fax: 7-095-7190740 E-mail: valman@socio.msk.su	Valery Mansurov
Slovak Sociological Association	Klemensova 19 813 64 Bratislava SLOVAKIA Tel.: 421-7-326321 Fax: 421-7-361312 E-mail: sociolog@klemens.savba.sk http://nic.savba.sk/sav/svs/sss/	Ladislav Machacek
Sociedad Chilena de Sociologia	Nueva York 9, piso 12 Santiago CHILE Tel.: 56-2-6333836 Fax: 56-2-6334411	

Name and Year Admitted Into the ISA	Contact Information	President
Sociedade Brasileira de Sociologia	c/o Cesar Barreira Rua Pereira Vorente 1194 Ap-800 Fortaleza-Ceara Cep 60160-250 BRASIL Tel.: 55-85-2444450 Fax: 55-85-2815223 E-mail: cbarrerira@secrel.com.br	José Vicente Tavares dos Santos
Société Française de Sociologie (1963)	59-61 rue Pouchet 75849 Paris Cedex 17 FRANCE Tel.: 33-140251099 Fax: 33-142289544 Secrétaire: Monique Bidault bidault@iresco.fr	Claude Dubar
Sociological Association of Aotearoa (1990)	Department of Sociology and Social Policy Victoria University of Wellington Box 600 Wellington NEW ZEALAND Tel.: 64-4-4635676 Fax: 64-4-4955041 E-mail: allison.kirkman@vuw.ac.nz http://saanz.science.org.nz/	Allison Kirkman allison.kirkman@vuw.ac.nz
Sociological Association of Ireland	Dept. Political Science & Sociology University College Galway IRELAND Tel.: 353-91-24411 Fax: 353-91-25700	
Sociological Association of Trinidad and Tobago (1999)	Department of Behavioral Sciences University of West Indies St. Augustine Campus Trinidad TRINIDAD-TOBAGO Tel.: 1-868-662002 Fax: 1-868-6634948 E-mail: fssuwisa@carib-link.net	Ronald Marshall
Sociological Association of Ukraine	International Institute of Sociology 2 Skovoroda Str 252145 Kiev 145 UKRAINE Tel.: 380-44-4166053 Fax: 380-44-2280875	
South African Sociological Association (1993)	Dept. Sociology University of Durban-Westville PB X54001 Durban 4000 SOUTH AFRICA Tel.: 27-31-8202526 Fax: 27-31-2044949	Dasarath Chetty

(continued)

Name and Year Admitted Into the ISA	Contact Information	President
Sveriges Sociologförbund/ Swedish Sociological Association (1965)	Department of Sociology University of Göteborg Skanstorget 18 41122 Göteborg SWEDEN Tel.: 46-31-7734788 Fax: 46-31-7734764 E-mail: Klas.Borell@soa.mh.se www.sam.kau.se/sociologi/svsocfb.html	
Swiss Sociological Association	Research Institute of Sociology University of St. Gallen Tigerbergstr. 2 9000 St. Gallen SWITZERLAND Tel.: 41-71-2242929 Fax: 41-71-2242928 E-mail: sgs@unisg.ch http://www-sagw.unine.ch/members/sgs/	Thomas S. Eberle thomas.eberle@unisg.ch
Taiwanese Sociological Association	c/o Institute of Sociology Academia Sinica Nankang, Taipei 11529 TAIWAN Tel.: 886-2-3514239 Fax: 886-2-3514461 E-mail: ethw@gate.sinica.edu.tw	Ly-Yun Chang
The Westermarck Society— The Finnish Sociological Association (1950)	Post Box 124 20521 Turku FINLAND Tel.: 358-2-333 6322 Fax: 358-2-333 5080	
Yugoslav Sociological Association	Studentski trg. 1 11000 Belgrade YUGOSLAVIA Tel.: 381-11-637115 Fax: 381-11-637115 E-mail: ysa@afrodita.rcub.bg.ac.yu	

Regional Sociological Associations

Name and Year Admitted Into the ISA	Contact Information	President
Asia Pacific Sociological Association	Ryukoku University Otsu Seta Oe-cho Yokotani 1-5 JAPAN 520-2194 pauline@world.ryukoku.ac.jp www.geocities.com/Athens/Cyprus/2004/ index.html	Professor Kenji Kosaka

Name and Year Admitted Into the ISA	Contact Information	President
Asociación Latinoamericana de Sociología (1994)	Departamento de Sociología Universidad de Concepción Barrio Universitario s/n Concepción CHILE Tel.: 56-41-215860 Fax: 56-41-204766 E-mail: alas@udec.cl www.udec.cl/%7Ealas/alas.html	Eduardo Aquevedo eaqueve@udec.cl
Asociación Latinoamericana de Sociología del Trabajo, ALAST	Largo de São Francisco, 1 sala 418 Rio de Janeiro, RJ 20051-070 BRAZIL Fax: 55-21-2248965 E-mail: alast@ifcs.ufrj.br	Alice Rangel de Paiva Abreu
Association Internationale des Sociologues de Langue Française, AISLF (1964)	Université de Toulouse - Le Mirail 5 Allées Antonio Machado 31058 Toulouse Cedex FRANCE Tel.: 33-561-504374 Fax: 33-561-504660 E-mail: aislf@univ-tlse2.fr	Liliane Voyé
Association Arabe de Sociologie	7 Marouf St., Flat 5 Cairo EGYPT Fax: 202-2428789	
Association du Sociologues du Tiers Monde	BP 11.142 Case Postale 17 Dakar SENEGAL	
The European Association for Advancement in Social Sciences	ICCR Schottenfeldgasse 69/1 1070 Vienna AUSTRIA Tel.: 43-1-5241393100 Fax: 43-1-5241393200 E-mail: office@iccr.co.at	
International Association for the Study of Persian-Speaking Societies (1999)	Department of Sociology SUNY Stony Brook, NY 11794-4356 USA Tel.: 1-516-2469775 Fax: 1-516-6324361 E-mail: sarjoman@notes.cc.sunysb.edu	Saïd Amir Arjomand

Other International Supporting Organization and Institutions

Name	Contact Information
Associaçao de Antropólogos e Sociólogos de Angola	CP 16.648 Luanda ANGOLA
Associaçao Portuguesa de Profissionais em Sociologia Industrial, das Organizaçoes e do Trabalho	APSIOT Rua de Santa Justa 38 - 3 andar 1100 Lisboa PORTUGAL Tel.: 351-213476622 Fax: 351-213476982 E-mail: apsiot@mail.telepac.pt www.uninova.pt/CRI/GSIA/APSIOT/apsiot.html
Centro de Investigaciones Sociológicas (CIS)	Montalban, 8 28014 Madrid SPAIN Tel.: 34-915807600 Fax: 34-915807619 www.cis.es
Centre d'études Sociologiques	Blvd du Jardin Botanique, 431000 Bruxelles BELGIUM Tel.: 32-2-2117970 Fax: 32-2-2117995 E-mail: ces@fusl.ac.be www.fusl.ac.be/Files/General/ces/home.html
Cntr Brasileiro de Analise e Planejamento (CEBRAP)	Rua Morgado de Mateus 615 São Paulo, SP 04015-902 BRAZIL Tel.: 55-11-5740399 Fax: 55-11-5745928 E-mail: cebrap@internetcom.com.br
Cntr de Estudios Rurais e Urbanos	Av Prof Luciano Gualberto 315-S 20 São Paulo, SP 05508-900 BRAZIL Tel.: 55-11-8183735 Fax: 55-11-2112096 E-mail: mccampos@spider.usp.br
Cntr de Estudios Sociologicos El Colegio de Mexico	Camino al Ajusco 20 Pedregal de Santa Teresa Delegación Magdalena Contreras 01000 Mexico DF MEXICO Tel.: 52-5-6455955 Fax: 52-5-6450464 E-mail: zapata@colmex.mx
Cntr de Estudios y Promocion del Desarrollo (DESCO)	León de la Fuente 110 Lima 17 PERU E-mail: olivia@desco.org.pe

Name	Contact Information
Cntr de Investigaciones en Ciencias Sociales (CISOR)	Apartado 5894 1010 Caracas VENEZUELA Tel.: 58-2-4724401 Fax: 58-2-4716036 E-mail: cisor@conicit.ve
Cntr de Recherche en Economie Applique pour le Developpement	20 rue Chahid Khalef Mustapha Ben Aknoun ALGERIA Tel.: 213-2-784292
Cntr de Recherches Sociologiques de Toulouse	Université de Toulouse - Le Mirail 5 Allées Antonio Machado 31058 Toulouse Cedex FRANCE
Cntr Estudios Constitucionales	Plaza de la Marina Española 92807 1 Madrid SPAIN Tel.: 34-915415000 Fax: 34-915478549
Cntr Nazionale di Prevenzione e Difensa Sociale	Piazza Castello 3 20121 Milano ITALY Tel.: 39-02-86460714 Fax: 39-02-72008431 E-mail: cnpds.ispac@iol.it
Cntr voor Rechtssociologie	Universiteit Antwerpen, UFSIA Grote Kauwenberg 18 2000 Antwerpen BELGIUM Tel.: 32-3-2204316 Fax: 32-3-2204325
Colegio Doctores y Licenciados Ciencias Politicas y Sociologia	Quintana 29 28008 Madrid SPAIN Tel.: 34-915473480 Fax: 34-915592373 E-mail: colpolsoc@fct.fidelca.es
Danish National Institute of Social Research	Herluf Trolles Gade 11 1052 Copenhagen K DENMARK Tel.: 45-33480800 Fax: 45-33480833 E-mail: imv@smsfi.dk
Federaçao Nacional dos Sociologos FNS Brasil	Rua Tamandaré, 348 - 2 liberdade 01525-000 SP BRAZIL Tel.: 55-11-2793811 Fax: 55-11-2790662 E-mail: fednasoc@uol.com.br http://sites.uol.com.br/fednasoc

(continued)

Name	Contact Information
Forschungsinstitut für Soziologie	Universität zu Köln Greinstrasse 250939 Köln GERMANY Tel.: 49-221-4702409 Fax: 49-221-4705180 E-mail: friedrichs@wiso.uni-koeln.de www.rrz.uni-koeln.de
Foundation for Mediterranean Studies	2 Lycabettus Str 106 71 Athens GREECE Tel.: 30-1-3636026
Housing Research Centre	Univ. Ulster at Magee College Londonderry BT48 7JL Northern Ireland UNITED KINGDOM E-mail: ct.paris@ulst.ac.uk
Indian Institute of Youth & Development	Kalinga Phulbani, Orissa 762 022 INDIA Tel.: 91-6847-6514
Indian Statistical Institute	Att: CHIEF LIBRARIAN 203 Barrackpore Trunk Road Calcutta 700 035 INDIA Tel.: 91-33-5568085 Fax: 91-33-5566680 E-mail: library@isical.ernet.in
Inst. de Economia y Geografia	C.S.I.C. Pinar 25 28006 Madrid SPAIN Tel.: 34-914112220 Fax: 34-915625567
Inst. de Investigaciones Sociales	Universidad de Costa Rica Ciudad Universitaria Rodrigo Facio Código 2060, San José COSTA RICA Tel.: 506-535323 Fax: 506-249367
Inst. de Sociologia Aplicada	Claudio Coello 141, 4° 28006 Madrid SPAIN Tel.: 34-915620239
Inst. Internacional de Sociología Jurídica (IISL)	Antigua Universidad de Oñati AP 28 20560 Oñati SPAIN Tel.: 34-943783064 Fax: 34-943783147 E-mail: onati@sc.ehu.eswww.iisj.es

Name	Contact Information
Inst. Musiksoziologie	Schubertring 14 A-1010 Wien AUSTRIA Tel.: 43-1-5137620 Fax: 43-1-5137642 E-mail: t0031daa@vm.univie.ac.at
Inst. Recherche Sociétés Contemporaines	CNRS-IRESCO 59-61 rue Pouchet 75849 Paris Cedex 17 FRANCE Tel.: 33-140251133 Fax: 33-140251135 E-mail: brault@iresco.frwww.iresco.fr
Inst. Universitario de Pesquisas Rio de Janeiro	Rua de Matriz, 82 Botafogo Rio de Janeiro, RJ 22260-100 BRAZIL Tel.: 55-21-2860996 Fax: 55-21-2867146
Int'l Inst. of Sociology	Via Mazzini 13 34170 Gorizia ITALY Tel.: 39-481-533632 Fax: 39-481-532094
Int'l Inst. Sociology	University of Kansas Gerontology Center 4089 Dole Lawrence, KS 66045 USA
Istituto di Filosofia e Sociologia del Diritto	Facoltá di Giurisprudenza Univ degli Studi di Milano Via Festa del Perdono 720122 Milano ITALY Tel.: 39-2-58352621 Fax: 39-2-58312599
Istituto di Sociologia	Facoltà di Scienze dell'Educazione Univ Salesiana Piazza Ateneo Salesiano 1 00139 Roma ITALY Tel.: 39-6-87290349 Fax: 39-6-87290658
Istituto di Sociologia Università Centrale	Facoltà di Lettere e Filosofia Corso Umberto 1 Napoli ITALY Fax: 39-81-5521076
Istituto di Studi Sociali	Univ degli Studi di Firenze Via Cavour 82 50129 Firenze ITALY Tel.: 39-55-2757749 Fax: 39-55-2757750

(continued)

Name	Contact Information
Japanese Association of Sociology of Law	Faculty of Law The University of Tokyo 9-3-1, Hongo, Bunkyo-ku Tokyo JAPAN Tel.: 81-3-38122111
Laboratoire d'Economie et de Sociologie du Travail CNRS)	Atn: BIBLIOTHEQUE 35 Avenue Jules Ferry 13626 Aix-en-Provence Cedex FRANCE Tel.: 33-42-378500 Fax: 33-42-267937
Laboratoire de Recherches en Sciences Sociales (LARES)	4 Place St. Melaine 35000 Rennes FRANCE Tel.: 33-99-631918 Fax: 33-99-635758
Laboratoire Travail et Mobilités	Université Paris X - Nanterre 200, av. de la République, Bt. 6505 92001 Nanterre Cedex FRANCE
Mannheimer Zentrum für Europäische Sozialforschung (MZES)	Bibliothek, L7, 1univ Mannheim 68131 Mannheim GERMANY Tel.: 49-621-2921745 E-mail: direkt@mzes.sowi.uni-mannheim www.sowi.uni-mannheim.de
Observatori Català de la Joventut	Secretaria General de Joventut Departament de Presidencia de la Generalitat de Catalunya Calabria, 147 08015 Barcelona SPAIN Tel.: 34-934838383 Fax: 34-934838300 E-mail: observatori_catjov@presidencia.gencat.es
Research Center for Greek Society	Academy of Athens 84 Solonos Str 106 80 Athens GREECE Tel.: 30-1-3603028 Rural Sociological Society
Rural Sociological Society	Dept. Sociology, Rm. 510 Western Washington University Arntzen Hall Bellingham, WA 98225-9081 USA Tel.: 1-360-6507571 Fax: 1-360-6507295 E-mail: burdge@cc. wwu.eduwww.ruralsociology.org

Name	Contact Information
School of Social Sciences	Univ. Teesside Middlesbrough TS1 3BA UNITED KINGDOM Tel.: 44-1642-342301 Fax: 44-1642-34299 E-mail: pamela.abbott@tees.ac.uk
Service de la recherche en éducation	12, quai du Rhöne 1205 Genève SWITZERLAND Tel.: 41-22-3275711 Fax: 41-22-3275718
Sezione di Sociologia	Dept. di Studi Politici e Sociali Univ. degli Studi di Pavia Strada Nuova, 106/C 27100 Pavia, PV ITALY
Sociological Abstracts Inc.	POB 22206 San Diego, CA 92192-0206 USA Tel.: 1-619-6958803 Fax: 1-619-6950416 E-mail: info@mail.socabs.com www.socabs.org/
Sociologisch Onderzoeksinstitut	Dept. Soziologie Katholieke Universität Leuven E. van Evenstraat 2C 3000 Leuven BELGIUM Tel.: 32-16-283111 Fax: 32-16-323365
Soziologisches Institut	Universität Zürich Rämistrasse 69 8001 Zürich SWITZERLAND
Spolecnost pro socialni badani	Malebná 1043 149 00 Praha 4 CZECH REPUBLIC Tel. & Fax: 420-2-7934119

BIBLIOGRAPHY OF METHODS GUIDES 5.23

5.23.1 Documents

Allport, Gordon. (1942). *The use of personal documents in psychological science.* New York: Social Science Research Council.

Armstrong, J., & Jones, S. (1987). *Business documents: Their origins, sources and uses in historical research.* New York: Continuum International Publishing Group.

Bertaux, Daniel. (1998, July). *Life stories as documents for ethnosociological research.* Paper presented at the annual meeting of the International Sociological Association, Montreal.

Garrow, Patrick H. (1986). Public documents as primary sources for ethnohistorical research: The Mattamuskeet model. *Studies in Third World Societies, 35,* 1-23.

Harrington, Stuart A. (1999). Maintaining research documents with database management software. *Computers in the Schools, 15,* 67-80.

Lunsford, Andrea, Connors, Robert, & Muth, Marcia. (1999). *The new St. Martin's pocket guide to research and documentation.* New York: St. Martin's.

Mohapatra, Urmila. (1996). *Asian Indian culture in America: A bibliography of research documents. A research report.* Terre Haute: Indiana State University, Department of Political Science.

Troyka, Lynn Q. (1996). *Simon and Schuster handbook for writers* (4th ed.). Upper Saddle River, NJ: Prentice-Hall.

White, John H. (1997). *From research to printout: Effective technical documents.* New York: ASME Press.

Whiteman, Darrell L. (1983). Missionary documents and anthropological research. *Studies in Third World Societies, 25,* 295-322.

5.23.2 Content Analysis

Berelson, Bernard. (1952). *Content analysis in communication research.* New York: Free Press.

Carpenter, Sandra. (1998). Content analysis project for research novices. *Teaching of Psychology, 25,* 43-44.

Lee, Fiona, & Peterson, Christopher. (1997). Content analysis of archival data. *Journal of Consulting and Clinical Psychology, 65,* 959-969.

Holsti, Ole R. (1969). *Content analysis for the social sciences and humanities.* Reading, MA: Addison-Wesley.

Krippendorff, Klaus. (1980). *Content analysis: An introduction to its methodology.* Beverly Hills, CA: Sage.

Naccarato, John L., & Neuendorf, Kimberly A. (1998). Content analysis as a predictive methodology: Recall, readership, and evaluations of business-to-business print advertising. *Journal of Advertising Research, 38,* 19-23.

Potter, W. James, & Levine-Donnerstein, Deborah. (1999). Rethinking validity and reliability in content analysis. *Journal of Applied Communication Research, 27,* 258-284.

Reis, Harry T., & Judd, Charles M. (Eds.). (2000). *Handbook of research methods in social and personality psychology.* New York: Cambridge University Press.

Riffe, Daniel, Lacy, Stephen, & Fico, Frederick G. (1998). *Quantitative content analysis.* Mahwah, NJ: Lawrence Erlbaum.

Rosengren, Karl Erik. (Ed.). (1981). *Advances in content analysis.* Beverly Hills, CA: Sage.

Ruby, C. L., & Brigham, John C. (1997). The usefulness of the criteria-based content analysis technique in distinguishing between truthful and fabricated allegations: A critical review. *Psychology, Public Policy, and Law, 3,* 705-737.

Ruby, Charles, & Brigham, John C. (1998). Can criteria-based content analysis distinguish between true and false statements of African-American speakers? *Law and Human Behavior, 22,* 369-388.

Stone, Phillip J., & others. (1966). *The general inquirer: A computer approach to content analysis.* Cambridge: MIT Press.

Tarnai, Christian, & Bos, Wilfried. (Eds.). (1999). Content analysis in educational research. *International Journal of Educational Research, 31,* 657-734.

Wang, HsingChi A. (1998, April). *Science textbook studies reanalysis: Teaches "friendly" content analysis methods?* Paper presented at the annual meeting of the National Association for Research in Science Teaching, San Diego, CA.

Weber, Robert P. (1990). *Basic content analysis.* Newbury Park, CA: Sage.

5.23.3 Conversation Analysis

Bossard, James H. S. (1944). Family table talk: An area for sociological study. *American Sociological Review, 8,* 295-301.

Conner, Linton Jeff. (1993). The problem of solutions: Two cautionary cases for applying conversation analysis to business. *Issues in Applied Linguistics, 4,* 271-282.

Have, Paul. (1999). Doing conversation analysis: A practical guide. Thousand Oaks, CA: Sage.

Heritage, John. (1999). Conversation analysis at century's end: Practices of talk-in-interaction, their distributions, and their outcomes. *Research on Language and Social Interaction, 32,* 69-76.

Hutchby, Ian. (1999). Beyond agnosticism?: Conversation analysis and the sociological agenda. *Research on Language and Social Interaction, 32,* 85-93.

Hutchby, Ian, & Wooffitt, Robin. (1999). *Conversation analysis: Principles, practices and applications.* Malden, MA: Blackwell.

Kottler, Amanda E., & Swartz, Sally. (1993). Conversation analysis: What is it, can psychologists use it? *South African Journal of Psychology, 23,* 103-110.

Markee, Numa. (2000). *Conversation analysis.* Mahwah, NJ: Lawrence Erlbaum.

Sanders, William B. (1976). Conversation analysis. In *The sociologist as detective: An introduction to research methods* (Rev. ed.). New York: Praeger.

Schiffrin, Deborah. (1990). Conversation analysis. *Annual Review of Applied Linguistics, 11,* 3-16.

Tapsell, Linda. (2000). Using applied conversation analysis to teach novice dietitians history taking skills. *Human Studies, 23,* 281-307.

Wieder, D. Lawrence. (1999). Ethnomethodology, conversation analysis, microanalysis, and the ethnography of speaking (EM-CA-MA-ES): Resonances and basic issues. *Research on Language and Social Interaction, 32,* 163-171.

5.23.4 Questionnaire Construction

Bailey, Kenneth D. (1999). *Methods of social research.* Collingdale: Diane.

Bauman, Laurie J., & Adair, Elissa Greenberg. (1992). The use of ethnographic interviewing to inform questionnaire construction. *Health Education Quarterly, 19,* 9-23.

Jenkins, Stephen, & Solomonides, Tony. (1999). Automating questionnaire design and construction. *International Journal of Market Research, 42,* 79-94.

Saunders, Shaun, & Munro, Don. (2000). The construction and validation of a consumer orientation questionnaire (SCOI) designed to measure Fromm's (1995) "marketing character" in Australia. *Social Behavior and Personality, 28,* 219-240.

Yamada, Naoko. (1999). Error proneness questionnaire: Construction, reliability and validity. *Japanese Journal of Educational Psychology, 47,* 501-510.

5.23.5 Interview Construction

Connaway, Lynn Silipigni. (1996). Focus group interviews: A data collection methodology. *Library Administration and Management, 10,* 231-239.

Dorio, Marc. (2000). *Complete idiot's guide to the perfect interview.* Indianapolis: Macmillan.

Geiselman, R. Edward. (1999). Commentary on recent research with the cognitive interview. *Psychology, Crime and Law, 5*, 197-202.

Frey, James H. (1983). *Survey research by telephone.* Beverly Hills, CA: Sage.

Gillham, Bill. (2000). *The research interview.* New York: Continuum International.

Ginsburg, Herbert P. (1997). *Entering the child's mind: The clinical interview in psychological research and practice.* New York: Cambridge University Press.

Menard, Katherine A. (1996, April). *Interviews as method or data: Paradigmatic vs. narrative approaches to the study of returning adult students.* Paper presented at the annual meeting of the American Educational Research Association, New York.

Ornstein, Peter A. (1996). To interview a child: Implications of research on children's memory. *Monography of the Society for Research in Child Development, 61*, 215-222.

Siegel, Gilbert B., & Clayton, Ross. (1996). *Mass interviewing and the marshalling of ideas to improve* performance: The Crawford slip method. Lanham, MD: University Press of America.

Wester, Fred. (1996). Telephone polls in social research: Methods, techniques, interview practice. *Communications, 21*, 507-508.

Wilson, John Preston, & Keane, Terence Martin. (Eds.). (1997). *Assessing psychological trauma and PTSD.* New York: Guilford.

5.23.6 Index and Scale Construction

Bauer, Raymond A. (Ed.). (1966). *Social indicators.* Cambridge: MIT Press.

Dwyer, Evelyn E. (1993). *Attitude scale construction: A review of the literature* (ERIC Document Service No. ED359 201).

Edirisooriya, Gunapala. (1997, March). *A different approach to attitude scale construction.* Paper presented at the annual meeting of the American Educational Research Association, Chicago.

Edwards, Allen. (1957). *Technique of attitude scale construction.* New York: Appleton-Century-Crofts.

Fulcher, Glenn. (1996). Does thick description lead to smart tests? A data-based approach to rating scale construction. *Language Testing, 13*, 208-238.

Horiguchi, Toshihiro, & Sasaki, Tokio. (1998). Rorschach study of borderline personality disorder: Construction of borderline personality disorder index. *Journal of Mental Health, 44*, 69-74.

Spector, Paul E. (1992). *Summated rating scale construction: An introduction.* Newbury Park, CA: Sage.

Tuck, Kathy D. (1995). Assessment of the continuous progress report for the early learning years (an examination of scale construction). Washington, DC: District of Columbia Public Schools, Research Branch.

5.23.7 The Sample Survey

Barnett, V. (1991). *Sample survey principles and methods.* New York: Oxford University Press.

Bateson, Nicholas. (1984). *Data construction in social surveys.* Winchester, MA: Allen & Unwin.

Bhatti, M. Ishaq. (1995). *Testing regression models based on sample survey data.* Brookfield, VT: Avebury.

Converse, Jean M. (1987). *Survey research in the United States: Roots and emergence, 1960-1980.* Berkeley: University of California Press.

Dignan, Mark B. (1992). A brief review of sample survey methods for research in health education and health promotion. *Health Values: The Journal of Health Behavior, Education, and Promotion, 16*, 58-61.

Fink, Arlene, & Kosecoff, Jacqueline. (1985). *How to conduct surveys: A step-by-step guide.* Beverly Hills, CA: Sage.

Hansen, Morris H., Hurwitz, William N., & Madow, William G. (1993). *Sample survey methods and theory* (2 vols.). New York: John Wiley and Sons.

Hess, Irene. (1985). *Sampling for social research surveys, 1947-1980.* Ann Arbor: University of Michigan, Institute for Social Research.

Hyman, Herbert. (1955). *Survey design and analysis: Principles, cases, and procedures.* Glencoe, IL: Free Press.

Lee, Eun Sul, Forthofer, Ronald N., & Lorimor, Ronald J. (1986). Analysis of complex sample survey data: Problems and strategies. *Sociological Methods and Research, 15,* 69-100.

Patterson, Blossom Hansen. (1999). Latent class analysis of sample survey data. *Dissertation Abstracts International, 60,* 716A.

Perry, Patricia D. (1993, April). *High dimensional empirical Bayes canonical/interbattery methods applied in a small sample survey of adolescent alcohol use.* Paper presented at the annual meeting of the American Educational Research Association, Atlanta, GA.

Reviere, Rebecca, & Berkowitz, Susan. (Eds.). (1996). *Needs assessment: A creative and practical guide for social scientists.* Philadelphia: Taylor and Francis.

Wang, Lin, & Fan, Xitao. (1998, April). *Six criteria for survey sample design evaluation.* Paper presented at the annual meeting of the American Educational Research Association, San Diego, CA.

5.23.8 Direct Observation

Arnold, David H., Homrok, Susan, Ortiz, Camilo, & Stowe, Rebecca M. (1999). Direct observation of peer rejection acts and their temporal relation with aggressive acts. *Early Childhood Research Quarterly, 14,* 183-196.

Bales, Robert F. (1949). *Interaction process analysis.* Reading, MA: Addison-Wesley.

Bramlett, Ronald K., & Barnett, David W. (1993). The development of a direct observation code for use in preschool settings. *School Psychology Review, 22,* 49-62.

Bustion, Marifran, Eltinge, J., & Harer, J. (1992). On the merits of direct observation of periodical usage: An empirical study. *College and Research Libraries, 53,* 537-550.

Confessore, Sharon J. (1993). What direct observation discloses about who is best served in the multi-age classroom. *Continuing Higher Education Review, 57,* 58-71.

Cost, Hollie Anderson Campbell. (1999). Examining the concurrent validity between behavior rating scales and direct observation of student behavior. *Dissertation Abstracts International, 59,* 4103A.

Gardner, Frances. (2000). Methodological issues in the direct observation of parent-child interaction: Do observational findings reflect the natural behavior of participants? *Clinical Child and Family Psychology Review, 3,* 185-198.

Leutner, Detley, & Plass, Jan L. (1998). Measuring learning styles with questionnaires versus direct observation of preferential choice behavior in authentic learning situations: The Visualizer/Verbalizer Behavior Observation Scale (VV-BOS). *Computers in Human Behavior, 14,* 543-557.

Shapiro, Edward Steven, & Kratochwill, Thomas R. (Eds.). (2000). *Behavioral assessment in schools: Theory, research, and clinical foundations.* New York: Guilford.

Shapiro, Edward, & Kratochwill, Thomas R. (Eds.). (2000). *Conducting school-based assessments of child and adolescent behavior.* New York: Guilford.

5.23.9 Historical and Theoretical Methods in Research

Backs, Richard W., & Boucsein, Wolfram. (Eds.). (2000). *Engineering psychophysiology: Issues and applications.* Mahwah, NJ: Lawrence Erlbaum.

Boss, Pauline G., & Doherty, William J. (Eds.). (1993). *Sourcebook of family theories and methods: A contextual approach.* New York: Plenum.

Burstyn, Joan N. (1993, April). *New tools for multicultural education: A response to Patricia Seed's "Multiculturalism and the Predicament of the Comparative Method in Historical and Social Science Research and Teaching."* Paper presented at the annual meeting of the American Educational Research Association, Atlanta, GA.

Connor, Jennifer L. (1993). Medical text and historical context: Research issues and methods in history and technical communication. *Journal of Technical Writing and Communication, 23,* 211-232.

Ferris, Gerald R., & Rowland, Kendrith M. (Eds.). (1990). *Theoretical and methodological issues in human resources research.* Stanford, CA: JAI.

Grant, Don C. (1994). The historical method in psychiatric research. *Australian and New Zealand Journal of Psychiatry, 28,* 342.

Harvey, Charles, & Press, Jon. (1996). *Databases in historical research: Theory, methods, and applications.* New York: St. Martin's.

Henggeler, Scott W., Smith, Bradley H., & Schoenwald, Sonja K. (1994). Key theoretical and methodological issues in conducting treatment research in the juvenile justice system. *Journal of Clinical Child Psychology, 23,* 143-150.

Parry Jones, William L. (1992). Historical research in child and adolescent psychiatry: Scope, methods and application. *Journal of Child Psychology and Psychiatry and Allied Disciplines, 33,* 803-811.

5.23.10 Participant Observation

Ashworth, Peter D. (1995). The meaning of "participation" in participant observation. *Qualitative Health Research, 5,* 366-387.

Drury, John, & Stott, Clifford. (2001). Bias as a research strategy in participant observation: The case of intergroup conflict. *Field Methods, 13,* 47-67.

Fine, Gary, & Sandstrom, Kent L. (1988). *Knowing children: Participant observation with minors.* Newbury Park, CA: Sage.

Glaser, James M. (1996). The challenge of campaign watching: Seven lessons of participant-observation research. *Political Science and Politics, 29,* 533-537.

Havens, Leston L. (1993). *Participant observation: The psychotherapy schools in action.* Northvale, NJ: Jason Aronson.

Jorgensen, Danny L. (1989). *Participant observation: A methodology for human studies.* Newbury Park, CA: Sage.

Kolesar, Rastislav. (1998). Participant observation: A research and assessment approach for multiply disabled populations. *McGill Journal of Education, 33,* 253-264.

Spradley, James P. (1980). *Participant observation.* Fort Worth, TX: Harcourt College Publishers.

Tindale, Joseph A. (1993). Participant observation as a method for evaluating a mental health promotion program with older persons. *Canadian Journal on Aging, 12,* 200-215.

5.23.11 Secondary Research Analysis

Beatty, Alexandra S., Ramirez, Francisco O., National Research Council Board on International Comparative Studies in Education, & National Research Council Board on Testing and Assessment. (1999). *Next steps for TIMSS: Directions for secondary analysis.* Washington, DC: National Academy Press.

Clark, Rich, & Maynard, Marc. (1998). Research methodology: Using online technology for secondary analysis of survey research data—"Act Globally, Think Locally." *Social Science Computer Review, 16,* 58-71.

Freeman, Howard E., & Corey, Christopher R. (1994). *Health insurance and access to medical services: A secondary analysis of three years of NCHS health interview surveys.* Collingdale, PA: Diane.

Jacob, Herbert. (1984). *Using published data: Errors and remedies.* Beverly Hills, CA: Sage.

Kiecolt, K. Jill, & Nathan, Laura E. (1985). *Secondary analysis of survey data.* Newbury Park, CA: Sage.

Roberts, Brian A. (1996). Secondary analysis in qualitative research: Thoughts on data obsolescence. *Bulletin of the Council for Research in Music Education, 130,* 44-51.

Stewart, David W. (1984). *Secondary research: Information sources and methods.* Beverly Hills, CA: Sage.

5.23.12 Use of Informants

Dedmon, Angela M. M. (2000). The availability, use, and participation of multiple informants in the assessment of child and adolescent psychopathology in research and practice. *Dissertation Abstracts International, 60,* 4215B.

Hart, Elizabeth L., & others. (1994). Criterion validity of informants in the diagnosis of disruptive behavior disorders in children: A preliminary study. *Journal of Consulting and Clinical Psychology, 62,* 410-414.

McDonald, Skye, & Togher, Leanne. (Eds.). (1999). *Communication disorders following traumatic brain injury* (Brain Damage, Behaviour and Cognition Series). Hove, England: Psychology Press/Taylor and Francis.

Seidler, John. (1974). On using informants: A technique for collecting quantitative data and controlling measurement error in organizational analysis. *American Sociological Review, 39,* 816-831.

Tomada, Giovanna, & Schneider, Barry H. (1997). Relational aggression, gender, and peer acceptance: Invariance across culture, stability over time, and concordance among informants. *Developmental Psychology, 33,* 601-609.

5.23.13 Field Methods for Studying Social Organizations

Baeriswyl, D. (Ed.). (1990). *Applications of statistical and field theory methods to condensed matter.* Norwood, NJ: Kluwer Academic.

Bailey, Carol A. (1995). *A guide to field research.* Boston: Pine Forge.

Burgess, Robert G. (1984). *In the field: An introduction to field research.* New York: Routledge.

Dresch, Paul, James, Wendy, & Parkin, David J. (2001). *Anthropologists in a wider world: Essays on field research.* New York: Berghahn Books.

Emerson, Robert M. (Ed.). (1988). *Contemporary field research: A collection of readings.* Prospect Heights, IL: Waveland.

Orlans, F. Barbara (Ed.). (1988). *Field research guidelines: Impact on animal care and use committees.* Greenbelt, MD: Scientists Center for Animal Welfare.

Smith, Carolyn D., & Kornblum, William. (Eds.). (1996). *In the field: Readings on the field research experience.* Westport, CT: Greenwood.

Wixon, Dennis, & Ramey, Judith. (Eds.). (1996). *Field methods casebook for software design.* New York: John Wiley and Sons.

5.24   A COMMENT ON THE INTERNET

The use of the Internet as a part of university, public, and private research is ubiquitous, but this handbook is not the place for a review of Internet basics or e-mail fundamentals.

Perhaps the most important and increasingly used tools available on the Internet are newsgroups. Newsgroups are discussion groups focused on a particular topic. To help manage the flow of articles, news sites are managed, moderated, administered, and censored by system administrators. Not all newsgroups reach each potential site or everyone who has access to an Internet site. The newsgroups from which you can select news are those that the system administrator makes available. The following is a list of major newsgroups, the general area they cover, and examples of what they contain.

Newsgroup	General Area	Examples
Alt	Everything that doesn't fit anywhere else, and certainly lots of stuff out of the ordinary	Alt.actors.dustin-hoffman Alt.amazon.women Alt.anything
Comp	Information about computers, computer science, and software, as well as general interest computer topics	Comp.ai (artificial intelligence) Comp.compression (a discussion of ways to compress or reduce files) Comp.software engineering (chip design)
News	Information about news, newsgroups, and the newsgroup network	News.admin.censorships (all about what should and shouldn't be on the Net) News.admin.net-abuse.email (about junk e-mail) News.announce.conferences (conferences on the Internet)
Biz	Information about business	Biz.healthcare (the business of health care) Biz.books.technical (new publications about business) Biz.comp.accounting (accounting practices and procedures)
Newsgroup	General Area	Examples
K12	Information about education from kindergarten through grade 12	K-12.ed.science (teaching science from kindergarten through 12th grade) K-12.library (especially for librarians) K-12.lang.francais (mais oui!)
Bionet	Information about biology	Bionet.biophysics Bionet.jobs (job hunting) Bionet.journals (publishing in biology)
Rec	Information about recreation, hobbies, the performing arts, and fun stuff	Rec.sport.swimming Rec.bicycles.racing Rec.skydiving
Sci	Information about science, scientific research and discoveries, engineering, and some social science stuff	Sci.astro (astronomy) Sci.cognitive (cognitive studies)
Soc	Information about the social sciences	Soc.couples (people getting along) Soc.penpals (why people write to one another)

With increasing numbers of newsgroups, new domain names are constantly being considered for addition to the existing structure. For more information about domain names, see the home page for The Internet Corporation for Assigned Names and Numbers at www.icann.org/.

Six new domains were under consideration as of August, 2001. They are the following:

Aero:	Air transport industry
Coop:	Cooperatives
Info:	Unrestricted use
Museum:	Museums
Prof:	Accountants, physicians, and lawyers
Name:	For registration by individuals

GUIDE TO STATISTICAL ANALYSIS
OF SOCIAL SCIENCE DATA

Part 6 of the *Handbook of Research Design and Social Measurement* includes guides that should prove useful to researchers as they seek information on which statistical tools to test hypotheses and how they can use personal computers to collect, analyze, and interpret data. Superior research studies can be completed only when the researcher has the required knowledge of research design and an understanding of the full scope of statistical tools that are available, as well as the skills to use those tools via the personal computer. When these conditions are realized, research options of maximum effectiveness open to stir the creative imagination.

Qualitative and quantitative variables both require appropriate statistical tools to provide tests of a research hypothesis. The first sections of this chapter briefly review statistical tests and delineate the distinction between parametric and nonparametric statistics, also discussing how they are used to draw inferences from samples. Also included is a brief review of commonly used tests of differences between groups and tests of association.

Computations being done in the social sciences today use increasingly powerful personal computers, with mainframes being left for the analysis of huge databases and associated analyses. Computer technology has advanced rapidly in the past several decades, creating powerful desktop and laptop machines. Because this technology is so widespread, familiarity with it is essential for the researcher and graduate student. With easily accessible off-site Internet connection capabilities, researchers can now work from their homes and complete the same type of sophisticated analyses that previously required travel to a campus and use of its mainframe computer.

Use of these tools is expected of students and researchers, so they must develop a knowledge of both basic and advanced statistics. Computers can be used, for example, to generate formal models of social systems; to simulate the behavior of persons, groups, or nations; and to retrieve large amounts of documentary material such as abstracts of journal articles (as explained in Part 5).

Because statistical planning is such an integral part of research, the sooner a researcher can devote attention to this research activity, the better. After the problem, theory, study design, and hypotheses are chosen, the time for statistical planning has arrived. Researchers cannot wait until they are in the process of gathering or analyzing data because how one analyzes data is closely tied to the research question being asked and the type of data that are collected. Young and inexperienced researchers in particular should begin statistical planning well before any experimental work or fieldwork begins.

The article that follows should sharpen researchers' awareness of the dimensions of their hypotheses as they prepare to test them. As Lurie puts it:

> It is the scientist's responsibility to decide exactly what his hypotheses are, what these hypotheses are about, and how sure he wants to be of their correctness. . . . And the more the scientist becomes aware of his responsibilities, and takes them into account in his work, so much more accurate and valid will his conclusions be, and so much more properly related to the reality with which he deals.

▶ **The Impertinent Questioner:**
The Scientist's Guide to the Statistician's Mind

William Lurie

Prologue

It has become fashionable to ornament science with statistical embellishments. No equation is complete without at least a double summation sign somewhere in it, sub-ij's attach themselves to familiar Xs, Ys, and Zs; and phrases like "polymodal distribution," "inverse reciprocal correlation," and "multivariate deviations" now can be seen on practically every other page of "The Journal of the Society for Thus-and-So," "The Transactions of the Association for Such-and-Such," and "The Proceedings of the Symposium on Etc., Etc."

But in addition to providing mathematical and linguistic ornamentation for these publications, the statistician, if he is really to assist the scientist, must perform a necessary, but irritatingly annoying task: he must ask the scientist impertinent questions. Indeed, the questions, if bluntly asked, may appear to be not only impertinent but almost indecently prying—because they deal with the foundations of the scientist's thinking. By these questions, unsuspected weaknesses in the foundations may be brought to light, and the exposure of weaknesses in one's thinking is a rather unpleasant occurrence.

The statistician will, then, if he is wise in the ways of human beings as well as learned in statistics, ask these questions diplomatically, or even not ask them as questions at all. He may well guide the discussion with the scientist in such a way that the answers to the questions will be forthcoming without the questions having been even explicitly asked.

And if happily the scientific and statistical disciplines reside within one mind, and it is the scientist's statistical conscience that asks him these questions, instead of impertinent questioning there is valid scientific soul-searching.

Regardless, then, of whether these questions arise inside or outside the scientist's own mind, what are they? These:

1. With respect to the experiment you are performing, just what are your ideas?
2. With respect to the scientific area to which these ideas refer, just what are they about?
3. How sure do you want to be of the correctness of these ideas?

In order to understand the statistician's reasons for asking these questions, let us first see how the scientist's activities look to the statistician.

From the statistician's point of view, what the scientist does, is: performs experiments and/or makes observations to obtain data relating to *an idea he has* about the organization of *that portion of the world he is interested in*, so that he can decide *whether his idea was correct or not*.

For each of these italicized aspects of the scientist's activity, there is a corresponding question.

Let us, then, examine each of these aspects of the scientist's activities, and the purpose for and consequences of the question concerning it.

An Idea He Has

The impertinent questioner must take the risk of appearing to imply that the scientist is not thinking clearly. And, of course, even an implication to this effect is not calculated to endear the implier to the heart of the implyee. But it is exactly this implication that, perhaps innocently, is associated with the question, "Just what are your ideas?"

Why does the statistician ask this impertinent question? Because it is a precondition for the statistician's being able to help the scientist accomplish his objective. A hazily formulated idea not only can be discussed, at best, with difficulty, but further, it is practically impossible to test its correctness. Therefore, the statistician has a rule, his name for which is: EXPLICIT HYPOTHESIZATION. This rule expresses the requirement that the idea, whose correctness is to be determined by the experiment, should be stated in as clear, detailed, and explicit form as possible, preferably before the experiment is conducted. This idea can relate either to the influence of one factor or to the influence of several factors, or to the numerical characterization of a property (or properties) of whatever is being experimented on. In the early stages of an investigation, where what are being sought are the influential factors (i.e., those which, when they are at varying levels, give rise to sufficiently varied results), the idea (or hypothesis) need not be specific, but it must be explicit. The hypothesis can be broad, but it must be explicitly broad—that is, even though it is not a hypothesis about details, its boundary must be sharply delineated.

For example, "Factors, A, B, C, and D individually influence the results," "Factors A and B, acting in conjunction, influence the results differently than would be expected from the effects of A alone and B alone," "Factors A, B, and C, acting in conjunction, etc., etc." Or later in the investigation, and more specifically, "The measurement of the effect of factor A at level a_1, will result in the numerical value $N \pm n$."

To emphasize unmistakably the requirement for explicit hypothesization, let us use an obviously exaggerated example dealing with a particular subject: the task of an industrial psychologist who has been given the job of finding out why the accounting clerks are making too many errors in addition. (The problem of deciding how many errors are "too many" is another statistical problem, which will not be considered here.)

The psychologist, for the purposes of this example, may say to himself: "My training as a psychologist tells me that the situation in which a person operates affects his behavior. So let me find out what the situation is that is causing the clerks to make these errors." If the formulation of the psychologist's idea goes no further than this, he can obviously continue to attempt to find out what the situation is, from now on forever, since "The Situation" has no boundaries.

It might, for example, not only include the working circumstances of the clerks, but their home circumstances, their childhood histories, their dream life; and it is seen that the possibilities are unlimited. As then is obvious, the hypothesis has not been sufficiently explicitly formulated, nor the situation covered by it clearly enough delineated, for a decision to be able to be arrived at as to the correctness of the hypothesis.

But now, let the psychologist's statistical conscience awaken, and his ideas begin to crystallize out of their original diffuseness. "The Situation?—Well, to be more specific, let's just consider the office situation. And within the office situation, I'll pick three factors that I believe affect the performance of the clerks. The factors I'm selecting to study for their effects are: Temperature, Humidity, and Noise. And now, my explicit hypothesis: It makes a difference what the levels of temperature, humidity, and noise are with respect to the number of errors in addition made by the accounting clerks." The hypothesis could (and probably should) have been even more explicitly formulated (e.g., including as factors Illumination Level, Desk Space per employee, etc.) but the direction of the path to statistical virtue has been pointed out, and further travel along that path is left to the reader.

Now, assuming that the hypothesis has been sufficiently explicitly formulated, the scientist and statistician can together review the plan (or design) of the experiment, and assure themselves that such data will be obtained as will be sufficient to determine the correctness (or noncorrectness) of the scientist's idea.

That Portion of the World He Is Interested In

Again, the impertinent questioner must be careful in asking: "Just what are your ideas about?" Even though one may admit that his ideas are not as clearly and explicitly formulated as he would like, the question "Just what are your ideas about?" carries with it, to the person being asked, the implication that he isn't clear about the subject-matter of his ideas, surely not a flattering implication. The statistician has a reason for his implied aspersion on the basis of the scientist's self-esteem. The statistician's reason can be stated to the scientist thus: "It's for your own good. If I am to help you decide, on the basis of the experimental facts, whether your ideas are correct or not, I have to know, as explicitly as possible, not only what your ideas are, but *what they are about*. My name for this requirement is: MODEL FORMULATION." Technically, model formulation establishes the requirement that a clear differentiation be made as to whether the scientist's ideas are intended to be applicable only to the conditions of the experiment (the narrower range of application) or to conditions (i.e., levels of the factors) other than those specific ones under which the experiment is being conducted (the broader range of application). Why the necessity for this differentiation? Because, when the experimental data have been obtained, the analysis of the data is carried on in different ways, depending on whether the hypotheses are intended to have the broader or narrower range of application.

Let us again, for exemplification, return to our industrial psychologist. And, let us say, his experimental conditions are, for temperature, 40°, 55°, and 70°F; for humidity, 40, 55, and 70 percent; and for noise level, 40, 55, and 70 decibels.

It may well make a difference in the way the experimental data are analyzed to arrive at conclusions (i.e., decisions as to correctness of ideas), and whether any conclusions can be arrived at, and, if so, what they are, depending on whether the scientist wants his conclusions to apply only to the three levels of temperature, humidity, and noise level that have been used in the experiment, or also to other (unspecified) temperature, humidity, and noise levels. Data that support narrow conclusions may not be sufficient to support broader conclusions. Therefore, the scientist must have clearly in mind what his hypotheses are about, and whether, consequently, his conclusions will be broad or narrow; and the statistician's effort to assure that the scientist does have this clearly in mind, may well, to the scientist, appear to be impertinent.

Whether His Idea Was Correct or Not

The statistician's third question—"How sure do you want to be of the correctness of your ideas?"—is the least important of the three. This question, unlike the other two, does not probe the foundations of the scientist's thinking, but rather requests him to quantify a previously unquantified aspect of it. (In fact, the request is in accordance with the scientist's own predilection for quantitative data.) This aspect is that dealing with levels of assurance, for which ordinary language supplies us with qualitatively descriptive terms (somewhat sure, rather sure, quite sure, extremely sure). But these terms are not sufficiently explicit for scientific use. Therefore, the statistician asks the scientist to decide upon and express his desired level of assurance in quantitative terms, so that it can be determined, by analysis of the quantitative data, whether the desired level of assurance of the conclusions has been achieved. The statistician's name for the choice and quantitative expression of the desired level of assurance is: SIGNIFICANCE LEVEL SELEC-

TION. And how does the statistician help the scientist choose the desired level of assurance? By bringing to the forefront of the scientist's consciousness his already unconscious awareness of the inherent variability of events (i.e., that, because of chance alone, no repetition of an experiment will give exactly the same results); by helping the scientist decide what assurance is desired that the hypothesis has not been "confirmed" just by the operation of chance alone; and by furnishing the mathematical tools to decide, on the basis of the experimental data, whether the desired level of assurance has been attained. Say, for example, in the temperature–humidity–noise level experiment, when all the data have been accumulated, and the scientist is preparing them for analysis so that he may decide whether his hypotheses were correct or not, the statistician will then say to him: "You know, of course, that if you did the experiment over, under as near the same conditions as possible, you'd get slightly, or even somewhat different results. The results might even, just by chance, be different enough to lead you to believe that temperature does affect accuracy, even though it really doesn't. Or even if you didn't do the experiment over again, the particular experiment you've just done might be the one in which the data are such that you'd believe temperature has an effect though it really doesn't. *But I can test these data of yours.* I can assure you that when you state the conclusion, say, that temperature does affect accuracy, you'll have only a 5 percent, or 1 percent, or 1/10th of 1 percent chance of being wrong, as a result of that off chance I told you about. Now—what chance do you want to take? If you select a very small chance of being wrong in saying there is a temperature effect when there really isn't you're taking a bigger chance of saying there isn't a temperature effect when there really might be. I can figure this out for you also. So again, what chance do you want to take?"

When the scientist has selected the chance he is willing to take of being wrong (or what is equivalent, how sure he wants to be that he is correct) in his conclusions, the statistician can analyze the data and tell the scientist what conclusions he can validly draw (i.e., what decisions he can make about the correctness of his ideas).

Epilogue

One final word. *It is the statistician's responsibility to ask these questions, not to answer them.* It is the scientist's responsibility to decide exactly what his hypotheses are, what these hypotheses are about, and how sure he wants to be of their correctness.

The statistician, in asking his impertinent questions, is just explicitly bringing to the scientist's attention responsibilities that the scientist may not have been aware that he had. And the more the scientist becomes aware of his responsibilities, and takes them into account in his work, so much more accurate and valid will his conclusions be, and so much more properly related to the reality with which he deals.

SOURCE: From William Lurie (1958), "The Impertinent Questioner: The Scientist's Guide to the Statistician's Mind," *American Scientist, 46,* 57-61. Reprinted by permission of the author and publisher.

6.2 FOUR LEVELS OF MEASUREMENT AND THE STATISTICS APPROPRIATE TO EACH LEVEL

Part 7 of this volume includes scales that measure a wide variety of social and behavioral variables. These scales may have their basis in *nominal, ordinal, interval,* or *ratio* types of data. This classification of levels of measurement was first proposed by S. S. Stevens (1951).

Table 6.1	FOUR LEVELS OF MEASUREMENT		
Level	Qualities	Examples	Defining Characteristic
Nominal	Assignment of labels to categories	Preference (like or dislike) Voting record (for or against)	Each observation belongs in its own category
Ordinal	Assignment of relative values along some continuum	Rank in college Social class relative to others	One observation is ranked above or below another
Interval	Equal distances between points	Intelligence test scores Temperature	One score differs from another on some measure that has equal-appearing intervals
Ratio	Absolute zero point	Age Weight Time	Ratios of scale values are meaningful, so that one value can be said to be twice as large as another or have some other ratio, and it is possible for none of the quantity measured to exist

- *Nominal* or *classificatory* scales use labels, numbers, or other symbols simply to classify an object, person, or characteristic (e.g., high or low, rural or urban). This level of measurement characterizes variables that are categorical in nature. For example, social class (in category), gender, and neighborhood all can be considered variables at the nominal level of measurement.

- *Ordinal* or *ranking scales* involve a level of measurement in which objects in various categories of a scale stand in some kind of *relation* to the categories (e.g., class rank, higher or lower). Given a group of equivalence classes, if the relation *greater than* holds between some but not all pairs of classes, we have a partially ordered scale. If the relation *greater than* holds for all pairs of classes so that a complete rank ordering of classes arises, we have an ordinal scale.

- *Interval scales* have all the characteristics of ordinal scales, and in addition the distances between any two numbers on the scale are of known size (e.g., number correct on a test). Measurement considerably stronger than ordinality can be achieved with interval scales. Thurstone's equal-appearing interval scale is an example. This type of scale characterizes many social and behavior assessments. At times, some liberty is taken to assign a measure as such.

- *Ratio scales* have all the characteristics of interval scales, and in addition they have true zero points as their origins (e.g., the Centigrade temperature scale). The ratio of any two scale points is independent of the unit of measurement. There are few, if any, scales in the social and behavioral sciences because there are few characteristics of which any one person or institution possesses none (a true zero point).

Table 6.1 presents a comparison of these types of measurement.

Each of these types of scales has defining relations that make particular statistical tests appropriate. In general, nominal and ordinal scales require nonparametric tests, whereas interval and ratio scales require the use of parametric tests. (There are exceptions, such as when nonparametric statistics are used with interval data.) Because most indexes and scales are ordinal, nonparametric tests are of special importance, and it is necessary to match the appropriate statistic with the defining characteristics of the scale.

It is necessary to keep two things in mind regarding levels of measurement and the selection of variables in a research setting. First, as the scale type moves from nominal toward ratio, precision of measurement is increased. When the nominal level of measurement might allow us to conclude that two groups are different, a ratio level would allow us to conclude the magnitude of the difference. Second, the science might not exist for a researcher to declare a variable at the interval level of measurement, but there tends to be a somewhat liberal attitude regarding this assignment.

<table>
<tr><td>6.3</td><td>

THE MEANING AND USE OF STATISTICAL SIGNIFICANCE

</td></tr>
</table>

Regardless of whether you use parametric or nonparametric procedures, the goal of *inferential* statistics (as opposed to *descriptive* statistics) is to reach a conclusion regarding the probability of an outcome being attributed to chance rather than to some hypothesized cause.

Statistical significance is a central theme in this rationale. The excerpt from Thompson that follows discusses some of the most important aspects of that concept and its application.

Further Reading on Statistical Methods

Bechhofer, Robert E., Santner, Thomas J., & Goldsman, David M. (1995). *Design and analysis of experiments for statistical selection, screening, and multiple comparison.* New York: John Wiley & Sons.

▶ The Concept of Statistical Significance Testing

Bruce Thompson

Too few researchers understand what statistical significance testing does and doesn't do, and consequently their results are misinterpreted. Even more commonly, researchers understand elements of statistical significance testing, but the concept is not integrated into their research. For example, the influence of sample size on statistical significance may be acknowledged by a researcher, but this insight is not conveyed when interpreting results in a study with several thousand subjects.

This article will help you better understand the concept of significance testing. The meaning of probabilities, the concept of statistical significance, arguments against significance testing, misinterpretation, and alternatives are discussed.

What Are Those Probabilities in Statistical Significance Testing?

Researchers may invoke statistical significance testing whenever they have a random sample from a population, or a sample that they believe approximates a random, representative sample. Statistical significance testing requires subjective judgment in setting a predetermined acceptable probability (ranging between 0 and 1.0) of making an inferential error caused by the sampling error—getting samples with varying amounts of "flukiness"—inherent in sampling. Sampling error can only be eliminated by gathering data from the entire population.

One probability (p), the probability of deciding to reject a null hypothesis (e.g., a hypothesis specifying that $Mean_1 = Mean_2 = Mean_3$, or $R^2 = 0$) when the null hypothesis is actually true in the population, is called "alpha," and also $p_{(CRITICAL)}$. When we pick an alpha level, we set an upper limit on the probability of making this erroneous decision, called a Type I error. Therefore, alpha is typically set small, so that the probability of this error will be low. Thus, $p_{(CRITICAL)}$ is selected based on subjective judgment regarding what the consequences of Type I error would be in a given research situation, and given personal values regarding these consequences.

A second probability, $p_{(CALCULATED)}$ (which, like all p's, ranges between .0 and 1.0), is calculated. Probabilities can only be calculated in the context of assumptions sufficient to constrain the computations such that a given problem has only one answer.

What's the probability of getting mean IQ scores of 99 and 101 in two sample groups? It depends, first, on the actual statistical parameters (e.g., means) in the populations from which the samples were drawn. These two sample statistics ($Mean_1 = 99$ and $Mean_2 = 101$) would be most probable (yielding the highest $p_{(CALCULATED)}$) if the population means were respectively 99 and 101. These two sample statistics would be less likely (yielding a smaller $p_{(CALCULATED)}$) if the population means were both 100. Since the actual population parameters are not known, we must assume what the parameters are, and in statistical significance testing we assume the parameters to be correctly specified by the null hypothesis, i.e., we assume the null hypothesis to be exactly true for these calculations.

A second factor that influences the calculation of p involves the sample sizes. Samples (and thus the statistics calculated for them) will potentially be less representative of populations ("flukier") as sample sizes are smaller. For example, drawing two samples of sizes 5 and 5 may yield "flukier" statistics (means, r's, etc.) than two samples of sizes 50 and 50. Thus, the $p_{(CALCULATED)}$ computations also must (and do) take sample size influences into account. If the two samples both of size 5 had means of 100 and 90, and the two samples both of size 50 also had means of 100 and 90, the test of the null that the means are equal would yield a smaller $p_{(CALCULATED)}$ for the larger samples, because assuming the null is exactly true, unequal sample statistics are increasingly less likely as sample sizes increase. Summarizing, the $p_{(CALCULATED)}$ probability addresses the question:

> Assuming the sample data came from a population in which the null hypothesis is (exactly) true, what is the probability of obtaining the sample statistics one got for one's sample data with the given sample size(s)?

Even without calculating this p, we can make logical judgments about $p_{(CALCULATED)}$. In which one of each of the following pairs of studies will the $p_{(CALCULATED)}$ be smaller?

- In two studies, each involving three groups of 30 subjects: in one study the means were 100, 100, and 90; in the second study the means were 100, 100, and 100.
- In two studies, each comparing the standard deviations (SDs) of scores on the dependent variable of two groups of subjects, in both studies $SD_1 = 4$ and $SD_2 = 3$, but in study one the sample sizes were 100 and 100, while in study two the sample sizes were 50 and 50.
- In two studies involving a multiple regression prediction of Y using predictors X_1, X_2, and X_3, and both with sample sizes of 75, in study one $R^2 = .49$ and in study two $R^2 = .25$.

What Does Statistical Significance Really Tell Us?

Statistical significance addresses the question:

> "Assuming the sample data came from a population in which the null hypothesis is (exactly) true, and given our sample statistics and sample size(s), is the calculated probability of our sample results less than the acceptable limit ($p_{(CRITICAL)}$) imposed regarding a Type I error?"

When $p_{(CALCULATED)}$ is less than $p_{(CRITICAL)}$, we use a decision rule that says we will "reject" the null hypothesis. The decision to reject the null hypothesis is called a "statistically significant" result. All the decision means is that we believe our sample results are relatively unlikely, given our assumptions, including our assumption that the null hypothesis is exactly true.

However, though it is easy to derive $p_{(CRITICAL)}$, calculating $p_{(CALCULATED)}$ can be tedious. Traditionally, test statistics (e.g., F, t, χ squared) have been used as equivalent (but more convenient) reexpressions of p's, because Test Statistics$_{(CALCULATED)}$ are easier to derive. The TS$_{(CRITICAL)}$ exactly equivalent to a given $p_{(CRITICAL)}$ can be derived from widely available tables; the tabled value is found given alpha and the sample size(s). Different TS$_{(CALCULATED)}$ are computed depending on the hypothesis being tested. The only difference in invoking test statistics in our decision rule is that we reject the null (called "statistically significant") when TS$_{(CALCULATED)}$ is greater than TS$_{(CRITICAL)}$. However, comparing p's and TS's for a given data set will always yield the same decision.

Remember, knowing sample results are relatively unlikely, assuming the null is true, may not be helpful. An improbable result is not necessarily an important result, as Shaver (1985, p. 58) illustrates in his hypothetical dialogue between two teachers:

Chris: . . . I set the level of significance at .05, as my thesis advisor suggested. So a difference that large would occur by chance less than five times in a hundred if the groups weren't really different. An unlikely occurrence like that surely must be important.

Jean: Wait a minute. Remember the other day when you went into the office to call home? Just as you completed dialing the number, your little boy picked up the phone to call someone. So you were connected and talking to one another without the phone ever ringing. . . . Well, that must have been a truly important occurrence then?

Why Not Use Statistical Significance Testing?

Statistical significance testing may require an investment of effort that lacks a commensurate benefit. Science is the business of isolating relationships that (re)occur under stated conditions, so that knowledge is created and can be cumulated. But statistical significance does not adequately address whether the results in a given study will replicate (Carver, 1978). As scientists, we must ask (a) what the magnitudes of sample effects are and (b) whether these results will generalize; statistical significance testing does not respond to either question (Thompson, in press). Thus, statistical significance may distract attention from more important considerations.

Misinterpreting Statistical Significance Testing

Many of the problems in contemporary uses of statistical significance testing originate in the language researchers use. Several names can refer to a single concept (e.g., "SOS$_{(BETWEEN)}$" = "SOS$_{(EXPLAINED)}$" = "SOS$_{(MODEL)}$" = "SOS$_{(REGRESSION)}$"), and different meanings are given to terms in different contexts (e.g., "univariate" means having only one dependent variable but potentially many predictor variables, but may also refer to a statistic that can be computed with only a single variable).

Overcoming three habits of language will help avoid unconscious misinterpretations:

- **Say "statistically significant" rather than "significant."** Referring to the concept as a phrase will help break the erroneous association between rejecting a null hypothesis and obtaining an important result.
- **Don't say things like "my results approached statistical significance."** This language makes little sense in the context of the statistical significance testing logic. My favorite response to this is offered by a fellow editor who responds, "How did you know your results were not trying to avoid being statistically significant?"

- **Don't say things like "the statistical significance testing evaluated whether the results were 'due to chance.'"** This language gives the impression that replicability is evaluated by statistical significance testing.

What Analyses Are Preferred to Statistical Significance Testing?

Two analyses should be emphasized over statistical significance testing (*Journal of Experimental Education*, 1993). First, effect sizes should be calculated and interpreted in all analyses. These can be *r* squared-type effect sizes (e.g., *R* squared, eta squared, omega squared) that evaluate the proportion of variance explained in the analysis, or standardized differences in statistics (e.g., standardized differences in means), or both.

Second, the replicability of results must be empirically investigated, either through actual replication of the study, or by using methods such as cross-validation, the jackknife, or the bootstrap (see Thompson, in press).

Recommended Readings

Carver, R. P. (1978). The case against statistical significance testing. *Harvard Educational Review, 48,* 378-399.

Cohen, J. (1990). Things I have learned (so far). *American Psychologist, 45*(12), 1304-1312.

Journal of Experimental Education. (1993). Special Issue—"The role of statistical significance testing in contemporary analytic practice: Alternatives with comments from journal editors." Washington, DC: Heldref Publications. (Available from ERIC/AE).

Rosnow, R. L., & Rosenthal, R. (1989). Statistical procedures and the justification of knowledge in psychological science. *American Psychologist, 44,* 1276-1284.

Shaver, J. (1985). Chance and nonsense. *Phi Delta Kappan, 67*(l), 57-60.

Thompson, B. (in press). The pivotal role of replication in psychological research: Empirically evaluating the replicability of sample results. *Journal of Personality.*

From Bruce Thompson (1994), "The Concept of Statistical Significance Testing," *Practical Assessment, Research & Evaluation,* 4(5). Retrieved September 3, 2001, from http://ericae.net/pare/getvn.asp?v=4&n=5. Reprinted with permission.

SUMMARY OF COMMON MEASURES OF ASSOCIATION AND GROUP DIFFERENCES   6.4

Statistical methods enable us to study and to describe precisely averages, differences, and relationships and to assign the probability that outcomes are due to chance or some other factor (such as the manipulation of the independent variable).

The number of statistical tests available has risen considerably in the past 30 years and has become so large that even professional statisticians can't keep all of them at their fingertips. (See Kanji [1993], for more information.) As these tests have become more numerous, both the degree of precision has improved and the kinds of hypotheses that can be tested have increased in number.

In the next two sections of Part 6, we will review some of the common tests used to examine associations between variables and differences between groups. We'll then move on to computation guides for the most common and simple of these: the Pearson *r*, the *t* value, and the *F* test. The guide to calculating and using these statistics discusses both manual and computer procedures. In all these cases, students who wish to become competent at using and understanding these statistical tools will need specific coursework in these areas. For further information about the use of these tests, see Salkind (2000).

References

Kanji, Gopal K. (1993). *100 Statistical tests*. Thousand Oaks, CA: Sage.

Salkind, Neil. J. (2000). *Statistics for people who (think they) hate statistics*. Thousand Oaks, CA: Sage.

6.5 AN OVERVIEW OF MEASURES OF ASSOCIATION

The more common measures of association include Pearson's product-moment r, the correlation ratio eta, gamma (Γ), Spearman's rank difference coefficient rho (ρ), lambda (Λ), and the multiple correlation R. Consult the bibliography in Section 6.12.

Table 6.2 summarizes common measures of association. Because a major object of scientific inquiry is to discover relationships, it has become standard training for scientists to learn how to use these measures.

6.5.1 The Pearson Product-Moment Correlation Coefficient

The Pearson product-moment correlation coefficient is computed through examination of the proportion of variance that is shared by variables. The raw score formula is

$$r_{xy} = \frac{N\sum XY - \sum X \sum Y}{\sqrt{\left[N\sum X^2 - (\sum X)^2\right]\left[N\sum Y^2 - (\sum Y)^2\right]}}$$

where

r_{xy}	= the correlation coefficient between X and Y
N	= the size of the sample
X	= the individual's score on the X variable
Y	= the individual's score on the Y variable
XY	= the product of each X score and its corresponding Y score
X^2	= the individual X score, squared
Y^2	= the individual Y score, squared

6.5.1.1 Interpretation of r_{xy}

Correlations of any type are easily misinterpreted because association is often seen to be synonymous with causality. The fact that two variables can change concurrently is often misunderstood to mean that a change in one causes a change in the other. This is a serious error often made by beginning researchers. Some other guidelines for interpreting the correlation coefficient follow.

.00-.20	little or no relationship
.20-.40	some slight relationship
.40-.60	substantial relationship
.60-.80	strong useful relationship
.80-1.00	strong relationship

Table 6.2   COMMON MEASURES OF ASSOCIATION

Measure of Association	Symbol	Level of Measurement	When It Is Used
Pearson product-moment correlation, r	r_{xy}	Interval	To measure relationships between two variables when both are continuous and the relationship is linear. The coefficient of correlation is most reliable when it is based on a large number of pairs of observations.
Correlation ratio, eta	η_{xy}	Interval	To measure relationships between two continuous variables that are related in a curvilinear fashion.
Spearman's rank difference coefficient, rho	ρ_{xy}	Ordinal	To measure the association between two rankings. It is used primarily when rankings of individual cases on two variables are available so that rankings range from 1 to N for each variable.
Lambda	λ_{xy}	Nominal	To measure the association between two bivariate distributions when both variables are interpreted to be nominal.
Multiple correlation coefficient, R	R_{123}	Interval	To measure the maximum relationship that may be obtained between a combination of several continuous (independent) variables and some other continuous (dependent) variable.
Partial correlation coefficient, r	$r_{12 \cdot 3}$	Interval	To measure the relationship between two continuous variables with the effects of a third continuous variable held constant.
Biserial correlation coefficient	r_{bi}	Ordinal	To measure relationships when one variable is recorded in terms of a dichotomy and the other is continuous, when it is assumed that the variable underlying the dichotomy is continuous and normal.
Point biserial correlation coefficient	r_{pbi}	Nominal	To measure the relationship between a two-categoried dichotomous variable and a continuous variable.
Contingency coefficient	C	Nominal	To measure the association between two variables that can be classified in two or more categories, but when the categories themselves are not quantitative.
Phi coefficient	ϕ	Nominal	To measure the association between two variables that are truly dichotomous.

The usefulness of a correlation is determined by its size, not its sign. The sign has no bearing on the strength of the relationship. It determines only the direction of the relationship: positive or direct versus negative or inverse.

The square of the correlation coefficient, known as the coefficient of determination (r_{xy}^2), provides the best indicator of the meaningfulness or significance of a correlation coefficient. It identifies the amount of variance in one variable accounted for by the variance in another variable. An r_{xy} of 1.0 or a perfect relationship has a coefficient of determination of 1, or 100%, and a correlation half as strong ($r_{xy} = .50$) has a coefficient of determination of 25%. A significant correlation means that the variables in the population from which the data were drawn probably do not have a zero correlation; that is, they are related.

6.5.1.2 Using the Computer to Compute the Pearson Product-Moment Correlation

For the behavioral and social sciences, SPSS® is one of the leading statistical and data analysis packages. Throughout the *Handbook of Research Design and Social Measurement*, examples of use of a computer to calculate statistics will be based on SPSS. The example shown in Figure 6.1 uses a simple data set of 20 sets of observations, with the two variables being income in dollars and level of education. The output for a bivariate correlation appears as shown in the figure below.

Correlations

		INCOME	EDUC
INCOME	Pearson Correlation	1.000	.574**
	Sig. (2-tailed)	.	.008
	N	20	20
EDUC	Pearson Correlation	.574**	1.000
	Sig. (2-tailed)	.008	.
	N	20	20

**Correlation is significant at the 0.01 level

Figure 6.1. SPSS Output for Computation of the Correlation Coefficient

6.6 AN OVERVIEW OF TESTS OF THE DIFFERENCE BETWEEN MEANS

A summary of the more common measures of testing for group differences would include a simple *t* test for a pair of independent or dependent means and an *F* test for evaluating the difference between more than two means. The *F* test (named after R. A. Fisher) is also called analysis of variance (ANOVA).

6.6.1 The *t* Value for a Test of Independent Means

The *t* value is computed through comparing the variance that is attributable to between-group variance to that attributable to within-group variance. The raw score formula for a test of independent groups, where two different groups are tested, is as follows:

$$t = \frac{\overline{X}_1 - \overline{X}_2}{\sqrt{\frac{(n_1 - 1)s_1^2 + (n_2 - 1)s_2^2}{n_1 + n_2 - 2} \quad \frac{n_1 + n_2}{n_1 n_2}}}$$

where

$\overline{X}_1$ = the mean for group 1

$\overline{X}_2$ = the mean for group 2

n_1 = the number of participants in group 1

n_2 = the number of participants in group 2

s_1^2 = the variance for group 1

s_2^2 = the variance for group 2

6.6.2 The *t* Value for a Test of Dependent Means

The *t* value for dependent means is computed through comparing the variance that is attributable to between-subject variance to that attributable to within-subject variance. The raw score formula for a test of dependent groups, where one group is tested twice, is as follows:

$$t = \frac{\sum D}{\sqrt{\dfrac{n \sum D^2 - (\sum D^2)}{(n-1)}}}$$

where

$\sum D$ = the sum of all the differences between groups

$\sum D^2$ = the sum of the squares of the differences between groups

n = the sample size

6.6.2.1 *Interpretation of t*

In all cases, the *t* value is the obtained or test value, which is traditionally compared to a table or an expected value given that the null hypothesis

H_0: μ_1 = μ_2 (in the case of independent means) or

H_0: D = 0 (in the case of dependent means)

is true.

When the obtained value exceeds the critical or tabled value, one can conclude that the probability of the obtained value occurring by chance alone is very small. Alternatively, the *t* value is interpreted using the results of a statistical package such as SPSS and the exact associated probability assigned to the obtained value.

6.6.2.2 *Using the Computer to Compute the t Value*

For the example shown in Figure 6.2 here, a simple data set is used, consisting of 60 observations (from two independent groups) and with the dependent variable being attitude. Using SPSS, the output for a comparison of independent means appears as shown in Figure 6.2.

Independent Samples Test

| | | Levene's Test for Equality of Variances | | t test for Equality of Means | | | | | | |
| | | F | Sig. | t | df | Sig. (2-tailed) | Mean Difference | Std. Error Difference | 95% Confidence Interval of the Difference | |
									Lower	Upper
ATTITUDE	Equal variances assumed	4.994	.029	–.137	58	.891	–1.00E-01	.73	–1.56	1.36
	Equal variances not assumed			–.137	47.635	.892	–1.00E-01	.73	–1.57	1.37

Figure 6.2. The Results of a *t* Test of Independent Means Produced by SPSS

Figure 6.2 shows SPSS computes probabilities. In this example, the exact probability of the differences between the two groups being due to chance is .891. Notice how it is unnecessary, when such output is available, to use traditional tables of significance levels and critical values.

6.6.3 Computing the F Value for a Test of More Than Two Means

Computing the F value for an overall test of the difference between more than two means (be they between or within groups) is done through comparing the variance that is attributable to between-group variance to that attributable to within-group variance. The raw score formula for an F test is as follows:

$$F = \frac{MS_{Between\ Groups}}{MS_{Within\ Groups}}$$

where

$MS_{Between\ Groups}$ = the variability due to between-group differences
$MS_{Within\ Groups}$ = the variability due to within-group differences

6.6.3.1 Interpretation of F

The F value is the obtained or test value, which traditionally is compared to the tabled or expected value given that the null hypothesis

$$H_0: \mu_1 = \mu_2 = \mu_3$$

is true. When the obtained value exceeds the critical or tabled value, one can conclude that the probability of the obtained value occurring by chance alone is very small. Alternatively, the F value is interpreted using the results of a statistical package such as SPSS and the exact probability assigned to the obtained value.

6.6.3.2 Using the Computer to Compute the F Value

For the example in this section, a simple data set is used consisting of 60 observations (from three independent groups) with the grouping variable being time in program and the dependent variable being reduction in juvenile crimes. The output for an overall comparison of the three independent means appears as shown in Figure 6.3.

ANOVA

CRIME

	Sum of Squares	df	Mean Square	F	Sig.
Between Groups	1133.067	2	566.533	8.799	.001
Within Groups	1738.400	27	64.385		
Total	2871.467	29			

Figure 6.3. ANOVA Output Using SPSS

6.7 CAUSATION AND MULTIVARIATE ANALYSIS: FROM UNIVARIATE AND BIVARIATE PROBLEMS TO MULTIVARIATE ANALYSIS OF SOCIAL BEHAVIOR

It was once generally thought that for every effect there existed only one cause, and if several causes were discovered, it was assumed there must really be more than one effect. The history of social theory is largely a series of statements asserting that one factor is the sole cause of social change. These notions have been called "determinisms"; they include geographic, physical, racial, psychological, religious, political, economic, technological, and familial factors, among many more.

It is characteristic of all these notions of determinism to assert that the sole factor operates according to its own inherent laws, independently of all factors, including human will and desires. These single-factor theories were relatively simple to understand and appealed to scholars and laypersons alike. They seemed to draw truth from the complex phenomena presented by social problems. But in their oversimplification, the single-factor theories distorted reality and foisted a great amount of mischief and misery on people. For example, racial determinism bred prejudice and discrimination in every country of the world.

Contemporary humans know better, although single-factor theories still abound. The contemporary approach involves allowing for and expecting a number of different causes for a single effect.

6.7.1 Four Manifestations of Causes

Causes may manifest themselves in a *sequence*, as a *convergence* or cluster, as producing *dispersion* effects, or as a *complex network*.

1. Causes may occur in a *sequence*, like the links on a chain. Some of these causes are direct and immediate; others are indirect and remote. Thus, a decline in worker motivation and sense of personal responsibility may be due to the direct fact that much labor is performed in large corporations on highly repetitive jobs. The remote causes are the factory system and mass market, which in turn were brought about by the steam engine, the electric motor, and machine tools.

2. Several causes may *converge* to produce a change. Thus, electric power and several transportation and communication inventions have converged to augment the decentralization of industry. These converging causes are often called a cluster.

3. The effects of a single cause may be *dispersed* outward into many different sectors of a society. Thus, the average increase of formal education that is being acquired by Americans has many different effects on family, church, community, military organization, and labor relations.

4. The phenomena of convergence and of dispersion may be tied in with the phenomena of sequence to produce a *complex network* of causes. This is a very common manifestation, but the complexity can be simplified by recognizing that causes vary in importance, and important causes may be identified that account for a large part of the effects observed.

6.7.2 The Statistical World of Multivariate Analysis

Multivariate analysis has now developed techniques for dealing with more than three variables or attributes at a time. The type of analysis to use in attempting to unravel a complex of variables in a real-life situation depends on what will best bring out the essential relationships under scrutiny. Multivariate analysis may give increased precision to prediction problems (the relation of a number of predictor variables to a criterion), offer greater control of interfering or confounding variables (holding more variables constant), and furnish guiding principles in the development of attitude scales, rating scales, psychological tests, and criterion measures (finding dimensions of behavior). Some of the most important multivariate techniques include the following:

- Multiple correlation and classification analysis
- Path analysis
- Factor analysis
- Partial correlation analysis
- Analysis of variance and covariance
- Multiple discriminant analysis

Full descriptions of these techniques are beyond the scope and purpose of this volume.

Computer technology is advancing at a rapid rate and is an indispensable adjunct to multivariate analysis. An introduction to the computer is presented in Section 6.9 for those who are seeking guidance in using computer programs. Descriptions of multiple correlation and classification analysis (Section 6.7.3), path analysis (Section 6.7.4), and factor analysis (Section 6.7.5) are also set out to provide an introduction to these forms of multivariate analysis now so common to sociological research.

Further Readings on Multivariate Statistics

Algina, James, & Keselman, H. J. (1997). Detecting repeated measures effects with univariate and multivariate statistics. *Psychological Methods, 2*, 208-218.

Bray, James H., Maxwell, Scott E., & Cole, David. (1995). Multivariate statistics for family psychology research. *Journal of Family Psychology, 9*, 144-150.

Grimm, Laurence G., & Yarnold, Paul R. (Eds.). (1995). *Reading and understanding multivariate statistics.* Washington, DC: American Psychological Association.

Johnson, Richard Arnold, & Wichern, Dean W. (1998). *Applied multivariate statistical analysis* (4th ed.). Upper Saddle River, NJ: Prentice Hall.

Mulaik, Stanley A. (1993). Objectivity and multivariate statistics. *Multivariate Behavioral Research, 28*, 171-203.

Sheu, Ching Fan, & O'Curry, Suzanne. (1996). Implementation of nonparametric multivariate statistics with S. *Behavior Research Methods, Instruments and Computers, 28*, 315-318.

Stevens, James. (2001). *Applied multivariate statistics for the social sciences* (3rd ed.). Mahwah, NJ: Lawrence Erlbaum.

Stevenson, Jim. (1993). Multivariate statistics: V. The use of factor scores in psychiatric research. *Nordic Journal of Psychiatry, 47*, 169-178.

Streinger, David L. (1993). An introduction to multivariate statistics. *Canadian Journal of Psychiatry, 38*, 9-13.

6.7.3 Multiple Correlation, Regression, and Classification Analysis

The multiple correlation ($R_{1.234}$) is simply the correlation between the actual scores on a single dependent variable and the scores derived from any linear combination of independent variables. The multiple correlation, like the simple product-moment correlation (r), has a range of -1 to $+1$. The smaller the coefficient (in absolute value), the poorer the correlation; the larger the coefficient, the stronger the correlation. The multiple correlation can be interpreted by squaring it. R^2 is called the coefficient of multiple determination and expresses the proportion of the variation in the dependent variable that is explained by the regression equation.

Further Readings on Multicollinearity Problems

Allen, Michael Patrick. (1997). *Understanding regression analysis.* New York: Plenum.

Bartolini, Stefano. (1993). On time and comparative research. *Journal of Theoretical Politics, 5,* 131-167.

Cortina, Jose M. (1993). Interaction, nonlinearity, and multicollinearity: Implications for multiple regression. *Journal of Management, 19,* 915-922.

Ganzach, Yoav. (1998). Nonlinearity, multicollinearity and the probability of Type II error in detecting interaction. *Journal of Management, 24,* 615-622.

Morrow-Howell, Nancy. (1994). The M word: Multicollinearity in multiple regression. *Social Work Research, 18,* 247-251.

6.7.3.1 Scope of Application

The utility of R has been known for some time, but it was originally cumbersome to calculate when more than four or five independent variables (predictors) were introduced. The computer erased that limitation, but a second limitation intervened. The coefficient was adaptable only when the variables were continuous. Modern methods of *multiple classification analysis* have removed this limitation. Computer techniques can handle predictors with no better than nominal measurement and can analyze interrelationships of any form among predictors or between predictors or between a predictor and the dependent variable. Many of the most interesting analysis problems involve the simultaneous consideration of several predictor variables (i.e., "independent" variables) and their relationships to a dependent variable. Sometimes one wants to know *how well* all the variables together explain variation in the dependent variable. At other times, it is necessary to look at each predictor separately to see how it relates to the dependent variable, either considering or neglecting the effects of other predictors. A criterion for judging the predictive power of a variable that is used frequently is its contribution to reduction in unexplained variance or "error." Another is the extent to which its class means differ from the grand mean.

A different but related concern is the matter of predicted relations. Instead of asking *how well* one can predict, one sometimes asks *what level* (i.e., what particular value or score) one would predict for a person or other unit having a certain combination of characteristics. This is the classic problem to which multiple regression frequently is applied. Finally, one sometimes wants to know whether one's ability to predict is significantly better than chance.

The multiple classification analysis devised by Frank M. Andrews, James N. Morgan, John A. Sonquist, and Laura Klem (reported in this section) implements a multivariate technique that is relevant for all the above problems and that may be applied to many kinds of data for which the simpler forms of the traditional techniques would be inappropriate. Its chief advantages over conventional dummy variable regression are a more convenient input arrangement and understandable output that focuses on sets of predictors (such as occupation groups) and on the extent and direction of adjustments made for intercorrelations among the sets of predictors.

Further Readings on Multivariate Analysis

Bartholomew, D. J. (1997). Fifty years of multivariate analysis. *British Journal of Mathematical and Statistical Psychology, 50*, 205-214.

Carroll, J. Douglas, Green, Paul E., & Anil, Chaturvedi. (1997). *Mathematical tools for applied multivariate analysis* (Rev. ed.). San Diego: Academic Press.

Hromco, Joseph George. (1997). A multivariate analysis of patient presenting problem: Why patients seek psychotherapy. *Dissertation Abstracts International, 57*, 7227B.

Ruth, Edward Keith. (1996). A multivariate analysis of gender, age, and ethnicity as elements shaping technological attitudes, anxiety, and self-efficacy in workplace settings. *Dissertation Abstracts International, 57*, 2449A.

Seilheimer, Thomas A. (1995). Self-efficacy, quality of life domains, and residential satisfaction: A multivariate analysis of mental patients. *Disseration Abstracts International, 56*, 1121B.

6.7.3.2 *Dummy Variable Regression Analysis*

Dummy variables are dichotomous variables employed when the researcher is working with categorical or nominal variables. The binary nature of the computer makes it well suited to work with dummy variables that indicate the presence (scored 1) or absence (scored 0) of a certain characteristic for each individual respondent. For qualitative variables it is especially useful. For example, marital status can be coded using four dummy variables:

currently married:	$1 = yes, 0 = no$
never married:	$1 = yes, 0 = no$
widowed:	$1 = yes, 0 = no$
separated:	$1 = yes, 0 = no$
divorced:	pattern of 0, 0, 0, 0 would indicate a person is divorced; no dummy variable needed

If a person were widowed, rather than having a score of 3, he or she would have four scores, one on each of the four dummy variables: 0010.

These dummy variables all would be included in a typical multiple regression analysis. When a zero score appears for an individual on one of the dummy variables, that is the regression weight placed in the regression equation. Otherwise, the regression weight becomes the value assigned by the researcher to a particular status.

Dummy variables can be used as independent variables in standard score or raw score form, and they can be used in path analysis. Dummy variables are useful if a researcher wishes to "score" specific combinations of values of variables to search for expected statistical interaction in a multiple regression equation when otherwise, the model would assume an additive relationship among variables. These efforts are called *dummy variable regression analysis*.

Further Readings on Dummy Variables

Eisinga, Rob, Scheepers, Peer, & Van Snippenburg, Leo. (1991). The standardized effect of a compound of dummy variables or polynomial terms. *Quality and Quantity, 25*, 103-114.

Figart, Deborah M. (1997). Gender as more than a dummy variable: Feminist approaches to discrimination. *Review of Social Economy, 55*, 1-32.

Hardy, Melissa A. (1993). *Regression with dummy variables.* Newbury Park, CA: Sage.

Herrera-Hernandez, Maria Lucila, Merchan-Solano, Rafael, & Ortiz-Perez, Hildelisa. (1987). Application of the regression method with dummy variables for the determination of norms for quantity of workers. *Economia y Desarrollo, 100,* 72-79.

Sawyer, Richard. (1986). Using demographic subgroup and dummy variable equations to predict college freshman grade average. *Journal of Educational Measurement, 23,* 131-145.

6.7.4 Path Analysis as Causal Analysis

Path analysis has become popular as a form of data analysis because it provides possibilities for causal determination among sets of measured variables. A principal objective of science is to build theoretical explanations of social phenomena. Kaplan (1964) has said:

> Science is a search for constancies, for invariants. It is the enterprise of making those identifications in experience which prove to be most significant for the control of appreciation of the experience to come. The basic scientific question is "what the devil is going on around here?" (p. 85)

When the underlying assumptions of path analysis are met, theory and data may be related in situations where many variables are to be handled simultaneously. Path analysis is essentially a data-analytic technique using standardized multiple regression equations in examining theoretical models.

Extravagant hopes for causal explanations should not be entertained—at least not yet. The inability to deal with all variables in a social system, to measure and plot their exact interactions, makes the results in most problems only first approximations to causality. The power of the technique continues to challenge and intrigue researchers nevertheless, and its use is proliferating.

A researcher commonly wishes to discover the relationship of independent factors to a dependent variable. Simple and multiple correlations are utilized and often yield important relationships, but they never demonstrate causality. For example, if we wish to relate father's occupational status to son's occupational status, correlational techniques can determine their correlational relationship, but causality can only be inferred. Using path analysis, it is possible to postulate that such independent factors as father's educational attainment and occupational status are causal factors in the son's subsequent educational attainment, the status of the first job achieved, and the status of the current job.

Reference

Kaplan, Abraham. (1964). *The conduct of inquiry.* San Francisco: Chandler.

6.7.4.1 Six Steps in the Application of Path Analysis

1. Develop a causal scheme or model.
2. Establish a pattern of associations among the variables in the sequence.
3. Depict a path diagram.
4. Calculate path coefficients for the basic model.
5. Test for "goodness of fit" with the basic model.
6. Interpret the result.

Step 1: Develop a causal scheme. Path analysis allows the social theorist to state a theory in the form of a linear causal model. The crucial question has to do with the order of priority of the variables in the system in a causal or processual sequence. Causal models involve the construction of an over-

Table 6.3	SIMPLE CORRELATIONS FOR FIVE STATUS VARIABLES					
	Variable	Z	Y	X	B	A
Z	Son's current occupational status	—	.541	.596	.405	.322
Y	Son's first-job status		—	.538	.417	.332
X	Son's education			—	.438	.453
B	Father's occupational status				—	.516
A	Father's education					—

simplified model of social reality in the sense that the model takes into account only a very limited number of variables that are of interest in the specific research area. The most important variables are sought; all others are regarded as "residual." On the basis of results of past research and current theory, the social scientist constructs a representation of the process assumed to be in operation among the variables.

Let us suppose that we utilize stratification theory and research. We postulate that status changes in the life cycle of a cohort of males indicate that father's educational attainment (A) and father's occupational attainment (B) will determine the subsequent educational attainment of the son (X), his first job (Y), and his current job (Z). This is the linear statement or temporal order and may be written as follows:

$$(A \rightarrow B) \rightarrow X \rightarrow Y \rightarrow Z.$$

The earlier variables may affect a later one not only through intervening variables but also directly.

Step 2: Establish a pattern of associations between the variables in the sequence. The conceptual framework must be translated into quantitative estimates. This is done by establishing the pattern of association of the variables in the sequence. A correlation matrix is developed, utilizing the simple correlations for the five status variables in the model. An adaptation of Blau and Duncan (1967) shows the matrix of their occupational mobility study (see Table 6.3).

Simple correlation measures the gross magnitude of the effect of an antecedent variable on the consequent variable. The current job status is the expected outcome of all the other four antecedent variables. The first row of Table 6.3 shows that all four antecedent variables show a significant correlation with current job status, the highest being for the son's education ($r = .596$) and the next being for his first-job status ($r = .541$). As expected, father's occupational status and father's education are related in somewhat diminished magnitude ($r = .405$ and $r = .322$, respectively). The second row reports correlations with first-job status. The same pattern of relationship with father's occupation and education appears. The third row repeats expected relationships of son's education to father's occupational status and education. The fourth row demonstrates the high correlation of father's occupational status and education ($r = .516$).

Step 3: Construct a path diagram. Path diagrams generally are illustrated, as in Figure 6.4, by means of one-headed arrows connecting some of or all the variables included in the basic model. Variables are distributed from left to right, depending on their theoretical ordering. The first independent variables are placed at the extreme left. In this case, these are father's education and father's occupa-

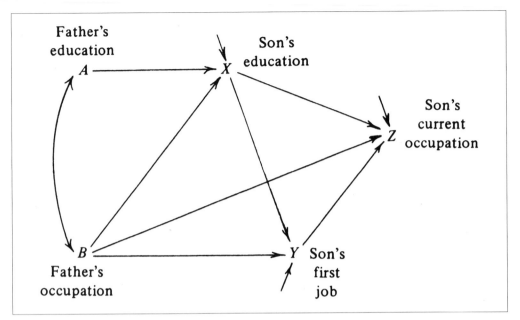

Figure 6.4. Basic Model of the Process of Stratification

SOURCE: Adapted with permission of the Free Press, a Division of Simon & Schuster, Inc., from Peter M. Blau and Otis Dudley Duncan (1967), *The American Occupational Structure* (New York: John Wiley). Copyright 1967 by Peter M. Blau and Otis Dudley Duncan.

NOTE: The algebraic representation of the causal scheme shown in the path model rests on a system of equations rather than the single equation more often employed in multiple regression analysis. This feature permits a flexible ordering of the inferred influences. Each line represents a search and a determination of direct (or net) influences. Note how much emphasis Blau and Duncan have given to the father's occupation as a causative factor—path coefficients are traced to son's education, first job, and current job. Father's education, on the other hand, is traced only through the son's education.

tion, and the link is shown as an arrowhead at both ends to distinguish it from other paths of influence. Variables not influenced by other variables in the model (with intercorrelations of zero order) are called *exogenous* variables. The term refers to all variables prior to and outside the model.

The remaining subset of variables (which may consist of only one variable) is assumed to consist of dependent variables. These variables are called *endogenous* (here, X, Y, and Z). As contrasted with the exogenous variables, this subset is considered totally determined by some combination of the variables in the system. The straight lines in Figure 6.4 running from one measured variable to another represent the direct influences of one variable upon another. There are also indirect influences, as illustrated in the diagram. Variables recognized as being affected by certain antecedent factors may, in turn, serve as causes for subsequent variables. For example, X is influenced by A and B and it in turn influences Y and Z. Thus, Y and Z are affected indirectly by both A and B, in addition to any direct effects.

Finally, residual paths must be drawn. These are the lines with no source indicated, carrying arrows to each of the endogenous or effect variables. Residuals are represented by the arrows coming from outside the system to X, Y, and Z. They are causes not recognized or measured, errors of measurement, and departures of the true relationships from additivity and linearity, properties that are assumed throughout the analysis.

Step 4: Calculate path coefficients. Path coefficients reflect the amount of direct contribution of a given variable on another variable when effects of other related variables are taken into account. Path coefficients are identical to partial regression coefficients (the betas) when the variables are measured

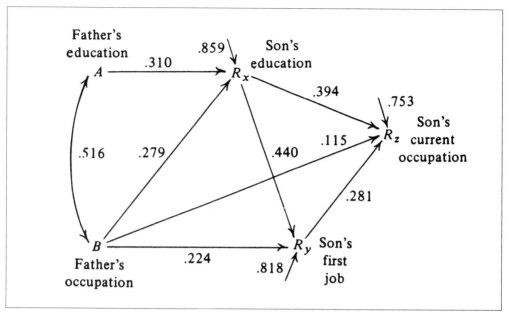

Figure 6.5. The Path Model for the Causal Scheme

SOURCE: Adapted with permission of the Free Press, a Division of Simon & Schuster, Inc., from Peter M. Blau and Otis Dudley Duncan (1967), *The American Occupational Structure* (New York: John Wiley). Copyright 1967 by Peter M. Blau and Otis Dudley Duncan.

in standard form. Two ways of computing path coefficients frequently are employed. The first uses regression programs that take raw data and compute partial coefficients from standardized input data. Both path coefficients and multiple correlation coefficients generally are provided by standard computer regression programs (for explanations of this procedure, see, e.g., Blau and Duncan [1967], pp. 171-177, or Loether and McTavish [1974], pp. 321-328). The second method uses only zero-order correlations among variables; a researcher can employ the "basic theorem" to compute the path coefficients (Nygreen, 1971).

In Figure 6.5, the path coefficients have been entered on the path diagram, with the exception of antecedent variables A and B. The basic model is now complete and awaits evaluation.

Step 5: Test for "goodness of fit" of the basic model. The crux of the analysis is the test for goodness of fit between the observed data and the basic model. Three general approaches may be made:

1. Examine the amount of *variation* in dependent variables that is *explained* by variables linked as specified in the model.
2. Examine the *size of path coefficients* to see whether they are large enough to warrant the inclusion of a variable or path in the model.
3. Evaluate the ability of the model to *predict correlation coefficients* that were not used in computation of the path coefficients themselves. (For further information, see Land [1969].)

An investigator usually contrasts the usefulness of the model in these three respects with the usefulness of alternative models. This is the heart of explanatory progress in any science.

The partial regression coefficients in standard form and the coefficients of determination for specified combinations of variables are essential for applying the first goodness-of-fit criterion. Table 6.4 is an adaptation of the Blau and Duncan data. It shows that the coefficient of determination for father's occupation, father's education, and son's education is .26, meaning that 26% of the variation in son's education can be accounted for by the father's occupation and education.

Table 6.4   PARTIAL REGRESSION COEFFICIENTS IN STANDARD FORM (BETA COEFFICIENTS) AND COEFFICIENTS OF DETERMINATION, FOR SPECIFIED COMBINATIONS OF VARIABLES

Dependent Variable	First Job	Son's Education	Father's Occupation	Father's Education	Coefficient of Determination (R^2)
Son's education			.279	.310	.26
First job		.433	.214	.026	.33
Current occupation	.282	.397	.120	−.014	.43

Similarly, 33% of the variation in son's first job can be accounted for by father's occupation, father's education, and son's education. Finally, 43% of the variation in son's current occupation is due to father's occupation, father's education, son's education, and son's first job. Note that father's education is not helpful in explaining this variance. The unexplained variation, $1 - R^2_{4,123} = .57$. The model leaves unexplained 57% of the variance in the son's current job. This is not as satisfactory as might be hoped. The "unexplained" variation is due to variables or measurement error not included in the model. For the sake of completeness, the square roots of these $(1 - R^2)$ values are ascribed to the residual variables, R_x, R_y, and R_z, as shown in Figure 6.5. These "residual" paths are large, and the investigator must reexamine his or her causal scheme. It should not be assumed, however, that the size of the residual is necessarily a measure of success in explaining the phenomenon under study. As Blau and Duncan (1967) state, "The relevant question about the residual is not really its size at all, but whether the unobserved factors it stands for are properly *represented as being uncorrelated* with the measured antecedent factors" (p. 175).

In terms of the second criterion of goodness of fit, the model fares well. Most of the path coefficients are significant. It turned out that the net regressions of both father's occupation and son's first job on father's education were so small as to be negligible; hence, father's education could be disregarded without loss of information (Blau & Duncan, 1967, p. 175). One might consider eliminating father's education as a factor because of its low coefficients and recompute path coefficients.

Third, one could examine the "fit" between observed correlations not previously used in formulas for calculating path coefficients and predictions of correlation coefficients that would be derived from the model. In this instance, the correlation between father's education and son's first job (as well as son's current job) was not used to estimate path coefficients.

The question of testing an alternative model involves a thorough reexamination of the basic model. Two possibilities present themselves: (a) substituting factors in the basic model believed to be more important and (b) adding new factors to the basic model. Whether a path diagram or the causal scheme it represents is judged to be adequate depends on both theoretical and empirical considerations. The causal scheme must be complete in the sense that all causes are accounted for, and unmeasured causes presumed to be uncorrelated with the dependent variable must be represented.

Step 6: Interpret the result.   The variables in the causal scheme may be studied for their direct and indirect effects. The direct effects of father's occupation on son's education, first job, and current occupation are shown by path coefficients of .279, .224, and .115, none of which is particularly large. The cumulative indirect effects nevertheless are significant. Father's occupation and education do influence son's education, and this in turn influences the son's first job, which in turn influences the son's current occupation. At the same time, many other factors of even greater influence clearly are operating to determine this last dependent variable of interest.

The technique of path analysis is not a method of discovering causal laws but instead a procedure for finding a quantitative interpretation of an assumed causal system as it operates within a given population.

References

Blau, Peter M., & Duncan, Otis Dudley. (1967). *The American occupational structure*. New York: John Wiley.

Land, Kenneth C. (1969). Principles of path analysis. In Edgar F. Borgatta (Ed.), *Sociological methodology 1969*, pp. 1-37. San Francisco: Jossey-Bass.

Loether, Herman J., & McTavish, Donald C. (1974). *Descriptive statistics for sociologists*. Boston: Allyn & Bacon.

Nygreen, G. T. (1971). Interactive path analysis. *American Sociologist, 6*, 37-43.

Further Readings on Path Analysis

Bishop, R. M., & Bieschke, K. J. (1998). Applying social cognitive theory to interest in research among counseling psychology doctoral students: A path analysis. *Journal of Counseling Psychology, 45*, 182-188.

Blalock, Hubert M., Jr. (1964). *Causal inferences in nonexperimental research*. Chapel Hill: University of North Carolina Press.

Boudon, Raymond. (1965). A method of linear causal analysis: Dependence analysis. *American Sociological Review, 30*, 365-374.

Cnann, Ram A., Hasenfeld, Yeheskel, Cnann, Avital, & Rafferty, Jane. (1993). Cross-cultural comparison of attitudes toward welfare-state programs: Path analysis with log-linear models. *Social Indicators Research, 29*, 123-152.

Costner, Herbert L., & Leik, Robert K. (1964). Deductions from "axiomatic theory." *American Sociological Review, 29*, 819-835.

Dellva, Wilfred L., Teas, R. Kenneth, & McElroy, James C. (1985). Leader behavior and subordinate role stress: A path analysis. *Journal of Political and Military Sociology, 13*, 183-193.

Ensminger, Margaret E., & Slusarcick, Anita L. (1992). Paths to high school graduation or dropout: A longitudinal study of a first-grade cohort. *Sociology of Education, 65*, 95-113.

Forbes, H. D., & Tufte, E. R. (1968). A note of caution in causal modelling. *American Political Science Review, 62*, 1258-1264.

Ganzeboom, Harry B. G., Treiman, Donald J., & Ultee, Wout C. (1991). Comparative intergenerational stratification research: Three generations and beyond. *Annual Review of Sociology, 17*, 277-302.

Haney, Colleen J., & Long, Bonita C. (1995). Coping effectiveness: A path analysis of self-efficacy, control, coping, and performance in sport competitions. *Journal of Applied Social Psychology, 25*, 17-26.

Heise, D. R. (1969). Problems in path analysis and causal inference. In Edgar F. Borgatta (Ed.), *Sociological methodology 1969* (pp. 38-71). San Francisco: Jossey-Bass.

Hemmings, Brian, Putai, Jin, & Low, Renae. (1997). Evaluating a theoretical model of school withdrawal using a qualitative analysis. *Asia Pacific Journal of Social Work, 7*, 77-96.

Holland, Paul W. (1988). Causal inference, path analysis, and recursive structural equations models. *Sociological Methodology, 18*, 449-484.

Hutchison, Steven. (1997). A path model of perceived organizational support. *Journal of Social Behavior and Personality, 12*, 159-174.

Israels, A. Z. (1987). Path analysis for mixed qualitative and quantitative variables. *Quality and Quantity, 21*, 91-102.

Krymkowski, Daniel H. (1991). The process of status attainment among men in Poland, the U.S., and West Germany. *American Sociological Review, 56*, 46-59.

Lee, Valerie E., & Frank, Kenneth A. (1990). Students' characteristics that facilitate the transfer from two-year to four-year colleges. *Sociology Education, 63*, 178-193.

Lewis, Michael. (1999). A path analysis of the effect of welfare on infant mortality. *Journal of Sociology and Social Welfare, 26*, 125.

Li, C. C. (1955). *Population genetics.* Chicago: University of Chicago Press.

Loehle, Craig. (1994). A critical path analysis of scientific productivity. *Journal of Creative Behavior, 28*, 33-47.

McDonald, Roderick P. (1994). The bilevel reticular action model for path analysis with latent variable. *Sociological Methods and Research, 22*, 399-413.

Simon, Herbert A. (1957). *Models of man.* New York: John Wiley.

Stinchcombe, Arthur. (1968). *Construction of social theories.* New York: Harcourt, Brace & World.

6.7.5 Factor Analysis: Explaining Relations Among Numerous Variables in Simpler Terms

The purpose of this introduction is to provide sociological researchers with a working knowledge of the basic concepts of factor analysis without burdening them with statistical details. It will be assumed in the following discussion, however, that the user has some grasp of the meaning of correlation and regression coefficients.

Factor analysis is a procedure for investigating the possibility that a large number of variables have a small number of factors in common that account for their intercorrelations. As Schuessler (1971) explains, "We observe that pupils who score high in reading tend to score high in spelling and arithmetic. We ascribe this consistency, or correlation, in pupils' marks to the general factors of intelligence" (p. 44). This principle holds that a circumstance common to a succession of categorically identical events, which otherwise have nothing in common, may be regarded as a cause of that event. Therefore, to discover the cause of an event, we search for the lone circumstance that is always present when the event occurs. In a similar manner, by means of factor analysis, we seek to isolate those common elements that are present in two or more variables and to which the intercorrelations among these variables may be attributed. It can be seen, then, that factor analysis is an arithmetical procedure for determining whether the intercorrelations among many variables could be due to a few common factors.

C may be considered as either a cause of both X and Y or simply an element present in both variables (see Figure 6.6). Factor analysis considers the possibility that X and Y are indicators of the same thing. From the observed correlation between X and Y, the inference can be drawn that they were produced by the same cause or that they are, in varying degrees, different aspects of the same thing.

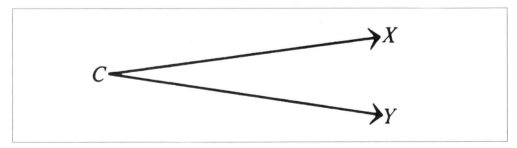

Figure 6.6. A Model of Causation

6.7.5.1 Underlying Factors

To distinguish the observed variables, which are manipulated, from the common variables, which are hidden components in them, it is customary to speak of the latter as factors rather than as variables. Thus for the simplest case of two variables, Z_1 and Z_2, where each is the sum of the two parts, one part common (A) and one part distinct to each variable (B_i), where

$$Z_1 = A + B_1$$
$$Z_2 = A + B_2.$$

Z is conventionally spoken of as a variable and A and B_i as factors. Before proceeding any further, it should be emphasized that factors are statistical variables in the usual sense in all respects: Factors possess both a mean and a variance, they may be symmetrically distributed, and they may also be correlated with other factors. The special term *factor* serves to maintain the distinction between the composite variable, which is observed, and its component parts, which are hypothetical.

Reference

Schuessler, Karl. (1971). *Analyzing social data.* Boston: Houghton Mifflin.

6.7.5.2 Reduction Capability of Factor Analysis

The single most distinctive characteristic of factor analysis is its data-reduction capability. Given an array of correlation coefficients for a set of variables, factor-analytic techniques enable the researcher to see whether some underlying pattern of relationships exists such that the data may be "rearranged" or reduced to a set of factors, smaller in number than the set of variables, that may be considered source variables accounting for the observed interrelations in the data. There are multiple uses for this statistical capability, but the most frequent applications of the method fall into one of the following three categories: (a) exploratory uses, the exploration and detection of patterning of variables with a view to the discovery of new concepts and a possible reduction of data; (b) confirmatory uses, the testing of hypotheses about the structuring of variables in terms of the expected number of significant factors and factor loadings; or (c) uses as a measuring device, the construction of indices to be used as new variables in later analysis (Nie, Bent, & Hull, 1970).

Reference

Nie, N. H., Bent, D. H., & Hull, C. H. (1970). *Statistical package for the social sciences.* New York: McGraw-Hill.

6.7.5.3 Factor Analysis as Research Design

Factor analysis is one of the few methods capable of teasing out what *would* happen through manipulation in situations where manipulation is impossible. It seeks conclusions through statistical techniques rather than through the more traditional experimental route of manipulative control.

6.7.5.4 Three Major Steps in Factor Analysis

Factor analysis includes a fairly large variety of statistical techniques, but there are basically three steps in a factor analysis procedure:

1. preparation of a correlation matrix,
2. extraction of the initial factors—the exploration of possible data reduction, and
3. rotation to a terminal solution—the search for simple and interpretable factors.

Major options at each of these three stages may be summed up by three dichotomies: R-type versus Q-type factor analysis in Step 1, defined versus inferred factors in Step 2, and orthogonal versus oblique in Step 3. These dichotomies are defined in detail in the treatments of factor analysis listed in the following bibliography.

Further Readings on Factor Analysis

Attias, H. (1999). Independent factor analysis. *Neural Computation, 11,* 803-851.

Cattell, Raymond B. (1952). *Factor analysis: An introduction and manual for the psychologist and social scientist.* New York: Harper & Row.

Crabtree, Craig. (1999). Critical factor analysis: An exploratory general model for understanding diverse systems. *World Futures, 53,* 213-227.

Dunlap, William P., & Landis, Ronald S. (1998). Interpretations of multiple regression borrowed from factor analysis and canonical correlation. *Journal of General Psychology, 125,* 397-407.

Fruchter, Benjamin. (1954). *Introduction to factor analysis.* Princeton, NJ: Van Nostrand.

Harman, Harry H. (1976). *Modern factor analysis* (3rd ed.). Chicago: University of Chicago Press.

Heck, Ronald H. (1998). Factor analysis: Exploratory and confirmatory approaches. In George Marcoulides (Ed.), *Modern methods for business research: Methodology for business and management* (pp. 177-215). Mahwah, NJ: Lawrence Erlbaum.

Hershberger, Scott L. (1998). Dynamic factor analysis. In George Marcoulides (Ed.), *Modern methods for business research: Methodology for business and management* (pp. 217-249). Mahwah, NJ: Lawrence Erlbaum.

Horst, Paul. (1965). *Factor analysis of data matrices.* New York: Holt, Rinehart & Winston.

Hutchinson, Susan R. (1998). The stability of post hoc model modifications in confirmatory factor analysis models. *Journal of Experimental Education, 66,* 361-380.

Jöreskog, K. G. (1979). *Advances in factor analysis and structural equation models.* Cambridge, MA: Abt.

Kim, Jae-on, & Mueller, Charles W. (1978). *Factor analysis: Statistical methods and practical issues.* Beverly Hills, CA: Sage.

MacCallum, Robert C., Widaman, Keith F., Zhang, Shaobo, & Hong, Sehee. (1999). Sample size in factor analysis. *Psychological Methods, 4,* 84-99.

Marsh, Herbert W., Hau, Kit Tai, Balla, John R., & Grayson, David. (1998). Is more ever too much? The number of indicators per factor in confirmatory factor analysis. *Multivariate Behavioral Research, 33,* 181-220.

Nie, N. H., Bent, D. H., & Hull, C. H. (1970). *Statistical package for the social sciences.* New York: McGraw-Hill.

Raykov, Tenko. (1998). On the use of confirmatory factor analysis in personality research. *Personality and Individual Differences, 24,* 291-293.

Raykov, Tenko, & Little, Todd D. (1999). A note on procrustean rotation in exploratory factor analysis: A computer intensive approach to goodness-of-fit evaluation. *Educational and Psychology Measurement, 59,* 47-57.

Rummel, Rudolph J. (1970). *Applied factor analysis.* Evanston, IL: Northwestern University Press.

Thurstone, Louis L. (1947). *Multiple factor analysis.* Chicago: University of Chicago Press.

Research Examples of Factor Analysis

Kalliath, Thomas J., Bluedorn, Allen C., & Gillespie, David F. (1999). A confirmatory factor analysis of the competing values instrument. *Educational and Psychology Measurement, 59,* 143-158.

Kranzler, John H., & Keith, Timothy Z. (1999). Independent confirmatory factor analysis of the Cognitive Assessment System. *School Psychology Review, 28,* 117-144.

Owens, Timothy J. (1993). Accentuate the positive and the negative: Rethinking the use of self-esteem. *Social Psychology Quarterly, 56,* 288-299.

Shevlin, M. E., & Lewis, Christopher Alan. (1999). The Revised Social Anxiety Scale: Exploratory and confirmatory factor analysis. *Journal of Social Psychology, 139,* 250-252.

Valtinson, Gale Rene. (1998). A multi-sample confirmatory factor analysis of work-family conflict. *Dissertation Abstracts International, Section B: The Sciences and Engineering.*

AN OVERVIEW OF OTHER STATISTICAL TECHNIQUES AND EXAMPLES OF THEIR APPLICATION 6.8

The concepts in this section are among those that commonly appear in the sociological research writing found in major journals. The explanations of them are attempts to state as simply as possible what these concepts mean. References are given after the discussion of each concept to indicate research applications. The aim of this section is to provide the reader with understanding but not to explain and formulate operational procedures.

6.8.1 Bayesian Methods: Bayesian Inference and Bayesian Statistics

Bayesians believe that scientists should qualify their opinions as probabilities before performing their experiments, do the experiments so as to collect data bearing on these opinions, and then use a Bayesian theorem formally to revise prior probabilities to yield new posterior probabilities. Posterior probabilities are scientists' opinions that have been revised in the light of information provided by the data. That is the key idea behind all Bayesian methods.

Statistically, a Bayesian inference is simply a conditional probability. It gives the probability of a cause (hypothesis) on condition that the effect (evidence) has occurred. The usual ordering of reasoning is reversed: from effect to cause rather than from cause to effect. In its emphasis on subjective beliefs, a Bayesian inference has the distinctive characteristic of refining one's probability.

Bayesian methods are seldom used in sociology, although they have been used advantageously in economics and psychology. A Bayesian approach would seem to have value to sociology whenever the social analyst works backward from effect to causes, as indicated in the method of analytical induction. In analytical induction, the cause must be present whenever the effect is present, and it must be absent whenever the effect is absent. Such statistical methods as Bayesian statistics utilize prior information (objective or subjective) about parameters. The term has also been applied to statistical methods based on the concept of subjective or personal probability.

Further Readings on Bayesian Methods

Arminger, Gerhard, & Muthen, Bengt O. (1998). A Bayesian approach to nonlinear latent variable models using the Gibbs Sampler and the Metropolis-Hastings. *Psychometrika, 63,* 271-300.

Bauwens, Luc., Lubrano, Michele, & Richard, Jean Francois. (2000). *Bayesian inference in dynamic econometric models.* New York: Oxford University Press.

Djafari, Ali M. (Ed.). (1998). *Bayesian inferences for inverse problems.* Bellingham, WA: SPIE International Society for Optical Engineering.

Gross, Alan L. (1997). Interval estimation of bivariate correlations with missing data on both variables: A Bayesian approach. *Journal of Educational and Behavioral Statistics, 22,* 407-424.

Kontsevich, Leonid L., & Tyler, Christopher W. (1999). Bayesian adaptive estimation of psychometric slope and threshold. *Vision Research, 39,* 2729-2737.

Lee, Peter M. (1997). *Bayesian statistics: An introduction.* New York: Oxford University Press.

Park, Young C., & Choi, Key Sun. (1996). Automatic thesaurus construction using Bayesian networks. *Information Processing and Management, 32,* 543-553.

van der Linden, Wim J. (1998). Bayesian item selection criteria for adaptive testing. *Psychometrika, 63,* 201-216.

Winkler, Robert L. (1993). Bayesian statistics: An overview. In Gideon Keren & Charles Lewis (Eds.), *A handbook for data analysis in the behavioral sciences: Statistical issues* (pp. 201-232). Hillsdale, NJ: Lawrence Erlbaum.

Zellner, Arnold. (1996). *An introduction to Bayesian inference in econometrics.* New York: John Wiley and Sons.

6.8.2 Canonical Correlation

The canonical correlation is the maximum correlation between two sets of independent and dependent variables. It can be compared to the simpler coefficient of multiple correlation, which provides the maximum correlation between a number of independent variables with a single dependent variable.

The basic idea of canonical correlation is that, through least squares analysis, two linear composites are formed, one for the independent variables, X_J, and one for the dependent variables, Y_N. The correlation between these two composites is the canonical correlation R_c. The square of the canonical correlation, R_c^2, is an estimate of the variance shared by the two composites.

Further Readings on Canonical Correlation

Alexander, Erika D. (2000). *Using canonical correlation to explore relationships between sets of variables: An applied example with interpretive suggestions.* Paper presented at the annual meeting of the Southwest Educational Research Association, Dallas, TX.

Arnold, Margery E. (1996). *The relationship of canonical correlation analysis to other parametric methods.* Paper presented at the annual meeting of the Southwest Educational Research Association, New Orleans, LA.

Cook, J. A., Razzano, L., & Cappelleri, S. (1996). Canonical correlation analysis of residential and vocational outcomes following psychiatric rehabilitation. *Evaluation and Program Planning, 19,* 351-363.

Fan, Xitao. (1997). Canonical correlation and structural equation modeling: What do they have in common? *Structural Equation Modeling, 4,* 65-79.

Fan, Xitao, & Wang, Lin. (1996). Comparability of jackknife and bootstrap results: An investigation for a case of canonical correlation analysis. *Journal of Experimental Education, 64,* 173-189.

Fung, Wing K., & Gu, Hong. (1998). The second order approximation to sample influence curve in canonical correlation analysis. *Psychometrika, 63,* 263-269.

Tanguma, Jesus. (1999). *Variable deletion strategies in canonical correlation analysis.* Paper presented at the annual meeting of the Mid-South Educational Research Association, Point Clear, AL.

6.8.3 Causal Analysis

Causal analysis is given high priority in all branches of social science. Causal judgments are made to *explain* the occurrence of events to understand *why* particular events occur. With causal knowledge it is often possible to predict events—and to exercise some measure of control over them. Marini and Singer (1988) provide an excellent bibliography on the topic.

Berk (1988) provides an excellent review of causal influence in sociology. His chapter is followed by an extensive bibliography. He points out that increased attention was focused on causality when Hubert M. Blalock and Otis Dudley Duncan introduced "structural equations" to serve as a model from which causal inferences could be drawn when experimental methods could not be employed. The description of path analysis as causal analysis is made in part 3 of Smelser's (1988) collection. The promises and limitations are pointed out. Bernett (1983) has observed, in his 70-year survey of causal terminology in American sociology, that in sociology, causality has proved to be a fragile core concept.

References

Berk, Richard A. (1988). Causal inference for sociological data. In Neil J. Smelser (Ed.), *Handbook of sociology* (pp. 155-171). Newbury Park, CA: Sage.

Bernett, Christopher. (1983). The career of causal analysis in American sociology. *British Journal of Sociology, 34*(2), 230-254.

Marini, Margaret M., & Singer, Burton. (1988). Causality in the social sciences. In Clifford C. Clogg (Ed.), *Sociological methodology 1988* (pp. 347-409). Washington, DC: American Sociological Association.

Smelser, Neil J. (Ed.). (1988). *Handbook of sociology.* Newbury Park, CA: Sage.

Further Readings on Causal Analysis

Finkel, Steven E. (1995). *Causal analysis with panel data.* Thousand Oaks, CA: Sage.

Kish, Leslie. (1987). *Statistical design for research.* New York: John Wiley.

Levine, Tamar, & Donitsa-Schmidt, Smadar. (1998). Computer use, confidence, attitudes, and knowledge: A causal analysis. *Computers in Human Behavior, 14,* 125-146.

McClendon, McKee J. (1994). *Multiple regression causal analysis.* Itasca, IL: F. E. Peacock.

Okraku, Ishmael O. (1998). Tavern-going in America: A causal analysis. *Leisure Sciences, 20,* 303-317.

Peyrot, Mark. (1996). Causal analysis: Theory and application. *Journal of Pediatric Psychology, 21,* 3-24.

Valette-Florence, Pierre. (1998). A causal analysis of means-end hierarchies in a cross-cultural context: Methodological refinements. *Journal of Business Research, 42,* 161-166.

Xiaoming, Li, Feigelman, Susan, Stanton, Bonita, Galbraith, Jennifer, & Huang, Weihua. (1998). Drug trafficking and drug use among urban African-American adolescents: A causal analysis. *Journal of Adolescent Health, 23,* 280-288.

Yates, Donald L., & Pillai, Vijayan K. (1996). Attitudes toward community policing: A causal analysis. *Social Science Journal*, *33*, 193-209.

6.8.4 Cluster Analysis

Cluster analysis is a method in which the researcher identifies items that "cluster" together, as shown by item intercorrelation. For example, we know that people choose jobs because of such factors as the ability to exercise originality and creativity, the opportunity to work with people, and the desire to earn a substantial sum of money and accumulate property. If various questions about job characteristics were posed to respondents, the researcher might find that items would fall into three general clusters. Each cluster would include items that are more highly intercorrelated with others in their cluster than with items outside that cluster.

A correlation matrix can be developed, with rows and columns of the matrix rearranged so that the more highly intercorrelated items form triangular "bunches" at different points along the diagonal. In this way, the nature of interacting forces can be revealed with precision.

Further Readings on Cluster Analysis

Bruehl, Stephen, Lofland, Kenneth R., Semenchuk, Elizabeth M., Rokicki, Lori A., & Penzien, Donald B. (1999). Use of cluster analysis to validate HIS diagnostic criteria for migraine and tension-type headache. *Headache*, *39*, 181-189.

Fleming, Jennifer M., Strong, Jenny, & Ashton, Roderick. (1998). Cluster analysis of self-awareness levels in adults with traumatic brain injury and relationship to outcome. *Journal of Head Trauma Rehabilitation*, *13*, 39-51.

Prior, Margot, Eisenmajer, Richard, Leekam, Susan, Wing, Lorna, Gould, Judith, Ong Ben, & Dowe, David. (1998). Are there subgroups within the autistic spectrum? A cluster analysis of a group of children with autistic spectrum disorders. *Journal of Child Psychology and Psychiatry and Allied Disciplines*, *39*, 893-902.

Roussos, Louis A., Stout, William F., & Marden, John I. (1998). Using new proximity measures with hierarchical cluster analysis to detect multidimensionality. *Journal of Educational Measurement*, *35*, 1-30.

Seifert, Timothy L. (1997). Academic goals and emotions: Results of a structural equation model and a cluster analysis. *British Journal of Educational Psychology*, *67*, 323-338.

6.8.5 Cohort Analysis

The term *cohort* refers to persons matched or nearly matched by age or other selected characteristics so that the defining characteristics can be held constant. A cohort analysis is the study of one or more cohorts in which designated variables are assessed. Such analysis is very valuable for occupational and industrial sociology because cohorts in the labor force are studied in both cross-sectional and longitudinal designs. Population, health sciences, criminology, gerontology, and many other fields frequently use cohort analysis.

Further Readings on Cohort Analysis

Birkett, Nicholas J. (1997). Trends in smoking by birth cohort for births between 1940 and 1975: A reconstructed cohort analysis of the 1900 Ontario Health Survey. *Preventive Medicine*, *26*, 534-541.

Glenn, Norval D. (1977). *Cohort analysis*. Beverly Hills, CA: Sage.

Greenberg, David F., & Larkin, Nancy J. (1996). Age-cohort analysis of arrest rates. In David F. Greenberg (Ed.), *Criminal careers* (Vol. 1, pp. 91-104). Aldershot, UK: Dartmouth.

Miller, Alan S., & Nakamura, Takashi. (1997). Trends in American public opinion: A cohort analysis of shifting attitudes from 1972-1990. *Behaviormetrika, 24*, 179-191.

Riley, Matilda W. (1973). Aging and cohort succession: Interpretations and misinterpretations. *Public Opinion Quarterly, 37*, 35-49.

Takei, Noriyoshi, Lewis, Glyn, Sham, Pak C., & Murray, Robin M. (1996). Age-period-cohort analysis of the incidence of schizophrenia in Scotland. *Psychological Medicine, 26*, 963-973.

Yoon, In Jin. (1997). A cohort analysis of Korean immigrants' class backgrounds and socioeconomic status in the United States. *Korea Journal of Population and Development, 26*, 61-81.

6.8.6 Communication Network Analysis

This is a method of research for identifying the communication network in a system. Much human behavior occurs in interactions through which one individual exchanges information with one or more other individuals. A communication network depicts the individuals who are linked by patterned communication flows. Analysis includes various research procedures, including identification of cliques; examination of specialized communication roles (liaisons, bridges, and isolates); and construction of communication structural indices such as communication connectedness for individuals, dyads, personal networks, cliques, or entire systems.

6.8.7 Decomposition of a Dependent Variable

Many social variables are composites. For example, population growth is the sum of natural increase and net migration. Each of those can be further decomposed: Natural increase can be calculated as births minus deaths, and net migration is the difference between in- and out-migration. When such decomposition is possible, it is of interest (a) to compute the relative contributions of the components to variation in the composite variable and (b) to ascertain how causes affecting the composite variables are transmitted through the respective components.

6.8.8 Decomposition of Effects in Causal Modeling

It is important to interpret patterns of direct and indirect causation in path models and other structural equation models. Such interpretation helps answer questions of the following forms:

- How does variable X affect variable Y?
- How much does mechanism Z contribute to the effect of X or Y?
- Does mechanism Z contribute as much to explaining the effect of X on Y in population A as in population B?

Causal modeling usually entails decomposing the total effect of the antecedent variable into direct and indirect components. The direct effect of one variable on another is simply that part of the total effect not transmitted via intervening variables. Indirect effects are those parts of a variable's total effect transmitted or mediated by variables intervening between the cause and effect of interest in a model. *Decomposition* here means calculating total, direct, and indirect effects in multiequation models.

Further Reading on Decomposition of Effects

Alwin, Duane F., & Hauser, Robert M. (1975). The decomposition of effects in pattern analysis. *American Sociological Review, 40*, 37-47.

6.8.9 The Delphi Technique

The Delphi technique is a forecasting methodology for generating expert opinion on any given subject. It was developed in the early 1950s by the RAND Corporation as an attempt to eliminate the influences of interpersonal feelings and actions that can arise as controlling variables when experts interact in meetings. The Delphi technique uses written answers rather than placing experts in a face-to-face meeting or conference. The written anonymity avoids possible domination by certain individuals in a group meeting. The technique is especially helpful when the experts are widely scattered and cannot easily meet in person. It also can be useful if respondents are hostile or antagonistic to one another.

Further Readings on the Delphi Technique

Martin, Andrew G., & Frick, Martin J. (1998). The Delphi technique: An informal history of its use in agricultural education research since 1984. *Journal of Agricultural Education, 39*, 73-79.

Passig, David. (1993). Reactions to experts' forecasts by a group of Jewish teenagers: An Imen-Delphi exercise—An applied social methodology-a variant of the Delphi-forecasting technique: I and II. *Dissertation Abstracts International, 54*, 480.

Petrina, Stephen, & Volk, Kenneth S. (1992). Policy making processes and the Delphi technique in STS curricula: A case study examining energy issues. *Bulletin of Science, Technology and Society, 12*, 299-303.

Stahl, Nancy N., & Stahl, Robert J. (1991). We can agree after all! Achieving consensus for a critical thinking component of a gifted program using the Delphi technique. *Roeper Review, 14*, 79-88.

Wicklein, Robert C. (1993). Identifying critical issues and problems in technology education using a modified-Delphi technique. *Journal of Technology Education, 5*, 54-71.

6.8.10 Discriminant (Function) Analysis

The discriminant function was originally proposed by R. A. Fisher (see the Further Readings at the end of this section). It was designed to aid in the classification of an individual observation into one of two groups. The discriminant function has been defined as a linear combination of a set of n variables that will classify into two different classes (or groups) the events or items for which the measurements of the n variables are available, and that will do so with the smallest possible proportion of misclassifications. It is useful, for example, in the problem of classifying persons into two social groups, such as culturally assimilated and culturally alienated.

Further Readings on Discriminant (Function) Analysis

D'Andrea, Livia M., & D'Andrea, Lester R. (1996). Prediction of treatment outcome using state-trait anxiety inventory scores: The use of discriminant analysis. *Journal of Addictions & Offender Counseling, 16*, 50-61.

Ermer, Julie, & Dunn, Winnie. (1998). The Sensory Profile: A discriminant analysis of children with and without disabilities. *American Journal of Occupational Therapy, 52*, 283-290.

Fisher, R. A. (1936). The use of multiple measurements in taxonomic problems. *Annals of Eugenics,* *7,* 179-188.

Huberty, Carl J., & Lowman, Laureen L. (1997). Discriminant analysis via statistical packages. *Educational and Psychological Measurement,* *57,* 759-784.

Lagana, Luciana. (1995). Older adults' expectations about mental health counseling: A multivariate and discriminant analysis. *International Journal of Aging & Human Development,* *40,* 297-316.

Pineda, David, Ardila, Alfredo, & Rosselli, Monica. (1999). Neuropsychological and behavioral assessment of ADHD in seven- to twelve-year-old children: A discriminant analysis. *Journal of Learning Disabilities,* *32,* 159-173.

6.8.11 Event History Analysis

Event history analysis uses methods for analyzing data on the number, timing, and sequencing of events experienced by persons and entities. Essentially, an event is a change of state, such as the change from being single to being married. Events are separated by time intervals. Marriage serves as an episode until divorce or death occurs. Events can also be analyzed for such entities as firms or nations, which experience firm failures, national wars, depressions, and revolutions.

The potential utility of event analysis for sociology is great. The procedures that have been developed make use of data on the order of the occurrence of events instead of exact dates. Sociologists and economists have found event analysis useful in the study of work histories and various problems of labor force dynamics. Sequential data are available for the study of annual fertility, the number of children in integrated schools, yearly costs of criminal victimization, and so on.

The general analytic approach for both persons and entities involves positing a stochastic model that relates the probability of no change in state, a change in state, or movement among various states. A sample of event histories is used to estimate the population parameters.

Further Readings on Event History Analysis

Allison, Paul D. (1985). *Event history analysis: Regression for longitudinal event data.* Beverly Hills, CA: Sage.

Fernandez, Elizabeth. (1999). Pathways in substitute care: Representation of placement careers of children using event history analysis. *Children & Youth Services Review,* *21,* 177-216.

Leiter, Jeffrey, & Johnsen, Matthew C. (1997). Child maltreatment and school performance declines: An event-history analysis. *American Educational Research Journal,* *34,* 563-589.

Myers, Daniel J. (1997). Racial rioting in the 1960s: An event history analysis of local conditions. *American Sociological Review,* *62,* 94-112.

Palmer, William R. T. (1997). Parole prediction using current psychological and behavioural predictors, a longitudinal criterion, and event history analysis. *Dissertation Abstracts International,* *58,* 2694B.

6.8.12 Log-Linear Modeling and Analysis

Log-linear modeling, a recent development in contingency table analysis, applies new techniques to analyzing multidimensional tables. In the past, purely categorical data were difficult to analyze, especially in the construction of multivariate models. Leo A. Goodman has said that log-linear models not only help one find bivariate relationships and higher-order interactions in complex tables but also can be viewed as analogous to the analysis of simultaneous equations. The promise is that the exploration of polls and surveys may have caught up with causal and path analysis. Some researchers caution that the same concepts they employ in studying interval-level data may not apply unambiguously in interpreting cross-classifications of categorical data.

Essential to log-linear modeling is building a model for the expected frequencies in a multidimensional population cross-classification by introducing so-called main and interaction effects. It is sometimes more convenient to work with the natural logarithms of the expected frequencies. A model is to be described by the set of "fitted marginals" tables used in estimating the expected frequencies under the model.

Further Readings on Log-Linear Modeling and Analysis

Keller, F., & Wolfersdorf, M. (1995). Changes in suicide numbers in psychiatric hospitals: An analysis using log-linear time-trend models. *Social Psychiatry and Psychiatric Epidemiology*, *30*, 269-273.

Knoke, David, & Burke, Peter J. (1980). *Log-linear models.* Beverly Hills, CA: Sage.

Miller, Todd Q., & Flay, Brian R. (1996). Using log-linear models for longitudinal data to test alternative explanations for stage-like phenomena: An example from research on adolescent substance abuse. *Multivariate Behavioral Research*, *31*, 169-196.

Rojewski, Jay W., & Bakeman, Roger. (1997). Log-linear modeling and analysis: Reflections on the use of multivariate categorical data in social science research. *Exceptionality*, *7*, 199-203.

Sobel, Michael E. (1998). Some log-linear and log-nonlinear models for ordinal scales with midpoints, with an application to public opinion data. *Sociological Methodology*, *28*, 263-292.

Vermunt, Jeroen K. (1997). *Log-linear models for event histories.* Thousand Oaks, CA: Sage.

6.8.13 Markov Chains

Markov chains are models predicting changes that take place over time. Imagine a problem of predicting the outcomes over time as some persons move from job to job while others stay on the same job. When confronting such a question and associated data, it is natural to wonder whether the observed frequencies might be accounted for by a simple probability law. Markov's law (simple) would account for a stationary, but not necessarily equal, division of movers and stayers toward the end of the time sequence. A Markov chain might be found for all kinds of change behavior stated in dichotomous terms: those who change their minds before election day and those who never change their minds, those whose morale changes daily and those whose morale remains fixed, and so on.

Further Readings on Markov Chains

Donhardt, G. L. (1995). Tracking student enrollments using the Markov chain, comprehensive tool for enrollment management. *Journal of College Student Development*, *36*, 457-462.

Humphreys, Keith. (1998). The latent Markov chain with multivariate random effects: An evaluation of instruments measuring labor market status in the British Household Panel Study. *Sociological Methods and Research*, *26*, 269-299.

Meiser, Thorsten, & Ohrt, Barbara. (1996). Modeling structure and chance in transitions: Mixed latent partial Markov-chain models. *Journal of Educational and Behavioral Statistics*, *21*, 91-109.

Yamaguchi, Kazuo. (1996). Some log-linear fixed-effect latent-trait Markov-chain models: A dynamic analysis of personal efficacy under the influence of divorce/widowhood. *Sociological Methodology*, *26*, 39-78.

6.8.14 Meta-Analysis

This term refers to analytical procedures for the cumulation of evidence on organizations—both within single research studies and across studies of the same phenomena—collected at different times by different researchers. It is a valuable analytic tool. The discussion by Lipsey and Wilson that follows, excerpted from their book *Practical Meta-Analysis*, highlights the usefulness and strengths as well as weaknesses of this tool.

Further Readings on Meta-Analysis

Furnham, Adrian, & Hayward, Robert. (1997). A study and meta-analysis of lay attributions of cures for overcoming specific psychological problems. *Journal of Genetic Psychology, 158*, 315-331.

Glass, Gene V., McGaw, Barry, & Smith, Mary Lee. (1981). *Meta-analysis in social research.* Beverly Hills, CA: Sage.

Hunger, John E., Schmidt, Frank C., & Jackson, Gregg B. (1984). *Meta-analysis: Cumulating research findings across studies.* Beverly Hills, CA: Sage.

McLaughlin-Cheng, Elissa. (1998). Asperger syndrome and autism: A literature review and meta-nalysis. *Focus on Autism and Other Developmental Disabilities, 13*, 234-245.

McNamara, James F., Morales, Pamilla, Yeonbee, Kim, & McNamara, Maryanne. (1998). Conducting your first meta-analysis: An illustrated guide. *International Journal of Educational Reform, 7*, 380-397.

Ping, Xin Yan, & Jitendra, Asha K. (1999). The effects of instruction in solving mathematical word problems for students with learning problems: A meta-analysis. *Journal of Special Education, 32*, 207-225.

Ross, Steven. (1998). Self-assessment in second language testing: A meta-analysis and analysis of experiential factors. *Language Testing, 15*, 1-20.

Wolf, Fredric M. (1986). *Meta-analysis: Quantitative methods for research synthesis.* Beverly Hills, CA: Sage.

▶ Practical Meta-Analysis

M. W. Lipsey and D. B. Wilson

Situations to Which Meta-Analysis Is Applicable

Meta-analysis can be understood as a form of survey research in which research reports, rather than people, are surveyed. A coding form (survey protocol) is developed, a sample or population of research reports is gathered, and each research study is "interviewed" by a coder who reads it carefully and codes the appropriate information about its characteristics and quantitative findings. The resulting data are then analyzed using special adaptations of conventional statistical techniques to investigate and describe the pattern of findings in the selected set of studies.

Meta-analysis is only one of many ways to summarize, integrate, and interpret selected sets of scholarly works in the various disciplines and it has an important, but somewhat circumscribed domain of applicability. First, meta-analysis applies only to empirical research studies; it cannot be used to summarize theoretical papers, conventional research reviews, policy proposals, and the like. Second, it applies only to research studies that produce quantitative findings, that is, studies using quantitative measurement of variables and reporting descriptive or inferential statistics to summarize the resulting data. This rules out qualitative forms of research such as case studies, ethnography, and "naturalistic" inquiry. Third, meta-analysis is a technique for encoding and analyzing the statistics that summarize research findings as they are typically presented in research reports. If the full data sets for the studies of interest are available, it will generally be more appropriate and informative to analyze them directly using conventional procedures rather than meta-analyze summary statistics.

In addition, because meta-analysis focuses on the aggregation and comparison of the findings of different research studies, it is necessary that those findings be of a sort that can be meaningfully compared. This means that the findings must (a) be conceptually comparable, that is, deal with the same constructs and relationships and (b) be configured in similar statistical forms. For instance, a set of studies of the effectiveness of treatment for depression could be meta-analyzed if the various treatments were judged to be appropriate for comparison with each other and if treatment findings were in the same basic form, e.g., measures of depression contrasted for a treatment and control group of respondents. It would not generally be appropriate to include studies of distinctly different topics in the same meta-analysis, e.g., studies of treatment for depression and studies of gender differences in spatial visualization. This is often referred to as the "apples and oranges" problem in meta-analysis—attempting to summarize or integrate over studies that do not really deal with the same constructs and relationships.

Similarly, it is not generally appropriate to combine study findings derived from different research designs and appearing in different statistical forms, even if they deal with the same topic. For instance, experimental studies of treatment for depression using treatment versus control group comparisons generally would not be combined with observational studies in which level of depression was correlated with level of service received. Though both types of study deal in some fashion with the relationship between treatment and depression, the differences in the research designs, the nature of the quantitative relationships constituting the findings, and the meaning of those findings are so great that they would be difficult to incorporate in the same meta-analysis. Of course, one might separately meta-analyze the experimental findings and correlational findings, using appropriate procedures for each, and then draw some conclusions across both meta-analyses.

The set of findings included in a meta-analysis must result from comparable research designs for practical reasons as well as conceptual ones. Meta-analysis represents each study's findings in the form of *effect sizes*. An effect size is a statistic that encodes the critical quantitative information from each relevant study finding. Different types of study findings generally require different effect size statistics. Studies that produce bivariate correlations, for instance, are typically meta-analyzed using a different effect size statistic than studies that compare groups of subjects on the mean values of dependent variables. Similarly, findings that report pre–post mean differences for a single subject sample use a still different effect size statistic, and there are others even more specialized.

Given comparable statistical forms, the definition of what study findings are conceptually comparable for purposes of meta-analysis is often fixed only in the eye of the beholder. Findings that appear categorically different to one analyst may seem similar to another. Glass's meta-analysis of the effectiveness of psychotherapy (Smith & Glass, 1977), for instance, was criticized for combining findings from distinctly different therapies, e.g., cognitive behavioral, psychodynamic, gestalt, etc. Glass claimed that his interest was in the overall effectiveness of the whole broad class of psychotherapies and in comparisons between the different types, hence all had to be represented in the meta-analysis. Another analyst might have a narrower interest and meta-analyze only study findings on, say, desensitization therapy for snake phobias. In either case, however, it is essential that the analyst have a definition of the domain of interest and a rationale for the inclusion and exclusion of studies from the meta-analysis. Others may criticize that definition and rationale but, as long as they are explicit, each reviewer can judge for him- or herself whether they are meaningful.

The Key Concept of Effect Size

Given a set of quantitative research findings judged to deal with the same topic and involve comparable research designs, a significant problem still remains for anyone who wants to encode those results into a database that can be meaningfully analyzed. With rare exceptions, such studies will not use the same operationalizations (measurement procedures) for their key variables. Say, for instance, we select comparison group studies of the effectiveness of treatment for depression. Some studies may use Beck's depression inventory as the outcome variable, some may use the Hamilton rating scale for depression, some may use therapists' ratings of depression, and some may have other idiosyncratic but reasonable measures of this construct. With these quite different measures yielding different numerical values that are meaningful only in relation to the specific operationalizations and scales used, how can their quantitative findings be encoded in a way that allows them to be statistically combined and compared?

The answer relates to an essential feature of meta-analysis, indeed, the feature that makes meta-analysis possible and provides the hub around which the entire process revolves. The various effect size statistics used to code different forms of quantitative study findings in meta-analysis are based on the concept of *standardization*. The effect size statistic produces a statistical standardization of the study findings such that the resulting numerical values are interpretable in a consistent fashion across all the variables and measures involved. Standardization in this context has much the same meaning it does when we speak of standardized scores in testing and measurement. For instance, we might convert mathematics achievement test scores to percentiles, or z-scores standardized on the standard deviation of a sample of scores, and thus be able to compare them meaningfully with a different variable, e.g., reading achievement scores. Johnny may be at the 85th percentile on math but only at the 60th percentile on reading.

In similar fashion, the most common effect size statistics in meta-analysis standardize on the variation in the sample distributions of scores for the measures of interest. Thus the mean difference between a treatment and a control group on the Beck's depression inventory can be represented in terms of standard deviation units, as can the mean ratings of therapists, and all such other quantitative measures of depression. In the metric of standard deviation units, one can combine and compare results across different measures and operationalizations. A study using Beck's depression inventory may show a difference of .30 standard deviations between treatment and control group while a study using therapists' ratings may show a difference of .42 standard deviations. Assuming the same underlying population from which the respective samples are drawn, we can compare these numbers, use them in statistical analysis to compute means, variances, correlations, and the like, and generally treat them as meaningful indicators of the same thing—in this case, differences between the amount of depression experienced by respondents in the treatment group and those in the control group relative to the estimated population variability on depression.

The key to meta-analysis, therefore, is defining an effect size statistic capable of representing the quantitative findings of a set of research studies in a standardized form that permits meaningful numerical comparison and analysis across the studies. There are many possibilities. The dichotomous categorization of study findings into those that are statistically significant and those that are not is a rudimentary form of effect size. A slightly more differentiated version is the p-value (e.g., $p = .03$, $p = .50$) for each statistical significance test (Becker, 1994). These, however, are not very good effect size statistics. The more desirable forms index both the *magnitude* and the *direction* of a relationship, not merely its statistical significance. In addition, they are defined so that there is relatively little confounding with other issues, such as sample size, which figures prominently in significance test results.

The meta-analyst should use an effect size statistic that provides appropriate standardization for the particular research design, form of quantitative finding, variables, and operationalizations presented in the set of studies under investigation. There are many effect size statistics that are workable for one circumstance or another but, in practice, only a few are widely used. Most empirical findings fall into one of several generic categories for which specific effect size statistics and related statistical procedures are developed and are widely recognized. A range of useful effect size statistics is defined in Chapter 3 along with the research situations to which they are most applicable.

The Strengths of Meta-Analysis

Why should one consider using meta-analysis to summarize and analyze a body of research studies rather than conventional research reviewing techniques? There are basically four reasons that constitute the primary advantages of meta-analysis.

First, meta-analysis procedures impose a useful discipline on the process of summarizing research findings. Good meta-analysis is conducted as a structured research technique in its own right and hence requires that each step be documented and open to scrutiny. It involves specification of the criteria that define the population of study findings at issue, organized search strategies to identify and retrieve eligible studies, formal coding of study characteristics and findings, and data analysis to support the conclusions that are drawn. By making the research summarizing process explicit and systematic, the consumer can assess the author's assumptions, procedures, evidence, and conclusions rather than take on faith that the conclusions are valid.

Second, meta-analysis represents key study findings in a manner that is more differentiated and sophisticated than conventional review procedures that rely on qualitative summaries or "vote-counting" on statistical significance. By encoding the magnitude and direction of each relevant statistical relationship in a collection of studies, meta-analysis effect sizes constitute a variable sensitive to findings of different strength across studies. By contrast, using statistical significance to differentiate studies that find effects from those that do not is potentially quite misleading. Statistical significance reflects both the magnitude of the estimated effect and the sampling error around that estimate, the latter almost entirely a function of sample size. Thus, studies with small samples may find effects or relationships of meaningful magnitude that are not statistically significant because of low statistical power (Lipsey, 1990; Schmidt, 1992, 1996).

Third, meta-analysis is capable of finding effects or relationships that are obscured in other approaches to summarizing research. Qualitative, narrative summaries of findings, while informative, do not lend themselves to detailed scrutiny of the differences between studies and associated differences in their findings. The systematic coding of study characteristics typical in meta-analysis, on the other hand, permits an analytically precise examination of the relationships between study findings and such study features as respondent characteristics, nature of treatment, research design, and measurement procedures. Furthermore, by estimating the size of the effect in each study and pooling those estimates across studies (giving greater weight to larger studies), meta-analysis produces synthesized effect estimates with considerably more statistical power than individual studies. Thus, meaningful effects and relationships upon which studies agree, and differential effects related to study differences, are both more likely to be discovered by meta-analysis than by less systematic and analytic approaches.

Fourth, meta-analysis provides an organized way of handling information from a large number of study findings under review. When the number of studies or amount of information extracted from each study passes a fairly low threshold, note-taking or coding on index cards cannot effectively keep track of all the details. The systematic coding procedures of meta-analysis and the construction of a computerized database to record the resulting information, by contrast, have almost unlimited capability for detailing information from each study and covering large numbers of studies. A meta-analysis conducted by one of the authors of this volume, for instance, resulted in a database of more than 150 items of information for each of nearly 500 studies (Lipsey, 1992). We hasten to add, however, that meta-analysis does not require large numbers of studies and, in some circumstances, can be usefully applied to as few as two or three study findings.

The Weaknesses of Meta-Analysis

Meta-analysis is not without disadvantages and it is the subject of harsh criticism from some quarters (Sharpe, 1997). One disadvantage of meta-analysis is simply the amount of effort and expertise it takes. Properly done, a meta-analysis with more than a handful of study findings is labor intensive and takes considerably more time than a conventional qualitative research review. Additionally, many aspects of meta-analysis require specialized knowledge, especially the selection and computation of appropriate effect sizes and the application of statistical analysis to them. The major objective of this book, of course, is to make that specialized knowledge available at a practical level to interested persons who wish to conduct, or understand, meta-analysis.

Another concern about meta-analysis relates to its structured and somewhat mechanical procedures, which, in other regard, can be viewed as strengths. For some applications (and some critics say for all applications), the relatively objective coding of data elements and effect sizes from research studies, and the type of analysis to which such data lend themselves, may not be sensitive to important issues, e.g., the social context of the study, theoretical influences and implications, methodological quality, more subtle or complex aspects of design, procedure, or results, and the like. To draw on the survey research analogy used earlier, meta-analysis is a structured, closed-ended questionnaire approach to summarizing research findings. Some survey applications require a more open-ended approach, e.g., unstructured interviews or focus groups, to deal with the complexity or subtlety of certain topics. It may well be that some research issues also require a more qualitative assessment and summary than meta-analysis can provide. Of course, there is no reason in principle why both meta-analytic and qualitative reviews cannot be done on the same body of research findings, with overall conclusions drawn from both. One approach to meta-analysis, what Slavin (1986, 1995) calls *best evidence synthesis*, attempts to do just that, combining qualitative and quantitative reviewing techniques in the same research review.

Perhaps the most persistent criticism of meta-analysis has to do with the mix of studies included (the apples and oranges issue mentioned earlier). Critics argue, with some justification, that mean effect sizes and other such summary statistics produced by meta-analysis are not meaningful if they are aggregated over incommensurable study findings. There would be little sense, for instance, in constructing the distribution of effect sizes for a mix of study findings on methadone maintenance for drug abusers, gender differences in social skills, and effects of unionization on employee morale. On the other hand, few would object to a meta-analysis of findings from virtual replications of the same study. Most of the criticism on this point, however, has been well short of such obvious extremes. The gray area in between becomes controversial when a meta-analyst includes study findings that are clearly not replications, but are claimed to relate to a broader theme. As noted earlier, Smith and Glass (1977) included a wide range of studies of psychotherapy in their pioneering meta-analysis on the grounds that the issue of interest to them was the overall effectiveness of psychotherapy. However, they were stridently criticized by researchers who saw vast differences between the different therapies and different outcome variables and felt it was misleading to report average effectiveness over such distinct approaches as behavioral therapy, psychodynamic therapy, and gestalt therapy and such diverse outcomes as fear and anxiety, self-esteem, global adjustment, emotional-somatic problems, and work and school functioning.

The problem comes in, of course, when the different types of study findings are averaged together in a grand mean effect size. Meta-analysts who wish to deal with broad topics are increasingly approaching their task as one of comparison rather than aggregation. Where distinctly different subcategories of study findings are represented in a meta-analysis, they can be broken out separately and the distribution of effect sizes and related statistics can be reported for each, permitting comparison among them. Additionally, technical advances in meta-analysis have made it possible to statistically test for homogeneity to determine if a grouping of effect sizes from different studies shows more variation than would be expected from sampling error alone. This provides an empirical test for whether studies show such disparate results that it may not be plausible to presume that they are comparable. Put differently, contemporary meta-analysis is increasingly attending to the variance of effect size distributions rather than the means of those distributions. That is, the primary question of interest often has to do with identifying the sources of differences in study findings, rather than aggregating results together into a grand average. This emphasis provides a more careful handling of distinctly different subgroups of study findings and runs less risk of vexing critics who are concerned about such differences.

A related and more troublesome issue is the mixing of study findings of different methodological quality in the same meta-analysis. Some critics argue that a research synthesis should be based only on findings from the highest quality studies and should not be degraded by inclusion of those from methodologically flawed studies. Indeed, some approaches to meta-analysis set very strict methodological criteria for inclusion, e.g., the best evidence synthesis method mentioned earlier (Slavin, 1986). What makes this point controversial is that there are problematic trade-offs and judgment calls whichever way the meta-analyst goes. One difficulty is that, aside from a few simple canons, there is relatively little agreement among researchers on what constitutes methodological quality. Moreover, few research areas provide studies that all reviewers would agree are methodologically impeccable in sufficient numbers to make a meaningful meta-analysis. Many areas of research, especially those that deal with applied topics, provide virtually no perfect studies and the ones closest to textbook standards may be conducted in circumstances that are unrepresentative of those in which the meta-analyst is most interested. For instance, methodologically rigorous studies of psychotherapy are more likely in demonstration projects and university clinics than in routine mental health practice (Weisz, Donenberg, Han, & Weiss, 1995; Weisz, Weiss, & Donenberg, 1992). Thus, much of the knowledge we have on some issues resides in studies that are methodologically imperfect and potentially misleading. The meta-analyst must decide how far to go with inclusion of findings from studies that are judged interpretable but flawed, knowing that relaxed methodological standards may result in a derisive reproach of "garbage in, garbage out," while stringent standards are likely to exclude much, or most, of the available evidence on a topic.

Two approaches have emerged on this issue. One is to keep the methodological criteria strict and accept the consequences in regard to the limitations thus imposed on the proportion of available and relevant study findings that may be included. In this instance, the meta-analyst has assurance that the synthesis is based on only the "best" evidence but its results may summarize only a narrow research domain and have little generality. The other approach is to treat methodological variation among studies as an empirical matter to be investigated as part of the meta-analysis (Greenland, 1994). In this case, less stringent methodological criteria are imposed, but the meta-analyst carefully codes methodological characteristics that may influence the study findings. One phase of statistical analysis then investigates the extent to which various methodological features are related to study findings (e.g., random vs. nonrandom assignment in treatment studies). If a questionable methodological practice has no demonstrable relationship to study findings, the corresponding findings are included in the final analysis, which thus gains the benefit of the evidence they contain. If, however, studies with the questionable practice show results significantly different from those without that problem, they can then be excluded from the final results or used only with statistical adjustments to correct for their bias.

Recent History and Contemporary Usage of Meta-Analysis

Published examples of the quantitative synthesis of findings from different studies can be found as far back as 1904 when Karl Pearson averaged the correlations between inoculation for typhoid fever and mortality for five separate samples (Cooper & Hedges, 1994). As mentioned at the beginning of this chapter, however, the modern era of meta-analysis began with the work of Glass on psychotherapy (Glass, 1976; Smith & Glass, 1977; Smith, Glass, & Miller, 1980), Schmidt and Hunter (1977) on validity coefficients for employment tests, and Rosenthal and Rubin (1978) on interpersonal expectancy effects.

Stimulated in large part by these intriguing applications, the next phase of development focused primarily on the methodological and statistical underpinnings of meta-analysis. This period, in the early 1980s, was marked by the publication of a number of book-length expositions of the concepts, methods, and statistical theory of various versions of meta-analysis (Glass, McGaw, & Smith, 1981; Hedges & Olkin, 1985; Hunter, Schmidt, & Jackson, 1982; Light & Pillemer, 1984; Rosenthal, 1984; Wolf, 1986). The practical and methodological guidance provided by these volumes, combined with the interest generated by the pioneering work, ignited a virtual explosion of meta-analytic applications and commentary upon those applications. Meta-analysis spread rapidly in the social sciences, especially education and psychology, and caught on with especial vigor in the health sciences where it has been virtually institutionalized as the preferred approach to integrating the findings of clinical trials research (Chalmers et al., 1987; Olkin, 1992; Sacks et al., 1987).

Meanwhile, another generation of more sophisticated methodological and statistical work has expanded and strengthened the foundations of meta-analysis (e.g., Cook et al., 1992; Cooper, 1989; Hunter & Schmidt, 1990; Rosenthal, 1991). The pinnacle of these efforts was the publication of *The Handbook of Research Synthesis* (Cooper & Hedges, 1994) under sponsorship of the Russell Sage Foundation, a compendium of 32 chapters covering virtually every aspect of meta-analysis and authored by an array of preeminent contributors to the field. Against this background, it is the task of the present volume to integrate and translate the most current methodological and statistical work into a practical guide for conducting state-of-the-art meta-analysis of empirical research findings in the social and behavioral sciences.

References

Becker, B. J. (1994). Combining significance levels. In H. Cooper & L. V. Hedges (Eds.), *The handbook of research synthesis* (pp. 215-230). New York: Russell Sage Foundation.

Chalmers, T. C., Berrier, J., Sack, H. S., Levin, H., Reitman, D., & Nagalingam, R. (1987). Meta-analysis of clinical trials as a scientific discipline. *Statistics in Medicine, 6*, 733-744.

Cook, T. D., Cooper, H., Cordray, D. S., Hartmann, H., Hedges, L. V., Light, R. J., Louis, T. A., & Mosteller, F. (1992). *Meta-analysis for explanation: A casebook.* New York: Russell Sage Foundation.

Cooper, H. M. (1989). *Integrating research: A guide for literature reviews* (2nd ed.). Newbury Park, CA: Sage.

Cooper, H., & Hedges, L. V. (Eds.). (1994). *The handbook of research synthesis.* New York: Russell Sage Foundation.

Glass, G. V. (1976). Primary, secondary and meta-analysis of research. *Educational Researcher, 5*, 3-8.

Glass, G. V., McGaw, B., & Smith, M. L. (1981). *Meta-analysis in social research.* Beverly Hills, CA: Sage.

Greenland, S. (1994). Invited commentary: A critical look at some popular meta-analytic methods. *American Journal of Epidemiology, 140*, 290-296.

Hedges, L. V., & Olkin, I. (1985). *Statistical methods for meta-analysis.* Orlando, FL: Academic Press.

Hunter, J. E., & Schmidt, F. L. (1990). *Methods of meta-analysis: Correcting error and bias in research findings.* Newbury Park, CA: Sage.

Hunter, J. E., Schmidt, F. L., & Jackson, G. B. (1982). *Meta-analysis: Cumulating research findings across studies.* Beverly Hills, CA: Sage.

Light, R. J., & Pillemer, D. B. (1984). *Summing up: The science of reviewing research.* Cambridge, MA: Harvard University Press.

Lipsey, M. W. (1990). *Design sensitivity: Statistical power for experimental research.* Newbury Park, CA: Sage.

Lipsey, M. W. (1992). Juvenile delinquency treatment: A meta-analytic inquiry into the variability of effects. In T. D. Cook, H. Cooper, D. S. Cordray, H. Hartmann, L. V. Hedges, R. J. Light, T. A. Louis, & F. Mosteller (Eds.), *Meta-analysis for explanation: A casebook* (pp. 83-127). New York: Russell Sage Foundation.

Olkin, I. (1992). Meta-analysis: Methods for combining independent studies. *Statistical Science, 7,* 226.

Rosenthal, R. (1984). *Meta-analytic procedures for social research.* Beverly Hills, CA: Sage.

Rosenthal, R. (1991). *Meta-analytic procedures for social research. Applied Social Research Methods Series* (Vol. 6). Thousand Oaks, CA: Sage.

Rosenthal, R., & Rubin, D. B. (1978). Interpersonal expectancy effects: The first 345 studies. *The Behavioral and Brain Sciences, 3,* 377-415.

Sacks, H. S., Berrier, J., Reitman, D., Axcona-Berk, V. A., & Chalmers, T. C. (1987). Meta-analyses of randomized controlled trials. *New England Journal of Medicine, 316,* 450-455.

Schmidt, F. L. (1992). What do data really mean? Research findings, meta-analysis, and cumulative knowledge in psychology. *American Psychologist, 47,* 1173-1181.

Schmidt, F. L. (1996). Statistical significance testing and cumulative knowledge in psychology: Implications for training of researchers. *Psychological Methods, 1,* 115-129.

Schmidt, F. L., & Hunter, J. E. (1977). Development of a general solution to the problem of validity generalization. *Journal of Applied Psychology, 62,* 529-540.

Sharpe, D. (1997). Of apples and oranges, file drawers and garbage: Why validity issues in meta-analysis will not go away. *Clinical Psychology Review, 17,* 881-901.

Slavin, R. E. (1986). Best-evidence synthesis: An alternative to meta-analytic and traditional reviews. *Educational Researcher, 15,* 5-11.

Slavin, R. E. (1995). Best evidence synthesis: An intelligent alternative to meta-analysis. *Journal of Clinical Epidemiology, 48,* 9-18.

Smith, M. L., & Glass, G. V. (1977). Meta-analysis of psychotherapy outcome studies. *American Psychologist, 32,* 752-760.

Smith, M. L., Glass, G. V., & Miller, T. I. (1980). *The benefits of psychotherapy.* Baltimore, MD: Johns Hopkins.

Weisz, J. R., Donenberg, G. R., Han, S. S., & Weiss, B. (1995). Bridging the gap between laboratory and clinic in child and adolescent psychotherapy. *Journal of Consulting and Clinical Psychology, 63,* 688-701.

Weisz, J. R., Weiss, B. D., & Donenberg, G. R. (1992). The lab versus the clinic: Effects of child and adolescent psychotherapy. *American Psychologist, 47,* 1578-1585.

Wolf, F. M. (1986). *Meta-analysis: Quantitative methods for research synthesis.* Beverly Hills, CA: Sage.

SOURCE: From M. W. Lipsey and D. B. Wilson (2001), *Practical Meta-Analysis* (Thousand Oaks, CA: Sage), pp. 1-11. Reprinted with permission.

6.8.15 Multiple Discriminant (Function) Analysis

The discriminant function technique has been extended by Fisher to include more than two groups (see Fisher [1938]). With the computer, it is now possible to study a large number of groups simultaneously across many variables.

Multiple discriminant function analysis provides three kinds of information:

1. It determines whether in fact certain groups really are distinct with respect to selected characteristics.
2. It tells on what factors the groups may be best discriminated.
3. It indicates whether an individual is like other individuals in the group to which he or she has been assigned. That is, it indicates the extent to which individuals have been theoretically misclassified.

Reference

Fisher, R. A. (1938). The statistical utilization of multiple measurements. *Annals of Eugenics, 13,* 376-386.

Further Readings on Multiple Discriminant (Function) Analysis

Azari, N. P., Pettigrew, K. D., Pietrini, P., Murphy, D. C., Horwitz, B., & Schapiro, M. B. (1995). Sex differences in patterns of hemispheric cerebral metabolism: A multiple regression/discriminant analysis of positron emission tomographic data. *International Journal of Neuroscience, 81*, 1-20.

Azari, N. P., Pietrini, P., Horwitz, B., Pettigrew, K. D., Leonard, H. L., Rapoport, J. L., Schapiro, M. B., & Swedo, S. E. (1993). Individual differences in cerebral metabolic patterns during pharmacotherapy in obsessive-compulsive disorder: A multiple regression/discriminant analysis of positron emission tomographic data. *Biological Psychiatry, 34*, 798-809.

Chen, T., Bruininks, R. H., Lakin, K. C., & Hayden, M. (1993). Personal competencies and community participation in small community residential programs: A multiple discriminant analysis. *American Journal on Mental Retardation, 98*, 390-399.

DeRose, Daryn. (1992). Comparing classification models from multinomial logistic regression and multiple discriminant analysis. *Dissertation Abstracts International, 52*, 6696.

Klecka, William R. (1980). *Discriminant analysis.* Beverly Hills, CA: Sage.

Le Blanc, Louis A., & Rucks, Conway T. (1996). A multiple discriminant analysis of vessel accidents. *Accident Analysis and Prevention, 28*, 501-510.

Oleckno, William A., & Blacconiere, Michael J. (1990). Multiple discriminant analysis of smoking status and health-related attitudes and behaviors. *American Journal of Preventive Medicine, 6*, 323-329.

Rettig, Solomon. (1964). Multiple discriminant analysis: An illustration. *American Sociological Review, 29*, 398-402.

6.8.16 Probit and Logit Models

These models are nonlinear regressions used as alternatives to the ordinary multivariate linear regression model; they are used to estimate a dichotomous dependent variable. Common examples of such dichotomous dependent variables are "succeeds" or "fails," "occurring" or "not occurring," "maintained parole" or "violated parole," and "remained in school" or "dropped out." Probit and logit methods are necessary because the ordinary least squares regression estimates with a dichotomous variable are misleading. A key assumption of the ordinary least squares model—constant variance of the error term across all observations—is violated.

Further Readings on Probit and Logit Models

Aldrich, John H., & Nelson, Forrest. (1984). *Linear probability, logit, and probit models.* Beverly Hills, CA: Sage.

Dey, Eric L., & Astin, Alexander W. (1993). Statistical alternatives for studying college student retention: A comparative analysis. *Research in Higher Education, 34*, 569-581.

Gibbons, R. D., & Lavigne, J. V. (1998). Emergence of childhood psychiatric disorders: A multivariate probit analysis. *Statistical Medicine, 17*, 2487-2499.

Hagle, Timothy M., Mitchell, Glenn E., II. (1992). Goodness-of-fit measures for probit and logit. *American Journal of Political Science, 36*, 762-784.

Rosenthal, James A., & Rosenthal, Donald H. (1991). Logit and probit models: A juvenile justice program evaluation. *Social Work Research and Abstracts, 27*, 16-21.

6.8.17 Smallest Space Analysis

This is a mapping technique, developed by James C. Lingoes and Louis F. Guttman, that depicts social phenomena in graphic terms. The social objects are graphed according to their proximity on selected social characteristics. Solutions may be applied in spaces with one, two, or three dimensions.

Further Readings on Smallest Space Analysis

Cheng, Man Tsun. (1992). A smallest-space analysis of employment changes in Japan. *Sociological Perspectives, 35,* 593-627.

Foisy, Pierre. (1994). Age-related deficits in intentional memory for spatial location in small-scale space: A meta-analysis and methodological critique. *Canadian Journal on Aging, 13,* 353-367.

Lingoes, James C. (1973). *The Guttman-Lingoes Non-metric program series.* New York: Academic Press.

Morrison, Paul, Burnard, Philip, & Hackett, Paul. (1991). A smallest space analysis of nurses' perceptions of their interpersonal skills. *Counselling Psychology Quarterly, 4, 119-125.*

Poreh, Amir, & Shye, Samuel. (1998). Examination of the global and local features of the Rey Osterrieth Complex Figure using faceted smallest space analysis. *The Clinical Neuropsychologist, 12,* 453-467.

6.8.18 Stochastic Processes

In the study of random processes, one is generally concerned with sequences of random variables, with special reference to their interdependence and limiting behavior. Random processes are governed at least in part by some random mechanism and may be expressed by a corresponding mathematical model.

Examples of random processes in physical nature are provided by the growth of populations such as bacterial colonies. Similarly, stochastic probability processes may be considered as models of human mobility, population growth, and migration.

Further Readings on Stochastic Processes

Balakrishnan, J. D. (1994). Simple additivity of stochastic psychological processes: Tests and measures. *Psychometrika, 59,* 217-240.

Fararo, Thomas J. (1970). Stochastic processes. In Edgar F. Borgatta & George W. Bohrnstedt (Eds.), *Sociological methodology 1969.* San Francisco: Jossey-Bass.

McClelland, James L. (1991). Stochastic interactive processes and the effect of context on perception. *Cognitive Psychology, 23,* 1-44.

McMillan, N. J., Sacks, J., Welch, W. J., & Gao, F. (1999). Analysis of protein activity data by Gaussian stochastic process models. *Journal of Biopharmacy Statistics, 9,* 145-160.

Newell, K. M., Slobounov, S. M., Slobounova, E. S., & Molennar, P. C. (1997). Stochastic processes in postural center-of-pressure profiles. *Experimental Brain Research, 113,* 158-164.

Parzen, Emanuel. (1962). *Stochastic processes.* San Francisco: Holden-Day.

Rumsey, Deborah Jean. (1994). Nonresponse models for social network stochastic processes. *Dissertation Abstracts International, 54,* 4236B.

6.8.19 Structural Equations and Structural Equation Models

Structural equations relate a dependent variable to various structural components believed to have causal influence on the dependent variable. Various *structural equation models* may be developed. Each "dependent" variable must be regarded explicitly as completely determined by some combination of variables in the system. For problems in which complete determination by measured variables does not hold, a residual variable uncorrelated with other determining variables must be introduced.

For example, let us posit a stratification system in which rewards ensure the placement and motivation of persons in various occupational positions within a social structure. Rewards may include prestige, income, leisure, and other amenities. Prestige may be designated dependent variable X_3, and other rewards such as income, leisure, and amenities may be designated as a second dependent variable, X_4. Now suppose we postulate that the rated functional importance of an occupation X_1 and required skill X_2 will deliver appropriate rewards of prestige, income, and leisure, and will draw the aspiring incumbent into an achieved status position.

Using X to stand for the standard score of a given variable, one could express the relationship as a path of influence in which

$$\text{prestige } X_3 = p_{31}X_1 + p_{32}X_2 + p_{3a}X_a \text{ and}$$
$$\text{other rewards } X_4 = p_{41}X_1 + p_{42}X_2 + p_{4b}X_b.$$

These structural equations correspond to multiple regression equations. In these equations, p is a path coefficient (path coefficients are identical to beta coefficients in the standard multiple regression equation), and the subscripts indicate the variable the path coefficient connects. X_a and X_b are included to reflect variables external to prestige (X_3) and income (X_4) as well as measurement errors that may influence the dependent variables. These are sometimes called *residual variables*. This is a "fully" recursive model because all the possible one-way arrows are drawn between four explicit variables: $X_1, X_2, X_3,$ and X_4.

The term *recursive* refers to a system of equations (as above) in which correlations between any pair of variables can be written in terms of paths leading from common antecedent variables. In path diagrams, this is represented by one-way arrows leading from each determining variable to each variable dependent upon it. Nonrecursive systems involve instantaneous reciprocal action of variables; thus, no path of influence can be plotted for such systems.

Further Readings on Structural Equations and Structural Equation Models

Bandalos, Deborah L. (1997). Assessing sources of error in structural equation models: The effects of sample size, reliability and model misspecification. *Structural Equation Modeling, 4*, 177-192.

De Jonge, Jan, & Schaufeli, Wilmar B. (1998). Job characteristics and employee well-being: A test of Warr's vitamin model in health care workers using structural equation modeling. *Journal of Organizational Behavior, 19*, 387-407.

Fan, Xitao, Thompson, Bruce, & Wang, Lin. (1999). Effects of sample size, estimation methods, and model specification on structural equation modeling fit indexes. *Structural Equation Modeling, 6*, 56-83.

Goldberger, Arthur S., & Duncan, Otis Dudley (Eds.). (1975). *Structural equation models in the social sciences.* New York: Academic Press.

Hui, Chun, Law, Kenneth S., & Chen, Zhen Xiong. (1999). A structural equation model of the effects of negative affectivity, leader-member exchange, and perceived job mobility on in-role and extra-role performance: A Chinese case. *Organizational Behavior and Human Decision Processes, 77*, 3-21.

Seifert, T. L. (1997). Academic goals and emotions: Results of a structural equation model and a cluster analysis. *British Journal of Educational Psychology, 67*, 323-343.

6.9 USING THE COMPUTER IN SOCIAL SCIENCE RESEARCH

The purpose of any data analysis procedure is to condense information contained in a body of data into a form that can be easily comprehended and interpreted. Sometimes this process is used simply to describe a body of empirical data, but it is far more common for the social scientist to use tools to search for meaningful patterns of relationships among sets of variables, that is, as a means to test empirical social theory. In its most simple form, such analysis could appear as a chart or some other visual display of information. The more complex forms, however, require computers to help us complete analysis in a timely and accurate fashion.

Computers are extremely useful for the processing of large quantities of data and reducing data to more manageable and easily understood forms. The need for large-scale processing led directly to the development of the computer, with the earliest applications being military in nature, with business and scientific applications following closely. Such processing of large data sets includes the classification, sorting, storing, retrieval, and analysis of data that have been presented to the computer in a suitable coded form.

Besides being a *data analysis device*, the computer is also used as a *communication device*. Computers can "talk" to other computers, and the ability of a computer to hook into other information storage systems and retrieve information is an extremely valuable asset. In many settings, it is the primary use of computer technology. Computer technology provides access to incredibly wide worlds of information (hence the World Wide Web, or www). Finally, the computer can be used as an *assisstive device*, helping perform otherwise mundane tasks such as word processing and the production of documents.

The trend from maxi- to mini- to microcomputers extends over a 10-year period that began in the mid-1960s and progressed into the mid-1970s. Minis and micros now have processing and storage capabilities greater than most of the commercial computers in use in the mid-1960s. In fact, a personal computer or Macintosh on an office desk has more computing power—by a factor of 100 or more—than the computer used on the Apollo moon missions during the 1960s.

The components and subsystems have not changed functionally; what has changed is that the components operate faster, have become significantly smaller, are better integrated, and are much less expensive. Regardless of these changes, any digital computer is still made up of five basic subsystems or components: the input and output devices, the system unit itself, storage devices, and communications devices. The following sections provide an overview of a modern microcomputer and these five subsystems.

Source

Microsoft computer dictionary (4th ed.). (1999). Redmond, WA: Microsoft Press.

6.9.1 The Modern Personal Computer[1]

The principal commodity of any personal computer is information in the form of data. Those bits of data are acted upon by a series of components including input devices, output devices, a systems unit or "box," storage devices, and communications devices.

Input devices allow the scientist to enter data and send commands to the computer to perform certain types of operations. The computer's keyboard is the most common type of input device; the mouse and other pointing devices are others. Scanners to encode pictures or text for use by the computer are now fairly common. Graphic tablets and voice recognition are slowly catching up.

Output devices allow the user to see the results of the computer's operations. The printer and monitor are the most common output devices. Another is a speaker that allows the user to hear output. Many personal computer users are willing to invest heavily in output devices, and they will get the largest monitor with the best resolution they can afford, because it is the monitor on which their eyes focus for the majority of their workday.

The *systems unit* consists of a "box" that contains all the elements that make a computer what it is. This box contains the central processing unit (CPU), the brains of the computer. The CPU contains the vital operating system and its instructions. All inside the box are the memory chips, silicon-based electronic wonders that hold data and provide the space for the computer to "think" and perform necessary operations. This space is expressed as random access memory (RAM). The more memory the CPU holds and the faster the operating speed, the more efficient a computer will be.

Storage devices, used to store information, can take the form of floppy or hard (also called fixed) disk drives; CD-ROM and DVD-ROM drives are gaining popularity but still are less common than disk drives. These different types of storage devices have different capacities and different uses. For example, the first microcomputers used 5.25" floppy (or flexible) disks that stored up to 360,000 bits of information. These were quickly replaced by 3.5" disks that could store up to 1,440,000 bits. Storage capability has increased dramatically, with capacities for tape drives exceeding 5 billion bits of information (or five gigabytes). Internal hard drives now have capacities reaching 100 gigabytes, and technological advances offer the promise of even greater capacity.

Finally, *communications devices* allow computers (and people, of course) to communicate with one another. The hardware comes in the form of modems (telephone or cable modems, Ethernet cards) that can be internal or external. The devices use telephone lines or cable to transmit information.

6.9.1.1 The System

The term *system* generally refers to the personal computer itself plus all connected peripheral equipment dedicated to its use. For example, a personal computer, a monitor, a dedicated (to that computer) printer, and a modem all combine to make one system. To be effective, all components of the system must function together to meet the needs of the software programs, or applications, that the personal computer executes.

For example, to run some of the large data analysis programs such as SAS and SPSS, a significant amount of internal memory (such as 128 megabytes of RAM, or random access memory) is necessary. To multitask, which means having more than one application open and available for use simultaneously, places great demands on the available memory.

Personal computer systems can assume many different configurations and come in all different price ranges—it is truly a buyer's market, with thousands of companies competing for business both on- and offline.

Before you select a micro computer system, the first step is to define what you want the computer to do. In some cases, the first step is to find the software that you want to use and then look at its requirements. You can find guidance and answers to purchasers' questions at Dave's Guides (www.css.msu.edu/PC-Guide/) or Tips on Buying or Upgrading a Personal Computer Using the Internet (www.buinc.com/pc-net.htm). You'll find just about everything you need to know about buying a computer as well as some terrific technical information about computers in general.

6.9.1.2 The Microprocessor, Chip, or CPU (Central Processing Unit)

A "chip"—a generic name for an integrated circuit (IC)—is a complex assembly of ultraminiature electronic circuits, constructed on a tiny flat square of silicon, a highly refined form of glass introduced in 1971. Packaged in ceramic or plastic, these integrated circuits are wired to metallic legs that can be either soldered in place on a circuit board or plugged into a matching IC socket.

Many types of chips perform the various functions in a microcomputer. Some chips help control the number of colors available and the resolution on a monitor. Memory chips have the sole purpose of "remembering" pieces of information, whereas microprocessor chips contain the instructions necessary to run the computer.

There have been dramatic improvements in the speed at which these chips can process information, with the speed doubling about every 18 months (Moore's Law). The only real constraints on reaching a faster threshold of processing information are the size of the chip and the technical challenge of effectively dissipating the heat that these chips generate when active.

6.9.1.3 Memory

A microcomputer cannot function without memory. Microcomputer memory usually takes the form of different types of chips. The two types of memory chips are read-only memory (ROM) and random-access memory (RAM). ROM chips are stable, and the contents usually do not change. Once data are written to ROM, the data cannot be lost, even if power to the computer is turned off. Programmed by the computer manufacturer, ROM chips typically house the data that execute the central processing unit's instructions and invoke, from disk storage, the software needed to operate the system. These instructions literally tell the computer what to do when the electricity is turned on.

ROM is essential to a personal computer's operation, but most of the memory is RAM. RAM chips are not stable, and data stored in RAM is lost when power to the computer is turned off. It's a temporary place to store information while it is being worked on, much like a vast temporary scratchpad, and as the computer goes about executing programs and performing other necessary tasks. For example, when you highlight and copy a paragraph from one document to another, the text is stored in RAM until you paste it in its destination. The computer stores this data as electrical charges and uses a series of memory locations to create a sequential binary code and then later retrieve that code when the information is needed again.

The binary code used to store data is represented by the digits 1 and 0. It can take as few as eight of these binary digits, or "bits," to create a single character, or "byte." For example, the character "A" is represented in computer memory as 01000001, a sequence of eight bits, or a single byte. The more bits and bytes that a computer can access, the faster it can function and the more efficiently information can be processed.

Memory is measured in units called kilobytes, or K (or k) for short. Each kilobyte of memory can hold 1,024, or 2^8, characters of information. A block of 1,024 kilobytes is called a megabyte, or MB for short. Memory sizes in early personal computers ranged from 16K to 640K, but memory in today's personal computers has expanded greatly, with machines commonly boasting 64 or 128 megabytes of RAM, an incredible increase, but surprisingly enough, sometimes not enough for the demands that users place on the machine.

6.9.1.4 Central Processing Unit (CPU)

The CPU is a specialized chip that is the focal point of the personal computer. The CPU is also referred to as a *microprocessor* or simply as the *processor*. Its job is to interpret and execute software instructions.

CPUs vary in the number of bits they can process at one time, as well as in the length of time the CPU requires to process those bits. A CPU that can process more information faster will provide improved performance.

6.9.1.5 Printer

The printer is an output device that meets a critical need—the generation of a hard (paper) copy of information. No matter how good the documents you create, if they cannot be printed out, it may be impossible to share them with others. A wide variety of printers are available, with prices for these devices steadily decreasing.

6.9.1.6 Monitor

The monitor is the television-like device through which the computer relays information to the operator. Most systems require (and come with) a monitor-specific display adapter or *video board* (also called a graphics card) that converts the digital information provided by the computer to analog information so that it appears as an image on the monitor screen.

Almost every computer system comes with a color monitor these days. The difference between monitors is resolution: The higher the resolution, the more distinct and clear the image on the monitor screen. Resolution is expressed as a measure of how many pixels (picture elements) can be shown on the monitor screen. For example, a low resolution monitor will display 640 (horizontally) by 480 (vertically) pixels on the screen. A high resolution monitor will display 1,280 (horizontally) by 1,024 (vertically) pixels on the screen. Other concerns regarding the quality of a monitor are *dot pitch* (the horizontal distance between pixels on the screen) and *refresh rate* (how quickly a monitor screen refreshes itself, avoiding flickering of the image). A final concern is the screen size: Larger screens are easier on the eyes and allow easier viewing of small parts and details of the image on the screen.

As monitor technology becomes more sophisticated, the huge, deep monitors of today are being replaced with flat panel displays that provide a clearer picture with less distortion and take up perhaps 3 inches of desk space as opposed to 15 to 18 inches.

6.9.1.7 Keyboard

Along with the mouse, the keyboard (with about 100 keys) serves as a primary input device by which the operator enters data into the computer. The keys on modern keyboards are organized in the traditional typewriter configuration, often called a QWERTY keyboard. This arrangement derives its name from the six letter keys in the upper left corner of the keyboard. Other, less common, key arrangements are also available, such as the Dvorak keyboard, which has the most frequently used characters placed toward the middle of the keyboard. Most keyboards also include several additional function keys and numeric keypads similar to those found on adding machines or calculators. For example, most keyboards that come with a Windows-ready system have a "Windows" key, which, when pressed, opens the Start menu.

New keyboards are also being introduced to the marketplace. Addressing significant concerns of ergonomics and the worker-workplace interface, keyboards have been redesigned to be tilted or split down the middle.

6.9.1.8 The Mouse

Almost all modern computers of almost every type, regardless of operating system or size, have some capability of using a mouse. A mouse is so useful because it takes advantage of the fully graphical interface represented by such operating systems as Windows or that on the Macintosh.

Table 6.5   A COMPARISON OF DIFFERENT STORAGE MEDIA

Type	Storage Capacity	Best Use
Floppy disk	360K to 120 MB	Transferring data from one computer to another
Fixed or hard drive	6 GB to 40 GB	Long-term storage of data
Removable storage	100 MB to 2 GB	Long-term storage of data and transferring data from one computer to another
Optical drive (CD-ROM and DVD-ROM)	700 MB to 20 GB	Long-term storage of data
Flash RAM	16K to 32K	Used in notebooks and handheld computers to store data

The mouse is a hand-sized device that is rolled across the desktop. The movement of the mouse (and the small ball on its bottom side) corresponds to the movement of the pointer on the monitor screen. Buttons on the mouse can be specially programmed. The mechanical mouse just described is the most popular. The optical mouse (with no moving parts and no problem with dirt and debris) scans the surface on which it is and translates the movements into action.

Other types of tools used to control the mouse pointer on the screen are trackballs (an upside-down mouse, with the ball moved by the operator's fingers), touch pads (where a finger is used to move the position of the cursor), joysticks (used mostly for entertainment), and even pens (attached to the computer through a cable). These diverse input devices provide an especially attractive array for interacting directly with the computer.

6.9.1.9 Disk Drives

Unlike microcomputer system RAM chips that lose all stored data the moment power is switched off, disks provide stable, long-term storage of data files. The disk drive, a device that spins disks to read and write information on them, falls into three categories: floppy, fixed (or hard), and optical (including CD-ROM and DVD).

Floppy disks typically are used for moving software and data between machines. They also can be used strictly for data storage. Common to all floppy disks is a thin plastic disk with a magnetic coating on which the disk drive stores information. Flexible 5.25″ floppy disks were popular for many years, but now 3.5″ hard-cased floppy disks have become standard for most modern microcomputers. In the past, floppy disks could be used only on machines that used the same operating system as the machine on which they were formatted, but some manufacturers are introducing disk drives and software that can read disks formatted by otherwise incompatible systems. Super floppy drives hold up to 1.2 megabytes of data.

Fixed or hard disk drives evolved to meet the need for larger volumes of data storage. A fixed disk drive is a self-contained unit that holds at least one metal "platter" upon which data can be stored. This platter is encased in an airtight chamber to prevent contamination by dust and moisture. Early fixed disk drives offered 5 to 10 megabytes of data storage; today, fixed disk drives can store up to 100 gigabytes.

Optical disk drives, which use laser technology to store data on a removable disk, much like an audio compact disc, are the standard today (but only supplement the floppy and fixed systems). Optical drives combine the portability of a floppy disk with the mass storage capability of a fixed disk drive, with CD-ROMs able to store about 700 MB of information. That is nowhere near the capacity of a DVD-ROM, which can store from 4 to 17 gigabytes (a gigabyte, or GB, is 1,024 MB). Table 6.5 provides a brief overview of different disk types, their capacity, and their uses.

6.9.1.10 Modems

Telephone modems allow digital computer signals to be converted to analog audio tones (and vice versa), enabling two or more computers to exchange data over telephone wires. Modems derive their name from their function: they *mod*ulate and *dem*odulate signals. They can be incorporated into microcomputer systems either as external devices or as internal add-on boards.

The speed at which a telephone modem can send and receive data is referred to as its baud rate. Early modems operated at 300 baud, regarded as painfully slow by today's standards. Today speeds between 28,800 and 56,000 baud are standard.

Relatively new is the use of cable modems, which have a direct connection to the Internet with speeds up to 100 times as fast as telephone modems. These high-speed connections were used almost exclusively by businesses for several years, but with the installation of cable TV in many homes, home computer cable connections are gaining ground. They cost about as much as an additional telephone line. DSL (digital subscriber line) uses established telephone lines and is competitive in speed and cost with a cable modem.

6.9.1.11 Scanners

Another useful input device is the scanner, a flat, boxlike device that "reads" documents and converts them into digital information. An optical flatbed scanner is a light-sensing device that looks like a copy machine. The material to be scanned is placed on the glass window. Specialized software then detects the image on the page and converts it to a graphic image or text that can then be used by some of the more popular software programs.

As with monitors, the higher the resolution with which the scanner can operate, the more is precise the image that results. The accuracy of a scanner, regardless of image, depends almost primarily on the type of software used to scan the material. Even with the best optical character recognition software, an accuracy rate of 99% means that for a 10-page document with 2,500 words, there are likely to be 250 character errors, so that the document still requires a careful proofreading by the creator.

Note

1. Sections 6.9.1 through 6.9.11 are based heavily on Eric J. Schlene (1990), "Inside a Microcomputer," *University Computing Times* (September-October), pp. 14-17; published by the Wrubel Computing Center, Indiana University, Bloomington, IN 47405. Adapted with permission. Material has been updated for use in this handbook.

6.9.1.12 Operating Systems

The default operating system (or OS) is Windows, which is now available in several different versions. Although the Microsoft Corporation has worked for years to make Windows the default (available on 90% of new computers), other systems also are popular.

The Macintosh OS (now in version Mac OS X) has engendered extraordinary loyalty, perhaps for its ease of use and rarity of system crashes. Unfortunately, the Apple Corporation (the manufacturers of the Mac OS) elected not to license the Mac OX system, thereby preventing competition among companies for Mac clones. Licensing was the strategy that Bill Gates chose for Microsoft (among some serious controversy), and the success of Microsoft is evidence that the strategy worked well.

Table 6.6	COMMON NETWORK ELEMENTS

Network Element	What It Does
Servers	Provide shared resources to clients (network users)
Clients	Users of the network
Media	The type of connection between computers on the network, such as cables
Shared data	Files that are provided by servers across the entire network and are available to all clients
Resources	Files, printers, or other items to be used by clients

Finally, the Linux operating system is an open source platform (the code for which is available for anyone to examine and enhance) that has become increasingly popular. It is easy to use (but not to install), is free, and is designed to be relatively immune to system crash problems. With increasing frequency, the various models of Linux now come with interfaces that resemble Windows.

6.9.1.13 Networks

About a decade ago, the personal computer used by the researcher was a stand-alone device, not connected to any other computers. Today, with the Internet and electronic mail as popular research tools, networks have become increasingly important. A *network* is simply a collection of computers or peripheral devices (such as printers) that are connected to one another, with software applications and data documents readily shared. The need for networks arose out of the need to share information in a timely and efficient fashion. The concept of sharing resources is called *networking*. The largest network in the world is the Internet; it is a network of networks.

Most networks, regardless of the type of network and how they are used, operate using a server (which distributes data) and clients (those locations that receive and use that data). All networks have certain components, functions, and features in common, as shown in Table 6.6.

On any network, each computer or peripheral device has its own unique address (so it can be found). These addresses come in two forms: a numeric address, known as the IP (or Internet Protocol) address, and a name. The IP address is a set of four numbers separated by periods, such as 24.124.51.31, which has a corresponding name of njs@falcon.cc.ukans.edu. These addresses are organized as a type of hierarchy. For example,

- njs represents the specific user
- falcon represents the computer in which the user files are stored and transferred
- cc represents the computer center
- ukans represents the University of Kansas
- edu represents an educational institution

Further Reading on Computer Networks

Rice, Ronald E. (1994). Network analysis and computer-mediated communication systems. In Stanley Wasserman & Joseph Galaskiewicz (Eds.), *Advances in social network analysis: Research in the social and behavioral sciences* (pp. 167-203). Thousand Oaks, CA: Sage.

6.9.1.14 Local Area Networks

Initially, networks were small, with only a few computers connected to one another. The available technology limited the size of the network, in terms of both the number of computers connected and the physical distance that could be covered by the network. For example, only 20 years ago, the most popular method of networking computers allowed for only 30 users. This is fine for a small group of people working together, but that limitation hampered the networking of buildings on a school campus or of institutions with operations around the world.

This limited type of network is known as a LAN, or local area network. The wide area network or WAN was developed in response to the limits that LANs imposed and the increasing needs of most growing institutions. With a WAN, individuals separated by thousands of miles can stay connected through signals transmitted via telephone lines, cable, and satellite.

Further Readings on Computers

Bigelow, Stephen J. (1998). *Bigelow's build your own PC pocket guide* (Bigelow's Pocket Reference Series). New York: McGraw-Hill.

Biow, Lisa. (1998). *How to use computers: Visually and in full color.* Indianapolis, IN: Sams.

Biow, Lisa, & Temple, Bob. (2001). *How to use computers* (5th ed., Betsy Brown & Jon Steever, Eds.). Indianapolis, IN: Sams.

Chen, A. Y., & Looi, C. K. (1999). Teaching, learning and inquiry strategies using computer technology. *Journal of Computer Assisted Learning, 15,* 162-172.

Editors of *Consumer Guide.* (1999). *Computer buying guide: Rating the best computers, peripherals & software.* Skokie, IL: Publications International.

> This title has been published annually since 1984.

Garson, G. David, & Nagel, Stuart S. (Eds.). *Advances in social science and computers: A research annual* (Vol. 4). Greenwich, CT: JAI.

> Earlier volumes in this series were published in 1989, 1991, and 1993.

Maran, Ruth. (1998). *Computers simplified* (4th ed.). Foster City, CA: IDG Books.

Minasi, Mark. (2001). *The complete PC upgrade & maintenance guide* (12th ed.). San Francisco: Sybex.

Mishra, S. K., & Binwal, J. C. (1992). *Computer in social science research.* Columbia, MO: South Asia Books.

Norman, Donald A. (1999). *Invisible computer: Why good products can fail, the personal computer is so complex, and information appliances are the solution.* Cambridge, MA: MIT Press.

O'Donnell, Bob. (1999). *Personal computer secrets.* Foster City, CA: IDG Books Worldwide.

Russell, Deborah, & Gangemi, G. T., Sr. (1991). *Computer security basics.* Sebastopol, CA: O'Reilly and Associates.

Schoning, U., & Pruim, R. (1998). *Gems of theoretical computer science.* New York: Springer-Verlag.

Steinberg, Esther R. (1991). *Computer-assisted instruction: A synthesis of theory, practice, and technology.* Hillsdale, NJ: Erlbaum.

Stephens, Robert, with Burg, Dale Reeves. (1999). *The geek squad guide to solving any computer glitch: The technophobe's guide to troubleshooting, equipment, installation, maintenance, and saving your data in almost any personal computing crisis.* New York: Simon & Schuster.

> Illustrated by Steve Mark and with poetry by Martha Rose Reeves.

Stigliani, Joan. (1995). *The computer user's survival guide.* Sebastopol, CA: O'Reilly & Associates.

Tanenbaum, Andrew S. (1996). *Computer networks* (3rd ed.). Upper Saddle River, NJ: Prentice Hall.

White, Ron. (1998). *How computers work* (4th ed.). Indianapolis, IN: Que.

> Includes interactive CD-ROM. Illustrated by Timothy Edward Downs, Sarah Ishida, and Stephen Adams.

White, Ron. (1999). *How computers work, millennium edition.* Indianapolis, IN: Macmillan Computer Publishing.

6.10 SOFTWARE APPLICATIONS FOR THE COMPUTER

The term *software* refers to the detailed instructions or programs that tell a computer what to do. What follows is a brief review of some of the programs available to social and behavior scientists for data analysis. Be sure to see the review of programs used to analyze qualitative data in Part 4, especially Part 4.9.

6.10.1 Selecting the Perfect Statistics Software

No matter what statistics program is used, it needs to meet certain criteria. What follows is a general guide to selecting data analysis software.

1. Whether the software program is expensive (like SYSTAT) or not (like Ecstatic), be sure you try it out before you buy it. Almost every one of the programs listed below has a demo that you can download, and in some cases you can even ask the company to send you a demo version on disk or CD. These versions are often fully featured and last for up to 30 days, giving you plenty of time to try before you buy.

2. Buying directly from the manufacturer might be the most expensive way to go. University bookstores usually offer a discount, and a mail order company might offer a better price.

3. Many of the vendors who produce statistical analysis software offer several versions, including a commercial version and an academic version. They usually are identical or close to it but differ (sometimes dramatically) in price. Before you choose the academic version, be sure that it is the same as the fully featured commercial version. The academic version is often less expensive, with the company offering a low price in the hope that it can get and retain new customers.

4. It's hard to know exactly what you'll need before you get started. Some packages come in modules, and you don't have to buy all of them to get the tools you need for your purposes. Read the company's brochures and call to ask questions.

5. "Shareware" is another option, with plenty of programs available. Shareware is a method of distributing software in which users pay for it only if they like it. The prices are almost always very reasonable, and often the shareware is better than the commercial product. If you do pay, you help ensure that the clever author will continue efforts to deliver new versions that are even better than the one you have.

6. Don't buy any software that does not offer telephone technical support or, at the least, some type of e-mail contact.

7. Almost all the big stats packages do the same things—the difference is in the way that they do them. For example, SPSS, MiniTab, and JMP all do a nice job of analyzing data and are acceptable. It's the little things that might make a difference. For example, MiniTab allows you to have more than one file open at once, but SPSS does not.

8. Make sure you have the hardware to run the program you want to use. For example, most software is not limited by the number of cases and variables you want to analyze. The limit instead usually is the size of your hard drive, which you'll use to store the data files. Be sure you have the hardware you need to run a program before you download the demo.

Further Readings on Computer Software

Bernard, Coulange, & Craig, I. (1997). *Software reuse.* New York: Springer-Verlag.

Constantine, Larry L., & Lockwood, Lucy A. (1999). *Software for use: A practical guide to the models and methods of usage-centered design.* Reading, MA: Addison-Wesley.

Hamilton, Marc. (1999). *Software development: Building reliable systems.* Upper Saddle River, NJ: Prentice Hall.

Jacobson, Ivar, Booch, Grady, & Rumbaugh, James. (1999). *The unified software development process* (Addison-Wesley Object Technology Series). Reading, MA: Addison-Wesley.

Kaner, Cem, Nguyen, Hung Quoc, & Falk, Jack. (1999). *Testing computer software.* New York: John Wiley & Sons.

Maguire, Steve, McCarthy, Jim, & McConnell, Steve. (1998). *Software engineering classics: Vol. 3. Software project survival guide/debugging the development process/dynamics of software development.* Redmond, WA: Microsoft Press.

McConnell, Steve C. (1997). *Software project survival guide.* Redmond, WA: Microsoft Press.

Pressman, Roger S. (1996). *Software engineering: A practitioner's approach.* New York: McGraw-Hill.

Royce, Walker. (1998). *Software project management: A unified framework* (Addison-Wesley Object Technology Series). Reading, MA: Addison-Wesley.

Shigeichi, Moriguchi. (1997). *Software excellence: A total quality management guide.* Portland, OR: Productivity Press.

6.10.2 A Sampling of Data Analysis Programs

More statistical analysis programs are available than you would ever need. What follows is a listing of some of the most popular ones and their outstanding features. Remember that many of these do the same thing. If at all possible, try before you buy to see which programs best suit your needs and desires for particular features. Note that all prices shown are current as of September 2001 and are subject to change.

6.10.2.1 JMP

JMP operates on a Mac and Windows platform and is billed as "statistical discovery software that can help you explore data, fit models, discover patterns, and discover points that don't fit patterns."

One of the product's main selling points is that when graphics are used, discoveries and relationships between data are more likely to be revealed. Using these discoveries, you can more easily understand the results of your work.

One feature of JMP is to present a graph accompanying every statistic so you can always see the results of the analysis both as statistical text and as a graphic. All this is done automatically, without a request from the user.

- **More information:** www.jmpdiscovery.com/
- **Cost:** $895 for the commercial version, with discounts for quantity purchases. The student version, JMPIN, is $395 and is available from Duxbury/Thomson Learning.

6.10.2.2 Minitab

This is one of the first programs that was available for the personal computer. It is now in version 13, which means that it has seen its share of changes over the years in response to users' needs. Some of the outstanding features of this new version are the following.

- One file holds all the work created in a session, including data, results, and graphs.
- More than one worksheet can be open at the same time (an advantage over many other programs).
- Graphs are OLE objects, which means they can be exported easily to other applications.
- *Meet Minitab*, an introductory book for beginners.

Figure 6.7 shows a sample of what Minitab output looks like for a correlation and a regression analysis—neat and nicely organized.

- **More information:** www.minitab.com/
- **Cost:** $995 for the commercial version. The educational version varies in price depending on licensing arrangements and quantity purchased.

6.10.2.3 StatView

This statistical analysis program comes from people who bring you SAS and JMP (the SAS Institute). StatView is a bit less ambitious than the monster SAS system but still very comprehensive. It is designed for both the Mac and Windows operating systems.

StatView works like some other statistical software. It has two types of windows. In the data set window, you enter, manage, and transform data. In the view window, you can analyze, examine results, and use the drawing tools to prepare a presentation. StatView offers several outstanding features, including its spreadsheet-like operation that allows for precise and powerful manipulation of data. For example, formulas are easy to create and are dynamic—when values change in the formula, so do the values in connected cells.

Figure 6.8 shows numerous StatView windows and the spreadsheet-like data entry system. There's also a sample correlation matrix that shows the correlation between the fat content and calories in candy bars.

Other nice features include Mac and Windows compatibility, lots of regression tools, and improved tools for analysis of variance.

- **More information:** www.sas.com/
- **Cost:** $695 for commercial users and $350 for academic users, with quantity discounts applied.

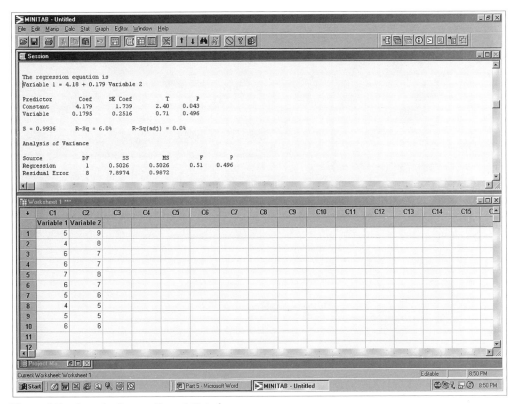

Figure 6.7. Sample Output From Minitab

6.10.2.4 Statistica

StatSoft offers a collection of Statistica products for Windows as well as Statistica for the Mac. Some particularly nice features of this powerful program are the self-prompting dialog boxes (you click OK and Statistica tells you what to enter) and the ability to use macros to automate tasks. A nice bonus at the Web site is an Electronic Statistical Textbook, which you can download in its entirety.

■ **More information:** www.statsoftinc.com/
■ **Cost:** $795 for the basic commercial version and $250 for the basic academic version, which has fewer functions than the commercial version. A more inclusive package adds capabilities for advanced linear and nonlinear models as well as multivariate explanatory models; it sells for $1,585 for the commercial version and $350 for the academic.

6.10.2.5 SPSS: Mac, Windows, MS-DOS, OS/2, UNIX, VMS, and MVS-VM/CMS

SPSS may be the most popular statistical package. It comes with a variety of different modules that cover all aspects of statistical analysis, including both basic and advanced statistics. A version exists for almost every platform.

One of the nicer new features included in version 9 (released in 1999) is that you can easily, with one mouse click, create a graph from any tabled data. Then you can use the Chart Editor to modify what you produced. Also featured is a powerful report writer. Figure 6.9 shows one such graph, created with one right click and selection of the type of graph desired (in this case, it was a line graph).

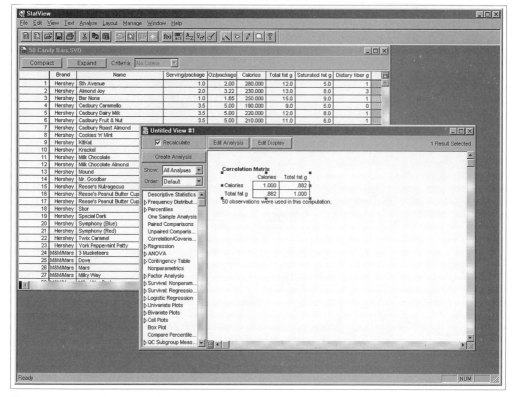

Figure 6.8. Sample Screens From StatView

- **More information:** www.spss.com/Products/SpssProd.html
- **Cost:** $999 for the commercial version and $599 for the academic version

6.10.2.6 SYSTAT

- SYSTAT is produced by the same company that offers SPSS and is just as powerful, but it tends to be used by researchers in the biological and physical sciences rather than the social and behavior sciences, which tend to use SPSS. It's available for more operating systems than most other software packages, including DOS, Windows, OS/2, Mac, and Unix. It supports a strong command language, so analysis can be fine-tuned to users' needs. The beginner can use these features, but they are more appropriate for advanced students or professionals.
- **More information:** www.spss.com/software/science/systat/
- **Cost:** $1,299 for the commercial version and $799 for the academic version.

6.10.2.7 STATISTIX for Windows

STATISTIX is as powerful as the other programs described here but also offers publication-quality custom-titled and legend graphs that can be exported to bitmap, Postscript, and HPGL file formats. This is a big plus for those interested in creating their own publications or reports based on STATISTIX output. Another nice feature is a 330-page manual (real paper, believe it or not). When

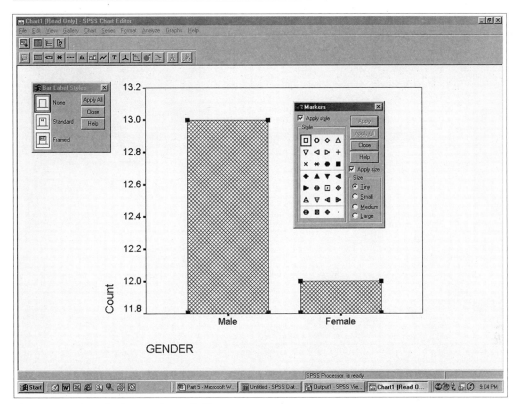

Figure 6.9. Sample Output From SPSS

you call technical support, you talk with the programmers. Figure 6.10 shows some STATISTIX output from a one-tailed *t* test.

- **More information:** www.sigma-research.com/bookshelf/
- **Cost:** $495 for the commercial version. It appears that no academic version is offered.

6.10.2.8 EcStatic

Both the Windows and DOS versions of EcStatic are by far the least expensive of those reviewed here, and you get much more than you pay for in comparison with the huge programs described above. Some of the features it offers are listed below.

Analysis of variance
Breakdown
Convert scores
Correlation
Cross-tabulation and chi-square
Frequency distributions and histograms
Nonparametric statistics
Regression
Scatterplot
Summary statistics

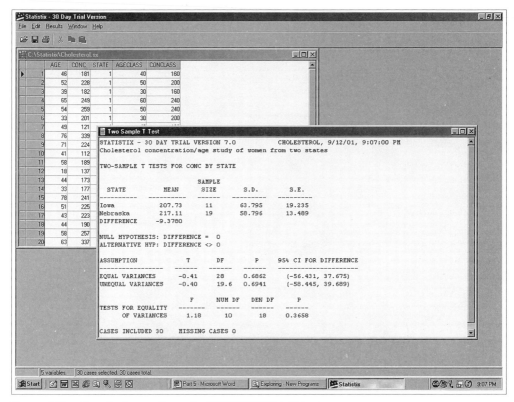

Figure 6.10. Sample Output From the STATISTIX Trial Version

Transformations

t test

■■ **More information:** www.somewareinvt.com/ecstatic.htm
■■ **Cost:** $89.95, with a discount on 10 copies or more ($49.95).

6.11 A GUIDE TO COMPUTER PERIODICALS AND OTHER PUBLICATIONS

The number of computing magazines is overwhelming and continues to grow. Targeted niches now include everything from families to data analysts to air controllers.

The major advantage of these periodicals is that they are far more current than any book can be. It may be advisable to subscribe to one or more to keep up to date in a particular area. Be sure to select a magazine that fits your level of technical understanding. You usually can get the "flavor" of such a publication by going to its Web site and reading sample articles, if not entire issues, online.

As a supplement to periodicals, do not ignore major newspaper coverage of technology. *The Wall Street Journal* and *The Washington Post*, for example, offer regular columns, and *The New York Times* publishes an entire section called Circuits (www.nyt.com) each Thursday. Circuits, in and of itself, resembles a major publication.

Listed on the following pages are some of the more popular computer-related periodicals and publishers.

Adobe Magazine	www.adobe.com/publications/adobemag/
Advisor magazines	www.advisor.com/
Australian Personal Computer	http://apcmag.com/
Boardwatch Magazine	http://boardwatch.internet.com/
Byte Magazine	www.byte.com/
c|net	www.cnet.com/
CADALYST	www.cadonline.com/
CIO	www.cio.com/
Computer Bits	www.computerbits.com/
Computer Currents	www.currents.net/magazine/national/national.html
Computer Dealer News	www.plesman.com/cdn/index.html
Computer Edge	www.computoredge.com/sandiego/
Computer Gaming World	http://cgw.gamespot.com/
Computer News Daily	http://computernewsdaily.com/
Computer Paper	www.tcp.ca/
Computer Post	www.cpost.mb.ca/
Computer Reseller News	www.crn.com
Computer Retail Week	www.crw.com/
Computer Shopper	www.zdnet.com/computershopper/
Computer Times Singapore	www.asia1.com.sg/computertimes/
Computerworld	www.computerworld.com/
Computing Japan	http://cjmag.co.jp/magazine/magazine.html
Crossroads: The ACM Student Magazine	www.acm.org/crossroads/
D-Lib Program	www.dlib.org
Data Communications Magazine	www.data.com/
Data Management Review	www.dmreview.com/
Datamation	www.datamation.com/
Dr. Dobb's Journal	www.ddj.com/
Ebiz (Business Week)	www.ebiz.ebusinessweek.com
EDN Access	www.ednmag.com/
EE Times	www.eetimes.com/
Embedded Systems Programming	www.embedded.com/mag.shtml
Entropy Gradient Reversals	www.rageboy.com/
Family PC	www.zdnet.com/familypc/
Federal Computer Week	www.fcw.com/pubs/fcw/fcwhome.htm
FEED	www.feedmag.com/
First Monday	www.firstmonday.dk
Government Computer Canada	www.govcomp.com/
Government Technology Magazine	www.govtech.net/publications/publications.shtm
Industry Standard	www.thestandard.net/
InfoWorld	www.infoworld.com/
The Institute (IEEE)	www.institute.ieee.org/INST/ti.html
Intelligent Enterprise	www.intelligententerprise.com/
Interactive Week	www.interactiveweek.com
Internet Shopper	www.internet-shopper.com/
Internet Week	www.internetwk.com
Internet World	www.iw.com/
I.T. Web site	http://it.mycareer.com.au/
Java Pro	www.java-pro.com/
JavaWorld	www.javaworld.com/

Linux Journal	www.ssc.com/lj/
Linux Today	www.linuxtoday.com/
MacAddict	www.macaddict.com/
MacCentral	www.maccentral.com/
MacOSRumors	www.macosrumors.com/
MacWeek	www.macweek.com/
Macworld	www.macworld.com/
Maximum PC	www.maximumpc.com/
Microprocessor Report	www.chipanalyst.com/report/mpr.html
Net Guide	www.netguide.com/
Network Computing	www.networkcomputing.com/
Network Magazine	www.networkmagazine.com/
Network World Fusion	www.nwfusion.com
New Media News	www.newmedianews.com/
News.com	news.com/
Oracle Magazine	www.oramag.com/
PC Computing	www.zdnet.com/pccomp/
PC Magazine	www.pcmag.com/
PC Novice & Smart Computing	www.smartcomputing.com/
PC World	www.pcworld.com/
Red Herring	www.redherring.com/
The Register	www.theregister.co.uk/
SCO World: UNIX Business Solutions	www.scoworld.com/
Service News	www.servicenews.com/
Shift	www.shift.com/shiftstd/html/core.asp
SunWorld Online	www.sun.com/sunworldonline/index.html
Tech Web	www.techweb.com/
Technology Review	www.techreview.com/
tele.com	www.teledotcom.com/
Think Leadership (IBM)	www.ibm.com/thinkmag/
TidBITS	www.tidbits.com/
Ugeek	www.geek.com/
Upside	www.upside.com/
User Friendly Online	www.userfriendlyonline.com/
Visual C++ Developers Journal	www.vcdj.com/
WebBusiness Magazine	http://webbusiness.cio.com/
Web Developer	www.webdeveloper.com/
Web Developer's Journal	www.webdevelopersjournal.com/
Web Marketing Today	www.wilsonweb.com/wmt/
Web Reference	www.webreference.com/
Web Review	http://webreview.com/wr/pub
Web Techniques	www.webtechniques.com/
Webserver Online	http://webserver.cpg.com/
Win98 Magazine	www.win98mag.com/
Windows Magazine	www.winmag.com/
Windows NT Magazine	www.winntmag.com/
Wired	www.wired.com/wired/current.html
WWWiz Magazine	http://wwwiz.com/
Yahoo! Internet Life	www.zdnet.com/yil/
ZDNet	www.zdnet.com/

BIBLIOGRAPHY ON STATISTICAL METHODS   **6.12**

Basilevsky, A. (1994). *Statistical factor analysis and related methods: Theory and applications.* New York: John Wiley and Sons.

Bickel, P. J., & Doksum, K. A. (2000). *Mathematical statistics: Basic ideas and selected topics* (2nd ed., Vol. 1). Paramus, NJ: Prentice Hall.

Blossfeld, H., Hamerle, A., & Mayer, K. U. (1989). *Event-history analysis: Statistical theory and application in the social sciences.* Mahwah, NJ: Lawrence Erlbaum.

Chow, S. L. (1996). *Statistical significance: Rationale, validity and unity.* Thousand Oaks, CA: Sage.

Cohen, J., & Cohen, P. (1984). *Applied multiple regression/correlation analysis for the behavioral sciences* (2nd ed.). Mahwah, NJ: Lawrence Erlbaum.

Diekhoff, G. M. (1992). *Statistics for the social and behavioral sciences: Univariate, bivariate, and multivariate.* Madison, WI: Brown and Benchmark.

Everitt, B. S., Landau, S., & Leese, M. (2001). *Cluster analysis* (4th ed.). New York: Oxford University Press.

Gelman, A., Carlin, J. B., Stern, H. S., & Rubin, D. B. (1995). *Bayesian data analysis.* Boca Raton, FL: CRC Press.

Glenn, N. D. (1977). *Cohort analysis.* Beverly Hills, CA: Sage.

Gorsuch, R. L. (1983). *Factor analysis.* Mahwah, NJ: Lawrence Erlbaum.

Harman, H. H. (1976). *Modern factor analysis.* Chicago: University of Chicago Press.

Keppel, G., & Zedeck, S. (1989). *Data analysis for research designs: Analysis-of-variance and multiple regression/correlation approaches.* New York: W. H. Freeman and Company.

Kim, J., & Mueller, C. W. (1979). *Factor analysis: Statistical methods and practical issues.* Beverly Hills, CA: Sage.

Knoke, D., & Burke, P. J. (1980). *Log-linear models.* Beverly Hills, CA: Sage.

Kuebler, R. R., & Smith, H. (1976). *Statistics: A beginning.* New York: John Wiley and Sons.

Liebetrau, A. M. (1983). *Measures of association.* Beverly Hills, CA: Sage.

Lockyer, K. G. (1969). *Introduction to critical path analysis* (3rd ed.). London: Pitman.

Mendenhall, W. (1993). *Beginning statistics A to Z.* Belmont, CA: Wadsworth.

Moore, D. S. (1999). *The basic practice of statistics* (2nd ed.). New York: W. H. Freeman and Company.

Retherford, R. D., & Choe, M. K. (1993). *Statistical models for causal analysis.* New York: John Wiley and Sons.

Revuz, D. (1984). *Markov chains* (Rev. ed.). New York: North-Holland.

Salkind, N. J. (2000). *Statistics for those who (think they) hate statistics.* Thousand Oaks, CA: Sage.

Shipley, B. (2000). *Cause and correlation in biology: A user's guide to path analysis, structural equations and causal inference.* New York: Cambridge University Press.

Sprinthall, R. C. (1999). *Basic statistical analysis* (6th ed.). Boston: Allyn & Bacon.

Tabachnich, B. G., & Fidell, L.S. (2000). *Using multivariate statistics* (4th ed.). Boston: Allyn & Bacon.

Thompson, B. (1985). *Canonical correlation analysis: Uses and interpretation.* Beverly Hills, CA: Sage.

6.13 CONTENTS OF SOCIOLOGICAL METHODOLOGY, 1994 THROUGH 2000

Sociological Methodology is an official publication of the American Sociological Association. It is a series of books published annually that began in 1969 and was designed to keep social scientists abreast of methodological changes and innovations in all areas of sociological inquiry. Because of its importance in defining the cutting edge of the discipline, the contents are reproduced here to provide a ready reference for the researcher. All volumes are published by

Blackwell Publishers, Inc.
350 Main Street
Malden, MA 02148
United States
Tel.: +1-781-388-8200; Fax: +1-781-388-8210
E-mail: subscrip@blackwellpub.com

1994: Peter V. Marsden, Ed.

1. "Updating Occupational Prestige and Socioeconomic Scores: How the New Measures Measure Up" by Keiko Nakao and Judith Treas
2. "Survey Pretesting: Do Different Methods Produce Different Results?" by Stanley Presse and Johnny Blair
3. "From Words to Numbers: A Set Theory Framework for the Collection, Organization, and Analysis of Narrative Data" by Roberto Franzosi
4. "Identification of Simple Measurement Models With Multiple Latent Variables and Correlated Errors" by Robert M. O'Brien
5. "Measuring Local Association: An Introduction to the Correlation Curve" by Stephen James Blyth
6. "Logit Models for Sets of Ranked Items" by Paul D. Allison and Nicholas A. Christakis
7. "Analysis of Cross-Classifications of Counts Using Models for Marginal Distributions: An Application to Trends in Attitudes on Legalized Abortion" by Mark P. Becker
8. "Some Accelerated Failure-Time Regression Models Derived From Diffusion Process Models: An Application to a Network Diffusion Analysis" by Kazuo Yamaguchi
9. "Log-Multiplicative Models for Discrete-Time, Discrete-Covariate Event-History Data" by Yu Xie
10. "Discrete-Time Bivariate Hazards With Unobserved Heterogeneity: A Partially Observed Contingency Table Approach" by Robert D. Mare

1995: Peter V. Marsden, Ed.

1. "Discovering Theory Dynamics by Computer Simulation: Experiments on State Legitimacy and Imperialist Capitalism" by Robert A. Hanneman, Randall Collins, and Gabriele Mordt
2. "On the Reliability of Unitizing Continuous Data" by Klaus Krippendorff
3. "Item Nonresponse in Organizational Surveys" by Donald Tomaskovic-Devey, Jeffrey Leiter, and Shealy Thompson
4. "Bayesian Model Selection in Social Research" by Adrian E. Raftery
5. "Discussion: Avoiding Model Selection in Bayesian Social Research" by Andrew Gelman and Donald B. Rubin
6. "Better Rules for Better Decisions" by Robert M. Hauser

7. "Rejoinder: Model Selection Is Unavoidable in Social Research" by Adrian E. Raftery
8. "A New Index of Structure for the Analysis of Models for Mobility Tables and Other Cross-Classifications" by Clifford C. Clogg, Tamás Rudas, and Liwen Xi
9. "Structural Equation Models That Are Nonlinear in Latent Variables: A Least-Squares Estimator" by Kenneth A. Bollen
10. "Exact Variance of Indirect Effects in Recursive Linear Models" by Paul D. Allison
11. "Complex Sample Data in Structural Equation Modeling" by Bengt O. Muthén and Albert Satorra
12. "Models for Interdependent Event-History Data: Specification and Estimation" by Trond Petersen
13. "Specification and Estimation of Heterogeneous Diffusion Models" by Henrich R. Greve, David Strang, and Nancy Brandon Tuma
14. "Statistical Inference for Apparent Populations" by Richard A. Berk, Bruce Western, and Robert E. Weiss
15. "Discussion: Apparent and Nonapparent Significance Tests" by Kenneth A. Bollen
16. "Will Bayesian Inference Help? A Skeptical View" by Glenn Firebaugh
17. "Bayes, Neyman, and Calibration" by Donald B. Rubin
18. "Reply to Bollen, Firebaugh, and Rubin" by Richard A. Berk, Bruce Western, and Robert E. Weiss

1996: Adrian E. Raftery, Ed.

1. "Clifford Collier Clogg, 1949-1995: A Tribute to His Life and Work" by Michael E. Sobel
2. "Some Log-Linear Fixed-Effect Latent-Trait Markov-Chain Models: A Dynamic Analysis of Personal Efficacy Under the Influence of Divorce/Widowhood" by Kazuo Yamaguchi
3. "Multiple Group Association Models With Latent Variables: An Analysis of Secular Trends in Abortion Attitudes, 1972-1988" by Allan L. McCutcheon
4. "Negative Multinomial Regression Models for Clustered Event Counts" by Guang Guo
5. "Characterizing Latent Structure: Factor Analytic and Grade of Membership Models" by Margaret Mooney Marini, Xiaoli Li, and Pi-Ling Fan
6. "Vague Theory and Model Uncertainty in Macrosociology" by Bruce Western
7. "The Structure of Social Exchange Networks: A Game-Theoretic Reformulation of Blau's Model" by James D. Montgomery

1997: Adrian E. Raftery, Ed.

Formal Analysis of Qualitative Data: A Symposium

1. "The Niche Hikers Guide to Population Ecology: A Logical Reconstruction of Organization Ecologies Niche Theory" by Gábor Péli
2. "Sequence Comparison via Alignment and Gibbs Sampling: A Formal Analysis of the Emergence of the Modern Sociological Article" by Andrew Abbott and Emily Barman
3. "A Generic Semantic Grammar for Quantitative Text Analysis: Applications to East and West Berlin Radio News Content From 1979" by Carl W. Roberts

Socioeconomic Indices

4. "Socioeconomic Indexes for Occupations: A Review, Update, and Critique" by Robert M. Hauser and John Robert Warren
5. "A Dual-Source Indicator of Consumer Confidence" by Gordon G. Bechtel

Estimating Treatment Effects

6. "Matching With Multiple Controls to Estimate Treatment Effects in Observational Studies" by Herbert L. Smith

Event-History Analysis

7. "The Neighborhood History Calendar: A Data Collection Method Designed for Dynamic Multilevel Modeling" by William G. Axinn, Jennifer S. Barber, and Dirgha J. Ghimire
8. "Adjusting for Attrition in Event-History Analysis" by Daniel H. Hill
9. "Dynamic Discrete-Time Duration Models: Estimation via Markov Chain Monte Carlo" by Ludwig Fahrmeir and Leonhard Knorr-Held

Longitudinal and Multilevel Modeling

10. "Latent Variable Modeling of Longitudinal and Multilevel Data" by Bengt Muthén

1998: Adrian E. Raftery, Ed.

Linking Qualitative and Quantitative Methods

1. "Linking Life Histories and Mental Health: A Person-Centered Strategy" by Burton Singer, Carol D. Ryff, Deborah Carr, and William J. Magee

Comparing Distributions

2. "Relative Distribution Methods" by Mark S. Handcock and Martina Morris

Estimating Treatment Effects

3. "Bounding Disagreements About Treatment Effects: A Case Study of Sentencing and Recidivism" by Charles F. Manski and Daniel S. Nagin

Categorical Data Analysis

4. "Estimating Two-Sided Logit Models" by John Allen Logan
5. "Statistical Methods and Graphical Displays for Analyzing How the Association Between Two Qualitative Variables Differs Among Countries, Among Groups, and Over Time: A Modified Regression-Type Approach" by Leo A. Goodman and Michael Hout
6. "Some Log-Linear and Log-Nonlinear Models for Ordinal Scales With Midpoints, With an Application to Public Opinion Data" by Michael E. Sobel
7. "Latent Class Marginal Models for Cross-Classifications of Counts" by Mark P. Becker and Ilsoon Yang

Event History Analysis

8. "Mover-Stayer Models for Analyzing Event Nonoccurrence and Event Timing With Time-Dependent Covariates: An Application to an Analysis of Remarriage" by Kazuo Yamaguchi

Structural Equation Models

9. "Structural Equation Modeling With Robust Covariances" by Ke-Hai Yuan and Peter M. Bentler

1999: *Michael E. Sobel and Mark P. Becker, Eds.*

1. "Ecometrics: Toward a Science of Assessing Ecological Settings, With Application to the Systematic Social Observation of Neighborhoods" by Stephen W. Raudenbush and Robert J. Sampson
2. "Simulating the Micro-Macro Link: New Approaches to an Old Problem and an Application to Military Coups" by Nicole J. Saam
3. "A Goodness-of-Fit Test for the Latent Class Model When Expected Frequencies Are Small" by Mark Reiser and Yiching Lin
4. "Algebraic Representations of Beliefs and Attitudes: Partial Order Models for Item Responses" by John Levi Martin and James A. Wiley
5. "On a Relation Between Joint Correspondence Analysis and Latent Class Analysis" by Peter G. M. van der Heijden, Zvi Gilula, and L. Andries van der Ark
6. "A General Class of Nonparametric Models for Ordinal Categorical Data" by Jeroen K. Vermunt
7. "Testing Transitivity in Digraphs" by Martin Karlberg
8. "Logit Models for Affiliation Networks" by John Skvoretz and Katherine Faust
9. "A New Model for Information Diffusion in Heterogeneous Social Networks" by Vincent Buskens and Kazuo Yamaguchi

2000: *Michael E. Sobel and Mark P. Becker, Eds.*

1. "Regression Analysis of Multivariate Binary Response Variables Using Rasch-Type Models and Finite-Mixture Models" by Gerhard Arminger, Clifford C. Clogg, and Tzuwei Cheng
2. "Random Effects Modeling of Categorical Response Data" by Alan Agresti, James Booth, James P. Hobert, and Brian Caffo
3. "Log-Multiplicative Association Models as Latent Variable Models for Nominal and/or Ordinal Data" by Carolyn J. Anderson and Jeroen K. Vermunt
4. "Algebraic Representations of Beliefs and Attitudes II: Microbelief Models for Dichotomous Belief Data" by John Levi Martin and James A. Wiley
5. "Three Likelihood-Based Methods for Mean and Covariance Structure Analysis With Nonnormal Missing Data" by Ke-Hai Yuan and Peter M. Bentler
6. "Discrete-Time Multilevel Hazard Analysis" by Jennifer S. Barber, Susan Murphy, William G. Axinn, and Jerry Maples
7. "Systemic Patterns of Zero Exposures in Event-History Analysis" by Jan M. Hoem
8. "The Self as a Fuzzy Set of Roles, Role Theory as a Fuzzy System" by James D. Montgomery

2001: *Michael E. Sobel and Mark P. Becker, Eds.*

1. "Statistics in Sociology, 1950-2000: A Selective Review" by Adrian E. Raftery
2. "A Framework for the Study of Individual Behavior and Social Interactions" by Steven N. Durlauf
3. "Analysis of Categorical Response Profiles by Informative Summaries" by Shelby J. Haberman and Zvi Gilula
4. "Statistical Methods and Graphical Displays for Analyzing How the Association Between Two Qualitative Variables Differs Among Countries, Among Groups, or Over Time: Part II. Some Exploratory Techniques, Simple Models, and Simple Examples" by Leo A. Goodman and Michael Hout
5. "Latent Class Factor and Cluster Models, Bi-Plots and Related Graphical Displays" by Jay Magidson and Jeroen K. Vermunt

6. "Covariance Models for Latent Structure in Longitudinal Data" by Marc A. Scott and Mark S. Handcock

7. "The Cohesiveness of Blocks in Social Networks: Connectivity and Conditional Density" by Douglas White and Frank Harary

8. "The Statistical Evaluation of Social Network Dynamics" by Tom A. B. Snijders

PART 7

ASSESSING SOCIAL VARIABLES: SCALES AND INDEXES

There are literally thousands of scales and indexes to measure social variables. Social scientists have often elected to construct new measures even when scales of high reliability and validity have been available. This practice is wasteful of time, energy, and money. In addition, it makes replication and accumulation of research findings difficult if not impossible. The selection of scales to be included in this handbook was based on such criteria as validity, reliability, and utility. The variables most commonly used in social measurement were studied, and measures for them were sought. Those with the highest reliability and validity were selected. It is hoped that his handbook will encourage greater use of these scales or stimulate the search for better ones.

In general, three groups of variable factors need to be observed and measured in any research design that seeks to test a basic hypothesis or social relationship. First is the *dependent variable*, the effect we wish to observe and describe. Second is the *independent variable* (or variables) designated as the causal factor(s). Sometimes the independent variable(s) must be broken down into component parts, which operate more or less as a unit pattern. Third are *intervening* or other variables that must be controlled lest they obscure the relationship we wish to measure by use of experimental design.

Scales have been constructed in substantial numbers to facilitate quantitative description of various factors in human relations. Three areas of social measurement can be identified.

1. *Psychometric and social psychological scales.* These include intelligence scales, personality tests and scales, and attitude tests and scales. Examples of such scales are the Minnesota Multiphasic Personality Inventory and attitude scales to measure leisure satisfaction, community attitudes, achievement orientation, and alienation.

2. *Demographic scales.* These scales measure the forms or results of social behavior in large units such as the community, state, or nation. Examples include community rating scales, scales of community service activity and citizen political activity, and a community solidarity index.

3. *Sociometric scales.* These are used to measure social structures and processes. Examples include sociometric tests to measure informal friendship constellations and measurements of such concepts as social participation, social distance, and group cohesiveness. Other scales assess marital adjustment and group dimensions.

Keep in mind increases in the number of qualitative and, more recently, quantitative assessment tools (see Part 3). If you do not find a scale that fits your particular research interest, consult the articles and measures used in the *Annual Review of Sociology* (section 5.2.9) and *American Sociological Review* (section 5.2.10), as well as other periodicals such as *Social Psychology Quarterly*, the *American Journal of Sociology*, and empirical journals of the kind listed in Table 5.3, this volume.

Scale construction yields four types of scales, which reflect the different levels of measurement first identified by experimental psychologist S. S. Stevens: the *nominal* scale, consisting simply of distinguishable categories with no implication of more or less of an item being measured; the *ordinal* scale, on which positions can be identified in a rank order but with no implication as to the distance between positions; the *interval* scale, which has equal distance between any two adjacent positions on the continuum; and the *ratio* scale, which has not only equal intervals but also an absolute zero (implying the absence of a trait or characteristic). (See Table 6.1 for a review of these types of scales.)

Ideally, every scale would be a ratio scale, but with the possible exception of the procedures for measuring certain psychophysical phenomena, none of the measurement techniques currently used fits the requirements for a ratio scale. The nominal scale permits neither rank ordering nor a metric scale. It is so elemental as a classification scheme that such scales generally are regarded as first approximations toward the quantification of a social variable, with variables being measured as either present or absent. The result is that ordinal and interval scales are the types most frequently used. Considerable disagreement exists concerning whether an ordinal or an interval scale provides the most appropriate model for social data. Some writers have taken the view that few, if any, of the techniques now in use provide data that can be considered appropriate to more than ordinal scales. Others believe that various types of scales may properly be treated as conforming to the definition of interval scales. Still others have taken the position that although most of the measurements used do not go beyond ordinal scales, little harm is done in applying statistics to them that are appropriate for use with interval scales.

The result is that statistics appropriate to interval scales continue to be widely used in the analysis of social data, whether the assumptions of interval scaling are met or not. There is also an increasing use of statistics that are specifically appropriate to ordinal scales. The statistical tools included in Part 4 of this volume are for the use of ordinal and interval scales.

The selection of a good scale involves weighing a number of criteria. Frequency of use is one useful criterion for choice of a scale. Using a frequently used scale leads to maximizing accumulated research in the test of hypotheses—the current study will build on a larger body of accumulated research. A search of the literature for key words identifying the scale will result in a rough approximation of frequency of use.

Frequency is by far not the only determinant of fitness, or even the most important. The most important single consideration is validity; that is, does the scale measure what it purports to measure? How much and what kind of evidence is available, and does the scale fit the problem selected for study?

Other considerations include reliability (which is implied by the validity of a scale), precision, simplicity, and ease of administration. Recent years have witnessed considerable emphasis on unidimensionality. The Guttman technique enables the researcher to identify the construct scales of a single dimension. This may be important in increasing the precision and predictability of a given variable; however, two qualifications must be kept in mind. Such a scale may not be the most effective either for measuring attitudes toward complex objects or for making predictions about behavior in relation to such objects. It must also be remembered that a given scale may be unidimensional for one group of individuals but not for another.

The scales and assessment tools assembled in this part of the handbook include those constructed by arbitrary or judgmental ranking, by item analysis techniques, by Thurstone's equal-appearing interval method, by Guttman's technique of scale analysis, and by factor analysis. Regardless of the method used in construction, what the researcher seeks is the scale that best fits his or her problem, has the highest reliability and validity, is precise, and is relatively easy to apply.[1] As the researcher selects a scale for use, he or she must be aware of the statistical techniques that subsequently will be applied. Generally, nonparametric statistics will be used for ordinal scales and parametric statistics for interval scales and for those ordinal scales that do not deviate too far from the assumptions of randomness and normal distribution.

Note

1. For excellent discussions of these criteria, see Paul F. Lazarsfeld and Morris Rosenberg, *The Language of Social Research* (Glencoe, IL: Free Press, 1955), and Hans Zeisel, *Say It With Figures* (5th ed.) (New York: Harper, 1968), pp. 76-102. See also George W. Bohrnstedt, "A Quick Method for Determining the Reliability and Validity of Multiple-Item Scales," *American Sociological Review*, 34 (1969), 542-548.

7.1.1 Books

Bishop, Lloyd, & Lester, Paula E. (Eds.). (1993). *Instrumentation in education: An anthology.* New York: Garland.

Davis, Clive M. (1998). *Handbook of sexuality-related measures.* Thousand Oaks, CA: Sage.

Goldman, Bert Arthur, Mitchell, David F., & Egelson, Paula. (1997). *Directory of unpublished experimental measures: 1990-1995* (Vol. 7). Washington, DC: American Psychological Association.

Johnson, Orval G. (1976). *Tests and measurements in child development: Handbook II* (2 vols.). San Francisco: Jossey-Bass.

Maddox, Taddy. (1997). *Tests: A comprehensive reference for assessments in psychology, education, and business* (4th ed.). Austin, TX: Pro-Ed.

Murphy, Linda, Plake, Barbara S., & Impara, James C. (Ed.). (1995). *Tests in print V: An index to tests, test reviews, and the literature on specific tests.* Lincoln: Buros Institute of Mental Measurements, University of Nebraska at Lincoln.

Robinson, John P., Shaver, Phillip R., & Wrightsman, Lawrence S. (Eds.). (1991). *Measures of personality and social psychological attitudes.* New York: Academic Press.

Robinson, John P., Shaver, Phillip R., & Wrightsman, Lawrence S. (Eds.). (1998). *Measures of political attitudes.* New York: Academic Press.

Touliatos, John, Perlmutter, Barry F., & Straus, Murray A. (Eds.). (2001). *Handbook of family measurement techniques.* Thousand Oaks, CA: Sage.

7.1.2 Publishers and Test Providers

American Guidance Service
4201 Woodland Road
Circle Pines, MN 55014-1796
800-328-2560
www.agsnet.com

Association of Test Publishers
1201 Pennsylvania Avenue
Suite 300
Washington, DC 20004
202-857-8444
www.testpublishers.org

Consulting Psychologists Press, Inc.
Davies-Black Publishing
3803 East Bayshore Road
P.O. Box 10096
Palo Alto, CA 94303
650-969-8901
www.cpp-db.com

ETS Test Collection
Educational Testing Service
Princeton, NJ 08541
609-734-5686
www.ets.org

Health and Psychosocial Instruments (HAPI)
Behavior Measurement Database Services
P.O. Box 110287
Pittsburgh, PA 15232-0787
412-687-6850

MultiHealth Systems
P.O. Box 950
North Tonawanda, NY 14120-0950
800-456-3003

NCS Pearson
Operations Center
Atrium E 80, Route 4
Paramus, NJ 07652-2622
201-291-0233
www.ncs.com

Psychological Assessment Resources, Inc.
16204 N. Florida Ave.
Lutz, FL 33549
813-968-3003
www.parinc.com

The Psychological Corporation
19500 Bulverde
San Antonio, TX 78259
800-872-1726
www.psychcorp.com

PsycINFO Database
American Psychological Association
750 First Street
Washington, DC 20002
202-336-5500
www.apa.org/psycinfo/

Riverside Publishing
425 Spring Lake Drive
Itasca, IL 60143-9921
800-323-9540

SCALES ASSESSING SOCIAL STATUS 7.2

Social class or status is one of the most important variables in social research. The socioeconomic position of a person affects his or opportunities for education, income, occupation, marriage, health, and friends, and it even can affect life expectancy. The variable has proved difficult to measure in a pluralistic, egalitarian, and fluid society such as exists in the United States. Many researchers nevertheless have tried to identify the social strata and to measure variables associated with them. Occupation has been shown to be the best single predictor of social status, and overall occupational prestige ratings have been found to be highly stable. A number of factors act in tandem in the relationship between occupation and social status. Both individual income and educational attainment are known to be correlated with occupational ranks. Education is a basis for entry into many occupations, and for most persons, income is derived from occupation. House type and dwelling area constitute other highly correlated factors.

Six scales are presented here for the researcher to review and possibly to use in research. They vary in length and in the number of factors included in the scale. The scales are

1. Duncan's Socioeconomic Index,
2. Siegel's (NORC) Prestige Scores,
3. Treiman's Standard International Occupational Prestige Scale,
4. the Nam-Powers Socioeconomic Status Scores,
5. Hollingshead's Index of Social Position, and
6. the Educational Scale.

7.2.1 Duncan's Socioeconomic Index

Variable measured. This socioeconomic index relates such basic characteristics as occupational prestige, education, and income.

Description. This measure was developed with two objectives in mind: (a) to extend the North-Hatt (National Opinion Research Center, or NORC) occupational prestige scores from 90 to 446 occupations in the detailed classification of the 1950 Census of Population and (b) to obtain a socioeconomic index to measure the relationship between the NORC prestige ratings and socioeconomic characteristics of the population. This index has face validity, in terms of its constituent variables, and sufficient predictive efficiency with respect to the NORC occupational prestige ratings.

Where published. Initial scale: Albert J. Reiss, with O. D. Duncan, Paul K. Hatt, and C. C. North, *Occupations and Social Status* (Glencoe, IL: Free Press, 1961). Revised scale: Robert M. Hauser and David L. Featherman, *The Process of Stratification: Trends and Analysis* (New York: Academic Press, 1977). Revised scale: David L. Featherman and Gillian Stevens updated the Duncan Socioeconomic Index in 1982 using more recent measures of income and educational attainments of the labor force, providing a better approximation of the prestige measure as well as considering attributes of both the male and total labor force. The revision was published as "A Revised Socioeconomic Index of Occupational Status: Application in Analysis of Sex Differences in Attainment," chapter 7 in *Social Structure and Behavior: Essays in Honor of William Hamilton Sewell* (New York: Academic Press).

Reliability. Reliability problems emerge as a respondent's description of his or her occupation is translated into an occupational code number using the U.S. Census Index of Occupations and Industries or the *Dictionary of Occupational Titles* published by the U.S. Department of Labor.

Validity.   The prestige variable is highly related to each predictor—with education, $r = .84$, and with income, $r = .85$. *The multiple correlation among the three variables,* $R_{1(23)}$, is $.91$. Overall occupational ratings have been found to be highly stable over time ($r = .99$ from 1947 to 1963) and across social systems (Hodge, Siegel, & Rossi, 1964).

Hauser and Featherman (1977) present many validating coefficients between Duncan SEI scores and father's education, father's occupation, son's education, son's first job, and son's current occupation. A moderate correlation ($r = .74$) was found between the August Hollingshead's Two-Factor Index of Social Position and the Duncan SEI; however, these scales are constructed differently and the correlation can be explained (Hollingshead, 1971). It is of consequence, however, that the two leading measures of social status express such a variance.

Utility.   The basic data required are subjects' descriptions of their occupations. These must then be translated into occupational codes by the researcher, and the occupational titles then converted into preexisting Duncan SEI scores (or NORC transformed Prestige Scores, if desired). There are many subtleties in the art of occupation coding, especially for blue-collar occupations. The researcher should reserve adequate time for training and cross-checking. Anyone planning detailed occupation coding should consult the Bureau of Labor Statistics Standard Occupational Classification System.

References

Hauser, Robert M., & Featherman, David L. (1977). *The process of stratification: Trends and Analysis.* New York: Academic Press.

Hodge, Robert W., Siegel, Paul M., & Rossi, Peter R. (1964). Occupational prestige in the United States, 1925-1963. *American Journal of Sociology, 70,* 286-302.

Hollingshead, August B. (1971). Commentary on "The indiscriminate state of social class measurement." *Social Forces, 49,* 563-567.

Research Applications

Airsman, Linda A., & Sharda, Bam Dev. (1993). A comparative study of the occupational attainment processes of white men and women in the United States: The effects of having ever married, spousal education, children and having ever divorced. *Journal of Comparative Family Studies, 24,* 171-187.

Caston, Richard J. (1989). Dimensions of occupational inequality and Duncan's Socioeconomic Index. *Sociological Forum, 4,* 329-348.

Davey, Lynn F. (1993, March). *Developmental implications of shared and divergent perceptions in the parent-adolescence relationship.* Paper presented at the biennial meeting of the Society for Research in Child Development, New Orleans, LA.

Dworkin, Rosalind J. (1981). Prestige ranking of the housewife occupation. *Sex Roles, 7*(1), 59-63.

Ell, Kathleen, Larson, David, Finch, Wilbur, Sattler, Fred, et al. (1989). Mental health services among ambulatory patients with human immunodeficiency syndrome infections. *Journal of Health and Social Policy, 1*(1), 3-17.

Ganzeboom, Harry B. G., De Graaf, Paul M., & Treiman, Donald J. (1992). A standard international socio-economic index of occupational status. *Social Science Research, 21*(1), 1-56.

Giudicatti, V., & Stening, B. W. (1980). Socioeconomic background and children's cognitive abilities in relation to television advertisements. *Journal of Psychology, 106*(2), 153-155.

Gottfried, Allen W. (1985). Measures of socioeconomic status in child development research: Data and recommendations. *Merrill-Palmer Quarterly, 31*(1), 85-92.

Graham, Sandra, & Long, Anna. (1986). Race, class, and the attributional process. *Journal of Educational Psychology*, *78*(1), 4-13.

Hanson, Sandra L. (1982). The effects of rural residence on the socio-economic attainment process of married females. *Rural Sociology*, *47*(1), 91-113.

Hirschman, Charles, & Kraly, Ellen Percy. (1990). Racial and ethnic inequality in the United States, 1940 and 1950: The impact of geographic location and human capital. *International Migration Review*, *24*(1), 4-33.

Hodge, Robert W. (1981). The measurement of occupational status. *Social Science Research*, *10*, 396-415.

Lin, Yangjing, & Vogt, W. Paul. (1996). Occupational outcomes for students earning two-year college degrees: Income, status, and equity. *Journal of Higher Education*, *67*(4), 446-475.

Markides, Kyriakos S., Martin, Harry W., & Sizemore, Mark. (1980). Psychological distress among elderly Mexican Americans and Anglos. *Ethnicity*, *7*, 298-309.

Mueller, Charles W., & Parcel, Toby L. (1981). Measures of socioeconomic status: Alternatives and recommendations. *Child Development*, *52*(1), 13-30.

Mutchler, Jan E., & Poston, Dudley L. (1983). Do females necessarily have the same occupational status scores as males? A conceptual and empirical examination of the Duncan Socioeconomic Index and Nam-Powers Occupational Status Scores. *Social Science Research*, *12*, 353-362.

Stevens, Gillian, & Featherman, David L. (1981). A revised socioeconomic index of occupational status. *Social Science Research*, *10*, 364-395.

7.2.2 Siegel's (NORC) Prestige Scores

Variable measured.   An index measuring the prestige of a stratification system.

Description.   The North-Hatt NORC study of occupational prestige appeared in 1947 and thereafter was widely used in research on prestige. Prestige scores were obtained for 90 occupations through a national sample of the American adult population. In 1963, under a National Science Foundation grant to the National Opinion Research Center, a replication was undertaken to provide definitive prestige scores for a more representative sample of occupations and to uncover some of the characteristics of occupations that generate their prestige scores. As in the 1947 study, occupational ratings were elicited by asking respondents to judge an occupation as having excellent, good, average, somewhat below average, or poor standing (along with a "don't know" option) in response to this item stem: "For each job mentioned, please pick out the statement that best gives your own personal opinion of the general standing that such a job has."

One indicator of prestige position is the proportion of respondents (among those rating an occupation) giving a response of either excellent or good. Another measure can be derived from a matrix of ratings by occupation by weighting the various responses with arbitrary numerical values. Assigning to an excellent rating a numerical average of these arbitrarily assigned values over all respondents rating the occupation yields the NORC prestige score. This latter measure has received rather widespread use, despite arbitrariness in the numerical weights assigned to the five possible ratings.

The NORC Occupational Prestige Ratings of 1963 were limited to 90 occupations (compared with the more than 500 occupation scores available in the Duncan SEI). By 1970, this limitation had been removed, as Hodge, Siegel, and Rossi (1964) established prestige scores on more than 400 occupations. More recently, Wisconsin researchers have transformed the 1964 65 NORC Prestige Scores (reported in Siegel, 1971, for the 1960 census detailed occupational titles) into the 1970 classification system.

Where published.   P. M. Siegel, *Prestige in the American occupational structure* (PhD dissertation, University of Chicago, Department of Sociology, 1971).

Reliability.   The respondent's own social status and familiarity with various occupations have been found to affect scores. Hatt found internally homogeneous scales with eight occupational groups: political, professional, business, recreation, agriculture, manual, military, and service.

Validity.   A correlation of .87 was reported by Siegel (1971) between Duncan's SEI scores (1960) and NORC Prestige Scores. The correlation between NORC Prestige Scores and Treiman's Standard International Occupational Prestige Scale scores is .95. The Duncan SEI seems to underrate clergy, farmers, and certain blue-collar workers (e.g., machinist, carpenter) while overrating entertainers, newspaper personnel, and sanitation workers. NORC scores show discrepant ratings of these occupations when compared with Duncan ratings, and the researcher may prefer to substitute NORC ratings for these occupations (Robinson, Athanasiou, & Head, 1969, p. 337).

Because of the way they were created (weights used in combining income and education were those that maximized scale scores with prestige), Duncan's scores have often been treated as estimates of the relative prestige of occupations, but in fact the correlations between Duncan scores and actual prestige scores are far from perfect. Some significant discrepancies have been pointed out, but the best demonstrated finding is that prestige scores *in toto* are less valid indicators of the dimension of status that underlies occupational mobility than are Duncan SEI scores. Prestige measures may be more responsive to nonsocioeconomic occupational dimensions (Houser & Featherman, 1977, pp. 37, 50).

Utility.   The best strategy is to code occupations in alternative ways and investigate differences in the results obtained. If the researcher wishes to settle on a single occupational status index for American data, there are two advantages to the Duncan index: It is the most widely used and offers opportunities for comparative analysis, and it will capture more joint variance with education and income than would a prestige scale. When other information on socioeconomic status is available for individuals, the NORC prestige ratings will avoid artificially inflated correlations with income and education (Treiman, 1977, pp. 311-312).

References

Hauser, Robert M., & Featherman, David L. (1977). *The process of stratification: Trends and analysis.* New York: Academic Press.

Hodge, Robert W., Siegel, Paul M., & Rossi, Peter H. (1964). Occupational prestige in the United States, 1925-1963. *American Journal of Sociology, 70,* 286-302.

Robinson, John P., Athanasiou, Robert, & Head, Kendra B. (1969). *Measures of occupational attitudes and occupational characteristics.* Ann Arbor: University of Michigan, Institute for Social Research.

Siegel, P. M. (1971). *Prestige in the American occupational structure.* PhD dissertation, University of Chicago Department of Sociology.

Treiman, Donald J. (1977). *Occupational prestige in comparative perspective.* New York: Academic Press.

Research Applications

Bose, Christine E., & Rossi, Peter H. (1983). Gender and jobs: Prestige standings of occupations as affected by gender. *American Sociological Review, 48,* 316-330.

Featherman, David L., & Hauser, Robert M. (1976). Prestige or socioeconomic scales in the study of occupational achievement? *Sociological Methods and Research, 4,* 403-422.

Glenn, Norval D. (1975). The contribution of white collars to occupational settings. *Sociological Quarterly*, 16(2), 184-189.

Kamieniecki, Sheldon, & O'Brien, Robert. (1984). Are social class measures interchangeable? *Political Behavior*, 6(1), 41-59.

Moreland, Carol P. (1978). *Sex and occupational attainment: A comparison of black males and females.* Paper presented at the meeting of the Mid-South Sociological Association.

Nilson, Linda Burzotta. (1978). The social standing of a housewife. *Journal of Marriage and the Family*, 40, 541-547.

Rytina, Steven L. (n.d.). *Scaling the intergenerational continuity of occupation: Is occupational inheritance ascriptive after all?* Unpublished manuscript, Department of Sociology, Harvard University.

Spaeth, Joe L. (1978). Measures of occupational status in a special population. *Social Science Research*, 7(1), 48-60.

Sullivan, Teresa A. (1983, April). *The occupational prestige of women immigrants: A comparison of Cubans and Mexicans.* Paper prepared for presentation at the annual meeting of the Population Association of America, Pittsburgh, PA.

Villemez, Wayne J., & Silver, Burton B. (1977). Occupational situs as horizontal social position: A reconsideration. *Sociology and Social Research*, 61, 320-336.

7.2.3 Treiman's Standard International Occupational Prestige Scale

Variable measured.   A standardized prestige measure that can be used to code occupations in any country and to make cross-national comparisons.

Description.   The scale consists of prestige scores for 509 occupations, 288 unit groups, 84 minor groups, and 11 major categories. The scale has a range of 92 points, from "chief of state" (with a score of 90) to "gatherer" (with a score of –2). The mean scale score computed over the 509 occupations is 43.3.

Where published.   Donald J. Treiman, *Occupational Prestige in Comparative Perspective* (New York: Academic Press, 1977).

Reliability.   The scale has been shown to be highly reliable. The average intercountry correlation based on seven countries is .97.

Validity.   The Standard Scale is extremely highly correlated with prestige hierarchies of 55 countries. The mean correlation of intercountry correlations with the Standard Scale is .91, computed across the 55 countries with pure prestige data. Of the 55 countries, only 7 exhibit correlations with the Standard Scale smaller than .87. For the United States and Great Britain, the correlations exceed .96.

Utility.   Because of the basic similarity of prestige evaluations in all societies, Donald Treiman has been able to produce the first prestige scale that can be used validly to assign prestige scores to occupations in any country.

Research Applications

Ganzeboom, Harry B. G., & Treiman, Donald J. (1996). Internationally comparable measures of occupational status for the 1988 International Standard Classification of Occupations. *Social Science Research*, 25(3), 201-239.

Sharda, Bam Dev, & Elder, Joseph W. (1975, August). *Industrialization and the processes of stratification in rural societies: A comparison of rural India and rural United States.* Paper presented at the annual meeting of the American Sociological Association.

Spaeth, Joe L. (1978). Measures of occupational status in a special population. *Social Science Research*, 7(1), 48-60.

Treiman, Donald J. (1975). Problems of concept and measurement in the comparative study of occupational mobility. *Social Science Research*, 4(3), 183-230.

Treiman, Donald J. (1976). A standard occupational prestige scale for use with historical data. *Journal of Interdisciplinary History*, 7(2), 283-304.

Wolf, Christof. (1997). The ISCO-88 International Standard Classification of Occupations in cross-national survey research. *Bulletin de Methodologie Sociologique*, 54, 23-40.

Yogev, Abraham. (1980). Validating the applicability of the Standard International Occupational Prestige Scale: Illustrations from Costa Rica and Israel. *International Review of Modern Sociology*, 10(1), 15-35.

7.2.4 The Nam-Powers Socioeconomic Status Scores

Variables measured. This is a multiple-item measure that averages scores for the component items of occupation, education, and family income. A companion measure of status consistency also is available.

Description. In the 1960s, Charles B. Nam, Mary G. Powers, and their associates worked at the U.S. Bureau of the Census, where they devised socioeconomic status scores for occupations (without use of prestige ratings) based on 1960 census data for income and education. The Census Bureau's group decided that homogeneity could best be achieved not only by stratifying occupations per se but also by developing a multiple-item index of socioeconomic status that combined independent ratings of education and income with ratings of occupations.

The procedure employed to compute the scores is similar to that used by Duncan, but with these differences: (a) median education and income, rather than percentages of specified education and income levels, were used; (b) Duncan indirectly standardized scores by age; and (c) Duncan used the 1947 NORC prestige ratings in deriving rights for census characteristics. The similarity between the census index and Duncan's index is attested, however, by the Pearson coefficient of .97, as previously reported. In planning for the 1970 census, the Census Bureau decided to drop the practice of generating socioeconomic scores using any procedure.

Nam and Powers take cognizance of the controversy between the pure prestige approach (Siegel's [NORC] Prestige Scores) and the socioeconomic status (SES) determination of prestige of occupations. They believe a third option, the direct measurement of SES without reference to prestige, deserves a more careful assessment. This approach was used in the work of August B. Hollingshead and Frederick C. Redlich (1958) and that of Peter M. Blau and Otis Dudley Duncan (1967). This orientation begins with the notion that often a researcher wants a measure of class or life chances or of objective status conditions; any of these criteria for valuing occupations leads one to pure socioeconomic indicators of occupational rankings. This third, purely socioeconomic approach has been evident in work produced by the U.S. Bureau of the Census for the past century.

Nam and Terrie have continued to generate new Nam-Powers occupational status scores based on 1980 census data. A rationale for their pure socioeconomic multiple-item measure is presented in Nam and Powers (1983).

Where published. Initial work on 1960 census data appears in U.S. Bureau of the Census, *Methodology and Scores of Socioeconomic Status* (Working Paper No. 15) (Washington, DC: Government Printing Office, 1963), and U.S. Bureau of the Census, *U.S. Census of Population, 1960, Socioeconomic Status, Final Report PC(2)-5C* (Washington, DC: Government Printing Office, 1967). Work on the 1970 census incorporated SES scores for males, females, full-time year-round female workers, and both sexes. These scores are shown in Charles B. Nam, John LaRocque, Mary G. Powers, and Joan Holmberg, "Occupational Status Scores: Stability and Change," *Proceedings of the American Statistical Association, Social Statistics Section* (1975), pp. 570-575.

Reliability. When Nam and Powers compared the full list of detailed occupations for men for 1950 and 1960, they calculated a correlation coefficient between the two sets of scores of .96. The 1950-1960 correlation coefficient using the 126 occupations is .95. The calculation for men in the 126 occupations in 1960 and 1970 provides a correlation coefficient of .97, indicating that an extremely high degree of stability in status scores has been maintained. The correlation coefficient between scores for men in 1950 and 1970 is .91. For all women, the coefficient for 1960-1970 is .85, reasonably high but much lower than for men. In 1980, an increasing similarity of scores for men and women was observed, such that a single set of scores for men and women combined is now indicated.

Validity. Measured against prestige measures (from Duncan or Siegel), very high correlations are reported. Although these two dimensions, socioeconomic status and prestige, are highly associated, there is a tendency for occupational status to vary more over time than does occupational prestige (Pavalko, 1971, pp. 132 and 140).

Utility. Women have become increasingly involved in the labor force, and it is increasingly uncommon to label occupations as exclusively men's or women's.

References

Blau, Peter M., & Duncan, Otis Dudley. (1967). *The American occupational structure.* New York: John Wiley.

Hollingshead, August B., & Redlich, Frederick C. (1958). *Social class and mental illness: A community study.* New York: John Wiley.

Nam, Charles B., & Powers, Mary G. (1983). *The socioeconomic approach to status measurement.* Houston: Cap & Gown.

Pavalko, Ronald M. (1971). *Sociology of occupations and professions.* Itasca, IL: Peacock.

Research Applications

Broman, Sarah H., Nichols, Paul L., & Kennedy, Wallace A. (1975). *Preschool IQ: Prenatal and early developmental correlates.* New York: John Wiley.

Chiricos, Theodore G., & Waldo, Gordon P. (1975). Socioeconomic status and criminal sentencing: An empirical assessment of a conflict proposition. *American Sociological Review, 40,* 753-772.

Myrianthopoulos, N. C., & French, K. S. (1968). An application of the U.S. Bureau of the Census socioeconomic index to a large, diversified patient population. *Social Science and Medicine, 2,* 283-299.

Nam, Charles B. (1968). Changes in the relative status level of workers in the United States, 1950-1960. *Social Forces, 47*(December), 167-170.

Nam, Charles B., & Powers, Mary G. (1965). Variations in socioeconomic structure by race, residence, and the life cycle. *American Sociological Review*, *30*(February), 97-103.

Nam, Charles B., Powers, Mary G., & Glick, Paul C. (1964). *Socioeconomic characteristics of the population: 1960* (Current Population Reports, series P-23, no. 12). Washington, DC: Government Printing Office.

Powers, Mary G., & Holmberg, Joan J. (1978). Occupational status scores: Changes introduced by the inclusion of women. *Demography*, *15*, 183-204.

7.2.5 Hollingshead's Index of Social Position

Variable measured.   Positions individuals occupy in the status structure.

Description.   Both two- and three-factor forms of the index have been used extensively. The two-factor index is composed of an occupational scale and an educational scale. The three-factor index includes a residential scale. Because the residential scale was based on sociological analysis concerning New Haven, Connecticut, many communities would not be amenable until residential areas were mapped into a six-position scale. The two-factor index requires only knowledge of occupation and education.

The occupational scale is a 7-point scale representing a modification of the Edwards system of classifying occupations into socioeconomic groups. The Edwards system does not differentiate among kinds of professionals or the size and economic strength of businesses. The Hollingshead Index of Social Position ranks professions into different groups and ranks businesses by their size and value.

The educational scale is also divided into seven positions. In the two-factor index, occupation is given a weight of 7 and education is given a weight of 4. If one were to compute a score for the manager of a Kroger grocery store who had completed high school and one year of business college, the procedure would be as follows:

Factor	Scale Score	+	Factor Weight	=	Partial Score
Occupation	3		7		21
Education	3		4		12
		Index of Social Position Score			33

Where published.   August B. Hollingshead, *Two Factor Index of Social Position* (copyright 1957), privately printed 1965, Yale Station, New Haven, CT. August B. Hollingshead and Frederick C. Redlich, *Social Class and Mental Illness: A Community Study* (New York: John Wiley, 1958), 387-397.

Hollingshead's account of the background and rationale for the two-factor scale appears in August B. Hollingshead (1971), "Commentary on 'The Indiscriminate State of Social Class Measurement,'" *Social Forces*, *49*, 563-567.

Reliability and validity of Index of Social Position.   High correlation is reported between the Hollingshead and Redlich measure and the index of class position devised by Ellis, Lane, and Olesen (1963).

Various combinations of the scale score for occupation and education are reproducible in the Guttman sense because there is no overlap between education-occupation combinations. If an individual's education and occupation are known, one can calculate his or her score; if one knows an individual's score, one can calculate both occupational and educational level.

Hollingshead and Redlich reported a correlation of judged class with education and occupation as $R_{1(23)} = .906$. For judged class correlation with residence, education, and occupation, $R_{.(234)} = .942$. Hollingshead and others conducted extensive studies of the reliability of scoring and validity of the index on more than 100 variables.

Slomczynski, Miller, and Kohn (1981) report that use of the Hollingshead index of occupational status for research in the United States is validated by longitudinal measurement models that show the Hollingshead index to be as strong an indicator of occupational status as is Treiman's International Prestige Scale, the Hodge-Siegel Index, or the Duncan Socioeconomic Index.

Utility. Because of the difficulty in obtaining residential information where adequate ecological maps do not exist, the two-factor variation of the Index of Social Position has been used widely. Only occupation and education are needed, and these data are relatively easy to obtain. The scale score can be computed quickly and individual social position established.

References

Ellis, R., Lane, W., & Olesen, V. (1963). The Index of Class Position: An improved intercommunity measure of stratification. *American Sociological Review, 28*, 271-277.

Slomczynski, Kazimierz M., Miller, Joanne, & Kohn, Melvin L. (1981). Stratification, work, and values: A Polish-United States Comparison. *American Sociological Review, 46*, 720-744.

7.2.5.1 Hollingshead's Two-Factor Index of Social Position

The following two scales, the occupational and educational scales of the two-factor Index of Social Position, are reprinted by permission from August B. Hollingshead and Frederick C. Redlich, *Social Class and Mental Illness: A Community Study* (New York: John Wiley, 1958). Copyright 1958 by John Wiley and Sons, Inc.

The Occupational Scale

1. Higher Executives of Large Concerns, Proprietors, and Major Professionals

   A. *Higher Executives (Value of corporation $500,000 and above as rated by Dun and Bradstreet)*

Bank	Business
Presidents	Vice-presidents
Vice-Presidents	Assistant vice-presidents
Assistant vice-presidents	Executive secretaries
	Research directors
	Treasurers

   B. *Proprietors (Value over $100,000 by Dun and Bradstreet)*

Brokers	Farmers
Contractors	Lumber dealers
Dairy owners	

C. *Major Professionals*

Accountants (CPA)
Actuaries
Agronomists
Auditors
Architects
Artists, portrait
Astronomers
Bacteriologists
Chemical engineers
Chemists
Clergymen (professional trained)
Dentists
Economists
Engineers (college graduates)
Foresters
Geologists

Judges (superior courts)
Lawyers
Metallurgists
Military: commissioned officers, major and
   above
Officials of the executive branch of
   government, federal, state, local: e.g.,
   Mayor, City manager, City plan director,
   Internal Revenue director
Physicians
Physicists, research
Psychologists, practicing
Symphony conductor
Teachers, university, college
Veterinarians (veterinary surgeons)

2. Business Managers, Proprietors of Medium-Sized Businesses, and Lesser Professionals

   A. *Business Managers in Large Concerns (Value $500,000)*

Advertising directors
Branch managers
Brokerage salesmen
Directors of purchasing
District managers
Executive assistants
Export managers, international concerns
Government officials, minor, e.g.,
   Internal Revenue agents

Manufacturer's representatives
Office managers
Personnel managers
Police chief; Sheriff
Postmaster
Production managers
Sales engineers
Sales managers, national concerns
Store managers

   B. *Proprietors of Medium-Sized Businesses (Value $35,000-$100,000)*

Advertising
Clothing store
Contractors
Express company
Farm owners
Fruits, wholesale
Furniture business

Jewelers
Poultry business
Real estate brokers
Rug business
Store
Theater

   C. *Lesser Professionals*

Accountants (not CPA)
Chiropodists
Chiropractors
Correction officers
Director of Community House
Engineers (not college graduate)
Finance writers
Health educators
Labor relations consultants
Librarians

Military: commissioned officers, lieutenant,
   captain
Musicians (symphony orchestra)
Nurses
Opticians
Optometrists, D.O.
Pharmacists
Public health officers (MPH)
Research assistants, university (full-time)
Social workers

3. Administrative Personnel, Owners of Small Businesses, and Minor Professionals

A. *Administrative Personnel*

Advertising agents	Sales representatives
Chief clerks	Section heads, federal, state, and local
Credit managers	governmental offices
Insurance agents	Section heads, large businesses and industries
Managers, departments	Service managers
Passenger agents, railroad	Shop managers
Private secretaries	Store managers (chain)
Purchasing agents	Traffic managers

B. *Small Business Owners*

Art gallery	Furniture
Auto accessories	Garage
Awnings	Gas station
Bakery	Glassware
Beauty shop	Grocery, general
Boatyard	Hotel protection
Brokerage, insurance	Jewelry
Car dealers	Machinery brokers
Cattle dealers	Manufacturing
Cigarette machines	Monuments
Cleaning shops	Music
Clothing	Package stores (liquor)
Coal businesses	Paint contracting
Contracting businesses	Poultry
Convalescent homes	Real estate
Decorating	Records and radios
Dog supplies	Restaurant
Dry goods	Roofing contractor
Engraving business	Shoe
Feed	Signs
Finance companies, local	Tavern
Fire extinguishers	Taxi company
Five and dime	Tire shop
Florist	Trucking
Food equipment	Trucks and tractors
Food products	Upholstery
Foundry	Wholesale outlets
Funeral directors	Window shades

C. *Semiprofessionals*

Actors and showmen	Dispatchers, railroad
Appraisers (estimators)	Interior decorators
Army, master sergeant	Interpreters, courts
Artists, commercial	Laboratory assistants
Clergymen (not professionally trained)	Landscape planners
Concern managers	Morticians
Deputy sheriffs	Navy, chief petty officer

Oral hygienists
Physiotherapists
Piano teachers
Publicity and public relations
Radio, TV announcers
Reporters, court

Reporters, newspapers
Surveyors
Title searchers
Tool designs
Travel agents
Yard masters, railroad

D. *Farmers*
Farm owners

4. Clerical and Sales Workers, Technicians, and Owners of Small Businesses

A. *Clerical and Sales Workers*

Bank clerks and tellers
Bill collectors
Bookkeepers
Business machine operators, offices
Claims examiners
Clerical or stenographic
Conductors, railroad
Factory storekeepers

Factory supervisors
Post office clerks
Route managers
Sales clerks
Sergeants and petty officers, military services
Shipping clerks
Supervisors, utilities, factories
Supervisors, toll stations

B. *Technicians*

Dental technicians
Draftsmen
Driving teachers
Expediter, factory
Experimental tester
Instructors, telephone company, factory
Inspectors, weights, sanitary, railroad,
    factory
Investigators
Laboratory technicians
Locomotive engineers

Operators, PBX
Proofreaders
Safety supervisors
Supervisors of maintenance
Technical assistants
Telephone company supervisors
Timekeepers
Tower operators, railroad
Truck dispatchers
Window trimmers (stores)

C. *Owners of Little Businesses ($3,000-$6,000)*

Flower shop
Grocery

Newsstand
Tailor shop

D. *Farmers*
Owners

5. Skilled Manual Employees

Auto body repairers
Bakers
Barbers
Blacksmiths
Bookbinders
Boilermakers
Brakemen, railroad

Brewers
Bulldozer operators
Butchers
Cabinet makers
Cable splicers
Carpenters
Casters (founders)

Cement finishers
Cheese makers
Chefs
Compositors
Diemakers
Diesel engine repair and maintenance
   (trained)
Diesel shovel operators
Electricians
Engravers
Exterminators
Firemen, city
Firemen, railroad
Fitters, gas, steam
Foremen, construction, dairy
Gardeners, landscape (trained)
Glass blowers
Glaziers
Gunsmiths
Gauge makers
Hair stylists
Heat treaters
Horticulturists
Linemen, utility
Linoleum layers (trained)
Linotype operators
Lithographers
Locksmiths
Loom fixers
Machinists (trained)
Maintenance foremen
Masons
Masseurs

Mechanics (trained)
Millwrights
Moulders (trained)
Painters
Paperhangers
Patrolmen, railroad
Pattern and model makers
Piano builders
Piano tuners
Plumbers
Policemen, city
Postmen
Printers
Radio, television maintenance
Repairmen, home appliances
Rope splicers
Sheetmetal workers (trained)
Shipsmiths
Shoe repairmen (trained)
Stationery engineers (licensed)
Stewards, club
Switchmen, railroad
Tailors (trained)
Teletype operators
Tool makers
Track supervisors, railroad
Tractor-trailer trans.
Typographers
Upholsterers (trained)
Watchmakers
Weavers
Welders
Yard supervisors, railroad

Small Farmers
   Owners

Tenants who own farm equipment

6. Machine Operators and Semiskilled Employees

Aides, hospital
Apprentices, electricians, printers, steam
   fitters, toolmakers
Assembly line workers
Bartenders
Bingo tenders
Bridge tenders
Building superintendents (construction)
Bus drivers
Checkers
Coin machine fillers

Cooks, short order
Deliverymen
Dressmakers, machine
Elevator operators
Enlisted men, military services
Filers, sanders, buffers
Foundry workers
Garage and gas station attendants
Greenhouse workers
Guards, doorkeepers, watchmen
Hairdressers

Housekeepers

Meat cutters and packers

Meter readers

Operators, factory machines

Oilers, railroad

Practical nurses

Pressers, clothing

Pump operators

Receivers and checkers

Roofers

Setup men, factories

Shapers

Signalmen, railroad

Solderers, factory

Sprayers, paint

Steelworkers (not skilled)

Farmers
   Smaller tenants who own little equipment

Standers, wire machines

Strippers, rubber factory

Taxi drivers

Testers

Timers

Tire moulders

Trainmen, railroad

Truck drivers, general

Waiters-waitresses ("better placed")

Weighers

Welders, spot

Winders, machine

Wiredrawers, machine

Wine bottlers

Wood workers, machine

Wrappers, stores and factories

7. Unskilled Employees

Amusement park workers
   (bowling alleys, pool rooms)

Ash removers

Attendants, parking lots

Cafeteria workers

Car cleaners, railroad

Carriers, coal

Countermen

Dairy workers

Deck hands

Domestics

Farm helpers

Fishermen (clam diggers)

Freight handlers

Garbage collectors

Gravediggers

Hod carriers

Hog killers

Hospital workers, unspecified

Hostlers, railroad

Janitors (sweepers)

Laborers, construction

Laborers, unspecified

Laundry workers

Messengers

Platform men, railroad

Peddlers

Porters

Relief, public, private

Roofer's helpers

Shirt folders

Shoe shiners

Sorters, rag and salvage

Stage hands

Stevedores

Stock handlers

Street cleaners

Struckmen, railroad

Unemployed (no occupation)

Unskilled factory workers

Waitresses ("hash houses")

Washers, cars

Window cleaners

Woodchoppers

Farmers
   Sharecroppers

7.2.6 The Educational Scale

The educational scale is premised upon the assumption that men and women who possess similar educations will tend to have similar tastes and similar attitudes, and will also tend to exhibit similar behavior patterns.

The educational scale is divided into seven positions:

1. *Graduate professional training:* Persons who completed a recognized professional course that led to the receipt of a graduate degree were given scores of 1.
2. *Standard college or university graduation:* All individuals who had completed a 4-year college or university course leading to a recognized college degree were assigned the same scores. No differentiation was made between state universities and private colleges.
3. *Partial college training:* Individuals who had completed at least 1 year but not a full college course were assigned this position.
4. *High school graduation:* All secondary school graduates, whether from a private preparatory school, public high school, trade school, or parochial school, were given this score.
5. *Partial high school:* Individuals who had completed the 10th or 11th grades but had not completed high school were given this score.
6. *Junior high school:* Individuals who had completed the 7th grade through the 9th grade were given this position.
7. *Less than 7 years of school:* Individuals who had not completed the 7th grade were given the same score irrespective of the amount of education they had received.

Research Applications

Beck, Frances W. (1984, November). *Incidence of moderate and severe retardation.* Paper presented at the annual conference of the Mid-South Educational Research Association, New Orleans, LA.

Derogatis, Leonard R., et al. (1975). Social class, psychological disorder, and the nature of the psychopathologic indicator. *Journal of Consulting and Clinical Psychology, 43,* 183-191.

Evans, Charles S. (1982). Moral stage development and knowledge of Kohlberg's theory. *Journal of Experimental Education, 51*(1), 14-17.

Gray-Ray, Phyllis, & Ray, Melvin C. (1990). Juvenile delinquency in the black community. *Youth and Society, 22,* 67-84.

Healey, Gary W., & DeBlassie, Richard R. (1974). A comparison of Negro, Anglo, and Spanish American adolescents' self concepts. *Adolescence, 33,* 15-24.

Kelley, Eleanor, et al. (1974). Working-class adolescents' perceptions of the role of clothing in occupational life. *Adolescence, 34,* 185-198.

Morrison, J. W., Ispa, J., & Thornburg, K. (1994). African American college students' psychosocial development as related to care arrangements during infancy. *Journal of Black Psychology, 20,* 418-429.

Raph, Jane, et al. (1971, February). *Influences of a Piaget-oriented curriculum on intellectual functioning of lower-class kindergarten children.* Paper presented at the annual meeting of the American Educational Research Association, New York, NY.

Rosenbaum, Sarah C. (1998). Gender differences in fear of power: The relationship between internal representations of mothers and attitudes toward authority. *Dissertation Abstracts International, 59,* 2431B.

Sherman, William Joseph. (1996). Role development in adult children of alcoholics: An experimental design. *Dissertation Abstracts International, 57,* 2164B.

7.3 SCALES ASSESSING GROUP STRUCTURE AND DYNAMICS

This section contains a discussion of five scales, each of which measures a different variable relating to group structure and dynamics.

1. Hemphill's Index of Group Dimensions, which ascertains 13 dimensions of a group, is the most ambitious attempt to measure the structural properties of groups.
2. Bales's Interaction Process Analysis is a nominal scale widely used to assess the characteristics of personal interaction in problem-solving groups.
3. Seashore's Group Cohesiveness Index provides a measure of the strength of a group used to maintain its identity and to persist.
4. The Sociometry Scales of Spontaneous Choice and Sociometric Preference reveal the interpersonal attractions of members in groups. These scales may be widely adapted to suit many different situations. They are useful not only to researchers seeking basic relationships but also to action researchers or social workers. New groupings of individuals can be arranged quickly, and new measurements of morale or productivity can be made.
5. The Bogardus Social Distance Scale also may be adapted to many different purposes. The social distance between two persons, between a person and a group, or between groups can be measured in such diverse situations as that involving an out-group member and a country, a community, or an organization.

7.3.1 Hemphill's Index of Group Dimensions

Variable measured. The index is designed to measure group dimensions of characteristics.

Description. The index is built upon 13 comparatively independent group dimensions: autonomy, control, flexibility, hedonic tone, homogeneity, intimacy, participation, permeability, polarization, potency, stability, stratification, and viscidity. The 150 items are answered on a 5-point scale. The dimensions were selected from a list of group adjectives used by authorities. Items were suggested from a free-response–type questionnaire administered to 500 individuals, and five judges then put the items into the dimensional categories.

Where published. John K. Hemphill, *Group Dimensions: A Manual for Their Measurement* (Research Monograph No. 87) (Columbus: Ohio State University, Bureau of Business Research, 1956).

Reliability. Split-half reliabilities range from .59 to .87. The relationship between an item and high-low categories ranges from .03 to .78 (with a median of .36) on the keyed items and from .01 to .36 (with a median of .12) on the randomly selected items. Intercorrelation of dimension scores ranges from –.54 to .81, with most within +.29 (which has a .01 significance level). Agreement between different reporters of the same group ranges from .53 to .74.

Validity. The dimension scores describing the characteristics of two quite different groups vary accordingly, whereas those describing the characteristics of two similar groups are quite similar.

Utility. The index can be useful in studying the relationships between the behavior of leaders and characteristics of groups in which they function. Although fairly long, it is comparatively easy to administer and score.

7.3.1.1 Group Dimensions Descriptions Questionnaire

Questionnaire Directions

Record your answer to each of the items on the answer sheet for the group you are describing. Make no marks on the question booklet itself.

In considering each item go through the following steps:

1. Read the item carefully.
2. Think about how well the item tells something about the group you are describing.
3. Find the number on the answer sheet that corresponds with the number of the item you are considering.
4. After each number on the answer sheet you will find five pairs of dotted lines lettered A, B, C, D, or E.

   If the item you are considering tells something about the group that is definitely true, blacken the space between the pair of dotted lines headed by A.

   If the item you are considering tells something that is mostly true, blacken the space between the pair of lines headed by B.

   If the item tells something that is to an equal degree both true and false, or you are undecided about whether it is true or false, blacken the space between the pair of lines headed by C.

   If the item you are considering tells something that is mostly false, blacken the space between the pair of lines headed by D.

   If the item you are considering tells something about the group that is definitely false, blacken the space between the pair of dotted lines headed by E.
5. When blackening the space between a pair of lines, fill in all the space with a heavy black line. If you should make an error in marking your answer, erase thoroughly the mark you made and then indicate the correct answer.
6. In rare cases where you believe that an item does not apply at all to the group or you feel that you do not have sufficient information to make any judgment concerning what the item tells about the group, leave that item blank.
7. After you have completed one item, proceed to the next one in order.

You may have as long as you need to complete your description. Be sure the number on the answer sheet corresponds with the number of the item being answered in the booklet.

Questions

The questions that follow make it possible to describe objectively certain characteristics of social groups. The items simply describe characteristics of groups; they do not judge whether the characteristic is desirable or undesirable. Therefore, in no way are the questions to be considered a test either of the groups or of the person answering the questions. We simply want an objective description of what the group is like.

1. The group has well understood but unwritten rules concerning member conduct.
2. Members fear to express their real opinions.
3. The only way a member may leave the group is to be expelled.
4. No explanation need be given by a member wishing to be absent from the group.
5. An individual's membership can be dropped should he fail to live up to the standards of the group.
6. Members of the group work under close supervision.
7. Only certain kinds of ideas may be expressed freely within the group.

8. A member may leave the group by resigning at any time he wishes.
9. A request made by a member to leave the group can be refused.
10. A member has to think twice before speaking in the group's meetings.
11. Members are occasionally forced to resign.
12. The members of the group are subject to strict discipline.
13. The group is rapidly increasing in size.
14. Members are constantly leaving the group.
15. There is a large turnover of members within the group.
16. Members are constantly dropping out of the group but new members replace them.
17. During the entire time of the group's existence no member has left.
18. Each member's personal life is known to other members of the group.
19. Members of the group lend each other money.
20. A member has the chance to get to know all other members of the group.
21. Members are not in close enough contact to develop likes or dislikes for one another.
22. Members of the group do small favors for one another.
23. All members know each other very well.
24. Each member of the group knows all other members by their first names.
25. Members are in daily contact either outside or within the group.
26. Members of the group are personal friends.
27. Certain members discuss personal affairs among themselves.
28. Members of the group know the family backgrounds of other members of the group.
29. Members address each other by their first names.
30. The group is made up of individuals who do not know each other well.
31. The opinions of all members are considered as equal.
32. The group's officers hold a higher status in the group than other members.
33. The older members of the group are granted special privileges.
34. The group is controlled by the actions of a few members.
35. Every member of the group enjoys the same group privileges.
36. Experienced members are in charge of the group.
37. Certain problems are discussed only among the group's officers.
38. Certain members have more influence on the group than others.
39. Each member of the group has as much power as any other member.
40. An individual's standing in the group is determined only by how much he gets done.
41. Certain members of the group hold definite office in the group.
42. The original members of the group are given special privileges.
43. Personal dissatisfaction with the group is too small to be brought up.
44. Members continually grumble about the work they do for the group.
45. The group does its work with no great vim, vigor, or pleasure.
46. A feeling of failure prevails in the group.
47. There are frequent intervals of laughter during group meetings.
48. The group works independently of other groups.
49. The group has support from outside.
50. The group is an active representative of a larger group.
51. The group's activities are influenced by a larger group of which it is part.
52. People outside the group decide on what work the group is to do.
53. The group follows the examples set by other groups.
54. The group is one of many similar groups that form one large organization.
55. The things the group does are approved by a group higher up.
56. The group joins with other groups in carrying out its activities.
57. The group is a small part of a larger group.
58. The group is under outside pressure.
59. Members are disciplined by an outside group.
60. Plans of the group are made by other groups above it.
61. The members allow nothing to interfere with the progress of the group.

62. Members gain a feeling of being honored by being recognized as one of the group.
63. Membership in the group is a way of acquiring general social status.
64. Failure of the group would mean little to individual members.
65. The activities of the group take up less than ten percent of each member's waking time.
66. Members gain in prestige among outsiders by joining the group.
67. A mistake by one member of the group might result in hardship for all.
68. The activities of the group take up over ninety percent of each member's waking time.
69. Membership in the group serves as an aid to vocational advancement.
70. Failure of the group would mean nothing to most members.
71. Each member would lose his self-respect if the group should fail.
72. Membership in the group gives members a feeling of superiority.
73. The activities of the group take up over half the time each member is awake.
74. Failure of the group would lead to embarrassment for members.
75. Members are not rewarded for effort put out for the group.
76. There are two or three members of the group who generally take the same side on any group issue.
77. Certain members are hostile to other members.
78. There is constant bickering among members of the group.
79. Members know that each one looks out for the other one as well as for himself.
80. Certain members of the group have no respect for other members.
81. Certain members of the group are considered uncooperative.
82. There is a constant tendency toward conniving against one another among parts of the group.
83. Members of the group work together as a team.
84. Certain members of the group are responsible for petty quarrels and some animosity among other members.
85. There are tensions among subgroups that tend to interfere with the group's activities.
86. Certain members appear to be incapable of working as part of the group.
87. There is an undercurrent of feeling among members that tends to pull the group apart.
88. Anyone who has sufficient interest in the group to attend its meetings is considered a member.
89. The group engages in membership drives.
90. New members are welcomed to the group on the basis "the more the merrier."
91. A new member may join only after an old member resigns.
92. A college degree is required for membership in the group.
93. A person may enter the group by expressing a desire to join.
94. Anyone desiring to enter the group is welcome.
95. Membership is open to anyone willing to further the purpose of the group.
96. Prospective members are carefully examined before they enter the group.
97. No applicants for membership in the group are turned down.
98. No special training is required for membership in the group.
99. Membership depends upon the amount of education an individual has.
100. People interested in joining the group are asked to submit references which are checked.
101. There is a high degree of participation on the part of members.
102. If a member of the group is not productive he is not encouraged to remain.
103. Work of the group is left to those who are considered most capable for the job.
104. Members are interested in the group but not all of them want to work.
105. The group has a reputation for not getting much done.
106. Each member of the group is on one or more active committees.
107. The work of the group is well divided among members.
108. Every member of the group does not have a job to do.
109. The work of the group is frequently interrupted by having nothing to do.
110. There are long periods during which the group does nothing.
111. The group is directed toward one particular goal.
112. The group divides its efforts among several purposes.
113. The group operates with sets of conflicting plans.

114. The group has only one main purpose.
115. The group knows exactly what it has to get done.
116. The group is working toward many different goals.
117. The group does many things that are not directly related to its main purpose.
118. Each member of the group has a clear idea of the group's goals.
119. The objective of the group is specific.
120. Certain members meet for one thing and others for a different thing.
121. The group has major purposes which to some degree are in conflict.
122. The objectives of the group have never been clearly recognized.
123. The group is very informal.
124. A list of rules and regulations is given to each member.
125. The group has meetings at regularly scheduled times.
126. The group is organized along semimilitary lines.
127. The group's meetings are not planned or organized.
128. The group has an organization chart.
129. The group has rules to guide its activities.
130. The group is staffed according to a table of organization.
131. The group keeps a list of names of members.
132. Group meetings are conducted according to Robert's Rules of Order.
133. There is a recognized right and wrong way of going about group activities.
134. Most matters that come up before the group are voted upon.
135. The group meets at any place that happens to be handy.
136. The members of the group vary in amount of ambition.
137. Members of the group are from the same social class.
138. Some members are interested in altogether different things than other members.
139. The group contains members with widely varying backgrounds.
140. The group contains whites and Negroes.
141. Members of the group are all about the same ages.
142. A few members of the group have greater ability than others.
143. A number of religious beliefs are represented by members of the group.
144. Members of the group vary greatly in social background.
145. All members of the group are of the same sex.
146. The ages of members range over a period of at least 20 years.
147. Members come into the group with quite different family backgrounds.
148. Members of the group vary widely in amount of experience.
149. Members vary in the number of years they have been in the group.
150. The group includes members of different races.

Scoring Key and Directions for Scoring

A subject's score for a particular dimension is the sum of the item scores for that dimension. For example, the raw score for the dimension "Control" is the sum of the scores for items 1 to 12 inclusive. The total (raw) score for this dimension can range from 12 to 60.

Occasionally a respondent may fail to indicate an answer. Such omissions are scored as C responses (neither true nor false). However, if the number of omitted items exceeds half the total number of items assigned to a given dimension, no score for that dimension is assigned. In general, experience has shown that few respondents deliberately omit items.

Scoring Keys

Control	A	B	C	D	E						
1	5	4	3	2	1	37	5	4	3	2	1
2	5	4	3	2	1	38	5	4	3	2	1
3	5	4	3	2	1	39	1	2	3	4	5
4	1	2	3	4	5	40	5	4	3	2	1
5	5	4	3	2	1	41	5	4	3	2	1
6	5	4	3	2	1	Hedonic tone	A	B	C	D	E
7	5	4	3	2	1	43	5	4	3	2	1
8	1	2	3	4	5	44	1	2	3	4	5
9	5	4	3	2	1	45	1	2	3	4	5
10	5	4	3	2	1	46	1	2	3	4	5
11	5	4	3	2	1	47	5	4	3	2	1
12	5	4	3	2	1	Autonomy	A	B	C	D	E
Stability	A	B	C	D	E	48	5	4	3	2	1
13	1	2	3	4	5	49	1	2	3	4	5
14	1	2	3	4	5	50	1	2	3	4	5
15	1	2	3	4	5	51	1	2	3	4	5
16	1	2	3	4	5	52	1	2	3	4	5
17	5	4	3	2	1	53	1	2	3	4	5
Intimacy	A	B	C	D	E	54	1	2	3	4	5
18	5	4	3	2	1	55	1	2	3	4	5
19	5	4	3	2	1	56	1	2	3	4	5
20	5	4	3	2	1	57	1	2	3	4	5
21	1	2	3	4	5	58	1	2	3	4	5
22	5	4	3	2	1	59	1	2	3	4	5
23	5	4	3	2	1	60	1	2	3	4	5
24	5	4	3	2	1	Potency	A	B	C	D	E
25	5	4	3	2	1	61	5	4	3	2	1
26	5	4	3	2	1	62	5	4	3	2	1
27	5	4	3	2	1	63	5	4	3	2	1
28	5	4	3	2	1	64	1	2	3	4	5
29	5	4	3	2	1	65	1	2	3	4	5
30	1	2	3	4	5	66	5	4	3	2	1
Stratification	A	B	C	D	E	67	5	4	3	2	1
31	1	2	3	4	5	68	5	4	3	2	1
32	5	4	3	2	1	69	5	4	3	2	1
33	5	4	3	2	1	70	1	2	3	4	5
34	5	4	3	2	1	71	5	4	3	2	1
35	1	2	3	4	5	72	5	4	3	2	1
36	5	4	3	2	1	73	5	4	3	2	1
						74	5	4	3	2	1
						75	1	2	3	4	5

Viscidity	A	B	C	D	E
76	1	2	3	4	5
77	1	2	3	4	5
78	1	2	3	4	5
79	5	4	3	2	1
80	1	2	3	4	5
81	1	2	3	4	5
82	1	2	3	4	5
83	5	4	3	2	1
84	1	2	3	4	5
85	1	2	3	4	5
86	1	2	3	4	5
87	1	2	3	4	5
Permeability	A	B	C	D	E
88	5	4	3	2	1
89	5	4	3	2	1
90	5	4	3	2	1
91	1	2	3	4	5
92	1	2	3	4	5
93	5	4	3	2	1
94	5	4	3	2	1
95	5	4	3	2	1
96	1	2	3	4	5
97	5	4	3	2	1
98	5	4	3	2	1
99	1	2	3	4	5
100	1	2	3	4	5
Participation	A	B	C	D	E
101	5	4	3	2	1
102	5	4	3	2	1
103	1	2	3	4	5
104	1	2	3	4	5
105	1	2	3	4	5
106	5	4	3	2	1
107	5	4	3	2	1
108	1	2	3	4	5
109	1	2	3	4	5
110	1	2	3	4	5
Polarization	A	B	C	D	E
111	5	4	3	2	1
112	1	2	3	4	5

113	1	2	3	4	5
114	5	4	3	2	1
115	5	4	3	2	1
116	1	2	3	4	5
117	1	2	3	4	5
118	5	4	3	2	1
119	5	4	3	2	1
120	1	2	3	4	5
121	1	2	3	4	5
122	1	2	3	4	5
Flexibility	A	B	C	D	E
123	5	4	3	2	1
124	1	2	3	4	5
125	1	2	3	4	5
126	1	2	3	4	5
127	5	4	3	2	1
128	1	2	3	4	5
129	1	2	3	4	5
130	1	2	3	4	5
131	1	2	3	4	5
132	1	2	3	4	5
133	1	2	3	4	5
134	1	2	3	4	5
135	5	4	3	2	1
Homogeneity	A	B	C	D	E
136	5	4	3	2	1
137	1	2	3	4	5
138	1	2	3	4	5
139	1	2	3	4	5
140	1	2	3	4	5
141	5	4	3	2	1
142	1	2	3	4	5
143	1	2	3	4	5
144	1	2	3	4	5
145	5	4	3	2	1
146	1	2	3	4	5
147	1	2	3	4	5
148	1	2	3	4	5
149	1	2	3	4	5
150	1	2	3	4	5

Group Dimensions Profile and Face Sheet

Name _____ Age _____ Date _____

Name of group _____

Length of your membership _____ No. of group members _____

General purpose of the group _____

	Dimension	Stanine score								
		1	2	3	4	5	6	7	8	9
A	Autonomy	.	.	.	.	.	.	.	.	.
B	Control	.	.	.	.	.	.	.	.	.
C	Flexibility	.	.	.	.	.	.	.	.	.
D	Hedonic Tone	.	.	.	.	.	.	.	.	.
E	Homogeneity	.	.	.	.	.	.	.	.	.
F	Intimacy	.	.	.	.	.	.	.	.	.
G	Participation	.	.	.	.	.	.	.	.	.
H	Permeability	.	.	.	.	.	.	.	.	.
I	Polarization	.	.	.	.	.	.	.	.	.
J	Potency	.	.	.	.	.	.	.	.	.
K	Stability	.	.	.	.	.	.	.	.	.
L	Stratification	.	.	.	.	.	.	.	.	.
M	Viscidity	.	.	.	.	.	.	.	.	.

Research Applications

Hemphill, John K. (1949). *Situational factors in leadership* (Bureau of Educational Research Monograph No. 32). Columbus: Ohio State University

Hemphill, John K. (1956). *Group dimensions: A manual for their measurement* (Research Monograph No. 87). Columbus: Ohio State University, Bureau of Business Research.

Hemphill, John K., & Westie, Charles M. (1950). The measurement of group dimensions. *Journal of Psychology, 29,* 325-342.

Pheysey, Diana C., & Payne, Roy L. (1970). The Hemphill Group Dimensions Description Questionnaire: A British industrial application. *Human Relations, 23,* 473-497.

7.3.2 Bales's Interaction Process Analysis

Variable measured.   Group interaction.

Description.   This index consists of 12 categories—shows solidarity, shows tension release, agrees, gives suggestion, gives opinion, gives orientation, asks for orientation, asks for opinion, asks for suggestion, disagrees, shows tension, shows antagonism. Scoring is made by designating each person in the group with a number. All interaction is analyzed according to the category and marked in the fashion of 1-5 or 1-0 as the interaction takes place. After observation, a summary or profile can be constructed and inferences made to describe the underlying workings of the group.

A slightly revised version of the categories has been developed by Bales (1970). A new interpersonal behavior rating system is organized around the dimensions of up/down, forward/back, and positive/negative. Category 1 is now labeled Seems Friendly and category 12 Seems Unfriendly; category 2 is now Dramatizes, and categories 6 and 7 are Gives Information and Asks for Information. Contents of other categories (except 3, 8, and 10) also have been changed.

Although Bales's scheme is not widely used today in its original form, it remains the model in its field. It did much to aid early development of small group analysis.

Where published.   R. F. Bales, *Interaction Process Analysis: A Method for the Study of Small Groups* (Cambridge, MA: Addison-Wesley, 1950).

Reliability.   With competent and trained observers, an interobserver correlation of between .75 and .95 can be obtained.

Validity.   Face validity. Consult the critique by Lake, Miles, and Earle (1973).

Utility.   This is a general-purpose, standard set of categories well suited for the observation and analysis of small groups. The chief disadvantage is that the training of observers requires a great deal of practice. Frequent retraining is also necessary.

1	SHOWS SOLIDARITY, raises others' status, gives help, reward:					
2	SHOWS TENSION RELEASE, jokes, laughs, shows satisfaction:					
3	AGREES, shows passive acceptance, understands, concurs, complies:					
4	GIVES SUGGESTION, direction, implying autonomy for other:					
5	GIVES OPINION, evaluation, analysis, expresses feeling, wish:					
6	GIVES ORIENTATION, information, repeats, clarifies, confirms:					
7	ASKS FOR ORIENTATION, information, repetition, confirmation:					
8	ASKS FOR OPINION, evaluation, analysis, expression of feeling:					
9	ASKS FOR SUGGESTION, direction, possible ways of action:					
10	DISAGREES, shows passive rejection, formality, withholds help:					
11	SHOWS TENSION, asks for help, withdraws "Out of Field":					
12	SHOWS ANTAGONISM, deflates other's status, defends or asserts self:					

References

Bales, R. F. (1970). *Personality and interpersonal behavior.* New York: Holt, Rinehart & Winston.

Lake, Dale G., Miles, Mathew B., & Earle, Ralph B. (1973). *Measuring human behavior.* New York: Teachers College Press.

Research Applications

Allen, William R., Comerford, Robert A., & Ruhe, John A. (1989). Factor analytic study of Bales' Interaction Process Analysis. *Educational and Psychological Measurement*, 49, 701-707.

Bell, Lorna. (2001). Patterns of interaction in multidisciplinary child protection teams in New Jersey. *Child Abuse and Neglect, 25*(1), 65-80.

De Grada, Eraldo, Kruglanski, Arie W., Mannetti, Lucia, & Pierro, Antonio. (1999). Motivated cognition and group interaction: Need for closure affects the contents and processes of collective negotiations. *Journal of Experimental Social Psychology, 35*, 346-365.

Jacobs, Janis E., & Bennett, M. A. (1993). Family decision-making during the transition into adolescence. *Journal of Early Adolescence, 13*, 245-266.

Martinez, I. M., Orengo, V., & Prieto, Fernando. (1998). Development phases of task groups in videoconference communication. *Revista de Psicologia Social Aplicada, 8*(2), 91-107.

Mpofu, D.J.S., Lanphear, J., Stewart, T., Das, M., Ridding, P., & Dunn, E. (1998). Facility with the English language and problem-based learning group interaction: Findings from an Arabic setting. *Medical Education, 32*, 479-485.

Pierro, Antonio, Sensales, Gilda, & Perez, Michela. (1998). Role differentiation in small groups: The effects of the sex composition of the group on expressive and instrumental behaviors. *Rassegna di Psicologia, 15*(1), 153-162.

Sells, James Nathan. (1995). The relationship between supervisor and trainee gender and their interactional behavior. *Dissertation Abstracts International, 56*, 874A.

7.3.3 Seashore's Group Cohesiveness Index

Index of Group Cohesiveness

Variable measured.   The index measures group cohesiveness, defined as attraction to the group or resistance to leaving.

Description.   The test consists of three questions: "Do you feel that you are really a part of your work group?" "If you had a chance to do the same kind of work for the same pay, in another work group, how would you feel about moving?" and "How does your work group compare with other work groups at Midwest on each of the following points?" The last question has three areas of comparison: the way people get along together, the way people stick together, and the way people help each other on the job. The first two questions can be answered by five degrees, and the three items of the third question are answered by four degrees.

Where published.   Stanley E. Seashore, *Group Cohesiveness in the Industrial Work Group* (Ann Arbor: University of Michigan, Institute for Social Research, Survey Research Center, 1954).

Reliability.   Intercorrelations among mean scale values for the groups on scales constituting the index of cohesiveness ranged from .15 to .70.

Validity.   The variance found among groups on this scale was significant beyond the .001 level.

Utility.   As the questions are phrased, the index is especially set up for an industrial situation. It can probably, with a few changes, be adapted to almost any situation where an index of group cohesiveness is required. The test takes very little time to administer. The subject should be assured that replies will be kept confidential.

Research applications.   The study of 228 section-shift groups in a company manufacturing heavy machinery, described in the Seashore monograph identified in the "Where published" section above.

"Do you feel that you are really a part of your work group?"

- ☐ Really a part of my work group
- ☐ Included in most ways
- ☐ Included in some ways, but not in others
- ☐ Don't feel I really belong
- ☐ Don't work with any one group of people
- ☐ Not ascertained

"If you had a chance to do the same kind of work for the same pay, in another work group, how would you feel about moving?"

- ☐ Would want very much to move
- ☐ Would rather move than stay where I am
- ☐ Would make no difference to me
- ☐ Would rather stay where I am than move
- ☐ Would want very much to stay where I am
- ☐ Not ascertained

"How does your work group compare with other work groups at Midwest on each of the following points?"

	Better than most	About the same as most	Not as good as most	Not ascertained
The way people get along together	☐	☐	☐	☐
The way people stick together	☐	☐	☐	☐
The way people help one another on the job	☐	☐	☐	☐

7.3.4 Sociometry Scales of Spontaneous Choice and Sociometric Preference

Variable measured.   The degree to which individuals are accepted in a group, interpersonal relationships that exist among individuals, and structure of the group.

Description.   Results are most satisfactory for small, cohesive groups. The sociometric technique consists of asking each individual in a group to state with whom among the members of the group he or she would prefer to associate for specific activities or in particular situations. Criteria (selected areas that should include different aspects of possible association: work, play, visiting) range in number from 1 to 8 or more; choices, from 1 to as many as desired by the researcher.

Where published.   J. L. Moreno, *Who Shall Survive? A New Approach to the Problem of Human Relationships* (Beacon, NY: Beacon House, 1934).

Reliability.   Loeb's correlations ranging from .53 to .85, test-retest reliability $r = .74$.

Validity.   Eugene Byrd's (1946) comparison of sociometric choice with actual choice and then an 8-week interval retest shows $r = .76, .80, .89$. Gronlund's (1951) comparison of judgment of teachers versus testing shows $r = .59$.

References

Byrd, Eugene. (1946). A study of validity and constancy of choices in a sociometric test. *Sociometry*, *9*(2-3), 21.

Gronlund, N. (1951). *Accuracies of teachers' judgments concerning the sociometric status of sixth grade pupils* (Sociometry Monograph No. 25). Beacon, NY: Beacon House.

Research Applications

Andrews, David, & Krantz, Murray. (1982). The effects of reinforced cooperative experience on friendship patterns of preschool children. *Journal of Genetic Psychology, 140*(2), 197-205.

Bukowski, William M., Hoza, Betsy, & Newcomb, Andrew F. (1994). Using rating scale and nomination techniques to measure friendship and popularity. *Journal of Social and Personal Relationships, 11*, 485-488.

Fjeld, Stanton P. (1965). A longitudinal study of sociometric choice and the communication of values. *Journal of Social Psychology, 66*, 297-306.

Herz, Joan A., et al. (1983, April). *Preschool children's concepts of their peers.* Paper presented at the biennial meeting of the Society for Research in Child Development, Detroit, MI.

Maras, Pam, & Brown, Rupert. (2000). Effects of different forms of school contact on children's attitudes toward disabled and non-disabled peers. *British Journal of Educational Psychology, 70*, 337-351.

Pettit, Gregory S., Bakshi, Anuradha, Dodge, Kenneth A., & Coie, John D. (1990). The emergence of social dominance in young boys' play groups: Developmental differences and behavioral correlates. *Developmental Psychology, 26*, 1017-1025.

Steiner, Ivan D., & Field, William L. (1960). Role assignment and interpersonal influence. *Journal of Abnormal and Social Psychology, 61*, 239-245.

Tagiuri, Renato, & Kogan, Nathan. (1957). The visibility of interpersonal preferences. *Human Relations, 10*, 385-390.

Tripathi, R. B. (1970). A sociometric study for the selection of section commander in "SICP" cadets. *Indian Psychological Review, 6*(2), 104-106.

Wait, Robert F., & Burke, Peter J. (1984). *Task performance factors and social-emotional leadership in small groups.* Paper presented at the meeting of the North Central Sociological Association.

Spontaneous Choice Test

Opposite each name, check how you feel about persons in your group.

	Like	*Dislike*	*Indifferent*
Mary J.			
James F.			
John J.			
Sam E.			
Etc.			

Sociometric Preference Test

Choose five persons you would most like to work with.[a] Mark 1st, 2nd, 3rd, 4th, 5th choice.

Mary J.			
James F.			
John J.			
Sam E.			
Etc.			

a. Many criteria may be employed. For example, to have in a discussion group, to have in your neighborhood, to play bridge with, to work on a project with, etc.

7.3.5 Bogardus's Social Distance Scale

Variable measured. The social distance or degree of social acceptance that exists between given persons and certain social groups. The scale may be adapted to measure the social distance between two persons or between two or more social groups. The method has been applied to racial distance, regional distance, sex distance, age distance, parent-child distance, educational distance, class distance, occupational distance, religious distance, and international distance.

Description. Typically, a group of persons is asked to rank a series of social types with respect to the degrees of social distance on seven attributes, starting with "acceptance to close kinship by marriage" and concluding with "would exclude from my country." A group of 100 people acting as judges have identified these 7 attributes among 60 as those ordered on a continuum of social distance.

Where published. Emory S. Bogardus, *Social Distance* (Yellow Springs, OH: Antioch, 1959).

Reliability. Split-half reliability coefficient reported at .90 or higher.

Validity. Theodore Newcomb reports high validity if one uses agreement with other scales that in certain particulars are more exact. Application of the known-group method is advocated in determination of validity. This involves finding groups known to be favorable toward some of the ethnic types and unfavorable toward others. If the responses of these groups fit the requisite pattern, evidence for validity may be accepted.

Scoring. Several scoring methods have been used. A simple method that has been found to be as reliable as more complex ones is that of counting the numbers of the nearest column that is checked. That is, if the racial distance quotient (RDQ) of a number of persons is desired, then the arithmetic mean of the total number of the nearest columns that are checked by all the subjects for each race is obtained. If the RDQ of a person is sought, then the arithmetic mean of the total numbers of the nearest column for each race is obtained.

Utility. The Bogardus scale may be used to estimate the amount of potential and real conflict existing between any cultural groups, anywhere in industrial, political, racial, religious, and other phases of life. It also helps to determine the extent of the trend toward conflict or toward cooperation between groups. The test is easy to administer and to score. It can be adapted easily to other problems of social distance.

Research Applications

Brooks, Thomas Daniel. (2000). Differences in ethnic identity and social distance in White and Native Americans. *Dissertation Abstracts International, 60,* 3959A.

Fox, Louise W. (1984, April). *College students' attitudes towards social, physical and political deviancy.* Paper presented at the annual meeting of the Eastern Psychological Association, Baltimore, MD.

Howe, Esther. (1999). Reducing interethnic social distance among adolescents through participation in life-skills groups. *International Journal of Adolescent Medicine and Health, 11,* 411-428.

Kleg, Milton, & Yamamoto, Kaoru. (1995). Ethnic and racial social distance: Seven decades apart. *Psychological Reports, 76*(1), 65-66.

Kunz, Phillip R., & Yaw, Oheneba-sakyi. (1989). Social distance: A study of changing views of young Mormons toward Black individuals. *Psychological Reports, 65*(1), 195-200.

Lee, Sai Quon. (2000). Ethnic conflict: Social distance and trait attribution perspectives within four Southeast Asian ethnic groups in the United States. *Dissertation Abstracts International*, *60*, 5836B.

Meyer-Lee, Elaine E. (1999). Understanding change in White adult students' racial identity and attitudes: The contribution of a developmental-contextual approach. *Dissertation Abstracts International*, *60*, 3002B.

Oddou, Gary, & Clavijo, Fabio. (1983, August). *Teaching culture: The effects on attitude change and perceived similarity.* Paper presented at the annual convention of the American Psychological Association, Anaheim, CA.

Owen, Carolyn A., Eisner, Howard L., & McFaul, Thomas R. (1981). A half-century of social distance research: National replication of the Bogardus studies. *Sociology and Social Research*, *66*(1), 80-98.

Rapp, Adrian. (1983). Prejudice and discrimination among community college students. *Community College Social Science Journal*, *4*(3), 63-66.

7.3.5.1 Bogardus's Racial Distance Scale

Race is defined here largely as a cultural group.

Directions

1. Remember to give your *first feeling* reactions in every case.
2. Give your reactions to each race as a *group*. Do not give your reactions to the best or to the worst members that you have known, but think of the picture or stereotype that you have of the whole race.
3. Put a cross after each race in as many of the five rows as your feeling dictates.

Category	English	Swedes	Poles	Koreans	Etc.
1. To close kinship by marriage					
2. To my club as personal chums					
3. To my street as neighbors					
4. To employment in my occupation					
5. To citizenship in my country					

SOCIAL INDICATORS 7.4

The role of social indicators known as *social reporting*, *social systems accounting*, and *social intelligence* is set forth in the following definition: Social indicators—statistics, statistical series, and all other forms of evidence—are summary measures that enable policymakers and other decision makers to assess various social aspects of an ongoing society and to evaluate specific programs and determine their impacts. Social indicators help experts and laypersons alike to understand better their own and other societies with respect to values and goals and the nature of social change. Stuart Rice (1967) has provided a compact statement:

> Social Indicators . . . are needed to find pathways through the maze of society's interconnections. They delineate social states, define social problems, and trace social trends, which by social engineering may hopefully be guided toward social goals formulated by social planning. (p. 173)

The potential scope of social indicators is very broad. The question of goals must be resolved before the appropriate scope can be determined. The final answer may best be given by the needs of a society and the requests of policymakers for information about problems they must meet and solve.

Reference

Rice, Stuart A. (1967). Social accounting and statistics for the Great Society. *Public Administration Review, 27*, 169-174.

7.4.1 Definitions of Social Indicators

Whatever social indicators are used on community, state, national, or internal levels, there tends to be a high level of agreement of what each indicator represents. What follows is a list/glossary of some of the most common terms used as social indicators, adapted from the Web site www.socwatch. org.uy/indicators/Glossary.htm. It is adapted with permission from the Third World Institute, Uruguay. Terms in bold type within definitions have listings of their own.

AIDS: AIDS cases per 100,000 people.

Area: Land area (in square kilometers) is a country's total area, excluding area under inland water bodies. In most cases the definition of inland water bodies includes major rivers and lakes.

Assistance as percentage of GNP (donors): Assistance disbursed as percentage of donor countries' GNP.

Assistance as percentage of GNP (receivers): Assistance as percentage of receiver countries' GNP.

Assistance in dollars (donors): Assistance disbursed by donors in millions of dollars.

Assistance in dollars (receivers): Assistance received in millions of dollars.

Assistance per capita (receivers): Assistance received (per capita) in dollars.

Assistance to LDC (donors, $): Total net **official development assistance (ODA)** disbursed by DAC to Least Developed Countries (millions of dollars).

Assistance to LDC (donors, % GNP): Total net **official development assistance (ODA)** disbursed by DAC to Least Developed Countries (as percentage of donor GNP).

Births attended: The percentage of births attended by physicians, nurses, midwives, trained primary health care workers, or trained traditional birth attendants.

Calories: Daily calorie supply per capita shows the equivalent in calories of the net daily supply of food in a country divided by the population.

Child mortality (under 5): Under-5 mortality rate shows the annual number of deaths of children under 5 years of age per 1,000 live births. More specifically, it shows the probability of dying between birth and exactly 5 years of age expressed per 1,000 live births.

Contraceptives: Contraceptive prevalence rate is the percentage of women who are practicing, or whose sexual partners are practicing, any form of contraception. It is usually measured for married women age 15-49 only.

Convention on Civil and Political Rights: International Covenant on Civil and Political Rights, 1966.

Convention on Economic, Social and Cultural Rights: International Covenant on Economic, Social and Cultural Rights, 1966.

Convention on Political Rights of Women: Convention on the Political Rights of Women, 1953.

Convention on Racial Discrimination: International Covenant on the Elimination of All Forms of Racial Discrimination, 1969.

Convention on Refugees Status: Convention Relating to the Status of Refugees, 1954.

Convention on Rights of Children: Convention on the Rights of Children, 1989.

Convention on Women Discrimination: Convention on the Elimination of All Forms of Discrimination Against Women, 1979.

Defense (as % of GNP): Military expenditures as a percentage of GNP. Military expenditures for NATO countries are based on the NATO definition, which covers military-related expenditures of the defense ministry (including recruiting, training, construction, and the purchase of military supplies and equipment) and other ministries. Civilian-type expenditures of the defense ministry are excluded. Military assistance is included in the expenditures of the donor country, and purchases of military equipment on credit are included at the time the debt is incurred, not at the time of payment. Data for other countries generally cover expenditures of the ministry of defense (excluded are expenditures on public order and safety, which are classified separately).

Defense (as % of health and education): Military expenditures as a percentage of health and education expenditures. *See* **defense (as % of GNP)** for further information.

Defense (as % of total expenditures): Military expenditures as a percentage of total expenditures. *See* **defense (as % of GNP)** for further information.

Deforestation: Annual rate of deforestation (1,000 ha per year). The permanent clearing of forest lands for shifting cultivation, permanent agriculture, or settlements; it does not include other alterations such as selective logging.

Doctors per 100,000 people: Doctors are defined as graduates of any facility or school of medicine who are working in the country in any medical field (practice, teaching, research).

Earned income share (female): Percentage of total income earned by women. PNUD calculations are based on estimates from the following: for real GDP per capita (PPP$), World Bank; for share of economically active population, ILO; and for female wages as percentage of male wages, ILO, UN, and Psacharopoulos and Tzannatos.

Earned income share (male): Percentage of total income earned by men. *See* **earned income share (female)** for further information.

Education (expenditure): Public expenditure on education as percentage of GNP.

Education expenditure (primary and secondary): Public expenditure on primary and secondary education as percentage of expenditure on all education levels.

Expected years of schooling: Average number of years of formal schooling that a child is expected to receive, including university education and years spent in repetition. It may also be interpreted as an indicator of the total education resources, measured in school years, that a child will require over the course of his or her "lifetime" in school. May be measured separately for male and female children.

Exports: Exports in millions of dollars. Exports of goods and services represent the value of all goods and other market services provided to the world. Included is the value of merchandise, freight, insurance, travel, and other nonfactor services. Factor and property income (formerly called factor services), such as investment income, interest, and labor income, are excluded. Data are in current U.S. dollars.

External debt (% of GNP): Total external debt is debt owed to nonresidents repayable in foreign currency, goods, or services. Total external debt is the sum of public, publicly guaranteed, and private nonguaranteed long-term debt, use of IMF credit, and short-term debt. Short-term debt includes all debt having an original maturity of 1 year or less and interest in arrears on long-term debt. Data are in current U.S. dollars.

External debt (total in millions of dollars): *See* **external debt (% of GNP)** for further information.

Fertility: Total fertility rate represents the number of children that would be born to a woman were she to live to the end of her childbearing years and bear children at each age in accordance with prevailing age-specific fertility rates. The data are a combination of observed, interpolated, and projected estimates and usually are expressed as "children per woman."

Foreign direct investment: Foreign direct investment is net inflows of investment to acquire a lasting management interest (10% or more of voting stock) in an enterprise operating in an economy other than that of the investor. It is the sum of equity capital, reinvestment of earnings, other long-term capital, and short-term capital as shown in the balance of payments. Data are in current U.S. dollars.

Gender-related Development Index (GDI): The GDI uses the same variables as the **Human Development Index (HDI)** but adjusts the average achievement of each country in life expectancy, educational attainment, and income in accordance with the disparity in achievement between women and men.

Gender Empowerment Measure (GEM): The GEM index indicates whether women are able to actively participate in economic and political life. It focuses on participation, measuring gender inequality in key areas of economic and political participation and decision making. It thus differs from the **Gender-related Development Index (GDI)**, an indicator of gender inequality in basic capabilities.

Gender Empowerment Measure (rank): Shows the country position in the world ranking according with the **Gender Empowerment Measure (GEM)** index value.

Gini index: A summary measure of the extent to which the actual distribution of income or consumption differs from a hypothetical uniform distribution in which each person or household receives an identical share. The Gini index has a maximum value of 100%, indicating that one person or household receives everything, and a minimum value of zero, indicating absolute equality. A Lorenz curve plots the cumulative percentages of total income received against the cumulative percentage of recipients, starting with the poorest individual or household. The Gini index measures the area between the Lorenz curve and a hypothetical line of absolute equality, expressed as a percentage of the maximum area under the line.

Gross national product (GNP) (growth): Annual growth rate of GNP at market prices based on constant 1987 local currency. The GNP consists of the total internal and external aggregate value produced by residents, without calculating deductions for depreciation. It includes gross domestic product (GDP) plus net factorial income from abroad, which is the income collected from abroad by residents for factorial services (labor and capital) less analogous payments made to nonresidents who contribute to the national economy.

Gross national product (GNP) per capita: Shows the per capita GNP. *See* **gross national product (GNP) growth** for further information.

Gross national product (GNP) per capita (growth): Shows the annual growth rate of the per capita GNP. *See* **gross national product (GNP) growth** for further information.

Health (expenditure): Shows the total national health expenditure related to gross domestic product (GDP). This indicator is defined as the share of GDP devoted to health expenditure. It includes public and private expenditures.

Health (services): Access to health services, measured as the percentage of the population that can reach local health services by the usual means of transportation in no more than 1 hour. Note that facilities tend to be concentrated in urban areas. In some cases, rural areas may have a much lower level of access.

Human Development Index (HDI): A composite index, the HDI measures the average achievements in a country through three basic dimensions of human development: longevity, knowledge, and a decent standard of living. The variables used to show these dimensions are life expectancy, educational attainment, and real gross domestic product per capita.

Human Development Index (HDI) (rank): Shows the country position in the world ranking according with the HDI value. *See* **Human Development Index (HDI)** for further information.

Illiteracy (adult): The adult illiteracy rate is the proportion of adults aged 15 and above who cannot, with understanding, read or write a short, simple statement about their everyday life.

Immunization (BCG): Shows the percentage of the eligible population that have received BCG immunization according to national immunization policies. Definitions of immunization include three components: (a) the proportion of children immunized against diphtheria, pertussis, and tetanus (DPT); measles; poliomyelitis; tuberculosis; BCG; and hepatitis B before their first birthday; (b) the proportion of children immunized against yellow fever in affected countries of Africa; and (c) the proportion of women of childbearing age immunized against tetanus.

Immunization (DPT): Shows the percentage of the eligible population that have been immunized against diphtheria, pertussis, and tetanus (DPT) according to national immunization policies. See **immunization (BCG)** for further information.

Immunization (measles): Shows the percentage of the eligible population that have been immunized against measles according to national immunization policies. See **immunization (BCG)** for further information.

Immunization (polio): Shows the percentage of the eligible population that have been immunized against polio according to national immunization policies. See **immunization (BCG)** for further information.

Imports: Imports of goods and services represent the value of all goods and other market services provided from the rest of the world. Included is the value of merchandise, freight, insurance, travel, and other nonfactor services. Factor and property income (formerly called factor services), such as investment income, interest, and labor income, are excluded. Data are in current U.S. dollars.

Income (20% highest): Percentage share of income or consumption of the 20% highest is the share that accrues to population in the highest quintile. Data on personal or household income or consumption come from nationally representative household surveys. Where the original data from the household survey were available, they have been used to directly calculate the income (or consumption) shares by quintile. Otherwise, shares have been estimated from the best available grouped data. The distribution indicators for low- and middle-income economies have been adjusted for household size, providing a more consistent measure of income or consumption per capita. No adjustment has been made for geographic differences in the cost of living within countries, because the data needed for such calculations generally are unavailable. Because the underlying household surveys differ in method and in the type of data collected, the distribution indicators are not strictly comparable across countries. These problems are diminishing as survey methods improve and become more standardized, but strict comparability is still impossible. Whenever possible, consumption has been used rather than income. Households have been ranked by consumption or income per capita in forming the percentiles, and the percentiles are based on population, not households. Data on distribution for low- and middle-income economies are compiled by the Poverty and Human Resources Division of the World Bank's Policy Research Department, using primary household survey data obtained from government statistical agencies and World Bank country departments. Data for high-income economies are from national sources, supplemented by the Luxembourg Income Study 1990 database, the Eurostat statistical yearbook, and the United Nations' *National Accounts Statistics: Compendium of Income Distribution Statistics* (1985).

Income (20% lowest): Percentage share of income or consumption for the 20% lowest is the share that accrues to population in the lowest quintile. *See* **income (20% highest)** for further information.

Income (ratio 20% high/low): Income share of highest 20% of households to income of lowest 20%, a measure of the distribution of income or expenditure (or share of expenditure) accruing to percentile groups of households ranked by total household income, by per capita income, or by expenditure. Shares of population quintiles and the top decile in total income or consumption expenditure are used in calculating income shares. The data sets for these countries are drawn mostly from nationally representative household surveys conducted in different years during the reference period. The data sets for the high-income OECD economies are based on information from the Statistical Office of the European Union (Eurostat), the Luxemburg Income Study, and the OECD. Data should be interpreted with caution owing to differences between income studies in the use of income and consumption expenditures to estimate living standards.

Infant mortality: The infant mortality rate is the number of deaths of infants under 1 year of age per thousand live births in a given year. More precisely, it is the probability of dying between birth and the exact moment of the first birthday, multiplied by 1,000. The data are a combination of observed values and interpolated and projected estimates. A few countries, such as the economies of the former Soviet Union, employ an atypical definition of live births that reduces the reported infant mortality rate relative to the standard (World Health Organization) definition.

Labor force: Shows the percentage of the population in the labor force. The total labor force comprises people who meet the International Labour Organization definition of the economically active population: all people who supply labor for the production of goods and services during a specified period. It includes both the employed and the unemployed. Although national practices vary in the treatment of such groups as the armed forces and seasonal or part-time workers, in general the labor force includes the armed forces, the unemployed, and first-time job-seekers but excludes homemakers and other unpaid caregivers and workers in the informal sector.

Labor force (women): The female labor force as a percentage of the total shows the extent to which women are active in the labor force. *See* **labor force** for further information.

Life expectancy: The number of years a newborn infant would live if prevailing patterns of mortality at the time of birth were to stay the same throughout the child's life.

Low birth weight: The percentage of children weighing less than 2,500 grams at birth.

Malaria: Malaria cases per 100,000 people.

Malnutrition (under 5): The percentage of children under age 5 who are more than two standard deviations below the median birth weight for age of the reference population.

Maternal mortality: The maternal mortality ratio refers to the number of female deaths that occur during pregnancy and childbirth per 100,000 live births. Because deaths during childbirth are defined more widely in some countries to include complications of pregnancy or the period after childbirth or of abortion, and because many pregnant women die from lack of suitable health care, maternal mortality is difficult to measure consistently and reliably across countries. Clearly, many maternal deaths go unrecorded, particularly in countries with remote rural populations. This may account for some low estimates, especially for several African countries. The data are official estimates from administrative records, survey-based indirect estimates, or estimates derived from a demographic model developed by the World Health Organization (WHO) and the United Nations Children's Fund (UNICEF).

Official development assistance (ODA): Net grants or loans to countries and territories on Part I of the Development Assistance Committee (DAC) List of Aid Recipients (developing countries) that are undertaken by the official sector, with promotion of economic development and welfare as the main objective—and at concessional financial terms (if a loan, at least 25% grant element). Figures for total net ODA disbursed are based on OECD data for DAC member countries, multilateral organizations, and Arab countries.

Nurses per 100,000 people: All persons who have completed a program of basic nursing education and are qualified and registered or authorized by the country's authorities to provide responsible and competent service for the promotion of health, prevention of illness, care of the sick, and rehabilitation.

Population: Total population is based on the de facto definition of population, which counts all residents regardless of legal status or citizenship. Refugees not permanently settled in the country of asylum are generally considered to be part of the population of their country of origin.

Population (% urban): Percentage of the population living in urban areas according to the national definition used in the most recent population census. The percentage rural also is calculated.

Poverty (international line): A poverty line set at $1 a day per person is used by the World Bank for international comparison. This poverty line is based on consumption of goods and services. A poverty line of $2 a day is suggested for Latin America and the Caribbean. For Eastern Europe and the republics of the former Soviet Union, a poverty line of $4 a day has been used. For comparison among industrialized countries, a poverty line corresponding to the U.S. poverty line of $14.40 a day per person has been used.

Poverty (national line): Developing countries that have set national poverty lines have generally used the "food poverty" method. These lines indicate insufficient economic resources to meet basic minimum food needs. In industrialized countries, national poverty lines are used to measure relative poverty. The European Commission has suggested a poverty line for these countries as half of the median for adjusted personal income.

Poverty (rural): Shows the percentage of rural population living under the national poverty line. *See* **poverty (national line)** for further information.

Poverty (urban): Shows the percentage of urban population living under the national poverty line. *See* **poverty (national line)** for further information.

Pregnant women attended: Shows the percentage of women attended during pregnancy.

Primary school (children reaching grade 5): Percentage of children starting primary school who eventually attain grade 5 (grade 4 if the duration of primary school is 4 years). The estimate is based on the Reconstructed Cohort Method, which uses data on enrollment and repeaters for two consecutive years.

Pupils per teacher: The primary school pupil-teacher ratio is the number of pupils enrolled in primary school divided by the number of primary school teachers (regardless of their teaching assignment).

Radios: The estimated number of radio receivers in use for broadcasts to the general public, per 1,000 people.

Safe water: Access to safe water is the share of the population with reasonable access to an adequate amount of safe water (including treated surface water and untreated but uncontaminated water, such as from springs, sanitary wells, and protected boreholes). An "adequate" amount of water is that needed to satisfy metabolic, hygienic, and domestic requirements, usually about 20 liters of safe water per person per day. The definition of safe water has changed over time.

Sanitation: Access to sanitation refers to the percentage of population with at least adequate excreta-disposal facilities that can effectively prevent human, animal, and insect contact with excreta.

School enrollment (primary, gross): Gross primary school enrollment ratio. Primary school enrollment data are estimates of the ratio of children of all ages enrolled in primary school to the country's population of primary school–age children. Although many countries consider primary school age to be 6 to 11 years, others use different age groups. For countries with universal primary education, the gross enrollment ratios may exceed 100% because some pupils are younger or older than the country's standard primary school age.

School enrollment (primary, net): Net primary school enrollment ratio. This is the proportion of the population of the official age for primary education (according to national regulations) who are enrolled in primary schools. This indicator is used in monitoring the level of participation in primary education and in identifying the non-enrolled school-age population. Net enrollment ratios approaching 100% indicate availability of adequate primary school capacities and active enrollment of school-age children. Low net enrollment ratios signal inadequacies in universalizing participation in primary education, as a result of either the lack of school places or other factors that prevent children from enrolling in school. This indicator, when disaggregated by sex, highlights the extent of gender disparities. The relevance of this indicator in many developed countries is limited because primary school is compulsory, with an enrollment ratio usually near or even above 100% (because of enrollment of students outside the usual age range). If the enrollment is lower, it usually indicates a data problem.

School enrollment (secondary, gross): The gross secondary school enrollment ratio shows the total enrollment in secondary education as a proportion of the population of secondary school age according to national regulations.

School enrollment (secondary, net): The net secondary school enrollment ratio is the proportion of the population of the official age for secondary education (according to national regulations) who are actually enrolled in secondary schools.

School enrollment (tertiary, gross): The tertiary gross enrollment ratio is calculated by dividing the number of pupils enrolled in all postsecondary schools and universities by the population in the 20-24 age group. Pupils attending vocational schools, adult education programs, 2-year community colleges, and distant education centers (primarily correspondence courses) are included. The distribution of pupils across these different types of institutions varies among countries. A definition of the youth population as those 20 to 24 years of age has been adopted by UNESCO as the denominator because it represents an average tertiary level cohort, although people above and below this age group may be registered in tertiary institutions.

Scientists and technicians: Shows the number of scientists and technicians per 1,000 people. "Scientists" refers to scientists and engineers with scientific or technological training (usually completion of third-level education) in any field of science who are engaged in professional work in research and development activities, including administrators and other high-level personnel who direct the execution of research and development activities. "Technicians" refers to persons engaged in scientific research and development activities who have received vocational or technical training for at least 3 years after the first stage of second-level education.

Secondary school enrollment ratio: Shows the total enrollment in secondary education as a proportion of the population of secondary school-age according to national regulations.

Social expenditure: National social services expenditure comprises expenditures on health, education, housing, welfare, social security, and community amenities. These categories also cover compensation for loss of income to the sick and temporarily disabled; payments to the elderly, the permanently disabled, and the unemployed; family, maternity, and child allowances; and the cost of welfare services, such as care of the aged, the disabled, and children. Many expenditures relevant to environmental defense, such as pollution abatement, water supply, sanitary affairs, and refuse collection, are included indistinguishably in this category.

Telephones: Telephone main lines are telephone lines connecting a customer's equipment to the public switched telephone network. Data are presented per 1,000 people for the entire country.

Televisions: Number of television sets in use, per 1,000 people.

Tertiary students (female): Female tertiary students per 100,000 women.

Unemployment: All persons above a specified age who are not in paid employment or self-employed, but are available and have taken specific steps to seek paid employment or self-employment.

Unemployment benefits expenditure: Unemployment benefits expenditure as percentage of total government expenditure.

Unemployment incidence (12 months): Incidence of long-term unemployment (more than 12 months), expressed as a percentage.

Women (salaries): Women per 100 men in the labor force. The ratio measures men and women's respective shares in the labor force.

Women who breastfeed: Percentage of women who breastfeed for 6 months.

Youth unemployment: The ratio of unemployed young people to the total youth labor force. *See* **unemployment** for further information.

Research Applications

Boardman, Anthony P., Hodgson, Richard E., Lewis, Martyn, & Allen, Keith. (1997). Social indicators and the prediction of psychiatric admission in different diagnostic groups. *British Journal of Psychiatry, 171*, 457-462.

Bomalaski, Susan Huyler. (1999). Effects of counseling services with homeless women: Social indicators and intrapersonal outcomes. *Dissertation Abstracts International, 60*, 1842B.

Brown, Brett, Kirby, Gretchen, & Botsko, Christopher. (1997). *Social indicators of child and family well-being: A profile of six state systems* (Institute for Research on Poverty Special Report No. 72). Madison: Institute for Research on Poverty, Publications Department, University of Wisconsin–Madison.

Delgado, Melvin, & Barton, Keva. (1998). Murals in Latino communities: Social indicators of community strengths. *Social Work, 43*, 346-356.

Herman-Stahl, Mindy, Wiesen, Christopher A., Flewelling, Robert L., Weimer, BeLinda J., Bray, Robert M., & Rachal, J. Valley. (2001). Using social indicators to estimate county-level substance use intervention and treatment needs. *Substance Use and Misuse, 36*, 501-521.

Mammo, Abate, & French, John F. (1998). Using social indicators to predict addiction. *Substance Use and Misuse, 33*, 2499-2513.

Mazumdar, Krishna. (2000). Inter-country inequality in social indicators of development. *Social Indicators Research, 49*, 335-345.

Moore-Greene, Gracie. (2000). Standardizing social indicators to enhance medical case management. *Social Work in Health Care, 30*(3), 39-53.

Ryan, John A., Abdelrahman, A. I., French, John F., & Rodriguez, Gloria. (1999). Social indicators of substance abuse prevention: A need-based assessment. *Social Indicators Research, 46*(1), 23-60.

Zanders, Harry L. G. (1998). Social indicators. In Pieter J. D. Drenth, Henk Thierry, & Charles de Wolff (Eds.), *Handbook of work and organizational psychology. Vol. 2. Work psychology* (2nd ed., pp. 283-298). Hove, England: Psychology Press/Erlbaum.

7.4.2 Human Development Indicators

The United Nations Development Program has prepared an extensive summary of data from the 1999 *Human Development Report* by Mark Malloch Brown and Richard Jolly (New York: Oxford University Press). The table of contents is reprinted below.

7.4.2.1 Human Development Index

The Human Development Index (HDI), one of many different indices available at www.undp.org/hdro/indicators.html#industrial, is a composite score of many different variables that assess general quality of life. Table 7.1 shows the rankings of the countries with the highest HDI.

7.4.2.2 United Nations Social Indicators

The United Nations Statistics Division produces the following statistics as social indicators. Current data can be found at the Web site www.un.org/Depts/unsd/social/index.htm.

Population

Estimated population (thousands)
  Male
  Female
Sex ratio (males per 100 females)
Average annual rate of change of population (%)

Youth and Elderly Populations

Percentage of total population under age 15
Percentage of male population aged 60+
Percentage of female population aged 60+
Sex ratio (men per 100 women) in the population aged 60+

Table 7.1 RANKINGS OF COUNTRIES ON VARIOUS HUMAN DEVELOPMENT INDICATORS

Rank	Country	Life Expectancy at Birth, 1995 (years)	Adult Literacy Rate (%)	1995 Combined First-, Second-, and Third-Level Gross Enrollment Ratio (%)	1995 Real GDP per Capita (PPP$)[a]	1995 Adjusted Real GDP per Capita (PPP$)[a]	Life Expectancy Index, 1995	Education Index	Human Development Index, 1995
1	Canada	79.1	99	100	21,916	6,230.98	.9008	.9933	.96
2	France	78.7	99	89	21,176	6,229.37	.8948	.9567	.946
3	Norway	77.6	99	92	22,427	6,231.96	.8758	.9667	.943
4	United States	76.4	99	96	26,977	6,259.29	.8562	.98	.943
5	Iceland	79.2	99	83	21,064	6,229.11	.9028	.9367	.942
6	Finland	76.4	99	97	18,547	6,218.88	.8563	.9833	.942
7	Netherlands	77.5	99	91	19,876	6,225.7	.8747	.9633	.941
8	Japan	79.9	99	78	21,930	6,231	.9142	.92	.94
9	New Zealand	76.6	99	94	17,267	6,197.05	.8607	.9733	.939
10	Sweden	78.4	99	82	19,297	6,223.42	.8895	.9333	.936
11	Spain	77.7	97.1	90	14,789	6,187.12	.8783	.9473	.935
12	Belgium	76.9	99	86	21,548	6,230.21	.8652	.9467	.933
13	Austria	76.7	99	87	21,322	6,229.71	.8617	.95	.933
14	United Kingdom	76.8	99	86	19,302	6,223.44	.864	.9467	.932
15	Australia	78.2	99	79	19,632	6,224.81	.886	.9233	.932
16	Switzerland	78.2	99	76	24,881	6,254.05	.887	.9133	.93
17	Ireland	76.4	99	88	17,590	6,198.1	.856	.9533	.93
18	Denmark	75.3	99	89	21,983	6,231.11	.8388	.9567	.928

(continued)

◀ 493

Table 7.1 Continued

Rank	Country	Life Expectancy at Birth, 1995 (years)	Adult Literacy Rate (%)	1995 Combined First-, Second-, and Third-Level Gross Enrollment Ratio (%)	1995 Real GDP per Capita (PPP$)[a]	1995 Adjusted Real GDP per Capita (PPP$)[a]	Life Expectancy Index, 1995	Education Index	Human Development Index, 1995
19	Germany	76.4	99	81	20,370	6,227.27	.8572	.93	.925
20	Greece	77.9	96.7	82	11,636	6,140.28	.8813	.918	.924
21	Italy	78	98.1	73	20,174	6,226.68	.8828	.8973	.922
22	Israel	77.5	95	75	16,699	6,195.11	.8755	.8833	.913
23	Cyprus	77.2	94	79	13,379	6,178.34	.8703	.8897	.913
24	Barbados	76	97.4	77	11,306	6,135.82	.8502	.9054	.909
25	Hong Kong, China	79	92.2	67	22,950	6,232.88	.9007	.8379	.909
26	Luxembourg	76.1	99	58	34,004	6,286.9	.851	.8533	.9
27	Malta	76.5	91	76	13,316	6,177.83	.8588	.86	.899
28	Singapore	77.1	91.1	68	22,604	6,232.28	.8687	.8325	.896
29	Antigua and Barbuda	75	95	76	9,131	6,102.08	.8333	.8867	.895
30	Korea, Republic of	71.7	98	83	11,594	6,139.72	.779	.9298	.894
31	Chile	75.1	95.2	73	9,930	6,115.55	.8355	.8765	.893
32	Bahamas	73.2	98.2	72	15,738	6,191.43	.8028	.8958	.893
33	Portugal	74.8	89.6	81	12,674	6,171.35	.8305	.8673	.892
34	Costa Rica	76.6	94.8	69	5,969	5,968.72	.8603	.8613	.889

35	Brunei Darussalam	75.1	88.2	74	31,165	6,282.54	.8347	.8363	.889
36	Argentina	72.6	96.2	79	8,498	6,090.16	.7938	.9045	.888
37	Slovenia	73.2	96	74	10,594	6,125.71	.8035	.8867	.887
38	Uruguay	72.7	97.3	76	6,854	6,048.8	.7943	.9016	.885
39	Czech Republic	72.4	99	70	9,775	6,113.04	.7897	.8933	.884
40	Trinidad and Tobago	73.1	97.9	65	9,437	6,107.42	.8017	.8702	.88
41	Dsominica	73	94	77	6,424	6,031.66	0.8	.8833	.879
42	Slovakia	70.9	99	72	7,320	6,062.94	.7657	0.9	.875
43	Bahrain	72.2	85.2	84	16,751	6,195.29	.7868	.8474	.872
44	Fiji	72.1	91.6	78	6,159	6,015.99	.7845	.8709	.869
45	Panama	73.4	90.8	72	6,258	6,022.74	.8065	.8439	.868
46	Venezuela	72.34	91.1	67	8,090	6,081.66	.7885	.829	.86
47	Hungary	68.9	99	67	6,793	6,046.67	.7317	.8833	.857
48	United Arab Emirates	74.4	79.2	69	18,008	6,209.19	.8235	.7592	.855
49	Mexico	72.1	89.6	67	6,769	6,045.81	.7853	.8213	.855
50	Saint Kitts and Nevis	69	90	78	10,150	6,119	.7333	.86	.854
	Average	73.5	95.7	78.7	16,241	6,193	.8087	.9002	.896

SOURCE: Data from which this table was constructed can be found at the Web site www.undp.org/hdro/98hd1.htm. See also Mark Malloch Brown and Richard Jolly (1999), *Human Development Report* (New York: Oxford University Press).

NOTE: PPP$ = purchasing power parity dollars, an adjustment to reflect differences in the cost of goods among countries.

Human Settlements

Population distribution (% rural vs. urban)
Average annual rate of change of population (%)
    Urban
    Rural

Water Supply and Sanitation

Percentage of population with access to improved drinking water sources
    Total
    Urban
    Rural
Percentage of population with access to improved sanitation facilities
    Total
    Urban
    Rural

Housing

Average number of persons per room
    Total
    Urban
    Rural

Health

Life expectancy at birth (years)
    Male
    Female
Infant mortality rate
Child mortality rate
    Male
    Female

Childbearing

Total fertility rate
Estimated maternal mortality ratio
Contraceptive prevalence among married women of childbearing age (%)
    Any method
    Modern method

Education

School life expectancy (expected number of years of formal schooling)
    Total
    Male
    Female

Literacy

Estimated adult (15+) illiteracy rate (%)
   Men
   Women
Illiteracy rate (%)
   Ages 15-24 (calculated as total and for men and women separately)
   Ages 25+ (calculated as total and for men and women separately)

Income and Economic Activity

Per capita gross domestic product ($US)
Adult economic activity rate (%)
   Male
   Female
Unemployment (% unemployed)
   Total
   Male
   Female

7.4.3 National Social Indicators

Following are selected social indicators used by various social agencies at the U.S. federal government level.

1. Population and the Family

Lifetime births expected by wives 18 to 34 years old, by race, selected years

Satisfaction with family life and attitudes toward older persons sharing home with their grown children, marital happiness, and ease of divorce

1a. Population growth and composition

Population growth, selected years

Average annual rate of population change, selected years

Population, by sex and age

Population, by race and age

Components of population change, selected years

Fertility rates, by age of mother

Cumulative fertility rates for selected cohort groups

Immigrants admitted, by major occupation group, selected years

Average annual migration rate, by metropolitan status

Average annual migration rate in counties not adjacent to Standard Metropolitan Statistical Areas (SMSAs), by population density

1b. Family size and composition

Families, by type, selected years

Average size of families, by age of members, selected years

Families, by type and race

Marital status of women maintaining families with no husband present, by race

Families, by number of own children under 18 years old and race

Families, by size and race

1c. *Living arrangements*

Family status of persons, by age and sex

Living arrangements of unrelated individuals, by age and sex

Children under 18 years old in families, by presence of parents and race of children

1d. *Marital status and stability*

Marital status of the population 14 years old and over, by sex, selected years

Married women 14 years old and over, by selected age group, selected years

First marriages, divorces, and remarriages of women

Divorced persons per 1,000 married persons with spouse present, by race, sex, and age, selected years

Divorce decrees involving children, by number of children involved

Marital dissolution based on divorce and death rates

Divorce rates for first and second marriages, by sex and selected cohort groups

1e. *International comparisons*

Population growth, by region of the world

Years required to double population, by region of the world

Population growth, selected countries

Years required to double population, selected countries

Total fertility rate for selected countries, selected years

Index of aging and dependency ratio, by region of the world

Index of aging and dependency ratio for selected countries, selected years

2. *Health and Nutrition*

2a. *Public perceptions*

Self-assessment of health, by age and income

Selected opinion items relating to the health area

2b. *Health resources, utilization, and costs*

Primary care physicians and practicing dentists by location

Visits to physicians and dentists, by sex, age, and family income of patients

Discharges from short-stay hospitals and average length of stay, by age, sex, and family income of patients

Inpatient and outpatient care episodes in mental health facilities

New admissions to state and county mental hospitals, by primary diagnosis and sex of patients

Admissions to outpatient mental health services, by primary diagnosis and by race and sex of patients

National and personal expenditures for health care, by source of payment, selected years

Consumer price indexes for selected medical care expenses, selected years

2c. Life chances

Life expectancy at birth, by race and sex

Life expectancy at ages 20 and 65, by race and sex

Death rates due to heart disease and malignant neoplasm, persons 50 years old and over, selected years

Death rates for children and teenagers, selected causes and years

Infant mortality rates, by race

2d. Health status

Days of disability, by type, and by sex and family income of patient, selected years

Prevalence of selected chronic diseases, by selected population characteristics

Adults who have had hypertension, by sex, race, and age

Adults who had a blood pressure check within the past year, by sex, race, and age

2e. Prevention and nutrition

Children 1 to 4 years old immunized against measles, rubella, dpt, and polio, by race

Persons who smoke, by sex, race, and selected age group, selected years

Average daily consumption of 0.501 ounces or more of absolute alcohol by persons 18 years old or over, by selected characteristics

Persons 20 to 74 years old who were determined by skinfold measurement to be obese, by sex, race, age, and poverty status

Persons 17 years old and over who assessed themselves as overweight, by sex

Persons 12 to 74 years old on diets for weight reduction, by selected characteristics

Mean iron intake of persons, by sex, race, poverty level, and age

Initiation of prenatal care, by trimester, and by race and age of mother

Adults with high cholesterol, by age and sex

Per capita consumption of major food commodities

2f. International comparisons

Life expectancy at birth, by sex, selected countries

Infant mortality rates, selected countries

3. Housing and the Environment

3a. Public perceptions

Evaluation of housing units, by location and tenure

Evaluation of neighborhood, by location and tenure

3b. Housing inventory and facilities

Changes in housing inventory, by geographic area and region

Selected characteristics of occupants of all housing units and units built since 1970 in SMSA central cities, by tenure

Changes in housing occupancy, by race and geographic area

Housing problems, selected years

Increase in housing prices and family income

Comparative rental costs of subsidized and nonsubsidized housing

Type of home heating fuel in occupied units, by region, selected years

3c. *Trends in housing demand*

Population increase, by region
Projected housing demand, by type of unit and source

3d. *Community services and amenities*

Inadequate neighborhood services, by tenure and location
Wish to move, by inadequate neighborhood services, tenure, and location
Selected undesirable neighborhood conditions, by tenure

3e. *Environmental quality*

Selected sources of neighborhood pollution, by tenure
Estimated air pollutant emissions, by source, selected years
Estimated pollutant discharges to waterways, by source and region
Federal expenditures to improve and protect the environment
Evaluation of expenditures to improve and protect the environment

3f. *International comparisons*

Rooms per dwelling and persons per household, selected countries, latest available year
Persons per room and dwelling units with 1.5 or more persons per room, selected countries, latest available year
Dwelling units with selected household amenities, selected countries, latest available year

4. *Transportation*

4a. *Public perceptions*

Selected inadequate neighborhood services
Selected undesirable neighborhood transportation-related conditions
Satisfaction with means of travel to work as compared with last year
Satisfaction with change in means of travel to work
Views toward selected transportation concerns
Conditions and future needs of selected transportation facilities

4b. *The role of transportation in American life*

Importance of transportation to U.S. economy
Related economic and transportation trends
Freight and transportation expenditures, selected years

4c. *Intercity travel*

Intercity travel by type of carrier
Intercity passengers carried by public carrier
Passenger car use, by purpose
Changes in automobile use
Automobiles in operation, by age, selected years
Motor vehicle fuel consumption and miles per gallon

4d. Social costs and impacts

Motor vehicle mileage and mileage death rates
Personal consumption expenditures for transportation
Atmospheric pollutants, by type
Average atmospheric pollutants, by type and source

4e. Transportation energy

Consumption of energy, by end-use sector, selected years
Energy consumption for transportation
Gross national product and gross energy consumption per capita, selected years
Fuel efficiency of U.S. passenger cars

4f. International comparisons

Motor vehicle registrations, selected countries and years
Motor vehicle fatality rates, by selected countries

5. Public Safety

5a. Public perceptions

Persons afraid to walk alone at night, selected years
Attitudes toward treatment of criminals by the courts, selected years

5b. Resource commitments

Police protection expenditures, by level of government, selected fiscal years
Per capita expenditures for police protection, by state
Per capita expenditures for police protection, selected cities
Full-time police protection employees, selected cities
Personal crimes of violence and theft, selected cities

5c. Crime and its victims

Violent crimes reported to the Federal Bureau of Investigation, by type
Property crimes reported to the Federal Bureau of Investigation, by type
Victims of homicide, by race and sex
Personal crimes of violence and theft, by type
Personal crimes of violence and theft, by sex, race, and Hispanic origin of victims
Personal crimes of violence and theft, by age of victims
Household crimes, by race of victims and type of crime
Household crimes, by race and tenure of victims and type of crime
Household crimes, by family income of victims and type of crime
Household crimes, by race and family income of victims and by type of crime
Victimizations reported to the police, by type of crime
Victimizations reported to the police, by race of victims and type of crime

5d. Other public safety indicators

Deaths due to transportation accidents, by type
Deaths due to fire

Deaths due to fire, by sex and race

Deaths and injuries due to fire, by age and sex

5e. *International comparisons*

Unexpected deaths due to transport accidents and to natural factors, selected countries

Unexpected deaths due to industrial accidents, homicides, and other causes, selected countries

Deaths due to motor vehicle accidents, selected countries

Deaths due to homicides, selected countries

Deaths due to fires, selected countries

6. *Education and Training*

6a. *Public perceptions*

Educational aspirations and expectations of parents for their elementary school children

Perceptions of the level of expenditures to improve the nation's educational system and confidence in people running that system

Importance of a college education, by race, educational attainment, and income level of respondents

6b. *Resource commitments*

Public and private schools, by level, selected years

Classroom teachers employed in public and private elementary and secondary schools, selected years

Pupil-teacher ratios in public and private elementary and secondary schools

Resident instructional staff in institutions of higher learning

Expenditures for education, health, and defense as a percentage of gross national product (GNP)

State and local expenditures by type, selected years

Expenditures per pupil for elementary and secondary education, selected years

Expenditures of public and private institutions of higher learning, by source of revenue, selected years

6c. *Enrollment and attainment*

School enrollment of persons 3 to 34 years old, by level of school

High school graduation rates among persons 18 years old, by state

College enrollment of persons 18 to 24 years old, by sex and race

College enrollment of persons 18 to 34 years old, by race and ethnicity

College enrollment of dependent family members 18 to 24 years old, by family income

Educational attainment of persons 25 years old and over, by sex and race

6d. *Performance and achievement*

Students 8 to 17 years old enrolled below model grade, selected years

National assessment of educational progress for 9-year-olds, by subject and selected characteristics of participants

Change in science achievement of 9-, 13-, and 17-year-olds, by type of exercise

Median income of year-round, full-time workers 25 to 34 years old, by sex and educational attainment

Underemployment of bachelor's degree recipients, by sex and selected college field

6e. Adult education and training

Participation in adult education of persons 17 years old and over who were not enrolled in full-time elementary school, high school, or college, by educational attainment

Participation in adult education of persons 17 years old and over who were not enrolled full-time in high school or college, by type of provider

Participants in basic and secondary adult education, by age, race, and ethnicity

6f. International comparisons

Full-time school enrollment of persons 15 to 24 years old, selected countries

Expenditures for education as a percentage of GNP, selected countries

7. Work

7a. Public perceptions

Commitment to work

Relative importance of selected job characteristics

Overall job satisfaction, by selected characteristics of respondents

Indicators of job satisfaction

7b. Labor resources

Workers, by sex, and nonworkers, by age

Nonworkers per 100 workers, by age

Population and labor force, by sex

Total labor force, by sex and age

Labor force with 8 years or less of school completed, by sex and race

Labor force with 4 years or more of college completed, by sex and race

Educational attainment of employed workers, by sex, race, and occupation

Labor force participation of selected cohort groups, by sex and years of school completed

Persons not in labor force, by desire for job and reason for nonparticipation

7c. Employment and unemployment

Persons who worked, by duration and sex, selected years

Occupational distribution of employed workers, by sex and race

Married women, husband present, in labor force, by presence and age of children, selected years

Employment status of married men, by employment status of other family members, selected years

Self-employed and civilian government workers

Government employment and employment resulting from government enterprises and purchases of goods and services, selected years

Unemployment of persons 16 years old and over, by duration

Unemployment rates of persons 16 to 34 years old, by selected characteristics, selected years

Labor force and employment status of persons 16 to 19 years old, not enrolled in school, by sex

7d. Conditions and quality of work

Spendable average weekly earnings, by industry

New employment and occupational mobility rates of employed persons, by selected characteristics

Labor turnover rates in manufacturing

Current job tenure of employed workers 35 years old and over, by age, sex, and race

Average weekly hours of work

Work time lost, by reason

Workers engaged in shift work

Persons with two or more jobs, by sex and race

Black and Hispanic employment, by sex and occupation

Work stoppages and days idle

7e. *International comparisons*

Labor force participation rates, by sex, selected countries

Unemployment rates, selected countries

Employment by economic sector, selected countries and years

8. *Social Security and Welfare*

8a. *Public perceptions*

Attitudes toward spending on social issues

8b. *Resource commitments*

Public and private expenditures for selected social welfare purposes, selected years

Per capita social welfare expenditures, by public program area, selected years

Personal income other than wages and salaries, selected years

8c. *Protection provided*

OASDHI cash benefits, by type of beneficiary, selected years

Population age 65 and over receiving OASDHI cash benefits, SSI Payments, or both, selected years

Sources of income for persons age 65 and over, by marital status and sex, selected years

Median income of OASDHI beneficiaries age 65 and over, by marital status and sex, selected years

Hospital insurance claims paid to the elderly by Medicare, selected years

Employees covered by social insurance programs, selected years

Protection against income loss from short-term sickness, selected years

Workers covered by specified employee-benefit plans, selected years

Coverage and beneficiaries of private pension and deferred profit-sharing plans, selected years

Contributions to private pension and deferred profit-sharing plans, selected years

Average monthly payments per recipient, selected public assistance programs and years

Average monthly AFDC payments per family, by state

Recipients of AFDC, by status of father, selected years

Medical vendor payments (Medicaid), selected years

Recipients of Title XX social services, by category

8d. *International comparisons*

Expenditures for selected social welfare programs, selected countries

Change in social security pensions, wages, and prices, selected countries and years

7.4.4 Social Indicators at the State and Local Community Levels

The social indicator movement has not neglected the state level. The public welfare assistance load, infant mortality, crime, educational deficiency, and other issues are cited as problem areas. Statistics similar to those collected at the national level, listed in section 7.4.3, provide clues to social problems that require social action for their resolution.

Community social indicators should meet the same criteria as do national and state indicators. They should demonstrate measurability, tap social importance and shared goals, have policy importance, and fit into a model that explicates the most important relationships between the indicator and empirically associated variables.

7.4.5 A Directory of General and Specific Social Indicators and Current Developments

Hundreds of sources provide information about social indicators, and different organizations have designed their own sets useful in monitoring their own objectives. Table 7.2 provides a list of 11 such sources.

Table 7.2 SOURCES OF SOCIAL INDICATORS	
Source	*URL*
Health, United States, 2000	www.cdc.gov/nchs/products/pubs/pubd/hus/hus.htm
United Nations Statistics Division—Social Indicators	www.un.org/Depts/unsd/social/
World Bank Social Indicators	www.ciesin.org/lw-kmn/guides/sid.html
World Tables Dataset	www.ciesin.org/IC/wbank/wtables.html
The Social Indicators Site	www.ccsd.ca/soc_ind.html
Monthly Economic and Social Indicators	www.aph.gov.au/library/pubs/mesi/
Social Statistics Briefing Room	www.whitehouse.gov/fsbr/ssbr.html
International Sociological Association Working Group on Social Indicators	www.ucm.es/info/isa/wg06.htm
Indicators of Social Justice	www.aminso.com/index.html
Social Indicators Survey Center	www.columbia.edu/cu/ssw/projects/surcent/
European System of Social Indicators	www.gesis.org/en/social_monitoring/social_indicators/ EU_Reporting/eusi.htm

7.4.6 *Social Indicators Network News*

The International Society for Quality-of-Life Issues publishes *SINET*, the *Social Indicators Network News* (www.soc.duke.edu/dept/sinet/). This publication regularly contains information about the importance and use of social indicators. The contents page of the summer 2000 issue is reproduced on the next page as a sample of the publication's content.

Social Reports and Trends
  Has the Recent Epidemic in Adolescent Drug Use in the United States Peaked?
  Some Recent Findings from the *Monitoring the Future* Study
Social Indicators
  Indicators of Environmental Trends of Our World
Brief Reports
  Positive Psychology and the Quality of Life—A Conference Report
  New Country and Region Demographic Data
  Photos from the 3rd Annual ISQOLS Conference in Girona, Spain
Announcements
  The International Society for Quality-of-Life Studies
  The 2001 ISQOLS Conference—Call for Participation in Organizing Tracks
  Journal of Happiness Studies, Call for Papers
  The Citizenship Studies Journal
  Website for the EuReporting Project
  SINET World Wide Web Homepage

7.5 NATIONAL ECONOMIC INDICATORS

Economic conditions are a subset of social conditions, and economic indicators can provide insight into social conditions. National governments and research institutes collect data on a variety of economic indicators, a representative sampling of which is presented below.

Total Output, Income, and Spending

  Gross domestic product
  Real gross domestic product
  Implicit price deflators for gross domestic product
  Gross domestic product and related price measures: Indexes and percentage changes
  Nonfinancial corporate business: Output, price, costs, and profits
  National income
  Real personal consumption expenditures
  Sources of personal income
  Disposition of personal income
  Farm income
  Corporate profits
  Real gross private domestic investment
  Real private fixed investment by type
  Business investment

Employment, Unemployment, and Wages

  Status of the labor force
  Selected unemployment rates
  Selected measures of unemployment and unemployment insurance programs
  Nonagricultural employment

Average weekly hours, hourly earnings, and weekly earnings: Private nonagricultural industries

Employment cost index: Private industry

Productivity and related data, business sector

Production and Business Activity

Industrial production and capacity utilization

Industrial production: Major market groups and selected manufactures

New construction

New private housing and vacancy rates

Business sales and inventories: Manufacturing and trade

Manufacturers' shipments, inventories, and orders

Prices

Producer prices

Consumer prices: All urban consumers

Changes in producer prices for finished goods

Changes in consumer prices: All urban consumers

Prices received and paid by farmers

Money, Credit, and Security Markets

Money stock and debt measures

Components of money stock

Aggregate reserves and monetary base

Bank credit at all commercial banks

Sources and uses of funds, nonfarm nonfinancial corporate business

Consumer credit

Interest rates and bond yields

Common stock prices and yields

Federal Finance

Federal receipts, outlays, and debt

Federal receipts by source and outlays by function

Federal sector, national income accounts basis

International Statistics

Industrial production and consumer prices: Major industrial countries

U.S. international trade in goods and services

U.S. international transactions

MEASURES OF ORGANIZATIONAL STRUCTURE 7.6

A number of basic facts about organizational measurement should be considered in sociological studies:

1. A large number of structural attributes and interpersonal relationships exists both within a single organization and across different organizations.
2. Development of organizational measurement has come a long way in recent years, but serious shortcomings remain.
3. There is little standardization of the measures used in studying organizations. The lack of standardization hinders development of organizational theory and forces the researcher to use a high degree of judgment in selecting an organizational measure.
4. Although the measurement and description of structure is an interesting process and exercise in its own right, important research problems are centered on the correlation of various structural arrangements in organizations.
5. Correlates will range from such internal factors as morale and decision making to the impact of structure on external relationships such as cooperative, defensive, and competitive postures vis-à-vis other organizations. Interrelationships of structural relationships themselves reveal much about the character of the organization as a collective unit.
6. Some consensus about the most important structural variables is emerging. These include size, formalization, and centralization. Whatever else may be of interest, these variables usually cannot be ignored in research designs.
7. Researchers are highly interested in many other variables, including absenteeism, administrative staff, alienation, autonomy, bases of power, communication, complexity, consensus, coordination, dispersion, distributive justice, effectiveness, innovation, mechanization, motivation, routinization, satisfaction, span of control, specialization, and succession.
8. Two different sets of measures exist to assess many of these variables. One set represents the institutional approach, which relies on documents and informants; the other set relies on the survey approach, which is characterized by the use of questionnaire and interview schedules.
9. Measures for the three variables believed most important in analyzing correlations between these three variables and others—size, formalization, and centralization—have been selected. One social psychological measure, the Index of Job-Related Tensions in Organizations, is discussed in section 7.6.4.2.

Research Applications

Ashkenas, Ron, Jick, Todd, Ulrich, Dave, & Kerr, Steve. (1995). *The boundaryless organization: Breaking the chains of organizational structure*. San Francisco: Jossey-Bass.

Fritz, Robert. (1996). *Corporate tides: The inescapable laws of organizational structure*. San Francisco: Berrett-Koehler.

MacKenzie, Donald, & Rogers, Vernon. (1997). The full service school: A management and organizational structure for 21st century schools. *Community Education Journal, 25*(3-4), 9-11.

Oliver, Barry D. (1989). *SDA organizational structure: Past, present, and future*. Berrien Springs, MI: Andrews University Press.

Person, Ruth. (1994). Organizational structure at the crossroads. *Educational Record, 75*(3), 42-46.

Pollard, George. (1995). Job satisfaction among newsworkers: The influence of professionalism, perceptions of organizational structure, and social attributes. *Journalism and Mass Communication Quarterly, 72*, 682-697.

Sauer, Mavis Anne Cheney. (2001). The mindful conduit: Organizational structure, climate and individual characteristics related to stress, communication and decision processes. *Dissertation Abstracts International, 61*, 2807A.

Sciulli, Lisa M. (1998). *Innovations in the retail banking industry: The impact of organizational structure and environment on the adoption process*. New York: Garland.

Stanley, Kay, & Reiboldt, J. Max. (1999). *IPA management: Organizational structure and strategic planning*. New York: McGraw-Hill.

Underwood, James C., & Hammons, James O. (1999). Past, present, and future variations in community college organizational structure. *Community College Review, 26*(4), 39-60.

7.6.1 *The Organizational Measurement Manual*

The best available guide for the design and selection of an organizational measure is *The Organizational Measurement Manual* by David Wealleans (Burlington, VT: Gower, 2001). The table of contents is reproduced below.

PART 1: THE CONCEPT OF MEASUREMENT

PART 2: ESTABLISHING A PROCESS MEASUREMENT PROGRAMME

7.6.2 Size of Organization

Definition.   Size is the scale of operations of an organization. Measures of size include the number of personnel, the amount of assets, and the degree of expenditures. In organizational research, size generally is expressed as the number of employees, even though the number of employees is not necessarily the best way to measure the scale of operations. A firm may be quite large, but because of a very high degree of mechanization it may have relatively few personnel. Still, as an operating index the number of employees remains the most common measure.

Measurement.   Advice to a researcher about the measurement of size would be conditioned by the design of the research. Will it involve few or many organizations? Will these organizations be small, intermediate, or large in size? What breakdowns will be needed? By department, division, total organization? What sensitivity about data may be involved because of the nature of the organizations to be studied—health, governmental, industrial? What resources are available? Only funds to write? Or telephone? Funds to make a personal interview?

Organizations do not usually give out information casually. They make some information public as a matter of custom or law, and needed data may be available from the last annual report of the organization. The researcher should try the annual report first if all he or she needs is figures on total employment.

Numbers of employees in industrial and commercial organizations can be found in the following volumes. *Standard & Poor's Register of Corporations* provides important business facts on more than 100,000 leading public and private corporations worldwide, including current address, financial and marketing information, and a listing of officers and directors with positions and departments. A sample record for a company is shown in Figure 7.1.

DIALOG(R)File 527:S&P's Register-Corp.

	0018401
/CO, CO=	BLACK & DECKER CORP.
	701 E. Joppa Rd.
CY=, ST=, ZP=	Towson, MD 21204
TE=	TELEPHONE: 301-583-3900
/DE	BUSINESS: Consumer & professional power tools, household &
	outdoor products & accessories
S2=. P2=, PC=, SC=	PRIMARY SIC: 3546
S2=, SC=	SECONDARY SIC(S): 3423; 3524; 3541; 3545; 3634; 3635; 3639
YR=	YEAR STARTED: 1910
SA=	SALES: $1.94 Bil
EM=	EMPLOYEE TOTAL: 19,700
TY=	MARKET TERRITORY: NATIONAL INTERNATIONAL
SF=	THIS IS: A PUBLIC COMPANY An S&P 500 Company Included in Corporate Descriptions (File 133)
EX=	STOCK EXCHANGE: NYS; BST; PAC; MID; CIN; PSE CUSIP NUMBER: 091797
CU=	BANK: Morgan Guaranty Trust Co. of New York, New York, NY
AC=	ACCOUNTING FIRM: Ernst & Whinney, Baltimore, MD
LF=	LAW FIRM: Miles & Stockbridge
DO=, /DO, NA=, /NA	EXECUTIVES AND DIRECTORS: * Chrm, Pres & Chief Exec Officer Archibald, Nolan D
PO=	Chairman, Chief Executive Officer, President, Inside Director
DP=	Administration, Operations
	* Exec V-P Stevens, William E. Vice President-Executive, Inside Director Administration
	Sr V-P (Worldwide Inf Serv) Barcus, James F. Jr. Vice President-Senior Administration
	Sr V-P (Power Tools Group) Sherman, George M Vice President-Senior Administration

Figure 7.1.   A Sample Record from *Standard & Poor's Register of Corporations*

(continued)

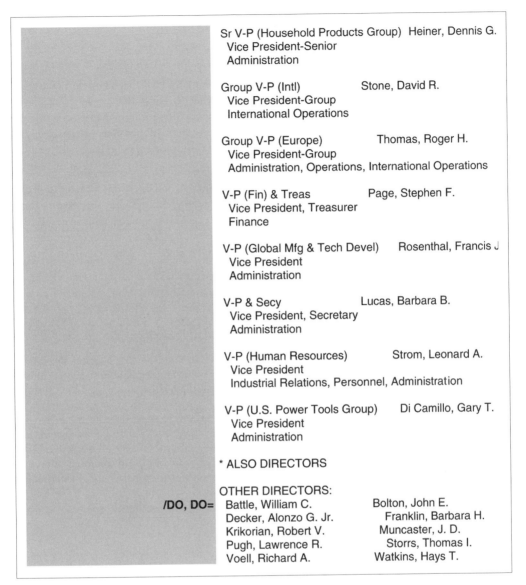

Sr V-P (Household Products Group) Heiner, Dennis G.
Vice President-Senior
Administration

Group V-P (Intl)   Stone, David R.
Vice President-Group
International Operations

Group V-P (Europe)   Thomas, Roger H.
Vice President-Group
Administration, Operations, International Operations

V-P (Fin) & Treas   Page, Stephen F.
Vice President, Treasurer
Finance

V-P (Global Mfg & Tech Devel)   Rosenthal, Francis J
Vice President
Administration

V-P & Secy   Lucas, Barbara B.
Vice President, Secretary
Administration

V-P (Human Resources)   Strom, Leonard A.
Vice President
Industrial Relations, Personnel, Administration

V-P (U.S. Power Tools Group)   Di Camillo, Gary T.
Vice President
Administration

* ALSO DIRECTORS

OTHER DIRECTORS:

/DO, DO=   Battle, William C.   Bolton, John E.
Decker, Alonzo G. Jr.   Franklin, Barbara H.
Krikorian, Robert V.   Muncaster, J. D.
Pugh, Lawrence R.   Storrs, Thomas I.
Voell, Richard A.   Watkins, Hays T.

Figure 7.1 Continued

If the needed information is not available publicly, the researcher should send a letter, place a telephone call, or pay a visit to the industrial relations director or personnel director, stating the needs, reasons, and sponsorship of the research. This official may be able to provide what is needed as expressed in department and division breakdowns. (The researcher should be sure to indicate what he or she can do with the data that may be useful to the organization.) Another strategy is to contact the marketing or public relations department, which is always interested in spreading news about almost any (positive) facet of the company's history and activities.

In most companies, the employment or personnel department stores personal records and the payroll department has an official payroll printout. The latter record may be the more accurate of the two. Of course, payroll (and personnel) often fluctuate greatly during the course of a year. It is important for the researcher to indicate how his or her computations take this into account.

7.6.2.1 Validity of Size as an Independent Factor in Organization Structuring and Dynamics

A summary of research on size and its correlates is provided by Hall (1972, esp. pp. 112-139). This summary points out that the size factor has led to rather contradictory conclusions in the determination of the form of the organization. There is, however, growing consensus that larger organizations tend to have more specialization, more standardization, and more formalization than smaller organizations. A lack of relationship between size and the remaining structural dimensions—that is, concentration of authority and line control of work flows—is equally striking. Hall, Haas, and Johnson (1967), using data on 75 North American organizations, report on the conclusions of their findings:

The most immediate implication of these findings is that neither complexity nor formalization can be implied from organizational size. A social scientist conducting research in a large organization would do well to question the frequent assumption that the organization under study is necessarily highly complex and formalized. . . . He will need to examine empirically, for each organization, the level of complexity and formalization extant at that time. (p. 911)

In Hall's (1972) review of research on size, conclusions are drawn about correlates with technology, professionalization, work flow, administrative components, the individual, the organization, and society (p. 138). The most important conclusions may be stated as follows:

1. The size factor is greatly modified by the technology or technologies employed by the organization.
2. The administrative component in relation to overall size of the organization displays a curvilinear relationship: The administrative component tends to decrease in size as organizational size increases; however, in very large organizations, the relative size of the administrative component again increases with overall size.
3. Large size has an impact on the individuals in the organization: There is more stress, and the depersonalization process can lead to discomfort for many members. Negative consequences are partially alleviated by the presence of informal friendship groups found in all organizations.
4. Large size creates difficulties in organizational control, coordination, and communications; at the same time, it gives the organization more power over its environment, more resources for planning, and less dependence on particular individuals.
5. The concentration of power in large organizations may in turn concentrate power in the society, with resulting threats to democratic processes.

References

Hall, Richard H. (1972). *Organizations: Structures and process.* Englewood Cliffs, NJ: Prentice-Hall.

Hall, Richard H., J. Eugene Haas, & Johnson, Norman J. (1967). Organizational size, complexity, and formalization. *American Sociological Review, 32*, 903-912.

7.6.3 Formalization

Definition. Formalization represents the use of rules in an organization. Some organizations carefully describe the specific authority, responsibilities, duties, and procedures to be followed in every job and then supervise job occupants to ensure conformity to the job definitions. A penalty system may be spelled out in writing for impartial monitoring of discipline for infractions. Other organizations have loosely defined jobs and do not carefully control work behavior.

The two dimensions of formalization may be specified as job codification, or the degree of work standardization, and rule leniency, or the measure of the latitude of behavior that is tolerated from standards.

Measurement. Extensive research on formalization has been done by Aiken and Hage (1966; Hage & Aiken, 1967a, 1967b, 1970), as well as by Richard Hall and his associates and other groups. Aiken and Hage have relied on the traditional type of survey. Hall and others have relied more on documentary data. Both approaches are recommended, but for economy the Aiken-Hage measure is reproduced.

7.6.3.1 Hage and Aiken Formalization Inventory

The data are collected by means of interviews. Fifteen questions are used.

Directions

I'm going to read a series of statements that may or may not be true for your job in [name of organization]. For each item I read, please answer as it applies to you and your organization, using the answer categories on this card.

1. definitely true
2. more true than false
3. more false than true
4. definitely false

		Definitely True	More True Than False	More False Than True	Definitely False
1.	First, I feel that I am my own boss in most matters.	___	___	___	___
2.	A person can make his own decisions here without checking with anybody else.	___	___	___	___
3.	How things are done around here is left pretty much up to the person doing the work.	___	___	___	___
4.	People here are allowed to do almost as they please.	___	___	___	___
5.	Most people here make their own rules on the job.	___	___	___	___
6.	The employees are constantly being checked on for rule violations.	___	___	___	___
7.	People here feel as though they are constantly being watched to see that they obey all the rules.	___	___	___	___
8.	There is no rules manual.	___	___	___	___
9.	There is a complete written job description for my job.	___	___	___	___
10.	Whatever situation arises, we have procedures to follow in dealing with it.	___	___	___	___
11.	Everyone has a specific job to do.	___	___	___	___
12.	Going through the proper channels is constantly stressed.	___	___	___	___
13.	The organization keeps a written record of everyone's job performance.	___	___	___	___
14.	We are to follow strict operating procedures at all times.	___	___	___	___

SOURCE: From Michael Aiken and Jerald Hage (1966), "Organizational Alienation," *American Sociological Review, 31,* 497-507. A minor adaptation of this inventory has been made by James L. Price.

Computation.   The five following measures are constructed from the 14 questions: job codification (questions 1-5), rule observation (questions 6-7), rule manual (question 8), job descriptions (question 9), and specificity of job descriptions (questions 10-15). Replies to these 15 questions are scored from 1 (*definitely true*) to 4 (*definitely false*). A mean is constructed for each respondent for each of the five measures of formalization. The higher the mean (4 is the highest mean), the higher the formalization. The researchers report no ranges from the means of the five measures. Each respondent is then classified by social position, and based on the first mean, a second mean is computed for each social position in the organization for each of the five measures. A social position is defined by the level or stratum in the organization and by the department or type of professional activity. For example, if an agency's professional staff consists of psychiatrists and social workers, each divided into the hierarchical levels, the agency has four social positions: supervisory psychiatrists, psychiatrists, supervisory social workers, and social workers. The organizational scores for each of the five measures are determined by computing an average of all social position means in the organization.

Where published.   Michael Aiken and Jerald Hage (1966), "Organizational Alienation," *American Sociological Review*, *31*, 497-507. Scale and data on reliability and validity are reproduced in James L. Price, *Handbook of Organizational Measurement* (Lexington, MA: D. C. Heath, 1972), pp. 108-111.

Reliability.   The study contains no data relevant to reliability.

Validity.   Formalization is positively related to alienation. The greater the degree of formalization in the organization, the greater the likelihood of alienation from work. There is great dissatisfaction with work in those organizations in which jobs are rigidly structured. Strict enforcement of rules was strongly related to work dissatisfaction; social relations are also disturbed when rules are strictly enforced. Significant positive relationships are found between routine work and rule manual, job description, and specificity of job descriptions.

Utility.   The interview can be conducted in less than 5 minutes in most cases.

References

Aiken, Michael, & Hage, Jerald. (1966). Organizational alienation. *American Sociological Review*, *31*, 497-507.

Hage, Jerald, & Aiken, Michael. (1967a). Program change and organizational properties. *American Journal of Sociology*, 72, 503-519.

Hage, Jerald, & Aiken, Michael. (1967b). Relationship of centralization in other structural properties. *Administrative Science Quarterly*, 12, 72-92.

Hage, Jerald, & Aiken, Michael. (1970). *Social change in complex organizations.* New York: Random House.

7.6.4 Centralization

Definition.   Centralization is the degree to which power is concentrated in an organization. Power is an important component in every organization. The distribution of power has major consequences for the performance of an organization and the behavior of its members.

An important consideration in dealing with power is the manner in which it is distributed. The maximum degree of centralization would exist if all power were exercised by a single individual; the minimum degree of centralization would exist if all power were exercised equally by all members of the organization. Most organizations fall between these two extremes.

Various problems are generated by the degree of centralized power and the manner in which actors wield their power and influence over superordinate, coordinate, and subordinate members of the organization. The following topics are commonly generated by problems of power stratification: participation-management, industrial democracy, group decision making, employee representation, collective bargaining, alienation, and organizational conflict.

Measurement.   As with most measures, centralization may be assessed by the institutional approach, using documents and informants, or by the use of the survey approach, with questionnaires and interview schedules as the principal instruments.

Research Applications

Bohannan, Paul. (1994). The rise and fall of centralization. *Human Organization, 53*, 395-398.

Cullen, John B., & Perrewe, Pamela L. (1981). Decision making configurations: An alternative to the centralization/decentralization conceptualization. *Journal of Management, 7*(2), 89-103.

Dallago, Bruno, & Mittone, Luigi. (Eds.). (1996). *Economic institutions, markets and competition: Centralization and decentralization in the transformation of economic systems.* Northampton, MA: Edward Elgar.

Edelson, Paul J. (1995). Historical and cultural perspectives on centralization/decentralization in continuing education. *Continuing Higher Education Review, 59*(3), 143-156.

Hall, Richard H., Jiang, Shanhe, Loscocco, Karyn A., & Allen, John K. (1993). Ownership patterns and centralization: A China and U.S. comparison. *Sociological Forum, 8*, 595-608.

Hetherington, Robert W., & Hewa, Soma. (1998). The consequences of centralization for performance in departments of a multihospital system. *International Journal of Contemporary Sociology, 35*(1), 28-56.

Huber, G. P., Miller, C. C., & Glick, W. H. (1990). Developing more encompassing theories about organizations: The centralization-effectiveness relationship as an example. *Organization Science, 1*(1), 11-40.

Piankoff, Janette. (1999). The effects of centralization, formalization and innovation norms on organizational commitment. *Dissertation Abstracts International, 60*, 1898B.

Prechel, Harland. (1994). Economic crisis and the centralization of control over the managerial process: Corporate restructuring and neo-Fordist decision-making. *American Sociological Review, 59*, 723-745.

Van Buren, Mark Everett. (1996). Technology fulcrums: Information technology, the centralization of decision-making, and performance in commercial banking. *Dissertation Abstracts International, 56*, 4170A.

7.6.4.1 Aiken and Hage Scale of Personal Participation in Decision Making and Hierarchy of Authority

The questions for the index of actual participation are as follows.

---

1. How frequently do you usually participate in the decision to hire new staff?

____ Never	____ Often
____ Seldom	____ Always
____ Sometimes	

2. How frequently do you usually participate in the decisions on the promotion of any of the professional staff?
3. How frequently do you participate in decisions on the adoptions of new policies?
4. How frequently do you participate in the decisions on the adoptions of new programs?

The questions for the scale of hierarchy of authority are as follows:

1. There can be little action taken here until a supervisor approves a decision.

____ Definitely false	____ True
____ False	____ Definitely true

2. A person who wants to make his or her own decisions would be quickly discouraged here.
3. Even small matters have to be referred to someone higher up for a final decision.
4. I have to ask my boss before I do almost anything.
5. Any decision I make has to have my boss's approval.

Computation. The computations differ for the two types of decisions. For the index of actual participation, the five responses are assigned numbers from 1 (*low participation*) to 5 (*high participation*). A *never* response receives a 1; at the other extreme, an *always* response receives a 5. An average score on these five questions is computed for each respondent. Each respondent is then classified by social position and a second mean is computed for each social position in the organization. A social position, according to Aiken and Hage, is defined by the level or stratum in the organization and the department or type of professional activity. For example, if an agency's professional staff consists of psychiatrists and social workers, each divided into two hierarchical levels, the agency has four social positions: supervisory psychiatrists, psychiatrists, supervisory social workers, and social workers. The organizational score is determined by computing the average of all social position means in the organization.

Computations for the hierarchy of authority scale are similar to those for the index of actual participation. The responses are assigned numbers from 1 (*definitely false*) to 4 (*definitely true*). As with the index of actual participation, the organizational scores for the hierarchy of authority scale are based on social position means, which in turn are based on the means for each respondent.

Where published. M. Aiken and J. Hage (1968), "Organizational Interdependence and Intraorganizational Structure," *American Sociological Review*, 33, 912-930. Reprinted by permission of the American Sociological Association and the authors.

Reliability. No relevant data are provided by Aiken and Hage.

Validity. Organizations in which the decisions were made by only a few people at the top relied on rules and close supervision as a means of ensuring consistent performance by the workers. These organizations were also characterized by a less professional staff. The presence of a well-trained staff is related to a reduced need for extensive rules. Pennings (1973) reports that organizations that are highly autonomous tend to have a nonparticipative internal decision structure. The greater the autonomy, the larger the executive's span of control.

Reference

Pennings, Johannes. (1973). Measures of organizational structures: A methodological note. *American Journal of Sociology*, 79, 686-704.

7.6.4.2 Index of Job-Related Tensions in Organizations

Variable measured. This index purports to measure the amount of tension experienced by an individual as a result of his or her job.

Description. The index consists of 15 statements describing what the authors judge to be symptoms of conflict or ambiguity. Respondents are asked to estimate how often they are bothered by each type of symptom on a 5-point Likert-type scale.

Where published. Robert L. Kahn and Donald M. Wolfe, *Organizational Stress: Studies in Role Conflict and Ambiguity* (New York: John Wiley, 1964), pp. 424-425.

Reliability. No test-retest reliability value is indicated, but an intercorrelation analysis of the items was performed on a national sample of 725 employed adults; in addition, an intensive survey was taken of 53 supervisory personnel. On the whole, the average interitem correlation appears to be in the middle .70s. The intercorrelation matrix figures for the intensive sample are quite close to those found in the national sample.

Validity. The survey utilized an open-ended question to elicit information about the number, content, and intensity of job-related worries. These were shown to be closely related to the tension index. Some indirect relationships between tension and satisfaction were found.

Utility. Time required for test administration is estimated at less than 15 minutes. The scale is equally applicable to employees and supervisory personnel. It is a diagnostic instrument as well as a measurement index. The diagnostic capacity of the index to identify major tensions may be its most significant attribute.

Scoring. The respondent answers each item by choosing one of six fixed responses: *never bothered, rarely bothered, sometimes bothered, bothered rather often, bothered nearly all the time*, and *does not apply.* Scores of 1 to 5 are assigned to the first five responses. The respondent's total score is his or her average score over all the items, except those to which he or she responded "does not apply." Scores can range between 0 and 5.

Index of Job-Related Tensions in Organizations

All of us occasionally feel bothered by certain kinds of things in our work. I am going to read a list of things that sometimes bother people, and I would like you to tell me how frequently you feel bothered by each of them. You are to indicate your response by choosing one of the six alternative answers provided each item.

1. Feeling that you have too little authority to carry out the responsibilities assigned to you.
   1. never bothered
   2. rarely bothered
   3. sometimes bothered
   4. bothered rather often
   5. bothered nearly all the time
   6. does not apply

2. Being unclear on just what the scope and responsibilities of your job are.
   1. never bothered
   2. rarely bothered
   3. sometimes bothered
   4. bothered rather often
   5. bothered nearly all the time
   6. does not apply

3. Not knowing what opportunities for advancement or promotion exist for you.
   1. never bothered
   2. rarely bothered
   3. sometimes bothered
   4. bothered rather often
   5. bothered nearly all the time
   6. does not apply

(continued)

4. Feeling that you have too heavy a work load, one that you can't possibly finish during an ordinary workday.
   1. never bothered
   2. rarely bothered
   3. sometimes bothered
   4. bothered rather often
   5. bothered nearly all the time
   6. does not apply

5. Thinking that you'll not be able to satisfy the conflicting demands of various people over you.
   1. never bothered
   2. rarely bothered
   3. sometimes bothered
   4. bothered rather often
   5. bothered nearly all the time
   6. does not apply

6. Feeling that you're not fully qualified to handle your job.
   1. never bothered
   2. rarely bothered
   3. sometimes bothered
   4. bothered rather often
   5. bothered nearly all the time
   6. does not apply

7. Not knowing what your supervisor thinks of you, how he evaluates your performance.
   1. never bothered
   2. rarely bothered
   3. sometimes bothered
   4. bothered rather often
   5. bothered nearly all the time
   6. does not apply

8. The fact that you can't get information needed to carry out your job.
   1. never bothered
   2. rarely bothered
   3. sometimes bothered
   4. bothered rather often
   5. bothered nearly all the time
   6. does not apply

9. Having to decide things that affect the lives of individuals, people that you know.
   1. never bothered
   2. rarely bothered
   3. sometimes bothered
   4. bothered rather often
   5. bothered nearly all the time
   6. does not apply

10. Feeling that you may not be liked and accepted by the people you work with.
    1. never bothered
    2. rarely bothered
    3. sometimes bothered
    4. bothered rather often
    5. bothered nearly all the time
    6. does not apply

11. Feeling unable to influence your immediate supervisor's decisions and actions that affect you.
    1. never bothered
    2. rarely bothered
    3. sometimes bothered
    4. bothered rather often
    5. bothered nearly all the time
    6. does not apply

12. Not knowing just what the people you work with expect of you.
    1. never bothered
    2. rarely bothered
    3. sometimes bothered
    4. bothered rather often
    5. bothered nearly all the time
    6. does not apply

13. Thinking that the amount of work you have to do may interfere with how well it gets done.
    1. never bothered
    2. rarely bothered
    3. sometimes bothered
    4. bothered rather often
    5. bothered nearly all the time
    6. does not apply

14. Feeling that you have to do things on the job that are against your better judgment.
    1. never bothered
    2. rarely bothered
    3. sometimes bothered
    4. bothered rather often
    5. bothered nearly all the time
    6. does not apply

15. Feeling that your job tends to interfere with your family life.
    1. never bothered
    2. rarely bothered
    3. sometimes bothered
    4. bothered rather often
    5. bothered nearly all the time
    6. does not apply

SOURCE: Adapted from Robert L. Kahn and Donald M. Wolfe (1964), *Organizational Stress: Studies in Role Conflict and Ambiguity* (New York: John Wiley), pp. 424-425. Adapted with permission.

COMMUNITY 7.7

Measures of community variables are limited. One of the first attempts to secure measures of the goodness of a city was made by E. L. Thorndike. His research monograph *Our City* (1939) provided the first careful attempt to evaluate the quality of American cities. Ratings of 310 American cities with populations of more than 30,000 were made. In his *144 Smaller Cities* (1940), Thorndike applied his "goodness" rating to cities with populations between 20,000 and 30,000. The method requires the gathering of statistics on factors not easily obtained. Paul B. Gillen (1951), in *The Distribution of Occupations as a City Yardstick*, presents a shorter technique based on the occupational distribution of the city.

The past several decades have witnessed a growing interest in what is now called quality of life, or well-being. Numerous researchers and research organizations are seeking to measure quality of life in different communities. Part of this interest reflects the importance of attracting industry. Interested agencies, which sometimes can play roles in attracting industry, include the local chamber of commerce, the state's economic development agency, and numerous other interested parties. Local pride alone is sufficient to provide impetus to the measurement of community achievements.

The measurement of quality of life in communities, comparative evaluations, and trend patterns represents an excellent area for applied sociology.

References

Gillen, Paul B. (1951). *The distribution of occupations as a city yardstick*. New York: Columbia University Press.

Thorndike, E. L. (1939). *Our city*. New York: Harcourt, Brace.

Thorndike, E. L. (1940). *144 smaller cities*. New York: Harcourt, Brace.

Research Applications

Haskitz, Alan. (1996). A community service program that can be validated. *Phi Delta Kappan, 78*(2), 163-164.

LeSourd, Sandra J. (1997). Community service in a multicultural nation. *Theory into Practice, 36*(3), 157-163.

Loupe, Diane. (2000). Community service: Mandatory or voluntary? *School Administrator, 57*(7), 32-34, 36-39.

Morton, Keith, & Saltmarsh, John. (1997). Addams, Day, and Dewey: The emergence of community service in American culture. *Michigan Journal of Community Service Learning, 4*(Fall), 137-149.

Neururer, Julie, & Rhoads, Robert A. (1998). Community service: Panacea, paradox, or potentiation. *Journal of College Student Development, 39*, 321-330.

Peterson, Elizabeth A. (1997). What can adults learn from community service? Lessons learned from AmeriCorps. *Community Education Journal, 25*(1-2), 45-46.

Skinner, Rebecca, & Chapman, Chris. (1999). Service-learning and community service in K-12 public schools. *Education Statistics Quarterly, 1*(4), 51-59.

White, Glen W. (1992). National and community service. *Journal of Disability Policy Studies, 3*(2), 75-84.

Yates, Miranda, & Youniss, James. (1996). Community service and political-moral identity in adolescents. *Journal of Research on Adolescence*, 6, 271-284.

Yates, Miranda, & Youniss, James. (1997, April). *Engendering civic identity through community service.* Paper presented at the biennial meeting of the Society for Research on Child Development, Washington, DC.

7.7.1 Community Attitude Scale

Variable measured. The degree of progressive attitude evidenced in such areas of community life as general community improvement, living conditions, business and industry, health and recreation, education, religion, youth programs, utilities, and communications.

Description. A cross section of a wide range of groups in various communities defined the meaning of progress by submitting a number of statements that they designated as progressive or unprogressive. These statements provided 364 items that were placed in a 5-point Likert-type format. A representative panel of leaders independently designated each item as progressive or unprogressive. Various tests showed that 60 items were most discriminating. These 60 items were compiled into three subscales with 20 items each. These scales are identified as Community Integration, Community Services, and Civic Responsibilities.

Where published. A PhD dissertation by Claud A. Bosworth, submitted to the University of Michigan, 1954.

Reliability. 60-item scale, $r = .56$.

Validity. Total mean scores discriminated significantly between a progressive and an unprogressive group at the .025 level. It was also found that those citizens who endorsed the scale items designed to measure attitudes toward other phases of community progress also voted for a sewer extension plan.

Utility. The scale is easily administered either in an interview or by questionnaire. Approximate time required is 20 minutes.

Community Attitude Scale

	Strongly Agree	Agree	?	Disagree	Strongly Disagree
(Community Services Subscale)					
1. The school should stick to the 3 R's and forget about most of the other courses being offered today.	____	____	____	____	____
2. Most communities are good enough as they are without starting any new community improvement programs.	____	____	____	____	____
3. Every community should encourage more music and lecture programs.	____	____	____	____	____
4. This used to be a better community to live in.	____	____	____	____	____
5. Long-term progress is more important than immediate benefits.	____	____	____	____	____
6. We have too many organizations for doing good in the community.	____	____	____	____	____
7. The home and the church should have all the responsibility for preparing young people for marriage and parenthood.	____	____	____	____	____

	Strongly Agree	Agree	?	Disagree	Strongly Disagree

(Community Services Subscale)

8. The responsibility for older people should be confined to themselves and their families instead of the community. _____ _____ _____ _____ _____
9. Communities have too many youth programs. _____ _____ _____ _____ _____
10. Schools are good enough as they are in most communities. _____ _____ _____ _____ _____
11. Too much time is usually spent on the planning phases of community projects. _____ _____ _____ _____ _____
12. Adult education should be an essential part of the local school program. _____ _____ _____ _____ _____
13. Only the doctors should have the responsibility for the health program in the community. _____ _____ _____ _____ _____
14. Mental illness is not a responsibility of the whole community. _____ _____ _____ _____ _____
15. A modern community should have the services of social agencies. _____ _____ _____ _____ _____
16. The spiritual needs of the citizens are adequately met by the churches. _____ _____ _____ _____ _____
17. In order to grow, a community must provide additional recreation facilities. _____ _____ _____ _____ _____
18. In general, church members are better citizens. _____ _____ _____ _____ _____
19. The social needs of the citizens are the responsibility of themselves and their families and not of the community. _____ _____ _____ _____ _____
20. Churches should be expanded and located in accordance with population growth. _____ _____ _____ _____ _____

(Community Integration Subscale)

21. No community improvement program should be carried on that is injurious to a business. _____ _____ _____ _____ _____
22. Industrial development should include the interest in assisting local industry. _____ _____ _____ _____ _____
23. The first and major responsibility of each citizen should be to earn dollars for his own pocket. _____ _____ _____ _____ _____
24. More industry in town lowers the living standards. _____ _____ _____ _____ _____
25. The responsibility of citizens who are not actively participating in a community improvement program is to criticize those who are active. _____ _____ _____ _____ _____
26. What is good for the community is good for me. _____ _____ _____ _____ _____
27. Each one should handle his own business as he pleases and let the other businessmen handle theirs as they please. _____ _____ _____ _____ _____
28. A strong Chamber of Commerce is beneficial to any community. _____ _____ _____ _____ _____
29. Leaders of the Chamber of Commerce are against the welfare of the majority of the citizens in the community. _____ _____ _____ _____ _____
30. A community would get along better if each one would mind his own business and others take care of theirs. _____ _____ _____ _____ _____
31. Members of any community organization should be expected to attend only those meetings that affect him personally. _____ _____ _____ _____ _____
32. Each of us can make real progress only when the group as a whole makes progress. _____ _____ _____ _____ _____

	Strongly Agree	Agree	?	Disagree	Strongly Disagree
33. The person who pays no attention to the complaints of the persons working for him is a poor citizen.	____	____	____	____	____
34. It would be better if we would have the farmer look after his own business and we look after ours.	____	____	____	____	____
35. All unions are full of Communists.	____	____	____	____	____
36. The good citizens encourage the widespread circulation of all news including that which may be unfavorable to them and their organizations.	____	____	____	____	____
37. The good citizen should help minority groups with their problems.	____	____	____	____	____
38. The farmer has too prominent a place in our society.	____	____	____	____	____
39. A citizen should join only those organizations that will promote his own interests.	____	____	____	____	____
40. Everyone is out for himself at the expense of everyone else.	____	____	____	____	____

(Civic Responsibilities Subscale)

	Strongly Agree	Agree	?	Disagree	Strongly Disagree
41. Busy people should not have the responsibility for civic programs.	____	____	____	____	____
42. The main responsibility for keeping the community clean is up to the city officials.	____	____	____	____	____
43. Community improvements are fine if they don't increase taxes.	____	____	____	____	____
44. The younger element have too much to say about our community affairs.	____	____	____	____	____
45. A progressive community must provide adequate parking facilities.	____	____	____	____	____
46. Government officials should get public sentiment before acting on major municipal projects.	____	____	____	____	____
47. A good citizen should be willing to assume leadership in a civic improvement organization.	____	____	____	____	____
48. Progress can best be accomplished by having only a few people involved.	____	____	____	____	____
49. Community improvement should be the concern of only a few leaders in the community.	____	____	____	____	____
50. A community would be better if less people would spend time on community improvement projects.	____	____	____	____	____
51. Only those who have the most time should assume the responsibility for civic programs.	____	____	____	____	____
52. Living conditions in a community should be improved.	____	____	____	____	____
53. A good citizen should sign petitions for community improvement.	____	____	____	____	____
54. Improving slum areas is a waste of money.	____	____	____	____	____
55. The police force should be especially strict with outsiders.	____	____	____	____	____
56. The paved streets and roads in most communities are good enough.	____	____	____	____	____
57. The sewage system of a community must be expanded as it grows even though it is necessary to increase taxes.	____	____	____	____	____
58. Some people just want to live in slum areas.	____	____	____	____	____
59. The main problem we face is high taxes.	____	____	____	____	____

SOURCE: Scale created by Claud A. Bosworth.

7.7.2 Scorecard for Community Services Activity

Variable measured.   Individual participation in community services.

Description.   The scorecard is an arbitrary index to assess individual participation in community services. Fifteen possible behavioral items are presented as those that compose the bulk of community service activity. Scores of 0 to 15 may be recorded, as each participation item is given a weight of one.

Where published.   Previously unpublished except in earlier editions of the *Handbook of Research Design and Social Measurement*.

Reliability.   No tests have been made.

Validity.   Rests on face validity.

Scoring.   Cutting points were based on a random sample of 100 adults in a middle-class community. They are as follows.

   10-15, outstanding community member

   6-9, average member

   0-5, low-participating member

Utility.   Administration of the scorecard takes less than 4 minutes. It provides for both individual and group assessment.

Scorecard for Community Services Activity

Score one point for each "yes."

FINANCIAL SUPPORT—Did you, in the past year,
   _____   contribute money to a community chest campaign?
   _____   contribute money to a church?
   _____   contribute money for other charitable purposes?
GENERAL ACTIVITY—Did you, in the past year,
   _____   serve on any board responsible for civic programs?
   _____   serve on any committee working to improve civic life?
   _____   assume leadership of any civic action program?
COMMUNITY ISSUES AND PROBLEMS—Did you, in the past year,
   _____   inform yourself about civic issues and problems?
   _____   discuss civic problems frequently with more than one person?
   _____   persuade others to take a particular position?
   _____   get advice from others?
   _____   speak to key leaders about problems?
   _____   visit community organizations or board meetings to inform yourself?
   _____   write letters, or circulate literature, or hold home meetings?
GROUP ACTION—Did you, in the past year,
   _____   belong to one or more organizations that takes stands on community issues and problems?
   _____   make group visits or invite visits of community officials to your organization?
   _____   Total Score

Scoring: 10-15 points, an outstanding community member
         6-9 points, an average member
         0-5 points, a low-participating member

SOURCE: Scale constructed by Delbert C. Miller.

7.8 SOCIAL PARTICIPATION

This section includes information on Chapin's Social Participation Scale, a general scale of participation in voluntary organizations of all kinds—professional, civic, and social. It is used when the total participation pattern is an important variable. The Leisure Participation and Enjoyment Scale enables the researcher to get a detailed picture of leisure patterns and also to get a score for each respondent on both participation and enjoyment.

A measure of neighborhood participation is included. Wallin's Women's Neighborliness Scale is a Guttman-type scale that has exhibited unidimensionality on the samples of respondents that have been tested. It is designed to be answered by women respondents only.

7.8.1 Chapin's Social Participation Scale

Variable measured. Degree of a person's or family's participation in community groups and institutions.

Description. This is a Guttman-type scale with reproducibility coefficients of .92 or .97 for groups of leaders. High scores (18 and above) represent titular leader achievement. The five components are as follows:

1. member,
2. attendance,
3. financial contributions,
4. member of committees, and
5. offices held.

These components measure different dimensions: The first component measures extent of participation, whereas the other four measure intensity of participation. Rejection-acceptance in formal groups is measured by components 1, 4, and 5, for which the intercorrelations are found to be of the order of $r_{14} = .53$ to .58, $r_{15} = .36$ to .40, and $r_{45} = .36$ to .40. Social participation is measured by components 2 and 3, with intercorrelations of $r_{23} = .80$ to .89. Other intercorrelations among the components have been found to be of the order of $r_{12} = .88$, $r_{13} = .89$, $r_{24} = .60$, $r_{34} = .40$, $r_{35} = .35$, and $r_{45} = .50$ to .58.

Where published. F. Stuart Chapin, *Experimental Designs in Sociological Research* (New York: Harper, 1955), Appendix B, pp. 275-278.

Reliability. $r = .89$ to .95.

Validity. With Chapin's social status scale scores, $r = .62$ to .66; with income class, $r = .52$; with occupational groups, $r = .63$; with years of formal education, $r = .54$; between husband and wife, $r = .76$.

Standard scores. Mean scores for occupational groups are as follows:

1. Professional, 20
2. Managerial and proprietary, 20
3. Clerical, 16
4. Skilled, 12
5. Semiskilled, 8
6. Unskilled, 4

Social Participation Scale

Address _____   Case No. _____

Husband*

Age _____ Education _____   Race or Nationality _____

Occupation _____   Income _____

Name of Organization	1. Member[a]	2. Attendance	3. Financial contributions	4. Member of committees (not name)	5. Offices held
1.					
2.					
3.					
4.					
5.					
6.					
7.					
8.					
9.					
10.					
Totals					

Date _____   Investigator _____

SOURCE: University of Minnesota Press, Minneapolis. Copyright 1938 by the University of Minnesota.

a. Enter L if purely local group; enter N if a local unit of a state or national organization.

*A similar form is filled out by the wife.

◀ 527

Utility   One sheet is used for entries on each group affiliation of subject recorded, with five entries under five columns, in reply to questions answered by the subject. It takes 10 to 15 minutes to fill in the subject's answers. The scale also can be self-administered.

Research Applications

Bach, Mary L. (1961). Factors related to student participation in campus social organizations. *Journal of Social Psychology, 54*, 337-348.

Buck, Roy C. (1960). The extent of social participation among public school teachers. *Journal of Educational Sociology, 33*, 311-319.

de Man, Anton F., & Efraim, Danielle P. (1988). Selected personality correlates of social participation in university students. *Journal of Social Psychology, 128*(2), 265-267.

Mayo, Selz C. (1951). Social participation among the older population in rural areas of Wake County, North Carolina. *Social Forces, 30*, 53-59.

7.8.1.1 Social Participation Scale

Directions

1. List by name the organizations with which the husband and wife are affiliated (at the present time) as indicated by the five types of participation No. 1 to No. 5 across the top of the schedule. It is not necessary to enter the date at which the person became a member of the organization. It is important to enter *L* if the membership is in a purely local group, and to enter *N* if the membership is in a local unit of some state or national organization.
2. An organization means some active and organized grouping, usually but not necessarily in the community or neighborhood of residence, such as club, lodge, business or political or professional or religious organization, labor union, etc.; subgroups of a church or other institution are to be included separately *provided they are organized* as more or less independent entities.
3. Record under attendance the mere fact of attendance or nonattendance without regard to the number of meetings attended (corrections for the number attended have not been found to influence the final score sufficiently to justify such labor).
4. Record under contributions the mere fact of financial contributions or absence of contributions, and *not the amount* (corrections for amount of contributions have not been found to influence the final score sufficiently to justify such labor).
5. Previous memberships, committee work, offices held, etc., should *not be* counted or recorded or used in computing the final score.
6. Final score is computed by counting each membership as 1, each attended as 2, each contributed to as 3, each committee membership as 4, and each office held as 5. If both parents are living regularly in the home, add their total scores and divide the sum by two. The result is the mean social participation score of the family. In case only one parent lives in the home, as widow, widower, etc., the sum of that one person's participation is the score for the family (unless it is desired to obtain scores on children also).

SOURCE: This is the 1952 edition of the scale, published in F. Stuart Chapin (1955), *Experimental Designs in Sociological Research* (New York: Harper), Appendix B, pp. 275-278.

7.8.2 Leisure Participation and Enjoyment

Variable measured.   The customary use of and degree of enjoyment of leisure time.

Description. The scale includes 47 items that are activities in which one might be expected to participate. Each item is ranked on two 5-point scales. Leisure participation is scaled according to frequency of participation (1 = *never*, 2 = *rarely*, 3 = *occasionally*, 4 = *fairly often*, and 5 = *frequently*). Leisure enjoyment is scaled according to likes (1 = *dislike very much*, 2 = *dislike*, 3 = *indifferent*, 4 = *like*, and 5 = *like very much*). The appropriate degree on each scale is circled for each item. No ranking on the like-dislike scale is given for those items in which the individual never participates.

Where published. C. R. Pace, *They Went to College: A Study of 951 Former University Students* (Minneapolis: University of Minnesota, 1941).

Reliability. Not known.

Validity. Leisure participation: With income, $r = .019$, with sociocivic activities scale, $r = .40$, with cultural status, $r = .039$.

Standard scores. A summary of responses to the questionnaire on the Minnesota study is included in Pace (1941, pp. 142-145).

	1924-25		1928-29	
	Graduates	*Nongraduates*	*Graduates*	*Nongraduates*
Median leisure participation for men	125.00	123.24	132.29	131.72
Median leisure enjoyment for men	169.83	167.53	171.67	170.65
Median leisure participation for women	137.90	137.50	133.97	
Median leisure enjoyment for women	177.73	178.75	180.38	176.87

Utility. This scale is easily administered and may be self-administered; it also is easy to score. It takes little time to administer. Both leisure participation and leisure enjoyment scores are derived, and data can be compared.

Reference

Pace, C. R. (1941). *They went to college: A study of 951 former university students.* Minneapolis: University of Minnesota Press.

Research Applications

Anderssen, Norman, & Wold, Bente. (1992). Parental and peer influences on leisure-time physical activity in young adolescents. *Research Quarterly for Exercise and Sport, 63*, 341-348.

Berg, Ellen C., Trost, Melanie, Schneider, Ingrid E., & Allison, Maria T. (2001). Dyadic exploration of the relationship of leisure satisfaction, leisure time, and gender to relationship satisfaction. *Leisure Sciences, 23*(1), 35-46.

Bittman, Michael, & Wajcman, Judy. (2000). The rush hour: The character of leisure time and gender equity. *Social Forces, 79*, 165-189.

Crespo, Carlos J., Smit, Ellen, Carter-Pokras, Olivia, & Andersen, Ross. (2001). Acculturation and leisure-time physical inactivity in Mexican American adults: Results from NHANES III, 1988-1994. *American Journal of Public Health, 91*, 1254-1257.

Lindstroem, Martin, Hanson, Bertil S., & Oestergren, Per Olof. (2001). Socioeconomic differences in leisure-time physical activity: The role of social participation and social capital in shaping health related behaviour. *Social Science and Medicine, 52,* 441-451.

Martinez Gonzalez, Miguel Angel, Varo, Jose Javier, Santos, Jose Luis, De Irala, Jokin, Gibney, Michael, Kearney, John, et al. (2001). Prevalence of physical activity during leisure time in the European Union. *Medicine and Science in Sports and Exercise, 33,* 1142-1146.

Schooler, Carmi, & Mulatu, Mesfin Samuel. (2001). The reciprocal effects of leisure time activities and intellectual functioning in older people: A longitudinal analysis. *Psychology and Aging, 16,* 466-482.

Shebilske, Laura Jo. (2000). Affective quality, leisure time, and marital satisfaction: A 13-year longitudinal study. *Dissertation Abstracts International, 60,* 3545A.

Thrane, Christer. (2000). Men, women, and leisure time: Scandinavian evidence of gender inequality. *Leisure Sciences, 22*(2), 109-122.

Yeager, Kimberly K., et al. (1993). Socioeconomic influences on leisure-time sedentary behavior among women. *Health Values: The Journal of Health Behavior, Education and Promotion, 17*(6), 50-54.

7.8.2.1 Your Leisure-Time Activities

The use of leisure time is supposed to be an increasingly important social problem. We want to know how people usually spend their leisure time. Here is a list of activities. On the left side of the page put a circle around the number that tells how often you do these things now, using the key at the top of the column. On the right side of the page put a circle around the number that tells how well you like these things, using the key at the top of the column. If you never do the activity mentioned, circle number one in the left column to indicate no participation, and circle no number on the right side of the page. Try not to skip any item.

How Often Do You Do These Things		How Well Do You Like These Things
1. Never		1. Dislike very much
2. Rarely		2. Dislike
3. Occasionally		3. Indifferent
4. Fairly often		4. Like
5. Frequently		5. Like very much
1 2 3 4 5	1. Amateur dramatics	1 2 3 4 5
1 2 3 4 5	2. Amusement parks and halls	1 2 3 4 5
1 2 3 4 5	3. Art work (individual)	1 2 3 4 5
1 2 3 4 5	4. Attending large social functions (balls, benefit bridge, etc.)	1 2 3 4 5
1 2 3 4 5	5. Attending small social entertainments (dinner parties, etc.)	1 2 3 4 5
1 2 3 4 5	6. Book reading for pleasure	1 2 3 4 5
1 2 3 4 5	7. Conventions	1 2 3 4 5
1 2 3 4 5	8. Conversations with family	1 2 3 4 5
1 2 3 4 5	9. Card playing	1 2 3 4 5
1 2 3 4 5	10. Church and related organizations	1 2 3 4 5
1 2 3 4 5	11. Dancing	1 2 3 4 5
1 2 3 4 5	12. Dates	1 2 3 4 5
1 2 3 4 5	13. Entertaining at home	1 2 3 4 5

How Often Do You Do These Things						*How Well Do You Like These Things*				
1. *Never*						1. *Dislike very much*				
2. *Rarely*						2. *Dislike*				
3. *Occasionally*						3. *Indifferent*				
4. *Fairly often*						4. *Like*				
5. *Frequently*						5. *Like very much*				

1	2	3	4	5		1	2	3	4	5
1	2	3	4	5	14. Fairs, exhibitions, etc.	1	2	3	4	5
1	2	3	4	5	15. Informal contacts with friends	1	2	3	4	5
1	2	3	4	5	16. Informal discussions, e.g., "bull sessions"	1	2	3	4	5
1	2	3	4	5	17. Indoor team recreation or sports—basketball, volleyball	1	2	3	4	5
1	2	3	4	5	18. Indoor individual recreation or sports—bowling, gym, pool, billiards, handball	1	2	3	4	5
1	2	3	4	5	19. Knitting, sewing, crocheting, etc.	1	2	3	4	5
1	2	3	4	5	20. Lectures (not class)	1	2	3	4	5
1	2	3	4	5	21. Listening to radio or TV	1	2	3	4	5
1	2	3	4	5	22. Literary writing—poetry, essays, stories, etc.	1	2	3	4	5
1	2	3	4	5	23. Magazine reading (for pleasure)	1	2	3	4	5
1	2	3	4	5	24. Movies	1	2	3	4	5
1	2	3	4	5	25. Newspaper reading	1	2	3	4	5
1	2	3	4	5	26. Odd jobs at home	1	2	3	4	5
1	2	3	4	5	27. Organizations or club meetings as a member	1	2	3	4	5
1	2	3	4	5	28. Organizations or club meetings as a leader (as for younger groups)	1	2	3	4	5
1	2	3	4	5	29. Outdoor individual sports—golf, riding, skating, hiking, tennis	1	2	3	4	5
1	2	3	4	5	30. Outdoor team sports—hockey, baseball, etc.	1	2	3	4	5
1	2	3	4	5	31. Picnics	1	2	3	4	5
1	2	3	4	5	32. Playing musical instrument or singing	1	2	3	4	5
1	2	3	4	5	33. Shopping	1	2	3	4	5
1	2	3	4	5	34. Sitting and thinking	1	2	3	4	5
1	2	3	4	5	35. Spectator of sports	1	2	3	4	5
1	2	3	4	5	36. Symphony or concerts	1	2	3	4	5
1	2	3	4	5	37. Telephone visiting	1	2	3	4	5
1	2	3	4	5	38. Theater attendance	1	2	3	4	5
1	2	3	4	5	39. Traveling or touring	1	2	3	4	5
1	2	3	4	5	40. Using public library	1	2	3	4	5
1	2	3	4	5	41. Visiting museums, art galleries, etc.	1	2	3	4	5
1	2	3	4	5	42. Volunteer work—social service, etc.	1	2	3	4	5
1	2	3	4	5	43. Writing personal letters	1	2	3	4	5
1	2	3	4	5	44. Special hobbies—stamps, photography, shop work, gardening, and others not included above	1	2	3	4	5
1	2	3	4	5	45. Fishing or hunting	1	2	3	4	5
1	2	3	4	5	46. Camping	1	2	3	4	5
1	2	3	4	5	47. Developing and printing pictures	1	2	3	4	5

SOURCE: Adapted from C. R. Pace (1941), *They Went to College* (Minneapolis: University of Minnesota Press). Copyright © 1941 by the University of Minnesota. Reprinted with permission.

7.9 LEADERSHIP IN THE WORK ORGANIZATION

This section contains two leadership scales that may be widely used in work organizations. The first scale, the Leadership Opinion Questionnaire, is designed to find answers to the question, "What *should you* as a supervisor do?" The second scale, the Supervisory Behavior Description, is designed to find answers to the question, "What does *your own supervisor* actually do?" Note that these two scales make it possible to get measures of two levels of leadership in an organization. The relationship of a supervisor to his or her immediate superior has been shown to be a very important one. The use of both questionnaires makes it possible to secure a comparison between the two levels.

Each scale may be used for the specific purpose for which it was designed. Use the Leadership Opinion Questionnaire whenever a measure of a leader's personal orientation is desired. Use the Supervisory Behavior Description when it is desirable to get the perceptions of a supervisor held by those who report to him or her. This scale can be given to employees or any group of supervisors or managers. These two scales have been subjected to repeated refinement and may be considered highly reliable and valid in terms of present progress in scale construction.

Many measures of organizational performance might be included. Space prevents their addition, but the following measures are annotated for the consideration of the organizational researcher.

The Executive Position Description contains 191 items to determine the basic characteristics of executive positions in business and industry. Part 1 covers position activities; part 2, position responsibilities; part 3, position demands and restrictions; and part 4, position characteristics (Hemphill, 1960).

The Responsibility, Authority, and Delegation Scales were designed to measure different degrees of perceived responsibility, authority, and delegation as exhibited by individuals who occupy administrative or supervisory positions (Stogdill & Shartle, 1955).

The Multirelational Sociometric Survey measures interpersonal variables surrounding work activities. Five dimensions are included: the prescribed, the perceived, the actual, the desired, and the rejected (Tannenbaum, Weschler, & Massarik, 1961).

A Method for the Analysis of the Structure of Complex Organizations is an application of sociometric analysis based on work contacts. The method enables the researcher to depict the organization coordination structure as established through the activities of liaison persons and the existence of the contacts between groups (Weiss & Jacobson, 1955).

References

Hemphill, John K. (1960). *Dimensions of executive positions.* Columbus: Ohio State University, Bureau of Business Research.

Stogdill, Ralph M., & Shartle, Carroll L. (1955). *Methods in the study of administrative leadership.* Columbus: Ohio State University, Bureau of Business Research.

Tannenbaum, Robert, Weschler, Irving W., & Massarik, Fred. (1961). *Leadership and organization: A behavioral science approach.* New York: McGraw-Hill.

Weiss, Robert S., & Jacobson, Eugene. (1955). A method for the analysis of the structure of complex organizations. *American Sociological Review, 20,* 661-668.

7.9.1 Leadership Opinion Questionnaire

Variable measured. The questionnaire measures a leader's orientation around two major factors: structure and consideration. Structure (S) reflects the extent to which an individual is likely to define and structure his or her own role and those of subordinates toward goal attainment. A high score on this dimension characterizes individuals who play a more active role in directing group activities through planning, communicating information, scheduling, trying out new ideas, and so on. Consideration (C) reflects the extent to which an individual is likely to have job relationships characterized by mutual trust, respect for subordinates' ideas, and consideration of their feelings. A high score is indicative of a climate of good rapport and two-way communication. A low score indicates that the superior is likely to be more impersonal in relations with group members.

Description.   This is a 40-item questionnaire divided into the two factors Structure and Consideration. Each factor is tested by 20 items. The items are presented with a 5-point continuum with scoring weights of 0 to 4, depending on the item's orientation to the total dimension.

Where published.   Available at the Reid London House Web site at www.reidlondonhouse.com/reidlondonhouse/tests/loq.htm; tel. 1-800-221-8378 or 847-292-1900; fax 847-292-3402; e-mail reidlondonhouse@ncs.com. Copyright © 1960 by Science Research Associates, Inc. The scale was first presented to social scientists in Ralph M. Stogdill and Alvin E. Coons, eds. (1957), *Leader Behavior: Its Description and Measurement* (Columbus: Ohio State University, Bureau of Business Research), pp. 120-133.

Reliability.   Test-retest coefficients for 31 foremen, after a 3-month interval, showed the following: $r = .80$ on Consideration and $r = .74$ on Initiating Structure. For 24 Air Force NCOs, $r = .77$ on Consideration and $r = .67$ on Initiating Structure. Split-half reliability estimates for Consideration and Initiating Structure were found to be .69 and .73, respectively.

Validity.   Validity was evaluated through correlations with independent leadership measures, such as merit rating by supervisors, peer ratings, forced-choice performance reports by management, and leaderless group situation tests. Relatively low validities were found for the particular criteria employed, although a few statistically significant correlations were found. Correlations with other measures revealed that scores on the Leadership Opinion Questionnaire were independent of the intelligence of the supervisor, an advantage not achieved by other available leadership attitude questionnaires.

The questionnaire scores have been found to be sensitive for discriminating reliably between leadership attitudes in different situations as well as for evaluating the effects of leadership training.

Scoring.   This assessment tool offers a variety of scoring options, such as hand-scored carbon format or Quanta™ Software for Windows®, and optical scanning. Answer sheets can be scored using optical mark reading, on site or mailed to Reid London House for scoring.

Utility.   The scale is easily administered in 10-15 minutes and is easily scored.

Reference

Fleishman, Edwin A. (1960). *A manual for administering the Leadership Opinion Questionnaire.* Chicago: Science Research Associates.

Research Applications

Dapra, Richard A., Zarrillo, Deirdre L., Carlson, Thomas K., & Teevan, Richard C. (1985). Fear of failure and indices of leadership utilized in the training of ROTC cadets. *Psychological Reports*, 56(1), 27-30.

Dukes, David Jefferson. (1996). Brain topography of leadership: Neurophysiological correlates of the Leadership Opinion Questionnaire. *Dissertation Abstracts International*, *56*, 7082B.

Fok, Lillian Y., Hartmann, Sandra J., Crow, Stephen M., & Moore, Alger. (1995). Use of the Leadership Opinion Questionnaire to predict managerial success in organizations: A longitudinal study. *Organization Development Journal*, *13*(1), 23-32.

Kaurala, Earl B. (1997). Leader attitudes and leader stress: Is there a connection? *Dissertation Abstracts International*, *57*, 3765A.

Kuntonbutr, Chanongkorn. (1999). A comparative study between Thai and American subordinates' perception of managerial values in the banking industry. *Dissertation Abstracts International*, *59*, 4473A.

Oakland, Thomas, Falkenberg, Bradd A., & Oakland, Christopher. (1996). Assessment of leadership in children, youth and adults. *Gifted Child Quarterly*, *40*(3), 138-146.

Schippmann, Jeffery S., & Prien, Erich P. (1986). Individual difference correlates of two leadership styles. *Psychological Reports*, *59*(2, Pt. 2), 817-818.

Tharenou, Phyllis, & Lyndon, John T. (1990). The effect of a supervisory development program on leadership style. *Journal of Business and Psychology*, *4*, 365-373.

Thomas, Veronica G., & Littig, Lawrence W. (1985). A typology of leadership style: Examining gender and race effects. *Bulletin of the Psychonomic Society*, *23*(2), 132-134.

Trewatha, Robert L., & Vaught, Bobby C. (1987). The role of preferred leader behavior, managerial demographics, and interpersonal skills in predicting leadership style. *Journal of Behavioral Economics*, *16*(1), 99-107.

7.9.1.1 The Leadership Opinion Questionnaire

This questionnaire contains 40 items when presented as a complete scale. The items that follow exemplify those found in the longer questionnaire. They are presented here so that the researcher may evaluate them for possible use of the complete scale.

Structure

Assign people in the work group to particular tasks.
    1. always   2. often   3. occasionally   4. seldom   5. never

Stress being ahead of competing work groups.
    1. a great deal   2. fairly much   3. to some degree   4. comparatively little   5. not at all

Criticize poor work.
    1. always   2. often   3. occasionally   4. seldom   5. never

Emphasize meeting of deadlines.
    1. a great deal   2. fairly much   3. to some degree   4. comparatively little   5. not at all

Consideration

Put suggestions made by people in the work group into operation.
    1. always   2. often   3. occasionally   4. seldom   5. never

Help people in the work group with their personal problems.
    1. often   2. fairly often   3. occasionally   4. once in a while   5. seldom

Get the approval of the work group on important matters before going ahead.
    1. always   2. often   3. occasionally   4. seldom   5. never

---

7.9.2 Supervisory Behavior Description

Variable measured.   Perceptions of subordinates of the leadership behavior demonstrated by their immediate superior. Factor analysis revealed that Initiating Structure and Consideration items are the most significant factors in distinguishing leadership performance. Initiating Structure reflects the extent to which the supervisor facilitates group interaction toward goal attainment; Consideration reflects the extent to which the supervisor is considerate of the feelings of subordinates. All questions are worded in terms of the question, "What does your own supervisor actually do?"

Description.   This is a 48-item questionnaire divided into two independent areas of leadership: Initiating Structure and Consideration. The first area includes 20 items, and the second contains the other 28 items. The items are presented with a 5-point continuum answer scale that has scoring weights of 0 to 4, depending on the item orientation to the total dimension. The highest possible score is 112 on Consideration and 80 on Initiating Structure.

Where published.   Edwin A. Fleishman, "A Leader Behavior Description for Industry," in *Leader Behavior: Its Description and Measurement*, ed. Ralph M. Stogdill and Alvin E. Coons (Columbus: Ohio State University, Bureau of Business Research, 1957), pp. 103-119.

Reliability.   Test-retest reliability coefficients based on numerous samples range from .46 to .87. Split-half reliabilities are reported for samples as between .68 and .98.

Validity.   The correlation between Consideration and Initiating Structure was found to be −.02 when based on replies of 122 foremen. The intercorrelation was shown to be −.33 when administered to 394 workers who described the 122 foremen. The correlation between the two scales was shown to be −.05 when administered to 176 Air Force and Army ROTC students who described their superior officers. The independence of the two factors appears to be confirmed.

Correlations have been obtained between descriptions of foremen's behavior and independent indexes of accident rates, absenteeism, grievances, and turnover among the foremen's own work groups. In production departments, high scores on the Consideration scale were predictive of low ratings of proficiency by the foreman's supervisor but also of low absenteeism among the workers. A high score on Initiating Structure was predictive of a high proficiency rating as well as high absenteeism and labor grievances.

Standard scores.   Standard scores were obtained from several studies, with the results shown below.

| | Dimension | | | |
| | Consideration | | Initiating Structure | |
Sample	M	S.D.	M	S.D.
Descriptions of 122 foremen	79.8	14.5	41.5	7.6
Descriptions of 31 foremen	71.5	13.2	37.5	6.3
Descriptions of 31 foremen	73.0	12.7	40.7	7.3
Descriptions of 8 civil service supervisors	75.1	17.6	37.3	9.6
Descriptions of 60 general foremen	82.3	15.5	51.5	8.8

Utility. The questionnaire may be administered in 10-15 minutes. When used in group application, it is very efficient. By using this questionnaire in conjunction with the Leader Behavior Description, it is possible to get a view of how a supervisor thinks he or she should lead and compare this view with an assessment by the supervisor's subordinates of his or her actual leadership performance. The best summary of research is found in Fleishman (1957). Much of the research has been done by E. A. Fleishman in plants of the International Harvester Company.

Reference

Fleishman, Edwin A. (1957). A leader behavior description for industry. In Ralph M. Stogdill & Alvin E. Coons (Eds.), *Leader behavior: Its description and measurement* (pp. 103-119). Columbus: Ohio State University, Bureau of Business Research.

Research Applications

Asher-Shultz, Nancy R. (1990). A comparison between observer ratings of supervisory behavior and the perceptions of supervisors and subordinates. *Dissertation Abstracts International, 51,* 2603B.

Brodhead, Sheila A. (1992). The effect of role stress and social support on supervisory behavior. *Dissertation Abstracts International, 52,* 3934B.

Bryant, Scott E., & Gurman, Ernest B. (1996). Contingent supervisory behavior: A practical predictor of performance. *Group and Organization Management, 21,* 404-413.

Cherniss, Cary. (1988). Observed supervisory behavior and teacher burnout in special education. *Exceptional Children, 54,* 449-454.

Childers, Terry L., Dubinsky, Alan J., & Skinner, Steven J. (1990). Leadership substitutes as moderators of sales supervisory behavior. *Journal of Business Research, 21,* 363-382.

Giacalone, Robert A., & Pollard, Hinda G. (1990). Acceptance of managerial accounts for unethical supervisory behavior. *Journal of Social Psychology, 130*(1), 103-109.

Kennebrew, Johnny L., & Sistrunk, Walter E. (1989, November). *Principals' supervisory behavior and school climate.* Paper presented at the annual meeting of the Mid-South Educational Research Association, Little Rock, AR.

Kohli, Ajay K. (1989). Effects of supervisory behavior: The role of individual differences among salespeople. *Journal of Marketing, 53*(4), 40-50.

Maroldo, Georgette K. (1988). Private shyness, social loneliness, and supervisory behavior. *Organization Development Journal, 6*(3), 56-62.

Pullen, Deborah B., & Sistrunk, Walter E. (1990, November). *Ideal and actual supervisory behavior as perceived by Mississippi Community College vocational instructors and their supervisors.* Paper presented at the annual conference of the Mid-South Educational Research Association, New Orleans, LA.

7.9.2.1 Revised Form of the Supervisory Behavior Description

Item Number	Item
	Consideration: revised key
1.	He refuses to give in when people disagree with him.
2.	He does personal favors for the foremen under him.
3.	He expresses appreciation when one of us does a good job.

Item Number	Item
4.	He is easy to understand.
5.	He demands more than we can do.
6.	He helps his foremen with their personal problems.
7.	He criticizes his foremen in front of others.
8.	He stands up for his foremen even though it makes him unpopular.
9.	He insists that everything be done his way.
10.	He sees that a foreman is rewarded for a job well done.
11.	He rejects suggestions for changes.
12.	He changes the duties of people under him without first talking it over with them.
13.	He treats people under him without considering their feelings.
14.	He tries to keep the foremen under him in good standing with those in higher authority.
15.	He resists changes in ways of doing things.
16.	He "rides" the foreman who makes a mistake.
17.	He refuses to explain his actions.
18.	He acts without consulting his foremen first.
19.	He stresses the importance of high morale among those under him.
20.	He backs up his foremen in their actions.
21.	He is slow to accept new ideas.
22.	He treats all his foremen as his equal.
23.	He criticizes a specific act rather than a particular individual.
24.	He is willing to make changes.
25.	He makes those under him feel at ease when talking with him.
26.	He is friendly and can be easily approached.
27.	He puts suggestions that are made by foremen under him into operation.
28.	He gets the approval of his foremen on important matters before going ahead.

Initiating Structure: revised key

1.	He encourages overtime work.
2.	He tries out his new ideas.
3.	He rules with an iron hand.
4.	He criticizes poor work.
5.	He talks about how much should be done.
6.	He encourages slow-working foremen to greater effort.
7.	He waits for his foremen to push new ideas before he does.
8.	He assigns people under him to particular tasks.
9.	He asks for sacrifices from his foremen for the good of the entire department.
10.	He insists that his foremen follow standard ways of doing things in every detail.
11.	He sees to it that people under him are working up to their limits.
12.	He offers new approaches to problems.
13.	He insists that he be informed on decisions made by foremen under him.
14.	He lets others do their work the way they think best.
15.	He stresses being ahead of competing work groups.
16.	He "needles" foremen under him for greater effort.

Item Number	Item
17.	He decides in detail what shall be done and how it shall be done.
18.	He emphasizes meeting of deadlines.
19.	He asks foremen who have slow groups to get more out of their groups.
20.	He emphasizes the quantity of work.

SOURCE: Reprinted from Edwin A. Fleishman (1957), "A Leader Behavior Description for Industry," in Ralph M. Stogdill & Alvin E. Coons (Eds.), *Leader Behavior: Its Description and Measurement* (Columbus: Ohio State University, Bureau of Business Research), pp. 103-119. Reprinted with permission.
NOTE: Most items were answered as 1, always; 2, often; 3, occasionally; 4, seldom; 5, never.

7.10 MORALE AND JOB SATISFACTION

Morale is only one of many words we use to try to express a person's outlook on society and his or her frame of mind. Many scales have been constructed to express the diverse attitudes encompassed by such terms. Karl Schuessler has examined most of these scales and the items appearing in them. *Morale* and other terms seemed too narrow to define the area; Schuessler uses *social life feelings*, a term broad enough to capture what the items have in common. Item correlations indicated significant dimensions that can be seen in the Schuessler Social Life Feelings Scales, which follow.

Nancy Morse and associates have constructed a set of subscales to measure intrinsic job satisfaction, pride in performance, company involvement, and financial and job status. The researcher should use the Morse Scales if short scales are needed to tap these dimensions.[1]

For more information on the reliability and validity of specific questionnaire items, the serious researcher will consult *Some Questionnaire Measures of Employee Motivation and Morale* (Patchen, 1966), a monograph that evaluates the reliability and validity of questionnaire items associated with job motivation, interest in work innovation, willingness to express disagreement with supervisors, attitude toward changes in the job situation, and identification with the work organization.

Note

1. For a critical review of general job satisfaction scales, see Robinson, Athanasiou, and Head (1969, pp. 99-103).

References

Patchen, Martin, with Pelz, Donald C., & Allen, Craig W. (1966). *Some questionnaire measures of employee motivation and morale: A report on their reliability and validity.* Ann Arbor: University of Michigan, Institute for Social Research.

Robinson, John P., Athanasiou, Robert, & Head, Kendra B. (1969). *Measures of occupational attitudes and occupational characteristics.* Ann Arbor: University of Michigan, Institute for Social Research.

7.10.1 Schuessler's Social Life Feelings Scales

Variables measured. Doubt about self-determination, doubt about trustworthiness of people, feeling down, job satisfaction, faith in citizen involvement, feeling up, people cynicism, disillusionment with government, future outlook, economic self-determination, feeling demoralized, and career concerns. Social life feelings items were selected from a domain of more than 100 such items appearing in more than 100 scales used in American sociology during the last 50 years. Using Response Analysis, Inc., of Princeton, New Jersey, 187 interviewers tested 237 items with a national sample of adult respondents from 1,522 randomly drawn households.

Based on the highest correlations found in various item clusters, 12 individual scales were identified. Each scale can be considered to represent a common dimension based on high intercorrelations between constituent items as identified using factor analysis.

Where published.   Karl F. Schuessler, *Measuring Social Life Feelings* (San Francisco: Jossey-Bass, 1982).

Reliability.   General ratings were based on six categories: alpha reliability, Tucker-Lewis reliability, missing response rate, relation to social background, simplicity of measuring, and number of proxies (number of scales dropped in its favor). Eight scales were rated as good, and four were rated as fair.

Validity.   Efforts have been made to establish validity by examining the three best items of each scale, the closest author scale, closest topic scale, and closest subject-class scale; then what Schuessler takes it to be measuring (in a word or two) and a rating of that interpretation as simple or complex. Both face and criterion validities were investigated.

Administration.   Scales may be utilized in questionnaire form or be administered by interview. The authors worked with Response Analysis, Inc., and set up three ways of presenting scale items. In all three ways, the respondent is asked "whether you mostly agree or mostly disagree with each statement." The three methods of administering the scales employed by the researchers were (a) reading the statements to respondents, (b) handing the respondents the questionnaire and reading brief instructions, and (c) handing respondents a deck of cards, each of which contains one of the statements, and asking respondents to sort the cards according to their level of agreement with the statement on each card.

Method of administration.   Each method was applied to each item about 500 times, and to each respondent approximately 67 times. Results indicate that for most items, patterns of responding and techniques of testing were statistically independent.

7.10.1.1 SLFS1: Doubt About Self-Determination

Statement

1. There are few people in this world you can trust, when you get right down to it.
2. What happens in life is largely a matter of chance.
3. If the odds are against you, it's impossible to come out on top.
4. I have little influence over the things that happen to me.
5. I sometimes feel that I have little control over the direction my life is taking.
6. Nowadays a person has to live pretty much for today and let tomorrow take care of itself.
7. I've had more than my share of troubles.
8. For me one day is no different from another.
9. The world is too complicated for me to understand.
10. I regret having missed so many chances in the past.
11. It's unfair to bring children into the world with the way things look for the future.
12. The future is too uncertain for a person to plan ahead.
13. I find it difficult to be optimistic about anything nowadays.
14. No right or wrong ways to make money, only easy and hard.

7.10.1.2   SLFS2: Doubt About Trustworthiness of People

Statement

1. It is hard to figure out who you can really trust these days.
2. There are few people in this world you can trust, when you get right down to it.
3. Most people can be trusted.
4. Strangers can generally be trusted.
5. Most people are fair in their dealings with others.
6. Most people don't really care what happens to the next fellow.
7. Too many people in our society are just out for themselves and don't really care for anyone else.
8. Many people are friendly only because they want something from you.

7.10.1.3   SLFS3: Feeling Down

Statement

1. I feel that I'm not a part of things.
2. I feel somewhat apart even among friends.
3. I sometimes feel forgotten by friends.
4. At times I feel that I am a stranger to myself.
5. I just can't help feeling that my life is not very useful.
6. Very lonely or remote from other people.*
7. Depressed or very unhappy.*
8. Bored.*
9. So restless you couldn't sit long in a chair.*
10. Vaguely uneasy about something without knowing why.*

*O = often; S = sometimes.

7.10.1.4   SLFS4: Job Satisfaction

Statement

1. There is too little variety in my job.
2. I tend to get bored on the job.
3. There must be better places to work.
4. I would like more freedom on the job.
5. I have too small a share in deciding matters that affect my work.
6. My job means more to me than just money.
7. I am satisfied with the work I do.
8. My job gives me a chance to do what I do best.
9. People feel like they belong where I work.

7.10.1.5   SLFS5: Faith in Citizen Involvement

Statement

1. The public has little control over what politicians do in office.
2. The average person can get nowhere by talking to public officials.
3. The average citizen has considerable influence on politics.
4. The average person has much to say about running local government.

5. People like me have much to say about government.
6. The average person has a great deal of influence on government decisions.
7. The government is generally responsive to public opinion.
8. I am usually interested in local elections.
9. By taking an active part in political and social affairs the people can control world events.
10. Taking everything into account, the world is getting better.

7.10.1.6 SLFS6: Feeling Up

Statement

1. I sometimes feel I have little control over the direction my life is taking.
2. When I make plans, I am almost certain that I can make them work.
3. I was happier as a child than I am now.
4. I couldn't be much happier.
5. I get a lot of fun out of life.
6. I am satisfied with the way things are working out for me.
7. The future looks very bright to me.
8. Things get better for me as I get older.
9. I have a great deal in common with most people.
10. I seem to be marking time these days.
11. There is much purpose to what I am doing at present.

7.10.1.7 SLFS7: People Cynicism

Statement

1. In a society where almost everyone is out for himself, people soon come to distrust each other.
2. Most people know what to do with their lives.
3. Too many people in our society are just out for themselves and don't really care for anyone else.
4. Many people in our society are lonely and unrelated to their fellow human beings.
5. Many people are friendly only because they want something from you.
6. Many people don't know what to do with their lives.

7.10.1.8 SLFS8: Disillusionment With Government

Statement

1. Most supermarkets are honestly run.
2. We are slowly losing our freedom to the government.
3. Most politicians are more interested in themselves than in the public.
4. I have little confidence in the government today.
5. The government is run by a few people in power.
6. There's little use writing to public officials because they often aren't really interested in the problems of the average man.
7. Public officials work for the people and not just for themselves.
8. Our local government costs the taxpayer more than it is worth.
9. In my opinion, this country is sick.

7.10.1.9 SLFS9: Future Outlook

Statement

1. We are slowly losing our freedom to the government.
2. I have little confidence in the government today.
3. Many things our parents stood for are going down the drain.
4. Although things keep changing all the time, one still knows what to expect from one day to another.
5. The lot of the average man is getting worse, not better.
6. The future looks very bleak.
7. More people will be out of work in the next few years.
8. Friends are easy to find.
9. The future of this country is very uncertain.
10. The future looks very bright to me.
11. Taking everything into account, the world is getting better.
12. In my opinion, this country is sick.

7.10.1.10 SLFS10: Economic Self-Determination

Statement

1. Individuals are poor because of the lack of effort on their part.
2. Anyone can raise his standard of living if he is willing to work at it.
3. Most people have a good deal of freedom in deciding how to live.
4. Poor people could improve their lot if they tried.
5. Our country has too many poor people who can do little to raise their standard of living.

7.10.1.11 SLFS11: Feeling Demoralized

Statement

1. I have little influence over the things that happen to me.
2. I consider myself to be in good physical condition.
3. The world is too complicated for me to understand.
4. Compared to others, my life is not too good.
5. I find it difficult to be optimistic about anything nowadays.
6. I seem to be marking time these days.
7. I can't do much for other people.
8. On top of the world.
9. Pleased about having accomplished something.

7.10.1.12 SLFS12: Career Concerns

Question: How often was each of these things on your mind in the last few weeks?

1. Money
2. Work
3. Marriage
4. Getting ahead
5. Bringing up children
6. Future

Scoring. All negative statements are scored 1. Negative statements are shown as "agree," "often," or "sometimes." Positive statements answered as "disagree," "seldom," or "never" receive a score of 2.[1] Norms, means, medians, and standard deviations were determined for each of the 12 scales on a representative adult U.S. national sample of 1,522 respondents (as carried out by Response Analysis, Inc.).

Utility. These scales represent the best short scales available to measure the given variable. Any single scale can be answered easily in less than 2 to 3 minutes. The researcher can use any scales that best fit his or her research design. Use of two or more of these scales can be arranged to establish profiles of individuals and groups. Profiles can show comparative rankings or means.

Note

1. For the rationale for 2-point scales (agree/disagree), see Schuessler (1982, pp. 11-41).

References

Schuessler, Karl F. (1982). How social background influences people's responses. In *Measuring social life feelings*. San Francisco: Jossey-Bass, pp. 73-78. Reprinted with permission of the author.

Research Applications

Krebs, Dagmar, & Schuessler, Karl. (1989). Life feeling scales for use in German and American samples. *Social Indicators Research*, *21*, 113-131.

Lucke, Joseph F., & Schuessler, Karl. (1987). Scaling social life feelings by factor analysis of binary variables. *Social Indicators Research*, *19*, 403-428.

Newton, Rae R., Prensky, David, & Schuessler, Karl. (1982). Form effect in the measurement of feeling states. *Social Science Research*, *11*, 301-317.

Reiser, Mark, Wallace, Michael, & Schuessler, Karl. (1986). Direction-of-wording effects in dichotomous social life feeling items. *Sociological Methodology*, *16*, 1-25.

Schuessler, Karl. (1982). How social background influences people's responses. In *Measuring social life feelings* (pp. 73-87). San Francisco: Jossey-Bass.

SCALES OF ATTITUDES, VALUES, AND NORMS 7.11

This section includes selected attitude and value scales that revolve around current interests and concerns. In the 1960s and early 1970s, as the counterculture movement gained momentum, much attention was focused on alienation. Sociologists responded to demand, and research interest increased using the Srole Anomia Scale, the Dean Alienation Scale, and many others still in use today. Although the interest in alienation has lessened, related feelings of powerlessness remain as big government, big business, big religion, big labor, and big cities seem to dominate human life. For this reason, the Neal and Seaman Powerlessness Scale has been selected as representative of one of the dimensions in the alienation of persons and groups from major social institutions.

Researchers looking for more information on the innumerable scales that now exist should check the contents tables of *Measures of Occupational Attitudes and Occupational Characteristics* (1969), *Measures of Political Attitudes* (1969), and *Measures of Social Psychological Attitudes* (1973) by John P. Robinson and his coworkers.

References

Robinson, John P., Athanasiou, Robert, & Head, Kendra B. (1969). *Measures of occupational attitudes and occupational characteristics.* Ann Arbor: University of Michigan, Institute for Social Research.

Robinson, John P., Rusk, Jerrold G., & Head, Kendra B. (1969). *Measures of political attitudes.* Ann Arbor: University of Michigan, Institute for Social Research.

Robinson, John P., & Shaver, Phillip R. (1973). *Measures of social psychological attitudes* (Rev. ed.). Ann Arbor: University of Michigan, Institute for Social Research.

7.11.1 The Measurement of Alienation and Anomie

The "rediscovery of alienation," as Daniel Bell has put it, has encouraged scientists to develop scales to measure these phenomena.[1] Research has demonstrated that a number of independent factors may be identified. Melvin Seeman (1959) set forth a fivefold classification: powerlessness, meaninglessness, normlessness, isolation, and self-estrangement. The scales that have been produced have sought to isolate such factors and measure them. The first element, powerlessness, was suggested by Georg Wilhelm Friedrich Hegel, Karl Marx, and Max Weber in their discussions of the workers' separation from effective control over their economic destiny, of their helplessness, and of their being used for purposes other than their own. Weber argued that in the industrial society, the scientist, the civil servant, and the professor are likewise separated from control over their work.

Dwight Dean has developed three subscales to measure powerlessness, normlessness, and social isolation. He combined the three subscales to make up an alienation scale. He believes that the pattern of intercorrelations demonstrates that alienation can be treated as a composite concept, but that there appears to be enough independence among the subscales to warrant treating them as independent variables. Arthur G. Neal and Solomon Rettig (1963), using factor analysis, have found empirical evidence for the structural independence of powerlessness, normlessness, and Srole's Anomia Scale. The subscales should be utilized when the greatest precision is desired. There is great variety in the scales being used, and consensus is low.

The researcher wishing to consult the Srole and Dean scales should see Srole (1956) and Dean (1961). The researcher may wish to examine other scales purporting to measure alienation and anomie, including McClosky and Schaar's "Psychological Dimensions of Anomie" (McClosky & Schaar, 1965) and Nettler's "A Measure of Alienation" (Nettler, 1957). For a more thorough listing and appraisal, see John P. Robinson and Phillip R. Shaver (1973, esp. pp. 254-294).

Note

1. See, for example, Roberts and Rokeach (1956), Nettler (1957), and Srole (1956). The concepts of alienation and anomie not only have become widely used but also are among the most misused terms in the field. Researchers need to be especially cautious in estimating the size of the alienated segment of the population when using various scales.

References

Dean, Dwight G. (1961). Alienation: Its meaning and measurement. *American Sociological Review,* 26, 753-758.

McClosky, Herbert, & Schaar, John H. (1965). Psychological dimensions of anomie. *American Sociological Review,* 30, 14-40.

Neal, Arthur G., & Rettig, Solomon. (1963). Dimensions of alienation among manual and non-manual workers. *American Sociological Review, 28*, 599-608.

Nettler, Gwynn. (1957). A measure of alienation. *American Sociological Review, 22*, 670-677.

Roberts, Allan H., & Rokeach, Milton. (1956). Anomie, authoritarianism, and prejudice: A replication. *American Journal of Sociology, 61*, 355-358.

Robinson, John P., & Shaver, Phillip R. (1973). *Measures of social psychological attitudes* (Rev. ed.). Ann Arbor: University of Michigan, Institute for Social Research.

Seeman, Melvin. (1959). On the meaning of alienation. *American Sociological Review, 24*, 783-791.

Srole, Leo. (1956). Social integration and certain corollaries: An exploratory study. *American Sociological Review, 21*, 709-716.

Research Applications

Furst, Edward J. (1975). *Measuring human-relations attitudes and values with situational inventories.* Fayetteville: Arkansas University, College of Education.

Gable, Robert K. (1993). *Instrument development in the affective domain: Measuring attitudes and values in corporate and school settings.* Norwood, NJ: Kluwer Academic.

Hullett, Craig R., & Boster, Franklin J. (2001). Matching messages to the values underlying value-expressive and social-adjustive attitudes: Reconciling an old theory with a contemporary measurement approach. *Communication Monographs, 68*, 133-153.

Kerlinger, Fred N. (1972, April). *The study and measurement of values and attitudes.* Paper presented at the American Educational Research Association, Chicago, IL.

Larkin, Caroline M. (1971). A longitudinal analysis of changes in attitudes and values during the undergraduate years as measured by the college student questionnaires. *Dissertation Abstracts International, 32*, 1880A.

Linn, Lawrence S., DiMatteo, M. Robin, Cope, Dennis W., & Robbins, Alan. (1987). Measuring physicians' humanistic attitudes, values, and behaviors. *Medical Care, 25*, 504-515.

Penn, John R. (1973). Values and attitudes as measures of intergenerational differences. *Dissertation Abstracts International, 33*, 4531A-4532A.

Schumacher, Joseph E. (1992). Decision error tolerance and attitudes toward crime control: Measuring values toward judicial decisions. *Dissertation Abstracts International, 52*, 4961B-4962B.

Suich, Paul S. (1992). Social interest: Triangulating the construct with measures of rational attitudes, communal values, and cooperative behavior. *Dissertation Abstracts International, 52*, 4988B.

Watral, David M. (1979). Relationships among values structure, attitudes and measured personality. *Dissertation Abstracts International, 39*, 5599B.

FAMILY AND MARRIAGE   7.12

Marital adjustment has been one of the most widely used concepts in family research. Students have tried to improve both conceptual and methodological levels of measurement. A very popular tool is the Dyadic Adjustment Scale (DAS), developed by Graham B. Spanier and Erik E. Filsinger. It provides a standardized assessment of the relationship of couples, both married and unmarried. Although developed out of a family sociological research orientation, the DAS can be used meaningfully within a wide range of therapeutic situations. It has been crafted carefully to achieve high reliability and validity.

7.12.1 The Dyadic Adjustment Scale

Variable measured.   Marital adjustment is a process, the outcome of which is determined by the degree of (a) troublesome marital differences, (b) interspousal tensions and personal anxiety, (c) marital satisfaction, (d) dyadic cohesion, and (e) consensus on matters of importance to marital functioning. DAS subcomponents include Dyadic Satisfaction, Dyadic Cohesion, Dyadic Consensus, and Affectional Expression.

Description.   The DAS is a 32-item, primarily Likert-style questionnaire utilizing 5-, 6-, and 7-point responses. The DAS was drawn from an initial pool format of 300 items, all of which were used in previous scales of marital adjustment. New items were added to tap areas of adjustment ignored in previous measures. Duplicate items were eliminated. Three judges examined the items for content validity against the definition of marital adjustment as given above. By consensus among the judges, numerous items were eliminated. A questionnaire was constructed using 225 items along with some demographic items.

The questionnaire was administered to a purposive sample of 218 married persons in central Pennsylvania. Questionnaires also were sent to every person who obtained a divorce decree in Centre Country, Pennsylvania, during the 12 months previous to the mailing. Tests were made of the scoring means of the married couples and divorced couples. Items not significantly different at the .001 level were eliminated. Forty remaining variables were factor analyzed. A final 32 items remained.

Factor analysis produced four interrelated dimensions: Dyadic Consensus (the degree to which the couple agrees on matters of importance to the relationship), Dyadic Cohesion (the degree to which the couple engages in activities together), Dyadic Satisfaction (the degree to which the couple is satisfied with the present state of the relationship and is committed to its continuance), and Affectional Expression (the degree to which the couple is satisfied with the expression of affection and sex in the relationship). The subscales are indicated in the DAS as shown. More than 1,000 reported studies have used the DAS. More than 90% of these studies have involved married persons.

Where published.   Multi-Health Systems, 908 Niagara Falls Blvd., North Tonawanda, NY, 14120-2060, phone 1-800-456-3003, Webs site www.mhs.com. The scale earlier appeared in Graham Spanier and Erik E. Filsinger (1983), "The Dyadic Adjustment Scale," chapter 8 in Erik E. Filsinger (Ed.), *Marriage and Family Assessment: A Source Book for Family Therapy* (Beverly Hills, CA: Sage).

Reliability.   Coefficient alphas for internal consistency reliability have been reported by Spanier as Dyadic Adjustment, .96; Dyadic Consensus, .90; Dyadic Cohesion, .86; Dyadic Satisfaction, .94; and Affectional Expression, .73. Cronbach's alpha is reported to be .96 for the overall DAS.

Similar coefficient alpha levels were reported by Filsinger and Wilson (1983, 1984) for husbands and wives, respectively: Dyadic Adjustment, .94, .93; Dyadic Consensus, .91, .88; Dyadic Cohesion, .85, .80; Dyadic Satisfaction, .82, .84; and Affectional Expression, .73, .73.

Validity.   Judges determined content validity based on the theoretical dimensions. The scale discriminated between married and divorced samples. The scale also discriminated between distressed and nondistresed samples.

The DAS has the construct validity conforming to a theoretical structure. The correlation between the DAS and the Locke-Wallace Marital Adjustment Scale (Locke & Wallace, 1959) is reported to be .86 among married couples and .88 among divorced respondents.

Utility. The DAS is a measure of the individual's adjustment to marriage but also has been used to study the adjustment of the couple to marriage. The scale also can be used to measure the adjustment of persons in nonmarried dyads. It can be used in diagnosing relationships as distressed or not, in identifying potential problems in the relationship, and in evaluating the effectiveness of treatment by comparing intake scores with posttreatment scores. It also can be used for long-term follow-up. The DAS has been translated into several languages for use with various nationalities and cultural groups.

Administration. The DAS can be given to the couple at any time; however, it probably would be useful to have them fill it out at intake or during an early session. The clients should complete the form separately and should not discuss their answers with each other before completing the scale. The form also should not be discussed with the therapist until he or she has the opportunity to examine and score it.

Scoring. The DAS is scored by assigning numbers to each response. The score for the individual is the sum of the numbers for each item. The total scale score is the most meaningful indicator for both researchers and therapists, but the responses to the subscales and to individual items also can be examined for clues as to the origins of problems. Mean scale scores reported by the authors for married and divorced samples were 114.8 and 70.7, respectively.

Couple scores can be derived in a number of ways—for example, by adding the individual scores or taking the difference between them—but these practices have not been empirically or theoretically justified. At this point in time there are no aids to interpreting couple scores.

References

Filsinger, E. E., & Wilson, M. R. (1983). Social anxiety and marital adjustment. *Family Relations, 32,* 513-519.

Filsinger, E. E., & Wilson, M. R. (1984). Religiosity, socioeconomic rewards, and family development: Predictors of marital adjustment. *Journal of Marriage and the Family, 46,* 663-670.

Locke, Harvey J., & Wallace, Karl M. (1959). Short marital-adjustment and prediction tests: Their reliability and validity. *Marriage and Family Living, 21,* 251-255.

Research Applications

Bernard, Vicki Renee. (1999). Perceptions of sex role egalitarianism and dyadic adjustment among African-American couples. *Dissertation Abstracts International, 59,* 4291A.

Casas, J. Manuel, & Ortiz, Silvia. (1985). Exploring the applicability of the Dyadic Adjustment Scale for assessing level of marital adjustment with Mexican Americans. *Journal of Marriage and the Family, 47,* 1023-1027.

Crane, D. Russell, Middleton, Kenneth C., & Bean, Roy A. (2000). Establishing criterion scores for the Kansas Marital Satisfaction Scale and the Revised Dyadic Adjustment Scale. *American Journal of Family Therapy, 28*(1), 53-60.

Deleonardo, Lisa A. (2000). An investigation of identity development, ego strength, and dyadic adjustment in lesbian women. *Dissertation Abstracts International, 61,* 1077B.

Fisiloglu, Huerol, & Demir, Ayhan. (2000). Applicability of the Dyadic Adjustment Scale for measurement of marital quality with Turkish couples. *European Journal of Psychological Assessment, 16*(3), 214-218.

Hackney, Harold, & Bernard, Janine M. (1990). Dyadic adjustment processes in divorce counseling. *Journal of Counseling and Development, 69*(2), 134-143.

Hunsley, John, Best, Marlene, Lefebvre, Monique, & Vito, Diana. (2001). The seven-item short form of the Dyadic Adjustment Scale: Further evidence for construct validity. *American Journal of Family Therapy, 29*(4), 325-335.

Lim, Ben K., & Ivey, David. (2000). The assessment of marital adjustment with Chinese populations: A study of the psychometric properties of the Dyadic Adjustment Scale. *Contemporary Family Therapy: An International Journal, 22*, 453-465.

Prouty, Anne M., Markowski, Edward Mel, & Barnes, Howard L. (2000). Using the Dyadic Adjustment Scale in marital therapy: An exploratory study. *Family Journal: Counseling and Therapy for Couples and Families, 8*(3), 250-257.

Wilson, Stephan M., Larson, Jeffry H., McCulloch, B. Jan, & Stone, Katherine L. (1997). Dyadic adjustment: An ecosystemic examination. *American Journal of Family Therapy, 25*(4), 291-306.

7.12.2 The PREPARE Inventory

Variables measured. Major problems related to personal, interpersonal, and external issues in relationships among premarital couples.

Description. PREPARE is a self-report questionnaire containing 165 Likert-style items and utilizes a 5-point response format (*strongly disagree* to *strongly agree*). The main purpose is to serve as a diagnostic tool in assessing relationship problems. PREPARE covers marriage expectations, personality issues, communication, conflict resolution, financial management, leisure activities, sexual expectations, children and parenting, family and friends, role relationship, spiritual beliefs, couple closeness, family closeness, couple flexibility, and family flexibility. PREPARE and PREPARE-MC help engaged couples identify issues unique to their own relationships so that they can begin more realistic assessment of their upcoming marriages.

Where published. The manual and materials for PREPARE are available from Life Innovations, Inc., at P.O. Box 190, Minneapolis, MN 55440-0190, Web site www.lifeinnovations.com.

Reliability. Cronbach's alpha for a nationwide sample of 5,718 individuals ranged from .49 to .88.

Research Applications

Fowers, Blaine J. (1991). His and her marriage: A multivariate study of gender and marital satisfaction. *Sex Roles, 24*(3-4), 209-221.

Fowers, Blaine J., Montel, Kelly H., & Olson, David H. (1996). Predicting marital success for premarital couple types based on PREPARE. *Journal of Marital and Family Therapy, 22*(1), 103-119.

Fowers, Blaine J., & Olson, David H. (1992). Four types of premarital couples: An empirical typology based on PREPARE. *Journal of Family Psychology, 6*(1), 10-21.

Greeff, Abraham P., & Malherbe, Hildegarde L. (2001). Intimacy and marital satisfaction in spouses. *Journal of Sex and Marital Therapy, 27*(3), 247-257.

Larsen, Andrea S., & Olson, David H. (1989). Predicting marital satisfaction using PREPARE: A replication study. *Journal of Marital and Family Therapy, 15*(3), 311-322.

Montel, Kelly Huott. (1996). Predicting marital status outcome and satisfaction based on an empirical typology of engaged couples. *Dissertation Abstracts International, 56*, 7097B.

Rosen Grandon, Jane R. (1998). The relationship between marital characteristics, marital interaction processes, and marital satisfaction. *Dissertation Abstracts International*, *59*, 1792A.

7.12.3 The Life Innovations Scales

Life Innovations, Inc. (www.lifeinnovations.com) is a Minneapolis-based research and counseling center that focuses on designing tools to be used in the assessment, diagnosis, and treatment of couples preparing for marriage as well as those who are already married. The creative company is run by well-trained family and psychological counselors. In addition to the PREPARE Inventory, it produces many other scales worth considering when examining family dynamics, including a large number of research-based tools such as couples scales, family scales, and a set of observation scales. All these scales are available from Life Innovations, Inc., at P.O. Box 190, Minneapolis, MN 55440-0190, or the Web site provided above.

7.12.3.1 ENRICH Couple Satisfaction Scale

The 17-item Couple Satisfaction Scale was authored by David Olson. It contains 10 items on satisfaction and 7 items on idealism.

The Marital Satisfaction scale provides a global measure of satisfaction by surveying 10 areas of the couple's marriage. These areas include the major categories in the ENRICH program: communication, conflict resolution, roles, financial concerns, leisure time, sexual relationship, parenting, family, friends, and religion.

The Idealistic Distortion scale measures the extent to which the person is being optimistic, realistic, or pessimistic in answering the questions. This scale can be a useful reference point in understanding the perceptual biases of a person. Premarital couples tend to be overly optimistic in describing their relationship, whereas unhappy couples tend to be overly pessimistic and married couples tend to be more realistic.

Scale reliability (alpha).   There is very good evidence of scale reliability ($r = .86$).

Validity.   Very good evidence of content validity comes from outside observers' assessments of the individual items. There is also very good construct validity, demonstrated by factor analysis of the scale.

Sample Item

I am unhappy with our communication and feel my partner does not understand me.

7.12.3.2 ENRICH Couple Scales

The ENRICH Couple Scales by David H. Olson, David G. Fournier, and Joan M. Druckman contain three 10-item subscales that can be used for research: Marital Satisfaction, Communication, and Conflict Resolution. There is also a 7-item Idealistic Distortion Scale.

The Marital Satisfaction scale provides a global measure of satisfaction by surveying nine areas of the couple's marriage. These areas include the major categories in ENRICH: personality, role responsibilities, communication, conflict resolution, financial concerns, management of leisure time, sexual relationship, parental responsibilities, relationships with family and friends, and religious orientation.

The Communication scale is concerned with an individual's feelings, beliefs, and attitudes about the communication in his or her relationship. Items focus on the level of comfort felt by both partners in being able to share important emotions and beliefs with each other, the perception of a partner's way of giving and receiving information, and the respondent's perception of how adequately he or she communicates with his or her partner.

The Conflict Resolution scale assesses an individual's attitudes, feelings, and beliefs about the existence and resolution of conflict in his or her relationship. Items focus on the openness of partners to recognizing and resolving issues, the strategies and procedures used to end arguments, and their satisfaction with the way problems are resolved.

The Idealistic Distortion scale measures the extent to which the person is being optimistic, realistic, or pessimistic in answering the questions. This scale can be a useful reference point in understanding the perceptual biases of a person. Premarital couples tend to be overly optimistic in describing their relationship, whereas unhappy couples tend to be overly pessimistic and married couples tend to be more realistic.

Scale reliability (alpha).   There is very good evidence of scale reliability for the Marital Satisfaction scale ($r = .86$), Communication scale ($r = .82$), and Conflict Resolution scale ($r = .84$).

Validity.   Very good evidence of content validity comes from outside observers' assessments of the individual items. There is also very good construct validity, demonstrated by factor analysis of the scales. Concurrent validity was shown in comparisons with the Locke-Wallace Marital Adjustment Scale.

Sample Items

I am very happy with how we make decisions and resolve conflict. (Marital Satisfaction item)

I can express my true feelings to my partner. (Communication item)

To end an argument, I tend to give in too quickly. (Conflict Resolution item)

7.12.3.3   FACES II

The Family Adaptability and Cohesion Scales by David H. Olson, Joyce Portner, and Yoav Lavee is used for research with families. The 30-item self-report instrument assesses the two major dimensions of the Circumplex Model, family cohesion and family adaptability (flexibility). It is designed to be administered to families across the life cycle. FACES II can be used with the Parent-Adolescent Communication scale or the Marital Communication scale to measure all three dimensions of the Circumplex Model.

Scale reliability (alpha).   There is very good evidence for scale reliability on both cohesion ($r = .87$) and flexibility ($r = .78$).

Validity.   Very good evidence of construct and concurrent validity comes from many studies.

Sample Items

Family members feel closer to people outside the family than to other family members. (cohesion item)

Our family tries new ways of dealing with problems. (flexibility item)

7.12.3.4 FACES III

The Family Adaptability and Cohesion Scales by David H. Olson, Joyce Portner, and Yoav Lavee are recommended for clinical work with families. The 20-item self-report instrument assesses the two major dimensions of the Circumplex Model, family cohesion and family adaptability (flexibility). It is designed to be administered to families across the life cycle. FACES III can be used with the Parent-Adolescent Communication scale or the Marital Communication scale to measure all three dimensions of the Circumplex Model. FACES II is recommended over FACES III because FACES II has better reliability and validity. FACES III is recommended for clinical work because it contains fewer items.

Scale reliability (alpha).   There is good evidence for scale reliability on both cohesion ($r = .77$) and flexibility ($r = .62$).

Validity.   Very good evidence of construct and concurrent validity comes from many studies.

Sample Items

Family members like to spend free time with each other. (cohesion item)
Our family changes its way of handling tasks. (flexibility item)

7.12.3.5 Family Satisfaction

Scale reliability (alpha).   There is very good evidence for scale reliability on both cohesion ($r = .85$) and flexibility ($r = .84$).

Validity.   Very good evidence of content validity comes from outside observers' assessments of the individual items. Very good construct validity is demonstrated by factor analysis of the scale.

Sample Items

How satisfied are you with how close you feel to the rest of the family? (cohesion item)
How satisfied are you with your ability to say what you want in your family? (flexibility item)

7.12.3.6 Parent-Adolescent Communication

The Parent-Adolescent Communication scale by Howard Barnes and David H. Olson is a 20-item self-report scale that assesses the perceptions of adolescents and their parents regarding communication with each other. Two subscales, Open Family Communication and Problems in Family Communication, were designed to measure both positive and negative aspects of parent-adolescent communication.

Scale reliability (alpha).   There is very good evidence of scale reliability for the subscales of Open Family Communication ($r = .87$) and Problems in Family Communication ($r = .78$), as well as for the total scale ($r = .88$).

Validity.   Very good evidence of content validity comes from outside observers' assessments of the individual items. Very good construct validity is demonstrated by factor analysis of the scale.

Sample Items

I am sometimes afraid to ask my mother for what I want.
My father is always a good listener.
My child can tell how I'm feeling without asking.

7.12.3.7 Family Strengths

The Family Strengths Scale by David H. Olson, A. S. Larson, and Hamilton I. McCubbin is designed to measure family strengths on the dimensions of pride and accord. It contains 12 items.

Scale reliability (alpha). There is very good evidence of scale reliability on the subscales of Pride ($r = .88$) and Accord ($r = .72$), as well as on the total scale ($r = .83$).

Validity. Very good evidence of content validity comes from outside observers' assessments of the individual items. Very good construct validity is demonstrated by factor analysis of the scale.

Sample Item

There are many conflicts in our family.

7.12.3.8 Quality of Life

Scale reliability (alpha). There is very good evidence of scale reliability for both the parent form ($r = .92$) and the adolescent form ($r = .86$).

Validity. Very good evidence of content validity comes from outside observers' assessments of the individual items. Very good construct validity is demonstrated by factor analysis of the scale.

Sample Items

How satisfied are you with your family?
How satisfied are you with the amount of money you have to spend?

7.12.3.9 Clinical Rating Scale

The Clinical Rating Scale by David H. Olson and Elinor Killorin is designed primarily for use by therapists. It can be used to rate the family's behavior on the dimensions of cohesion, adaptability (flexibility), and communication. It is then possible to assess location of the couple or family on the Circumplex Model. This is an observation scale, not a self-report scale.

Scale reliability (alpha). There is solid evidence for scale reliability on all three subscales: cohesion ($r = .95$), adaptability ($r = .94$), and communication ($r = .97$).

Interrater reliability. High levels of interrater reliability have been shown for the subscales of cohesion (95%), adaptability (91%), and communication (97%).

Validity. Very good evidence of content validity comes from outside observers' assessments of the individual items. Very good construct validity is demonstrated by factor analysis of the scale.

PERSONALITY MEASUREMENTS 7.13

Of the hundreds of existing personality inventories, only one is selected for presentation here. The Minnesota Multiphasic Personality Inventory-2™, or MMPI, is described but not reproduced. It is a battery of scales containing 550 statements. It is thorough and so well constructed that it has generally won the confidence of researchers as the best scale to use in probing the personality. The research applications included in the description of the instrument attest its use.

7.13.1 Minnesota Multiphasic Personality Inventory

Variables measured   The MMPI includes 8 validity scales, 10 clinical scales, 15 content scales, 27 content component scales, 20 supplementary scales, 5 PSY-5 scales (part of the supplementary scales), 31 clinical subscales (Harris-Lingoes and social introversion subscales), 5 superlative self-presentations subscales, and various special or setting-specific indices.

Description.   The MMPI is designed primarily to provide, in a single test, scores on all the more clinically important phases of personality. The instrument itself comprises 550 true-false statements covering a wide range of subject matter, from the physical condition of the individual being tested to his or her morale and social attitude. For administration of the inventory, the subject is asked to respond to all statements, which are in the first person, with response options of "true," "false," and "cannot say."

Where published.   Starke R. Hathaway, PhD, and J. C. McKinley, MD, were on the faculty of the University of Minnesota hospitals when the MMPI instrument was published in 1942. Authors of the current test are Yossef S. Ben-Porath, James N. Butcher, W. Grant Dahlstrom, John R. Graham, and Auke Tellegen.

Reliability. $r = .71$ to $.83$.[1]

Validity.   Hathaway and McKinley maintain that the chief criterion of excellence has been the valid prediction of clinical cases against the neuropsychiatric staff diagnosis, rather than statistical measures of reliability and validity.

Note

1. See Hathaway and McKinley (1951), along with Gough (1947) and Weisgerber (1951).

References

Gough, Harrison G. (1947). Simulated patterns on the Minnesota Multiphasic Personality Inventory. *Journal of Abnormal and Social Psychology, 42,* 215-225.

Hathaway, Starke R., & McKinley, J. Chamley. (1951). *Manual for the Minnesota Multiphasic Personality Inventory* (Rev. ed.). New York: Psychological Corporation.

Weisgerber, Charles A. (1951). The predictive value of the Minnesota Multiphasic Personality Inventory with student nurses. *Journal of Social Psychology, 33,* 3-11.

Research Applications and Further Readings

Archer, R. P., Maruish, M., Imhof, E. A., & Piotrowski, C. (1991). Psychological test usage with adolescent clients: 1990 survey findings. *Professional Psychology: Research and Practice, 22,* 247-252.

Bagby, R. Michael, et al. (1997). Does clinical training facilitate feigning schizophrenia on the MMPI-2? *Psychological Assessment, 9*(2), 106-112.

Ben-Porath, Y. S., & Butcher, J. N. (1989). Psychometric stability of rewritten MMPI items. *Journal of Personality Assessment, 53,* 645-653.

Butcher, J. N. (1987). Computerized clinical and personality assessment using the MMPI. In J. N. Butcher (Ed.), *Computerized psychological assessment: A practitioner's guide* (pp. 161-197). New York: Basic Books.

Butcher, J. N. (1990). *MMPI-2 in psychological treatment.* New York: Oxford University Press.

Butcher, James Neal. (Ed.). (2000). *Basic sources on the MMPI-2.* Minneapolis: University of Minnesota Press.

Butcher, J. N., Graham, J. R., Dahlstrom, W. G., & Bowman, E. (1990). The MMPI-2 with college students. *Journal of Personality Assessment, 54,* 1-15.

Butcher, J. N., & Owen, P. L. (1978). Objective personality inventories: Recent research and some contemporary issues. In B. Wolman (Ed.), *Clinical diagnoses of mental disorders* (pp. 475-546). New York: Plenum.

Caldwell, A. B. (1991). MMPI-2 content scales: What you say is what you get? *Contemporary Psychology, 6,* 560-561.

Cloak, Nancy L., Kirklen, Leonard E., Strozier, Anne L., & Reed, James R. (1997). Factor analysis of Minnesota Multiphasic Personality Inventory-1 (MMPI-1) validity scale items. *Measurement and Evaluation in Counseling and Development, 30*(1), 40-49.

Dana, Richard H. (1995). Culturally competent MMPI assessment of Hispanic populations. *Hispanic Journal of Behavioral Sciences, 17,* 305-319.

Friedman, A. R., Webb, J. T., & Lewak, R. (1989). *Psychological assessment with the MMPI.* Hillsdale, NJ: Lawrence Erlbaum Associates.

Graham, J. R. (1990). *MMPI-2: Assessing personality in psychopathology.* New York: Oxford University Press.

Graham, J. R., Timbrook, R. E., Ben-Porath, Y. S., & Butcher, J. N. (in press). Code-type congruence between MMPI and MMPI-2: Separating fact from artifact. *Psychological Assessment: A Journal of Consulting and Clinical Psychology.*

Greene, R. L. (1991). *The MMPI-2-MMPI: An interpretive manual.* Boston: Allyn & Bacon.

Hostetler, K., Ben-Porath, Y. S., Butcher, J. N., & Graham, J. R. (1989, April). *New MMPI-2 subscales.* Paper presented at the annual meeting of the Society for Personality Assessment, New York, NY.

Jackson, D. N. (1989). *Basic Personality Inventory.* Port Huron, MI: Sigma Assessment Systems.

Levitt, E. E. (1990). A structural analysis of the impact of MMPI-2 on MMPI-1. *Journal of Personality Assessment, 55,* 562-577.

Long, K. A., Graham, J. R., & Timbrook, R. E. (1994). Socioeconomic status and MMPI-2 interpretation. *Measurement and Evaluation in Counseling and Development, 27*(3), 158-177.

Megargee, Edwin I. (2001). *Classifying criminal offenders with the MMPI-2: The Megargee system.* Minneapolis: University of Minnesota Press.

Nichols, D. S. (in press). New MMPI-2 content scales. *Journal of Personality Assessment.*

Pancoast, D. L., & Archer, R. P. (1989). Original adult MMPI norms in normal samples: A review with implications for future developments. *Journal of Personality Assessment, 53,* 376-395.

Schlenger, W. E., & Kulka, R. A. (1987, August). *Performance of the Keane-Fairbank MMPI scale and other self-report measures in identifying posttraumatic stress disorder.* Paper presented at the 95th Annual Convention of the American Psychological Association, New York, NY.

Sturmer, Paul J., & Gerstein, Lawrence H. (1997). MMPI profiles of black Americans: Is there a bias? *Journal of Mental Health Counseling, 19*(2), 114-129.

Tellegen, A. M. (1988, August). *Derivation of uniform T-scores for the restandardized MMPI.* Symposium presentation at the 96th Annual Convention of the American Psychological Association, Atlanta, GA.

Tsai, David C., & Pike, Patricia L. (2000). Effects of acculturation on the MMPI-2 scores of Asian American students. *Journal of Personality Assessment, 74*(2), 216-230.

Wrobel, Nancy Howells, & Lachar, David. (1995). Racial differences in adolescent self-report: A comparative validity study using homogeneous MMPI content measures. *Psychological Assessment, 7*(2), 140-147.

CITATIONS, FOCUS, AND PURPOSE OF STUDIES REPORTED IN THE PAST FIVE YEARS IN THE AMERICAN JOURNAL OF SOCIOLOGY, THE AMERICAN SOCIOLOGICAL REVIEW, AND SOCIAL PSYCHOLOGY QUARTERLY | 7.14

The *American Journal of Sociology*, established in 1895 as the first U.S. scholarly journal in its field, publishes analysis and research in the social sciences, with a focus on theory, methods, practice, and history of sociology. The *American Sociological Review* was founded in 1936 and is published by the American Sociological Association. It publishes original works of interest to the discipline in general, new theoretical developments, results of research, and methodological innovations. *Social Psychology Quarterly* publishes theoretical and empirical papers on the link between the individual and society, including the study of the relations of individuals to one another, to groups, to collectivities, and to institutions. It also includes the study of intra-individual processes. Table 7.3 lists the articles published in these three leadings journals in the past 5 years. They are organized alphabetically by primary topic.

(text continues on p. 605)

Table 7.3   CITATIONS, FOCUS, AND PURPOSE OF STUDIES REPORTED IN THE PAST 5 YEARS OF THE AMERICAN JOURNAL OF SOCIOLOGY, THE AMERICAN SOCIOLOGICAL REVIEW, AND SOCIAL PSYCHOLOGY QUARTERLY

Locus of Study and/or Assessment	Citation	Purpose or Intent
American Journal of Sociology		
Activism	Conell, Carol, and Samuel Cohn. (1995). "Learning From Other People's Actions: Environmental Variation and Diffusion in French Coal Mining Strikes, 1890-1935." 101:366-403.	Shows the role of imitation in producing social protests.
Altruism	Healy, Kieran. (2000). "Embedded Altruism: Blood Collection Regimes and the European Union's Donor Population." 105:1633-1657.	A comparative study of blood collection regimes in Europe.
Associationalism	Kaufman, Jason. (1999). "Three Views of Associationalism in 19th-Century America: An Empirical Examination." 104:1296-1345.	Three different theoretical conceptions of associationalism are examined with respect to cross-sectional data on municipal expenditure and voter participation in American cities for the fiscal year 1880: a "neo-Tocquevillian" perspective, a "social movements" perspective, and a "social capital" perspective.
Career opportunities	Yamagata, Hisashi, Kuang S. Yeh, Shelby Stewman, and Hiroko Dodge. (1997). "Sex Segregation and Glass Ceilings: A Comparative Static Model of Women's Career Opportunities in the Federal Government Over a Quarter Century." 103:566-632.	Examines new linkages between sex segregation and glass ceilings, two elements of sex segregation (composition and captivity), and two elements of glass ceilings (pathways inside and outside one's original ILM.)
Civil rights	Kelly, Erin, and Frank Dobbin. (1999). "Civil Rights Law at Work: Sex Discrimination and the Rise of Maternity Leave Policies." 105:455-492.	Charts the spread of maternity leave policies between 1955 and 1985 in a sample of 279 organizations. Sex discrimination law played a key role in the rise of maternity leave policies. Building on neoconstitutional theory, this article explores how the separation of powers shapes employer response to law.
Class analysis	Sorensen, Aage B. (2000). "Toward a Sounder Basis for Class Analysis." 105:1523-1558.	Using a broad conception of property rights, the article proposes to base class concepts on personal wealth, that is, the assets a person controls.
Communications	Zaret, David. (1996). "Petitions and the 'Invention' of Public Opinion in the English Revolution." 101:1497-1555.	This empirical account explains the transition in political communication from norms of secrecy to appeals to public opinion.
Communications	Giordano, Peggy C. (1995). "The Wider Circle of Friends in Adolescence." 101:661-697.	The author contrasts the style and content of the communications directed to close friends and other youths characterized by varying degrees of "nearness and remoteness."

Corporate governance	Davis, Gerald F., and Henrich R. Greve. (1997). "Corporate Elite Networks and Governance Changes in the 1980s." 103:1-37.	The authors compare the spreads of two governance innovations adopted in response to the 1980s takeover wave: poison pills (which spread rapidly through a board-to-board diffusion process) and golden parachutes (which spread slowly through geographic proximity).
Cultural dynamics	Jacobs, Ronald N. (1996). "Civil Society and Crisis: Culture, Discourse, and the Rodney King Beating." 101:1238-1272.	Narrative methods are used to analyze the cultural dynamics of civil society through a comparison of African American and "mainstream" newspaper coverage of the Rodney King crisis in Los Angeles.
Drugs	Engen, Rodney L., and Sara Steen. (2000). "The Power to Punish: Discretion and Sentencing Reform in the War on Drugs." 105:1357-1395.	Addresses whether and how organizational processes and the exercise of discretion affect the relationship between sentencing reforms and sentencing outcomes.
Economic growth	Dixon, William J., and Terry Boswell. (1996). "Look at Foreign Capital Penetration." 102:543-562.	The authors show that foreign capital dependence diminishes economic growth, enhances income inequality, and very probably impairs domestic capital formation, all irrespective of denominator effects.
Economics	Bernhardt, Annette, Martina Morris, and Mark S. Handcock. (1995). "Women's Gains or Men's Losses? A Closer Look at the Shrinking Gender Gap in Earnings." 101:302-328.	The authors develop a decomposition that allows them to test how distributional changes in men's and women's earnings combine to yield changes in women's economic status.
Economics	Hicks, Alexander, and Lane Kenworthy. (1998). "Cooperation and Political Economic Performance in Affluent Democratic Capitalism." 103:1631-1672.	Explores the idea that cooperative economic institutions provide a key to understanding comparative political economic performance among capitalist democracies.
Economics	Zhou, Xueguang. (2000). "Economic Transformation and Income Inequality in Urban China: Evidence From Panel Data." 105:1135-1174.	Using panel data of 4,730 urban residents drawn from 20 cities in China, this article examines changes in income determinants between the prereform and reform eras.
Education	Biblarz, Timothy J., and Adrian E. Raftery. (1999). "Family Structure, Educational Attainment, and Socioeconomic Success: Rethinking the 'Pathology of Matriarchy.'" 105:321-365.	The authors assess whether discrepancies observed in the literature can be accounted for by change over time in the effects of alternative families or by differences in researchers' decisions about which independent variables to include and leave out of models.
Education	Gerber, Theodore P., and Michael Hout. (1995). "Educational Stratification in Russia During the Soviet Period." 101:611-660.	A national survey of educational stratification in Russia reveals substantial inequality of educational attainments throughout the Soviet period. Parents' education, main earner's occupation, and geographical origin contributed to these inequalities.

(continued)

Table 7.3   Continued

Locus of Study and/or Assessment	Citation	Purpose or Intent
Education	Ishida, Hiroshi, Walter Muller, and John M. Ridge. (1995). "Class Origin, Class Destination, and Education: A Cross-National Study of Ten Industrial Nations." 101:145-193.	Examines three themes concerning the relationships among class origin, education, and class destination in 10 industrial nations: (a) differential access to education for different class origins, (b) the allocation of class positions by education, and (c) the role of education in class reproduction and mobility.
Educational attainment	Deng, Zhong, and Donald J. Treiman. (1997). "The Impact of the Cultural Revolution on Trends in Educational Attainment in the People's Republic of China." 103:391-428.	Examines the effects of social origins on educational attainment, using data from the 1982 census of the People's Republic of China.
Employment	Birkelund, Gunn Elisabeth, Leo A. Goodman, and David Rose. (1996). "The Latent Structure of Job Characteristics of Men and Women." 102:80-113.	Describes how the underlying latent variables associated with men's job characteristics differ from the corresponding variables associated with women's job characteristics.
Employment	Cotter, David A., JoAnn DeFiore, Joan M. Hermsen, Brenda Marsteller Kowalewski, and Reeve Vanneman. (1998). "The Demand for Female Labor." 103:1673-1712.	The authors construct a measure of the demand for female labor and use it to examine effects on labor market inequality, educational attainment, family structure, political representation, and gender role attitudes across 261 metropolitan areas.
Employment	Gerber, Theodore P., and Michael Hout. (1998). "More Shock Than Therapy: Market Transition, Employment, and Income in Russia, 1991-1995." 104:1-50.	Sixteen predictions from market transition theory are assessed using survey data on employment, earnings, and income in Russia, during the first 5 years of market reform.
Employment	Logan, John Allen. (1996). "Opportunity and Choice in Socially Structured Labor Markets." 102:114-160.	Presents a new approach to studying the factors that determine employment outcomes. It develops a statistical technique, two-sided logit (TSL), directly from a model of the preferences and resources of employers and workers.
Expectations and expectation theory	Fisek, M. Hamit, Joseph Berger, and Robert Z. Norman. (1995). "Evaluations and the Formation of Expectations." 101:721-746.	Presents a theoretical formulation that integrates two theories within the expectation states program—status characteristics and expectation states theory and source theory.
Expectations and expectation theory	Troyer, Lisa, and C. Wesley Younts. (1997). "Whose Expectations Matter? The Relative Power of First- and Second-Order Expectations in Determining Social Influence." 103:692-732.	Develops a theoretical framework describing interaction both when one's own expectations are consistent with those held by others and when one's own expectations conflict with those held by others.
Foreign investment	Kentor, Jeffrey. (1998). "The Long-Term Effects of Foreign Investment Dependence on Economic Growth, 1940-1990." 103:1024-1046.	Analyzes models similar to those tested in previous research but with data from earlier time periods to examine the long-term effects of foreign capital penetration.

Funding	Alexander, Victoria D. (1996). "Pictures at an Exhibition: Conflicting Pressures in Museums and the Display of Art." 101:797-839.	Examines the format and content of exhibitions from large American museums to gauge the effect of funding.
Gender and gender role	Lieberson, Stanley, Susan Dumais, and Shyon Baumann. (2000). "The Instability of Androgynous Names: The Symbolic Maintenance of Gender Boundaries." 105:1249-1287.	Analysis of the accidental ways in which androgynous names develop, their special characteristics, and their asymmetric growth patterns leads to viewing the androgynous process as collective behavior that can be fruitfully examined through the perspective of the Schelling residential segregation model.
Gender and gender role	Manza, Jeff, and Clem Brooks. (1998). "The Gender Gap in U.S. Presidential Elections: When? Why? Implications?" 103:1235-1266.	Using survey data for 11 elections since 1952, this study develops a systematic analysis of the gender gap in presidential elections.
Gender and gender role	Yamaguchi, Kazuo. (2000). "Multinomial Logit Latent-Class Regression Models: An Analysis of the Predictors of Gender-Role Attitudes Among Japanese Women." 105:1702-1740.	Describes the method and application of multinomial logit latent-class regression models in sociological research.
Government reform	Soule, Sarah A., and Yvonne Zylan. (1997). "Runaway Train? The Diffusion of State-Level Reform in ADC/AFDC Eligibility Requirements, 1950-1967." 103:733-762.	The authors use diffusion models to examine how two sets of processes affected the rate of enactment of work requirements.
Incarceration	Jacobs, David, and Ronald E. Helms. (1996). "Toward a Political Model of Incarceration: A Time-Series Examination of Multiple Explanations for Prison Admission Rates." 102:323-357.	Examines yearly shifts in prison admissions since 1950. The effects of political and economic determinants are investigated using measures of economic inequality, political variables, and unemployment.
Income, distribution of	Korzeniewicz, Roberto Patricio, and Timothy Patrick Moran. (1997). "World-Economic Trends in the Distribution of Income, 1965-1992." 102:1000-1039.	By identifying these trends, the article is able to explain past discrepancies and recent shifts in the relevant empirical and theoretical literature.
Institutional change	DiPrete, Thomas A., and Patricia A. McManus. (1996). "Institutions, Technical Change, and Diverging Life Chances: Earnings Mobility in the United States and Germany." 102:34-79.	Argues that important institutional effects are countrywide and demonstrates the effect of country-level institutional differences by comparing recent earnings dynamics in the United States and Germany.
Institutional change	Nee, Victor. (1996). "The Emergence of a Market Society: Changing Mechanisms of Stratification in China." 101:908-949.	Examines the effect of institutional change—the shift from redistribution to markets—in altering the mechanisms of stratification.
International relations	Yamagishi, Toshio, Karen S. Cook, and Motoki Watabe. (1998). "Uncertainty, Trust, and Commitment Formation in the United States and Japan." 104:165-194.	Provides further empirical support for the theory of trust proposed by Yamagishi and his associates.

(continued)

Table 7.3 Continued

Locus of Study and/or Assessment	Citation	Purpose or Intent
Interpersonal conflict and exchange	Jacobs, David, and Katherine Woods. (1999). "Interracial Conflict and Interracial Homicide: Do Political and Economic Rivalries Explain White Killings of Blacks or Black Killings of Whites?" 105:157-190.	Studies the determinants of disaggregated interracial killing rates in 165 U.S. cities by testing economic, political, and social control accounts.
Interpersonal conflict and exchange	Mulford, Matthew, John Orbell, Catherine Shatto, and Jean Stockard. (1998). "Physical Attractiveness, Opportunity, and Success in Everyday Exchange." 103:1565-1592.	The role perceived physical attractiveness plays in everyday exchange is addressed using a laboratory paradigm that examines both play-versus-not-play and cooperate-versus-defect choices in an ecology of available Prisoner's Dilemma games.
Labor	Western, Bruce, and Katherine Beckett. (1999). "How Unregulated Is the U.S. Labor Market? The Penal System as a Labor Market Institution." 104:1030-1060.	Argues that the U.S. state made a large and coercive intervention into the labor market through expansion of the penal system.
Leadership	Robnett, Belinda. (1996). "African-American Women in the Civil Rights Movement, 1954-1965: Gender, Leadership, and Micromobilization." 101:1661-1693.	Through an analysis of gender in the civil rights movement, this article illustrates that the conceptualization of social movement leadership requires expansion.
Living conditions	Barkey, Karen, and Ronan Van Rossem. (1997). "Networks of Contention: Villages and Regional Structure in the Seventeenth-Century Ottoman Empire." 102:1345-1382.	The authors argue that peasant contention results from the position of the village in the regional structure, with village-level organization providing the means for contention.
Marital quality, configuration, and marital status	Gillis, A. R. (1996). "So Long as They Both Shall Live: Marital Dissolution and the Decline of Domestic Homicide in France, 1852-1909." 101:1273-1305.	Suggests that the growth of European states, the decline of families, and the rise of individualism generated the institutionalization of judicial separation and divorce.
Marital quality, configuration, and marital status	Hao, Lingxin, and Mary C. Brinton. (1997). "Productive Activities and Support Systems of Single Mothers." 102:1305-1344.	Using 14 waves of data from the National Longitudinal Survey of Youth, the article shows that kin coresidence facilitates young single mothers' entry into productive activities but does not play a significant role in sustaining participation.
Marital quality, configuration, and marital status	Webster, Pamela S., Terri L. Orbuch, and James S. House. (1995). "Effects of Childhood Family Background on Adult Marital Quality and Perceived Stability." 101:404-432.	The authors examine the effect of various single-parent childhood family structures on adult marital quality and perceived stability.

Migration patterns	Quillian, Lincoln. (1999). "Migration Patterns and the Growth of High-Poverty Neighborhoods, 1970-1990." 105:1-37.	Using geocoded data from the Panel Study of Income Dynamics, this article examines why the number of high-poverty neighborhoods in American cities has increased since 1970.
Mobility	Sobel, Michael E., Mark P. Becker, and Susan M. Minick. (1998). "Origins, Destinations, and Association in Occupational Mobility." 104:687-721.	Nonlinear models of association are combined with linear models for logits of marginal distributions, resulting in models with parameters directly interpretable in terms of association or structural mobility.
Nationalism	Gorski, Philip S. (2000). "The Mosaic Moment: An Early Modernist Critique of Modernist Theories of Nationalism." 105:1428-1468.	Drawing on primary and secondary evidence from the Netherlands, England, and other early modern polities, the article documents the existence of movements and ideologies that must be classified as national and nationalist by the modernists' own criteria. It is then argued that some nationalist discourses had medieval roots and that they were no less nationalistic than the nationalisms of the French Revolution. In the conclusion, the theoretical premises of the modernist position are subjected to critical examination.
Neighborhood influences and issues	Grannis, Rick. (1998). "The Importance of Trivial Streets: Residential Streets and Residential Segregation." 103:1530-1564.	Argues that racial similarity among neighborhoods emerges primarily from their relational connections via tertiary streets rather than as a result of geographic proximity. Analyzing tertiary streets can better predict racial composition than can spatial considerations.
Neighborhood influences and issues	Green, Donald P., Dara Z. Strolovitch, and Janelle S. Wong. (1998). "Defended Neighborhoods, Integration, and Racially Motivated Crime." 104:372-403.	Investigates demographic and macroeconomic correlates of racially motivated antiminority crime in New York City (1987-1995).
Neighborhood influences and issues	Sampson, Robert J., and Stephen W. Raudenbush. (1999). "Systematic Social Observation of Public Spaces: A New Look at Disorder in Urban Neighborhoods." 105:603-651.	Highly reliable scales of social and physical disorder for 196 neighborhoods are constructed on the basis of videotaping and systematic rating of more than 23,000 street segments in Chicago.
Neighborhood influences and issues	South, Scott J., and Kyle D. Crowder. (1997). "Escaping Distressed Neighborhoods: Individual, Community, and Metropolitan Influences." 102:1040-1084.	Links longitudinal data from the Panel Study of Income Dynamics with information on respondents' census tracts to examine patterns of annual residential mobility between poor and nonpoor neighborhoods.
Networking	Fernandez, Roberto M., Emilio J. Castilla, and Paul Moore. (2000). "Social Capital at Work: Networks and Employment at a Phone Center." 105:1288-1356.	Argues that a common organizational practice—the hiring of new workers via employee referrals—provides key insights into the notion of social capital.
Organizations and organizational issues	Chaves, Mark. (1996). "Ordaining Women: The Diffusion of an Organizational Innovation." 101:840-873.	Extensive loose coupling between formal policy and actual practice concerning female access to positions within religious organizations highlights the symbolic importance of rules about women's ordination. This article focuses on these rules via an event-history analysis of U.S. Christian denominations' official adoption of women's ordination.

(continued)

Table 7.3 Continued

Locus of Study and/or Assessment	Citation	Purpose or Intent
Organizations and organizational issues	Guthrie, Douglas. (1997). "Between Markets and Politics: Organizational Responses to Reform in China." 102:1258-1304.	Using data from a random sample of firms in Shanghai, the article discusses two common situations: economic instability, with weak firms struggling to survive in the rapidly changing market system, and administrative instability, with large firms that were the most protected now being forced to handle the responsibilities that were previously handled by the state.
Organizations and organizational issues	Keister, Lisa A. (1998). "Engineering Growth: Business Group Structure and Firm Performance in China's Transition Economy." 104:404-440.	Analyzes the effect of business group structure on the financial performance and productivity of the groups' member firms using 1988-1990 panel data on China's 40 largest business groups and their 535 member firms.
Organizations and organizational issues	Kono, Clifford, Donald Palmer, Roger Friedland, and Matthew Zafonte. (1998). "Lost in Space: The Geography of Corporate Interlocking Directorates." 103:863-911.	The authors hypothesize that interlocks are spatial phenomena, with spatial attributes and spatial determinants.
Parental investment	Freese, Jeremy, and Brian Powell. (1999). "Sociobiology, Status, and Parental Investment in Sons and Daughters: Testing the Trivers-Willard Hypothesis." 104:1704-1743.	Although some dismiss sociobiological theories as untestable, post hoc explanations, this article argues that sociologists should instead increase their efforts to identify and engage those theories that have novel empirical implications.
Parent-child relationships	Silverstein, Merril, and Vern L. Bengtson. (1997). "Intergenerational Solidarity and the Structure of Adult Child-Parent Relationships in American Families." 104:429-460.	The authors investigate the structure of intergenerational cohesion by examining social-psychological, structural, and transactional aspects of adult child-parent relations.
Prison	Goldstone, Jack A., and Bert Useem. (1999). "Prison Riots as Microrevolutions: An Extension of State-Centered Theories of Revolution." 104:985-1029.	Explores the applicability of state-centered theories of revolution to the phenomena of prison riots.
Protest movements	Zhao, Dingxin. (2000). "State-Society Relations and the Discourses and Activities of the 1989 Beijing Student Movement." 105:1592-1632.	Argues that the 1989 movement's traditionalist outlook can be explained by three structural conditions, all involving state-society relations.
Racial attitudes and integration	Quillian, Lincoln. (1996). "Group Threat and Regional Change in Attitudes Toward African-Americans." 102:816-860.	Using survey data from the General Social Survey 1972-1991, the author assesses several possible causes of regional differences and temporal change in white racial attitudes.
Racial attitudes and integration	Sigelman, Lee, Timothy Bledsoe, Susan Welch, and Michael W. Combs. (1996). "Making Contact? Black-White Social Interaction in an Urban Setting." 101:1306-1332.	Drawing on a survey of residents of the Detroit area, this article probes to what extent and in what manner interracial contact (a) has changed over the past quarter century and (b) is shaped by propinquity and personal characteristics.

Racial minorities	Minkoff, Debra C. (1999). "Bending With the Wind: Strategic Change and Adaptation by Women's and Racial Minority Organizations." 104:1666-1703.	Provides an integrated analysis of social movement organizational change and survival based on the activities of national women's and racial minority organizations during the 1955-1985 period.
Religion	Davis, Nancy J., and Robert V. Robinson. (1996). "Are the Rumors of War Exaggerated? Religious Orthodoxy and Moral Progressivism in America." 102:756-787.	The authors argue, along with Wuthnow and Hunter, that religion is an important source of political division in the United States, but that the effect of this religious division is primarily on gender- and family-related issues of children's schooling, sexuality, reproductive rights, and women's involvement in the family and workplace.
Religion	Manza, Jeff, and Clem Brooks. (1997). "The Religious Factor in U.S. Presidential Elections, 1960-1992." 103:38-81.	Analyzes the relationship between religion and political behavior in recent U.S. presidential elections.
Religion and economic justice	Davis, Nancy J., and Robert V. Robinson. (1999). "Their Brothers' Keepers? Orthodox Religionists, Modernists, and Economic Justice in Europe." 104:1631-1665.	Through analyses of national surveys of 21 European countries and Israel, the authors test the conventional wisdom in Europe that modernists are to the left of the religiously orthodox on economic justice concerns.
Retirement	Han, Sin-Kap, and Phyllis Moen. (1999). "Clocking Out: Temporal Patterning of Retirement." 105:191-236.	Draws on life history data of the cohorts of recent U.S. retirees to examine the temporal patterning of retirement.
Self-esteem	Yabiku, Scott T., William G. Axinn, and Arland Thornton. (1999). "Family Integration and Children's Self-Esteem." 104:1494-1524.	Introduces the concept of family integration to describe the way in which family social organization affects individuals.
Sex segregation	Chang, Mariko Lin. (2000). "The Evolution of Sex Segregation Regimes." 105:1658-1701.	Addresses issues of cross-national convergence in patterns of occupational sex segregation in the context of a new typology that distinguishes between substantive-egalitarian, formal-egalitarian, traditional family-centered, and economy-centered systems.
Social attitudes	DiMaggio, Paul, John Evans, and Bethany Bryson. (1996). "Have Americans' Social Attitudes Become More Polarized?" 102:690-755.	The authors find little evidence of polarization over the past two decades, with attitudes toward abortion and opinion differences between Republican and Democratic party identifiers the exceptional cases.
Social capital	Paxton, Pamela. (1999). "Is Social Capital Declining in the United States? A Multiple Indicator Assessment." 105:88-127.	Improves upon previous research by providing a model of social capital that has explicit links to theories of social capital and that analyzes multiple indicators of social capital over a 20-year period.
Social communications	Ansell, Christopher K. (1997). "Symbolic Networks: The Realignment of the French Working Class, 1887-1894." 103:359-390.	Argues that organizational cohesion emerges through the interplay between powerful symbols, political discourse, and social or interorganizational networks.
Social exchange	Molm, Linda D., Nobuyuki Takahashi, and Gretchen Peterson. (2000). "Risk and Trust in Social Exchange: An Experimental Test of a Classical Proposition." 105:1396-1427.	Develops theoretical implications and reports on an experimental test that compares levels of both trust and commitment in two forms of direct exchange, negotiated and reciprocal.

(continued)

Table 7.3 Continued

Locus of Study and/or Assessment	Citation	Purpose or Intent
Status	Lovaglia, Michael J., Jeffrey W. Lucas, Jeffrey A. Houser, Shane R. Thye, and Barry Markovsky. (1998). "Status Processes and Mental Ability Test Scores." 104:195-228.	The authors predict that status processes, including status differences and the differences in rewards and costs that result, will produce differences in ability test scores between high-status and low-status individuals.
Violence	Jacobs, David, and Robert M. O'Brien. (1998). "The Determinants of Deadly Force: A Structural Analysis of Police Violence." 103:837-862.	Assesses the determinants of the rate of killings committed by the police in 170 U.S. cities.
Violence	Liska, Allen E., and Paul E. Bellair. (1995). "Violent-Crime Rates and Racial Composition: Convergence Over Time." 101:578-610.	Using a sample of U.S. cities, the authors examine the reciprocal effects of racial composition and violent-crime rates over the last 40 years.
Violence	O'Brien, Robert M., Jean Stockard, and Lynne Isaacson. (1999). "The Enduring Effects of Cohort Characteristics on Age-Specific Homicide Rates, 1960-1995." 104:1061-1095.	The authors explain the relative increase in youth homicides in comparison to those for people age 25 and over without invoking an explanation specific to the period after the mid-1980s.
Violence	Tolnay, Stewart E., Glenn Deane, and E. M. Beck. (1996). "Vicarious Violence: Spatial Effects on Southern Lynchings, 1890-1919." 102:788-815.	Considers what effect lynchings in one location had on lynchings elsewhere.
Volunteerism	Popular, Pamela A., and J. Miller McPherson. (1995). "On the Edge or in Between: Niche Position, Niche Overlap, and the Duration of Voluntary Association Memberships." 101:698-720.	The authors analyze an event-history data set, generated by the life-history calendar approach, of 2,813 voluntary association membership polls.
Wages	Petersen, Trent, and Laurie A. Morgan. (1995). "Separate and Unequal: Occupation-Establishment Sex Segregation and the Gender Wage Gap." 101:329-365.	The authors report the first large-scale empirical investigation of within-job wage differences between men and women in the same occupation and establishment, using data first on blue-collar and clerical employees from 16 U.S. industries in 1974-1983 and second on employees in 10 professional and administrative occupations.
Wages	Tam, Tony. (1997). "Sex Segregation and Occupational Gender Inequality in the United States: Devaluation or Specialized Training?" 102:1652-1692.	Examines two hypotheses of the wage effects of occupational sex composition in the United States: the devaluation and the specialized human capital hypotheses.
Wages	Xie, Yu, and Emily Hannum. (1996). "Regional Variation in Earnings Inequality in Reform-Era Urban China." 101:950-992.	Studies regional variation in earnings inequality in contemporary urban China, focusing on the relationship between the pace of economic reforms and earning determination.

Topic	Citation	Description
War	Centeno, Miguel Angel. (1997). "Blood and Debt: War and Taxation in Nineteenth-Century Latin America." 102:1565-1605.	Using data from 11 Latin American countries, this article challenges the universality of the positive relationship between war and state making.
Welfare	DiPrete, Thomas A., Paul M. de Graaf, Ruud Luijkx, Michael Tahlin, and Hans-Peter Blossfeld. (1997). "Collectivist Versus Individualist Mobility Regimes? Structural Change and Job Mobility in Four Countries." 103:318-358.	Develops a synthesis of labor market and welfare state theory to account for cross-national differences in the labor market response to changing occupational and industrial distributions.
Welfare	Lichter, Daniel T., Diane K. McLaughlin, and David C. Ribar. (1997). "Welfare and the Rise in Female-Headed Families." 103:112-143.	Provides a bridge between recent marriage market research and studies of a welfare incentive effect on U.S. family formation.

American Sociological Review

Topic	Citation	Description
Achievement	Mouw, Ted, and Yu Xie. (1999). "Bilingualism and the Academic Achievement of First- and Second-Generation Asian Americans: Accommodation With or Without Assimilation?" 64:232-252.	The authors use data on first- and second-generation Asian American students to assess whether the effect of bilingualism on academic achievement is transitional rather than cognitive or cultural.
Adolescent work	Entwisle, Doris R., Karl L. Alexander, and Linda Steffel Olson. (2000). "Early Work Histories of Urban Youth." 65:279-297.	The authors investigate how social constraints bear on the timing and quality of adolescents' work by summarizing detailed life course data on the paid work and schooling experiences of a panel of urban adolescents followed prospectively from the time their formal schooling began.
Assessment	Bollen, Kenneth A., and Pamela Paxton. (1998). "Detection and Determinants of Bias in Subjective Measures." 63:465-478.	Demonstrates the feasibility of investigating biases in subjective measures under a broad range of research designs.
Attitudes and values	MacIntosh, Randall. (1998). "Global Attitude Measurement: An Assessment of the World Values Survey Postmaterialism Scale." 63:452-464.	Uses the World Values Survey to develop a postmaterialism scale.
Attitudes toward social problems	Phelan, Jo, Bruce G. Link, Ann Stueve, and Robert E. Moore. (1995). "Education, Social Liberalism, and Economic Conservatism: Attitudes Toward Homeless People." 60:126-140.	The authors use attitude data on a social problem with both economic and social components of homelessness to help resolve the question of whether education influences political attitudes through personality and cognitive development, socialization, or ideological refinement.
Authority	Boyd, Elizabeth A. (1998). "Bureaucratic Authority in the 'Company of Equals': The Interactional Management of Medical Peer Review." 63:200-224.	Examines the negotiation of treatment decisions and the management of professional relationships during medical peer review.

(continued)

Table 7.3 Continued

Locus of Study and/or Assessment	Citation	Purpose or Intent
Birth order	Freese, Jeremy, Brian Powell, and Lala Carr Steelman. (1999). "Rebel Without a Cause or Effect: Birth Order and Social Attitudes." 64:207-231.	The authors use contemporary data to test Sulloway's contention that firstborn adults are more conservative, supportive of authority, and "tough-minded" than laterborns.
Birth weight, long-term effects of	Conley, Dalton, and Neil G. Bennett. (2000). "Is Biology Destiny? Birth Weight and Life Chances." 65:458-467.	Addresses questions regarding the intersection of socioeconomic status, biology, and low birth weight over the life course using data from the Panel Study of Income Dynamics for the years 1968 through 1992.
Bureaucracy and growth	Evans, Peter, and James E. Rauch. (1999). "Bureaucracy and Growth: A Cross-National Analysis of the Effects of 'Weberian' State Structures on Economic Growth." 64:748-765.	Uses a recent and original data set to examine the characteristics of core state economic agencies and the growth records of a sample of 35 developing countries for the 1970-1990 period.
Business decisions	Grant, Don Sherman, II. (1995). "The Political Economy of Business Failures Across the American States, 1970-1985: The Impact of Reagan's New Federalism." 60:851-873.	Extends Gordon, Edwards, and Reich's historical model of social structures of accumulation to analyze state differences in business failure rates between 1970 and 1985.
Business decisions	Romo, Frank P., and Michael Schwawiz. (1995). "The Structural Embeddedness of Business Decisions: The Migration of Manufacturing Plants in New York State, 1960-1985." 60:874-907.	Presents a sociological analysis of regional political economies, specifically examining industrial migration in New York State.
Career advancement and institutional quality	Ishida, Hiroshi, Seymour Spilerman, and Kuo-Hsien Su. (1997). "Educational Credentials and Promotion Chances in Japanese and American Organizations." 62:866-882.	Examines how the process of career advancement in organizations is affected by the quality of educational institutions previously attended by the employees and by employees' specializations in college.
Career paths	Walder, Andrew G., Bobai Li, and Donald J. Treiman. (2000). "Politics and Life Chances in a State Socialist Regime: Dual Career Paths Into the Urban Chinese Elite, 1949 to 1996." 65:191-209.	The authors use life history data from a nationally representative 1996 survey of urban Chinese adults to test the finding that party membership and education may have had different effects in administrative and professional careers.
Child rearing	Wilcox, W. Bradford. (1998). "Conservative Protestant Childrearing: Authoritarian or Authoritative?" 63:796-809.	Suggests that this subculture is characterized both by strict discipline and by an unusually warm and expressive style of parent-child interaction.
Child rearing and parents' networks	Munch, Allison, J. Miller McPherson, and Lynn Smith-Lovin. (1997). "Gender, Children, and Social Contact: The Effects of Childrearing for Men and Women." 62:509-520.	Investigates the impact of child rearing on men's and women's social networks, using a probability sample of residents of 10 Great Plains towns.

Childbearing	Guthrie, Doug, and Louise Marie Roth. (1999). "The State, Courts, and Maternity Policies in U.S. Organizations: Specifying Institutional Mechanisms." 64:41-63.	Analyzes the dynamic interaction of state institutions and organizational policies through an analysis of leave benefits in U.S. organizations.
Childbearing	Sucoff, Clea A., and Dawn M. Upchurch. (1998). "Neighborhood Context and the Risk of Childbearing Among Metropolitan-Area Black Adolescents." 63:571-585.	Examines whether neighborhood racial composition or poverty is the more important predictor of premarital adolescent childbearing among metropolitan-area blacks, and how family socioeconomic status moderates these neighborhood influences.
Children's namings	Lieberson, Stanley, and Kelly S. Mikelson. (1995). "Distinctive African American Names: An Experimental, Historical, and Linguistic Analysis of Innovation." 60:928-946.	Analyzes innovative naming patterns used in the past 75 years and then considers both the influence of African heritage in America and the thrust toward African roots in recent decades.
Church and state	Gorski, Philip S. (2000). "Historicizing the Secularization Debate: Church, State, and Society in Late Medieval and Early Modern Europe, ca. 1300 to 1700." 65:138-167.	The author puts the old paradigm and the new paradigm of religious development to the test through a detailed examination of religious life in Western Europe before and after the Reformation.
Church culture	Pattillo-McCoy, Mary. (1998). "Church Culture as a Strategy of Action in the Black Community." 63:767-784.	The author uses social constructionism as an analytical approach to bridge social movement and cultural theory.
Civil rights	Crenshaw, Edward M. (1995). "Democracy and Demographic Inheritance: The Influence of Modernity and Proto-Modernity on Political and Civil Rights, 1965 to 1980." 60:702-718.	Tests a hypothesis concerning the relationship between political democracy and preindustrial social structure.
Class and voting behavior	Hout, Michael, Clem Brooks, and Jeff Manza. (1995). "The Democratic Class Struggle in the United States, 1948-1992." 60:805-828.	Presents evidence of a historic realignment in the relationship between class and voting behavior in U.S. presidential elections in the postwar period.
Class conflict	Kelley, Jonathan, and M.D.R. Evans. (1995). "Class and Class Conflict in Six Western Nations." 60:157-178.	Suggests that materialist forces and reference-group processes jointly shape people's subjective images of class and class conflict, with important political consequences.
Cohabitation	Raley, R. Kelly. (1996). "A Shortage of Marriageable Men? A Note on the Role of Cohabitation in Black-White Differences in Marriage Rates." 61:973-983.	Using the National Survey of Families and Households, the author explores the role of cohabitation in differences between blacks and whites in union formation.
Cohesion	Brines, Julie, and Kara Joyner. (1999). "The Ties That Bind: Principles of Cohesion in Cohabitation and Marriage." 64:333-355.	The authors aim to see whether the principles governing stability in relationships differ by type of union and to address the implications of these differences for theory and research on modern couples.
Cohort and age effects	Alwin, Duane F., and Ryan J. McCammon. (1999). "Aging Versus Cohort Interpretations of Intercohort Differences in GSS Vocabulary Scores." 64:272-286.	The authors investigate the plausibility of aging versus cohort interpretations of cohort-linked differences in vocabulary knowledge using data from 13 General Social Survey data sets covering a 22-year period.

(continued)

Table 7.3 Continued

Locus of Study and/or Assessment	Citation	Purpose or Intent
Collective efficacy	Sampson, Robert J., Jeffrey D. Morenoff, and Felton Earls. (1999). "Beyond Social Capital: Spatial Dynamics of Collective Efficacy for Children." 64:633-660.	The authors propose a theoretical framework on the structural sources and spatially embedded nature of three mechanisms that produce collective efficacy for children.
Collective labor actions	Heckathorn, Douglas D. (1996). "The Dynamics and Dilemmas of Collective Action." 61:250-277.	The author proposes a theoretically exhaustive inventory of the dilemmas arising in collective action systems and shows that five games, including the Prisoner's Dilemma, can underlie collective action.
Collective memory and culture	Olick, Jeffrey K., and Daniel Levy. (1997). "Collective Memory and Cultural Constraint: Holocaust Myth and Rationality in German Politics." 62:921-936.	Uses a case study of official representations of the Holocaust in the Federal Republic of Germany to address the ways in which collective memory constrains political claim-making.
Colonialism	Adams, Julia. (1996). "Principals and Agents, Colonialists and Company Men: The Decay of Colonial Control in the Dutch East Indies." 61:12-28.	Argues that network structures mediated principal/agent relationships among early modern European colonialists.
Commemoration	Olick, Jeffrey K. (1999). "Genre Memories and Memory Genres: A Dialogical Analysis of May 8, 1945 Commemorations in the Federal Republic of Germany." 64:381-402.	Takes an integrated approach that includes the politics of commemoration, the history of commemoration, and the memory of commemoration, illuminating a subtle yet crucial feature of the 50th anniversary commemoration of May 8, 1945.
Communications	Clayman, Steven E., and Ann Reisner. (1998). "Gatekeeping in Action: Editorial Conferences and Assessments of Newsworthiness." 63:178-199.	Studies how newspaper editors, in conference meetings, jointly determine which stories will appear on the front page.
Communications	Greatbatch, David, and Robert Dingwall. (1997). "Argumentative Talk in Divorce Mediation Sessions." 62:151-170.	Analyzes the management of arguments in sessions recorded at a divorce mediation agency.
Communications	Lawler, Edward J., and Jeongkoo Yoon. (1996). "Commitment in Exchange Relations: Test of a Theory of Relational Cohesion." 61:89-108.	Develops and tests a theory of relational cohesion that predicts how and when people in exchange become committed to their relationship.
Conflict	Cooney, Mark. (1997). "From Warre to Tyranny: Lethal Conflict and the State." 62:316-338.	Reviews the cross-cultural and cross-national evidence on the impact of the state on the most common form of extreme violence—lethal conflict.
Conflict	Pescosolido, Bernice A., Elizabeth Grauerholz, and Melissa A. Milkie. (1997). "Culture and Conflict: The Portrayal of Blacks in U.S. Children's Picture Books Through the Mid- and Late-Twentieth Century." 62:443-464.	Documents changes in racial images and examines the relationships between culture, gatekeeping, and conflict in society.

Consumer behavior	DiMaggio, Paul, and Hugh Louch. (1998). "Socially Embedded Consumer Transactions: For What Kinds of Purchases Do People Most Often Use Networks?" 63:619-637.	Documents high levels of within-network exchanges using data from the economic sociology module of the 1996 General Social Survey.
Corporate acquisitions	Palmer, Donald, Brad M. Barber, Xueguang Zhou, and Yasemin Soyal. (1995). "The Friendly and Predatory Acquisition of Large U.S. Corporations in the 1960s: The Other Contested Terrain." 60:469-499.	Explores the factors that led large corporations to be acquired through friendly and predatory means in the 1960s.
Corporations and mergers	Brewster Stearns, Linda, and Kenneth D. Allan. (1996). "Economic Behavior in Institutional Environments: The Corporate Merger Wave of the 1980s." 61:699-718.	Develops a theoretical model that centers on the actors who promote the mergers and on those changes in the political and economic environments that provide the resources these actors need to act.
Crime	Horney, Julie, D. Wayne Osgood, and Ineke Haen Marshall. (1995). "Criminal Careers in the Short Term: Intra-Individual Variability in Crime and Its Relation to Local Life Circumstance." 60:655-673.	The authors fill an important gap in knowledge about change in criminal behavior during adulthood.
Criminology	Grattet, Ryken, Valerie Jenness, and Theodore R. Curry. (1998). "The Homogenization and Differentiation of Hate Crime Law in the United States, 1978 to 1995: Innovation and Diffusion in the Criminalization of Bigotry." 63:286-307.	Investigates the patterns of innovation and diffusion that characterize hate crime laws.
Criminology	Laub, John H., Daniel S. Nagin, and Robert J. Sampson. (1998). "Trajectories of Change in Criminal Offending: Good Marriages and the Desistance Process." 63:225-238.	The authors draw an analogy between changes in criminal offending spurred by the formation of social bonds and an investment process.
Cultural practices	Mackie, Gerry. (1996). "Ending Footbinding and Infibulation: A Convention Account." 61:999-1017.	The author seeks to show that footbinding and infibulation are closely equivalent practices and that the successful campaign to end footbinding in China has lessons for the efforts to end infibulation in Africa.
Cultural revolution	Zhou, Xueguang, and Liren Hou. (1999). "Children of the Cultural Revolution: The State and the Life Course in the People's Republic of China." 64:12-36.	Examines the life experiences of children of the Cultural Revolution: those youths who entered the labor force during this period.
Cultural taste	Bryson, Bethany. (1996). "'Anything But Heavy Metal': Symbolic Exclusion and Musical Dislikes." 61:884-899.	Using data on musical dislikes from the 1993 General Social Survey, the author links literatures on taste, racism, and democratic liberalism by showing that people use cultural taste to reinforce symbolic boundaries between themselves and categories of people they dislike.

(continued)

Table 7.3   Continued

Locus of Study and/or Assessment	Citation	Purpose or Intent
Demographic transition theory	Crenshaw, Edward M., Matthew Christenson, and Doyle Ray Oakey. (2000). "Demographic Transition in Ecological Focus." 65:371-391.	The authors argue that human ecology and evolutionary theory can help respecify and revitalize demographic transition theory.
Deviant behavior	Osgood, D. Wayne, Janet K. Wilson, Patrick M. O'Malley, Jerald G. Bachman, and Lloyd D. Johnston. (1996). "Routine Activities and Individual Deviant Behavior." 61:635-655.	The authors extend the routine activity perspective's situational analysis of crime to individual offending and to a broad range of deviant behaviors.
Disadvantaged men and women	Sampson, Robert J., and John H. Laub. (1996). "Socioeconomic Achievement in the Life Course of Disadvantaged Men: Military Services as a Turning Point, Circa 1940-1965." 61:347-367.	Linking historical context with macro-social opportunity over the life course, the authors examine the social mechanisms by which military service in the World War II era fostered long-term socioeconomic achievement.
Divorce	Diekmann, Andreas, and Henriette Engelhardt. (1999). "The Social Inheritance of Divorce: Effects of Parent's Family Type in Postwar Germany." 64:783-793.	Investigates the intergenerational transmission of divorce risk among German first marriages using multivariate event-history techniques.
Divorce	Peterson, Richard R. (1996). "A Re-Evaluation of the Economic Consequences of Divorce." 61:528-536.	The author replicates The Divorce Revolution's (1985) analysis and demonstrates that the estimates reported in the book are inaccurate.
Divorce	Smock, Pamela J., Wendy D. Manning, and Sanjiv Gupta. (1999). "The Effect of Marriage and Divorce on Women's Economic Well-Being." 64:794-812.	The authors focus on the question of whether divorced women would experience the same absolute levels of economic well-being by staying married as women who remain married experience. They also examine the argument that all women are economically vulnerable once marriage ends.
Economic determinants	Muller, Edward N. (1995). "Economic Determinants of Democracy." 60:966-982.	Hypothesizes that income inequality affects democracy, and this effect often counteracts the positive influence of economic development.
Economic hardship	Mirowsky, John, and Catherine E. Ross. (1999). "Economic Hardship Across the Life Course." 64:548-569.	Tests two hypotheses about the relationship between age and reported difficulty paying bills or buying things the family needs.
Economic markets	Fligstein, Neil. (1996). "Markets as Politics: A Political-Cultural Approach to Market Institutions." 61:656-673.	Develops a conceptual view of the social institutions that comprise markets, discusses a sociological model of action, and discusses how markets and states are intimately linked.
Economic segregation	Jargowsky, Paul A. (1996). "Take the Money and Run: Economic Segregation in U.S. Metropolitan Areas." 61:984-998.	Presents a methodological critique of the measure of economic segregation used by Massey and Eggers and argues that their measure confounds changes in the income distribution with spatial changes.

Economics	Tomaskovic-Devey, Donald, and Vincent J. Roscigno. (1996). "Racial Economic Subordination and White Gain in the U.S. South." 61:565-589.	The authors argue that competition and exploitation perspectives are theoretically limited because they neglect the historically and structurally contingent nature of distributional struggles and political-economic development.
Economics and agriculture	Emigh, Rebecca Jean. (1997). "The Spread of Sharecropping in Tuscany: The Political Economy of Transaction Costs." 62:423-442.	Examines the spread of sharecropping in late medieval and early modern Tuscany.
Economics and economic growth	Crenshaw, Edward M., Ansari Z. Ameen, and Matthew Christenson. (1997). "Population Dynamics and Economic Development: Age-Specific Population Growth Rates and Economic Growth in Developing Countries, 1965 to 1990." 62:974-984.	The authors regress the annual average percentage change in real gross domestic product per capita from 1965 to 1990 on demographic models that incorporate either total population growth rates and labor force growth rates or age-specific population growth rates.
Economies and capitalism	Collins, Randall. (1997). "An Asian Route to Capitalism: Religious Economy and the Origins of Self-Transforming Growth in Japan." 62:843-865.	The author proposes a neo-Weberian model in which the initial breakout from agrarian-coercive obstacles took place within the enclave of religious organizations, with monasteries acting as the first entrepreneurs.
Education	Smits, Jeroen, Wout Ultee, and Jan Lammers. (1998). "Educational Homogamy in 65 Countries: An Explanation of Differences in Openness Using Country-Level Explanatory Variables." 63:264-285.	Uses log-linear analysis to assess the degree of educational homogamy in 65 countries.
Education and health	Ross, Catherine E., and Chia-Ling Wu. (1995). "The Links Between Education and Health." 60:719-745.	Replicates analyses with two samples, cross-sectionally and over time, using two health measures (self-reported health and physical functioning).
Education and labor	Sakamota, Arthur, and Daniel A. Powers. (1995). "Education and the Dual Labor Market for Japanese Men." 60:222-246.	Investigates the relationship between educational attainment and primary-sector employment among Japanese men.
Education and private schools	Arum, Richard. (1996). "Do Private Schools Force Public Schools to Compete?" 61:29-46.	Demonstrates that public school students in states with large private school sectors have better educational outcomes.
Educational attainment	Darnell, Alfred, and Darren E. Sherkat. (1997). "The Impact of Protestant Fundamentalism on Educational Attainment." 62:306-315.	Examines how fundamentalist Protestant cultural orientations discourage educational pursuits.
Educational attainment and cultural careers	Aschaffenburg, Karen, and Ineke Maas. (1997). "Cultural and Educational Careers: The Dynamics of Social Reproduction." 62:573-587.	Uses data from the Surveys of Public Participation in the Arts to analyze the relationship between cultural careers and educational careers.
Emotion	Lawler, Edward J., and Jeongkoo Yoon. (1998). "Network Structure and Emotion in Exchange Relations." 63:871-894.	The authors apply their theory of relational cohesion to propose network effects on the development of cohesive exchange relations.

(continued)

Table 7.3   Continued

Locus of Study and/or Assessment	Citation	Purpose or Intent
Employment	D'Alessio, Stewart J., and Lisa Stolzenberg. (1995). "Unemployment and the Incarceration of Pretrial Defendants." 60:350-359.	Using longitudinal data and a Box-Jenkins Autoregressive-Integrated Moving Average (ARIMA) modeling method, the authors investigate the effect of unemployment rates on pretrial incarceration rates.
Employment	Huber, Evelyne, and John D. Stephens. (2000). "Partisan Governance, Women's Employment, and the Social Democratic Service State." 65:323-342.	Analyzes the expansion of, and the cross-national variation in the expansion of, welfare state goods and services.
Employment	Kalleberg, Arne L., Barbara F. Reskin, and Ken Hudson. (2000). "Bad Jobs in America: Standard and Nonstandard Employment Relations and Job Quality in the United States." 65:256-278.	The authors examine the relationship between nonstandard employment and exposure to bad job characteristics, using data from the 1996 Current Population Survey.
Employment	Portes, Alejandro, and Min Zhou. (1996). "Self-Employment and the Earnings of Immigrants." 61:219-230.	Examines economic returns to immigrants engaged in self-employment.
Employment	Sanders, Jimy M., and Victor Nee. (1996). "Immigrant Self-Employment: The Family as Social Capital and the Value of Human Capital." 61:231-249.	Examines how self-employment among Asian and Hispanic immigrants is affected by family composition and human capital/class resources.
Employment	Reskin, Barbara F., and Debra Branch McBrier. (2000). "Why Not Ascription? Organizations' Employment of Male and Female Managers." 65:210-233.	Examines the effects of organizations' employment practices on sex-based ascription in managerial jobs.
Employment and personal contacts	Fernandez, Roberto M., and Nancy Weinberg. (1997). "Sifting and Sorting: Personal Contacts and Hiring in a Retail Bank." 62:883-902.	Uses data from a large retail bank to investigate the theoretical mechanisms by which preexisting social ties affect the hiring process.
Employment transitions	DiPrete, Thomas A., and Patricia A. McManus. (2000). "Family Change, Employment Transitions, and the Welfare State: Household Income Dynamics in the United States and Germany." 65:343-370.	The authors argue that a society's structure of household income mobility depends on four components: (a) the rate of events that trigger income change, (b) the direct financial impact of these events, (c) the tax and social welfare programs that modify this direct impact in the short and longer terms, and (d) the rate of subsequent events that cause the original effect to intensify or decay.
Environment	Frank, David John, Ann Hironaka, and Evan Schofer. (2000). "The Nation-State and the Natural Environment Over the Twentieth Century." 65:96-116.	Tests a view of a top-down causal imagery that hinges on a global redefinition of the "nation-state" to include environmental protection as a basic state responsibility.

Evaluation	Heimer, Carol A., and Lisa R. Staffen. (1995). "Interdependence and Reintegrative Social Control: Labeling and Reforming 'Inappropriate' Parents in Neonatal Intensive Care Units." 60:635–654.	The authors argue that the process of sorting and evaluating parents of NICU patients varies with the gender, age, and race of the parents and depends on what those characteristics are taken to mean in the context of the organization.
Family configuration	Powell, Brian, and Douglas B. Downey. (1997). "Living in Single-Parent Households: An Investigation of the Same-Sex Hypothesis." 62:521–539.	Examines the social scientific evidence regarding one question increasingly addressed in legal scholarship and in custody cases: Are children who live with their same-sex parent in a better situation than their peers who live with an opposite-sex parent?
Family configuration	South, Scott J., and Kyle D. Crowder. (1999). "Neighborhood Effects on Family Formation: Concentrated Poverty and Beyond." 64:113–132.	The authors use longitudinal data from the Panel Study of Income Dynamics, in conjunction with decennial census data, to examine the impact of neighborhood socioeconomic disadvantage on young women's risk of premarital childbearing and the timing of their transition to first marriage.
Family size and parental resources	Downey, Douglas B. (1995). "When Bigger Is Not Better: Family Size, Parental Resources, and Children's Educational Performance." 60:746–761.	Provides a framework for conceptualizing parental resources and specifies tests of the model's implications.
Family stability	Tolnay, Stewart E., and Kyle D. Crowder. (1999). "Regional Origin and Family Stability in Northern Cities: The Role of Context." 64:97–112.	Examines the effects of metropolitan-level distress on urban black family patterns and explores whether group differences in exposure to these contextual conditions can explain the greater stability of migrant families.
Feminization	Rosenfeld, Rachel A., David Cunningham, and Kathryn Schmidt. (1997). "American Sociological Association Elections, 1975 to 1996: Exploring Explanations for 'Feminization.'" 62:746–759.	Examines possible factors behind the trend of increased proportions of women in American Sociological Association governance positions and the trend that women candidates for ASA offices and the ASA Council have been over-represented and generally have had higher odds of winning than male candidates.
Fertility and population factors	Tolnay, Stewart E. (1995). "The Spatial Diffusion of Fertility: A Cross-Sectional Analysis of Counties in the American South, 1940." 60:299–308.	Examines the impact of diffusion on variation in fertility levels in the American South in 1940, near the end of the transition to lower fertility.
Fertility and population factors	Yamaguchi, Kazuo, and Linda R. Ferguson. (1995). "The Stopping and Spacing of Childbirths and Their Birth-History Predictors: Rational-Choice Theory and Event-History Analysis." 60:272–298.	Using data on women from the 1985 Current Population Survey, the authors analyze the distinct effects of covariates on birth stopping and birth spacing.
Financial capital	Uzzi, Brian. (1999). "Embeddedness in the Making of Financial Capital: How Social Relations and Networks Benefit Firms Seeking Financing." 64:481–505.	Investigates how social embeddedness affects an organization's acquisition and cost of financial capital in middle-market banking, a lucrative but understudied financial sector.

(continued)

Table 7.3 Continued

Locus of Study and/or Assessment	Citation	Purpose or Intent
Foreign investment	de Soysa, Indra, and John R. Oneal. (1999). "Boon or Bane? Reassessing the Productivity of Foreign Direct Investment." 64:766-782.	Assesses the effects of foreign and domestic capital on economic growth using the latest data and better models of economic growth than those previously used.
Friendship	Kadushin, Charles. (1995). "Friendship Among the French Financial Elite." 60:202-221.	Demonstrates the role of friendship in determining elite political alignments and corporate board overlap.
Gender	Cohen, Lisa E., Joseph P. Broschak, and Heather A. Haveman. (1998). "And Then There Were More? The Effect of Organizational Sex Composition on the Hiring and Promotion of Managers." 63:711-727.	The authors study how organizational sex composition influences the intraorganizational mobility of male and female managers.
Gender	Gornick, Janet C., and Jerry A. Jacobs. (1998). "Gender, the Welfare State, and Public Employment: A Comparative Study of Seven Industrialized Countries." 63:688-710.	Explores the influence of government employment on the gender gap in earnings in seven countries using data from the Luxembourg Income Study.
Gender	Kay, Fiona M., and John Hagan. (1998). "Raising the Bar: The Gender Stratification of Law-Firm Capital." 63:728-743.	Investigates issues of gender disparity in partnership attainment.
Gender	Martin, Karin A. (1998). "Becoming a Gendered Body: Practices of Preschools." 63:494-511.	Examines one way that everyday movements, comportment, and use of physical space become gendered, using semistructured observation in five preschool classrooms.
Gender	McCall, Leslie. (2000). "Gender and the New Inequality: Explaining the College/Non-College Wage Gap." 65:234-255.	Uses the 1990 5-percent Public Use Microdata Samples, independent sources of macro data, and controls for individual human capital characteristics and examines the association between the college/non-college wage gap and key aspects of local economic conditions for women and men.
Gender and gender inequality	Ridgeway, Cecilia L. (1997). "Interaction and the Conservation of Gender Inequality: Considering Employment." 62:218-235.	Describes interactional gender mechanisms and then discusses the role they play in mediating the persistence of gender inequality in employment.
Gender and gender inequality	Sorensen, Annemette, and Heike Trappe. (1995). "The Persistence of Gender Inequality in Earnings in the German Democratic Republic." 60:398-406.	Examines women's disadvantage in pay at the time of entry into the labor force and at the end of 1989, just before the state socialist regime collapsed.
Gender and gender role	Amato, Paul R., and Alan Booth. (1995). "Changes in Gender Role Attitudes and Perceived Marital Quality." 60:58-66.	Uses longitudinal survey data from a national sample of married persons to examine how changes in gender role attitudes over an 8-year period are related to reported changes in marital quality.

Gender and the gender gap	Wright, Erik Olin, and Janeen Baxter, with Gunn Elisabeth Birkelund. (1995). "The Gender Gap in Workplace Authority: A Cross-National Study." 60:407-435.	Explores a range of issues concerning the gender gap in workplace authority in seven countries (the United States, Canada, the United Kingdom, Australia, Sweden, Norway, and Japan).
Gender and values	Beutel, Ann M., and Margaret Mooney Marini. (1995). "Gender and Values." 60:436-448.	Examines gender differences in the fundamental value orientations of U.S. adolescents.
Gender construction	Udry, J. Richard. (2000). "Biological Limits of Gender Construction." 65:443-457.	Tests the hypothesis that the effect on women of their childhood gender socialization is constrained by the biological process that produces natural behavior predispositions.
Gender gap and wage earners	Marini, Margaret Mooney, and Pi-Ling Fan. (1997). "The Gender Gap in Earnings at Career Entry." 62:588-604.	Takes the structure of jobs and wages as a characteristic of the economy that is given at the time individuals enter the labor market, and seeks to determine how individuals are sorted, or matched, to different jobs.
Gender role	Haney, Lynne. (1996). "Homeboys, Babies, Men in Suits: The State and the Reproduction of Male Dominance." 61:759-778.	A theoretically based ethnography of the gender practices of two state institutions.
General Accounting Office	Basu, Onker N., Mark W. Dirsmith, and Parveen P. Gupta. (1999). "The Coupling of the Symbolic and the Technical in an Institutionalized Context: The Negotiated Order of the GAO's Audit Reporting Process." 64:506-526.	The authors examine the relationship between the work an organization actually performs backstage and the image it presents to external parties through a qualitative field study of the U.S. General Accounting Office's audit reporting process.
Group dynamics	Friedkin, Noah E. (1999). "Choice Shift and Group Polarization." 64:856-875.	Develops a social structural perspective on the choice shifts that individuals make within groups and argues that choice shifts are a ubiquitous product of the inequalities of interpersonal influence that emerge during discussions of issues.
Group dynamics	Lovaglia, Michael J., and Jeffrey A. Houser. (1996). "Emotional Reactions and Status in Groups." 61:867-883.	The authors propose that emotional reactions compatible with status characteristics reduce status differences among group members, while incompatible emotional reactions increase status differences.
Group solidarity	Gould, Roger V. (1999). "Collective Violence and Group Solidarity: Evidence From a Feuding Society." 64:356-380.	Proposes and tests the argument that group violence occurs because groups are plagued by the tension between collective interest and individual interest, and because participants in conflict are conscious of this tension.
Group tenure composition	Sorensen, Jesper B. (2000). "The Longitudinal Effects of Group Tenure Composition on Turnover." 65:298-310.	Analyzes the effect of group tenure heterogeneity over time on managers' turnover rates.
Health data, utility of	Ferraro, Kenneth F., and Melissa M. Framer. (1999). "Utility of Health Data From Social Surveys: Is There a Gold Standard for Measuring Morbidity?" 64:303-315.	The authors compare self-reported morbidity with indicators of morbidity from physicians' evaluations and examine the predictive validity of each indicator on self-assessed health and mortality in adulthood.

(continued)

Table 7.3 Continued

Locus of Study and/or Assessment	Citation	Purpose or Intent
Identity theory	Burke, Peter J. (1997). "An Identity Model for Network Exchange." 62:134-150.	Introduces a dynamic model of the exchange process in which network nodes are based on a model of identity processes as given by identity theory.
Immigrant groups	Alba, Richard D., John R. Logan, Brian J. Stults, Gilbert Marzan, and Wenquan Zhang. (1999). "Immigrant Groups in the Suburbs: A Reexamination of Suburbanization and Spatial Assimilation." 64:446-460.	The authors use Public Use Microdata from the 1980 and 1990 U.S. censuses to examine the link between suburban residence and life-cycle, socioeconomic, and assimilation characteristics for 11 racial/ethnic groups, including those growing most from contemporary immigration as well as non-Hispanic whites.
Immigration	Bergesen, Albert, and Max Herman. (1998). "Immigration, Race, and Riot: The 1992 Los Angeles Uprising." 63:39-54.	Tests the hypothesis that the 1992 Los Angeles race riot represented backlash violence in response to recent Latino and Asian immigration into African American neighborhoods.
Income	Alderson, Arthur S., and Francois Nielsen. (1999). "Income Inequality, Development, and Dependence: A Reconsideration." 64:606-631.	Reconsiders the role of foreign investment in income inequality in the light of recent critiques that question the results of quantitative cross-national research on foreign capital penetration.
Income	Gustafsson, Bjorn, and Mats Johansson. (1999). "In Search of Smoking Guns: What Makes Income Inequality Vary Over Time in Different Countries?" 64:585-605.	Investigates the forces affecting the distribution of income by analyzing an unbalanced panel of information for 16 industrialized countries for the years 1966 through 1994.
Income	Nielsen, Francois, and Arthur S. Alderson. (1997). "The Kuznets Curve and the Great U-Turn: Income Inequality in U.S. Counties, 1970 to 1990." 62:12-33.	Examines the determinants of inequality in the distribution of family income in approximately 3,100 counties of the United States in 1970, 1980, and 1990.
Income and wage inequality	LaFree, Gary, and Kriss A. Drass. (1996). "The Effect of Changes in Intraracial Income Inequality and Educational Attainment on Changes in Arrest Rates for African Americans and Whites, 1957 to 1990." 61:614-634.	The authors reexamine the link between postwar trends in economic well-being, educational attainment, and crime among African Americans and whites.
Indian identity	Nagel, Joane. (1995). "American Indian Ethnic Renewal: Politics and the Resurgence of Identity." 60:947-965.	Examines the phenomenon of ethnic identity change and the role of politics in prompting the reconstruction of individual ethnicity.
Individualism	Frank, David John, John W. Meyer, and David Miyahara. (1995). "The Individualist Policy and the Prevalence of Professionalized Psychology: A Cross-National Study." 60:360-377.	Demonstrates cross nationally the empirical connection between variations in levels of institutionalized individualism and the prevalence of professionalized psychology.

Industrialization	Alderson, Arthur S. (1999). "Explaining Deindustrialization: Globalization, Failure, or Success?" 64:701-721.	Examines the link that has been been drawn between globalization and the deindustrialization of the advanced industrial societies, employing a data set of pooled time series of cross sections that combines observations on 18 OECD nations across the 1968-1992 period.
Institutionalism	Kraatz, Matthew S., and Edward J. Zajac. (1996). "Exploring the Limits of the New Institutionalism: The Causes and Consequences of Illegitimate Organizational Change." 61:812-836.	The authors analyze longitudinal data from 1971 to 1986 for 631 private liberal arts colleges facing strong institutional and increasingly strong technical environments.
International development	Van Rossem, Ronan. (1996). "The World System Paradigm as General Theory of Development: A Cross-National Test." 61:508-527.	Tests the world system paradigm as a general theory of development by focusing on three central constructs: world system role, dependency, and development.
Iranian Revolution	Rasler, Karen. (1996). "Concessions, Repression, and Political Protest in the Iranian Revolution." 61:132-152.	Investigates how and why the shah's policies of accommodation and repression escalated the revolutionary mobilization of the Iranian population.
Job changes	Zhou, Xueguang, Nancy Brandon Tuma, and Phyllis Moen. (1997). "Institutional Change and Job-Shift Patterns in Urban China, 1949 to 1994." 62:339-365.	The authors examine job-shift patterns across types of organizations and economic sectors in urban China throughout the entire history of Communist rule, 1949 to 1994, thereby establishing a baseline for examining changes in China's redistributive economy.
Justice indexes	Jasso, Guillermina. (1999). "How Much Injustice Is There in the World? Two New Justice Indexes." 64:133-167.	Explores the possibility of constructing justice indexes, measures that would quantify the amount of perceived injustice in a society and thus enable comparison of the amount of injustice across societies and over time.
Labor	Babb, Sarah. (1996). "A True American System of Finance: Frame Resonance in the U.S. Labor Movement, 1866 to 1886." 61:1033-1052.	Examines labor-greenbackism in order to address the theoretical question of what happens when a social movement's ideology does not fit the perceptions of its constituents.
Labor	Caspi, Avshalom, Bradley R. Entner Wright, Terrie E. Moffitt, and Phil A. Silva. (1998). "Early Failure in the Labor Market: Childhood and Adolescent Predictors of Unemployment in the Transition to Adulthood." 63:424-451.	Investigates the childhood and adolescent predictors of youth unemployment in a longitudinal study of young adults who have been studied for the 21 years since their births in 1972-1973.
Labor and labor markets	DiPrete, Thomas A., and K. Lynn Nonnemaker. (1997). "Structural Change, Labor Market Turbulence, and Labor Market Outcomes." 62:386-404.	Develops a model of mobility that includes the macro forces of turbulence and change and includes individual-level attributes.
Labor and labor markets	Eliason, Scott R. (1995). "An Extension of the Sørensen-Kalleberg Theory of the Labor Market Matching and Attainment Processes." 60:247-271.	Advances the theory of the labor market matching and attainment processes outlined by Sørensen and Kalleberg and provides an empirical test of the new specification.

(continued)

Table 7.3   Continued

Locus of Study and/or Assessment	Citation	Purpose or Intent
Labor and women	Lee, Ching Kwan. (1995). "Engendering the Worlds of Labor: Women Workers, Labor Markets, and Production Politics in the South China Economic Miracle." 60:378-397.	A comparative ethnographic study of two gendered regimes of production in two factories in the south China manufacturing region.
Labor markets	Bielby, William T., and Denise D. Bielby. (1999). "Organizational Mediation of Project-Based Labor Markets: Talent Agencies and the Careers of Screenwriters." 64:64-85.	The authors examine how organizations that mediate "life-of-project" employment segment the labor market in a culture industry.
Labor participation	Browne, Irene. (1997). "Explaining the Black-White Gap in Labor Force Participation Among Women Heading Households." 62:236-252.	Compares three explanations of the black-white gap in labor force participation among female household heads: lack of human capital, lack of opportunities resulting from industrial restructuring, and disarticulation from mainstream institutions as described by theories of the underclass.
Language proficiency	Espenshade, Thomas J., and Haishan Fu. (1997). "An Analysis of English-Language Proficiency Among U.S. Immigrants." 62:288-305.	Examines factors that influence the process by which foreign-born persons whose mother tongue is not English acquire English-language proficiency.
Legal issues	Sutton, John R., and Frank Dobbin. (1996). "The Two Faces of Governance: Responses to Legal Uncertainty in U.S. Firms, 1955 to 1985." 61:794-811.	The authors carry the analysis of due-process governance forward by showing that legalization in the workplace has two aspects that reflect distinctly different governance strategies and images of the worker, focusing on legalization in private for-profit firms, and offering more complex specifications of the neoinstitutional model.
Life after death	Greeley, Andrew M., and Michael Hout. (1999). "Americans' Increasing Belief in Life After Death: Religious Competition and Acculturation." 64:813-835.	The authors assess the relative contributions of internal and external sources of belief change after examining the magnitude of changing beliefs and reviewing the conditions of religious competition around the turn of the 20th century.
Marital status and education	Thornton, Arland, William G. Axinn, and Jay D. Teachman. (1995). "The Influence of School Enrollment and Accumulation on Cohabitation and Marriage in Early Adulthood." 60:762-774.	Empirically, the authors evaluate the influence of education on cohabitation and marriage using data from a panel study of young adults and their mothers.
Market	Spenner, Kenneth I., Olga O. Suhomlinova, Sten A. Thore, Kenneth C. Land, and Derek C. Jones. (1998). "Strong Legacies and Weak Markets: Bulgarian State-Owned Enterprises During Early Transition." 63:599-616.	Examines the factors affecting the performance of state-owned enterprises during early transition to a market economy.

Market transitions	Bian, Yanjie, and John R. Logan. (1996). "Market Transition and the Persistence of Power: The Changing Stratification System in Urban China." 61:739–758.	Examines the trend in income inequality and changing stratification mechanisms in one major city from 1978 to 1993.
Markets, international	Baker, Wayne E., Robert R. Faulkner, and Gene A. Fisher. (1998). "Hazards of the Market: The Continuity and Dissolution of Interorganizational Market Relationships." 63:147–177.	The authors analyze the dissolution of interorganizational market ties between advertising agencies and their clients as a function of three forces: competition, power, and institutional forces.
Marriage	Ermakoff, Ivan. (1997). "Prelates and Princes: Aristocratic Marriages, Canon Law Prohibitions, and Shifts in Norms and Patterns of Domination in the Central Middle Ages." 62:405–422.	Explores the processes whereby, at the turn of the 12th century, European aristocrats acknowledged clerics' prohibitions of divorce and close-kin marriages.
Measurement of norms	Jasso, Guillermina, and Karl-Dieter Opp. (1997). "Probing the Character of Norms: A Factorial Survey Analysis of the Norms of Political Action." 62:947–964.	The authors' purposes are to contribute to the methodology for measuring norms and to measure the norms of political action among a sample of respondents in Leipzig, in the former East Germany, in 1993.
Memory	Schwartz, Barry. (1996). "Memory as a Cultural System: Abraham Lincoln in World War II." 61:908–927.	Compares and contrasts memory as a cultural system with constructionist theories of collective memory and discusses it in the light of the erosion of American society's grand narratives.
Mental health	Cherlin, Andrew J., P. Lindsay Chase-Lansdale, and Christine McRae. (1998). "Effects of Parental Divorce on Mental Health Throughout the Life Course." 63:239–249.	The authors examine the long-term effects of parental divorce on individuals' mental health after the transition to adulthood using data from a British birth cohort that has been followed from birth to age 33.
Mental illness	Rosenfield, Sarah. (1997). "Labeling Mental Illness: The Effects of Received Services and Perceived Stigma on Life Satisfaction." 62:660–672.	Directly compares the effects of the receipt of services versus perceptions of stigma on the subjective quality of life for people with chronic mental illness.
Mobility	Breen, Richard. (2000). "Class Inequality and Social Mobility in Northern Ireland, 1973 to 1996." 65:392–406.	Uses data from 1973 and 1996 to examine changes in the class structures and patterns of social mobility of Catholic and Protestant men in Northern Ireland.
Mobility	Cress, Daniel M., and David A. Snow. (1996). "Mobilization at the Margins: Resources, Benefactors, and the Viability of Homeless Social Movement Organizations." 61:1089–1108.	Using data from ethnographic fieldwork on 15 homeless SMOs in eight U.S. cities, the authors construct an empirically grounded typology of resources and assess the combinations of resources necessary for the viability of homeless SMOs.
Mobility	Diani, Mario. (1996). "Linking Mobilization Frames and Political Opportunities: Insights From Regional Populism in Italy." 61:1053–1069.	Drawing on the case of the Northern League in Italy, the author provides a framework for systematically relating insights from two major currents of recent research on collective action: framing processes and political opportunity structures.

(continued)

Table 7.3   Continued

Locus of Study and/or Assessment	Citation	Purpose or Intent
Mobility	Herting, Jerald R., David B. Grusky, and Stephen E. Van Rompaey. (1997). "The Social Geography of Interstate Mobility and Persistence." 62:267-287.	The authors introduce a new model of geographic mobility that maps the underlying contours of sociocultural space after purging the confounding effects of distance, inertia, contiguity, and population size.
Mobility	McCarthy, John D., and Mark Wolfson. (1996). "Resource Mobilization by Local Social Movement Organizations: Agency, Strategy, and Organization in the Movement Against Drinking and Driving." 61:1070-1088.	Data from local social movement organizations opposing drinking and driving are used to assess the roles of agency (i.e., amount of effort), strategy, organizational structure, and nature of national affiliation in the mobilization of resources.
Mobility	Myers, Dowell, and Cynthia J. Cranford. (1998). "Temporal Differentiation in the Occupational Mobility of Immigrant and Native-Born Latina Workers." 63:68-93.	Estimates changes over time in the occupational participation of Latina workers.
Mobility	South, Scott J., and Kyle D. Crowder. (1998). "Leaving the 'Hood: Residential Mobility Between Black, White, and Integrated Neighborhoods." 63:17-26.	Uses data from the Panel Study of Income Dynamics to explore patterns and determinants of residential mobility between census tracts with varying racial composition.
Mobility	Walder, Andrew G. (1995). "Career Mobility and the Communist Political Order." 60:309-328.	Offers a model of selective political screening and incorporation, using survey data from urban China to demonstrate the existence of two distinct career paths that lead to a divided elite.
Negotiating	Molm, Linda D. (1997). "Risk and Power Use: Constraints on the Use of Coercion in Exchange." 62:113-133.	Investigates how risk and fear of loss constrain the use of coercive power in nonnegotiated social exchange relations.
Neighborhoods	Harris, David R. (1999). "'Property Values Drop When Blacks Move in Because . . .': Racial and Socioeconomic Determinants of Neighborhood Desirability." 64:461-479.	Assesses the magnitude and motivations of racial aversion by conducting a hedonic price analysis of geocoded data from the Panel Study of Income Dynamics.
Networking	Bian, Yanjie. (1997). "Bringing Strong Ties Back In: Indirect Ties, Network Bridges, and Job Searches in China." 62:366-385.	Makes distinctions between information and influence that flow through networks during job searches and between direct ties and indirect ties used by job-seekers.
Networks	Smith, Thomas S., and Gregory T. Stevens. (1999). "The Architecture of Small Networks: Strong Interaction and Dynamic Organization in Small Social Systems." 64:403-420.	Discusses a theoretical model that provides a nonreductionistic understanding of how biological forces constrain social interaction and yield effects that propagate beyond dyads into wider social networks.

Topic	Citation	Description
Networks and relationships	Podolny, Joel M., and James N. Baron. (1997). "Resources and Relationships: Social Networks and Mobility in the Workplace." 62:673-693.	The authors examine how the structure and content of individuals' networks in the workplace affect intraorganizational mobility.
Organization by governments	Boli, John, and George M. Thomas. (1997). "World Culture in the World Polity: A Century of International Non-Government Organizations." 62:171-190.	Analyzes the growth of international nongovernmental organizations between 1875 and 1973 using a data set on almost 6,000 organizations.
Organizational characteristics	Ranger-Moore, James. (1997). "Bigger May Be Better, But Is Older Wiser? Organizational Age and Size in the New York Life Insurance Industry." 62:903-920.	Explores the effects of organizational size and age on failure rates among New York life insurance companies between 1813 and 1985.
Organizational evolution	Hannan, Michael T., Glenn R. Carroll, Elizabeth A. Dundon, and John Charles Torres. (1995). "Organizational Evolution in a Multinational Context: Entries of Automobile Manufacturers in Belgium, Britain, France, Germany, and Italy." 60:509-525.	The authors examine the entry of firms into the automobile manufacturing industry in Europe from 1886 through 1981.
Organizational populations	Barron, David N. (1999). "The Structuring of Organizational Populations." 64:421-445.	The author constructs theoretical models of the founding, failure, and growth of organizations that, when combined, constitute an explanation of the process by which the number of organizations in a population declines from a peak, while at the same time the population mass continues to increase.
Organizations	Baron, James N., Michael T. Hannan, and M. Diane Burton. (1999). "Building the Iron Cage: Determinants of Managerial Intensity in the Early Years of Organizations." 64:527-547.	The authors examine how founding conditions shape the proliferation of management and administration in a sample of young technology start-up companies in California's Silicon Valley.
Organizations and economics	Uzzi, Brian. (1996). "The Sources and Consequences of Embeddedness for Economic Performance of Organizations: The Network Effect." 61:674-698.	Attempts to advance the concept of embeddedness beyond the level of programmatic statement by developing a formulation that specifies how embeddedness and network structure affect economic action.
Organizations and size	Kalleberg, Arne L., and Mark E. Van Buren. (1996). "Is Bigger Better? Explaining the Relationship Between Organization Size and Job Rewards." 61:47-66.	The authors attempt to advance the understanding of the organizational bases of stratification by examining the links between size and pecuniary and nonpecuniary job rewards.
Parenting	Nock, Steven L. (1998). "The Consequences of Premarital Fatherhood." 63:250-263.	Examines the socioeconomic consequences of premarital fatherhood using the first 15 years of the National Longitudinal Survey of Youth.
Personality/self-esteem	Rosenberg, Morris, Carmi Schooler, Carrie Schoenbach, and Florence Rosenberg. (1995). "Global Self-Esteem and Specific Self-Esteem: Different Concepts." 60:141-156.	The authors aim to shed light on the nature and relevance of global and specific self-esteem and their relationship to each other.

(continued)

Table 7.3   Continued

Locus of Study and/or Assessment	Citation	Purpose or Intent
Political realignment	Brooks, Clem, and Jeff Manza. (1997). "The Social and Ideological Bases of Middle-Class Political Realignment in the United States, 1972 to 1992." 62:191-208.	The authors address unresolved questions about the political alignments of the middle class through an investigation of change in voting behavior among two of its principal segments: managers and professionals.
Postmodernism	Pescosolido, Bernice A., and Beth A. Rubin. (2000). "The Web of Group Affiliations Revisited: Social Life, Postmodernism, and Sociology." 65:52-76.	The authors address current debates about the future of society and the future of sociology.
Post-Communism	Szelenyi, Szonja, Ivan Szelenyi, and Winifred R. Poster. (1996). "Interests and Symbols in Post-Communist Political Culture: The Case of Hungary." 61:466-477.	Examines the dynamics of the transition to democracy in post-Communist Hungary.
Poverty	Duncan, Greg J., W. Jean Yeung, Jeanne Brooks-Gunn, and Judith R. Smith. (1998). "How Much Does Childhood Poverty Affect the Life Chances of Children?" 63:406-423.	Uses whole-childhood data from the Panel Study of Income Dynamics to relate children's completed schooling and nonmarital fertility to parental income during middle childhood, adolescence, and early childhood.
Power	Berger, Joseph, Cecilia L. Ridgeway, M. Hamit Fisek, and Robert Z. Norman. (1998). "The Legitimation and Delegitimation of Power and Prestige Orders." 63:379-405.	The authors construct a set of assumptions that describe how the legitimation and delegitimation of informal power and prestige orders can be created in task-oriented situations.
Power	Molm, Linda D., Gretchen Peterson, and Nobuyuki Takahashi. (1999). "Power in Negotiated and Reciprocal Exchange." 64:876-890.	Analyzes how the form of social exchange affects the distribution of power in exchange networks.
Power	Yamaguchi, Kazuo. (1996). "Power in Networks of Substitutable and Complementary Exchange Relations: A Rational-Choice Model and an Analysis of Power Centralization." 61:308-332.	Introduces a new measure of power in exchange networks under substitutable/complementary exchange relations.
Prejudices	Quillian, Lincoln. (1995). "Prejudice as a Response to Perceived Group Threat: Population Composition and Anti-Immigrant and Racial Prejudice in Europe." 60:586-611.	Tests the group-threat theory using a multilevel model that combines population data with survey results on attitudes toward immigrants and racial minorities from Eurobarometer Survey 30.
Premarital births	Wu, Lawrence L. (1996). "Effects of Family Instability, Income, and Income Instability on the Risk of a Premarital Birth." 61:386-406.	In this study, the author uses prospective income histories and retrospective parental histories from the National Longitudinal Survey of Youth to determine if the effect of family instability on premarital births is an artifact of low, unstable, or declining family income.

Topic	Citation	Description
Press coverage	Mueller, Carol. (1997). "International Press Coverage of East German Protest Events, 1989." 62:820-832.	Uses a model developed by Snyder and Kelly to test the validity of newspaper coverage of U.S. racial protests and disorders in the 1960s.
Profitability, effects of	Lincoln, James. R., Michael L. Gerlach, and Christina L. Ahmadjian. (1996). "Keiretsu Networks and Corporate Performance in Japan." 61:67-88.	Using data on 197 large Japanese firms over a 24-year period, the authors study how profitability is affected by firm integration in horizontal keiretsu networks.
Protest	McCarthy, John D., Clark McPhail, and Jackie Smith. (1996). "Images of Protest: Dimensions of Selection Bias in Media Coverage of Washington Demonstrations, 1982 to 1991." 61:478-499.	The authors study the problem of media bias regarding protests by comparing police records of demonstrations in Washington, D.C., in 1982 and 1991 with media coverage of the events in three major newspapers and on three national television networks.
Public education	Walters, Pamela Barnhouse, David R. James, and Holly J. McCammon. (1997). "Citizenship and Public Schools: Accounting for Racial Inequality in Education in the Pre- and Post-Disfranchisement South." 62:34-52.	The authors use the specific case of the U.S. South from 1890 to 1910 to explore how local governments allocate educational opportunities, how the availability of educational opportunities affects children's use of educational opportunities, and, how changes in citizenship rights change the way local governments allocate the social right to educational services.
Race	Taylor, Marylee C. (1998). "How White Attitudes Vary With the Racial Composition of Local Populations: Numbers Count." 63:512-535.	Focuses on whites' reactions to the racial composition of the local population.
Race and gender inequality	Beggs, John J. (1995). "The Institutional Environment: Implications for Race and Gender Inequality in the U.S. Labor Market." 60:612-633.	Links institutionalism in organizational theory with research on stratification and document the effects of the institutional environment, a non-economic variable, on economic inequality.
Race and racism	Bonilla-Silva, Eduardo. (1997). "Rethinking Racism: Toward a Structural Interpretation." 62:465-480.	Reviews traditional approaches and alternative approaches to the study of racism, then discusses their limitations and advances a structural theory of racism.
Racial and ethnic concepts	Van Ausdale, Debra, and Joe R. Feagin. (1996). "Using Racial and Ethnic Concepts: The Critical Case of Very Young Children." 61:779-793.	Examines the racial and ethnic concepts and related actions of very young children in a preschool setting.
Racial and ethnic differences	Ainsworth-Darnell, James W., and Douglas B. Downey. (1998). "Assessing the Oppositional Culture Explanation for Racial/Ethnic Differences in School Performance." 63:536-553.	Provides a test of the oppositional culture explanation using a large sample of African American, Asian American, and non-Hispanic white high school sophomores from the first follow-up of the National Education Longitudinal Study.
Racial disparities	Bridges, George S., and Sara Steen. (1998). "Racial Disparities in Official Assessments of Juvenile Offenders: Attributional Stereotypes as Mediating Mechanisms." 63:554-570.	Explores how attributions about the causes of crime, as reflected in written narratives, explain the race-punishment relationship.

(continued)

Table 7.3 Continued

Locus of Study and/or Assessment	Citation	Purpose or Intent
Racial group competition	Bobo, Lawrence, and Vincent L. Hutchings. (1996). "Perceptions of Racial Group Competition: Extending Blumer's Theory of Group Position to a Multiracial Social Context." 61:951-972.	The authors hypothesize that perceptions of threat are driven by a group's feelings of racial alienation within the larger social order.
Racial inequality	Schuman, Howard, and Maria Krysan. (1999). "A Historical Note on Whites' Beliefs About Racial Inequality." 64:847-855.	Examines shifts in the beliefs about sources of the socioeconomic disadvantage suffered by blacks using two survey questions asked by the Gallup organization.
Racial influences	Hughes, Michael, and Melvin E. Thomas. (1998). "The Continuing Significance of Race Revisited: A Study of Race, Class, and Quality of Life in America, 1972 to 1996." 63:785-795.	Shows that quality of life continues to be worse for African Americans than it is for whites, although anomie and mistrust have increased a little more rapidly in recent years for whites than for blacks.
Racial relations	Myers, Daniel J. (1997). "Racial Rioting in the 1960's: An Event History Analysis of Local Conditions." 62:94-112.	Uses event-history analysis to investigate the effects of local conditions on city-level hazard rates of rioting, using Spilerman's data on the timing and locations of race riots from 1961 to 1968.
Racial relations	Olzak, Susan, Suzanne Shanahan, and Elizabeth H. McEneaney. (1996). "Poverty, Segregation, and Race Riots: 1960 to 1993." 61:590-613.	Tests arguments that residential segregation incites racial unrest, using event histories of 154 race riots in 1960 to 1993 in 55 of the largest SMSAs in the United States.
Religion	Pearce, Lisa D., and William G. Axinn. (1998). "The Impact of Family Religious Life on the Quality of Mother-Child Relations." 63:810-828.	Investigates the impact of family religious life on a vital human relationship: the mother-child bond.
Religion	Presser, Stanley, and Linda Stinson. (1998). "Data Collection Mode and Social Desirability Bias in Self-Reported Religious Attendance." 63:137-145.	Examines the impact of misreporting on the correlates of church attendance.
Religion	Smith, Tom W. (1998). "A Review of Church Attendance Measures." 63:131-136.	Reviews several new studies of church attendance rates and reports on new experiments conducted on the 1996 General Social Survey.
Religion and family context	Myers, Scott M. (1996). "An Interactive Model of Religiosity Inheritance: The Importance of Family Context." 61:858-866.	Uses an intergenerational data set suited for estimating the magnitude of religiosity inheritance.
Religion and religious participation	Stolzenberg, Ross M., Mary Blair-Loy, and Linda J. Waite. (1995). "Religious Participation in Early Adulthood: Age and Family Life Cycle Effects on Church Membership." 60:84-103.	The authors integrate, elaborate, and test hypotheses about the ways in which religious participation depends on age, family formation, and attitudes toward marriage and family.

Topic	Citation	Description
Religious beliefs	Kelley, Jonathan, and Nan Dirk De Graaf. (1997). "National Context, Parental Socialization, and Religious Belief: Results From 15 Nations." 62:639-659.	The authors propose that one source of the durability of religious belief is the religious context of the nation as a whole.
Religious pluralism	Finke, Roger, Avery M. Guest, and Rodney Stark. (1996). "Mobilizing Local Religious Markets: Religious Pluralism in the Empire State, 1855 to 1865." 61:203-218.	Examines whether pluralism generated higher levels of religious participation in 19th-century America.
School effects	Morgan, Stephen L., and Aage B. Sorensen. (1999). "Parental Networks, Social Closure, and Mathematics Learning: A Test of Coleman's Social Capital Explanation of School Effects." 64:661-681.	Examines Coleman's explanation for why Catholic schools produce more learning than public schools through an analysis of gains in mathematics achievement between the 10th and 12th grades for respondents to the National Education Longitudinal Study of 1988.
Scientific activities	Baldi, Stephane. (1998). "Normative Versus Social Constructivist Processes in the Allocation of Citations: A Network-Analytic Model." 63:829-846.	Assesses competing arguments on the determinants of scientists' citation patterns by developing a new approach to the multivariate study of citations that builds upon a network-analytic model.
Selection bias	Stolzenberg, Ross M., and Daniel A. Relles. (1997). "Tools for Intuition About Sample Selection Bias and Its Correction." 62:494-507.	Provides mathematical tools to assist intuition about selection bias in concrete empirical analyses.
Self-esteem	Jang, Sung Joon, and Terence P. Thornberry. (1998). "Self-Esteem, Delinquent Peers, and Delinquency: A Test of the Self-Enhancement Thesis." 63:585-598.	Tests Kaplan's self-enhancement thesis, which argues that self-esteem is negatively related to delinquency but that delinquency is positively related to later self-esteem.
Self-esteem	Oates, Gary L. (1997). "Self-Esteem Enhancement Through Fertility? Socioeconomic Prospects, Gender, and Mutual Influence." 62:965-973.	Analyzes data from the National Longitudinal Survey of Youth to examine whether having children influences one's self-esteem, whether the effect of children on self-esteem is stronger among the less socioeconomically privileged and among women, and whether there is evidence of mutual influence in the relationship between having children and self-esteem.
Sex differences	Mirowsky, John, and Catherine E. Ross. (1995). "Sex Differences in Distress: Real or Artifact?" 60:449-468.	Examines whether women genuinely experience greater distress than men, suggesting a heavier burden of hardship and constraint.
Sex differences	Pampel, Fred C. (1998). "National Context, Social Change, and Sex Differences in Suicide Rates." 63:744-758.	Examines a hypothesis of institutional adjustment in which the sex differential in suicide rates first narrows and then widens with continued societal change.
Sex differences	Xie, Yu, and Kimberlee A. Shauman. (1998). "Sex Differences in Research Productivity: New Evidence About an Old Puzzle." 63:847-870.	The authors examine changes in observed sex differences in research productivity over a 24-year period and then apply multivariate negative binomial models in an attempt to uncover explanations for the observed sex differences.
Sex segregation	Chan, Tak Wing. (1999). "Revolving Doors Reexamined: Occupational Sex Segregation Over the Life Course." 64:86-96.	Reexamines the revolving doors thesis using career history data from Great Britain.

(continued)

Table 7.3   Continued

Locus of Study and/or Assessment	Citation	Purpose or Intent
Sexual contact, effects of	Browning, Christopher R., and Edward O. Laumann. (1997). "Sexual Contact Between Children and Adults: A Life Course Perspective." 62:540-560.	The authors adjudicate between two competing models of the long-term effects on women of sexual contact in childhood.
Siblings and intellectual development	Guo, Guang, and Leah K. VanWey. (1999). "Sibship Size and Intellectual Development: Is the Relationship Causal?" 64:169-187.	The authors measure child quality by intellectual development, which is in turn measured by three standardized cognitive tests administered in the National Longitudinal Survey of Youth.
Social capital	Hagan, John, Ross MacMillan, and Blair Wheaton. (1996). "New Kid in Town: Social Capital and the Life Course Effects of Family Migration on Children." 61:368-385.	The authors build on past studies of residential and geographic mobility by incorporating insights from the life course paradigm.
Social cleavages	Brooks, Clem, and Jeff Manza. (1997). "Social Cleavages and Political Alignments: U.S. Presidential Elections, 1960 to 1992." 62:937-946.	Analyzes the magnitude of and interrelationship among four major social cleavages of race, religion, class, and gender in U.S. presidential elections since 1960.
Social composition	McPherson, J. Miller, and Thomas Rotolo. (1996). "Testing a Dynamic Model of Social Composition: Diversity and Change in Voluntary Groups." 61:179-202.	The authors test a dynamic model of the social composition of voluntary groups.
Social differentiation	Mark, Noah. (1998). "Beyond Individual Differences: Social Differentiation From First Principles." 63:309-330.	Seeks to explain the emergence of social differentiation by developing a theory of information and social structure.
Social movement theory	Kurzman, Charles. (1996). "Structural Opportunity and Perceived Opportunity in Social-Movement Theory: The Iranian Revolution of 1979." 61:153-170.	Examines the implications of a mismatch between structural opportunities and perceived opportunities using participant and eyewitness accounts of the Iranian revolutionary movement of 1977 to 1979.
Social movements	Andrews, Kenneth T. (1997). "The Impacts of Social Movements on the Political Process: The Civil Rights Movement and Black Electoral Politics in Mississippi." 62:800-819.	Examines the relationship between social movements and political outcomes.
Social movements	Edwards, Bob, and Sam Marullo. (1995). "Organizational Mortality in a Declining Social Movement: The Demise of Peace Movement Organizations in the End of the Cold War Era." 60:908-927.	The authors examine the U.S. peace movement at the end of the Cold War (1988 to 1992).

Social movements	Goodwin, Jeff. (1997). "The Libidinal Constitution of a High-Risk Social Movement: Affectual Ties and Solidarity in the Huk Rebellion, 1946 to 1954." 62:53-69.	The author explores the effects of affectual and sexual relationships on the Communist-led Huk rebellion in the Philippines.
Social movements	Kim, Hyojoung, and Peter S. Bearman. (1997). "The Structure and Dynamics of Movement Participation." 62:70-93.	Develops a dynamic network model of collective action that explains how collective action can arise in the absence of selective incentives or disincentives from the voluntary action of rational actors in large groups.
Social movements	Minkoff, Debra C. (1997). "The Sequencing of Social Movements." 62:779-799.	Argues that the expansion of social movement organizations, or organizational density, is also an essential component of protest cycles.
Social movements	Whittier, Nancy. (1997). "Political Generations, Micro-Cohorts, and the Transformation of Social Movements." 62:760-778.	Analyzes change and continuity in a social movement, then proposes a generational approach that draws on theory about political generations and cohort replacement.
Social networks	Hagan, Jacqueline Maria. (1998). "Social Networks, Gender, and Immigrant Incorporation: Resources and Constraints." 63:55-67.	Presents a dynamic and variable portrayal of networks to demonstrate how they gradually assume different forms and functions for women and for men that differentially affect settlement outcomes, particularly opportunities to become legal residents.
Social organization	Biggart, Nicole Woolsey, and Mauro F. Guillen. (1999). "Developing Difference: Social Organization and the Rise of the Auto Industries of South Korea, Taiwan, Spain, and Argentina." 64:722-747.	The authors argue that neither a critical factor nor a single path leads to economic development; viable paths vary.
Social relations	Maynard, Douglas W. (1996). "On 'Realization' in Everyday Life: The Forecasting of Bad News as a Social Relation." 61:109-131.	The author uses a collection of bad news narratives to address the interactional work of forecasting and compares it to two other strategies involved in conveying bad news: being blunt and stalling.
Social relations	Umberson, Debra, Meichu D. Chen, James S. House, Kristine Hopkins, and Ellen Slaten. (1996). "The Effect of Social Relationships on Psychological Well-Being: Are Men and Women Really So Different?" 61:837-857.	The authors assess evidence for gender differences across a range of relationships and consider whether the form and quality of these relationships affect the psychological functioning of men and women differently.
Social security	Hicks, Alexander, Joya Misra, and Tang Nah Ng. (1995). "The Programmatic Emergence of the Social Security State." 60:329-349.	Using a theoretical framework that stresses political institutions, the authors examine the consolidation of income-security programs during the formation of the welfare state around the turn of the century.
Social security	Meyer, Madonna Harrington. (1996). "Making Claims as Workers or Wives: The Distribution of Social Security Benefits." 61:449-465.	Demonstrates that benefits linked to marital status are potentially as exclusionary as benefits linked to contributions.

(continued)

Table 7.3	Continued	
Locus of Study and/or Assessment	Citation	Purpose or Intent
Social status	Peterson, Richard A., and Roger M. Kern. (1996). "Changing Highbrow Taste: From Snob to Omnivore." 61:900-907.	Using comparable 1982 and 1992 surveys, the authors test the hypothesized change in tastes associated with high status.
Social status	Ridgeway, Cecilia L., Elizabeth Heger Boyle, Kathy J. Kuipers, and Dawn T. Robinson. (1998). "How Do Status Beliefs Develop? The Role of Resources and Interactional Experience." 63:331-350.	The authors conduct an experimental test using dyadic, same-sex encounters between participants who differ in pay level and a "mere difference" attribute.
Social status	Webster, Murray, Jr., and Stuart J. Hysom. (1998). "Creating Status Characteristics." 63:351-378.	The authors generalize Ridgeway's pathbreaking theory of status construction in three stages, note some parallels with other theorists' work, suggest some independent tests, and consider theoretical and applied implications of this work.
Social stratification	Warren, John Robert, and Robert M. Hauser. (1997). "Social Stratification Across Three Generations: New Evidence From the Wisconsin Longitudinal Study." 62:561-572.	The authors ask whether grandparents' characteristics have significant and direct effects on their grandchildren's outcomes when the characteristics of the parents are held constant.
Social structure	Lomborg, Bjorn. (1996). "Nucleus and Shield: The Evolution of Social Structure in the Iterated Prisoner's Dilemma." 61:278-307.	The basic question of whether social order can evolve in a Hobbesian world is approached using a micro-based simulation that explains macro-outcomes and can handle the macro-level's ensuing effects on micro-decisions.
Social structure and personality	Kohn, Melvin L., Kazimierz M. Slomczynski, Krystyna Janicka, Valeri Khmelko, Bogdan W. Mach, Vladimir Paniotto, Wojciech Zaborowski, Roberto Gutierrez, and Cory Heyman. (1997). "Social Structure and Personality Under Conditions of Radical Social Change: A Comparative Analysis of Poland and Ukraine." 62:614-638.	The authors conducted surveys in Poland and Ukraine to determine if the relationship between social structure and personality during times of apparent social stability obtain as well under conditions of radical social change.
Socialism	Kogut, Bruce, and Udo Zander. (2000). "Did Socialism Fail to Innovate? A Natural Experiment of the Two Zeiss Companies." 65:169-190.	The authors trace the technological contributions of Zeiss Jena in the German Democratic Republic and Zeiss Oberkochen in the Federal Republic of Germany.
Societal fragmentation	Orbell, John, Langche Zeng, and Matthew Mulford. (1996). "Individual Experience and the Fragmentation of Societies." 61:1018-1032.	Uses computer simulations to show how social fragmentation and consequent social loss can result from six innocuous cognitive and behavioral assumptions.
Sociology of the black working class	Horton, Hayward Derrick, Beverlyn Lundy Allen, Cedric Herring, and Melvin E. Thomas. (2000). "Lost in the Storm: The Sociology of the Black Working Class." 65:128-137.	The authors attempt to empirically document changes in the black working class from 1850 to 1990.

Status value theory	Thye, Shane R. (2000). "A Status Value Theory of Power in Exchange Relations." 65:407-432.	Introduces and tests a new status value theory of power.
Stratification	Ferree, Myra Marx, and Elaine J. Hall. (1996). "Rethinking Stratification From a Feminist Perspective: Gender, Race, and Class in Mainstream Textbooks." 61:929-950.	Using a sample of textbooks from 1983 through 1988, the authors examine "mainstream" sociology; that is, the sociology that teachers, students, and textbook publishers have treated as nonproblematic.
Stress	Turner, R. Jay, Blair Wheaton, and Donald A. Lloyd. (1995). "The Epidemiology of Social Stress." 60:104-125.	Examines the social distribution of exposure to stress to test the hypothesis that differences in stress exposure are one factor in sociodemographic variations in mental health.
Suffrage rights	Ramirez, Francisco O., Yasemin Soysal, and Suzanne Shanahan. (1997). "The Changing Logic of Political Citizenship: Cross-National Acquisition of Women's Suffrage Rights, 1890 to 1990." 62:735-745.	The authors analyze the acquisition of women's suffrage in 133 countries from 1890 to 1990.
Suicide	Thorlindsson, Thorolfur, and Thoroddur Bjarnason. (1998). "Modeling Durkheim on the Micro Level: A Study of Youth Suicidality." 63:94-110.	In this study, family integration and parental regulation are operationalized as independent constructs and tested in relation to anomie, suicidal suggestion, and suicidality.
Suicide and Durkheim's theory	van Poppel, Frans, and Lincoln H. Day. (1996). "A Test of Durkheim's Theory of Suicide—Without Committing the 'Ecological Fallacy.'" 61:500-507.	The current analysis, which tests Durkheim's theory of suicide, is based on death rates calculated from data on cause of death recorded simultaneously with the deceased individual's sex, age, and religious affiliation.
Trade globalization	Chase-Dunn, Christopher, Yukio Kawano, and Benjamin D. Brewer. (2000). "Trade Globalization Since 1795: Waves of Integration in the World-System." 65:77-95.	The authors study one type of economic globalization over the past two centuries: the trajectory of international trade as a proportion of global production.
Trust	Macy, Michael W., and John Skvoretz. (1998). "The Evolution of Trust and Cooperation Between Strangers: A Computational Model." 63:638-660.	Uses computer simulation to show how trust and cooperation between strangers can evolve without formal or informal social controls.
Unemployment	Petterson, Stephen M. (1997). "Are Young Black Men Really Less Willing to Work?" 62:605-613.	Argues against the popular view that young black men experience more joblessness than their white counterparts because they have priced themselves out of the labor market.
Union activities	Stepan-Norris, Judith, and Maurice Zeitlin. (1995). "Union Democracy, Radical Leadership, and the Hegemony of Capital." 60:829-850.	The authors attempt to show that both union democracy and radical union leadership foster the imposition of limits on capital's power in the sphere of production.

(continued)

Table 7.3   Continued

Locus of Study and/or Assessment	Citation	Purpose or Intent
Union and unionization trends	Western, Bruce. (1995). "A Comparative Study of Working-Class Disorganization: Union Decline in Eighteen Advanced Capitalist Countries." 60:179-201.	Describes recent unionization trends in 18 OECD countries and outlines explanations tracing waning labor organization to adverse world economic conditions, preexisting levels of unionization, and labor passivity.
Values	Inglehart, Ronald, and Wayne E. Baker. (2000). "Modernization, Cultural Change, and the Persistence of Traditional Values." 65:19-51.	Tests the thesis that economic development is linked with systematic changes in basic values.
Verbal ability	Wilson, James A., and Walter R. Gove. (1999). "The Intercohort Decline in Verbal Ability: Does It Exist?" 64:253-266.	The authors argue that Alwin's and Glenn's analyses confuse cohort effects with aging effects.
Violence	Link, Bruce G., John Monahan, Ann Stueve, and Francis T. Cullen. (1999). "Real in Their Consequences: A Sociological Approach to Understanding the Association Between Psychotic Symptoms and Violence." 64:316-331.	The authors propose a sociologically inspired explanation for the association between mental illness and violence by referring to the Thomas Theorem that if situations are defined as real, they are real in their consequences.
Violence	Liska, Allen E., John R. Logan, and Paul E. Bellair. (1998). "Race and Violent Crime in the Suburbs." 63:27-38.	The authors examine the reciprocal effects of racial composition and crime rates.
Volunteering	Wilson, John, and Marc Musick. (1997). "Who Cares? Toward an Integrated Theory of Volunteer Work." 62:694-713.	The authors estimate a model in which formal volunteering and informal helping are reciprocally related but connected in different ways to different forms of capital.
Voter turnout	Kanazawa, Satoshi. (2000). "A New Solution to the Collective Action Problem: The Paradox of Voter Turnout." 65:433-442.	Uses pooled data from seven separate waves of the General Social Survey to test the stochastic learning theory of voter turnout.
Wage and wage inequality	Nielsen, Francois, and Arthur S. Alderson. (1995). "Income Inequality, Development, and Dualism: Results From an Unbalanced Cross-National Panel." 60:674-701.	The authors investigate the mechanisms that produce the inverted-U shape of the relationship between income inequality and economic development.
Wages	Waldfogel, Jane. (1997). "The Effect of Children on Women's Wages." 62:209-217.	Uses data from the 1968-1988 National Longitudinal Survey of Young Women to investigate the lower wages of mothers.
Wages and earnings	Morgan, Laurie A. (1998). "Glass Ceiling Effect or Cohort Effect? A Longitudinal Study of the Gender Earnings Gap for Engineers, 1982 to 1989." 63:479-493.	Investigates whether what appears to be a glass ceiling in cross-sectional analyses of the gender earnings gap for engineers results instead from a cohort effect, using longitudinal data from the Survey of Natural and Social Scientists and Engineers.

Topic	Reference	Description
Wages and gender equality	Cotter, David A., JoAnn DeFiore, Joan M. Hermsen, Brenda Marsteller Kowalewski, and Reeve Vanneman. (1997). "All Women Benefit: The Macro-Level Effect of Occupational Integration on Gender Earnings Equality." 62:714-734.	The authors investigate macro-level effects of processes that transfer many of the income benefits of occupational integration to all women in the labor market and not just to those women who enter predominantly male occupations.
Wages and racial differences	Cancio, A. Silvia, T. David Evans, and David J. Maume, Jr. (1996). "Reconsidering the Declining Significance of Race: Racial Differences in Early Career Wages." 61:541-556.	The authors test Wilson's assertion that race was declining in significance as a determinant of economic rewards by comparing the net effect of race on hourly wages for two cohorts of young workers. The authors also decomposed the racial gap in hourly wages into a discrimination component and a nondiscrimination component.
Welfare	Cauthen, Nancy K., and Edwin Amenta. (1996). "Not for Widows Only: Institutional Politics and the Formative Years of Aid to Dependent Children." 61:427-448.	The authors argue and demonstrate that Aid to Dependent Children, the central welfare program in the United States, marked a fundamental departure from previous U.S. efforts to aid families without breadwinning fathers.
Welfare	Chaves, Mark. (1999). "Religious Congregations and Welfare Reform: Who Will Take Advantage of 'Charitable Choice'?" 64:836-846.	Uses data from the National Congregations Study to address two questions: To what extent will congregations seek government support for social service activity? and Which subsets of congregations are most likely to take advantage of these new opportunities?
Welfare	Edin, Kathryn, and Laura Lein. (1997). "Work, Welfare, and Single Mothers' Economic Survival Strategies." 62:253-266.	The authors argue that because some survival strategies are more compatible with work than others, the strategies a mother employs may affect her ability to move from welfare to work.
Welfare	Harris, Kathleen Mullan. (1996). "Life After Welfare: Women, Work, and Repeat Dependency." 61:407-426.	Examines the process by which single mothers who have ever experienced and ended a spell on welfare return to welfare for further economic support.
Welfare	Korpi, Walter, and Joakim Palme. (1998). "The Paradox of Redistribution and Strategies of Equality: Welfare State Institutions, Inequality, and Poverty in the Western Countries." 63:661-687.	Examines the different types of social policy programs operating in capitalist democracies and evaluates their effectiveness in reducing inequality and poverty.
Work and family	Burstein, Paul, R. Marie Bricher, and Rachel L. Einwohner. (1995). "Policy Alternatives and Political Change: Work, Family, and Gender on the Congressional Agenda, 1945-1990." 60:67-83.	Examines the ideas on the congressional agenda from 1945 through 1990 on a particularly important issue: What, if anything, should Congress do to regulate gender and family roles in the labor market?
Workplace dignity	Hodson, Randy. (1996). "Dignity in the Workplace Under Participative Management: Alienation and Freedom Revisited." 61:719-738.	Uses a model of workplace organizations that combines elements from Blauner's technology-based model and Edwards's labor-control model to evaluate workers' experiences of alienation and freedom across different systems of production.

(continued)

Table 7.3 Continued

Locus of Study and/or Assessment	Citation	Purpose or Intent
Social Psychology Quarterly		
Attitude	Schultz, P. Wesley, and Stuart Oskamp. (1996). "Effort as a Moderator of the Attitude-Behavior Relationship: General Environmental Concern and Recycling." 59:375-383.	The authors propose that the amount of effort required for a behavior functions as an impediment to action and that overcoming higher barriers requires stronger attitudes.
Attitudes and homelessness	Phelan, Jo, Bruce G. Link, Robert E. Moore, and Ann Stueve. (1997). "The Stigma of Homelessness: The Impact of the Label 'Homeless' on Attitudes Toward Poor Persons." 60:323-337.	The authors use a vignette experiment designed to directly compare attitudes toward a homeless and domiciled poor man and to compare the effects of being labeled homeless with those of being labeled mentally ill.
Attraction	Sprecher, Susan. (1998). "Insiders' Perspectives on Reasons for Attraction to a Close Other." 61:287-300.	The author conducted three studies with college students to examine how "insiders" view the importance of various factors as reasons for their attraction to a close other.
Attractiveness and competence	Jackson, Linda A., Jonh E. Hunter, and Carole N. Hodge. (1995). "Physical Attractiveness and Intellectual Competence: A Meta-Analytic Review." 58:108-122.	The authors use meta-analyses to test hypotheses about the relationship between physical attractiveness and intellectual competence.
Authority, influence of	Johnson, Cathryn, Jody Clay-Warner, and Stephanie J. Funk. (1996). "Effects of Authority Structures and Gender on Interaction in Same-Sex Task Groups." 59:221-236.	Examines the possible effects of the social composition of authority structures on interaction in same-sex task groups in organizations.
Authority and intersubjectivity	Perakyla, Anssi. (1998). "Authority and Intersubjectivity: The Delivery of Diagnosis in Primary Health Care." 61:301-320.	Draws on a database of more than 100 videotaped and transcribed medical consultations to analyze the balance between authority and accountability in delivering diagnostic news in interactions between doctors and patients in Finnish primary health care.
Balance scale	Macintosh, Randall. (1998). "A Confirmatory Factor Analysis of the Affect Balance Scale in 38 Nations: A Research Note." 61:83-91.	Applies confirmatory factor analysis to assess the validity of the positive and negative subscales for use in cross-national research.
Behavioral styles	Shackelford, Susan, Wendy Wood, and Stephen Worchel. (1996). "Behavioral Styles and the Influence of Women in Mixed-Sex Groups." 59:284-293.	Hypothesizes that women who adopt group-oriented or attention-getting styles will be more influential than those who adopt neutral or ambiguous behavioral styles that do not clearly demonstrate group-oriented motivation or attract high levels of attention.

Carpooling	Van Vugt, Mark, Paul A. Am. Van Lange, Ree M. Meertens, and Jeffrey A. Joireman. (1996). "How a Structural Solution to a Real-World Social Dilemma Failed: A Field Experiment on the First Carpool Lane in Europe." 59:364-374.	Examines the impact of a carpool lane on attitudes and preferences relevant to commuting alone or by carpool.
Choice	Gray, Louis N., and Irving Tallman. (1996). "Cost Equalization as a Determinant of Behavioral Allocation: The Case of Binary Choice." 59:154-161.	Proposes that the process of determining which action to choose requires the assessment of potential costs of the alternative courses of action.
Communications	Johnson, Cathryn, Stephanie Funk, and Jody Clay-Warner. (1998). "Organizational Contexts and Conversation Patterns." 61:361-371.	Investigates whether the larger organizational context affects conversation patterns in informal same-sex task groups.
Communications	Lundgren, David C., and Donald J. Rudawsky. (2000). "Speaking One's Mind or Biting One's Tongue: When Do Angered Persons Express or Withhold Feedback in Transactions With Male and Female Peers?" 63:253-263.	The authors examine when angered individuals express feedback and when they withhold it.
Communications and interaction	Lerner, Gene H. (1996). "Finding 'Face' in the Preference Structures of Talk-in-Interaction." 59:303-321.	Connects the concept of "face" to interactionally characterizable locations in conversation and to a specific speaking practice use there.
Conflict and authority	Johnson, Cathryn, and Rebecca Ford. (1996). "Dependence Power, Legitimacy, and Tactical Choice." 59:126-139.	Examines the impact of dependence power and legitimate authority on evaluations of various tactics in a two-party conflict.
Conflict resolution	Lawler, Edward J., Rebecca Ford, and Michael D. Large. (1999). "Unilateral Initiatives as a Conflict Resolution Strategy." 62:240-256.	The authors argue that under equal power, unilateral initiatives will be more credible and will foster more positive impressions.
Control	Mirowsky, John. (1995). "Age and the Sense of Control." 58:31-43.	Examines the cross-sectional association between age and the sense of control.
Cooperation	Macy, Michael W. (1995). "PAVLOV and the Evolution of Cooperation: An Experimental Test." 58:74-87.	Uses empirical research to test PAVLOV's behavioral assumptions, using laboratory experiments with human subjects.
Cooperation	Paese, Paul W., and Spencer J. Stang. (1998). "Adaptation-Level Phenomena and the Prevalence of Cooperation." 61:172-183.	The authors conducted a computer simulation study to examine the relation between an individual-level decision process and the prevalence of self-sacrificial cooperation in large groups of interacting "individuals."
Cost equalization	Gray, Louis N., Irving Tallman, Dean H. Judson, and Candan Duran-Aydintug. (1998). "Cost-Equalization Applications to Asymmetric Influence Processes." 61:259-269.	The authors attempt to describe quantitatively the interaction structures that emerge in task-oriented groups in which the initiation of problem-solving attempts is unrestricted.

(continued)

Table 7.3   Continued

Locus of Study and/or Assessment	Citation	Purpose or Intent
Death and dying	Kutfey, Karen, and Douglas Maynard. (1998). "Bad News in Oncology: How Physician and Patient Talk About Death and Dying Without Using Those Words." 61:321-341.	The authors focus on the socialization of patients to the process of death and dying by examining actual interactions among medical practitioners, patients, and their family members.
Deliberations	Manzo, John F. (1996). "Taking Turns and Taking Sides: Opening Scenes From Two Jury Deliberations." 59:107-125.	The author is concerned with the organization of turn taking in the opening rounds of two actual deliberations, one civil and one criminal.
Dialogicality	Josephs, Ingrid E., and Jaan Valsiner. (1998). "How Does Autodialogue Work? Miracles of Meaning Maintenance and Circumvention Strategies." 61:68-82.	Presents a process model of dialogicality that occurs within a person's self-system in the context of two kinds of tasks.
Domestic violence	Felson, Richard B., and Steven F. Messner. (2000). "The Control Motive in Intimate Partner Violence." 63:86-94.	The authors apply multivariate statistical modeling to examine whether violence by men against their female partners is more likely than other violence to involve a control motive.
Emotion	Heise, David R., and Cassandra Calhan. (1995). "Emotion Norms in Interpersonal Events." 58:223-240.	The authors use a graphically structured adjective checklist to assess prescriptive and reactive norms of emotion in 128 social events.
Emotional control	Whalen, Jack, and Don H. Zimmerman. (1998). "Observations on the Display and Management of Emotion in Naturally Occurring Activities: The Case of 'Hysteria' in Calls to 9-1-1." 61:141-159.	The authors focus on a particular type of emotional display known in the vernacular as "hysteria" and on the "socio-logic" of such an affective state.
Emotions	Conway, Michael, Roberto Difazio, and Shari Mayman. (1999). "Judging Others' Emotions as a Function of the Others' Status." 62:291-305.	The authors address expectancies concerning the emotion-eliciting conditions experienced by individuals of differing status, the emotions experienced and displayed by these individuals, and the norms dictating their display of emotions.
Empathy	Schieman, Scott, and Karen Van Gundy. (2000). "The Personal and Social Links Between Age and Self-Reported Empathy." 63:152-174.	Examines the relationship between age and self-reported empathy.
Equality versus equity	Meeker, Barbara F., and Gregory C. Elliott. (1996). "Reward Allocations, Gender, and Task Performance." 59:294-301.	Examines choice of equality versus equity, dollar amount allocated, perception of relative value of workers, social orientation, and task orientation.
Ethnicity and control	Sastry, Jaya, and Catherine E. Ross. (1998). "Asian Ethnicity and the Sense of Personal Control." 61:101-120.	Examines both the relationship between Asian culture and the sense of personal control and the impact of perceived control on depression and anxiety among Asians and non-Asians.

Topic	Reference	Description
Exchange orientation	Sprecher, Susan. (1998). "The Effect of Exchange Orientation on Close Relationships." 61:220-231.	Examines two types of exchange orientation for their associations with quality and stability of relationships.
Exchange regulation	Bonacich, Phillip, and Noah E. Friedkin. (1998). "Unequally Valued Exchange Relations." 61:160-171.	The authors relax the usual constraint of uniform relations and evaluate the applicability of current theoretical approaches to structures of unequally valued exchange relations.
Expectations	Balkwell, James W. (1995). "Strong Tests of Expectation-States Hypotheses." 58:44-51.	Presents a procedure for assessing the distinctive predictions of a model, which concern group members' locations in a hierarchy.
Expectations	Foschi, Martha. (1996). "Double Standards in the Evaluation of Men and Women." 59:237-254.	Presents the results from two expectation-states studies on gender and double standards for task competence.
Friendship	Kubitschek, Warren N., and Maureen T. Hallinan. (1998). "Tracking and Students' Friendships." 61:1-15.	The authors investigate the means by which academic tracking influences students' friendship choices.
Gender	LaFrance, Marianne, Hiram Brownell, and Eugene Hahn. (1997). "Interpersonal Verbs, Gender, and Implicit Causality." 60:138-152.	Describes a series of studies investigating whether women and men are regarded as equivalently able to cause outcomes in social interaction.
Gender	Smoreda, Zbigniew, and Christian Licoppe. (2000). "Gender-Specific Use of the Domestic Telephone." 63:238-252.	The authors focus on the correlation between the observed duration of phone calls and the gender of callers and receivers, using a study on the uses of the telephone in 317 French homes.
Gender	Stets, Jan E., and Peter J. Burke. (1996). "Gender, Control, and Interaction." 59:193-220.	Examines gender as status, and gender and control as identities, by analyzing negative and positive behavior of married couples whose task was to resolve disagreements in their marriage.
Gender and problem solving	Balkwell, James W., and Joseph Berger. (1996). "Gender, Status, and Behavior in Task Situations." 59:273-283.	Investigates the relative empirical adequacy of four hypotheses using experimental data on mixed-sex problem-solving discussions entailing feminine, gender-neutral, and masculine tasks.
Gender and public goods	Sell, Jane. (1997). "Gender, Strategies, and Contributions to Public Goods." 60:254-265.	Examines factors affecting cooperation in public goods settings involving relatively small groups.
Gender development	Langford, Tom, and Neil J. Mackinnon. (2000). "The Affective Bases for the Gendering of Traits: Comparing the United States and Canada." 63:34-48.	Reconsiders the relationships between gender stereotypes and the three universal dimensions of affective meaning.
Gender differences	Heimer, Karen. (1996). "Gender, Interaction, and Delinquency: Testing a Theory of Differential Social Control." 59:39-61.	Develops an interactionist explanation of gender differences in the processes leading to juvenile delinquency.

(continued)

Table 7.3   Continued

Locus of Study and/or Assessment	Citation	Purpose or Intent
Gender differences	Ibarra, Herminia. (1997). "Paving an Alternative Route: Gender Differences in Managerial Networks." 60:91-102.	Uses the network-analytic concepts of homophily, tie strength, and range to explore gender differences in characteristics of middle managers' information and career support networks.
Gender differences	Rippl, Susanne, and Christian Seipel. (1999). "Gender Differences in Right-Wing Extremism: Intergroup Validity of a Second-Order Construct." 62:381-393.	The authors use the case of gender differences in right-wing extremism as an example to demonstrate the advantage of applying the methodological reasoning of cross-cultural research to intergroup comparison in a single culture.
Gender differences	Wickrama, Kas, Rand D. Conger, Frederick O. Lorenz, and Lisa Mathews. (1995). "Role Identity, Role Satisfaction, and Perceived Physical Health." 58:270-283.	Tests gender differences in the relationships between job, marital and parental satisfaction, and perceived physical health.
Gender gap	Jasso, Guillermina, and Murray Webster, Jr. (1999). "Assessing the Gender Gap in Just Earnings and Its Underlying Mechanisms." 62:367-380.	Reports new theoretical and empirical developments of the gender gap in just earnings, estimating both the gap and the mechanisms by which just earnings are produced.
Gender harassment	Miller, Laura L. (1997). "Not Just Weapons of the Weak: Gender Harassment as a Form of Protest for Army Men." 60:32-51.	Describes men's resistance in the form of gender harassment and then examines who is likely to oppose expanded or even current roles for women soldiers, and why gender harassment is a product of this opposition.
Gender inequality	Foddy, Margaret, and Michael Smithson. (1999). "Can Gender Inequalities Be Eliminated?" 62:307-324.	The authors argue that the theory of status characteristics and expectation states can be employed to increase understanding of the process by which category-based beliefs are combined with specific or individuating information.
Gender stratification	Rosenfield, Sarah, Jean Vertefuille, and Donna D. McAlpine. (2000). "Gender Stratification and Mental Health: An Exploration of Dimensions of the Self." 63:208-223.	Reviews theories and research that link gender stratification to dimensions of the self and, through this, to gender differences in disorders.
Gender-role socialization	Walker, Henry A., Barbara C. Ilardi, Anne M. McMahon, and Mary L. Fennell. (1996). "Gender, Interaction, and Leadership." 59:255-272.	Uses data from laboratory studies of single-gender and mixed-gender groups to test gender-role socialization, status characteristic, and legitimation arguments.
Group cooperation	Yamagishi, Toshio, and Toko Kiyonari. (2000). "The Group as the Container of Generalized Reciprocity." 63:116-132.	Examines results of an experiment with 91 Japanese participants in the Prisoner's Dilemma game to see if they would cooperate more with the in-group or out-group depending on if the game was sequential or simultaneous.

Topic	Reference	Description
Group dynamics	Oakes, Penelope J., S. Alexander Haslam, Brenda Morrison, and Diana Grace. (1995). "Becoming an In-Group: Reexamining the Impact of Familiarity on Perceptions of Group Homogeneity." 58:52-61.	Reports a field study investigating the relationship between familiarity and perceived in-group homogeneity.
Group processes	Ridgeway, Cecilia L., and James W. Balkwell. (1997). "Group Processes and the Diffusion of Status Beliefs." 60:14-31.	Presents a formal model of status belief diffusion that incorporates the most important group processes proposed by the theory.
Homelessness	Wright, Bradley R. Entner. (1998). "Behavioral Intentions and Opportunities Among Homeless Individuals: An Extension of the Theory of Reasoned Actions." 61:271-286.	Applies the social psychological theory of reasoned action to processes of homelessness, extending the breadth of the theory and illuminating the study of homelessness.
Identity	Ellemers, Naomi, and Wendy Van Rijswik. (1997). "Identity Needs Versus Social Opportunities: The Use of Group-Level and Individual-Level Management Strategies." 60:52-65.	Investigates how relative group size and group status affect the use of direct and indirect identity management strategies.
Identity	Francis, Linda E. (1997). "Ideology and Interpersonal Emotion Management: Redefining Identity in Two Support Groups." 60:153-171.	Demonstrates the process by which people's emotions are constructed not only by themselves but also by others.
Identity	Riley, Anna, and Peter J. Burke. (1995). "Identities and Self-Verification in the Small Group." 58:61-73.	Examines the relationship between the meanings contained in one's identity and the meanings attributed to one's behavior by both oneself and others in small-group interaction.
Identity theory	Large, Michael D., and Kristen Marcussen. (2000). "Extending Identity Theory to Predict Differential Forms and Degrees of Psychological Distress." 63:49-59.	Proposes an explanation of how identities influence the way people experience distress.
Identity theory	Lee, Lichang, Jane Allyn Piliavin, and Vaughn R. A. Call. (1999). "Giving Time, Money, and Blood: Similarities and Differences." 62:276-290.	Reports research testing the applicability of an identity theory model, developed with samples of blood donors, to two other forms of institutional helping: volunteering and charitable donation.
Identity theory	Stets, Jan E., and Peter J. Burke. (2000). "Identity Theory and Social Identity Theory." 63:224-237.	Presents core components of identity theory and social identity theory and argues that although differences exist between the two theories, they are more different in emphasis than in kind, and that linking the two theories can establish a more fully integrated view of the self.
Identity theory	Stryker, Sheldon, and Peter J. Burke. (2000). "The Past, Present, and Future of an Identity Theory." 63:284-297.	Reviews each strand of identity theory and then discusses ways in which the two relate to and complement one another.
Individualism and self-sacrifice	Lois, Jennifer. (1999). "Socialization to Heroism: Individualism and Collectivism in a Voluntary Search and Rescue Group." 62:117-135.	Examines the tension between self-interested individualism and norms of self-sacrifice in a volunteer search and rescue group in the western United States.

(continued)

Table 7.3 Continued

Locus of Study and/or Assessment	Citation	Purpose or Intent
Instrumentalism	Mirowsky, John, Catherine E. Ross, and Marieke Van Willigen. (1996). "Instrumentalism in the Land of Opportunity: Socioeconomic Causes and Emotional Consequences." 59:322-337.	The authors analyze the relationship between the sense of control over one's own life and the belief that most Americans control their lives and create their own good or bad outcomes.
Interpersonal interaction	Cohen, Dov, Joseph Vandello, Sylvia Puente, and Adrian Rantilla. (1999). "When You Call Me That, Smile!' How Norms for Politeness, Interaction Styles, and Aggression Work Together in Southern Culture." 62:257-275.	The authors examine how styles of interpersonal interaction and strong norms regarding politeness and conflict resolution can perpetuate violence in the U.S. South, rather than lessening it.
Intimate relationships	Longmore, Monica A., and Alfred DeMaris. (1997). "Perceived Inequity and Depression in Intimate Relationships: The Moderating Effect of Self-Esteem." 60:172-184.	Examines the moderating effect of self-esteem on the relationship between perceived equity/inequity and depression.
Job satisfaction	Randall, Christina A., and Charles W. Mueller. (1995). "Extensions of Justice Theory: Justice Evaluations and Employees' Reactions in a Natural Setting." 58:178-194.	The authors test a series of hypotheses about the effects of justice evaluations on job satisfaction, organizational commitment, intent to stay with an employer, and turnover.
Justice	Mueller, Charles W., and Jean E. Wallace. (1996). "Justice and the Paradox of the Contented Female Worker." 59:338-349.	The authors empirically evaluate the hypotheses stated by Phelan and focus on the degree to which perceptions of justice are responsible for the paradox.
Justice, understanding of	Hegtvedt, Karen A., and Cathryn Johnson. (2000). "Justice Beyond the Individual: A Future With Legitimation." 63:298-311.	The authors argue that inclusion of legitimacy, which is fundamentally a collective process, augments understanding of justice.
Labor	Kroska, Amy. (1997). "The Division of Labor in the Home: A Review and Reconceptualization." 60:304-322.	Reviews and synthesizes the literature on the division of labor in the home, noting some theoretical omissions and advancing a model that may account for findings in the literature.
Labor market	Dunifon, Rachel, and Greg J. Duncan. (1998). "Long-Run Effects of Motivation on Labor-Market Success." 61:33-48.	Examines the relationship between motivation and labor-market success using a sample from the Panel Study of Income Dynamics.
Leisure activity	Fine, Gary Alan, and Lori Holyfield. (1996). "Secrecy, Trust, and Dangerous Leisure: Generating Group Cohesion in Voluntary Organizations." 59:22-38.	Employs an ethnographic examination of a leisure activity involving risk to analyze how voluntary leisure groups maintain members' allegiance and affiliation, thus creating cohesion.
Life expectancy	Mirowsky, John, and Catherine E. Ross. (2000). "Socioeconomic Status and Subjective Life Expectancy." 63:133-151.	The authors test the hypothesis that the higher the achieved socioeconomic status of American adults, the longer they expect their lives to be.

Marital conflict	Tallman, Irving, Louis N. Gray, Vicki Kullberg, and Debra A. Henderson. (1999). "The Intergenerational Transmission of Marital Conflict: Testing a Process Model." 62:219-239.	The authors describe and test a sequential process model derived from socialization theory and designed to expand on previous explanations of the transmission of marital conflict across generations.
Marital interaction	Stets, Jan E. (1997). "Status and Identity in Marital Interaction." 60:185-217.	Examines the effects of gender as status in newly formed marriages as well as the status characteristics of age, education, and occupation.
Maternal and paternal roles	Milkie, Melissa A., Robin W. Simon, and Brian Powell. (1997). "Through the Eyes of Children: Youths' Perceptions and Evaluations of Maternal and Paternal Roles." 60:218-237.	The authors explore children's perceptions and evaluations of maternal and paternal roles by content analyzing more than 3,000 essays in which children explain why their parent is the "best" mother or father.
Media images	Milkie, Melissa A. (1999). "Social Comparisons, Reflected Appraisals, and Mass Media: The Impact of Pervasive Beauty Images on Black and White Girls' Self-Concepts." 62:190-210.	Provides a way to bridge perspectives that argue either that media content is powerful or that people are powerful in interpreting media.
Medial interaction	Gill, Virginia Teas. (1998). "Doing Attributions in Medical Interaction: Patients' Explanations for Illness and Doctors' Responses." 61:342-360.	Presents an analysis of the process of offering and responding to attributions in social interaction.
Mental health	Keyes, Corey Lee M., and Carol D. Ryff. (2000). "Subjective Change and Mental Health: A Self-Concept Theory." 63:264-279.	Investigates the consequences of perceived improvements and perceived declines in life domain functioning..
Networks	Friedkin, Noah E. (1995). "The Incidence of Exchange Networks." 58:213-221.	Advances a line of work on an expected-value model of social exchange, in which a power structure indicates opportunities for exchange and a sample space of exchange networks.
Networks	Skvoretz, John, and Michael J. Lovaglia. (1995). "Who Exchanges With Whom: Structural Determinants of Exchange Frequency in Negotiated Exchange Networks." 58:163-177.	The authors outline and evaluate three explanations for exchange frequencies.
Networks	Szmatka, Jacek, and David Willer. (1995). "Exclusion, Inclusion, and Compound Connection in Exchange Networks." 58:123-132.	The authors extend network exchange theory to networks with compound inclusion-exclusion connections.
Norms	Jimerson, Jason B. (1999). "'Who Has Next?' The Symbolic, Rational, and Methodical Use of Norms in Pickup Basketball." 62:136-156.	Analyzes an entire conversation between people waiting to play an informal game of basketball to illustrate how a combination of perspectives emphasizing the internalization of norms, rational use of norms, and talk about norms can inform a description of norm usage that is plausible to participants and observers.
Organizational principles	Mueller, Charles W., and Edward J. Lawler. (1999). "Commitment to Nested Organizational Units: Some Basic Principles and Preliminary Findings." 62:325-346.	The authors identify several basic principles for understanding what produces different levels of employee commitment to the nested units.

(continued)

Table 7.3 Continued

Locus of Study and/or Assessment	Citation	Purpose or Intent
Parent identity	Tsushima, Teresa, and Peter J. Burke. (1999). "Levels, Agency, and Control in the Parent Identity." 62:173-189.	The authors examine how parents relate standards higher in the identity hierarchy with standards lower in the hierarchy.
Peer groups	Ridgeway, Cecilia L., David Diekema, and Cathryn Johnson. (1995). "Legitimacy, Compliance, and Gender in Peer Groups." 58:298-311.	The authors turn to the special theoretical issues raised by peer groups and present new data for such groups, allowing the predictions about them to be tested as well.
Perception of scientists	Lee, James Daniel. (1998). "Which Kids Can 'Become' Scientists? Effects of Gender, Self-Concepts, and Perceptions of Scientists." 61:199-219.	Uses identity theory to examine links between gender, self-concepts, and perceptions of scientific others, focusing on how these contribute to students' interests and the resulting educational trajectories.
Power	Ford, Rebecca, and Cathryn Johnson. (1998). "The Perception of Power: Dependence and Legitimacy in Conflict." 61:16-32.	Extends previous research by considering how additional information on legitimate authority shapes power estimates in an intraorganizational conflict.
Professional socialization	Cahill, Spencer E. (1999). "Emotional Capital and Professional Socialization: The Case of Mortuary Science Students (and Me)." 62:101-116.	An ethnographic study of an accredited mortuary science program serves as a basis to describe a variety of ways in which this program and its students' social lives normalize work with and around the dead.
Public goods	Sell, Jane, and Yeongi Son. (1997). "Comparing Public Goods With Common Pool Resources: Three Experiments." 60:118-137.	The authors examine whether public good and common pool resources generate equivalent levels of cooperation when payoffs are the same.
Public goods	Van Vugt, Mark. (1997). "Concerns About the Privatization of Public Goods: A Social Dilemma Analysis." 60:355-367.	The author advances a social dilemma analysis to examine the role of self-interested and prosocial concerns in the approval of a real-life structural solution.
Race and ethnicity	Hunt, Matthew, Pamela Braboy Jackson, Brian Powell, and Lala Carr Steelman. (2000). "Color-Blind: The Treatment of Race and Ethnicity in Social Psychology." 63:352-364.	The authors explore the extent to which race and ethnicity have been incorporated in social psychological scholarship and argue that social psychologists should, and can, do better in this regard.
Racial and ethnic attitudes	Huddy, Leonie, and David O. Sears. (1995). "Opposition in Bilingual Education: Prejudice or the Defense of Realistic Interests?" 58:133-143.	The authors further research on the dynamics of racial and ethnic polity attitudes by reviewing the underlying premises and central measures of the prejudice and realistic interest theories and by extending their application beyond a consideration of whites' racial policy attitudes to an examination of Anglos' attitudes toward bilingual education programs.
Racial divide	Johnson, Monica Kirkpatrick, and Margaret Mooney Marini. (1998). "Bridging the Racial Divide in the United States: The Effect of Gender." 61:247-258.	The authors use data for national samples of high school seniors between 1976 and 1992 to examine gender differences in racial attitudes in the United States.

Racial equality	Krysan, Maria. (1999). "Qualifying a Quantifying Analysis on Racial Equality." 62:211-218.	Examines two survey questions about support for government involvement in two important areas of race: housing and employment.
Racial perceptions	Ford, Thomas E. (1997). "Effects of Stereotypical Television Portrayals of African-Americans on Person Perception." 60:266-275.	Tests the hypothesis that stereotypical television portrayals of African Americans increase the likelihood that whites will make negative social perception judgments of an African American (but not a white) target person.
Relationships	Cox, Chante L., Michael O. Wexler, Caryl E. Rusbult, and Stanley O. Gaines, Jr. (1997). "Prescriptive Support and Commitment Processes in Close Relationships." 60:79-90.	The authors examine associations of commitment with both forms of prescriptive support and traditional investment-model variables.
Reward allocation	Rusbult, Caryl E., Chester A. Insko, and Yuan-Huei W. Lin. (1995). "Seniority-Based Reward Allocation in the United States and Taiwan." 58:13-30.	Investigates the manner in which members' seniority influences reward allocation in formal groups.
School transitions	Corsaro, William A., and Luisa Molinari. (2000). "Priming Events and Italian Children's Transition From Preschool to Elementary School: Representations and Actions." 63:16-33.	The authors report on the Italian component of an ethnographic study of children's transition from preschool to elementary school in Italy and the United States.
Self-esteem	Elliott, Marta. (1996). "Impact of Work, Family, and Welfare Receipt on Women's Self-Esteem in Young Adulthood." 59:80-95.	Analyzes the impact of work, family, and welfare on chance in white women's self-esteem from 1980, when women were age 15-23, to 1987, when they were 22-30.
Self-esteem	Roberts, Robert E. L., and Vern L. Bengtson. (1996). "Affective Ties to Parents in Early Adulthood and Self-Esteem Across Twenty Years." 59:96-106.	The authors address the question "Do relations with parents during the transition from adolescence to adulthood have long-term consequences for self-esteem?"
Self-identification	Kinket, Barbara, and Maykel Verkuyten. (1997). "Levels of Ethnic Self-Identification and Social Context." 60:338-354.	The authors examine three forms of ethnic self-identification in relation to their school class among Dutch and Turkish children age 10-13.
Self-image	Peck, B. Mitchell, and Howard B. Kaplan. (1995). "Adolescent Self-Rejection and Adult Political Activity: The Mediating Influence of Achieved Social Status." 58:284-297.	The authors estimate a series of models to address the relationship between adolescent negative self-attitudes and adult political participation.
Sexual identity	Ponticelli, Christy M. (1999). "Crafting Stories of Sexual Identity Reconstruction." 62:157-172.	Draws from field research with one former gay ministry affiliated with Exodus International and Exodus literature to analyze the process used by lesbian members to reconstruct their sexual identities.
Small groups	Harrington, Brooke, and Gary Alan Fine. (2000). "Opening the 'Black Box': Small Groups and Twenty-First-Century Sociology." 63:312-323.	The authors bring together the key pieces that small group research has contributed to sociological knowledge, in an effort to make the case for a renewed interest in studying groups in their own right.

(continued)

Table 7.3   Continued

Locus of Study and/or Assessment	Citation	Purpose or Intent
Social change	Kohn, Melvin L., Wojciech Zaborowski, Krystyna Janicka, Bogdan W. Mach, Valeriy Khmelko, Kazimierz M. Slomczynski, Cory Heyman, and Bruce Podobnik. (2000). "Complexity of Activities and Personality Under Conditions of Radical Social Change: A Comparative Analysis of Poland and Ukraine." 63:187-207.	The authors use a comparative analysis of Poland and Ukraine to extend the often-confirmed hypothesis that the substantive complexity of work in paid employment substantially affects fundamental dimensions of personality.
Social context and identity	Ellemers, Naomi, Cathy van Dyck, Steve Hinkle, and Annelieke Jacobs. (2000). "Intergroup Differentiation in Social Context: Identity Needs Versus Audience Constraints." 63:60-74.	The authors investigate intergroup differentiation in different social contexts.
Social distance	Verkuyten, Maykel, and Barbara Kinket. (2000). "Social Distances in a Multiethnic Society: The Ethnic Hierarchy Among Dutch Preadolescents." 63:75-85.	The authors focus on preferences for contact with members of different ethnic minority groups and on contextual variables as well as individual characteristics.
Social identity	Grant, Peter R., and Rupert Brown. (1995). "From Ethnocentrism to Collective Protest: Responses to Relative Deprivation and Threats to Social Identity." 58:195-211.	Examines the hypotheses that both collective relative deprivation and perceived threat to social identity increase the intention to engage in collective protest actions and expressions of ethnocentrism.
Social identity	Kalkhoff, Will, and Christopher Barnum. (2000). "The Effects of Status-Organizing and Social Identity Processes on Patterns of Social Influence." 63:95-115.	The authors explore the joint effect of status and social identity.
Social inequities	Hollander, Jocelyn A., and Judith A. Howard. (2000). "Social Psychological Theories on Social Inequalities." 63:338-351.	The authors analyze patterns in social psychology's approach to social inequalities, which they argue have been characterized by neglect, a focus on difference rather than on similarity, a tendency toward essentialism, and a lack of attention to social context and power.
Socialization	Adler, Patricia A., and Peter Adler. (1995). "Dynamics of Inclusion and Exclusion in Preadolescent Cliques." 58:145-162.	Draws on longitudinal participant observation and on depth interviews with advanced elementary-school children to explore the central feature of clique dynamics: the techniques of inclusion and exclusion.
Stability and change in gender	Burke, Peter J., and Alicia D. Cast. (1997). "Stability and Change in the Gender Identities of Newly Married Couples." 60:277-290.	Uses identity theory as a multilevel control system to investigate stability and change in identities.

Topic	Citation	Description
Stability theory	Ardelt, Monika. (2000). "Still Stable After All These Years? Personality Stability Theory Revisited." 63:392-405	Examines the claim of personality stability theory that personality remains basically stable after age 30.
Status and personality attributions	Gerber, Gwendolyn L. (1996). "Status in Same-Gender and Mixed-Gender Police Dyads: Effects on Personality Attributions." 59:350-363.	Tests whether external status characteristics affect the personality dispositions attributed to police team members.
Status and power	Massey, Kelly, Sabrina Freeman, and Morris Zelditch. (1997). "Status, Power, and Accounts." 60:238-253.	Reports the results of three experiments studying the effects of status, power, and validity of justifications for the propriety of acts by an actor who violated expectations, with untoward consequences for another.
Status-characteristic theory	Walker, Henry A., and Brent T. Simpson. (2000). "Equating Characteristics and Status-Organizing Processes." 63:175-185.	Uses the graph-theoretic interpretation of status-characteristic theory to examine the question of whether actors use equal status information in status-generalizing processes.
Stereotypes	Ford, Thomas E., and George R. Tonander. (1998). "The Role of Differentiation Between Groups and Social Identity in Stereotype Formation." 61:372-384.	Tests the hypothesis that when social identity is threatened, the social perceiver will form stereotypes of the in-group and the out-group that reflect the in-group's inferiority along that dimension, but will alter the structure of those emerging stereotypes.
Structural theory	Bonacich, Phillip. (1998). "A Behavioral Foundation for a Structural Theory of Power." 61:185-198.	Proposes structural criteria for power based on simple and valid assumptions about how individuals in exchange networks make decisions.
Task groups	Wilke, Henk, Heather Young, Ingeborg Mulders, and Dick de Gilder. (1995). "Acceptance of Influence in Task Groups." 58:312-320.	The authors investigated acceptance of influence in task groups by means of an experiment with a 2 X 2 within-subjects factorial design.
Task orientation	Robinson, Dawn T., and James W. Balkwell. (1995). "Density, Transitivity, and Diffuse Status in Task-Oriented Groups." 58:241-254.	The authors investigate the structure of precedence relations, including whether these relations are dense, whether they are transitive, and whether they are structured in any obvious way by diffuse status characteristics.
Task performance	Foddy, Margaret, and Michael Smithson. (1996). "Relative Ability, Paths of Relevance, and Influence in Task-Oriented Groups." 59:140-153.	Examines the relative impact of three aspects of task performance on the inference of ability.
Transsexuals	Mason-Schrock, Douglas. (1996). "Transsexuals' Narrative Construction of the 'True Self.'" 59:176-192.	The author studies preoperative transsexuals, who are preparing for a radical identity change, to observe the interactive processes through which stories are used to construct a new self.
Trust	Burke, Peter J., and Jan E. Stets. (1999). "Trust and Commitment Through Self-Verification." 62:347-366.	Examines how self-processes and trust influence the development of commitment in society, thereby making social order possible.

(continued)

◀ 603

Table 7.3   Continued

Locus of Study and/or Assessment	Citation	Purpose or Intent
Urban alienation	Geis, Karlyn J., and Catherine E. Ross. (1998). "A New Look at Urban Alienation: The Effect of Neighborhood Disorder on Perceived Powerlessness." 61:232-246.	The authors propose that the environment in which an individual lives affects his or her sense of control versus powerlessness.
Values and gender	Prince-Gibson, Eetta, and Shalom H. Schwartz. (1998). "Value Priorities and Gender." 61:49-67.	Uses theories of gender and research on values to generate hypotheses about the impact on value priorities of gender differences and of interactions of gender with possible sociodemographic moderators of gender experience.
Values and religiosity	Schwartz, Shalom H., and Sipke Huismans. (1995). "Value Priorities and Religiosity in Four Western Religions." 58:88-107.	The authors study the relations of value priorities to degree of commitment to religion.
Wages	Gartrell, C. David, and Bernard E. Paille. (1997). "Wage Cuts and the Fairness of Pay in a Worker-Owned Plywood Cooperative." 60:103-117.	The authors apply the justice theories formulated by Jasso and Markovsky in a worker-owned plywood cooperative where founding workers were responsible for a decision to take substantial wage cuts and accept a wage freeze.
Wages	Jasso, Guillermina, and Murray Webster, Jr. (1997). "Double Standards in Just Earnings for Male and Female Workers." 60:66-78.	The authors conduct two analyses that focus on the double standard and the mechanisms by which the double standard operates.
Well-being	Keyes, Corey Lee M. (1998). "Social Well-Being." 61:121-140.	The authors investigate the theoretical structure, construct validity, and social structural sources of the dimensions of social well-being.
Well-being	Orbuch, Terri L., James S. House, Richard P. Mero, and Pamela S. Webster. (1996). "Marital Quality Over the Life Course." 59:162-171.	The authors argue that objective changes in family composition and in social and economic conditions in middle and later life may explain the later-life increase in well-being.
Work-family conflict	Matthews, Lisa S., Rand D. Conger, and K.A.S. Wickrama. (1996). "Work-Family Conflict and Marital Quality: Mediating Processes." 59:62-79.	The authors use a sample of 337 couples derived from a longitudinal study of families living in the rural Midwest to examine the influence of work-family conflict on marital quality and marital stability as it is mediated through psychological distress and quality of marital interaction.
Working parents	Whitbeck, Les B., Ronald L. Simons, Rand D. Conger, K.A.S. Wickrama, Kevin A. Ackley, and Glen H. Elder, Jr. (1997). "The Effects of Parents' Working Conditions and Family Economic Hardship on Parenting Behaviors and Children's Self-Efficacy." 60:291-303.	Investigates the effects of parents' working conditions and family economic hardship on parenting behaviors, and their subsequent effects on the self-efficacy of adolescent children.

This book, published in 1991, is Volume 1 in the Measures of Social Psychological Attitudes series by Academic Press. Its editors are John P. Robinson, Phillip R. Shaver, and Lawrence S. Wrightsman. The main items in the table of contents are reproduced below. Most chapters contain reference sections and directions for future research.

7.16 THE BUROS INSTITUTE AND THE BUROS MENTAL MEASUREMENTS YEARBOOK

The most useful resource for locating a very large collection of test reviews is available from the Buros Institute of Mental Measurements (www.unl.edu/buros/), affiliated with the University of Nebraska. The Web site mirrors a print publication series, the Mental Measurements Yearbook. The *Fourteenth Mental Measurements Yearbook*, edited by Barbara Plake and James C. Impara, was published in 2001 by the Buros Institute of Mental Measurements, University of Nebraska at Lincoln.

More than 2,000 reviews are available online through SilverPlatter (www.silverplatter.com), a database company whose products are available at most college and university libraries. Table 7.4 is a truncated sample review.

Table 7.4 SAMPLE ENTRY FROM SILVERPLATTER

Minnesota Multiphasic Personality Inventory-2

Hathaway-S; R; McKinley-J; C; Butcher-James-N

75: 7 Validity Indicators: Cannot Say (?), Lie (L), Infrequency (F), Correction (K), Back F (FB), Variable Response Inconsistency (VRIN), True Response Inconsistency (TRIN) (last 3 are supplementary validity scales); 10 Clinical Scales: Hypochondriasis (Hs), Depression . . .

PB: Published by University of Minnesota Press; distributed by National Computer Systems Inc Professional Assessment Services Division PO Box 1416 Minneapolis MN 55440 . . .

Purpose

"Designed to assess a number of the major patterns of personality and emotional disorders."

Review of the Minnesota Multiphasic Personality Inventory-2 by ROBERT P. ARCHER, Professor of Psychiatry and Behavioral Sciences, Eastern Virginia Medical School, Norfolk, VA:

Stark Hathaway reported that he encountered substantial difficulty, including several rejections, before successfully finding a publisher for the Minnesota Multiphasic Personality Inventory (MMPI) in the early 1940s (Dahlstrom and Welsh, 1960). From this humble beginning, the MMPI's climb in popularity was nothing less than phenomenal. Surveys of test usage conducted in 1946 listed the MMPI among the 20 most widely used psychological tests (Louttit and Browne, 1947). A survey conducted in 1959 showed the MMPI to be among the 10 leading tests, and the only objective personality assessment instrument included in this group (Sundberg, 1961). By 1982, a national survey of patterns of psychological test usage found the MMPI to rank second overall (behind the Wechsler Adult Intelligence Scale) among clinicians' reports of tests they had used, and first overall when ratings were adjusted for . . .

Review of the Minnesota Multiphasic Personality Inventory-2 by DAVID S. NICHOLS, Supervising Clinical Psychologist, Department of Psychology, Dammasch State Hospital, Wilsonville, OR:

The original Minnesota normal sample consisted of 724 relatives and other visitors at the University of Minnesota Hospitals. The data from this sample provided the needed contrast for the original criterion groups from which the clinical scales of the Minnesota Multiphasic Personality Inventory (MMPI) were developed. But this use made the normal sample unsuitable for the establishment of test norms. Unfortunately, funds that would have been required to gather a normative sample of adequate size and representation were unavailable. . . .

Summary. So far as the standard validity and clinical scales are concerned, the statistical properties of the MMPI-2 with respect to reliability, validity, and standard error are those of its predecessor, for better or worse. The provision of uniform T-scores is a significant . . .

What follows are the names of the tests listed in the Mental Measurements Yearbook, listed alphabetically within the 19 categories into which the tests are organized. The edition of the yearbook in which the review is located follows the test name. If you are interested in considering one of these tests in your research, go to the most current volume of the MMY or use the online service and read the review. You can then request a sample from the publisher and make a more complete evaluation. Note that many of these tests, particularly in the fields of personality and intelligence, are available only to trained professionals such as licensed clinical social workers, school psychologists, and clinical psychologists.

7.16.1 Achievement

ACER Tests of Basic Skills—Blue Series, 12th MMY

ACER Tests of Basic Skills—Green Series, 12th MMY

Achievement Test for Accounting Graduates, 13th MMY

Adult Basic Learning Examination, Second Edition, 11th MMY

Aprenda: La Prueba de Logros en Español, 13th MMY

Aprenda: La Prueba de Logros en Español—Segunda edicion, 14th MMY

Assessment and Placement Services for Community Colleges, 11th MMY

Basic Achievement Skills Individual Screener, 9th MMY

Basic Educational Skills Test, 9th MMY

Basic Skills Inventory, 9th MMY

Brigance Diagnostic Comprehensive Inventory of Basic Skills, 9th MMY

BRIGANCE Diagnostic Comprehensive Inventory of Basic Skills, Revised, 14th MMY

Brigance Diagnostic Inventory of Basic Skills, 9th MMY

Brigance Diagnostic Inventory of Essential Skills, 9th MMY

BRIGANCE Diagnostic Life Skills Inventory, 14th MMY

Bristol Achievement Tests, 9th MMY

California Achievement Tests, Fifth Edition, 13th MMY

Canadian Achievement Survey Tests for Adults, 14th MMY

Canadian Achievement Tests, Second Edition, 13th MMY

Canadian Tests of Basic Skills, Forms 7 and 8, 11th MMY

Closed High School Placement Test, 14th MMY

College Basic Academic Subjects Examination, 11th MMY

College Board Scholastic Aptitude Test, 9th MMY

Collegiate Assessment of Academic Proficiency, 13th MMY

Comprehensive Testing Program III, 13th MMY

Comprehensive Tests of Basic Skills, Fourth Edition, 11th MMY

CTB Portfolio Assessment System, 13th MMY

Curriculum Frameworks Assessment System, 14th MMY

Developing Skills Checklist, 12th MMY

Diagnostic Achievement Battery, Second Edition, 12th MMY

Diagnostic Achievement Test for Adolescents, Second Edition, 13th MMY

Diagnostic Screening Test: Achievement, 9th MMY

Differential Ability Scales, 11th MMY

Distar Mastery Tests, 9th MMY

Early School Assessment, 12th MMY

Test of Academic Performance, 13th MMY

Tests of Achievement and Proficiency, Forms K, L, and M, 14th MMY

Tests of Adult Basic Education, Forms 7 & 8, 13th MMY

Tests of Adult Basic Education Work-Related Foundation Skills, 13th MMY

Tests of General Educational Development [The GED Tests], 11th MMY

Wechsler Individual Achievement Test, 13th MMY

Wide Range Achievement Test 3, 12th MMY

Wonderlic Basic Skills Test, 13th MMY

Woodcock-McGrew-Werder Mini-Battery of Achievement, 13th MMY

7.16.2 Behavior Assessment

AAMR Adaptive Behavior Scale—Residential and Community, Second Edition, 13th MMY

AAMR Adaptive Behavior Scale—School, Second Edition, 13th MMY

Aberrant Behavior Checklist, 12th MMY

Achieving Behavioral Competencies, 13th MMY

Adaptive Behavior Evaluation Scale, 12th MMY

Adaptive Behavior Evaluation Scale, Revised, 14th MMY

Adaptive Behavior Inventory, 10th MMY

Adaptive Behavior Inventory for Children, 9th MMY

ADD-H: Comprehensive Teacher's Rating Scale, Second Edition, 12th MMY

AD/HD Comprehensive Teacher's Rating Scale, Second Edition [1998 Revision], 14th MMY

Adjustment Scales for Children and Adolescents, 14th MMY

Adult Attention Deficit Disorder Behavior Rating Scale, 13th MMY

Adult Attention Deficit Disorders Evaluation Scale, 14th MMY

Assessment of Adaptive Areas, 14th MMY

Attention Deficit Disorder Behavior Rating Scales, 13th MMY

Attention Deficit Disorders Evaluation Scale, Second Edition, 12th MMY, 14th MMY

Attention Deficit Disorders Evaluation Scale Secondary-Age Student (The), 14th MMY

Attention-Deficit/Hyperactivity Disorder Test, 14th MMY

Attention-Deficit Scales for Adults, 14th MMY

BASC Monitor for ADHD, 14th MMY

Bay Area Functional Performance Evaluation, Second Edition, 12th MMY

Behavior Analysis Forms for Clinical Intervention, 9th MMY

Behavior Assessment System for Children, 13th MMY

Behavior Assessment System for Children [Revised], 14th MMY

Behavior Dimensions Rating Scale, 11th MMY

Behavior Dimensions Scale, 14th MMY

Behavior Disorders Identification Scale, 12th MMY

Behavior Evaluation Scale—2, 12th MMY

Behavior Rating Profile, Second Edition, 12th MMY

Behavioral and Emotional Rating Scale: A Strength-Based Approach to Assessment, 14th MMY

Brown Attention-Deficit Disorder Scales, 14th MMY

Burks' Behavior Rating Scales, 11th MMY

Camelot Behavioral Checklist, 9th MMY

Caregiver-Teacher Report Form, 14th MMY

Parent Behavior Form, 11th MMY

Portland Problem Behavior Checklist—Revised, 14th MMY

Pre-Referral Intervention Manual [Revised and Updated Second Edition], 13th MMY

Preschool and Kindergarten Behavior Scales, 13th MMY

Preschool Behavior Rating Scale, 10th MMY

Pyramid Scales (The), 10th MMY

REHAB: Rehabilitation Evaluation (Hall and Baker), 14th MMY

Responsibility and Independence Scale for Adolescents, 12th MMY

Revised Behavior Problem Checklist, 11th MMY

Scales of Independent Behavior—Revised, 14th MMY

School Function Assessment, 14th MMY

School Social Behavior Scales, 13th MMY

Scorable Self-Care Evaluation (Revised), 14th MMY

Social Behavior Assessment Inventory, 12th MMY

Social Competence and Behavior Evaluation, Preschool Edition, 14th MMY

Social Skills Rating System, 12th MMY

Spadafore Attention Deficit Hyperactivity Disorder Rating Scale, 14th MMY

Sutter-Eyberg Student Behavior Inventory, 11th MMY

Systematic Screening for Behavior Disorders, 13th MMY

Test of Variables of Attention, 13th MMY

Test of Variables of Attention (Version 7.03), 14th MMY

Transition Behavior Scale, 12th MMY

Transition Planning Inventory, 14th MMY

Work Readiness Profile, 14th MMY

Young Adult Behavior Checklist and Young Adult Self-Report, 14th MMY

7.16.3 Developmental Assessment

ABC Inventory to Determine Kindergarten and School Readiness (The), 10th MMY

Adolescent and Adult Psychoeducational Profile, 11th MMY

Ages and Stages Questionnaires, 14th MMY

AGS Early Screening Profiles, 12th MMY

Assessment for Persons Profoundly or Severely Impaired, 11th MMY

Assessment in Infancy: Ordinal Scales of Psychological Development, 9th MMY

Assessment in Nursery Education, 9th MMY

A.S.S.E.T.S.: A Survey of Students' Educational Talents and Skills, 10th MMY

Autism Screening Instrument for Educational Planning, Second Edition, 13th MMY

Bangs Receptive Vocabulary Checklist (The), 11th MMY

Basic School Skills Inventory, Third Edition, 9th MMY, 14th MMY

Basic School Skills Inventory—Screen, 9th MMY

Battelle Developmental Inventory, 10th MMY

Battelle Developmental Inventory Screening Test, 11th MMY

Bayley Infant Neurodevelopmental Screener, 13th MMY

Behavioral Characteristics Progression, 11th MMY

Bilingual Home Inventory, 11th MMY

Birth to Three Assessment and Intervention System, 11th MMY

Block Survey and S.L.I.D.E. (The), 12th MMY

Bracken Basic Concept Scale, 10th MMY

Bracken Basic Concept Scale—Revised, 14th MMY

BRIGANCE Early Preschool Screen for Two-Year-Old and Two-and-a-Half-Year-Old Children, 11th MMY

BRIGANCE K & 1 Screen for Kindergarten and First Grade Children [Revised], 12th MMY

Brigance Preschool Screen, 10th MMY

Bury Infant Check, 10th MMY

Caregiver's School Readiness Inventory, 12th MMY

Chicago Early Assessment and Remediation Laboratory, 11th MMY

Child Development Inventory, 13th MMY

Child Development Review, 14th MMY

Children at Risk Screener: Kindergarten and Preschool, 13th MMY

Children's Adaptive Behavior Scale, Revised, 10th MMY

Clinical Observations of Motor and Postural Skills, 14th MMY

Cognitive Control Battery, 11th MMY

Comprehensive Identification Process [Revised], 14th MMY

Dallas Pre-School Screening Test, 11th MMY

Denver II, 12th MMY

Developmental Activities Screening Inventory—II, 10th MMY

Developmental Assessment for the Severely Handicapped, 9th MMY

Developmental Assessment of Life Experiences [1986 Edition], 12th MMY

Developmental Assessment of Young Children, 14th MMY

Developmental Indicators for the Assessment of Learning, Third Edition, 14th MMY

Developmental Indicators for the Assessment of Learning—Revised/AGS Edition, 12th MMY

Developmental Observation Checklist System, 13th MMY

Developmental Profile II, 10th MMY

Developmental Tasks for Kindergarten Readiness—II, 9th MMY, 14th MMY

Diagnostic Inventory for Screening Children, 13th MMY

Early Child Development Inventory, 11th MMY

Early Intervention Developmental Profile, 13th MMY

Early Learning: Assessment and Development, 9th MMY

Early School Inventory, 13th MMY

Early Screening Inventory—Revised, 11th MMY, 14th MMY

Early Years Easy Screen, 12th MMY

ECOScales, 12th MMY

Egan Bus Puzzle Test (The), 10th MMY

Einstein Assessment of School-Related Skills, 11th MMY

Erhardt Developmental Prehension Assessment, 12th MMY

FirstSTEP: Screening Test for Evaluating Preschoolers, 13th MMY

Fisher-Landau Early Childhood Screening [Experimental Version], 14th MMY

Five P's (Parent/Professional Preschool Performance Profile) [Revised] (The), 13th MMY

Gesell Child Developmental Age Scale (The), 12th MMY

Gesell Preschool Test, 9th MMY

HELP Checklist (Hawaii Early Learning Profile), 11th MMY

Help for Special Preschoolers ASSESSMENT CHECKLIST: Ages 3-6, 11th MMY

High/Scope Child Observation Record for Ages 2 1/26, 14th MMY

Howell Prekindergarten Screening Test, 10th MMY

Humanics National Child Assessment Form [Revised], 11th MMY

Infant Development Inventory, 14th MMY

Infant Developmental Screening Scale, 14th MMY

Infant Screening, 10th MMY

Infant-Toddler Developmental Assessment, 13th MMY

Is This Autism? A Checklist of Behaviours and Skills for Children Showing Autistic Features, 12th MMY

Keele Pre-School Assessment Guide, 9th MMY

Kent Inventory of Developmental Skills [1996 Standardization], 14th MMY

Kindergarten Readiness Test, 12th MMY

Kindergarten Screening Inventory, 10th MMY

Learning Behaviors Scale, Research Edition, 11th MMY

Learning Inventory of Kindergarten Experiences, 12th MMY

Lexington Developmental Scales, 9th MMY

MacArthur Communicative Development Inventories, 13th MMY

Metropolitan Readiness Tests, Sixth Edition, 12th MMY, 14th MMY

Milani-Comparetti Motor Development Screening Test, 11th MMY

Miller Assessment for Preschoolers, 9th MMY

Missouri Kindergarten Inventory of Developmental Skills, Alternate Form, 11th MMY

Movement Assessment Battery for Children, 14th MMY

Mullen Scales of Early Learning: AGS Edition, 14th MMY

Neonatal Behavioral Assessment Scale, 3rd Edition, 14th MMY

Neurobehavioral Assessment of the Preterm Infant, 13th MMY

Oral-Motor/Feeding Rating Scale, 12th MMY

PACE, 12th MMY

Parents' Evaluation of Developmental Status, 14th MMY

Pediatric Early Elementary Examination—II, 13th MMY

Pediatric Evaluation of Disability Inventory, 14th MMY

Pediatric Examination of Educational Readiness at Middle Childhood [Revised], 10th MMY, 14th MMY

Pediatric Extended Examination at Three, 11th MMY

Phelps Kindergarten Readiness Scale, 12th MMY

Pictorial Scale of Perceived Competence and Social Acceptance for Young Children (The), 11th MMY

Play Observation Scale (The), 13th MMY

Pragmatics Profile of Early Communication Skills (The), 12th MMY

Pre-School Behavior Checklist, 11th MMY

Preschool Development Inventory, 13th MMY

Preschool Developmental Profile, 13th MMY

Preschool Evaluation Scale (The), 13th MMY

Preschool Language Scale, 13th MMY

Preschool Screening Test, 12th MMY

Preschool Skills Test, 14th MMY

Pre-Verbal Communication Schedule, 11th MMY

Printing Performance School Readiness Test, 12th MMY

Program for the Acquisition of Language with the Severely Impaired, 11th MMY

Psychoeducational Profile Revised, 12th MMY

Revised BRIGANCE Diagnostic Inventory of Early Development, 12th MMY

Revised Denver Prescreening Developmental Questionnaire, 12th MMY

Schedule of Growing Skills (The), 11th MMY

Screening Test for Educational Prerequisite Skills, 12th MMY

Sequenced Inventory of Communication Development, Revised Edition, 10th MMY

Southern California Ordinal Scales of Development (The), 10th MMY

Spatial Orientation Memory Test, 11th MMY

Speech-Ease Screening Inventory (K-1), 12th MMY

Study of Children's Learning Behaviors, Research Edition, 11th MMY

Survey of Students' Educational Talents and Skills. *See* A.S.S.E.T.S.: A Survey of Students' Educational Talents and Skills

Symbolic Play Test, Second Edition, 12th MMY

System to Plan Early Childhood Services, 12th MMY

TARC Assessment System (The), 11th MMY

Teacher's School Readiness Inventory, 12th MMY

Test of Kindergarten/First Grade Readiness Skills, 13th MMY

Test of Sensory Functions in Infants, 11th MMY

Toddler and Infant Motor Evaluation, 14th MMY

Transdisciplinary Play-Based Assessment, Revised Edition, 13th MMY

Vineland Social-Emotional Early Childhood Scales, 14th MMY

Vulpe Assessment Battery—Revised, 14th MMY

Wisconsin Behavior Rating Scale, 11th MMY

7.16.4 Education

Academic Advising Inventory, 10th MMY

Achievement Identification Measure—-Teacher Observation, 11th MMY

ACT Evaluation/Survey Service (The), 12th MMY

ACT Study Skills Assessment and Inventory (College Edition), 12th MMY

Adaptive Style Inventory, 13th MMY

Analytic Learning Disability Assessment, 9th MMY

Assessment of School Needs for Low-Achieving Students: Staff Survey, 11th MMY

Class Activities Questionnaire (The), 9th MMY

Classroom Communication Screening Procedure for Early Adolescents: A Handbook for Assessment and Intervention, 11th MMY

Classroom Environment Scale, Second Edition, 10th MMY

College Major Interest Inventory, 12th MMY

College Outcome Measures Program, 13th MMY

College Student Experiences Questionnaire, 10th MMY

Community College Goals Inventory, 9th MMY

Community College Student Experiences Questionnaire, 12th MMY

Community College Student Experiences Questionnaire, Second Edition, 14th MMY

Comprehensive Assessment of School Environments, 11th MMY

NTE Programs, 9th MMY

Oetting Michaels Anchored Ratings for Therapists, 14th MMY

Our Class and Its Work, 10th MMY

PEEK—Perceptions, Expectations, Emotions, and Knowledge About College, 14th MMY

Performance Levels of a School Program Survey, 10th MMY

Prescriptive Teaching Series, 11th MMY

Program Self-Assessment Service, 10th MMY

Rating Inventory for Screening Kindergartners (A), 12th MMY

Scales for Effective Teaching (The), 13th MMY

Scales for Predicting Successful Inclusion, 14th MMY

School Archival Records Search, 13th MMY

School Assessment Survey, 12th MMY

School Effectiveness Questionnaire, 13th MMY

School Environment Preference Survey, 10th MMY

School Situation Survey, 12th MMY

School Social Skills Rating Scale, 12th MMY

School-Age Care Environment Rating Scale, 14th MMY

SCREEN [Senf-Comrey Ratings of Extra Educational Need], 11th MMY

Screening Children for Related Early Educational Needs, 11th MMY

Secondary School Admission Test, 11th MMY

Student Goals Exploration, 13th MMY

Student Rights Scales, 10th MMY

Study Attitudes and Methods Survey [Revised Short Form], 14th MMY

Styles of Training Index, 10th MMY

Survey of Student Opinion of Instruction, 10th MMY

Surveys of Problem-Solving and Educational Skills, 11th MMY

Teacher Evaluation Rating Scales, 11th MMY

Teacher Evaluation Scale, 12th MMY

Teacher Role Survey (Revised), 10th MMY

Test of Attitude Toward School, 11th MMY

Thinking About My School, 10th MMY

Vocational Learning Styles, 12th MMY

7.16.5 English

ACO. *See* Assessment of Conceptual Organization (ACO): Improving, Writing, Thinking, and Reading Skills

Adolescent Language Screening Test, 10th MMY

Adult Language Assessment Scales, 14th MMY

Adult Rating of Oral English, 14th MMY

Alberta Essay Scales: Models, 9th MMY

Alphabet Mastery, 9th MMY

Analyzing the Communication Environment, 14th MMY

Assessing Motivation to Communicate, 14th MMY

Assessment of Children's Language Comprehension, 1983 Revision, 10th MMY

Assessment of Conceptual Organization (ACO): Improving, Writing, Thinking, and Reading Skills, 12th MMY

Bankson Language Test—2, 11th MMY

Basic English Skills Test, 11th MMY

Basic Inventory of Natural Language, 9th MMY

Basic Language Concepts Test, 10th MMY

Beery Picture Vocabulary Test and Beery Picture Vocabulary Screening Series, 12th MMY

Bristol Language Development Scales, 12th MMY

British Ability Scales: Spelling Scale, 12th MMY

California Achievement Tests Writing Assessment System, 11th MMY

CAP Assessment of Writing, 12th MMY

CAT/5 Listening and Speaking Checklist, 13th MMY

Clark-Madison Test of Oral Language, 10th MMY

Classroom Communication Skills Inventory: Listening and Speaking Checklist (The), 13th MMY

Clinical Evaluation of Language Fundamentals, Third Edition—Observational Rating Scales, 14th MMY

Clinical Evaluation of Language Fundamentals-3 Screening Test, 13th MMY

Communication Abilities Diagnostic Test, 12th MMY

Communication Skills Profile, 14th MMY

Competent Speaker Speech Evaluation Form (The), 14th MMY

Comprehension of Oral Language, 9th MMY

Comprehensive Receptive and Expressive Vocabulary Test, 13th MMY

Comprehensive Receptive and Expressive Vocabulary Test—Adult, 14th MMY

Computer-Based Test of English as a Foreign Language and Test of Written English, 14th MMY

Conversational Skills Rating Scale: An Instructional Assessment of Interpersonal Competence (The), 14th MMY

CTB Writing Assessment System, 13th MMY

Descriptive Tests of Language Skills, 11th MMY

Diagnostic Achievement Test in Spelling (A), 10th MMY

Diagnostic Screening Test: Language, Second Edition, 9th MMY

Diagnostic Screening Test: Spelling, Third Edition, 9th MMY

Diagnostic Spelling Potential Test, 9th MMY

Diagnostic Spelling Test, 9th MMY

Dos Amigos Verbal Language Scales, 14th MMY

Early Language Milestone Scale, Second Edition, 13th MMY

English as a Second Language Oral Assessment, Revised, 11th MMY

English Language Skills Assessment in a Reading Context, 11th MMY

English Skills Assessment, 9th MMY

ERB Writing Assessment, 13th MMY

ESL/Adult Literacy Scale, 11th MMY

ETS Tests of Applied Literacy Skills, 13th MMY

Expressive Vocabulary Test, 14th MMY

Figurative Language Interpretation Test, 12th MMY

First Words and First Sentences Tests, 14th MMY

Fullerton Language Test for Adolescents, Second Edition (The), 10th MMY

Graded Word Spelling Test, 12th MMY

Graded Word Spelling Test, Second Edition, 14th MMY

Grammatical Analysis of Elicited Language—Simple Sentence Level, Second Edition, 11th MMY

Group Literacy Assessment, 9th MMY

Henderson-Moriarty ESL/Literacy Placement Test, 10th MMY

Houston Test for Language Development, Revised Edition (The), 11th MMY

IDEA Oral Language Proficiency Test, 14th MMY

IDEA Reading and Writing Proficiency Test, 13th MMY

Independent Mastery Testing System for Writing Skills, 11th MMY

Informal Writing Inventory, 11th MMY

Integrated Literature and Language Arts Portfolio Program, 12th MMY

Integrated Writing Test, 14th MMY

Inventory of Language Abilities, 9th MMY

Inventory of Language Abilities, Level II, 10th MMY

Kindergarten Language Screening Test, Second Edition, 14th MMY

Language Arts Assessment Portfolio, 13th MMY

Language Assessment Battery, 9th MMY

Language Assessment Scales—Oral, 12th MMY

Language Assessment Scales, Reading and Writing, 12th MMY

Language Facility Test, 9th MMY

Language Imitation Test, 9th MMY

Language Processing Test, 10th MMY

Language Proficiency Test, 9th MMY

Language Sampling, Analysis, and Training, Revised Edition, 9th MMY

Language Sampling, Analysis, and Training—Third Edition, 14th MMY

Learning Through Listening, 9th MMY

Listen Up: Skills Assessment, 14th MMY

Listening Comprehension Test, 12th MMY

Listening Styles Profile, 14th MMY

MAC Checklist for Evaluating, Preparing, and/or Improving Standardized Tests for Limited English Speaking Students, 10th MMY

Mather-Woodcock Group Writing Tests, 14th MMY

Michigan English Language Assessment Battery, 14th MMY

Michigan Prescriptive Program in English, 9th MMY

Miller-Yoder Language Comprehension Test (Clinical Edition), 11th MMY

Multilevel Informal Language Inventory, 10th MMY

Oral and Written Language Scales: Listening Comprehension and Oral Expression, 14th MMY

Oral and Written Language Scales: Written Expression, 14th MMY

Oral Language Evaluation, Second Edition, 12th MMY

Parallel Spelling Tests, 12th MMY

Parallel Spelling Tests, Second Edition, 14th MMY

PRE-LAS English, 11th MMY

Preliminary Test of English as a Foreign Language, 11th MMY

Primary Language Screen (The), 12th MMY

Progressive Achievement Tests of Listening Comprehension [Revised], 13th MMY

Quick Informal Assessment, 13th MMY

7.16.6 Fine Arts

Advanced Measures of Music Audiation, 12th MMY

Group Tests of Musical Abilities, 12th MMY

Instrument Timbre Preference Test, 10th MMY

Iowa Tests of Music Literacy, Revised, 13th MMY

Measures of Musical Abilities, 10th MMY

Music Achievement Tests 1, 2, 3, and 4, 12th MMY

Musical Aptitude Profile [1988 Revision], 12th MMY

7.16.7 Foreign Languages

Ber-Sil Spanish Test (The), 10th MMY

Bilingual Syntax Measure, 9th MMY

Chinese Proficiency Test, 13th MMY

Chinese Speaking Test, 13th MMY

El Circo, 9th MMY

Hausa Speaking Test, 14th MMY

Hebrew Speaking Test, 13th MMY

Indonesian Speaking Test, 13th MMY

LOTE Reading and Listening Tests, 12th MMY

Portuguese Speaking Test, 12th MMY

Spanish Computerized Adaptive Placement Exam (A), 12th MMY

7.16.8 Intelligence and Scholastic Aptitude

ACCUPLACER: Computerized Placement Tests, 13th MMY

ACER Advanced Test B40, 9th MMY

ACER Advanced Test B90: New Zealand Edition, 12th MMY

ACER Advanced Tests AL and AQ (Second Edition) and BL-BQ, 9th MMY

ACER Intermediate Test G, 9th MMY

ACER Test of Reasoning Ability, 12th MMY

ACER Word Knowledge Test, 11th MMY

Adaptation of the Wechsler Preschool and Primary Scale of Intelligence for Deaf Children (An), 11th MMY

AH1 Forms X and Y, 9th MMY

AH6 Group Tests of High Level Intelligence, 10th MMY

Alternate Uses, 9th MMY

Arlin Test of Formal Reasoning, 9th MMY

Assessment of Individual Learning Style: The Perceptual Memory Task, 11th MMY

Bateria Woodcock-Munoz—Revisada, 13th MMY

Bilingual Verbal Ability Tests, 14th MMY

Boehm Test of Basic Concepts—Preschool Version, 11th MMY

Boehm Test of Basic Concepts—Revised, 10th MMY

British Ability Scales (The), 9th MMY

California Critical Thinking Dispositions Inventory (The), 12th MMY

California Critical Thinking Skills Test, 12th MMY

Canadian Cognitive Abilities Test, Form 7, 12th MMY

Canadian Test of Cognitive Skills, 13th MMY

Children's Abilities Scales, 10th MMY

Children's Category Test, 13th MMY

CID Preschool Performance Scale, 12th MMY

Cognitive Abilities Scale, 10th MMY

Cognitive Abilities Test, Form 5, 13th MMY

Cognitive Diagnostic Battery, 9th MMY

Cognitive Observation Guide, 12th MMY

Comprehensive Adult Student Assessment System, 13th MMY

Comprehensive Scales of Student Abilities: Quantifying Academic Skills and School-Related Behavior Through the Use of Teacher Judgments, 13th MMY

Comprehensive Test of Nonverbal Intelligence, 13th MMY

Continuous Visual Memory Test [Revised], 12th MMY, 14th MMY

Cornell Critical Thinking Tests (The), 11th MMY

Cree Questionnaire, 9th MMY

Critical Reasoning Tests, 12th MMY

Das-Naglieri Cognitive Assessment System, 14th MMY

Deductive Reasoning Test, 9th MMY

Detroit Tests of Learning Aptitude, Fourth Edition, 12th MMY, 14th MMY

Detroit Tests of Learning Aptitude—Adult, 12th MMY

Detroit Tests of Learning Aptitude—Primary, Second Edition, 12th MMY

Developing Cognitive Abilities Test [Second Edition], 11th MMY

Drumcondra Verbal Reasoning Test 1, 11th MMY

Edinburgh Picture Test, 12th MMY

Ennis-Weir Critical Thinking Essay Test, 10th MMY

Expressive One-Word Picture Vocabulary Test, Revised, 12th MMY

Extended Merrill-Palmer Scale (The), 12th MMY

Fuld Object-Memory Evaluation, 9th MMY

General Ability Measure for Adults, 14th MMY

General Processing Inventory, 14th MMY

Gifted and Talented Scale, 10th MMY

Gifted Evaluation Scale, 12th MMY

Gifted Evaluation Scale, Second Edition, 14th MMY

Graduate and Managerial Assessment, 10th MMY

Graduate Management Admission Test, 9th MMY

Graduate Record Examinations—General Test (The), 9th MMY

Hammill Multiability Intelligence Test, 14th MMY

Harding Skyscraper, 9th MMY

Henmon-Nelson Ability Test, Canadian Edition, 12th MMY

Jenkins Non-Verbal Test, 1986 Revision, 12th MMY

Kaufman Adolescent and Adult Intelligence Test, 12th MMY

Kaufman Assessment Battery for Children, 9th MMY

Kaufman Brief Intelligence Test, 12th MMY

Kaufman Infant and Preschool Scale, 9th MMY

Teacher Observation Scales for Identifying Children with Special Abilities, 14th MMY

Test of Cognitive Skills, Second Edition, 13th MMY

Test of Learning Ability, 12th MMY

Test of Memory and Learning, 13th MMY

Test of Nonverbal Intelligence, Third Edition, 11th MMY, 14th MMY

Test of Relational Concepts, 11th MMY

Test on Appraising Observations Tests of Adult Basic Education Work-Related Problem Solving, 13th MMY

Thinking Creatively in Action and Movement, 9th MMY

Thinking Creatively With Sounds and Words, Research Edition, 9th MMY

Torrance Tests of Creative Thinking, 9th MMY

Universal Nonverbal Intelligence Test, 14th MMY

USES General Aptitude Test Battery for the Deaf, 13th MMY

Watson-Glaser Critical Thinking Appraisal, Form S, 13th MMY

Wechsler Abbreviated Scale of Intelligence, 14th MMY

Wechsler Adult Intelligence Scale—Third Edition, 14th MMY

Wechsler Intelligence Scale for Children, Third Edition, 12th MMY

Wechsler Memory Scale III, 11th MMY, 14th MMY

Wechsler Preschool and Primary Scale of Intelligence—Revised, 11th MMY

Wide Range Assessment of Memory and Learning, 11th MMY

Wiesen Test of Mechanical Aptitude (The), 14th MMY

Wisconsin Card Sorting Test, Revised and Expanded, 14th MMY

Wonderlic Personnel Test and Scholastic Level Exam, 11th MMY, 14th MMY

Woodcock-Johnson Psycho-Educational Battery—Revised, 12th MMY

7.16.9 Mathematics

American High School Mathematics Examination, 11th MMY

American Invitational Mathematics Examination, 11th MMY

American Junior High School Mathematics Examination, 11th MMY

Arithmetic Skills Assessment Test, 14th MMY

Assessment in Mathematics, 9th MMY

Basic Number Diagnostic Test, 9th MMY

Basic Number Screening Test, 9th MMY

Booker Profiles in Mathematics: Numeration and Computation, 13th MMY

Buswell-John Diagnostic Test for Fundamental Processes in Arithmetic, 9th MMY

California Diagnostic Mathematics Tests, 11th MMY

Class Achievement Test in Mathematics, 11th MMY

Collis-Romberg Mathematical Problem Solving Profiles, 12th MMY

Descriptive Tests of Mathematics Skills, 11th MMY

Diagnostic Mathematics Profiles, 12th MMY

Diagnostic Screening Test: Math, Third Edition, 9th MMY

Diagnostic Test of Arithmetic Strategies, 9th MMY

Early Mathematics Diagnostic Kit, 11th MMY

ENRIGHT Diagnostic Inventory of Basic Arithmetic Skills, 10th MMY

Group Mathematics Test, Second Edition, 9th MMY

Independent Mastery Testing System for Math Skills, 10th MMY

Iowa Algebra Aptitude Test, Fourth Edition, 12th MMY

KeyMath Revised: A Diagnostic Inventory of Essential Mathematics, 11th MMY

KeyMath Revised: A Diagnostic Inventory of Essential Mathematics [1998 Normative Update], 14th MMY

Mathematical Olympiads, 11th MMY

Mathematics Anxiety Rating Scale, 11th MMY

Mathematics Attitude Inventory, 9th MMY

Mathematics Competency Test, 14th MMY

Mathematics 7, 11th MMY

Mathematics Topic Pre-Tests, 13th MMY

Practical Maths Assessments, 12th MMY

Profiles of Problem Solving, 13th MMY

Progressive Achievement Test of Mathematics [Revised], 12th MMY

Progressive Achievement Tests in Mathematics, 11th MMY

Ramsay Corporation Job Skills—Office Arithmetic Test, 13th MMY

Sequential Assessment of Mathematics Inventories: Standardized Inventory, 11th MMY

Stanford Diagnostic Mathematics Test, Fourth Edition, 13th MMY

Target Mathematics Tests, 14th MMY

Test of Cognitive Style in Mathematics, 12th MMY

Test of Early Mathematics Ability, Second Edition, 11th MMY

Test of Mathematical Abilities, Second Edition, 13th MMY

Test of Mathematical Abilities for Gifted Students, 14th MMY

7.16.10 Miscellaneous

ACCESS—A Comprehensive Custody Evaluation Standard System, 14th MMY

Achievement Identification Measure, 10th MMY

Ackerman-Schoendorf Scales for Parent Evaluation of Custody, 12th MMY

ACT Study Power Assessment and Inventory, 12th MMY

Adaptive Behavior: Street Survival Skills Questionnaire, 11th MMY

Adaptive Functioning Index, 9th MMY

Adolescent Diagnostic Interview, 12th MMY

Adult Growth Examination, 11th MMY

Aggregate Neurobehavioral Student Health and Educational Review. *See* ANSER System-Aggregate Neurobehavioral Student Health and Educational Review

Ahr's Individual Development Survey, 9th MMY

Alcohol Clinical Index, 13th MMY

Alcohol Use Disorders Identification Test, 14th MMY

American Drug and Alcohol Survey (The), 12th MMY

Ann Arbor Learning Inventory, 11th MMY

ANSER System-Aggregate Neurobehavioral Student Health and Educational Review (The), 9th MMY

Arizona Battery for Communication Disorders of Dementia (The), 12th MMY

ASIST: A Structured Addictions Assessment Interview for Selecting Treatment, 13th MMY

Family Environment Scale, Second Edition, 12th MMY
Family Risk Scales, 13th MMY
Fast Health Knowledge Test, 1986 Revision, 10th MMY
Food Choice Inventory, 10th MMY
Functional Fitness Assessment for Adults over 60 Years, 13th MMY
Functional Performance Record, 12th MMY
Functional Time Estimation Questionnaire, 12th MMY
Golombok Rust Inventory of Marital State (The), 12th MMY
Goodman Lock Box (The), 9th MMY
Grandparent Strengths and Needs Inventory, 13th MMY
Gregorc Style Delineator, 12th MMY
Group Environment Scale, Second Edition, 10th MMY
GROW—The Marriage Enrichment Program, 10th MMY
Health and Daily Living, 10th MMY
Health Problems Checklist, 10th MMY
Herrmann Brain Dominance Instrument, 11th MMY
Herrmann Brain Dominance Instrument [Revised], 14th MMY
Home Environment Questionnaire, HEQ-2R and HEQ-1R, 10th MMY
Home Observation for Measurement of the Environment, 9th MMY
Home Screening Questionnaire, 9th MMY
How Am I Doing? A Self-Assessment for Child Caregivers, 13th MMY
Identi-Form System for Gifted Programs (The), 10th MMY
Individual Service Strategy Portfolio, 13th MMY
Infant/Toddler Environment Rating Scale, 12th MMY
Influence Strategies Exercise, 13th MMY
Interpersonal Conflict Scale, 9th MMY
Inventory for Client and Agency Planning, 10th MMY
Inventory of Drinking Situations, 13th MMY
Inventory of Drug-Taking Situations, 14th MMY
I-SPEAK Your Language: A Survey of Personal Styles, 13th MMY
Jordan Left-Right Reversal Test (1990 Edition), 12th MMY
Kilmann-Saxton Culture-Gap Survey [Revised], 13th MMY
Kohlman Evaluation of Living Skills (The), 14th MMY
Krantz Health Opinion Survey, 9th MMY
Language-Structured Auditory Retention Span Test, 11th MMY
Lawrence Psychological Forensic Examination (The), 10th MMY
Learning Environment Inventory, 9th MMY
Level of Service Inventory—Revised (The), 14th MMY
Life Experiences Checklist, 12th MMY
Life Stressors and Social Resources Inventory—Adult Form, 13th MMY
Life Stressors and Social Resources Inventory—Youth Form, 13th MMY
Lifestyle Assessment Questionnaire, 13th MMY
Listening Comprehension, 9th MMY
Love Attitudes Inventory (A), 9th MMY
Marital Check-Up Kit, 13th MMY

Marital Evaluation Checklist, 10th MMY

Marriage and Family Attitude Survey (The), 11th MMY

Marriage Evaluation (A), 9th MMY

Marriage Expectation Inventories (The), 9th MMY

Marriage Role Expectation Inventory (A), 9th MMY

Matching Person and Technology, 14th MMY

Mathematics Self-Efficacy Scale, 14th MMY

Medical Ethics Inventory, 10th MMY

Michigan Alcoholism Screening Test, 14th MMY

Military Environment Inventory, 11th MMY

Multidimensional Health Profile, 14th MMY

Multiphasic Environmental Assessment Procedure, 12th MMY

My Class Inventory, 9th MMY

Older Persons Counseling Needs Survey, 14th MMY

Opinions About Deaf People Scale, 14th MMY

Organizational Climate Exercise II, 13th MMY

Organizational Culture Inventory, 12th MMY

Pain Assessment Battery, Research Edition, 14th MMY

Parent Perception of Child Profile, 12th MMY

Parent-Adolescent Communication Scale, 12th MMY

Parent/Family Involvement Index, 10th MMY

Parenting Satisfaction Scale, 14th MMY

Perceptions of Parental Role Scales, 11th MMY

Personal Assessment of Intimacy in Relationships, 11th MMY

Personal Communication Plan (The), 12th MMY

Personal Experience Inventory for Adults, 13th MMY

Personal Experience Screening Questionnaire, 12th MMY

Personal Relationship Inventory, 12th MMY

Pollack-Branden Inventory, 11th MMY

PREPARE/ENRICH, 14th MMY

Prevocational Assessment and Curriculum Guide (The), 12th MMY

Prison Inmate Inventory, 14th MMY

Productivity Environmental Preference Survey, 13th MMY

Project Implementation Profile, 13th MMY

Psychosocial Pain Inventory [Revised], 14th MMY

Quality of Life Inventory, 14th MMY

Quality Potential Assessment, 14th MMY

Quickview Social History, 13th MMY

RAND-36 Health Status Inventory, 14th MMY

Rating Scale of Communication in Cognitive Decline, 12th MMY

Recovery Attitude and Treatment Evaluator, 14th MMY

Rehabilitation Compliance Scale, 14th MMY

Relating to Each Other: A Questionnaire for Students, 13th MMY

Relating with Colleagues: A Questionnaire for Faculty Members, 13th MMY

Retirement Activities Card Sort Planning Kit, 13th MMY

7.16.11 Multi-Aptitude Batteries

Armed Services Vocational Aptitude Battery [Forms 18/19], 9th MMY

Comprehensive Ability Battery, 9th MMY

Differential Aptitude Tests, Fifth Edition, 12th MMY

Differential Aptitude Tests—Computerized Adaptive Edition, 12th MMY

Differential Aptitude Tests for Personnel and Career Assessment, 12th MMY

Perceptual-Motor Assessment for Children & Emotional/Behavioral Screening Program, 12th MMY

Quick Cognitive Inventory, 11th MMY

USES General Aptitude Test Battery, 9th MMY

USES Nonreading Aptitude Test Battery, 1982 Edition, 9th MMY

7.16.12 Neuropsychological

Adult Neuropsychological Questionnaire, 12th MMY

Aphasia Diagnostic Profiles, 13th MMY

Apraxia Battery for Adults, 9th MMY

Bedside Evaluation and Screening Test of Aphasia, 11th MMY

Bedside Evaluation Screening Test, Second Edition, 14th MMY

Behavior Change Inventory, 11th MMY

Behavioural Assessment of the Dysexecutive Syndrome, 14th MMY

Booklet Category Test, Second Edition (The), 9th MMY, 14th MMY

Brief Neuropsychological Cognitive Examination, 14th MMY

Brief Test of Head Injury, 13th MMY

Burns Brief Inventory of Communication and Cognition, 14th MMY

California Computerized Assessment Package, 14th MMY

California Verbal Learning Test, Children's Version, 13th MMY

California Verbal Learning Test, Research Edition, Adult Version, 13th MMY

CERAD (Consortium to Establish a Registry for Alzheimer's Disease) Assessment Battery, 12th MMY

Child Neuropsychological Questionnaire, 12th MMY

Children's Auditory Verbal Learning Test-2, 12th MMY

Children's Memory Scale, 14th MMY

Clifton Assessment Procedures for the Elderly, 9th MMY

Clock Test (The), 14th MMY

Closed Head Injury Screener, 14th MMY

Cognistat (The Neurobehavioral Cognitive Status Examination), 14th MMY

Cognitive Behavior Rating Scales, 11th MMY

Cognitive Symptom Checklists, 14th MMY

CogScreen Aeromedical Edition, 14th MMY

Comprehensive Test of Visual Functioning, 12th MMY

Computerized Assessment of Response Bias: Revised Edition, 14th MMY

Consortium to Establish a Registry for Alzheimer's Disease Assessment Battery. *See* CERAD (Consortium to Establish a Registry for Alzheimer's Disease) Assessment Battery

Contextual Memory Test, 14th MMY

Dementia Rating Scale, 11th MMY

Digit Vigilance Test, 14th MMY

Digital Finger Tapping Test, 12th MMY

Discourse Comprehension Test, 13th MMY

Functional Linguistic Communication Inventory, 13th MMY

Halstead Russell Neuropsychological Evaluation System, 12th MMY

Halstead-Reitan Neuropsychological Test Battery, 9th MMY

Human Information Processing Survey, 10th MMY

Infanib (The), 14th MMY

Intermediate Booklet Category Test, 14th MMY

Kaufman Short Neuropsychological Assessment Procedure, 13th MMY

Learning and Memory Battery, 14th MMY

Learning Disabilities Diagnostic Inventory, 14th MMY

Loewenstein Occupational Therapy Cognitive Assessment, 13th MMY

Luria-Nebraska Neuropsychological Battery: Children's Revision, 11th MMY

Luria-Nebraska Neuropsychological Battery: Forms I and II, 11th MMY

McCarron-Dial System, 11th MMY

MicroCog: Assessment of Cognitive Functioning, 13th MMY

Mini Inventory of Right Brain Injury, 11th MMY

Minnesota Test for Differential Diagnosis of Aphasia, 13th MMY

National Adult Reading Test, Second Edition, 12th MMY

NEPSY: A Developmental Neuropsychological Assessment, 14th MMY

Neurobehavioral Cognitive Status Examination. *See* Cognistat (The Neurobehavioral Cognitive Status Examination)

Neurological Dysfunctions of Children, 9th MMY

Neuropsychological Impairment Scale (The), 14th MMY

Neuropsychological Questionnaire, 9th MMY

Neuropsychology Behavior and Affect Profile, 14th MMY

Ohio Functional Assessment Battery: Standardized Tests for Leisure and Living Skills, 14th MMY

Philadelphia Head Injury Questionnaire, 12th MMY

Portable Tactual Performance Test, 11th MMY

Portland Digit Recognition Test, 12th MMY

Quick Neurological Screening Test, 2nd Revised Edition, 14th MMY

Repeatable Battery for the Assessment of Neuropsychological Status, 14th MMY

Rey Auditory Verbal Learning Test: A Handbook, 14th MMY

Rey Complex Figure Test and Recognition Trial, 14th MMY

Rivermead Behavioural Memory Test [Second Edition] (The), 14th MMY

Rivermead Perceptual Assessment Battery, 11th MMY

Ross Information Processing Assessment, Second Edition, 14th MMY

Ross Information Processing Assessment—Geriatric, 14th MMY

Scales of Adult Independence, Language and Recall, 14th MMY

Scales of Cognitive Ability for Traumatic Brain Injury, 13th MMY

Screening Test for the Luria-Nebraska Neuropsychological Battery: Adult and Children's Forms, 11th MMY

Sensory Integration and Praxis Tests, 12th MMY

Severe Cognitive Impairment Profile, 14th MMY

Short Category Test, Booklet Format, 11th MMY

Sklar Aphasia Scale, Revised 1983, 10th MMY

Stroop Color and Word Test, 9th MMY

Stroop Neuropsychological Screening Test, 11th MMY

Test of Memory Malingering, 14th MMY

Test of Oral and Limb Apraxia, 13th MMY

Test of Orientation for Rehabilitation Patients, 13th MMY

Visual Search and Attention Test, 12th MMY

WAIS-R NI, 14th MMY

Word Memory Test (The), 14th MMY

7.16.13 Personality

Abuse Risk Inventory for Women, Experimental Edition, 11th MMY

ACDI-Corrections Version and Corrections Version II, 14th MMY

Achievement Motivation Profile, 14th MMY

Additional Personality Factor Inventory—2, 9th MMY

Adjective Check List (The), 9th MMY

Adolescent Apperception Cards, 14th MMY

Adolescent Coping Scale, 13th MMY

Adolescent Dissociative Experiences Scale, 14th MMY

Adolescent Drinking Index, 12th MMY

Adolescent Psychopathology Scale, 14th MMY

Adolescent Separation Anxiety Test, 9th MMY

Adult Personality Inventory, 12th MMY

Adult Personality Inventory [Revised], 14th MMY

Adult Self Expression Scale, 9th MMY

Adult Suicidal Ideation Questionnaire, 12th MMY

Affective Perception Inventory, 9th MMY

Affective Perception Inventory/College Level (The), 11th MMY

Age Projection Test, 12th MMY

Alcadd Test, Revised Edition (The), 11th MMY

Alcohol Dependence Scale, 10th MMY

Alcohol Use Inventory, 12th MMY

Anomalous Sentences Repetition Test (The), 12th MMY

APT Inventory (The), 13th MMY

Arousal Seeking Tendency Scale, 13th MMY

Assessment of Core Goals, 12th MMY

Assessment of Qualitative and Structural Dimensions of Object Representations, Revised Edition, 9th MMY

Athletic Motivation Inventory, 12th MMY

Attentional and Interpersonal Style Inventory (The), 14th MMY

Attitudes Toward Mainstreaming Scale, 12th MMY

Attitudes Toward Working Mothers Scale, 9th MMY

Balanced Emotional Empathy Scale (The), 13th MMY

Barclay Classroom Assessment System (The), 9th MMY

BarOn Emotional Quotient Inventory, 14th MMY

Basic Living Skills Scale, 10th MMY

Basic Personality Inventory, 12th MMY

BASIS-A Inventory [Basic Adlerian Skills for Interpersonal Success—Adult Form], 13th MMY

Battery for Health Improvement, 14th MMY

Beck Anxiety Inventory [1993 Edition], 13th MMY

Beck Depression Inventory—II, 13th MMY, 14th MMY

Beck Hopelessness Scale [Revised], 13th MMY

Beck Scale for Suicide Ideation, 13th MMY

Behavior Rating Scale, 9th MMY

Behavioral Academic Self-Esteem, 9th MMY

Behaviour Problems: A System of Management, 11th MMY

Bell Object Relations and Reality Testing Inventory, 14th MMY

Bem Sex-Role Inventory, 9th MMY

Bessell Measurement of Emotional Maturity Scales, 9th MMY

BEST Instruments, 13th MMY

Biographical and Personality Inventory, Series II, 11th MMY

Biographical Inventory Form U, 9th MMY

Bloom Sentence Completion Survey, 9th MMY

BrainMap (The), 11th MMY

Butcher Treatment Planning Inventory, 14th MMY

California Child Q-Set (The), 9th MMY

California Psychological Inventory, Revised Edition, 11th MMY

California Q-Sort (Revised Adult Set), 14th MMY

California Test of Personality, 9th MMY

Callahan Anxiety Pictures, 9th MMY

Campbell Leadership Index, 12th MMY

Canfield Instructional Styles Inventory, 11th MMY

Canfield Learning Styles Inventory, 11th MMY

Career Beliefs Inventory, 12th MMY

Carey Temperament Scales, 14th MMY

Carlson Psychological Survey, 9th MMY

Carroll Depression Scales, 14th MMY

Chart of Initiative and Independence, 9th MMY

Charteris Reading Test, 12th MMY

Child Abuse Potential Inventory, Form VI (The), 10th MMY

Child and Adolescent Adjustment Profile, 9th MMY

Child Anxiety Scale, 9th MMY

Childhood Autism Rating Scale (The), 11th MMY

Children of Alcoholics Screening Test, 10th MMY

Children's Academic Intrinsic Motivation Inventory, 10th MMY

Children's Apperception Test [1991 Revision], 13th MMY

Children's Apperceptive Story-Telling Test, 12th MMY

Children's Depression Inventory, 11th MMY

Children's Depression Rating Scale, Revised, 14th MMY

Children's Depression Scale [Second Research Edition], 12th MMY

Children's Inventory of Self-Esteem, 12th MMY

Children's Personality Questionnaire, 1985 Edition, 13th MMY

Children's Problems Checklist, 10th MMY

Children's Role Inventory, 13th MMY

Christensen Dietary Distress Inventory, 13th MMY

Clinical Analysis Questionnaire, 9th MMY

Clyde Mood Scale, 9th MMY

College Adjustment Scales, 13th MMY

Communication Response Style: Assessment, 11th MMY

Composite International Diagnostic Interview, 13th MMY

Comprehensive Assessment of Symptoms and History, 12th MMY

Comprehensive Personality Profile, 14th MMY

Conflict Management Appraisal, 12th MMY

Conflict Management Survey, 12th MMY

Conflict Style Inventory, 14th MMY

Coolidge Axis II Inventory, 14th MMY

Coopersmith Self-Esteem Inventories, 9th MMY

Coping Inventory for Stressful Situations, 14th MMY

Coping Resources Inventory, 12th MMY

Coping Responses Inventory—Adult and Youth, 14th MMY

Coping Resources Inventory for Stress, 13th MMY

Coping with Stress, 12th MMY

Couples BrainMap (The), 11th MMY

Couple's Pre-Counseling Inventory, Revised Edition, 1987, 11th MMY

CPF [Second Edition], 12th MMY

Creative Behavior Inventory, 11th MMY

Creative Reasoning Test (The), 11th MMY

Creatrix Inventory (The), 11th MMY

Cross-Cultural Adaptability Inventory, 14th MMY

Crown-Crisp Experiential Index, 9th MMY

Culture-Free Self-Esteem Inventories, Second Edition, 12th MMY

Custody Quotient (The), 11th MMY

Daily Stress Inventory, 11th MMY

Dating Problems Checklist, 9th MMY

Davidson Trauma Scale, 14th MMY

Decision Making Inventory, 10th MMY

Defense Mechanisms Inventory [Revised], 13th MMY

Defining Issues Test, 11th MMY

Denver Community Mental Health Questionnaire—Revised, 9th MMY

Depression and Anxiety in Youth Scale, 13th MMY

Derogatis Affects Balance Scale [Revised], 14th MMY

Derogatis Psychiatric Rating Scale, 13th MMY

Derogatis Sexual Functioning Inventory, 9th MMY

Derogatis Stress Profile, 13th MMY

Description of Body Scale, 9th MMY

Devereux Scales of Mental Disorders, 14th MMY

Diagnostic Interview for Borderline Patients, 10th MMY

Mental Status Checklist for Children, 11th MMY
Meta-Motivation Inventory, 9th MMY
Meyer-Kendall Assessment Survey, 12th MMY
Miller Motivation Scale, 10th MMY
Millon Adolescent Clinical Inventory, 12th MMY
Millon Clinical Multiaxial Inventory—III [Manual Second Edition], 14th MMY
Millon Clinical Multiaxial Inventory—III [Second Edition], 13th MMY
Millon Index of Personality Styles, 13th MMY
MindMaker6, 11th MMY
Miner Sentence Completion Scale, 11th MMY
Minnesota Multiphasic Personality Inventory-Adolescent, 12th MMY
Minnesota Multiphasic Personality Inventory-2, 11th MMY
Mother-Child Relationship Evaluation, 1980 Edition (The), 12th MMY
Motivation Analysis Test, 12th MMY
Motivational Patterns Inventory, 12th MMY
Motives, Values, Preferences Inventory, 14th MMY
Multidimensional Addictions and Personality Profile (The), 14th MMY
Multidimensional Anxiety Scale for Children, 14th MMY
Multidimensional Assessment and Planning Form, 9th MMY
Multidimensional Self Concept Scale, 12th MMY
Multidimensional Self-Esteem Inventory (The), 11th MMY
Multiple Affect Adjective Check List, Revised, 10th MMY
Multiscore Depression Inventory, 11th MMY
Multiscore Depression Inventory for Children, 14th MMY
Murphy-Meisgeier Type Indicator for Children, 12th MMY
Mutually Responsible Facilitation Inventory, 9th MMY
Myers-Briggs Type Indicator, 10th MMY
Myers-Briggs Type Indicator, Form M, 14th MMY
NEEDS Survey, 14th MMY
NEO-4, 14th MMY
North American Depression Inventories for Children and Adults, 11th MMY
NPF [Second Edition], 12th MMY
Observational Emotional Inventory—Revised, 11th MMY
Occupational Personality Questionnaire, 11th MMY
Occupational Stress Indicator, 11th MMY
Occupational Stress Inventory, 11th MMY
Occupational Stress Inventory—Revised Edition, 14th MMY
Occupational Type Profile, 14th MMY
Oetting's Computer Anxiety Scale, 10th MMY
Offer Self-Image Questionnaire, Revised, 12th MMY
Oliver Organization Description Questionnaire, 11th MMY
Pain Patient Profile, 14th MMY
P.A.R. Admissions Test, 11th MMY
Parent as a Teacher Inventory [Revised], 13th MMY
Parent Awareness Skills Survey, 12th MMY
Parent-Child Relationship Inventory, 13th MMY

Parenting Stress Index, Third Edition, 13th MMY
Partner Relationship Inventory (Research Edition), 12th MMY
Perception of Ability Scale for Students, 12th MMY
Perception-of-Relationships-Test, 12th MMY
Personal Experience Inventory, 11th MMY
Personal History Checklist for Adults, 11th MMY
Personal Inventory of Needs, 12th MMY
Personal Orientation Dimensions, 14th MMY
Personal Problems Checklist—Adult, 10th MMY
Personal Problems Checklist for Adolescents, 10th MMY
Personal Profile System, 10th MMY
Personal Resource Questionnaire, 11th MMY
Personal Skills Map, 13th MMY
Personal Stress Assessment Inventory, 14th MMY
Personal Style Assessment, 11th MMY
Personal Style Assessment, Jung-Parry Form, 13th MMY
Personal Style Indicator , 13th MMY
Personal Style Inventory, 14th MMY
Personal Styles Inventory [PSI-120], 13th MMY
Personal Values Questionnaire, 13th MMY
Personality Adjective Check List, 12th MMY
Personality Assessment Inventory, 12th MMY
Personality Assessment Screener, 14th MMY
Personality Disorder Interview-IV: A Semistructured Interview for the Assessment of Personality
   Disorders, 14th MMY
Personality Inventory for Children, Revised Format, 10th MMY
Personality Inventory for Youth, 13th MMY
Personality Research Form, 3rd Edition, 10th MMY
PERSONALYSIS, 12th MMY
Phase II Profile Integrity Status Inventory and Addendum, 10th MMY
Piers-Harris Children's Self-Concept Scale (The Way I Feel About Myself), 9th MMY
Porteous Problem Checklist, 10th MMY
Positive and Negative Syndrome Scale, 12th MMY
Posttraumatic Stress Diagnostic Scale, 14th MMY
Problem Experiences Checklist, 12th MMY
Problem Solving Inventory (The), 11th MMY
Problem-Solving Decision-Making Style Inventory, 10th MMY
Prout-Strohmer Personality Inventory, 11th MMY
Psychap Inventory (The), 11th MMY
Psychiatric Content Analysis and Diagnosis, 14th MMY
Psychiatric Diagnostic Interview—Revised, 11th MMY
Psychosocial Adjustment to Illness Scale, 10th MMY
Psychotherapy Outcome Kit (Including Quality of Emotional Life Self-Report), 14th MMY
Quality of Life Enjoyment and Satisfaction Questionnaire, 14th MMY
Quality of Life Questionnaire, 11th MMY
Questionnaire Measure of Individual Differences in Achieving Tendency (A), 10th MMY

Questionnaire Measure of Trait Arousability (Or Its Converse, Stimulus Screening), 13th MMY

Questionnaire on Resources and Stress, 11th MMY

Racial Attitude Test, 11th MMY

Reid Report, 12th MMY

Reiss-Epstein-Gursky Anxiety Sensitivity Index, 11th MMY

Revised Children's Manifest Anxiety Scale, 10th MMY

Revised Hamilton Rating Scale for Depression, 13th MMY

Revised NEO Personality Inventory me, 12th MMY

Reynolds Adolescent Depression Scale, 11th MMY

Reynolds Child Depression Scale, 11th MMY

Reynolds Depression Screening Inventory, 14th MMY

Roberts Apperception Test for Children [with new Interpretive Handbook], 14th MMY

Rokeach Value Survey, 12th MMY

Rorschach, 14th MMY

Rotter Incomplete Sentences Blank, Second Edition, 12th MMY

Rust Inventory of Schizotypal Cognitions, 13th MMY

Sales Personality Questionnaire, 12th MMY

Sales Transaction Audit, 14th MMY

Salience Inventory (The), 11th MMY

SAQ-Adult Probation III, 14th MMY

Scale for Assessing Emotional Disturbance, 14th MMY

Scale for the Assessment of Negative Symptoms, 12th MMY

Scale for the Assessment of Positive Symptoms, 12th MMY

Scale of Social Development, 11th MMY

Schedule for Affective Disorders and Schizophrenia, Third Edition, 12th MMY

Schedule for Nonadaptive and Adaptive Personality, 14th MMY

Schedule of Recent Experience (The), 10th MMY

School Attitude Measure, Second Edition, 11th MMY

Search Institute Profiles of Student Life, 11th MMY

Self Worth Inventory, 13th MMY

Self-Awareness Profile, 11th MMY

Self-Description Questionnaire—I, II, III, 13th MMY

Self-Esteem Index, 11th MMY

Self-Perception Inventory: Nursing Forms, 11th MMY

Self-Perception Profile for College Students, 11th MMY

Senior Apperception Technique [1985 Revision] (The), 13th MMY

Sentence Completion Series, 14th MMY

Severity and Acuity of Psychiatric Illness Scales—Adult Version (The), 14th MMY

Sexual Adjustment Inventory, 14th MMY

Shapiro Control Inventory, 13th MMY

Singer-Loomis Inventory of Personality, Experimental Edition (The), 10th MMY

Singer-Loomis Type Deployment Inventory, 14th MMY

SIPOAS: Styles in Perception of Affect Scale, 14th MMY

Sixteen Personality Factor Questionnaire, Fifth Edition, 12th MMY

Social Phobia and Anxiety Inventory, 14th MMY

Social Reticence Scale, 11th MMY

Social Skills Inventory, Research Edition, 11th MMY
Social Styles Analysis, 11th MMY
Social-Emotional Dimension Scale, 11th MMY
SPECTRUM-I: A Test of Adult Work Motivation, 12th MMY
Spiritual Well-Being Scale, 12th MMY
Staff Burnout Scale for Health Professionals, 9th MMY
Stanton Inventory (The), 9th MMY
Stanton Survey and the Stanton Survey Phase II (The), 9th MMY
State Trait-Depression Adjective Check Lists, 13th MMY
State-Trait Anger Expression Inventory [1996 Edition], 13th MMY, 14th MMY
Stokes/Gordon Stress Scale, 13th MMY
Strength Deployment Inventory, 14th MMY
Stress Analysis System, 10th MMY
Stress Audit, 10th MMY
Stress Impact Scale, 12th MMY
Stress Index for Parents of Adolescents, 14th MMY
Stress Management Questionnaire, 10th MMY
Stress Resiliency Profile, 13th MMY
Stress Response Scale, 11th MMY
Structured Clinical Interview for DSM-IV Axis I Disorders: Clinician Version, 14th MMY
Structured Clinical Interview for DSM-IV Axis II Personality Disorders, 14th MMY
Structured Interview of Reported Symptoms, 12th MMY
Structured Pediatric Psychosocial Interview, 10th MMY
Student Adaptation to College Questionnaire, 11th MMY
Student Adjustment Inventory, 12th MMY
Student Developmental Task and Lifestyle Inventory, 11th MMY
Student Referral Checklist, 11th MMY
Student Self-Concept Scale, 13th MMY
Student Styles Questionnaire, 14th MMY
Student Talent and Risk Profile, 12th MMY
Study Process Questionnaire, 11th MMY
Style of Learning and Thinking, 11th MMY
Substance Abuse Life Circumstance Evaluation, 14th MMY
Substance Abuse Subtle Screening Inventory, 12th MMY
Suicidal Ideation Questionnaire, 11th MMY
SUPER Star Profiles, 13th MMY
Supervisory Human Relations, 11th MMY
Survey of Organizational Climate, 11th MMY
Survey of Organizational Culture, 11th MMY
Survey of Personal Values, 10th MMY
Survey of Work Values, Revised, Form U, 12th MMY
Symptom Assessment-45 Questionnaire, 14th MMY
Symptom Checklist-90-Revised, 9th MMY
Symptom Scale—77, 14th MMY
Taylor-Johnson Temperament Analysis [1992 Edition], 13th MMY, 14th MMY

Teacher Attitude Inventory: Identifying Teacher Positions in Relation to Educational Issues and Decisions (A), 10th MMY

Teacher Stress Inventory, 11th MMY

Team Development Survey, 13th MMY

TEMAS (Tell-Me-A-Story), 11th MMY

Temperament Assessment Battery for Children, 11th MMY

Tennessee Self-Concept Scale, Second Edition, 13th MMY

Test Anxiety Profile, 9th MMY

Test Attitude Inventory, 9th MMY

Test for Creative Thinking—Drawing Production, 14th MMY

Themes Concerning Blacks, 9th MMY

Thomas-Kilmann Conflict Mode Instrument, 10th MMY

Tiffany Control Scales, 14th MMY

Time Perception Inventory, 11th MMY

TMJ Scale, 12th MMY

Trait Pleasure-Displeasure Scale (The), 13th MMY

Trauma Symptom Inventory, 14th MMY

Treatment Intervention Inventory, 14th MMY

Understanding and Managing Stress, 12th MMY

Validity Indicator Profile, 14th MMY

Values Scale, Second Edition (The), 13th MMY

Victoria Symptom Validity Test, 14th MMY

VITAL Checklist and Curriculum Guide, 11th MMY

Waksman Social Skills Rating Scale, 10th MMY

Walker-McConnell Scale of Social Competence and School Adjustment, 11th MMY

Ways of Coping Questionnaire, Research Edition, 11th MMY

Weinberg Depression Scale for Children and Adolescents, 14th MMY

What Do You Say?, 12th MMY

Whitaker Index of Schizophrenic Thinking, 11th MMY

Wide Range Interest-Opinion Test, 9th MMY

Work Personality Profile, 11th MMY

7.16.14 Reading

ACER Applied Reading Test, 12th MMY

Assessing Reading Difficulties: A Diagnostic and Remedial Approach, 9th MMY

Bader Reading and Language Inventory, 10th MMY

Basic Reading Inventory, Seventh Edition, 12th MMY, 14th MMY

Bench Mark Measures, 9th MMY

Boder Test of Reading-Spelling Patterns (The), 9th MMY

Burns/Roe Informal Reading Inventory: Preprimer to Twelfth Grade, Third Edition, 12th MMY

Burns/Roe Informal Reading Inventory: Preprimer to Twelfth Grade, Fifth Edition, 14th MMY

Burt Word Reading Test, New Zealand Revision, 9th MMY

California Diagnostic Reading Tests, 11th MMY

CHILD Center Operational Assessment Tool (The), 9th MMY

Classroom Reading Inventory, Seventh Edition, 10th MMY

Cloze Reading Tests 1-3, Second Edition, 9th MMY

Clymer-Barrett Readiness Test, Revised Edition, 9th MMY

Content Inventories: English, Social Studies, Science, 9th MMY

Corrective Reading Mastery Tests, 9th MMY

Croft Readiness Assessment in Comprehension Kit, 9th MMY

Decoding Skills Test, 10th MMY

Degrees of Reading Power, 12th MMY

Degrees of Reading Power [Revised], 14th MMY

Degrees of Word Meaning, 13th MMY

Diagnostic Assessments of Reading, 12th MMY

Diagnostic Reading Scales, 9th MMY

Diagnostic Screening Test: Reading, Third Edition, 9th MMY

Durrell Analysis of Reading Difficulty, Third Edition, 9th MMY

Dyslexia Screening Instrument, 14th MMY

Dyslexia Screening Survey (The), 10th MMY

Edinburgh Reading Tests, 9th MMY

Ekwall/Shanker Reading Inventory—Third Edition, 13th MMY

GAP Reading Comprehension Test, Third Edition, 10th MMY

Gates-MacGinitie Reading Tests, Canadian Edition, 9th MMY

Gates-MacGinitie Reading Tests, Third Edition, 11th MMY

Gates-McKillop-Horowitz Reading Diagnostic Test, Second Edition, 9th MMY

Gray Oral Reading Tests, Third Edition, 12th MMY

Gray Oral Reading Tests—Diagnostic, 11th MMY

Group Diagnostic Reading Aptitude and Achievement Tests, Intermediate Form, 12th MMY

Group Reading Test, Third Edition, 12th MMY

Group Reading Test, Fourth Edition, 14th MMY

Industrial Reading Test-Infant Reading Tests (The), 9th MMY

Informal Reading Comprehension Placement Test [Revised], 13th MMY

IOX Basic Skills Word List (The), 9th MMY

Johnston Informal Reading Inventory, 12th MMY

Laurita-Trembley Diagnostic Word Processing Test (The), 9th MMY

Lollipop Test: A Diagnostic Screening Test of School Readiness—Revised (The), 11th MMY

London Reading Test, 9th MMY

Macmillan Diagnostic Reading Pack (The), 9th MMY

Macmillan Graded Word Reading Test, 10th MMY

Macmillan Group Reading Test, 10th MMY

Maryland/Baltimore County Design for Adult Basic Education, 9th MMY

McCall-Crabbs Standard Test Lessons in Reading, 9th MMY

McCarthy Individualized Diagnostic Reading Inventory, Revised Edition, 9th MMY

Murphy-Durrell Reading Readiness Screen, 11th MMY

Neale Analysis of Reading Ability, Revised British Edition, 11th MMY

Nelson Reading Skills Test, Forms 3 and 4 (The), 9th MMY

Nelson-Denny Reading Test, Forms G and H, 13th MMY

New Macmillan Reading Analysis, 10th MMY

NewGAP, 12th MMY

Progressive Achievement Tests in Reading: Reading Comprehension and Reading Vocabulary Tests, 11th MMY

Progressive Achievement Tests of Reading [Revised], 12th MMY

Ramsay Corporation Job Skills—Health Care Reading Test, 13th MMY

Ramsay Corporation Job Skills—Office Reading Test, 13th MMY

Ramsay Corporation Job Skills—Supervisory Reading Test, 13th MMY

Reading Ability Series, 11th MMY

Reading Comprehension Battery for Aphasia, Second Edition, 14th MMY

Reading Comprehension Inventory, 11th MMY

Reading Comprehension Test DE, 10th MMY

Reading Evaluation Adult Diagnosis (Revised), 11th MMY

Reading Evaluation Adult Diagnosis, Fifth Edition, 14th MMY

Reading Evaluation and Diagnostic Screen, 10th MMY

Reading Style Inventory, 11th MMY

Reading Test AD, 10th MMY

Reading Test SR-A and SR-B, 10th MMY

Reversals Frequency Test (The), 11th MMY

Revised PSB—Reading Comprehension Examination, 13th MMY

Roswell-Chall Diagnostic Reading Test of Word Analysis Skills, Revised and Extended, 14th MMY

School Readiness Test, 12th MMY

Secondary & College Reading Inventory, Second Edition, 13th MMY

Shortened Edinburgh Reading Test, 14th MMY

Slosson Oral Reading Test [Revised], 12th MMY

Slosson Test of Reading Readiness, 12th MMY

SPAR Spelling and Reading Tests, Second Edition, 12th MMY

SPAR Spelling and Reading Tests, Third Edition, 14th MMY

Standardized Reading Inventory, 10th MMY

Standardized Reading Inventory, Second Edition, 14th MMY

Stanford Diagnostic Reading Test, Fourth Edition, 13th MMY

STAR Reading, 14th MMY

Stieglitz Informal Reading Inventory: Assessing Reading Behaviors from Emergent to Advanced Levels (The), 13th MMY

Suffolk Reading Scale, 11th MMY

Test of Awareness of Language Segments, 11th MMY

Test of Early Reading Ability—2, 11th MMY

Test of Early Reading Ability—Deaf or Hard of Hearing, 12th MMY

Test of Inference Ability in Reading Comprehension, 13th MMY

Test of Initial Literacy, 11th MMY

Test of Reading Comprehension, Third Edition, 13th MMY

Tests of Reading Comprehension, 11th MMY

Watson-Glaser Critical Thinking Appraisal, 9th MMY

Wide-Span Reading Test, 10th MMY

Woodcock Diagnostic Reading Battery, 14th MMY

Woodcock Reading Mastery Tests—Revised [1998 Normative Update], 14th MMY

Woodcock Reading Mastery Tests—Revised [1998 Norms], 10th MMY

Word Recognition and Phonic Skills, 14th MMY

7.16.15 Science

Scientific Orientation Test, 14th MMY

Tapping Students' Science Beliefs: A Resource for Teaching and Learning, 13th MMY

7.16.16 Sensorimotor

Basic Visual-Motor Association Test, 9th MMY

Bender-Gestalt Test, 11th MMY

Benton Visual Retention Test, Fifth Edition, 13th MMY

Bruininks-Oseretsky Test of Motor Proficiency, 9th MMY

Carrow Auditory-Visual Abilities Test, 9th MMY

City University Colour Vision Test, Second Edition 1980 (The), 13th MMY

DeGangi-Berk Test of Sensory Integration, 10th MMY

Developmental Test of Visual Perception, Second Edition, 12th MMY

Developmental Test of Visual-Motor Integration [Third Revision], 12th MMY

Developmental Test of Visual-Motor Integration, 4th Edition, Revised, 14th MMY

Dysphagia Evaluation Protocol, 14th MMY

Erhardt Developmental Vision Assessment, 12th MMY

Evaluating Movement and Posture Disorganization in Dyspraxic Children, 12th MMY

Gibson Spiral Maze, Second Edition, 14th MMY

Grooved Pegboard Test, 12th MMY

Hill Performance Test of Selected Positional Concepts, 9th MMY

Hooper Visual Organization Test (The), 12th MMY

Infant/Toddler Symptom Checklist, 14th MMY

Inventory of Perceptual Skills, 12th MMY

Kent Visual Perception Test, 14th MMY

Lateral Preference Schedule, 11th MMY

McDowell Vision Screening Kit, 14th MMY

McGill Pain Questionnaire (The), 14th MMY

Minnesota Manual Dexterity Test, 12th MMY

Modified Version of the Bender-Gestalt Test for Preschool and Primary School Children (The), 11th MMY

Motor Skills Inventory, 11th MMY

Motor-Free Visual Perception Test—Revised, 14th MMY

Motor-Free Visual Perception Test—Vertical, 14th MMY

OSOT Perceptual Evaluation, 12th MMY

Pin Test (The), 11th MMY

Sensory Evaluation Kit, 13th MMY

Sensory Integration Inventory—Revised for Individuals with Developmental Disabilities, 14th MMY

Test of Visual-Motor Integration, 14th MMY

Test of Visual-Motor Skills, 13th MMY

Wide Range Assessment of Visual Motor Abilities, 14th MMY

7.16.17 Social Studies

Basic Economics Test, 11th MMY

Cultural Literacy Test, 12th MMY

Test of Economic Knowledge, 11th MMY

Test of Economic Literacy, Second Edition, 12th MMY

Test of Understanding in College Economics, Third Edition, 13th MMY

7.16.18 Speech and Hearing

Adapted Sequenced Inventory of Communication Development, 12th MMY

Apraxia Profile: A Descriptive Assessment Tool for Children (The), 14th MMY

Arizona Articulation Proficiency Scale, Second Edition, 11th MMY

Assessing and Teaching Phonological Knowledge, 14th MMY

Assessing Linguistic Behaviors: Assessing Prelinguistic and Early Linguistic Behaviors in Developmentally Young Children, 11th MMY

Assessment of Aphasia and Related Disorders, Second Edition (The), 10th MMY

Assessment of Fluency in School-Age Children, 10th MMY

Assessment of Intelligibility of Dysarthric Speech, 10th MMY

Assessment of Phonological Processes—Revised (The), 12th MMY

Auditory Continuous Performance Test, 13th MMY

Auditory Discrimination and Attention Test (The), 12th MMY

Bankson-Bernthal Test of Phonology, 12th MMY

Bedside Evaluation of Dysphagia, 14th MMY

Behavior Analysis Language Instrument, 11th MMY

Boston Assessment of Severe Aphasia, 12th MMY

Children's Articulation Test, 12th MMY

CID Phonetic Inventory, 11th MMY

CID Picture SPINE, 11th MMY

Clinical Evaluation of Language Fundamentals, Third Edition, 13th MMY

Clinical Evaluation of Language Fundamentals—Preschool, 13th MMY

Communication Activities of Daily Living, Second Edition, 14th MMY

Communication and Symbolic Behavior Scales, 13th MMY

Communication Profile: A Functional Skills Survey, 14th MMY

Communicative Abilities in Daily Living, 10th MMY

Comprehensive Screening Tool for Determining Optimal Communication Mode, 10th MMY

Computer Managed Articulation Diagnosis, 11th MMY

Computer Managed Screening Test, 11th MMY

Cooper Assessment for Stuttering Syndromes, 14th MMY

Denver Audiometric Screening Test, 9th MMY

Draw A Person: A Quantitative Scoring System, 11th MMY

Dysarthria Examination Battery, 14th MMY

Dysarthria Profile, 11th MMY

Early Speech Perception Test, 12th MMY

Elicited Articulatory System Evaluation, 11th MMY

Examining for Aphasia, Third Edition, 13th MMY

Fluharty Preschool Speech and Language Screening Test, 9th MMY

Frenchay Aphasia Screening Test, 11th MMY

Frenchay Dysarthria Assessment, 12th MMY

Goldman-Fristoe Test of Articulation, 10th MMY

Hearing Measurement Scale (The), 9th MMY

Hundred Pictures Naming Test (The), 12th MMY

INteraction CHecklist for Augmentative Communication, Revised Edition, 13th MMY

Iowa's Severity Rating Scales for Speech and Language Impairments, 12th MMY

Joliet 3-Minute Preschool Speech and Language Screen, 14th MMY

Joliet 3-Minute Speech and Language Screen (Revised), 13th MMY

Jones-Mohr Listening Test (The), 9th MMY

Khan-Lewis Phonological Analysis, 10th MMY

Lindamood Auditory Conceptualization Test, Revised Edition, 9th MMY

Metaphon, 12th MMY

Multilingual Aphasia Examination, Third Edition, 14th MMY

Northwestern Syntax Screening Test, 9th MMY

Oral Motor Assessment and Treatment: Improving Syllable Production, 10th MMY

Oral Speech Mechanism Screening Examination, Third Edition, 14th MMY

Oral Speech Mechanism Screening Examination—Revised, 11th MMY

PACS Pictures: Language Elicitation Materials, 11th MMY

Patterned Elicitation Syntax Test with Morphonemic Analysis (The), 13th MMY

Phonological Assessment of Child Speech, 10th MMY

Phonological Process Analysis, 12th MMY

Phonological Processes Assessment and Intervention, 11th MMY

Photo Articulation Test, Third Edition, 14th MMY

Prosody-Voice Screening Profile, 12th MMY

Quick Screen of Phonology, 12th MMY

Receptive-Expressive Emergent Language Test, Second Edition, 12th MMY

Revised Edinburgh Functional Communication Profile, 12th MMY

Revised Evaluating Acquired Skills in Communication, 12th MMY

Roswell-Chall Auditory Blending Test, 14th MMY

Scales of Early Communication Skills for Hearing-Impaired Children, 12th MMY

SCAN: A Screening Test for Auditory Processing Disorders, 11th MMY

SCAN-A: A Test for Auditory Processing Disorders in Adolescents and Adults, 13th MMY

Screening Instrument for Targeting Educational Risk, 12th MMY

Screening Test for Developmental Apraxia of Speech, 11th MMY

Slosson Articulation Language Test with Phonology, 12th MMY

Smit-Hand Articulation and Phonology Evaluation, 14th MMY

Speech and Language Evaluation Scale, 12th MMY

STIM/CON: Prognostic Inventory for Misarticulating Kindergarten and First Grade Children, 11th MMY

Structured Photographic Articulation Test Featuring Dudsberry, 12th MMY

Stuttering Severity Instrument for Children and Adults, Third Edition, 13th MMY

Temple University Short Syntax Inventory, 12th MMY

Test for Auditory Comprehension of Language, Revised Edition, 10th MMY

Test for Examining Expressive Morphology, 10th MMY
Test of Articulation in Context, 14th MMY
Test of Auditory-Perceptual Skills, 13th MMY
Test of Oral Structures and Functions, 12th MMY
Test of Phonological Awareness, 13th MMY
Test of Pragmatic Language, 12th MMY
Voice Assessment Protocol for Children and Adults (A), 11th MMY
Wepman's Auditory Discrimination Test, Second Edition, 11th MMY
Wiig Criterion Referenced Inventory of Language, 13th MMY

7.16.19 Vocations

Access Management Survey, 12th MMY
Accounting Aptitude Test, 13th MMY
Accounting Program Admission Test, 12th MMY
Adult Career Concerns Inventory, 12th MMY
Allied Health Professions Admission Test, 12th MMY
American Occupational Therapy Association, Inc. Fieldwork Evaluation for the Occupation Therapist (The), 12th MMY
Applied Knowledge Test, 9th MMY
Aptitude Interest Inventory, 13th MMY
Armed Services-Civilian Vocational Interest Survey, 10th MMY
Ashland Interest Assessment, 14th MMY
ASPIRE (A Sales Potential Inventory for Real Estate), 12th MMY
ASSESS Personality Battery [Expert System Version 5.X], 14th MMY
Assessing Specific Competencies, 12th MMY
Assessing Your Team: Seven Measures of Team Success, 14th MMY
Assessment Inventory for Management, 13th MMY
Assessment of Career Decision Making, 10th MMY
Assessment of Competencies for Instructor Development, 11th MMY
Automated Office Battery, 11th MMY
Ball Aptitude Battery, 9th MMY
Becker Work Adjustment Profile, 11th MMY
Belbin Team-Roles Self-Perception Inventory, 14th MMY
BENCHMARKS, 12th MMY
Bennett Mechanical Comprehension Test, 11th MMY
BRIGANCE Diagnostic Employability Skills Inventory, 14th MMY
Business Analyst Skills Evaluation, 10th MMY
Campbell Interest and Skill Survey, 13th MMY
Campbell Organizational Survey, 12th MMY
Campbell-Hallam Team Development Survey, 14th MMY
Canadian Occupational Interest Inventory, 9th MMY
Candidate Profile Record (The), 12th MMY
Career Anchors: Discovering Your Real Values, Revised Edition, 13th MMY
Career Assessment Inventory, Second Edition (Vocational Version), 11th MMY
Career Assessment Inventory—The Enhanced Version, 10th MMY

Career Attitudes and Strategies Inventory: An Inventory for Understanding Adult Careers, 13th MMY

Career Decision Scale, 9th MMY

Career Decision-Making Self-Efficacy Scale, 14th MMY

Career Development Inventory [Consulting Psychologists Press, Inc.], 13th MMY

Career Directions Inventory, 10th MMY

Career Exploration Inventory (The), 13th MMY

Career Exploration Series, 1992 Revision, 13th MMY

Career Factors Inventory, 14th MMY

Career Guidance Inventory, 11th MMY

Career Interest Inventory, 13th MMY

Career Interests Test, 9th MMY

Career IQ Test, 14th MMY

Career Occupational Preference System—Professional Level Interest Inventory, 14th MMY

Career Problem Check List, 9th MMY

Career Profile System, Second Edition (The), 13th MMY

Career Thoughts Inventory, 14th MMY

Career Values Card Sort, 13th MMY

Change Abilitator, 14th MMY

Chronicle Career Quest, 12th MMY

Clerical Abilities Battery, 11th MMY

Clerical Staff Selector, 10th MMY

Coaching Process Questionnaire, 13th MMY

Common-Metric Questionnaire (The), 13th MMY

Communication Knowledge Inventory, 11th MMY

Communications Profile Questionnaire, 10th MMY

Competency-Based Performance Improvement: Organizational Assessment Package, 14th MMY

Computer Programmer Aptitude Battery, 11th MMY

Computer Programmer Test Package, 11th MMY

Cosmetology Student Admissions Evaluation, 11th MMY

Dental Admission Test, 12th MMY

Developing the High-Performance Workplace, 14th MMY

Developmental Challenge Profile: Learning from Job Experiences, 13th MMY

Devine Inventory (The), 12th MMY

Diversity Management Survey (The), 14th MMY

Electrical Maintenance Trainee, 13th MMY

Electromechanical Vocational Assessment Manuals, 13th MMY

Electronic and Instrumentation Technician Test, 10th MMY

Electronics Test—Form G2, 13th MMY

Employability Inventory (The), 12th MMY

Employability Maturity Interview, 11th MMY

Employee Aptitude Survey, Second Edition, 14th MMY

Employee Effectiveness Profile, 12th MMY

Employment Screening Test and Standardization Manual, 11th MMY

Employment Values Inventory, 14th MMY

Kuder General Interest Survey, Form E, 12th MMY

Kuder Occupational Interest Survey, Revised (Form DD), 1985, 10th MMY

Law Enforcement Assessment and Development Report, 10th MMY

Law Enforcement Candidate Record, 13th MMY

Law School Admission Test, 13th MMY

Leader Behavior Analysis II, 12th MMY

Leader Behavior Questionnaire, Revised, 14th MMY

Leadership Practices Inventory—Delta, 14th MMY

Leadership Skills Inventory [Consulting Resource Group], 13th MMY

Learning Organization Practices Profile, 14th MMY

Leatherman Leadership Questionnaire [Revised], 12th MMY

Leatherman Leadership Questionnaire: 360 Degree Leadership Profile, 14th MMY

Leisure Search Inventory, 13th MMY

Life Style Questionnaire, 9th MMY

Lore Leadership Assessment, 14th MMY

Maintest, 13th MMY

Major-Minor-Finder, 1986-1996 Edition (The), 10th MMY

Management and Graduate Item Bank, 11th MMY

Management & Leadership Systems, 14th MMY

Management Appraisal Survey, 10th MMY

Management Change Inventory, 11th MMY

Management Interest Inventory, 11th MMY

Management Inventory on Leadership, Motivation and Decision-Making, 12th MMY

Management Inventory on Modern Management, 10th MMY

Management Style Inventory [Hanson Silver Strong & Associates], 13th MMY

Management Styles Inventory, 12th MMY

Management Styles Questionnaire, 10th MMY

Manager Profile Record, 11th MMY

Manager Style Appraisal, 12th MMY

Manager/Supervisor Staff Selector, 10th MMY

Managerial and Professional Job Functions Inventory, 11th MMY

Managerial Assessment of Proficiency MAP, 11th MMY

Managerial Competence Index, 11th MMY

Managerial Style Questionnaire, 10th MMY

MAPP: Motivational Appraisal of Personal Potential, 14th MMY

MbM Questionnaire: Managing by Motivation, Third Edition (The), 14th MMY

MDS Vocational Interest Exploration System, 13th MMY

Measurement of Counselor Competencies: A Self-Assessment, 10th MMY

MecTest (A Test for Maintenance Mechanics), 13th MMY

Microcomputer User Aptitude Test, 11th MMY

Minnesota Clerical Assessment Battery, 14th MMY

Minnesota Clerical Test, 9th MMY

Minnesota Importance Questionnaire, 11th MMY

Minnesota Spatial Relations Test, Revised Edition, 9th MMY

Modern Occupational Skills Tests, 12th MMY

Welding Test, 13th MMY

Word Processor Assessment Battery, 10th MMY

Work Adjustment Inventory, 13th MMY

Work Adjustment Scale (The), 13th MMY

Work Aptitude: Profile and Practice Set, 10th MMY

Work Experience Survey (The), 14th MMY

Work Performance Assessment, 13th MMY

Work Skills Series Production, 12th MMY

Work Temperament Inventory, 13th MMY

Worker Rehabilitation Questionnaire, 14th MMY

Working—Assessing Skills, Habits, and Style, 14th MMY

7.17 HOW RESEARCHERS CREATE THEIR OWN SCALES: AN ACTIVITY OF LAST RESORT

A researcher constructs a new scale if (a) after a literature search, he or she does not find a scale that fits the problem, or (b) the available scales are poorly constructed. Any constructed scale should be good enough to invite future researchers to use it in the ongoing process of accumulating research findings. Putting some items together and assigning arbitrary weights to them does not produce this kind of scale. An acceptable scale will cover an important theoretical construct and meet evaluative criteria discussed below.

Some researchers, caught up in the desire to produce instruments that address their particular research interests, construct scales without sufficient attention to psychometric qualities such as reliability and validity. The obvious difficulty is that when such scales are used to test a research hypothesis, a null result precludes a clear and unbiased test of the research question.

7.17.1 Checklist of Evaluative Criteria for Assessing a Scale

The following checklist is adapted from one constructed by Robert Athanasiou and Kendra B. Head (Robinson, Athanasious, & Head, 1969, pp. 4-13).

I. Item Construction Criteria
   1. Selected items reflect accurately the universe of items encompassed by the variable to be measured
   2. Items are simply worded so that they can be easily understood by the population to whom the scale is to be administered
   3. Item analysis demonstrates that each item is closely related to the selected variable, with techniques of item analysis including the following
      a. Item-intercorrelation matrix
      b. Factor analysis
      c. Complex multidimensional analysis
      d. Item correlation with external criteria
   4. Pretest and eliminate or revise undesirable items

II. Response Set Criteria
  1. Avoid response set bias resulting from acquiescence (subservient syndrome), using the following techniques, among others
     a. Discard simple affirmative items
     b. Switch response alternatives occasionally between positive and negative
     c. Use forced-choice items: Two or more replies to a question are listed, and the respondent is asked to choose only one
  2. Avoid response set bias resulting from social desirability (good impression syndrome), using the following techniques, among others
     a. Use forced-choice items in which the alternatives have been equated on the basis of social desirability ratings
     b. Pretest items in social desirability, and drop or revise alternative pairings (or item pairings) that do not prove to be equated
  3. Analyze and eliminate efforts of respondents to fake responses according to some image that the respondent wishes to convey
  4. Analyze and eliminate spurious replies that result from respondents wanting to appear too consistent, to use few or many categories in replies, or to choose extreme alternatives

III. Scale Metric Criteria
  1. Representative sampling: Sampling methods accurately produce a miniature population that reflects the universe under study
  2. Adequate normative information: To ensure that the meaning of responses secured in research can be interpreted correctly, the researcher should calculate the following measures for the constructed scale
     a. Mean scale score and standard deviation for the sample on which it was constructed
     b. Means and standard deviations for certain well-defined groups
     c. Item means and standard deviations
  3. Reliability: A reliable scale measures consistently what it is supposed to measure, with "reliability" referring to the following three major criteria
     a. High correlation between a person's score on the same items at two separate points in time
     b. High correlation between two different sets of items at the same time (these sets may be presented as parallel forms with items in a separate format or as a split half when all items are presented together)
     c. High correlation between the scale items for all people who answer the items[1]
  4. Homogeneity: A homogeneous scale agrees with itself, and homogeneity refers to the internal consistency of a scale, a property that is crucial in scale construction because only a homogeneous scale can present a common attribute; techniques to test homogeneity include the following
     a. Split-half correlation
     b. Parallel forms and interitem indices of internal homogeneity (Cronbach's alpha)
     c. Guttman scaling technique
  5. Validity: A valid scale measures what it is supposed to measure, and validity (best tested by the correlation achieved with an external criterion) implies predictive power beyond the immediate range of factors in the scale; techniques to test validity include the following
     a. Discrimination between known groups
     b. Double cross-validation
     c. Multitrait, multimethod matrix
     d. Correlation of scale scores with one or more independent criteria of the phenomena being measured

Note

1. It is widely agreed by experts that the test-retest index is the best measure of reliability. Many insist that measures b and c are actually indices of homogeneity and not reliability, which is a term commonly used in an ambiguous fashion. The test-retest reliability level can be approximated from indices of homogeneity, but there is no substitute for actual test-retest data.

Reference

Robinson, John P., Athanasiou, Robert, & Head, Kendra B. (1969). *Measures of occupational attitudes and occupational characteristics*. Ann Arbor: University of Michigan, Survey Research Center.

PART 8

RESEARCH PROPOSAL, FUNDING, BUDGETING, REPORTING, AND CAREER PLANNING

The end product of research designing is generation of a proposal. The student setting forth on his or her first independent research and the professional with a lifetime of research achievement both face the same requirement: They must produce an acceptable proposal. Other professionals will critically examine the proposal and decide if it is acceptable. The planning and submission of proposals may take a year or more—always longer than expected—and the competition for research funding is often intense. Almost always, more proposals are rejected than are accepted because of the limited amount of resources available. A promising development is the increasing number of places to apply for support. The researcher must know where the money is and develop the skill of research negotiation.

Section 8.1, "The Research Grant Proposal," describes the preliminary planning of a proposal and offers a few useful hints that are especially appropriate in regard to how such proposals are evaluated. A general outline of a research proposal is included.

Section 8.2, "Research Funding," lists various guides to major research agencies.

Section 8.3 lists major sources of funding information.

Section 8.4 identifies major reasons why proposals are rejected.

Section 8.5 provides readings and other information sources on grantsmanship and proposal writing.

Sections 8.6 through 8.11 present detailed discussions of selected federal government agencies and private organizations offering fellowships and grants. For example, funding opportunities are described for two of the largest federal funding sources, the National Science Foundation and the National Institutes of Health.

◀ 661

Section 8.12 discusses the difficult task of setting budgets. Most researchers have never had formal training (in graduate school) in this aspect of research, and they acquire their knowledge through experience and the process of trial and error. Most researchers drastically underestimate the time and effort required to complete their proposals, and almost everyone experiences unforeseen hindrances and delays. These delays are costly, but without some previous experience, it can be difficult to estimate how expensive.

Section 8.13, "Research Reporting," discusses planning for the research report and reviews both the specifications for a report and a set of criteria that can be used for evaluation.

Sections 8.14 through 8.16 are devoted to the process of publishing research reports in books and journals.

A professional research life includes professional communication and reporting to professional meetings. Section 8.17 describes the leading sociological associations and the role they play in professional socialization.

Finally, section 8.18, "Planning for a Career in the Social Sciences," provides guides for job applicants in sociology and other behavioral sciences.

8.1.1 Preliminary Planning

The purpose of a research proposal is to provide a statement establishing the objectives and scholarly significance of the proposed activity, the technical qualifications of the project director/principal investigator and his or her organization, and the level of funding required.

The proposal should contain sufficient information to convince both the professional staff of the agency and members of the scholarly community that the proposed activity is sound and worthy of support under the agency's criteria for the selection of projects or under specific criteria specified in the applicable proposal-generating mechanism. The proposal should be both succinct and complete.

Writing a proposal, like writing any other request, is a challenge in effective persuasion. Every agency and foundation has its own method for selecting proposals it wants to fund. Whatever the method used, individuals at the agency will read the proposal to determine how it fits into the agency's funding pattern and how cogently the applicant has presented it.

A few hints are especially appropriate in regard to evaluation of the proposal by judges or readers, or by a committee of them.

1. A clearly written abstract is essential. Readers may be evaluating numerous proposals in a limited amount of time, and they may dismiss some on the basis of their abstracts. You cannot expect a positive review if your ideas, as presented in the abstract, are unclear. To convey the meaning and significance of complex topics, writing and organization must be crystal clear.
2. A statement of previous work serves to validate the ability of the applicant to get into his or her research quickly without false starts and to carry out the proposed research successfully.
3. The availability of the research population is important. Weight is added to a proposal by evidence from pretests that shows that the population is responsive.
4. The availability of research facilities also is important. If matching funds or supporting facilities are needed, it is important for the committee to know that they are forthcoming.
5. Clear, professionally defined budgets that cover the entire time period of the research are imperative. The committee must be convinced that the size of the grant is appropriate and that the money will be spent wisely. Members want to know if the applicant's plans are realistic.
6. Especially important is evidence that convinces the committee that the applicant is able to and will carry the research to completion. Such evidence should include a biographical sketch, a statement of ongoing research, current letters of recommendation, and published material relevant to the proposal.

Each funding source has its own rules for grant applications. Some seek very short statements, perhaps limited to 5-10 pages; others prefer longer statements. Some provide forms that prescribe precisely what is wanted; others afford latitude. The researcher must be flexible.

Whatever the differences between agencies or foundations, all are greatly concerned with elements of the research design. In general, they include those shown in this volume in section 2.1, "Basic Guide for the Design of a Social Research Proposal."

8.1.2 The Elements of a Research Grant Proposal

When an agency has a set of forms and/or instructions, the researcher should use them and follow them rigorously. For example, the National Institutes of Health (http://grants.nih.gov/grants/index.cfm) has a Grants Page offering hundreds of forms and documents (such as those in Figure 8.1, the National Science Foundation form NSF 1030A). Almost all funding institutions (both government or private) have such forms available on the Internet.

(SEE INSTRUCTIONS BEFORE COMPLETING) **USE ONLY**

SUMMARY PROPOSAL BUDGET

Attachment D

FOR NSF

ORGANIZATION	PROPOSAL NO.	DURATION (MONTHS) Proposed | Granted
PRINCIPAL INVESTIGATOR/PROJECT DIRECTOR	AWARD NO.	

A. SENIOR PERSONNEL: PI/PD and Other Senior Associates (List each separately with title, A.6, show number in brackets)	NSF Funded Person-mos. CAL	Funds Requested By Proposer	Funds Granted By NSF (If Different)
1.		$	$
2.			
3.			
4.			
5.			
6. ( ) OTHERS (LIST INDIVIDUALLY ON BUDGET EXPLANATION PAGE)			
7. ( ) TOTAL SENIOR PERSONNEL (1-5)			
B. OTHER PERSONNEL (SHOW NUMBERS IN BRACKETS)			
1. ( ) POSTDOCTORAL ASSOCIATES			
2. ( ) OTHER PROFESSIONALS (TECHNICIAN, PROGRAMMER, ETC.)			
3. ( ) GRADUATE STUDENTS			
4. ( ) UNDERGRADUATE STUDENTS			
5. ( ) SECRETARIAL - CLERICAL			
6. ( ) OTHER			
TOTAL SALARIES AND WAGES (A+B)			
C. FRINGE BENEFITS (IF CHARGED AS DIRECT COSTS)			
TOTAL SALARIES, WAGES AND FRINGE BENEFITS (A+B+C)			
D. PERMANENT EQUIPMENT (LIST ITEM AND DOLLAR AMOUNT FOR EACH ITEM EXCEEDING $5,000.) (Do not use for Phase I) **TOTAL PERMANENT EQUIPMENT**			

Figure 8.1. The National Science Foundation Summary Budget Form

E. TRAVEL 1. DOMESTIC (INCL. CANADA AND U.S. POSSESSIONS)		$	$
2. FOREIGN (Do not use for Phase I)			

F. PARTICIPANT SUPPORT COSTS

1. STIPENDS $

2. TRAVEL $

3. SUBSISTENCE $

4. OTHER $

( ) TOTAL PARTICIPANT COSTS			
G. OTHER DIRECT COSTS			
1. MATERIALS AND SUPPLIES			
2. PUBLICATION COSTS/DOCUMENTATION/DISSEMINATION			
3. CONSULTANT SERVICES			
4. COMPUTER (ADPE) SERVICES			
5. SUBAWARDS			
6. OTHER			
TOTAL OTHER DIRECT COSTS			
H. TOTAL DIRECT COSTS (A THROUGH G)			

I. INDIRECT COSTS (SPECIFY RATE AND BASE)

RATE = BASE =

TOTAL INDIRECT COSTS

J. TOTAL DIRECT AND INDIRECT COSTS (H+I)			
K. FEE (If requested; maximum equals 7% of J)			
L. TOTAL COST AND FEE (J + K)		$	$

PI/PD TYPED NAME & SIGNATURE	DATE	**FOR NSF USE ONLY**		
		INDIRECT COST RATE VERIFICATION		
CO. REP. TYPED NAME & SIGNATURE	DATE	Date Checked	Date of Rate Sheet	Initials-DGA

NSF FORM 1030A (SBIR) (2/97)   (End of Form)   (Page 2 of 2)

(NOTE: Budget form pages 1 of 2 & 2 of 2 together count as only one page)

In the absence of any specific instructions from a funding agency, this general outline of parts of a proposal may be helpful. Remember, however, that each institution has its own desired way of preparing materials, its own set of due dates and deadlines, and its own preferred way that a research budget should be constructed. A proposal that does not adhere to these instructions may not get a fair chance of being considered and may even be disqualified.

The following sections discuss 11 elements found in nearly all research proposals.

8.1.2.1 The Title Page

Many sponsoring agencies have their own format for the title page, with the format usually self-explanatory. In the absence of a specified format, the title or face page should include most of or all the following items: the agency to which the proposal is to be submitted; the name and address of the institution submitting the proposal; the title of the proposed work; the name, title, phone number, e-mail address, and mailing address of the project director; the period of time over which the proposed research will take place; the requested amount of funds; the date of the proposal; and endorsements. Minimum endorsement should be arranged for signature of the project director and the authorizing official of the submitting institution.

8.1.2.2 The Abstract

Although the abstract appears at the front of the proposal, it should be written last, as a concise summary of the material presented in the proposal. The abstract usually includes the major objectives of the proposal and the procedures to be used to meet these objectives. These materials are condensed to a page or less (specific lengths sometimes are given in guidelines). If the proposal is awarded funding, the abstract will be printed in national data banks (such as ERIC, see section 5.12.2.2). The abstract serves several purposes: (a) The reviewer usually reads it first to acquire a perspective on the study and its expected significance; (b) the reviewer uses it as a reference to the nature of the study when the project comes up for discussion; and (c) it sometimes will be the only part of the proposal that is read by those reviewing a panel's recommendation or the field readers' consensus.

To meet these uses, it is important that the abstract be prepared with the utmost care and that objectives and procedures are paraphrased using general but precise statements. Key concepts presented in the body of the proposal are highlighted in the abstract to alert the reviewer to look for them in the body of the proposal.

8.1.2.3 The Table of Contents

A brief proposal does not necessarily need a table of contents. The convenience of the reader should be the guiding consideration in deciding whether to provide one. When included, the table of contents should list all major parts and divisions of the proposal.

8.1.2.4 The Introduction

The introduction should be well written and clear, so that it can be understood by an educated but possibly naïve reader. It should provide enough background to enable the reader to place the proposal in a context of common knowledge, and it should show how the proposed activities will advance the field or be important to the solution of the problem.

8.1.2.5 Background

The background should present a review of what has been accomplished in the field, demonstrate the researcher's competence in connection with the problem, and show what he or she will add to the existing field of knowledge. This usually is the physically largest part of a grant proposal and is also referred to as the review of literature.

8.1.2.6 Description of Proposed Research

The proposal should present a detailed description of the work to be undertaken. The objectives and significance should be stated clearly and specifically. Research methods or operating procedures should be detailed, and the general plan of work should be outlined, including the broad design of experiments and the plan for analysis of the results.

8.1.2.7 Evaluation

The proposal should provide an evaluation component designed to determine how effective the research program is in reaching the objectives established and in solving the problems with which it deals. If possible, the evaluation should also be designed to allow for appropriate changes and adjustments in a program as it proceeds. In some experimental settings, such an evaluation may not be necessary.

8.1.2.8 Description of Relevant Institutional Resources

Available facilities and major items of equipment especially adapted to the proposed project should be described. These facilities could include libraries, computer centers, other recognized centers, and any special but relevant equipment.

8.1.2.9 Vitae

Most sponsoring agencies require a curriculum vitae and list of publications for each applicant and senior professional staff member in the project.

8.1.2.10 Personnel

All personnel who will participate in the proposed project should be identified by name, title, and expected amount of time to be devoted to the project. Unfilled positions should be identified as "vacant" or "to be appointed" (TBA). If the individuals involved have exceptional qualifications that would merit special consideration in the evaluation of the proposal, this information should be included.

8.1.2.11 *Budget*

A checklist for budget items should include at least the following categories.

▪▪ Salaries and wages
Academic personnel during academic year
Academic personnel during summer
Research associates
Research assistants
Technicians
Secretarial staff
Hourly help
▪▪ Fringe benefits
▪▪ Consultants
Fees
Travel expenses
▪▪ Equipment, including installation and freight
▪▪ Supplies
Photocopying costs
Office supplies
▪▪ Travel
Domestic
Foreign
▪▪ Physical alterations and renovation
▪▪ Other costs
Trainee costs
Telephone
Equipment rental
Information and data processing
Postage
Subcontracts
Indirect costs

The competition for external support is intense (because it often serves to support many non–revenue-producing institutional activities), so many organizations employ grant research officers to assist researchers in writing proposals. The grant researcher's help and counsel should be sought. The preparation of any proposal, and especially the budget, requires all the planning skill that can be mustered. Shortcomings in this stage of the research augur problems later.

8.2 RESEARCH FUNDING

Obtaining funding for research is a major activity of almost all sociologists and other social and behavior scientists. Funding might be internal, through a home institution, or external, such as that obtained through the federal government or a foundation. Funding often provides the resources not only to conduct research but also to staff teaching and administrative positions. The last aspect makes funding vital to the health of a college or university where research is emphasized.

8.2.1 Major Funding Agencies for Social Science Research

8.2.1.1 Federal Agencies

For additional information about any federal agency and what types of funding it provides, visit the FEDIX Web site (http://content.sciencewise.com/fedix/). Addresses and contact information for some of the main federal agencies are shown here. In addition, thousands of state and local agencies support funding for a variety of projects.

National Science Foundation
4201 Wilson Boulevard
Arlington, VA 22230
703-292-5111
www.nsf.gov/

National Institute of Mental Health
Parklawn Building
5600 Fisher's Lane
Rockville, MD 20857
www.nih.gov/

U.S. Department of Justice
950 Pennsylvania Avenue, NW
Washington, DC 20530-0001
202-353-1555
www.usdoj.gov/

U.S. Department of Education
400 Maryland Avenue, SW
Washington, DC 20202-0498
800-872-5327
www.ed.gov

U.S. Department of Labor
200 Constitution Avenue
Washington, DC 20210
202-693-1999
www.dol.gov

National Endowment for the Humanities
1100 Pennsylvania Avenue, NW
202-606-8400
www.neh.fed.us

U.S. Department of Defense
1000 Defense Pentagon
Washington, DC 20301-1000
www.defenselink.mil/

U.S. Agency for International Development
Information Center
Ronald Reagan Building
Washington, DC 20523-0016
202-712-4810
www.usaid.gov/

U.S. Department of Agriculture
14th & Independence Ave., SW
Washington, DC 20250
202-720-2791
www.usda.gov

National Aeronautics and Space Administration
Washington, DC
www.nasa.gov

Department of Transportation
400 Seventh Street, SW
Washington, DC 20590
202-366-4000
www.dot.gov

8.2.1.2 Private and Other Foundations

For detailed information about more than 61,000 nongovernmental organizations and what types of projects they fund, refer to The Foundation Center (http://fdncenter.org/). The Web site provides information about specific foundations (such as that given later in this section). You can search by private foundations, corporate grant makers, grant-making public charities, and community foundations. In addition, you can search by sector to further refine your results. You can even subscribe to

Table 8.1 THE 25 LARGEST U.S. GRANT-MAKING FOUNDATIONS

Name	URL	Total Giving ($)
The Ford Foundation	www.fordfound.org/	652,091,000
Lilly Endowment Inc.	www.lilly.com/about/community/ foundation/endowment.html	583,890,521
Bill & Melinda Gates Foundation	www.gatesfoundation.org/	549,432,864
The David and Lucile Packard Foundation	www.packfound.org/	391,568,231
The Robert Wood Johnson Foundation	www.rwjf.org/index.jsp	290,249,646
The Pew Charitable Trusts	www.pewtrusts.com/	211,053,071
Robert W. Woodruff Foundation, Inc.	www.woodruff.org/	191,355,356
The California Endowment	www.calendow.org/	189,663,220
W. K. Kellogg Foundation	www.wkkf.org/	186,605,961
The Andrew W. Mellon Foundation	www.mellon.org/	161,501,133
John D. and Catherine T. MacArthur Foundation	www.macfdn.org/	158,582,350
Open Society Institute	www.soros.org/	152,974,312
The Rockefeller Foundation	www.rockfound.org/	149,343,068
The Starr Foundation	http://fdncenter.org/grantmaker/starr/index.html	143,822,676
The Annenberg Foundation	www.whannenberg.org/	133,487,973
The New York Community Trust	www.nycommunitytrust.org/	130,680,652
Charles Stewart Mott Foundation	www.mott.org/	116,137,110
California Community Foundation	www.calfund.org/	113,449,501
The Kresge Foundation	www.kresge.org/	112,710,216
Arthur S. DeMoss Foundation		104,283,341
Robert R. McCormick Tribune Foundation	www.rrmtf.org/	104,000,582
The Annie E. Casey Foundation	www.aecf.org/	103,944,570
Ford Motor Company Fund	www.ford.com/servlet/ecmcs/ford/index.jsp	97,789,429
The McKnight Foundation	www.mcknight.org/	93,949,623
Bank of America Foundation, Inc.	www.bankofamerica.com/foundation/	90,999,532

The Foundation Directory Online for $19.95 per month (as of October 2001). This service provides links to foundations, tax returns filed by private foundations, monthly updates, and more.

8.2.1.3 Major Foundation Sources of Funding

Table 8.1 lists the 25 largest U.S. grant-making foundations, ranked by total giving (which includes grants, scholarships, employee matching gifts, and other amounts). Each listing includes the organization's URL or Web site address when available. For further information about applying for funding from any of these foundations, go to its Web site.

MAJOR SOURCES OF FUNDING INFORMATION **8.3**

Obtaining information is the first step in securing funding for a research project. The following sections discuss a variety of sources and how to contact funders and apply for funds.

8.3.1 *Annual Register of Grant Support*

The 35th edition (2002) of this annual volume is organized by 11 major subject areas and 61 specific subcategories. More than 3,500 granting organizations are listed. A description of the book and reviewer comments can be found at www.bowker.com/bowkerweb/catalog2001/prod.00088.htm. The publisher's contact information is listed below.

R. R. Bowker
RENP Building
121 Chanlon Road
New Providence, NJ 07974
U.S. contact: Susan Towne
www.bowker.com

8.3.2 Federal Funding Sources for Rural Areas

Information on federal funding sources for rural areas can be found at the Federal Funding Sources for Rural Areas Web site, www.nal.usda.gov/ric/ricpubs/funding/federalfund/ff.html, which contains a collection of resources from the *Catalog of Federal Domestic Assistance* (1998), compiled by the Rural Information Center Program of the National Agricultural Library. That catalog can be accessed free of charge at www.cfda.gov. The agency's contact information is listed below.

Rural Information Center
National Agricultural Library
10301 Baltimore Ave., Rm. 304
Beltsville, MD 20705
800-633-7701

8.3.3 Federal Funding Tools and Information Sources

The Web site www.lib.msu.edu/harris23/grants/federal.htm provides Web links to federal databases, newsletters, and Web sites.

8.3.4 *Action Guide to Government Grants, Loans, and Giveaways*

This book, by George Chelekis (Perigee Books, 1993). contains 510 pages of comprehensive information on grants, loan guarantees, loans, and other financial help available from federal and state government sources.

8.3.5 *Guide to Federal Funding for Governments and Nonprofits*

This annual publication is produced by Government Information Services. The 1998 edition consists of two looseleaf volumes. It describes federal funding opportunities for state and local governments, public agencies, nonprofit entities, and community organizations, covering in detail more than 750 federal programs. Each program description provides detailed information on who is eligible, uses of the funds, how to apply, program restrictions, funding, and program contacts. Chapter topics include new programs, community development, economic development, energy, environment, transportation, public justice and victims' services, social services, health, child care and early childhood development, senior citizens, job training and employment, housing, and aid for the homeless.

8.3.6 Federal Government Contract Research

Any academic institution seriously interested in contract research should keep current on *Commerce Business Daily* (www.cbd-net.com/), a daily list of government procurement invitations, contract awards, subcontracting leads, sales of surplus properties, and foreign business opportunities. Research institutions usually have one or more people who read *Commerce Business Daily* regularly and then refer relevant announcements to interested faculty. Subscriptions are $299 per year. The publisher's contact information is as follows.

Nepac, Inc.
55 Maple Avenue
Suite 304
Rockville Centre, NY 11570
1-800-932-7761
online@cbdweb.com

8.4 COMMON REASONS FOR REJECTION OF GRANT PROPOSALS

Although each granting agency has its own set of criteria for evaluating a proposal (a good reason to talk with agency personnel as you prepare your application), some general guidelines are useful in preparing applications. This section presents a collection of common reasons why grants are rejected.

8.4.1 Mechanical Reasons for Rejection

1. Deadline for submission was not met.
2. Guidelines for proposal content, format, and length were not followed exactly.
3. The proposal was not absolutely clear in describing one or several elements of the study.
4. The proposal was not absolutely complete in describing one or several elements of the study.
5. The author(s) took highly partisan positions on issues and thus became vulnerable to the prejudices of the reviewers.
6. The quality of writing was poor—for example, sweeping and grandiose claims, convoluted reasoning, excessive repetition, or unreasonable length.
7. The proposal document contained an unreasonable number of mechanical defects that reflected carelessness and the author's unwillingness to attend to detail. The risk that the same attitudes might attend execution of the proposed study may not be acceptable to the reviewers, leading to rejection of the proposal.

8.4.2 Methodological Reasons for Rejection

1. The proposed question, design, and method were completely traditional, with nothing that could strike a reviewer as unusual, intriguing, or clever.
2. The proposed method of study was unsuited to the purpose of the research.

8.4.3 Personnel Reasons for Rejection

1. As revealed in the review of literature, the author(s) simply did not know the territory.
2. The proposed study appeared to be beyond the capacity of the author(s) in terms of training, experience, and available resources.

8.4.4 Cost-Benefit Reasons for Rejection

1. The proposed study was not an agency priority for *this* year.
2. The budget was unrealistic in terms of estimated requirements for equipment, supplies, and personnel.
3. The cost of the proposed project appeared to be greater than any possible benefit to be derived from its completion.

FURTHER READINGS ON GRANTSMANSHIP AND PROPOSAL WRITING 8.5

8.5.1 Proposal Writing

Brown, William F., & Kirby, Jane E. (1983). *Proposal preparation manual.* Washington, DC: U.S. Dept. of Transportation, Research and Special Programs Administration, Office of University Research.

Coley, Soraya M., & Scheinberg, Cynthia A. (2000). *Proposal writing.* Thousand Oaks, CA: Sage.

Friedland, Andrew J., & Folt, Carol L. (2000). *Writing successful science proposals.* New Haven, CT: Yale University Press.

Geever, Jane C. (2001). *The Foundation Center's guide to proposal writing.* New York: Foundation Center.

Haliman, Jack Parker, & Strier, Karen B. (1997). *Planning, proposing, and presenting science effectively: A guide to graduate students and researchers in behavioral science and biology.* New York: Cambridge University Press.

Hall, Mary K. S. (1988). *Getting funded: A complete guide to proposal writing* (3rd ed.). Continuing Education Publications, Portland State University.

Hamper, Robert J., & Baugh, L. Sue. (1996). *Handbook for writing proposals.* Chicago: NTC Publishing Group.

Locke, Lawrence F., Spirduso, Waneen Wyrick, & Silverman, Stephen J. (2000). *Proposals that work: A guide for planning dissertations and grant proposals* (4th ed.). Newbury Park, CA: Sage.

Meador, Roy. (1985). *Guidelines for preparing proposals: A manual on how to organize winning proposals for grants, venture capital, R&D projects and other proposals.* Chelsea, MI: Lewis.

Miner, Lynn E. (1998). *Directory of biomedical and health care grants 1998. With a guide of proposal planning and writing* (12th ed.). Phoenix, AZ: Oryx Press.

Peterson, Susan Louise. (1998). *The research writer's phrase book: A guide to proposal writing and research phraseology.* San Francisco: International Scholars Publications.

Stewart, Rodney D., & Stewart, Ann L. (1984). *Proposal presentations.* New York: Wiley.

8.5.2 Grantsmanship

Blaine, Lawrence. (1981). *Grant proposal: A practical guide to planning, funding, and managing.* Mill Valley, CA: Psyon.

Browning, Bev. (in press). *Grant writing for dummies.* New York: Hungry Minds.

Burke, Jim, & Prater, Carol Ann. (2000). *I'll grant you that: A step-by-step guide to finding funds, designing winning projects, and writing powerful proposals.* Woburn, MA: Heinemann.

Carlson, Mim, & Support Centers of America Staff. (1995). *Winning grants step by step.* San Francisco: Jossey-Bass.

Crombie, Iain K., & Florey, Charles D. (Eds.). (1998). *The pocket guide to grant applications.* London: BMJ.

Gilpatrick, Eleanor G. (1989). *Grants for nonprofit organizations: A guide to funding and grant writing.* New York: Praeger.

Gitlin, Laura N., & Lyons, Kevin J. (1996). *Successful grant writing: Strategies for health and human service professionals.* Heidelberg, Germany: Springer.

Hale, Phale D., Jr. (1997). *Writing grant proposals that win.* Gaitherburg, MD: Aspen.

Illes, Judy. (1999). *The strategic grant-seeker: A guide to conceptualizing fundable research in the brain and behavioral sciences.* Mahwah, NJ: Lawrence Erlbaum.

Lauffer, Armand. (1984). *Grantsmanship and fundraising.* Beverly Hills, CA: Sage.

Oryx Press Staff. (1996). *Directory of grants in the humanities 1996-1997: With a guide to proposal planning and writing.* Phoenix, AZ: Oryx Press.

Reif-Leher, Liane. (1982). *Writing a successful grant application.* Boston: Science Books International.

Reif-Leher, Liane. (1995). *Grant application writer's handbook.* Boston: Jones and Bartlett.

Sultz, Harry A., & Sherwin, Frances S. (1981). *Grant writing for health professionals.* Boston: Little, Brown.

White, Virginia (Ed.). (1983). *Grant proposals that succeeded.* New York: Plenum.

8.5.3 Other Sources of Information

8.5.3.1 GrantsNet

GrantsNet is an Internet application tool created by the Office of Grants Management (OGM) at the Department of Health and Human Services (DHHS) for finding and exchanging information about federal grant programs. GrantsNet serves the general public, the grantee and grantors such as state and local governments, educational institutions, nonprofit organizations, and commercial businesses. GrantsNet provides a variety of department-wide grants policies that govern the awarding and administration of grant activities, publishing these in grants policy directives, regulations, and/or manuals.

8.5.3.2 *Additional Web Sites for Foundations, Grant Writing, and Funding Sources*

The following Web sites may prove useful to grant seekers.

Announcements of Grants From the *Federal Register* at
www.ed.gov/legislation/FedRegister/

Federally Funded Research at
http://login.cos.com/loginForm?request_uri=http%3A%2F%2Ffundedresearch%2Ecos%2Ecom%2F&message=

Funding Opportunities From U.S. Government Information Sources gathered by the National Guide to U.S. Department of Education Programs and Resources at
http://web99.ed.gov/GTEP/Program2.nsf

Grant Opportunities from the University of Pittsburgh at
www.pitt.edu/~ian/resource/grants.htm

Grants Link, Inc. at
www.grantslink.com/

Grantsmanship Center at
www.tgci.com/

GrantsNet (for biomedical sciences and undergraduate science education) at
www.grantsnet.org/

A Guide for Proposal Writing (from the National Science Foundation) at
www.ehr.nsf.gov/EHR/DUE/documents/general/9783/proposal.htm

Hints for preparing funding proposals and grant applications (from Indiana University, Purdue University, Indianapolis) at
www.science.iupui.edu/wilson/Grantweb/home.html

Money Matters (from the U.S. Department of Education) at
www.ed.gov/funding.html

NonProfit Gateway (federal government grant and related information) at
www.nonprofit.gov/

Proposal Writer's Guide (from the University of Michigan) at
www.research.umich.edu/research/proposals/proposal_dev/pwg/PWGCONTENTS.HTML

Proposal Writing Short Course (from the Foundation Center) at
http://fdncenter.org/learn/shortcourse/prop1.html

THE NATIONAL SCIENCE FOUNDATION (NSF)

The National Science Foundation is an independent U.S. government agency responsible for promoting science and engineering through programs that invest more than $3.3 billion per year in almost 20,000 research and education projects in science and engineering. NSF receives approximately

30,000 proposals each year for research, education, and training projects, of which approximately 10,000 are funded. In addition, it receives several thousand applications for graduate and postdoctoral fellowships. NSF grants typically are awarded to universities, colleges, academic consortia, nonprofit institutions, and small businesses. NSF also supports cooperative research between universities and industry, U.S. participation in international scientific efforts, and educational activities at every academic level.

NSF is structured much like a university, with funding divisions for the various disciplines and fields of science and engineering, and for science, mathematics, engineering, and technology education. NSF also uses a variety of management mechanisms to coordinate research in areas that cross traditional disciplinary boundaries. NSF is helped by advisers from the scientific community who serve on formal committees or as ad hoc reviewers of proposals. This advisory system, which focuses on both program directions and specific proposals, involves approximately 50,000 scientists and engineers each year. NSF staff members who are experts in a certain field or area make award recommendations; proposers get unattributed verbatim copies of peer reviews.

Information may be obtained by writing to the foundation, and informal communication with the foundation's staff is encouraged prior to formal submission of a proposal.

Among a variety of forms of foundation support, the activities of greatest interest to sociologists are as follows.

1. Grants for *basic scientific research*, or for related activities, such as research conferences, construction of specialized research facilities, and travel to selected meetings of international scientific organizations of major importance. In addition, social science dissertation research grants provide funds for research expenses (not stipends) to improve the quality and significance of dissertations and reduce the time required for their completion. All these programs seek basic scientific understanding of behavioral and social processes and improved research methods. Support is provided for research that seeks to discover and test scientific generalizations. Criteria for the selection of research projects include (a) competent performance of the research, (b) intrinsic merit of the research, (c) utility or relevance of the research, and (d) effect of the research on the infrastructure of science and engineering.

2. *Computer research* including theoretical computer science, software systems, intelligent systems, and societal issues in computer science, including privacy and security, social and economic impact, and new directions in computer science and applications.

3. *Measurement methods and data resources* including survey operations research; methods and models for the quantitative analysis of social data; improvements in the scientific adequacy and accessibility of social statistical data, including those generated by government and by the academic research community; and development and testing of new social indicators.

4. *Institutional programs*, which include support of small college faculty in research at large institutions, and support for research workshops, symposia, publications and monographs, conferences, the purchase of scientific equipment for research purposes, the operation of specialized research facilities, and the improvement of research collections. The foundation has been encouraging working linkages between industry and universities in research activity (university cooperative research centers).

5. *International cooperative research programs*, which support research in health sciences, natural sciences, energy, and social and behavioral sciences.

6. *Socioeconomic aspects of science and technology* are supported by programs of the Societal Dimensions of Engineering, Science, and Technology, or SDEST (www.cep.unt.edu/EVS.html). SDEST folds together two former NSF programs, Ethics and Values Studies (EVS) and Research on Science and Technology (RST), in the Division of Social, Behavioral and Economic Research. EVS was originally called Ethics and Values in Science and Technology (EVIST). SDEST is the only U.S. government program that regularly seeks proposals and regularly funds projects in environmental ethics. The EVS component focuses on developing and transmitting knowledge about ethical and value dimensions associated with the conduct and impacts of science, engineering, and technology. The RST component supports research to improve approaches and information for decision making concerning management and direction of research, science, and technology.

Over the past few years, NSF has made approximately 40 new awards each year in these areas, with a budget of about $2.3 million. The overarching goals are to improve approaches to research and information for and from research in these fields; to make research results of broad use in educational, policy, and other settings; and to consider the implications of research results for the actions of a wide range of individuals and groups, as well as for theories and methods in all scientific and engineering fields.

You can easily find out the types of projects to which NSF is awarding funds by consulting the Award Data page at www.nsf.gov/home/grants/grants_awards.htm) and search by the following terms:

- List of recent awards
- List of awards by program
- List of awards by institution
- List of awards by state

A search in this site is an excellent way to find out if your ideas are consistent with NSF's mission. To search by a specific area, go to the Awards Abstract Database at www.fastlane.nsf.gov/a6/A6 AwardSearch.htm and enter keywords in a topic area. For example, Figure 8.2 shows the results of a search on social class.

8.6.1 Guide to National Science Foundation Programs

With respect to the social and behavior sciences, NSF makes grants and awards for social, behavioral, and economic research that builds fundamental knowledge of human behavior, interaction, and social and economic systems, organizations, and institutions. Most of this research is supported through the NSF divisions described in the following sections.

8.6.1.1 Division of Social and Economic Sciences (SES)

The Division of Social and Economic Sciences (SES) supports research to develop and advance scientific knowledge focusing on economic, legal, political, and social systems, organizations, and institutions. In addition, SES supports research on the intellectual and social contexts that govern the development and use of science and technology. SES programs also encourage and support interdisciplinary projects, which are evaluated through joint review among programs in SES as well as joint review with programs in other divisions, as well as in NSF-wide multidisciplinary panels as appropriate.

All programs in SES consider proposals for research projects, conferences, and workshops. Some programs also consider proposals for doctoral dissertation improvement assistance, the acquisition of specialized research and computing equipment, group international travel, and large-scale data

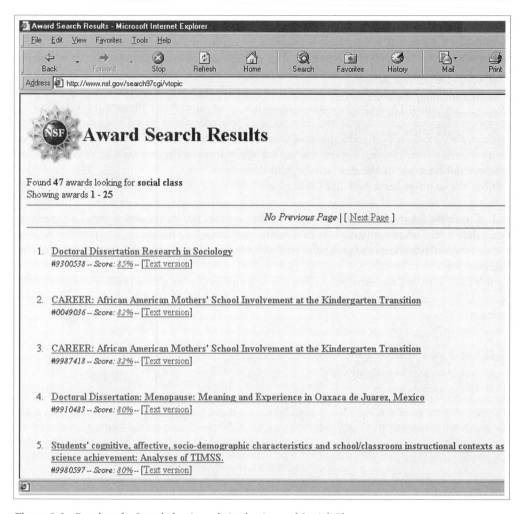

Figure 8.2. Results of a Search for Awards in the Area of Social Class

collection. SES participates in special initiatives and competitions on a number of topics, including human dimensions of global change and infrastructure to improve data resources, data archives, collaboratories, and centers.

Research support is available in the Division of Social and Economic Sciences through the following clusters of programs:

- Economic, Decision, and Management Sciences Cluster
- Methods, Cross-Directorate, and Science and Society Cluster
- Social and Political Sciences Cluster

For more information, see the Web site at www.nsf.gov/sbe/ses/start.htm.

The programs in the economic, decision, and management sciences cluster consist of the following:

- Decision, Risk, and Management Science
- Economics
- Innovation and Organizational Change

For more information, see the Web site mentioned above.

Particularly relevant to social and behavior scientists is the Methods, Cross-Directorate, and Science and Society cluster. This cluster of programs within the SES is composed of the following:

- Cross-Directorate Activities
- Methodology, Measurement, and Statistics
- Science and Technology Studies
- Societal Dimensions of Engineering, Science, and Technology: Ethics and Values Studies, Research on Science and Technology

For more information, see the Web site mentioned above, www.nsf.gov/sbe/ses/start.htm. More detail about these programs is provided below.

1. *Cross-Directorate Activities* provides information about various cross-directorate programs in which the Social, Behavioral, and Economic Sciences Directorate participates. For activities related to the social and behavioral sciences, the program administers the Research Experiences for Undergraduates Sites and Minority Postdoctoral Research Fellowships programs, and it coordinates the Faculty Early Career Development, Presidential Early Career Awards for Scientists and Engineers, and Small Business for Innovative Research programs. Also in the areas of social and behavioral sciences, the program officers for Cross- Directorate Activities can provide information about special opportunities NSF offers for minority and women investigators and for education initiatives.

2. *Methodology, Measurement, and Statistics* supports fundamental research on the development, application, and extension of formal models and methodologies for social and behavioral research, including methods for improving measurement and research on statistical methodology or statistical modeling that has direct implications for one or more of the social and behavioral sciences. Also supported are research on methodological aspects of new or existing procedures for data collection; research to evaluate or compare existing databases and data collection procedures; the collection of unique databases with cross-disciplinary implications, especially when paired with developments in measurement or methodology; and the methodological infrastructure of social and behavioral research.

3. *Science and Technology Studies* supports historical, philosophical, cognitive, and social research regarding the character and development of science and technology, the nature of theory and evidence in different fields, and the social and intellectual construction of science and technology. Support is also given to research that examines the relationship among science, government, and other social institutions and groups, and to research on processes of scientific innovation and change.

4. *Societal Dimensions of Engineering, Science, and Technology: Ethics and Values Studies, Research on Science and Technology* includes Ethics and Values Studies (EVS) and Research on Science and Technology (RST). The EVS component focuses on improving knowledge about ethical and value dimensions in science, engineering, and technology. The RST component focuses on improving approaches and information for decision making about investment in science, engineering, and technology.

The Social and Political Sciences cluster of programs within the SES consists of the following:

- Law and Social Science
- Political Science
- Sociology

More information is available at the Web site mentioned earlier, www.nsf.gov/sbe/ses/start.htm. More detail concerning this cluster follows.

1. *Law and Social Science* supports social science studies of law and lawlike systems of rule, institutions, processes, and behavior. These studies may include research designed to enhance the scientific understanding of the impact of law; human behavior and interaction as they relate to law; the dynamics of legal decision making; and the nature, source, and consequence of variation and change in legal institutions. The primary consideration is that the research shows promise of advancing the scientific understanding of law and legal process. Within this framework, the program has an "open window" for diverse theoretical perspectives, methods, and contexts for study.

2. *Political Science* supports scientific research that advances knowledge and understanding of citizenship, government, and politics. Research proposals are expected to be theoretically motivated, conceptually clear, methodologically rigorous, and empirically oriented. Substantive areas for research proposals include American government and politics, comparative government and politics, international relations, political behavior, political economy, and political institutions. In recent years, program awards have supported research projects on bargaining processes; campaigns and elections, electoral choice, and electoral systems; citizen support in emerging and established democracies; democratization, political change, and regime transitions; domestic and international conflict; international political economy; party activism; and political psychology and political tolerance. On occasion, program awards also have supported research experiences for undergraduate students, methodological advances in political science, and infrastructural improvements through conference activities.

3. *Sociology* supports scientific research on all forms of human social organization: societies, institutions, groups, and demography. The program encourages theoretically focused empirical investigations of social processes and social structures. It welcomes research that will build connections with other disciplines. Recent awards supported by the program include research on assimilation, crime and delinquency, democratization, education, family, gender, group processes, migration and immigration, organizations and organizational behavior, race and ethnic relations, religion, science and technology, social movements, social networks, stratification and mobility, voluntary organizations, and work and labor markets. The program also promotes doctoral research through Dissertation Improvement Grants.

8.6.1.2 *Division of Behavioral and Cognitive Sciences (BCS)*

The Division of Behavioral and Cognitive Sciences (BCS) supports research to develop and advance scientific knowledge focusing on human cognition, language, social behavior, and culture, as well as research on the interactions between human societies and the physical environment. BCS programs also encourage and support interdisciplinary projects, which are evaluated through joint review among programs in BCS, as well as joint review with programs in other divisions and through NSF-wide multidisciplinary panels, as appropriate.

All programs in BCS consider proposals for research projects, conferences, and workshops. Some programs also consider proposals for doctoral dissertation improvement assistance, the acquisition of specialized research and computing equipment, group international travel, and large-scale data collection. BCS participates in special initiatives and competitions on a number of topics, including the human dimensions of global change, cognitive science and intelligent systems, and infrastructure to improve data resources, data archives, and centers.

Research support is available in BCS through the following clusters of programs:

■■ Anthropological and Geographic Sciences Cluster
■■ Cognitive, Psychological, and Language Sciences Cluster

For more information, see the Web site at www.nsf.gov/sbe/bcs/start.htm.

The Cognitive, Psychological, and Language Sciences cluster of programs, perhaps the cluster most closely related to what social and behavioral scientists do, is composed of the following.

■■ Child Learning and Development
■■ Human Cognition and Perception
■■ Linguistics
■■ Social Psychology

Because these different program areas are so closely related to the interests of social and behavioral scientists, they are described in detail below.

1. *Child Learning and Development* supports research on cognitive, social, and biological processes related to children's and adolescents' learning in formal and informal settings. Priority is given to supporting research on learning and development that incorporates multidisciplinary, multimethod, microgenetic, and longitudinal approaches; develops new methods and theories; examines transfer of knowledge from one domain to another; assesses peer relations, family interactions, social identities, and motivation; examines the impact of family, school, and community resources; assesses adolescents' preparation for entry into the workforce; and investigates the role of demographic and cultural characteristics in children's learning and development.

2. *Human Cognition and Perception* supports research on human perceptual and cognitive processes, including the development of these processes. Emphasis is on research strongly grounded in theory. Research topics include vision, audition, haptic perception, attention, object recognition, language processing, spatial representation, motor control, memory, reasoning, and concept formation. The program encompasses a wide range of theoretical perspectives such as experimental computation, connectionism, and ecological perception, as well as a variety of methodologies such as experimental studies and computational modeling. Research involving acquired or developmental deficits is appropriate if the results speak to basic issues in the study of normal perception or cognition.

3. *Linguistics* supports theoretically informed scientific research that focuses on human language as an object of investigation. The program encompasses a wide range of theoretical perspectives and a variety of methodologies, including experimental studies and computational modeling. Research topics include the properties of individual languages and of language in general; language acquisition; the psychological processes involved in the use of language; social and cultural factors in language use, variation, and change; the acoustics of speech and speech production and perception; and the biological bases of language in the central nervous system.

4. *Social Psychology* supports research on human and social behavior, including cultural influences and development over the life span. Research topics include aggression; altruism; attitude formation and change; attitudes and behavior; attributional processes; emotion; environmental psychology; group decision making, performance, and process; intergroup relations; interpersonal attraction and relations; nonverbal communication; person perception; personality processes; prejudice; the self; social cognition; social comparison; social influence; and stereotyping.

8.6.1.3 Division of Graduate Education

The Division of Graduate Education (DGE) provides support for graduate students, postdoctoral fellows, and graduate education programs to ensure the strength, diversity, and vitality of the science and engineering workforce in the United States. DGE aims to enhance the flexibility and appropriateness of graduate programs at various levels in order to maintain the preeminence of American science, mathematics, and engineering, as well as to strengthen the U.S. economy. Activities supported by the division fortify the links between higher education and K-12 education; recognize and support a diverse pool of outstanding individuals in their pursuit of advanced science, mathematics, engineering, and technology education; and support innovative models of graduate education. DGE supports research and education through the following programs and activities:

- Graduate Research Fellowships
- Graduate Teaching Fellowships in K-12 Education
- Integrative Graduate Education and Research Traineeships
- NSF-NATO Postdoctoral Fellowships in Science and Engineering
- Travel Grants for NATO Advanced Study Institutes

More information is available at the Web site www.ehr.nsf.gov/EHR/DGE/dge.htm.

8.6.1.4 Division of Human Resource Development

The Division of Human Resource Development (HRD) has primary responsibility for broadening the participation of groups underrepresented at the K-12, undergraduate, and graduate levels in science, mathematics, engineering, and technology, as well as for improving the research infrastructure of minority institutions. The division operates and coordinates a range of programs that focus on increasing the presence of underrepresented minorities, women and girls, and persons with disabilities in science and engineering. HRD supports programs and activities in the following focus areas:

- Minorities and Minority-Serving Institutions
- Women and Girls
- Persons With Disabilities

For more information, see the Web site at www.ehr.nsf.gov/EHR/HRD/default.asp.

8.6.1.5 Division of Research, Evaluation, and Communication

The Division of Research, Evaluation, and Communication provides a research-based foundation for teaching and learning in science, mathematics, engineering, and technology (SMET), using the results of research in technology utilization, content, pedagogy, assessment, and policy-oriented studies and indicators. This division supports projects that investigate the learning process and integrate research with educational practices, including those that provide the groundwork for the effective use of technology. The division provides support for NSF's participation in the Interagency Education Research Initiative and for participation of the Directorate for Education and Human Resources in the agency-wide Faculty Early Career Development Program.

For more information, see the Web site at www.ehr.nsf.gov/EHR/REC.

8.6.1.6 Division of Undergraduate Education

The Division of Undergraduate Education serves as the focal point for NSF's efforts in undergraduate education. Whether preparing students to participate as citizens in a technological society, enter the workforce with 2- or 4-year degrees, continue their formal education in graduate school, or further their education in response to new career goals or workplace expectations, undergraduate education provides the critical link between the nation's secondary schools and a society increasingly dependent on science and technology.

The Division of Undergraduate Education supports the following programs and activities:

- Advanced Technological Education
- Course, Curriculum, and Laboratory Improvement
- NSF Computer Science, Engineering, and Mathematics Scholarships
- National Science, Mathematics, Engineering, and Technology Education Digital Library

For more information, see the Web site at www.ehr.nsf.gov/EHR/DUE/.

8.6.2 Funding Opportunities

What follows is a description of programs and funding opportunities available through NSF that are relevant to social and behavioral scientists.

8.6.2.1 Programs at the Undergraduate Level

Activities to enhance undergraduate education in science and engineering are supported throughout NSF. In particular, the Division of Undergraduate Education (DUE) in the Directorate of Education and Human Resources offers focused programs for the education of technologists, primarily through community colleges, and for the education of future teachers (see www.nsf.gov/home/crssprgm/reu/start.htm). On a broader scale, DUE supports course, curriculum, and laboratory improvement aimed at all undergraduate students, both majors in science and engineering and those not majoring in those fields. In addition, some of NSF's disciplinary directorates offer programs in support of course development. Information on these can be found within the directorate sections of this guide.

NSF is committed to the education of a science and engineering workforce drawn broadly from the nation's talent pool. To increase diversity at the undergraduate level, NSF offers the Louis Stokes Alliances for Minority Participation. To provide opportunities for participation in research, NSF supports the Research Experiences for Undergraduates program, which in turn supports active research participation by undergraduate students in any of the research areas funded by NSF. These projects involve students in meaningful ways in ongoing research programs or in research projects specially designed to involve them in research activities.

8.6.2.2 Programs at the Graduate and Postdoctoral Levels

NSF is a major supporter of graduate and postdoctoral education in science and engineering. The majority of this support is embedded in research awards to institutions, with the funds used to support graduate research assistants and postdoctoral associates. NSF also supports fellowships and traineeships in the following programs:

- Graduate Research Fellowships
- Integrative Graduate Education and Research Traineeship (IGERT) Program
- NSF Graduate Teaching Fellows in K-12 Education

8.6.2.3 Postdoctoral Fellowships

In addition to supporting postdoctoral associates through NSF research awards to institutions, NSF offers a number of postdoctoral fellowship programs in specific disciplines. For more information, contact the National Science Foundation at:

4201 Wilson Blvd., Rm. 615
Arlington, VA 22230
703-292-8470.

8.6.2.4 Programs for Faculty and Institutional Development

One of NSF's core strategies is the integration of research and education into the career development of faculty. NSF also encourages research by faculty members of predominantly undergraduate institutions by supporting their substantial contributions to research and education. Special research opportunities are available for these faculty as well as for faculty who are underrepresented minorities. Such research opportunities are available from NSF through the following programs:

- Faculty Early Career Development
- NSF Component of the Presidential Early Career Awards for Scientists and Engineers
- Research in Undergraduate Institutions and Research Opportunity Awards
- Minority Research Planning Grants and Career Advancement Awards
- Presidential Awards for Excellence in Science, Mathematics, and Engineering Mentoring

1. The *Faculty Early Career Development (CAREER)* program, which ranges across NSF, supports junior faculty within the context of their overall career development. More information is available at www.eng.nsf.gov/career/.

2. Each year, NSF selects up to 20 nominees for the *NSF Component of the Presidential Early Career Awards for Scientists and Engineers (PECASE)*. Nominees are selected from among the most meritorious first-year awardees supported by the Faculty Early Career Development (CAREER) Program (see description of CAREER above). More information is available at www.nsf.gov/home/crssprgm/pecase/start.htm.

3. The *Research in Undergraduate Institutions (RUI)* activity supports research by faculty members from predominantly undergraduate institutions through funding individual and collaborative research projects, the purchase of shared-use research instrumentation, and Research Opportunity Awards for work with NSF-supported investigators from other institutions. All NSF directorates participate in the RUI activity. RUI proposals are evaluated and funded by the NSF program in the disciplinary area of the proposed research. The objectives of RUI are to support high-quality research, strengthen the research environment in academic departments that are oriented primarily toward undergraduate instruction, and promote the integration of research and education. More information is available at www.ehr.nsf.gov/crssprgm/rui/program.shtm.

4. The *Minority Research Planning Grants and Career Advancement Awards* are part of NSF's overall effort to give members of minority groups that are underrepresented in science and engineering greater access to scientific research support. The program includes Minority Research Planning Grants and Minority Career Advancement Awards.

5. *Presidential Awards for Excellence in Science, Mathematics, and Engineering Mentoring* are administered by NSF on behalf of the White House. The program seeks to identify outstanding mentoring efforts and programs that are designed to enhance the participation of groups traditionally underrepresented in science, mathematics, and engineering. For more information, see www.ehr.nsf.gov/ehr/hrd/paesmem.asp.

NSF emphasizes developing the research capacity of faculty across a range of institutions, including the predominantly undergraduate institutions previously mentioned as well as institutions that have had low participation in NSF programs in the past. The Experimental Program to Stimulate Competitive Research (EPSCoR) is an example of this emphasis. The following are two examples of specialized programs aimed at the enhancement of research and education in institutions that serve student populations with heavy minority representation:

- Historically Black Colleges and Universities—Undergraduate Program
- Centers for Research Excellence in Science and Technology

8.6.2.5 *Programs for Groups Underrepresented in Science and Engineering*

NSF has a number of special programs that address members of groups underrepre- sented in science. Activities are aimed at increasing the participation of underrepresented minorities, including American Indians/Alaskan Natives, Blacks, Hispanics, and Pacific Islanders; improving the recruitment and retention of women and girls in science and engineering careers; and ensuring that persons with disabilities have the opportunity to participate fully in NSF-supported projects. Although not all these initiatives have immediate importance to the social or behavioral science, most NSF divisions accept applications that focus on these areas and should be considered by aspiring researchers.

Some of these program and activities are identified below. Information about them can be obtained through a search on the main NSF Internet site, www.nsf.gov.

Directorate for Biological Sciences

- Minority Postdoctoral Research Fellowships and Supporting Activities

Directorate for Computer and Information Science and Engineering

- CISE Minority Institutions Infrastructure
- Information Technology Workforce Program

Directorate for Education and Human Resources

- Alliances for Graduate Education and the Professorate
- Centers of Research Excellence in Science and Technology
- Historically Black Colleges and Universities Undergraduate Program
- Louis Stokes Alliances for Minority Participation
- Presidential Awards for Excellence in Science, Mathematics, and Engineering Mentoring
- Program for Gender Equity in Science, Mathematics, Engineering, and Technology
- Program for Persons with Disabilities

Directorate for Engineering

▪▪ Biomedical Engineering and Research to Aid Persons with Disabilities
▪▪ Supplemental Funding for Support of Women, Minorities, and Physically Disabled Engineering Research Assistants

NSF-Wide Activities

▪▪ Minority Research Planning Grants and Career Advancement Awards
▪▪ Facilitation Awards for Scientists and Engineers with Disabilities

8.6.3 How to Apply to the NSF for Funding

The following are typical steps in applying for NSF funding.

1. Investigate the funding opportunities at NSF that may be available to you. See the current and new opportunities at the main NSF site (www.nsf.gov); also review the generic eligibility categories specified in the Grant Proposal Guide.
2. Select the funding area that best represents your field by visiting the corresponding Web site to review current funding opportunities. It is vital to check whether there are any special programmatic requirements and that you carefully follow the instructions in the program announcement.
3. Review the target dates and deadlines for the program you have selected.
4. Contact the relevant program officer(s) if you have any questions or need additional information.
5. Read chapter 2 in the Grant Proposal Guide for instructions on how to prepare and submit a proposal to NSF. Then read the Guide to Getting Started on FastLane for additional guidance on preparing your proposal for electronic submission. The NSF FastLane system (see the Web site www.fastlane.nsf.gov/a1/newinst.htm) uses Internet technology to facilitate the way NSF works with research, education, and related communities. Effective October 1, 2000, use of the NSF FastLane system is required for proposal preparation, submission and status checking, project reporting, and post-award administrative activities. All this information is available at the main Web site (www.nsf.gov).
6. Most organizations have a sponsored research office (SRO) or equivalent administrative entity that is authorized to submit proposals for the organization. Work closely with that office as you prepare your proposal, especially on budget and cost issues.
7. Submit your proposal using FastLane (at www.fastlane.nsf.gov/a1/newinst.htm). Use of FastLane is mandatory as of October 1, 2000.

8.6.3.1 Deadlines and Target Dates

Information about most deadlines can be found in the NSF *E-Bulletin*, an electronic publication available at www.nsf.gov/home/ebulletin/. Individual program announcements and solicitations also carry deadline and target date information, as do NSF Division Web sites. A list of all deadlines sorted by date and by program area is available at www.nsf.gov/home/deadline/deadline.htm.

8.6.3.2 Eligibility Requirements

Except where a program solicitation establishes more restrictive eligibility criteria, individuals and organizations in the following categories may submit proposals to NSF:

- *Universities and colleges:* U.S. universities and 2- and 4-year colleges (including community colleges) acting on behalf of their faculty members. Keep in mind that it is the sponsoring institution that is awarded the research funding and not the individual.

- *Nonprofit, non-academic organizations:* Independent museums, observatories, research laboratories, professional societies, and similar organizations in the United States that are directly associated with education or research activities.

- *For-profit organizations:* U.S. commercial organizations, especially small businesses with capabilities in scientific or engineering research and education.

- *State and local governments:* State educational offices or organizations and local school districts may submit proposals intended to broaden the impact and increase the effectiveness of improvements in science, mathematics, and engineering education in both K-12 and postsecondary levels.

- *Unaffiliated individuals:* Scientists, engineers, and educators in the United States and U.S. citizens may be eligible for support, provided that the individual is not employed by or affiliated with an organization.

8.6.3.3 Merit Review Criteria for the Selection of Research and Education Projects

Funding decisions on proposals are made through the process of merit review, in which expert evaluation by external peer reviewers contributes to recommendations by NSF program managers. NSF receives more than 170,000 external reviews each year from approximately 50,000 scientists and engineers. Reviews consider such questions as the following:

- What is the intellectual merit of the proposed activity?
- How important is the proposed activity to advancing knowledge and understanding within its own field or across different fields?
- How well qualified is the proposer (individual or team) to conduct the project?
- To what extent does the proposed activity suggest and explore creative and original concepts?
- How well conceived and organized is the proposed activity?
- Is there sufficient access to resources?
- What are the broader impacts of the proposed activity?
- How well does the activity advance discovery and understanding while promoting teaching, training, and learning?
- How well does the proposed activity broaden the participation of underrepresented groups (e.g., groups defined by gender, ethnicity, disability, or geography)?
- To what extent will it enhance the infrastructure for research and education, such as facilities, instrumentation, networks, and partnerships?
- Will the results be disseminated broadly to enhance scientific and technological understanding?
- What may be the benefits of the proposed activity to society?

Note: Information in this section is adapted from information found at the Web site www.nsf.gov.

8.6.4 NSF Publications

The *NSF E-Bulletin* is a Web publication, updated daily, that announces current deadline and target dates for the submission of proposals to NSF. A print-on-demand monthly edition is available for those without Internet access. The *E-Bulletin* can be found at www.nsf.gov/home/ebulletin/.

8.6.4.1 How to Obtain NSF Publications

NSF strongly encourages electronic dissemination of its documents and offers several ways of obtaining publications electronically. The Online Document System (ODS) includes all forms and publications available electronically from NSF. The ODS offers a search capability that allows searches by document type, publication title, form number, and keyword. The ODS home page is at www.nsf.gov/cgi-bin/pubsys/browser/odbrowse.pl. For a list of current NSF documents available in electronic format, visit the ODS Index at www.nsf.gov/pubsys/index.htm.

8.6.4.2 The Nine Most Popular NSF Publications

The Web site www.nsf.gov/home/pubinfo/popular.htm lists the most requested publications from NSF. All are available electronically. A sample from a listing posted in 2001 follows.

- Grant Proposal Guide—NSF 01-2 ADDENDUM, Effective June 1, 2001
- Guide to Programs, Fiscal Year 2001
- Small Business Innovation Research and Small Business Technology Transfer Programs, Phase I Solicitation FY-2001
- Faculty Early Career Development Program
- Grant Proposal Guide—NSF 01-2
- A Guide for Proposal Writing
- Course, Curriculum, and Laboratory Improvement Program Solicitation
- NSF Graduate Teaching Fellows in K-12 Education
- Elementary, Secondary, and Informal Education Program Solicitation and Guidelines

8.7 NATIONAL INSTITUTES OF HEALTH (NIH)

Begun as a one-room Laboratory of Hygiene in 1887, the National Institutes of Health today is one of the world's foremost medical research centers and is the federal focal point for medical research in the United States. NIH is now part of the Department of Health and Human Services, but it is treated here as a distinct entry because it provides so much research funding.

The NIH mission is to uncover new knowledge that will lead to better health for everyone by

- Conducting research in its own laboratories
- Supporting the research of non-federal scientists in universities, medical schools, hospitals, and research institutions throughout the country and abroad
- Helping in the training of research investigators and fostering communication of medical information

NIH is one of eight health agencies of the Public Health Service. As of 2001, NIH was composed of 27 separate components, mainly institutes and centers. In all, NIH had 75 buildings on more than 300 acres in Bethesda, Maryland. From a total of about $300 in 1887, the NIH budget had grown to more than $20.3 billion in 2001. Approximately 10% of the budget goes to NIH's Intramural Research Programs, the more than 2,000 projects conducted mainly in its own laboratories. About 8% of the budget is for research support costs associated with both intramural and extramural research.

8.7.1 NIH Institutes of Interest to Social and Behavioral Scientists

Of the 27 separate institutes, centers, and offices of NIH, the following are likely to be of greatest interest for social and behavioral scientists seeking funding for their research.

8.7.1.1 The National Institute of Aging (NIA)

The National Institute on Aging (NIA) leads an effort to understand the nature of aging and to extend the healthy, active years of human life. The NIA's mission is to improve the health and well-being of older Americans through research, and specifically to

- Support and conduct high-quality research on aging processes, age-related diseases, and special problems and needs of the aged
- Train and develop skilled research scientists from all population groups
- Develop and maintain resources to accelerate research progress
- Disseminate information and communicate with the public and interested groups on health, research advances, and new directions for research

For more information, contact NIA at

National Institute on Aging
Building 31, Room 5C27
31 Center Drive, MSC 2292
Bethesda, MD 20892
301-496-1752
www.nih.gov/nia/

8.7.1.2 The National Institute on Alcohol Abuse and Alcoholism (NIAAA)

The National Institute on Alcohol Abuse and Alcoholism (NIAAA) supports and conducts biomedical and behavioral research on the causes, consequences, treatment, and prevention of alcoholism and alcohol-related problems. It focuses on these topics by

- Conducting and supporting research directed at determining the causes of alcoholism, discovering how alcohol damages the organs of the body, and developing prevention and treatment strategies for application in the nation's health care system
- Supporting and conducting research across a wide range of scientific areas including genetics, neuroscience, medical consequences, medication development, prevention, and treatment
- Conducting policy studies that have implications for prevention of alcohol-related problems, treatment of these problems, and rehabilitation activities
- Conducting epidemiological studies
- Maintaining continuing relationships with international, national, state, and local officials, institutions, professional associations, and voluntary agencies and organizations engaged in alcohol-related work
- Disseminating research findings to health care providers, researchers, policymakers, and the public

For more information, contact NIAAA at

National Institute on Alcohol Abuse and Alcoholism
6000 Executive Boulevard—Willco Building
Bethesda, MD 20892-7003
www.niaaa.nih.gov/

8.7.1.3 *National Institute of Child Heath and Human Development (NICHD)*

The National Institute of Child Health and Human Development (NICHD) seeks to ensure that every individual is born healthy and wanted, that women suffer no adverse consequence from the reproductive process, and that all children have the opportunity to fulfill their potential for a healthy and productive life unhampered by disease or disability.

NICHD conducts and supports laboratory, clinical, and epidemiological research on the reproductive, neurobiologic, developmental, and behavioral processes that determine and maintain the health of children, adults, families, and populations. It administers a multidisciplinary program of research, research training, and public information, nationally and within its own facilities.

For more information, contact NICHD at

National Institute of Child Health and Human Development
Bldg. 31, Room 2A32, MSC 2425
31 Center Drive
Bethesda, MD 20892-2425
www.nichd.nih.gov/

8.7.1.4 *The National Institute of Mental Health (NIMH)*

The mission of the National Institute of Mental Health (NIMH) is to conduct research aimed at diminishing the burden of mental illness. Meeting this public health mandate demands the harnessing of powerful scientific tools to achieve better understanding, treatment, and—eventually—prevention of mental illness.

For more information, contact NIMH at

NIMH Public Inquiries
6001 Executive Blvd., Rm. 8184, MSC 9663
Bethesda, MD 20892-9663
301-443-4513; fax: 301-443-4279
http://www.nimh.nih.gov/

8.7.2 Office of Extramural Research Funding Opportunities

NIH has both an intramural and an extramural funding program. About 10% of the resources available for funding are dedicated to the intramural (in-house) research activities. The examining 90% is dedicated to extramural programs housed in universities and research centers that are unaffiliated with NIH.

8.7.2.1 NIH Academic Research Enhancement Award (AREA) Grants

AREA grants support individual research projects in the biomedical and behavioral sciences. These projects, which involve undergraduate students, are conducted by faculty who are located in schools for health professionals and other academic components that have not been major recipients of NIH research grant funds.

8.7.2.2 NIH Investigator-Initiated Interactive Research Project Grant (IRPG)

The Interactive Research Project Grant (IRPG) program provides support for formal, investigator-initiated, collaborative relationships.

8.7.2.3 NIH Career Development Awards

Numerous Career Development Awards are available to researchers. The Career Award Wizard (at http://grants.nih.gov/training/kwizard/index.htm) leads the user through a series of questions to help determine which is the best individual career award to apply for.

8.7.2.4 Research Supplements for Individuals With Disabilities

The President's Task Force on Women, Minorities, and the Handicapped in Science and Technology has documented a low participation rate in the science and engineering workforce for Americans with disabilities. To address this, NIH and its awarding components have developed an initiative that is designed to extend opportunities to individuals with qualifying disabilities who are capable of entering or resuming research careers. Under this initiative, NIH offers supplemental awards to certain ongoing research grants to encourage individuals with disabilities to pursue research careers in the biomedical, behavioral, clinical, or social sciences.

For more information, refer to the Web site at

http://grants.nih.gov/grants/guide/pa-files/PA-01-080.html

8.7.2.5 NIH National Research Service Award (NRSA) Institutional Research Training Grants

NIH awards National Research Service Award (NRSA) Institutional Research Training Grants to eligible institutions to develop or enhance research training opportunities for individuals, selected by the institution, who are training for careers in specified areas of biomedical and behavioral research. The purpose of the NRSA program is to help ensure that a diverse and highly trained workforce is available to assume leadership roles related to the nation's biomedical and behavioral research agenda. Accordingly, the NRSA program supports predoctoral, postdoctoral, and short-term research training experiences.

For more information, see the Web site at

http://grants.nih.gov/grants/guide/pa-files/PA-00-103.html

8.7.2.6 National Research Service Award Short-Term Institutional Research Training Grants

NIH awards National Research Service Awards (NRSA) Short-Term Institutional Research Training Grants to eligible institutions to develop or enhance research training opportunities for individuals interested in careers in biomedical and behavioral research. Many of the NIH institutes and centers use this grant mechanism exclusively to support intensive, short-term research training experiences for students in schools for health professionals during the summer.

For more information, see the Web site at

http://grants.nih.gov/grants/guide/notice-files/not98-027.html

8.7.2.7 Predoctoral Fellowship Awards for Minority Students

This is a relatively new type of award from the NIH, also under the NRSA program. Individual Predoctoral Fellowships for Minority Students will provide up to 5 years of support for research training leading to the PhD or equivalent research degree, the combined MD/PhD degree, or other combined professional doctorate/research PhD degrees in the biomedical or behavioral sciences.

For more information, see the Web site at

http://grants.nih.gov/grants/guide/pa-files/PA-95-029.html

8.7.2.8 Predoctoral Fellowship Awards for Students With Disabilities

These fellowships will provide up to 5 years of support for research training leading to the PhD or equivalent research degree, the combined MD/PhD degree, or other combined professional doctorate/research PhD degrees in the biomedical or behavioral
sciences. Support is not available for individuals enrolled in medical or other professional schools unless they are enrolled in a combined professional doctorate/PhD degree program in biomedical or behavioral research.

For more information, see the Web site at

http://grants.nih.gov/grants/guide/pa-files/PA-00-068.html

8.7.3 Applying for an NIH Grant

If you are interested in applying for an NIH grant or fellowship, the best way to begin the process is by talking to a program official whose responsibilities lie in the scientific area in which you are interested in doing your research. To find out whom to talk to, try starting with the NIH home page (www.nih.gov) or calling the Grants Information Office (301-435-0714) in the NIH Center for Scientific Review (CSR). Grant applications should be submitted using the standard application form PHS 398, available from the office of sponsored research at most institutions or from the CSR, which can be contacted at the phone number above. NIH is currently developing a system for electronic application submission, but as of 2001 applications were required to be submitted on paper.

Once your proposal is submitted, it undergoes a two-level process of peer review before becoming eligible for funding. It typically takes at least 9 months from the time an application is received until the time a grant award can be made. Certain types of grants and fellowships are reviewed and awarded on a faster schedule that takes about 6 months. These schedules reinforce the idea that the researcher must be very well organized and plan well ahead.

The first step in processing a grant application is assignment. Scientists in the CSR assign each application to both an initial review group and an NIH institute or center. The review group is composed of scientists and others with expertise in a given subject area and is administered by a scientist known as a Scientific Review Administrator. Most investigator-initiated grant applications are reviewed by standing committees, known as study sections or initial review groups. These are administered by the CSR. Each of these committees meets three times a year to evaluate the scientific/technical merit of each application assigned to it. In addition to the CSR-based review groups, each of the NIH institutes and centers also administers at least one initial review group. These committees review other types of applications, such as many program projects, training grants, or centers.

In all cases, the conclusions of the review committee are recorded in a written evaluative statement, known as a summary statement. For applications whose quality is considered to be in the upper half of applications reviewed, a priority score is assigned as a quantitative measure of the reviewers' opinion of the proposal.

Finally, a percentile score is calculated to indicate the relative ranking of the application within the larger group of applications reviewed by that review group at its last three meetings. Review groups also make recommendations about the budget and length of support requested. (Currently, as part of attempts to "streamline" the NIH grant award process, NIH is evaluating a system in which the investigator would not have to submit detailed budget information or certain other supporting material until it is clear that his or her application is being considered for funding.)

The summary statement and scores are provided to the applicant, as well as to appropriate officials in the institute or center to which the application has been assigned. Within most institutes at NIH, scored applications then receive a second level of review, carried out by the institute's or center's National Advisory Council (NAC). This committee, composed of scientists and members of the public, provides the institute with programmatic and policy advice about the institute's programs. By law, a grant application must receive NAC approval to be eligible for funding.

Once an NAC has approved an application, it becomes eligible for funding. Funding decisions are made by institute staff, taking into account many factors, including the scientific merit of the application, its program relevance, and the budget of the institute.

8.7.3.1 Preparing an NIH Proposal

Applications should be submitted to the Center for Scientific Review (CSR), at the NIH, on the appropriate application form (usually PHS form 398). The form is available at the office of sponsored research at many institutions and can be downloaded from the World Wide Web at http://grants. nih.gov/grants/funding/funding.htm. The CSR assigns each application to an NIH institute or center and to an Initial Review Group (IRG), such as Health Promotion and Disease Prevention. (An applicant may request, in a cover letter, the assignment of his or her application to a particular institute and/or IRG. The CSR usually honors such requests and considers them helpful.)

If you have been in contact with program staff in the process of developing your application, mention this and provide the contact person's name and telephone number. You should also indicate on the face page of the application that it is in response to a particular program announcement or an RFA when this is appropriate. The assignment to an institute and an IRG is the first official step in the 9-month review process. You can obtain preliminary feedback about 4 to 5 months after the submission of your application by contacting program staff. In addition, a summary of critiques of your application will be sent to you as soon as it is available.

The IRGs are the main evaluating groups for applications and form the core of the peer review system. A secondary review is conducted by the respective institute's Advisory Council. IRGs review applications for scientific merit in terms of novelty, originality, and feasibility of the approach; the training, experience, and research competence of the investigators; the adequacy of the research design; the suitability of the facilities; and the appropriateness of the requested budget to the proposed work.

Reviewers are asked to identify applications that they judge noncompetitive and to designate these applications as nonscored. Applications so designated are deemed to be not competitive for funding when compared to other applications. Although a summary statement still is prepared, it is only a compilation of reviewers' comments and does not contain budget recommendations.

There is no further review at the level of Advisory Council. Applicants are free to revise and resubmit their applications after taking into account the reviewers' comments. Only applications that are deemed to be competitive are discussed by the review group and assigned priority scores. These applications are compared to all the applications assigned to the review group, not just those actually reviewed. The institute's decision to fund or not to fund an application is based primarily on the evaluations of the scientific merit made by the IRG.

8.7.3.2 Planning Your Application

You should keep some key steps and deadlines in mind prior to, during, and after your application is prepared.

1. The standard deadlines for new NIH grant applications are February 1, June 1, and October 1.
2. The deadlines for Requests for Applications (RFAs) may differ. The review and award process of applications submitted to NIH takes, on average, about 9 months.
3. Read the program announcement or RFA in detail. Before you start writing your grant application, read the pertinent instructions carefully and become thoroughly familiar with all the requirements and certifications necessary. If necessary, find someone who, based on his or her experience, can assist you in understanding and completing the requirements. Incomplete applications are returned without review.
4. Establish investigators' own deadlines for preparation of the grant application, particularly when collaborating investigators are involved. Be aware of institutional deadlines that could affect your application.
5. Do not hesitate to request technical assistance from the funding agency or your institution. Contact the scientific review administrator who will coordinate the peer review process or the program officer who will manage your award for advice on scientific and technical issues. Seek advice from the NIH grants management specialist on administrative issues.
6. When your application is completed, proofread it, then have someone else read and comment on it. Make sure someone has final editing responsibilities.
7. If available, have senior scientists (for example, successful grantees or objective experts) review your application. Keep in mind, however, that professional colleagues or close associates may not be as critical as the scientific reviewers at NIH.
8. Inquire about funding priorities of funding agencies and ascertain from the program officer whether your application falls within the scope of agencies' established priorities.
9. When submitting a revision of an application that originally responded to an RFA, keep in mind that the application must provide all scientific rationale, significance, potential contribution, and other merits because it will go to a review group different from the one that originally reviewed the application. Some aspects of the application intended to match the original RFA may not be acceptable to the new review group.
10. Feel free to consult NIH staff with specific questions.

8.7.3.3. *Preparation of Your Grant Application*

Remember, as you prepare a grant application, that you are writing primarily to an IRG. Given this fact, what can you do to improve your chances of a favorable review?

Although there are no substitutes for good ideas and well-planned studies, IRGs are influenced by how these ideas and plans are presented. Much of the following advice may appear to be self-evident, but a surprising number of applications run into difficulties because they do not follow these simple principles.

1. Contact institute program staff. They can help in the proposal phase. They should be your first and primary contacts with the institute, during the review process, and after an award is made. They are most likely to understand your perspective and needs because they have research experience themselves, as well as knowledge and understanding of how the NIH system works.

2. Follow the directions provided with the grant application kit. The instructions call for a particular organization of the materials, and reviewers are accustomed to finding information in specific places. Avoid antagonizing them by making them hunt through your proposal for information they expect to see in a certain place. Do not exceed the specified page limits or use type sizes other than those in the guidelines. Failure to follow guidelines will lead the CSR to return your application without its being reviewed.

3. Be brief, concise, and clear. Make your points as directly as possible. Use diagrams to help the reviewers understand complex models, relationships among variables, or design features.

4. Present your proposal in an organized and logical manner. Many applications fail because the reviewers cannot follow the thought process of the applicant or because parts of the application do not fit together. For example, an outstanding literature review may not lead logically to the hypotheses and design of the proposed study. Provide an analysis plan that relates the research questions to specific data and appropriate analytic techniques.

5. Show how your work goes beyond previous research. What contribution will your study make to the field? State this as clearly as possible.

6. Be complete, and be certain not to omit vital information. If a piece of information is important for reviewers to understand, provide it even if it appears to you to be implicit or obvious. (Keep in mind, however, that you should be brief and concise, so not all potentially useful information can be provided.) Provide an adequate literature review and details of the study design, sampling procedure, and data analysis.

7. Whenever possible, provide background on pilot instruments and data. Such information helps convince reviewers that you know what you are doing and that the proposed research project is feasible.

8. Be careful in the use of appendixes. Given the seemingly contradictory advice to be both concise and complete, it is tempting to rely heavily on appendixes to provide required details. You should be aware that only the two primary reviewers of your application receive both the main body and the appendixes.

9. Consider dual assignment of your application: You may request that your application be assigned to more than one institute as potential funders (for example, NIMH and NSF). Although dual assignment does not influence the review of your application by an IRG, it does provide you with a second chance for funding at no cost to you. If the primary institute is unable to fund your approved application, the secondary one may be able to.

10. Submit your application to other potential funders, such as private foundations. Be sure to inform them of such multiple submissions and of any other funding offers by other agencies.

After following these guidelines, be prepared to revise and resubmit. Given the competition for funds, it is common practice to submit a revised application. Few applications are funded after the first round of reviews.

8.7.3.4 *Computer Retrieval of Information on Scientific Projects (CRISP)*

Computer Retrieval of Information on Scientific Projects (CRISP) is a tool with which to search for topics that have been funded through NIH and its various institutes. CRISP, located at the Web site http://www-commons.cit.nih.gov/crisp/, is a searchable database of federally funded biomedical research projects conducted at universities, hospitals, and other research institutions. The database, maintained by the Office of Extramural Research at the National Institutes of Health (NIH), includes projects funded by NIH, Substance Abuse and Mental Health Services Administration (SAMHSA), the Health Resources and Services Administration (HRSA), the Food and Drug Administration (FDA), the Centers for Disease Control and Prevention (CDCP), the Agency for Health Care Policy Research (AHCPR), and the Office of Assistant Secretary of Health (OASH).

8.8 DEPARTMENT OF HEALTH AND HUMAN SERVICES

8.8.1 Office of Adolescent Pregnancy Programs

The Office of Adolescent Pregnancy Programs (OAPP) was established in 1978 and began awarding research grants in fiscal year (FY) 1982. (For further information on this office, see the Web site http://opa.osophs.dhhs.gov/titlexx/oapp.html.) Like the Office of Family Planning (discussed in the next section), OAPP has begun issuing a general research announcement to stimulate investigator-initiated proposals in areas of agency interest. OAPP is primarily responsible for administering the Adolescent Family Life Act (AFL), enacted by Congress in 1981 as Title XX of the Public Health Service Act. Language contained in the act permits OAPP to spend up to one third of AFL funds for research, although the agency has not chosen to utilize that amount to date.

OAPP supports demonstration and evaluation projects for delivery of services to prevent adolescent pregnancy and to care for pregnant adolescents, as well as research on topics including adolescent sexual activity, parenting, and childbearing. A fundamental basis of the AFL (and thus of the research program) is to encourage the delay of sexual activity among adolescents, rather than to promote use of contraceptives. The AFL budget for FY 2001 provided funding for three areas:

1. Care demonstration projects
2. Prevention demonstration projects
3. Research projects

Approximately 300 care and prevention demonstration projects and 65 research projects had been supported by the program from its inception to 2001. Care demonstration projects serve pregnant adolescents, adolescent parents, their infants, male partners, and their families. AFL care projects are required to provide comprehensive health, education, and social services, either directly or through partnerships with other community agencies, and to evaluate new approaches for implementation of these services. AFL care projects are based within a variety of settings, such as universities, hospitals, schools, public health departments, and community agencies. They provide a youth development approach to services. Many provide home visiting services, and all have partnerships with diverse community agencies. A major focus of AFL care projects is a case management approach in which each adolescent works one-on-one with a case manager throughout the pregnancy and early parenting period to address her needs, as well as those of her infant, male partner, and family.

Prevention demonstration projects serve preadolescents, adolescents, and their families. The major focus of AFL prevention projects is, by statute, to develop and test abstinence-based programs designed to delay the onset of sexual activity and thus reduce the incidence of adolescent pregnancy,

STD transmission, and HIV/AIDS. These projects also focus on risk behaviors and address such issues as drugs, alcohol, tobacco, and violence. Projects are based in both schools and communities. They generally provide basic sexuality education as well as training in life skills, social skills, and negotiation skills in various combinations. These projects have a holistic approach to adolescent health, well-being, resiliency, and self-respect.

A new series of abstinence education grants was funded by the OAPP in FY 1997. By 2001, 55 of these programs were in their fourth year of project activity and 17 programs were entering their second year of program activity. All 72 abstinence education grants are required to conform to the definition of abstinence education contained in the welfare reform legislation (PL-104-193) and have developed and tested diverse curricula and educational materials, which many programs not funded through AFL are using. These educational materials are medically accurate and constantly revised to include new information and statistics. OAPP staff review and approve all such materials prior to their use in the AFL projects.

All AFL care and prevention projects include an independent assessment conducted by an evaluator associated with a college or university in the grantee's home state. Care/prevention projects have developed programs that address education, life and career planning, job training, safe housing, decision making, and social skills, as well as the medical and health education services traditionally associated with pregnancy prevention and pregnancy management. The OAPP has conducted training programs for project staff in the field in such areas as child sexual abuse, cultural sensitivity, family and male involvement, abstinence education, curriculum development, and sexually transmitted diseases. OAPP is also conducting training for project staff in such areas as adolescent psychology, adolescent health, communication, and the use of both curricula and teaching methods in reaching preadolescents and adolescents. The program also supports research projects intended to improve understanding of the issues surrounding adolescent sexuality, pregnancy, and parenting. Projects have examined factors that influence adolescent sexual, contraceptive, and fertility behaviors; the nature and effectiveness of care services for pregnant and parenting adolescents; and why adoption is a little-used alternative among pregnant adolescents.

8.8.1.1 The OAPP Program

Five research topics identified as of interest to OAPP are as follows:

1. influences on adolescent premarital sexual behavior (demographic, economic, social, and psychological characteristics; family, peer, and media influence; adolescent decision-making processes; different patterns of influence for males and females);
2. consequences of adolescent premarital sexual behavior (differing effects on development of males and females, including psychological, social, educational, and moral factors; differing consequences for major population subgroups);
3. the adoption option for unmarried adolescent mothers (social, psychological, legal, and service factors; role of counseling; social attitudes toward single parenthood; family involvement);
4. parenting by unmarried adolescent mothers (role of the extended family, factors influencing parenting behavior, role of the father); and
5. adolescent pregnancy services (scope and impact of public and private sector services and policies, evaluations of strategies to eliminate adolescent premarital sexual relations, evaluations of strategies that might enhance service delivery).

8.8.1.2 Budget

OAPP spent about $25 million for extramural research in FY 2001.

8.8.2 Office of Family Planning

The National Family Planning Program was created in 1970 as Title X of the Public Health Service Act (PL 91-572). The mission of Title X is to provide individuals with the information and means to exercise personal choice in determining the number and spacing of their children. Grants made under this section provide funding for comprehensive family planning and preventive reproductive health service.

The Title X program, funded at $238.9 million for FY 2000, is administered—like the OAPP—by the Office of Family Planning within the Office of Population Affairs. (For further information on the Office of Family Planning, see the Web site http://opa.osophs.dhhis.gov/titleX/ofp.html.) Services are provided through a network of 4,600 clinics nationwide.

Family planning plays a key role in the prevention of unintended pregnancy, including some adolescent pregnancies. Preventing unintended pregnancy reduces the incidence of abortion and improves birth outcomes. Family planning information, education, and services reduce both the incidence and the impact of sexually transmitted infections through screening and treatment.

Title X family planning service funds are allocated to the 10 Department of Health and Human Services Regional Offices, which solicit applications, manage a competitive review process, make awards, and monitor program performance. Grantees include states, family planning councils, Planned Parenthood affiliates, and other public and private entities that provide family planning services. Almost two thirds of the Title X service funds are awarded to state health departments.

8.9 NATIONAL INSTITUTE OF JUSTICE (NIJ)

The National Institute of Justice (NIJ) is a research branch of the Department of Justice. NIJ's mission is to develop knowledge about crime, its causes, and its control. Priority is given to policy-relevant research that can yield approaches and information that state and local agencies can use in preventing and reducing crime.

NIJ reorganized its extramural program in FY 1986 in an effort to provide a more sustained, coordinated support base. The new Sponsored Research Program solicits proposals in several broad areas, with specific priorities established in each area. In addition, support is available through visiting fellowships, graduate research fellowships, and summer research fellowships. Unsolicited proposals may be submitted, but because the targeted priority areas are so broad, most unsolicited proposals can be placed in one or more of the designated programs. All NIJ programs are appropriate for social and behavioral scientists. Goals of the various programs are

1. controlling the serious offender (including crime control theory and policy; offender classification and prediction of criminal behavior; violent criminal behavior; and drugs, alcohol, and crime),
2. aiding the victims of crime (including legislation and other changes affecting victims, police assistance to victims, and family violence and child sex abuse),
3. crime prevention (including partnerships among police agencies, neighborhood actions against crime, and programs within the private sector focusing on prevention of specific crimes), and
4. improving the criminal justice system (including police efficiency and effectiveness, police response to spouse assault, court effectiveness, corrections, and the system of criminal justice).

FEDERAL GOVERNMENT AGENCIES AND PRIVATE ORGANIZATIONS OFFERING FELLOWSHIPS AND GRANTS 8.10

Research programs of interest to social and behavioral scientists are listed in this section. More information about funding opportunities within the various programs can be found at the Web site www.ojp.usdoj.gov/fundopps.htm.

American Association for the Advancement of Science
AAAS Science and Technology Policy Fellowships Program
1200 New York Avenue, NW
Washington, DC 20005
E-mail: science_policy@aaas.org

Department of Justice Web Site:
www.usdoj.gov
202-326-6700
Fax: 202-289-4950

American Association of Retired Persons
Andrus Foundation
601 E Street, NW
Washington, DC 20049
www.andrus.org
800-775-6776 or 202-434-6190
Fax: 202-434-6483
E-mail: andrus@aarp.org

Selected Fellowship and Grant Programs: Yearly grants with the U.S. Department of Justice Headquarters in Washington, D.C. Areas of prospective study include the Environment and Natural Resources Division, the Federal Bureau of Investigation, the Justice Management Division, the Office of Policy Development, and the Office of Justice Programs. One of the senior prospective Fellows must have a PhD or equivalent doctoral-level degree at the time of application (January of each year). Individuals with a master's degree in engineering and at least 3 years of post-degree professional experience may also apply. All applicants must be U.S citizens. Federal employees are not eligible for the fellowships.

Description: The AARP Andrus Foundation creates positive differences in the lives of older adults across the nation through funding aging-related research and educational grants. "As one of the few grant making foundations continuing to focus solely on aging issues, our goal is simple; to provide the public with aging-related information that can positively impact their quality of life." The organization's board meets three times a year (January, May, and September). Once a proposal is funded, researchers will be expected to start the project within 2 months of notification.

Contact: Leah Rege, Manager of Prospect Research and Donor Database, 202-434-6179, lrege@aarp.org; or Sandra E. Fauriol, CFRE Director of Development, 202-434-6188, e-mail: sfauriol@aarp.org.

Selected Fellowship and Grant Programs: The current priority areas for research funding are living with chronic health conditions and aging, and living environments. The goals of the AARP Andrus Foundation are achieved through four grant programs: The Research Grant Program, the Innovations Grant Program, the Dissemination Grant Program, and the Education and Training Grant Program.

(continued)

American Association of University Women Educational Foundation
1111 Sixteenth Street, NW
Washington, DC 20036
E-mail: info@aauw.org
800-326-AAUW (800-326-2289)
Fax: 202-872-1425
TDD: 202-785-7777

Description: The American Association of University Women (AAUW) is a national organization that endorses equal educational opportunities for all women and girls. Commitment to these issues is reflected in public policy efforts, programs, and diversity initiatives. AAUW is made up of three groups: the Association, the AAUW Educational Foundation, and the AAUW Legal Advocacy Fund.

Contact: Sharon Schuster, Foundation President.

Selected Fellowship and Grant Programs: Scholar in Residence Awards, American Fellowships, Career Development Grants, Community Action Grants, Eleanor Roosevelt Teacher Fellowships, International Fellowships, and Selected Professions Fellowships.

American Council of Learned Societies
228 East 45th Street
New York, NY 10017-3398
URL: www.acls.org
212-697-1505
Fax: 212-949-8058

The American Council of Learned Societies (ACLS) is a private, nonprofit federation of 63 national scholarly organizations. Its mission is "the advancement of humanistic studies in all fields of learning in the humanities and the social sciences and the maintenance and strengthening of relations among the national societies devoted to such studies."

Contact: Ruth Waters, Executive Assistant for Fellowships and Grants.

Selected Fellowship and Grant Programs: Fredrick Burkhardt Residential Fellowships for Recently Tenured Scholars, ACLS Fellowships, Library of Congress Fellowships in International Studies, Contemplative Practice Fellowships, and Art and the CSCC China Program.

American Philosophical Society
104 South Fifth Street
Philadelphia, PA 19106-3387
URL: www.amphilsoc.org
215-440-3400
Fax: 215-440-3436

Description: The American Philosophical Society is a scholar-based organization that "promotes useful knowledge in the sciences and humanities through excellence in scholarly research, publications, library resources, professional meetings and community outreach."

Contact: eroach@amphilsoc.org

Selected Fellowship and Grant Programs: Franklin Research Grants, Daland Fellowships in Clinical Investigation, Phillips Fund grants for Native American Research, Sabbatical Fellowship for the Humanities and Social Sciences, Slater Fellowship in the History of the Twentieth-Century Physical Sciences, and Library Resident Research Fellowships.

American Sociological Association
1307 New York Avenue, NW
Suite 700
Washington, DC 20005-4701
URL: www.asanet.org
202-383-9005
Fax: 202-638-0882
TDD: 202-872-0486

Description: The American Sociological Association (ASA) is a nonprofit membership association whose mission is to further sociology as a scientific discipline and profession serving the community's interests. ASA has approximately 13,000 members and includes sociologists who are faculty members at colleges and universities, researchers, practitioners, and students.

Contact: Carla B. Howery, Program Director for Academic and Professional Affairs.

Selected Fellowship and Grant Programs: ASA Small Grants Program: Teaching Enhancement Fund, Minority Fellowship Program, 2000 Mass Media Science Fellow Program, 2000 Community Action Research Initiative, 2000 ASA Congressional Fellowship, and Fund for the Advancement of the Discipline.

American Sociological Association Minority Fellowship Program
1722 N Street, NW
Washington, DC 20036-2981
E-mail: minority.affairs@asanet.org
URL: www.asanet.org
202-833-3410 x322

Description: For American citizens and permanent residents who are beginning or continuing work in sociology or related fields and who have a commitment to teaching, research, and service careers in sociological aspects of mental health. Awards consist of a $10,000 annual stipend plus allowance for books and supplies. The application deadline is December 31.

The Lynde and Harry Bradley Foundation
P.O. Box 510860
Milwaukee, WI 53203-0153

Description: This private, independent organization, established in 1985, is dedicated to creating grants directed to supporting research and education. The foundation mainly funds scholarly studies and academic achievement. Its board of directors meets four times a year, in February, May or June, August, and November. Proposals should be submitted by the following dates: December 1, March 1, July 1, and September 1.

The Century Foundation (formerly known as Twentieth Century Fund)
41 East 70th Street
New York, NY 10021
URL: www.tcf.org
212-535-4441
Fax: 212-535-7534

Description: The Century Foundation supports critical analyses of major economic, political, and social institutions and issues in the areas of domestic policies, politics, and economics; communications, science, and technology; urban economic and social issues; and U.S. policy in the international arena. Projects are expected to be book-length manuscripts.

Congressional Hispanic Leadership Opportunity/Graduate Fellowship Program
Congressional Hispanic Caucus Institute Inc.
504 C Street, NE
Washington, DC 20002
E-mail: chci@chci.org
URL: www.chci.org
800-EXCELDC (800-392-3532)

Description: The graduate fellowship program offers Hispanic students enrolled in graduate public policy programs or policy-related fields the opportunity to participate in the making of national public policy. Applicants must be currently enrolled in an accredited university and be working toward a graduate degree in public policy or a related field. Applicants should be committed to taking a leadership position in the Hispanic community. The monthly stipend is $1,550. The application deadline is April 14.

The Danforth Foundation
One Metropolitan Square
211 North Broadway, Suite 2390
St. Louis, MO 63102
URL: www.info.csd.org
314-588-1900
Fax: 314-588-0035

Description: The Danforth Foundation aims to enhance the "humane dimensions of life." Activities of the foundation traditionally have emphasized improving the quality of teaching and learning.

Selected Fellowship and Grant Programs: Currently, the Danforth Foundation funds national and metropolitan St. Louis programs and projects in precollegiate public education. The foundation also funds special activities that provide unique contributions to the St. Louis community. The foundation funds one higher education program, the Dorothy Danforth Compton Fellowships.

Ford Foundation (Headquarters)
320 East 43rd Street
New York, NY 10017
212-573-5000
Fax: 212-351-3677

Description: The modern Ford Foundation was founded in 1936, when it expanded to national and international scope. Since its inception, it has been an independent, nonprofit, nongovernmental organization. It has provided slightly more than $10 billion in grants and loans.

Selected Fellowship and Grant Programs: Asset Building and Community Development Education; Media; Arts and Culture; and Peace and Social Justice.

(continued)

Fulbright-Hays Doctoral Dissertation Research Abroad Program
U.S. Department of Education
1990 K Street, NW
Washington, DC 20006-8521
202-502-7700

Description: This program provides grants to colleges and universities to fund individual doctoral students to conduct research in other countries, in the areas of modern foreign languages and area studies, for periods of 6 to 12 months. Proposals focusing on Western Europe are not eligible.

Contact: Karla Ver Bryck Block, 202-502-7632, e-mail: karla_verbryckblock@ed.gov.

The Harry Frank Guggenheim Foundation
527 Madison Avenue
New York, NY 10022-4304
URL: www.gf.org
212-644-4907

Description: The Harry Frank Guggenheim Foundation (HFG) sponsors scholarly research on problems of violence, aggression, and dominance. The foundation provides both research grants to established scholars and dissertation fellowships to graduate students during the dissertation-writing year. (HFG does not support institutions, programs, or pure interventions.) In addition, the foundation sponsors small, interdisciplinary conferences on various topics related to violence, aggression, and dominance. The HFG Review, containing research studies, is published annually.

John Simon Guggenheim Memorial Foundation
90 Park Avenue
New York, NY 10016
E-mail: fellowships@gf.org
URL: www.gf.org
212-687-4470
Fax: 212-697-3248

Description: This Guggenheim Foundation was founded in 1925. It provides fellowships for advanced professionals in natural sciences, social sciences, humanities, and creative arts (except the performing arts). Fellowships are not available for students. The foundation supports only individuals; it does not make grants to institutions or organizations. In 2000, the foundation awarded 182 U.S. and Canadian fellowships for a total of $6,345,000 (an average grant of $34,862). There were 2,927 applicants. In 2000, the foundation awarded 33 Latin American and Caribbean fellowships for a total of $1,155,000 (an average grant of $35,000). There were 428 applicants.

The Alexander von Humboldt Foundation
Jean-Paul-St. 12
D-53173 Bonn
Germany
URL: www.avh.de/en/index.htm
(+49) 0228-833-0
Fax: (+49) 0228-833-199

Description: The foundation is a nonprofit organization under private law, established by the Federal Republic of Germany. It enables highly qualified foreign scholars holding doctorates to carry out long-term research projects in Germany.

Selected Fellowship and Grant Programs: The foundation grants research fellowships and research awards to highly qualified foreign scholars, enabling them to undertake periods of research in Germany, as well as research fellowships to highly qualified German scholars, enabling them to spend periods of research at the institutes of former Humboldt guest-researchers abroad. Research grants to both non-German and German scholars are mainly for doctoral candidates.

International Research & Exchanges Board
1616 H Street, NW, 6th Floor
Washington, DC 20006
E-mail: irex@irex.org
URL: www.irex.org
202-628-8188
Fax: 202-628-8189

Description: The International Research & Exchanges Board (IREX) is a U.S.-based nonprofit organization committed to international education in its broadest sense. IREX's efforts encompass academic research, professional training, institution building, technical assistance, and policy programs conducted between the United States and the countries of Eastern Europe, the new independent states of the former Soviet Union, Asia, and the Near East.

Selected Fellowship and Grant Programs: Mongolia Research Fellowship Program, ECA Alumni Small Grants Program, and Individual Advanced Research Opportunities.

Institute for European Studies
120 Uris Hall
Cornell University
Ithaca, NY 14853
URL: www.ies.admin.is.cornell.edu
607-255-7592
Fax: 607-255-1565

Description: The Einaudi Chair sponsors various grants and fellowships for Cornell graduate and undergraduate students interested in conducting field research in Europe.

Contact: Susan Tarrow, Associate Director of Institute for European Studies, 607-255-7592.

Selected Fellowship and Grant Programs: The Frederic Conger Wood Fellowship for Research in Europe, Foreign Language and Area Studies Fellowship, Michele Sicca Summer Research Grants, Manon Michels Einaudi Summer Travel Grant, Luigi Einaudi Graduate Fellowship, and Mario Einaudi Graduate Fellowship.

Institute for the Study of World Politics
1755 Massachusetts Avenue, NW
Washington, DC 20036

Selected Fellowship and Grant Programs: The Dorothy Danforth-Compton Fellowship makes approximately 20 awards for African American, Hispanic American, and Native American students pursuing degrees related to careers in world affairs and politics. Awards are made to doctoral candidates doing dissertation research as well as to graduate students at earlier stages of their academic programs. The application deadline is February 15.

The Japan Foundation
New York Office
Carnegie Hall Tower
152 West 57th Street, 39th Floor
New York, NY 10019
URL: www.cgp.org
212-489-0299
Fax: 212-489-0409

Description: The Japan Foundation began in 1972 with the purpose of promoting international cultural exchange and mutual understanding between Japan and other countries. The foundation conducts a wide range of programs worldwide, including support for Japanese studies, Japanese language instruction, arts and cultural events, intellectual exchange, and the exchange of persons.

Selected Fellowship and Grant Programs: Available programs include publication and translation assistance, artists' fellowships, support for exhibitions abroad, and support for film production. Japanese language–related programs are reviewed by a committee of specialists and language center staff.

W. K. Kellogg Foundation
One Michigan Avenue East
Battle Creek, MI 49017-4058

Description: The W. K. Kellogg Foundation is a nonprofit organization whose mission is to "apply knowledge to solve the problems of people."

Contact: Supervisor of Proposal Processing.

Selected Fellowship and Grant Programs: Areas of interest include health, philanthropy and volunteerism, food systems and rural development, and youth and education.

Lilly Endowment, Inc.
P.O. Box 88068
Indianapolis, IN 46208
URL: www.lilly.com/about/community/
    foundation/endowment.html
317-924-5471
Fax: 317-926-4431

Description: The Lilly Endowment was established in 1937 by members of the Lilly family as a vehicle through which to pursue their personal philanthropic interests.

Selected Fellowship and Grant Programs: Public Policy Research, Academic Relations.

(continued)

Josiah Macy, Jr. Foundation
44 E. 64th Street
New York, NY 10021
E-mail: nickrjmacy@aol.com
URL: www.josiahmacyfoundation.org/
  jmacy1.html
212-486-2424
Fax: 212-644-0765

Description: Since the mid-1960s, the foundation has focused its resources specifically on improving the education of health professionals, particularly physicians. The foundation concentrates most of its funds on medical science and the clinical decision-making process.

Selected Fellowship and Grant Programs: The foundation has supported programs at medical schools and research institutions that encouraged doctoral candidates in biomedical science to pursue careers in research relevant to human disease by providing them with special programs in human pathology and physiology.

The National Endowment for the Humanities
1100 Pennsylvania Avenue, NW
Washington, DC 20506
E-mail: info@neh.gov
ULR: www.neh.fed.us
202-606-8400

Description: The National Endowment for the Humanities is an independent grant-making agency of the U.S. government dedicated to supporting research, education, and public programs in the humanities.

Contact: Robert Anderson, Grants Office.

National Institute for Mental Health
6001 Executive Boulevard
Rm. 8184, MSC 9663
Bethesda, MD 20892-9663
E-mail: nimhinfo@nih.gov
301-443-4513
Fax: 301-443-4279

Description: The information provided by the National Institute for Mental Health (NIMH) is intended to help people better understand mental health and mental disorders as well as to diminish the burden of mental illness through research. This public health mandate demands harnessing powerful scientific tools to achieve better understanding, treatment, and eventually prevention of mental illness.

Contact: Assigned Contracting Officer or David Eskenazi, Branch Chief, e-mail: de5d@nih.gov

National Institute of Health
Center for Scientific Review
6701 Rockledge Drive, Rm. 1040,
  MSC 7710
Bethesda, MD 20892-7710
Bethesda, MD 20817 (for express/courier
  service)

Grants Information
Division of Extramural Outreach and
  Information Resources
Office of Extramural Research
E-mail: grantsinfo@nih.gov
URLs: www.grants.nih.gov/grants/
  welcome.htm
and
www.grants.nih.gov/grants/guide/pa-files/
  PA-99-087.html
301-435-0714
Fax: 301-480-0525

Description: The National Institute of Health (NIH) aims to protect and improve human health by conducting and supporting basic, applied, and clinical and health services research to understand the processes underlying human health and to acquire new knowledge to help prevent, diagnose, and treat human diseases and disabilities.

National Research Council
Fellowship Office
2101 Constitution Avenue
Washington, DC 20418
E-mail: infofell@nas.edu
URL: http://national-academies.org/osep/fo
202-334-2860 or 202-334-2872
Fax: 202-334-2759

Selected Fellowship and Grant Programs: Ford Foundation Predoctoral and Dissertation Fellowships for Minorities. The predoctoral program is open to students beginning their doctoral work who are American Indian (Native, Eskimo, Aleut), African American, Mexican American/Chicano, and Puerto Rican. Studies must be research-based, in the areas of behavioral and social sciences, humanities, engineering, mathematics, or the physical and biological sciences. The predoctoral award is for 3 years and includes a stipend of $14,000 plus tuition. The Dissertation Award is a 1-year fellowship for approximately 100 candidates and has a stipend of $21,500. The application deadline is November 3.

National Science Foundation
4201 Wilson Boulevard
Arlington, VA 22230
URL: www.nsf.gov
703-292-5111
TDD: 703-292-5090

Description: The National Science Foundation (NSF) is an independent U.S. government agency responsible for promoting science and engineering through programs that invest more than $3.3 billion per year in almost 20,000 research and education projects in science and engineering.

Selected Fellowship and Grant Programs: Research areas include biology, computers, information sciences, crosscutting, education, engineering, geosciences, international studies, math, physical sciences, polar research, and social, behavioral, and economic sciences.

Population Council
Social Science Fellowships Program
Policy Research Division
One Dag Hammarskjold Plaza
New York, NY 10017
E-mail: ssfellowship@popcouncil.org
URL: www.popcouncil.org/opportunities/
socscifellowships.html
212-339-0671
Fax: 212-755-6052

Description: The Population Council Fellowships in the Social Sciences, administered by the Policy Research Division, support work leading to a doctoral degree, postdoctoral research, or midcareer training in the population field. The fellowships are for 1 year of research, except in the case of postdoctoral fellowships, which are made for 2 years.

Contact: Fellowship Coordinator.

Selected Fellowship and Grant Programs: Fellowships are awarded for advanced training in population studies, including demography and public health, in combination with a social science discipline, such as economics, sociology, anthropology, or geography. Awards are made only to applicants whose proposals deal with the developing world.

Radcliffe Institute for Advanced Study
(formerly known as Radcliffe College)
10 Garden Street
Cambridge, MA 02138
URL: www.radcliffe.edu
617-495-8601
Fax: 617-496-4640

Description: The institute is committed to the study of women, gender, and society. It is an interdisciplinary center where leading scholars can promote learning and scholarship across a broad array of academic and professional fields within the setting of a major university.

Selected Fellowship and Grant Programs: Research support is given for postdoctoral research in humanities and the social and behavioral sciences. Resources include the Arthur and Elizabeth Schlesinger Library on the History of Women in America and the Henry A. Murray Research Center. Scholarships and grants range from $100 to $2,000. The application deadline is February 1.

(continued)

The Rockefeller Foundation
420 Fifth Avenue
New York, NY 10018-2702
URL: www.rockefellerfound.org
212-869-8500

Description: The foundation supports several categories of research fellowships and grants, including a fellowship program in environmental affairs, fellowships in conflict in international relations, and the Rockefeller and Ford Foundation program in the support of public policy research in the social sciences.

Contact: Lynda Mullen, Secretary.

Selected Fellowship and Grant Programs: Community development, economic development, education, and environment. In 1993, 961 grants were awarded, ranging from $98 to more than $75,845. The board of directors meets in March, June, September, and December. There are no formal deadlines for applications.

Russell Sage Foundation
112 East 64th Street
New York, NY 10021
URL: www.russellsage.org
212-750-6000
Fax: 212-371-4761

Description: The foundation's purpose is to strengthen the methods, data, and theoretical core of the social sciences as a means of improving social policies.

Selected Fellowship and Grant Programs: This foundation's main interests are in the future of work with respect to the causes and consequences of the decline and demand for low-skill workers in the advanced economy, immigration, cultural conflict, and increasing literacy. Awards currently average about $100,000, with a range running roughly from $20,000 to $300,000. There are no formal application deadlines, but the foundation has an outside peer review committee that meets in May and November of each year.

Social Behavioral and Economic Sciences International Programs
Western Europe (WE) Program, Suite 935
Division of International Programs
National Science Foundation
4201 Wilson Boulevard
Arlington, VA 22230
URL: www.nsf.gov
703-292-8702
Fax: 703-292-9177

Description: The aim of the Western Europe Program (WE) is to provide access to new research collaborations between the United States and Western Europe, an area of world-class research capabilities in all fields supported by the National Science Foundation.

Contact: Jeanne Hudson, Regional Coordinator, jhudson@nsf.gov

Social Science Research Council
810 Seventh Avenue
New York, NY 10019
URL: www.ssrc.org
212-377-2700
Fax: 212-377-2727

Description: The Social Science Research Council (SSRC) is a private, not-for-profit international association dedicated to the promotion of interdisciplinary research in the social sciences. It pursues this goal by offering an array of interdisciplinary workshops and conferences, fellowships and grants, summer training institutes, scholarly exchanges, and publications.

Contact: Mary Byrne McDonnell, Executive Director, ext. 420, e-mail: mcdonnel@ssrc.org.

Selected Fellowship and Grant Programs: International Predissertation Fellowship Program (IPFP); Eastern Europe Dissertation Fellowships; Fellowships on Conflict, Peace, and Social Transformations; International Migration Dissertation Fellowships; and Near/Middle East Dissertation Research Fellowships in the Social Sciences and Humanities.

Social Sciences and Humanities Research Council of Canada
350 Albert Street
Box 1610
Ottawa, ON, K1P 6G4 Canada
URL: www.sshrc.ca
613-992-0691
Fax: 613-992-1787

Description: The Social Sciences and Humanities Research Council of Canada (SSHRC) is Canada's federal funding agency for university-based research and graduate training in the social sciences and humanities.

Selected Fellowship and Grant Programs: In 1998-1999, SSHRC's total program budget was about $96.4 million in support of research, research training, and research communication.

The Society for the Psychological Study of Social Issues
SPSSI Central Office
P.O. Box 1248
Ann Arbor, MI 48106-1248
E-mail: spssi@spssi.org
734-662-9130
Fax: 734-662-5607

Description: The Society for the Psychological Study of Social Issues (SPSSI) is an international group of more than 3,500 psychologists, allied scientists, students, and others who team together to discuss and analyze research on the psychological aspects of important social issues.

Selected Fellowship and Grant Programs: Applied Social Issues Internship, Clara Mayo Grants Program, Grants-in-Aid Program, Gordon Allport Prize, Louise Kidder Award, Otto Klineberg Award, Social Issues Dissertation Award, and SAGES Grants Program.

Society for Research in Child Development
505 E. Huron, Suite 301
Ann Arbor, MI 48104-1567
E-mail: srcd@umich.edu
734-998-6578
Fax: 734-998-6569

Description: The Society for Research in Child Development (SRCD) is a "multidisciplinary, not-for-profit professional association with an international membership of approximately 5,000 researchers, practitioners, and human development professionals."

Contact: Lauren Fasig, 750 First Street, NW, Washington, DC 20002-4242, 202-336-6153.

Selected Fellowship and Grant Programs: There are currently two types of fellowships: Congressional and Executive Branch. Both programs focus on research regarding child development and public policy. Deadlines are around December 15 of each year.

The Spencer Foundation
875 North Michigan Avenue, Suite 3930
Chicago, IL 60611-1803
URL: www.spencer.org/fellows/index.htm
312-337-7000
Fax: 312-337-0282

Description: The Spencer Foundation is a private foundation that provides grant funds for the support of research that contributes to the understanding of education and improvement of its practice.

Selected Fellowship and Grant Programs: The Dissertation Fellowship Program for Research Related to Education assists young scholars interested in educational research in the completion of the doctoral dissertation, thus helping to ensure a continued growth of able researchers in the field. Annually, the Dissertation Fellowship Program supports 30 to 35 Fellows by providing monetary assistance ($20,000) and opportunities for professional development.

SOURCES OF INFORMATION FOR OTHER FELLOWSHIPS AND GRANT OPPORTUNITIES 8.11

The following lists contain books and Web sites useful for researchers and students seeking grants and other funding. The lists are representative and contain some of the best resources, but they are by no means exhaustive.

8.11.1 Books

Annual Register for Grant Support 2001: A Directory of Founding Sources (34th ed.). New Providence, NJ: R. R. Bowker, 2001.

> Part of the section on educational research is devoted to scholar aid programs (all disciplines). Typical entries include name, address, Web site, phone number of grant-making organization, and description of the aid program, including eligibility and application requirements, average amount of financial support awarded, number of applications received, and number of awards made annually.

Chronicle Financial Aid Guide (2000-2001): Scholarships and Loans for High School Students, College Undergraduates, Graduates and Adult Learners. Monrovia, NY: Chronicle Guidance Publications, 2001. www.chronicleguidance.com

> Provides information on numerous financial aid programs available to high school students, undergraduate and graduate students, and adult learners. Programs include those offered by private corporations and associations, non-collegiate organizations, labor unions, the federal government, and state higher education agencies. Revised annually.

The College Blue Book (27th ed., 5 vols). New York: Macmillan, 1999.

> The volume titled *Scholarships, Fellowships, Grants, and Loans* lists and describes awards offered by corporations, labor unions, foundations, professional societies, and federal and state governmental agencies. Several indexes list awards by title of the award (e.g., paraprofessional, community college, college, professional, postdoctoral, seminary) and by subject. Addresses are given for persons to contact for further information.

Dan Cassidy's Worldwide Graduate Scholarship Directory (5th ed.). Daniel J. Cassidy. Franklin Lakes, NJ: Career Press, 2000.

> This book contains information on thousands of grants, scholarships, loans, fellowships, and internships from colleges, foundations, corporations, trust funds, associations, religious and fraternal groups, and private philanthropists.

Directory of Financial Aid for Minorities 1995-1997. Gail Ann Schlachter and R. David Weber. Santa Barbara, CA: Reference Service Press, 1995.

> Describes scholarships, fellowships, loans, grants, awards, internships, and state sources of educational benefits for minorities in general, Asian Americans, African Americans, Hispanic Americans, and Native Americans.

Directory of Financial Aids for Women 1997-1999. Gail Ann Schlachter, ed. San Carlos, CA; Reference Service Press, 2000.

> Lists more than 1,700 funding sources for women and contains an annotated bibliography of 60 key directories that identify other financial aid opportunities.

DRG: Directory of Research Grants. Scottsdale, AZ: Oryx. Annual.

> Describes thousands of potential sources of funding for research-related projects within specific disciplines and subject areas. Awards for graduate study not limited by subject area are indexed under "Dissertations and Scholarships." Others are under specific subjects; for example, art (dissertation support), economics (scholarships and fellowships).

Foundation Grants to Individuals (12th ed.). Phyllis Edelson, ed. New York: Foundation Center, 2001.

> Undergraduate and graduate sources are categorized under general and specific requirements. Also listed are fellowships, residencies, internships, and grants by U.S. foundations to foreign nationals and citizens and company-sponsored aid.

Funding for United States Study: A Guide for International Students and Professionals. Marie O'Sullivan and Sara Steen, eds. Stockholm, Sweden: Institute of International Education, 1996.

> Detailed descriptions of more than 600 fellowships, scholarships, and paid internships for undergraduates, graduate students, and working professionals. The sponsors of all the listed awards welcome applications from foreign nationals, and many of the awards are intended for international scholars. Sponsors include U.S. and foreign governments, colleges, universities, educational associations, libraries, research centers, foundations, corporations, and other organizations.

Graduate Study in Psychology and Associated Fields (Rev. ed.). Washington, DC: American Psychological Association, 1996 (with 1997 addendum).

> This text offers concise and usable information about 550 psychology programs in the United States and Canada. This edition provides current facts about programs and degrees offered, admission requirements, application information, financial aid, tuition, and housing. Cross-referenced indexes allow users to find an institution by state, by area of study, or alphabetically. This reference is suitable for students, counselors, libraries, and department offices in psychology, education, and other related fields.

The Grants Register 2001 (19th ed.). Sarah Hackwood, ed. Houndmills, Basingstoke, Hampshire, England: Palgrave, 2000.

> A comprehensive and practical guide to funding and a leading source for current information on the availability of and eligibility for postgraduate and professional funding. Each entry gives details of subject area, eligibility, purpose, numbers of awards offered, frequency, value, length of study, and application procedures. Full contact details appear with each awarding organization or individual award.

Need a Lift? To Educational Opportunities, Careers, Loans, Scholarships, Employment (49th ed.). Indianapolis, IN: American Legion Educational Program, 2000. www.americanlegion.org

> An annually revised guide, of interest to any student in need of aid for postsecondary education. Sources of funds are listed and described in separate sections for undergraduates only, for graduates, and for both. Other units contain information relative to state educational benefits, financial assistance for veterans and their dependents, and sources of loans. The list price is only $3.00.

Peterson's Grants for Graduate and Postdoctoral Study (5th ed.). Princeton, NJ: Peterson Guides, 1998.

> Covers more than 1,900 grants, scholarships, awards, fellowships, and prizes directed mainly to graduate students, postdoctoral scholars, and beginning researchers.

Scholarships, Fellowships, and Loans: A Guide to Education-Related Financial Aid Programs for Students and Professionals (13th ed.). Valerie J. Webster, ed. Farmington Hills, MI: Gale, 2000.

> Contains data on funding sources available to researchers and students at all levels of postsecondary education.

The 2000 Catalog of Federal Domestic Assistance. Baton Rogeu, LA: Claitors, 2000. http://aspe.os.dhhs.gov/cfda/

> A comprehensive listing and description of federal programs that provide benefits to the American public. Gives information on grants, loans, scholarships, and other types of financial assistance, with addresses of offices to contact for additional information and application procedures. Several indexes are provided, with the subject index providing such headings as fellowships, scholarships, traineeships, and education. Kept reasonably current by annual editions updated 6 months after publication.

8.11.2 Web Sites

The Chronicle of Philanthropy. www.philanthropy.com

> Web site of *The Chronicle of Philanthropy*, a newspaper published every other week that, according to the Web site, is the primary news source for charity leaders, fund-raisers, grant makers, and other people involved in philanthropic enterprises.

Financial Resources for International Study: A Guide for U.S. Students and Professionals. Stockholm, Sweden: Institute of International Education, 1996.

> A helpful resource for study and research abroad, includes detailed descriptions of nearly 700 fellowships, grants, scholarships, and paid internships for undergraduates, graduate students, and postdoctoral students as well as working professionals.

Social, Behavioral and Economic Sciences International Programs: Western Europe. www.nsf.gov/sbe/int/w_europe.

> From the Web site: "The goal of WE is to provide access for new research collaborations between the US and Western Europe, a region of world class research capabilities in all fields supported by the National Science Foundation." Regional coordinator Jeanne Hudson can be reached at jhudson@nsf.gov.

8.12 ESTIMATING RESEARCH COSTS

How much does it cost to conduct a research project? One writer says that such a question can be answered no better or more precisely than a question about how much it costs to go on a vacation. There are simply too many variables.

One major cost is the overhead charges of the sponsoring agency or the indirect costs charged by universities to grants (especially federal grants), which commonly are in the 50%-60% range of the total grant. Other major variables influencing costs include the size of population or sample involved, the mode of collecting data, the amount of assistance required, and the size of salaries needed for the principal investigator(s) and assistants.

Our purpose here is to enable various researchers working under different conditions to make cost estimates that apply to their own designs. Table 8.2, a general form to apply to any research project, is

Table 8.2   A COST-ESTIMATION WORKSHEET

Activity	Week Ending	Week Ending	Week Ending	Total
1. Total				
Personnel hours	_____	_____	_____	_____
Cost ($)	_____	_____	_____	_____
% of total completed	_____	_____	_____	_____
2. Planning				
Personnel hours	_____	_____	_____	_____
Cost ($)	_____	_____	_____	_____
% of total completed	_____	_____	_____	_____
3. Pilot study and pretests				
Personnel hours	_____	_____	_____	_____
Cost ($)	_____	_____	_____	_____
% of total completed	_____	_____	_____	_____
4. Drawing sample				
Personnel hours	_____	_____	_____	_____
Cost ($)	_____	_____	_____	_____
% of total completed	_____	_____	_____	_____
5. Preparing observational materials				
Personnel hours	_____	_____	_____	_____
Cost ($)	_____	_____	_____	_____
% of total completed	_____	_____	_____	_____
6. Selection and training				
Personnel hours	_____	_____	_____	_____
Cost ($)	_____	_____	_____	_____
% of total completed	_____	_____	_____	_____
7. Trial run				
Personnel hours	_____	_____	_____	_____
Cost ($)	_____	_____	_____	_____
% of total completed	_____	_____	_____	_____
8. Revising plans				
Personnel hours	_____	_____	_____	_____
Cost ($)	_____	_____	_____	_____
% of total completed	_____	_____	_____	
9. Collecting data				
Personnel hours	_____	_____	_____	_____
Cost ($)	_____	_____	_____	_____
% of total completed	_____	_____	_____	_____
10. Processing data				
Personnel hours	_____	_____	_____	_____
Cost ($)	_____	_____	_____	_____
% of total completed	_____	_____	_____	_____
11. Preparing final report				
Personnel hours	_____	_____	_____	_____
Cost ($)	_____	_____	_____	_____
% of total completed	_____	_____	_____	_____

SOURCE: Adapted from Russell K. Ackoff (1953), *Design for Social Research* (Chicago: University of Chicago Press), p. 347. Copyright © 1953 by the University of Chicago. Adapted with permission of the University of Chicago Press.

a budget-time schedule summary setting forth major activities that may be necessary and that will incur costs. (The form is general and suggestive only; individual projects may have different activities in different order, and they may extend over more or fewer than 3 weeks.) One of the principal requirements to use this form is information about the costs associated with various modes of collecting data. Section 8.12.1 presents a guide to costs associated with mail questionnaires. This is followed in section 8.12.2 by a guide to comparative costs of telephone surveys and personal interviews. (Refer to section 5.13, pp. 309-312 in this volume, for information about the relative merits of different types of data collection.)

8.12.1 Guide to Costs of a Mail Questionnaire

Data collection by mail is relatively inexpensive; in general, costs will be substantially lower than those for data collected from personal interviews or telephone surveys. Dillman (1978) studied mail questionnaire costs over a 10-year period. The minimum first-class mailing rate was 6 cents in 1970, 8 cents in 1971, 13 cents in 1977, 15 cents in 1980, and 20 cents in 1981—a 233% increase in just over a decade. The first-class mailing rate went to 25 cents in 1988 and to 29 cents in 1991. At this writing, it is 34 cents. Keep in mind that researchers who use mail as a tool often arrange for a bulk rate permit or use e-mail, both of which can reduce costs substantially.

The researcher must make projections of costs, sometimes using extrapolations from past data on costs. Dillman (1978) has provided itemized costs for questionnaire surveys using his total design method; the figures are updated here to reflect present costs. The costs shown are for general public surveys of Washington residents in 1982. The cost specifications include the following:

- 12-page questionnaires mailed for the minimum first-class postage in 1982 (20 cents)
- Machine scoring at $.05 per sheet
- Data analysis costs
- Labor costs calculated at the prevailing rate ($6.50 per hour) for part-time clerical help
- Professional supervision costs based on the number of hours actually spent by the principal investigator providing direct supervision of data collection activities

Table 8.3 shows costs by general expenditure area, followed by phases of the study. The reader will note that costs are shown for one large statewide survey of the general public (4,500 questionnaires) and a smaller survey (450 questionnaires). The bottom line is a mean cost for each potential respondent of $5.44 for the larger sample and $28.28 for the smaller.

The researcher seeking estimates for a proposed mail questionnaire survey can utilize Table 8.3 by estimating the percentage of expenditure required using the data given for the survey more nearly comparable to his or her own sample. A determination of inflationary costs since 1982 must be projected to the year of administration selected.

Reference

Dillman, Don A. (1982). Mail and other self-administered questionnaires. In Peter Rossi, James Wright, & Andy Anderson (Eds.), *Handbook of survey research*. New York: Academic Press.

8.12.2 Guide to Comparative Costs of the Telephone Survey and Personal Interviews

Groves and Kahn of the Survey Research Center of the University of Michigan undertook a study in 1976 to identify certain basic characteristics of telephone surveys and compare them to corresponding features of personal interview surveys. A comparison of costs was an important objective. Even

Table 8.3 SAMPLE BUDGETS FOR MAIL SURVEYS

	Large Survey (n = 4,500)	Small Survey (n = 450)	Your Survey (n = ?)
General Costs			
Purchase systematic samples from broker or other sample source	$2,000	$200	____
Purchase mailout envelopes	$275	$28	____
Purchase business reply envelopes	$185	$19	____
Print questionnaires	$1,620	$162	____
Graphics design for cover	$250	$250	____
Telephone (toll charges)	$325	$325	____
Supplies (miscellaneous)	$600	$150	____
Subtotal	$5,255	$1,134	____
First Mailout			
Print cover letter	$250	$35	____
Address letters and envelopes	$2,000	$2,000	____
Postage for mailout	$3,600	$360	____
Prepare mailout packets	$825	$115	____
Postage for returned questionnaires (business reply envelopes)	$360	$360	____
Process and precode returns	$375	$55	____
Subtotal	$10,650	$3,645	____
Postcard Follow-Up			
Purchase postcards	$990	$99	____
Print postcards	$245	$25	____
Address postcards (run labels)	$150	$150	____
Prepare mailout	$225	$50	____
Process and precode returns	$400	$350	____
Postage for returned questionnaires	$1,664	$166	____
Subtotal	$3,674	$840	____
Third Mailout			
Print cover letter	$300	$30	____
Address letters and envelopes	$560	$56	____
Prepare mailout packets	$300	$30	____
Postage for mailout	$3,333	$333	____
Process and precode returns	$150	$15	____
Postage for returned questionnaires	$1,667	$167	____
Subtotal	$6,060	$631	____
Fourth Mailout			
Print cover letter	$75	$20	____
Address letters and envelopes	$240	$24	____
Prepare mailout packets	$200	$20	____
Postage for mailout (certified)	$2,500	$250	____
Process and precode returns	$100	$10	____
Postage for returned questionnaires	$1,000	$100	____
Subtotal	$4,615	$424	____
Professional supervision	$7,500	$7,500	____
Clerical staff	$2,250	$750	____
Grand total	$30,254	$14,924	____
Mean cost per potential respondent	$6.72	$33.16	____

SOURCE: Adapted from Don A. Dillman (1982), "Mail and Other Self-Administered Questionnaires," in Peter Rossi, James Wright, and Andy Anderson (Eds.), *Handbook of Survey Research* (New York: Academic Press), chap. 12. Adapted with permission. Mailing costs have been adjusted to reflect costs of postage in 2001.

Table 8.4 A COMPARISON OF COSTS FOR TELEPHONE SURVEYS AND PERSONAL INTERVIEWS[a]

Task	Telephone Survey (N = 1,618) 2001	1976 Cost	1976 Percentage of Total	Personal Interview (N = 1,584) 2001	Cost	Percentage of Total
1. Sampling costs	$2,311.75	$955.27	2.5	$20,684.10	$8,547.15	10.1
2. Pretesting	$1,750.75	$723.45	1.9	$2,693.70	$1,113.10	1.3
3. Training and prestudy work	$5,000.54	$2,066.34	5.4	$23,047.14	$9,523.61	11.2
4. Materials	$3,327.40	$1,374.96	3.6	$8,857.56	$3,660.15	4.3
5. Ann Arbor head-quarters field office salaries: adminis-trative and clerical (typing)	$3,375.27	$1,394.74	3.7	$10,065.80	$4,159.42	4.9
6. Field salaries: supervisory and interviewer	$30,358.15	$12,544.69	33.1	$78,112.57	$32,277.92	38.0
7. Field staff travel	$0.00	$0.00	0	$40,692.57	$16,815.11	19.8
8. Communications	$38,220.51	$15,793.60	41.6	$14,472.35	$5,980.31	7.0
9. Control function	$2,910.17	$1,202.55	3.2	$2,137.39	$883.22	1.0
10. Postinterview activities						
a. Interviewer evaluation/ debriefing	$597.06	$246.72	0.6	$680.72	$281.29	0.3
b. Verification	$1,228.22	$507.53	1.3	$2,120.84	$876.38	1.0
c. Report to respondents	$2,734.45	$1,129.94	3.0	$1,805.95	$746.26	0.9
Total	$91,814.27	$37,939.79		$205,370.69	$84,863.92	
Per-interview costs	$56.75	$23.45		$132.67	$54.82	
Per-interview average hours required			3.3			8.7

SOURCE: Adapted from Robert M. Groves and Robert L. Kahn (1979), *Surveys by Telephone: A National Comparison With Personal Interviews* (New York: Academic Press, 1979), pp. 189, 193. Adapted with permission.
NOTE: Costs are adjusted to reflect 2001 prices by multiplying by a factor of 2.42.

today, 25 years later, these differences hold true (in a relative, if not absolute, sense) and are important for researchers to consider when planning data collection.

The cost data shown in Table 8.4 are based on two national surveys: a telephone survey sample of 1,618 persons using random digit dialing and a personal interview sample of 1,584 persons. These surveys include the following cost items and are adjusted to reflect 2001 pricing.

The telephone survey is substantially less expensive in terms of both time and money than the personal interview. Selection of the more appropriate mode depends, however, on a complete evaluation of the advantages and disadvantages of the two methods. That evaluation will reflect researchers' belief as to which method would best answer the question(s) being asked.

RESEARCH REPORTING 8.13

The professional code contains many mores concerning the reporting of research. Beyond the mundane pressures to publish, there is an underlying normative prescription: *Let the world know what you have found. Add to the storehouse of knowledge. Try to write so that you connect past research with your findings and so that other scholars can build upon your work in the future.*

In this section, both oral and written reporting are described. Research reporting usually takes place in a rather closed world, where professionals interact with one another either in professional meetings or through learned journals. Some important attributes of this subculture will be described.

The subsections that follow include material on specifications for sociological report rating, a form for sociological report rating, and a guide to sociological journals and related publications. Also discussed are where and how (and why) sociologists publish their findings, information on professional communication and reporting, and annual meetings held by various sociological and kindred societies. Lists are provided of journals sponsored by the American Sociological Association and the American Psychological Association; major journals in political science and public administration, anthropology, and education; and those used by organizational and behavioral researchers in business and by journalism and communication researchers.

8.13.1 Specifications for Sociological Report Rating

The form shown in Table 8.5 can be used to evaluate manuscripts before they are submitted for publication review. You might also benefit from using this form to evaluate your own manuscripts prior to submitting them, but even greater benefit comes from having a colleague do the review. Even though the form is almost 50 years old, it is a wonderful screening tool to obtain a general idea as to the scientific integrity and viability of a study report.

8.13.2 Evaluating Sociological Manuscripts

The evaluation form in Table 8.6 can be used to incorporate the categories and their descriptions presented in Table 8.5.

A GUIDE TO PUBLICATIONS 8.14

There are literally thousands of publications in hundreds of disciplines that publish research reports in the general areas of sociology. The following sections describe some of them, but you should be aware that new publications arise frequently and that some established ones cease publication. Check Web sites or a recent printed copy of the journal before submitting anything for publication. (Table 5.3, pp. 205-238 of this volume, contains a list of journals of interest to sociologists. This section discusses a smaller number of journals in more detail.)

Table 8.5 RATING OF SOCIOLOGICAL REPORTS

	Defective	*Substandard*	*Standard*	*Superior*
Statement of Problem				
1. Clarity of statement	Statement is ambiguous, unclear, biased, inconsistent, or irrelevant to the research.	Problem must be inferred from incomplete or unclear statement.	Statement is unambiguous and includes precise description of research objectives.	Statement is unambiguous and includes formal propositions and specifications for testing them.
2. Significance of problem	No problem stated, or problem is meaningless, unsolvable, or trivial.	Solution of the problem would be of interest to a few specialists.	Solution of the problem would be of interest to many sociologists.	Solution of the problem would be of interest to most sociologists.
3. Documentation	No documentation to earlier work, or documentation is incorrect.	Documentation to earlier work is incomplete or contains errors of citation or interpretation.	Documentation to earlier work is reasonably complete.	Documentation shows in detail the evolution of the research problem from previous research findings.
Description of Method				
4. Appropriateness of method	Problems cannot be solved by this method.	Only a partial or tentative solution can be obtained by this method.	Solution of the problem by this method is possible, but uncertain.	Problem is definitely solvable by this method.
5. Adequacy of sample or field	Sample is too small, or not suitable, or biased, or of unknown sampling characteristics.	The cases studied are meaningful, but findings cannot be projected.	Findings are projectable, but with errors of considerable, or of unknown, magnitude.	Results are projectable with known small errors, or the entire universe has been enumerated.
6. Replicability	Not replicable.	Replicable in substance, but not in detail.	Replicable in detail with additional information from the author(s).	Replicable in detail from the information given.
Presentation of Results				
7. Completeness				
8. Comprehensibility	Results are incomprehensible, or enigmatic.	Comprehension of results requires special knowledge or skills.	Relevant results are presented, partly in detail, partly in summary form.	Relevant details are presented in detail.
9. Yield	No contribution to solution of problem.	Useful hints or suggestions toward solution of problem.	Tentative solution of problem.	Definitive solution of problem.

	Defective	Substandard	Standard	Superior
Interpretation				
10. Accuracy	Errors of calculation, transcription, dictation, logic, or fact detected.	Errors likely with the procedures used. No major errors detected.	Errors unlikely with the procedures used. No errors detected.	Positive checks of accuracy included in the procedures.
11. Bias	Evident bias in presentation of results and in interpretation.	Some bias in interpretation, but not in presentation of results.	No evidence of bias.	Positive precautions against bias included in procedures.
12. Usefulness	Not useful.	Possible influence on some future work in this area.	Probable influence on some future work in this area.	Probable influence on all future work in this area.

SOURCE: Theodore Caplow designed this form. It was tested by the Committee on Research, American Sociological Society. See "Official Reports and Proceedings," *American Sociological Review, 23* (December 1958), 704-711.

Table 8.6 FORM FOR EVALUATION OF SOCIOLOGICAL MANUSCRIPTS

Author _____

Title _____

Publication Reference _____

Rater _____

Date _____

Check (√) Appropriate Columns	Defective 0	Substandard 1	Standard 2	Superior 3
Statement of problem:				
1. Clarity of statement	_____	_____	_____	_____
2. Significance of problem	_____	_____	_____	_____
3. Documentation	_____	_____	_____	_____
Description of method:				
4. Appropriateness of method	_____	_____	_____	_____
5. Adequacy of sample or field	_____	_____	_____	_____
6. Replicability	_____	_____	_____	_____
Presentation of results:				
7. Completeness	_____	_____	_____	_____
8. Comprehensibility	_____	_____	_____	_____
9. Yield	_____	_____	_____	_____
Interpretation:				
10. Accuracy	_____	_____	_____	_____
11. Bias	_____	_____	_____	_____
12. Usefulness	_____	_____	_____	_____
Enter number of checks in each column in appropriate blanks; weight as indicated, and add for Total Rating	__ × 0 = 0	__ × 1 = __ [Total Rating] [ ]	__ × 2 = __	__ × 3 = __

SOURCE: Adapted from Theodore Caplow's original form. Test reliabilities appear in "Official Reports and Proceedings," *American Sociological Review, 23* (December 1958): 704-711. See also the reports of the Educational Testing Service, Princeton, NJ, for ingenious rating scales on a large variety of subjects.

8.14.1 Guide to Major Journals in Sociology

8.14.1.1 Journals Sponsored by the American Sociological Association

The *American Sociological Review* is the official journal of the American Sociological Association (ASA), publishing articles of major concern to social scientists. This journal is noted for original research and works that promote greater understanding and introduce the newest developments in the field of sociology. All areas of sociology are accepted. The journal is based on mutual interest and high quality articles. (Section 5.2.10 discusses this journal and lists its contents for the years 1995-2000.)

Editorial information: Glenn Firebaugh, Editor, Department of Sociology, 206 Oswald Tower, The Pennsylvania State University, University Park, PA 16802, 814-863-3733, e-mail: asr@pop.psu.edu. Published in February, April, June, August, October, and December.

Contemporary Sociology is dedicated to reviews and critical discussions of recent works in sociology and related disciplines of interest to sociologists. It does not accept unsolicited reviews. Editorial information: Barbara J. Risman and Donald Tomaskovic-Devey, Co-editors, Department of Sociology, Box 8107, North Carolina State University, Raleigh, NC 27695-8107, 919-515-9022, fax: 919-513-8118, e-mail: contemporarysoc@ncsu.edu. Published in January, March, May, July, September, and November.

The *Journal of Health and Social Behavior* (formerly *Journal of Health and Human Behavior*) publishes articles that link sociological ideas and methods to the understanding of health, illness, and medicine in a social context. It "publishes research on social causes and consequences of physical health, social causes and consequences of mental health, medical professions, practices and organizations, development, life-course and aging as they relate to health and well-being, deviance and risky behavior related to health and well-being and cultural and symbolic aspects of health" (*Journal of Health and Social Behavior*'s mission statement).

Editorial information: John Mirowsky, Editor, Department of Sociology, Ohio State University, 300 Bricker Hall, 190 North Oval Mall, Columbus, OH 43210-1353, 614-688-8673, fax: 614-292-6687, e-mail: jhsb@osu.edu. Published in March, June, September, and December.

Social Psychology Quarterly (formerly *Sociometry*), a quarterly journal of research in social psychology, publishes both theoretical and empirical papers on the association between the individual and society. *Social Psychology Quarterly* is truly interdisciplinary, publishing works of sociologists and psychologists.

Editorial information: Linda Molm and Lynn Smith-Lovin, Co-editors, University of Arizona, Department of Sociology, Tucson, AZ 85721, 520-626-6499, fax: 520-621-9875, e-mail: spq@arizona.edu. Published in March, June, September, and December.

Sociological Methodology is published annually and contains articles on methods of research in the social sciences. Its mission is to "disseminate material that advances empirical research in sociology and related disciplines."

Editorial information: Co-editors are Mark Becker, University of Michigan, and Michael Soebel, University of Arizona, Department of Sociology, Tucson, AZ 85721, 520-621-3531 (Michael Soebel at University of Arizona) or 734-647-6233 (Mark Becker at University of Michigan), e-mail: soebel@arizona.edu or mbecker@umich.edu. Published annually in August.

Sociological Theory publishes articles in all areas of social thought, including new substantive theories, history of theory, metatheory, formal theory construction, and syntheses of existing bodies of theory.

Editorial information: Craig J. Calhoun, Editor, Joe Karaganis, Managing Editor, Department of Sociology, New York University, 269 Mercer Street, Room 400, New York, NY 10003, 212-998-8349, fax: 212-995-4865, e-mail: sociologicaltheory@nyu.edu. Published in March, July, and November.

Sociology of Education is a forum for social scientists and educators seeking to advance sociological knowledge about education. The journal serves as a significant medium for the application of this knowledge to major issues of educational policy and practice. It is published quarterly.

Editorial information: Pamela Barnhouse Walters, Editor, Indiana University, Department of Sociology, Indiana University, Ballantine Hall, Bloomington, IN 47405, 812-855-6969, e-mail: soe@indiana.edu. (Aaron M. Pallas, Editor-Elect, 437 Erickson Hall, Michigan State University, East Lansing, MI 48824-1034, 517-355-6682, e-mail: ampallas@pilot.msu.edu.) Published in January, April, July, and October.

The quarterly *Teaching Sociology* publishes information aimed at the discipline's teachers. Articles of analysis synthesize the issues in an area and highlight the implications for teaching sociology. Research articles report on studies of specific aspects of teaching sociology.

Editorial information: Jeffery Chin, LeMoyne College, Syracuse, NY 13214-1399, 315-445-4671, fax: 315-445-6024, e-mail: ts_editor@maple.lemoyne.edu. Published in January, April, July, and October.

8.14.1.2 ASA Publications

A list of publications of professional interest to sociologists and students majoring in sociology is available from the American Sociological Association, 1307 New York Avenue, NW, Suite 700, Washington, DC 20005. It also can be ordered through the ASA Web site, www.asanet.org.

8.14.1.3 The Ten Major Journals in Sociology

The following 10 journals are viewed by many sources as the most influential because of their content, readership, or other factors.

1. *American Journal of Sociology*
2. *American Sociological Review*
3. *The American Sociologist*
4. *Contemporary Sociology*
5. *Journal of Health and Social Behavior*
6. *Social Forces*
7. *Social Psychology Quarterly*
8. *Sociological Methods*
9. *Sociological Theory*
10. *Sociology of Education*

An author and subject index is available for each of these journals. Each entry contains the name of the journal, volume, year, month of issue, and article page ranges. Author entries contain the first and last names of articles' authors. The cumulative index can be ordered from the American Sociological Association, 1307 New York Avenue, NW, Suite 700, Washington, DC 20005. The current price is $25.00 for ASA members and $40.00 for nonmembers. The Web site is at www.asanet.org/forms/pubord.html.

8.14.1.4 Other Important Publications Issued Regularly

Footnotes of the American Sociological Association is the organ for the official reports and proceedings of the ASA. It invites opinion on such matters as the state of undergraduate education, the future employment of sociologists, the status of women and minorities in sociology, the linkage of sociology to social policy, alternative modes of graduate training, broadening the world perspective of American sociology, and adding to the knowledge base of the discipline.

The Arnold Rose Monograph Series is published by the Russell Sage Foundation Press. It provides an opportunity for members and student members of the ASA to publish short research monographs (100-300 typed pages) in any subject matter field in sociology that normally is beyond the scope of publication in a regular academic journal. Numerous volumes have been published since establishment of the series in 1968. It is published for the ASA by Rutgers University Press, P.O. Box 5062, New Brunswick, NJ 08903-5062.

Employment Bulletin is published monthly and contains current position vacancies for sociologists.

The *Annual Review of Sociology*, established in 1975, summarizes the progress of development in various fields of sociology.

Current Contents/Social & Behavioral Sciences provides access to complete bibliographic information from articles, editorials, meeting abstracts, commentaries, and all other significant items in recently published editions of approximately 1,596 of the world's leading social and behavioral sciences journals and books.

The Educational Resources Information Center (ERIC) of the National Institute of Education (NIE) publishes a monthly abstract journal, *Resources in Education* (RIE), which announces research reports and other nonjournal literature of interest to the educational community. These documents are cataloged, abstracted, and indexed by subject, author or investigator, and responsible institution. *Resources in Education* started publication in November 1966, and can be purchased in single copies or on subscription from the Superintendent of Documents, U.S. Government Printing Office, Washington, DC 20402.

Oryx Press publishes *Current Index of Journals in Education* (CIJE), which indexes articles in more than 700 journals. These journals represent the core of periodical/serial literature in the field of education. Oryx publishes the monthly and semiannual editions of CIJE, the *Thesaurus of ERIC Descriptors*, the *ERIC Identifier Authority List* (IAL), the *Semiannual Index of Resources in Education* (RIE), the *Resources in Education Annual Cumulation Abstracts*, and the *Resources in Education Annual Cumulation Index*. Oryx Press can be reached at P.O. Box 33889, Phoenix, AZ 85067-3889, 602-265-2651, e-mail: info@oryxpress.com, and Web site www.oryxpress.com.

Individual monthly volumes and yearly cumulations of *Resources in Education* and *Current Index to Journals in Education* are available in many college and university libraries, as well as in some special library collections. Most of these libraries are open to the public for on-site reference, and many also have complete ERIC microfiche collections and/or computers to access the ERIC Web site. *Resources in Education* also is available in the offices of many school systems at the state and local levels. All routine searches for documentary material should begin with *Resources in Education*.

ERIC was originally conceived in the U.S. Office of Education in the mid-1960s as a system for providing ready access to recent educational research and other educational related literature. The ERIC Processing and Reference Facility is a centralized information processing facility serving central ERIC and 16 decentralized clearinghouses, each specializing in a branch of knowledge. For further information, contact ERIC at ERIC's main address:

Educational Resources Information Center
National Library of Education
Office of Educational Research and Improvement
U.S. Department of Education
400 Maryland Ave., SW
Washington, DC 20202-5721
800-424-1616
eric@inet.ed.gov
www.accesseric.org/

Thousands of journals devoted to the social and behavioral sciences are related to the direct teaching and research efforts of sociologists. What follows is a list of related journals, some more directed to sociologists' efforts in general than others. All, however, contain information that sociologists have defined as within their scope of interest.

Other information (some of it overlapping) is available at Julian Dierkes's Sociology Links at Princeton Collection (www.princeton.edu/~sociolog/links.html), a collection including associations, journals, mailing lists, libraries, archives, and institutions. Loyola University Chicago has a collection of sociology links (at www.luc.edu/depts/sociology/soclinks.html) as does Sinclair College at its Web site for sociologists (www.sinclair.edu/departments/soc/links.htm). For listings of international electronic journals and magazines, see www.pscw.uva.nl/sociosite/ and click on Journals. This Web site contains a large list of international journals and their descriptions.

The following is a partial list of relevant journals.

Acta Sociologica
Addiction and Recovery: The Alcohol and Drug Publication
Administration in Social Work
Adolescence
Advances in Experimental Social Psychology
Advances in Group Processes
Advocate
Ageing and Society
Ageing International
Aging
Alchohol Health and Research World
Alcohol and Alcoholism: International Journal of the Medical Center on Alcoholism
Alcohol Research and Health: The Journal of the National Institute on Alcohol Abuse and Alcoholism
American Annals of the Deaf
American City and Country
American Family
American Jails: The Magazine of the American Jail Association
American Journal of Drug and Alcohol Abuse
American Journal of Police: An Interdisciplinary Journal of Theory and Research
American Journal of Sociology
American Sociological Review
American Sociologist
Ampo, Japan-Asia Quarterly Review
Annals of Human Genetics
Annals of Regional Science
Annals of Sex Research
Annual Review of Sociology
Archives Europeennes de Sociologie/European Journal of Sociology
Archives of Sexual Behavior: An Interdisciplinary Research Journal
Asia Pacific Journal of Social Work
Asia-Pacific Journal of Public Health
Australian and New Zealand Journal of Criminology

Australian and New Zealand Journal of Family Therapy
Australian and New Zealand Journal of Sociology
Australian Disability Review: Journal of the Disability Advisory Council of Australia
Australian Family/The Australian Family Association
Australian Feminist Studies
Australian Journal of Marriage and Family
Australian Journal of Regional Studies: Journal of the Australian and New Zealand Regional Science Association
Australian Journal on Ageing
Australian Planner: Journal of the Royal Australian Planning Institute
Australian Social Work
Australian Victimology: Journal of the Australia Society of Victimology
Basic and Applied Social Psychology
Behavioral Health Management
Berkeley Journal of Sociology
Berkeley Planning Journal
BIPR Bulletin/Bureau of Immigration and Population Research
Bottom Line on Alcohol in Society
British Journal of Addiction
British Journal of Criminology
British Journal of Sociology
Broadsheet: New Zealand Feminist Magazine
Bulletin on Narcotics
Canadian Journal of Criminology
Canadian Journal of Regional Science
Canadian Journal of Sociology
Canadian Journal of Women and the Law
Canadian Review of Sociology and Anthropology
Canadian Women Studies
Careers and the Disabled
Child: Care, Health, Development
Child Abuse and Neglect
Child and Adolescent Social Work Journal
Child and Family

Child and Youth Care Forum
Child and Youth Care Quarterly
Child and Youth Services
Child Care information Exchange
Child Development
Child Welfare
Children and Youth Services Review
Children Australia
Children Today
Children's Environments
Children's House, Children's World
Children's Voice
Chinese Sociology and Anthropology
Cities
City and Society
City Limits
Cityscape: A Journal of Policy Development and
    Research/U.S. Department of Housing and Urban
    Development
CJ Europe, A Criminal Justice Newsletter
Clinical Gerontologist
Clinical Social Work Journal
Community Alternatives
Community Care
Community Development Journal
Community Quarterly: A Journal Focusing on
    Community Issues
Comparative Social Research
Comparative Urban and Community Research
Computers, Environment, and Urban Systems:
    An International Journal
Computers in Human Services
Connexions
Contemporary Crises
Continuity and Change
Contrasts: Journal of the Probation and Parole
    Officers' Association of NSW (Inc.)
Contributions to Indian Sociology
Corrections Management Quarterly
Corrections Today
Counseling Across Australia
Creative Women
Crime and Delinquency
Crime and Justice
Crime Laboratory Digest/U.S. Department of Justice,
    FBI
Crime, Law, and Social Change
Criminal Justice and Behavior
Criminal Justice Ethics
Criminal Justice History
Criminal Justice Policy Review
Criminology
Criminology Australia
Crisis: The Journal of Early Intervention and Suicide
    Prevention

Critical Matrix
Critical Sociology
Cultural Dynamics
Cultural Studies
Current Issues in Criminal Justice
Current Perspectives in Social Theory
Current Perspectives on Aging and the Life Cycle
Current Research on Occupations and Professions
Day Care and Early Education
Deviant Behavior
Differences
Disability and Society
Disability, Handicap and Society
Disaster Management
Disasters
Drug and Alcohol Review
Drugs and Society
Early Child Development and Care
Economic Development Commentary
Economic Development Horizon/Center for
    International Business and Economic
    Development
Education and Training in Mental Retardation
Education and Training in Mental Retardation and
    Development Disabilities
Education of the Visually Handicapped: The Official
    Publication of Association for Education of the
    Visually Handicapped
Eighteenth Century Life
Empathy
Environment and Behavior
Environment and Planning
Environment and Urbanization
Environments
Ethnic and Racial Studies
European Journal of Social Psychology
European Sociological Review
Evaluation Review
Families
Families in Society: The Journal of Contemporary
    Human Service
Family Futures
Family Life Educator
Family Perspectives
Family Planning Perspectives
Family Relations
Family Safety and Health
Federal Prisons Journal
Feminism and Psychology
Feminisms
Feminist Arts News
Feminist Collections
Feminist Economics
Feminist Issues
Feminist Review

Feminist Studies: FS
Focus on Exceptional Children
Free Inquiry in Creative Sociology
Frontiers
Future Choices: Toward a National Youth Policy
Future of Children/Center for the Future of Children
Gallup Poll Monthly
Gender and History
Gender and Society: Official Publication of
  Sociologists for Women in Society
Gender Issues
Generations: A Journal of the Western Gerontological
  Society
Gerontologist
Global Journal on Crime and Criminal Law
Group and Organization Management
Group and Organization Studies
Growth and Change
Guru Nanak Journal of Sociology
Health and Social Work
Health Matrix
Histoire Sociale
Howard Journal of Criminal Justice
Human Ecology Forum
Human Life Review
Human Services in the Rural Environment
Humanity and Society
Indian Journal of Social Work
Information and Referral: The Journal of the Alliance
  of Information and Referral Systems
Innovations in Aging
Interaction
International Family Planning Perspectives
International Journal of Aging and Human
  Development
International Journal of Comparative and Applied
  Criminal Justice
International Journal of Comparative Sociology
International Journal of Contemporary Sociology
International Journal of Group Tensions
International Journal of Moral and Social Studies
International Journal of Offender Therapy and
  Comparative Criminology: Official Organ of the
  Association for Psychiatric Treatment of Offenders
  (APTO)
International Journal of Public Opinion Research
International Journal of Sociology
International Journal of Sociology of the Family
International Journal of Urban and Regional
  Research/Revue Internationale de Recherche
  Urbaine et Regionale
International Public Relations Review
International Regional Science Review
International Review of Modern Sociology

International Review of Social History
International Review of Women and Leadership
International Social Work
International Sociology: Journal of the International
  Sociological Association
Interrace
Iowa Woman
Issues in Child Abuse Accusations
Journal for the Theory of Social Behavior
Journal of Addictive Diseases
Journal of Adolescent Research
Journal of Adult Development
Journal of Aging and Identity
Journal of Aging Studies
Journal of Alcohol and Drug Education
Journal of Analytic Social Work
Journal of Applied Communication Research
Journal of Applied Gerontology: The Official Journal
  of the Southern Gerontological Society
Journal of Applied Social Behavior
Journal of Applied Social Psychology
Journal of Applied Social Sciences
Journal of Applied Sociology
Journal of Baccalaureate Social Work
Journal of Biosocial Science
Journal of Child and Youth Care
Journal of Child Sexual Abuse
Journal of Children and Poverty
Journal of Children in Contemporary Society
Journal of Community and Applied Social Psychology
Journal of Community Practice
Journal of Comparative Family Studies
Journal of Contemporary Criminal Justice
Journal of Contemporary Ethnography
Journal of Crime and Justice (sponsored by the
  Society of Police and Criminal Psychology)
Journal of Criminal Justice
Journal of Criminal Justice Education
Journal of Criminal Law and Criminology
Journal of Cross-Cultural Gerontology
Journal of Developmental and Physical Disabilities
Journal of Disability Policy Studies
Journal of Divorce and Remarriage
Journal of Drug Education
Journal of Drug Issues
Journal of Early Adolescence
Journal of Elder Abuse and Neglect
Journal of English and Germanic Philology
Journal of European Social Policy
Journal of Experimental Social Psychology
Journal of Family and Economic Issues
Journal of Family History
Journal of Family Issues
Journal of Family Social Work

Journal of Family Studies
Journal of Family Violence
Journal of Feminist Studies in Religion
Journal of Gay and Lesbian Social Services
Journal of Gay, Lesbian, and Bisexual Identity
Journal of Gerontological Social Work
Journal of Historical Sociology
Journal of Human Behavior in the Social
    Environment
Journal of Intercultural Studies
Journal of Interdisciplinary Gender Studies: JIGS
Journal of Intergroup Relations
Journal of Interpersonal Violence
Journal of Law and Social Work
Journal of Marriage and the Family
Journal of Mathematical Sociology
Journal of Men's Studies
Journal of Multicultural Social Work
Journal of Offender Counseling, Services and
    Rehabilitation (changed to Journal of Offender
    Rehabilitation)
Journal of Offender Rehabilitation
Journal of Personality and Social Psychology
Journal of Police Science and Administration
Journal of Political and Military Sociology
Journal of Progressive Human Services
Journal of Psychohistory
Journal of Public Relations Research
Journal of Quantitative Criminology
Journal of Refugee Studies
Journal of Research in Crime and Delinquency
Journal of Research on Adolescence
Journal of Rural Studies
Journal of Safety Research
Journal of Security Administration
Journal of Sex Education and Therapy
Journal of Sex Research
Journal of Social and Personal Relationships
Journal of Social Distress and the Homeless
Journal of Social History
Journal of Social Issues
Journal of Social Justice Studies Special Issue Series
Journal of Social Policy
Journal of Social Psychology
Journal of Social Service Research
Journal of Social Work Education
Journal of Sociology and Social Welfare
Journal of Teaching in Social Work
Journal of Technology in Human Services
Journal of the American Deafness and Rehabilitation
    Association
Journal of the British Association of Teachers of the
    Deaf

Journal of the Community Development Society
Journal of the Forensic Science Society
Journal of the History of Sexuality
Journal of the Home Economics Institute of Australia
Journal of the North-East India Council for Social
    Science Research
Journal of the Urban and Regional Information
    Systems Association/URISA
Journal of Urban Affairs
Journal of Urban Economics
Journal of Urban History
Journal of Visual Impairment and Blindness
Journal of Volunteer Administration
Journal of Women and Aging
Journal of Women's History
Journal of Youth and Adolescence
Journal of Planning Education and Research
    (Association of Collegiate Schools of Planning)
Just Policy: A Journal of Australian Social Policy
Justice Quarterly: Academy of Criminal Justice
    Sciences
Juvenile Justice (U.S. Department of Justice, Office
    of Justice Programs, Office of Juvenile Justice and
    Delinquency Prevention)
Korean Social Science Journal
Law and Order
Loss, Grief, and Care
Mainstream
Marriage and Family
Marriage and Family Review
Media, Culture & Society
Media Report to Women
Merrill-Palmer Quarterly
Michigan Feminist Studies
Mid-American Review of Sociology
Milbank Quarterly
Modern Maturity
Mortality
Motorcyclist
National Institute of Justice Journal
National Sheriff
Netherlands' Journal of Social Sciences
New Choices: Living Even Better After 50
New Choices for Retirement Living
New Choices for the Best Years
New England Journal of Human Services
New Man
New Social Worker
New Studies on the Left
New Woman
News—Women's International Network
NIJ Reports: A Selective Notification of Information
    Program of the National Institute of Justice

Nonprofit and Voluntary Sector Quarterly
NWSA Journal: A Publication of the National
  Women's Studies Association
On the Issues/Choices
Organization: The Interdisciplinary Journal of
  Organization, Theory, and Society
Papers in Regional Science: The Journal of the
  Regional Science Association International
Peace Review
Personal Relationships/Journal of the International
  Society for the Study of Personal Relationships
Perspective on Aging
Perspectives for Teachers of the Hearing Impaired
Perspectives in Education and Deafness
Perspectives on Social Problems
PETA News/People for the Ethical Treatment of
  Animals
Philanthropy Monthly
Philosophy and Social Action
Planned Giving Today
Planning and Design
Play and Culture
Plural Societies
Pointer: For Special Class Teachers and Parents of the
  Handicapped
Police Chief
Police Journal
Police Studies: The International Review of Police
  Development
Policing
Policy and Practice of Public Human Services
Policy and Research Report/The Urban Institute
Preventing School Failure
Prison Journal
Prison Service Journal
Psychoanalytic Social Work
Psychology of Women Quarterly
Public Opinion Quarterly
Public Perspective: A Roper Center Review of Public
  Opinion and Polling
Public Relations Journal
Public Relations Quarterly
Public Relations Review
Public Welfare
Qualitative Sociology
Quality Progress
Race and Class
Race, Gender, and Class: An Interdisciplinary and
  Multicultural Journal
Race, Poverty, and the Environment
Re: View
Reclaiming Children and Youth: A Journal of
  Emotional and Behavioral Problems

Refractory Girl: A Women's Studies Journal
Refugees
Regional Development Dialogue
Regional Studies
Representative Research in Social Psychology
Research in Developmental Disabilities
Research in the Sociology of Organizations
Research in Urban Economics
Research on Aging
Research on Social Work Practice
Resources for Feminist Research/Documentation sur
  la recherche féministe
Response to the Victimization of Women and Children
  (Center for Women Policy Studies)
Revue Française de Sociologie
Rural Development Perspectives (U.S. Department
  of Agriculture, Economic Research Service;
  later titled *Rural America*)
Rural History: Economy, Society, Culture
Rural Society
Rural Sociologist: A Publication of the Rural
  Sociological Society
Rural Sociology
SA: Sociological Analysis
Samya Shakti: A Journal of Women's Studies
Scarlet Woman
Science and Justice
Sex Roles
Sexualities
Sexuality and Culture
Sexuality and Disability
Sheriff: The Magazine of the National Sheriffs'
  Association
SIECUS Report
Sign Language Studies
Signs: A Journal of Women in Culture and Society
Small Group Behavior
Small Group Research
Small Town
Smith College Studies in Social Work
Social Action
Social Alternatives
Social Analysis
Social and Economic Studies
Social Behavior and Personality
Social Biology
Social Casework
Social Change
Social Development
Social Development Issues
Social Forces
Social History
Social Indicators Research

Social Justice
Social Networks
Social Pathology: A Journal of Reviews
Social Policy
Social Problems
Social Psychology Quarterly
Social Scientist
Social Service Review
Social Studies: Irish Journal of Sociology
Social Text
Social Welfare
Social Work
Social Work Education
Social Work in Health Care
Social Work Research
Social Work Research and Abstracts
Social Work Today
Social Work With Groups
Social Worker/Travailleur Social
Sociologia Ruralis
Sociological Bulletin
Sociological Focus
Sociological Forum
Sociological Inquiry
Sociological Methods and Research
Sociological Perspectives (official publication of the
    Pacific Sociological Association)
Sociological Practice
Sociological Practice Review
Sociological Quarterly
Sociological Research
Sociological Review
Sociological Spectrum
Sociological Theory
Sociologus
Sociology
Sociology and Social Research
Sociology of Religion
Sojourn: Journal of Social Issues in Southeast Asia
Solidarity
Southeast Asian Journal of Social Science
Sri Lanka Journal of Social Sciences
Sterilization of Australia/Sterilizing Research and
    Advisory Council of Australia
Studies in Conflict and Terrorism
Studies in Family Planning
Studies in Symbolic Interaction
Survey of Regional Literature
Symbolic Interaction
Teaching Sociology
Terrorism and Political Violence

Terrorism: An International Journal
Theory and Society
Third World Planning Review
Town and Country Planning (a journal of the Town
    and Country Planning Association [United
    Kingdom])
Traffic Safety
Trouble and Strife
Turn of the Century Women
Urban Affairs Quarterly
Urban Affairs Review
Urban Anthropology and Studies of Cultural Systems
    and World Economic Development
Urban Design International
Urban Ecologist: The Journal of Urban Ecology
Urban Futures
Urban History
Urban History Review
Urban Policy and Research: A Guide to Australian
    Urban Affairs
Urban Studies
US-Japan Women's Journal: English Supplement
Violence Against Women
Violence and Victims
Visibilities
Volta Review
Volta Voices
Voluntary Action Leadership
War and Society
WE International
Without Prejudice
Woman of Power
Women
Women and Criminal Justice
Women and Environments
Women and Politics
Women and Revolution
Women in Action
Women of China
Women of Vietnam
Women: A Cultural Review
Women's Studies
Women's Studies Forum
Women's Studies International Forum
Women's Studies Quarterly
Women's View
Work and Occupations
Working Mother
Working Woman
XY: Men, Sex, Politics
Youth and Society

8.14.2 Guide to Journals Sponsored by the American Psychological Association

The following is a list of journals published by the American Psychological Association (www.apa. org). Such journals often are helpful to sociologists, especially as the contents relate to areas such as social psychology.

American Psychologist is the official journal of the American Psychological Association. The monthly journal publishes the official papers of the association and substantive articles on psychology.

Contemporary Psychology is a bimonthly journal of reviews—critical reviews of books, films, and other material in the field of psychology.

The quarterly *Journal of Abnormal Psychology* is devoted to basic research and theory in the broad area of abnormal behavior.

The *Journal of Applied Psychology*, published bimonthly, gives primary consideration to original quantitative investigations of value to people interested in the following broad areas: personnel research; industrial working conditions; research on opinion and morale factors; job analysis and classification research; marketing and advertising research; and vocational and educational prognosis, diagnosis, and guidance at the secondary and college levels.

The bimonthly *Journal of Comparative Psychology* publishes original research reports in the field of comparative psychology, including animal learning, conditioning, and sensory processes.

The bimonthly *Journal of Consulting and Clinical Psychology* is devoted to the area of clinical psychology, both child and adult.

The *Journal of Counseling Psychology*, published quarterly, serves as a primary publication medium for research on counseling theory and practice.

The quarterly *Journal of Educational Psychology* publishes original investigations and theoretical papers dealing with problems of learning and teaching, and with the psychological development, relationships, and adjustment of the individual.

The *Journal of Personality and Social Psychology*, published monthly, is devoted to basic research and theory in the broad areas of social interaction and group processes. Specifically, it deals with interpersonal perception and attitude change, the psychological aspects of formal social systems and less structured collective phenomena, the socialization process at both child and adult levels, social motivation and personality dynamics, the structure of personality, and the relationship of personality to group process and social systems.

Psychological Abstracts publishes concise abstracts of the world's literature in psychology and pertinent allied subjects. All titles and abstracts of foreign material are translated into English. It is published monthly.

Psychological Bulletin is concerned with research reviews and methodological contributions in the field of psychology. One of the principal functions of this bimonthly journal is to publish critical, evaluative summaries of research. The methodological articles are directed toward people who might or do make practical use of such information and are intended to bridge the gap between the technical statistician and the typical research psychologist. Articles feature the application of new methodology as well as the creative application of more familiar methodology.

Psychological Review is the major journal of articles of theoretical significance to any area of scientific endeavor in psychology. It is published quarterly.

Other journals sponsored by the American Psychological Association include the following:

Behavioral Neuroscience

Clinician's Research Digest

Consulting Psychology Journal

Cultural Diversity and Ethnicity

Developmental Psychology

Emotion

European Psychology

Experimental and Clinical Psychopharmacology

Group Dynamics: Theory, Research and Practice

Health Psychology

History of Psychology

Journal of Educational Psychology (JEP)

    Animal Behavior Processes

JEP Applied

JEP General

JEP Human Perception and Performance

JEP Learning, Memory and Cognition

Journal of Family Psychology

Journal of Occupational Health Psychology

Minority Psychology

Neuropsychological Prevention and Treatment

Practice and Research

Professional Psychology: Research and Practice

Psychoanalytic Psychology

Psychological Methods

Psychology and Aging

Psychology of Addictive Behaviors

Psychology of Men and Masculinity

Psychology, Public Policy and Law

Rehabilitation Psychology

Review of General Psychology

8.14.3 Guide to Major Journals in Political Science and Public Administration

American Journal of Political Science. Journals Division, University of Wisconsin Press, 2537 Daniels St., Madison, WI 53718. Published quarterly, in the months of January, April, July, and October.

American Political Science Review. American Political Science Association, 1527 New Hampshire Avenue, NW, Washington, DC 20036, www.apsanet.org/.

Annals of the American Academy of Political and Social Science. Sage Periodicals Press, Sage Publications, Inc., 2455 Teller Road, Thousand Oaks, CA 91320.

Foreign Affairs. Council of Foreign Relations Publications, Box 420235, Palm Coast, FL 32142-0235.

Journal of Politics. Southern Political Science Association. Published by Blackwell Publishers, 108 Cowley Road, Oxford, OX4 1JF United Kingdom, www.blackwellpub.com/.

Midwest Journal of Political Science. Midwest Political Science Association, 1100 E. Seventh St., Woodburn Hall #210, Bloomington, IN 47405.

Political Science Quarterly. The Academy of Political Science, Political Science Quarterly, 475 Riverside Drive, Suite 1274, New York, NY 10115-1274, www.psqonline.org/.

Public Administration Review. Levin College of Urban Affairs, Cleveland State University, Cleveland, OH 44115, par@urban.csuohio.edu.

Review of Politics. P.O. Box B, Notre Dame, IN 46556-0762.

Social Research. New School University, 65 Fifth Avenue, Room 354, New York, NY 10003.

World Politics. Johns Hopkins University Press, 2715 North Charles Street, Baltimore, MD 21218-4319, www.press.jhu.edu/.

8.14.4 Guide to Major Journals in Anthropology

American Anthropologist. 4350 North Fairfax Drive, Suite 640, Arlington, VA 22203-1620.

Current Anthropology. University of Chicago Press, P.O. Box 37005, Chicago, IL 60637.

Human Organization. P.O. Box 24083, Oklahoma City, OK 73124.

8.14.5 Guide to Major Research Journals in Education

American Educational Research Journal (American Educational Research Association, www.www.aera.net)

American Journal of Education (www.journals.uchicago.edu)

British Journal of Educational Studies (www.blackwellpublishers.co.uk)

Child Development (www.srcd.org)

Child Development Abstracts & Bibliography (www.blackwellpublishers.co.uk/srcd/)
Educational and Psychological Measurement (www.sagepub.co.uk)
Educational Policy Analysis Archives (www.epaa.asu.edu)
ERIC Clearinghouse on Assessment and Evaluation (www.ericae.net)
Journal of Educational Measurement (www.ncme.org)
Journal of Educational Policy
Journal of Educational Research (*www.heldref.org/*)
Journal of Experimental Education (www.heldref.org/)
National Black Child Development Institute (www.nbcdi.org)
Review of Educational Research (www.aera.net)

8.14.6 Guide to Major Journals Used by Organizational and Behavioral Researchers

Academy of Management Journal
Administrative Science Quarterly
Decision Sciences
Human Relations
Journal of Applied Psychology
Organization and Administrative Sciences
Organizational Behavior and Human Performance
Social Psychology Quarterly

8.14.7 Guide to Major Journals Used by Journalism and Communication Researchers

American Communication Journal (www.americancomm.org)
Canadian Journal of Communication (www.cjc-online.ca)
International Journal of Communications Law and Policy (www.digital-law.net)
Journal of Computer Mediated Communication (www.ascusc.org)
Journal of Visual Communication and Image Representation (www.apnet.com)
Journalism and Mass Communication Quarterly (http://scolar.vsc.edu)
Public Opinion Quarterly (www.journals.uchicago.edu)

8.14.8 Other Journals of Interest to Sociologists

The following journals of interest to sociologists are published by Sage Publications.

Communication Abstracts
Communication Research
Discourse & Society
Discourse Studies
Ethnicities
European Journal of Communication
European Journal of Cultural Studies
Feminist Theory
Gazette
The Harvard International Journal of Press/Politics
International Journal of Cultural Studies
Journal of Business and Technical Communication
Journal of Communication Inquiry
Journal of Consumer Culture

Journal of Language and Social Psychology
Journal of Social and Personal Relationships
Journal of Visual Culture
Journalism
Journalism and Mass Communication Resources
Management Communication Quarterly
Media, Culture & Society
New Media & Society
Organization
Science Communication
Television & New Media
The Iowa Guide
Theory, Culture & Society
Visual Communication

8.14.9 Books of Interest in Sociology and Related Fields

Educating for Freedom: The Paradox of Pedagogy, by Donald L. Finkle and William Ray Arney. 1995, 260 pages, $48.00 cloth.

Flesh Peddlers and Warm Bodies: The Temporary Help Industry and Its Workers, by Robert E. Parker. 1994, 187 pages, $40.00 cloth/$14.00 paper.

Gender Differences in Science Careers: The Project Access Study, by Gerhard Sonnert with Gerald Holton, foreword by Robert K. Merton. 1995, 200 pages, $50.00 cloth.

Identity Designs: The Sights and Sounds of a Nation, by Karen A. Cerulo. 1995, 264 pages, $50.00 cloth.

Organizing for Equality: The Evolution of Women's and Racial-Ethnic Organizations in America, 1955-1985, by Debra C. Minkoff. 1995, 150 pages, $48.00 cloth.

Macrodynamics: Toward a Theory on the Organization of Human Populations, by Jonathan H. Turner. 1995, 242 pages, $50.00 cloth.

Relations Into Rhetorics: Local Elite Structure in Norfolk, England, 1540-1640, by Peter S. Bearman. 1993, 208 pages, $40.00 cloth.

The Social Control of Religious Zeal: A Study of Organizational Contradictions, by Jon Miller. 1994, 240 pages, $48.00 cloth.

Supermarkets Transformed, by John P. Walsh. 1993, 180 pages, $36.00 cloth.

A Weberian Theory of Human Society: Structure and Evolution, by Walter L. Wallace. 1994, 335 pages, $59.00 cloth.

8.15 WHERE PRESTIGIOUS SOCIOLOGISTS PUBLISH AND WHY

Sociologists publish research manuscripts with numerous publishing companies and university presses, and they publish research articles in many different journals (some of which are listed in the preceding sections). Many trade outlets serve as additional outlets, such as *Harper's Magazine*, *The Atlantic*, *Commentary*, *The New Yorker*, and *New Republic*.

In addition, sociologists write in newspapers, prepare pamphlets, and distribute mimeographed and printed materials to selected audiences. They write to secure tenure and promotion, to secure merit increases in pay, to increase their status, and because they just like to write and "get their work out." They, like many academics, are driven by an ethic that impels them to "make their work known" so that their knowledge will be preserved and transmitted.

Of all the motives that drive scholars to write, the most universal and persistent is the desire for status. This is expressed first as a desire to become "known" and then as the desire to rank even higher in prestige. It is appropriate, therefore, for scholars to know which journals rank high in prestige.

8.15.1 Publication Characteristics Among Leading Sociological Journals

Table 8.7 identifies the major journals in sociology and provides information (current as of 2001) on the following variables:

- ▪▪ Types of items published
- ▪▪ Publication lag (from submission to appearance in print)
- ▪▪ Gender and minority status of reviewers
- ▪▪ Gender and minority status of editorial board members

Table 8.7 GENERAL INFORMATION ABOUT LEADING SOCIOLOGICAL JOURNALS

	American Sociological Review	Contemporary Sociology	Journal of Health and Social Behavior	Social Psychology Quaarterly	Sociological Methodology	Sociological Theory	Sociology of Education	Teaching Sociology
Types of items published								
Articles	42	33	27	25	9	13	12	16
Book reviews	0	448	0	0	0	0	0	26
Symposium reviews	0	0	0	0	0	0	0	0
Review essays	0	26	0	0	0	0	0	0
Comments	12	16	0	0	0	4	0	2
Other	0	0	1	0	0	1	0	19
Publication lag								
Editorial (in weeks)	9.1	24.0	12.1	10.3	15.3	9.0	15.6	10.0
Production (in months)	7.3	7.0	4.5	5.7	NA	2.0	3.0	6.0
Time from review to publication (in months)	9.6	13.0	7.5	8.3	NA	4.3	6.9	8.5
Gender and minority status of reviewers								
Male	488	164	NA	105	33	190	85	NA
Female	262	129	NA	69	2	55	58	NA
Minorities	NA	NA	NA	NA	1	NA	NA	NA

NA = not available.

8.16 GETTING PUBLISHED

Few academics know all the ins and outs of publishing. This is not surprising, because the rules governing publishing are not a few, easily learned principles but instead a multitude of various considerations, any one of which can work for or against a researcher. Each form of publishing has its own set of particular requirements.

Being well prepared is surely the first step. The American Sociological Association's preparation checklist for submitting manuscripts to publications serves a useful role in becoming well prepared. Even though this checklist is complete, almost every journal has (usually printed on the inside front or inside back cover) guidelines that are specific to that journal. These also should be consulted before sending a manuscript for review.

8.16.1 The All-Important ASA Checklist

Below is the preparation checklist for manuscripts submitted to journals published by the American Sociological Association (ASA). Following these guidelines will ensure that the reviewer will not reject a manuscript simply because of format inconsistencies. Reprinted with permission of the ASA.

Format

- All pages must be typed or printed (12-point type size preferred), double-spaced (including footnotes and references) on 8-½ by 11-inch white paper.
- Margins must be at least 1-¼ inches on all four sides to allow room for editor's or copy editor's notes.

Title Page

- Includes the full title of the article, the author(s)'s name(s) and institution(s) (listed vertically if there is more than one author), a running head (60 characters or less), the approximate word count for the manuscript, and a title footnote.
- An asterisk (*) by the title refers to the title footnote at the bottom of the title page. The title footnote includes the name and address of the corresponding author, acknowledgments, credits, and/or grant numbers.

Abstract

- The abstract appears on a separate page headed by the title. It should be a brief (one paragraph of 150 to 200 words) and descriptive summary of the most important contributions in your paper.

Text

- **Content.** As you make changes in your text, read it objectively—from your reader's point of view. Use terminology consistently throughout your text. Referring to a variable by one name at one time and by another name later or in your tables can confuse your readers. And remember, "active" writing ("I discovered that . . .") is more concise, accurate, and interesting than "passive" writing ("It was discovered that . . .").
- **Subheadings.** Generally, three levels of subheadings are sufficient to indicate the organization of the content. See recent issues of the *ASR* for subheading formats.

■ **Text citations.** Include the last name of the author and year of publication. Include page numbers when you quote directly from a work or refer to specific passages. Cite only those that provide evidence for your assertions or that guide readers to important sources on your topic. Examples follow:

If author's name is in the text, follow the name with the year of publication in parentheses—". . . Duncan (1959)"; if author's name is not in the text, enclose both the last name and year in parentheses—". . . (Gouldner 1963)."

Pagination follows the year of publication after a colon—". . . (Ramirez and Weiss 1979:239-40)."

Give both last names for joint authors—". . . (Martin and Bailey 1988)."

For works with three authors, list all last names in the first citation in the text; thereafter use "et al."—". . . (Carr, Smith, and Jones 1962)"; and later, ". . . (Carr et al. 1962)." For more than three authors, use "et al." throughout.

For institutional authorship, supply minimum identification from the complete citation—". . . (U.S. Bureau of the Census 1963:117)."

Separate a series of references with semicolons—". . . (Burgess 1968; Marwell et al. 1971)."

For unpublished materials, use "forthcoming" to indicate material scheduled for publication. For dissertations and unpublished papers, cite the date. If no date, use "n.d." in place of the date—". . . Smith (forthcoming) and Jones (n.d.)."

For machine-readable data files, cite authorship and date—". . . (Institute for Survey Research 1976)."

Equations

■ Equations in the text should be typed or printed. Use consecutive Arabic numerals in parentheses at the right margin to identify important equations. Align all expressions and clearly mark compound subscripts and superscripts. Please clarify all unusual characters or symbols. Use italic type for variables in equations and in the text; use bold type for vectors.

Footnotes/Endnotes

■ Use footnotes/endnotes only when necessary. Notes, in general, and long notes, in particular, distract the reader and are expensive to print. As alternatives, consider (a) stating in the text that information is available from the author, or (b) adding an appendix.

■ Begin each note with the superscript numeral to which it is keyed in the text. Notes can (a) explain or amplify text, or (b) cite materials of limited availability.

■ Notes should be typed or printed, double-spaced, either as footnotes at the bottom of the page or in a separate "Endnotes" section following the references.

Reference List

■ All references cited in the text must be listed in the reference list, and vice versa. Double check spelling and publication details—ASA journals are not responsible for the accuracy of your reference list.

■ List references in alphabetical order by authors' last names. Include full names of all authors. Use first name, or initials only if the author used initials in the original publication.

■ For multiple authorship, only the name of the first author is inverted (e.g., "Jones, Arthur B., Colin D. Smith, and Barrie Thorne").

▪▪ For two or more references by the same author(s), list them in order of the year of publication. Use six hyphens and a period (———.) in place of the name when the authorship is the same as in the preceding citation.

▪▪ To list two or more works by the same author(s) from the same year, distinguish them by adding letters (a, b, c, etc.) to the year or to "Forthcoming" (e.g., 1992a, Forthcoming a). List in alphabetical order by title.

A few examples of references styles follow. See recent issues of any ASA journal for further examples:

Books

Bernard, Claude. [1865] 1957. *An Introduction to the Study of Experimental Medicine.* Translated by H. C. Greene. New York: Dover.

Mason, Karen O. 1974. *Women's Labor Force Participation and Fertility.* Research Triangle Park, NC: National Institutes of Health.

U.S. Bureau of the Census. 1960. *Characteristics of Population.* Vol. 1. Washington, DC: U.S. Government Printing Office.

Periodicals

Conger, Rand D. Forthcoming. "The Effects of Positive Feedback on Direction and Amount of Verbalization in a Social Setting." *Sociological Perspectives.*

Goodman, Leo A. 1947a. "The Analysis of Systems of Qualitative Variables When Some of the Variables Are Unobservable. Part I-A Modified Latent Structure Approach." *American Journal of Sociology* 79:1179-1259.

Collections

Clausen, John A. 1972. "The Life Course of Individuals." Pp. 457-514 in *Aging and Society*, vol. 3, *A Sociology of Age Stratification*, edited by M. W. Riley, M. Johnson, and A. Foner. New York: Russell Sage.

Elder, Glen H. 1975. "Age Differentiation and the Life Course." Pp. 165-90 in *Annual Review of Sociology*, vol. 1, edited by A. Inkeles, J. Coleman, and N. Smelser. Palo Alto, CA: Annual Reviews.

Dissertations

Charles, Maria. 1990. "Occupational Sex Segregation: A Log-Linear Analysis of Patterns in 25 Industrial Countries." Ph.D. dissertation, Department of Sociology, Stanford University, Stanford, CA.

Machine-Readable Data File

American Institute of Public Opinion. 1976. *Gallup Public Opinion Poll #965* [MRDF]. Princeton, NJ: American Institute of Public Opinion [producer]. New Haven, CT: Roper Public Opinion Research Center, Yale University [distributor].

Foreign Language Books/Journals/Articles

Kardelj, Edvard. 1960. *Razvoj Slovenackog Nacionalnog Pitanja* (Development of the Slovenian National Question). Beograd, Yugoslavia: Kultura.

Biography

Include a short biography (five or six lines) for each author. Each biography should include the author's name, title, department, and institution, and a brief description of current research interests, publications, or awards.

Tables, Figures, and Appendices

Include tables, figures, and appendices only when they are critical to the reader's understanding. As an alternative, consider inserting a statement in the text stating that the information is available from the author.

Tables

Number tables consecutively throughout the text. Type or print each table on a separate page at the end of your paper. Insert a note in the text to indicate table placement (e.g., "Table 2 About Here").

Each table must include a descriptive title and headings for all columns and rows (see recent ASA journal issues for examples).

For clarity, always use the same variable names in your tables as you use in your text.

Standard errors, standard deviations, t statistics, and so on should appear in parentheses under the means or coefficients in the tables.

Gather general notes to tables as "Note:" or "Notes:" at the bottom of the table; use [a], [b], [c], etc., for table footnotes.

Use asterisks *, **, and/or *** to indicate statistical significance at the $p < .05$, $p < .01$, and $p < .001$ levels, respectively; note if tests are one-tailed or two-tailed. Generally, only those results significant at the $p < .05$ level or better should be indicated as significant in tables or text.

Figures and Other Artwork

Number figures or illustrations consecutively throughout the text. Each should include a title. Insert a note in the text to indicate placement (e.g., "Figure 1 About Here").

If your manuscript is accepted for publication, you must submit figures and illustrations in camera-ready form or on floppy disk. Camera-ready artwork must be produced by computer or by a graphic artist in black ink on white paper with clear lines. All labels on figures and illustrations must be typeset.

IMPORTANT: Before you submit a figure or illustration for publication, please contact the journal editorial office to discuss size specifications and/or disk and file formats. All artwork and type must be legible when reduced or enlarged to fit one or two column widths, 2-9/16 and 5-5/16 inches wide respectively (standard column widths for ASA journals).

Author(s) must secure permission to publish any copyrighted figure, illustration, or photograph.

Appendices

Appendices appear at the end of your article and should be labeled "Appendix A," "Appendix B," etc.

When you have completed the final changes to your manuscript, run your computer spell-checker to correct misspelled words. You can also use the spell-checker to cross-check author names cited in your text with author names in the reference list.

8.16.2 Finding a Publisher for Articles

Each journal has its own goals and its own preferred style. It may have its own definition of "appropriate length" for a manuscript as well. Most important will be the standards of quality the journal's editors impose upon the articles accepted for publication. The more accurately the writer gauges these considerations, the greater his or her chance of acceptance. (Contributors should always follow the guidelines for the specific journal, as discussed in section 8.16.1.)

The way to acquire such background information is to become thoroughly familiar with the journal in which you hope to publish. If you want to publish in the most prestigious journals, you should not send them any work that fails to meet the standards exhibited in the issues you read. You should be aware that the competition is intense and that the acceptance rate ranges each year between 10% and 20% of the articles received. This rate includes articles that initially were rejected, then accepted after substantial revisions had been made to meet editors' criticisms. Each article is read by two or more professional readers, whose evaluations are subsequently weighed by the editor.

It is generally a good idea to have colleagues read a manuscript for their comments and input before you send it out to a journal. Writers who get published usually write tentative drafts and ask for the advice of colleagues. They are willing to accept criticism and willing to rewrite, rewrite, and rewrite if necessary. In some cases, your colleagues may be as qualified as the reviewers that the journal uses. The final draft, incorporating colleagues comments, should be as close to perfect as possible, with all style requirements matched against the format of the journal to which the manuscript will be submitted.

Whatever the fate of the papers submitted, researchers must remember that writing is an art, even for scientific work—and art is subject to taste, so rejection from one journal does not mean that another journal will not choose to publish an article. The writer who wants to be published keeps writing and submitting work. There are numerous journals, and most work of reasonable quality can be published somewhere. In the exercise of the art, the writer learns the ins and outs of both writing and the placement of work. If a writer seeks prestige, he or she will aim for the prestigious journals only when the work merits it and when the writing commends it.

If a manuscript is rejected by the leading journal (and perhaps not invited for resubmission after changes have been made), take into account the lengthy review that usually accompanies the editorial decision. Following the advice of experts in the field, as expressed in the review, can only help in the redraft of the document.

8.16.3 Finding a Publisher for Books

A writer may achieve higher prestige and notoriety for publishing a book rather than one or more journal articles. In addition, books (especially textbooks) can generate revenue. Decisions about whether to publish monographs, texts, edited books, or readings require balancing motives and skills. The decisions also should be timed to appropriate stages in the researcher's professional career.

A beginning assistant professor will want to concentrate on establishing his or her academic reputation. That reputation is not enhanced by writing a textbook, even though the textbook might bring notice (and potentially revenue) to the author. At many major research universities, a textbook does not carry a significant amount of weight when it comes to promotion and tenure considerations, and it may even hurt the candidate.

A few general rules for finding a publisher for books have been set forth by Carolyn Mullins.

When and How?

The ideal time to begin interesting publishers in a research monograph is when you begin the research or receive funds to support it. If a text or trade book is on your mind, start looking for a publisher as soon as you get the idea for it.

Texts are usually intended for classroom use only. Rarely do they have scholarly interest. Trade books . . . have a nonacademic market in addition to whatever student or professional market they may have. Monographs are usually intended for faculty use; many have some utility in graduate seminars, and a few are useful in advanced undergraduate courses. Publishers, naturally, are delighted when a genuine research monograph also has obvious text and/or trade markets. Publishers (some university presses excepted) usually show greater interest in texts and trade books than in monographs because the former are more likely to make money. It follows, then, that competition is more likely to develop if you are trying to interest publishers in a text or trade book than if a monograph is your intended product.

Edited collections—whether of previously published papers or of unpublished papers—can fall into any category. They present many different and specialized problems. These have to do with obtaining permissions, pricing, keeping them within reasonable size limits, getting several contributors to cooperate and meet deadlines, trying to set contract obligations and rewards equitably, and so forth. They are also less popular now than they used to be, partly because of the high permission cost that is often involved. (Mullins, 1975, pp. 2-3)[1]

Charles Kadushin explains that he was besieged for advice after the publication of *Books: The Culture and Commerce of Publishing* (1982), written with Lewis A. Coser and Walter W. Powell.

Colleagues want to know how to deal with editors and publishers, what different kinds of publishers there are, how to get editors and publishers to pay attention to your work, what kinds of manuscripts are appropriate for whom, how to negotiate a contract, and one hundred and one tactical and practical questions about scholarly communications in print. I now have an immediate answer to almost any question. First read *Scholarly Writing and Publishing*. Chances are that your question is answered in that slim volume. (Kadushin, 1987, pp. 857-858)[2]

Further words of wisdom from Kadushin (1987) include the following:

- The kind of organization, style, and presentation of a dissertation are anathema to publishers and journal reviewers.
- Potential authors of college texts should be forewarned that they are about to enter into a complex system that has more in common with mass media business than with academic scholarship.
- The major means of communication among scholars remains, for better or worse, the journal article.
- Amitai Etzioni once said that the way to reach your colleagues is to write them a letter.
- Authors need to take a much more active role in the publishing process, especially in book promotion. If the scholarly author does not know, by name, the 3,000 or so persons who *must* read her book, then she does not know enough to have written it.

Notes

1. This quotation is used by permission of the author. Writing books and finding a publisher for monographs and textbooks is discussed more fully in C. J. Mullins, *Writing and Publishing in the Social and Behavioral Sciences* (New York: Wiley-Interscience, 1977).

2. The work Kadushin cites is Mary Frank Fox, editor, *Scholarly Writing and Publishing: Issues, Problems, and Solutions* (Boulder, CO: Westview, 1985).

References

Kadushin, Charles. (1987). How not to perish in the publishing process. *Contemporary Sociology,* *16*, 857-858.

Mullins, Carolyn J. (1975, February). *Everything you always wanted to know about book publishing.* Paper presented at Indiana University.

8.16.4 How to Take Rejection

The probability is far higher that your learned paper will receive a rejection from a major journal than that it will be accepted for publication. There are many reasons for this, including the ones discussed below. If you cannot learn how to adjust to having your submissions rejected, then you will have a particularly difficult time learning from the process of sharing research findings with your colleagues. Rejection happens to everyone.

Lack of space. The *American Sociological Review* receives upward of 500 manuscripts a year, and *Contemporary Sociology* almost 1,800. Obviously, only a fraction of the submitted papers can be accepted because the number of pages available are limited.

Errors of judgment made by competent reviewers and editors. Let us assume that no biases exist in the review process and that the same level of measurement efficiency exists as in other measurement processes that are based on coding of qualitative materials. Given these assumptions, Stinchcombe and Ofshe (1969) estimated the validity of a judgment of article quality to be about .70. They then set forth a model providing an estimate of the proportion of acceptance of papers of different quality at the acceptance level of 16%. If the quality of the papers is approximately normal, papers *judged* to be one standard deviation or more above the mean of the papers submitted will be accepted. For papers at different points of *true quality*, the researchers calculated what proportion would be judged to be above the acceptance level of one standard deviation above the mean. They computed the conditional distribution of *judged* quality for a given value of *true* quality. They applied the resulting model to a random 100 papers submitted for publication, with the following results: Of 84 submitted papers that were truly below the acceptance level, 77 (92%) were rejected and only 7 (8%) were accepted. Of 16 papers truly above the cutoff point, 9 (56%) were accepted and 7 (44%) were rejected. "In terms of numbers of papers, there are about equal numbers of distinguished papers mistakenly rejected and mediocre papers mistakenly accepted" (Stinchcombe & Ofshe, 1969, p. 116).

Many editors would dispute this finding and would contend that good reviewers and editors are better judges than the validity coefficient (.70) allows. Stinchcombe and Ofshe (1969) contend that the virtue of their model does not "take a conspiracy theory of journal editing to account for the rejection of a great many good papers and the publishing of a large number of mediocre papers" (p. 117).[1] Of course, because the cutoff level is 16%, 84 out of every 100 papers are, on average, rejected.

Reviewer and editor incompetence and bias. There is a widespread suspicion (but no proof) that considerable incompetence exists among referees and editors (Freese, 1979). It is possible that such suspicion is based on the understandable reaction that "*my* paper was of such high quality that only poor reviewing failed to discern its merit." Wounded egos aside, it must be remembered that most reviewers are *volunteers* (the exceptions are paid editorial assistants, when they exist) and that they sometimes give their valuable time grudgingly and unevenly. Almost no reviewers have been specifically trained to review. It is like college teaching: They are expected to learn this as a by-product of other training. Some reviewers get an "ego trip" out of overcritical behavior, some just do a lazy "once over," and some simply are not competent to handle particular papers. Furthermore, some react with ideological or methodological bias rather than giving a decision based on balanced judgment.

It is up to the editor to catch this kind of misconduct, but journal editors, too, have human frailties. As professionals, they must budget their time, and there is just so much time to give to the reviewing process of the journal. In defense of editors, the following may be said:

- Editors often lack information about many reviewers' work and lack resources to identify the ablest reviewers.
- Editors must persuade busy professionals to give up valuable time to get the best reviews; failing to get the best, editors often must take second or third best if a review is to be made at all.

Table 8.8   A TYPOLOGY OF REVIEWERS

The Lazy	The Ego Aggrandizer	The Ego Projectionist	The Competent	The Compassionate
Gives the paper a hasty examination	Wants to parade his or her critical and superior faculties	Wants the author to write just as he or she, the reviewer, would do	Studies carefully and conscientiously prepares a balanced critique	Does a competent review and takes added care in pointing out ways of improving the article

- Editors cannot read every paper and every review if their journals attract large numbers of papers.
- Most editors are specialists in particular fields and cannot be expected to judge wisely on papers in large number of fields.

Inherent difficulty of judging social research. Finally, for editor and reviewer alike, ascertaining the "quality" of a paper is more difficult in sociology and the other social sciences than in the physical sciences. Standards are difficult to apply. In the physical sciences, criteria for quality can be established more easily, and rejection rates in physical science journals are much lower than in the major sociological journals.

Don't Blow Your Cool

There are sensitive egos in any profession. Professionals have worked many years and have surmounted many barriers to prove their right to hold degrees and to practice. A professional ego gets a jolt when an "excellent" paper fares badly. The range of emotions runs from disappointment and despondence to humiliation to anger and explosive vehemence. One editor writes

> In my judgment, authors' distress with the review process is more a function of the rejection of submitted articles than the quality of reviews; the two are not necessarily related. . . . Nothing so infuriates an author as to be told that little fault can be found with an article but that it cannot be accepted for publication. (Stryker, 1979, p. 238)

In the world of "publish or perish," with tenure, promotion, and merit increases at stake, there is ample impetus to raise both adrenalin and blood pressure in the human organism.

The Adaptive Response

You can "stew in your juices" or take a new look at your paper and at the reviews. (Ordinarily, the editor will send copies of the review in whole or in part.) Maybe you will be asked to revise and resubmit. Now is the time to apply some social insight. What kind of reviewers did you have? A typology of reviewers is provided (Table 8.8) so that you can make a judgment.

This typology may give you some clues as to the quality of your reviewers and help you make up your mind as to the worth of and future prospects for your paper. You may want to dig deeper into the motivations of the anonymous persons who judged your paper. If you do this, it is suggested that you examine some basic orientations of social researchers. This is the age of diversity, and professionals come in all colors. Look at the classification in Table 8.9 and examine carefully the radicals, the humanists, and the positivists. Did you get caught in an ideological bias that helped to reject your paper? Where do you fit in these orientations? What is the dominant orientation of the journal to which you offered your paper? It is entirely possible that your reviewers may have "liked your paper but found weaknesses in your method." This may mean that their methodological biases are showing. A look at methodological bias is in order (see Table 8.10).

Table 8.9   ORIENTATIONS OF REVIEWERS

Radical			Humanist		Positivist	
(personality and organizational change oriented)			*(historical, theoretical, value-oriented)*		*(measurement oriented)*	
Concern With Rapid Social Change			*Concern with Current Social Problems*		*Concern With Sociological Problems*	
Marxist ideologist	Ideologically uncommitted but critical of established institutions	Active intervention in social problems	Monitoring of crisis	Eschews any interest in applied work; concerned only with theoretical and value implications	Favors placing method secondary to the cumulation of new knowledge around central persistent sociological themes	Favors rigorous empirical treatment with emphasis on sophisticated mathematical methods

Table 8.10   METHODOLOGICAL PREDISPOSITIONS OF REVIEWERS

Introspection	Theory	Observation	Measurement
Likes evidence of capable intuitive identification of personal and social processes	Likes demonstration of interrelated theoretical propositions ranging from global to middle range according to reviewer's preference	Gives special significance to the manner of observation, ranging from archival and documentary work to fieldwork to laboratory work	Gives favor to the rigor of measurement, ranging from qualitative to quantitative methodology

Make Decisions, Then Act

You are now ready to reevaluate your paper. Go over the reviewer's criticisms and look at your paper as if you are a critic. Your choices are these:

1. Submit a revised version of your paper with an accompanying letter to the editor setting out your dispute with points used in the initial rejection. Ask the editor to bring your revised paper and notes to the attention of the previous reviewers in order to get a reappraisal.
2. Try another publication channel. They are numerous. Look at section 8.14, which lists journals not only in sociology but also in related fields. If your paper has something to offer, it will get published. Keep trying.
3. Have the guts to admit that the paper is seriously flawed and get on with new work.[2]

Notes

1. A symposium in *Contemporary Sociology* reviews in detail the *American Journal of Sociology*, *American Sociological Review*, and *Social Forces* for 1975-1979; see *Contemporary Sociology, 8,* 789-824, which includes discussions by Jerry Gaston, Norbert Wiley, Walter B. Grove, Everett K. Wilson, Morris Zelditch, Jr., James L. McCartney, Samuel A. Mueller, and Duncan Lindsey. Critiques and suggestions for improvement of the review process abound. This symposium is the most thorough analysis made to date.

For further research and discussion, see Hargens (1988) and note the appendix on page 150 showing annual acceptance rates and submissions for 30 journals during the late 1960s and early 1980s. This is followed by a provocative paper by Cole, Cole, and Simon (1988) and a reply by Hargens.

2. For a discussion of behavior response to failure, see Crittenden and Wiley (1980). Authors' attributions to rejections in the referred journals *Sociology of Work* and *Sociological Quarterly* are studied using regression procedures. The authors find that the behavioral response is directly influenced by past experience. It makes a difference in confidence whether one attributes the rejection to variable causes or to stable causes. Women, especially, are prone to attribute rejection to stable causes.

References

Cole, Stephen, Cole, Jonathan R., & Simon, Gary. (1988). Do journal rejection rates index consensus? *American Sociological Review, 53,* 152-156.

Crittenden, Kathleen S., & Wiley, Mary G. (1980). Causal attribution and behavioral response to failure. *Social Psychology Quarterly, 43,* 353-358.

Freese, Lee. (1979). On changing some role relationships in the editorial review process. *American Sociologist, 14,* 231-238.

Hargens, Lowell L. (1988). Scholarly consensus and journal rejection rates. *American Sociological Review, 53,* 139-151.

Stinchcombe, Arthur L., & Ofshe, Richard (1969). On journal editing as probabilistic process. *American Sociologist, 4*(2), 116-117.

Stryker, Sheldon. (1979). On the editorial review process. *American Sociologist, 14,* 238.

PROFESSIONAL MEMBERSHIPS AND ORGANIZATIONS · 8.17

A professional research life is an ongoing process of research investigation, reading research journals, preparing scientific papers, and reading papers before professional audiences of various learned societies, and finally publishing articles and monographs.[1] For them to command attention, it is necessary for researchers to make themselves and their work known to colleagues in local, state, regional, national, and international circles.

The North American sociologist who wishes to be known in national and international circles will join the American Sociological Association (ASA) and may affiliate with one or both of the leading international sociological associations: the International Sociological Association and Institut International de Sociologie.

Of all the many circles in which the researcher may move and find outlets, no forums are more important than annual meetings of the ASA and publication in the *American Sociological Review*. If you are a young sociologist, you should join the ASA as soon as you make a commitment to professional life. You should begin reading the *ASR*, which will provide research examples of high-quality work as well as names of leaders in the field. For the aspiring sociologist, the *ASR* should stimulate participation in the annual meetings and encourage growth of research interests.

One of the first steps to professionalization is to know the research in your fields of interest and the leading researchers who are at the cutting edge of the discipline. Another step to be taken early, and the most important, is to join this circle through participation, achievement, and recognition.

The ASA is a voluntary association of individual members with many categories of membership. Full membership in the ASA requires the holding of a PhD degree in sociology or in some related field, or the completion of 3 years of graduate study in such field. Students are encouraged to join as associates at low fees. An earlier survey showed that 8 out of 10 members were employed in colleges and universities and another 2 out of 10 members worked in nonacademic settings. Of the total membership, 11,000 came from the United States and 1,400 came from outside the United States. Approximately 30% of the members were women, and their proportion has risen steadily.

Regional associations are part of the contact and communication pattern and often represent the first professional experience of a young scholar. Regional meetings are smaller, and the competition for acceptance of papers is less intense. This is a good place for the young scholar to start on the journey toward becoming a professional. Numerous local and regional associations exist. Some of the larger associations and typical activities at associational meetings are discussed in the following sections.

8.17.1 American Sociological Association

For information about annual meetings of the American Sociological Association and other sociological societies, contact

American Sociological Association
1307 New York Avenue, NW
Suite 700
Washington, DC 20005
202-383-9005
www.asa.org/

8.17.2 Topics Common at Annual ASA Meetings

What follows is a list of topics that are discussed at most annual meetings of the American Sociological Association.

Aging	Divorce, Consequences of
Altruism	Economic Sociology
Applied Research and Evaluation	Education, Sociology of
At-Risk Youth	Emotions, Sociology of
Bioethics	Environmental Sociology
Biosocial Interactions	Ethnic Conflict and the New Civil Wars
Children and Youth	Family and Kinship
Collective Behavior	Feminist Theory
Community Development	Food, Sociology of
Comparative/Cross-Cultural Sociology	Gay and Lesbian Studies
Consequences of Affirmative Action	Gender, Sociology of
Consumers and Consumption	Gender and Work
Conversation Analysis and Ethnomethodology	Genocide
Criminology	Global Warming
Culture and Cognition	Globalization
Culture and Identity	Globalization and Citizenship
Culture and Inequity	Group Processes
Culture, Sociology of	Hate Crimes
Death, Dying, and Bereavement	Health and Well-Being
Development and Indigenous Peoples	Health Policy
Development of Sociology	Historical Sociology
Deviance and Social Control	History of Sociology
Disability and Social Life	Homelessness
Disaster	Human Ecology

Human-Animal Interaction
Immigrants, Second Generation
Immigration
Informal Economy
Integrating Quantitative and Qualitative
   Methodologies
Intergroup Relations
Internet and Social Interaction
Interracial Marriage and Multiracialism
Knowledge, Sociology of
Labor
Labor Markets
Law and Society
Mathematical Sociology
Media, Sociology of the
Medical Care, Social Organization of
Medical Sociology
Mental Health
Methodology, Qualitative
Methodology, Quantitative
Military, Sociology of the
Millennial Movements
Nations and Nationalism
New Age Religions, Sociology of
New Family Form
Occupations and Professions
Organizations
Perspective
Political Sociology
Popular Culture
Population Processes
Postmodern Theory
Poverty
Prisons and Prisoners
Public Opinion
Race and Ethnicity
Race, Class, and Gender
Race, Gender, Class, and Sexualities: A
   Multicultural Urban Community

Rational Choice
Reconceptualizing Race
Religion, Sociology of
Religious Right, Sociology of the
Reproduction, Sociology of
Retailing and the Urban World
Risk, Social Aspects of
Rural Sociology
Science, Sociology of
Sexuality, Sociology of
Social Capital and the City
Social Dimensions of AIDS
Social Implications of Population Aging
Social Movements
Social Networks
Social Policy
Social Psychology
Social Stratification and Inequality
Social Theory
Sociolinguistics
Sociology and Cultural Studies
Sociology of Affluence
Sociology of the Body
Sport, Sociology of
Substance Use, Abuse, and Treatment
Symbolic Interaction
Teaching Sociology
Technology and Social Change
Transnational Corporations
Urban Agriculture in Cities of the Future
Urban Sociology
Violence
Voluntary and Non-Profit Organizations
Women and Development
Work and the Workplace
World Systems

The specialized sections listed below meet concurrently with those above.

Aging and the Life Course
Community and Urban Sociology
Comparative Historical Sociology
Computers and Sociology
Culture
Economic Sociology
Education
Environment and Technology
Family
International Migration
Knowledge and Science Network
Labor and Labor Movements

Law
Marxist Sociology
Mathematical Sociology
Medical Sociology
Organizations, Occupations, and Work
Peace, War, and Social Conflict
Political Economy of the World System
Political Sociology
Section on Sex and Gender
Social Psychology
Sociological Practice

8.17.3 International Sociological Association

For information about meetings of the International Sociological Association (ISA) and other socio-logical societies, contact

International Sociological Association
Secretariat: Facultad C.C. Políticas y Sociología
Universidad Complutense
28223 Madrid
Spain
(34)-91352-76-50
www.ucm.es/info/isa/

8.17.3.1 Research Topics Within the ISA

The scientific activities of the ISA are organized in research committees, where scholars who wish to pursue comparative research become part of a network of scientific research, intellectual debate, and professional exchange. The 53 topics (as of 2001) are as follows. More information about any of the committees can be obtained by clicking on its link at www.ucm.es/info/isa/rc.htm.

Aging
Agriculture and Food
Alienation Theory and Research
Armed Forces and Conflict Resolution
Arts
Biography and Society
Childhood
Clinical Sociology
Communication, Knowledge, and Culture
Community Research
Comparative Sociology
Conceptual and Terminological Analysis
Deviance and Social Control
Disasters
Economy and Society
Education
Environment and Society
Ethnic, Race, and Minority Relations
Family Research
Futures Research
Health
History of Sociology
Housing and Built Environment
Labor Movements
Law
Leisure
Logic and Methodology

Mental Health and Illness
Migration
Organization
Participation and Self-Management
Political Sociology
Population
Poverty, Social Welfare, and Social Policy
Protected Groups
Rational Choice
Regional and Urban Development
Religion
Science and Technology
Social Classes and Social Movements
Social Movements, Collective Action, and Social
    Change
Social Practice and Transformation
Social Psychology
Sociocybernetics
Sociolinguistics
Sociotechnics and Sociological Practice
Sport
Stratification
Theory
Tourism, International
Women in Society
Work
Youth

8.17.3.2 *Members of the ISA*

Members of the ISA can be found at www.ucm.es/info/isa/colmemb/colmemb.htm, with links to the particular national association.

8.17.3.3 *ISA Publications*

Besides a newsletter, the ISA publishes the following. Additional information is available about each of these publications at www.ucm.es/info/isa/.

International Sociology is published four times a year

Current Sociology is published four times a year

Sage Studies in International Sociology is a book series edited by the International Sociological Association and published by Sage Publications

Sage Studies in International Sociology is a monograph series published jointly with *Current Sociology*

8.17.4 American Anthropological Association

The American Anthropological Association can be reached at

4350 North Fairfax Drive
Suite 640
Arlington, VA 22203-1620
703-528-1902
Fax: 703-528-3546
www.aaanet.org

8.17.4.1 *Common Section Topics at American Anthropological Association Annual Meetings*

The following excerpt from the 2001 American Anthropology Association Web site (www.aaanet.org/mtgs/html) identifies common topics of interest:

Sessions might examine anthropologists' changing relationship to our informants, the emergence of human rights as an anthropological concern, ongoing dialogues between humanistic and scientific points of view within anthropology and the emergence of new theoretical frameworks. Additional panels could address the hidden histories of women and people of color, disciplinary reframing of categories, shifting notions of culture, race and gender, methodological transformations, the history of anthropology's clandestine involvement in intelligence activities and new approaches toward understanding the colonial enterprise.

A list of meeting sections and interest groups follows.

American Ethnological Society	Association of Black Anthropologists
Anthropology and Environment Section	Association of Latina and Latino Anthropologists
Anthropology of Religion Section	Association of Senior Anthropologists
Archeology Division	Biological Anthropology Section
Association for Africanist Anthropology	Central States Anthropological Society
Association for Feminist Anthropology	Council for Museum Anthropology
Association for Political and Legal Anthropology	Council on Anthropology and Education
	Council on Nutritional Anthropology

Culture and Agriculture

East Asia Section

General Anthropology Division

Middle East Section

National Association for the Practice of
Anthropology

National Association of Student Anthropologists

Society for Anthropology in Community
Colleges

Society for Cultural Anthropology

Society for Humanistic Anthropology

Society for Latin American Anthropology

Society for Linguistic Anthropology

Society for Medical Anthropology

Society for Psychological Anthropology

Society for Urban, National, and
Transnational/Global Anthropology

Society for Visual Anthropology

Society for the Anthropology of Consciousness

Society for the Anthropology of Europe

Society for the Anthropology of North America

Society for the Anthropology of Work

Society of Lesbian and Gay Anthropologists

8.17.5 American Psychological Association

This association can be contacted at

750 First Street, NE
Washington, DC 20002-4242
800-374-2721
Fax: 202-336-5500
www.apa.org

8.17.5.1 Common Section Topics at American Psychological Association Annual Meetings

1   Addictive Behavior
2   AIDS
3   Art/Music/Literature
4   Behavior Analysis
5   Behavioral Neuroscience
6   Child Abuse
7   Clinical/Counseling/Consulting
    7.1   adolescent
    7.2   assessment/diagnosis
    7.3   child clinical/pediatric
    7.4   geriatric
    7.5   interaction/communication
    7.6   process/outcome
    7.7   professional
    7.8   psychopathology
        7.8.1   organic
        7.8.2   personality/behavior disorders
        7.8.3   schizophrenia
    7.9   psychotherapy/treatment-methods
        7.9.1   behavioral/cognitive
        7.9.2   dynamic/psychoanalytic
        7.9.3   existential
        7.9.4   humanistic

54 Psycholinguistics
55 Psychology Policy Issues
    55.1 ethics
    55.2 professional issues
    55.3 public policy
    55.4 scientific issues
    55.5 training and education
56 Psychophysiology
57 Religion
58 Rural
59 School
60 Sensation/Perception
61 Sexual Behavior/Functioning
62 Social
    62.1 attitude/attitude change
    62.2 attribution
    62.3 conflict resolution
    62.4 decision making
    62.5 group processes
    62.6 sex roles
    62.7 social cognition
63 Sports
64 Stress
65 Substance Abuse
66 Teaching of Psychology
67 Violence/Aggression
    67.1 assault
    67.2 homicide
    67.3 suicide
68 Women's Studies
69 Work/Employment/Careers
    69.1 academic
    69.2 business/government
    69.3 practice/research

8.17.6 Other Associations of Interest

American Association for the Advancement of Science
1200 New York Avenue, NW
Washington, DC 20005
202-326-6400
www.aaas.org

American Political Science Association
1527 New Hampshire Avenue, NW
Washington, DC 20036-1206
202-483-2512
Fax: 202-483-2657
www.apsanet.org/

American Public Health Association
800 I Street, NW
Washington, DC 20001-3710
202-777-2742
www.apha.org

American Statistical Association
1429 Duke Street
Alexandria, VA 22314-3402
703-684-1221
888-231-3473 (toll-free)
www.amstat.org

The Canadian Sociology and Anthropology Association
Concordia University/SB-323
1455 de Maisonneuve West
Montreal, Quebec
Canada H3G 1M8
514-848-8780
http://alcor.concordia.ca/~csaa1/csaa.htm

Population Association of America
8630 Fenton Street
Suite 722
Silver Spring, MD 20910-3812
301-565-6710
www.popassoc.org

8.18   PLANNING FOR A CAREER IN THE SOCIAL SCIENCES

8.18.1 The *Occupational Outlook Handbook*

The *Occupational Outlook Handbook*, revised every 2 years, is a source of career information prepared by the Department of Labor. It is designed to provide assistance to individuals making decisions about their future work lives by describing what workers in different occupations do on the job, working conditions, the training and education needed, earnings, and expected job prospects in a wide range of occupations.

What follows in sections 8.18.1 through 8.18.1.7 is material adapted from the *Occupational Outlook Handbook* (at http://stats.bls.gov/oco/ocos054.htm) on social scientists, edited to remove information not relevant to sociologists.

8.18.1.1 *Nature of the Work*

The major social science occupations covered in this statement include anthropologists, geographers, historians, political scientists, and sociologists. (Economists, psychologists, and urban and regional planners are covered elsewhere in the *Occupational Outlook Handbook*.)

Social scientists study all aspects of society—from past events and achievements to human behavior and relationships between groups. Their research provides insights that help us understand different ways in which individuals and groups make decisions, exercise power, and respond to change. Through their studies and analyses, social scientists suggest solutions to social, business, personal, governmental, and environmental problems.

Research is a major activity for many social scientists. They use various methods to assemble facts and construct theories. Applied research usually is designed to produce information that will enable people to make better decisions or manage their affairs more effectively. Interviews and surveys are widely used to collect facts, opinions, or other information. Information collection takes many forms, including living and working among the population being studied, field investigations, the analysis of historical records and documents, experiments with human or animal subjects in a laboratory, administration of standardized tests and questionnaires, and preparation and interpretation of maps and computer graphics. The work of the major specialties in social science—other than psychologists, economists, and urban and regional planners—varies greatly. Specialists in one field, however, often find that their research overlaps work being conducted in another discipline.

Sociologists study society and social behavior by examining the groups and social institutions people form, as well as various social, religious, political, and business organizations. They also study the behavior and interaction of groups, trace their origin and growth, and analyze the influence of group activities on individual members. They are concerned with the characteristics of social groups, organizations, and institutions; the ways individuals are affected by each other and by the groups to which they belong; and the effect of social traits such as sex, age, or race on a person's daily life. The results of sociological research aid educators, lawmakers, administrators, and others interested in resolving social problems and formulating public policy.

Most sociologists work in one or more specialties, such as social organization, stratification, and mobility; racial and ethnic relations; education; family; social psychology; urban, rural, political, and comparative sociology; sex roles and relations; demography; gerontology; criminology; or sociological practice.

8.18.1.2 Working Conditions

Most social scientists have regular hours. Generally working behind a desk, either alone or in collaboration with other social scientists, they read and write research reports. Many experience the pressures of writing and publishing articles, with deadlines and tight schedules. Sometimes they must work overtime, for which they usually are not reimbursed. Social scientists often work as an integral part of a research team, in which good communications skills are important. Travel may be necessary to collect information or attend meetings. Social scientists on foreign assignment must adjust to unfamiliar cultures, climates, and languages.

Some social scientists do fieldwork. For example, anthropologists, archaeologists, and geographers often travel to remote areas, live among the people they study, learn their languages, and stay for long periods at the site of their investigations. They may work under rugged conditions, and their work may involve strenuous physical exertion.

Social scientists employed by colleges and universities usually have flexible work schedules, often dividing their time among teaching, research and writing, consulting, or administrative responsibilities.

8.18.1.3 Employment

Social scientists held about 50,000 jobs in 1998. Many worked as researchers, administrators, and counselors for a wide range of employers, including federal, state, and local governments; educational institutions; social service agencies; research and testing services; and management consulting firms. Other employers include international organizations, associations, museums, and historical societies.

Many additional individuals with training in a social science discipline teach in colleges and universities and in secondary and elementary schools. (For more information, see the *Occupational Outlook Handbook* statements on college and university faculty and on kindergarten, elementary, and secondary school teachers.) The proportion of social scientists that teach varies by specialty—for example, the academic world usually is a more important source of jobs for graduates in history than for graduates in other fields of study.

8.18.1.4 *Training, Other Qualifications, and Advancement*

Educational attainment of social scientists is among the highest of all occupations. The PhD or equivalent degree is a minimum requirement for most positions in colleges and universities and is important for advancement to many top-level nonacademic research and administrative posts. Graduates with master's degrees in applied specialties usually have better professional opportunities outside colleges and universities, although the situation varies by field. Graduates with a master's degree in a social science qualify for teaching positions in junior colleges. Bachelor's degree holders have limited opportunities and in most social science occupations do not qualify for "professional" positions. The bachelor's degree does, however, provide a suitable background for many different kinds of entry-level jobs, such as research assistant, administrative aide, or management or sales trainee. With the addition of sufficient education courses, social science graduates also can qualify for teaching positions in secondary and elementary schools.

Training in statistics and mathematics is essential for many social scientists. Mathematical and quantitative research methods are increasingly used in geography, political science, and other fields. The ability to use computers for research purposes is mandatory in most disciplines.

Depending on their jobs, social scientists may need a wide range of personal characteristics. Because they constantly seek new information about people, things, and ideas, intellectual curiosity and creativity are fundamental personal traits. The ability to think logically and methodically is important to a political scientist comparing, for example, the merits of various forms of government. Objectivity, open-mindedness, and systematic work habits are important in all kinds of social science research. Perseverance is essential for an anthropologist, who might spend years accumulating artifacts from an ancient civilization. Excellent written and oral communication skills are essential for all these professionals.

8.18.1.5 *Job Outlook*

Overall employment of social scientists is expected to grow about as fast as the average for all occupations through 2008. Prospects are best for those with advanced degrees and usually are better in disciplines such as sociology and geography that offer more opportunities in nonacademic settings.

Government agencies, social service organizations, marketing research and consulting firms, and a wide range of other businesses seek social science graduates, although often in jobs with titles unrelated to their academic discipline. Social scientists will face stiff competition for academic positions; however, the growing importance and popularity of social science subjects in secondary schools is strengthening the demand for social science teachers at that level.

Candidates seeking positions as social scientists can expect to encounter competition in many areas of social science. Some social science graduates, however, will find good employment opportunities in areas outside traditional social science, often in related jobs that require good research, communication, and quantitative skills.

8.18.1.6 Earnings

Median annual earnings of social scientists (excluding economists, psychologists, and urban and regional planners) were $38,990 in 1998. The middle 50% earned between $28,950 and $56,550 a year. The lowest 10% earned less than $21,530, and the highest 10% earned more than $80,640 a year. Median annual earnings of all other social scientists in 1997 were $53,700 in the federal government and $37,300 in state government, except education and hospitals.

In the federal government, social scientists with a bachelor's degree and no experience could start at $20,600 or $25,500 a year in 1999, depending on their college records. Those with a master's degree could start at $31,200, and those with a PhD degree could begin at $37,700. Some individuals with experience and an advanced degree could start at $45,200. Beginning salaries were slightly higher in selected areas of the country where the prevailing local pay level was higher.

8.18.1.7 Related Occupations

A number of occupations requiring training and personal qualities similar to those of social scientists are covered elsewhere in the *Occupational Outlook Handbook*. These include lawyers, statisticians, mathematicians, computer programmers, computer scientists, computer engineers, computer systems analysts, reporters and correspondents, social workers, college and university faculty, and counselors.

8.18.2 Careers for Sociology Degree Holders in Academic and Nonacademic Markets

Each of the three degrees in sociology—the BA, the MA, and the PhD—offers a varying range of opportunities. The PhD degree usually is required for full-time teaching in a college or university and for work in some of the different social and behavioral science positions in government.

8.18.2.1 Careers for Students With a BA Degree

The BA is not considered a professional or "terminal" degree in any of the social science fields such as history, political science, economics, human geography, social psychology, and social anthropology. The BA holder in sociology usually seeks entry-level jobs in social work; in nonprofit or religious organizations; in federal, local, or state government; or in business and industry. The American Sociological Association states:

> There are still very few employers who are looking for sociology BA's in the same sense in which they might look for BA's in engineering, nursing, accounting, etc. Sociology BA's will often find themselves competing with other liberal arts students who have majored in English, history, psychology, etc. Here, a strong undergraduate program in sociology can conceivably produce a competitive advantage. For example, students interested in business careers after the BA might emphasize courses in industrial sociology and complex organization; students seeking work with public welfare agencies might concentrate their course work in areas such as stratification, race and ethnic relations, sociology of the family, and urban sociology.

Regardless of one's special interests, many students would do well to emphasize research methods and statistics. It is precisely these courses that are cited as most valuable by persons already employed in non-academic jobs who are asked to reconsider their education with the wisdom of hindsight. Statistics is not as difficult as many students fear and it often provides the most valuable and marketable career skills. This is especially true for the student who plans to stop with the BA. (American Sociological Association, 1975, p. 14)

BAs in sociology and social work might examine job opportunities with the federal government. The following list is from The Career Center (www.magiclink.com/web/jobcofji/list188.htm):

Community planner
Correctional officer
Criminal investigator
Foreign affairs officer

Geographer
Outdoor recreation planner
Park ranger
Treasury enforcement

Western Washington University offers a more comprehensive list (below) of job possibilities (at www.ac.wwu.edu/~socad/jobtitles.html) for undergraduates in sociology.

Business and Industry
Administrative assistant
Advertising staffer
Banker
Business manager
Computer analyst
Consumer relations worker
Consumer researcher
Control engineer
Data entry manager
Human resources manager
Insurance agent
Labor relations analyst
Market analyst/researcher
Marketing/sales representative
Merchandiser/purchaser
Planning assistant
Production manager
Project manager
Public relations specialist
Publishing staffer
Quality control manager
Real estate agent
Technical writer
Telemarketer
Trainer
Training assistant

Justice System
Correctional counselor
Corrections officer
Criminal investigator
Criminal justice specialist
Juvenile court worker
Parole officer
Police officer
Rehabilitation counselor

Special agent
State trooper

Community and Social Service
Case manager
Caseworker/aide
Charities administrator
Child development technician
Community organizer
Environmental organizer
Family planner
Fund-raising assistant/director
Gerontologist
Group home worker
Homeless/housing worker
Hospital administrator
Housing coordinator
Medical records clerk
Occupational/career counselor
Park/forest ranger
Public administration assistant
Public assistance worker
Public health supervisor
Rehabilitation program worker
Resident planning aide
Substance abuse counselor
Volunteer program coordinator
Youth outreach worker

Government
Affirmative action worker
Census worker
Employee specialist
Foreign service officer
Human rights officer
Information officer
International worker
Legislative aide

Peace Corps volunteer
Personnel coordinator
Program supervisor
Special agent

Education
Admissions counselor
Affirmative action assistant
Alumni relations officer
College placement specialist
Extension service specialist
Student personnel

Public health educator
Teacher

Research
Consultant
Economic analyst
Interviewer
Market researcher
Population analyst
Researcher
Statistician
Surveyor

Reference

American Sociological Association. (1975). *Careers in sociology.* Washington, DC: Author.

8.18.2.2 *Careers for Students With a Master's Degree*

The holder of an MA or MS degree in sociology often teaches in a junior or other 2-year college. Many are "on their way" to a PhD. This educational background offers occupations with public agencies and private businesses. The MA is often sought for technical skill in social research.

8.18.2.3 *Careers for Students With a PhD*

The "best" jobs in sociology and related fields usually go to holders of a PhD. The PhD makes it much easier to find a teaching position in a university at the undergraduate or graduate level. Research and administration jobs at higher levels become available as experience is gained and competence is demonstrated. A sociology PhD finds a place in the wider market of behavioral scientists from many disciplines.

8.18.3 The Market for Sociologists in the United States

The current status of jobs for sociologists (and other behavioral scientists) is bright, and it looks promising for the future. According to the American Sociological Association's 1999 Survey of Doctorate Recipients, sociologists and other social and behavioral scientists benefited from a strong labor market and experienced unemployment rates of only about 1% in 1999. About 9 out of 10 sociologists were in the labor market (including the 1% who were unemployed). This labor force participation rate is similar to PhDs in all the behavioral and social science disciplines. Of the remaining one tenth of sociologists who are not in the labor market, most are retired. About 1 out of 20 sociologists who report that they are working are employed part-time because they could not find what they considered to be a suitable job for a sociologist.

The unemployment rates for doctoral social and behavioral scientists in 1999 were as follows, for selected disciplines. (Data are from the Web site www.asanet.org/members/employ1.html, and updates can be obtained there.)

Economics	1.1%
Political and related sciences	1.1%
Sociology	1.2%
Other social sciences	1.2%
Psychology	1.2%

8.18.4 Roles of Academic and Nonacademic Markets

Professional sociologists with PhDs usually have trained for college or university teaching and hope to find the opportunity to do their own research as a part of their total responsibilities. In fact, two out of three professional sociologists do just that. Research and its publication are nearly obligatory for tenure and promotions at major universities.

With teaching opportunities increasing (in part because of the increase in retirement of baby boom professors), it is becoming more difficult to be granted tenure. The university structure finds it more efficient to hire adjunct professors who teach for a much-decreased cost, rather than awarding tenure and making a long-term financial commitment to any one person. The nonacademic market therefore is becoming more important; in fact, it has provided the majority of jobs for BA and MA degree holders in sociology.

8.18.4.1 Education as a Factor That Facilitates Entry Into the Nonacademic Market

A sociology student not intent on a career in academia can improve employment prospects through the means listed below.

1. *Master existing knowledge.* Acquire a substantial store of knowledge about social problems and theories. This is the resource that will provide the best source for attacking problems. Many nonacademic researchers are not scholars; some are little more than technicians. The majority of administrators in nonacademic institutions have limited opportunities to do systematic reading in the broad field of social knowledge. Someone who is able to inform them about knowledge in a particular field may have an immediate value. Holders of a bachelor's degree, a master's degree, or a PhD have opportunities for more important responsibilities.
2. Do everything possible to *improve your basic writing and quantitative skills.* Seek opportunities to write papers for credit. Select courses in statistics and computer science that can give you marketable skills for many entry-level positions.
3. *Consider a double major* and interdisciplinary programs such as sociology and communications (or economics, urban planning, statistics, computer science, journalism, or business administration), or especially information technology.
4. *Seek opportunities for student-originated research* at the undergraduate level and research support at the graduate level.
5. *Locate opportunities for internships and work experience.* Make your summer and college work count. If at all possible, find work that can be used later as "good experience for an entry-level job."
6. *Develop an understanding of the job market* in your college town as well as your home community. Talk with professionals about careers and technical expertise such as writing and editorial skills, experience in computer programming, statistical knowledge, graphic skills, and interviewing.
7. Remember, regardless of whether you obtain a bachelor's degree, a master's degree, or a PhD, the nonacademic market has *not* been structured to fit your social science major. You must *fit your major study to the market*, under whatever name or title you find a job related to your knowledge and skills.

8.18.5 Finding Where the Jobs Are

In the early stages of a career, a job applicant may have to search hard and long for jobs. Later, jobs may come to the experienced worker. It is entirely possible that the first job is the only one that must be seriously searched for. For the young worker eager for employment, this is little consolation, but people are willing to help. The applicant must find such helpers. What follows are some step-by-step hints.

Step 1: *Use the resources of your college's sociology department.* Provide faculty members with résumés and ask their counsel.

Step 2: *Use your college's employment office.* Find out which interviewers are coming to the college and talk with as many as possible.

Step 3: *Attend the annual meetings of your regional sociological society and the American Sociological Association.* All annual meetings have employment services where registrants seeking jobs and employers seeking applicants can get together. The ASA has a nonacademic roster. Ask to see this, and use employed sociologists to assist you in locating jobs and arranging interviews. Try to get face-to-face contact with possible employers. Employers want to see you in person!

Step 4: *Read the Chronicle of Higher Education and other publications that regularly list jobs in the field of higher education, such as the American Psychology Association's* Monitor *and* The New York Times *(Sunday edition).* The *Chronicle of Higher Education,* widely read in higher-education circles, has an extensive listing of available college and university teaching, research, counseling, and administrative positions. Ordinarily, 40-50 pages of each issue are devoted to the paid advertisements of college employers. Positions available are indexed by occupational titles and by geographic location.

Step 5: *Try the shotgun approach.* Write to any organizations or institutions you would be willing to work for and very clearly state your assets and why you would be a positive addition to the organization. You can begin doing this by learning how to write a good résumé (there are hundreds of books on this at the library or your local bookstore). You might want to ask several of your faculty members for their résumés, so that you can model yours after one or more of them.

This approach necessitates writing *lots* of "blind" letters in which you apply for jobs that may or may not exist. The following suggestions may be helpful.

1. Create a well-written, succinct, and to-the-point one-page letter introducing yourself and your intentions.
2. Include a summary or a draft of your dissertation. Indicate when it will be finished, if it is not already.
3. Send the letter out to as many schools as you might like. Although many faculty disapprove of this approach, it shows some degree of determination, and one never knows what the outcome will be. In many cases, a good job resulted from such a letter when there was actually no vacancy, but one opened shortly thereafter.
4. Don't let preconceptions of geographical locations limit your search. If you have not been to a particular part of the country or to a large urban area, don't preclude it until you visit and have a firsthand opportunity to explore the area.

Step 6: *Take advantage of online announcements.* One of the most popular activities on the Internet is seeking jobs. Such major job search sites as Monster.com regularly have more than 1,000,000 jobs advertised. A recent search on Monster.com revealed eight jobs in the area of sociology, with four of them full- or part-time opportunities in higher education. If you have a specific school in mind where you might like to teach, don't hesitate to explore its Web site.

Other online sites include careerbuilder (at www.careerbuilder.com), jobs.com (at www.jobs.com), and HotJobs.com (at www.hotjobs.com). Government jobs can be searched for online at Federal Jobs Net (at http://federaljobs.net), Government Job Sites (at www.jmu.edu/polisci/mpa/jobsites.htm), and Government Jobs (at www.govtjobs.com/).

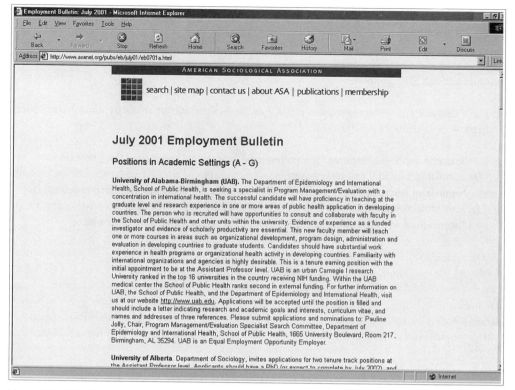

Figure 8.3. The American Sociological Association Employment Bulletin Web Page

Finally, academic positions can be reviewed at the Academic Employment Network (at www.academploy.com/), where you can post your résumé, check job listings, and even advertise (if you want to post a job opening).

8.18.5.1 *Employment Links for Sociologists*

Regularly check the American Sociological Association's employment bulletin (at www.asanet.org/members/employlk.html). Figure 8.3 shows a sample page from that Web site.

8.18.6 Salary and Salary Comparisons

More often than not, taking a job means leaving one location and moving to another. The Salary Wizard (at www.careerbuilder.com/salary/salary.html) allows you to pick a job category and a region, then quickly find median salaries by position. The site also contains news on compensation and benefit trends.

8.18.7 Checklist for University Faculty Job Seekers Who Make Research a High Priority

If you elect to pursue a university-related position, you can use the following list as you prepare for job interviews. Most faculty interviewers inquire about the following subjects and how well you fit with the university regarding each. You should also be concerned about how any job that is offered meets your professional plans and desires.

■■ Research Elements

Research/teaching/service orientation of the department and the institution generally

Types and scopes of research encouraged

Research budget for department or division (dollars per faculty member) if available; if none is available directly, does the university offer internal competition for research funds?

Assistance available in securing grants

Research facility: computer capabilities, editorial or computer assistance, a supportive institute of social research

Number of hours per week of secretarial help for each professor (research requires great secretarial support)

Photoreproduction support (access to machines, type and number of machines)

Computer availability (you should expect a personal computer in your office as part of the employment agreement)

Research assistant availability (criteria for obtaining assistants)

■■ Teaching Policy

Teaching load and demands on time

Class size to expect

Number of preparations per term

Number of *new* preparations per semester or quarter

Availability of summer school teaching

Day/night schedule

Travel time committed to teaching

Graduate program: seminar teaching opportunities, number and quality of graduate students

Fellow faculty members, especially in area of interest; also research emphasis, compatibility, competence of faculty

Travel money for national and international professional conferences

■■ Salary and Financial Issues

Check the salary report at the American Association of University Professors Web site (www.aaup.org) for a recent report on the economic status of the profession, showing the salary rating of the institution in which you are interested

If the information is available to the public (as it will be for most state universities and colleges), check the budget to confirm salaries (such documentation usually is available through the main library)

Summer salary available, moving expenses provided, life insurance, and health insurance

Cost of housing and other living expenses in the area

■■ Research Facilities

Office space

Office equipment

Library facility, including extent and quality of holdings

■■ University Environment

Number of undergraduate and graduate majors in the department

Tenure rules

Promotion procedures

Retirement program

Morale of the faculty; history of faculty mobility in the department

Relationships across departments and schools

Quality and character of the administration, especially the chair of the department and the dean

History and current status of the financing of the institution

Faculty governance and rules (ask for faculty handbook)

8.18.8 Other Employment Resources

The following are some of the more popular job preparation and employment-related books.

Beatty, Richard H. (1997). *The five-minute interview.* New York: John Wiley.

Bolles, Richard Nelson. (2001). *What color is your parachute? A practical manual for job-hunters and career-changers.* San Francisco: Ten Speed Press.

Dorio, Marc A., & Myers, William. (2000). *The complete idiot's guide to the perfect interview.* Indianapolis: Alpha Books.

Fry, Ronald W. (2001). *101 great answers to the toughest interview questions.* Franklin Lakes, NJ: Career Press.

Ireland, Susan. (2000). *The complete idiot's guide to the perfect resume.* Indianapolis: Alpha Books.

Schmidt, Frances. (n.d.). *Getting hired in any job market.* Available at www.iUniverse.com.

Stafford, Diane. (1998). *Your job: Getting it, keeping it, improving it, changing it.* Kansas City, MO: Kansas City Star Books.

AUTHOR INDEX

SUBJECT INDEX

ABOUT THE AUTHORS

Delbert C. Miller (1913-1998) was Professor of Sociology and Business Administration at Indiana University, Bloomington. He was the author of numerous research articles in scholarly journals, and his books include *Industrial Sociology* (1st, 2nd, and 3rd editions) and *Industry, Labor, and Community,* (both with William H. Form). His research monographs, *International Community Power Structures* and *Leadership and Power in Bos-Wash Megalopolis,* describe large-scale team research projects that he directed. He served for many years as a supervisory training specialist and as an arbitrator for the American Arbitration Association and the state of Indiana.

Neil J. Salkind is Professor of Psychology and Research in Education at the University of Kansas, where he has taught child development and research methods for the past 29 years. His primary research interests are in policy analysis and policies affecting young children. He received his Ph.D. from the University of Maryland and is a member of the American Psychological Association and the Society for Research in Child Development. He has served as editor of Child Development Abstracts and Bibliography for 13 years.